EDUCATION IN THE UNITED STATES
A DOCUMENTARY HISTORY

Edited by
SOL COHEN

UNIVERSITY OF
CALIFORNIA
LOS ANGELES

VOLUME 5

Random House New York

Reference Series Editors:

Fred L. Israel
William P. Hansen

Acknowledgments for use of material covered by
Copyright Conventions appear on pages 3395–99.

Art´spots courtesy of Dover Pictorial Archives

FIRST EDITION

9 8 7 6 5 4 3 2 1

Copyright © 1974 by Random House, Inc.
All rights reserved under International and Pan-American
Copyright Conventions. Published in the United States by
Random House, Inc., New York, and simultaneously in Canada
by Random House of Canada Limited Toronto.

MANUFACTURED IN THE UNITED STATES OF AMERICA

Library of Congress Cataloging in Publication Data
Cohen, Sol, comp.
Education in the United States: a documentary history.
1. Education—United States—History—Sources.
1. Title.
LA205.C53   370.973   73-3099
ISBN 0-394-49443-1 (v. 5)

Designed by Marsha Picker
for computer typesetting by Volt Information Sciences, Inc.

VOLUME V
CONTENTS

THE
PROFESSION
OF
EDUCATION

Teacher Training

THE COURSE OF STUDY AT TEACHERS COLLEGE, COLUMBIA
UNIVERSITY (1899)   From James E. Russell, "The Organization and Administration of
Teachers College," *Teachers College Record*, vol. I, pp. 46–51.

Courses of Study in Teachers College

The courses of study offered in Teachers College fall naturally into three groups:

A. Graduate Courses:

(1) A course for teachers in normal schools, and for principals, supervisors, and superintendents of schools. This course is intended to fit teachers of superior ability and of special academic attainments for the work of training teachers in colleges and normal schools, and for positions in the public-school service requiring a high degree of professional insight and technical skill. It leads to the Higher Diploma, the highest honor granted in the College. Candidates for the Higher Diploma must spend at least one year in residence and pursue courses in one major and two minor subjects. The choice of subjects is entirely optional, except that at least the major subject must be education. Candidates for a higher diploma must be graduates of an approved institution of learning—a college, engineering school, or normal school, or the equivalent of one of these,—and must present satisfactory evidence of a high degree of professional ability, as a result of the study of education or experience in teaching. The real test of fitness, however, is the ability of the candidate to undertake research and investigation. No definite course, therefore, is prescribed. The minimum period of residence is fixed at one year; but the necessity of completing some special task, in line with the major subject, and putting the results in form for publication makes it difficult for the student, however well prepared, to secure the diploma in the minimum time.

The graduate courses are designed not only to give advanced professional training but also to promote research and investigation in the field of education. Hence certain courses in Teachers College properly fall within the jurisdiction of the University Faculty of Philosophy, under which Education holds a co-ordinate place with other philosophic and linguistic subjects. Graduate students of Teachers College, therefore, who conform to the general regulations of the University Council, may thus pursue at the same time, with no additional expense, courses leading to a Teachers College diploma and to a University degree. Teachers College students who thus become candidates for the degree of Master of Arts or Doctor of

Philosophy must make Education their major subject; their minor subjects may be selected in any other department of the University, subject to the approval of the Dean of Teachers College.

(2) A course for teachers in secondary schools and instructors in colleges.

Candidates for admission to this course must hold a Bachelor's degree from some American college in good standing, except that, under the general regulations of Columbia University, students in Columbia College and Barnard College may enter this course in their senior collegiate year. It leads to a diploma in one or more of the subjects commonly taught in secondary schools and colleges. Candidates for the diploma in secondary teaching must spend at least one year in residence, devoting themselves exclusively to acadmeic and professional study of the subjects which they intend to teach. Students who have already taken the baccalaureate degree may combine the work of this course according to the regulations above-mentioned, with the requirements for the degree of Master of Arts or Doctor of Philosophy.

The course of study designed for intending teachers in secondary schools is one to which Teachers College can point with pride. Despite the fact that in the popular mind any one of the above-named qualifications suffices for eligibility to teach in the American high school, we have planned a course which requires as much in each respect as is generally required in any one. For example, in the State of New York about thirty-two per cent of the teachers in secondary schools have a college degree, approximately thirty-nine per cent are normal-school graduates, and the remainder, it is to be presumed, have been selected because of their special scholarship or success in teaching. Candidates for the Teachers College diploma in secondary teaching must, first of all, be college graduates (at least when they complete the course); they must be able to demonstrate a high degree of special scholarship in every subject in which the diploma is sought—at least the equivalent of three years of university work, three hours per week; they must pass satisfactory examinations in the history and principles of education and in psychology and its applications in teaching; and, finally, they are required to pursue courses specially designed to afford practice in the selection and arrangement of materials for instruction and in the actual teaching of the subjects which they elect.

However one may question the expediency of a university's undertaking the training of teachers for the elementary grades, no doubt can arise as to the desirability of bringing such immediate and direct support to higher education. This is work that cannot well be done outside of a college or a university. The general culture demanded is that which colleges aim to supply; the special scholarship must be the product of university study; and the professional knowledge which should be acquired differs, both in degree and in kind, from that which properly pertains to the teaching of infants and children. The instinct of self-preservation, therefore, should lead the university to do all in its power to support the secondary schools, and especially to provide them with teachers capable of intelligent service.

B. General Undergraduate Courses:

(1) A course for teachers in elementary schools.[1]

This course is intended to fit teachers for the more responsible positions in the elementary grades of the public schools and to provide graduates of state normal schools with opportunities for further professional study. Candidates for admission to the course leading to the diploma in elementary teaching must be graduates of an approved secondary school. They are required to spend four years in residence and pursue a prescribed course of study, except that advanced standing is granted to professionally trained teachers.

(2) A course for teachers in the kindergarten.[2]

The purpose of this course is to train teachers through four years of undergraduate study for work in public and private kindergartens. Graduates of approved secondary schools are admitted to the first year of the course. Such advanced standing as may be warranted is granted to experienced kindergartners and graduates of recognized kindergarten training schools.

Under present economic conditions, the normal schools of the country can require for admission, at most, only a high-school training of those who intend to teach in the elementary grades. Teachers College ought not in any sense to enter into competition with the normal schools; for its purpose is to supplement their work and carry it to its highest development. Hence, it insists upon two years' academic study, beyond the college preparatory course, in English, history, biology, geography and geology, physical science, freehand drawing and music, for all students who have not had a good normal training. Another important reason for prolonging the period of academic training is the need that students shall bring to the study of educational principles the best mental equipment of which they are capable. Teachers who expect to rise to commanding positions in the kindergarten and elementary school can well afford to spend two or three years beyond the period of minimum requirement.

C. Departmental Undergraduate Courses:

(1) A two-year course for teachers and supervisors of art and drawing.[3]

---

[1] The prescribed studies of this course are as follows (the hours given with each subject indicate the number of lessons or exercises a week throughout the academic year, i. e., from the last week in September to the first week in June inclusive; the figures in parentheses indicate the number of hours of work required as distinguished from the hours of credit granted—two hours of laboratory or shop-work counting as one credit hour):

First Year—English literature and composition, 3 hours; mediæval and modern history, 3 hours; biological nature study, 2 (3) hours; physics and chemistry, 3 (5) hours; freehand drawing, 2 (4) hours; music, 2 hours; physical training, 1 (2) hour; elective, 2 hours.

Second Year—English literature and analysis, 3 hours; United States history, 3 hours; physiology and hygiene, 2 (3) hours; general geography, 3 hours; applied freehand drawing, 2 (4) hours; music, 2 hours; physical training, 1 (2) hour; elective, 2 hours.

Third Year—Psychology and applications in teaching, 3 hours; child study, 2 hours; methods of teaching English, 3 (half-year) hours; methods of teaching mathematics, 3 (half-year) hours; music, 2 hours; elective, 8 hours.

Fourth Year—History of education, 2 hours; principles of education, 2 hours; observation and practice-teaching, 2 hours or more; elective, 12 hours. Students who intend to teach in the lower grades of elementary school are required to elect primary manual training, 2 (3) hours, and kindergarten methods, 1 (2) hour.

[2] The requirements of this course during the first two years are practically the same as in the first and second years of the course for elementary teachers; the rest of the course is as follows:

Third Year—Psychology and its applications in teaching, 3 hours; child study, 2 hours; gifts and occupations, 3 hours; songs and games, 2 (3) hours; stories, 1 1/2 hours; music, 2 hours elective, 4 1/2 hours.

Fourth Year History of education, 2 hours; principles of education, 2 hours; kindergarten principles, 2 (half-year) hours; program and gift work, 2 hours; games, 1 (2) hour; observation and practice teaching, 4 (8) hours; elective, 6 hours.

[3] The prescribed course in art and drawing is as follows:

First Year—Psychology and its applications in teaching, 3 hours; studio work, 4 (8) hours; sketch class, 2 (4) hours; clay modeling, 1 (2) hour; art interpretation, 1 (2) hour; mechanical drawing, 2 (4) hours; elective, 4 hours.

Second Year—History of education, 2 hours; principles and methods in art teaching, 2 (4) hours; water-color and oil painting, 4 (8) hours; advanced sketch class, 2 (4) hours; advanced design, 2 (3) hours; applied design, 2 (4) hours; history of art, 1 hour; elective, 3 hours.

(2) A two-year course for teachers and supervisors of domestic art.[4]
(3) A two-year course for teachers and supervisors of domestic science.[5]
(4) A two-year course for teachers and supervisors of manual training.[6]

Candidates for admission to these courses must give evidence of (a) technical ability or experience in teaching, and (b) academic training equivalent to graduation from a secondary school.

TEACHER-TRAINING AT TEACHERS COLLEGE, COLUMBIA UNIVERSITY (1899)   From James E. Russell, "The Function of the University In the Training of Teachers," *Columbia University Quarterly,* vol. I, pp. 335–40.

The chief factors in a teacher's equipment are: (1) general culture, (2) special scholarship, (3) professional knowledge and (4) technical skill. The first of these qualifications is so elusive that it can hardly be measured except in terms of academic training. It is taken for granted that a teacher should know what he is to

[4]The prescribed course in domestic art is as follows:
First Year—Psychology and its applications in teaching, 3 hours; physiology and hygiene, 2 (3) hours; sewing, 1 (2) hour; textiles, 2 hours; drafting and making garments, 3 (4) hours; principles and methods, 2 hours; design, 1 (2) hour; industrial evolution of society, 1 hour; elective, 3 hours.
Second Year—History of education, 2 hours; observation and practice teaching, 2 (or more) hours; equipment and management, 2 hours; household art and design, 2 (3) hours, conference, 1 hour; advanced design, 2 (3) hours; art interpretation, 1 (2) hour; social reform movements, 1 hour; elective, 5 hours (or less if observation and practice teaching counts more than 2 hours).

[5]The prescribed course in domestic science is as follows:
First Year—Psychology and its applications in teaching, 3 hours; physiology and hygiene, 2 (3) hours; foods, 4 (7) hours, food production and manufacture, 3 (5) hours; bacteriology, 1 hour; household chemistry, 2 (4) hours; industrial evolution of society, 1 hour; elective, 2 hours.
Second Year—History of education, 2 hours; observation and practice teaching, 2 (or more) hours; foods, advanced course, 4 (7) hours, home sanitation and management, 2 (3) hours; methods of teaching domestic science, 2 hours; elective, 6 hours (or less if observation and practice teaching counts more than 2 hours).

[6]The prescribed course in manual training for elementary schools is as follows:
First Year—Psychology and its applications in teaching, 3 hours; knife-work for elementary schools, 2 (4) hours; wood-working for elementary schools, 3 (6) hours; mechanical drawing, 2 (4) hours; principles and methods, 2 (3) hours; elementary freehand drawing, 2 (4) hours; design, 1 (2) hour; elective, 3 hours.
Second Year—History of education, 2 hours; organization and supervision of manual training, 2 (3) hours; wood-working for secondary schools, 5 (10) hours; mechanical drawing, 3 (6) hours; applied freehand drawing, 2 (4) hours; elective, 4 hours.
The course prescribed for teachers of manual training in secondary schools is as follows:
First Year—Psychology and its applications in teaching, 3 hours; wood-working for secondary schools, 5 (10) hours; mechanical drawing, 2 (4) hours; principles and methods, 2 (3) hours; elementary freehand drawing, 2 (4) hours; design, 1 (2) hour, elective, 3 hours.
Second Year—History of education, 2 hours; organization and supervision of manual, training, 2 (3) hours, turning and pattern-making, 4 (8) hours, and moulding and foundry practice, 2 (4) hours; or forging, 6 (12) hours; or machine work, 6 (12) hours; mechanical drawing, 3 (6) hours; elective, 5 hours.

teach; but it is not so generally recognized that to know a subject to the extent of being qualified to teach it presupposes, not only familiarity with the particular branch, but also an understanding of its relations to other subjects and its place in the general domain of knowledge. No amount of general culture and special scholarship will, however, make a person competent to teach who does not have the skill to use the means at his command in the attainment of rational ends. The great problem in the training of teachers is to combine these four characteristics in due proportions. . . .

Under present economic conditions, the normal schools of the country can require for admission, at most, only a high-school training of those who intend to teach in the elementary grades. Teachers College ought not in any sense to enter into competition with the normal schools; for its purpose is to supplement their work and carry it to its highest development. Hence, it insists upon two-years' academic study, beyond the college preparatory course, in English, history, biology, geography and geology, physical science, free-hand drawing and music for all students who have not had a good normal training. Another important reason for prolonging the period of academic training is the need that students shall bring to the study of educational principles the best mental equipment of which they are capable. Teachers who expect to rise to commanding positions in the kindergarten and elementary school can well afford to spend two or three years beyond the period of the minimum requirement.

In the courses for teachers and supervisors of art and drawing, domestic art, domestic science and manual training, it is difficult to keep a satisfactory balance between the requirements. These subjects are so technical in their nature, and the progress of the student depends so largely upon natural talents and special training, that it is impossible to insist upon the same degree of academic preparation as for the more general courses. In this case, technical skill and special scholarship must outweigh other considerations. Hence, in these courses the requirements in both academic and professional subjects are somewhat lightened, to give more time for specialization along technical lines.

The course of study designed for intending teachers in secondary schools is one to which Teachers College can point with pride. Despite the fact that in the popular mind any one of the above-named qualifications suffices for eligibility to teach in the American high school, we have planned a course which requires as much in each respect as is generally required in any one. For example, in the State of New York about 32 per cent. of the teachers in secondary schools have a college degree, approximately 39 per cent. are normal school graduates and the remainder, it is to be presumed, have been selected because of their special scholarship or success in teaching. Candidates for the Teachers College diploma in secondary teaching must, first of all, be college graduates (at least, when they complete the course); they must be able to demonstrate a high degree of special scholarship in every subject in which the diploma is sought—at least the equivalent of three years of university work, three hours per week; they must pass satisfactory examinations in the history and principles of education and in psychology and its applications in teaching; and, finally, they are required to pursue courses specially designed to afford practice in the selection and arrangement of materials for instruction and in the actual teaching of the subjects which they elect.

However one may question the expediency of a university's undertaking the training of teachers for the elementary grades, no doubt can arise as to the desirability of bringing such immediate and direct support to higher education. This is work that cannot well be done outside of a college or a university. The general culture demanded is that which colleges aim to supply; the special scholarship must be the product of university study; and the professional knowledge which should be acquired differs, both in degree and in kind, from that which properly pertains to the teaching of infants and children. The instinct of self-preservation, therefore, should lead the university to do all in its power to support the secondary schools, and especially to provide them with teachers capable of intelligent service.

The graduate courses leading to the higher diploma are specially intended for teachers of the science and art of education in colleges and normal schools, and for principals, supervisors and superintendents of schools. The choice of subjects is entirely optional, except that at least one minor must be in the theory and practice of teaching. Candidates for the higher diploma must be graduates of an approved institution of learning—a college, engineering school or normal school, or the equivalent of one of these—and must present satisfactory evidence of a high degree of professional ability, as a result of the study of education or experience in teaching. The real test of fitness, however, is the ability of the candidate to undertake research and investigation. No definite course, therefore, is prescribed. The minimum period of residence is fixed at one year; but the necessity of completing some special task, in line with the major subject, and putting the results in form for publication makes it difficult for the students, however well prepared, to secure the diploma in the minimum time. The attainments of graduate students in Teachers College, accordingly, are all that can be secured under any faculty of the University.

The work peculiar to Teachers College is that which is technically educational. This consists of courses in the history and philosophy of education, in child study, in school economy, and in the theory and practice of teaching.

Psychology, physiology and child-study stand first in order among the required subjects of a technical nature. The special aim in these courses is to know the child; to become familiar with the physical and psychical characteristics of infancy, childhood and youth; to gain some insight into the influences of heredity and environment; and to understand the processes of the normal, adult mind. The course in child-study is supplementary to the prescribed courses in systematic and applied psychology. It is designed to present the facts, so far as they have been scientifically determined, concerning the nature and the development of the mind during childhood and adolescence, with special reference to the meaning of these facts to the teacher. It seeks to provide the student with sound criteria for estimating theories about the child's mind and to give practice in right methods of observation and experiment.

The general course in the history of education aims to ascertain what standards of culture—what ideals of life and what methods of training the young to assume the duties of life—have prevailed in the past or now exist among various peoples. It shows the growth of civilization and discloses some of the causes of progress; it reveals instances of arrested development and suggests means of obviating it; it is Kultur-Geschichte, with special reference to educational needs and educational problems. In the first half-year of this course the chief types of ancient education— Egyptian, Chinese, Hebrew, Greek and Roman—are presented in the light of the history of civilization; the continuation of the course in the second half-year gives special attention to the interaction of Greek, Roman and Christian influences, in forming the educational ideals and shaping the school systems of mediaeval and modern times. A part of the course is devoted to the reading and discussion of selections from the classics and the works of later writers on education.

The course on the principles of education aims to lay the basis for a scientific theory of education, considered as a human institution. The process of education is explained from the standpoint of the doctrine of evolution, and the fundamental principles thus arrived at are applied from the threefold standpoint of the history of civilization, the developing powers of the child and the cultivation of individual and social efficiency. The courses in the history and philosophy of education thus seek to establish reliable foundations for all educational practice.

The prescribed courses in the theory and practice of teaching are concerned with both the science and the art of education—with the science, so far as it is dependent upon the laws of mental development; with the art, so far as it involves the application of these laws in observing, planning and teaching a series of lessons. The introductory course, which grows directly out of the course in general psychology, has as its special aim the development of a scientific method of the recitation and the application of the principles of method to various studies of the elementary school. Then follows a period of training, under actual class-room conditions, for all students who are not experienced teachers.

The classes of the Horace Mann School, from the kindergarten up through the high school, are open to students who are qualified to undertake systematic study of the courses of instruction or to engage in actual teaching under the guidance and criticism of the school instructors. It is not the purpose of the Horace Mann School, however, to provide means for practice and experimentation except along lines already demonstrated as safe and reliable. The proving ground, both for pupil-teachers and for untried methods of instruction, is a series of special classes, under the immediate direction of the professor of the theory and practice of teaching. These classes, now embracing the kindergarten and first primary grades, will ultimately be extended to include the entire elementary school.

All other courses of the department are either optional or required only of candidates for diplomas in special subjects. Under the head of the theory and practice of teaching the following courses are offered: kindergarten methods, primary teaching, and the principles and methods of teaching English, French, German, Greek, Latin, history, mathematics, biology, geography and geology, chemistry, physics, art and drawing, domestic economy and manual training. In speaking of these courses as "method courses," I am using the term in its broadest sense. In dealing with mature students, there is little need of putting exceptional stress upon technical devices and formal classroom procedure. . . .

JOHN DEWEY ON THE RELATION OF THEORY TO PRACTICE IN TEACHER TRAINING (1904) From John Dewey, "The Relation of Theory to Practice in Education," as quoted in National Society for the Study of Education, *Thirty-third Yearbook, Part I* (Bloomington, Ill., 1904), pp. 9–15.

It is difficult, if not impossible, to define the proper relationship of theory and practice without a preliminary discussion, respectively, (1) of the nature and aim of theory; (2) of practice.[1]

[1]This paper is to be taken as representing the views of the writer, rather than those of any particular institution in an official way; for the writer thought it better to discuss certain principles that seem to him fundamental, rather than to define a system of procedure.

A. I shall assume without argument that adequate professional instruction of teachers is not exclusively theoretical, but involves a certain amount of practical work. The primary question as to the latter is the aim with which it shall be conducted. Two controlling purposes may be entertained so different from each other as radically to alter the amount, conditions, and method of practice work. On one hand, we may carry on the practical work with the object of giving teachers in training working command of the necessary tools of their profession; control of the technique of class instruction and management; skill and proficiency in the work of teaching. With this aim in view, practice work is, as far as it goes, of the nature of apprenticeship. On the other hand, we may propose to use practice work as an instrument in making real and vital theoretical instruction; the knowledge of subject-matter and of principles of education. This is the laboratory point of view.

The contrast between the two points of view is obvious; and the two aims together give the limiting terms within which all practice work falls. From one point of view, the aim is to form and equip the actual teacher; the aim is immediately as well as ultimately practical. From the other point of view, the *immediate* aim, the way of getting at the ultimate aim, is to supply the intellectual method and material of good workmanship, instead of making on the spot, as it were, an efficient workman. Practice work thus considered is administered primarily with reference to the intellectual reactions it incites, giving the student a better hold upon the educational significance of the subject-matter he is acquiring, and of the science, philosophy, and history of education. Of course, the *results* are not exclusive. It would be very strange if practice work in doing what the laboratory does for a student of physics or chemistry in way of securing a more vital understanding of its principles, should not at the same time insure some skill in the instruction and management of a class. It would also be peculiar if the process of acquiring such skill should not also incidentally serve to enlighten and enrich instruction in subject-matter and the theory of education. None the less, there is a fundamental difference in the conception and conduct of the practice work according as one idea or the other is dominant and the other subordinate. If the primary object of practice is acquiring skill in performing the duties of a teacher, then the amount of time given to practice work, the place at which it is introduced, the method of conducting it, of supervising, criticising, and correlating it, will differ widely from the method where the laboratory ideal prevails; and *vice versa.*

In discussing this matter; I shall try to present what I have termed the laboratory, as distinct from the apprentice idea. While I speak primarily from the standpoint of the college, I should not be frank if I did not say that I believe what I am going to say holds, *mutatis mutandis,* for the normal school as well.

I. I first adduce the example of other professional schools. I doubt whether we, as educators, keep in mind with sufficient constancy the fact that the problem of training teachers is one species of a more generic affair—that of training for professions. Our problem is akin to that of training architects, engineers, doctors, lawyers, etc. Moreover, since (shameful and incredible as it seems) the vocation of teaching is practically the last to recognize the need of specific professional preparation, there is all the more reason for teachers to try to find what they may learn from the more extensive and matured experience of other callings. If now we turn to what has happened in the history of training for other professions, we find the following marked tendencies:

1. The demand for an increased amount of scholastic attainments as a

prerequisite for entering upon professional work.

2. Development of certain lines of work in the applied sciences and arts, as centers of professional work; compare, for example, the place occupied by chemistry and physiology in medical training at present, with that occupied by chairs of "practice" and of *materia medica*'' a generation ago.

3. Arrangement of the practical and quasi-professional work upon the assumption that (limits of time, etc., being taken into account) the professional school does its best for its students when it gives them typical and intensive, rather than extensive and detailed, practice. It aims, in a word, at *control of the intellectual methods* required for personal and independent mastery of practical skill, rather than at turning out at once masters of the craft. This arrangement necessarily involves considerable postponement of skill in the routine and technique of the profession, until the student, after graduation, enters upon the pursuit of his calling.

These results are all the more important to us because other professional schools mostly started from the same position which training schools for teachers have occupied. Their history shows a period in which the idea was that students ought from the start to be made as proficient as possible in practical skill. In seeking for the motive forces which have caused professional schools to travel so steadily away from this position and toward the idea that practical work should be conducted for the sake of vitalizing and illuminating *intellectual* methods two reasons may be singled out:

a) First, the limited time at the disposal of the schools, and the consequent need of economy in its employ. It is not necessary to assume that apprenticeship is of itself a bad thing. On the contrary, it may be admitted to be a good thing; but the time which a student spends in the training school is short at the best. Since short, it is an urgent matter that it be put to its most effective use; and, relatively speaking, the wise employ of this short time is in laying scientific foundations. These cannot be adequately secured when one is doing the actual work of the profession, while professional life does afford time for acquiring and perfecting skill of the more technical sort.

b) In the second place, there is inability to furnish in the school adequate conditions for the best acquiring and using of skill. As compared with actual practice, the best that the school of law or medicine can do is to provide a somewhat remote and simulated copy of the real thing. For such schools to attempt to give the skill which comes to those adequately prepared, insensibly and unavoidably in actual work, is the same sort of thing as for grammar schools to spend months upon months in trying to convey (usually quite unsuccessfully) that skill in commercial arithmetic which comes, under penalty of practical failure, in a few weeks in the bank or counting-house.

It may be said that the analogy does not hold good for teachers' training schools, because such institutions have model or practice departments, supplying conditions which are identical with those which the teacher has to meet in the actual pursuit of his calling. But this is true at most only in such normal schools as are organized after the Oswego pattern—schools, that is to say, where the pupil-teacher is given for a considerable period of time the entire charge of instruction and discipline in the class-room, and does not come under a room critic-teacher. In all other cases, some of the most fundamentally significant features of the real school are reduced or eliminated. Most "practice schools" are a compromise. In theory they approximate ordinary conditions. As matter of fact, the "best interests of the children" are so safeguarded and supervised that the situation approaches learning to swim without going *too* near the water.

There are many ways that do not strike one at first glance, for removing the conditions of "practice work" from those of actual teaching. Deprivation of responsibility for the discipline of the room; the continued presence of an expert ready to suggest, to take matters into his own hands; close supervision; reduction of size of group taught; etc., etc., are some of these ways. The topic of "lesson plans" will be later referred to in connection with another topic. Here they may be alluded to as constituting one of the modes in which the conditions of the practice-teacher are made unreal. The student who prepares a number of more or less set lessons; who then has those lesson plans criticised; who then has his actual teaching criticised from the standpoint of success in carrying out the prearranged plans, is in a totally different attitude from the teacher who has to build up and modify his teaching plans as he goes along from experience gained in contact with pupils.

It would be difficult to find two things more remote from each other than the development of subject-matter under such control as is supplied from actual teaching, taking effect through the teacher's own initiative and reflective criticism, and its development with an eye fixed upon the judgment, presumed and actual, of a superior supervisory officer. Those phases of the problem of practice teaching which relate more distinctly to responsibility for the discipline of the room, or of the class, have received considerable attention in the past; but the more delicate and far-reaching matter of intellectual responsibility is too frequently ignored. Here centers the problem of securing conditions which will make practice work a genuine apprenticeship.

II. To place the emphasis upon the securing of proficiency in teaching and discipline *puts the attention of the student-teacher in the wrong place, and tends to fix it in the wrong direction*—not wrong absolutely, but relatively as regards perspective of needs and opportunities. The would-be teacher has some time or other to face and solve two problems, each extensive and serious enough by itself to demand absorbing and undivided attention. These two problems are:

1. Mastery of subject-matter from the standpoint of its educational value and use; or, what is the same thing, the mastery of educational principles in their application to that subject-matter which is at once the material of instruction and the basis of discipline and control;

2. The mastery of the technique of class management.

This does not mean that the two problems are in any way isolated or independent. On the contrary, they are strictly correlative. *But the mind of a student cannot give equal attention to both at the same time.*

The difficulties which face a beginning teacher, who is set down for the first time before a class of from thirty to sixty children, in the responsibilities not only of instruction, but of maintaining the required order in the room as a whole, are most trying. It is almost impossible for an old teacher who has acquired the requisite skill of doing two or three distinct things simultaneously—skill to see the room as a whole while hearing one individual in one class recite, of keeping the program of the day and, yes, of the week and of the month in the fringe of consciousness while the work of the hour is in its center—it is almost impossible for such a teacher to realize all the difficulties that confront the average beginner.

There is a technique of teaching, just as there is a technique of piano-playing. The technique, if it is to be educationally effective, is dependent upon principles. But it is possible for a student to acquire outward form of method without capacity to put it to genuinely educative use. As every teacher knows, children have an inner and an outer attention. The inner attention is the giving of the mind without reserve or qualification to the subject in hand. It is the first-hand and personal play of mental powers. As such, it is a fundamental condition of mental growth. To be able to keep track of this mental play, to recognize the signs of its presence or absence, to know how it is initiated and maintained, how to test it by results attained, and to test *apparent* results by it, is the supreme mark and criterion of a teacher. It means insight into soul-action, ability to discriminate the genuine from the sham, and capacity to further one and discourage the other.

External attention, on the other hand, is that given to the book or teacher as an independent object. It is manifested in certain conventional postures and physical attitudes rather than in the movement of thought. Children acquire great dexterity in exhibiting in conventional and expected ways the *form* of attention to school work, while reserving the inner play of their own thoughts, images, and emotions for subjects that are more important to them, but quite irrelevant.

Now, the teacher who is plunged prematurely into the pressing and practical problem of keeping order in the schoolroom has almost of necessity to make supreme the matter of external attention. The teacher has not yet had the training which affords psychological insight—which enables him to judge promptly (and therefore almost automatically) the kind and mode of subject-matter which the pupil needs at a given moment to keep his attention moving forward effectively and healthfully. He does know, however, that he must maintain order; that he must keep the attention of the pupils fixed upon his own questions, suggestions, instructions, and remarks, and upon their "lessons." The inherent tendency of the situation therefore is for him to acquire his technique in relation to the outward rather than the inner mode of attention.

III. Along with this fixation of attention upon the secondary at the expense of the primary problem, *there goes the formation of habits of work which have an empirical, rather than a scientific, sanction.* The student adjusts his actual methods of teaching, not to the principles which he is acquiring, but to what he sees succeed and fail in an empirical way from moment to moment; to what he sees other teachers doing who are more experienced and successful in keeping order than he is; and to the injunctions and directions given him by others. In this way the controlling habits of the teacher finally get fixed with comparatively little reference to principles in the psychology, logic, and history of education. In theory, these latter are dominant; in practice, the moving forces are the devices and methods which are picked up through blind experimentation; through examples which are not rationalized; through precepts which are more or less arbitrary and mechanical; through advice based upon the experience of others. Here we have the explanation, in considerable part at least, of the dualism, the unconscious duplicity, which is one of the chief evils of the teaching profession. There is an enthusiastic devotion to certain principles of lofty theory in the abstract—principles of self-activity, self-control, intellectual and moral—and there is a school practice taking little heed of the official pedagogic creed. Theory and practice do not grow together out of and into the teacher's personal experience.

Ultimately there are two bases upon which the habits of a teacher as a teacher may be built up. They may be formed under the inspiration and constant criticism of intelligence, applying the best that is available. This is possible only where the would-be teacher has become fairly saturated with his subject-matter, and with his psychological and ethical philosophy of education. Only when such things have become incorporated in mental habit, have become part of the working tendencies of observation, insight, and reflection, will these principles work automatically, unconsciously, and hence promptly and effectively. And this means that practical work should be pursued primarily with reference to its reaction upon the professional pupil in making him a thoughtful and alert student of education, rather than to help him get immediate proficiency.

THE MOVE TO TRANSFORM NORMAL SCHOOLS INTO COLLEGES

(1912)   From *Seventh Annual Report of the Carnegie Foundation for the Advancement of Teaching* (New York, 1912), pp. 149–52.

How great a part personal and institutional ambition has played in the development of educational politics it would be difficult to say, but the results of it can be seen in every state where the divided institution exists. These appear usually in two forms: first, the endeavor of each institution to cover the whole field of education and the consequent duplications which ensue; secondly, the widespread tendency to drop the legitimate work for which the institution was founded in order to take up some other work, which appeals to the ambitions of its president, or of its board of trustees, or of its faculty or alumni.

Examples of the first sort have just been alluded to. Other examples in the educational history of Iowa, Colorado, Michigan, and various other states will readily occur to the reader. . . .

Where three or four state institutions exist, this rivalry has inevitably led to much commerce with the legislature, to overlapping institutions, and in nearly all cases to a strenuous struggle for students. The three-cornered rivalry between the university, the agricultural and mechanical college, and the normal school in the states like Iowa and Kansas are typical instances of the results of such a regime.

A singular outcome of this situation in recent years has been the effort of the normal school in many states to transform itself into an arts college. The normal school is at best a singular institution, seldom related logically to the educational system of its state. Its weakness from the educational point of view lies in the fact that it undertakes to make a teacher of a man or woman whose education is so limited as to afford slender basis for a teacher's training. From the time of Horace Mann, however, it has been the agency upon which our states have come more and more to depend for the training of teachers for the elementary schools, and particularly for the rural elementary schools, since the larger cities have in many cases provided agencies to train teachers for their own schools. Notwithstanding its educational isolation, some such agency as the normal school seems necessary at the present stage of our educational organization, and probably will be necessary for many years to come. When one considers that in many of the middle western states not more than ten per cent of all the public school teachers had had the equivalent of a high school education, one realizes that in order to obtain the necessary teachers for the common schools of the country, some agency must for a long time prepare a large number as best it may. One may well hope that the low standards of training for rural teachers now in use in many states may be raised, and that the necessary number of teachers may be forthcoming at a continually higher level, and that school teachers may soon be themselves fairly educated men and women. In any case the function of the normal school in our present situation is definite, clear, and of immense importance. It is therefore little less than astounding to find normal schools in so many states ready to turn aside from this definite and important work, in the effort to transform themselves into weak colleges, and this, too, in states where the number of such colleges is already larger than the ability of the population to sustain. This movement has arisen in some cases out of the ambitions of the heads of these institutions and of their faculties, who somehow have the mistaken feeling that the work of the college is more honorable and more desirable. In some cases it has been undertaken with the honest belief that the two institutions, college and normal school, would grow side by side, a result which would be against all our educational experience; but from whatever motive undertaken, it has inevitably involved these schools in politics.

An illustration of such legislation is found in the measure passed by the last session of the Wisconsin legislature to the following effect: "The Board of Normal School regents may extend the course of instruction in any normal school so that any course, the admission to which is based upon graduation from an accredited high school or its equivalent, may include the substantial equivalent of the instruction given in the first two years of a college course. Such course of instruction shall not be extended further than the substantial equivalent of the instruction given in such college course without the consent of the legislature."

This language is capable of at least two interpretations. It might mean the extension of the normal school course for two years along normal school and pedagogical lines equivalent in intellectual demand to the corresponding years in college, thereby training a better teacher, or it might mean the superimposing on the normal school of two years of ordinary college work. Apparently both of these ideas were in the minds of those interested in the legislation. As a matter of fact, however, the normal schools have immediately translated this legislation into the authority for establishing the first two years of an arts college.

It requires no prophet to see whither this movement leads. Under the arrangement college students and normal school students are in the same classes. It will not be long before there is an attempt to so extend the curriculum that the equivalent of four college years will be given. Already the normal schools are introducing technical studies and asking for credit for the first half of curricula in agriculture and engineering. There are in Wisconsin eight state normal schools, and more are in prospect. This movement means the transformation of these schools from institutions primarily designed for the training of teachers to colleges having the ordinary college atmosphere with all the distractions which differentiate the American college from the professional school. It may be wise for these professional schools to be transformed into colleges, but if this is to be done, it should come only after a fair and full discussion of the whole matter from the educational point of view. There are those who contend that the atmosphere and spirit of the present day college can be successfully grafted upon the professional school. Perhaps this is true, although the evidence would seem to be against it. The result of such a mixture is likely to be an institution lacking the best qualities of both. But in any case, such legislation should not be enacted until those responsible for it have had a full discussion of the whole matter by men familiar with educational problems and who are not directly interested in the problems either of the Wisconsin normal schools or the Wisconsin endowed colleges. Wisconsin has in many respects led the way among American commonwealths in the intelligent use of experts in the solution of legislative problems. This question is one which ought not to be legislated upon without the light of expert and unbiased educational judgment. To legislate on such a technical question in the absence of an expert survey of the problem is to legislate in the dark.

GEORGE COUNTS ON THE RIDDLE OF CONTROL OF THE SCHOOL
(1928) From George S. Counts, *School and Society in Chicago* (New York, 1928), pp. 349, 351–54, 357–58.

What solution may be offered to the problem that has been raised? How should these complicated systems of education be controlled in an industrial society? Perhaps there is no solution. Perhaps there is no wholly satisfactory method of controlling the school. One might even argue that there is no problem. It is conceivable that the brand of educational control that Chicago has had is the brand that the people of Chicago want. If this be true, then why should a stranger feel concern over the situation there? Moreover, for ages educational reformers have insisted that the relationship between the school and society should be intimate. Clearly no one would question the intimacy of the relationship in Chicago today. Yet, as one reviews the recent history of education in this city, one feels that the contacts between the people and their schools are superficial, spasmodic, and unsymmetrical. The remedy therefore would not seem to lie in the withdrawal of the school from society, but rather in the development of a more stable, enduring, and balanced connection. A form of control is desired which will protect the school against the assaults of selfish interests and the passions of the mob, but which at the same time will make it responsive to the more fundamental changes in society and the more solid advances in professional knowledge.

✻   ✻   ✻

If the city of Chicago were converted into a half dozen or a dozen separate units, the heterogeneity of the social medium would no doubt be considerably reduced; but the lines of division would of necessity be more or less arbitrary and would perhaps create more difficulties than they would resolve. Before the rise of the great systems of education the American city experimented sufficiently with this type of organization to discover its defects. The other proposal, that the unit be enlarged, possibly possesses certain merits from the standpoint of administration and the equalization of opportunity between the more needy and the more opulent communities, but it could hardly be defended in terms of the simplification of the social situation. If the size of the unit of control were increased, certain petty influences which agitate the schools at present might drop out of the picture, but only because of the emergence of an array of forces on a larger scale. The suggestion that a mere change in the area embraced by a single administrative organization is sufficient seems to be derived from an inadequate analysis of the problem.

Because of the brazen attack of the political machine on Mr. McAndrew and many of his predecessors in Chicago, as well as because of similar attacks on his colleagues in other cities, numerous students of education have argued that the road to freedom in the schools lies in the direction of the increase of the power of the superintendent. . . .

*　*　*

But the proposals advanced thus far seem to reflect an inadequate grasp of the question. They appear to imply that the major task before us is that of insulating the school from corrupt political influences. This may be the negative aspect of the task, but the present survey of the Chicago situation shows that the problem strikes much deeper. One of the most disconcerting conclusions emerging from a first-hand study of the schools in this city is the conviction that the great body of persons, regardless of the side on which they fight, are entirely honest and sincere. Some of the forces which play upon the schools are selfish, dishonest, and corrupt, but to assume that the question is merely a moral question is grievously to misread the facts. If the willfully vicious factor were ruled out entirely, the situation would be simplified but little. The competitive struggles of group, sect, race, class, and occupation, as well as the indifference and ignorance of great numbers of citizens, would still remain.

Moreover, unless the term *politics* is to carry exclusively the invidious connotation of the subordination of the public interest to the personal fortunes of politicians, to say that politics should be kept out of the schools is fatuous. It is worse. It is to admit that the impulses which created the American nation have spent themselves. Nothing could render public education more sterile than to remove from it the very forces which a century ago gave it the breath of life. When politics have become so evil that their touch defiles the school, then indeed have both school and society begun to decay. Such a condition means that the purposes of the social order have been achieved and that the future holds no promise. Therefore, rather than seek refuge in the cautious counsel of removing the school from politics, we should move forward under the assumption that the real business of politics is to provide the channels through which the living energies of society may flow into new forms and patterns. The great desideratum, as already stated, is to devise some means of making the school responsive to the more fundamental social realities and of enabling it at the same time to maintain an even keel amid the clash and roar of the contending elements.

There is, of course, no proposal that can be advanced with even a fair measure of optimism. In charting his course through the mazes of industrialism the boldest mariner must experience a feeling of profound timidity, for society has never been this way before. There are no familiar stars to show the way, the compass seems to have lost its precision, and even the magnetic pole appears to be shifting its position from moment to moment. Yet the situation is not without its ray of hope. From a study of the condition of public education in Chicago or any great American city, as well as from other sources, including the experience of foreign countries, come two suggestions which seem to possess some merit. According to the one, the more important points of view found in the community should be frankly recognized and given representation on the board of education; according to the other, the authority of the professional staff should be greatly increased. The argument in favor of each of these proposals is fairly plain.

*　*　*

Let the employing groups, the working-classes, the women's clubs, the more important religious sects, and other groups have their representatives on the board. Recourse to the methods of indirection would then be unnecessary, and genuine differences would be brought out into the clear sunlight of discussion. Since such an arrangement would in a sense merely regularize practices already in existence, it is much less radical than it may appear. It would create no new forces. Rather it would provide channels through which forces now at work might function more honestly and effectively. The representatives of capital and labor, for example, instead of speaking to each other through the columns of the daily press or the idle chatter of the street, would sit face to face across the conference table. It would likewise lay the pious fiction that no real differences exist in society, and at the same time it would make impossible the imposition of a single point of view upon the schools or the use of the system of public education as an instrument of narrow indoctrination. What methods should be employed in selecting the representatives of the different interests is a practical question which does not concern us here. The major consideration is to insure to each major legitimate interest in the city an opportunity to make itself heard. Thus the play of social forces upon the school, which today is constantly disrupting the program of instruction, might be turned to a useful purpose and be made to contribute to the formulation of a stable but ever-growing policy of public education.

The creation of a genuinely representative board of control, however, does not in itself insure the development of a satisfactory relationship between school and society. The task is but half completed. Only one of the two partners to the enterprise of public education has been considered. To be sure, if the system of instruction were simple, as it was in the old agrarian civilization, no difficulty would remain. But the school has changed with the changing society. The little red schoolhouse with its one teacher has evolved into the great city system. Moreover, the business of education has become so complicated that its successful management requires the services of specially trained persons. While the layman must continue to bear the burden of formulating general policies, the translation of these policies into educational programs and procedures is the responsibility of the teaching profession.

RECOMMENDATIONS OF THE AMERICAN HISTORICAL ASSOCIATION FOR A NEW TEACHER TRAINING (1934)   From American Historical Association, Report of the Commission on the Social Studies, *Conclusions and Recommendations* (New York, 1934), pp. 107, 110–14.

1. The kind of training which is appropriate for the teacher depends upon how the function of teaching is conceived. If it is conceived in terms of the practice of a narrow technique which is to be mastered in all of its rigid detail, the pattern of training to be followed should be like that of one of the more exact professions, such as mechanical engineering; but if it is conceived in terms of the application of broad and diverse fields of knowledge, thought, and ideal to the physical, intellectual, and moral growth of the child and to the transformation and

enrichment of culture, then the pattern of training to be followed should be like that suited to the education of the artist, the poet, the statesman, the spiritual leader of mankind.

2. The Commission takes this second conception of teaching; its members have argued at various places in their individual reports that education should be regarded as involving a peculiarly high and disinterested form of leadership.

*　　*　　*

7. If teachers of the social sciences in the schools are to be prepared for the performance of the tasks outlined in the present report, this old breach must be healed; students of the social sciences will have to view education as one of the main channels through which their work may find fruition; and persons engaged in teacher training will have to become earnest students of human society. Fortunately a movement in this direction is already discernible.

8. For great university departments to refuse to relate their work to the tasks of education will scarcely be tolerated in a closely integrated economy managed in the interests of society; for teacher training institutions to fail to make full use of social knowledge and thought in the formulation of their policies should be regarded as a gross neglect of duty.

9. The Commission, refusing to take sides in this struggle of vested interests in higher education, proposes: (a) a vigorous searching of hearts by specialists in subject matter and in methodology; (b) a reunion in both instances of specialty with the living tree of knowledge and thought; and (c) a revaluation of subject matter and methodology with reference to social purpose rather than in terms of abstract logic and schemes of organization.

10. In practical outcome, this will mean: (a) a drastic reduction in the number of highly specialized courses in history, politics, economics, and sociology offered to teachers in colleges and universities; (b) the establishment of general and balanced courses in these subjects for teachers; (c) the organization of seminars in which teachers may receive rigorous training in those methods of research, bibliographical operations, analysis, verification, synthesis, and criticism indispensable to the advancement of learning and effective instruction.

11. In the field of teacher training this will mean: (a) a drastic curtailment in the number of courses—often thin, arid, and duplicating—offered in the principles and methods of education; (b) an insistence that persons engaged in training teachers in various branches of learning shall, first of all, be competent scholars in these fields; (c) the abandonment of the conception of a distinct "science of education" and the reunion of education with the great streams of human knowledge, thought, and aspiration—empirical, ethical, and aesthetic.

12. These proposals imply the dominance neither of that anomalous profession known as "subject matter specialists" nor of that equally anomalous group called "educational specialists"; they imply a radical reformation of both traditions and a close co-operation among the individuals in both groups who possess some sense of humor, some breadth of view, some capacity for thinking through and around their own operations, and some feeling of responsibility to the society which nourishes them and to the world in which they live.

13. These proposals imply further that the old division between colleges and universities, on the one side, and normal schools and teachers' colleges, on the other, must be abolished and the two institutions of thought and training united.

The weaker normal schools and teachers' colleges should be closed, while the remainder should become centers, not of pedagogy as traditionally conceived, but of knowledge and thought devoted to the organization and conduct of education as a focal point in the evolution of culture. Social science departments in the colleges and universities, besides discharging their other obligations to society, should turn their attention to the preparation of teachers and to the organization of materials of instruction for use in the schools.

14. When the philosophy, program, and purpose of instruction in the social sciences are thus clearly recognized and provisions made for the thorough preparation of teachers in knowledge and thought, the various forms of pedagogical prestidigitation, such as the unit method, the correlation method, the radiation method, the fusion method, the concomitant method, the dioptric method, and the penetralia method, appear in their true light as empty formalisms.

15. In summary, an institution for the preparation of social science teachers should be a center for introducing young men and women to a realistic knowledge of the trends, tensions, and conflicts of American society in its world setting, for bringing them into close and living connection with all the great systems of social thought—ancient, modern, and contemporary,—and for revealing to them the magnificent potentialities of science in the realization of the finest dreams of mankind.

AN ACCOUNT OF THE PASSING OF THE TEACHERS COLLEGE

(1957)   From Karl W. Bigelow, "The Passing of the Teachers College," *Teachers College Record*, vol. LVIII, pp. 409–12.

In 1938 the American Association of Teachers Colleges was approximately at the height of its position as a representative of the teachers colleges of America. To be sure it still included at one end of the scale a small number of normal schools, and at the other an even smaller number of university schools and colleges of education. The former were a reminder of the past, the latter—as it was to turn out—a harbinger of the future. The remaining normal schools would soon themselves become teachers colleges. But the number of schools of education in the AATC would increase steadily until, with the creation of the American Association of Colleges for Teacher Education in 1948, this body would become as representative of them as of the teachers colleges.

Two significant future developments, however, were only beginning to make themselves felt in 1938. The implications of one were, I think, wholly unrecognized. This was the presence in the membership list of a single, lonely college of liberal arts. Today the AACTE has a considerable and steadily growing representation from liberal arts circles, but I doubt if any AATC leaders in 1938 foresaw that development.

Of the second development, already under way at that time, there was much greater awareness. This one was represented by the member institutions from California and Ohio. Both sets, in general, had been founded as normal schools and had later become teachers colleges. But those in California had already, by 1938, dropped the word "teachers" from their titles, had become "state colleges," and had begun to offer at least liberal arts or general curricula in addition to those designed for teacher education. The Ohio institutions had made similar program changes, but called themselves "state universities."

In 1938 this kind of movement was viewed apprehensively by AATC leaders, almost all of whom were heads of institutions that had teacher education as their sole and exclusive business. The normal school had been a single-purpose institution and it had learned to emphasize the advantages of such an arrangement. The teachers colleges, which emerged from the normal school chrysalis, naturally maintained this same point of view. The way to prepare teachers was to catch them young and bring them up in an atmosphere in which teacher education was the dominant—preferably, indeed, the exclusive—concern of everyone with whom they would come in contact. It was inevitable that strong criticism should be aroused when some teachers colleges began to expand their functions, particularly when they dropped from their titles all words suggestive of their traditional job.

In the AATC membership list of 1938—leaving out of account the one college of liberal arts and the handful of full-fledged universities—93 percent of the member institutions had names that included the word "normal," or "teachers," or "education." Only 4 per cent called themselves "state colleges," and only 3 per cent just plain "institutes," "colleges," or "universities." The AATC was an organization of institutions which were, with rare exceptions, exclusively devoted to teacher education.

The teachers colleges of course had developed from normal schools. Everybody knows that to be the case. But not everybody is aware how rapidly that change took place. Because I was planning to compare the AATC membership list of 1938 with the AACTE list of 1956, eighteen years later, it struck me that it would be interesting to take a look at the situation eighteen years earlier, that is in 1920. The list of institutions on which I focused my attention was made up of all those that belonged to the AATC in 1938 which were still members of the AACTE in 1956, excluding—as I noted above—the one 1938 liberal arts member and the handful of big university members of that same date. These exclusions left a population of 164 institutions, which can be considered to include the bulk of all those American institutions that have ever been considered "teachers colleges."

As late as 1920, however—the first of my three years of comparison—only about one-sixth of this group of institutions had achieved degree-granting status. Four-fifths were still normal schools, the remainder not having yet even come into existence. But in the eighteen years between 1920 and 1938 the proportions were reversed—by the latter date only about one tenth *remained* normal schools. The great majority—about three-quarters—now both were and called themselves "teachers colleges," while the addition of those institutions which preferred the names "normal college" or "university" on the one hand, or "college of education" on the other, brought the proportion of four-year, degree-granting institutions specializing in teacher education up to 82 per cent. The change that had taken place in less than two decades had been enormous. Moreover, as I have already suggested, there was an all but universal feeling that the new situation would and should prove relatively permanent. The teachers colleges, it was assumed, had come to stay.

But now let us take a look at what has happened to our 164 institutions during the eighteen years *since* 1938. None, of course, remains a normal school, and only three retain the word "normal" in their titles—now "normal college" or "university." But the word "teachers" has also proved to be only a temporary part of many institutional names. I just stated that in 1938 about three-quarters of the institutions I have been studying "both were and called themselves 'teachers colleges.' " By 1956 the proportion using that title had fallen below one-half and the proportion actually limiting themselves to teacher education considerably below that. Moreover, the name "college of education" had not caught on—a few more normal schools had adopted this as their new title, but almost as many of the earlier "colleges of education" had dropped the qualifying phrase—had become plain "colleges."[1]

As a matter of fact it is the flight from qualifying words and phrases, such as "normal," "teachers," and "education," that is particularly striking. Only slightly over one-half of the 164 institutions still employed them in 1956—and I have no doubt that that proportion has decreased in the past year. The popular move has been to the name "state college," although even the word "state" is increasingly dispensed with.

Now I do not want to make too much of changes in names, it being notorious that function cannot safely be inferred from the title of an American institution of higher education. So let me turn to evidence respecting function. This is readily attainable—for 1956 with some exactness through use of the classification provided by the United States Office of Education. The results of inquiry regarding function more than confirm the implications of our study of changing nomenclature. In 1920, 98 per cent of my 164 institutions were classifiable as "primarily teacher-preparatory"; in 1938 that proportion had fallen only very slightly, to 92 per cent; but by 1956 the figure had plummeted to 38 per cent. This was only slightly larger than the percentage of the whole group classified last year, as to curricula, as "Both liberal arts and general *and* teacher-preparatory," which in turn only slightly exceeded the proportion offering, in addition to that combination, one or more other professional or vocational courses of study.

On the basis of all this evidence I have reached the conclusion that the teachers college—in the strict sense of that term—is going to turn out to have been a temporary phenomenon in American higher education. Let me drive my point home in another way. Forty-five states in the Union were represented in the AACTE in 1956. In only twenty-six were any "state teachers colleges" or "colleges of education" still listed—and in only twenty-two (less than half of the total) were a majority of institutions that had originally been exclusively teacher-preparatory still called by such names.

To repeat my conclusion, the teachers college as we knew it twenty years ago is on the way to oblivion. It is proving to have been a way-station between the normal school and the state college—whether or not so called—a multi-purpose institution for which teacher education is only one among several functions. I venture to prophesy that in another couple of decades the name "state teachers college" will have disappeared except, possibly, in a few backward states like New York which, even as late as 1938, was resisting letting its normal schools grow up. (And even Massachusetts, New Jersey, New York, and Pennsylvania, demonstrably among the most backward states in the use of public funds for the provision of higher educational opportunity for their young citizens, may well have their hands forced when the prospective enormous increase in population of college age materializes.)

[1] An instructive example is the institution that was established in Kalamazoo as Western State Normal School in 1903. It became Western State Teachers College in 1927; Western Michigan College of Education in 1941; and Western Michigan College in 1955. The name is now Western Michigan University.

My prophecy as to the prospective disappearance of the teachers college is not made with any particular satisfaction. It did not take long, after my first association with those colleges in 1938, for me to become deeply appreciative of their devotion to the cause of teacher education—to which I myself was so deeply committed—and of their great merits as institutions of higher education. For sentimental reasons, certainly, the prospect of their passing saddens me. I am not prepared to declare that what is happening to them represents forward movement in any positive sense. But the prospect has suddenly become perfectly clear to me—and we shall have to make our calculations and plans accordingly.

ORGANIZATION OF A NATIONAL ACADEMY OF EDUCATION

(**1965**) From *National Academy of Education: Background, Activities, Constitution, Membership* (Syracuse, 1969), pp. 22–23, 30–35.

Constitution[1]

Article I

NAME

The name of this corporation shall be "The National Academy of Education."

Article II

PURPOSE

The purpose of the National Academy of Education shall be to promote scholarly inquiry and discussion concerning the ends and means of education, in all of its forms, in the United States and abroad. To this end, the Academy shall serve as a forum for conversation, debate, and mutual instruction; a rostrum for the communication of accurate information and informed opinion; and a stimulus for imaginative and fruitful research. The Academy may also, to the extent it deems wise and feasible, serve as a source of counsel for such public and private agencies as require and request it.

Article III

MEMBERSHIP

Section 1: The Academy shall consist of a maximum of fifty members, including those named in the Act of Incorporation, and such others, citizens of the United States, as shall from time to time be elected to membership.

Section 2: The Members of the Academy shall be predominately persons whose

[1]As amended May 19, 1968.

scholarly and scientific writings bearing on the subject of education are judged outstanding. The Members shall be arranged in four Sections, each of which shall have a maximum enrollment of ten: (1) The History and Philosophy of Education; (2) The Politics, Economics, Sociology and Anthropology of Education; (3) The Psychology of Education; and (4) The Study of Educational Practice. In addition, a maximum of ten persons, whose accomplishments in the field of education are judged outstanding but whose writings need not identify them with one of the Sections, may be elected Members-at-Large.

OFFICERS

Section 3: Upon reaching the age of 70, a Member shall become a Member Emeritus in the Academy, and his place on the roster of Membership shall be declared vacant by the Secretary. Members Emeriti shall have the privilege of attending the meetings of the Academy and taking part in its business (without vote), of reading and communicating papers to it, and of receiving its publications, but shall not be subject to its assessments. In exceptional circumstances, the Academy may, upon nomination of the Council, elect Members directly to Emeritus status.

Section 4: The Academy may elect not more than twenty-five Foreign Associates, who shall have the privilege of attending the meetings of the Academy, of reading and communicating papers to it, and of receiving its publications, but who shall take no part in its business, and shall not be subject to its assessments. Upon reaching the age of 70, a Foreign Associate shall assume Emeritus status in the Academy, and his place on the roster of Foreign Associates shall be declared vacant by the Secretary; but he shall continue to enjoy all of his former privileges. In exceptional circumstances, the Academy may, upon nomination by the Council, elect Foreign Associates directly to Emeritus status.

*   *   *

ACADEMY MEMBERSHIP, SPRING 1969

JAMES E. ALLEN, JR.
Member-at-Large
Elected 1968

Commissioner of Education
The University of the State
of New York; Commissioner
Designate, United States Office
of Education

SIR ERIC ASHBY
Foreign Associate
Elected 1966

Master, Clare College
Cambridge, England

STEPHEN K. BAILEY
(Secretary-Treasurer)
Member, Section II
Founding Member

Chairman, Policy Institute
Syracuse University Research
Corporation and Maxwell
Professor of Political Science
Syracuse University

BERNARD BAILYN
Member, Section I
Founding Member

Winthrop Professor of History
Harvard University

GARY S. BECKER
Member, Section II
Founding Member

Professor of Economics
Columbia University

BRUNO BETTELHEIM
Member, Section III
Founding Member

Stella M. Rowley Professor of
Education and Professor in the
Department of Psychology and
Psychiatry, University of Chicago
and Principal of the Orthogenic
School, University of Chicago

BENJAMIN S. BLOOM
(Chairman, Section III)
Elected 1966

Professor of Education
University of Chicago

JEROME S. BRUNER
Member, Section III
Founding Member

Professor of Psychology
Harvard University

SIR CYRIL L. BURT
Foreign Associate Emeritus
Elected 1966

Professor Emeritus of Psychology
University College, London

ROALD F. CAMPBELL
Member, Section IV
Founding Member

William Claude Reavis Professor
and Chairman, Department of
Education, Dean, Graduate School
of Education, University of Chicago

JOHN B. CARROLL
Member, Section III
Founding Member

Senior Research Psychologist
Educational Testing Service

JOHN L. CHILDS
Member Emeritus
Elected 1966

Professor of Education Emeritus
Teachers College, Columbia
University

KENNETH B. CLARK
Member, Section IV
Elected 1968

President, Metropolitan Applied
Research Center, Professor of
Psychology, City College of the
City University of New York

JAMES S. COLEMAN
Member, Section II
Elected 1966

Professor of Social Relations
The Johns Hopkins University

JAMES B. CONANT
Member Emeritus
Elected 1965

President Emeritus
Harvard University

LAWRENCE A. CREMIN
(Chairman, Section I)
Founding Member

Frederick A.P. Barnard Professor
of Education, Teachers College
Columbia University

GEORGE S. COUNTS
Member Emeritus
Elected 1965

Distinguished Visiting Professor
College of Education
Southern Illinois University

LEE J. CRONBACH
Member, Section III
Founding Member

Vida Jacks Professor of Education
Stanford University

ERIK H. ERIKSON
Member, Section III
Elected 1967

Professor of Human Development
Lecturer in Psychiatry
Harvard University

JOHN H. FISCHER
Member-at-Large
Elected 1968

President
Teachers College
Columbia University

WILLIAM K. FRANKENA
Member, Section I
Founding Member

Professor of Philosophy
University of Michigan

JOHN W. GARDNER
Member-at-Large
Elected 1968

Chairman
The Urban Coalition

ARTHUR I. GATES
Member Emeritus
Elected 1965

Professor Emeritus
Teachers College
Columbia University

J. W. GETZELS
(Chairman, Section IV)
Elected 1967

Professor of Education and
Psychology, University of Chicago

JOHN I. GOODLAD
Member, Section IV
Founding Member

Dean, Graduate School of Education
University of California at
Los Angeles

FREDERICK H. HARBISON
Member, Section II
Elected 1967

Director, Industrial Relations
Section
Professor of Economics, Princeton
University

[1] Deceased

JACQUES MARITAIN
Foreign Associate Emeritus
Elected 1966

Professor Emeritus
Princeton University

MARK A. MAY
Member Emeritus
Elected 1966

Professor Emeritus of Educational
Psychology
Yale University

T. R. MC CONNELL
Member, Section IV
Founding Member

Chairman, Center for the Study of
Higher Education
University of California, Berkeley

ROBERT K. MERTON
Member, Section II
Founding Member

Giddings Professor of Sociology
Columbia University

RICHARD S. PETERS
Foreign Associate
Elected 1966

Professor of Philosophy of
Education
University of London
Institute of Education

JEAN PIAGET
Foreign Associate Emeritus
Elected 1966

Professor of Child Psychology
and History of Scientific Thought
Geneva University

SIDNEY L. PRESSEY
Member Emeritus
Elected 1965

Professor of Psychology (Emeritus)
College of Education
Ohio State University

DAVID RIESMAN
Member, Section II
Founding Member

Henry Ford II Professor of Social
Sciences
Harvard University

LORD ROBBINS
Foreign Associate Emeritus
Elected 1966

Lecturer in Economics
London School of Economics

ISRAEL SCHEFFLER
(Second Vice President)
Member, Section I
Founding Member

Victor S. Thomas Professor of
Education and Philosophy
Harvard University

THEODORE W. SCHULTZ
Member, Section II
Founding Member

Professor of Economics
University of Chicago

PATRICK SUPPES
Member, Section IV
Founding Member

Professor of Philosophy and
Statistics
Stanford University

THE HARVARD REPORT ON THE GRADUATE STUDY OF EDUCATION

(1966) From Theodore R. Sizer, "Foreword," *The Graduate Study of Education*
(Cambridge, Mass., 1966), pp. V–VI, VIII–IX.

A curious quality of education is that, while most persons experience it intimately, few study it in any serious way at all. In our hurry to purvey or consume it, we pause infrequently to question what we are up to. We are alternately too brash and too reactionary and always, it seems, too busy to decide which and why. More importantly, we are too caught up with pressing numbers and immediate crises to decide what we should be doing in the first place. So we stumble on, giving and receiving schooling without full reflection on the truly sophisticated and ethical practice it involves.

Presumably it is one function of universities to illumine the purposes and practices of the institutions of society, schools among them. Schools of education would seem to bear this responsibility, but casual inspection finds most of them not only overwhelmed with the magnitude of merely keeping the schools staffed, but also confused over how, even if there were time, resources, and imagination, to organize themselves to study the enterprise which they service. Further inquiry shows that schools of education differ widely in size, tradition, setting, and stated purpose. Clearly no single answer will solve for all of them the dual problem of responsibility for great numbers of students and confusion of purpose. Each institution or group of similar institutions must find its own solutions to these and other problems.

It was with these concerns that the Committee on the Graduate Study of Education was appointed at Harvard in 1964. The committee was charged to ask how this faculty of education, with its own set of strengths and weaknesses, could

THE
PROFESSION
OF EDUCATION

2685

best use its resources to study and improve the quality of education. It was asked to set priorities and provide a focus that would make sense for this particular university at this particular time. The faculty actions that followed (which, it should be noted, did not necessarily conform to the suggestions of the committee) are now made available to the community at large, as perhaps a useful example of how one school of education has assessed its function. The report does not recommend a particular detailed national blueprint; quite the contrary. It does suggest, however, an approach to the analysis of the problem faced by the committee. It speaks to Harvard and presumes little more. Yet it does speak, if with restraint, to the general question of how the study of education might be construed anywhere.

*   *   *

In many respects the Harvard report can be called remarkably conservative. It does not offer a new conception of "education": it deliberately disavows "education" as some kind of science or discipline. It suggests no radical pattern of organization or areas to be approached. It is an argument for balance and improvement of the best we know now. It is, thus, more a blueprint for reaching adequately our present goals than a statement of new direction. Given the popularity of educational "innovation" in these days, this conservative nature of the report may indeed be radical!

Appendix B outlines the details of faculty action on the report. Most important was the endorsement of an increased emphasis on doctoral studies and scholarship. While, owing to inadequate time, the committee did not specify the details of doctoral work to the extent of those for the master's degree, faculty committees have made progress on these matters during the 1965–66 academic year, as described in Appendix C. A much strengthened "clinical" master's degree has been approved, though in a more flexible form than the committee recommended. Key to this in an emphasis on a well-supervised, paid internship of up to a year's duration. Studies at Harvard would be of one year's length. Postdoctoral programs (or, more appropriately, "midcareer" sabbatical programs) and short-term nondegree institutes focused on currently critical areas have been endorsed.

The committee's rejection of a "discipline" of education is best symbolized by the adoption of six "areas" of faculty organization: teaching, guidance, administration, humanities, social sciences, and psychology. The first three focus on "clinical" problems: the teaching of the various subjects (the natural sciences, languages, and so forth), counseling, administration. The latter three include faculty from the traditional disciplines who are working through these to illumine and find solutions for problems in education. The areas overlap, and faculty have assumed membership in two or more; they differ from traditional "departments" in this sense and in the sense that the areas do not have budgetary responsibilities. Further, the areas symbolize the faculty's commitment both to applied and theoretical fields, to a carefully contrived wedding of theory and practice both in inquiry into the nature of the enterprise and in the training of practitioners. They imply a plan to maintain both the perspective of aloofness and the leavening of involvement, the wisdom gained both from detachment and commitment. The search for this mix is nothing new, but no institution has so far achieved it. The committee attempted to find an approach for this particular community, but the power of its argument should provoke useful consideration elsewhere.

The following report is, really, an affirmation that university schools of education can make a significant difference not only in supplying the raw material for the nation's schools but also the significant ideas upon which education must rest. It rests now with the faculty to see that this optimism was not misplaced.

*   *   *

Theodore R. Sizer
Dean, Harvard Graduate School of Education

Cambridge, Massachusetts
May 1966

The Teacher

ROBERT AND HELEN LYND ON THE TEACHER IN MIDDLETOWN
(1929) From Robert S. Lynd and Helen Lynd, *Middletown* (New York, 1929), pp. 206–10.

In the school as in the home, child-training is largely left to the womenfolk. Four-fifths of Middletown's teachers are women, the majority of them unmarried women under forty.[1] This is not the result of a definite policy, although the general sentiment of the community probably accords with at least the first half of the local editorial statement in 1900 that teaching is "an occupation for which women seem to have a peculiar fitness and a greater adaptability than men; but whether from their qualities of gentleness or from superior mental endowment is open to question." Actually, however, here as at so many other points in the city's life, money seems to be the controlling factor; more money elsewhere draws men away from teaching, rather than special fitness attracting women. Middletown pays its teachers more than it did thirty-five years ago,[2] but even the $2,100 maximum paid to grade school principals and high school teachers, the $3,200 paid to the high school principal, and the $4,900 to the Superintendent of Schools are hardly enough to tempt many of the abler men away from business in a culture in which everything hinges on money.

One becomes a teacher by doing a certain amount of studying things in books. All teachers today must have graduated from high school and have spent at least nine months in a recognized teacher-training college, while at least two years more of normal training or a college degree are necessary to teach in the high school. In 1890 the common practice was for new teachers to secure a license simply by passing an examination and then to begin by teaching in rural schools, whence they eventually graduated to city grade schools, and from them in turn moved up to the high school; today it is not uncommon for teachers who have had no experience in teaching, save possibly "practice teaching" in connection with normal school work,

---

[1] Twenty-one percent of 273 teachers (247 academic teachers, 15 principals, 6 supervisors, and 5 physical directors) in 1923–24 were men. Only two of the thirty-four teachers in 1889–90 were men. The increase in the proportion of men is largely accounted for by the introduction of vocational work and the greater use of men as principals of grade schools.

Between 1880 and 1914 the percentage of male teachers in the United States was more than halved, dropping from 43 per cent. to 20 per cent. (Ernest C. Moore, *Fifty Years of American Education: 1867–1917*, Boston; Ginn, 1918, pp. 60–61.) The percentage of men teachers in Middletown at present corresponds closely to the national figure.

[2] Cf. Lynd, Ch. VIII for rise in teachers' salaries since 1890 in relation to rise in cost of living.

to teach even in high school. For the most part, teachers in Middletown's schools today have more formal book training and less experience of dealing with children than those of a generation ago.[3] One sees in the high school young people, caught in the crosscurrents of a period of rapid change in many deep-lying institutional habits, being trained by teachers many of whom are only slightly older and less bewildered than their pupils. The whole situation is complicated by the fact that these young teachers go into teaching in many cases not primarily because of their ability or great personal interest in teaching; for very many of them teaching is just a job. The wistful remark of a high school teacher, "I just wasn't brought up to do anything interesting. So I'm teaching!" possibly represents the situation with many.

Cultural in-breeding is a dominant factor in the selection of teachers; for the most part, children are taught by teachers brought up in the same state. Preference tends to be given to Middletown's own teachers' training college and, failing that, to colleges in the state. A bill was even introduced into the legislature in 1924 providing that teachers' licenses be issued only to graduates of public high schools in the state. Of the 156 teachers and principals in 1923-24 who held a college or normal school diploma, degree, or certificate, only twenty-nine, less than a fifth, had received them from institutions outside the state.[4]

Two shifts in the general conditions surrounding teaching operate variously to lessen or to increase the handicaps of teachers selected and trained in the above fashion. On the one hand, class units are usually considerably smaller today; in 1923-24 there were thirty pupils per teacher as against fifty-eight in 1889-90.[5] Congestion in 1889-90 was greatest in the early years, some first-year classes numbering as many as eighty.

At the same time, a second trend operates to render it unnecessary for each teacher to spread herself over as much subject matter as formerly, but at the same time to allow her less contact with the individual student. From the fourth or fifth year on, a teacher becomes a specialized teacher of one subject to many groups instead of teaching a single group all their subjects for two years as was formerly the case; by the time a child reaches high school he has as many teachers as he has subjects. This becomes significant in view of the fact that in a period when the home is losing some of its close control of the child's activities to the school, the latter is likewise diminishing rather than increasing the former status of the teacher *in loco parentis*, through the teacher's having to concentrate more and more upon teaching subjects rather than upon teaching children. This situation is being met somewhat in the high school, as noted earlier, by the creation of a new type of teacher known as the "dean of girls"; the freeing of grade school principals of

[3] Of sixteen women teachers in the grades in 1889-90 of whose training some record could be found, ten had high school training, one had high school plus two years of normal training, three had high school plus six or twelve weeks of normal, one had a few weeks of normal but no high school, one had neither high school nor normal; of three high school teachers one, the principal, a man, was a graduate of the state university, and the other two of the high school. Of 268 teachers, principals, and supervisors in 1923-24 (excluding the five physical directors), fifty-six have college degrees; eight, college diplomas; three, college certificates; thirty have normal degrees; twenty-six, normal diplomas; thirty-three, normal certificates; 112 have no degree, diploma, or certificate from either college or normal, but are all high school graduates.

[4] A few of the others, following their first degree, had received some summer school or other professional training outside the state.

[5] Figures on the basis of the number of pupils enrolled. The number of teachers in 1923-24 is taken as 252, i.e., all teachers exclusive of principals and special supervisors. Principals are included in the thirty-four teachers of 1889-90, since they all taught; special supervisors were then a thing unknown.

teaching responsibility operates, theoretically at least, to the same end. This growing impersonality of teacher-pupil relationships is responsible, in part, for such observed phenomena as the heavy relative drop in space devoted to the faculty in the high school annual, noted below; one no longer finds tributes to teachers such as those printed in 1894:

> "The influence of her beautiful life will be felt by her pupils in after years, and make them stronger and better fitted for the realities of life."
>
> And "one of the brightest and dearest of our teachers . . . her persistent efforts have been rewarded in the love and respect which her pupils have for her, and her life is one which should be a criterion to all."

It seems unlikely that such appreciations could have been entirely perfunctory. Pupils today are apparently inclined to take their teachers more casually, unless the latter happen to be basket-ball enthusiasts or fraternity brothers or have some other extra-teaching hold upon them.

Indeed, few things about education in Middletown today are more noteworthy than the fact that the entire community treats its teachers casually. These more than 250 persons to whom this weighty responsibility of training the young is entrusted are not the wise, skilled, revered elders of the group. In terms of the concerns and activities that preoccupy the keenest interests of the city's leaders, they are for the most part nonentities; rarely does one run across a teacher at the weekly luncheons of the city's business men assembled in their civic clubs; nor are many of them likely to be present at the social functions over which the wives of these influential men preside. Middletown pays these people to whom it entrusts its children about what it pays a retail clerk, turns the whole business of running the schools over to a School Board of three business men appointed by the political machine, and rarely stumbles on the individual teacher thereafter save when a particularly interested mother pays a visit to the school "to find out how Ted is getting along." The often bitter comments of the teachers themselves upon their lack of status and recognition in the ordinary give and take of local life are not needed to make an observer realize that in this commercial culture the "teacher" and "professor" do not occupy the position they did even a generation ago.

Furthermore, as Middletown every year is confronted with an increasing number of children to be educated at public expense and as a growing number of more highly paid occupations are drawing men and women from teaching, emphasis almost inevitably comes to be laid upon the perfection of the system rather than upon the personality or qualifications of the individual teacher. The more completely a teacher is a part of the accepted school system in terms of his own training, the more he is valued and the more salary he receives. As in so many other aspects of Middletown's life, criticism of individuals or creakings in the system are met primarily not by changes in its foundations but by adding fresh stories to its superstructure. If teaching is poor, supervisors are employed and "critic teachers" are added; in 1890 the only person in the entire school system who did not teach was the superintendent, while between superintendent and teacher today is a galaxy of principals, assistant principals, supervisors of special subjects, directors of vocational education and home economics, deans, attendance officers, and clerks, who do no teaching but are concerned in one way or another with keeping the system going; in 1924 the office of superintendent itself was bifurcated into a superintendent of schools and a business director. Thus, in personnel as well as in textbooks and courses of study, strains or maladjustments in education are being met by further elaboration and standardization.

A REPORT ON THE EDUCATIONAL LEVEL OF TEACHERS (1930–31)
From Edward S. Evenden, "National Survey of the Education of Teachers: Summary and Evaluation," as quoted in U.S. Office of Education, *Bulletin no. 10* (Washington, D.C., 1933), pp. 36, 39–42.

In presenting the picture of the amount of educational preparation of elementary teachers five questions are of interest alike to the school patron and to those responsible for State programs for the education of teachers.

1. How many teachers are now teaching whose formal education has not gone beyond 4 years of high school?

2. How many teachers have less education than the generally accepted minimum of 2 years of college or normal school work beyond the completion of a standard high-school course?

3. How many teachers barely meet the minimum standard of 2 years of college or normal school work?

4. How many have more than the minimum education by 1 or 2 years?

5. How many elementary teachers have had 1 or more years of graduate work?

*　　*　　*

Approximately 1 out of every 20 elementary teachers in the United States in 1930–31 had no schooling beyond the high school. This is the surprising answer to the first of the questions just asked. The rural schools had the largest percentage of their teachers in this group, but on the other hand, the cities, and even the largest cities, had 3 or more percent of their teachers with this inexcusably meager preparation—inexcusable because, even though many of them were older teachers who entered teaching 20 or more years ago when standards were lower, they should not have been permitted to remain in teaching during that time without adding to their educational preparation.

The answer to the second question is equally disquieting. One-fifth of the elementary teachers of the United States who had completed high school reported 1 year or less in college as the highest level of their training. This group and those with 4 years of high school or less make a total of more than a fourth of America's elementary teachers who in 1930–31 had not had the minimum of 2 years of education beyond the completion of a 4-year high-school course. One out of four elementary teachers had less education than is represented by the completion of the junior college which, according to many estimates, represents about the same level of intellectual maturity as the completion of the secondary schools of Europe.

It is clear that most of these undereducated teachers were teaching in the rural schools, the consolidated schools, and the villages—the locations in which the work of teaching is most difficult and where the need for the highest type of teaching service is probably greatest. The selection of the most poorly qualified teachers in the rural and small village schools is an unfortunate continuation of one element in the vicious circle of inadequately prepared teachers, poor teaching, ineffective schools, low educational standards, resulting in the selection of inadequately prepared teachers and the beginning of another circle. Thus it continues from school generation to school generation in circles of ever-narrowing educational opportunities.

The situation just presented is both unjustifiable and challenging. Something should be done to remedy it, and done immediately. Some States in which corrective action is imperative may not be stimulated by the national situation just pictured. Such States may not recognize how much of the national situation is due to their low standards. A careful study . . . of this report will rather effectively remove any doubt as to the States in which this problem needs prompt, vigorous, and State-wide attention. For example, of the rural school teachers reporting in 1930–31, the following 9 States had 20 percent or more—a fifth or more—with 4 years of high-school education or less: Arkansas, Florida, Georgia, Iowa, Kansas, Kentucky, Mississippi, Nebraska, and New York. In one of these States more than half (53.8 percent) of the rural teachers reported no more than high-school education.

The answer to the third question concerning the number of teachers who barely meet the minimum standard of educational preparation is that in 1930–31 approximately half of the elementary teachers belonged in that group. About half (46.2 percent) of the elementary teachers had had 2 years' work above high school in a normal school, teachers college, junior college, college, or university. The size of this group affords a basis for encouragement if one looks backward a few years, but the encouragement should disappear when it is realized that nearly three-fourths of our elementary teachers (72.4 percent) had no more than the minimum educational preparation when that minimum was as low as only 2 years above high school. The number of teachers in the 2 years of college-work group may help justify the impression that many persons now teaching took no more preservice education than was required for admission to teaching. For many of those persons the only sure way to increase their education would be to raise the minimum standard by regulation, since it is unlikely that they will do it voluntarily.

That such a criticism does not apply to all teachers in the elementary schools is evidenced in the percentages of elementary teachers who had 1 or more years of education above the minimum and the number who had had 1 or more years of graduate work. While these two groups represented only a tenth of the rural school teachers, they comprised more than two-fifths (42.9 percent) of the elementary teachers in the largest cities and more than one-fourth of the total elementary group. To be sure, not all of the education above the 2 years of college level represents voluntary improvement. Several States extended their normal-school courses from 2 to 3 years, and other States and a number of cities have required the completion of 4 years of preservice education for admission to teaching. Even though these requirements would account for some of the individuals being in this group, there is no doubt that most of the preparation obtained above the "2 years' minimum" was obtained either because of a professional desire to be better prepared for teaching or because additional education was an advantage in meeting the increased competition for teaching positions which has developed during the 7 or 8 years just past.

The answer to the fifth question—the number with 1 or more years of graduate work affords little comfort to those who believe that teaching should be comparable with the so-called "learned professions" in the educational equipment of its members or to those who believe that teachers in the elementary schools should be as well educated as the teachers in the high schools. Not 1 in every 200 rural school teachers had done a year's graduate work when the data were collected in 1930–31 and even in the largest cities where competition for placement is keenest and tenure longest only 1 elementary teacher in each 20 reported a year or more of graduate work. To be sure, small as these percentages are, they are better than nothing especially if they show the beginning of a movement toward adequate education of elementary teachers. They are relatively very small when compared with those for high-school teachers in this country or for either elementary or high-school teachers in some European countries.

The problem of raising the level of education of elementary teachers can be understood more clearly in the light of some hypothetical problems in connection with the data presented. . . .

1. Suppose that the sorry plight of the rural schools should attract attention enough so that a concerted attack were made to bring all the rural school teachers up to a minimum of 2 years of college work. This would affect 61.8 percent of the rural teachers in 1- and 2-teacher schools and if successful would lower the percentage of elementary teachers in the United States with less than the minimum of 2 years of college work from 26.4 percent to 10.2 percent and raise the percent with the minimum amount of education from 46.2 percent to 61.4 percent. The other groups would remain the same.

2. If all the elementary teachers in the entire country were required to meet the 2 years of college work minimum there would be no teachers with less than that amount and the percent in the minimum group would be 72.4, the other groups remaining unchanged.

3. As a third problem, suppose that within the next 5 years all elementary teachers in the country with less than 2 years of college work could be required to meet this standard and that all other elementary teachers with less than 1 year of graduate work could be required to increase their educational preparation by at least 1 year—what would be the result? . . . The 5.7 percent with 4 years of high school or less and the 20.5 percent with 1 year of college or less would disappear and there would be no elementary teachers with less than 2 years of education beyond high school. The group which barely met the minimum would be 26.2 percent instead of 46.2 percent. The remaining groups would be: 3 years of college work, 46.2 percent; 4 years of college work, 15.5 percent; and 1 year or more of graduate work, 12.1 percent. While this distribution would still not be all that is desirable it would present a very much better picture than the one that represented the education of our elementary teachers in 1930–31.

It is readily admitted that these problems are hypothetical and the solutions proposed unreal and impractical. They are inserted for only two purposes. In the first place they show that any improvement in standards, especially in bringing all teachers up to an accepted minimum, has a marked effect upon the total picture even if the increase is only in one group. In the second place they show that a relatively small amount of additional preparation, if obtained by all teachers, makes a very large difference in the number who meet acceptable standards. The problem of raising the educational level of elementary teachers in the United States is quite clearly a threefold one of cutting off the lower end of the distribution, raising the educational level of the total group, and increasing the number at the upper end of the distribution. The solution implies the elimination or upgrading of the teachers with less than an approved minimum amount of education (certainly not less than 2 years beyond high school), the upgrading of all elementary teachers with less than 4 years of college-level work and the encouragement of greater numbers of elementary teachers to continue their educational preparation into the graduate level for 1 or more years.

Highest Level of Training of Junior High School Teachers in 1930–31

The highest level of training of junior high school teachers in the United States for the year 1930–31 was determined in the same way as for elementary teachers. The answers may therefore be used for comparisons between the junior high school and the elementary school teachers as well as for an analysis of the education of the group itself. Because of the smaller numbers in the groups and also because some preliminary tabulations showed that the preparation of secondary teachers was not as much affected by the size of the communities in which the schools were located, the junior and senior high school groups were not distributed according to size of community.

. . . It is clearly apparent that in the matter of the education of its teachers the junior high school stood between the other two groups—distinctly better than the elementary group and decidedly poorer than the senior high school group. The explanation is probably due to the fact that the junior high school is a relatively new type of school organization. When it was started it was not clear in the minds of many school people whether it was an intermediate school, an upward extension of the elementary school, or a downward extension of the high school. As a result of that confusion the prevailing standards for the training of teachers for both the elementary and the secondary schools were applied in staffing the first junior high schools; in fact, many of those first schools were staffed by transferring successful teachers from the elementary schools to the junior high schools. At the time this was done it was quite generally accepted that high-school teachers should be college graduates. If the junior high school in its beginning could have been clearly classed as a secondary school and the standards of secondary schools applied to it, its teachers would probably have been, because of the recency of its development, a better educated group than the teachers of the senior high schools.

OBSERVATIONS ON THE TEACHER'S STATUS IN THE COMMUNITY
(1932)   From Willard Waller, *The Sociology of Teaching* (New York, 1932), pp. 49–50, 58–60.

Enough has been said to mark out the general position of the teacher in the community. It will be readily understandable that the teacher is usually more or less isolated in the community in which he lives. He is isolated because he is often an outsider hired to mediate certain skills and certain specialized lores to the young of the community. He is mentally isolated from the rest of the community by his own set of attitudes. But, most important of all, he is isolated because the community isolates him. This the community does by making him the carrier of certain super-mundane values, and by imposing upon him certain humbling restrictions. The community can never know the teacher because it insists upon regarding him as something more than a god and something less than a man. In short, the teacher is psychologically isolated from the community because he must live within the teacher stereotype.

The teacher stereotype is a thin but impenetrable veil that comes between the teacher and all other human beings. The teacher can never know what others are really like because they are not like that when the teacher is watching them. The community can never know what the teacher is really like because the community does not offer the teacher opportunities for normal social intercourse. The cessation of spontaneous social life at the entry of the teacher, and the substitution for it of highly artificial and elegant conversation, is very evident in the following record:

> I was listening to a group telling jokes customarily heard in a barber shop, when a man approached the door. At once the barber stopped working and said, "Sh! Sh! Boys, the principal of the high school is coming in." All was quiet. The principal entered and sat down. The barber broke the spell by saying, "Well, I suppose, professor, you are glad school will soon be out?"
>
> "Yes," he replied.
>
> The barber remarked, "If you are as anxious as that boy of mine is for it to let out, why it can't be too soon." The principal had come to pay a bill. He started out. The barber said, "Professor, you need not hurry off. There is just one ahead of you and then you're next. Won't be over twenty minutes."
>
> "Oh, I'll be back later," the principal remarked.
>
> "All right, come in about twelve-fifteen. Business is lax at that time and I can fix you out right away."
>
> After the principal had left the barber turned to the group and said, "Boys, I enjoy a good story myself but this is a public place and we've got to treat such men as the one that left with respect. *Besides that I have many women customers.* It is embarrassing to them and, too, it throws the responsibility upon me. You understand what I mean. All right, now go on with your jokes and stories!" The barber laughed. (Unpublished manuscript by Charles Zaar, *The Social Psychology of the Barber Shop*, stenographic report of conversation.)

The constant use of the title "Professor," the obviously artificial conversation, the lack of interest of the teacher in those banal remarks that he had heard so many times before, the assimilation of the teacher to the female character ideal, the suppression of normal activity when the teacher entered the room—all these things make the above stand out as an interesting and significant incident. It has been said that no woman and no negro is ever fully admitted to the white man's world. Possibly we should add men teachers to the list of the excluded.

But it is not only in his public appearances that the teacher feels the gulf between himself and other men. When the teacher must live in a private home, the teacher stereotype still isolates him from the people with whom he lives. A woman teacher narrates the following incident:

> Soon supper time came and the family and I were seated at the table. There was a small boy of three in the family and much conversation was directed to him in which the mother and the father remarked that he must behave because the teacher was watching him. The fact that I was the teacher seemed to be foremost in the minds of these people. That barrier between the teacher and the rest of society was much in evidence. I was the teacher. Towards me there was a somewhat strained attitude. I didn't see much of the family, for as soon as they were through eating they had chores to do and when the chores were finished they all went to bed. (Student paper, *My First Year of Teaching*.)

Concerning the low social standing of teachers much has been written. The teacher in our culture has always been among the persons of little importance, and his place has not changed for the better in the last few decades. Fifty years or more ago it used to be argued that teachers had no standing in the community because they whipped little children, and this was undoubtedly an argument that contained some elements of truth. But flogging, and all the grosser forms of corporal punishment, have largely disappeared from the modern school, and as yet there is little indication that the social standing of the profession has been elevated. It has also been argued that the social standing of any profession is a pretty accurate mirror of its economic standing, and that therefore the low financial rewards of teaching are a sufficient cause of its being considered one of the less honorable pursuits. This, however, is an explanation that may not be pushed very far; it holds some truth, but there are other facts that limit it. In the smaller communities, the superintendent of schools often occupies a financial position far superior to that of most of the villagers, and yet the villagers both pity him and condescend to him (the while, perhaps, they envy him his easy means of livelihood). And it happens that the group among the teachers who are most respected in the world at large, the college and university professors, are but little better-to-do in most cases, and in some cases are much poorer, than secondary school executives, who nevertheless, except in the larger cities, have less social standing. The Lynds have a simpler sort of economic explanation, which is that there is simply no place in this commercial culture for the teacher and the professor.

In analyzing the opinion people have of teachers, it is necessary to reckon with the teacher stereotype which partly reflects and partly determines that opinion. This stereotype apparently represents a caricature of the methods used by the teacher to maintain control over children, and of the personality worked out by the teacher as a solution for the problem of control. This problem of control arises, of course, out of the supposed necessity of conducting schools along the lines of teacher domination and pupil subordination. From the means which the teacher has to use to obtain control and to keep it arises a generalized conception of the school teacher which perdures in the minds of all the graduates of the school. This is an idealized and not a factual portrait, because the memory will not hold all the flesh and blood of human beings for so long a time; the general impression remains, but details fade. The idealized conception tends to become a caricature, and an unpleasant and belittling caricature, because a real enmity exists between teacher and taught, and this enmity transmutes the work of memory into irony. In accordance with this theory, each generation of teachers pays in its turn for the sins of the generation that has gone before; it would require some decades of sensible and friendly teaching to remove the stigma from the occupation. There are some indications that this process has already begun, but antagonism toward teachers is still widespread. It is a hostility not unmixed with a certain respect, but it is a real hostility, and apparently it is as universal as is the school itself. A passage in *The Road Back*,[1] in which the mayor and some other villagers endeavor to make the new teachers drunk, might well have been, with certain changes, a passage in *The Hoosier Schoolmaster.*

[1] Remarque, Erich Maria, *The Road Back* (translation), pp. 227 ff., Little, Brown, & Co., Boston, 1931.

Teachers lack respect in the community because of the teacher stereotype which comes between them and other persons. The stereotype is something of a caricature, and its distinguishing features arise from the fact that the teacher must be a despot ruling over the petty concerns of children. Where the relation between the teacher and the taught is unfriendly, the caricature may be sharp, and this is one basis for the argument that popular opinion of teachers will rise as the schools come to use less arbitrary and cruel means of enforcing discipline. However sound this reasoning may be, this principle has only a limited applicability, for there is another cause, and a deeper one, that operates to cut the teacher off from commerce with his fellow men. And the more successful the teacher is, the more he is cut off. The teacher must live in a universe of adolescent attitudes and values. He can teach, it is true, and remain essentially adult, but to do that he must interpose between himself and his students an immense distance, and then the teacher-pupil relationship becomes one of dominance and subordination in its strictest form. If the teacher is to control understandingly it must be by the sacrifice of some of his own adulthood. This is not to say that an individual with sufficient insight might not be able to have his cake and eat it too, in this case, to make adjustments to boys on a boyish level, and to adults on a slightly different level; but this is insight which is rare, and it could lead to the complete isolation, in feeling, of the individual from society.

The teacher must talk to boys of the things in which boys are interested. He must understand adolescent roles, and live vividly roles of his own not wholly incompatible with the roles of adolescence. The persons who are happiest in these roles, and perhaps most successful in playing them, are individuals who have never wholly made the transition from their own adolescence, the college heroes, the football players, the track stars, and the debaters who have never quite forgotten their undergraduate conception of themselves. These persons are able to live adolescent roles vividly because there is no discontinuity in those roles in their own lives. More introspective teachers may resent the parts they have to play. But the teacher must always take very seriously the social system designed for the edification and control of children. He must speak seriously and even prayerfully of examinations, grades, credits, promotions, demerits, scoldings, school rituals, making good, etc. And it is difficult for the teacher to take such things seriously and yet keep them from entering his soul. In the main, the better a teacher he becomes, the further they will enter.

It is not only that the teacher must have social traits which enable him to enter a little way into the society of boys, but that these same traits exclude him from the society of men. A banker and a lawyer may converse together with interest and profit, because they live in the same universe of values, but any contact between either of these and the professional teacher must be more difficult. Of what is the teacher to talk? When teachers meet they talk shop, but that is excluded when the teacher and the banker meet. After the introductory commonplaces, the conversation may go on to platitude, possibly to politics; very likely it languishes. Individual teachers learn to transcend these boundaries, but for teachers as a class they continue to exist.

The situation is made somewhat worse by the fact that much of the communion of men in general is on the level of certain vices, or certain sporting interests which are more or less taboo for the teacher. One who does not smoke, drink, swear, or tell risqué stories is excluded from the confraternity of men in general, from all barber shop, pool room, and men's club fellowship.

Critics

**ABRAHAM FLEXNER'S REPORT ON AMERICAN SCHOOLS OF
EDUCATION (1930)**   From *Universities: American, English, German* (New York,
1930), pp. 96–103.

The American school or faculty of education has made an unquestionable
contribution of genuine value to American, perhaps one might add without
exaggeration, to modern education. A generation ago elementary and secondary
schools were a treadmill. The curricula were dead; the discipline was unintelligent;
the world of reality and action hardly existed for the schools. Rousseau and Froebel
and Pestalozzi had dreamed dreams of immense inspirational importance. They had
had no general effect. A tremendous change in practice has, however, recently taken
place though, to be sure, not in America alone. The curricula, especially in the
elementary school, are alive. This wholesome transformation has not been
accomplished wholly through colleges of education; but they have been important,
perhaps the main agencies, in bringing it about. There are so many problems,
specifically educational closely bound up with psychology, philosophy, economics,
and government—without falling into any one of these categories—that education
may make some claim to constituting a profession with cultural roots and high
ideals in the university sense of the term. In this American development Teachers
College at Columbia led the way; others—at Chicago, at Harvard, and at the state
universities—have followed. For their accomplishment in vitalizing elementary and
high schools they deserve high commendation.

Unfortunately, like the universities to which they belong, faculties of education
have lost their heads. In the first place, in discarding what was dead or irrelevant,
they have lost sight of much that was alive and relevant. They have failed to heed
the fact that, as human beings mature, schools must shift the emphasis from the
individual to the task itself. "Respect for persons," writes Professor Woodbridge, "is
what the old education neglected. It would be a pity, would it not, if the new
should neglect respect for learning?"

"Past" and "dead" are very different words. More and more, philosophy,
scholarship, and history have tended to fade much too far into the background;
technique, administration, "socialization" have more and more come to the fore;
more and more, by means of "combined degrees" and otherwise the need of taking
courses in "education" interferes with the mastery of subject-matter. Because one
type of discipline was barren and repellent, it does not follow that "ease,"
"spontaneity," "self-expression" are sound guides. Civilization is an artificial thing;
it is inseparable from ideals deliberately adopted; these ideals often involve effort

THE
PROFESSION
OF EDUCATION

2699

that runs against the stream. Without ideals, without effort, without scholarship, without philosophical continuity, there is no such thing as education, no such thing as culture. The college for teachers has become less and less sensitive to these considerations. It has run into all kinds of excesses, all kinds of superficiality and immediacy, all kinds of "rabbit paths." It is undertaking to tell "how" to persons who mainly do not know "what." Of course, there are profound individual differences impelling individuals in different directions, and these must be respected. But, the choice once made, the individual who at the high school, college, or university stage, requires that his teachers employ an insinuating technique so as to guide him happily and painlessly towards the mastery of a subject belongs not in school but somewhere else. Teachers will, of course, vary in their powers and methods of presentation and inspiration. That seems to me, at the higher levels, of relatively slight importance, if they are masters of their respective subjects. Let the onus rest mainly on the student, for there it belongs and thus only will his powers be brought out. The very acme of absurdity has been attained at the Johns Hopkins in the creation of a professorship of chemical education.[1] Remsen was a distinguished chemist. His influence was felt throughout the entire country. What might he not have accomplished, had he possessed as running mate a mediocre or unsuccessful investigator who would have been professor of chemical education? But, hold! If the university professor of chemistry needs at his side a professor of chemical education, so do physics, mathematics, history, English, Greek, Latin, and other chairs. American universities, all under-financed, and few in weaker financial condition than the Johns Hopkins, must thus create, parallel with chairs of subject-matter, professorships of education. Truly the Johns Hopkins has once more opened a new vista—even if in the wrong direction!

One is thus led to ask whether schools of education are capable of coordination in the university with such professions as law and medicine. The American teachers college has not yet proved the affirmative. And it seems on the whole less impressive at the moment than when it was proposed a generation ago. And this, because the American college of education, not wholly, but largely oblivious of the really important, is devoting itself more and more to the technical, trivial, and sometimes absurd. In education, there are things that require doing, but it does not follow that it is the business of the university to do them all. The members of the first teachers colleges in the United States were themselves scholars; but scholars and scientists are now scarce, very scarce, in these faculties. In their place, one finds hordes of professors and instructors possessing meagre intellectual background whose interests centre in technique and administration viewed in a narrow ad hoc fashion. The staff of Teachers College, Columbia University, requires 26 pages for mere enumeration: the roster contains 303 instructors;[2] the catalogue lists over 19,000 "students" of one kind or another. A few instructors offer courses in educational philosophy, in foreign or comparative education; problems of elementary and secondary education are not slighted. But why do not these substantial and interesting fields suffice? Why should not an educated person, broadly and deeply versed in educational philosophy and experience, help himself from that point on? Why should his attention be diverted during these pregnant years to the trivialities and applications with which common sense can deal adequately when the time

[1] The official description is as follows: "This course will cover theory, observation, and practice in the teaching of chemistry. It is especially designed for students who are planning to teach chemistry in universities, colleges, or large high schools."

[2] Not including scores of teachers in the Extension Department, Summer School, etc.

comes? Most of 200 pages, filled with mere cataloguing, are devoted to trivial, obvious, and inconsequential subjects, which could safely be left to the common sense or intelligence of any fairly well educated person. Atomistic training—the provision of endless special courses, instead of a small number of opportunities that are at once broad and deep—is hostile to the development of intellectual grasp. A Negro preacher in a popular play declares: "The Lord expects us to figure out a few things for ourselves;" but Teachers College is organized on the opposite principle. Thus in this huge institution thousands are trained "ad hoc," instead of being educated and encouraged to use their wits and their senses. Among the hundreds of courses thus offered, I cite as fair examples "manuscript writing," "teaching of educational sociology," "administrative procedures in curriculum construction," "research in the history of school instruction in history," "music for teachers of literature and history," "methods used in counseling individuals," "research in college administration," "psychology of higher education," "teaching English to foreigners," "teaching the individual," "extra-curricular activities, including school clubs, excursions, athletic insignia, class parties and dances, extra-curricular finances, and a record card for pupil activity"!

The School of Education of the University of Chicago is a more modest affair: it has a teaching staff of only 33 and about 800 students, and its list of courses occupies only 40 pages. I find one course devoted to "educational progress in Europe and the United States from 1400 to the present." As for the rest, the School avoids the detailed absurdities in which the Columbia list abounds and pays relatively far more attention to psychological problems. But absurdities and trivialities are not absent, as, for example, separate courses in "the supervision of the teaching staff," "duties of school officers," "awareness of situations and planning of behaviour," "reflective thought as a basis for teaching method," "supervision of instruction" under eight separate heads, "study and supervision of the high school girl," etc. In the main, however, its attention is devoted to tests, measurements, organization, administration—including administration of the teaching staff and how to organize for planning the curriculum! Of testing, the psychologists appear to have practically lost control. It may have a limited field of usefulness; but the length to which it may go is shown in a formula devised at the University of Chicago, showing "the relation of scholarship to a combination of all tests":

$$R_{S}.12345678$$
$$\frac{}{\sqrt{1-(1-R^{2}S_{1})(1-R^{2}S_{2.1})(1-R^{2}S_{.4.123})(1-RS_{.6.12345})}}$$
$$(1-R^{2}S_{7.123456})(1-R^{2}S_{8.1234567})$$

Thus neatly and simply can a tester dispose of all the personal factors on which good teaching really depends!

By the side of this formula, Professor Spaulding's is a very modest one indeed:[2]

If A_r = average of class-enrolments in required subjects
X = the number of hours of combined classes
T = the total number of class-hours
G = the average number of pupils per grade, then
$A_r = \dfrac{X.2G + (T-X).G}{T}$ and $X = T . \dfrac{A_r - G}{G}$

[2]Francis T. Spaulding, *The Small Junior High School* (Harvard Studies in Education, Volume IX, Harvard University Press, 1927), p. 31.

The Harvard Graduate School of Education has a staff of 37 instructors, a few devoting themselves to large fundamental issues, while most of them deal with simple practical problems, which would quickly yield to experience, reading, common sense, and a good general education. Among the latter are special courses in the teaching of different subjects, courses for specialists in play and recreation, supervisors of recreation parks, social centres, summer camps, festivals, pageants, commercial education, community recreation, and singing in schools and communities. Obviously, Harvard, too, leaves as little as possible to intelligence, individual initiative, chance, and technical non-university training, and is at least partially blind to the significance of history and philosophy.

The calibre of the persons who are attracted to this sort of thing and its upshot may be gathered from the trivial and uninteresting character of educational periodicals and the subjects of the dissertations submitted for higher degrees. The topics discussed in the current literature are so unimportant as compared with the subjects discussed by physicists, chemists, or political scientists that it may well seem as though they were devised to frighten off intelligence. And that the unconscious effort to frighten away intelligence is usually quite successful is demonstrated by the theses which crown the student with the A.M. or Ph.D. degree. At random I select from the Chicago and Columbia lists: "The City School District," "The Experience Variables: A Study of the Variable Factors in Experience Contributing to the Formation of Personality," "Measuring Efficiency in Supervision and Teaching," "City School Attendance Service," "Pupil Participation in High School Control," "Administrative Problems of the High School Cafeteria," "Personnel Studies of Scientists in the United States," "Suggestion in Education," "Social Background and Activities of Teachers College Students,"[3] "Qualities Related to Success in Teaching," "The Technique of Estimating School Equipment Costs," "Public School Plumbing Equipment," "An Analysis of Janitor Service in Elementary Schools,"[4] "The Equipment of the School Theatre," "Concerning our Girls and What They Tell Us," "Evidences of the Need of Education for Efficient Purchasing," "Motor Achievements of Children of Five, Six, and Seven Years of Age," "A Scale for Measuring Antero-Posterior Posture of Ninth Grade Boys," "A Study of School Postures and Desk Dimensions," "The Technique of Activity and Trait Analysis Applied to Y. M. C. A. Executive Secretaries as a Basis for Curricular Materials," and "Statistical Methods for Utilizing Personal Judgments to Evaluate Activities for Teacher Training Curricula." Harvard is in danger of following the same course: it has recently bestowed the Ph.D. degree for theses on "Vocational Activities and Social Understanding in the Curriculum for Stenographer-Clerks," "Guidance in Colleges for Women."

[3]In this production, the author of which is a dean of women at a teachers college, account is taken of whether in the homes from which the students came there is a lawn mower, a desk set, a rag carpet, a built-in bookcase, potted plants, company dishes. Among the leisure activities investigated are "shopping," "heart-to-heart talks," "just sit alone," "think and dream," "going to picnics," "idle conversation (talking about just anything)," "having 'dates' with men," "telling jokes," "teasing somebody," "doing almost anything so you are with the gang," "reading."

[4]I pause for a moment to contemplate the thesis on "An Analysis of Janitor Service in Elementary Schools." Why elementary? There are reasons: first, obviously, the title suggests other theses—and new subjects are in demand, as students multiply—the duties of a junior high school janitor, of a high school janitor, of a college janitor, etc. "Are these really different subjects?" I once asked a professor of school administration.
"Oh, yes," he replied, "the lavatory problem, for example, is with small boys quite different from the same problem at the high school level!"

AMERICAN COUNCIL ON EDUCATION CALLS FOR IMPROVEMENT OF TEACHER EDUCATION (1946)

From American Council on Education, *The Commission on Teacher Education, The Improvement of Teacher Education* (Washington, D.C., 1946), pp. 82–88, 101–02.

The Commission does not consider that its experience, within and beyond the cooperative study, equips it to speak with authority regarding all of the issues connected with the matter of general education. It believes that many of these must for some time continue to be the subject of debate among educators and that such debate should be encouraged, especially among members of the same faculty. There is no doubt that dissatisfaction with the present chaotic situation with respect to general education is powerful and widespread. Conflicting educational philosophies and the usual preoccupation of individual faculty members with responsibilities that are not general—with, for example, their own departmental specialties—make agreement difficult. At the same time, however, interest in the achievement of greater unity is insistent, as is the desire to make general education more vitally concerned with the related needs of man and society.

The Commission's own judgments respecting the general education of teachers may be summarized as follows:

1. Teachers should receive the best possible general education, not only in order that they may share in what ought to be the birthright of all young Americans today, but also because to them is entrusted considerable responsibility for the general education of all young Americans tomorrow.

2. The aim of general education should be to enable young men and women to meet effectively the most important and widespread problems of personal and social existence; in the case of prospective teachers such education should seek to further the development of knowledge, skills, attitudes, and interests that are fundamentally related to needs and responsibilities shared with contemporaries destined for other vocations.

3. While general education may be usefully contrasted with special or vocational education, it ought not, as conducted, to ignore the implications of the special or vocational purposes of students; nor should professional education be carried on wholly without reference to students' more general needs: an integration of general and professional education should be sought.

4. At least three-eighths of the college experience of a prospective teacher should have as its primary objectives those properly ascribable to general education.

5. While elements of general education may well predominate during the first two college years they should neither monopolize nor be limited to this period: some educational experiences related to vocational purposes should be provided as soon as the latter are formed; and the idea that general education may be considered as "completed" at some particular time should not be encouraged.

6. The contemporary trend toward balance and integration in general education is significant and deserves support. This implies a basic pattern of broad courses, each developed with the special purposes of general education in mind, each requiring a fairly substantial block of time, and all planned in relation to one another.

7. The trend toward the use of more in the way of nonverbal methods of instruction and student expression also deserves encouragement. Firsthand experience, as well as motion pictures and the radio, should supplement books as tools for

learning, and students should be helped to express what they have learned not only in words but through the arts and social action.

8. General education should be concerned with the body and the emotions as well as with the intellect.

9. Students should be given a more active, responsible role in the planning and carrying out of their own general education. This implies that instruction should be flexibly administered to provide for responsiveness to individual differences.

10. A leading aim of college programs of general, or for that matter of professional, education should be to make it probable that graduates will continue their growth in understanding and competence after they have become teachers.

11. The development of superior programs of general education on particular campuses requires local group endeavor: faculty unity is prerequisite to curricular unity.

12. Such shared effort should be designed to reveal and clarify existing differences of opinion, to increase general understanding of the needs of students and society, and to obtain open-minded consideration of educational thought and action as expressed and carried out elsewhere.

13. Helpful in facilitating improvements in general education have been faculty group discussions, special studies, interviews with students and alumni, community and service-area surveys, visits to schools and to other colleges, use of consultants, and participation in general education workshops.

14. Willingness to sanction the testing of new ideas respecting general education by experimental-minded staff members working with special groups of students has often helped to resolve differences of speculative opinion and led to an extension of sound reforms.

Advanced Subject-Matter Preparation

In several of the universities with which the Commission was associated special attempts were made to improve the advanced subject-matter preparation of teachers for the secondary schools. These efforts were in each case carried on by committees representing both the schools or departments of education and the appropriate subject-matter faculties. The attacks were invariably made with reference to teachers for particular fields—for example, English, social studies, natural science, or vocational agriculture—but the general implications of recommendations were borne in mind. In most cases, indeed, the committees found themselves concerned with questions of general education before they were through.

These efforts were not unaccompanied with difficulties, and in most instances less progress in the way of reform was made during the course of the study than optimists in the several situations had hoped for; but the work done resulted in distinctly better mutual understanding, cleared a good deal of ground, brought some significant changes, and laid a substantial basis for further advance. The fact is, of course, that there is ordinarily such distance·between educationists and subject-matter professors that it is inevitable that considerable time and energy must be expended before genuine agreement between them as to principles and desirable changes respecting teacher education can be expected. The work of the committees mentioned was successful in greatly increasing the area of such agreement.

*   *   *

The Commission may now summarize some of its own general conclusions regarding the role of subject-matter instruction, over and above that which may be considered as falling within the area of general education, in the preparation of a teacher:

1. There can be no doubt that a high degree of scholarly competence is essential in a teacher; such competence requires not only knowledge and personal skill but also the ability to use both effectively in the teaching relationship.

2. It is essential that subject-matter instructors whose students are preparing to teach should be sympathetic to their purpose and informed as to the problems they will face when they enter upon their professional careers.

3. It is also important that such instructors should work more closely and realistically with representatives of schools and departments of education in identifying the needs of prospective teachers and planning curricula in which both subject-matter and professional elements will be functionally combined.

4. The familiar major-minor pattern of subject-matter preparation is being desirably paralleled in many colleges by arrangements that provide for more integration and greater attention to bearings on personal and social needs. For example, divisional as contrasted with departmental majors are increasingly available to undergraduates. Such arrangements offer particular advantages to students who are preparing to teach in modern elementary and secondary schools.

GILBERT HIGHET ON THE ART OF TEACHING (1950)   From Gilbert Highet, *The Art of Teaching* (New York, 1950), pp. 14, 18–20.

Now, it is natural for a pupil to resist his teacher. It is healthy, and it can be invigorating for them both. The best works of art are created in difficult media: it is harder to shape marble than wax. Yet when the resistance is never broken down, but hardens into hostility, and when the teacher finds the same hostility—or at best a sniggering indifference—year after year, there is something very far wrong. Sometimes the pupils are wrong. Sometimes the teacher is wrong. Sometimes there is a deep-seated dislocation in the community to which they both belong, and their hostility reflects it. (We shall be discussing this a little later, when we come to discipline.) But whatever its cause may be, it is a sore trial to the teacher. It is one of the two worst drawbacks in the job. It is bitter to be poor; but it is torture to spend your life's energy, year after year, trying to awaken understanding and appreciation of genuinely important things in what seems to be a collection of spoiled, ill-mannered boobies, smirking or scowling, yawning or chattering, whose ideals are gangsters, footballers, and Hollywood divorcees. It is like giving a blood transfusion, and then seeing your precious blood spilt on the ground and trodden into mud.

This can happen, in certain conditions, even to a good teacher. But it is more likely to happen to bad teachers. How can it be avoided?

In other words, what are the qualities of a good teacher?

✻   ✻   ✻

First, and most necessary of all, he must know the subject. He must know what he teaches. This sounds obvious; yet it is not always practiced. It means that, if his job is teaching chemistry, he must know chemistry. It is not enough for a chemistry teacher to know just that amount of chemistry which is taught in schools and required for the final examinations. He must really understand the science of chemistry. Its upper regions must be clear to him, at least in outline; and he should know what are the most important new discoveries made every year. If a boy shows a gift for chemistry, the master must be able to encourage him, by throwing open window after window into the future, showing him what he can learn at the university, what types of chemistry are most vital in peace and war, which big problems still remain to be solved, and (this is always important) how the great chemists of the past and present have lived and worked.

Therefore teaching is inseparable from learning. Every good teacher will learn more about his subject every year—every month, every week if possible. If a girl chooses the career of teaching French in school, she should not hope to commit the prescribed texts and grammars to memory and then turn her mind to other things. She should dedicate part of her life to the French language, to the superb literature of France, to French art and history and civilization. To become a good teacher of French, she will build up a growing library of her own French books, spending one year (for instance) reading Balzac, the next year reading Proust, the next with Moliere, and the next with Giraudoux, Cocteau, Romains, and the other modern playwrights. She will visit France, if and when she can save up enough money to do so—which will be fearfully difficult with salaries at their present low level. She may take summer courses in French at a university. Certainly she will see every available French film, and learn to enjoy Raimu's rich Marseillais accent, to guffaw with Fernandel. For it will not all be serious work and planned self-improvement. It will be living, and therefore it will contain enjoyments, and even frivolities, like the latest records by Lucienne Boyer and Charles Trenet. But it will be learning at the same time, and it will make better teaching.

You may ask why this is necessary. Why can a teacher not simply learn the rudiments of the subject, master them thoroughly, and then stop? A postman does not learn every street in the city. He learns only his own area. A French teacher in a small town may never have a pupil who will be able to understand Proust. Why should she trouble to read Proust's novels? Why should a schoolmaster teaching elementary chemistry keep up to date with the latest discoveries? The elements of chemistry are limited in number, and do not change.

There are two answers to this. The first is that one cannot understand even the rudiments of an important subject without knowing its higher levels—at least, not well enough to teach it. Every day the grossest and most painful blunders are made not only by teachers but by journalists and radio commentators and others who have the public ear, because they confidently state a half-truth which they have read in an encyclopedia article, or because they lay down as gospel a conjecture once uttered by an authority they admired. And many teachers, trying to explain certain problems in their own subject, fall into explanations suggested to them by a colleague or thrown up by their own imagination, which are nevertheless totally wrong, and which an extending knowledge of the field would have corrected long ago.

The second answer is that the human mind is infinitely capacious. We know the minimum diet which will keep a child alive. We know the maximum quantity of food he can absorb. But no one knows, no one can even guess how much knowledge a child will want and, if it is presented to him in the right way, will digest. Therefore

it is simply useless to teach a child even the elements of a subject, without being prepared to answer his questions about the upper ranges and the inner depths of the subject. And from the teacher's point of view it is far more difficult to do so. A limited field of material stirs very few imaginations. It can be learnt off by heart, but seldom creatively understood and never loved.A subject that carries the mind out in limitless journeys will, if it is well taught, make the learner eager to master all the preliminary essentials and press on.

Young people hate grown-ups for many reasons. One of the reasons is that they feel grown-ups' minds are fixed and limited. Whenever they meet a man or a woman who does not always say what they expect, who tells them novel stories about strange aspects of the world, who throws unexpected lights on what they sadly know as ordinary dull life, who seems as completely alive, sensitive, energetic, and zestful as they themselves, they usually admire him or her. It is true that we cannot all be fountains of energy and novelty throughout every day, but we ought, if we are teachers, to be so keen on our own subjects that we can talk interestingly about unusual aspects of them to young people who would otherwise have been dully neutral, or—worse—eager but disappointed. A teacher must believe in the value and interest of his subject as a doctor believes in health.

The neglect of this principle is one of the chief reasons for the bad teaching that makes pupils hate schools and universities and turn away from valuable fields of knowledge. . . .

The first essential of good teaching, then, is that the teacher must know the subject. That really means that he must continue to learn it.

The second essential is that he must like it. The two are connected, for it is almost impossible to go on learning anything year after year without feeling a spontaneous interest in it. . . .

The third essential of good teaching is to like the pupils. If you do not actually like boys and girls, or young men and young women, give up teaching.

It is easy to like the young because they are young. They have no faults, except the very ones which they are asking you to eradicate: ignorance, shallowness, and inexperience. The really hateful faults are those which we grown men and women have. Some of these grow on us like diseases, others we build up and cherish as though they were virtues. Ingrained conceit, calculated cruelty, deep-rooted ·cowardice, slobbering greed, vulgar self-satisfaction, puffy laziness of mind and body—these and the other real sins result from years, decades of careful cultivation. They show on our faces, they ring harsh or hollow in our voices, they have become bone of our bone and flesh of our flesh. The young do not sin in those ways. Heaven knows they are infuriatingly lazy and unbelievably stupid and sometimes detestably cruel—but not for long, not all at once, and not (like grown-ups) as a matter of habit or policy. They are trying to be energetic and wise and kind. When you remember this, it is difficult not to like them.

REPORT ON THE DIVISION BETWEEN ACADEMICIANS AND PROFESSIONAL EDUCATORS (1960) From "A Report on the Conferences of the National Commission on Teacher Education and Professional Standards," *ACLS Newsletter*, vol. XI, pp. 1-5.

D uring the past three years the ACLS [American Council of Learned Societies] has served as one of the co-sponsors of the annual national conferences of the National Commission on Teacher Education and Professional Standards (TEPS). These conferences were designed to bring together representatives of all types of schools and all levels of education to discuss the philosophy, content, and standards of teacher preparation, in the hope that general agreement might be reached on ways to improve teacher education.

Considering the widely divergent opinions and sense of distrust which had long existed between the two major segments of the educational world, it was admittedly a gamble to introduce humanists, scientists, and social scientists into an annual conference of professional educators and hope to achieve any semblance of unity. There had already been isolated examples of cooperative effort on college campuses, however, and it was believed, if this could be extended to a national scale, that state and local authorities might be encouraged to initiate needed revisions in the preparation of elementary and secondary school teachers.

The ACLS has now compiled the comments it has received from scholars in the humanities and social sciences who participated in one or more of these conferences, and this report attempts to summarize their reactions and to analyze their estimates of the results achieved.

The first conference, at Bowling Green, Ohio, in 1958, was a surprisingly effective beginning. Many of the scholars had gone expecting to be overwhelmed by sheer numbers and believing that little could be accomplished under such circumstances. Most came away deeply impressed by the experience. They found their opposite numbers not only willing to listen to their views but also genuinely interested in uniting to work out joint recommendations. This, indeed, was the most significant result of the conference, for it demonstrated that a frank exchange of ideas could allay hostilities, even though concrete agreement on specific issues might be difficult to reach.

The Bowling Green conference was not intended to probe very deeply into the issues that might divide academicians and professional educators. It was rather an occasion to explore the extent to which they shared similar goals and philosophies of education and, once it became apparent that each side was prepared to join in this effort, considerable mutual understanding and respect developed.

This does not mean that all were in accord on the meaning and results of the conference. There were some lingering suspicions about the ease with which compromises were made and some doubts about whether there was a great deal of substance to the agreements reached, considering the terminology in which certain resolutions were couched. Nevertheless, most of the liberal arts people were encouraged to learn that professional educators not only viewed the intellectual development of the child as the primary concern of the schools but also seemed prepared, as an earnest of this conviction, to give subject-matter specialists a strong voice in all phases of teacher education.

Some scholars, in their new-found enthusiasm, immediately reported these views to their deans in the hope of swift and concrete action, but those with more experience in such affairs cautioned against such optimism; a big job was yet to be done in changing basic attitudes on the part of a great many people at all levels of education. All agreed, however, that a breakthrough had apparently been effected in the "eternal dichotomy." Large numbers of people, who had never heard any views other than their own discussed at the annual meetings of their professional associations, had been exposed to new ideas at Bowling Green. The barriers to mutual understanding had been lowered, and the atmosphere appeared conducive to consider the following year what should constitute the subject-matter preparation of prospective teachers.

The conference at Lawrence, Kansas, in 1959, provided this opportunity. It was intended as a practical implementation of the previous year's more generalized and theoretical approach, with the content of teacher education as the subject of discussion. This was a more professional meeting than the first one, and more moderated in tone, and the participants found the atmosphere conducive to solid work on the hard issues confronting them. The agreements of 1958 remained reasonably intact, so that little time was spent in rehashing old issues. The discussions, as a result, generated less heat and more light than had those of the previous year.

This did not mean that accord was easily reached. Indeed, subject-matter specialists and professors of education were little inclined to yield to each other where differences of opinion existed on specific items in the curriculum. It did not take long, however, for both groups to subscribe to the general proposition that the initial requirement for a teacher should be high intellectual attainment and that proficiency in one's subject matter was absolutely necessary. The scholars were then willing to concede that the intangible factors of personality, drive, and desire to teach were essential, and that some professional education courses were desirable. Considerable support was also given to the demand that all prospective school teachers, whether elementary or secondary, should have the equivalent of a liberal arts degree with a strong academic major.

When, however, discussion turned to just what the term "general education" meant, what should be included in methods courses, and how to measure qualitatively the preparation required in English and foreign languages, the two sides could do little more than agree to disagree. As a result, the most that could be done was to establish a ceiling on professional preparation and a floor under academic preparation—each stated in terms of hours of credit.

The liberal arts professors left this conference with mixed feelings. The ease with which agreements had been reached on general principles and theories, combined with the reluctance to make concessions on specific issues, led a good many of them to reserve judgment until they saw how the new agreements were going to be implemented. Several of those who had returned from the 1958 conference prepared to work closely with their own education faculties found little indication that Bowling Green had had any impact at the college level. Others reported the same type of situation prevailing at regional and state TEPS meetings, and they wondered what steps were being taken below the national level to insure academic participation in teacher education. TEPS officials and co-sponsoring organizations, therefore, joined to urge directors of state and regional meetings to broaden their base of participation, for it was evident that the success of the national TEPS conferences would depend upon the extent to which recommendations were translated into action at the working level.

Some of the liberal arts professors who had been at Lawrence, on the other hand, doubted the wisdom of pressing for action on the basis of agreements reached at the second conference. They did not believe that enough had been accomplished on the question of curriculum to move on, as had been planned, to a discussion of certification in 1960. There was an uneasy feeling that setting curricular patterns in quantitative terms, as had been done at Lawrence, rather than in qualitative terms, was artificial and meaningless. The conviction existed, in other words, that real agreement on the importance of intellectual standards must precede a discussion of certification requirements. This was, of course, a measure of the scholars' sincere intention that the TEPS conferences should achieve concrete results, and the Steering Committee took the matter under advisement. It was reluctantly decided, however, that the proposed change was inadvisable, and that the third and final conference must deal with certification as scheduled.

This decision, in retrospect, appears to have been a mistake. Whereas the majority of liberal arts people had been enthusiastic about the first conference and were cautiously optimistic about the second, a good many left San Diego in 1960 with more than a little sense of frustration. Suggestions that there might be more than one acceptable method of certification, or that it might be possible to issue certificates to people well prepared in subject-matter areas but lacking in required professional courses, frequently met vocal opposition. This was often interpreted to mean that educators by and large consider it less damaging to have teachers unprepared in academic fields than in the professional aspects of their training. This construction might well have been avoided had a firm agreement been reached on the importance of intellectual standards before licensure requirements were discussed.

Certification is a difficult and complex process, and the scholars went to the third conference prepared to listen and learn. Generally, however, they report that the learning was primarily on their side, that the outcome of the debate sometimes seemed to have been settled before the conference opened, and that at least some of the educators appeared to be in a mood to nullify the concessions that had been made in 1958 and 1959.

It would be entirely incorrect to suggest, however, that all of the liberal arts professors viewed the results of the conference in such a discouraging light. Many were encouraged by the fact that the more rigid, and generally the most vocal, of the educators did not reflect the views of the profession as a whole. Classroom teachers, for example, seemed to be much more inclined to approve strong subject-matter programs and to insist upon endorsed certificates than were the superintendents and principals who are trapped in the mesh of the current teacher shortage. Professors of education and state certification officers likewise, in public or in private, indicated that they would like to see a certification system which would prevent teachers from giving courses in which they were not fully qualified. For this reason alone, a number of scholars, who were otherwise disappointed with the immediate results at San Diego, believed that something positive had been accomplished. Their very presence had furnished support for those who had previously felt inhibited about expressing their convictions.

The impressions the individual scholars took away with them from San Diego were in large part dependent upon the particular groups to which they were assigned. In one or two cases they felt themselves regarded as interlopers whose ideas were unwelcome. Others believed they had at least achieved negative results by acting as a brake on the extremists. In several groups, however, there was a good deal of sentiment in favor of giving liberal arts representatives a voice in the establishment of certification standards.

Unfortunately, a good many of the ACLS delegates who attended all three conferences are not as prepared to believe as they once were that such general recommendations will ever be translated into action. They have noted little change in attitude in their own departments of education or in state TEPS meetings, and they feel that San Diego failed to provide the impetus necessary to bring action on the local level. Moreover, the New Horizons Report issued by the TEPS Commission the week after the San Diego conference proved to be disheartening to every scholar who hoped for positive results from these conferences.

*   *   *

Large national conferences may be able to discuss general ideas, but the associations of subject-matter disciplines must take up the task of improving the program of teacher education. The overwhelming majority of the reports stressed this point. By establishing criteria for teacher training programs, by insisting on representation in accrediting agencies and on certification boards, and by establishing committees to work out model curricula for teacher education, the learned societies can exert great influence at all levels.

The scholars realize that the leaders in teacher education must be convinced and converted before anything can be accomplished, but they believe that the classroom teachers, if given sound texts and programs, and adequate support, can do much to effect this conversion. The TEPS officials, by inviting liberal arts representatives to this series of conferences, and by giving them a fair opportunity to express their views, performed a service which the professional associations of the academic disciplines cannot ignore.

JAMES CONANT ON NEW METHODS OF TRAINING AND CERTIFYING TEACHERS (1963)   From James B. Conant, *The Education of American Teachers* (New York, 1963), pp. 209–16.

I began this volume by introducing the reader to a long-standing quarrel among educators. I close by collecting in one chapter my recommendations, whose acceptance I believe might end the quarrel. If my findings are correct, neither side in the conflict has developed as coherent and consistent a position as the battle cries would lead the hearer to expect. In any discussion about the idea of a liberally educated man, one encounters differences of opinion as to what this expression means; and there is a great variety of programs reflecting these diverse opinions. A cynic might be tempted to define a liberal education as a four-year exposure to an experience prescribed by a group of professors, each of whom has prime allegiance to his own academic discipline. The programs in many institutions seem to have been developed not by careful consideration of a group but by a process that might be called academic logrolling. (I am not unfamiliar with the bargaining between departments when it comes to dividing up a student's time.) In any event, one finds a complete lack of agreement on what constitutes a satisfactory general education program for future teachers. As to the education in a specific field which the college student expects to teach, there is a far greater degree of unanimity. But about the amount of time to be devoted to such studies in college and the level of competence to be demanded, opinions differ.

When one examines the courses in education, one finds almost as much confusion as exists in general education. Here the cynic might well say that the professors are jealous of their share of the student's time but are ill prepared to use it well.

Academic professors and professors of education are in complete agreement only on one point: that practice teaching, if well conducted, is important. Aside from

THE
PROFESSION
OF EDUCATION

practice teaching and the accompanying methods course, there is little agreement among professors of education on the nature of the corpus of knowledge they are expected to transmit to the future teacher.

In view of the great diversity of opinions and practices to be found in the leading institutions, I conclude that neither a state authority nor a voluntary accrediting agency is in a position to specify the amount of time to be devoted to either academic or educational courses. What is needed is on the one hand for the state to allow freedom for institutions to experiment, and on the other for the academic professors and professors of education in each institution to take joint responsibility for the reputation of their college or university in training teachers.

Recognizing that the 27 recommendations distributed throughout various chapters of the book may be difficult to recall, I have arranged them in five categories according to the persons most likely to be involved in bringing about their adoption.

Group A. Recommendations Requiring Action Either by a Chief State School Officer, a State Board of Education or a Legislature

1. CERTIFICATION REQUIREMENTS

For certification purposes the state should require only (a) that a candidate hold a baccalaureate degree from a legitimate college or university, (b) that he submit evidence of having successfully performed as a student teacher under the direction of college and public school personnel in whom the state Department has confidence, and in a practice-teaching situation of which the state Department approves, and (c) that he hold a specially endorsed teaching certificate from a college or university which, in issuing the official document, attests that the institution as a whole considers the person adequately prepared to teach in a designated field and grade level.

5. PROGRAMS OF PRACTICE TEACHING

The state should approve programs of practice teaching. It should, working cooperatively with the college and public school authorities, regulate the conditions under which practice teaching is done and the nature of the methods instruction that accompanies it. The state should require that the colleges and public school systems involved submit evidence concerning the competence of those appointed as cooperating teachers and clinical professors.

6. STATE INFORMATION SERVICE

State Departments of Education should develop and make available to local school boards and colleges and universities data relevant to the preparation and employment of teachers. Such data may include information about the types of teacher-education programs of colleges or universities throughout the state and information concerning supply and demand of teachers at various grade levels and in various fields.

7. ASSIGNMENT OF TEACHERS BY LOCAL BOARDS

The state education authorities should give top priority to the development of regulations insuring that a teacher will be assigned only to those teaching duties for which he is specifically prepared, and should enforce these regulations rigorously.

10. CERTIFICATION RECIPROCITY AMONG STATES

Whenever a teacher has been certified by one state under the provisions of Recommendations 1 and 2, his certificate should be accepted as valid in any other state.

Group B. Recommendations Involving Appropriations by State Legislatures

4. STATE FINANCIAL RESPONSIBILITY FOR PRACTICE TEACHING

The state should provide financial assistance to local boards to insure high-quality practice teaching as part of the preparation of teachers enrolled in either private or public institutions.

12. LOAN POLICY FOR FUTURE TEACHERS

Each state should develop a loan policy for future teachers aimed at recruiting into the profession the most able students; the requirements for admission to the teacher-training institutions within the state should be left to the institution, but the state should set a standard for the recipients in terms of scholastic aptitude; the amount of the loan should be sufficient to cover expenses, and the loan should be cancelled after four or five years of teaching in the public schools of the state.

Group C. Recommendations Requiring Action by a Local School Board, Either Acting Alone or in Conjunction with State Action

3. COOPERATING TEACHERS IN PRACTICE TEACHING

Public school systems that enter contracts with a college or university for practice teaching should designate, as classroom teachers working with practice teaching, only those persons in whose competence as teachers, leaders, and evaluators they have the highest confidence, and should give such persons encouragement by reducing their work loads and raising their salaries.

11. INITIAL PROBATIONARY PERIOD OF EMPLOYMENT

During the initial probationary period, local school boards should take specific steps to provide the new teacher with every possible help in the form of: (a) limited teaching responsibility; (b) aid in gathering instructional materials; (c) advice of experienced teachers whose own load is reduced so that they can work with the new teacher in his own classroom; (d) shifting to more experienced teachers those pupils who create problems beyond the ability of the novice to handle effectively; and (e) specialized instruction concerning the characteristics of the community, the neighborhood, and the students he is likely to encounter.

23. REVISION OF SALARY SCHEDULE BY LOCAL BOARDS

School boards should drastically revise their salary schedules. There should be a large jump in salary when a teacher moves from the probationary status to tenure. Any salary increments based on advanced studies should not be tied to course credits earned (semester hours), but only to the earning of a master's degree, based normally on full-time residence or four summer sessions in which the program is directed toward the development of the competence of the teacher as a teacher. Such a salary increment should be made mandatory by state law.

24. FINANCIAL ASSISTANCE TO TEACHERS FOR STUDY IN SUMMER SCHOOLS

School boards or the state should provide financial assistance so that teachers may attend summer school after enrolling in a graduate school for the purpose of completing a program of the type stated in Recommendation 23.

25. LEAVES OF ABSENCE FOR FURTHER EDUCATION OF TEACHERS

School boards should provide leave of absence with salary for a full-time semester residence at a university to enable teachers to study toward a master's program, provided this program is designed to increase the competence of the teacher; state funds should be available for this purpose.

27. IN-SERVICE EDUCATION OF TEACHERS

To insure that the teachers are up to date, particularly in a period of rapid change (as in mathematics and physics), a school board should contract with an educational institution to provide short-term seminars (often called workshops) during the school year so that all the teachers, without cost to them, may benefit from the instruction. Such seminars or workshops might also study the particular educational problems of a given school or school district. (No credit toward salary increases would be given.)

Group D. Recommendations Requiring Action by the Faculties, Administrative Officers and Trustees of an Institution Engaged in Educating Teachers for the Public Elementary and Secondary Schools

2. COLLEGIATE OR UNIVERSITY RESPONSIBILITY

Each college or university should be permitted to develop in detail whatever program of teacher education it considers most desirable, subject only to two conditions: first, the president of the institution in behalf of the entire faculty involved—academic as well as professional—certifies that the candidate is adequately prepared to teach on a specific level or in specific fields, and second, the institution establishes in conjunction with a public school system a state-approved practice-teaching arrangement.

13. THE ALL-UNIVERSITY APPROACH TO TEACHER TRAINING

If the institution is engaged in educating teachers, the lay board trustees should ask the faculty or faculties whether in fact there is a continuing and effective all-university (or interdepartmental) approach to the education of teachers; and if not, why not?

14. REQUIREMENTS FOR COLLEGIATE OR UNIVERSITY TEACHER-EDUCATION PROGRAMS

The board of trustees should ask the faculty to justify the present requirements for a bachelor's degree for future teachers with particular reference to the breadth of the requirements and to spell out what in fact are the total educational exposures (school and college) demanded now in the fields of (a) mathematics, (b) physical science, (c) biological science, (d) social science, (e) English literature, (f) English composition, (g) history, (h) philosophy.

15. FOREIGN LANGUAGE PREPARATION

If courses are required in a foreign language, evidence of the degree of mastery obtained by fulfilling the minimum requirement for a degree should be presented to the board of trustees.

16. THE ESTABLISHMENT OF "CLINICAL PROFESSORS"

The professor from the college or university who is to supervise and assess the practice teaching should have had much practical experience. His status should be analogous to that of a clinical professor in certain medical schools.

17. BASIC PREPARATION OF ELEMENTARY TEACHERS

(a). The program for teachers of kindergarten and grades 1, 2, and 3 should prepare them in the content and methodology of all subjects taught in these early school years. Depth in a single subject or cluster of subjects is not necessary.
(b). The program for teachers of grades 4, 5, and 6 should provide depth of content and methods of teaching in a specific subject or cluster of subjects normally taught in these grades, with only an introduction to the remaining elementary school subjects.

18. PRACTICE TEACHING FOR ELEMENTARY TEACHERS

All future elementary teachers should engage in practice teaching for a period of at least 8 weeks, spending a minimum of 3 hours a day in the classroom; the period must include at least 3 weeks of full responsibility for the classroom under the direction of a cooperating teacher and the supervision of a clinical professor.

19. ADEQUATE STAFFING OF SMALL COLLEGES TRAINING ELEMENTARY TEACHERS

Those responsible for financing and administering small colleges should consider whether they can afford to maintain an adequate staff for the preparation of elementary school teachers. Unless they are able to employ the equivalent of three or four professors devoting their time to elementary education, they should cease attempting to prepare teachers for the elementary schools.

20. SINGLE FIELD DIPLOMA FOR SECONDARY SCHOOL TEACHERS

An institution should award a teaching certificate for teachers in grades 7 to 12 in one field only.

21. CLINICAL PROFESSORS IN INSTITUTIONS EDUCATING SECONDARY TEACHERS

Every institution awarding a special teaching certificate for secondary school teachers should have on the staff a clinical professor for each field or combination of closely related fields.

22. TEACHING DIPLOMA FOR ART, MUSIC AND PHYSICAL EDUCATION TEACHERS

An institution offering programs in art or music or physical education should be prepared to award a teaching diploma in each of these fields without grade designation; institutional programs should not attempt to develop competency in more than one field in four years.

26. MASTER'S DEGREE PROGRAMS

The graduate schools of education or their equivalent (in universities organized without such separate degree-granting schools) should devise a program for increasing the competence of teachers as teachers with the following characteristics:

(1) It should be open to any graduate of the same institution in the same field of endeavor (e.g., elementary education, secondary school social studies, etc.).

(2) Courses should be allowed for credit toward the 30 semester hours whether or not the courses are of an elementary nature, provided they are clearly courses needed to increase the competence of the teacher.

(3) No credit toward the degree should be given for extension courses or courses taken on campus while the teacher is engaged on a full-time teaching job.

(4) Passing of a comprehensive examination should be required for the master's degree, as is now the case in some institutions.

(5) The summer-school sessions should be arranged so that four summer residences will complete the degree requirements, or two summers plus one full-time semester residence.

(6) If the offering in the arts and sciences is not wide enough to provide meaningful work in the summer session (as it would not be in some state colleges), arrangements should be made for the transfer of credit from a university summer school with a good offering of courses in subject-matter fields.

(7) For elementary teachers, the degree should be master of education in elementary education; for secondary teachers, master of education in English (or science, or social science or modern languages or mathematics).

Academic Freedom

DECISION ON THE TEACHING OF ANY SUBJECT EXCEPT IN ENGLISH
(1919)   From *Meyer* v. *State of Nebraska,* 262 U.S. 390.

The challenged statute forbids the teaching in school of any subject except in English; also the teaching of any other language until the pupil has attained and successfully passed the eighth grade, which is not usually accomplished before the age of twelve. The Supreme Court of the State has held that "the so-called ancient or dead languages" are not "within the spirit or the purpose of the act" . . . Latin, Greek, Hebrew are not proscribed; but German, French, Spanish, Italian and every other alien speech are within the ban. Evidently the legislature has attempted materially to interfere with the calling of modern language teachers, with the opportunities of pupils to acquire knowledge, and with the power of parents to control the education of their own.

It is said the purpose of the legislation was to promote civic development by inhibiting training and education of the immature in foreign tongues and ideals before they could learn English and acquire American ideals; and "that the English language should be and become the mother tongue of all children reared in this State." It is also affirmed that the foreign born population is very large, that certain communities commonly use foreign words, follow foreign leaders, move in a foreign atmosphere, and that the children are thereby hindered from becoming citizens of the most useful type and the public safety is imperiled.

That the State may do much, go very far, indeed, in order to improve the quality of its citizens, physically, mentally and morally, is clear; but the individual has certain fundamental rights which must be respected. The protection of the Constitution extends to all, to those who speak other languages as well as to those born with English on the tongue. Perhaps it would be highly advantageous if all had ready understanding of our ordinary speech, but this cannot be coerced by methods which conflict with the Constitution—a desirable end cannot be promoted by prohibited means.

*   *   *

The desire of the legislature to foster a homogeneous people with American ideals prepared readily to understand current discussions of civic matters is easy to appreciate. Unfortunate experiences during the late war and aversion toward every characteristic of truculent adversaries were certainly enough to quicken that aspiration. But the means adopted, we think, exceed the limitations upon the power of the State and conflict with rights assured to plaintiff in error. The interference is plain enough and no adequate reason therefore in time of peace and domestic tranquility has been shown.

The power of the state to compel attendance at some school and to make reasonable regulations for all schools, including a requirement that they shall give instructions in English, is not questioned. Nor has challenge been made of the state's power to prescribe a curriculum for institutions which it supports. Those matters are not within the present controversy. Our concern is with the prohibition approved by the Supreme Court. . . . No emergency has arisen which renders knowledge by a child of some language other than English so clearly harmful as to justify its inhibition with the consequent infringement of rights long freely enjoyed. We are constrained to conclude that the statute as applied is arbitrary and without reasonable relation to any end within the competency of the state.

As the statute undertakes to interfere only with teaching which involves a modern language, leaving complete freedom as to other matters, there seems no adequate foundation for the suggestion that the purpose was to protect the child's health by limiting his mental activities. It is well known that proficiency in a foreign language seldom comes to one not instructed at an early age, and experience shows that this is not injurious to the health, morals or understanding of the ordinary child.

The judgment of the court below must be reversed and the cause remanded for further proceedings not inconsistent with this opinion.

Reversed.

MR. JUSTICE HOLMES AND MR. JUSTICE SUTHERLAND, DISSENT.

TENNESSEE OUTLAWS TEACHING OF DARWINISM (1925) From *Session Laws of Tennessee,* 1925, pp. 50–51.

SECTION 1

Be it enacted by the general assembly of the State of Tennessee, That it shall be unlawful for any teacher in any of the universities, normals and all other public schools of the state which are supported in whole or in part by the public school funds of the state to teach any theory that denies the story of the divine creation of man, as taught in the Bible and to teach instead that man has descended from a lower order of animals.

SECTION 2

Be it further enacted, That any teacher found guilty of the violation of this act, shall be guilty of a misdemeanor and upon conviction shall be fined not less than one hundred dollars and not more than five hundred dollars for each offense.

Be it further enacted, That this act take effect from and after its passage, the public welfare requiring it.

A DIALOGUE CONCERNING THE TEACHER AND MAJORITY RULE
(**1928**)   From Walter Lippmann, *American Inquisitors: A Commentary on Dayton and Chicago* (New York, 1928), pp. 96–99, 106–11.

Dialogue In America: Concerning Majority Rule

I shall suppose that the teacher finds himself in a community like Dayton or Chicago, where an effective majority of the voters is insisting that he shall make the schools safe for some kind of fundamentalism.

SOCRATES: The question you are asking yourself is what respect you ought to have in your own mind for the wishes of a majority. What then do you mean by wishes?

TEACHER: I mean the wish that in teaching science I shall not impugn revelation and that in teaching history I shall not impugn tradition.

SOCRATES: You being yourself one who accepts the authority of reason?

TEACHER: Yes.

SOCRATES: Then you cannot accept the authority of revelation or of tradition?

TEACHER: No. But I am employed by people a majority of whom do accept it.

SOCRATES: Have you complete confidence in reason?

TEACHER: In reason, yes.—In my reasoning, no.

SOCRATES: You feel that you may be wrong, and that the majority may be right.

TEACHER: Surely that is possible.

SOCRATES: Do you feel that the opinions of the majority may be right because they are the opinions of the majority?

TEACHER: Sometimes. But not always. The difficulty is to know when. There is some kind of wisdom in numbers.

SOCRATES: Your task then is to find out, if you can, what kind of wisdom there is in numbers.

TEACHER: Yes. It is plain, I think, that the majority is often wrong. It is equally plain that the educated minority has often been wrong.

SOCRATES: Then perhaps being right or wrong has nothing to do with majorities and minorities.

TEACHER: I am not satisfied with that. There are times, I believe, when an opinion is entitled to particular respect because it is the opinion of the majority.

SOCRATES: It would have to be the kind of opinion about which the majority was competent to have an opinion. Would it not?

TEACHER: Obviously.

SOCRATES: Is the majority competent to have an opinion about physics and biology?

TEACHER: I am sure it is not. You cannot settle scientific controversies by the election returns.

SOCRATES: But you settle great human problems by the election returns. And these problems are more important in your lives than any problem in physics or biology.

TEACHER: We do not settle great human problems by the election returns. We find out which party is the stronger. We decide between two or more courses of action.

SOCRATES: Then what you can learn from the majority is what the majority intends to do or consents to have done.

TEACHER: That is about what political democracy amounts to. Power today resides in numbers. It is necessary, therefore, for governments to satisfy numbers.

SOCRATES: Regardless of whether the majority is right or wrong?

TEACHER: In government it is necessary to know what the majority wants and what it will tolerate before you can know what is right or wrong. To act without that is to invite revolution.

SOCRATES: Then what the majority knows is what the majority wants. The people are experts on the subject of their own desires.

TEACHER: Not so very expert at that. They often do not know what they want. Less often do they know what they will want.

SOCRATES: Is it not so that they at least know at any particular moment what they think they want?

TEACHER: That much not even Mr. Mencken would deny.

SOCRATES: Pardon me, did I hear you say "Mr. Mencken"? I haven't met him.

TEACHER: A charming fellow, I assure you. You'll meet him soon.

TEACHER: We have not gotten much further.

SOCRATES: Your conclusion then is that this mystic wisdom of the people is most likely to appear in small groups dealing with their own affairs?

TEACHER: It is not likely to appear when they are dealing with other people's affairs, though most men seem to think so nowadays. And it is not likely to appear in large groups dealing with matters they know only by hearsay and can't very well understand. There can't be much wisdom in that.

SOCRATES: You are not, however, opposed to political democracy?

TEACHER: Am I opposed to the weather? On cold rainy days I am. The fact of democracy is as little subject to discussion in the modern world as the weather. Even dictators have to consult or cajole the people. There are two kinds of muddleheadedness in our own age on this question: there are the muddleheaded people who think the people are wise and the muddleheaded people who think they are foolish. Now Mr. Mencken—

SOCRATES: You were sorry the last time you mentioned him.

TEACHER: I won't mention him though it is a little like trying not to think of a white elephant for ten consecutive minutes.

SOCRATES: You were not talking about Mr. Mencken or about white elephants. You were talking of muddleheaded people.

TEACHER: Yes, and I was about to say that they are muddleheaded because they judge democracy from the point of view of what is wise and of what is unwise, when as a matter of fact political democracy is a matter of finding out who intends to have the last word, and then of having the government behave accordingly.

SOCRATES: Then to the expressions of political democracy you give no inward respect whatever?

TEACHER: Ought I to?

SOCRATES: The majority is sovereign. Ought the sovereign not to be respected?

TEACHER: We have already discussed the difficulties, have we not?

SOCRATES: Yes, but your conclusion is a little puzzling. You have no inward respect for the opinions of most majorities. Can you obey a sovereign whose opinions you do not respect?

TEACHER: Can I serve that sovereign if I do respect his opinions?

SOCRATES: Never mind the paradoxes.

TEACHER: The relation of an individual to democracy is a paradox. If everyone respected the opinions of the majority, those opinions would never improve. If everybody defied the opinions of the majority, there would be no government. And therefore no use in trying to improve the opinions of the majority.

SOCRATES: Your sovereign under democracy is a peculiar person.

TEACHER: He is not a person. He is many persons and not the same ones every day.

SOCRATES: Perhaps that is where your paradoxes arise. This democratic sovereign is not a person. It is a changing array of individuals. You may be part of the sovereign power one day and not the next.

TEACHER: Precisely.

SOCRATES: On the day when you are not part of it, you are one of the Outs hoping to become one of the Ins?

TEACHER: Or at least hoping to teach the Ins some better sense.

SOCRATES: Then whether you are out or in you are always helping to create the sovereign in a democracy?

TEACHER: In a manner of speaking.

SOCRATES: When you join the crowd you add to its force. When you resist the crowd, what happens to you?

TEACHER: I may lose my job. I may be pushed aside. I may be trampled upon.

SOCRATES: Is that the only fate of those who resist the crowd?

TEACHER: A very few become the leaders of the crowd.

SOCRATES: Is that all?

TEACHER: A few are cranks and fools.

SOCRATES: Is that all?

TEACHER: A few are martyrs and geniuses.

SOCRATES: What about those who go with the crowd. Are they all fools?

TEACHER: Certainly not.

SOCRATES: Are they all wise men?

TEACHER: Obviously not.

SOCRATES: Then to go with the crowd or against it is in itself no sign of wisdom or folly?

TEACHER: But we started out to see whether a man should respect or defy the crowd.

SOCRATES: And we have concluded that the majority is entitled to no particular respect. And that it is entitled to no particular disrespect. And that wise men may go with it. And that wise men may defy it. And that fools go with it. And that fools defy it. Is your question not answered?

TEACHER: How is it answered?

SOCRATES: Why, by saying that the rebellion of a wise man is wise and that the rebellion of a fool is foolish.

TEACHER: I am not sure whether this is a paradox or a truism.

SOCRATES: It is neither. Whether a man shall conform or rebel is largely an accident of his temperament and his circumstances. But whether in his rebellion or conformity a man is wise or foolish, whether he knows what he is doing and why, and where he is going and how fast, and what the consequences are, what are the risks and the costs, what lies behind and ahead and in between—those are the questions on which everything depends.

TEACHER: Is there then no rule of conduct in these matters?

SOCRATES: Your Washington was willing to shed blood in order to defy the constituted authorities. Your Lincoln was willing to shed blood to uphold the constituted authorities. They have both been justified. There can be no rule of conduct. That which brave men do with wisdom lesser men make rules to justify.

A Broad Generalization

To those who are seeking a simpler clue amidst these perplexities, I can offer only this suggestion: The advancement of human liberty has as a matter of practical politics consisted in building up centers of resistance against the absolutism of the reigning sovereign. For experience has shown that liberty is most ample if power is distributed, checked, and limited up to the point where it is paralyzed and is unable to maintain order. The struggles for liberty have consisted, therefore, in restraining the power of the Ins by the power of the Outs, in limiting the power of the king by the resistance of the nobles, or in limiting the power of the nobles by strengthening the power of the king. Whoever the sovereign, the program of liberty is to deprive him of arbitrary and absolute power.

In our age the power of majorities tends to become arbitrary and absolute. And therefore, it may well be that to limit the power of majorities, to dispute their moral authority, to deflect their impact, to dissolve their force, is now the most important task of those who care for liberty.

CALIFORNIA LOYALTY OATH FOR TEACHERS (1931)   From State of California Laws, chap. 71 (1943), p. 533.

Section 12009. Except as provided in this section, no credential shall be granted to any person unless and until he has subscribed to the following oath or affirmation:

"I solemnly swear (or affirm) that I will support the constitution of the United States of America, the constitution of the State of California, and the laws of the United States and the State of California, and will by precept and example, promote respect for the flag and the statutes of the United States and of the State of California, reverence for law and order, and undivided allegiance to the government of the United States of America."

The oath or affirmation shall be subscribed before any person authorized to administer oaths or before any member of a board of trustees or any board of education of the state and filed with the state board of education. Any person who is a citizen or subject of any country other than the United States, and who is employed in any capacity in any of the public schools of the state shall, before entering upon the discharge of his duties, subscribe to an oath to support the institutions and policies of the United States during the period of his sojourn within the state. Upon the violation of any of the terms of the oath or affirmation, the state board of education shall suspend or revoke the credential which has been issued.

NEW YORK TEACHERS' OATH (1934)   From *New York Education Law,* Section 709.

Section 709. After October first, nineteen hundred thirty-four, it shall be unlawful for any citizen of the United States to serve as teacher, instructor or professor in any school or institution in the public school system of the state or in any school, college, university or other educational institution in this state, whose real property or any part of it is exempt from taxation, under section four of the tax law unless and until he or she shall have taken and subscribed the following oath or affirmation:

"I do solemnly swear (or affirm) that I will support the constitution of the United States of America and the constitution of the state of New York, and that I will faithfully discharge, according to the best of my ability, the duties of the position of . . . . (title of position and name or designation of school, college, university or institution to be here inserted), to which I am now assigned."

The oath required by this section shall be administered by the president or other head of such school, college, university or institution, or by the officer or person, or in the case of a board or body by a member of the board or body, having authority to employ such person as a teacher, instructor or professor in such school, college, university or institution, and each is hereby authorized to administer it. The officer, person or member administering such oath shall cause a record or notation of the fact to be made in the books or records of the school, college, university or institution, and forthwith transmit the oath as taken and subscribed to the commissioner of education, who shall file it in his office, where it shall be subject to public inspection. It shall be unlawful for an officer, person or board having control of the employment, dismissal or suspension of teachers, instructors or professors in such a school, college, university or institution, to permit a person to serve in any such capacity therein in violation of the provisions of this section. This section shall not be construed to require a person to take such oath more than once during the time he or she is employed in the same school, college, university or institution, though there be a change in the title or duties of the position.

The provisions of section thirty of the civil service law shall not apply to a person who is required to take the oath prescribed by this section.

OPPOSITION OF THE AMERICAN ASSOCIATION OF UNIVERSITY PROFESSORS TO LOYALTY OATHS FOR TEACHERS (1937) From American Association of University Professors *Bulletin,* vol. XXIII, p. 7.

Whereas loyalty oath laws for teachers are futile in effecting the legitimate aims of such laws, that is an understanding of and loyalty towards American ideals; and whereas these laws can easily be used as an instrument to promote intolerance, restrict our civil liberties and the freedom of teaching, and to accentuate propaganda against democratic ideals; and whereas, these laws cast an undeserved aspersion on the integrity and loyalty of the teaching profession. Be it resolved, therefore, that our chapters and all citizens are urged to oppose the enactment of such laws, and to work for their repeal in states where such laws are already on the statute books.

DECISION ON STATE QUALIFICATIONS OF TEACHERS (1952) From *Adler v. Board of Education of New York,* 342 U.S. 485 (1952).

Appeal from the Court of Appeals of New York.

MR. JUSTICE MINTON DELIVERED THE OPINION OF THE COURT.

It is first argued that the Feinberg Law and the rules promulgated thereunder constitute an abridgment of the freedom of speech and assembly of persons employed or seeking employment in the public schools of the State of New York.

It is clear that such persons have the right under our law to assemble, speak, think and believe as they will. . . . It is equally clear that they have no right to work for the State in the school system on their own terms. . . . They may work for the school system upon the reasonable terms laid down by the proper authorities of New York. If they do not choose to work on such terms, they are at liberty to retain their beliefs and associations and go elsewhere. Has the State thus deprived them of any right to free speech or assembly? We think not. Such persons are or may be denied, under the statutes in question, the privilege of working for the school system of the State of New York because, first, of their advocacy of the overthrow of the government by force or violence, or, secondly, by unexplained membership in an organization found by the school authorities, after notice and hearing, to teach and advocate the overthrow of the government by force or violence, and known by such persons to have such purpose.

The constitutionality of the first proposition is not questioned here. . . .

As to the second, it is rather subtly suggested that we should not follow our recent decision in *Garner* v. *Los Angeles Board,* 341 U.S. 716. We there said:

We think that a municipal employer is not disabled because it is an agency of the State from inquiring of its employees as to matters that may prove relevant to their fitness and suitability for the public service. Past conduct may well relate to present fitness; past loyalty may have a reasonable relationship to present and future trust. Both are commonly inquired into in determining fitness for both high and low positions in private industry and are not less relevant in public employment. . . .

We adhere to that case. A teacher works in a sensitive area in a schoolroom. There he shapes the attitude of young minds toward the society in which they live. In this, the state has a vital concern. It must preserve the integrity of the schools. That the school authorities have the right and the duty to screen the officials, teachers, and employees as to their fitness to maintain the integrity of the schools as a part of ordered society, cannot be doubted. One's associates, past and present, as well as one's conduct, may properly be considered in determining fitness and loyalty. From time immemorial, one's reputation has been determined in part by the company he keeps. In the employment of officials and teachers of the school system, the state may very properly inquire into the company they keep, and we know of no rule, constitutional or otherwise, that prevents the state, when determining the fitness and loyalty of such persons, from considering the organizations and persons with whom they associate.

If, under the procedure set up in the New York law, a person is found to be unfit and is disqualified from employment in the public school system because of membership in a listed organization, he is not thereby denied the right of free speech and assembly. His freedom of choice between membership in the organization and employment in the school system might be limited, but not his freedom of speech or assembly, except in the remote sense that limitation is inherent in every choice. Certainly such limitation is not one the state may not make in the exercise of its police power to protect the schools from pollution and thereby to defend its own existence.

It is next argued by appellants that the provision in §3022 directing the Board of Regents to provide in rules and regulations that membership in any organization listed by the Board after notice and hearing, with provision for review in accordance with the statute, shall constitute prima facie evidence of disqualification, denies due process, because the fact found bears no relation to the fact presumed. In other words, from the fact found that the organization was one that advocated the overthrow of government by unlawful means and that the person employed or to be employed was a member of the organization and knew of its purpose, to presume that such a member is disqualified for employment is so unreasonable as to be a denial of due process of law. We do not agree. . . .

Membership in a listed organization found to be within the statute and known by the member to be within the statute is a legislative finding that the member by his membership supports the thing the organization stands for, namely, the overthrow of government by unlawful means. We cannot say that such a finding is contrary to fact or that "generality of experience" points to a different conclusion. Disqualification follows therefore as a reasonable presumption from such membership and support. Nor is there here a problem of procedural due process. The presumption is not conclusive but arises only in a hearing where the person against whom it may arise has full opportunity to rebut it. . . .

Where, as here, the relation between the fact found and the presumption is clear and direct and is not conclusive, the requirements of due process are satisfied. . . .

It is also suggested that the use of the word "subversive" is vague and indefinite. But the word is first used in §1 of the Feinberg Law, which is the preamble to the

Act, and not in a definitive part thereof. When used in subdivision 2 of § 3022, the word has a very definite meaning, namely, an organization that teaches and advocates the overthrow of the government by force or violence.

We find no constitutional infirmity in   12-a of the Civil Service Law of New York or in the Feinberg Law which implemented it, and the judgment is

Affirmed.

MR. JUSTICE BLACK, DISSENTING.

This is another of those rapidly multiplying legislative enactments which make it dangerous—this time for school teachers—to think or say anything except what a transient majority happen to approve at the moment. Basically these laws rest on the belief that government should supervise and limit the flow of ideas into the minds of men. The tendency of such governmental policy is to mould people into a common intellectual pattern. Quite a different governmental policy rests on the belief that government should leave the mind and spirit of man absolutely free. Such a governmental policy encourages varied intellectual outlooks in the belief that the best views will prevail. This policy of freedom is in my judgment embodied in the First Amendment and made applicable to the states by the Fourteenth. Because of this policy public officials cannot be constitutionally vested with powers to select the ideas people can think about, censor the public views they can express, or choose the persons or groups people can associate with. Public officials with such powers are not public servants; they are public masters.

I dissent from the Court's judgment sustaining this law which effectively penalizes school teachers for their thoughts and their associates.

MR. JUSTICE FRANKFURTER, DISSENTING.

We are asked to pass on a scheme to counteract what are currently called "subversive" influences in the public school system of New York. The scheme is formulated partly in statutes and partly in administrative regulations, but all of it is still an unfinished blueprint. We are asked to adjudicate claims against its constitutionality before the scheme has been put into operation, before the limits that it imposes upon free inquiry and association, the scope of scrutiny that it sanctions, and the procedural safeguards that will be found to be implied for its enforcement have been authoritatively defined. I think we should adhere to the teaching of this Court's history to avoid constitutional adjudications on merely abstract or speculative issues and to base them on the concreteness afforded by an actual, present, defined controversy, appropriate for judicial judgment, between adversaries immediately affected by it. In accordance with the settled limits upon our jurisdiction I would dismiss this appeal.

JUSTICE DOUGLAS, WITH WHOM MR. JUSTICE BLACK CONCURS, DISSENTING.

I have not been able to accept the recent doctrine that a citizen who enters the public service can be forced to sacrifice his civil rights. I cannot for example find in our constitutional scheme the power of a state to place its employees in the category of second-class citizens by denying them freedom of thought and expression. The Constitution guarantees freedom of thought and expression to everyone in our society. All are entitled to it; and none needs it more than the teacher.

The public school is in most respects the cradle of our democracy. The increasing role of the public school is seized upon by proponents of the type of legislation represented by New York's Feinberg law as proof of the importance and need for keeping the school free of "subversive influences." But that is to misconceive the effect of this type of legislation. Indeed the impact of this kind of censorship on the public school system illustrates the high purpose of the First Amendment in freeing speech and thought from censorship.

The present law proceeds on a principle repugnant to our society—guilt by association. A teacher is disqualified because of her membership in an organization found to be "subversive." The finding as to the "subversive" character of the organization is made in a proceeding to which the teacher is not a party and in which it is not clear that she may even be heard. To be sure, she may have a hearing when charges of disloyalty are leveled against her. But in that hearing the finding as to the "subversive" character of the organization apparently may not be reopened in order to allow her to show the truth of the matter. The irrebuttable charge that the organization is "subversive" therefore hangs on as an ominous cloud over her own hearing. The mere fact of membership in the organization raises a prima facie case of her own guilt. She may, it is said, show her innocence. But innocence in this case turns on knowledge; and when the witch hunt is on, one who must rely on ignorance leans on a feeble reed.

The very threat of such procedure is certain to raise havoc with academic freedom. Youthful indiscretions, mistaken causes, misguided enthusiasms—all long forgotten—become the ghosts of a harrowing present. Any organization committed to a liberal cause, any group organized to revolt against an hysterical trend, any committee launched to sponsor an unpopular program becomes suspect. These are the organizations into which Communists often infiltrate. Their presence infects the whole, even though the project was not conceived in sin. A teacher caught in that mesh is almost certain to stand condemned. Fearing condemnation, she will tend to shrink from any association that stirs controversy. In that manner freedom of expression will be stifled.

But that is only part of it. Once a teacher's connection with a listed organization is shown, her views become subject to scrutiny to determine whether her membership in the organization is innocent or, if she was formerly a member, whether she has *bona fide* abandoned her membership.

The law inevitably turns the school system into a spying project. Regular loyalty reports on the teachers must be made out. The principals become detectives; the students, the parents, the community become informers. Ears are cocked for telltale signs of disloyalty. The prejudices of the community come into play in searching out the disloyal. This is not the usual type of supervision which checks a teacher's competency; it is a system which searches for hidden meanings in a teacher's utterances.

footer labelTHE
PROFESSION
OF EDUCATION

DECISION ON STATES' RIGHT TO INQUIRE INTO FITNESS OF TEACHERS TO TEACH (1958)   From *Beilan v. Board of Education of Philadelphia,* 357 U.S. 399 (1958).

Certiorari to the Supreme Court of Pennsylvania.

MR. JUSTICE BURTON DELIVERED THE OPINION OF THE COURT.

By engaging in teaching in the public schools, petitioner did not give up his right to freedom of belief, speech or association. He did, however, undertake obligations of frankness, candor and cooperation in answering inquiries made of him by his employing Board examining into his fitness to serve it as a public school teacher.

"A teacher works in a sensitive area in a schoolroom. There he shapes the attitude of young minds toward the society in which they live. In this, the state has a vital concern. It must preserve the integrity of the schools. That the school authorities have the right and the duty to screen the officials, teachers, and employees as to their fitness to maintain the integrity of the schools as a part of ordered society, cannot be doubted." *Adler* v. *Board of Education,* 342 U.S. 485, 493.

As this Court stated in *Garner* v. *Board of Public Works,* 341 U.S. 716, 720, "We think that a municipal employer is not disabled because it is an agency of the State from inquiring of its employees as to matters that may prove relevant to their fitness and suitability for the public service."

The question asked of petitioner by his Superintendent was relevant to the issue of petitioner's fitness and suitability to serve as a teacher. Petitioner is not in a position to challenge his dismissal merely because of the remoteness in time of the 1944 activities. It was apparent from the circumstances of the two interviews that the Superintendent had other questions to ask. Petitioner's refusal to answer was not based on the remoteness of his 1944 activities. He made it clear that he would not answer any question of the same type as the one asked. Petitioner blocked from the beginning any inquiry into his Communist activities, however relevant to his present loyalty. The Board based its dismissal upon petitioner's refusal to answer any inquiry about his relevant activities—not upon those activities themselves. It took care to charge petitioner with incompetency, and not with disloyalty. It found him insubordinate and lacking in frankness and candor—it made no finding as to his loyalty.

We find no requirement in the Federal Constitution that a teacher's classroom conduct be the sole basis for determining his fitness. Fitness for teaching depends on a broad range of factors. The Pennsylvania tenure provision specifies several disqualifying grounds, including immorality, intemperance, cruelty, mental derangement and persistent and willful violation of the school laws, as well as "incompetency." However, the Pennsylvania statute, unlike those of many other States, contains no catch-all phrase such as "conduct unbecoming a teacher," to cover disqualifying conduct not included within the more specific provisions. Consequently, the Pennsylvania courts have given "incompetency" a broad interpretation. . . .

In the instant case, the Pennsylvania Supreme Court has held that "incompetency" includes petitioner's "deliberate and insubordinate refusal to answer the questions of his administrative superior in a vitally important matter pertaining to his fitness." . . . This interpretation is not inconsistent with the Federal Constitution.

Petitioner complains that he was denied due process because he was not sufficiently warned of the consequences of his refusal to answer his Superintendent. The record, however, shows that the Superintendent, in his second interview, specifically warned petitioner that his refusal to answer "was a very serious and a very important matter and that failure to answer the questions might lead to his dismissal." That was sufficient warning to petitioner that his refusal to answer might jeopardize his employment. Furthermore, at petitioner's request, his Superintendent gave him ample opportunity to consult counsel. There was no element of surprise.

Affirmed.

MR. CHIEF JUSTICE WARREN, DISSENTING.

I believe the facts of record . . . compel the conclusion that Beilan's plea of the Fifth Amendment before a sub-committee of the House Committee on Un-American Activities was so inextricably involved in the Board's decision to discharge him that the validity of the Board's action cannot be sustained without consideration of this ground. The clearest indication of this is the fact that for 13 months following petitioner's refusal to answer the Superintendent's questions, he was retained as a school teacher and continually rated "satisfactory," yet five days after his appearance before the House subcommittee petitioner was suspended. Since a plea of the Fifth Amendment before a congressional committee is an invalid basis for discharge from public employment, *Slochower* v. *Board of Higher Education,* 350 U.S. 551, I would reverse the judgment approving the petitioner's dismissal.

MR. JUSTICE DOUGLAS, WITH WHOM MR. JUSTICE BLACK CONCURS, DISSENTING.

Among the liberties of the citizens that are guaranteed by the Fourteenth Amendment are those contained in the First Amendment. . . . These include the right to believe what one chooses, the right to differ from his neighbor, the right to pick and choose the political philosophy that he likes best, the right to associate with whomever he chooses, the right to join the groups he prefers, the privilege of selecting his own path to salvation. . . .

We deal here only with a matter of belief. We have no evidence in either case that the employee in question ever committed a crime, ever moved in treasonable opposition against this country. The only mark against them—if it can be called such—is a refusal to answer questions concerning Communist Party membership. This is said to give rise to doubts concerning the competence of the teacher in the *Beilan* case and doubts as to the trustworthiness and reliability of the subway conductor in the *Lerner* case.

Our legal system is premised on the theory that every person is innocent until he is proved guilty. In this country we have, however, been moving away from that concept. We have been generating the belief that anyone who remains silent when interrogated about his unpopular beliefs or affiliations is guilty. I would allow no inference of wrongdoing to flow from the invocation of any constitutional right. I would not let that principle bow to popular passions. For all we know we are dealing here with citizens who are wholly innocent of any wrongful action. That must indeed be our premise. When we make the contrary assumption, we part radically with our tradition.

If it be said that we deal not with guilt or innocence but with frankness, the answer is the same. There are areas where government may not probe. Private citizens, private clubs, private groups may make such deductions and reach such conclusions as they choose from the failure of a citizen to disclose his beliefs, his philosophy, his associates. But government has no business penalizing a citizen merely for his beliefs or associations. . . .

If we break with tradition and let the government penalize these citizens for their beliefs and associations, the most we can assume from their failure to answer is that they were Communists. Yet, as we said in *Wieman* v. *Updegraff*, 344 U.S. 183, 190, membership in the Communist Party "may be innocent." The member may have thought that the Communist movement would develop in the parliamentary tradition here, or he may not have been aware of any unlawful aim, or knowing it, may have embraced only the socialist philosophy of the group, not any political tactics of violence and terror. Many join associations, societies, and fraternities with less than full endorsement of all their aims.

We compound error in these decisions. We not only impute wrongdoing to those who invoke their constitutional rights. We go further and impute the worst possible motives to them. . . .

In sum, we have here only a bare refusal to testify; and the Court holds that sufficient to show that these employees are unfit to hold their public posts. That makes qualification for public office turn solely on a matter of belief—a notion very much at war with the Bill of Rights.

When we make the belief of the citizens the basis of government action, we move toward the concept of *total security*. Yet *total security* is possible only in a totalitarian regime—the kind of system we profess to combat.
Mr. Justice Brennan, dissenting.

✳   ✳   ✳

STATE MAY NOT INTERFERE WITH ASSOCIATION OF FREEDOM OF TEACHERS (1960) From *Shelton V. Tucker,* 364 U.S. 479 (1960).

Appeal From The U.S. District Court For The Eastern District Of Arkansas. Certiorari to The Supreme Court of Arkansas.

MR. JUSTICE STEWART DELIVERED THE OPINION OF THE COURT.

An Arkansas statute compels every teacher, as a condition of employment in a state-supported school or college, to file annually an affidavit listing without limitation every organization to which he has belonged or regularly contributed within the preceding five years. . . .

Teachers there are hired on a year-to-year basis. They are not covered by a civil service system, and they have no job security beyond the end of each school year. The closest approach to tenure is a statutory provision for the automatic renewal of a teacher's contract if he is not notified within ten days after the end of a school year that the contract has not been renewed. . . .

The plaintiffs in the Federal District Court (appellants here) were B. T. Shelton, a teacher employed in the Little Rock Public School System, suing for himself and others similarly situated, together with the Arkansas Teachers Association and its Executive Secretary, suing for the benefit of members of the Association. Shelton had been employed in the Little Rock Special School District for twenty-five years. In the spring of 1959 he was notified that, before he could be employed for the 1959–1960 school year, he must file the affidavit required by Act 10, listing all his organizational connections over the previous five years. He declined to file the affidavit, and his contract for the ensuing school year was not renewed. At the trial the evidence showed that he was not a member of the Communist Party or of any organization advocating the overthrow of the Government by force, and that he was a member of the National Association for the Advancement of Colored People. The court upheld Act 10, finding the information it required was "relevant," and relying on the several decisions of this Court. . . .

The plaintiffs in the state court proceedings (petitioners here) were Max Carr, an associate professor at the University of Arkansas, and Ernest T. Gephardt, a teacher at Central High School in Little Rock, each suing for himself and others similarly situated. Each refused to execute and file the affidavit required by Act 10. Carr executed an affirmation in which he listed his membership in professional organizations, denied ever having been a member of any subversive organization, and offered to answer any questions which the University authorities might constitutionally ask touching upon his qualifications as a teacher. Gephardt filed an affidavit stating that he had never belonged to a subversive organization, disclosing his membership in the Arkansas Education Association and the American Legion, and also offering to answer any questions which the school authorities might constitutionally ask touching upon his qualifications as a teacher. Both were advised that their failure to comply with the requirements of Act 10 would make impossible their re-employment as teachers for the following school year. The Supreme Court of Arkansas upheld the constitutionality of Act 10, on its face and as applied to the petitioners. . . .

There can be no doubt of the right of a State to investigate the competence and fitness of those whom it hires to teach in its schools, as this Court before now has had occasion to recognize. . . .

It is not disputed that to compel a teacher to disclose his every associational tie is to impair that teacher's right of free association, a right closely allied to freedom of speech and a right which, like free speech, lies at the foundation of a free society. . . . Such interference with personal freedom is conspicuouly accented when the teacher serves at the absolute will of those to whom the disclosure must be made—those who any year can terminate the teacher's employment without bringing charges, without notice, without a hearing, without affording an opportunity to explain.

The statute does not provide that the information it requires be kept confidential. Each school board is left free to deal with the information as it wishes. The record contains evidence to indicate that fear of public disclosure is neither theoretical nor groundless. Even if there were no disclosure to the general public the pressure upon a teacher to avoid any ties which might displease those who control his professional destiny would be constant and heavy. Public exposure, bringing with it the possibility of public pressures upon school boards to discharge teachers who belong to unpopular or minority organizations, would simply operate to widen and aggravate the impairment of constitutional liberty.

*　　*　　*

The question to be decided here is not whether the State of Arkansas can ask certain of its teachers about all their organizational relationships. It is not whether the State can ask all of its teachers about certain of their associational ties. It is not whether teachers can be asked how many organizations they belong to, or how much time they spend in organizational activity. The question is whether the State can ask every one of its teachers to disclose every single organization with which he has been associated over a five-year period. The scope of the inquiry required by Act 10 is completely unlimited. The statute requires a teacher to reveal the church to which he belongs, or to which he has given financial support. It requires him to disclose his political party, and every political organization to which he may have contributed over a five-year period. It requires him to list, without number, every conceivable kind of associational tie—social, professional, political, avocational, or religious. Many such relationships could have no possible bearing upon the teacher's occupational competence or fitness.

In a series of decisions this Court has held that, even though the governmental purpose be legitimate and substantial, that purpose cannot be pursued by means that broadly stifle fundamental personal liberties when the end can be more narrowly achieved. . . .

The unlimited and indiscriminate sweep of the statute now before us brings it within the ban of our prior cases. The statute's comprehensive interference with associational freedom goes far beyond what might be justified in the exercise of the State's legitimate inquiry into the fitness and competency of its teachers. The judgments in both cases must be reversed.

MR. JUSTICE FRANKFURTER, DISSENTING.

As one who has strong views against crude intrusions by the state into the atmosphere of creative freedom in which alone the spirit and mind of a teacher can fruitfully function, I may find displeasure with the Arkansas legislation now under review. But in maintaining the distinction between private views and constitutional restrictions, I am constrained to find that it does not exceed the permissible range of state action limited by the Fourteenth Amendment. . . .

If I dissent from the Court's disposition in these cases, it is not that I put a low value on academic freedom. . . . It is because that very freedom, in its most creative reaches, is dependent in no small part upon the careful and discriminating selection of teachers. This process of selection is an intricate affair, a matter of fine judgment, and if it is to be informed, it must be based upon a comprehensive range of information. I am unable to say, on the face of this statute, that Arkansas could not reasonably find that the information which the statute requires—and which may not be otherwise acquired than by asking the question which it asks—is germane to that selection. Nor, on this record, can I attribute to the State a purpose to employ the enactment as a device for the accomplishment of what is constitutionally forbidden. Of course, if the information gathered by the required affidavits is used to further a scheme of terminating the employment of teachers solely because of their membership in unpopular organizations, that use will run afoul of the Fourteenth Amendment. It will be time enough, if such use is made, to hold the application of the statute unconstitutional. . . .

DECISION ON NEW YORK STATE'S LOYALTY OATH (1967)   From *Keyishan v. Board of Regents of the University of the State of New York,* 385 U.S. 589 (1967).

*Appeal from the U.S. District Court for
the Western District of New York.*

MR. JUSTICE BRENNAN DELIVERED THE OPINION OF THE COURT.

Appellants in this case timely asserted below the unconstitutionality of all these sections on grounds of vagueness and that question is now properly before us for decision. Moveover, to the extent that *Adler* sustained the provision of the Feinberg Law constituting membership in an organization advocating forceful overthrow of government a ground for disqualification, pertinent constitutional doctrines have since rejected the premises upon which that conclusion rested. *Adler* is therefore not dispositive of the constitutional issues we must decide in this case. . . .

* * *

We do not have the benefit of a judicial gloss by the New York courts enlightening us as to the scope of this complicated plan. In light of the intricate administrative machinery for its enforcement, this is not surprising. The very intricacy of the plan and the uncertainly as to the scope of its proscriptions make it a highly efficient *in terrorem* mechanism. It would be a bold teacher who would not stay as far as possible from utterances or acts which might jeopardize his living by enmeshing him in this intricate machinery. The uncertainty as to the utterances and acts proscribed increases that caution in "those who believe that written law means what it says." . . . The result must be to stifle "that free play of the spirit which all teachers ought especially to cultivate and practice, . . ." That probability is enhanced by the provisions requiring an annual review of every teacher to determine whether any utterance or act of his, inside the classroom or out, came within the sanctions of the laws. . . .

There can be no doubt of the legitimacy of New York's interest in protecting its education system from subversion. But "even though the governmental purpose be legitimate and substantial, that purpose cannot be pursued by means that broadly stifle fundamental personal liberties when the end can be more narrowly achieved." . . .

* * *

Our Nation is deeply committed to safeguarding academic freedom, which is of transcendent value to all of us and not merely to the teachers concerned. That freedom is therefore a special concern of the First Amendment, which does not tolerate laws that cast a pall of orthodoxy over the classroom. "The vigilant protection of constitutional freedoms is nowhere more vital than in the community of American schools." . . . The classroom is peculiarly the "marketplace of ideas." The Nation's future depends upon leaders trained through wide exposure to that robust exchange of ideas which discovers truth "out of a multitude of tongues, [rather] than through any kind of authoritative selection." . . . In *Sweezy* v. *New Hampshire*, 354 U.S. 234, 250, . . . we said:

"The essentiality of freedom in the community of Amercian universities is almost self-evident. No one should underestimate the vital role in a democracy that is played by those who guide and train our youth. To impose any strait jacket upon the intellectual leaders in our colleges and universities would imperil the future of our Nation. No field of education is so thoroughly comprehended by man that new discoveries cannot yet be made. Particularly is that true in the social sciences, where few, if any, principles are accepted as absolutes. Scholarship cannot flourish in an atmosphere of suspicion and distrust. Teachers and students must always remain free to inquire, to study and to evaluate, to gain new maturity and understanding; otherwise our civilization will stagnate and die."

We emphasize once again that "[p]recision of regulation must be the touchstone in an area so closely touching our most precious freedoms." . . . New York's complicated and intricate scheme plainly violates that standard. When one must guess what conduct or utterance may lose him his position, one necessarily will "steer far wider of the unlawful zone. . . ." The danger of that chilling effect upon the exercise of vital First Amendment rights must be guarded against by sensitive tools which clearly inform teachers what is being proscribed. . . .

The regulatory maze created by New York is wholly lacking in "terms susceptible of objective measurement." . . . Vagueness of wording is aggravated by prolixity and profusion of statutes, regulations, and administrative machinery, and by manifold cross-references to inter-related enactments and rules. . . .

*   *   *

Appellants have also challenged the constitutionality of the discrete provisions of subdivision 1(c) of § 105 and subdivision 2 of the Feinberg Law, which make Communist Party membership, as such, prima-facie evidence of disqualification. . . .

Here again constitutional doctrine has developed since *Adler*. Mere knowing membership without a specific intent to further the unlawful aims of an organization is not a constitutionally adequate basis for exclusion from such positions as those held by appellants. . . .

*   *   *

Measured against this standard, both Civil Service Law § 105, subd. 1(c), and Education Law § 3022, subd. 2, sweep overbroadly into association which may not be proscribed. The presumption of disqualification arising from proof of mere membership may be rebutted, but only by (a) a denial of membership, (b) a denial that the organization advocates the overthrow of government by force, or (c) a denial that the teacher has knowledge of such advocacy. . . . Thus proof of nonactive membership or a showing of the absence of intent to further unlawful aims will not rebut the presumption and defeat dismissal. This is emphasized in official administrative interpretations. . . .

Thus § 105, subd. 1(c), and § 3022, subd. 2, suffer from impermissible "overbreadth." . . . They seek to bar employment both for association which legitimately may be proscribed and for association which may not be proscribed consistently with First Amendments rights. Where statutes have an overbroad sweep, just as where they are vague, "the hazard of loss or substantial impairment of those previous rights may be critical," . . . since those covered by the statute are bound to limit their behavior to that which is unquestionably safe. . . .

The judgment of the District Court is reversed.

MR. JUSTICE CLARK WITH WHOM MR. JUSTICE HARLAN,
MR. JUSTICE STEWART, AND MR. JUSTICE WHITE JOIN, DISSENTING.

It is clear that the Feinberg Law, in which this Court found "no constitutional infirmity" in 1952, has been given its death blow today. Just as the majority here finds that there "can be no doubt of the legitimacy of New York's interest in protecting its education system from subversion" there can also be no doubt that "the be-all and end-all" of New York's effort is here. And, regardless of its correctness, neither New York nor the several States that have followed the teaching of *Adler* v. *Board of Education*, . . . for some 15 years, can ever put the pieces together again. No court has ever reached out so far to destroy so much with so little. . . .

This Court has again and again, since at least 1951, approved procedures either identical or at the least similar to the ones the Court condemns today. . . .

The majority makes much over the horribles that might arise from subdivision l(*b*) of § 105 which condemns the printing, publishing, selling, etc., of matter containing such doctrine. But the majority fails to state that this action is condemned only *when and if* the teacher also personally advocates, advises, teaches, etc., the necessity or propriety of adopting such doctrine. This places this subdivision on the same footing as l(*a*). And the same is true of subdivision l(*c*) where a teacher organizes, helps to organize or becomes a member of an organization which teaches or advocates such doctrine, for *scienter* would also be a necessary ingredient under our opinion in *Garner, supra*. Moreover, membership is only prima-facie evidence of disqualification and could be rebutted, leaving the burden of proof on the State. Furthermore, all of these procedures are protected by an adversary hearing with full judicial review.

In the light of these considerations the strained and unbelievable suppositions that the majority poses could hardly occur. . . . Where there is doubt as to one's intent or the nature of his activities we cannot assume that the administrative boards will not give him full protection. Furthermore, the courts always sit to make certain that this is done.

The majority says that the Feinberg Law is bad because it has an "overbroad sweep." I regret to say—and I do so with deference— that the majority has by its broadside swept away one of our most precious rights, namely, the right of self-preservation. Our public educational system is the genius of our democracy. The minds of our youth are developed there and the character of that development will determine the future of our land. Indeed, our very existence depends upon it. The issue here is a very narrow one. It is not freedom of speech, freedom of thought, freedom of press, freedom of assembly, or of association, even in the Communist Party. It is simply this: May the State provide that one who, after a hearing with full judicial review, is found to have wilfully and deliberately advocated, advised, or taught that our Government should be overthrown by force or violence or other unlawful means; or to have wilfully and deliberately printed, published, etc., any book or paper that so advocated *and to have personally* advocated such doctrine himself; or to have wilfully and deliberately become a member of an organization that advocates such doctrine, is prima-facie disqualified from teaching in its university? My answer, in keeping with all of our cases up until today, is "Yes!" I dissent.

TEACHERS HAVE RIGHT TO FREEDOM OF SPEECH (1968)   From
Pickering v. *Board of Education of Township High School,* 391 U.S. 563 (1968).

Appeal from the Supreme Court of Illinois.

MR. JUSTICE MARSHALL DELIVERED THE OPINION OF THE COURT.

Appellant Marvin L. Pickering, a teacher in Township High School District 205, Will County, Illinois, was dismissed from his position by the appellee Board of Education for sending a letter to a local newspaper in connection with a recently proposed tax increase that was critical of the way in which the Board and the district superintendent of schools had handled past proposals to raise new revenue for the schools. Appellant's dismissal resulted from a determination by the Board, after a full hearing, that the publication of the letter was "detrimental to the efficient operation and administration of the schools of the district. . . ."

Appellant's claim that his writing of the letter was protected by the First and Fourteenth Amendments was rejected. Appellant then sought review of the Board's action in the Circuit Court of Will County, which affirmed his dismissal on the ground that the determination that appellant's letter was detrimental to the interests of the school system was supported by substantial evidence and that the interests of the schools overrode appellant's First Amendment rights. On appeal, the Supreme Court of Illinois, two Justices dissenting, affirmed the judgment of the Circuit Court. . . .

In February of 1961 the appellee Board of Education asked the voters of the school district to approve a bond issue to raise $4,875,000 to erect two new schools. The proposal was defeated. Then, in December of 1961, the Board submitted another bond proposal to the voters which called for the raising of $5,500,000 to build two new schools. This second proposal passed and the schools were built with the money raised by the bond sales. In May of 1964 a proposed increase in the tax rate to be used for educational purposes was submitted to the voters by the Board and was defeated. Finally, on September 19, 1964, a second proposal to increase the tax rate was submitted by the Board and was likewise defeated. It was in connection with this last proposal of the School Board that appellant wrote the letter to the editor . . . that resulted in his dismissal.

Prior to the vote on the second tax increase proposal a variety of articles attributed to the District 205 Teachers' Organization appeared in the local paper. These articles urged passage of the tax increase and stated that failure to pass the increase would result in a decline in the quality of education afforded children in the district's schools. A letter from the superintendent of schools making the same point was published in the paper two days before the election and submitted to the voters in mimeographed form the following day. It was in response to the foregoing material, together with the failure of the tax increase to pass, that appellant submitted the letter in question to the editor of the local paper.

The letter constituted, basically, an attack on the School Board's handling of the 1961 bond issue proposals and its subsequent allocation of financial resources between the school's educational and athletic programs. It also charged the superintendent of schools with attempting to prevent teachers in the district from opposing or criticizing the proposed bond issue.

The Board dismissed Pickering for writing and publishing the letter. Pursuant to Illinois law, the Board was then required to hold a hearing on the dismissal. At the hearing the Board charged that numerous statements in the letter were false and that the publication of the statements unjustifiably impugned the "motives, honesty, integrity, truthfulness, responsibility and competence" of both the Board and the school administration. The Board also charged that the false statements damaged the professional reputations of its members and of the school administrators, would be disruptive of faculty discipline, and would tend to foment "controversy, conflict and dissension" among teachers, administrators, the Board of Education, and the residents of the district. Testimony was introduced from a variety of witnesses on the truth or falsity of the particular statements in the letter with which the Board took issue. The Board found the statements to be false as charged. No evidence was introduced at any point in the proceedings as to the effect of the publication of the letter on the community as a whole or on the administration of the school system in particular, and no specific findings along these lines were made.

The Illinois courts reviewed the proceedings solely to determine whether the Board's findings were supported by substantial evidence and whether, on the facts as found, the Board could reasonably conclude that appellant's publication of the letter was "detrimental to the best interests of the schools." Pickering's claim that his letter was protected by the First Amendment was rejected on the ground that his acceptance of a teaching position in the public schools obliged him to refrain from making statements about the operation of the schools "which in the absence of such position he would have an undoubted right to engage in." . . .

To the extent that the Illinois Supreme Court's opinion may be read to suggest that teachers may constitutionally be compelled to relinquish the First Amendment rights they would otherwise enjoy as citizens to comment on matters of public interest in connection with the operation of the public schools in which they work, it proceeds on a premise that has been unequivocally rejected in numerous prior decisions of this Court. . . . At the same time it cannot be gainsaid that the State has interests as an employer in regulating the speech of its employees that differ significantly from those it possesses in connection with regulation of the speech of the citizenry in general. The problem in any case is to arrive at a balance between the interests of the teacher, as a citizen, in commenting upon matters of public concern and the interest of the State, as an employer, in promoting the efficiency of the public services it performs through its employees.

*   *   *

What we do have before us is a case in which a teacher has made erroneous public statements upon issues then currently the subject of public attention, which are critical of his ultimate employer but which are neither shown nor can be presumed to have in any way either impeded the teacher's proper performance of his daily duties in the classroom or to have interfered with the regular operation of the schools generally. In these circumstances we conclude that the interest of the school administration in limiting teachers' opportunities to contribute to public debate is not significantly greater than its interest in limiting a similar contribution by any member of the general public.

The public interest in having free and unhindered debate on matters of public importance—the core value of the Free Speech Clause of the First Amendment—is so great that it has been held that a State cannot authorize the recovery of damages by a public official for defamatory statements directed at him except when such statements are shown to have been made either with knowledge of their falsity or with reckless disregard for their truth or falsity. *New York Times Co. v. Sullivan*, 376 U.S. 254 (1964). . . . It is therefore perfectly clear that, were appellant a member of the general public, the State's power to afford the appellee Board of Education or its members any legal right to sue him for writing the letter at issue here would be limited by the requirement that the letter be judged by the standard laid down in *New York Times*.

This Court has also indicated, in more general terms, that statements by public officials on matters of public concern must be accorded First Amendment protection despite the fact that the statements are directed at their nominal superiors. . . .

While criminal sanctions and damage awards have a somewhat different impact on the exercise of the right to freedom of speech from dismissal from employment, it is apparent that the threat of dismissal from public employment is nonetheless a potent means of inhibiting speech. We have already noted our disinclination to make an across-the-board equation of dismissal from public employment for remarks critical of superiors with awarding damages in a libel suit by a public official for similar criticism. However, in a case such as the present one, in which the fact of employment is only tangentially and insubstantially involved in the subject matter of the public communication made by a teacher, we conclude that it is necessary to regard the teacher as the member of the general public he seeks to be.

In sum, we hold that, in a case such as this, absent proof of false statements knowingly or recklessly made by him, a teacher's exercise of his right to speak on issues of public importance may not furnish the basis for his dismissal from public employment. Since no such showing has been made in this case regarding appellant's letter, . . . his dismissal for writing it cannot be upheld and the judgment of the Illinois Supreme Court must, accordingly, be reversed and the case remanded for further proceedings not inconsistent with this opinion.

DECISION ON STATE'S ROLE IN CURRICULUM MAKING (1968) From *Epperson v. Arkansas*, 393 U.S. 97 (1968).

Appeal from the Supreme Court of Arkansas.

MR. JUSTICE FORTAS DELIVERED THE OPINION OF THE COURT.

This appeal challenges the constitutionality of the "anti-evolution" statute which the State of Arkansas adopted in 1928 to prohibit the teaching in its public schools and universities of the theory that man evolved from other species of life.

The statute was a product of the upsurge of "fundamentalist" religious fervor of the twenties. The Arkansas statute was an adaptation of the famous Tennessee "monkey law" which that State adopted in 1925. The constitutionality of the Tennessee law was upheld by the Tennessee Supreme Court in the celebrated *Scopes* case in 1927.

The Arkansas law makes it unlawful for a teacher in any state-supported school or university "to teach the theory or doctrine that mankind ascended or descended from a lower order of animals," or "to adopt or use in any such institution a textbook that teaches" this theory. Violation is a misdemeanor and subjects the violator to dismissal from his position.

The present case concerns the teaching of biology in a high school in Little Rock. According to the testimony, until the events here in litigation, the official textbook furnished for the high school biology course "did not have a section on the Darwinian Theory." Then, for the academic year 1965–1966, the school administration, on recommendation of the teachers of biology in the school system, adopted and prescribed a textbook which contained a chapter setting forth "the theory about the origin . . . of man from a lower form of animal."

Susan Epperson, a young woman who graduated from Arkansas' school system and then obtained her master's degree in zoology at the University of Illinois, was employed by the Little Rock school system in the fall of 1964 to teach 10th grade biology at Central High School. At the start of the next academic year, 1965, she was confronted by the new textbook (which one surmises from the record was not unwelcome to her). She faced at least a literal dilemma because she was supposed to use the new textbook for classroom instruction and presumably to teach the statutorily condemned chapter; but to do so would be a criminal offense and subject her to dismissal.

She instituted the present action in the Chancery Court of the State, seeking a declaration that the Arkansas statute is void and enjoining the State and the defendant officials of the Little Rock school system from dismissing her for violation of the statute's provisions. . . .

The Chancery Court, in an opinion by Chancellor Murray O. Reed, held that the statute violated the Fourteenth Amendment to the United States Constitution. The court noted that this Amendment encompasses the prohibitions upon state interference with freedom of speech and thought which are contained in the First Amendment. Accordingly, it held that the challenged statute is unconstitutional because, in violation of the First Amendment, it "tends to hinder the quest for knowledge, restrict the freedom to learn, and restrain the freedom to teach." In this perspective, the Act, it held, was an unconstitutional and void restraint upon the freedom of speech guaranteed by the Constitution.

On appeal, the Supreme Court of Arkansas reversed. . . . It sustained the statute as an exercise of the State's power to specify the curriculum in public schools. It did not address itself to the competing constitutional considerations. . . .

Only Arkansas and Mississippi have such "anti-evolution" or "monkey" laws on their books. There is no record of any prosecutions in Arkansas under its statute. It is possible that the statute is presently more of a curiosity than a vital fact of life in these States. Nevertheless, the present case was brought, the appeal as of right is properly here, and it is our duty to decide the issues presented.

At the outset, it is urged upon us that the challenged statute is vague and uncertain and therefore within the condemnation of the Due Process Clause of the Fourteenth Amendment. The contention that the Act is vague and uncertain is supported by the language in the brief opinion of Arkansas' Supreme Court. That court, perhaps reflecting the discomfort which the statute's quixotic prohibition necessarily engenders in the modern mind, stated that it "expresses no opinion" as to whether the Act prohibits "explanation" of the theory of evolution or merely forbids "teaching that the theory is true." Regardless of this uncertainty, the court held that the statute is constitutional.

On the other hand, counsel for the State, in oral argument in this Court, candidly stated that, despite the State Supreme Court's equivocation, Arkansas would interpret the statute "to mean that to make a student aware of the theory . . . just to teach that there was such a theory" would be grounds for dismissal and for prosecution under the statute; and he said "that the Supreme Court of Arkansas' opinion should be interpreted in that manner." He said "If Mrs. Epperson would tell her students that 'Here is Darwin's theory, that man ascended or descended from a lower form of being,' then I think she would be under this statute liable for prosecution."

In any event, we do not rest our decision upon the asserted vagueness of the statute. On either interpretation of its language, Arkansas' statute cannot stand. It is of no moment whether the law is deemed to prohibit mention of Darwin's theory, or to forbid any or all of the infinite varieties of communication embraced within the term "teaching." Under either interpretation, the law must be stricken because of its conflict with the constitutional prohibition of state laws respecting an establishment of religion or prohibiting the free exercise thereof. The overriding fact is that Arkansas' law selects from the body of knowledge a particular segment which it proscribes for the sole reason that it is deemed to conflict with a particular religious doctrine; that is, with a particular interpretation of the Book of Genesis by a particular religious group.

The antecedents of today's decision are many and unmistakable. They are rooted in the foundation soil of our Nation. They are fundamental to freedom.

Government in our democracy, state and national, must be neutral in matters of religious theory, doctrine, and practice. It may not be hostile to any religion or to the advocacy of no-religion; and it may not aid, foster, or promote one religion or religious theory against another or even against the militant opposite. The First Amendment mandates governmental neutrality between religion and religion, and between religion and non-religion.

As early as 1872, this Court said: "The law knows no heresy, and is committed to the support of no dogma, the establishment of no sect." . . . This has been the interpretation of the great First Amendment which this Court has applied in the many and subtle problems which the ferment of our national life has presented for decision within the Amendment's broad command.

Judicial interposition in the operation of the public school system of the Nation raises problems requiring care and restraint. Our courts, however, have not failed to apply the First Amendment's mandate in our educational system where essential to safeguard the fundamental values of freedom of speech and inquiry and of belief. By and large, public education in our Nation is committed to the control of state and local authorities. Courts do not and cannot intervene in the resolution of conflicts which arise in the daily operation of school systems and which do not directly and sharply implicate basic constitutional values. On the other hand, "[t]he vigilant protection of constitutional freedoms is nowhere more vital than in the community of American schools."

✽   ✽   ✽

The earliest cases in this Court on the subject of the impact of constitutional guarantees upon the classroom were decided before the Court expressly applied the specific prohibitions of the First Amendment to the States. But as early as 1923, the Court did not hesitate to condemn under the Due Process Clause "arbitrary" restrictions upon the freedom of teachers to teach and of students to learn. In that year, the Court, in an opinion by JUSTICE MCREYNOLDS, held unconstitutional an Act of the State of Nebraska making it a crime to teach any subject in any language other than English to pupils who had not passed the eighth grade. The State's purpose in enacting the law was to promote civic cohesiveness by encouraging the learning of English and to combat the "baneful effect" of permitting foreigners to rear and educate their children in the language of the parents' native land. The Court recognized these purposes, and it acknowledged the State's power to prescribe the school curriculum, but it held that these were not adequate to support the restriction upon the liberty of teacher and pupil. The challenged statute, it held, unconstitutionally interfered with the right of the individuals, guaranteed by the Due Process Clause, to engage in any of the common occupations of life and to acquire useful knowledge. *Meyer* v. *State of Nebraska*, 262 U.S. 390 (1923). . . .

For purposes of the present case, we need not re-enter the difficult terrain which the Court, in 1923, traversed without apparent misgivings. . . . Today's problem is capable of resolution in the narrower terms of the First Amendment's prohibition of laws respecting an establishment of religion or prohibiting the free exercise thereof.

There is and can be no doubt that the First Amendment does not permit the State to require that teaching and learning must be tailored to the principles or prohibitions of any religious sect or dogma. . . .

While study of religions and of the Bible from a literary and historic viewpoint, presented objectively as part of a secular program of education, need not collide with the First Amendment's prohibition, the State may not adopt programs or practices in its public schools or colleges which "aid or oppose" any religion. . . . This prohibition is absolute. It forbids alike the preference of a religious doctrine or the prohibition of theory which is deemed antagonistic to a particular dogma. As Mr. Justice Clark stated in *Joseph Burstyn, Inc.* v. *Wilson*, "the state has no legitimate interest in protecting any or all religions from views distasteful to them . . . ." 343 U.S. 495, 505 (1952). . . .

The State's undoubted right to prescribe the curriculum for its public schools does not carry with it the right to prohibit, on pain of criminal penalty, the teaching of a scientific theory or doctrine where that prohibition is based upon reasons that violate the First Amendment. It is much too late to argue that the State may impose upon the teachers in its schools any conditions that it chooses, however restrictive they may be of constitutional guarantees. . . .

In the present case, there can be no doubt that Arkansas has sought to prevent its teachers from discussing the theory of evolution because it is contrary to the belief of some that the Book of Genesis must be the exclusive source of doctrine as to the origin of man. No suggestion has been made that Arkansas' law may be justified by considerations of state policy other than the religious views of some of its citizens. It is clear that fundamentalist sectarian conviction was and is the law's reason for existence. Its antecedent, Tennessee's "monkey law," candidly stated its purpose: to make it unlawful "to teach any theory that denies the story of the Divine Creation of man as taught in the Bible, and to teach instead that man has descended from a lower order of animals." Perhaps the sensational publicity attendant upon the *Scopes* trial induced Arkansas to adopt less explicit language. It eliminated Tennessee's reference to "the story of the Divine Creation of man" as taught in the Bible, but there is no doubt that the motivation for the law was the same: to suppress the teaching of a theory which, it was thought, "denied" the divine creation of man.

Arkansas' law cannot be defended as an act of religious neutrality. Arkansas did not seek to excise from the curricula of its schools and universities all discussion of the origin of man. The law's effort was confined to an attempt to blot out a particular theory because of its supposed conflict with the Biblical account, literally read. Plainly, the law is contrary to the mandate of the First, and in violation of the Fourteenth, Amendment to the Constitution.

The judgment of the Supreme Court of Arkansas is

Reversed.

MR. JUSTICE BLACK, *concurring.*

*　　*　　*

21

HIGHER
EDUCATION

The Colleges and Universities

DESCRIPTION OF THE ELECTIVE SYSTEM AT HARVARD (1901)   From
Charles S. Moore, "The Elective System at Harvard." *Harvard Graduate Magazine,* vol. XI,
pp. 530-34.

The following facts (with many others) were obtained from a detailed examination of the programs of study of 448 members of the Class of 1901. This examination was made by the Pedagogical Seminary (Education 20a) under the guidance of Professor Hanus in the winter of 1900–1901, and in particular by a committee of four, whose partial reports were discussed by the Seminary, and who made a final report upon the subject at the close of the academic year.

During the winter of 1901–1902 this report was revised, enlarged, and entirely rewritten by the writer of this article, who had general charge of the work of the committee. The purpose from the start has been to secure the facts, and then to present them without bias. It is hoped that the entire data, embodied in about 35 tables accompanied by explanatory text may, at no distant date, be published. No similar detailed study of the actual working of the Elective System has been made since Pres. Eliot, in his Report of 1886, presented the programs of 350 members of the classes of 1884 and 1885. Dean Briggs in his report for 1899–1900 gives "certain statistics of the use to which the Elective System was put by the various college classes between and including the classes of 1886 and 1900." The work of the Seminary, it will be seen, carried on, but with more detail, the studies already made of the Elective System at Harvard.

Some objections to the Elective System at Harvard imply that the choice of studies thereunder is practically unrestricted. It should, however, be understood that the choice of the Freshmen is practically limited to certain specified elementary courses, comprising only about 20 per cent of all the courses offered to undergraduates, and that a Freshman cannot take more than two courses in any one subject. Besides, English, and either French or German, must be taken by almost all Freshmen. Freshmen and Special Students must secure the approval of their choices by specially appointed advisers. Elementary courses must, of course, be taken prior to more advanced courses in the same subject, and a large number of the courses offered may be taken only in case the applicants satisfy the instructors in those courses of their fitness to take them. Furthermore, the whole body of courses offered is divided into about 14 examination groups, and no two courses in the same group may be taken at the same time. No more than six courses may be taken at a time, the requirement being five courses for a Freshman, and four for upper classmen with an extra half course in English Composition for those whose work in Freshman English was not satisfactory.

Let us now see what general lines of choice are followed at Harvard, the facts being obtained from an examination of the programs of study of 448 members of the Class of 1901. Of 33 subjects offered for choice, the first 14 that were chosen (the order being based upon the number of students making the choice and also substantially, upon the number of courses taken in each subject) were as follows:—

English (facile princeps), History, Economics, German, French, Philosophy, Fine Arts, Chemistry, Latin, Geology, Government, Greek, Mathematics, and Physics.

Arranged according to the average number of courses taken by each student, the first 14 are English, History, Music, Economics, Engineering, Chemistry, Philosophy, German, French, Architecture, Greek, Fine Arts, Latin, and Spanish. Mathematics drops to the 19th place, Geology and Government to the 22nd, Physics to the 26th. While relatively few students chose Music, Engineering, and Architecture, each of those students took a large number of courses, and while relatively many took Geology, Government, and Physics, each one took but little in each subject. . . .

Examining the 448 programs for evidence of evasion of hard work, we find 20 that show from six to eight choices (out of a total of about 20 choices) among courses having the reputation to a greater or less degree of being "snap" courses. Several of these are the programs of men of high rank who graduated with a *magna cum*. Fewer than one eighth of the choices of the entire class were made from such courses, and but a few programs (only five indisputably) show a preponderance of "snap" and elementary, *i.e.* introductory, courses.

It is to be recognized that the term "snap" is a very inexact term, and also that a number of lecture courses of an introductory character are essential both for later work, and also for general culture. It would be unfortunate should the Elective System, through its marked tendency to increase the standard of work, change the character of such courses.

Let us consider next the extent to which the Elective System has led to specialization. We are met at once by the necessity of defining specialization. Dean Briggs, in his Report for 1899–1900, presents a table "of those who began to specialize not later than the Sophomore year, that is, of those who after the Freshman year took at least half of their work in one department." It seems useful, however, for our purposes, to recognize the fact that there may be specialization for but one year or for but two years, and to construct a definition to include this element of time. The following is offered as the basis upon which the programs in question have been classified with regard to specialization. A student is regarded as specializing who has taken 2 full courses or more in one department (*i.e.* Greek, Latin, Mathematics) in one year or 3 1/2 full courses or more in one department in two years, or 5 full courses or more in one department in three years, or 6 full courses or more in one department in four years, with not less than 1 1/2 courses in any one year.

The definition will be more complete if groups of kindred departments be included, as, the Classics, History, Government, and Modern Languages. So we will

say in addition to the above definition that a student is regarded as specializing who has taken

3 full courses or more in one *group* in one year,

5 full courses or more in one *group* in two years,

7 full courses or more in one *group* in three years,

8 1/2 full courses or more in one *group* in four years, with not less than two courses in any one year.

The tables show that of the four-year men 6 per cent have specialized throughout the four years; 12 per cent more for three years; and 19 per cent failed to specialize even for one year.

It is interesting to note that of the men who completed the four years' work in three years, but 4 per cent specialized throughout the three years, while on the other hand but 12 per cent failed to specialize even for one year. Three fourths of the men who, coming from other colleges, were admitted to the senior class, specialized during their one year.

Nearly one half of the men who specialized during three and four years, did so in English, one sixth in Modern Languages (except English), and less than one eighth in the Classics, and also in History and Government.

If we seek out the programs that show such specialization every year, or for some part of the time that the work was confined to a narrow field, we find that there are 29 which appear open to the charge of showing undue specialization. This is 7.8 per cent of the 372 who did the full work for a diploma at Harvard. Of these 29, 14 specialized in History and Political Science, and nine of the 14 are now studying Law. Ten specialized in History and Modern Languages, of whom two are studying Law, and two are teaching Modern Languages. Three specialized in the Classics, two now being candidates for the doctor's degree, and one studying for the Ministry. Of the remaining two, one specialized in Engineering and is now studying Engineering, and one in Psychology, and is now studying Medicine. Nine of the 29 were three-year men.

If we examine the data to see to what extent there was a lack of proper concentration of energy, we find 17 students (or 4 1/2 per cent of the 372 who did full work at Harvard) whose programs show a small amount of work in any one subject or group together with a wide range of subjects or groups. The work of these 17 is so scattered that thoroughness seems impossible; yet three of them received the A.B. *magna cum laude*, one of them being a Phi Beta Kappa man, and one received the A.B. *cum laude*.

There is another point of view which should be taken in studying the actual working of the Elective System. A program should be well-balanced, that is, should include some work in each of, say, three groups of subjects, Languages, Social Studies, and Science. It seems a reasonable requirement that each of these groups should be represented by at least 15 per cent of the total work of the student. This would leave 55 per cent for distribution according to interest, aptitude, or future needs. It might be stated in this way, that the presence of this minimum of 15 per cent would save a program from condemnation as ill-balanced. Turning now to the actual programs of the three hundred and seventy-two who completed their work at Harvard, we find that there was no one who failed to take some work in the Linguistic group, but two who failed to take some work in the Sociological group, and sixteen who failed to take some work in the Scientific group, while three failed to take the minimum of 15 percent in the Linguistic group, twenty-one in the sociological, and one hundred and ninety in the Scientific.

Taking into consideration individual subjects, we find that of the 372 who completed at Harvard all the requirements for the degree of A.B. 254 (68%) took no Physics; 250 (67%) took no Mathematics; 247 (66%) took no Greek; 215 (58%) took no Chemistry; 178 (48%) took no Latin; 147 (39%) took no Fine Arts; 140 (37%) took no Philosophy; 137 (36%) took neither Greek nor Latin; 87 (23%) took neither Latin nor Mathematics; 29 (8%) took no Science of any kind; 8 (2%) took neither

Physics nor Chemistry; 60 (16%) took neither Botany, Zoology, Mineralogy, nor Hygiene.

These facts are interesting, and are given without comment as evidence of the actual working of the Elective System as at present administered at Harvard. The writer has at his command similar sets of statistics from Wellesley, Dartmouth, and Radcliffe, which may be made public at a later date.

MARTHA CAREY THOMAS ON THE HIGHER EDUCATION OF WOMEN

(**1901**)   From Martha Carey Thomas, "Should the Higher Education of Women Differ from That of Men?" *Educational Review*, vol. XXI, pp. 1–10.

$\mathbf{A}$ subject like this fairly bristles with possibilities of misunderstanding. To get a firm grip of it we must resolutely turn our minds from all side issues and endeavor to put the question in so precise a form as to make sure that we at least mean the same thing. Stripped of its non-essentials we shall find that the real question at issue has very seldom been seriously argued. Not, of course, because of its unimportance—it is all-important—but because its approaches are set round about with our dearest prejudices, especially if we are men. Logical pitfalls lie on all sides of us; controversies past and present darken the air; our path leads us thru hard-won battlefields. If we are women, our almost irresistible impulse is to slay again the slain; if we are men, the graves of our dead comrades provoke an equally irresistible desire to send a scattering volley into some weak side-encampment of the enemy instead of lining up squarely for the last logical trial of arms. I have contrasted men and women advisedly, because this is one of the very few questions on which most educated men and women are to be found in opposite sides of the camp. If it were possible to discuss it dispassionately, I believe men and women could reach substantial agreement.

I will try, first of all, to state the subject of discussion so that there may be no possibility of our misunderstanding each other in regard to it; next, I will make an attempt to clear the way of prejudices and prejudgments that have really nothing at all to do with the argument; and finally, I will address myself to the argument itself. Higher education means generally any education above the high-school grade; that is, the education given in the technical and professional school as well as in the college.

In regard to technical and professional education there should, it seems to me, be little, if any, serious difference of opinion, and I shall therefore begin with that. We may differ as to whether it is desirable for a college course to precede, and be presupposed in, the course of a technical or professional school, but we cannot think that men students of law or medicine or architecture, for example, should be college-bred, while women students of law, medicine, or architecture should not. Personally I am confident that in ten years' time after graduation, physicians, and lawyers, and architects, whether men or women, whose parents have been able to send them to college, will be found to have outstripped their non-college-bred competitors both in reputation and in income. But, however we decide this matter, it must be decided in the same way for men and women. Sex cannot affect the question of the best preliminary preparation for professional and technical study.

So also with professional and technical courses themselves. Once granted that women are to compete with men for self-support as physicians or lawyers, whether wisely or unwisely does not now concern us, being merely one of the many side issues that have in the past so obscured our judgment of the main argument; indeed, if women are not to compete there will be, of course, no women in medical schools and law schools and no reason for argument at all—the question is simply, what is the best attainable training for the physician or the lawyer, man or woman? There is no reason to believe that typhoid or scarlet fever or phthisis can be successfully treated by a woman physician in one way and by a man physician in another way. There is indeed every reason to believe that unless treated in the best way the patient may die, the sex of the doctor affecting the result less even than the sex of the patient. The question needs only to be put for us to feel irrevocably sure that there is no special woman's way of dealing with disease. And so in law, in architecture, in electricity, in bridge-building, in all mechanic arts and technical sciences, our effort must be for the most scientific instruction, the broadest basis of training that will enable men and women students to attain the highest possible proficiency in their chosen profession. Given two bridge-builders, a man and a woman, given a certain bridge to be built, and given as always the unchangeable laws of mechanics in accordance with which this special bridge and all other bridges must be built, it is simply inconceivable that the preliminary instruction given to the two bridge-builders should differ in quantity, quality, or method of presentation because while the bridge is building one will wear knickerbockers and the other a rainy-day skirt. You may say you do not think that God intended a woman to be a bridge-builder. You have, of course, a right to this prejudice; but as you live in America, and not in the interior of Asia or Africa, you will probably not be able to impose it on women who wish to build bridges. You may say that women's minds are such that they cannot build good bridges. If you are right in this opinion you need concern yourselves no further—bridges built by women will, on the whole, tend to fall down, and the competition of men who can build good bridges will force women out of the profession. Both of these opinions of yours are side issues, and, however they may be decided hereafter, do not in the remotest degree affect the main question of a common curriculum for men and women in technical and professional schools. But you may say that men and women should study bridge-building and medicine and law in separate schools, and not together. You may be foolish enough, and wasteful enough, to think that all the expensive equipment of our technical and professional schools should be duplicated for women, when experience and practice have failed to bring forward a single valid objection to professional coeducation, and when the present trend of public opinion is overwhelmingly against you; and for the sake of argument let us grant that beside every such school for men is to be founded a similar school for women. But this duplication of professional schools for women leaves us just where we were in regard to the curriculum of professional study to be taught in such women's schools. So long as men and women are to compete together, and associate together, in their professional life, women's preparation for the same profession cannot safely differ from men's. If men's preparation is better, women, who are less well prepared, will be left behind in the race; if women's is better, men will suffer in competition with women. What is best in medical training for men will be best in medical training for women; what has bad results in medical training for men will be found to have the same bad results in women's medical training. Whatever we may think of

HIGHER EDUCATION

women's right to gain a livelihood in any given occupation, we must all agree that, if they are to compete successfully with men engaged in this same occupation, they must receive as thoro and prolonged a preparation for it as men. Even if we hold that women's minds differ from men's, this too is a side issue, for we must all recognize that for the purposes of successful competition it is desirable to minimize this difference by giving the *same* and not a different preparation. The greater the natural mental difference between the sexes the greater the need of a men's curriculum for professional women, if they are to hold their own in professional life after leaving the university.

The above argument applies with equal force to the training given by the university graduate school of arts and sciences. Statistics indicate that an overwhelmingly large majority of men and women graduate students are fitting themselves for the profession of higher teaching, that over one-third of all graduate students in the United States are women, and that the annual increase of women graduate students is greater than that of men. In the lower grades of teaching, men have almost ceased to compete with women; in the higher grade, that is, in college teaching, women are just beginning to compete with men, and this competition is beset with the bitterest professional jealousy that women have ever had to meet, except perhaps in medicine. There are in the United States only eleven independent colleges for women of at all the same grade as the three hundred and thirty-six coeducational colleges where women and men are taught together, yet only in these separate colleges for women have women an opportunity of competing with men for professors' chairs. It is very rare indeed for coeducational colleges to employ any women instructors, and even then only so many women are as a rule employed as are needed to look after the discipline or home life of the women students. Where women are teaching in coeducational colleges side by side with men their success is regarded by men teachers with profound dislike, and on account of this sex jealousy college presidents and boards of trustees (all of whom are, as a rule, men) cannot, even if they would, materially add to the number of women teachers or advance them. The working of the elective system, however, permits us to see that men students show no such jealousy, but recognize the able teaching of women by overcrowding their classes. Women have succeeded so brilliantly, on the whole so much better than men, as primary and secondary teachers, that they will undoubtedly repeat this success in their college teaching so soon as artificial restrictions are removed. No one could seriously maintain that, handicapped as women now are by prejudice in the highest branches of a profession peculiarly their own, they should be further hampered by a professional training different from men's. Indeed, one-half of the pupils to be taught by them in schools and in colleges, if they succeed in gaining admission on an equal footing into college faculties, are boys or men who should, according to this theory, receive a training different from that of their teachers. And, further, unless we could prove that in future all women students will be taught in separate women's colleges in a different way from men students and only by differently trained women professors, we should deprive women professors who were trained differently from men in the graduate school of the power to compete successfully with men, even for chairs in women's colleges. As in medicine, law, and bridge-building, so in arts and sciences the professional work of the graduate school must from the very nature of the case be the same for men and women. Science and literature and philology are what they are and inalterable, and the objects of competition are one and the same for both men and women— instructorships and professors' chairs, scholarly fame, and power to advance, however little, the outposts of knowledge.

We have, I think, then reached substantial agreement as to the subdivision of higher education that concerns itself with professional and technical training. We are prepared to admit that when women are to compete with men in the practice of the same trade or profession, there should be as little difference as possible in their preliminary education. Further than this, I think most of us will agree that coeducation in professional and technical schools is the only economical and feasible method of educating women.

But this line of reasoning will be incomplete unless we ask ourselves whether there are not some subjects peculiar to women in which we must maintain special women's technical schools. There are certainly three professional schools where women students already largely outnumber men: normal schools, including normal departments of universities, schools of nursing, and schools for library study. If cooking and domestic service ever become lucrative professions, and more especially if men of wealth ever come to choose their wives for culinary and sanitary lore instead as at present for social and intellectual charm, such schools will tend to spring up and, like normal schools, will undoubtedly be attended almost exclusively by women. They will beyond question be taught exactly in the same way as if they were to be attended exclusively by men. The method of teaching cooking is one and the same and does not depend on the sex of the cooks. In this sense even the higher education of women in cooking will not differ from that of men. There are, however, not enough elements of intellectual growth in cooking or housekeeping to furnish a very serious or profound course of training for really intelligent women. Likewise I do not think highly of the acumen of those people who predict the coming of schools of professional training for wifehood or motherhood. What requires the harmonious balance of all our human faculties can scarcely be taught in a professional school, nor is the intellectual side sufficiently prominent to be made the subject of prolonged training.

The burden of proof is with those who believe that the college education of men and women should differ. For thirty years it has been as nearly as possible the same, with brilliantly satisfactory results, so far as concerns women. College women have married as generally as their non-college-bred sisters, and have as a rule married better than their sisters, because they have chosen a larger proportion of professional men; they have not died in childbirth, as was predicted; they have borne their proper proportion of children, and have brought up more than the usual proportion of those born; they have made efficient housekeepers and wives as well as mothers; their success as teachers has been so astonishingly great that already they are driving non-college-bred women teachers out of the field. There is, in short, not a word to be said against the success and efficiency and healthfulness of these women educated by men's curriculum.

Indeed, except practice on the piano and violin and banjo and other musical instruments, which we might have believed that women would wish in a college course, (altho most happily they do not), let us ask ourselves what other subjects peculiar to women could be introduced in a college curriculum? I have never heard more than three suggested: infant psychology, to which there is no special objection as an elective in a college curriculum (I believe, however, that as many men as women will be foolish enough—I am expressing my own point of view—to elect it, and, after all, as many college men will become fathers as college women will become mothers); chemistry with special reference to cooking, and food values and domestic science generally, which is already introduced in some coeducational colleges and will never, in my opinion, be largely elected because it lacks the wider outlook of the more general sciences and belongs rather in the technical school; and physiology with special reference to motherhood and wifehood, which is never likely to be elected voluntarily by women college students who do not know whether they will marry; nor is it, in my opinion, desirable that it should be elected. It would certainly lead to much unhappiness in married life if such courses were elected by women and not by the men they marry also. These subjects, even if we grant (which I do not) that they are especially desirable for women to study in college, would not constitute a woman's curriculum. They would simply form three electives out of many to be introduced as occasion serves into such colleges as are open to women.

Undoubtedly the life of most women after leaving college will differ from that of men. About one-half will marry in a rather deliberate fashion, choosing carefully, and on the whole living very happily a life of comparative leisure, not of self-support; about one-third will become professional teachers, probably for life; and the greater part of the remainder will lead useful and helpful lives as unmarried women of leisure. And just because after leaving college only one-third, and that in the peculiarly limited profession of teaching, are to get the wider training of affairs that educates men engaged in business and in the professions all their lives thru, women while in college ought to have the broadest possible education. This college education should be the same as men's, not only because there is, I believe, but one best education, but because men and women are to live and work together as comrades and dear friends and married friends and lovers, and because their effectiveness and happiness and the welfare of the generation to come after them will be vastly increased if their college education has given them the same intellectual training and the same scholarly and moral ideals.

WILLIAM JAMES ON "THE Ph.D. OCTOPUS" (1903)   From *Educational Review*, vol. LV, pp. 149–57.

Some years ago we had at our Harvard Graduate School a very brilliant student of philosophy, who, after leaving us and supporting himself by literary labor for three years, received an appointment to teach English literature at a sister institution of learning. The governors of this institution, however, had no sooner communicated the appointment than they made the awful discovery that they had enrolled upon their staff a person who was unprovided with the Ph.D. degree. The man in question had been satisfied to work at philosophy for her own sweet (or bitter) sake, and had disdained to consider that an academic bauble should be his reward.

His appointment had thus been made under a misunderstanding. He was not the proper man; and there was nothing to do but to inform him of the fact. It was notified to him by his new President that his appointment must be revoked, or that a Harvard doctor's degree must forthwith be procured.

Although it was already the spring of the year, our subject, being a man of spirit, took up the challenge, turned his back upon literature (which in view of his approaching duties might have seemed his more urgent concern) and spent the weeks that were left him, in writing a metaphysical thesis and grinding his psychology, logic and history of philosophy up again, so as to pass our formidable ideals.

When the thesis came to be read by our committee, we could not pass it. Brilliancy and originality by themselves won't save a thesis for the doctorate; it must also exhibit a heavy technical apparatus of learning; and this our candidate had neglected to bring to bear. So, telling him that he was temporarily rejected, we advised him to pad out the thesis properly, and return with it next year, at the same time informing his new President that this signified nothing as to his merits, that he was of ultra Ph.D. quality, and one of the strongest men with whom we had ever had to deal.

To our surprise we were given to understand in reply that the quality *per se* of the man signified nothing in this connection, and that three magical letters were the thing seriously required. The College had always gloried in a list of faculty members who bore the doctor's title, and to make a gap in the galaxy, and admit a common fox without a tail, would be a degradation impossible to be thought of. We wrote again, pointing out that a Ph.D. in philosophy would prove little anyhow as to one's ability to teach literature; we sent separate letters in which we outdid each other in eulogy of our candidate's powers, for indeed they were great; and at last, *mirabile dictu*, our eloquence prevailed. He was allowed to retain his appointment provisionally, on condition that at one year later at the farthest his miserably naked name should be prolonged by the sacred appendage, the lack of which had given so much trouble to all concerned.

Accordingly he came up here the following spring with an adequate thesis (known since in print as a most brilliant contribution to metaphysics), passed a first rate examination, wiped out the stain, and brought his college into proper relations with the world again. Whether his teaching, during that first year, of English Literature was made any better by the impending examination in a different subject, is a question which I will not try to solve.

I have related this incident at such length because it is so characteristic of American academic conditions at the present day. Graduate schools still are something of a novelty, and higher diplomas something of a rarity. The latter, therefore, carry a vague sense of preciousness and honor, and have a particularly "up-to-date" appearance, and it is no wonder if smaller institutions, unable to attract professors already eminent, and forced usually to recruit their faculties from the relatively young, should hope to compensate for the obscurity of the names of their officers of instruction by the abundance of decorative titles by which those names are followed on the pages of the catalogs where they appear. The dazzled reader of the list, the parent or student, says to himself, "this must be a terribly distinguished crowd—their titles shine like the stars in the firmament, Ph.D.'s, S.D.'s, and Litt.D.'s, bespangle the page as if they were sprinkled over it from a pepper caster."

Human nature is once for all so childish that every reality becomes a sham somewhere, and in the minds of Presidents and Trustees the Ph.D. degree is in point of fact already looked upon as a mere advertising resource, a manner of throwing dust in the Public's eyes. "No instructor who is not a Doctor" has become a maxim in the smaller institutions which represent demand; and in each of the larger ones which represent supply, the same belief in decorated scholarship expresses itself in two antagonistic passions, one for multiplying as much as possible the annual output of doctors, the other for raising the standard of difficulty in passing, so that the Ph.D. of the special institution shall carry a higher blaze of distinction than it does elsewhere. Thus we at Harvard are proud of the number of candidates whom we reject, and of the inability of men who are not *distingués* in intellect to pass our tests.

America is thus as a nation rapidly drifting toward a state of things in which no man of science or letters will be accounted respectable unless some kind of badge or diploma is stamped upon him, and in which bare personality will be a mark of outcast estate. It seems to me high time to rouse ourselves to consciousness, and to cast a critical eye upon this grotesque tendency. Other nations suffer terribly from the Mandarin disease. Are we doomed to suffer like the rest?

Our higher degrees were instituted for the laudable purpose of stimulating scholarship, especially in the form of "original research." Experience has proved that great as the love of truth may be among men, it can be made still greater by adventitious rewards. The winning of a diploma certifying mastery and marking a barrier successfully past, acts as a challenge to the ambitious; and if the diploma will help to gain bread-winning positions also, its power as a stimulus to work is tremendously increased. So far, we are on innocent ground; it is well for a country to have research in abundance, and our graduate schools do but apply a normal psychological spur. But the institutionizing on a large scale of any natural combination of need and motive always tends to run into technicality and to develop a tyrannical machine with unforeseen powers of exclusion and corruption. Observation of the workings of our Harvard system for twenty years past has brought some of these drawbacks home to my consciousness, and I should like to call the attention of the readers of the *Monthly* to this disadvantageous aspect of the picture, and to make a couple of remedial suggestions, if I may.

In the first place, it would seem that to stimulate study, and to increase the *gelehrtes Publikum*, the class of highly educated men in our country, is the only positive good, and consequently the sole direct end at which our graduate schools, with their diploma-giving powers, should aim. If other results have developed they should be deemed secondary incidents, and if not desirable in themselves, they should be carefully guarded against.

To interfere with the free development of talent, to obstruct the natural play of supply and demand in the teaching profession, to foster academic snobbery by the *prestige* of certain privileged institutions, to transfer accredited value from essential manhood to an outward badge, to blight hopes and promote invidious sentiments, to divert the attention of aspiring youth from direct dealings with truth to the passing of examinations—such consequences, if they exist, ought surely to be regarded as drawbacks to the system, and an enlightened public consciousness ought to be keenly alive to the importance of reducing their amount. Candidates themselves do seem to be keenly conscious of some of these evils, but outside of their ranks or in the general public no such consciousness, so far as I can see, exists; or if it does exist, it fails to express itself aloud. Schools, Colleges and Universities appear enthusiastic over the entire system, just as it stands, and unanimously applaud all its developments.

I beg the reader to consider some of the secondary evils which I have enumerated. First of all, is not our growing tendency to appoint no instructors who are not also doctors an instance of pure sham? Will anyone pretend for a moment that the doctor's degree is a guarantee that its possessor will be a successful teacher? Notoriously his moral, social and personal characteristics may utterly disqualify him for success in the classroom; and of these characteristics his doctor's examination is unable to take any account whatever. Certain bare human beings will always be better candidates for a given place than all the doctor-applicants on hand; and to exclude the former by a rigid rule, and in the end to have to sift the latter by private inquiry into their personal peculiarities among those who know them, just as if they were not doctors at all, is to stultify one's own procedure. You may say that at least you guard against ignorance of the subject by considering only the candidates who are doctors; but how then about making doctors in one subject teach a different subject? This happened in the instance by which I introduced this article, and it happens daily and hourly in all our colleges. The truth is that the Doctor-Monopoly in teaching, which is becoming so rooted an American custom, can show no serious grounds whatsoever for itself in reason. As it actually prevails and grows in vogue among us, it is due to childish motives exclusively. In reality it is but a sham, a bauble, a dodge whereby to decorate the catalogs of schools and colleges.

Next, let us turn from the general promotion of a spirit of academic snobbery to the particular damage done to individuals by the system.

There are plenty of individuals so well endowed by nature that they pass with ease all the ordeals with which life confronts them. Such persons are born for professional success. Examinations have no terrors for them, and interfere in no way with their spiritual or worldly interests. There are others, not so gifted, who nevertheless rise to the challenge, get a stimulus from the difficulty, and become doctors, not without some baleful nervous wear and tear and retardation of their purely inner life, but on the whole successfully and with advantage. These two classes form the natural Ph.D.'s for whom the degree is legitimately instituted. To be sure, the degree is of no consequence one way or the other for the first sort of man, for in him the personal worth obviously outshines the title. To the second set of persons, however, the doctor-ideal may contribute a touch of energy and solidarity of scholarship which otherwise they might have lacked, and were our candidates all drawn from these classes, no oppression would result from the institution.

But there is a third class of persons who are genuinely, and in the most pathetic sense, the institution's victims. For this type of character the academic life may become, after a certain point, a virulent poison. Men without marked originality or native force, but fond of truth and especially of books and study, ambitious of reward and recognition, poor often, and needing a degree to get a teaching position, weak in the eyes of their examiners—among these we find the veritable *chair à canon* of the wars of learning, the unfit in the academic struggle for existence. There are individuals of this sort for whom to pass one degree after another seems the limit of earthly aspirations. Your private advice does not discourage them. They will fail, and go away to recuperate, and then present themselves for another ordeal, and sometimes prolong the process into middle life. Or else, if they are less heroic morally they will accept the failure as a sentence of doom that they are not fit, and are broken-spirited men thereafter.

We of the university faculties are responsible for deliberately creating this new class of American social failures, and heavy is the responsibility. We advertise our "schools" and send out our degree requirements, knowing well that aspirants of all sorts will be attracted, and at the same time we set a standard which intends to pass no man who has not native intellectual distinction. We know that there is no test, however absurd, by which, if a title or decoration, a public badge or mark, were to be won by it, some weakly suggestible or hauntable persons would not feel challenged and remain unhappy if they went without it. We dangle our three magic letters before the eyes of these predestined victims, and they swarm to us like moths to an electric light. They come at a time of life when failure can no longer be repaired easily and when the wounds it leaves are permanent; and we say deliberately that mere work faithfully performed, as they perform it, will not by itself save them, they must in addition put in evidence the one thing they have not got, namely this quality of intellectual distinction. Occasionally, out of sheer human pity, we ignore our high and mighty standard and pass them. Usually, however, the standard, and not the candidate, commands our fidelity. The result is caprice, majorities of one on the jury, and on the whole, a confession that our pretensions about the degree can not be lived up to consistently. Thus, partiality in the favored cases; in the unfavored, blood on our hands; and in both a bad conscience—are the results of our administration.

The more widespread becomes the belief that our diplomas are indispensable hall-marks to show the sterling metal of their holders, the more widespread these corruptions will become. We ought to look to the future carefully, for it takes generations for a national custom, once rooted, to be grown away from. All the European countries are seeking to diminish the check upon individual spontaneity which state examinations with their tyrannous growth have brought in their train. We have had to institute state examinations too; and it will perhaps be fortunate if some day hereafter our descendants, comparing machine with machine, do not sigh with regret for old times and American freedom, and wish that the regime of the dear old bosses might be reinstalled, with plain human nature, the glad hand and the marble heart, liking and disliking, and man-to-man relations grown possible again. Meanwhile, whatever evolution our state examinations are destined to undergo, our universities at least should never cease to regard themselves as the jealous custodians of personal and spiritual spontaneity. They are, indeed, its only organized and recognized custodians in America today. They ought to guard against contributing to the increase of officialism and snobbery and insincerity as against a pestilence. They ought to keep truth and disinterested labor always in the foreground, treat degrees as secondary incidents, and in season and out of season make it plain that what they live for is to help men's souls, and not to decorate their persons with diplomas.

There seems to be three obvious ways in which the increasing hold of the Ph.D. Octopus upon American life can be kept in check.

The first way lies with the universities. They can lower their fantastic standards (which here at Harvard we are so proud of) and give the doctorate as a matter of course, just as they give the bachelor's degree, for a due amount of time spent in patient labor in a special department of learning, whether the man be a brilliantly gifted individual or not. Surely native distinction needs no official stamp, and should disdain to ask for one. On the other hand, faithful labor, however commonplace, and years devoted to a subject, always deserve to be acknowledged and requited.

The second way lies with both the universities and the colleges. Let them give up their unspeakably silly ambition to bespangle their lists of officers with these doctorial titles. Let them look more to substance and less to vanity and sham.

The third way lies with the individual student, and with his personal advisers in the faculties. Every man of native power, who might take a higher degree, and refuses to do so, because examinations interfere with the free following out of his more immediate intellectual aims, deserves well of his country, and in a rightly organized community, would not be made to suffer for his independence. With many men the passing of these extraneous tests is a very greivous interference indeed. Private letters of recommendation from their instructors, which in any event are ultimately needful, ought, in these cases, completely to off-set the lack of the bread-winning degree; and instructors ought to be ready to advise students against it upon occasions, and to pledge themselves to back them later personally in the market-struggle which they have to face.

It is indeed odd to see this love of titles—and such titles—growing up in a country of which the recognition of individuality and bare manhood have so long been supposed to be the very soul. The independence of the State, in which most of our colleges stand, relieves us of those more odious forms of academic politics which continental European countries present. Anything like the elaborate university machine of France, with its throttling influences upon individuals, is unknown here. The spectacle of the *Rath* distinction in its innumerable spheres and grades, with which all Germany is crawling today, is displeasing to American eyes; and displeasing also in some respects is the institution of knighthood in England, which, aping as it does an aristocratic title, enables one's wife as well as one's self so easily to dazzle the servants at the house of one's friends. But are we Americans ourselves destined after all to hunger after similar vanities on an infinitely more contemptible scale? And is individuality with us also going to count for nothing unless stamped and licensed and authenticated by some title-giving machine? Let us pray that our ancient national genius may long preserve vitality enough to guard us from a future so unmanly and so unbeautiful!

CHARLES VAN HISE ON THE UNIVERSITY OF WISCONSIN (1904)   From
Charles R. Van Hise, "Inaugural Address," as quoted in *Science*, vol. XX, pp. 194–205.

The catalogue of the present year shows an attendance of 3,105 students, and an instructional force of 228, while this commencement there will be conferred in course 361 degrees, of which 334 are bachelors, 17 masters and 10 doctors. If we contrast these numbers with those of fifty years ago, an instructional force of 4, 56 students and 2 baccalaureate graduates, is it surprising that we should cry: 'and ye shall hallow the fiftieth year. . . . A jubilee shall that fiftieth year be unto you'? And with our joyfulness there is a profound feeling of thankfulness to the state that has had the wisdom to be guided by men of such breadth of view as to provide liberally for the education of its children and of all others who care to share its educational hospitality.

*　　*　　*

If time permitted, I should be glad to consider the effect of university work upon the mind of the student, that is, work in which he takes a share as an investigator and during which he acquires the spirit of research. It would be easy to show that the qualities of mind gained by such work are those which best fit him for the struggle of life—which best fit him to handle difficult business, social and economic problems. In Germany the university scholar is a man of affairs. He is found in all important divisions of administration. Almost every prominent German and Austrian professor is an official adviser to the government. Already, in America, we see the beginning of this movement. University professors are asked to serve on tax commissions, in the valuation of railroads and in various other capacities.

Within the next half century the number of such men in these and similar positions will increase many fold. The college-trained man, and especially the university-trained man, is, directly or indirectly, to control the destinies of the nation.

But while the professor performs important service outside the university, his greatest service is his own creative work and the production of new scholars in the laboratory and seminary. I unhesitatingly assert that there is no investigation of matter or force or mind today in progress, but tomorrow may become of inestimable practical value. This could be illustrated by various investigations which have been made here. It is easy to show that the discoveries at the University of Wisconsin bring vastly more wealth to the state each year than the entire expenditure of the institution, but to tell of them might seem like placing too great emphasis upon our own achievements, and I, therefore, turn elsewhere for illustrations.

Scarcely more than a century since, Franklin began studies upon the nature of lightning. Later the character of electrical force was during many years investigated with remarkable power by Faraday. If, during these studies, some one had said: 'Of what practical value can be the discoveries of Franklin and Faraday?' no one could have given the answer. Had this work been paid for by the state it would have been easy to show to the legislature that such a foolish waste of money was wholly unwarranted. But out of the discoveries of Franklin and Faraday, and those who followed them, has come one of the greatest material advances that the world has known. Electricity has become the most docile of the forms of energy. It serves to carry to distant points the power of Niagara. It is the nerves which make all the world one body, which bring to us instantaneously all the happenings in every quarter of the globe, which puts in our ear the vibrations of the voice of our friend a thousand miles away. Through increased knowledge of nature the peoples of all nations are being made slowly, haltingly, with occasional disastrous wars, into one family. And this is largely the result of recondite studies upon subtle forces, which, even now, we can not define, but which we can utilize.

A striking case of the profound service of the investigator is furnished by the studies of Pasteur and Koch. If, a half century since, a legislator in France had wished to be humorous at the expense of the scientist, what better object of derision could he have found than his countryman, Pasteur, who was looking through a microscope at the minute forms of life, studying the nature and transformations of yeast and microbes? And yet, from the studies of Pasteur and Koch, and their successors, have sprung the most beneficent discoveries which it has been the lot of man to bestow upon his fellow men. The plague and cholera and yellow fever are controlled; the word diphtheria no longer whitens the cheek of the parent; even tuberculosis is less dreaded and may soon be conquered; aseptic surgery performs marvelous operations which, a few years ago, would have been pronounced impossible. The human suffering thus alleviated is immeasurable.

These illustrations are sufficient to show that no knowledge of substance or force or life is so remote or minute, although apparently indefinitely distant from present practise, but that tomorrow it may become an indispensable need. The practical man of all practical men is he who, with his face toward truth, follows wherever it may lead, with no thought but to get a deeper insight into the order of the universe in which he lives. It can not be predicted at what distant nook of knowledge, apparently remote from any practical service, a brilliantly useful stream may spring. It is certain that every fundamental discovery yet made by the delving student has been of service to man before a decade has passed.

Already at Wisconsin here and there a scholar has arisen whose most elemental thought is to see deeper into the order of nature. Let the university search well for such spirits and give them unbounded opportunity, for they are to be benefactors, not only of the state, but of the entire earth; for a new truth, a new principle, is not the property of any state, but instantly belongs to the world. May men of creative power, trained by Wisconsin, leave our doors in ever-increasing numbers, until they become a great enlightening influence in the state and the nation! The final and supreme test of the height to which a university attains is its output of creative men, not in science alone, but in arts, in literature, in ethics, in politics and in religion.

I, therefore, hold that the state university, a university which is to serve the state, must see to it that scholarship and research of all kinds, whether or not a possible practical value can be pointed out, must be sustained. A privately endowed institution may select some part of knowledge and confine itself to it, but not so a state university. A university supported by the state for all its people, for all its sons and daughters, with their tastes and aptitudes as varied as mankind, can place no bounds upon the lines of its endeavor, else the state is the irreparable loser.

Be the choice of the sons and daughters of the state, language, literature, history, political economy, pure science, agriculture, engineering, architecture, sculpture, painting or music, they should find at the state university ample opportunity for the pursuit of the chosen subject, even until they become creators in it. Nothing short of such opportunity is just, for each has an equal right to find at the state university the advanced intellectual life adapted to his need. Any narrower view is indefensible. The university should extend its scope until the field is covered from agriculture to the fine arts.

The barrenness of America in the creation and appreciation of literature, music and art is the point upon which Europe charges us with semi-barbarism. If the university does not become the center for the cultivation of the highest capacities of the human mind, where is the work to be done in this country? In America there is no other available agency. This work must be undertaken by the university, or else remain undone.

If the people of the United States are to cease being mere money getters, if they are to accomplish more than material advance, if they are to have proportional development, the university must give opportunity for training in all lines of human endeavor.

If the University of Wisconsin is to do for the state what it has a right to expect, it must develop, expand, strengthen creative work at whatever cost. Only by so doing is it possible for the university to serve the state in the highest way. For my part, I look forward with absolute confidence to the liberal support by the state of a school whose chief function is to add to the sum of human achievement. I am not willing to admit that a state university under a democracy shall be of lower grade than a state university under a monarchy. I believe that legislatures elected by all the people are as far-sighted as legislatures that represent an aristocracy. A great graduate school will be realized at some state university during this century. Is Wisconsin to have this preeminent position?

We are now able to suggest the ideal American university—one which has the best features of the English system with its dormitories, commons and union; one which includes the liberal and fine arts and the additions of science and applied science; and one which superimposes upon these an advanced school modeled upon the German universities, but with a broader scope. In such a university the student in the colleges of liberal and fine arts has opportunity to elect work in applied science, and thus broaden his education. He feels the inspiring influence of scholarship and research, and thus gains enthusiasm for the elementary work because it leads to the heights. The student in applied knowledge is not restricted to subjects which concern his future profession, but he has the opportunity to pursue the humanities and the fine arts, and thus liberalize his education. He, too, feels the stimulus of the graduate school, and, if one of the elect, may become an investigator and thus further ameliorate the lot of mankind by new applications of science to life. The student in the graduate school, primarily concerned with creative scholarship, may supplement a deficient basal training by work in the liberal arts and in the schools of applied knowledge. Thus the college of liberal arts, of applied knowledge and of creative scholarship interlock. Each is stronger and can do the work peculiar to itself better than if alone. This combination university is the American university of the future, and this the University of Wisconsin must become if it is to be the peer of the great universities of the nation.

Wisconsin is among the state universities which have this opportunity open to them. Many of the states have divided their grants among several foundations, supporting at different localities, schools of liberal arts, of agriculture, of medicine and of mining. In Wisconsin there is only one institution which attempts to do university work. Public and private funds alike, which are to go to a university, should come to that institution. This statement does not imply lack of appreciation of the excellent and very important work done by the colleges of the state. May they continue to thrive; may they continue to have the support of the citizens of the state; for the many thousands of students that during the next half century are continuously to demand a college education in this state can not be accommodated in one institution. Collegiate work should be done at several centers within the state, but professional and university work is so expensive and the different schools and colleges are so closely related, that the best opportunities can only be furnished in the various fields in the university. At a university of the first rank the opportunities for instruction in the fields strongly covered are superior to those which can be offered in an institution devoted to a single field. Wisconsin has fortunately escaped the fatal mistake of subdivision of its university effort. With the concentrated support of the state, public and private, there is no reason why the University of Wisconsin should not do in every line as high grade work as any in the country. My faith is such that I look forward with confidence to the future, with profound conviction that the breadth of vision, which has enabled this institution to grow from small beginnings to its present magnitude, will continue to guide the state, until a university is built as broad as human endeavor, as high as human aspiration.

PRESSURE ON DENOMINATIONAL COLLEGES (1907) From Carnegie
Foundation for the Advancement of Teaching, *Second Annual Report of the President and Treasurer* (New York, 1907), pp. 58–61.

In the First Annual Report to this board a brief statement was made of the difficulties involved in administering this trust so far as its relations to denominational institutions are concerned. The preceding pages throw light upon the nature of these difficulties and will serve to indicate to the trustees not only the problems of their own administration, but, to some extent, the viewpoint of those in charge of such institutions.

Originally there were admitted to the benefits of the Foundation some fifty institutions upon an examination of their academic standards and the evidences of their written charters. A longer experience has shown that in determining the denominational character of an institution many other things must be studied beside the printed charter or act of incorporation. During the past year but three institutions have been added to the list. The trustees and the executive officers find it difficult to use in many cases any criteria which do not seem arbitrary, and which admit some institutions and exclude others without apparent justification. It is to be remembered that the work of the Foundation is barely begun and that the trustees as a body have not as yet felt justified in translating the provisions of the charter with respect to denominational control into specific instructions to its executive committee. It has seemed wise, therefore, to proceed slowly. In the end, just and fair results will be arrived at only by a thorough discussion of all the matters involved. No institution can suffer harm by waiting for admission to the system of retiring allowances established under this board until those questions have been cleared.

The preceding pages may, I hope, make somewhat more clear the nature of the restrictions in the charter of the Foundation. The nature of these restrictions and their legal force in controlling the actions of the trustees have been often misunderstood. Among the records of the Foundation are numerous letters from college presidents and other academic authorities setting forth in detail the unsectarian spirit which prevails in the institution under their control. Accompanying such letters are sometimes complete lists of the students, of the faculty, and of the alumni of the institution arranged according to their religious preferences. Or, again, as in the case of one institution, a formal certificate of undenominationalism was forwarded to the Foundation signed by all of the pastors of the adjacent city, to prove that the university did not give itself to narrow sectarian views. One college president in whose institution a majority of the faculty must belong to a specified religious body wrote, after explaining the liberal spirit of the college: "Our college has always been liberal, why cannot the Carnegie Foundation be liberal, too?"

The fact that many colleges and universities are unsectarian in spirit, though controlled by a religious body, no one would deny. Trustees restricted to a particular denomination may govern their college as liberally as though the restrictions as to their religious faith did not exist. But that is quite beside the question. No court would entertain a suggestion that such liberality of action nullified the obligation under which the trustees of the Foundation are permitted to act.

A very common type of letter is one in which the writer states that his college is as free from denominational control as some institutions on the accepted list, which he generally declares belong by common knowledge to such and such churches.

In this matter also there is widespread misapprehension. For example, Princeton and Yale are the two institutions upon the accepted list which are most often referred to in this way, one as a Presbyterian, the other as a Congregational institution. As a matter of fact, neither of these institutions has any connection with a denomination. Such relationship as remains is one of tradition and sympathy and the Foundation is not concerned with the fact that a given college was founded under the auspices of a religious organization or that it retains to-day a sympathetic relation with it. Any institution will be at once eligible, so far as denominational considerations are concerned, which will put itself in the position of Princeton or of Yale.

Perhaps the most common form of inquiry which comes to the executive officers of the Foundation is, "Would you advise the amendment of our charter in such manner as to make our institution eligible to the benefits of the retiring allowance system?"

This question is, of course, one concerning which the authorities of each institution must make their own decision. Primarily, the college authorities in such a case ought to face fairly the question, "What does our denominational connection mean to us?" If it means a real gain to the spiritual and intellectual life of the college, or if its abrogation means the abandonment of obligations assumed in good faith, the inquiry can go no further. No gain in college support can compensate for a loss of college sincerity.

Even when these reasons do not exist, the traditions and aspirations of a religious body are so interwoven with the life of certain colleges that those in control may well hesitate to take such a step.

If such reasons are absent, the ground of financial support or of a student constituency may well be of such weight as to make a denominational connection desirable in the eyes of college authorities. All these questions are entirely in the hands of college officers. But it is fair that, at this epoch of our educational history, the grounds for such action as may be taken shall be made clear. If in denominational relationship there lies a possibility of higher service to education and to the country, if in denominational generosity there is a definite assurance of a fair support to higher education, these facts are most important to know.

On the other hand, it seems clear that, if no specific obligations rest upon the college authorities to retain a formal legal relation to a denomination, it is clearly their duty, in justice to their own teachers, to consider the question whether the substitution of a relation of sympathy and tradition in the place of formal legal relationship does not lie in the direction of true progress.

In some institutions the charters contain conditions as to the church membership of trustees or officers which are now completely obsolete. They belong to a period of earlier religious and social development and their retention would seem to be only a part of that inertia which goes with college traditions of growth. The retention of such limitations, after they are in practice obsolete, belongs rather to college self-consciousness than to scholarly courage and love of truth. Institutions which perfer to retain such conditions ought not to put the burden of their retention upon their professors, but should establish their own system of retiring allowances promptly and upon a generous plan. Until the respect for tradition takes this form, it will not be likely to contribute either to the reputation or to the upbuilding of the institution.

Such limitations in the charter of a great university seem more to be regretted than in the case of a modest college. And this arises not so much from the consequent narrowing in the choice of president or of trustees, though this may be serious. It lies rather in the fact that such restrictions are in direct contravention of that larger spirit of intellectual freedom for which a university exists. In proportion as an institution becomes a true university, taking its part in the life not only of the nation, but of the world, it finds such limitations embarrassing.

In most cases, charters or acts of incorporation can be amended without serious difficulty, once the nature of the amendments are agreed upon. When a special charter has been obtained from a legislature, that body is, in ordinary cases, willing to make any reasonable changes which those in control of the college may desire. A number of such revised charters have been granted during the past winter. Thus, the Legislature of Connecticut granted to Wesleyan University a charter making far-reaching changes in its denominational conditions and the Legislature of the State of Maine granted a new charter to Bates College, removing all denominational limitations.

In certain cases, such amendments present serious difficulties. For instance, Northwestern University has a special charter, which exempts from taxation all real estate it may own in the State of Illinois, including business property in the city of Chicago. This provision has been confirmed in a suit carried to the Supreme Court. The charter requires that a majority of the members of the board of trustees must belong to the Methodist Episcopal Church. Even if the university authorities desired to change their provision, they would not dare to risk such a charter in the uncertain sea of legislative amendment. Fortunately, an institution which possesses so large a financial advantage as this charter confers will be able to establish its own system of retiring allowances for professors.

There are other cases in which special agreements in the charter themselves either create contracts which must be carried out or contain other conditions which make amendment legally difficult. Thus, a denominational regulation at Hillsdale College in regard to both the trustees and the professors is expressly declared by the charter which contains the regulation not to be subject to change. The charter of the University of Chicago, after providing that the president of the university and the head of the college "which shall constitute its literary or undergraduate department," and two-thirds of the board of trustees of the university shall "at all times" be "members of regular Baptist churches," adds: "and as contributions of money and property have been and are being solicited, and have been and are being made, upon the condition last named, this charter shall not be amended or changed at any time hereafter so as to abrogate or modify the qualifications of two-thirds of the trustees and the president above mentioned, but in this particular this charter shall be forever unalterable."

As a number of institutions have at this time under consideration the question of a change in their charters, I venture to suggest that, in case of such change, the whole question of effective college organization—the size of the board of trustees, their powers and similar matters—be carefully considered, to the end that the new charter, if one is to be had, may look to the most effective college administration.

IRVING BABBITT'S DEFENSE OF HUMANISM (1908) From Irving Babbitt, *Literature and the American College* (Boston, 1908), pp. 8–10, 22–24, 258–63.

The humanist, then, as opposed to the humanitarian, is interested in the perfecting of the individual rather than in schemes for the elevation of mankind as a whole; and although he allows largely for sympathy, he insists that it be disciplined and tempered by judgment.

*   *   *

The true humanist maintains just balance between sympathy and selection. We moderns, even a champion of the past like Brunetière, tend to lay an undue stress on the element of sympathy. On the other hand, the ancients in general, both Greek and Roman, inclined to sacrifice sympathy to selection.

* * *

Ancient humanism is as a whole intensely aristocratic in temper; its sympathies run in what would seem to us narrow channels; it is naturally disdainful of the humble and lowly who have not been indoctrinated and disciplined. Indeed, an unselective and universal sympathy, the sense of the brotherhood of man, as we term it, is usually supposed to have come into the world only with Christianity. We may go farther and say that the exaltation of love and sympathy as supreme and all-sufficing principles that do not need to be supplemented by doctrine and discipline is largely peculiar to our modern or humanitarian era. . . .

* * *

Later on this humanistic ideal became more and more conventionalized and associated with a hierarchy of rank and privilege. The sense of intellectual superiority was reinforced by the sense of social superiority. The consequent narrowing of sympathy is what Amiel objects to in the English gentleman: "Between gentlemen, courtesy, equality, social proprieties; below that level, haughtiness, disdain, coldness, indifference. . . . The politeness of a gentleman is not human and general, but quite individual and personal." It is a pity, no doubt, that the Englishman is thus narrow in his sympathies; but it will be a greater pity, if, in enlarging his sympathies, he allows his traditional disciplines, humanistic and religious, to be relaxed and enervated. The English humanist is not entirely untrue to his ancient prototype even in the faults of which Amiel complains. There is a real relation, as Professor Butcher points out, between the English idea of the gentleman and scholar and the view of the cultivated man that was once held in the intensely aristocratic democracy of Athens.

* * *

We may perhaps venture to sum up the results of our search for a definition of humanism. We have seen that the humanist, as we know him historically, moved between an extreme of sympathy and an extreme of discipline and selection, and became humane in proportion as he mediated between these extremes. To state this truth more generally, the true mark of excellence in a man, as Pascal puts it, is his power to harmonize in himself opposite virtues and to occupy all the space between them (*tout l'entredeux*). By his ability thus to unite in himself opposite qualities man shows his humanity, his superiority of essence over other animals.

* * *

Man is a creature who is foredoomed to one-sidedness, yet who becomes humane only in proportion as he triumphs over this fatality of his nature, only as he arrives at that measure which comes from tempering his virtues, each by its opposite. The aim, as Matthew Arnold has said in the most admirable of his critical phrases, is to see life steadily and see it whole; but this is an aim, alas, that no one has ever attained completely—not even Sophocles, to whom Arnold applies it. After man has made the simpler adjustments, there are other and more difficult adjustments awaiting him beyond, and the goal is, in a sense, infinitely remote.

For most practical purposes, the law of measure is the supreme law of life, because it bounds and includes all other laws. It was doubtless the perception of this fact that led the most eminent personality of the Far East, Gotama Buddha, to proclaim in the opening sentence of his first sermon that extremes are barbarous. But India as a whole failed to learn the lesson. Greece is perhaps the most humane of countries, because it not only formulated clearly the law of measure ("nothing too much"), but also perceived the avenging nemesis that overtakes every form of insolent excess ($\nu\beta\rho\iota\varsigma$) or violation of this law.

Of course, even in Greece any effective insight into the law of measure was confined to a minority, though at times a large minority. The majority at any particular instant in Greece or elsewhere is almost sure to be unsound, and unsound because it is one-sided. We may borrow a homely illustration from the theory of commercial crises. A minority of men may be prudent and temper their enterprise with discretion, but the majority is sure to over-trade, and so unless restrained by the prudent few will finally bring on themselves the nemesis of a panic.

* * *

In general the humanist will not repudiate either sentimental or scientific naturalism; for this would be to attempt an impossible reaction. His aim is not to deny his age, but to complete it. Various modern tendencies have been freely criticised throughout these essays, especially the tendency to make utopian appeals to the principle of brotherhood when what is wanted is a submission to the discipline of common sense and humane standards.

* * *

Some of the duties that Plato assigns to his ideal ruler would seem to belong in our own day to the higher institutions of learning. Our colleges and universities could render no greater service than to oppose to the worship of energy and the frantic eagerness for action an atmosphere of leisure and reflection. It would seem that they might recognize the claims of the contemplative life without encouraging a cloistered seclusion or falling into the monastic abuses of the past. We should make large allowance in our lives for the "eventual element of calm," if they are not to degenerate into the furious and feverish pursuit of mechanical efficiency. The industrial democracy of which President Eliot speaks will need to temper its joy in work with the joy in leisure, if it is to be a democracy in which a civilized person would care to live. The tendency of an industrial democracy that took joy in work alone would be to live in a perpetual devil's sabbath of whirling machinery, and call it progress. Progress, thus understood, will prove only a way of retrograding toward barbarism. It is well to attain to the secret of power, but not at the sacrifice of the secret of peace. What is wanted is neither Oriental quietism, nor again the inhuman strenuousness of a certain type of Occidental; neither pure action nor pure repose, but a blending of the two that will occupy all the space between them,—that activity in repose which has been defined as the humanistic ideal. The serious advantage of our modern machinery is that it lightens the drudgery of the world and opens up the opportunities of leisure to more people than has hitherto been possible. We should not allow ourselves to be persuaded that the purpose of this machinery is merely to serve as point of departure for a still intenser activity. The present situation especially is not one that will be saved—if it is to be saved at all— by what we have called humanitarian hustling. We have already quoted the federal judge who exhorts the American people to combine ten per cent of thought with ninety per cent of action. If we ourselves ventured on an exhortation to the American people, it would rather be that of Demosthenes to the Athenians: "In God's name, I beg of you to think." Of action we shall have plenty in any case; but it is only by a more humane reflection that we can escape the penalties sure to be exacted from any country that tries to dispense in its national life with the principle of leisure.

ALEXANDER MEIKLEJOHN ON THE LIBERAL ARTS COLLEGE

(1912)   From Alexander Meiklejohn, "What the Liberal College Is," *The Liberal College* (Boston, 1920), pp. 30–42.

What do our teachers believe to be the aim of college instruction? Wherever their opinions and convictions find expression there is one contention which is always in the foreground, namely, that to be liberal a college must be essentially intellectual. It is a place, the teachers tell us, in which a boy, forgetting all things else, may set forth on the enterprise of learning. It is a time when a young man may come to awareness of the thinking of his people, may perceive what knowledge is and has been and is to be. Whatever light-hearted undergraduates may say, whatever the opinions of solicitous parents, of ambitious friends, of employers in search of workmen, of leaders in church or state or business,—whatever may be the beliefs and desires and demands of outsiders,—the teacher within the college, knowing his mission as no one else can know it, proclaims that mission to be the leading of his pupil into the life intellectual. The college is primarily not a place of the body, nor of the feelings, nor even of the will; it is, first of all, a place of the mind. . . .

*   *   *

In the conflict with the forces within the college our teachers find themselves fighting essentially the same battle as against the foes without. In a hundred different ways the friends of the college, students, graduates, trustees and even colleagues, seem to them so to misunderstand its mission as to minimize or to falsify its intellectual ideals. The college is a good place for making friends; it gives excellent experience in getting on with men; it has exceptional advantages as an athletic club; it is a relatively safe place for a boy when he first leaves home; on the whole it may improve a student's manners; it gives acquaintance with lofty ideas of character, preaches the doctrine of social service, exalts the virtues and duties of citizenship. All these conceptions seem to the teacher to hide or to obscure the fact that the college is fundamentally a place of the mind, a time for thinking, an opportunity for knowing. And perhaps in proportion to their own loftiness of purpose and motive they are the more dangerous as tending all the more powerfully to replace or to nullify the underlying principle upon which they all depend. . . .

How then shall we justify the faith of the teacher? What reason can we give for our exaltation of intellectual training and activity? To this question two answers are possible. First, knowledge and thinking are good in themselves. Secondly, they help us in the attainment of other values in life which without them would be impossible. Both these answers may be given and are given by college teachers. Within them must be found whatever can be said by way of explanation and justification of the work of the liberal college. . . .

In a word, men know with regard to thinking, as with regard to every other content of human experience, that it cannot be valued merely in terms of itself. It must be measured in terms of its relation to other contents and to human experience as a whole. Thinking is good in itself,—but what does it cost of other things, what does it bring of other values? Place it amid all the varied contents of our individual and social experience, measure it in terms of what it implies, fix it by means of its relations, and then you will know its worth not simply in itself but in that deeper sense which comes when human desires are rationalized and human lives are known in their entirety, as well as they can be known by those who are engaged in living them.

In this consideration we find the second answer of the teacher to the demand for justification of the work of the college. Knowledge is good, he tells us, not only in itself, but in its enrichment and enhancement of the other values of our experience. In the deepest and fullest sense of the words, knowledge pays. This statement rests upon the classification of human actions into two groups, those of the instinctive type and those of the intellectual type. By far the greater part of our human acts are carried on without any clear idea of what we are going to do or how we are going to do it. For the most part our responses to our situations are the immediate responses of feeling, of perception, of custom, of tradition. But slowly and painfully, as the mind has developed, action after action has been translated from the feeling to the ideational type; in wider and wider fields men have become aware of their own modes of action, more and more they have come to understanding, to knowledge of themselves and of their needs. And the principle underlying all our educational procedure is that on the whole, actions become more successful as they pass from the sphere of feeling to that of understanding. Our educational belief is that in the long run if men know what they are going to do and how they are going to do it, and what is the nature of the situation with which they are dealing, their response to that situation will be better adjusted and more beneficial than are the responses of the feeling type in like situations.

It is all too obvious that there are limits to the validity of this principle. If men are to investigate, to consider, to decide, then action must be delayed and we must pay the penalty of waiting. If men are to endeavor to understand and know their situations, then we must be prepared to see them make mistakes in their thinking, lose their certainty of touch, wander off into pitfalls and illusions and fallacies of thought, and in consequence secure for the time results far lower in value than those of the instinctive response which they seek to replace. The delays and mistakes and uncertainties of our thinking are a heavy price to pay, but it is the conviction of the teacher that the price is as nothing when compared with the goods which it buys. . . .

Within the limits of this general educational principle the place of the liberal college may easily be fixed. . . . But the college is called liberal . . . because the instruction is dominated by no special interest, is limited to no single human task, but is intended to take human activity as a whole, to understand human endeavors not in their isolation but in their relations to one another and to the total experience which we call the life of our people. . . . To give boys an intellectual grasp on human experience—this, it seems to me, is the teacher's conception of the chief function of the liberal college.

ABRAHAM FLEXNER ON REFORM OF MEDICAL EDUCATION

(1910) From Abraham Flexner, *Medical Education in the United States and Canada, a Report of the Carnegie Foundation for the Advancement of Teaching,* Bulletin no. 4, (New York, 1910), pp. 13–19, 23–27.

With the creation of the heterogeneous situation thus bequeathed to us, it is clear that consideration for the public good has had on the whole little to do; nor is it to be expected that this situation will very readily readjust itself in response to public need. A powerful and profitable vested interest tenaciously resists criticism from that point of view; not, of course, openly. It is too obvious that if the sick are to reap the full benefit of recent progress in medicine, a more uniformly arduous and expensive medical education is demanded. But it is speciously argued that improvements thus accomplished will do more harm than good: for whatever makes medical education more difficult and more costly will deplete the profession and thus deprive large numbers of all medical attention whatsoever, in order that a fortunate minority may get the best possible care. It is important to forestall the issue thus raised; otherwise it will crop out at every turn of the following discussion, in the effort to justify the existing situation and to break the force of constructive suggestion. It seems, therefore, necessary to refer briefly at this point to the statistical aspects of medical education in America, so far as they are immediately pertinent to the question of improvement and reform.

The problem is of course practical and not academic. Pending the homogeneous filling up of the whole country, inequalities must be tolerated. Man has been not inaptly differentiated as the animal with "the desire to take medicine." When sick, he craves the comfort of the doctor,—any doctor rather than none at all, and in this he will not be denied. The question is, then, not merely to define the ideal training of the physician; it is just as much, at this particular juncture, to strike the solution that, economic and social factors being what they are, will distribute as widely as possible the best type of physician so distributable. Doubtless the chaos above characterized is in part accounted for by crude conditions that laughed at regular methods of procedure. But this stage of our national existence has gone by. What with widely ramifying railroad and trolley service, improving roads, automobiles, and rural telephones, we have measurably attained some of the practical consequences of homogeneity. The experience of older countries is therefore suggestive, even if not altogether conclusive.

Professor Paulsen, describing in his book on the *German Universities* the increased importance of the medical profession, reports with some astonishment that "the number of physicians has increased with great rapidity so that now there is, in Germany, one doctor for every 2000 souls, and in the large cities one for every 1000.[1] What would the amazed philosopher have said had he known that in the entire United States there is already on the average one doctor for every 568 persons, that in our large cities there is frequently one doctor for every 400[2] or less, that many small towns with less than 200 inhabitants each have two or three physicians apiece.[3]

Over-production is stamped on the face of these facts; and if, in its despite, there are localities without a physician, it is clear that even long-continued over-production of cheaply made doctors cannot force distribution beyond a well marked point. In our towns health is as good and physicians probably as alert as in Prussia; there is, then, no reason to fear an unheeded call or a too tardy response, if urban communities support one doctor for every 2000 inhabitants. On that showing, the towns have now four or more doctors for every one that they actually require,—something worse than waste, for the superfluous doctor is usually a poor doctor. So enormous an overcrowding with low-grade material both relatively and absolutely decreases the number of well trained men who can count on the profession for a livelihood. According to Gresham's law, which, as has been shrewdly remarked, is as valid in education as in finance, the inferior medium tends to displace the superior. If then, by having in cities one doctor for every 2000 persons, we got four times as good a doctor as now when we provide one doctor for every 500 or less, the apothecaries would find time hanging somewhat more heavily on their hands. Clearly, low standards and poor training are not now needed in order to supply physicians to the towns.

Ohio:	Killbrook, population 307, has three doctors			
	Houston	"	227 " " "
Texas:	Wellington	"	87 " five "
	Whitt	"	378 " four "
	Whitney	"	766 " six "
Massachusetts:	Colerain	"	80 " two "
	Harding	"	100 " " "
Nebraska:	Eustin	"	232 " " "
	Crofton	"	46 " " "
Oregon:	Fossil	"	370 " " "
	Gaston	"	182 " " "

(From the American Medical Directory. 1909.)

In the country the situation follows one of two types. Assuming that a thousand people in an accessible area will support a competent physician, one of two things will happen if the district contains many less. In a growing country, like Canada or

[1] Thilly's translation, p. 400.

[2] New York, 1 : 460; Chicago, 1 : 580; Washington, 1 : 270; San Francisco, 1 : 370. These ratios are calculated on the basis of figures obtained from Polk's *Medical Register*, the *American Medical Directory*, and estimates prepared by the U. S. Census Bureau. The force of the figures as to the number of physicians cannot be broken by urging that many physicians no longer practise. Such have been carefully excluded by the compilers of the *American Medical Directory*. Figures used throughout this report were obtained from these sources.

[3] Examples may be cited at random from every section of the country in proof of the fact that overcrowding is general, not merely local or exceptional.

our own middle west, the young graduate will not hesitate to pitch his tent in a sparsely settled neighborhood, if it promises a future. A high-grade and comparatively expensive education will not alter his inclination to do this. The more exacting Canadian laws rouse no objection on this score. The graduates of McGill and Toronto have passed through a scientific and clinical discipline of high quality; but one finds them every year draining off into the freshly opened Northwest Territory. In truth, it is an old story. McDowell left the Kentucky backwoods to spend two years under Bell in Edinburgh; and when they were over, returned contentedly to the wilderness, where he originated the operation for ovarian tumor in the course of a surgical practice that carried him back and forth through Kentucky, Ohio, and Tennessee. Benjamin Dudley, son of a poor Baptist preacher, dissatisfied with the results first of his apprenticeship, then of his Philadelphia training, hoarded his first fees, and with them subsequently embarked temporarily in trade; he loaded a flat-boat with sundries, which he disposed of to good advantage at New Orleans, there investing in a cargo of flour, which he sold to the hungry soldiers of Wellington in the Spanish peninsula. The profits kept Dudley in the hospitals of Paris for four years, after which he came back to Lexington, and for a generation was the great surgeon and teacher of surgery in the rough country across the Alleghenies. The pioneer is not yet dead within us. The self-supporting students of Ann Arbor and Toronto prove this. For a region which holds out hope, there is no need to make poor doctors,—still less to make too many of them.

In the case of stranded small groups in an unpromising environment the thing works out differently. A century of reckless over-production of cheap doctors has resulted in general overcrowding; but it has not forced doctors into these hopeless spots. It has simply huddled them thickly at points on the extreme margin. Certain rural communities of New England may, for example, have no physician in their midst, though they are in most instances not inaccessible to one. But let never so many low-grade doctors be turned out, whether in Boston or in smaller places like Burlington or Brunswick, that are supposed not to spoil the young man for a country practice, these unpromising places, destined perhaps to disappear from the map, will not attract them. They prefer competition in some already over-occupied field. Thus, in Vermont, Burlington, the seat of the medical department of the University of Vermont, with a population of less than 21,000 has 60 physicians, one for every 333 inhabitants;[4] nor can these figures be explained away on the ground that the largest city in the state is a vortex which absorbs more than its proper share; for the state abounds in small towns in which several doctors compete in the service of less than a thousand persons: Post Mills, with 105 inhabitants, has two doctors; Jeffersonville, with 400, has two; Plainfield, with 341, has three. Other New England states are in the same case. It would appear, then, that over-production on a low basis does not effectually overcome the social or economic obstacles to spontaneous dispersion. Perhaps the salvation of these districts might, under existing circumstances, be better worked out by a different method. A large area would support one good man, where its separate fragments are each unable to support even one poor man. A physician's range, actual and virtual, increases with his competency. A well qualified doctor may perhaps at a central point set up a small hospital, where the seriously ill of the entire district may receive good care. The region is thus better served by one well trained man than it could possibly be even if over-production on a low basis ultimately succeeded in forcing an incompetent

[4]*American Medical Directory*; Polk (1908) gives 75 active physicians, a ratio of 1 : 280.

into every hamlet of five and twenty souls. This it cannot compel. It cannot keep even the cheap man in a place without a "chance;" it can only demoralize the smaller places which are capable of supporting a better trained man whose energies may also reach out into the more thinly settled surrounding country. As a last resort, it might conceivedly become the duty of the several states to salary district physicians in thinly settled or remote regions,—surely a sounder policy than the demoralization of the entire profession for the purpose of enticing ill trained men where they will not go.[5] We may safely conclude that our methods of carrying on medical education have resulted in enormous over-production at a low level, and that, whatever the justification in the past, the present situation in town and country alike can be more effectively met by a reduced output of well trained men than by further inflation with an inferior product.

The improvement of medical education cannot therefore be resisted on the ground that it will destroy schools and restrict output: that is precisely what is needed. The illustrations already given in support of this position may be reinforced by further examples from every section of the Union,—from Pennsylvania with one doctor for every 636 inhabitants, Maryland with one for every 658, Nebraska with one for every 602, Colorado with one for every 328, Oregon with one for every 646. It is frequently urged that, however applicable to other sections, this argument does not for the present touch the south, where continued tolerance of commercial methods is required by local conditions. Let us briefly consider the point. The section as a whole contains one doctor for every 760 persons. In the year 1908, twelve states[6] showed a gain in population of 358,837. If now we allow in cities one additional physician for every increase of 2000, and outside cities an additional one for every increase of 1000 in population,—an ample allowance in any event,—we may in general figure on one more physician for every gain of 1500 in total population. We are not now arguing that a ratio of 1 : 1500 is correct; we are under no necessity of proving that. Our contention is simply that, starting with our present overcrowded condition, production henceforth at the ratio of one physician to every *increase* of 1500 in population will prevent a shortage, for the next generation at least. In 1908 the south, then, needed 240 more doctors to take care of its increase in population. In the course of the same year, it is estimated that 500 vacancies in the profession were due to death.[7] If every vacancy thus arising must be filled, conditions will never improve. Let us agree to work towards a more normal adjustment by filling two vacancies due to death with one new physician,— once more, a decidedly liberal provision. This will prove sufficiently deliberate; it would have called for 250 more doctors by the close of the year. In all, 490 new men would have amply cared for the increase in population and the vacancies due to death. As a matter of fact, the southern medical schools turned out in that year 1144 doctors; 78 more southerners were graduated from the schools of Baltimore and Philadelphia. The grand total would probably reach 1300,—1300 southern doctors to compete in a field in which one-third of the number would find the making of a decent living already difficult. Clearly, the south has no cause to be

[5] These officials would combine the duties of county health officer with those now assigned in large towns to the city physician.

[6] This includes Kentucky, Virginia, Tennessee, North Carolina, South Carolina, Georgia, Florida, Alabama, Mississippi, Louisiana, Texas, Arkansas.

[7] Based on figures collected by the American Medical Association.

apprehensive in consequence of a reduced output of higher quality.[8] Its requirements in the matter of a fresh supply are not such as to make it necessary to pitch their training excessively low.

DISTRIBUTION

Place	Population	No. Drs.	Ratio	Place	Population	No. Drs.	Ratio
City of Henderson	17,500	27	1:644	Zion	250	3	1:84
Anthaston	24	1	1:24	Robards	500	3	1:167
Baskett	200	2	1:100	Niagara	100	3	1:34
Cairo	200	1	1:200	McDonald's Landing	25		
Corydon	1,000	4	1:250	Alzey	25	1	1:25
Dixie	300	1	1:300	Smith Mills	200	3	1:67
Geneva	100	2	1:50	Spottsville	700	3	1:234
Hebardsville	400	2	1:200				

Throughout the county there are doctors within five miles everywhere.

The rest of the country may be rapidly surveyed from the same point of view. The total gain in population, outside the southern states already considered, was 975,008,—requiring on the basis of one more doctor for every 1500 more people 650 doctors. By death, in the course of the year there were in the same area 1730 vacancies. Replacing two vacancies by one doctor, 865 men would have been required; in most sections public interest would be better cared for if they all remained unfilled for a decade to come. On the most liberal calculation, 1500 graduates would be called for, and 1000 would be better still. There were actually produced in that year, outside the south, 3497, *i.e.*, between two and three times as many as the country could possibly assimilate; and this goes on, and has been going on, every year.

It appears, then, that the country needs fewer and better doctors; and that the way to get them better is to produce fewer. To support all or most present schools at the higher level would be wasteful, even if it were not impracticable; for they cannot be manned. Some day, doubtless, posterity may reestablish a school in some place where a struggling enterprise ought now to be discontinued. Towards that remote contingency nothing will, however, be gained by prolonging the life of the existent institution.

The statistics just given have never been compiled or studied by the average medical educator. His stout asseveration that "the country needs more doctors" is based on "the letters on file in the dean's office," or on some hazy notion respecting conditions in neighboring states. As to the begging letters: selecting a thinly settled region, I obtained from the dean of the medical department of the University of Minnesota a list of the localities whence requests for a physician have recently come. With few exceptions, they represent five states:[9] fifty-nine towns in Minnesota want a doctor; but investigation shows that these fifty-nine towns have already one hundred and forty-nine doctors between them.[10] Forty-one places in North Dakota

[8] As Kentucky is one of the largest producers of low-grade doctors in the entire Union, it is interesting to observe conditions there. The following is the result of a careful study of Henderson County made for me by one thoroughly acquainted with it.
Total population, 35,000; number of doctors, 56; ratio, 1 : 624.

[9] The general distribution in these states shows that over-production prevails in new states as in old ones: Minnesota 1 : 981, South Dakota 1 : 821; Iowa 1 : 605; North Dakota 1 : 971; Wisconsin 1 : 936.

[10] Ten of the fifty-nine were without registered physicians; but of these ten, two are not to be found on the map, two more are not in the *Postal Guide*; of the other six, four are in easy reach of doctors; two, with a combined population of one hundred and fifty, are out of reach.

apply; they have already one hundred and twenty-one doctors. Twenty-one applications come from South Dakota, from towns having already forty-nine doctors; seven from Wisconsin, from places that had twenty-one physicians before their prayer for more was made; six from Iowa, from towns that had seventeen doctors at the time. It is clear that the files of the deans will not invalidate the conclusion which a study of the figures suggests. They are more apt to sustain it: for the requests in question are less likely to mean "no doctor" than poor doctors,[11]—a distemper which continued over-production on the same basis can only aggravate, and which a change to another of the same type will not cure. As to general conditions, no case has been found in which a single medical educator contended that his own vicinity or state is in need of more doctors: it is always the "next neighbor." Thus the District of Columbia, with one doctor for every two hundred and sixty two souls, maintains two low-grade medical schools. "Do you need more doctors in the District?" was asked of one of the deans. "Oh, no, we are making doctors for Maryland, Virginia, and Pennsylvania,"—for Maryland, with seven medical schools of its own and one doctor for every six hundred and fifty-eight inhabitants; for Virginia, with three medical schools of its own and one doctor for every nine hundred and eighteen; for Pennsylvania, with its eight schools and one doctor for every six hundred and thirty-six persons.

With the over-production thus demonstrated, the commercial treatment of medical education is intimately connected. Low standards give the medical schools access to a large clientele open to successful exploitation by commercial methods. The crude boy or the jaded clerk who goes into medicine at this level has not been moved by a significant prompting from within; nor has he as a rule shown any forethought in the matter of making himself ready. He is more likely to have been caught drifting at a vacant moment by an alluring advertisement or announcement, quite commonly an exaggeration, not infrequently an outright misrepresentation. Indeed, the advertising methods of the commercially successful schools are amazing.[12] Not infrequently advertising costs more than laboratories.[13] The school catalogues abound in exaggeration, misstatement, and half-truths.[14] The deans of these institutions occasionally know more about modern advertising than about modern medical teaching. They may be uncertain about the relation of the clinical laboratory to bedside instruction; but they have calculated to a nicety which "medium" brings the largest "return." Their dispensary records may be in hopeless disorder; but the card system by which they keep track of possible students is admirable. Such exploitation of medical education, confined to schools that admit students below the level of actual high school graduation, is strangely inconsistent with the social aspects of medical practice. The overwhelming importance of preventive medicine, sanitation, and public health indicates that in modern life the medical profession is an organ differentiated by society for its own highest purposes, not a business to be exploited by individuals according to their own fancy. There would be no vigorous campaigns led by enlightened practitioners against tuberculosis, malaria, and diphtheria, if the commercial point of view were tolerable in practice. And if not in practice, then not in education. The theory of state regulation covers that point. In the act of granting the right to confer degrees, the

[11]Occasionally these applications, which create the impression of a dearth, come from apothecaries who have a rear office to rent, a physician with a practice to sell, etc.

state vouches for them; through protective boards it still further seeks to safeguard the people. The public interest is then paramount, and when public interest, professional ideals, and sound educational procedure concur in the recommendation of the same policy, the time is surely ripe for decisive action.

*   *   *

Taking, then, modern medicine as an attempt to fight the battle against disease most advantageously to the patient, what shall we require of those who propose to enlist in the service? To get a somewhat surer perspective in dealing with a question around which huge clouds of dust have been beaten up, let us for a moment look elsewhere. A college education is not in these days a very severe or serious discipline. It is compounded in varying proportions of work and play; it scatters whatever effort it requires, so that at no point need the student stand the strain of prolonged intensive exertion. Further, the relation of college education to specific professional or vocational competency is still under dispute. It is clear, then, that a college education is less difficult, less trying, less responsible, than a professional education in medicine. It is therefore worth remarking that the lowest terms upon which a college education is now regularly accessible are an actual four-year high school training, scholastically determined, whether by examination of the candidate or by appraisement of the school.

Technical schools of engineering and the mechanic arts afford perhaps an even more illuminating comparison. These institutions began, like the college, at a low level; but they did not long rest there. Their instruction was too heavily handicapped by ignorance and immaturity. To their graduates, tasks involving human life and welfare were committed: the building of bridges, the installation of power plants, the construction of sewage systems. The technical school was thus driven to seek students of greater maturity, of more thorough preliminary schooling, and strictly to confine its opportunities to them. Now it is noteworthy that, though in point of intensive strain the discipline of the modern engineer equals the discipline of the modern physician, in one important respect, at least, it is less complex and exacting. The engineer deals mainly with measurable factors. His factor of uncertainty is within fairly narrow limits. The reasoning of the medical

---

[12] One school offers any graduate who shall have been in attendance three years a European trip.

[13] See chapter viii., "Financial Aspects of Medical Education," especially p. 135.

[14] A few instances may be cited at random:

Medical Department, University of Buffalo: "The dispensary is conducted in a manner unlike that usually seen. . . . Each one will secure unusually thorough training in taking and recording of histories" (p. 25). There are no dispensary records worthy the name.

Halifax Medical College: "First-class laboratory accommodation is provided for histology, bacteriology and practical pathology" (p. 9). One utterly wretched room is provided for all three.

Medical Department, University of Illinois: "The University Hospital . . . contains one hundred beds, and its clinical advantages are used exclusively for the students of this college" (p. 56). Over half of these beds are private, and the rest are of but limited use.

Western University (London, Ontario): Clinical instruction. "The Victoria Hospital . . . now contains two hundred and fifty beds, and is the official hospital of the City of London," etc. (p. 14). On the average, less than thirty of these beds are available for teaching.

The Medical Department of the University of Chattanooga: "The latest advances" are taught "in the most entertaining and instructive manner;" professors are "chosen for their proficiency;" "speculative research pertains" to the department of physiology; the department of pathology is "provided with a costly collection of specimens and generous supply of the best microscopes" (one, as a matter of fact); "the hospitals afford numerous cases of labor"!

student is much more complicated. He handles at one and the same time elements belonging to vastly different categories: physical, biological, psychological elements are involved in each other. Moreover, the recent graduate in engineering is not at once exposed to a decisive responsibility; to that he rises slowly through a lengthy series of subordinate positions that search out and complete his education.[15] Between the young graduate in medicine and his ultimate responsibility—human life—nothing interposes. He cannot nowadays begin with easy tasks under the surveillance of a superior; the issues of life and death are all in the day's work for him from the very first. The training of the doctor is therefore more complex and more directly momentous than that of the technician. Be it noted, then, that the minimum basis upon which a good school of engineering to-day accepts students is, once more, an actual high school education, and that the movement towards elongating the technical course to five years confesses the urgent need of something more.

There is another aspect of the problem equally significant. The curriculum of the up-to-date technical school is heavily weighted, to be sure; but except for mathematics, the essential subjects with which it starts are separate sciences that presuppose no prior mastery of contributory sciences. Take at random the College of Engineering of the University of Wisconsin. In the first year the science work is chemistry, and though the course is difficult, it demands no preceding acquaintance with chemistry itself or with any other science; second-year physics is in the same case, and the mechanics of the second semester looks back no further than to the physics of the first.

Very different is the plight of the medical school. There the earliest topics of the curriculum proper—anatomy, physiology, physiological chemistry—already hark back to a previous scientific discipline. Every one of them involves already acquired knowledge and manipulative skill. They are laboratory sciences at the second, not the primary, stage. Consider, for example, anatomy, the simplest and most fundamental of them all. It used to begin and end with the dissection of the adult cadaver. It can neither begin nor end there today; for it must provide the basis upon which experimental physiology, pathology, and bacteriology may intelligently be built up. Mere dissection does not accomplish this; in addition to gross anatomy, the student must make out under the microscope the normal cellular structure of organ, muscle, nerve, and blood-vessel; he must grasp the whole process of structural development. Histology and embryology are thus essential aspects of anatomical study. No treatment of the subject including these is possible within the time-limits of the modern medical curriculum unless previous training in general biology has equipped the student with the necessary fundamental conceptions, knowledge, and technical dexterity. It has just been stated that physiology presupposes anatomy on lines involving antecedent training in biology; it leans just as hard on chemistry and physics. The functional activities of the body propound questions in applied chemistry and applied physics. Nutrition and waste—what are these but chemical problems within the realm of biology? The mechanism of circulation, of seeing, of hearing—what are these but physical problems under the same qualifications? The normal rhythm of physiological function must then remain a riddle to students who cannot think and speak in biological, chemical, and physical language.

[15] It is interesting to observe the tendency towards conferring only a bachelor's degree in engineering at graduation instead of the degree of C.E., etc. The bachelor in engineering usually goes to work at laborer's wages; he is years reaching the degree of responsibility with which the graduate in medicine usually begins.

All this is, however, only preliminary. The physician's concern with normal process is not disinterested curiosity; it is the starting-point of his effort to comprehend and to master the abnormal. Pathology and bacteriology are the sciences concerned with abnormalities of structure and function and their causation. Now the agents and forces which invade the body to its disadvantage play their game, too, according to law. And to learn that law one goes once more to the same fundamental sciences upon which the anatomist and the physiologist have already freely drawn,—*viz.*, biology, physics, and chemistry.

Nor do these apparently recondite matters concern only the experimenting investigator, eager to convert patiently acquired knowledge of bacterial and other foes into a rational system of defense against them. For the practical outcome of such investigation is not communicable by rote; it cannot be reduced to prescriptions for mechanical use by the unenlightened practitioner. Modern medicine cannot be formulated in quiz-compends; those who would employ it must trouble to understand it. Moreover, medicine is developing with beneficent rapidity along these same biological and chemical lines. Is our fresh young graduate of five and twenty to keep abreast of its progress? If so, he must, once more, understand; not otherwise can he adopt the new agents and new methods issuing at intervals from each of a dozen fertile laboratories; for rote has no future: it stops where it is. "There can be no doubt," said Huxley, "that the future of pathology and of therapeutics, and *therefore of practical medicine*, depends upon the extent to which those who occupy themselves with these subjects are trained in the methods and impregnated with the fundamental truths of biology."[16] Now the medical sciences proper—anatomy, physiology, pathology, pharmacology—already crowd the two years of the curriculum that can be assigned to them; and in so doing, take for granted the more fundamental sciences—biology, physics, and chemistry—for which there is thus no adequate opportunity within the medical school proper. Only at the sacrifice of some essential part of the medical curriculum—and for every such sacrifice the future patients pay—can this curriculum be made to include the preliminary subjects upon which it presumes.

From the foregoing discussion, these conclusions emerge: By the very nature of the case, admission to a really modern medical school must at the very least depend on a competent knowledge of chemistry, biology,[17] and physics. Every departure from this basis is at the expense of medical training itself. From the exclusive standpoint of the medical school it is immaterial where the student gets the instruction. But it is clear that if it is to become the common minimum basis of medical education, some recognized and organized manner of obtaining it must be devised: it cannot be left to the initiative of the individual without greatly impairing its quality. Regular provision must therefore be made at a definite moment of normal educational progress. Now the requirement above agreed on is too extensive and too difficult to be incorporated in its entirety within the high school or to be substituted for a considerable portion of the usual high school course; besides, it demands greater maturity than the secondary school student can be credited with except towards the close of his high school career. The possibility of mastering the three sciences outside of school may be dismissed without argument. In the college or technical school alone can the work be regularly,

[16]Quoted by F. T. Lewis in "The Preparation for the Study of Medicine," *Popular Science Monthly*, vol. lxxv., no. 1, p. 66.

[17]Including botany.

efficiently, and surely arranged for. The requirement is therefore necessarily a college requirement, covering two years, because three laboratory courses cannot be carried through a briefer period,—a fortunate circumstance, since it favors the student's simultaneous development along other and more general lines. It appears, then, that a policy that at the outset was considered from the narrow standpoint of the medical school alone shortly involves the abandonment of this point of view in favor of something more comprehensive. The preliminary requirement for entrance upon medical education must therefore be formulated in terms that establish a distinct relation, pedagogical and chronological, between the medical school and other educational agencies. Nothing will do more to steady and to improve the college itself than its assumption of such definite functions in respect to professional and other forms of special training.

So far we have spoken explicitly of the fundamental sciences only. They furnish, indeed, the essential instrumental basis of medical education. But the instrumental minimum can hardly serve as the permanent professional minimum. It is even instrumentally inadequate. The practitioner deals with facts of two categories. Chemistry, physics, biology enable him to apprehend one set; he needs a different apperceptive and appreciative apparatus to deal with other, more subtle elements. Specific preparation is in this direction much more difficult; one must rely for the requisite insight and sympathy on a varied and enlarging cultural experience. Such enlargement of the physician's horizon is otherwise important, for scientific progress has greatly modified his ethical responsibility. His relation was formerly to his patient—at most to his patient's family; and it was almost altogether remedial. The patient had something the matter with him; the doctor was called in to cure it. Payment of a fee ended the transaction. But the physician's function is fast becoming social and preventive, rather than individual and curative. Upon him society relies to ascertain, and through measures essentially educational to enforce, the conditions that prevent disease and make positively for physical and moral well-being. It goes without saying that this type of doctor is first of all an educated man.

How nearly our present resources—educational and economic—permit us to approach the standards above defined is at bottom a question of fact to be investigated presently. We have concluded that a two-year college training, in which the sciences are "featured," is the minimum basis upon which modern medicine can be successfully taught. If the requisite number of physicians cannot at one point or another be procured at that level, a temporary readjustment may be required; but such an expedient is to be regarded as a makeshift that asks of the sick a sacrifice that must not be required of them a moment longer than is necessary. Before accepting such a measure, however, it is exceedingly important not to confuse the basis on which society can actually get the number of doctors that it needs with the basis on which our present number of medical schools can keep going. Much depends upon which end we start from.

THORSTEIN VEBLEN ON HIGHER LEARNING IN AMERICA (1918)   From
Thorstein Veblen, *The Higher Learning in America* (New York, 1918), pp. 219–25.

As in earlier passages, so here in speaking of profit and loss, the point of
view taken is neither that of material advantage, whether of the individuals
concerned or of the community at large, nor that of expediency for the common
good in respect of prosperity or of morals; nor is the appraisal here ventured upon
to be taken as an expression of praise or dispraise at large, touching this incursion
of business principles into the affairs of learning.

By and large, the intrusion of businesslike ideals, aims and methods into this
field, with all the consequences that follow, may be commendable or the reverse.
All that is matter for attention and advisement at the hands of such as aim to alter,
improve, amend or conserve the run of institutional phenomena that goes to make
up the current situation. The present inquiry bears on the higher learning as it
comes into this current situation, and on the effect of this recourse to business
principles upon the pursuit of learning.

Not that this learning is therefore to be taken as necessarily of higher and more
substantial value than that traffic in competitive gain and competitive spending
upon which business principles converge, and in which they find their consummate
expression,—even though it is broadly to be recognized and taken account of that
such is the deliberate appraisal awarded by the common sense of civilized mankind.
The profit and loss here spoken for is not profit and loss, to mankind or to any given
community, in respect of that inclusive complex of interests that makes up the
balanced total of good and ill; it is profit and loss for the cause of learning, simply;
and there is here no aspiration to pass on ulterior questions. As required by the
exigencies of such an argument, it is therefore assumed, *pro forma*, that profit and
loss for the pursuit of learning is profit and loss without reservation; very much as a
corporation accountant will audit income and outlay within the affairs of the
corporation, whereas, *qua* accountant, he will perforce have nothing to say as to the
ulterior expediency of the corporation and its affairs in any other bearing.

I

Business principles take effect in academic affairs most simply, obviously and
avowably in the way of a businesslike administration of the scholastic routine;
where they lead immediately to a bureaucratic organization and a system of
scholastic accountancy. In one form or another, some such administrative machinery
is a necessity in any large school that is to be managed on a centralized plan; as the
American schools commonly are, and as, more particularly, they aim to be. This
necessity is all the more urgent in a school that takes over the discipline of a large
body of pupils that have not reached years of discretion, as is also commonly the
case with those American schools that claim rank as universities; and the necessity
is all the more evident to men whose ideal of efficiency is the centralized control
exercised through a system of accountancy in the modern large business concerns.
The larger American schools are primarily undergraduate establishments,—with
negligible exceptions; and under these current American conditions, of excessive
numbers, such a centralized and bureaucratic administration appears to be
indispensable for the adequate control of immature and reluctant students; at the

same time, such an organization conduces to an excessive size. The immediate and visible effect of such a large and centralized administrative machinery is, on the whole, detrimental to scholarship, even in the undergraduate work; though it need not be so in all respects and unequivocally, so far as regards that routine training that is embodied in the undergraduate curriculum. But it is at least a necessary evil in any school that is of so considerable a size as to preclude substantially all close or cordial personal relations between the teachers and each of these immature pupils under their charge, as, again, is commonly the case with these American undergraduate establishments. Such a system of authoritative control, standardization, gradation, accountancy, classification, credits and penalties, will necessarily be drawn on stricter lines the more the school takes on the character of a house of correction or a penal settlement; in which the irresponsible inmates are to be held to a round of distasteful tasks and restrained from (conventionally) excessive irregularities of conduct. At the same time this recourse to such coercive control and standardization of tasks has unavoidably given the schools something of the character of a penal settlement.

As intimated above, the ideal of efficiency by force of which a large-scale centralized organization commends itself in these premises is that pattern of shrewd management whereby a large business concern makes money. The underlying business-like presumption accordingly appears to be that learning is a merchantable commodity, to be produced on a piece-rate plan, rated, bought and sold by standard units, measured, counted and reduced to staple equivalence by impersonal, mechanical tests. In all its bearings the work is hereby reduced to a mechanistic, statistical consistency, with numerical standards and units; which conduces to perfunctory and mediocre work throughout, and acts to deter both students and teachers from a free pursuit of knowledge, as contrasted with the pursuit of academic credits. So far as this mechanistic system goes freely into effect it leads to a substitution of salesmanlike proficiency—a balancing of bargains in staple credits—in the place of scientific capacity and addiction to study.

The salesmanlike abilities and the men of affairs that so are drawn into the academic personnel are, presumably, somewhat under grade in their kind; since the pecuniary inducement offered by the schools is rather low as compared with the remuneration for office work of a similar character in the common run of business occupations, and since businesslike employes of this kind may fairly be presumed to go unreservedly to the highest bidder. Yet these more unscholarly members of the staff will necessarily be assigned the more responsible and discretionary positions in the academic organization; since under such a scheme of standardization, accountancy and control, the school becomes primarily a bureaucratic organization, and the first and unremitting duties of the staff are those of official management and accountancy. The further qualifications requisite in the members of the academic staff will be such as make for vendibility,—volubility, tactful effrontery, conspicuous conformity to the popular taste in all matters of opinion, usage and conventions.

The need of such a businesslike organization asserts itself in somewhat the same degree in which the academic policy is guided by considerations of magnitude and statistical renown; and this in turn is somewhat closely correlated with the extent of discretionary power exercised by the captain of erudition placed in control. At the same time, by provocation of the facilities which it offers for making an impressive demonstration, such bureaucratic organization will lead the university management to bend its energies with somewhat more singleness to the parade of magnitude and statistical gains. It also, and in the same connection, provokes to a persistent and detailed surveillance and direction of the work and manner of life of the academic staff, and so it acts to shut off initiative of any kind in the work done.

Intimately bound up with this bureaucratic officialism and accountancy, and working consistently to a similar outcome, is the predilection for "practical efficiency"—that is to say, for pecuniary success—prevalent in the American community.[1] This predilection is a matter of settled habit, due, no doubt, to the fact that preoccupation with business interests characterizes this community in an exceptional degree, and that pecuniary habits of thought consequently rule popular thinking in a peculiarly uncritical and prescriptive fashion. This pecuniary animus falls in with and reinforces the movement for academic accountancy, and combines with it to further a so-called "practical" bias in all the work of the schools.

It appears, then, that the intrusion of business principles in the universities goes to weaken and retard the pursuit of learning, and therefore to defeat the ends for which a university is maintained. This result follows, primarily, from the substitution of impersonal, mechanical relations, standards and tests, in the place of personal conference, guidance and association between teachers and students; as also from the imposition of a mechanically standardized routine upon the members of the staff, whereby any disinterested preoccupation with scholarly or scientific inquiry is thrown into the background and falls into abeyance. Few if any who are competent to speak in these premises will question that such has been the outcome. To offset against this work of mutilation and retardation there are certain gains in expedition, and in the volume of traffic that can be carried by any given equipment and corps of employes. Particularly will there be a gain in the statistical showing, both as regards the volume of instruction offered, and probably also as regards the enrolment; since accountancy creates statistics and its absence does not.

ON THE CONTROL OF UNIVERSITIES BY LAYMEN (1920)   From A. Lawrence Lowell, "The Relation Between Faculties and Governing Boards," in *At War With Academic Traditions in America* (Cambridge, Mass., 1934), pp. 281–91.

If a university or college is a society or guild of scholars why does it need any separate body of trustees at all? Why more than learned societies, which are obviously groups of scholars, and have no such boards recruited outside their own membership? One reason is to be found in the large endowments of our institutions of learning that require for investment a wide knowledge and experience of business affairs. In fact, as already pointed out, the vast complexity of a modern university had compelled specialization of functions, and one aspect thereof is the

[1] So far has this predilection made its way in the counsels of the "educators" that much of the current discussion of *desideranda* in academic policy reads like controversial argument on "efficiency engineering,"—an "efficiency engineer" is an accountant competent to advise business concerns how best to increase their saleable output per unit of cost. And there has, indeed, been at least one tour of inspection of American universities by such an "efficiency engineer," undertaken in the service of an establishment founded with a view to academic welfare and governed by a board of university presidents. The report submitted by the inquiry in question duly conforms to the customary lines of "scientific management."

separation of the scholarly and business organs. Another reason is that higher education has assumed more and more of a public character; its importance has been more fully recognized by the community at large; it must therefore keep in touch with public needs, make the public appreciate its aims and the means essential to attain them; and for this purpose it must possess the influence and obtain the guidance of men conversant with the currents of the outer world.

There is a further reason more fundamental if less generally understood. Teaching in all its grades is a public service, and the administration of every public service must comprise both expert and lay elements. Without the former it will be ineffectual; without the latter it will become in time narrow, rigid, or out of harmony with its public object. Each has its own distinctive function, and only confusion and friction result if one of them strives to perform the function of the other. From this flows the cardinal principle, popularly little known but of well-nigh universal application, that experts should not be members of a non-professional body that supervises experts. One often hears that men with a practical knowledge of teaching should be elected to school boards, but unless they are persons of singlular discretion they are likely to assume that their judgment on technical matters is better than that of the teachers, with effects that are sometimes disastrous. Laymen should not attempt to direct experts about the method of attaining results, but only indicate the results to be attained. Many years ago the Board of Overseers, after a careful examination, came to the conclusion that the writing of English by Harvard undergraduates was sadly defective. In this they were acting wholly within their proper province, and the result was a very notable improvement in the teaching of English composition. But if they had attempted to direct how the subject should be taught they would have been hopelessly beyond their province. They would not have known, as the instructing staff did, how it should be done, and they would have exasperated and disheartened the teachers.

But another question may well be asked. Granted that there should be both expert and non-professional elements in the management of a university or college, why in a society or guild of scholars should the non-professional organ be the final authority? For this there are three reasons. In the first place, so far as the object is public—and where teaching is conducted on a large scale the object cannot fail to concern the public deeply—that object must in the final analysis be determined by public, that is by non-professional, judgment. In an endowed university the governing board does not, indeed, represent the public in the sense that it is elected by popular vote, but it is not on that account any less truly a trustee for the public.

In the second place, the non-professional board is responsible for the financial administration, and the body that holds the purse must inevitably have the final control.

Thirdly, the non-professional board is the only body, or the most satisfactory body, to act as arbiter between the different groups of experts. Everyone knows that in an American university or college there is a ceaseless struggle for the means of development between different departments, and someone must decide upon the relative merits of their claims. In a university with good traditions the professors would be more ready to rely on the fairness and wisdom of a well constituted board of trustees than on one composed of some of their own number each affected almost unavoidably by a bias in favor of his particular subject.

Let it be observed, however, that although the governing board is the ultimate authority it is not in the position of an industrial employer. It is a trustee not to earn dividends for stockholders, but of the purposes of the guild. Its sole object is to help the society of scholars to accomplish the object for which they are brought together. They are the essential part of the society; and making their work effective for the intellectual and moral training of youth and for investigation is the sole reason for the existence of trustees, of buildings, of endowments, and of all the elaborate machinery of a modern university. If this conception be fully borne in mind most of the sources of dissension between professors and governing boards will disappear. At Harvard it has, I believe, been borne in mind as a deep-seated traditional conviction.

The differences between the ordinary industrial employment and the conduct of a society or guild of scholars in a university are wide. In the industrial system of employment the employee is paid according to the value of his services; he can be discharged when no longer wanted; and his duties are prescribed as minutely as may be desired by the employer. In a university there is permanence of tenure; substantial equality of pay within each academic grade; and although the duties in general are well understood, there is great freedom in the method of performing them. It is not difficult to see why each of these conditions prevails, and is in fact dependent upon the others. Permanence of tenure lies at the base of the difference between a society of scholars in a university and the employees in an industrial concern. In the latter, under prevailing conditions, men are employed in order to promote its earning power. In a university the concern exists to promote the work of the scholars and of the students whom they teach. Therefore in the industrial concern an unprofitable employee is discharged; but in the university the usefulness of the scholar depends largely upon his sense of security, upon the fact that he can work for an object that may be remote and whose value may not be easily demonstrated. In a university, barring positive misconduct, permanence of tenure is essential for members who have passed the probationary period. The equality of pay goes with the permanence of tenure. In an industrial establishment the higher class of officials, those who correspond most nearly to the grade of professors, can be paid what they may be worth to the concern, and discharged if they are not worth their salaries. How valuable they are can be fairly estimated, and their compensation can be varied accordingly. But professors, whose tenure is permanent, cannot be discharged if they do not prove so valuable as they were expected to be. Moreover it is impossible to determine the value of scholars in the same way as that of commercial officials. An attempt to do so would create injustice and endless discontent; and it would offer a temptation to secure high pay, from their own or another institution, by a display wholly inconsistent with the scholarly attitude of mind. The only satisfactory system is that of paying salaries on something very close to a fixed scale, and letting every professor do as good work as he can. In an industrial concern the prospect of a high salary may be needed to induce the greatest effort; but indolence among professors is seldom found. They may, indeed, prefer a line of work less important than some other; a man may desire to do research who is better fitted for teaching, or he may prefer to teach advanced students when there is a greater need of the strongest men in more elementary instruction; but failure to work hard is rare.

The governing boards of universities having, then, the ultimate legal control in their hands, and yet not being in the position of industrial employers, it is pertinent to inquire what their relation to the professors should be. If we bear in mind the conception of a society or guild of scholars, that relation usually becomes in practice clear. The scholars, both individually and gathered into faculties, are to provide the expert knowledge; the governing board the financial management, the general coordination, the arbitral determinations, and the preservation of the general direction of public policy. In the words of a former member of the Harvard

Corporation, their business is to "serve tables." The relation is not one of employer and employed, or superior and inferior, of master and servant, but one of mutual cooperation for the promotion of the scholars' work. Unless the professors have confidence in the singleness of purpose and in the wisdom of the governing boards, and unless these in their turn recognize that they exist to promote the work of the society of scholars the relations will not have the harmony that they should. The relation is one that involves constant seeking of opinion, and in the main the university must be conducted, not by authority, but by persuasion. There is no natural antagonism of interests between trustees and professors. To suggest it is to suggest failure in their proper relation to one another; to suppose it is to provoke failure; to assume it is to ensure failure.

The question has often been raised whether nominations for appointments should be made by the faculties or their committees, or by the president. It would seem that the less formal the provisions the better. Any president of a university or college who makes a nomination to the governing board without consulting formally or informally the leading professors in the subject and without making sure that most of them approve of it, is taking a grave responsibility that can be justified only by a condition that requires surgery. The objection to a formal nomination by a faculty, or a committee thereof, is that it places the members in an uncomfortable position in regard to their younger colleagues, and that it creates a tendency for the promotion of useful rather than excellent men. A wise president will not make nominations without being sure of the support of the instructing staff, but he may properly, and indeed ought to, decline to make nominations unless convinced that the nominee is of the calibre that ought to be appointed.

Attempts have been made to define, and express in written rules, the relation between the faculties and the governing boards; but the best element in that relation is an intangible, an undefinable, influence. If a husband and wife should attempt to define by regulations their respective rights and duties in the household, that marriage could safely be pronounced a failure. The essence of the relation is mutual confidence and mutual regard; and the respective functions of the faculties and the governing boards—those things that each had better undertake, those it had better leave to the other, and those which require mutual concession—are best learned from experience and best embodied in tradition. Tradition has great advantages over regulations. It is a more delicate instrument; it accommodates itself to things that are not susceptible of sharp definition; it is more flexible in its application, making exceptions and allowances which it would be difficult to foresee or prescribe. It is also more stable. Regulations can be amended; tradition cannot, for it is not made, but grows, and can be altered only by a gradual change in general opinion, not by a majority vote. In short, it cannot be amended, but only outgrown.

MENTAL HYGIENE PROBLEMS OF COLLEGE STUDENTS (1929)   From

Lloyd J. Thompson, "Mental Hygiene In A University," *American Journal of Psychiatry, vol. LXXXV, pp. 1947–51.*

The mental hygiene problems found among college students are very similar to those found in other walks in life except that there are a few more or less minor factors peculiar to college life that may act as an added burden for the individual. Some of these added factors that are more or less peculiar to college life are as follows:

1. The rather acute and sudden emancipation from the home that occurs in many cases.

2. The adjustment to a large number of new acquaintances who are on an equal or superior plane in many ways.

3. Keener competition scholastically and in athletics.

4. The question of making a fraternity or club.

5. The necessity for developing within a short time the ability to stand on one's own feet.

However, after stripping away the more superficial problems of adjustment, we come to realize more and more that the fundamental problems are the same as are found in every other adolescent, namely, emancipation from the home and the establishment of healthy attitudes toward sex and social adjustments. These are more or less closely related and might be called the problem of maturing emotionally. For example, at the end of a term a student fails in enough work to cause his withdrawal from college. If there has been some physical illness as the cause of this failure it is easily recognized and can be dealt within a frank, open manner. If lack of intellectual ability has been the cause of his failure, this also can be determined fairly adequately by psychological tests, but it is safe to assume that most college students have the innate intellectual ability to complete college if they have a sufficiently good preparatory school record, college board record and psychological examination grade to be admitted to college in the upper half of the applicants. It usually means, then, that when a student fails scholastically without evident physical or intellectual handicaps the cause is to be found in his emotional life and the most common handicap found here is the retardation in the progress toward emotional maturity. Of course we cannot expect the college student to be emotionally mature, but he should have reached a certain level by the time he is in college that will enable him to adjust to the demands of college life. All the usual causes of retardation of development may be at work in this case or that case, but the most common factor in the group of college students seems to be the influence of the home.

The multiplicity of factors in any given case may be illustrated by a brief summary of a case record. A third-year man was asked to consult the psychiatrist because he wanted to leave college. The request for consultation came from his father who was the principal of a high school. At first the young man could give no particular reason for his desire to give up his college work, but later said that he wanted to leave so that he might build up his health. He knew that his health was not good simply because he had failed to make good in athletics. Further statements were not forthcoming for several visits and then it was found that he had always been more or less concerned about his health although numerous physical examinations had revealed no physical disease. His mother had been a chronic invalid with daily headaches for years and when she was not worrying about herself she was worrying about this only child. She was emotionally inhibited and her marital adjustments had not been at all satisfactory. It was quite evident that she was trying to find her emotional outlet through this boy and had done many things to keep him dependent upon her. When he entered elementary school he was kept in the open air class for four years without any apparent physical reason. During this time the idea was forced upon him that he was below par physically and that he could not compete with the other boys in their games. Apparently this acted as a strong conditioning factor and this attitude toward athletic competition persisted in his college life. Another rather common factor that entered the picture around the age of puberty was the problem of masturbation. In regard to this he was told the usual story, that it would cause him to develop tuberculosis or lose his mind. The thing that had the most effect on him was the statement that later on it would probably cause him to lose his manhood. From that time on he redoubled his efforts to build up his body, when at the same time he felt that he was not quite capable of entering competitive athletics. In fact he was afraid that it would take too much out of him and he felt that he should conserve all his so-called vital energy. He became the victim of many doubts and fears. First, he feared the classroom, then he developed fears of certain streets in the city because on these streets he had had a fear of falling. He became more and more particular about his health, would eat six apples every day and never fail to retire promptly at 9 p. m. He belonged to a fraternity but would not attend their dances because they kept him up too late. He also feared studying late at night and this interfered with his scholastic standing. No one in college or in his own family knew anything about his condition and he was considered a normal boy except that he was a little over-anxious about his health. It was necessary to resort to some dream analysis in order to get at some of these factors and some of the other factors that have not been mentioned. Finally, he came to understand how his reactions had many false premises. He decided to continue college work and by the end of the year was an honor student and had won his letter in track.

Another example that brings out some other factors is that of a young man who was referred to the Health Service by one of the athletic coaches because he complained of pain in his back. It was evident that the boy was not consciously giving an alibi for his failure because he was considered a very good athlete and had splendid prospects of making the team. It was quite true that two years previously he had had a back injury and later it had been discovered that there was a splintering of one of the spinus processes. It had been considered that this back injury had been well taken care of before he entered college in the fall and in the preceding summer he had been able to row a boat and swim without any return of symptoms. However, soon after entering college the pain in his back returned and there was no adequate physical basis for this except a possible over-compensation of the muscles of the back. From the very outset in life he had been handicapped by being the only child. His father had not been very successful; had not provided very well for the family and at times had more or less deserted them. The mother, of course, had turned to this only child and had hoped to work out through him all the ambitions which fate had denied her. She had over-protected and over-guided him and a strong emotional dependence had grown up between them, although the boy strenuously denied this and at times showed marked evidence of rebellious reaction toward his mother. His early life had been full of hardships and his social and educational opportunities were decidely limited before he entered college. He had never seen the inside of a school until he entered the second year of high school. He was definitely superior intellectually and his ambitions were unusually high. At the same time he had a tremendous feeling of inadequacy and was sensitive and shy. To make good in every way in college was, of course, paramount at the moment. He did not want to fail his mother, he wanted to raise the family standard above mediocrity, he wanted to show his father what a real man was, and it all depended upon him alone. He did not want to depend on the family financially and therefore was working his way through college. At first he maintained that sex matters had never interested him; that he never intended to marry, and that sex could not in any way be a factor in his case. After many talks he began to see that he had been inhibiting all conscious realization of sex desire and he was able to work out many causes for this inhibition. It seens, them, that his early life, especially as regards the family influence and his sex life were sufficient causes for a neurotic type of reaction.

The role of the situation that he faced upon entering college in the fall seems of considerable importance as a precipitating factor. At that time he had to compete scholastically with boys who were not working their way through college. He had competition in the job which he held. He wanted to make the swimming team and the crew. He also had to compete socially with boys who came from better families and who had already learned to make social adjustments much better than he. The fraternity rushing undoubtedly caused some conflict although he denied it. His final reaction gave a typical picture of an agitated depression with thoughts and threats of suicide. He recovered, however, just in time to take his final examinations and he passed with high marks.

These examples represent some of the more or less definite psychiatric problems that should be easily recognized by faculty and family, but much of the work is concerned with the so-called normal person who tells only the psychiatrist of his particular problem. With the so-called normal student and the superior student there seems to be a great field for the mental hygienist to add something to the general efficiency of these people. To classify cases seen among the students is a very difficult task becasue there is so much overlapping in any particular classification that may be adopted. The following classification gives a general idea of the problems encountered:

	Per cent
Frank mental disorder which includes mostly depressions and neurotic reactions	45
Scholastic difficulties	25
Sex problems	15
Personality problems	15

Each year over one hundred student cases have been treated in the Department. This usually means numerous consultations with the psychiatrist and consultations by either the psychiatrist or social service worker with the Health Service, various members of the faculty and the family. In all these consultations the confidences of the patient are safely guarded. It has been found that there is a definite place for a psychiatric social worker even in a men's college and much of the work done with the family falls to her lot. The department for obvious reasons has become interested in the student before he reaches college and efforts have been made to study situations in the preparatory schools and to spread the idea of mental hygiene to these schools. However, it is well recognized that the root of the problem that we find in the college student goes back, as in all cases, to the very early years of life and for that reason the college mental hygienist should be a psychiatrist well versed in the mental hygiene of all ages from infancy to maturity.

THE FLEXNER REPORT ON AMERICAN UNIVERSITIES (1930) From
Abraham Flexner, *Universities: American, English, German* (New York, 1930), pp. 45, 52–
59.

The term "university" is very loosely used in America; I shall not pause
to characterize the absurdities covered by the name. I propose, rather, to
concentrate attention on the most highly developed and prominent of American
institutions, to ask what they do, how they are constituted, how they fare from the
standpoint of the ideal which I have set up. As for the others—and they run into the
hundreds—it is impossible in this volume to take them into account; fine minds and
souls will be found here and there in them; many of them, more especially in the
South and West—though the East is not free—are hotbeds of reaction in politics,
industry, and religion, ambitious in pretension, meagre in performance, doubtful
contributors, when they are not actual obstacles, to the culture of the nation.

The great American universities which I shall discuss are composed of three
parts: they are secondary schools and colleges for boys and girls; graduate and
professional schools for advanced students; "service" stations for the general public.
The three parts are not distinct: the college is confused with the "service" station
and overlaps the graduate school; the graduate school is partly a college, partly a
vocational school, and partly an institution of university grade. For the sake of
simplicity, however, I shall examine each part separately; later we can observe the
strange ways in which they mingle and the effect of this intermingling.

VI

The number of students who seek to enter college is far in excess of the number
that can be admitted. Colleges therefore try to select. But it cannot be effectively
done. In the first place, the colleges do not know what they wish: do they wish
brains? do they wish industry? do they wish scholarship? do they wish character, or
they wish "qualities that fit for leadership"? They swing blindly and helplessly from
one to another. Even if they knew, they could not get what they wish. The high
school is such a welter of subjects and activities, the high school teaching staff is so
largely occupied in teaching subjects that the teachers themselves do not know,[1]
that grading and certificates are well-nigh meaningless. Unable to rely on high
school records of achievement or upon entrance examinations, lacking any reliable
contact with high schools at large, the colleges are now experimenting with
psychological tests. The experiments are regarded as hopeful and promising.
Perhaps. But American educators so commonly count unhatched chickens that it
may be well to wait before becoming too enthusiastic.

The collegiate function of the American university has to do with the group
which I have just described. They remain four years; they get during these four
years for the most part the same sort of education that they got in the high school,
though at a higher level, because they are older and know more. Another bargain-
counter period is lived through in the college. On the counter, the student finds
once more almost every imaginable article—Latin, Greek, history, science, business,
journalism, domestic arts, engineering, agriculture, military training, and a

[1] E. A. Fitzpatrick and P. W. Hutson, The Scholarship of Teachers in Secondary Schools
(New York, 1927).

miscellaneous aggregation of topics and activities that defy general characterization. Subject to a few more restrictions, latterly becoming in some institutions more rigid, and operating, though not always, at a higher level, he again nibbles at a confusing variety of "courses"—four months of this, six weeks of that, so many hours of this, so many hours of that, so many points here, so many there, with little, though happily increasing, continuity of purpose from year to year, until again, at the close of four years, he has won the number of "credits" or "points" that entitle him to the bachelor's degree. The sort of easy rubbish which may be counted towards an A.B. degree or the so-called combined degrees passes the limits of credibility. Education—college education, liberal education, call it what you will— should, one might suppose, concern itself primarily during adolescence and early manhood and womanhood with the liberation, organization, and direction of power and intelligence, with the development of taste, with culture—a perfectly good word that has unfortunately become odious in the ears of the professional educator in America—on the assumption that a trained mind, stored with knowledge, will readily enough find itself even in our complex world; that there are many things that do not require teaching at all; and that there are many things of technical nature which may require teaching, but surely not in a college or university.

I shall not fail to point out the fact that a reaction against quantitative measurements, according to which an hour spent in military drill is as educative as an hour spent on calculus, has set in and that there are happily colleges which, while thoroughly alive and progressive, have not lost sight of cultural distinctions. But for an overwhelming majority of colleges and college students the brief description I have given still holds.

VII

Once admitted to college, the student spends two years or more on work that should be included in a good high school—and is so included in countries whose secondary schools are soundly developed and staffed. Without, however, dwelling upon this point in this connection, I wish in the first place to emphasize the fact that an earnest student at, we will say, Columbia College, finds there ample opportunity to study science, mathematics, language, literature, history, philosophy, economics—indeed almost every imaginable subject of sound intellectual value— under competent and at times highly distinguished teachers and in reach of admirable laboratory and library facilities. To be sure, at the end of four years, when the students emerge as bachelors of arts or science, even those who have done their best usually betray signs of their inferior preliminary education or their barren environment. But in any event, Columbia College has done for the best of them all that it could. Here it should stop. Does it stop? By no means. The process of adulteration and dilution began, as I have pointed out, before the student entered: the undergraduate student may have been enabled to satisfy a considerable portion of the matriculation requirements by extension courses or by correspondence courses taken under the Home Study Department. Doubtless, now and then, an earnest student may safely dispense with continuous, full-time schooling; but it is absurd to suppose that to the hordes of extension and home study students registered at Columbia any such opportunity can be offered without lowering of standard, no matter what entrance examinations and psychological tests are subsequently employed. Abuse does not, however, end here. I have said that a student of Columbia College may study serious subjects in a serious fashion. But he may also complete the requirements for a bachelor's degree by including in his course of study "principles of advertising," "the writing of advertised copy," "advertising layouts,"* "advertising research," "practical poultry raising,"* "secretarial bookkeeping,"* "business English," "elementary stenography," "newspaper practice," "reporting and copy editing," "feature writing," "book reviewing," "wrestling, judo and self-defence."*If an advanced student in the School of Practical Arts, he may count towards a Columbia degree courses taken in Teachers College—an independent corporation belonging to Columbia—"in cookery—fundamental processes," "fundamental problems in clothing," "clothing decoration," "family meals," "recent research in cookery," "food etiquette and hospitality," "principles of home laundering," "social life of the home," "gymnastics and dancing for men including practice in clog dancing," and "instruction (elementary or advanced) in school orchestras and bands."

Is not this an appalling situation? By the hundreds, crude, poorly taught, eager boys and girls eighteen to twenty years of age resort to Columbia to be educated. In the main it is of no importance what they think they want. The question is—what do they need? They need a solid, cultural secondary education. It they cannot be educated in this sense, if they cannot be intellectually and spiritually aroused and directed, they have no business at Columbia at all; they had better be at work learning a trade or a craft—where or how, is not Columbia's concern. Columbia College is not a vocational school; vocational training may be ever so important, but the confusion of all sorts of training—vocational, domestic, scientific, cultural, in high school and college—harms all alike and harms the highest most of all. It is defended on the ground already mentioned that America is a democratic country, which, for large social reasons, ignores distinctions. But America does not ignore all distinctions. It simply ignores the real distinctions; and not all the weight of its wealth and numbers can place cooking and wrestling and typewriting on an intellectual par with music, science, literature, and economics, or make it sound educational procedure to jumble them together.

In so far as business or journalism is concerned, Columbia can do nothing for undergraduates that is worth their time and money. Both are worse than wasted. For undergraduates do not even learn the tricks of business and journalism, though, in so far as they try, they fail to make a profitable use of the real opportunities for education which Columbia undeniably possesses. Does Columbia University, embodiment and protector of intellectual and spiritual ideals, tell them this? Not at all! It takes their money, consumes their time, and at the end of three or four years bestows upon them a bachelor's degree that represents neither a substantial secondary education nor a substantial vocational training. To be sure, there are, I repeat, those who have not been misled—who have worked at subjects that are worth while, under teachers able and earnest, though the unit and credit system makes it incredibly difficult to do so. But how does that help those who have obtained undergraduate degrees by working at subjects not worth while, under teachers not themselves really educated? And what sort of contribution is Columbia making towards a clearer apprehension of what education really is on the part of this conglomerate nation of ours, so sorely in need of illumination as to relative and genuine values when it admits that cooking and typewriting are proper training for an undergraduate degree?

One might suppose that Columbia College would find its problems with campus

*Starred courses may be counted for degrees only if the approval of the dean or director has been previously obtained.

students of arts, business, and journalism sufficiently perplexing; for these problems have not been solved and are not even on the way to solution. But what of it? The University has an uneven teaching staff, an impossible and absurd teaching program, and inadequate funds. What is the remedy? Expansion! Achieving in New York City a limited success—the only sort of success, I grant, that is now possible—Columbia invades Brooklyn and requires the already over-burdened officers on Morningside Heights in New York to administer the newly formed Seth Low Junior College across the river, with a curriculum extensive enough to admit students after two years to any one of a dozen schools—professional, technical, or liberal—in the University itself. But not even thus is the administrative skill of the University officials or the pedagogical efficiency of the University ideals strained. Ninety-five miles from New York City an insignificant little college—St. Stephen's by name, one of hundreds scattered through the country, is gasping for breath. "The faculty and students wear the Oxford undergraduate gown to chapel, classes, and other official exercises"—the gown, by the way, must be purchased from the college store at the price of $8.00—a subtle compliment by which Oxford's cool heart may well be thrilled! This remote seat of college education, long isolated "on the top of hills, overlooking the Catskill Mountains," now nestles snugly in the capacious bosom of Columbia University. Since July 1, 1928, it has "become an undergraduate college of Columbia University on a parity with Columbia College and Barnard College. The bachelor's degree granted will be that of Columbia University." But it is expressly stipulated that "the University is under no implied obligation, responsibility, or liability of any kind whatsoever, for the maintenance, support, direction, or management of St. Stephen's College or for the disbursement of the income thereof." The Columbia degree is thus bestowed upon students belonging to a remote institution "for the maintenance, direction, or management" of which Columbia expressly repudiates all responsibility! And this degree is "on a parity" with the degrees conferred by Columbia University upon students who, so to speak, work under its nose in Barnard College and Columbia College! A New York newspaper,[1] commenting on Columbia's "Empire," intelligently remarks: "Columbia is already so various and conglomerate that one unit more or less cannot make much difference." And if Columbia's collegiate ideals, without financial or educational responsibility on the part of Columbia University, can thus subtly permeate remote colleges, one can readily understand that "there is not the least reason why a university should be confined to a single school of law, of medicine, or of engineering."[2] Not the least! Thus through Columbia and, as we shall see, the medical schools of the University of Chicago the "chain-store" concept enters the field of higher education in the United States.

VIII

Although Columbia is a flagrant, it is not by any means the only, offender. Fifteen "units" are required for admission to the Colleges of the University of Chicago, of which more than one-fourth (one, two, three, or four units) may be made up of stenography, typewriting, and bookkeeping—what a preparation for the intelligent use, cultural or professional, of four college years! Home economics and agriculture—as taught in high schools—are also "accepted." Now, to be frank, there is no more sense in "counting" stenography and bookkeeping towards college

[1] The New York Herald-Tribune.

[2] Columbia University Bulletin of Information, Report of the President, 1928, p. 25.

matriculation than there would be in counting manicuring, hair-bobbing, or toe-dancing. One has as much to do with intelligence and taste as another. . . .

COLUMBIA UNIVERSITY ON STRIKE (1932) James Wechsler, *Revolt on Campus* (New York, 1935), pp. 108–16.

$\mathbf{I}$f Kentucky had captured the imagination of thousands of American students, the expulsion of Reed Harris from Columbia University set free even more sweeping currents. It may have been less of a spectacle than the invasion into the land of Bourbon rule; yet the Harris case, localized, with a single Campus for background, indicated trouble close enough to home to atone for its conventional setting. Terror in the Kentucky coal regions was, to some extent at least, a remote consideration even to those aroused by the reports. However much they may have been astonished or chagrined by the fate of the student investigators, however intensely they might have become aware, for the first time, of such conditions, there were many who did not sense any genuine relation to the Campus.

But Harris was an American undergraduate, a member (in not very good standing) of the Phi Gamma Delta fraternity, the editor of a student newspaper at a major University. These were familiar items to any student, whatever his institution. Moreover, Harris was hardly unknown; a series of incidents prior to his expulsion had established his repute beyond the Columbia Campus. And finally, coming directly in the wake of the celebrated Kentucky furor, this episode found the Campus world already partially sensitized to the conflict of which it was a stormy sympton.

When the affair had at last subsided, Dr. John P. Neal, a Columbia alumnus of Knoxville, Tennessee, wrote that "this was the most significant event which has occurred in the colleges in a decade. . . . The students of Columbia have fired a shot which will be heard around the college world."

When Harris assumed the editorship of *The Spectator* in April, 1931, his unobtrusive arrival seemed no excuse for jubilation. The paper had always behaved in the best tradition of American college journalism: unhesitant pandering to the Administration, only intermittent and usually uninformed comment on affairs outside the realm of the University, devout catering to the institutions made sacred by Trustees, Alumni and their subordinates. The most illuminating example of this heritage has been furnished by Nicholas McD. McKnight, now associate dean of Columbia College but in 1920 a crusading editor of *The Spectator*. His ardor was directed most frequently against those who insisted upon witnessing football games from their dormitory rooms overlooking the field, rather than taking their places in the cheering section.

On October 28, 1920, he turned his virile pen upon these iconoclasts and wrote: "We also take the attitude that those dormites . . . are showing very poor college spirit. A man who comes to college should put something into it for what it gives him. And it certainly is not too much to ask him if he cannot play himself to at least lend his full support to the men who represent Columbia on the field of play.

"No matter how hard a man may exhort from Livingston or Hartley (dormitories), the team cannot hear him and he cannot help them. Where his cheer will help, is in the cheering section of South stand. And that is where he belongs if he is to call himself a Columbia man."

Whatever may have been the troubled state of the world two years after the war, no matter how infinite were the changes being wrought in certain patterns of civilization, the problem of indolent football rooters remained uppermost in the minds of the editorial department of *The Spectator*. But Mr. McKnight was not alone; he set the standard for a decade and his own prodigious efforts were equalled and often excelled by ensuing editors. The college press throughout the country was, on the whole, absorbed by topics of similar weight.

The background is important if we are to contemplate the outcries which greeted Harris' declarations. Mr. McKnight may have been apoplectic at the desecration of pages he once edited; there were hundreds of others accustomed to his treatises who must have been startled into confusion by these first rays of light.

In November, 1931, Harris questioned the eternal verities of high-pressure football, intimating that certain more valiant gridmen were receiving more than honor as their reward; whereupon Ralph Hewitt, quarterback par excellence, loudly offered to sock Mr. Harris in the eye. But when Harris asked for publication of the books of the Athletic Association to prove his charges, there was concerted silence in the camp of the enemy. (Now, four years later, despite efforts by every ensuing editor to achieve the same end, the books are still firmly shut.) From football Harris proceeded to evaluate critically the sacrosanct senior society, Nacoms, of which he was a member. Nacoms is a secret "honorary" body, addicted to all the mumbo-jumbo of such institutions and dedicated to the ideals of the better people. This attack was no small irritation to those Alumni whose very life was dependent on mumbo-jumbo. Anti-semitism, rife in almost every quarter of the University, was not, presumably a topic for public discussion; Harris discussed it fully and comprehensively. Although several high administrators were known to be in opposition to the Kentucky trip, Harris gave his editorial support and substantial news space. The awarding of jobs by the Appointments office, still an operation shrouded in considerable mystery, was probed for the first time. Nicholas Murray Butler, the highest monarch of all, was not immune to criticism. Nor did Harris confine himself to an estimate of institutions at Columbia. The world which his predecessors had so conveniently ignored was introduced as a subject of editorial analysis; the existence of R.O.T.C. units at other colleges was mercilessly attacked; repression in education became a field of inquiry. Finally, Harris approached more forbidden territory—the administration of the college dining halls, which had been mildly scrutinized the previous year. He merely reprinted the charge that the halls, ostensibly run for the service of students, were actually being manipulated for profit, and that student waiters were receiving far less than benevolent treatment. Citing these allegations, Harris demanded an investigation; and with this demand went his editorship of the paper. It becomes obvious, however, that his expulsion did not arise from that isolated incident but climaxed a series of Administrative grievances.

For Harris had broken the shell. Many of his writings—and those of Donald Ross, the editorial associate—might today be regarded as groping and undefined in terms of objectives; in 1931 he was speaking out amidst a dead silence. No wonder that one irate alumnus snapped: "Harris is too grown-up." His words summarized the view of the whole network of Columbia administrators. Accustomed to deal with the subservient and the credulous, who took what was offered without examining the contents, they were appalled by a critic who resisted them. Harris was marked for departure.

Dean Herbert E. Hawkes did not know, to his everlasting sorrow, that the Friday he expelled Reed Harris was the day of the election of Harris' successor. Had he But this sad lack of information about the affairs of his college was to plague him for the rest of his life. In the words of a prominent faculty man, he committed a bull.

On the last three days of March, 1932, *The Spectator* republished articles criticizing the preparation and serving of food in the John Jay dining hall, condemning the treatment of the student waiters and summarizing the results of previous investigations of the dining-room. On March 31 Harris was summoned to the Dean's office and substantiation of the charges was demanded—within the next twenty-four hours. Harris then wrote a letter of explanation to the Dean preceded by an expression of surprise at the Dean's dictatorial attitude. He said:

> Before submitting the explanation regarding a statement made in *The Spectator*, I want to protest against the manner in which I was "demanded" to produce an explanation. You have repeatedly said to me that my mode of presentation in my editorial column has been unmannerly. Surely the dictatorial tone you adopted yesterday was not an example for me to follow in changing the tone of that column. In spite of the fact that we have had, almost constantly, major differences of opinion, I believe that I have acted in a gentlemanly fashion while in your office during my term as editor of The Spectator. That you should have adopted a tone suited only to a sergeant in the Marine Corps surprises me.

The letter then outlined the basis of the accusations against the dining hall. Its contents should be observed because subsequently this document was used by the University as a last, desperate excuse for the ouster of Harris.

The following day, Harris, suddenly called to the Dean's office, was informed that he had been expelled. Startled by the abruptness of the pronouncement, he asked for a reason. Whereupon the Dean read him a statement prepared for the press, the substance of which was: "Material published in *The Spectator* during the last few days is a climax to a long series of discourtesies, innuendos and misrepresentations which have appeared in this paper during the current academic year and calls for disciplinary action."

Having explicitly informed Harris of his dismissal, Dean Hawkes then took him before the Committee on Instruction for a "hearing," although that committee had no authority to veto or modify the expulsion order. This was later explained by Harris, who quoted Dean Hawkes as saying that he had conferred with President Butler and the latter had cautioned him to give Harris "the pretense of a hearing." It was obvious, at any rate, despite Dean Hawkes' later repudiation of this statement, that there was to be no genuine hearing for the dissenting editor. And when the news appeared in the afternoon papers, Alumni, Trustee and administration rejoiced that the rebel was at last gone.

But his departure did not bring peace and quiet to the University. By the next morning the case had become a nationwide issue; any hope that Harris' ouster would still the waters he had troubled must have fled swiftly from Columbia's administrative halls.

So instantaneous and pronounced was the protest against the University's action that it became evident that her original defense would not suffice. The Dean had already admitted that more than a single editorial was involved in the expulsion, that Harris' whole editorial policy was the source of his discharge. Confronted with the dissatisfaction this explanation had caused, he reversed himself in mid-field—very likely after consultation with more authoritative groups. He informed a delegation of conservative students that Harris' "personal misconduct" prompted the ouster. To another delegation he gave the publication in *The Spectator* of the following paragraph as his reason:

> Waiters asserted that the personnel in charge of the dining room evidently were working only for profit, serving poor food, attracting organizations not strictly student in character and otherwise changing the character of the organization from one of student service to one of personal profit.

This was a tragic blunder which the Dean will not soon forget—and which was carelessly repeated by President Butler in an interview with another group. They had apparently been very negligent in preparing their alibis, for precisely that paragraph had been published in *The Spectator* a year before under a different editor and without any reprisals against him. The republication occurred in the course of an historical survey on previous inquiries into the dining-halls.

Neither Dean Hawkes nor Dr. Butler was ever able to explain why, if a previous editor could make this statement without punishment, Harris would have to be expelled for it. If all the other testimony could be forgotten, this phase alone would have demonstrated beyond dispute the real motivation behind the dismissal.

That was Dr. Butler's only direct statement on the case—his reference to "slanders" against the dining hall management. After that had proved a boomerang, he retired behind the scenes, resuming the attitude he had adopted on April 3 when interviewed by The Herald-Tribune:

> "Would you make a statement on the expulsion of Harris," Dr. Butler was asked. "Of whom?" he queried. "Harris, Reed Harris, editor of *The Spectator*." "Oh," said Dr. Butler, "I don't know anything about that. That hasn't come to me at all."

He was, by Dean Hawkes' earlier statement, not telling the truth. He had been consulted. Moreover, the event had been broadcast over the radio and spread over the newspapers; only a recluse could fail to have heard of it three days later.

Student indignation crystallized on the Monday after the expulsion, when a mass meeting was held on the Library Steps with more than 4,000 students present. Columbia had never witnessed—since the war years when R.O.T.C. men had held their review in exactly the same place—so impressive an outpouring of serious and determined students. And there, a University strike of major proportions was voted, to take place on Wednesday.

Since that time students in other colleges, faced with similar situations, have adopted the procedure of those thousands who massed on the Steps in the warm April afternoon. In 1931 that was a bold and almost unprecedented move.

Simultaneously the first hint of opposition developed. Its origin, tactics and appeal is worthy of note because, in subsequent years, almost every college has been visited by a similar bloc. At Columbia in 1931 the group styled itself "The Spartans"; later we are to see them as "Vigilantes" and even as "Silver Shirts." It was perhaps too early to comprehend their full meaning; yet some imitation of their later nature could be discerned.

Part of this opposition did not follow the action of "The Spartans" on the day of the strike when a meeting "to uphold the Dean" was held in front of his office under the auspices of that group. The "loyalists" preferred to attend the strike meeting, to hurl eggs, provoke fist-fights and attempt to disperse the assemblage. When one of their number was urged to express his sentiments verbally to the crowd, he rose and shouted: "I think it's a lot of boloney," then fled before the disgust of the audience. Another rose up to defend him, crying, "We all know what Harris said was true. But he didn't have to say it in public."

With these two eloquent contributions, the invaders, recruited primarily from the football team and Fraternity Row, then returned to their egg-throwing. At the meeting of "The Spartans," equally eloquent orators swore their fealty to the Dean and then devoted most of their time to a valiant assault on "communism." One of them later admitted the essence of his feeling on the matter: "The only way to run a corporation or a university or a government is to have discipline or authority vested in one person." He also confessed that, like most of his fellow-supporters of the Administration, he was an athlete, residing at the Manor House and otherwise enjoying a remunerative college career.

"The Spartans" and their sympathizers were plainly outnumbered. If a few hundred followed their leadership, close to seventy-five per cent of the 1800 students in the college, augmented by hundreds from other schools of the University, went on strike. The Dean's loyal lackeys could not carry the day despite the red menace, eggs and a substantial number of powerful football players.

On the steps of the Library several thousand students were demanding the reinstatement of Harris and a probe of the dining-halls.

The appearance and methods of the opposition was nevertheless ominous. It is equally significant that those who sought to break up the strike and provoke a riot were never censured by the Administration. They were its handmaidens and, if their tactics were crude, their intentions were noble. No sentimental Dean could have penalized such boyish devotion. They came from what we shall discover to be the accustomed seats of reaction—from Fraternity houses, from the athletic field and from that group which, in return for its willing and unquestioning loyalty, receives the numerous favors an Administration can afford to dispense.

Two days after the strike Dean Hawkes departed for a "long planned" trip to England. He told reporters at the boat that there was no possibility of Harris' reinstatement.

But the pressure did not cease. As one periodical wrote at the time, "This issue agitated the student body of the country for almost two weeks. From Maine to Texas, literally, letters and telegrams of protest came pouring into Columbia."

On April 20th prolonged negotiations between the Civil Liberties Union, representing Harris, and the University came to an end. Harris was reinstated. As he had originally intended, he immediately submitted his resignation to the University. In addition, he had previously sent a note of apology to the Dean for any personal injury the Dean may have experienced.

But, as the Civil Liberties Union commented in reviewing the case: "Columbia University's reinstatement of Reed Harris is a plain confession of error despite its face-saving conditions."

ROBERT HUTCHINS ON THE IDEAL EDUCATION (1936)   From Robert M. Hutchins, *The Higher Learning in America* (New Haven, 1936), pp. 77–87.

Let us avoid all questions of administration and method. Let us assume that we have an intelligible organization of education under which there is a four-year unit, beginning at about the beginning of the junior year in high school and ending at about the end of the sophomore year in college. Let us assume that we are going to try to teach in that unit everybody who can learn from books. Let us assume further that the conclusion of their work in this unit will mark the end of formal instruction for most students. They will not go on to the university. Nevertheless we must have a curriculum which will, in the main, do as well for those who are going on as those who are not. What shall this curriculum be?

We have excluded body building and character building. We have excluded the social graces and the tricks of trades. We have suggested that the curriculum should be composed principally of the permanent studies. We propose the permanent studies because these studies draw out the elements of our common human nature, because they connect man with man, because they connect us with the best that man has thought, because they are basic to any further study and to any understanding of the world. What are the permanent studies?

They are in the first place those books which have through the centuries attained to the dimensions of classics. Many such books, I am afraid, are in the ancient and medieval period. But even these are contemporary. A classic is a book that is contemporary in every age. That is why it is a classic. The conversations of Socrates raise questions that are as urgent today as they were when Plato wrote. In fact they are more so, because the society in which Plato lived did not need to have them raised as much as we do. We have forgotten how important they are.

Such books are then a part, and a large part, of the permanent studies. They are so in the first place because they are the best books we know. How can we call a man educated who has never read any of the great books in the western world? Yet today it is entirely possible for a student to graduate from the finest American colleges without having read any of them, except possibly Shakespeare. Of course, the student may have heard of these books, or at least of their authors. But this knowledge is gained in general through textbooks, and textbooks have probably done as much to degrade the American intelligence as any single force. If the student should know about Cicero, Milton, Galileo, or Adam Smith, why should he not read what they wrote? Ordinarily what he knows about them he learns from texts which must be at best second-hand versions of their thought.

In the second place these books are an essential part of general education because it is impossible to understand any subject or to comprehend the contemporary world without them. If we read Newton's *Principia*, we see a great genius in action; we make the acquaintance of a work of unexampled simplicity and elegance. We understand, too, the basis of modern science. The false starts, the backing and filling, the wildness, the hysteria, the confusion of modern thought and the modern world result from the loss of what has been thought and done by earlier ages. The Industrial Revolution begins our study of history and the social sciences. Philosophy begins with Descartes and Locke and psychology with Wundt and William James. Natural science originates with the great experimenters of the nineteenth century. If anything prior is mentioned, it is only as a reminder that our recent great achievements in these fields must, of course, have had some primitive beginnings in the dark earlier centuries. The classics, if presented at all, are offered in excerpts out of context, and for the most part for the sake of showing the student how far we have progressed beyond our primitive beginnings.

Yet we may with profit remember the words of Nicholas Murray Butler:

> Only the scholar can realize how little that is being said and thought in the modern world is in any sense new. It was the colossal triumph of the Greeks and Romans and of the great thinkers of the Middle Ages to sound the depths of almost every problem which human nature has to offer, and to interpret human thought and human aspiration with astounding profundity and insight. Unhappily, these deep-lying facts which should be controlling in the life of a civilized people with a historical background, are known only to a few, while the many grasp, now at an ancient and well-demonstrated falsehood and now at an old and well-proved truth, as if each had all the attractions of novelty.

You will note that Mr. Butler says that only a scholar can realize these things. Why should this insight be confined to scholars? Every educated person should know the colossal triumph of the Greeks and Romans and the great thinkers of the Middle Ages. If every man were educated—and why should he not be?—our people would not fall so easily a prey to the latest nostrums in economics, in politics, and, I may add, in education.

You will observe that the great books of the western world cover every department of knowledge. The *Republic* of Plato is basic to an understanding of the law; it is equally important as education for what is known as citizenship. The *Physics* of Aristotle, which deals with change and motion in nature, is fundamental to the natural sciences and medicine, and is equally important to all those who confront change and motion in nature, that is, to everybody. Four years spent partly in reading, discussing, and digesting books of such importance would, therefore, contribute equally to preparation for specialized study and to general education of a terminal variety. Certainly four years is none too long for this experience. It is an experience which will, as I have said, serve as preparation for advanced study and as general education designed to help the student understand the world. It will also develop habits of reading and standards of taste and criticism that will enable the adult, after his formal education is over, to think and act intelligently about the thought and movements of contemporary life. It will help him to share in the intellectual activity of his time.

In order to read books one must know how to do it. The degeneracy of instruction in English grammar should not blind us to the fact that only through grammatical study can written works be understood. Grammar is the scientific analysis of language through which we understand the meaning and force of what is written. Grammar disciplines the mind and develops the logical faculty. It is good in itself and as an aid to reading the classics. It has a place in general education in connection with the classics and independently of them. For those who are going to learn from books learning the art of reading would seem to be indispensable.

I do not suggest that learning the languages or the grammar in which the ancient classics were written is necessary to general education. Excellent translations of almost all of them now exist. Unless it can be shown that the study of Greek and Latin grammar is essential to the study of English grammar or that the mastery of the Greek and Latin languages is essential to mastery of our own, I see no reason for insisting on these languages as part of general education. The modern languages, of course, are no necessary part of it. Time should be allowed for students to acquire them; but the examinations reflecting general education should not contain them. They are an extracurriculum accomplishment or a tool for advanced work rather than a fundamental portion of general education.

I add to grammar, or the rules of reading, rhetoric and logic, or the rules of writing, speaking, and reasoning. The classics provide models of excellence; grammar, rhetoric, and logic are means of determining how excellence is achieved. We have forgotten that there are rules for speaking. And English composition, as it is commonly taught, is a feeble and debased imitation of the classical rules of writing, placing emphasis either on the most trivial details or on what is called self-expression. Self-expression as here understood is, of course, the exact reverse of the discipline which rhetoric in all ages up to the present was used to give. Logic is a statement in technical form of the conditions under which reasoning is rigorously demonstrative. If the object of general education is to train the mind for intelligent action, logic cannot be missing from it.

Logic is a critical branch of the study of reasoning. It remains only to add a study which exemplifies reasoning in its clearest and most precise form. That study is, of course, mathematics, and of the mathematical studies chiefly those that use the type of exposition that Euclid employed. In such studies the pure operation of reason is made manifest. The subject matter depends on the universal and necessary processes of human thought. It is not affected by differences in taste, disposition, or prejudice. It refutes the common answer of students who, conformable to the temper of the times, wish to accept the principles and deny the conclusions. Correctness in thinking may be more directly and impressively taught through mathematics than in any other way.[1] It is depressing that in high schools and junior colleges mathematics is not often taught in such a way as to achieve these ends. Arithmetic and geometry are there usually presented to the student as having great practical value, as of course they have.[2] But I have had students in the freshman year in college who had never heard that they had any other value, and who were quite unwilling to consider mathematical questions until their practical possibilities had been explained. To this pass has our notion of utility brought us.

We have then for general education a course of study consisting of the greatest books of the western world and the arts of reading, writing, thinking, and speaking, together with mathematics, the best exemplar of the processes of human reason. If our hope has been to frame a curriculum which educes the elements of our common human nature, this program should realize our hope. If we wish to prepare the young for intelligent action, this course of study should assist us; for they will have learned what has been done in the past, and what the greatest men have thought. They will have learned how to think themselves. If we wish to lay a basis for advanced study, that basis is provided. If we wish to secure true universities, we may look forward to them, because students and professors may acquire through this course of study a common stock of ideas and common methods of dealing with them. All the needs of general education in America seem to be satisfied by this curriculum.

---

[1] " 'You see, then, my friend,' said I, 'that this branch of study really seems to be indispensable for us, since it plainly compels the soul to employ pure thought with a view to truth itself.' " Plato, *Republic*, Book VII.

[2] Plato on geometers: "Their language is most ludicrous, though they cannot help it, for they speak as if they were doing something and as if all their words were directed toward action. For all their talk is of squaring and applying and adding and the like, whereas the real object of the entire study is pure thought." *Ibid.*, Book VII. See also Aristotle, *Ethics*, 1098a.

What, then, are the objections to it? They cannot be educational objections; for this course of study appears to accomplish the aims of general education. One objection may be that the students will not like it, which is, as we have seen, irrelevant. But even if it were relevant, it is not true. Since the proposed curriculum is coherent and comprehensible, and since it is free from the triviality that now afflicts our program, students will respond to it if the teachers will give them a chance to do it.

It may be said that the course of study is too difficult. It is not too difficult for students who can read or who can be taught to do so. For ease of reading, as well as other qualities, *The Federalist*, an American classic, is superior to some recent treatises on government and public administration; Herodotus is more sprightly than most modern historians of the ancient world; and Plato and Aristotle are as intelligible as contemporary philosophers.

No, the students can do the work if the faculties will let them. Will the faculties let them? I doubt it. The professors of today have been brought up differently. Not all of them have read all the books they would have to teach. Not all of them are ready to change the habits of their lives. Meanwhile they are bringing up their successors in the way they were brought up, so that the next crop will have the habits they have had themselves. And the love of money, a misconception of democracy, a false notion of progress, a distorted idea of utility, and the anti-intellectualism to which all these lead conspire to confirm their conviction that no disturbing change is needed. The times call for the establishment of a new college or for an evangelistic movement in some old ones which shall have for its object the conversion of individuals and finally of the teaching profession to a true conception of general education. Unless some such demonstration or some such evangelistic movement can take place, we shall remain in our confusion; we shall have neither general education nor universities; and we shall continue to disappoint the hopes of our people.

THE "G.I. BILL OF RIGHTS" (1944)   From *House Committee Print no. 371*, 80th Cong., 2d Sess. (Washington, D.C., 1948), pp. 7–10.

---

1. Any person who served in the active military or naval service on or after September 16, 1940, and prior to the termination of the present war, and who shall have been discharged or released therefrom under conditions other than dishonorable, and who either shall have served ninety days or more, exclusive of any period he was assigned for a course of education or training under the Army specialized training program or the Navy college training program, which course was a continuation of his civilian course and was pursued to completion, or as a cadet or midshipman at one of the service academies, or shall have been discharged or released from active service by reason of an actual service-incurred injury or disability, shall be eligible for and entitled to receive education or training under this part: *Provided,* That such course shall be initiated not later than four years after either the date of his discharge or the termination of the present war, whichever is

the later: *Provided further,* That no such education or training shall be afforded beyond nine years after the termination of the present war.

2. Any such eligible person shall be entitled to education or training at an approved educational or training institution for a period of one year plus the time such person was in the active service on or after September 16, 1940, and before the termination of the war, exclusive of any period he was assigned for a course of education or training under the Army specialized training program or the Navy college training program, which course was a continuation of his civilian course and was pursued to completion, or as a cadet or midshipman at one of the service academies, but in no event shall the total period of education or training exceed four years: *Provided,* That his work continues to be satisfactory throughout the period, according to the regularly prescribed standards and practices of the institution: *Provided further,* That wherever the period of eligibility ends during a quarter or semester and after a major part of such quarter or semester has expired, such period shall be extended to the termination of such unexpired quarter or semester.

3. (*a*) Such person shall be eligible for and entitled to such course of education or training, full time or the equivalent thereof in part-time training, as he may elect, and at any approved educational or training institution at which he chooses to enroll, whether or not located in the State in which he resides, which will accept or retain him as a student or trainee in any field or branch of knowledge which such institution finds him qualified to undertake or pursue: *Provided,* That, for reasons satisfactory to the Administrator, he may change a course of instruction: *And provided further,* That any such course of education or training may be discontinued at any time, if it is found by the Administrator that, according to the regularly prescribed standards and practices of the institution, the conduct or progress of such person is unsatisfactory.

(*b*) Any such eligible person may apply for a short, intensive post-graduate, or training course of less than thirty weeks: *Provided,* That the Administrator shall have the authority to contract with approved institutions for such courses if he finds that the agreed cost of such courses is reasonable and fair: *Provided further,* That (1) the limitation of paragraph 5 shall not prevent the payment of such agreed rates, but there shall be charged against the veteran's period of eligibility the proportion of an ordinary school year which the cost of the course bears to $500, and (2) not in excess of $500 shall be paid for any such course.

(*c*) Any such eligible person may apply for a course of instruction by correspondence without any subsistence allowance: *Provided,* That the Administrator shall have authority to contract with approved institutions for such courses if he finds that the agreed cost of such courses is reasonable and fair: *Provided further,* (1) That the provisions of paragraph 5 shall not apply to correspondence courses; (2) that one-fourth of the elapsed time in following such course shall be charged against the veteran's period of eligibility; and (3) that the total amount payable for a correspondence course or courses for any veteran shall not exceed $500; *And provided further,* That nothing herein shall be construed to preclude the use of approved correspondence courses as a part of institutional or job training, subject to regulations prescribed by the Administrator.

4. From time to time the Administrator shall secure from the appropriate agency of each State a list of the educational and training institutions (including industrial establishments), within such jurisdiction, which are qualified and equipped to furnish education or training (including apprenticeship, refresher or retraining and institutional on-farm training), which institutions, together with such additional

ones as may be recognized and approved by the Administrator, shall be deemed qualified and approved to furnish education or training to such persons as shall enroll under this part: *Provided,* That wherever there are established State apprenticeship agencies expressly charged by State laws to administer apprentice training, whenever possible, the Administrator shall utilize such existing facilities and services in training on the job when such training is of one year's duration or more.

5. The Administrator shall pay to the educational or training institution (including the institution offering institutional on-farm training), for each person enrolled in full time or part time course of education or training, the customary cost of tuition, and such laboratory, library, health, infirmary, and other similar fees as are customarily charged, and may pay for books, supplies, equipment, and other necessary expenses, exclusive of board, lodging, other living expenses, and travel, as are generally required for the successful pursuit and completion of the course by other students in the institution: *Provided,* That in no event shall such payments, with respect to any person, exceed $500 for an ordinary school year unless the veteran elects to have such customary charges paid in excess of such limitation, in which event there shall be charged against his period of eligibility the proportion of an ordinary school year which such excess bears to $500: *Provided further,* That no payments shall be made to institutions, business or other establishments furnishing apprentice training on the job: *And provided further,* That any institution may apply to the Administrator for an adjustment of tuition and the Administrator, if he finds that the customary tuition charges are insufficient to permit the institution to furnish education or training to eligible veterans, or inadequate compensation therefor, may provide for the payment of such fair and reasonable compensation as will not exceed the estimated cost of teaching personnel and supplies for instruction; and may in like manner readjust such payments from time to time.

6. While enrolled in and pursuing a course under this part, (including an institutional on-farm training course) such person, upon application to the Administrator, shall be paid a subsistence allowance of $65 per month, if without a dependent or dependents, or $90 per month, if he has a dependent or dependents, including regular holidays and leave not exceeding thirty days in a calendar year: Except, That (1) while so enrolled and pursuing a course of full-time institutional training, such person, shall be paid a subsistence allowance of $75 per month, if without a dependent or dependents, or $105 per month if he has one dependent or $120 per month if he has more than one dependent, and (2) while so enrolled and pursuing a course of part-time institutional training, including a course of institutional on-farm training, or other combination course, such person shall be paid, subject to the limitations of this paragraph, additional subsistence allowance in an amount bearing the same relation to the difference between the basic rates and the increased rates provided in (1) hereof as the institutional training part of such course bears to a course of full-time institutional training. Such person attending a course on a part-time basis, and such person receiving compensation for productive labor whether performed as part of his apprentice or other training on the job at institutions, business or other establishments, or otherwise, shall be entitled to receive such lesser sums, if any, as subsistence or dependency allowances as may be determined by the Administrator: *Provided,* That in no event shall the rate of such allowance plus the compensation received exceed $210 per month for a veteran without a dependent, or $270 per month for a veteran with one dependent, or $290 for a veteran with two or more dependents: *Provided further,* That only so much of the compensation as is derived from productive labor based on the

standard work-week for the particular trade or industry, exclusive of overtime, shall be considered in computing the rate of allowances payable under this paragraph.

7. Any such person eligible for the benefits of this part, who is also eligible for the benefit of Part VII, may elect either benefit or may be provided an approved combination of such courses: *Provided,* That the total period of any such combined courses shall not exceed the maximum period or limitations under the part affording the greater period of eligibility.

A REPORT ON GENERAL EDUCATION BY THE HARVARD COMMITTEE

(**1945**)   From *General Education in a Free Society* (Cambridge, Mass., 1945), pp. 43–47, 50, 57–58.

It was remarked at the end of the previous chapter that a supreme need of American education is for a unifying purpose and idea. As recently as a century ago, no doubt existed about such a purpose; it was to train the Christian citizen. Nor was there doubt how this training was to be accomplished. The student's logical powers were to be formed by mathematics, his taste by the Greek and Latin classics, his speech by rhetoric, and his ideals by Christian ethics. College catalogues commonly began with a specific statement about the influence of such a training on the mind and character. The reasons why this enviable certainty both of goal and of means has largely disappeared have already been set forth. For some decades the mere excitement of enlarging the curriculum and making place for new subjects, new methods, and masses of new students seems quite pardonably to have absorbed the energies of schools and colleges. It is fashionable now to criticize the leading figures of that expansive time for failing to replace, or even to see the need of replacing, the unity which they destroyed. But such criticisms, if just in themselves, are hardly just historically. A great and necessary task of modernizing and broadening education waited to be done, and there is credit enough in its accomplishment. In recent times, however, the question of unity has become insistent. We are faced with a diversity of education which, if it has many virtues, nevertheless works against the good of society by helping to destroy the common ground of training and outlook on which any society depends.

It seems that a common ground between some, though not all, of the ideas underlying our educational practice is the sense of heritage. The word heritage is not here taken to mean mere retrospection. The purpose of all education is to help students live their own lives. The appeal to heritage is partly to the authority, partly to the clarification of the past about what is important in the present. All Catholic and many Protestant institutions thus appeal to the Christian view of man and history as providing both final meaning and immediate standards for life. As observed at the outset, it is less than a century since such was the common practice of American education generally, and certainly this impulse to mold students to a pattern sanctioned by the past can, in one form or another, never be absent from education. If it were, society would become discontinuous.

In this concern for heritage lies a close similarity between religious education and education in the great classic books. Exponents of the latter have, to be sure, described it as primarily a process of intellectual discipline in the joint arts of word and number, the so-called *trivium* (grammar, logic, rhetoric) and *quadrivium* (arithmetic, geometry, astronomy, music). But, since the very idea of this discipline goes back to antiquity and since the actual books by which it is carried out are in fact the great books of the Western tradition, it seems fairer, without denying the disciplinary value of such a curriculum, to think of it as primarily a process of opening before students the intellectual forces that have shaped the Western mind. There is a sense in which education in the great books can be looked at as a secular continuation of the spirit of Protestantism. As early Protestantism, rejecting the authority and philosophy of the medieval church, placed reliance on each man's personal reading of the Scriptures, so this present movement, rejecting the unique authority of the Scriptures, places reliance on the reading of those books which are taken to represent the fullest revelation of the Western mind. But be this as it may, it is certain that, like religious education, education in the great books is essentially an introduction of students to their heritage.

Nor is the sense of heritage less important, though it may be less obvious, a part of education for modern democratic life. To the degree that the implications of democracy are drawn forth and expounded, to that degree the long-standing impulse of education toward shaping students to a received ideal is still pursued. Consider the teaching of American history and of modern democratic life. However ostensibly factual such teaching may be, it commonly carries with it a presupposition which is not subject to scientific proof: namely, the presupposition that democracy is meaningful and right. Moreover, since contemporary life is itself a product of history, to study it is to tread unconsciously, in the words of the hymn, where the saints have trod. To know modern democracy is to know something at least of Jefferson, though you have not read him; to learn to respect freedom of speech or the rights of the private conscience is not to be wholly ignorant of the *Areopagitica* or the *Antigone*, though you know nothing about them. Whether, as philosophers of history argue, being conditioned by the present we inevitably judge the past by what we know in the present (since otherwise the past would be unintelligible) or whether human motives and choices do not in reality greatly change with time, the fact remains that the past and the present are parts of the same unrolling scene and, whether you enter early or late, you see for the most part the still-unfinished progress of the same issues.

Here, then, in so far as our culture is adequately reflected in current ideals on education, one point about it is clear: it depends in part on an inherited view of man and society which is the function, though not the only function, of education to pass on. It is not and cannot be true that all possible choices are open to us individually or collectively. We are part of an organic process, which is the American, and, more broadly, the Western evolution. Our standards of judgment, ways of life, and form of government all bear the marks of this evolution, which would accordingly influence us, though confusedly, even if it were not understood. Ideally it should be understood at several degrees of depth which complement rather than exclude each other. To study the American present is to discern at best the aims and purposes of a free society animating its imperfections. To study the past is immensely to enrich the meaning of the present and at the same time to clarify it by the simplification of the writings and the issues which have been winnowed from history. To study either past or present is to confront, in some form or another, the philosophic and religious fact of man in history and to recognize the huge continuing influence alike on past and present of the stream of Jewish and Greek thought in Christianity. There is doubtless a sense in which religious education, education in the great books, and education in modern democracy may be mutually exclusive. But there is a far more important sense in which they work together to the same end, which is belief in the idea of man and society that we inherit, adapt, and pass on.

This idea is described in many ways, perhaps most commonly in recent times, as that of the dignity of man. To the belief in man's dignity must be added the recognition of his duty to his fellow men. Dignity does not rest on any man as a being separate from all other beings, which he in any case cannot be, but springs from his common humanity and exists positively as he makes the common good his own. This concept is essentially that of the Western tradition: the view of man as free and not as slave, an end in himself and not a means. It may have what many believe to be the limitations of humanism, which are those of pride and arise from making man the measure of all things. But it need not have these limitations, since it is equally compatible with a religious view of life. Thus it is similar to the position described at the end of the last chapter as cooperation without uniformity, agreement on the good of man at the level of performance without the necessity of agreement on ultimates. But two points have now been added. First, thus stated, the goal of education is not in conflict with but largely includes the goals of religious education, education in the Western tradition, and education in modern democracy. For these in turn have been seen to involve necessary elements in our common tradition, each to a great extent implied in the others as levels at which it can be understood. Certainly no fruitful way of stating the belief in the dignity and mutual obligation of man can present it as other than, at one and the same time, effective in the present, emerging from the past, and partaking of the nature not of fact but of faith. Second, it has become clear that the common ground between these various views—namely, the impulse to rear students to a received idea of the good— is in fact necessary to education. It is impossible to escape the realization that our society, like any society, rests on common beliefs and that a major task of education is to perpetuate them.

This conclusion raises one of the most fundamental problems of education, indeed of society itself: how to reconcile this necessity for common belief with the equally obvious necessity for new and independent insights leading to change. We approach here the one previously mentioned concept of education which was not included under the idea of heritage: namely, the views associated with the names of James and Dewey and having to do with science, the scientific attitude, and pragmatism. This is hardly the place to try to summarize this body of thought or even to set forth in detail its application by Mr. Dewey to education. To do so would be virtually to retrace the educational controversies of the last forty years. But, at the risk of some injustice to Mr. Dewey's thought as a whole, a few points can be made about it. It puts trust in the scientific method of thought, the method which demands that you reach conclusions from tested data only, but that, since the data may be enlarged or the conclusions themselves combined with still other conclusions, you must hold them only tentatively. It emphasizes that full truth is not known and that we must be forever led by facts to revise our approximations of it. As a feeling of commitment and of allegiance marks the sense of heritage, so a tone of tough-mindedness and curiosity and a readiness for change mark this pragmatic attitude.

Here, then, is a concept of education, founded on obedience to fact and well disposed, even hospitable, to change, which appears at first sight the antithesis of any view based on the importance of heritage. Such hostility to tradition well reflects one side of the modern mind. It is impossible to contemplate the changes even of the last decades, much less the major groundswell of change since the Renaissance, without feeling that we face largely new conditions which call for new qualities of mind and outlook. Moreover, it is obviously no accident that this pragmatic philosophy has been worked out most fully in the United States. Yet, in spite of its seeming conflict with views of education based on heritage, strong doubt exists whether the questioning, innovating, experimental attitude of pragmatism is in fact something alien to the Western heritage, or whether it is not, in the broadest sense of the word, a part of it.

*　　*　　*

Students of antiquity and of the Middle Ages can therefore rightly affirm that decisive truths about the human mind and its relation to the world were laid hold of then, and yet agree that, when new application of these truths was made through a more scrupulous attention to fact, their whole implication and meaning were immensely enlarged. Modern civilization has seen this enlargement of meaning and possibility; yet it is not a new civilization but the organic development of an earlier civilization. The true task of education is therefore so to reconcile the sense of pattern and direction deriving from heritage with the sense of experimentation and innovation deriving from science that they may exist fruitfully together, as in varying degrees they have never ceased to do throughout Western history.

Belief in the dignity and mutual obligation of man is the common ground between these contrasting but mutually necessary forces in our culture. As was pointed out earlier, this belief is the fruit at once of religion, of the Western tradition, and of the American tradition. It equally inspires the faith in human reason which is the basis for trust in the future of the democracy. And if it is not, strictly speaking, implied in all statements of the scientific method, there is no doubt that science has become its powerful instrument. In this tension between the opposite forces of heritage and change poised only in the faith in man, lies something like the old philosophic problem of the knowledge of the good. If you know the good, why do you seek it? If you are ignorant of the good, how do you recognize it when you find it? You must evidently at one and the same time both know it and be ignorant of it. Just so, the tradition which has come down to us regarding the nature of man and the good society must inevitably provide our standard of good. Yet an axiom of that tradition itself is the belief that no current form of the received ideal is final but that every generation, indeed every individual, must discover it in a fresh form. Education can therefore be wholly devoted neither to tradition nor to experiment, neither to the belief that the ideal in itself is enough nor to the view that means are valuable apart from the ideal. It must uphold at the same time tradition and experiment, the ideal and the means, subserving, like our culture itself, change within commitment.

*　　*　　*

It is most unfortunate if we envisage general education as something formless— that is to say, the taking of one course after another; and as something negative, namely, the study of what is not in a field of concentration. Just as we regard the courses in concentration as having definite relations to one another, so should we envisage general education as an organic whole whose parts join in expounding a ruling idea and in serving a common aim. And to do so means to abandon the view that all fields and all departments are equally valuable vehicles of general education. It also implies some prescription. At the least it means abandoning the usual attitude of regarding "distribution" as a sphere in which the student exercises a virtually untrammeled freedom of choice. It may be objected that we are proposing to limit the liberty of the student in the very name of liberal education. Such an objection would only indicate an ambiguity in the conception of liberal education. We must distinguish between liberalism in education and education in liberalism. The former, based as it is on the doctrine of individualism, expresses the view that the student should be free in his choice of courses. But education in liberalism is an altogether different matter; it is education which has a pattern of its own, namely, the pattern associated with the liberal outlook. In this view, there are truths which none can be free to ignore, if one is to have that wisdom through which life can become useful. These are the truths concerning the structure of the good life and concerning the factual conditions by which it may be achieved, truths comprising the goals of the free society.

Finally, the problem of general education is one of combining fixity of aim with diversity in application. It is not a question of providing a general education which will be uniform through the same classes of all schools and colleges all over the country, even were such a thing possible in our decentralized system. It is rather to adapt general education to the needs and intentions of different groups and, so far as possible, to carry its spirit into special education. The effectiveness of teaching has always largely depended on this willingness to adapt a central unvarying purpose to varying outlooks. Such adaptation is as much in the interest of the quick as of the slow, of the bookish as of the unbookish, and is the necessary protection of each. What is wanted, then, is a general education capable at once of taking on many different forms and yet of representing in all its forms the common knowledge and the common values on which a free society depends.

PRESIDENT HARRY TRUMAN'S COMMISSION CALLS FOR EXPANSION OF HIGHER EDUCATION (1947) From *Higher Education for Democracy: A Report of the President's Commission on Higher Education* (New York, 1947), vol. I, pp. 1, 25–29, 32–39.

The President's Commission on Higher Education has been charged with the task of defining the responsibilities of colleges and universities in American democracy and in international affairs—and, more specifically, with reexamining the objectives, methods, and facilities of higher education in the United States in the light of the social role it has to play.

*   *   *

Record of Growth

The expansion of the American education enterprise since the turn of the century has been phenomenal. The 700,000 enrollment in high schools in the school year 1900 was equal to only 11 percent of the youth of usual high-school age, 14 through 17 years old. This increased in 1940 to over 7,000,000 students representing 73 percent of the youth.

Almost as spectacular has been the increase in college attendance. In 1900 fewer than 250,000 students, only 4 percent of the population 18 through 21 years of age, were enrolled in institutions of higher education. By 1940 the enrollment had risen to 1,500,000 students, equal to a little less than 16 percent of the 18-21-year-olds. In 1947, enrollments jumped to the theretofore unprecedented peak of 2,354,000 although approximately 1,000,000 of the students were veterans, older than the usual college age because World War II had deferred their education. The situation in the fall of 1947 gives every indication that the school year 1948 will witness even larger enrollments. (See Chart I, "Growth of College Population.")

This record of growth is encouraging, but we are forced to admit nonetheless that the educational attainments of the American people are still substantially below what is necessary, either for effective individual living or for the welfare of our society.

According to the U. S. Bureau of the Census, almost 17,000,000 men and women over 19 years of age in 1947 had stopped their schooling at the sixth grade or less. Of these, 9,000,000 had never attended school or had stopped their schooling before completing the fifth grade. In 1947, about 1,600,000 or 19 percent of our high-school-age boys and girls were not attending any kind of school, and over two-thirds of the 18- and 19-year-old youths were not in school.

These are disturbing facts. They represent a sobering failure to reach the educational goals implicit in the democratic creed, and they are indefensible in a society so richly endowed with material resources as our own. We cannot allow so many of our people to remain so ill equipped either as human beings or as citizens of a democracy.

Great as the total American expenditure for education may seem, we have not been devoting any really appreciable part of our vast wealth to higher education. As table 1 shows, even though in the last 15 years our annual budget for education has risen in number of dollars, it has actually declined in relation to our increasing economic productivity.

The $1,000,000,000 we have put into our colleges and universities in 1947 was less than one-half of 1 percent of the gross national product, which is the market value of all the goods and services produced in the country in that year.

Barriers to Equal Opportunity

One of the gravest charges to which American society is subject is that of failing to provide a reasonable equality of educational opportunity for its youth. For the great majority of our boys and girls, the kind and amount of education they may hope to attain depends, not on their own abilities, but on the family or community into which they happened to be born or, worse still, on the color of their skin or the religion of their parents.

TABLE 5.—*Proportion of Young Persons Attending School, by Age and Color: April 1947* [1]

Age	Attending school	
	White	Nonwhites (about 95 percent Negro)
	Percent	*Percent*
6 years of age	67.8	63.4
7 to 9 years of age	97.1	89.2
10 to 13 years of age	98.2	93.7
14 to 17 years of age	82.5	71.9
18 to 19 years of age	28.2	24.2
20 to 24 years of age	11.3	6.7

[1] Source: U. S. Bureau of the Census.

Institutions which accept both Negro and non-Negro students do not maintain separate record systems for Negroes, and so data on enrollment of Negroes are restricted to those institutions—usually located in the South—which accept only Negro students. In recent years, since 1932, these institutions have almost tripled their enrollments whereas the institutions for whites or which are unsegregated only about doubled theirs:

TABLE 6.—*Enrollment of Institutions of Higher Education and Index of Change* [1]

Year	Enrollments in institutions accepting			
	Negroes only		All other	
	Number	Index of change (1932=100)	Number	Index of change (1932=100)
1932	21,880	100	1,132,237	100
1936	32,628	149	1,175,599	104
1940	41,839	191	1,452,364	128
1947 [2]	63,500	290	2,290,500	202

[1] Source is resident enrollment as reported by U. S. Office of Education.
[2] Estimated.

ECONOMIC BARRIERS

The old, comfortable idea that "any boy can get a college education who has it in him" simply is not true. Low family income, together with the rising costs of education, constitutes an almost impassable barrier to college education for many young people. For some, in fact, the barrier is raised so early in life that it prevents them from attending high school even when free public high schools exist near their homes.

Despite the upward trend in average per capita income for the past century and more, the earnings of a large part of our population are still too low to provide anything but the barest necessities of physical life. It is a distressing fact that in 1945, when the total national income was far greater than in any previous period in our history, half of the children under 18 were growing up in families which had a cash income of $2,530 or less. The educational significance of these facts is heightened by the relationship that exists between income and birth rate. Fertility is highest in the families with lowest incomes.

In the elementary and secondary schools the effects of these economic conditions are overcome to a considerable extent, though not entirely, by the fact that education is free and at certain ages is compulsory. But this does not hold true at the college level. For a number of years the tendency has been for the college student to bear an increasing share of the cost of his own education. Even in State-supported institutions we have been moving away from the principle of free education to a much greater degree than is commonly supposed.

Under the pressure of rising costs and of a relative lessening of public support, the colleges and universities are having to depend more and more on tuition fees to meet their budgets. As a result, on the average, tuition rates rose about 30 percent from 1939 to 1947.

Nor are tuition costs the whole of it. There are not enough colleges and universities in the country, and they are not distributed evenly enough to bring them within reach of all young people. Relatively few students can attend college in their home communities. So to the expense of a college education for most youth must be added transportation and living costs—by no means a small item.

This economic factor explains in large part why the father's occupation has been found in many studies to rank so high as a determining factor in a young person's college expectancy. A farm laborer earns less than a banker or a doctor, for instance, and so is less able to afford the costs of higher education for his children. The children, moreover, have less inducement to seek a college education because of their family background. In some social circles a college education is often considered a luxury which can be done without, something desirable perhaps, "but not for the likes of us."

The importance of economic barriers to post-high school education lies in the fact that there is little if any relationship between the ability to benefit from a college education and the ability to pay for it. Studies discussed in the volume of this Commission's report, "Equalizing and Expanding Individual Opportunity," show that among children of equally high ability those with fathers in higher-income occupations had greater probability of attending college.

By allowing the opportunity for higher education to depend so largely on the individual's economic status, we are not only denying to millions of young people the chance in life to which they are entitled; we are also depriving the Nation of a vast amount of potential leadership and potential social competence which it sorely needs.

BARRIER OF A RESTRICTED CURRICULUM

We shall be denying educational opportunity to many young people as long as we maintain the present orientation of higher education toward verbal skills and intellectual interests. Many young people have abilities of a different kind, and they cannot receive "education commensurate with their native capacities" in colleges and universities that recognize only one kind of educable intelligence.

Traditionally the colleges have sifted out as their special clientele persons possessing verbal aptitudes and a capacity for grasping abstractions. But many other aptitudes—such as social sensitivity and versatility, artistic ability, motor skill and dexterity, and mechanical aptitude and ingenuity—also should be cultivated in a society depending, as ours does, on the minute division of labor and at the same time upon the orchestration of an enormous variety of talents.

If the colleges are to educate the great body of American youth, they must provide programs for the development of other abilities than those involved in academic aptitude, and they cannot continue to concentrate on students with one type of intelligence to the neglect of youth with other talents.

RACIAL AND RELIGIOUS BARRIERS

The outstanding example of these barriers to equal opportunity, of course, is the disadvantages suffered by our Negro citizens. The low educational attainments of Negro adults reflect the cumulative effects of a long period of unequal opportunity. In 1940 the schooling of the Negro was significantly below that of whites at every level from the first grade through college. At the college level, the difference is marked; 11 percent of the white population 20 years of age and over had completed at least 1 year of college and almost 5 percent had finished 4 years; whereas for the nonwhites (over 95 percent of whom are Negroes) only a little more than 3 percent had completed at least 1 year of college and less than 1 1/2 percent had completed a full course.

Gains Have Been Made. Noteworthy advances have been made toward eliminating the racial inequalities which in large measure are responsible for this low level of educational achievement by the Negroes. Between 1900 and 1940 the percentage of Negroes 5 to 20 years of age attending school rose from 31.0 percent to 64.4 percent. And the percentage of Negro youth 15 to 20 years old attending school increased from 17.5 in 1900 to 33.8 in 1940.

Institutions which accept both Negro and non-Negro students do not maintain separate record systems for Negroes, and so data on enrollment of Negroes are restricted to those institutions—usually located in the South—which accept only Negro students. In recent years, since 1932, these institutions have almost tripled their enrollments whereas the institutions for whites or which are unsegregated only about doubled theirs. . . .

Inequalities Remain. But the numbers enrolled in school do not tell the whole story. Marked as has been the progress in Negro education in recent years, it cannot obscure the very great differences which still persist in educational opportunities afforded the Negro and the non-Negro.

In 17 states and the District of Columbia, segregation of the Negroes in education is established by law.[1] In the *Gaines* decision, the U. S. Supreme Court ruled that "if a State furnishes higher education to white residents, it is bound to furnish [within the State] substantially equal advantages to Negro students." Although segregation may not legally mean discrimination as to the quality of the facilities it usually does so in fact. The schools maintained for the Negroes are commonly much inferior to those for the whites. The Negro schools are financed at a pitifully low level, they are often housed in buildings wholly inadequate for the purpose, and many of the teachers are sorely in need of more education themselves. Library facilities are generally poor or lacking altogether, and professional supervision is more a name than a reality.

These facts are supported strongly by a recent study in the District of Columbia. The District's Superintendent of Schools in his 1946–47 report to the Board of Education states that the student-teacher ratios in the schools for Negroes were significantly and consistently higher than those for non-Negroes—from the kindergartens through the teachers' colleges.

Segregation lessens the quality of education for the whites as well. To maintain two school systems side by side—duplicating even inadequately the buildings, equipment, and teaching personnel—means that neither can be of the quality that would be possible if all the available resources were devoted to one system, especially not when the States least able financially to support an adequate educational program for their youth are the very ones that are trying to carry a double load.

It must not be supposed that Negro youth living in States in which segregation is not legalized are given the same opportunities as white youth. In these areas economic and social discrimination of various sorts often operates to produce

[1] In the case of *Mendez v. Westminster School District,* the segregation of students of Mexican ancestry in the Westminster, Calif., school district, on the alleged grounds that because of their ancestry such students have language difficulties, was held illegal. The U.S. district court which heard the case held that segregation is unconstitutional under the Federal constitution. On appeal by the Westminster school district, the U.S. circuit court of appeals limited its affirmance of the district court's decision by holding that the specific statutes involved were illegal under the California law.

segregation in certain neighborhoods, which are frequently characterized by poorer school buildings, less equipment and less able teachers.

Equality of education opportunity is not achieved by the mere physical existence of schools; it involves also the quality of teaching and learning that takes place in them.

The Quota System. At the college level a different form of discrimination is commonly practiced. *Many colleges and universities, especially in their professional schools, maintain a selective quota system for admission, under which the chance to learn, and thereby to become more useful citizens, is denied to certain minorities, particularly to Negroes and Jews.*

This practice is a violation of a major American principle and is contributing to the growing tension in one of the crucial areas of our democracy.

The quota, or *numerus clausus*, is certainly un-American. It is European in origin and application, and we have lately witnessed on that continent the horrors to which, in its logical extension, it can lead. To insist that specialists in any field shall be limited by ethnic quotas is to assume that the Nation is composed of separate and self-sufficient ethnic groups and this assumption America has never made except in the case of its Negro population, where the result is one of the plainest inconsistencies with our national ideal.

The quota system denies the basic American belief that intelligence and ability are present in all ethnic groups, that men of all religious and racial origins should have equal opportunity to fit themselves for contributing to the common life.

Moreover, since the quota system is never applied to all groups in the Nation's population, but only to certain ones, we are forced to conclude that the arguments advanced to justify it are nothing more than rationalizations to cover either convenience or the disposition to discriminate. The quota system cannot be justified on any grounds compatible with democratic principles.

CONSEQUENCES OF INEQUALITIES OF OPPORTUNITY

These various barriers to educational opportunity involve grave consequences both for the individual and for society.

From the viewpoint of the individual they are denying to millions of young people what the democratic creed assumes to be their birthright: an equal chance with all others to make the most of their native abilities. From the viewpoint of society the barriers mean that far too few of our young people are getting enough preparation for assuming the personal, social, and civic responsibilities of adults living in a democratic society.

It is especially serious that not more of our most talented young people continue their schooling beyond high school in this day when the complexity of life and of social problems means that we need desperately every bit of trained intelligence we can assemble. The present state of affairs is resulting in far too great a loss of talent—our most precious natural resource in a democracy.

In a country as vast as the United States, with all its regional differences in cultural patterns and economic resources, absolute equality of educational opportunity perhaps may not be reasonably expected. But today the differences that do exist are so great as to compel immediate action.

In communities where the birth rate is low, where the burden of caring for the nurture and education of the oncoming generation is relatively light, where the level of living is high, the advantages of education are extended to youth on more nearly equal terms. But in communities where the birth rate is high, where the economic structure is weak, where the level of living is low, where community and family resources contribute least to intellectual growth, there we support education in niggardly fashion, though at great effort.

If over the years we continue to draw the population reserves of the Nation from the most underprivileged areas and families and fail to make good the deficit by adequate educational opportunities, we shall be following a course that is sure to prove disastrous to the level of our culture and to the whole fabric of our democratic institutions.

We have proclaimed our faith in education as a means of equalizing the conditions of men. But there is grave danger that our present policy will make it an instrument for creating the very inequalities it was designed to prevent. If the ladder of educational opportunity rises high at the doors of some youth and scarcely rises at all at the doors of others, while at the same time formal education is made a prerequisite to occupational and social advance, then education may become the means, not of eliminating race and class distinctions, but of deepening and solidifying them.

It is obvious, then, that free and universal access to education, in terms of the interest, ability, and need of the student, must be a major goal in American education.

Toward Equalizing Opportunity

The American people should set as their ultimate goal an educational system in which at no level—high school, college, graduate school, or professional school—will a qualified individual in any part of the country encounter an insuperable economic barrier to the attainment of the kind of education suited to his aptitudes and interests.

This means that we shall aim at making higher education equally available to all young people, as we now do education in the elementary and high schools, to the extent that their capacity warrants a further social investment in their training.

Obviously this desirable realization of our ideal of equal educational opportunity cannot be attained immediately. But if we move toward it as fast as our economic resources permit, it should not lie too far in the future. Technological advances, that are already resulting in phenomenal increases in productivity per worker, promise us a degree of economic well-being that would have seemed wholly Utopian to our fathers. With wise management of our economy, we shall almost certainly be able to support education at all levels far more adequately in the future than we could in the past.

The Commission recommends that steps be taken to reach the following objectives without delay:

1. High school education must be improved and should be provided for all normal youth.

This is a minimum essential. We cannot safely permit any of our citizens for any reason other than incapacity, to stop short of a high school education or its equivalent. To achieve the purpose of such education, however, it must be improved in facilities and in the diversity of its curriculum. Better high school education is essential, both to raise the caliber of students entering college and to provide the best training possible for those who end their formal education with the twelfth grade.

2. The time has come to make education through the fourteenth grade available in the same way that high school education is now available.

This means that tuition-free education should be available in public institutions to all youth for the traditional freshman and sophomore years or for the traditional 2-year junior college course.

To achieve this, it will be necessary to develop much more extensively than at present such opportunities as are now provided in local communities by the 2-year junior college, community institute, community college, or institute of arts and sciences. The name used does not matter, though community college seems to describe these schools best; the important thing is that the services they perform be recognized and vastly extended.

Such institutions make post-high-school education available to a much larger percentage of young people than otherwise could afford it. Indeed, as discussed in the volume of this Commission's report, "Organizing Higher Education," such community colleges probably will have to carry a large part of the responsibility for expanding opportunities in higher education.

3. The time has come to provide financial assistance to competent students in the tenth through fourteenth grades who would not be able to continue without such assistance.

Tuition costs are not the major economic barrier to education, especially in college. Costs of supplies, board, and room, and other living needs are great. Even many high-school students are unable to continue in school because of these costs.

Arrangements must be made, therefore, to provide additional financial assistance for worthy students who need it if they are to remain in school. Only in this way can we counteract the effect of family incomes so low that even tuition-free schooling is a financial impossibility for their children. Only in this way can we make sure that all who are to participate in democracy are adequately prepared to do so.

4. The time has come to reverse the present tendency of increasing tuition and other student fees in the senior college beyond the fourteenth year, and in both graduate and professional schools, by lowering tuition costs in publicly controlled colleges and by aiding deserving students through inaugurating a program of scholarships and fellowships.

Only in this way can we be sure that economic and social barriers will not prevent the realization of the promise that lies in our most gifted youth. Only in this way can we be certain of developing for the common good all the potential leadership our society produces, no matter in what social or economic stratum it appears.

5. The time has come to expand considerably our program of adult education, and to make more of it the responsibility of our colleges and universities.

The crisis of the time and the rapidly changing conditions under which we live make it especially necessary that we provide a continuing and effective educational program for adults as well as youth. We can in this way, perhaps, make up some of the educational deficiencies of the past, and also in a measure counteract the pressures and distractions of adult life that all too often make the end of formal schooling the end of education too.

6. The time has come to make public education at all levels equally accessible to all, without regard to race, creed, sex or national origin.

If education is to make the attainment of a more perfect democracy one of its major goals, it is imperative that it extend its benefits to all on equal terms. It must renounce the practices of discrimination and segregation in educational institutions as contrary to the spirit of democracy. Educational leaders and institutions should take positive steps to overcome the conditions which at present obstruct free and equal access to educational opportunities. Educational programs everywhere should be aimed at undermining and eventually eliminating the attitudes that are responsible for discrimination and segregation—at creating instead attitudes that will make education freely available to all.[2]

Number Who Should Receive Higher Education

Achieving these immediate objectives necessarily will require a tremendous expansion of our educational enterprise at the college level.

It will be noted that many of the Commission's projects focus upon the year 1960. There are several important reasons why the Commission has chosen to look this far ahead. First of all, in the President's letter of appointment, the Commission was asked to direct its energies toward the investigation of long-term policy issues in American higher education. The Commission itself selected the terminal date of 1960 since it was felt that manageable data could be procured for studies up to this point. The basic consideration of population data weighed heavily in the selection. Individuals who will be enrolled in colleges in 1960 through 1964 have already been born, and thus the Commission has a tangible figure with which to make its projections.

The Commission believes that in 1960 a minimum of 4,600,000 young people should be enrolled in nonprofit institutions for education beyond the traditional twelfth grade. Of this total number, 2,500,000 should be in the thirteenth and fourteenth grades (junior college level); 1,500,000 in the fifteenth and sixteenth grades (senior college level); and 600,000 in graduate and professional schools beyond the first degree.

In thus appraising future enrollment in institutions of post-high school education, this Commission has not sought to project the future on the basis of the past nor to predict annual enrollments over the period 1948 to 1960. It frankly recognizes that such a forecast would be subject to unpredictable world-wide social and economic conditions.

A CRITIQUE OF THE PRESIDENT'S COMMISSION ON HIGHER EDUCATION (1949) From Seymour E. Harris, "Millions of B.A.'s But No Jobs," *The New York Times Magazine*, January 2, 1949, pp. 9–13.

In a bold and stimulating report, the President's Commission on Higher Education has proposed for 1960 an enrollment of 4.6 million students in American institutions of higher learning. Enrollment at the present time seems to be just

[2]The following Commission members wish to record their dissent from the Commission's pronouncements on "segregation," especially as these pronouncements are related to education in the South. Arthur H. Compton, Douglas S. Freeman, Lewis W. Jones, Goodrich C. White. A fuller statement, indicating briefly the basis for this dissent, will appear in volume II of the Commission's report.

about 2.5 millions and educators seem to be in agreement that universities and colleges will enroll 3 millions by the Fifties.

These are astronomical figures, which point up the rapid expansion of higher education in the United States. In 1870 our colleges graduated only 9,000 students. As late as 1900 the total enrollment in all institutions of higher learning was only 238,000. Now less than a generation and a half later we have more than ten times that number and the President's commission proposes to double the present output of college graduates within another twenty years.

This means a vast future increase in college graduates—an increase proportionately much greater than the gain in population. In 1940 the number of college graduates was nearly 4 million, or about 3 per cent of the population. At present-day enrollments we can expect at least 10 million people with college diplomas by the Nineteen Sixties.

At the rate of increase recommended by the President's commission the country would have, eighteen or twenty years from now, about 15 million graduates, or almost four times the present number. And it is not difficult to envision a "college-bred" population of 30 millions or even 45 millions, if one counts all those who have had as much as two years of college. Indeed, if all the recommendations of the President's commission were carried out, the time would come when we would be confronted with a college-graduate population of as much as 25 to 35 per cent of the nation's labor force.

At first thought this might seem an excellent thing. It is a generally accepted proposition that educational progress is linked to social and material progress. But there are long-range implications in the commission's proposals which must be considered. One problem is of primary importance. What do college graduates expect of the world and what do they get for their education? What opportunities are open to them?

The first question is a purely vocational one, but full of social, economic and political meaning. As a college teacher for almost thirty years who has observed undergraduates at close range. I am convinced that vocational reward is still the most important consideration prodding young men and women to go to college. They accept general education in large part because the subject-matter and the process of learning make them more fit to earn a living, because a college education increasingly is a passport to the most coveted openings.

In view of this preoccupation with increased income—and with the prestige attached to brain work—it is interesting to consider the part the college graduate plays in the labor market. His place in our present economy, or rather in the economy of 1940 when the last census was taken, is indicated by figures.

Nearly all of the college graduates belonged to the proprietorship-executive-managerial and professional classes, as those are defined by the census. The first group includes a large proportion of the employes in business. The professional group includes doctors, lawyers, teachers, scientists, engineers, Government workers and employes in the newspaper, radio, advertising, entertainment and many other fields. About 70 per cent of the graduates were in the professions, most of the remainder in the proprietorship-executive-managerial class. Only about 5 per cent of the jobs in the entire labor force require or attract college graduates.

If we assume that in the Nineteen Sixties college men and women would seek the same kinds of employment and in the same proportions as in 1940, definite conclusions may be drawn. There simply would be far more graduates than jobs. Nor could we expect Government and business to take up the slack. While college graduates seem to be increasingly interested in Government positions, the

Government depends mostly on non-college people for the bulk of its routine clerical tasks. And with the gradual depopulation of the farming areas and the growth of large business, the college graduate will not find many additional openings to his liking in the "executive" field.

The need for executives does not increase in proportion to the growth of population. From 1910 to 1940, while the population was increasing 36 per cent, the number of openings for executives was increased only 8 per cent. And from 1929 to 1946 the number of active proprietors of unincorporated enterprises (roughly, the field of small business) actually declined 2.6 per cent.

If we look at the professions, the employment picture is equally dark. On the basis of the proposed increase in graduates we could expect 7 million people with college diplomas looking for jobs in the professions by the Nineteen Sixties—a horde of would-be professional workers about four times as great as the number of professional jobs filled by college graduates in 1940.

A large proportion of these, perhaps 3.5 millions, would be teachers. It seems certain that most of them would not find teaching jobs of any kind. For the country supported only one million teachers in 1940 and these so inadequately that replacements could not be assured without a general lowering of qualifications. It would require a revolution in finance to increase teaching staffs by a mere 50 per cent within the next twenty years. Even then only three-sevenths of the anticipated number of teachers would be able to find jobs in that profession.

I continue to assume that the number seeking employment in each profession is determined by the ratio of college graduates in the profession in 1940. Thus if one-half of all college graduates were teachers in 1940, then if there promises to be 10 million graduates, there would be 5 million potential teachers.

In medicine the picture is not fundamentally different, though different problems are involved. There is, of course, a shortage of doctors and dentists. The nation might well use twice as many as it has now or a total of over 400,000. But it is not clear just what would happen to the remainder of the 1.6 million young men and women who would aspire to the medical profession under the expanded program, even if the country could use 400,000.

In 1940 the nation had about 338,000 scientists. Under the commission's proposals the universities and colleges could be expected to run the total up to 942,000, including engineers, within the next twenty years. This would involve certain complications. The commission itself points out that engineers face a saturated market by 1950.

Eight years ago there were some 180,000 lawyers in the United States. It could be argued that this number would be quite enough to handle all the legal work twenty years hence. Indeed, as the Committee on the Economic Status of the Legal Profession has said, lawyers could do more preventive work and could eliminate some people who should not be giving legal advice. Yet under the expanded college program it seems reasonable to expect 860,000 people trained for the law by the Nineteen Sixties, almost five times the present number.

All these estimates are based, of course, on the assumption that college people would choose the same profession in the same ratio that they did in 1940. This would not be true in all cases. Some people would be discouraged from entering the most crowded professions. Economic conditions might keep some students out of college or govern their choice of professions.

Yet, after all allowances are made and exceptions noted, we could still expect an outpouring of college graduates into an economy which probably would not be prepared to receive them. If there are basic changes due in the economy which would eliminate the problem one cannot imagine what they are.

What would be the result of a rapidly expanding proletariat of the A.B. and the Ph.D.? Obviously any new outpouring of young hopefuls, with their special brand of aspiration and disillusionment, is of vital importance to the American economy as well as to the college graduate himself. If American colleges and universities doubled or tripled their output within the course of a generation, it would be a significant social change. The change has already begun to occur.

University graduates have been accustomed to receive certain rewards in the form of income and station. In general the college graduate and the professional worker still earn more than the non-college graduate and the non-professional. But the overflow of high school and college graduates is beginning to be felt. It is reflected in the higher pay for craftsmen than for educated clerical and kindred workers; in the relative losses of white-collar workers over the last fifty years; in lower pay for school teachers than for factory workers or tradesmen.

Lower wages may serve the purpose of crowding some professional workers— not all of them underpaid, by any means—out of their chosen professions into other jobs where they may or may not be able to capitalize on their training. Is this not merely the principle of supply and demand at work in the field of education, it may be asked? One might call it that. But there is something wrong with a principle of supply and demand which steadily produces a flow of college-trained people who cannot be accommodated in their chosen professions. If, under an expanded program of higher learning, the candidates out-numbered the jobs five or six to one, serious complications might set in.

What are the likely results? Would we be compelled to change some of our attitudes toward higher learning? Would medical societies and bar associations meet the problem by recourse to more severe restrictionism? How would a college-graduate population five times as large as in 1932 react to a severe depression and mass unemployment?

Some of the results can be anticipated. Frustration. Anti-intellectualism. The bolstering of revolutionary forces by millions of college graduates who had hoped to be executives, college teachers, physicians and lawyers. Bumper crops of new graduates thrown into an economy unprepared to absorb them would certainly bring with them a bumper crop of disillusionment. Kotschnig, in his important study of "Unemployment in the Learned Professions," showed well the contributions of the disappointed intellectuals to the rise of fascism in Europe.

What is the answer to the problem?

With a greater surplus of college graduates, many non-college men and women would undoubtedly be squeezed out of some professions, retailing and other employments. Legislatures could pass laws setting up a college degree as a requirement for certain kinds of employment. But a diploma should not serve as a passport when education does not contribute to the productivity of a profession. Too much insistence upon a college degree excludes other worthy candidates from jobs and further accelerates the stampede to college.

Inadequate facilities and restrictionism do not constitute a good defense against an overflow of professional workers. The supply and demand for professional people is a public rather than a group-interest problem, and public need does not always coincide with the self-interests of medical societies, for example. The nation spent three times as much for medicine in 1946 as it did in 1932. During this same fourteen-year period the number of doctors and dentists increased by only 5 per cent, though the rise for the economy as a whole was 55 per cent. To open the doors of the medical profession a little wider, it might be necessary to make a frontal attack on restrictionism, overhaul the financing of medicine and establish a comprehensive program of federal aid and health insurance.

Clearly there is need for a thorough study of the supply and demand for college-trained men and women. President Conant of Harvard has asked for an inventory of jobs and job-seekers. Commissioner of Education Spaulding has requested a similar survey for New York State. I have made a provisional census of the market for educated men and women. A more searching study awaits the financial support of Government or some large research organization. We are spending about 10 per cent of our national income on education. (This estimate allows for income foregone.) Perhaps it is time to spend some money trying to determine the relationship between education and the national economy.

One of the other needs is for improved publicity on the part of colleges and Government. What are the objects of a college education? What can a college graduate expect in the labor market? And just what does he expect? Perhaps many high school graduates are rushing off to college who should have stayed at home or joined the labor market.

Then again our traditional attitudes toward higher learning may need to be re-examined. We profess to believe in higher learning for its own sake. Yet we expect a college degree to pay cash dividends, to open up greater economic opportunities. Perhaps we overstress the vocational gains.

*   *   *

It may be that we should stop putting so much emphasis in our own minds on the monetary value of a college education and put more emphasis on the intangible social and cultural values to be derived from learning. The time may be coming when we will have to start accepting the idea that education is life, not merely a preparation for it. As John Dewey put it, "Living has its own intrinsic quality and the business of education is with that quality." In any case, the graduates of the next generation will have to find more and more justification for their college education on other than economic grounds.

In the meantime it is up to college administrators and to the Government to clarify the situation. The boy or girl preparing for college has a right to know what to expect.

STATEMENT ACCOMPANYING FORD FOUNDATION'S GRANT TO HIGHER EDUCATION (1955)   From *The New York Times*, December 13, 1955.

To supplement and encourage the efforts of the American people in meeting problems affecting the progress of the whole nation, the trustees of the Ford Foundation have approved special appropriations of $500,000,000 for privately supported institutions in communities all over the land.

This sum is in addition to new appropriations for projects under the foundation's established program, the total of which was approximately $30,000,000.

The $500,000,000 appropriated for the special programs, which will be paid out over the next eighteen months, includes:

$210,000,000 for grants to 615 regionally accredited privately supported liberal arts and science colleges and universities in the United States to help them raise teachers' salaries. This supplements the $50,000,000 appropriated last spring for teachers' salaries.

$200,000,000 for approximately 3,500 privately supported hospitals to help them improve and extend their services to the public.

$90,000,000 for privately supported medical schools to help them strengthen their instruction.

In March, 1955, the trustees announced an appropriation of $50,000,000 to be spent in helping America's privately supported colleges and universities raise the level of their faculty salaries. In a statement at that time Henry Ford 2d, Chairman of the board of trustees said:

"All the objectives of higher education ultimately depend upon the quality of teaching. In the opinion of the foundation's trustees, private and corporate philanthropy can make no better investment of its resources than in helping to strengthen American education at its base—the quality of its teaching.

"Nowhere are the needs of the private colleges more apparent than in the matter of faculty salaries. Merely to restore professors' salaries to their 1939 purchasing power would require an average increase of at least 20 per cent. Even this would not bring teachers in our private colleges to their economic position before World War II in relation to that of other professions and occupations. They have not begun to share the benefits of the expanded productive power of this nation, and the whole educational system suffers from this fact.

"Industry, commerce, government, the arts, the sciences and the professions—indeed our whole way of life—depends heavily upon the quality of our education. Recognizing this fact, the trustees of the Ford Foundation want to do everything they can to emphasize the cardinal importance of the college teacher to our society."

Shortly after this announcement an advisory committee was formed to study the problem, recommend a list of colleges which should receive the grants, and suggest a method by which the funds could be most effectively allocated.

*   *   *

The program recommended by the advisory committee was approved by the Trustees and consists of two parts:

A sum approximating its 1954–55 payroll for instruction in the liberal arts and sciences would be given to each of the 615 private, regionally accredited, four-year colleges and universities in the United States. The income from the endowment grant would be used for increasing faculty salaries. The total amount appropriated for these grants is $210,000,000.

An additional sum approximating one-half of last year's faculty salaries in the liberal arts and sciences would be given to 126 institutions which have led the way in their regions in improving the status and compensation of American college teachers. Income from this additional grant could be spent by these institutions either for raising faculty salaries or for other pressing academic needs. The total sum appropriated for these grants is $50,000,000.

The schools to receive the additional grant were selected by the advisory committee on the basis of replies to questionnaires sent to every regionally accredited privately supported college and university in the country. The Committee emphasized that "it did not attempt to compare the caliber of these many different colleges, their general excellence or reputation. Indeed, our study confirms the belief so widely held that variety of excellence is a healthy aspect of our entire system of higher education, whether publicly or privately supported. This variety cannot be readily reduced to mathematical comparisons or scores.

HOW PERFORMANCE IS EVALUATED IN THE ACADEMIC MARKETPLACE (1958)   From Theodore Caplow and Bruce McGee, *The Academic Marketplace* (New York, 1958), pp. 68–73.

In any discussion of contemporary standards for the evaluation of academic men, the first, and major, point to be made is that there is a great deal of confusion in American universities with regard to the role of the professor in his institution and profession. As Logan Wilson pointed out some years ago,

> In view of the vague and conflicting criteria by which his work is judged, he is uncertain in the allocation of his energies. He knows that he is a competitor, but often is not clear regarding the terms of the competition.

The foremost element in this confusion is uncertainty about the relative importance accorded to the two fundamental academic activities; teaching and research. The problem of the professor who is not research-minded is a formidable one. Basically, he is playing against time, since he has only a limited number of years in which to meet the requirements for tenure and to be reasonably assured of a future in his chosen profession. If he is able to publish at all, however, he is not impossibly handicapped, since the actual number of publications necessary to meet tenure requirements at most universities is not large. Once having a tenure appointment, he may drop all serious effort (although not all pretense) at research and still hope to receive further promotion and emolument for other services rendered to the university.

"Publish or Perish"

For most members of the profession, the real strain in the academic role arises from the fact that they are, in essence, paid to do one job, whereas the worth of their services is evaluated on the basis of how well they do another. The work assignment, for which the vast majority of professors are paid, is that of teaching. There are a few—a very few—who are supported by full- or part-time regular research appointments, but their number is insignificant compared to the vast majority who are hired to teach, and in whose contracts no specification of research duties is made. Most professors contract to perform teaching services for their universities and are hired to perform those services. When they are evaluated, however, either as candidates for a vacant position, or as candidates for promotion, the evaluation is made principally in terms of their research contributions to their disciplines. The following quotation is an interesting case in point; note the aftereffects on the peers.

> Among other things, he coached the student group. He got canned by an ad hoc committee which split 4 to 3 in his favor, but it was decided to can him on the basis of the split. Some of us feel that this was a case of real campus politics. It may have been honest and it may not, but it was clear that his really tremendous work with this student group hadn't been weighted at all in the consideration of his promotion. He did a really tremendous job. It caused the rest of us to decide that if this kind of activity was not what was honored—and he'd led them to several national recognitions—then we'd do what was honored—namely, sitting in the library and writing weighty papers, and let their goddamned student group go to hell, which it has.

It is neither an overgeneralization nor an oversimplification to state that in the faculties of major universities in the United States today, the evaluation of performance is based almost exclusively on publication of scholarly books or articles in professional journals as evidence of research activity. Out of 371 responses to the question, "Do you think he has reached the peak of his productivity as yet?" 122 respondents define "productivity" unmistakably as research, or publication of research; only 14 refer either directly or indirectly to the teaching of students; and 11 of these 14 qualify the importance of teaching in some way. The other 235 responses are so worded that it is impossible to state what criteria are being used for productivity. Throughout the interviews, however, departures from the publication formula for productivity are rare indeed. The explicit definition of publication as the criterion of productivity is very common. In addition, respondents often specifically exclude from consideration other activities, such as teaching, administration, creative artistry, public service, or internal service to the university.

"Yes, he's getting involved with administration there, and that's the kiss of death for any research."

"It's my opinion that he will never be a productive scholar. He reads very widely and will be content to be a teacher and perhaps do a little creative writing—he used to write poetry—but he will never be a producing scholar."

"She hasn't been in positions where productivity was demanded or even permitted. She's always been a practicing clinician; in her current job there's no time for research. I would say that if this goes on, her peak has been reached."

"In his new job, he's going to be led into more superficial kinds of writing—for popular consumption—well, summaries for businessmen."

It has been suggested that the recent emphasis on team research in the social and physical sciences may be, in part, a protective device for the non-research-minded professor and for his counterpart who can do research but finds it difficult to put his results in publishable form. There is some evidence, of an admittedly speculative character, to support this contention. It appears that research teams are usually composed of one strong research worker, or "idea man," and a number of less brilliant colleagues working more or less under his direction. It is also commonly alleged that team research is somehow identified with qualitatively inferior work. These are only assertions, however, and there are many instances of brilliant results attributable to teams, and of research situations (*e.g.* high-energy nuclear physics) which require team effort. Certainly a team may provide the protection of joint publication for a man who would not otherwise see his name in print. Until quite recently, no such recourse was available, but, on the other hand, teaching had greater importance.

> He came here as a young man, and at the time the head of the department forbade research—said that it destroyed a man's capacity to teach.

It is interesting, after this echo of an older ethic, to realize that the criterion of publication is rationalized today by the argument that research activity is essential to effective teaching. Formerly, it was possible to make a career either in the university or in the discipline, and the man who chose a local career sustained himself through service to the institution and personal relationships in the faculty. The campus elder statesman is still a familiar figure on American university campuses, but it would seem that, as the present elders retire, there will not be many of a younger generation to take their places.

Today, a scholar's orientation to his institution is apt to disorient him to his discipline and to affect his professional prestige unfavorably. Conversely, an orientation to his discipline will disorient him to his institution, which he will regard as a temporary shelter where he can pursue his career as a member of the discipline. And he will be, as a matter of course, considerably more mobile than his institutionally oriented colleagues. In a handful of great universities, where many of the departments believed to be the best in their fields are found, a merger of orientations is possible. There a man may simultaneously serve an institution and a discipline and identify with both. But tensions exist between the two orientations everywhere. It is worthy of note that the publication requirements in the highest ranking departments are the most rigid, so that the men they select have already met the requirements imposed by the discipline.

Several respondents referred to the "guild aspect" of certain disciplines— especially mathematics and physics. Their comments seem to assert that, in these fields at least, for the successful professor the institutional orientation has entirely disappeared.

The Career Curve

We note in the responses of informants that peaks are always found, or assumed, in the academic career. It is a familiar fact that in different occupations careers tend to peak at different ages. This occurs within the academic profession as well, with considerable variation from one discipline to another. The extremes may be represented by history, a field in which men in their late forties are often referred to as "young," and by mathematics, where men are frequently said to have "burned out" (*i.e.,* completed their contributive careers) in their early thirties.

> I'd say he reached his mathematical peak years ago. There are damned few people that do any thinking after they're forty. I'm not competent to judge any other kind of peak. I'm no intellectual—neither was he.

There are many questions of superannuation which affect the contemporary academic labor market. A common theme is the dissatisfaction of younger men with the productivity of their elders. The following quotations illustrate the tone of a number of such responses.

"Yes, his leaving meant that there are no longer any nonproductive full professors. He had little sympathy for graduate work and research."

"He believed that conviviality and sociability were the prime qualities for a professor. We had parties twice a month, played golf, etc., all the time. We also had a lousy department. There have been some fundamental changes around here."

It is impossible to say just how much of the reported superannuation is due to a real decrease in research potential and how much to the encounter between the institutional orientation of the older men and the disciplinary orientation of the younger (with its increased stress on publication). It has been remarked before that prestige is, in part, a function of mobility or potential mobility, and that an older man's potential mobility is low.

An academic man's career is normally only half over at the age of fifty. Most academic men enter the labor market today at about thirty, upon receipt of the Ph.D., and since the usual age of compulsory retirement is about seventy, a man of fifty can still look forward to as many working years as lie behind him. Yet, unless he is widely known, his mobility after fifty is very, very limited. We can see two reasons for this. The first is that the retirement plans in effect at most institutions require a fairly long term of service for sizable benefits to accrue; the second is that evaluation by the criterion of research productivity tends to fix the market value of a man in proportion to the volume of future research expected from him. (We would expect, therefore, that the mobility potential of a middle-aged historian would be higher than that of a mathematician of the same age. The data of the study do not permit a test of this expectation.)

THE IDEA OF THE MULTIVERSITY (1963)   From Clark Kerr, *The Uses of the University* (New York, 1963), pp. 1, 18–19, 36–37, 41–45.

The university started as a single community—a community of masters and students. It may even be said to have had a soul in the sense of a central animating principle. Today the large American university is, rather, a whole series of communities and activities held together by a common name, a common governing board, and related purposes. This great transformation is regretted by some, accepted by many, gloried in, as yet, by few. But it should be understood by all.

The university of today can perhaps be understood, in part, by comparing it with what it once was—with the academic cloister of Cardinal Newman, with the research organism of Abraham Flexner. Those are the ideal types from which it has derived, ideal types which still constitute the illusions of some of its inhabitants. . . .

*   *   *

The Governance of the Multiversity

The multiversity is an inconsistent institution. It is not one community but several— the community of the undergraduate and the community of the graduate; the community of the humanist, the community of the social scientist, and the community of the scientist; the communities of the professional schools; the community of all the nonacademic personnel; the community of the administrators. Its edges are fuzzy—it reaches out to alumni, legislators, farmers, businessmen, who are all related to one or more of these internal communities. As an institution, it looks far into the past and far into the future, and is often at odds with the present. It serves society almost slavishly—a society it also criticizes, sometimes unmercifully. Devoted to equality of opportunity, it is itself a class society. A community, like the medieval communities of masters and students, should have common interests; in the multiversity, they are quite varied, even conflicting. A community should have a soul, a single animating principle; the multiversity has several—some of them quite good, although there is much debate on which souls really deserve salvation.

The multiversity is a name. This means a great deal more than it sounds as though it might. The name of the institution stands for a certain standard of performance, a certain degree of respect, a certain historical legacy, a characteristic quality of spirit. This is of the utmost importance to faculty and to students, to the government agencies and the industries with which the institution deals. . . .

✳ ✳ ✳

Academic government has taken the form of the Guild, as in the colleges of Oxford and Cambridge until recent times; of the Manor, as in Columbia under Butler; and of the United Nations, as in the modern multiversity. There are several "nations" of students, of faculty, of alumni, of trustees, of public groups. Each has its territory, its jurisdiction, its form of government. Each can declare war on the others; some have the power of veto. Each can settle its own problems by a majority vote, but altogether they form no single constituency. It is a pluralistic society with multiple cultures. Coexistence is more likely than unity. Peace is one priority item, progress another.

The president in the multiversity is leader, educator, creator, initiator, wielder of power, pump; he is *also* officeholder, caretaker, inheritor, consensus-seeker, persuader, bottleneck. But he is mostly a mediator.

The first task of the mediator is peace—how he may "the Two-and-Seventy jarring Sects confute." Peace within the student body, the faculty, the trustees; and peace between and among them. Peace between the "Two Cultures" and the "Three Cultures" and their subcultures; among all the ideas competing for support. Peace between the internal evironment of the academic community and the external society that surrounds and sometimes almost engulfs it. But peace has its attributes. There is the "workable compromise" of the day that resolves the current problem. Beyond this lies the effective solution that enhances the long-run distinction and character of the institution. In seeking it, there are some things that should not be compromised, like freedom and quality—then the mediator needs to become the gladiator. The dividing lines between these two roles may not be as clear as crystal, but they are at least as fragile.

The second task is progress; institutional and personal survival are not enough. A multiversity is inherently a conservative institution but with radical functions. There are so many groups with a legitimate interest in the status quo, so many veto groups; yet the university must serve a knowledge explosion and a population explosion simultaneously. The president becomes the central mediator among the values of the past, the prospects for the future, and the realities of the present. He is the mediator among groups and institutions moving at different rates of speed and sometimes in different directions; a carrier of change—as infectious and sometimes as feared as a "Typhoid Mary." He is not an innovator for the sake of innovation, but he must be sensitive to the fruitful innovation. He has no new and bold "vision of the end." He is driven more by necessity than by voices in the air. . . .

*   *   *

Life in the Multiversity

The "Idea of a University" was a village with its priests. The "Idea of a Modern University" was a town—a one-industry town—with its intellectual oligarchy. "The Idea of a Multiversity" is a city of infinite variety. Some get lost in the city; some rise to the top within it; most fashion their lives within one of its many subcultures. There is less sense of community than in the village but also less sense of confinement. There is less sense of purpose than within the town but there are more ways to excel. There are also more refuges of anonymity—both for the creative person and the drifter. As against the village and the town, the "city" is more like the totality of civilization as it has evolved and more an integral part of it; and movement to and from the surrounding society has been greatly accelerated. As in a city, there are many separate endeavors under a single rule of law.

The students in the "city" are older, more likely to be married, more vocationally oriented, more drawn from all classes and races than the students in the village; and they find themselves in a most intensely competitive atmosphere. They identify less with the total community and more with its subgroups. Burton R. Clark and Martin Trow have a particularly interesting typology of these subcultures: the "collegiate" of the fraternities and sororities and the athletes and activities majors; the "academic" of the serious students; the "vocational" of the students seeking training for specific jobs; and the "nonconformist" of the political activists, the aggressive intellectuals, and the bohemians. These subcultures are not mutually exclusive, and some of the fascinating pageantry of the multiversity is found in their interaction one on another.

The multiversity is a confusing place for the student. He has problems of establishing his identity and sense of security within it. But it offers him a vast range of choices, enough literally to stagger the mind. In this range of choices he encounters the opportunities and the dilemmas of freedom. The casualty rate is high. The walking wounded are many. *Lernfreiheit*—the freedom of the student to pick and choose, to stay or to move on—is triumphant.

Life has changed also for the faculty member. The multiversity is in the main stream of events. To the teacher and the researcher have been added the consultant and the administrator. Teaching is less central than it once was for most faculty members; research has become more important. This has given rise to what has been called the "non-teacher"—"the higher a man's standing, the less he has to do with students"—and to a threefold class structure of what used to be "the faculty": those who only do research, those who only teach (and they are largely in an auxiliary role), and those who still do some of both. In one university I know, the proportions at the Ph.D. level or its equivalent are roughly one researcher to two teachers to four who do both.

Consulting work and other sources of additional income have given rise to what is called the "affluent professor," a category that does include some but by no means all of the faculty. Additionally, many faculty members, with their research assistants and teaching assistants, their departments and institutes, have become administrators. A professor's life has become, it is said, "a rat race of business and activity, managing contracts and projects, guiding teams and assistants, bossing crews of technicians, making numerous trips, sitting on committees for government agencies, and engaging in other distractions necessary to keep the whole frenetic business from collapse."

The intellectual world has been fractionalized as interests have become much more diverse; and there are fewer common topics of conversation at the faculty clubs. Faculty government has become more cumbersome, more the avocation of active minorities; and there are real questions whether it can work effectively on a large scale, whether it can agree on more than preservation of the status quo. Faculty members are less members of the particular university and more colleagues within their national academic discipline groups.

But there are many compensations. "The American professoriate" is no longer, as Flexner once called it, "a proletariat." Salaries and status have risen considerably. The faculty member is more a fully participating member of society, rather than a creature on the periphery; some are at the very center of national and world events. Research opportunities have been enormously increased. The faculty member within the big mechanism and with all his opportunities has a new sense of independence from the domination of the administration or his colleagues; much administration has been effectively decentralized to the level of the individual professor. In particular, he has a choice of roles and mixtures of roles to suit his taste as never before. He need not leave the Groves for the Acropolis unless he wishes; but he can, if he wishes. He may even become, as some have, essentially a professional man with his home office and basic retainer on the campus of the multiversity but with his clients scattered from coast to coast. He can also even remain the professor of old, as many do. There are several patterns of life from which to choose. So the professor too has greater freedom. *Lehrfreiheit*, in the old German sense of the freedom of the professor to do as he pleases, also is triumphant.

What is the justification of the modern American multiversity? History is one answer. Consistency with the surrounding society is another. Beyond that, it has few peers in the preservation and dissemination and examination of the eternal truths; no living peers in the search for new knowledge; and no peers in all history among institutions of higher learning in serving so many of the segments of an advancing civilization. Inconsistent internally as an institution, it is consistently productive. Torn by change, it has the stability of freedom. Though it has not a single soul to call its own, its members pay their devotions to truth.

The multiversity in America is perhaps best seen at work, adapting and growing, as it responded to the massive impact of federal programs beginning with World War II. A vast transformation has taken place without a revolution, for a time almost without notice being taken. The multiversity has demonstrated how adaptive it can be to new opportunities for creativity; how responsive to money; how eagerly it can play a new and useful role; how fast it can change while pretending that nothing has happened at all; how fast it can neglect some of its ancient virtues. What are the current realities of the federal grant university?

Adult Education

THOMAS DAVIDSON ON THE "BREADWINNERS COLLEGE" OF NEW YORK CITY (1899), From "The Higher Education of the Breadwinners," as quoted in William Knight, ed. *Memorials of Thomas Davidson, the Wandering Scholar* (Boston, 1907), pp. 89–97.

It cannot be said of our people that they are backward or niggardly in the matter of education. In no country is so much money expended upon schools and colleges as in the United States. And yet our people are very far from being educated as they ought to be. Ignorance is still widespread, and not only the ignorant, but the whole nation suffers in consequence. In spite of our magnificent system of public schools and our numerous colleges and universities—over five hundred in all—the great body of our citizens lack the education necessary to give dignity and meaning to their individual lives, and to fit them for the worthy performance of their duties as members of the institutions under which they live. Our public schools stop short too soon, while our colleges do not reach more than one in a thousand of our population. Moreover, neither school nor college imparts that education which our citizens, as such, require—domestic, social, and civic culture. What is imparted is defective both in kind and in extent.

There are three kinds of education, which ought to be distinguished, but which at present we do not distinguish with sufficient care: (1) culture, that is, the education neccessary for every human being, in order that he may be able worthily to fulfill duties as a member of social institutions; (2) professional training, necessary for the earning of a livelihood; (3) erudition, demanded by those who would advance science, or give instruction in it. It is regrettable that both in our schools and in our colleges these are hopelessly mixed up, and that the first receives but scanty attention.

Even more regrettable is the fact that our schools and colleges, for the most part, confine their attention to persons who have nothing to do but study, who are not engaged in any kind of useful or porductive labor. This results in two evils: (1) education, for the great body of the people, must stop at an early age, since children of all but wealthy families must go to work as soon as possible, few of them reaching the high school, fewer yet the university, or professional training school; (2) education is withheld just from those who are in the best position to profit by it; for every teacher with sufficient experience knows that people who have a knowledge of practical life and its duties are far better and more encouraging pupils that those who have not.

It thus appears that social and civic culture is largely neglected in our educational institutions, and that it altogether fails to reach those who are best fitted to profit by it. In a word, the culture calculated to make the wise and good citizen is almost nonexistent. We have good artisans, good merchants, good doctors, good lawyers, etc., in abundance, but we have few persons of liberal culture, and still fewer who can worthily fill important offices in society and state, or who can even cast an intelligent vote for such. Fewest of all, those who understand how their lives affect the general welfare, whence the money they earn comes, and whether or not it is an equivalent for benefits conferred upon society.

Thus it comes to pass that the lives of the great mass of our citizens are unintelligent, narrow, sordid, envious, and unhappy, and that we are constantly threatened with popular uprisings and the overthrow of our free institutions. Thus, too, it comes that our politics are base, and our politicians venal and selfish. The laboring classes are, through want of education, easily cozened or bribed to vote in opposition to their own best interests, and so to condemn themselves to continued slavish toil and poverty, which means exclusion from all share in the spiritual wealth of the race.

There is, at the present time, perhaps no individual problem in our country [so pressing] as that of the higher education—the intellectual, moral, and social culture—of that great body of men and women, who, from a pretty early age, have to spend the larger portion of their time in earning a livelihood. These include not only the working classes so-called—the skilled and unskilled laborers—but also the great majority of the wage-earners of every sort, and not a few of the wage-givers. all these need a larger world, a more ideal outlook, such as education alone can give, not only to impart meaning and dignity to their life of toil, but also to enable them to contribute their share to the well-being of society, and prevent it from falling back into violence and barbarism.

It is true that, in the last few years, considerable efforts have been made to provide the breadwinners with opportunities both for professional training and for higher culture. In our larger cities "university extension" has been introduced, training schools have been opened, and evening schools and lectures on a large scale established. Of these efforts there is nothing but good to say. They are, however, a promise rather than a fulfillment, a beginning and little more. They must be greatly extended and systematized before they can meet the needs of the breadwinners. The training schools are, of course, an unmixed good, and we only require more of them; but the university extension, to a large extent, imparts a sort of education that is not demanded, and fails to give much that is demanded, while both it and the evening classes and lectures are deficient in system and unity of plan. Neither has a distinct aim, and neither sufficiently controls the work of the pupils. Worst of all, both exclude from their programmes some of the very subjects which it is most essential for the breadwinners to be acquainted with—economics, sociology, politics, religion, etc.

Of the three kinds of education, the breadwinners need only two—(1) technical training,[1] (2) intellectual and moral, or social training.[2] The breadwinner, if his

[1] A clear distinction should be drawn between manual training which should be imparted in the common schools to all children without distinction, as part of their general education—and technical training which should be given, as a preparation for a special profession, to those intending to follow that profession.

[2] I do not mean that any one should be shut out from erudition. I mean that erudition is not a necessity for the breadwinner. I think, too, that all distinction between liberal and illiberal professions should be blotted out.

work is to be effective, and equivalent to a decent livelihood, earnable with a moderate expenditure of time and energy, must have skill; otherwise he will have neither time nor energy left for any other sort of education. Spare time and energy are prime elements in the whole question. In any just order of society each member will receive from society a just equivalent for what he contributes to it. If he is so unskilled that his work is not equivalent to a livelihood, he has no right to complain when he suffers want. It must therefore be the aim of every one who would humanize and elevate the breadwinners to see that they have skill enough to earn their daily bread without depriving themselves of free time, and energy to devote to living and spiritual culture.

Supposing now that all the breadwinners were in this conditions that, being able to earn a living in, say, eight hours a day, they had considerable free time; they might still remain uncultured and sordid, their tastes vulgar or depraved. They might still have litttle rest and joy in life, little inspiring outlook. They might still not be valuable members of society. We have not done our whole duty by the breadwinners when we have made themm comfortable—we must go further and make them cultured and wise.

Now what must be the nature of such culture and wisdom? We may answer, Such as shall enable their recipients to play a worthy and generous part in all the relations of life and to enjoy those high satisfactions that come of such worthiness. We may express this otherwise, by saying that they must be such as to enable a man to know and understand his environment; to take an intelligent interest in all that goes on, or has gone on in the world; to enter into lofty personal relations, and to live clean, tasteful, useful, self-respecting lives. The relation for which culture should prepare are: (1) personal, (2) domestic, (3) social (including economic), (4) political. It would be possible to arrange a system of education on the basis of this classification; but it is necessary to do so. The different relations, however, ought to be kept in view in arranging any course of culture studies.

Perhaps the following curriculum, extending over three or four years, might meet the needs of the breadwinners in the present condition:

1. Evolution: its theory and history.
2. History of civilization.
3. The system of the sciences.
4. Sociology.
5. Political theory and history.
6. History of industry and commerce.
7. History of education (physhology).
8. History of science and philosophy.
9. History of ethical theory.
10. Comparative religion.
11. Comparative literature.
12. History and theory of the fine arts.

In following out this curriculum the greatest care should be taken to avoid any imposing of any special theory or doctrine—religious, political, economical, etc.—upon the pupils. All theories should be freely discussed without bias, party spirit, or passion, and every effort made to elicit the truth from the pupils themselves. The important thing is that they should learn to think for themselves, and thus become morally free. With a view to this the work of the teacher should consist mostly in direction and encouragement. The less he does himself, and the more his pupils do, the better. Lecturing should be resorted to only by way of introduction; then the seminary method should be followed. As a rule, some handy, compact, epochmaking book should be made the basis of work, for example, Aristotle's *Politics* for political theory and history; then a list of books should be given for the pupils to analyze, epitomize, and criticise in written essays, to be read and discussed before the class. Then when difficult points come up or deeper researches have to be made these should be assigned as subjects for special essays. In this way a wide knowledge of each subject and of its literature will be gained and a deep interest aroused.[3]

The curriculum as a whole will impart just the unitary views of the world and its agencies which will give meaning and zest to the individual life and make the good citizen.

At the close of each study the pupils should be asked to sum up, in a brief essay of not more than five hundred words, what they have learned from it. This will take the place of an examination.

Having settled what kind of culture is necessary for the breadwinners, we must next consider how it may be best brought with their reach. For this, two things above all are necessary: (1) that they should know what is proposed, and recognize its value; (2) that they should have spare time, energy, and convenience for continued study.

The former of these aims may be reached throught the public press— newspapers, magazines, etc.—and through lecturers, which are here in order. It is needless to dwell on the efficiency of the press in bringing things before the public: but a few words may be said about lectures. It would be of the utmost moment to arrange for a course of ten lectures, covering as many weeks, and given on some convenient evening[4] when most of the breadwinners of the neighborhood could attend. The following are suggested as titles for such lectures:

1. The present state of education among the breadwinners, and their opportunities for obtaining higher education. What the schools do.

2. The education needed by the breadwinners, and how it must differ from school and college education.

3. The education needed by the individual, in order to lift him above narrow, sordid ends.

4. The education needed for the ends of the family.

5. The education needed for the ends of civil society, for the tradesman, the merchant, etc. (1) Technical education. (2) Moral training.

6. The education needed by the citizen.

7. The need of unity, system,and aim in education. The defects of our present education in this respect.

8. How can education be carried into the home?

9. The state's duty in regard to the culture of the breadwinners.

10. A scheme for a breadwinners' culture institute, to be established in every township and in every city ward, to supplement our public schools.

I cannot but think that, if such a course of lectures were given at a convenient time by competent persons, carefully reported in the daily newspapers, and afterwards printed in the form of a cheap book, it would meet with a hearty response from the breadwinners.

It is necessary, not only that breadwinners should be brought to desire higher culture, but also that they should have the time, energy, and convenience to acquire

[3]I employed this method in my class last winter with considerable success.

[4]Or on Sunday afternoon. There could hardly be any more religious work than this.

it. How this is to be done is one of the great social questions of the day, and one that I do not purpose to answer here; but of two things I am morally certain: (1) that it cannot effectually be done by any legislation in favor of an eight-hour working day, or anything of that sort; and (2) that, if the breadwinners made it evident that they desired free time in order to devote it to self-culture, from which they are debarred by long hours of labor, public sentiment would soon insist that such time should be accorded them, and provisions made for such culture. One main reason why the demand for shorter hours meets with comparatively little response from the public, is the prevalent belief that a very large number of breadwinners would make a bad use of the spare time, spending it in saloons and other coarse resorts. Labor, it is said, is better or more profitable than idleness and saloon life. And there is some reason in this. Spare time demanded for culture would most certainly be accorded, and it will, I think, hardly ever be obtained on any other plea. I need hardly add that spare time would bring with it spare energy; for it is the long hours that exhaust the energies.

Along with time and energy the breadwinners must have home conveniences for study. Many of course have these, but many have not. In crowded rooms or apartments in tenement houses it is hard to find a quiet corner for study, and the public libraries and reading rooms offer conveniences for but a small number. This state of things must be remedied, and, I think would be remedied as soon as there was any genuine desire for culture. Persons inspired by this would refuse to live where they could not have conveniences for study, and would thus be brought to demand a higher standard of living, a thing altogether desirable. At the same time public reading rooms would doubtless increase.

At the present time we hear a great deal about saloon politics and the corruption that results from them; and manifold efforts are made to start rivals to the saloon, which a very reverend bishop has told us is the poor man's clubroom. It is sad to think that the bishop is right, and that the poor man has not been able, thus far, to establish any other sort of club room. It is my firm belief that the successful rival of the saloon will not be the coffee room, the reading room, the pool room, or the concert room, but the lecture room and the school room, with their various appurtenances and opportunities. I believe that we shall never be able to put a stop to the deleterious effects of the saloon upon individual, domestic, social, and political life, until we establish in every city ward and in every village a culture institute for the great body of the people who are engaged in business during the day,—an institute composed of three parts: (1) a technical school,[5] (2) a civic-culture school, and (3) a gymnasium. Such institutions must sooner or later be established by the state, and supported by public funds as part of the system of public education; but at present it is well that they should be undertaken by private effort, and their utility, yea, their necessity, clearly shown. The Educational Alliance is in a position to take an important step in this direction, and it can do so by establishing a system of evening classes with a programme such as I have sketched, and appealing to the breadwinners by a course of lectures of the nature I have indicated.

[5] An excellent model for this is the London Polytechnic (in Regent Street), which owes its existence to the energy and generosity of one man, W. Q. Hogg. It has several rivals in London now.

ADULT EDUCATION AT HULL HOUSE (1911) From Jane Addams, *Twenty Years at Hull-House* (New York, 1911), pp. 428–31, 434–38, 452–53.

Hull-House in the very beginning opened what we called College Extension Classes with a faculty finally numbering thirty-five college men and women, many of whom held their pupils for consecutive years. As these classes antedated in Chicago the University Extension and Normal Extension classes and supplied a demand for stimulating instruction, the attendance strained to their utmost capacity the spacious rooms in the old house. The relation of students and faculty to each other and to the residents was that of guest and hostess and at the close of each term the residents gave a reception to students and faculty which was one of the chief social events of the season. Upon this comfortable social basis some very good work was done.

In connection with these classes a Hull-House summer school was instituted at Rockford College, which was most generously placed at our disposal by the trustees. For ten years one hundred women gathered there for six weeks, in addition there were always men on the faculty, and a small group of young men among the students who were lodged in the gymnasium building. The outdoor classes in bird study and botany, the serious reading of literary masterpieces, the boat excursions on the Rock River, the cooperative spirit of doing the housework together, the satirical commencements in parti-colored caps and gowns, lent themselves toward a reproduction of the comradeship which college life fosters.

As each member of the faculty, as well as the students, paid three dollars a week, and as we had little outlay beyond the actual cost of food, we easily defrayed our expenses. The undertaking was so simple and gratifying in results that it might well be reproduced in many college buildings which are set in the midst of beautiful surroundings, unused during the two months of the year, when hundreds of people, able to pay only a moderate price for lodgings in the country, can find nothing comfortable and no mental food more satisfying than piazza gossip.

Every Thursday evening during the first years, a public lecture came to be an expected event in the neighborhood, and Hull-House became one of the early University Extension centers, first in connection with an independent society and later with the University of Chicago. One of the Hull-House trustees was so impressed with the value of this orderly and continuous presentation of economic subjects that he endowed three courses in a downtown center, in which the lectures were free to any one who chose to come. He was much pleased that these lectures were largely attended by workingmen who ordinarily prefer that an economic subject shall be presented by a partisan, and who are supremely indifferent to examinations and credits. They also dislike the balancing of pro and con which scholarly instruction implies, and prefer to be "inebriated on raw truth" rather than to sip a carefully prepared draught of knowledge.

Nevertheless Bowen Hall, which seats seven hundred and fifty people, is often none too large to hold the audiences of men who come to Hull-House every Sunday evening during the winter to attend the illustrated lectures provided by the faculty of the University of Chicago, and others who kindly give their services. These courses differ enormously in their popularity; one on European capitals and their social significance was followed with the most vivid attention and sense of participation indicated by groans and hisses when the audience was reminded of an unforgettable feud between Austria and her Slavic subjects, or when they wildly applauded a Polish hero endeared through his tragic failure.

In spite of the success of these Sunday evening courses, it has never been an easy undertaking to find acceptable lecturers.

❋   ❋   ❋

Therefore the residents of Hull-House place increasing emphasis upon the great inspirations and solaces of literature and are unwilling that it should ever languish as a subject for class instruction or for reading parties. The Shakespeare club has lived a continuous existence at Hull-House for sixteen years during which time its members have heard the leading interpreters of Shakespeare, both among scholars and players. I recall that one of its earliest members said that her mind was peopled with Shakespeare characters during her long hours of sewing in a shop, that she couldn't remember what she thought about before she joined the club, and concluded that she hadn't thought about anything at all. To feed the mind of the worker, to lift it above the monotony of his task, and to connect it with the larger world, outside of his immediate surroundings, has always been the object of art, perhaps never more nobly fulfilled than by the great English bard. Miss Starr has held classes in Dante and Browning for many years and the great lines are conned with never failing enthusiasm. I recall Miss Lathrop's Plato club and an audience who listened to a series of lectures by Dr. John Dewey on "Social Psychology," as genuine intellectual groups consisting largely of people from the immediate neighborhood, who were willing to make "that effort from which we all shrink, the effort of thought." But while we prize these classes as we do the help we are able to give to the exceptional young man or woman who reaches the college and university and leaves the neighborhood of his childhood behind him, the residents of Hull-House feel increasingly that the educational efforts of a Settlement should not be directed primarily to reproduce the college type of culture, but to work out a method and an ideal adapted to the immediate situation. They feel that they should promote a culture which will not set its possessor aside in a class with others like himself, but which will, on the contrary, connect him with all sorts of people by his ability to understand them as well as by his power to supplement their present surroundings with the historic background. Among the hundreds of immigrants who have for years attended classes at Hull-House designed primarily to teach the English language, dozens of them have struggled to express in the newly acquired tongue some of those hopes and longings which had so much to do with their emigration.

A series of plays was thus written by a young Bohemian; essays by a Russian youth, outpouring sorrows rivaling Werther himself and yet containing the precious stuff of youth's perennial revolt against accepted wrong; stories of Russian oppression and petty injustices throughout which the desire for free America became a crystallized hope; an attempt to portray the Jewish day of Atonement, in such wise that even individualistic Americans may catch a glimpse of that deeper national life which has survived all transplanting and expresses itself in forms so ancient that they appear grotesque to the ignorant spectator. I remember a pathetic effort on the part of a young Russian Jewess to describe the vivid inner life of an old Talmud scholar, probably her uncle or father, as of one persistently occupied with the grave and important things of the spirit, although when brought into sharp contact with busy and overworked people, he inevitably appeared self-absorbed and slothful. Certainly no one who had read her paper could again see such an old man in his praying shawl bent over his crabbed book, without a sense of understanding.

On the other hand, one of the most pitiful periods in the drama of the much-praised young American who attempts to rise in life, is the time when his educational requirements seem to have locked him up and made him rigid. He fancies himself shut off from his uneducated family and misunderstood by his friends. He is bowed down by his mental accumulations and often gets no farther than to carry them through life as a great burden, and not once does he obtain a glimpse of the delights of knowledge.

The teacher in a Settlement is constantly put upon his mettle to discover methods of instruction which shall make knowledge quickly available to his pupils, and I should like here to pay my tribute of admiration to the dean of our educational department, Miss Landsberg, and to the many men and women who every winter come regularly to Hull-House, putting untiring energy into the endless task of teaching the newly arrived immigrant the first use of a language of which he has such desperate need. Even a meager knowledge of English may mean an opportunity to work in a factory versus nonemployment, or it may mean a question of life and death when a sharp command must be understood in order to avoid the danger of a descending crane.

In response to a demand for an education which should be immediately available, classes have been established and grown apace in cooking, dressmaking, and millinery. A girl who attends them will often say that she "expects to marry a workingman next spring," and because she has worked in a factory so long she knows "little about a house." Sometimes classes are composed of young matrons of like factory experiences. I recall one of them whose husband had become so desperate after two years of her unskilled cooking that he had threatened to desert her and go where he could get "decent food," as she confided to me in a tearful interview, when she followed my advice to take the Hull-House courses in cooking, and at the end of six months reported a united and happy home.

* * *

Life in the Settlement discovers above all what has been called "the extraordinary pliability of human nature," and it seems impossible to set any bounds to the moral capabilities which might unfold under ideal civic and educational conditions. But in order to obtain these conditions, the Settlement recognizes the need of cooperation, both with the radical and the conservative, and from the very nature of the case the Settlement cannot limit its friends to any one political party or economic school.

The Settlement casts aside none of those things which cultivated men have come to consider reasonable and goodly, but it insists that those belong as well to that great body of people who, because of toilsome and underpaid labor, are unable to procure them for themselves. Added to this is a profound conviction that the common stock of intellectual enjoyment should not be difficult of access because of the economic position of him who would approach it, that those "best results of civilization" upon which depend the finer and freer aspects of living must be incorporated into our common life and have free mobility through all elements of society if we would have our democracy endure.

* * *

The educational activities of a Settlement, as well as its philanthropic, civic, and social undertakings, are but differing manifestations of the attempt to socialize democracy, as is the very existence of the Settlement itself.

A NIGHT SCHOOL FOR ADULT IMMIGRANTS: THE CASE OF MR. KAPLAN (1937) From Leonard Q. Ross, *The Education of Hyman Kaplan* (New York, 1937), pp. 3–12.

In the third week of the new term, Mr. Parkhill was forced to the conclusion that Mr. Kaplan's case was rather difficult. Mr. Kaplan first came to his special attention, out of the thirty-odd adults in the beginners' grade of the American Night Preparatory School for Adults ("English—Americanization— Civics—Preparation for Naturalization"), through an exercise the class had submitted. The exercise was entitled "Fifteen Common Nouns and Their Plural Forms." Mr. Parkhill came to one paper which included the following:

house	makes	houses
dog	"	dogies
libary	"	Public libary
cat	"	Katz

Mr. Parkhill read this over several times, very thoughtfully. He decided that here was a student who might, unchecked, develop into a "problem case." It was clearly a case that called for special attention. He turned the page over and read the name. It was printed in large, firm letters with red crayon. Each letter was outlined in blue. Between every two letters was a star, carefully drawn, in green. The multicolored whole spelled, unmistakably HYMAN KAPLAN.

This Mr. Kaplan was in his forties, a plump, red-faced gentleman, with wavy blond hair, two fountain pens in his outer pocket, and a perpetual smile. It was a strange smile, Mr. Parkhill remarked: vague, bland, and consistent in its monotony. The thing that emphasized it for Mr. Parkhill was that it never seemed to leave the face of Mr. Kaplan, even during Recitation and Speech period. This disturbed Mr. Parkhill considerably, because Mr. Kaplan was particularly bad in Recitation and Speech.

Mr. Parkhill decided he had not applied himself as conscientiously as he might to Mr. Kaplan's case. That very night he called on Mr. Kaplan first.

"Won't you take advantage of Recitation and Speech practice, Mr. Kaplan?" he asked, with an encouraging smile.

Mr. Kaplan smiled back and answered promptly, "Vell, I'll tell abot Prazidents United States. Fife Prazidents United States is Abram Lincohen, he was freeink de neegers; Hodding, Coolitch, Judge Vashington, an' Banjamin Frenklin."

Further encouragement revealed that in Mr. Kaplan's literary Valhalla the "most famous tree American wriders" were Jeck Laundon, Valt Viterman, and the author of "Hawk L. Barry-Feen," one Mocktvain. Mr. Kaplan took pains to point out that

HIGHER
EDUCATION

2835

he did not mention Relfvaldo Amerson because "He is a poyet, an' I'm talkink abot wriders."

Mr. Parkhill diagnosed the case as one of "inability to distinguish between 'a' and 'e'" He concluded that Mr. Kaplan would need special attention. He was, frankly, a little disturbed.

Mr. Kaplan's English showed no improvement during the next hard weeks. The orginality of his spelling and pronunciation, however, flourished—like a sturdy flower in the good, rich earth. A man to whom "Katz" is the plural of "cat" soon soars into higher and more ambitious endeavor. As a one-paragraph "Exercise in Composition," Mr. Kaplan submitted:

> When people is meating on the boulvard, on going away one is saying, "I am glad I mat you," and the other is giving answer, "Mutual."

Mr. Parkhill felt that perhaps Mr. Kaplan had overreached himself, and should be confined to the simpler exercises.

Mr. Kaplan was an earnest student. He worked hard, knit his brows regularly (albeit with that smile), did all his homework, and never missed a class. Only once did Mr. Parkhill feel that Mr. Kaplan might, perhaps, be a little more serious about his work. That was when he asked Mr. Kaplan to "give a noun."

"Door," said Mr. Kaplan, smiling.

It seemed to Mr. Parkhill that "door" had been given only a moment earlier, by Miss Mitnick.

"Y-es," said Mr. Parkhill. "Er—and another noun?"

"Another door," Mr. Kaplan replied promptly.

Mr. Parkhill put him down as a doubtful "C." Everything pointed to the fact that Mr. Kaplan might have to be kept on an extra three months before he was ready for promotion to Composition, Grammar, and Civics, with Miss Higby.

One night Mrs. Moskowitz read a sentence, from "English for Beginners," in which "the vast deserts of America" were referred to. Mr. Parkhill soon discovered that poor Mrs. Moskowitz did not know the meaning of "vast." "Who can tell us the meaning of 'vast'?" asked Mr. Parkhill lightly.

Mr. Kaplan's hand shot up, volunteering wisdom. He was all proud grins. Mr. Parkhill, in the rashness of the moment, nodded to him.

Mr. Kaplan rose, radiant with joy. "'Vast!' It's commink fromm diraction. Ve have four diractions: de naut, de sot, de heast, and de vast."

Mr. Parkhill shook his head. "Er—that is 'west,' Mr. Kaplan." He wrote "VAST" and "WEST" on the blackboard. To the class he added, tolerantly, that Mr. Kaplan was apparently thinking of "west," whereas it was "vast" which was under discussion.

This seemed to bring a great light into Mr. Kaplan's inner world. "So is 'vast' vat you eskink?"

Mr. Parkhill admitted that it was 'vast' for which he was asking.

"Aha!" cried Mr. Kaplan. "You minn 'vast,' not"—with scorn—"'vast.'"

"Yes," said Mr. Parkhill, faintly.

"Hau Kay!" said Mr. Kaplan, essaying the vernacular. "Ven I'm buyink a suit clothes, I'm gattink de cawt, de pents, an' de vast!"

Stunned, Mr. Parkhill shook his head, very sadly. "I'm afraid that you've used still another word, Mr. Kaplan."

Oddly enough, this seemed to give Mr. Kaplan great pleasure.

Several nights later Mr. Kaplan took advantage of Open Questions period. This ten-minute period was Mr. Parkhill's special innovation in the American Night

Preparatory School for Adults. It was devoted to answering any questions which the students might care to raise about any difficulties which they might have encountered during the course of their adventures with the language. Mr. Parkhill enjoyed Open Questions. He liked to clear up practical problems. He felt he was being ever so much more constructive that way. Miss Higby had once told him that he was a born Open Questions teacher.

"Plizz, Mr. Pockheel," asked Mr. Kaplan as soon as the period opened. "Vat's de minnink fromm—" It sounded, in Mr. Kaplan's rendition, like "a big department."

"'A big department,' Mr. Kaplan?" asked Mr. Parkhill, to make sure.

"Yassir!" Mr. Kaplan's smile was beauteous to behold. "In de stritt, ven I'm valkink, I'm hearink like 'I big de pottment.'"

It was definitely a pedagogical opportunity.

"Well, class," Mr. Parkhill began. "I'm sure that you have all—"

He told them that they had all probably done some shopping in the large downtown stores. (Mr. Kaplan nodded.) In these large stores, he said, if they wanted to buy a pair of shoes, for example, they went to a special part of the store, where only shoes were sold—a shoe department. (Mr. Kaplan nodded.) If they wanted a table, they went to a different part of the store, where tables were sold. (Mr. Kaplan nodded.) If they wanted to buy, say, a goldfish, they went to still another part of the store, where goldfish . . . (Mr. Kaplan frowned; it was clear that Mr. Kaplan had never bought a goldfish.)

"Well, then," Mr. Parkhill summed up hastily, "each article is sold in a different place. These different and special places are called departments." He printed "D-E-P-A-R-T-M-E-N-T" on the board in large, clear capitals. "And a big department, Mr. Kaplan, is merely such a department which is large—big!"

He put the chalk down and wiped his fingers.

"Is that clear now, class?" he asked, with a little smile. (It was rather an ingenious explanation, he thought; it might be worth repeating to Miss Higby during the recess.)

It was clear. There were thirty nods of approval. But Mr. Kaplan looked uncertain. It was obvious that Mr. Kaplan, a man who would not compromise with truth, did not find it clear.

"Isn't that clear now, Mr. Kaplan?" asked Mr. Parkhill anxiously.

Mr. Kaplan pursed his lips in thought. "It's a fine haxplination, Titcher," he said generously, "but I don' unnistand vy I'm herink de voids de vay I do. Simms to me it's used in annodder minnink."

"There's really only one meaning for 'a big department.'" Mr. Parkhill was definitely worried by this time. "If that's the phrase you mean." Kaplan nodded gravely. "Oh, dat's de phrase—ufcawss! It sonds like dat—or maybe a leetle more like 'I big de pottment.'"

Mr. Parkhill took up the chalk. ("I big department" was obviously a case of Mr. Kaplan's own curious audition.) He repeated the explanation carefully, this time embellishing the illustrations with a shirt department, a victrola section, and "a separate part of the store where, for example, you buy canaries, or other birds."

Mr. Kaplan sat entranced. He followed it all politely, even the part about "canaries, or other birds." He smiled throughout with consummate reassurance.

Mr. Parkhill was relieved, assuming, in his folly, that Mr. Kaplan's smiles were a testimony to his exposition. But when he had finished, Mr. Kaplan shook his head once more, this time with a new and superior firmness.

"Is the explanation still not clear?" Mr. Parkhill was genuinely concerned by this time.

"Is de haxplination clear!" cried Mr. Kaplan with enthusiasm. "Ha! I should live so! Soitinly! Clear like gold! So clear! An' netcheral too! But Mr. Pockheel—"

"Go on, Mr. Kaplan," said Mr. Parkhill, studying the white dust on his fingers. There was, after all, nothing more to be done.

"Vell! I tink it's more like 'I big de pottment.'"

"Go on, Mr. Kaplan, go on." (Domine, dirige nos.)

Mr. Kaplan rose. His smile was broad, luminous, transcendent; his manner was regal.

"I'm hearink it in de stritt. Sometimes I'm stendink in de stritt, talkink to a frand, or mine vife, mine brodder—or maybe only stendink. An' somvun is pessink around me. An' by hexident he's givink me a bump, you know, a poosh! Vell, he says, 'Axcuse me!' no? But sometimes, an' dis is vat I minn, he's sayink, 'I big de pottment!'"

Mr. Parkhill studied the picture of "Abram Lincohen" on the back wall, as if reluctant to face reality. He wondered whether he could reconcile it with his conscience if he were to promote Mr. Kaplan to Composition, Grammar, and Civics—at once. Another three months of Recitation and Speech might, after all, be nothing but a waste of Mr. Kaplan's valuable time.

THE RESPONSIBILITY OF COLLEGES AND UNIVERSITIES FOR ADULT EDUCATION (1947)   From *Higher Education For American Democracy: Report of the President's Commission On Higher Education* (New York, 1947), pp. 51–55.

The continuing education of the adult population is carried on by many agencies, by some as a deliberate aim, by others as a byproduct not always recognized as education. But the colleges and universities are the best equipped of all the agencies, from the standpoint of resources, to undertake the major part of the job. Education on a near adult level is their business, and they have, in some measure at least, the necessary teachers and facilities.

The present status of university extension services makes it painfully clear that the colleges and universities do not recognize adult education as their potentially greatest service to democratic society. It is pushed aside as something quite extraneous to the real business of the university.

This attitude is fostered by the necessities of adult education. It takes place outside regular college hours and usually off campus. It makes use of faculty members in other units of the university, and for these men extension or correspondence courses are usually extra chores they agree to add to their regular teaching load in order to supplement their inadequate incomes. In this frame of mind, many of them candidly get by with as little expenditure of energy as possible.

This state of affairs cannot be permitted to continue. The colleges and universities should elevate adult education to a position of equal importance with any other of their functions. The extension department should be charged with the task of channeling the resources of every teaching unit of the institution into the adult program.

Adult education, along with undergraduate and graduate education, should become the responsibility of every department or college of the university. It should be the duty of the English faculty or the physics faculty, for instance, to teach English or physics not just to those who come to the campus, but to everyone in the community or the State who wants to learn, or can be persuaded to want to learn, English or physics.

To this degree every college and university should become a "community college." Then extension teaching would be accounted a part of the regular teaching load and would receive its due share of faculty energy and interest.

Granted that this would increase the job of the institution many times over, that it would require more teachers, more manpower in administration, and a very considerable increase in the budget. The principal obstacle to acceptance of the program, nonetheless, is the limited concept that higher education still holds of its role in a free and democratic society.

It must broaden that concept. It must cease to be campus-bound. It must take the university to the people wherever they are to be found and by every available and effective means for the communication of ideas and the stimulation of intellectual curiosity. It must not hold itself above using all the arts of persuasion to attract consumers for the service it offers.

Adult education in the past has been much too inflexible, much too bound by traditional notions of proper educational procedures. Extension activities for years have been stultified by the idea that adult education consists merely of the transmission to mature people of campus courses developed to meet the needs of adolescents.

Fitting Method to Student

Adult students are not conscript classes. Already established as wage earners, most of them, they do not have to go to school; they have a wide range of activities from which to choose a way of spending their leisure. And adult education is, in most cases, a leisure time activity. The students come to the class or the correspondence lesson at the end of a full and probably tiring day. They want release from the tension of their jobs. They appreciate a much greater degree of informality in atmosphere and method than characterizes most campus classroom teaching.

The program of adult education must be fitted in content, methods, and aims to the adult student as he is, not as the college or the professor thinks he should be.

If adult students are to remain in the class, once enrolled, they must be stimulated and interested. There is nothing to prevent them from dropping a course that does not interest or benefit them, nothing to prevent them from walking out on a teacher who is dull, rambling, and irrelevant.

Adult interest in further education is not predominantly vocational. Many enroll in extension courses to fit themselves for a better job, but many others are motivated by a desire, often vague and fumbling, for self-improvement, which they think a course in literature or history or current events should give them. The majority of them will demand substance in the lecture or the discussion but they will not suffer gladly much academic or specialist jargon.

Courses by extension or by correspondence may not be the best means of educating adults; they certainly are not the only ones. Vigorous experimentation with new methods, however unorthodox, is called for.

With the demonstration constantly before us of the appeal and the effectiveness of motion pictures, higher education has been inexcusably slow in the development of visual education. That documentary and educational films could become teaching instruments of great power cannot be doubted. They are becoming so in the elementary and secondary schools.

But all too often the visual education department of the university is relegated to the status of a self-supporting service enterprise, along with the cafeteria or the bookstore, instead of being recognized as a vital educational unit worthy of a substantial budget and the encouragement of administration favor and interest. If use in the adult program brings visual education into its own, all of higher education will benefit.

The great influx of students into the universities and colleges immediately after the war has given much impetus to the development of visual education and other technical aids to learning. The considerable divergence in reading skills and achievement on the part of the students has made it necessary to find devices which make the teacher's presentation more vivid. The greater number of students per teacher and the lack of preparation on the part of many new teachers has augmented the need for effective training aids.

The experiences of the armed forces in World War II afford an excellent example for institutions of higher learning as they cope with the problems of mass education. During the war the service's training schools were faced with the necessity of evolving effective and rapid methods for mass instruction. With a practically unlimited budget they made marvelous strides in the development of motion pictures, strip films, transcriptions, mock-ups and other learning devices. The primary and successful application of these devices to wartime training purposes suggests the need for further exploration in an effort to develop similar devices for peacetime academic instruction.

There are currently certain handicaps to an extensive development of the use of technical aids at the college level. Primarily the meagerness of existing materials available for use in higher educational instruction retards this development. There is also a lack of information and centralized distribution of such materials as are presently in existence. Several institutions, notably Rutgers, Pennsylvania State College, the State University of Iowa, and Vassar, have developed effective materials for their own use. Doubtless these materials would have wider application and use in other institutions if a procedure for interchange of information and actual materials were developed.

This Commission recommends the establishment of a continuing committee devoted to the study, development, and utilization of technical aids to learning in higher education.

Such a committee should deal with four major areas of responsibility. In the first place, it should provide facilities for coordinating information on existing materials and develop a plan for the interchange of these materials among interested institutions. Secondly, the Committee should arrange for continued study of the special devices developed by the Navy, Army, and Air Corps to discover possible applications these developments may have for civilian instruction. Another important activity would be the stimulation of individual institutions or groups of institutions in a program of integrated effort at developing further basic-training aids. This committee should also assume responsibility for wide publicity on the advantages and objectives of technical aids in higher education.

The Commission is of the opinion that the work of such a committee would be most effective by having it attached to some existing educational organization which has sufficient prestige to challenge the serious consideration of institutions of higher education.

University owned and operated radio stations are another agency for adult education whose possibilities are all too seldom exploited. Their influence and appeal where they exist is widespread.

Yet here again the universities are niggardly and slow. The Federal Communications Commission has set aside twenty bands on the FM spectrum for use of educational institutions, but the colleges are not taking advantage of the opportunity thus offered them. They are repeating the mistake they made twenty years ago when they failed to take up the channels reserved for them in the AM spectrum. The FCC cannot be expected to hold out against the pressure of commercial interests that want these FM bands if the colleges and universities show no interest in making use of them.

Objectives of Adult Education

Whatever methods may prove best for reaching and instructing large numbers of the adult population, the purposes of the program are in large measure those of higher education in general. The adult program is not an additional objective of the college; it is one of the means by which the college can achieve its general objectives.

The knowledge, attitudes, and activities necessary for responsible citizenship in our free society cannot be left to the oncoming generation; they are needed now. The urgent necessities of world-wide understanding and cooperation cannot be postponed until the insight and good will on which they depend have been developed in a new generation; they call for thought and action now.

Higher education will not play its social role in American democracy and in international affairs successfully unless it assumes the responsibility for a program of adult education reaching far beyond the campus and the classroom.

THE U.S. ARMY AT SCHOOL (1964)   From Harold F. Clark and Harold S. Sloan, *Classrooms in the Military* (New York, 1964), pp. 5-6, 9-10.

Scattered over continental United States are more than 300 military schools located on some 126 Army, Navy, Air Force, and Marine Corps installations. . . . The schools are formal institutions, with classrooms, laboratories, workshops, study halls, and auditoriums. All those observed during the preparation of this report are superbly equipped with modern teaching aids such as projection machines, tape recorders, models, charts, mock-ups, closed-circuit television, and the like. The schools prepare their own text materials. The instructors are professionally trained

and are drawn from both military and civilian personnel. Each school is administered by what might be termed a department of education, which schedules classes,
supervises instruction, keeps student records, and so on, but is amenable to higher
authority. Collectively, all the schools within a given branch of the Armed Forces
present an integrated program geared to the needs of that particular branch. The
combined programs, in turn, form a vast educational complex which not only
performs a vital role in national security but also contributes, in no small measure,
to the intellectual life of the country.

If all these schools were placed on one contiguous campus, the area covered
would probably exceed that occupied by the three largest cities (in point of acreage)
in the United States—New York, Los Angeles, and Chicago. Thousands of buildings
housing classrooms, living quarters, administration equipment, and mess halls would
occupy many acres. Other acres would be given over to proving grounds, airfields,
firing ranges, drill centers, and recreational facilities. Some would be undeveloped,
awaiting further expansion, for education is a necessary corollary to technological
progress, and probably the age of technology has only just begun.

The gamut of subjects taught ranges all the way from the three R's to courses
required for a Ph.D. degree. Over 4,000 separate resident courses are listed in this
book. There are educational centers in every sizable Army post, and similar
facilities in Navy installations for recruits whose elementary education has been
interrupted. In the hundreds of service schools, nearly 2,500 separate jobs are
taught. Two technical schools offer curricula leading to baccalaureate and master's
degrees, and one grants a Ph.D. degree. In addition to the courses offered under
their own jurisdiction, these technical institutions have contractual relations with
universities and industries throughout the country, thus bringing the curricula of
hundreds of civilian educational institutions and the techniques and experience of
scores of industries within the orbit of the educational complex of the Armed
Forces.

Besides the resident schools of the Armed Forces, there are military hospitals
which provide internships and resident study as well as training for nurses and
medical technicians, and dental schools where graduate courses are conducted for
qualified personnel. Some 33 correspondence-school centers offer over 2,500 courses
and enroll nearly 1,000,000 students scattered all over the world. Courses in just
about every subject taught in elementary school, high school, and college are
available. Topping the educational hierarchy of the Armed Forces are 7 advanced
colleges for senior officers.

At any one time, as many as 300,000 military personnel may be attending school.
Indeed, an attendance figure for the year would be considerably higher because,
although many of the courses approximate the conventional college semester in
length, others are short and intensive, extending over a period of no more than a
week or a few weeks. The student turnover, therefore, is high. . . .

. . . Thus, unencumbered by academic traditions, standards of productivity in
teaching have been developed to an extent greater than is customarily found in
civilian institutions. Modern equipment, well-written textbooks, effective teacher
training, and close supervision have all contributed to this end. . . .

If the thousands of individual courses cuonducted by the Armed Forces are
analyzed for subject-matter content, nearly 1,400 civilian job classifications emerge.
In large part, therefore, the education and training to which career military
personnel are exposed can prove a valuable asset, in later life, to those who enlist or
who are inducted into the services for limited periods. This is a development of
recent decades and is a concomitant of the technological age. . . .

What do those who have been exposed to one or another phase of this complex educational program have to say about it? How effective did they find it? How did it compare with their previous educational experiences? Was there any carry-over to civilian life? These and similar questions were asked and answered in the course of interviews with men and women recently discharged from the Armed Services. . . .

Education stems from research. It is not surprising, therefore, to find the vast educational structure of the Armed Forces reinforced by equally imposing research institutions, and, just as there is considerable carry-over from the military to civilian life in the area of education, so military research is making notable contributions to peacetime activities. . . .

The present study concludes, on the note that the Armed Forces educational program is part of society's response to a technological age. As such, it is contributing liberally to the economic life of the nation. It can well serve as a model for developing a high level of technical competence among large numbers of the younger generation, and its efforts in this direction, together with those of other agencies, can help reduce the hard core of unemployment persisting in the United States.

The Junior Colleges

THE JUNIOR COLLEGE: FAD OR FIXTURE (1929) From Walter C. Eells, *Red Book Magazine*, vol. LIII, p. 6.

Education ever has been a subject close to the heart of America. Only sixteen years after the Pilgrims landed on the "bleak New England coast," they founded Harvard College—the beginning of higher education in America. But for over a century the education it furnished was for the professional classes. Secondary education for the masses was peculiarly the contribution of the nineteenth century.

Will collegiate education for the masses characterize the twentieth century? Already this century has witnessed an astonishing development of interest in higher education. The great universities of the country, institutions interested primarily in specialization and research, have found themselves swamped with thousands of immature youth, and parents are hesitating to lose their children in the university mass. Does higher education of masses necessarily imply education in masses?

The answer is the Junior College—a more widely diffused opportunity for two years of college in smaller units—an institution where closer contact is possible with instructors more interested in teaching than in research—an institution making transition easier from high school restrictions to university freedom.

According to the latest report of the American Association of Junior Colleges there are over four hundred Junior Colleges in the country with more than fifty thousand students. The movement is in its infancy but it is beginning to occupy a unique position in the American educational ladder—unmistakably higher than a glorified high school; distinctly lower than the scholarly specialization of the University.

Young men and women are finding they can secure adequate preparation for many life occupations in two years at Junior College. Others are finding excellent preparation under superior conditions for later specialization in the University.

How does the junior college graduate who wishes to continue his education compare with the university trained freshman and sophomore when they meet on common ground in the junior and senior years? At the convention of the Association of Junior Colleges at Forth Worth, Texas, last winter a detailed report was given by the writer based on the records of over three hundred graduates of thirty-seven different Junior Colleges who had entered Stanford University. They were compared with groups who had received their freshman and sophomore training at the University. After their first quarter the junior college group showed a distinct superiority in actual classroom accomplishments, a superiority which increased

HIGHER
EDUCATION

2845

regularly with each successive quarter until the end of the senior year. At graduation, twice as great a proportion of junior college students received final honors as the university trained students. Almost twice as many remained at the University for graduate work.

Another study from the athletic standpoint showed that a much greater proportion of students from Junior Colleges made places on varsity athletic squads than of those who entered the university as freshmen. This study was based upon the records of over seventy thousand students in California's three largest universities.

Such evidence indicates that the Junior College is making good, both scholastically and athletically. Unquestionably it is a permanent addition to higher education. Both educators and the general public are beginning to realize that here is a really major movement for improvement in American Education—the development of an institution which promises to popularize and democratize collegiate education. The Junior College is not a fad—it is a fixture!

PRESIDENT HARRY TRUMAN'S COMMISSION ON HIGHER EDUCATION CALLS FOR MORE COMMUNITY COLLEGES (1947) From *Higher Education for Democracy: Report of the President's Commission on Higher Education* (New York, 1947), vol. I, pp. 47–49.

To make sure of its own health and strength a democratic society must provide free and equal access to education for its youth, and at the same time it must recognize their differences in capacity and purpose. Higher education in America should include a variety of institutional forms and educational programs, so that at whatever point any student leaves school, he will be fitted, within the limits of his mental capacity and educational level, for an abundant and productive life as a person, as a worker, and as a citizen.

The Community College

As one means of achieving the expansion of educational opportunity and the diversification of educational offerings it considers necessary, this Commission recommends that the number of community colleges be increased and that their activities be multiplied.

Community colleges in the future may be either publicly or privately controlled and supported, but most of them, obviously, will be under public auspices. They will be mainly local or regional in scope and should be locally controlled, though they should be carefully planned to fit into a comprehensive State-wide system of higher education. They will derive much of their support from the local community, supplemented by aid from state funds.

Some community colleges may offer a full four years of college work, but most of them probably will stop at the end of the fourteenth grade, the sophomore year of the traditional college. In the latter case they should be closely articulated with the high school.

Whatever form the community college takes, its purpose is educational service to the entire community, and this purpose requires of it a variety of functions and programs. It will provide college education for the youth of the community certainly, so as to remove geographic and economic barriers to educational opportunity and discover and develop individual talents at low cost and easy access. But in addition, the community college will serve as an active center of adult education. It will attempt to meet the total post-high school needs of its community.

TERMINAL AND SEMIPROFESSIONAL EDUCATION

In the past the junior college has most commonly sought to provide within the local community the freshman and sophomore courses of the traditional college curriculum. With notable exceptions, it has concentrated on preparing students for further study in the junior and senior years of liberal arts colleges or professional schools.

But preparatory programs looking to the more advanced courses of the senior college are not complete and rounded in themselves, and they usually do not serve well the purpose of those who must terminate their schooling at the end of the fourteenth grade. Half the young people who go to college find themselves unable to complete the full 4-year course, and for a long time to come more students will end their formal education in the junior college years than will prolong it into the senior college. These 2-year graduates would gain more from a terminal program planned specifically to meet their needs than from the first half of a 4-year curriculum.

For this reason, the Commission recommends that the community college emphasize programs of terminal education.

These terminal programs should include both general education and vocational training. They should be designed both for young people who want to secure as good a general education as possible by the end of the fourteenth grade and for those who wish to fit themselves for semiprofessional occupations.

Semiprofessional training, properly conceived and organized, can make a significant contribution to education for society's occupational requirements. In not providing this sort of training anywhere in existing programs, the educational system is out of step with the demands of the twentieth century American economy.

Because of advancing technology, the occupational center of our economic system is shifting away from the major producing industries. The proportion of the working population engaged in these industries has decreased, while the proportion in the distributive and service trades has increased. In 1880, for instance, about one-half of all workers were engaged in agriculture; in 1947, less than one-seventh of the workers were so engaged.

One result of this development is a new and rapidly growing need for trained semiprofessional workers in these distributive and service occupations. To meet the needs of the economy our schools must train many more young people for employment as medical secretaries, recreational leaders, hotel and restaurant managers, aviators, salesmen in fields like life insurance and real estate, photographers, automotive and electrical technicians, and so on through a long list of positions in the business and professional world.

Education on the technician level—that is, the training of medical technicians, dental hygienists, nurses' aides, laboratory technicians—offers one practical solution for the acute shortage of professional personnel in medicine, dentistry, and nursing.

An adequate staff of well-trained assistants can substantially increase the number of patients one doctor, dentist, or nurse can handle.

For these semiprofessional occupations a full 4 years of college training is not necessary. It is estimated that in many fields of work there are *five* jobs requiring 2 years of college preparation for every *one* that requires 4 years. Training for these more numerous jobs is the kind the community college should provide.

If the semiprofessional curriculum is to accomplish its purpose, however, it must not be crowded with vocational and technical courses to the exclusion of general education. It must aim at developing a combination of social understanding and technical competence. Semiprofessional education should mix a goodly amount of general education for personal and social development with technical education that is intensive, accurate, and comprehensive enough to give the student command of marketable abilities.

COMMUNITY CENTER OF LEARNING

Post-high school education for youth is only one of the functions to be performed by the community college. One such college has been known to have a daytime junior college enrollment of 3,000 but an adult enrollment in the late afternoon and evening of 25,000.

The community college seeks to become a center of learning for the entire community, with or without the restrictions that surround formal course work in traditional institutions of higher education. It gears its programs and services to the needs and wishes of the people it serves, and its offerings may range from workshops in painting or singing or play writing for fun to refresher courses in journalism or child psychology.

If the health of the community can be improved by teaching restaurant managers something about the bacteriology of food, the community college sets up such a course and seeks to enroll as many of those employed in food services as it can muster. If the community happens to be a center for travelers from Latin America, the college provides classes in Spanish for salespeople, waitresses, bellboys, and taxicab drivers.

The potential effects of the community college in keeping intellectual curiosity alive in out-of-school citizens, of stimulating their zest for learning, of improving the quality of their lives as individuals and as citizens are limited only by the vision, the energy, and the ingenuity of the college staff—and by the size of the college budget. But the people will take care of the budget if the staff provides them with vital and worthwhile educational services.

IN RELATION TO THE LIBERAL ARTS COLLEGE

The Commission does not intend to suggest that the expansion of educational opportunity at the freshman-sophomore level should be limited to the community college. Part of the needed expansion can be achieved through existing 4-year colleges, part of it through the lower divisions of the universities.

Some of the established colleges may wish to institute terminal curriculums and contribute to the development of semiprofessional training. Others will prefer to concentrate on general education for students who plan to complete a 4-year course. Still others, especially the liberal arts colleges of universities, may welcome the opportunity to focus their energies on senior college programs.

In any case, the liberal arts college is so well established in the American educational tradition that it need not fear community colleges will weaken its own appeal. It should encourage the development of the community college, not oppose it. Experience indicates that these community institutions awaken intellectual curiosity and ambition in many youth who would not otherwise seek college education at all, and in many cases these students will be stimulated to continue their college careers if the 4-year colleges will meet them halfway with liberal admission policies.

There is little danger of lowered standards in this. We know now that ability to complete successfully the work of the last 2 years of college depends more upon the quality of mind and the mental habits a student brings to his work than upon the nature of the subject matter he has already covered. There is no reason to believe that community colleges, if they are adequately staffed, cannot do as good a job as the lower divisions of 4-year colleges in preparing students for advanced work in liberal and professional education.

While it favors the growth of community colleges, the Commission emphasizes that they must be soundly established with respect to financial support and student attendance. This calls for careful planning on a Statewide basis in determining location of the colleges and the curriculums to be offered. Simply to create more small, inadequately financed institutions would only retard the development of a sound program of post-high school education. . . .

A NEW ROLE FOR THE JUNIOR COLLEGE (1965)   From Richard C. Richardson, Jr. and Paul Elsner, *Junior College Journal*, vol. XXXVI, pp. 18–21.

A distinguishing feature of the community junior college has been its open door admission policy. The popularization of higher education has resulted in an influx of marginal students who increasingly view the junior college as a logical extension of the secondary school. The junior college, consequently, is torn between the necessity of maintaining standards to guarantee the employability and transfer-ability of its graduates, and the knowledge that it constitutes the last opportunity for formal education some of its students will ever have.

The problem of the marginal student is particularly acute in urban areas where poverty and de facto segregation generate discouraging numbers of educationally disadvantaged students who lack preparation for even the least rigorous technical programs offered by the junior college. Moreover, substantial numbers of these students fail to recognize their limitations and persist in enrolling in college transfer courses for status reasons to the mutual confoundment of themselves and their instructors.

Junior college educators have coined such phrases as the "revolving door" in criticizing existing programs for failing to meet the needs of from one-third to one-half of the total student population. . . .

The educationally disadvantaged student is coming to the open door community college in ever-increasing numbers. The recent trend toward increased college attendance by students falling below predetermined indexes of success criteria has probably resulted from (1) colleges and universities reaching into a wider range of social class structures for its students, (2) the need for higher level vocational and professional training on the part of an expanding future working force, and (3) The emerging of more comprehensive strata of collegiate institutions, such as the public junior college.

More recently, belated consideration is being given to the ethics of using the community college as a one-semester sieve. It appears likely that disadvantaged students will be present at least one semester and in many instances a full year. The question, then, becomes not whether such students will be educated but rather how they can best be educated.

Forest Park Community College of the Junior College District of St. Louis—St. Louis County has devoted extensive study to the problem of the educationally disadvantaged. A faculty committee reviewing the results of the college program for the fall session, 1964, found that of a total on-campus enrollment of 1,510, academic difficulty was experienced by 691 or 46 per cent. A total of 278 students were placed on enforced withdrawal, 318 were placed on academic probation, ninety-five withdrew officially, while an additional eighty-five simply stopped coming. The faculty committee recommended that an experimental program be established to attempt to meet the needs of the disadvantaged student. Specifically, the committee spelled out the following goals:

1. Meeting the needs of students in the lower range of the ability spectrum.

2. Improving standards in transfer courses by removing students incapable of making a contribution or of achieving significant benefit.

3. Providing educationally disadvantaged students with intensive counseling on an individual and group basis to: (a) minimize emotional factors inhibiting success; (b) aid students to assess realistically their potential and to relate this to vocational goals; and (c) identify students incapable of benefiting from any college program and refer them to community resources through accurate and complete knowledge of apprenticeship requirements, job openings, training courses such as those sponsored by the Manpower Development and Training Act, as well as other community resources.

4. Salvaging the academically able students from this group who might be upgraded to the point where they could be successful in regular technical or transfer programs.

It was not by accident that the salvage function of this program was placed last. The committee was determined that the program should be viewed as an end in and of itself, so that a student who never progressed beyond might nonetheless experience a feeling of success. Further, the committee determined that the emphasis of the program would be neither remedial nor vocational. Rather, an attempt would be made to structure a stimulating and challenging one-year program of general education on the students' level.

Since the salvage function was to be downgraded rather than excluded, some provision had to be made for providing students with the basic skills necessary for success in more demanding programs. The answer to this problem was found in the development of a programmed materials learning laboratory. Programmed materials and tutorial assistance would be provided in a learning center where the responsibility for mastery of the materials would rest primarily with the student. This center would supplement the organized general educational classes.

Concurrent with curriculum planning, intensive efforts were begun to study the characteristics of the student. Social workers, members of the Human Development Corporation, high school curriculum workers, and others met with the committee to convey the benefits of their experience.

It was agreed at an early point in the discussions that instructors must volunteer for the program and would have to be willing to accept full-time assignment.

Students would be grouped in divisions of 100, to which a five-person team would be assigned. Each team was to consist of one counselor, a learning laboratory coordinator (reading specialist backgrounds), and three representatives of academic divisions. The basic approach would involve an attempt to create a core curriculum organized around the social science area. In general, these considerations were central to planning the program:

1. A curriculum for the educationally disadvantaged should be concerned with the broader development of the person—this development would include his personal and emotional well-being as well as his intellectual development.

2. The program should assist the student in coping with his environment—his more immediate pressures would come from his academic environment but his ability to adjust to pressures of collegiate life would take on greater implication for total personal development as a citizen.

3. The program should not be delineated in terms of a specific curriculum or in terms of logically arranged course content: the courses should be wider in scope, less fixed—their content should be drawn from many more facets of human problems and they should emphasize the individual student's needs.

The Radicalized University

THE PORT HURON STATEMENT (1962)   From Students for a Democratic
Society, *The Port Huron Statement* (Chicago, 1962), pp. 3–13.

Agenda for a Generation

W e are people of this generation, bred in at least modest comfort,
housed in universities, looking uncomfortably to the world we inherit. . . . Our
work is guided by the sense that we may be the last generation in the experiment
with living. But we are a minority—the vast majority of our people regard the
temporary equilibriums of our society and the world as eternally-functional parts. In
this is perhaps the outstanding paradox: We ourselves are imbued with urgency, yet
the message of our society is that there is no viable alternative to the present.
Beneath the reassuring tones of the politicians, beneath the common opinion that
America will "muddle through," beneath the stagnation of those who have closed
their minds to the future, is the pervading feeling that there simply are no
alternatives, that our times have witnessed the exhaustion not only of Utopias, but
of any new departures as well. Feeling the press of complexity upon the emptiness
of life, people are fearful of the thought that at any moment things might thrust out
of control. They fear change itself, since change might smash whatever invisible
framework seems to hold back chaos for them now. For most Americans, all
crusades are suspect, threatening. The fact that each individual sees apathy in his
fellows perpetuates the common reluctance to organize for changes. The dominant
institutions are complex enough to blunt the minds of their potential critics, and
entrenched enough to swiftly dissipate or entirely repel the energies of protest and
reform, thus limiting human expectancies. Then, too, we are a materially improved
society, and by our own improvements we seem to have weakened the case for
change.

Some would have us believe that Americans feel contentment amidst prosperity—but might it not better be called a glaze above deeply-felt anxieties about their
role in the new world? And if these anxieties produce a developed indifference to
human affairs, do they not as well produce a yearning to believe there *is* an
alternative to the present, that something *can* be done to change circumstances in
the school, the workplaces, the bureaucracies, the government? It is to this latter
yearning, at once the spark and engine of change, that we direct our present appeal.
The search for truly democratic alternatives to the present, and a commitment to

HIGHER
EDUCATION

2853

social experimentation with them, is a worthy and fulfilling human enterprise, one which moves us and, we hope, others today. . . .

Values

Making values explicit—an initial task in establishing alternatives—is an activity that has been devalued and corrupted. The conventional moral terms of the age, the politician moralities ("free world," "people's democracies") reflect realities poorly, if at all, and seem to function more as ruling myths than as descriptive principles. But neither has our experience in the universities brought us moral enlightenment. Our professors and administrators sacrifice controversy to public relations; their curriculums change more slowly than the living events of the world; their skills and silence are purchased by investors in the arms race; passion is called unscholastic. The questions we might want raised—what is really important? can we live in a different and better way? if we wanted to change society, how would we do it?—are not thought to be questions of a "fruitful, empirical nature," and thus are brushed aside.

Unlike youth in other countries we are used to moral leadership being exercised and moral dimensions being clarified by our elders. But today, for us, not even the liberal and socialist preachments of the past seem adequate to the forms of the present. Consider the old slogans: Capitalism Cannot Reform Itself, United Front Against Fascism, General Strike, All Out on May Day. Or, more recently, No Cooperation with Commies and Fellow Travelers, Ideologies Are Exhausted, Bipartisanship, No Utopias. These are incomplete, and there are few new prophets. It has been said that our liberal and socialist predecessors were plagued by vision without program, while our own generation is plagued by program without vision. All around us there is astute grasp of method, technique—the committee, the ad hoc group, the lobbyist, the hard and soft sell, the make, the projected image—but, if pressed critically, such expertise is incompetent to explain its implicit ideals. It is highly fashionable to identify oneself by old categories, or by naming a respected political figure, or by explaining "how we would vote" on various issues.

Theoretic chaos has replaced the idealistic thinking of old—and, unable to reconstitute theoretic order, men have condemned idealism itself. Doubt has replaced hopefulness, and men act out a defeatism that is labelled realistic. The decline of utopia and hope is in fact one of the defining features of social life today. The reasons are various: The dreams of the older left were perverted by Stalinism and never recreated; the congressional stalemate makes men narrow their view of the possible; the specialization of human activity leaves little room for sweeping thought; the horrors of the twentieth century, symbolized in the gas ovens and concentration camps and atom bombs, have blasted hopefulness. To be idealistic is to be considered apocalyptic, deluded. To have no serious aspirations, on the contrary, is to be "tough-minded."

In suggesting social goals and values, therefore, we are aware of entering a sphere of some disrepute. Perhaps matured by the past, we have no sure formulas, no closed theories—but that does not mean values are beyond discussion and tentative determination. A first task of any social movement is to convince people that the search for orienting theories and the creation of human values is complex but worthwhile. We are aware that to avoid platitudes we must analyze the concrete conditions of social order. But to direct such an analysis we must use the guideposts of basic principles. Our own social values involve conceptions of human beings, human relationships, and social systems.

We regard *men* as infinitely precious and possessed of unfulfilled capacities for reason, freedom, and love. In affirming these principles we are aware of countering perhaps the dominant conceptions of man in the twentieth century: that he is a thing to be manipulated, and that he is inherently incapable of directing his own affairs. We oppose the depersonalization that reduces human beings to the status of things. If anything, the brutalities of the twentieth century teach that means and ends are intimately related, that vague appeals to "posterity" cannot justify the mutilations of the present. We oppose, too, the doctrine of human incompetence because it rests essentially on the modern fact that men have been "competently" manipulated into incompetence. We see little reason why men cannot meet with increasing skill the complexities and responsibilities of their situation, if society is organized not for minority participation but for majority participation in decision-making.

Men have unrealized potential for self-cultivation, self-direction, self-under-standing, and creativity. It is this potential that we regard as crucial and to which we appeal—not to the human potentiality for violence, unreason, and submission to authority. The goal of man and society should be human independence: a concern not with image or popularity but with finding a meaning in life that is personally authentic; a quality of mind not compulsively driven by a sense of powerlessness, nor one which unthinkingly adopts status values, nor one which represses all threats to its habits, but one which has full, spontaneous access to present and past experiences, one which easily unites the fragmented parts of personal history, one which openly faces problems which are troubling and unresolved—one with an intuitive awareness of possibilities, an active sense of curiosity, an ability and willingness to learn.

This kind of independence does not mean egoistic individualism; the object is not to have one's way so much as it is to have a way that is one's own. Nor do we deify man—we merely have faith in his potential.

Human relationships should involve fraternity and honesty. Human interdependence is contemporary fact; human brotherhood must be willed, however, as a condition of future survival and as the most appropriate form of social relations. Personal links between man and man are needed, especially to go beyond the partial and fragmentary bonds of function that bind men only as worker to worker, employer to employee, teacher to student, American to Russian.

Loneliness, estrangement, isolation describe the vast distance between man and man today. These dominant tendencies cannot be overcome by better personnel management, nor by improved gadgets, but only when a love of man overcomes the idolatrous worship of things by man.

As the individualism we affirm is not egoism, the selflessness we affirm is not self-elimination. On the contrary, we believe in generosity of a kind that imprints one's unique individual qualities in the relation to other men, and to all human activity. Further, to dislike isolation is not to favor the abolition of privacy; the latter differs from isolation in that it occurs or is abolished according to individual will.

In the last few years, thousands of American students demonstrated that they at least felt the urgency of the times. They moved actively and directly against racial injustices, the threat of war, violations of individual rights of conscience and, less frequently, against economic manipulation. They succeeded in restoring a small measure of controversy to the campuses after the stillness of the McCarthy period. They succeeded, too, in gaining some concessions from the people and institutions they opposed, especially in the fight against racial bigotry.

The significance of these scattered movements lies not in their success or failure in gaining objectives—at least not yet. Nor does the significance lie in the intellectual "competence" or "maturity" of the students involved—as some pedantic elders allege. The significance is in the fact that the students are breaking the crust of apathy and overcoming the inner alienation—facts that remain the defining characteristics of American college life.

If student movements for change are rarities still on the campus scene, what is commonplace there? The real campus, the familiar campus, is a place of private people, engaged in their notorious "inner emigration." It is a place of commitment to business-as-usual, getting ahead, playing it cool. It is a place of mass affirmation of the Twist, but mass reluctance toward the controversial public stance. Rules are accepted as "inevitable," bureaucracy as "just circumstances," irrelevance as "scholarship," selflessness as "martyrdom," politics as "just another way to make people, and an unprofitable one, too."

Almost no students value activity as a citizen. Passive in public, they are hardly more idealistic in arranging their private lives; Gallup concludes they will settle for "low success, and won't risk high failure." There is not much willingness to take risks (not even in business), no setting of dangerous goals, no real conception of personal identity except one manufactured in the image of others, no real urge for personal fulfillment except to be almost as successful as the very successful people. Attention is being paid to social status (the quality of shirt collars, meeting people, getting wives or husbands, making solid contacts for later on); much, too, is paid to academic status (grades, honors, the med school rat-race). But neglected generally is real intellectual status, the personal cultivation of the mind.

Look beyond the campus, to America itself. That student life is more intellectual, and perhaps more comfortable, does not obscure the fact that the fundamental qualities of life on the campus reflect the habits of society at large. The fraternity president is seen at the junior manager levels; the sorority queen has gone to Grosse Pointe; the serious poet burns for a place, any place, to work; the once-serious and never-serious poets work at the advertising agencies. The desperation of people threatened by forces about which they know little and of which they can say less, the cheerful emptiness of people giving up all hope of changing things, the faceless ones polled by Gallup who listed "international affairs" fourteenth on their list of problems but who also expected thermonuclear war in the next few years—in these and other forms, Americans are in withdrawal from public life, from any collective effort at directing their own affairs.

Some regard these national doldrums as a sign of healthy approval of the established order, but is it approval by consent or by manipulated acquiescence? Others declare that the people are withdrawn because compelling issues are fast disappearing; perhaps there are fewer breadlines in America, but is Jim Crow gone, is there enough work and is work more fulfilling, is world war a diminishing threat, and what of the revolutionary new peoples? Still others think the national quietude is a necessary consequence of the need for elites to resolve complex and specialized problems of modern industrial society. But, then, why should business elites help decide foreign policy, and who controls the elites anyway, and are they solving mankind's problems? Others finally shrug knowingly and announce that full democracy never worked anywhere in the past—but why lump qualitatively different civilizations together, and how can a social order work well if its best thinkers are skeptics, and is man really doomed forever to the domination of today?

There are no convincing apologies for the contemporary malaise. . . . The apathy is, first, subjective—the felt powerlessness of ordinary people, the resignation before the enormity of events. But subjective apathy is encouraged by the objective American situation—the actual separation of people from power, from relevant knowledge, from pinnacles of decision-making. Just as the university influences the student way of life, so do major social institutions create the circumstances in which the isolated citizen will try hopelessly to understand his world and himself.

The very isolation of the individual—from power and community and ability to aspire—means the rise of a democracy without publics. With the great mass of people structurally remote and psychologically hesitant with respect to democratic institutions, those institutions themselves attenuate and become, in a fashion of the vicious circle, progressively less accessible to those few who aspire to serious participation in social affairs. The vital democratic connection between community and leadership, between the mass and the several elites, has been so wrenched and perverted that disastrous policies go unchallenged time and again. . . .

The first effort, then, should be to state a vision: What is the perimeter of human possibility in this epoch? . . . The second effort, if we are to be politically responsible, is to evaluate the prospects for obtaining at least a substantial part of that vision in our epoch: What are the social forces that exist, or that must exist, if we are to be successful? And what role have we ourselves to play as a social force?

"Students don't even give a damn about apathy," one has said. Apathy toward apathy begets a privately constructed universe, a place of systematic study schedules, two nights each week for beer, a girl or two, and early marriage—a framework infused with personality, warmth, and under control, no matter how unsatisfying otherwise.

Under these conditions university life loses all relevance to some. Four hundred thousand of our classmates leave college each year.

But apathy is not simply an attitude; it is a product of social institutions, and of the structure and organization of higher education itself. The extracurricular life is ordered according to *in loco parentis* theory, which ratifies the administration as the moral guardian of the young. The accompanying "let's pretend" theory of student extracurricular affairs validates student government as a training center for those who want to spend their lives in political pretense, and discourages initiative from more articulate, honest, and sensitive students. The bounds and style of controversy are delimited before controversy begins. The university "prepares" the student for "citizenship" through perpetual rehearsals and, usually, through emasculation of what creative spirit there is in the individual.

The academic life contains reinforcing counterparts to the way in which extracurricular life is organized. The academic world is founded in a teacher-student relation analogous to the parent-child relation which characterizes *in loco parentis*. Further, academia includes a radical separation of student from the material of study. That which is studied, the social reality, is "objectified" to sterility, dividing the student from life—just as he is restrained in active involvement by the deans controlling student government. The specialization of function and knowledge, admittedly necessary to our complex technological and social structure, has produced an exaggerated compartmentalization of study and understanding. This has contributed to: an overly parochial view, by faculty, of the role of its research and scholarship; a discontinuous and truncated understanding, by students, of the surrounding social order; a loss of personal attachment, by nearly all, to the worth of study as a humanistic enterprise.

There is, finally, the cumbersome academic bureaucracy extending throughout the academic as well as extracurricular structures, contributing to the sense of outer complexity and inner powerlessness that transforms so many students from honest searching to ratification of convention and, worse, to a numbness to present and future catastrophes. The size and financing systems of the university enhance the permanent trusteeship of the administrative bureaucracy, their power leading to a shift to the value standards of business and administrative mentality within the university. Huge foundations and other private financial interests shape the under-financed colleges and universities, making them not only more commercial but less disposed to diagnose society critically, less open to dissent. Many social and physical scientists, neglecting the liberating heritage of higher learning, develop "human relations" or "morale-producing" techniques for the corporate economy, while others exercise their intellectual skills to accelerate the arms race.

The university is located in a permanent position of social influence. Its educational function makes it indispensable and automatically makes it a crucial institution in the formation of social attitudes. In an unbelievably complicated world, it is the central institution for organizing, evaluating, and transmitting knowledge. . . . Social relevance, the accessibility to knowledge, and internal openness—these together make the university a potential base and agency in the movement of social change.

1. Any new left in America must be, in large measure, a left with real intellectual skills, committed to deliberativeness, honesty, and reflection as working tools. The university permits the political life to be an adjunct to the academic one, and action to be informed by reason.

2. A new left must be distributed in significant social roles throughout the country. The universities are distributed in such a manner.

3. A new left must consist of younger people who matured in the post-war world, and must be directed to the recruitment of younger people. The university is an obvious beginning point.

4. A new left must include liberals and socialists, the former for their relevance, the latter for their sense of thoroughgoing reforms in the system. The university is a more sensible place than a political party for these two traditions to begin to discuss their differences and look for political synthesis.

5. A new left must start controversy across the land, if national policies and national apathy are to be reversed. The ideal university is a community of controversy, within itself and in its effects on communities beyond.

6. A new left must transform modern complexity into issues that can be understood and felt close-up by every human being. It must give form to the feelings of helplessness and indifference, so that people may see the political, social, and economic sources of their private troubles and organize to change society. In a time of supposed prosperity, moral complacency, and political manipulation, a new left cannot rely on only aching stomachs to be the engine force of social reform. The case for change, for alternatives that will involve uncomfortable personal efforts, must be argued as never before. The university is a relevant place for all of these activities.

But we need not indulge in illusions: The university system cannot complete a movement of ordinary people making demands for a better life. From its schools and colleges across the nation, a militant left might awaken its allies, and by beginning the process towards peace, civil rights, and labor struggles, reinsert theory and idealism where too often reign confusion and political barter. The power of students and faculty united is not only potential; it has shown its actuality in the South, and in the reform movements of the North.

To turn these possibilities into realities will involve national efforts at university reform by an alliance of students and faculty. They must wrest control of the educational process from the administrative bureaucracy. They must make fraternal and functional contact with allies in labor, civil rights, and other liberal forces outside the campus. They must import major public issues into the curriculum. . . . They must make debate and controversy, not dull pedantic cant, the common style for educational life. They must consciously build a base for their assault upon the loci of power.

As students for a democratic society, we are committed to stimulating this kind of social movement, this kind of vision and program in campus and community across the country. If we appear to seek the unattainable as it has been said, then let it be known that we do so to avoid the unimaginable.

PAMPHLET OF THE FREE SPEECH MOVEMENT AT THE UNIVERSITY OF CALIFORNIA, BERKELEY (1965) From FSM pamphlet distributed January 4, 1965, as quoted in Seymour Martin Lipset and Sheldon S. Wolin, eds., *The Berkeley Student Revolt: Facts and Interpretations* (Garden City, N.Y., 1965), pp. 209–15.

I. The Moral Impetus

Our stand *has* been moral. We feel, that to a great extent, our movement has accomplished something which so many of the movements of the past few generations have failed to accomplish. We have tried, in the context of a mass movement, to act politically with moral justification. We have tried to be sensitive to each of our supporters and the individual morality he has brought to the movement. This is what has been unique about our movement.

Although our issue has been free speech, our theme has been solidarity. When individual members of our community have acted, we joined together as a community to jointly bear the responsibility for their actions. We have been able to revitalize one of the most distorted, misused, and important words of our century: comrade. The concept of living cannot be separated from the concept of other people. In our practical, fragmented society, too many of us have been alone. By being willing to stand up for others, and by knowing that others are willing to stand up for us, we have gained more than political power, we have gained personal strength. Each of us who has acted, now knows that he is a being willing to act.

No one can presume to explain why so many thousands have become part of the Free Speech Movement. All we can say is what each of us felt: something was wrong; something had to be done. It wasn't just that student political rights had been abridged; much more was wrong. Something had to be done about political rights, and in actively trying to cope with political rights we found ourselves confronting the entire Berkeley experience. The Berkeley campus has become a new place since the beginning of the semester. Many are trying to tell us that what we are trying to do may destroy the university. We are fully aware that we are doing something which has implicit proportions so immense as to be frightening. We are frightened of our power as a movement; but it is a healthy fear. We must not allow our fear to lead us into believing that we are being destructive. We are beginning to *build* a great university. So long as the students stand united in firmness and dignity, and the faculty stands behind us, the university cannot be destroyed. As students, we have already demonstrated our strength and dedication; the faculty has yet to show it can do its share. Some faculty members have stated that if what they call "anarchy" continues, then they will leave the university to seek *employment* elsewhere. Such faculty members who would leave at this point would compromise themselves by an antiseptic solution to a problem of personal anguish, rather than stay and fight for a great university. There is reason to fear these professors, for *they* can destroy the university by deserting it.

And sadly there is reason to believe that even after all of the suffering which has occurred in our community, the overwhelming majority of faculty members have not been permanently changed, have not joined our community, *have not really listened to our voices*—at this late date. For a moment on December 8th, eight hundred and twenty-four professors gave us all a glimpse—a brief, glorious vision— of the university as a loving community. If only the Free Speech Movement could have ended that day! But already the professors have compromised away much for which they stood on that day. They have shamed themselves in view of the students and their colleagues all over the country. The ramparts of rationalization which our society's conditioning had erected about our professors' souls were breached by the relentless hammer-blows of conscience springing from thousands of students united in something called "FSM." But the searing light of their momentary courage became nakedness to them—too painful to endure. After December 8th most faculty members moved quickly to rebuild their justifications for years of barren compromise.

We challenge the faculty to be courageous. A university is a community of students and scholars: be equal to the position of dignity you should hold!! How long will you submit to the doorkeepers who have usurped your power? Is a university no more than a physical plant and an administration? The university cannot be destroyed unless its core is destroyed, and our movement is not weakening that core but strengthening it. Each time the FSM planned to act, it was warned that to act was to destroy. Each time, however, the campus community responded with new vigor. Too many people underestimate the resilience of a community fighting for a principle. Internally, the health of the university is improving. Communication, spirit, moral and intellectual curiosity, all have increased. The faculty has been forced to take the student body more seriously; it has begun to respect students. Furthermore, it has gained the opportunity to achieve a profound respect from the students. Those professors at Cal and other universities who love to teach, should be looking to Berkeley as the nation's greatest reservoir of students who embody the vital balance of moral integrity and high intellectual calibre. If the university community can maintain its courage, stand firmly together in the face of attacks from without, it will survive. Those who fearfully warn that we are destroying the university, are unwittingly weakening the FSM and the university. In the final analysis, only fear destroys!

II. Free Speech and the Factory

In our fight for free speech we said the "machine" must stop. We said that we must put our bodies on the line, on the machinery, in the wheels and gears, and that the "knowledge factory" must be brought to a halt. Now we must begin to clarify, for ourselves, what we mean by "factory."

We need to clarify this because the issues of free speech and the factory, of politics and education on the campus, are in danger of becoming separated. For example, the press has had the tendency to assert this separation when they insist that we return to our studies; that we are not in a center for political activity, but a center for education. Likewise, the faculty betrays the same tendency in its desire to settle the free speech issue as quickly and quietly as possible in order that we may return to the "normal conduct" of our "great university."

In contrast to this tendency to separate the issues, many thousands of *us*, the Free Speech Movement, have asserted that politics and education are inseparable, that the *political* issue of the First and Fourteenth Amendments and the *educational issue* cannot be separated. In place of "great university," we have said "impersonal bureaucracy," "machine," or "knowledge factory." If we emerge as victors from our long and still hard-to-be-won battle for free speech, will we then be returning to *less* than a factory? *Is* this a great university? If we are to take *ourselves* seriously we must define precisely what we meant when we said "knowledge factory."

The best way to identify the parts of our multiversity machinery is simply observe it "stripped down" to the bare essentials. In the context of a dazzling circus of "bait," which obscures our vision of the machinery, we get a four-year-long series of sharp staccatos: eight semesters, forty courses, one hundred twenty or more "units," ten to fifteen impersonal lectures *per week*, one to three oversized discussion meetings per week led by poorly paid graduate student "teachers." Over a period of four years the student-cog receives close to forty bibliographies; evaluation amounts to little more than pushing the test button, which results in over one hundred regurgitations in four years; and the writing of twenty to thirty-five "papers" in four years, in this context means that they are of necessity technically and substantially poor due to a lack of time for thought. The course-grade-unit system structure, resting on the foundation of departmentalization, produces knowledge for the student-cog which has been exploded into thousands of bits and is force-fed, by the coercion of grades. We all know what happens when we really get "turned on" by a great idea, a great man, or a great book: we pursue that interest at the risk of flunking out. The pursuit of thought, a painful but highly exhilarating process, requires, above all, the element of time.

Human nerves and flesh are transmuted under the pressure and stress of the university routine. It is as though we have become raw material in the strictly *in*organic sense. But the Free Speech Movement has given us an extraordinary taste of what it means to be part of something organic. Jumping off the conveyors, we have become a community of furiously talking, feeling, and thinking human beings. If we take seriously our common agreement that we stopped a "machine" how can we be accused of conspiring to destroy a "great university"? Where?

*   *   *

III. The Factory and the Society

The emotions expressed in the letter reflect the problems of the society as expressed in the multiversity as well as in a small prep school for girls in the East. The university has become grotesquely distorted into a "multiversity"; a public utility serving the purely technical needs of a society. In Clark Kerr's words, it is a factory for the production of knowledge and technicians to service society's many bureaucracies.

Current federal and private support programs for the university have been compared to classic examples of imperialism and neocolonialism. The government has invested in underdeveloped, capital-starved institutions, and imposed a pattern of growth and development upon them, which if disrupted, would lead to economic breakdown and political chaos.

Research and training replace scholarship and learning. In this system even during the first two years, the student is pressured to specialize or endure huge, impersonal lecture courses. He loses contact with his professors as they turn more to research and publishing, and away from teaching. His professors lose contact with one another as they serve a discipline and turn away from dialogue. Forms and structures stifle humane learning.

The student is powerless even to affect those aspects of the university supposedly closest to him. His student "government" by political castrates is a fraud permitted to operate only within limits imposed autocratically by the administration. Thus it is constitutionally mandated to serve the status quo. Likewise, the student has no power over the social regulations which affect his privacy, and little influence in shaping the character of the dormitories in which he lives. The university assumes the role of the parent.

As a human being seeking to enrich himself, the student has no place in the multiversity. Instead he becomes a mercenary, paid off in grades, status, and degrees, all of which can eventually be cashed in for hard currency on the job market. His education is not valued for its enlightenment and the freedom it should enable him to enjoy, but for the amount of money it will enable him to make. Credits for courses are subtly transformed into credit cards as the multiversity inculcates the values of the acquisitive society.

It has been written that "The main concern of the university should not be with the publishing of books, getting money from legislators, lobbying for federal aid, wooing the rich, producing bombs and deadly bacteria." Nor should it be with passing along the morality of the middle class, nor the morality of the white man, nor even the morality of the potpourri we call "western society." Nor should it be with acting as a second household or church for the young man away from home, nor as a playground for twisters, neophyte drinkers, and pledge classes. Already the parallels between the university and the habits of the society are many; the parallels between our academic and financial systems of credit, between competition for grades and for chamber of commerce awards, between cheating and price rigging, and between statements of "Attendance is a privilege, not a right," and "We reserve the right to refuse service to anyone."

In an article in the current *New York Review of Books*, Paul Goodman poignantly comments upon the plight of the modern student: "At present in the United States, students—middle class youth—are the major exploited class, (Negroes, small farmers, the aged are rather outcast groups; their labor is not needed and they are not wanted). The labor of intelligent youth is needed and they are accordingly subjected to tight scheduling, speedup and other factory exploitative methods. Then it is not surprising if they organize their CIO. It is frivolous to tell them to go elsewhere if they don't like the rules; for they have no choice but to go to college, and one factory is like another."

In saying these things it is important to avoid a certain misunderstanding. By identifying the parts of the machinery in our factory, the way in which we have described them, and their blending into our society of institutionalized greed, might lead people to assume that we have a fundamental bias against institutions as such; that we wish to destroy the structure altogether, to establish politics on the campus, and lash out against the power structure for the purposes of expressing a kind of collective orgasm of seething resentment against the "power structure." When we assert that free speech and the factory, or politics and education, are bound up together, we are again pointing to the obvious. In a twentieth-century industrial state, ignorance will be the definition of slavery. If centers of education fail, they will be the producers of the twentieth-century slave. To put it in more traditionally American terms, popular government cannot survive without education for the people. The people are more and more in the schools. But the pressure of the logistics of mass popular education combined with excessive greed has resulted in the machinery of the educational process having displaced the freedom to learn. We must now begin the demand of the right to know; to know the realities of the present world-in-revolution, and to have an opportunity to learn how to think clearly in an extended manner about that world. It is ours to demand meaning; we must insist upon meaning!

The Free University of California

The question of how to break down the machinery and build "intellectual communities worthy of the hopes and responsibilities of our people," is on the minds of many participants in the Free Speech Movement. No one supposes he has the answers, but they can come from the Berkeley community. Our task is to generate these answers and to discover how they can be implemented. The Free Speech Movement proposes that the Free University of California be formed. We are inviting prominent intellectual and political figures to address the university community. We would like to see seminars on the educational revolution and many other topics which are not considered in the university. In the near future we hope that discussions with students, faculty, and members of the community, will take place independent of the university community. Such discussions would deal with any topic in which a sufficient number of people are interested. We would like to establish the availability of a revolutionary experience in education. If we succeed, we will accomplish a feat more radical and significant than anything the Free Speech Movement has attempted. We will succeed in beginning to bring humanity back to campus.

THE STUDENT AS NIGGER (1967) From Jerry Farber, "Modern Slaves: The Student as Nigger," as quoted in the *Los Angeles Free Press*, March 3, 1967.

Students are niggers. When you get that straight, our schools begin to make sense. It's more important, though, to understand why they're niggers. If we follow that question seriously enough, it will lead us past the zone of academic bull—where dedicated teachers pass their knowledge on to a new generation, and into the nitty-gritty of human needs and hang-ups. And from there we can go on to consider whether it might ever be possible for students to come up from slavery.

First let's see what's happening now. Let's look at the role students play in what we like to call education.

Smiles & Shuffles

A student at Cal State is expected to know his place. He calls a faculty member "Sir" or "Doctor" or "Professor"—and he smiles and shuffles some as he stands outside the professor's office waiting for permission to enter. The faculty tell him what courses to take (in my department, English, even electives have to be approved by a faculty member); they tell him what to read, what to write, and, frequently, where to set the margins on his typewriter. They tell him what's true and what isn't. Some teachers insist that they encourage dissent but they're almost always jiving and every student knows it. Tell the man what he wants to hear or he'll fail your ass out of the course.

When a teacher says "jump," students jump. I know of one professor who refused to take up class time for exams and required students to show up for tests at 6:30 in the morning. And they did, by God! Another, at exam time, provides answer cards to be filled out—each one enclosed in a paper bag with a hole cut in the top to see through. Students stick their writing hands in the bags while taking the test. The teacher isn't a provo; I wish he were. He does it to prevent cheating. Another colleague once caught a student reading during one of his lectures and threw her book against the wall. Still another lectures his students into a stupor and then screams at them in a rage when they fall asleep.

Follow Orders

Even more discouraging than this Auschwitz approach to education is the fact that the students take it. They haven't gone through twelve years of public school for nothing. They've learned one thing and perhaps only one thing during those twelve years. They've forgotten their algebra. They're hopelessly vague about chemistry and physics. They've grown to fear and resent literature. They write like they've been lobotomized. But, Jesus, can they follow orders! Freshmen come up to me with an essay and ask if I want it folded and whether their name should be in the upper right hand corner. And I want to cry and kiss them and caress their poor tortured heads.

Students don't ask that orders make sense. They give up expecting things to make sense long before they leave elementary school. Things are true because the teacher says they're true. At a very early age we all learn to accept "two truths," as did certain medieval churchmen. Outside of class, things are true to your tongue, your fingers, your stomach, your heart. Inside class, things are true by reason of authority. And that's just fine because you don't care anyway. Miss Wiedemeyer tells you a noun is a person, place or thing. So let it be. You don't give a rat's ———, she doesn't give a rat's ———.

What school amounts to, then, for white and black kids alike, is a 12-year course in how to be slaves. What else could explain what I see in a freshman class? They've got that slave mentality: obliging and ingratiating on the surface but hostile and resistant underneath.

As do black slaves, students vary in their awareness of what's going on. Some recognize their own put-on for what it is and even let their rebellion break through to the surface now and then. Others—including most of the "good students"—have been more deeply brainwashed. They swallow the bullshit with greedy mouths. They honest-to-God believe in grades, in busy work, in General Education requirements. They're pathetically eager to be pushed around. They're like those old greyheaded house niggers you can still find in the South who don't see what all the fuss is about because Mr. Charlie "treats us real good."

Inward Anger

The saddest cases among both black slaves and student slaves are the ones who have so thoroughly introjected their masters' values that their anger is all turned inward. At Cal State these are the kids for whom every low grade is torture, who stammer and shake when they speak to a professor, who go through an emotional crisis every time they're called upon during class. You can recognize them easily at finals time. Their faces are festooned with fresh pimples; their bowels boil audibly across the room. If there really is a Last Judgement, then the parents and teachers who created these wrecks are going to burn in hell.

So students are niggers. It's time to find out why, and to do this, we have to take a long look at Mr. Charlie.

The teachers I know best are college professors. Outside the classroom and taken as a group, their most striking characteristic is timidity.

Forces a Split

I'm not sure why teachers are so chicken———. It could be that academic training itself forces a split between thought and action. It might also be that the tenured security of a teaching job attracts timid persons and, furthermore, that teaching, like police work, pulls in persons who are unsure of themselves and need weapons and the other external trappings of authority.

At any rate teachers ARE short on———. And, as Judy Eisenstein has eloquently pointed out, the classroom offers an artificial and protected environment in which they can exercise their will to power.

The grade is a hell of a weapon. It may not rest on your hip, potent and rigid like a cop's gun, but in the long run it's more powerful. At your personal whim—any time you choose—you can keep 35 students up for nights and have the pleasure of seeing them walk into the classroom pasty-faced and red-eyed carrying a sheaf of typewritten pages, with title page, MLA footnotes and margins set at 15 and 91.

The general timidity which causes teachers to make niggers of their students usually includes a more specific fear—fear of the students themselves. After all, students are different, just like black people. You stand exposed in front of them, knowing that their interests, their values and their language are different from yours. To make matters worse, you may suspect that you yourself are not the most engaging of persons. What then can protect you from their ridicule and scorn? Respect for Authority. That's what. It's the policeman's gun again.

'White Supremacy'

The teacher's fear is mixed with an understandable need to be admired and to feel superior, a need which also makes him cling to his "white supremacy." Ideally, a teacher should minimize the distance between himself and his students. He should encourage them not to need him—eventually or even immediately. But this is rarely the case. Teachers make themselves high priests of arcane mysteries. They become masters of mumbo-jumbo. Even a more or less conscientious teacher may be torn between the desire to give and the desire to hold them in bondage to him. I can find no other explanation that accounts for the way my own subject, literature, is generally taught. Literature, which ought to be a source of joy, solace and enlightenment, often becomes in the classroom nothing more than a source of anxiety—at best an arena for expertise, a ledger book for the ego.

Finally, there's the darkest reason of all for the master-slave approach to education. The less trained and the less socialized a person is, the more he constitutes a sexual threat and the more he will be subjugated by institutions, such as penitentiaries and schools.

Once a Nigger

So you can add sexual repression to the list of causes, along with vanity, fear and will to power, that turn the teacher into Mr. Charlie. You might also want to keep in mind that he was a nigger once himself and has never really gotten over it. And there are more causes, some of which are better described in sociological than in psychological terms. Work them out, it's not hard. But in the meantime what we've got on our hands is a whole lot of niggers. And what makes this particularly grim is that the student has less chance than the black man of getting out of his bag. Because the student doesn't even know he's in it. That, more or less, is what's happening in higher education. And the results are staggering.

For one thing damn little education takes place in the schools. How could it? You can't educate slaves; you can only train them. Or, to use an even uglier and more timely word, you can only program them.

At my school we even grade people on how they read poetry. That's like grading people on how they———. But we do it. In fact, God help me, I do it. I'm the Adolph Eichmann of English 323. Simon Legree on the poetry plantation. "Tote that iamb! Lift that spondee!" Even to discuss a good poem in that environment is potentially dangerous because the very classroom is contaminated. As hard as I may try to turn students on to poetry, I know that the desks, the tests, the IBM cards, their own attitudes toward school, and my own residue of UCLA method are turning them off.

Another result of student slavery is equally serious. Students don't get emancipated when they graduate. As a matter of fact, we don't let them graduate until they've demonstrated their willingness—over 16 years—to remain slaves. And for important jobs, like teaching, we make them go through more years, just to make sure. What I'm getting at is that we're all more or less niggers and slaves, teachers and students alike.

Intimidate or Kill

Educational oppression is trickier to fight than racial oppression. If you're a black rebel, they can't exile you; they either have to intimidate you or kill you. But in high school or college, they can just bounce you out of the fold. And they do. Rebel students and renegade faculty members get smothered or shot down with devastating accuracy. In high school, it's usually the student who gets it; in college, it's more often the teacher. Others get tired of fighting and voluntarily leave the system. This may be a mistake though. Dropping out of college, for a rebel, is a little like going North, for a Negro. You can't really get away from it so you might as well stay and raise hell.

Students, like black people, have immense unused power. They could, theoretically, insist on participating in their own education. They could make academic freedom bilateral. They could teach their teachers to thrive on love and admiration, rather than fear and respect, and to lay down their weapons. Students could discover community. And they could learn to dance by dancing on the IBM cards. They could make coloring books out of the catalogs and they could put the grading system in a museum. They could raze one set of walls and let life come blowing into the classroom. They could raze another set of walls and let education flow out and flood the streets. They could turn the classroom into where it's at—a "field of action" as Peter Marin describes it. And, believe it or not, they could study eagerly and learn prodigiously for the best of all possible reasons—their own reasons.

They could. Theoretically. They have the power. But only in a very few places, like Berkeley, have they even begun to think about using it. For students, as for black people, the hardest battle isn't with Mr. Charlie. It's with what Mr. Charlie has done to your mind.

RICHARD HOFSTADTER'S COMMENCEMENT REMARKS AT COLUMBIA UNIVERSITY (1968)   From Richard Hofstadter, "Columbia's Ordeal," as quoted in *Phi Delta Kappan*, vol. XL, pp. 15–17.

For a long time, Columbia University has been part of my life. I came here as a graduate student in 1937, returned as a member of the faculty in 1946, and have since remained. In these years, I have had at this university many admired and cherished colleagues, and many able students. In this respect I am but one of a large company of faculty members who, differing as they do on many matters, are alike in their sense of the greatness of this institution and in their affection for it. In this hour of its most terrible trial, it could surely have found a great many of us willing to speak. Quite frankly, I have never been very much interested in commencements, although I recognize their important symbolic function. But it seems to me entirely appropriate, and also symbolic, that on this unusual occasion a member of the faculty should have been asked to speak. Trustees, administrators, and students tend to agree that in ultimate reality the members of the faculty are the university, and we of the faculty have not been disposed to deny it.

Yet while I hope I am speaking in the interest of my university, it would be wrong to suggest that I am precisely speaking for it. It is in fact of the very essence of the conception of the modern university that I wish to put before you that no one is authorized to speak for it. A university is firmly committed to certain basic values of freedom, rationality, inquiry, discussion, and to its own internal order; but it does not have corporate views of public questions. Administrators and trustees are, of course, compelled by practical necessity to take actions that involve some assumptions about the course and meaning of public affairs; but they know that in so doing they are not expressing a corporate university judgment or committing other minds. Members of the faculties often express themselves vigorously on public issues, but they acknowledge the obligation to make it clear that they are not speaking in the name of their university. This fact of our all speaking separately is in itself a thing of great consequence, because in this age of rather overwhelming organizations and collectivities, the university is singular in being a collectivity that serves as a citadel of intellectual individualism.

Although I mean to say a few things about our prospects at Columbia, let me first suggest to you how I think the modern university as such ought to be regarded.

A university is a community, but it is a community of a special kind—a community devoted to inquiry. It exists so that its members may inquire into truths of all sorts. Its presence marks our commitment to the idea that somewhere in society there must be an organization in which anything can be studied or questioned—not merely safe and established things but difficult and inflammatory things, the most troublesome questions of politics and war, of sex and morals, of property and national loyalty. It is governed by the ideal of academic freedom, applicable both to faculty and students. The ideal of academic freedom does indeed put extraordinary demands upon human restraint and upon our capacity for disinterested thought. Yet these demands are really of the same general order as those we regard as essential to any advanced civilization. The very possibility of civilized human discourse rests upon the willingness of people to consider that they may be mistaken. The possibility of modern democracy rests upon the willingness of governments to accept the existence of a loyal opposition, organized to reverse some of their policies and to replace them in office. Similarly, the possibility of the modern free university rests upon the willingness of society to support and sustain institutions part of whose business it is to examine, critically and without stint, the assumptions that prevail in that society. Professors are hired to teach and students are sent to learn with the quite explicit understanding that they are not required to agree with those who hire or send them.

Underlying these remarkable commitments is the belief that in the long run the university will best minister to society's needs not alone through its mundane services but through the far more important office of becoming an intellectual and spiritual balance wheel. This is a very demanding idea, an idea of tremendous sophistication, and it is hardly surprising that we have some trouble in getting it fully accepted by society or in living up to it ourselves. But just because it is demanding we should never grow tired of explaining or trying to realize it. Nor should we too quickly become impatient with those who do not immediately grasp it.

We are very much impressed now not simply by the special character of the free university but also by its fragility. The delicate thing about freedom is that while it requires restraints, it also requires that these restraints normally be self-imposed, and not forced from outside. The delicate thing about the university is that it has a mixed character, that it is suspended between its position in the external world, with all its corruption and evils and cruelties, and the splendid world of our imagination. The university does in fact perform certain mundane services of instruction and information to society—and there are those who think it should aspire to nothing more. It does in fact constitute a kind of free forum—and there are those who want to convert it primarily into a center of political action. But above these aspects of its existence stands its essential character as a center of free inquiry and criticism—a thing not to be sacrificed for anything else. A university is not a service station. Neither is it a political society, nor a meeting place for political societies. With all its limitations and failures, and they are invariably many, it is the best and most benign side of our society insofar as that society aims to cherish the human mind. To realize its essential character, the university has to be dependent upon something less precarious than the momentary balance of forces in society. It has to pin its faith on something that is not hard-boiled or self-regarding. It has to call not merely upon critical intelligence but upon self-criticism and self-restraint. There is no group of professors or administrators, of alumni or students, there is no class or interest in our society that should consider itself exempt from exercising the self-restraint or displaying the generosity that is necessary for the university's support.

Some people argue that because the modern university, whether public or private, is supported by and is part of the larger society, it therefore shares in all the evils of society, and must be quite ruthlessly revolutionized as a necessary step in social reform, or even in social revolution. That universities do share in, and may even at some times and in some respects propagate, certain ills of our society seems to me undeniable. But to imagine that the best way to change a social order is to start by assaulting its most accessible centers of thought and study and criticism is not only to show a complete disregard for the intrinsic character of the university but also to develop a curiously self-destructive strategy for social change. If an attempt is made to politicize completely our primary centers of free argument and inquiry, they will only in the end be forced to lose their character and be reduced to centers of vocational training, nothing more. Total and pure neutrality for the university is in fact impossible, but neutrality should continue to define our aim, and we should resist the demand that the university espouse the political commitments of any of its members. This means, too, that the university should be extraordinarily chary of relationships that even suggest such a political commitment.

The university is the only great organization in modern society which considers itself obliged not just to tolerate but even to give facilities and protection to the very persons who are challenging its own rules, procedures, and policies. To subvert such a fragile structure is all too easy, as we now know. That is why it requires, far more than our political society, a scrupulous and continued dedication to the conditions of orderly and peaceable discussion. The technique of the forceable occupation and closure of a university's buildings with the intention of bringing its activities to a halt is no ordinary bargaining device—it is a thrust at the vitals of university life. It is a powerful device for control by a determined minority, and its continued use would be fatal to any university. In the next few years the universities of this country will have to find the effective strategy to cope with it and to distinguish it sharply and permanently from the many devices of legitimate student petition, demonstration, and protest.

This brings me to our own problem. Our history and situation, our own mistakes, have done a great deal to create this problem; but it must not be regarded as an isolated incident, since it is only the most severe, among American universities, of a number of such incidents. We are at a crisis point in the history of American education and probably in that of the Western world. Not only in New York and Berkeley, but in Madrid and Paris, in Belgrade and Oxford, in Rome, Berlin, and London, and on many college and university campuses throughout this country, students are disaffected, restive, and rebellious.

I cannot pretend to offer a theory that will pull together all these events in a single coherent pattern. Nothing could be more dissimilar, for example, than the intramural situation of students at Columbia and students at the Sorbonne—nor, for that matter, than the response of the community to their actions—and yet the common bond of dissatisfaction is obvious. It is easier to account for the general rise in activism on American campuses, for all our students are troubled today by two facts of the most fundamental consequence for all of us—the persistence at home of poverty and racial injustice, and abroad of the war in Vietnam. It is the first of these that we will have to live with the longest and address ourselves to much more fully, imaginatively, and generously than we have so far done. But in the short run the escalation of this cruel and misconceived venture in Vietnam has done more than any other thing to inflame our students, to undermine their belief in the legitimacy of our normal political processes, and to convince them that violence is the order of the day. I share their horror at this war, and I consider that the deep alienation it has inflicted on young Americans who would otherwise be well disposed toward their country is one of the staggering uncountable costs of the Vietnam undertaking. This war has already toppled a President; but its full effects on our national life have not yet been reckoned.

Here at Columbia, we have suffered a disaster whose precise dimensions it is impossible to state, because the story is not yet finished, and the measure of our loss still depends upon what we do. For every crisis, for every disaster, there has to be some constructive response. At Columbia the constructive response has been a call for university reform. I have spoken to no one who does not believe in its desirability, and I believe that the idea of reform commands an extraordinarily wide positive response in all bodies from trustees to students, though when we come to discussing particulars, we will surely differ sharply about them. Our foundation dates from the eighteenth century, and although we have made elaborate and ingenious improvisations upon it through the generations, we have never had a decisive, concerted moment of thorough and imaginative reconsideration of our procedures. Powers need to be redistributed. Some new organs of decision and communication need to be created. A greater participation of students in university decisions seems to me to be bound to come here and elsewhere. Some students call for student power—others shrink from the term because they have some sense of the arduous work, the sheer tedium, the high responsibilities that are always a part of administrative power. I would suggest that, except for certain areas in which student decision has proved workable, what students need and should have is influence, not power; but they also need formal channels to assure that their influence is in fact effective.

About university reform certain guiding principles ought to be observed. Columbia has been a distinguished university these many decades because it has been doing some things right. Plans for the future should be based upon an evolution from existing structures and arrangements, not upon a utopian scheme for a perfect university. The business of reforming a university takes time, requires a certain willingness to experiment and to retreat from experiment when it does not work, and indeed a willingness not to undertake too many interlocking experiments all at once. As reform demands time, it demands peace of mind, the ability to exchange views and proposals in a calm and deliberative spirit. It cannot be carried out, though it can be begun, in a moment of crisis. It cannot be carried out under duress.

What we need then is stability, peace, mutual confidence. The time will soon come when the first halting gestures toward conciliation can be multiplied and strengthened, when we can move more rapidly to reconstruct the frame of trust.

Friends outside the university who know how serious is the damage we have suffered have asked me: How can Columbia go on after this terrible wound? I can only answer: How can it not go on? The question is not whether it will continue but in what form. Will it fall into a decline and become a third- or fourth-rate institution, will it be as distinguished as it has been for generations past, or will it somehow be made even more distinguished? Columbia is a great—and in the way Americans must reckon time—an ancient university. In this immense, rich country, we have only a limited number of institutions of comparable quality. We are living through a period in which the need for teaching and research—for the services a university performs and the things it stands for—is greater than it ever was before. What kind of a people would we be if we allowed this center of culture and our hope to languish and fail?

Academic Freedom

ACADEMIC FREEDOM AT THE UNIVERSITY OF CHICAGO (1902) From William Rainey Harper, "The President's Report: Administration," *University of Chicago Decennial Publications*, 1st Series (Chicago, 1903), vol. 1, pp. XII–XXIV.

I . . . repeat . . . here a statement made at a recent Convocation. . . .

"Resolved, 1. That the principle of complete freedom of speech on all subjects has from the beginning been regarded as fundamental in the University of Chicago, as has been shown both by the attitude of the President and the Board of Trustees and by the actual practice of the President and the professors.

"2. That this principle can neither now nor at any future time be called in question.

"3. That it is desirable to have it clearly understood that the University, as such, does not appear as a disputant on either side upon any public question; and that the utterances which any professor may make in public are to be regarded as representing his opinions only.

"To this statement of the Congregation I wish to add, first, that whatever may or may not have happened in other universities, in the University of Chicago neither the Trustees, nor the President, nor anyone in official position has at any time called any instructor to account for any public utterances which he may have made. Still ·further, in no single case has a donor to the University called the attention of the Trustees to the teaching of any officer of the University as being distasteful or objectionable. Still further, it is my opinion that no donor of money to a university, whether that donor be an individual or the state, has any right, before God or man, to interfere with the teaching of officers appointed to give instruction in a university. . . . Neither an individual, nor the state, nor the church has the right to interfere with the search for truth, or with its promulgation when found. Individuals, or the state, or the church may found schools for propagating certain special kinds of instruction, but such schools are not universities, and may not be so denominated. A donor has the privilege of ceasing to make his gifts to an institution if, in his opinion, for any reason the work of the institution is not satisfactory; but as donor he has no right to interfere with the administration or the instruction of the university. The trustees in an institution in which such interference has taken place may not maintain their self-respect and remain trustees. They owe it to themselves and to the cause of liberty of thought to resign their places rather than to yield a principle the significance of which rises above all else in comparision. In order to be specific, and in order not to be misunderstood, I wish to say again that no donor of funds to the University—and I include in the number of donors the founder of the

University, Mr. Rockefeller—has ever by a single word or act indicated his dissatisfaction with the instruction given to students in the University, or with the public expression of opinion made by an officer of the University. I vouch for the truth of this statement, and I trust that it may have the largest possible publicity.

"Concerning the second subject, the use and abuse of the right of free expression by officers of the University staff: As I have said, an instructor in the University has an absolute right to express his opinion. If such an instructor is on an appointment for two or three or four years, and if during these years he exercises this right in such a way as to do himself and the institution serious injury, it is of course the privilege of the University to allow his appointment to lapse at the end of the term for which it was originally made. If an officer on permanent appointment abuses his privilege as a professor, the University must suffer and it is proper that it should suffer. This is only the direct and inevitable consequence of the lack of foresight and wisdom involved in the original appointment. The injury thus accruing to the University is, moreover, far less serious than would follow if, for an expression of opinion differing from that of the majority of the Faculty, or from that of the Board of Trustees, or from that of the President of the University, a permanent officer were asked to present his resignation. The greatest single element necessary for the cultivation of the academic spirit is the feeling of security from interference. It is only those who have this feeling that are able to do work which in the highest sense will be beneficial to humanity. Freedom of expression must be given the members of a university faculty, even though it be abused; for, as has been said, the abuse of it is not so great an evil as the restriction of such liberty. But it may be asked: In what way may the professor abuse his privilege of freedom of expression? Or, to put the question more largely: In what way does a professor bring reproach and injury to himself and to his institution? I answer: A professor is guilty of an abuse of his privilege who promulgates as truth ideas or opinions which have not been tested scientifically by his colleagues in the same department of research or investigation. A professor has no right to proclaim to the public a truth discovered which is yet unsettled and uncertain. A professor abuses his privilege who takes advantage of a class-room exercise to propagate the partisan views of one or another of the political parties. The university is no place for partisanship. From the teacher's desk should emanate the discussion of principles, the judicial statement of arguments from various points of view, and not the one-sided representations of a partisan character. A professor abuses his privilege who in any way seeks to influence his pupils or the public by sensational methods. A professor abuses his privilege of expression of opinion when, although a student and perhaps an authority in one department or group of departments, he undertakes to speak authoritatively on subjects which have no relationship to the department in which he was appointed to give instruction. A professor abuses his privilege in many cases when, although shut off in large measure from the world, and engaged within a narrow field of investigation, he undertakes to instruct his colleagues or the public concerning matters in the world at large in connection with which he has had little or no experience. A professor abuses his privilege of freedom of expression when he fails to exercise that quality ordinarily called common sense, which, it must be confessed, in some cases the professor lacks. A professor ought not to make such an exhibition of his weakness, or so many times, that the attention of the public at large is called to the fact. In this respect he has no larger liberty than other men.

"But may a professor do all of these things and yet remain an officer in the University? Yes. The professor in most cases is only an ordinary man. Perfection is not to be expected of him. like men in other professions, professors have their weaknesses. But will a professor under any circumstances be asked to withdraw from the University? Yes. His resignation will be demanded, and will be accepted, when, in the opinion of those in authority, he has been guilty of immorality, or when for any reason he has proved himself to be incompetent to perform the service called for. The public should be on its guard in two particulars: The utterance of a professor, however wise or foolish, is not the utterance of the University. No individual, no group of individuals, can speak for the University. A statement, by whomsoever made, is the statement of an individual.

THE CALL FOR A MEETING TO ORGANIZE THE AMERICAN ASSOCIATION OF UNIVERSITY PROFESSORS (1914) From *Bulletin of the American Association of University Professors,* vol. II, pp. 11–13.

The scientific and specialized interests of members of American university faculties are well cared for by various learned societies. No organization exists, however, which at once represents the common interests of the teaching staffs and deals with the general problems of university policy. Believing that a society, comparable to the American Bar Association and the American Medical Association in kindred professions, could be of substantial service to the ends for which universities exist, members of the faculties of a number of institutions have undertaken to bring about the formation of a national Association of University Professors. The general purposes of such an Association would be to facilitate a more effective cooperation among the members of the profession in the discharge of their special responsibilities as custodians of the interests of higher education and research in American; to promote a more general and methodical discussion of problems relating to education in higher institutions of learning; to create means for the authoritative expression of the public opinion of college and university teachers; to make collective action possible; and to maintain and advance the standards and ideals of the profession. The specific activities in which these general purposes may best find expression will, of course, become fully evident only through experience. There is, however, already manifest among university teachers an interest in such matters as the proper organization of departments, and their relation to one another; the relations of instruction and research, both in colleges and graduate schools; the adjustment of graduate to undergraduate instruction, and of professional studies to both; the possibility of cooperation between universities to prevent unnecessary duplication of effort; the effectiveness of the manner in which the university teaching profession is now recruited; the problem of graduate fellowships and scholarships; the desirability and practicability of an increased migration of graduate students; the suitable recognition of intellectual eminence, and the manner of awarding honorary degrees; the proper conditions of the tenure of the professorial office; methods of appointment and promotion, and the character of the qualifications to be considered in either case; the function of faculties in university government; the relations of facilities to trustees; the impartial determination of the facts in cases in which serious violations of academic freedom are alleged. It may be expected that the Association will from time to time take up the consideration of subjects of this character, will create committees for the purpose of ascertaining the experience and the existing practice of the American universities in such matters, and will, at its annual meetings, discuss the committees' reports and make recommendations upon the questions which these reports may raise. It would also appear desirable that the Association should, as soon as its financial condition makes this possible, establish an annual, semi-annual or quarterly periodical, devoted to the discussion of similar questions and to the interchange of information respecting the policies and activities of the different universities.

Those concerned in the organization of the Association do not, however, desire in any way to determine its programme in advance. What seems to them essential is that, in the working out of a national policy of higher education and research, the general body of university teachers shall exercise an effectual influence; that in the determination of the future of the profession, the profession itself shall have a voice; that issues hereafter arising which may seriously affect the work of the universities, or the usefulness, dignity, or standards of the professorate, shall be dealt with only after careful consideration and wide discussion. These essentials appear unlikely to be realized, unless there exist some organization fairly representative of the ideals, the interests and the point of view of the profession as such.

GENERAL DECLARATION OF PRINCIPLES OF THE AMERICAN ASSOCIATION OF UNIVERSITY PROFESSORS (1915) From American Association of University Professors, *Report of the Committee on Academic Freedom and Tenure* (n.p., 1915), pp. 6–29.

I. General Declaration of Principles

The term "academic freedom" has traditionally had two applications—to the freedom of the teacher and to that of the student, *Lehrfreiheit* and *Lernfreiheit*. It need scarcely be pointed out that the freedom which is the subject of this report is that of the teacher. Academic freedom in this sense comprises three elements: freedom of inquiry and research; freedom of teaching within the university or college; and freedom of extra-mural utterance and action. The first of these is almost everywhere so safeguarded that the dangers of its infringement are slight. It may therefore be disregarded in this report. The second and third phases of academic freedom are closely related, and are often not distinguished. The third, however, has an importance of its own, since of late it has perhaps more frequently been the occasion of difficulties and controversies than has the question of freedom of intra-academic teaching. All five of the cases which have recently been investigated by committees of this Association have involved, at least as one factor, the right of university teachers to express their opinions freely outside the university or to engage in political activities in their capacity as citizens. The general principles which have to do with freedom of teaching in both these senses seem to the committee to be in great part, though not wholly, the same. In this report, therefore, we shall consider the matter primarily with reference to freedom of teaching within the university, and shall assume that what is said thereon is also applicable to the freedom of speech of university teachers outside their institutions, subject to certain qualifications and supplementary considerations which will be pointed out in the course of the report.

An adequate discussion of academic freedom must necessarily consider three matters: (1) the scope and basis of the power exercised by those bodies having ultimate legal authority in academic affairs; (2) the nature of the academic calling; (3) the function of the academic institution or university.

*   *   *

3. THE FUNCTION OF THE ACADEMIC INSTITUTION

The importance of academic freedom is most clearly perceived in the light of the purposes for which universities exist. These are three in number:

A. To promote inquiry and advance the sum of human knowledge.

B. To provide general instruction to the students.

C. To develop experts for various branches of the public service.

Let us consider each of these. In the earlier stages of a nation's intellectual development, the chief concern of educational institutions is to train the growing generation and to diffuse the already accepted knowledge. It is only slowly that there comes to be provided in the highest institutions of learning the opportunity for the gradual wresting from nature of her intimate secrets. The modern university is becoming more and more the home of scientific research. There are three fields of human inquiry in which the race is only at the beginning: natural science, social science, and philosophy and religion, dealing with the relations of man to outer nature, to his fellow men, and to the ultimate realities and values. In natural science all that we have learned but serves to make us realize more deeply how much more remains to be discovered. In social science in its largest sense, which is concerned with the relations of men in society and with the conditions of social order and well-being, we have learned only an adumbration of the laws which govern these vastly complex phenomena. Finally, in the spiritual life, and in the interpretation of the general meaning and ends of human existence and its relation to the universe, we are still far from a comprehension of the final truths, and from a universal agreement among all sincere and earnest men. In all of these domains of knowledge, the first condition of progress is complete and unlimited freedom to pursue inquiry and publish its results. Such freedom is the breath in the nostrils of all scientific activity.

The second function—which for a long time was the only function—of the American college or university is to provide instruction for students. It is scarcely open to question that freedom of utterance is as important to the teacher as it is to the investigator. No man can be a successful teacher unless he enjoys the respect of his students, and their confidence in his intellectual integrity. It is clear, however, that this confidence will be impaired if there is suspicion on the part of the student that the teacher is not expressing himself fully or frankly, or that college and university teachers in general are a repressed and intimidated class who dare not speak with that candor and courage which youth always demands in those whom it is to esteem. The average student is a discerning observer, who soon takes the measure of his instructor. It is not only the character of the instruction but also the character of the instructor that counts; and if the student has reason to believe that the instructor is not true to himself, the virtue of the instruction as an educative force is incalculably diminished. There must be in the mind of the teacher no mental reservation. He must give the student the best of what he has and what he is.

The third function of the modern university is to develop experts for the use of the community. If there is one thing that distinguishes the more recent developments of democracy, it is the recognition by legislators of the inherent complexities of economic, social, and political life, and the difficulty of solving problems of technical adjustment without technical knowledge. The recognition of this fact has led to a continually greater demand for the aid of experts in these subjects, to advise both legislators and administrators. The training of such experts has, accordingly, in recent years, become an important part of the work of the universities; and in almost every one of our higher institutions of learning the professors of the economic, social, and political sciences have been drafted to an increasing extent into more or less unofficial participation in the public service. It is obvious that here again the scholar must be absolutely free not only to pursue his investigations but to declare the results of his researches, no matter where they may lead him or to what extent they may come into conflict with accepted opinion. To be of use to the legislator or the administrator, he must enjoy their complete confidence in the disinterestedness of his conclusions.

It is clear, then, that the university cannot perform its threefold function without accepting and enforcing to the fullest extent the principle of academic freedom. The responsibility of the university as a whole is to the community at large, and any restriction upon the freedom of the instructor is bound to react injuriously upon the efficiency and the *morale* of the institution, and therefore ultimately upon the interests of the community.

*   *   *

An inviolable refuge from such tyranny should be found in the university. It should be an intellectual experiment station, where new ideas may germinate and where their fruit, though still distasteful to the community as a whole, may be allowed to ripen until finally, perchance, it may become a part of the accepted intellectual food of the nation or of the world. Not less is it a distinctive duty of the university to be the conservator of all genuine elements of value in the past thought and life of mankind which are not in the fashion of the moment. Though it need not be the "home of beaten causes," the university is, indeed, likely always to exercise a certain form of conservative influence. For by its nature it is committed to the principle that knowledge should precede action, to the caution (by no means synonymous with intellectual timidity) which is an essential part of the scientific method, to a sense of the complexity of social problems, to the practice of taking long views into the future, and to a reasonable regard for the teachings of experience. One of its most characteristic functions in a democratic society is to help make public opinion more self-critical and more circumspect, to check the more hasty and unconsidered impulses of popular feeling, to train the democracy to the habit of looking before and after. It is precisely this function of the university which is most injured by any restriction upon academic freedom; and it is precisely those who most value this aspect of the university's work who should most earnestly protest against any such restriction. For the public may respect, and be influenced by, the counsels of prudence and of moderation which are given by men of science, if it believes those counsels to be the disinterested expression of the scientific temper and of unbiased inquiry. It is little likely to respect or heed them if it has reason to believe that they are the expression of the interests, or the timidities, of the limited portion of the community which is in a position to endow institutions of learning, or is most likely to be represented upon their boards of trustees. And a plausible reason for this belief is given the public so long as our universities are not organized in such a way as to make impossible any exercise of pressure upon professorial opinions and utterances by governing boards of laymen.

Since there are no rights without corresponding duties, the considerations heretofore set down with respect to the freedom of the academic teacher entail certain correlative obligations. The claim to freedom of teaching is made in the interest of the integrity and of the progress of scientific inquiry; it is, therefore, only those who carry on their work in the temper of the scientific inquirer who may justly assert this claim. The liberty of the scholar within the university to set forth his conclusions, be they what they may, is conditioned by their being conclusions gained by a scholar's method and held in a scholar's spirit; that is to say, they must be the fruits of competent and patient and sincere inquiry, and they should be set forth with dignity, courtesy, and temperateness of language. The university teacher, in giving instruction upon controversial matters, while he is under no obligation to hide his own opinion under a mountain of equivocal verbiage, should, if he is fit for his position, be a person of a fair and judicial mind; he should, in dealing with such subjects, set forth justly, without suppression or innuendo, the divergent opinions of other investigators; he should cause his students to become familiar with the best published expressions of the great historic types of doctrine upon the questions at issue; and he should above all, remember that his business is not to provide his students with ready-made conclusions, but to train them to think for themselves, and to provide them access to those materials which they need if they are to think intelligently.

*   *   *

It is, it will be seen, in no sense the contention of this committee that academic freedom implies that individual teachers should be exempt from all restraints as to the matter or manner of their utterances, either within or without the university. Such restraints as are necessary should in the main, your committee holds, be self-imposed, or enforced by the public opinion of the profession. But there may, undoubtedly, arise occasional cases in which the aberrations of individuals may require to be checked by definite disciplinary action. What this report chiefly maintains is that such action can not with safety be taken by bodies not composed of members of the academic profession. Lay governing boards are competent to judge concerning charges of habitual neglect of assigned duties, on the part of individual teachers, and concerning charges of grave moral delinquency. But in matters of opinion, and of the utterance of opinion, such boards cannot intervene without destroying, to the extent of their intervention, the essential nature of a university—without converting it from a place dedicated to openness of mind, in which the conclusions expressed are the tested conclusions of trained scholars, into a place barred against the access of new light, and precommitted to the opinions or prejudices of men who have not been set apart or expressly trained for the scholar's duties. It is, in short, not the absolute freedom of utterance of the individual scholar, but the absolute freedom of thought, of inquiry, of discussion and of teaching, of the academic profession, that is asserted by this declaration of principles. It is conceivable that our profession may prove unworthy of its high calling, and unfit to exercise the responsibilities that belong to it. But it will scarcely be said as yet to have given evidence of such unfitness. And the existence of this Association, as it seems to your committee, must be construed as a pledge, not only that the profession will earnestly guard those liberties without which it can not rightly render its distinctive and indispensable service to society, but also that it will with equal earnestness seek to maintain such standards of professional character, and of scientific integrity and competency, as shall make it a fit instrument for that service.

II. Practical Proposals

As the foregoing declaration implies, the ends to be accomplished are chiefly three:

First: To safeguard freedom of inquiry and of teaching against both covert and overt attacks, by providing suitable judicial bodies, composed of members of the academic profession, which may be called into action before university teachers are dismissed or disciplined, and may determine in what cases the question of academic freedom is actually involved.

Second: By the same means, to protect college executives and governing boards against unjust charges of infringement of academic freedom, or of arbitrary and dictatorial conduct—charges which, when they gain wide currency and belief, are highly detrimental to the good repute and the influence of universities.

Third: To render the profession more attractive to men of high ability and strong personality by insuring the dignity, the independence, and the reasonable security of tenure, of the professorial office.

The measures which it is believed to be necessary for our universities to adopt to realize these ends—measures which have already been adopted in part by some institutions—are four:

A. *Action by Faculty Committees on Reappointments.* Official action relating to reappointments and refusals of reappointment should be taken only with the advice and consent of some board or committee representative of the faculty. Your committee does not desire to make at this time any suggestion as to the manner of selection of such boards.

B. *Definition of Tenure of Office.* In every institution there should be an unequivocal understanding as to the term of each appointment; and the tenure of professorships and associate professorships, and of all positions above the grade of instructor after ten years of service, should be permanent (subject to the provisions hereinafter given for removal upon charges). In those state universities which are legally incapable of making contracts for more than a limited period, the governing boards should announce their policy with respect to the presumption of reappointment in the several classes of position, and such announcements, though not legally enforceable, should be regarded as morally binding. No university teacher of any rank should, except in cases of grave moral delinquency, receive notice of dismissal or of refusal of reappointment, later than three months before the close of any academic year, and in the case of teachers above the grade of instructor, one year's notice should be given.

C. *Formulation of Grounds for Dismissal.* In every institution the grounds which will be regarded as justifying the dismissal of members of the faculty should be formulated with reasonable definiteness; and in the case of institutions which impose upon their faculties doctrinal standards of a sectarian or partisan character, these standards should be clearly defined and the body or individual having authority to interpret them, in case of controversy, should be designated. Your committee does not think it best at this time to attempt to enumerate the legitimate grounds for dismissal, believing it to be preferable that individual institutions should take the initiative in this.

D. *Judicial Hearings Before Dismissal.* Every university or college teacher should be entitled, before dismissal[1] or demotion, to have the charges against him stated in writing in specific terms and to have a fair trial on those charges before a special or permanent judicial committee chosen by the faculty senate or council, or by the faculty at large. At such trial the teacher accused should have full opportunity to present evidence, and, if the charge is one of professional incompetency, a formal report upon his work should be first made in writing by the teachers of his own department and of cognate departments in the university, and, if the teacher concerned so desire, by a comittee of his fellow specialists from other institutions, appointed by some competent authority.

The above declaration of principles and practical proposals are respectfully submitted by your committee to the approval of the Association, with the suggestion that, if approved, they be recommended to the consideration of the faculties, administrative officers, and governing boards of the American universities and colleges.

EDWIN R. A. SELIGMAN, Chairman
Columbia University
CHARLES E. BENNETT,
Cornell University
JAMES Q. DEALEY,
Brown University
RICHARD T. ELY,
University of Wisconsin
HENRY W. FARNAM,
Yale University
FRANK A. FETTER,
Princeton University
FRANKLIN H. GIDDINGS,
Columbia University

CHARLES A. KOFOID,
University of California
ARTHUR O. LOVEJOY,
Johns Hopkins University
FREDERICK W. PADELFORD,
University of Washington
ROSCOE POUND,
Harvard University
HOWARD C. WARREN,
Princeton University
ULYSSES G. WEATHERLY,
University of Indiana

At the annual meeting of the American Association of University Professors held in Washington, D.C., on January 1, 1916, it was moved and carried that the report of the Committee on Academic Freedom and Academic Tenure be accepted and approved.

JOHN DEWEY,
President
A. O. LOVEJOY,
Secretary

[1]This does not refer to refusals of reappointment at the expiration of the terms of office of teachers below the rank of associate professor. All such questions of reappointment should, as above provided, be acted upon by a faculty committee.

OKLAHOMA LOYALTY OATH RULED UNCONSTITUTIONAL (1952) From
Weiman *v.* Updegraff, 344 U. S. 183.

Appeal from the Supreme Court of Oklahoma.

MR. JUSTICE CLARK DELIVERED THE OPINION OF THE COURT.

This is an appeal from a decision of the Supreme Court of Oklahoma upholding the validity of a loyalty oath prescribed by Oklahoma statute for all state officers and employees. . . . Appellants, employed by the state as members of the faculty and staff of Oklahoma Agricultural and Mechanical College, failed, within the thirty days permitted, to take the oath required by the Act. . . . Their objections centered largely on the following clauses of the oath:

". . . That I am not affiliated directly or indirectly . . . with any foreign political agency, party, organization or Government, or with any agency, party, organization, association, or group whatever which has been officially determined by the United States Attorney General or other authorized agency of the United States to be a communist front or subversive organization; . . . that I will take up arms in the defense of the United States in time of War, or National Emergency, if necessary; that within the five (5) years immediately preceding the taking of this oath (or affirmation) I have not been a member of . . . any agency, party, organization, association, or group whatever which has been officially determined by the United States Attorney General or other authorized public agency of the United States to be a communist front or subversive organization. . . ."

The purpose of the Act, we are told, "was to make loyalty a qualification to hold public office or be employed by the State." . . . During periods of international stress, the extent of legislation with such objectives accentuates our traditional concern about the relation of government to the individual in a free society. The perennial problem of defining that relationship becomes acute when disloyalty is screened by ideological patterns and techniques of disguise that make it difficult to identify. Democratic government is not powerless to meet this threat, but it must do so without infringing the freedoms that are the ultimate values of all democratic living. In the adoption of such means as it believes effective, the legislature is therefore confronted with the problem of balancing its interest in national security with the often conflicting constitutional rights of the individual. . . .

We are thus brought to the question . . . whether the Due Process Clause permits a state, in attempting to bar disloyal individuals from its employ, to exclude persons solely on the basis of organizational membership, regardless of their knowledge concerning the organizations to which they belonged. For, under the statute before us, the fact of membership alone disqualifies. If the rule be expressed as a presumption of disloyalty, it is a conclusive one.

But membership may be innocent. A state servant may have joined a proscribed organization unaware of its activities and purposes. In recent years, many completely loyal persons have severed organizational ties after learning for the first time of the character of groups to which they had belonged. . . . At the time of affiliation, a group itself may be innocent, only later coming under the influence of those who would turn it toward illegitimate ends. Conversely, an organization formerly subversive and therefore designated as such may have subsequently freed itself from the influences which orginally led to its listing.

There can be no dispute about the consequences visited upon a person excluded from public employment on disloyalty grounds. In the view of the community, the stain is a deep one; indeed, it has become a badge of infamy. Especially is this so in time of cold war and hot emotions when "each man begins to eye his neighbor as a possible enemy." Yet under the Oklahoma Act, the fact of association alone determines disloyalty and disqualification; it matters not whether association existed innocently or knowingly. To thus inhibit individual freedom of movement is to stifle the flow of democratic expression and controversy at one of its chief sources. . . . Indiscriminate classification of innocent with knowing activity must fall as an assertion of arbitrary power. The oath offends due process. . . .

We need not pause to consider whether an abstract right to public employment exists. It is sufficient to say that constitutional protection does extend to the public servant whose exclusion pursuant to a statute is patently arbitrary or discriminatory. . . .

Reversed. MR. JUSTICE BLACK, CONCURRING.

The Oklahoma oath statute is but one manifestation of a national network of laws aimed at coercing and controlling the minds of men. Test oaths are notorious tools of tyranny. When used to shackle the mind they are, or at least they should be, unspeakably odious to a free people. Test oaths are made still more dangerous when combined with bills of attainder which like this Oklahoma statute impose pains and penalties for past lawful associations and utterances.

Governments need and have ample power to punish treasonable acts. But it does not follow that they must have a further power to punish thought and speech as distinguished from acts. Our own free society should never forget that laws which stigmatize and penalize thought and speech of the unorthodox have a way of reaching, ensnaring and silencing many more people than at first intended. We must have freedom of speech for all or we will in the long run have it for none but the cringing and the craven. And I cannot too often repeat my belief that the right to speak on matters of public concern must be wholly free or eventually be wholly lost.

MR. JUSTICE FRANKFURTER, WHOM MR. JUSTICE DOUGLAS JOINS,
CONCURRING.

THE AMERICAN ASSOCIATION OF UNIVERSITY PROFESSORS ON THE RIGHTS AND FREEDOMS OF STUDENTS (1967) From "Joint Statement on Rights and Freedoms of Students," *AAUP Bulletin,* vol. LIII, pp. 365–68.

Preamble

Academic institutions exist for the transmission of knowledge, the pursuit of truth, the development of students, and the general well-being of society. Free inquiry and free expression are indispensable to the attainment of these goals. As members of the academic community, students should be encouraged to develop the capacity for critical judgment and to engage in a sustained and independent search for truth. Institutional procedures for achieving these purposes may vary from campus to campus, but the minimal standards of academic freedom of students outlined below are essential to any community of scholars.

Freedom to teach and freedom to learn are inseparable facets of academic freedom. The freedom to learn depends upon appropriate opportunities and conditions in the classroom, on the campus, and in the larger community. Students should exercise their freedom with responsibility.

The responsibility to secure and to respect general conditions conducive to the freedom to learn is shared by all members of the academic community. Each college and university has a duty to develop policies and procedures which provide and safeguard this freedom. Such policies and procedures should be developed at each institution within the framework of general standards and with the broadest possible participation of the members of the academic community. The purpose of this statement is to enumerate the essential provisions for student freedom to learn.

I. Freedom of Access to Higher Education

The admissions policies of each college and university are a matter of institutional choice provided that each college and university makes clear the characteristics and expectations of students which it considers relevant to success in the institution's program. While church-related institutions may give admission preference to students of their own persuasion, such a preference should be clearly and publicly stated. Under no circumstances should a student be barred from admission to a particular institution on the basis of race. Thus, within the limits of its facilities, each college and university should be open to all students who are qualified according to its admission standards. The facilities and services of a college should be open to all of its enrolled students, and institutions should use their influence to secure equal access for all students to public facilities in the local community.

II. In the Classroom

The professor in the classroom and in conference should encourage free discussion, inquiry, and expression. Student performance should be evaluated solely on an academic basis, not on opinions or conduct in matters unrelated to academic standards.

A. PROTECTION OF FREEDOM OF EXPRESSION

Students should be free to take reasoned exception to the data or views offered in any course of study and to reserve judgment about matters of opinion, but they are responsible for learning the content of any course of study for which they are enrolled.

B. PROTECTION AGAINST IMPROPER ACADEMIC EVALUATION

Students should have protection through orderly procedures against prejudiced or capricious academic evaluation. At the same time, they are responsible for maintaining standards of academic performance established for each course in which they are enrolled.

Information about student views, beliefs, and political associations which professors acquire in the course of their work as instructors, advisers, and counselors should be considered confidential. Protection against improper disclosure is a serious professional obligation. Judgments of ability and character may be provided under appropriate circumstances, normally with the knowledge or consent of the student.

III. Student Records

Institutions should have a carefully considered policy as to the information which should be part of a student's permanent educational record and as to the conditions of its disclosure. To minimize the risk of improper disclosure, academic and disciplinary records should be separate, and the conditions of access to each should be set forth in an explicit policy statement. Transcripts of academic records should contain only information about academic status. Information from disciplinary or counseling files should not be available to unauthorized persons on campus, or to any person off campus without the express consent of the student involved except under legal compulsion or in cases where the safety of persons or property is involved. No records should be kept which reflect the political activities or beliefs of students. Provisions should also be made for periodic routine destruction of noncurrent disciplinary records. Administrative staff and faculty members should respect confidential information about students which they acquire in the course of their work.

IV. Student Affairs

In student affairs, certain standards must be maintained if the freedom of students is to be preserved.

A. FREEDOM OF ASSOCIATION

Students bring to the campus a variety of interests previously acquired and develop many new interests as members of the academic community. They should be free to organize and join associations to promote their common interests.

1. The membership, policies, and actions of a student organization usually will be determined by vote of only those persons who hold bona fide membership in the college or university community.

2. Affiliation with an extramural organization should not of itself disqualify a student organization from institutional recognition.

3. If campus advisers are required, each organization should be free to choose its own adviser, and institutional recognition should not be withheld or withdrawn solely because of the inability of a student organization to secure an adviser. Campus advisers may advise organizations in the exercise of responsibility, but they should not have the authority to control the policy of such organizations.

4. Student organizations may be required to submit a statement of purpose, criteria for membership, rules of procedures, and a current list of officers. They should not be required to submit a membership list as a condition of institutional recognition.

5. Campus organizations, including those affiliated with an extramural organi-

HIGHER EDUCATION

2885

zation, should be open to all students without respect to race, creed, or national origin, except for religious qualifications which may be required by organizations whose aims are primarily sectarian.

B. FREEDOM OF INQUIRY AND EXPRESSION

1. Students and student organizations should be free to examine and discuss all questions of interest to them, and to express opinions publicly and privately. They should always be free to support causes by orderly means which do not disrupt the regular and essential operation of the institution. At the same time, it should be made clear to the academic and the larger community that in their public expressions or demonstrations students or student organizations speak only for themselves.

2. Students should be allowed to invite and to hear any person of their own choosing. Those routine procedures required by an institution before a guest speaker is invited to appear on campus should be designed only to insure that there is orderly scheduling of facilities and adequate preparation for the event, and that the occasion is conducted in a manner appropriate to an academic community. The institutional control of campus facilities should not be used as a device of censorship. It should be made clear to the academic and larger community that sponsorship of guest speakers does not necessarily imply approval or endorsement of the views expressed, either by the sponsoring group or the institution.

C. STUDENT PARTICIPATION IN INSTITUTIONAL GOVERNMENT

As constituents of the academic community, students should be free, individually and collectively, to express their views on issues of institutional policy and on matters of general interest to the student body. The student body should have clearly defined means to participate in the formulation and application of institutional policy affecting academic and student affairs. The role of the student government and both its general and specific responsibilities should be made explicit, and the actions of the student government within the areas of its jurisdiction should be reviewed only through orderly and prescribed procedures.

D. STUDENT PUBLICATIONS

Student publications and the student press are a valuable aid in establishing and maintaining an atmosphere of free and responsible discussion and of intellectual exploration on the campus. They are a means of bringing student concerns to the attention of the faculty and the institutional authorities and of formulating student opinion on various issues on the campus and in the world at large.

Whenever possible the student newspaper should be an independent corporation financially and legally separate from the university. Where financial and legal autonomy is not possible, the institution, as the publisher of student publications, may have to bear the legal responsibility for the contents of the publications. In the delegation of editorial responsibility to students the institution must provide sufficient editorial freedom and financial autonomy for the student publications to maintain their integrity of purpose as vehicles for free inquiry and free expression in an academic community.

Institutional authorities, in consultation with students and faculty, have a responsibility to provide written clarification of the role of the student publications, the standards to be used in their evaluation, and the limitations on external control of their operation. At the same time, the editorial freedom of student editors and managers entails corollary responsibilities to be governed by the canons of responsible journalism, such as the avoidance of libel, indecency, undocumented allegations, attacks on personal integrity, and the techniques of harassment and innuendo. As safeguards for the editorial freedom of student publications the following provisions are necessary:

1. The student press should be free of censorship and advance approval of copy, and its editors and managers should be free to develop their own editorial policies and news coverage.

2. Editors and managers of student publications should be protected from arbitrary suspension and removal because of student, faculty, administrative, or public disapproval of editorial policy or content. Only for proper and stated causes should editors and managers be subject to removal and then by orderly and prescribed procedures. The agency responsible for the appointment of editors and managers should be the agency responsible for their removal.

3. All university published and financed student publications should explicitly state on the editorial page that the opinions there expressed are not necessarily those of the college, university, or student body.

V. Off-Campus Freedom of Students

A. EXERCISE OF RIGHTS OF CITIZENSHIP

College and university students are both citizens and members of the academic community. As citizens, students should enjoy the same freedom of speech, peaceful assembly, and right of petition that other citizens enjoy and, as members of the academic community, they are subject to the obligations which accrue to them by virtue of this membership. Faculty members and administrative officials should insure that institutional powers are not employed to inhibit such intellectual and personal development of students as is often promoted by their exercise of the rights of citizenship both on and off campus.

B. INSTITUTIONAL AUTHORITY AND CIVIL PENALTIES

Activities of students may upon occasion result in violation of law. In such cases, institutional officials should be prepared to apprise students of sources of legal counsel and may offer other assistance. Students who violate the law may incur penalties prescribed by civil authorities, but institutional authority should never be used merely to duplicate the function of general laws. Only where the institution's interests as an academic community are distinct and clearly involved should the special authority of the institution be asserted. The student who incidentally violates institutional regulations in the course of his off-campus activity, such as those relating to class attendance, should be subject to no greater penalty than would normally be imposed. Institutional action should be independent of community pressure.

HIGHER
EDUCATION

2887

VI. Procedural Standards in Disciplinary
Proceedings

In developing responsible student conduct, disciplinary proceedings play a role substantially secondary to example, counseling, guidance, and admonition. At the same time, educational institutions have a duty and the corollary disciplinary powers to protect their educational purpose through the setting of standards of scholarship and conduct for the students who attend them and through the regulation of the use of institutional facilities. In the exceptional circumstances when the preferred means fail to resolve problems of student conduct, proper procedural safeguards should be observed to protect the student from the unfair imposition of serious penalties.

The administration of discipline should guarantee procedural fairness to an accused student. Practices in disciplinary cases may vary in formality with the gravity of the offense and the sanctions which may be applied. They should also take into account the presence or absence of an honor code, and the degree to which the institutional officials have direct acquaintance with student life, in general, and with the involved student and the circumstances of the case in particular. The jurisdictions of faculty or student judicial bodies, the disciplinary responsibilities of institutional officials and the regular disciplinary procedures, including the student's right to appeal a decision, should be clearly formulated and communicated in advance. Minor penalties may be assessed informally under prescribed procedures.

In all situations, procedural fair play requires that the student be informed of the nature of the charges against him, that he be given a fair opportunity to refute them, that the institution not be arbitrary in its actions, and that there be provision for appeal of a decision. The following are recommended as proper safeguards in such proceedings when there are no honor codes offering comparable guarantees.

A. STANDARDS OF CONDUCT EXPECTED OF STUDENTS

The institution has an obligation to clarify those standards of behavior which it considers essential to its educational mission and its community life. These general behavioral expectations and the resultant specific regulations should represent a reasonable regulation of student conduct but the student should be as free as possible from imposed limitations that have no direct relevance to his education. Offenses should be as clearly defined as possible and interpreted in a manner consistent with the aforementioned principles of relevancy and reasonableness. Disciplinary proceedings should be instituted only for violations of standards of conduct formulated with significant student participation and published in advance through such means as a student handbook or a generally available body of institutional regulations.

B. INVESTIGATION OF STUDENT CONDUCT

1. Except under extreme emergency circumstances, premises occupied by students and the personal possessions of students should not be searched unless appropriate authorization has been obtained. For premises such as residence halls controlled by the institution, an appropriate and responsible authority should be designated to whom application should be made before a search is conducted. The application should specify the reasons for the search and the objects or information

sought. The student should be present, if possible, during the search. For premises not controlled by the institution, the ordinary requirements for lawful search should be followed.

2. Students detected or arrested in the course of serious violations of institutional regulations, or infractions of ordinary law, should be informed of their rights. No form of harassment should be used by institutional representatives to coerce admissions of guilt or information about conduct of other suspected persons.

C. STATUS OF STUDENT PENDING FINAL ACTION

Pending action on the charges, the status of a student should not be altered, or his right to be present on the campus and to attend classes suspended, except for reasons relating to his physical or emotional safety and well-being, or for reasons relating to the safety and well-being of students, faculty, or university property.

D. HEARING COMMITTEE PROCEDURES

When the misconduct may result in serious penalties and if the student questions the fairness of disciplinary action taken against him, he should be granted, on request, the privilege of a hearing before a regularly constituted hearing committee. The following suggested hearing committee procedures satisfy the requirements of procedural due process in situations requiring a high degree of formality.

1. The hearing committee should include faculty members or students, or, if regularly included or requested by the accused, both faculty and student members. No member of the hearing committee who is otherwise interested in the particular case should sit in judgment during the proceeding.

2. The student should be informed, in writing, of the reasons for the proposed disciplinary action with sufficient particularity, and in sufficient time, to insure opportunity to prepare for the hearing.

3. The student appearing before the hearing committee should have the right to be assisted in his defense by an adviser of his choice.

4. The burden of proof should rest upon the officials bringing the charge.

5. The student should be given an opportunity to testify and to present evidence and witnesses. He should have an opportunity to hear and question adverse witnesses. In no case should the committee consider statements against him unless he has been advised of their content and of the names of those who made them, and unless he has been given an opportunity to rebut unfavorable inferences which might otherwise be drawn.

6. All matters upon which the decision may be based must be introduced into evidence at the proceeding before the hearing committee. The decision should be based solely upon such matters. Improperly acquired evidence should not be admitted.

7. In the absence of a transcript, there should be both a digest and verbatim record, such as a tape recording, of the hearing.

8. The decision of the hearing committee should be final, subject only to the student's right of appeal to the president or ultimately to the governing board of the institution.

THE
MINORITIES

Catholics

THE CATHOLIC SCHOOL: THE STRONGHOLD OF CHRISTIAN LIFE
(1919)   From "Pastoral Letter of the Archbishops and Bishops of the United States,"
Peter Guilday, editor, *The National Pastorals of the American Hierarchy, 1792-1919*
(Washington, D.C., 1923), pp. 280, 332-39.

The nursery of Christian life is the Catholic home; its stronghold, the Catholic school. . . . The interests of order and peace require that our domestic, social and national relations be established on the solid basis of principle. For the attainment of this end, much can be done by wise legislation and by organized effort on the part of associations. We are confident that such effort and enactment will hasten the desired result. With their practical sense and their love of fairness, the American people understand that our national life cannot develop normally without adequate protection for the rights of all and faithful performance of duty by every citizen. And as they united to secure freedom for other nations, they now will strive together to realize their country's ideals.

Once more, however, we must emphasize the need of laying a sure foundation in the individual mind and conscience. Upon the integrity of each, upon his personal observance of justice and charity, depends the efficacy of legislation and of all endeavor for the common good. Our aim, therefore, should be, not to multiply laws and restrictions, but to develop such a spirit as will enable us to live in harmony under the simplest possible form, and only the necessary amount, of external regulation. Democracy, understood as self-government, implies that the people as a whole shall rule themselves. But if they are to rule wisely, each must begin by governing himself, by performing his duty no less than by maintaining his right.

Inasmuch as permanent peace on a sound basis is the desire of all our people, it is necessary to provide for the future by shaping the thought and guiding the purpose of our children and youth toward a complete understanding and discharge of their duties. Herein lies the importance of education and the responsibility of those to whom it is entrusted. Serious at all times, the educational problem is now graver and more complex by reason of the manifold demands that are made on the school, the changes in our industrial conditions, and above all, by reason of the confusion and error which obscure the purpose of life and therefore of true education.

Nevertheless, it is mainly through education that our country will accomplish its task and perpetuate its free institutions. Such is the conviction that inspires much of the activity displayed in this field, whether by individuals or by organizations. Their

THE
MINORITIES

2893

confidence is naturally strengthened by the interest which is taken in the school, the enlarged facilities for instruction and the increased efficiency of educational work.

But these again are so many reasons for insisting that education shall move in the right direction. The more thorough it becomes, the greater is its power either for good or for evil. A trained intelligence is but a highly tempered instrument, whose use must depend on the character of its possessor. Of itself knowledge gives no guarantee that it will issue in righteous action, and much less than it will redound to the benefit of society. As experience too plainly shows, culture of the highest order, with abundance of knowledge at its command, may be employed for criminal ends and be turned to the ruin of the very institutions which gave it support and protection. While, therefore, it is useful to improve education by organizing the work of the schools, enriching the content of knowledge and refining the methods of teaching, it is still more necessary to insure that all educational activity shall be guided by sound principles toward the attainment of its true purpose.

The Church in our country is obliged, for the sake of principle, to maintain a system of education distinct and separate from other systems. It is supported by the voluntary contributions of Catholics who, at the same time, contribute as required by law to the maintenance of the public schools. It engages in the service of education a body of teachers who consecrate their lives to this high calling; it prepares, without expense to the State, a considerable number of Americans to live worthily as citizens of the Republic.

Our system is based on certain convictions that grow stronger as we observe the testing of all education, not simply by calm theoretic discussion, but by the crucial experience of recent events. It should not have required the pitiless searching of war to determine the value of any theory or system, but since that rude test has been so drastically applied and with such unmistakable results, we judge it opportune to restate the principles which serve as the basis of Catholic education.

First: The right of the child to receive education and the correlative duty of providing it, are established on the fact that man has a soul created by God and endowed with capacities which need to be developed for the good of the individual and the good of society. In its highest meaning therefore, education is a cooperation by human agencies with the Creator for the attainment of His purpose in regard to the individual who is to be educated, and in regard to the social order of which he is a member. Neither self-realization alone nor social service alone is the end of education, but rather these two in accordance with God's design, which gives to each of them its proportionate value. Hence it follows that education is essentially and inevitably a moral activity, in the sense that it undertakes to satisfy certain claims through the fulfilment of certain obligations. This is true independently of the manner and means which constitute the actual process; and it remains true, whether recognized or disregarded in educational practice, whether this practice include the teaching of morality, or exclude it, or try to maintain a neutral position.

Second: Since the child is endowed with physical, intellectual and moral capacities, all these must be developed harmoniously. An education that quickens the intelligence and enriches the mind with knowledge, but fails to develop the will and direct it to the practice of virtue, may produce scholars, but it cannot produce good men. The exclusion of moral training from the educative process is more dangerous in proportion to the thoroughness with which the intellectual powers are developed, because it gives the impression that morality is of little importance, and thus sends the pupil into life with a false idea which is not easily corrected.

Third: Since the duties we owe our Creator take precedence of all other duties, moral training must accord the first place to religion, that is, to the knowledge of God and His law, and must cultivate a spirit of obedience to His commands. The performance, sincere and complete, of religious duties, ensures the fulfilment of other obligations.

Fourth: Moral and religious training is most efficacious when it is joined with instruction in other kinds of knowledge. It should so permeate these that its influence will be felt in every circumstance of life, and be strengthened as the mind advances to a fuller acquaintance with nature and a riper experience with the realities of human existence.

Fifth: An education that unites intellectual, moral and religious elements, is the best training for citizenship. It inculcates a sense of responsibility, a respect for authority and a considerateness for the rights of others, which are the necessary foundations of civic virtue—more necessary where, as in a democracy, the citizen, enjoying a larger freedom, has a greater obligation to govern himself. We are convinced that, as religion and morality are essential to right living and to the public welfare, both should be included in the work of education.

There is reason to believe that this conviction is shared by a considerable number of our fellow-citizens who are not of the Catholic faith. They realize that the omission of religious instruction is a defect in education and also a detriment to religion. But in their view, the home and the church should give the needed training in morality and religion, leaving the school to provide only secular knowledge. Experience, however, confirms us in the belief that instead of dividing education among these several agencies, each of them should, in its own measure, contribute to the intellectual, moral and religious development of the child, and by this means become helpful to all the rest.

In order that the educative agencies may cooperate to the best effect, it is important to understand and safeguard their respective functions and rights. The office of the Church instituted by Christ is to "teach all nations," teaching them to observe whatsoever He commanded. This commission authorizes the Church to teach the truths of salvation to every human being, whether adult or child, rich or poor, private citizen or public official.

In the home with its limited sphere but intimate relations, the parent has both the right and the duty to educate his children; and he has both, not by any concession from an earthly power, but in virtue of a divine ordinance. Parenthood, because it means cooperation with God's design for the perpetuation of human kind, involves responsibility, and therefore implies a corresponding right to prepare for complete living those whom the parent brings into the world.

The schoool supplements and extends the educational function of the home. With its larger facilities and through the agency of teachers properly trained for the purpose, it accomplishes in a more effectual way the task of education, for which the parent, as a rule, has neither the time, the means nor the requisite qualifications. But the school cannot deprive the parent of his right nor absolve him from his duty, in the matter of educating his children. It may properly supply for certain deficiencies of the home in the way of physical training and cultivation of manners; and it must, by its discipline as well as by explicit instruction, imbue its pupils with habits of virtue. But it should not, through any of its administrations, lead the parent to believe that having placed his children in school, he is freed from responsibility, nor should it weaken the ties which attach the child to parent and home. On the contrary, the school should strengthen the home influence by developing in the child those traits of character which help to maintain the unity and happiness of family life. By this means it will cooperate effectually with the parent and worthily discharge its function.

Since the child is a member not only of the family but also of the larger social group, his education must prepare him to fulfil his obligations to society. The community has the right to insist that those who as members share in its benefits, shall possess the necessary qualifications. The school, therefore, whether private or public as regards maintenance and control, is an agency for social welfare, and as such it bears responsibility to the whole civic body.

While the social aspect of education is evidently important, it must be remembered that social righteousness depends upon individual morality. There are virtues, such as justice and charity, which are exercised in our relations with others; but there is no such thing as collective virtue which can be practiced by a community whose individual members do not possess it in any manner or degree. For this very reason, the attempt to develop the qualities of citizenship without regard for personal virtue, or to make civic utility the one standard of moral excellence, is doomed to failure. Integrity of life in each citizen is the only sure guarantee of worthy citizenship.

As the public welfare is largely dependent upon the intelligence of the citizen, the State has a vital concern in eduation. This is implied in the original purpose of our government which, as set forth in the preamble to the Constitution, is "to form a more perfect union, establish justice, ensure domestic tranquillity, provide for the common defense, promote the general welfare, and secure the blessings of liberty to ourselves and our posterity."

In accordance with these purposes, the State has a right to insist that its citizens shall be educated. It should encourage among the people such a love of learning that they will take the initiative and, without constraint, provide for the education of their children. Should they through negligence or lack of means fail to do so, the State has the right to establish schools and take every other legitimate means to safeguard its vital interests against the dangers that result from ignorance. In particular, it has both the right and the duty to exclude the teaching of doctrines which aim at the subversion of law and order and therefore at the destruction of the State itself.

The State is competent to do these things because its essential function is to promote the general welfare. But on the same principle, it is bound to respect and protect the rights of the citizen and especially of the parent. So long as these rights are properly exercised, to encroach upon them is not to further the general welfare but to put it in peril. If the function of government is to protect the liberty of the citizen, and if the aim of education is to prepare the individual for the rational use of his liberty, the State cannot rightfully or consistently make education a pretext for interfering with rights and liberties which the Creator, not the State, has conferred. Any advantage that might accrue even from a perfect system of State education, would be more than offset by the wrong which the violation of parental rights would involve.

In our country, government thus far has wisely refrained from placing any other than absolutely necessary restrictions upon private initiative. The result is seen in the development of our resources, the products of inventive genius and the magnitude of our enterprises. But our most valuable resources are the minds of our children; and for their development, at least the same scope should be allowed to individual effort as is secured to our undertaking in the material order.

The spirit of our people is in general adverse to State monopoly, and this for the obvious reason that such an absorption of control would mean the end of freedom and initiative. The same consequence is sure to follow when the State attempts to monopolize education; and the disaster will be greater inasmuch as it will affect, not simply the worldly interests of the citizen, but also his spiritual growth and salvation.

With great wisdom our American Constitution provides that every citizen shall be free to follow the dictates of his conscience in the matter of religious belief and observance. While the State gives no preference or advantage to any form of religion, its own best interests require that religion as well as education should flourish and exert its wholesome influence upon the lives of the people. And since education is so powerful an agency for the preservation of religion, equal freedom should be secured to both. This is the more needful where the State refuses religious instruction any place in its schools. To compel the attendance of all children at these schools, would be practically equivalent to an invasion of the rights of conscience, in respect of those parents who believe that religion forms a necessary part of education.

Our Catholic schools are not established and maintained with any idea of holding our children apart from the general body and spirit of American citizenship. They are simply the concrete form in which we exercise our rights as free citizens, in conformity with the dictates of conscience. Their very existence is a great moral fact in American life. For while they aim, openly and avowedly, to preserve our Catholic faith, they offer to all our people an example of the use of freedom for the advancement of morality and religion.

THE PHILOSOPHY OF CATHOLIC EDUCATION (1942) From William McGucken, S.J., "The Philosophy of Catholic Education," as quoted in National Society for the Study of Education, *Forty-first Yearbook, Part I. Philosophies of Education* (Chicago, 1942), pp. 251, 263–69, 287.

I. Introduction

To understand the philosophy of Catholic education it is necessary to understand—not necessary of course to accept—the Catholic philosophy of life which has its roots deep in the past. When Christianity came on the world scene, the revelation of Christ brought a completion of the Old Law; but not that merely, it also came as a completion, a correction often, of the thought of Greco-Roman civilization. The philosophy of Aristotle and Plato, for example, had an extraordinary influence on early Christian thought and thinkers. To the making of Christian philosophy many minds contributed: Aristotle and Plato, Augustine and Aquinas, and the great galaxy of philosophers and theologians of all ages aided in clarifying and defining the Christian view of life.

The essentials of Christian philosophy are found in the New Testament and the early writings of the Fathers of the Church. Augustine of Hippo and the American Catholic of today differ not at all with regard to essentials. Thomas Aquinas and the other medieval schoolmen, dispute though they did over the accidentals of that philosophy, were yet at one in basic principles. Through all the centuries from

Augustine to Aquinas to Suarez and Bellarmine to Newman and Chesterton and Pius XII there is seen a uniform pattern of the Christian philosophy of life, startling by reason of its uniformity. From that philosophy of life is derived the philosophy of Catholic education.

*   *   *

8. CATHOLIC THEORY OF EDUCATION UNCHANGEABLE

There has been acrimonious debate within the Catholic Church at various periods of history as to what the child should be taught, but the attitude of the Church in this matter of the child's nature has never changed. Every child born into this world is regarded as a child of Adam. Therefore, he comes into the world with Adam's inheritance, a lowlier estate because deprived of supernatural life than would have been his had it not been for the fall of Adam. Through the life, passion, death and resurrection of Christ, the Son of God, every one of the descendants of Adam can be restored to his rightful heritage as a child of God. The whole business of the Church is for this purpose, to give this new life to all the sons of men, to keep it alive and growing, bringing forth fruits. So, too, the educational work of the Church is precisely for that purpose. Her whole educational aim is to restore the sons of Adam to their high position as children of God, citizens of the kingdom of God.

*   *   *

9. THE SUPERNATURAL, THE BASIS OF THE CATHOLIC SYSTEM

The key of the Catholic system is the supernatural. Not only Catholic theology, but Catholic practice, the Catholic attitude toward life, and most of all, Catholic education are insoluble mysteries if we exclude an understanding of the supernatural. The Church holds that she is divinely commissioned by Christ to carry on His Work, to do what He did. "I am come that you may have life, that you may have it more abundantly." The Church continues that work, bringing this supernatural life to men who have not yet received it, surrounding it with safeguards that it may not be lost, restoring it once more to those who perversely cast it aside. The same is true of her educational system. Her primary purpose in establishing schools, kindergartens or universities is not merely to teach fractions or logarithms, biology or seismology, grammar or astronomy—these subjects are subordinate to her main purpose to inculcate the "eminent knowledge and love of Jesus Christ our Lord," a knowledge so intimate, a love so strong that it will lead necessarily to a closer following of Christ. Other-worldly? Yes, if you will; for strange as it may seem, the Church considers religion as more important than fractions. If it came to a point where a choice must be made between endangering faith by learning fractions or keeping the faith and not knowing fractions, there is only one answer.

Not, of course, that there is an essential conflict between fractions and the supernatural life, but man can create a factitious conflict. Let us suppose, for example, that the Nazis should conquer America, should establish a monopoly of schools, forcing all in its schools to accept the pagan ideology of Rosenberg with its cult of the state. To such a school no Catholic child could go, even though it meant that the child would grow up illiterate.

Since so much time has been spent elaborating the Catholic concept of man's nature, a concept derived from psychological dualism that man's nature is a unit, though composite, made up of body and soul, possessing intellect and free will, derived too from ethical theory with regard to man's origin, nature, and destiny, man's duties to God, his neighbor, and himself, the unchanging norm of morality based on man's composite, social and contingent nature, a concept of man's nature illuminated by revelation to include the supernatural, with all in theological science that is connoted by that term, it clearly follows that there is a certain hierarchy of values in Catholic education. Supernatural values, if the supernatural exists, are obviously of more importance than the natural; spiritual values of greater import than the bodily; and eternal of more significance than temporal.

✳   ✳   ✳

With this ultimate aim of Catholic education, there never has been, there can be no change. Given the Church's teaching about man's nature, and supernature, and man's supernatural destiny, it is impossible to see how there could be any change. Into this ultimate aim every type of Catholic educational institution must fit from kindergarten to graduate school; otherwise it has no right to be called a Catholic school. For no matter how poor the intellectual training it imparts, no matter how badly equipped academically the teachers may be, that school is a Catholic school which holds fast to its philosophy of supernaturalism. This is not to say that the school, *qua* school, must have as its specific concern the moral virtues as opposed to the intellectual virtues; that controversy will be referred to later.

Education is not confined to the school. There are other agencies concerned in the training of the child, the home and the Church to mention but two. Thus religious education, moral education, training in citizenship, courtesy, character education, even intellectual training, are not exclusively the perquisites of the school; they could not be. But the Catholic Church insists that each Catholic agency, the Catholic home, the Catholic school, place first things first, but that does not necessarily mean that the Church intends that character training, religious training and the rest should be the exclusive function of the school. It may well be doubted, however, whether character training, religious formation, can be imparted without a solid intellectual foundation. Some element of knowledge, varying in amount with the stage of development of the child, must enter into the formation of habit which is the basis of good character education and even of religious education. Obviously, habits cannot be properly established in a human being without his having some intellectual grasp of the motives upon which habits are based, of the standards by which their value is judged. Objectives of conduct are not attained by irrational, mechanical drill.

1. OBJECTIVES OF THE AMERICAN CATHOLIC ELEMENTARY SCHOOL

Dr. George Johnson of the Catholic University has stated what he regards as the aim of the Catholic elementary school.

The aim of the Catholic elementary school is to provide the child with those experiences which are calculated to develop in him such knowledge, appreciation, and habits as will yield a character equal to the contingencies of fundamental Christian living in American democratic society.[1]

American Catholics believe that America's tradition of democracy, her splendid struggle to achieve that democracy are of right taught every Catholic child in the elementary school together with his rich colorful Catholic heritage. In addition, of course, there must be training in the skills necessary to enable him to take his place as a useful citizen in America. To prepare the child to lead an intelligent Catholic life in contemporary American society it is necessary to impart training in processes that are needed for American Catholic citizenship. Further it is necessary to hand on the tradition of Catholicism and American democracy in such a fashion that knowledge will develop into an appreciation of that Catholic and American background. In a word, the elementary school aims to impart those knowledges and skills, habits and appreciative attitudes that will fit the child to be an intelligent practical Catholic, a good citizen, a good member of society, including the various groups to which he belongs, family, working group, neighborhood, and the like.

2. INDOCTRINATION

The Catholic educator does not hesitate to teach the rules of grammar, the multiplication tables, spelling, and the like. The child is given no choice in these matters. So, too, with regard to patriotism, love of country—a very noble Christian virtue—truths about God and God's law, he does not wait for the child to discover these important truths for himself, he helps him to discover them. As E. I. Watkin says,

> [This is] the justification of a religious education—no imposition of ideas upon the unreceptive and recalcitrant, but simply the showing what is actually there and what otherwise they might not see. For not only are individuals intellectually or spiritually colour-blind or sufferers from astigmatism; entire groups, races or epochs display particular faults of vision, which require correction by reference to a complete body of truth handed down through the ages and taught universally.[2]

3. OBJECTIVES OF THE AMERICAN CATHOLIC SECONDARY SCHOOL

The high school in America is a completion of education for some and a preparation of further education for others. The theory of universal secondary education, about which there probably is among Catholic as among other groups wide divergence of opinion, has brought about a multiplication of secondary schools and an amazing increase in the secondary-school population which unquestionably have produced a lowering of intellectual standards through adaptation of the curriculum to the needs of the students. Yet taking it as it is, the Catholic secondary school in America must find its objectives within the frame of reference that is common to all Catholic institutions—the supernatural. Therefore, its aims are a further and richer development of those knowledges and skills, habits and appreciations that will fit the pupil to be

a) an intelligent human being according to his capabilities;

[1] *National Catholic Educational Association Bulletin*, XXII (November, 1925), 458 ff.
[2] E. I. Watkin, *The Bow in the Clouds*, p. 8. New York: Macmillan Co., 1932.

b) an intelligent, practical Catholic, with all that these terms connote;

c) an intelligent, good American citizen;

d) an intelligent, helpful member of society and of these particular groups of which he is or will be a member—the family, professions, vocations, etc.

Therefore, the Catholic high school must cultivate in its pupils an intelligent appreciation of Catholicism and of the traditions of American democracy so as to bring about these ends.

✻ ✻ ✻

3. A FINAL WORD

The main difficulty for the reader of all the foregoing will be his inability to see what may be called the architectonic structure of Catholicism and Catholic education. The reason is that Catholics and non-Catholics have come to talk two different languages. The background of their thought is not the same. This is true not merely in the religious sphere but in the whole of life. Hence, the difficulty of understanding the Catholic theory of education.

There are two things particularly which set off the Catholic from the non-Catholic world. There is in the Catholic a singular unity of thought that springs from his totality of outlook that is particularly irritating to the non-Catholic. The Catholic never forgets at any time or place the totality of being—God, man, and cosmos. The other provocative feature of Catholic thought may be styled other-worldliness. This is not to imply that Catholics are necessarily holier than other people; still less that they are the only people who believe in the world to come. The modern non-Catholic feels sure of what he has; he is not sure—not *so* sure at all events—of what is to come. Therefore, quite logically he emphasizes living in this world. Probably, he reasons, there is another world, but let us make this one that we are sure about a better place to live in. For the Catholic on the other hand, the idea of the world to come looms large; it makes its presence felt in a greater number of spheres. To him the thing of ultimate importance is not here but hereafter. Not, of course, that the Catholic does not recognize values in this world; he enjoys, as any other, natural truth and beauty and goodness; the glory of this world, of mountain and sea and plain; the glow that comes from family life and human friendship finds an echo in his heart; they are good and true and beautiful but they lead him on to the Creator of all these manifold delights made for him. 'The heavens announce the glory of God.'

With his philosophy of supernaturalism, the Catholic rests his case for education and for everything else in the world. Reactionary he may be, even dangerous to modern life, but at least in the light of his first principles he believes that he is consistent.

CATHOLIC EDUCATION AFTER VATICAN II (1966) From John Cogley, "Catholic Education—After the Council," National Catholic Educational Association *Bulletin*, vol. LXIII, pp. 49–50, 52–57.

It is an extraordinary privilege to address so many educators. Let me begin, then, by thanking you for the opportunity. I deem it a great honor. At the same time, I am painfully conscious that, in your midst, I am an amateur—an educator of sorts, I suppose, but certainly not a professional educator.

My field has not been the classroom, the research library, or the laboratory of science. I have, rather, been at home in the noisy clatter of the open forum, the rough and tumble of public life, the table of argumentative political dialogue, the disputatious magazine office, and lately the pulsating city room of a metropolitan newspaper. Without fear of exaggeration, one might say that I was called to the active life. That combination of contemplation and activism which Aquinas tells us makes up the academic vocation was not for me.

Do not, then, turn to me as you would to one of your professional peers. I will bring you neither erudition nor academic expertise. I can bring you only the reactions of a man who is not only *in* the hurly-burly world but depressingly *of* it. In a word, I am something of an outsider here. It may be a tribute to your readiness to follow St. Thomas's advice and look for wisdom from unlikely sources that the invitation was issued.

Because I want to show my gratitude for this opportunity, I decided that the best thing I could do would be to speak candidly, from my particular and very personal perspective, about the topic assigned, "Catholic Education—After the Council."

I must admit, though, that I found your invitation flattering. The temptation has been to flatter you in return. I will try to resist the temptation. I will speak as forthrightly and critically as I know, or at least as I hope, you really want me to. At the same time it would be pleasant if what I have to say raises questions rather than temperatures, raises issues rather than blood pressures.

These days when you put a lay spokesman before a predominantly clerical audience, there is frequently an eruption. We will try to avoid anything like that. Nevertheless, it is my hope that each of you will take everything I say very personally. For if I have any ideas worth having, you are the only people who individually can put them into effect.

Catholic education—after the Council . . . It all depends, I suppose, on how profound one considers the changes wrought by Vatican II. Some take the view that the *aggiornamento* was a restatement of old Catholic positions in a contemporary idiom, it was merely a change in vocabulary. It was only a refurbishing of ecclesiastical furniture grown shabby, so to speak; the changes were superficial—at the very most, they amounted to the renewal of a flagging spirit.

And I will have to agree if you argue that this is how the Ecumenical Council was understood by some of the most important churchmen who participated in it. Till the end, there were prelates in Rome, and theologians too, who, against all the evidence, never granted that Catholicism was undergoing a revolutionary change.

They were wrong. For, among other things, this change in the Church amounted to a definite about-face in the Catholic attitude toward other Christians and other religions. It marked a definite reversal in attitudes toward contemporary culture and politics; toward science and modern philosophical thought; toward theology itself.

The foot-dragging ecclesiastics I have in mind had been led years ago to believe that on such matters the Church is practically changeless. They clung to that formula even after it had been clearly belied by the facts of the Council.

I believe, though, that it would be hard to exaggerate the revolutionary aspect or overstate the radical nature of Vatican II. Not that the full implications of what went on in Rome have yet been generally accepted—far from it. That would be expecting too much too soon. For a while yet we are going to hear tedious warnings, against magnifying the revolutionary impact of Vatican II; we are going to be assured periodically that nothing basic was changed. At the same time, however, the religious news columns will belie all the assurances.

Unless we return to the idea that nothing in the Catholic Church has truly happened until the event is approvingly acknowledged by higher authority, it is clear that something immense of a revolutionary nature is happening in the Church right now in our own country.

* * *

In the same way, it is clear that Catholic education will, or in any case should, never be quite the same again. An era has ended; a historic period has passed. Like all historic periods, it was on balance a mixture of magnificence and mistake, of benevolence and mischief, of accomplishment and stupidity. We can praise it or denounce it; but we cannot prolong it. It is over. A new day has dawned for the Church, and with it a new day for Catholic education.

* * *

Catholic education after the Council, then, willy-nilly, has to undergo a radical change. It will either be an instrument of revolution or the conductor of a deathwatch.

Now I am quite aware that the Catholic educational enterprise has not remained still for the past decade. There has been vast improvement all along the line, from the leap in academic standing of the major institutions of higher learning to the increased professionalism in the grade schools.

For that we must thank some of the critics who in the first instance were rejected as exaggerators and spoilsports. We must also thank the authorities, administrators, and superintendents all along the line. Despite the original defensiveness of some, they responded positively to criticism. And of course we have to thank the teachers on the firing line—the priests, religious, and lay-folk who have made increasingly more effective efforts to improve the schools.

* * *

The spirit of the Council is, of course, elusive. It is not easy to deal with. But one can try to talk about it in more or less concrete terms.

First of all, it is possible to say that before the new spirit (which might also be called the Johannine mood) can triumph, contradictory attitudes must be purged.

What makes this difficult is that some of these very attitudes were practically canonized among American Catholics less than a decade ago. A Catholic's orthodoxy, in fact, was frequently judged by how staunchly he upheld them.

One was the defensive spirit. The Catholic's vocation in the world was regarded as spending a lifetime defending the faith in a hostile, unfriendly environment. In this spirit, how many Catholic educators thought it their charge to provide students with "answers"—mechanical catechetical responses—to the difficulties that would supposedly confront them? However, some of the most percipient participants in the Vatican Council recognize that even the Fathers of the Council turned out to be short on "answers." The world's bishops actually raised more questions than they answered. And perhaps this, in the long run, is to their credit.

Another common habit of mind that needs purging, if it still survives anywhere, locates Catholicism as a vestige of another age. In this view the Catholic glories were to be celebrated as belonging to the past; "good Catholics" took a suspicious view of the present, of modernity. This antiquarianism once led to a lot of talk about Catholic renascences and literary revivals, and so on. It also distracted us from the need for reform and renewal.

We were, of course, stuck with modernity, the here-and-now, but the attitude suggested that the present was really no responsibility of ours. We were not to be blamed for its evils or implicated in its failures. If there was something wrong we knew where to locate the culprit. The blame was put solidly on the Communists, on the secularists, or, in some of the more rarified academic climes, on the Reformation, the rise of rationalism, or some other mischievous moment of history.

When it was clear that we were involved as a community in social evil—for instance, in racial segregation or connivance with political corruption—we had a wonderful way of getting out of it. We merely spouted the appropriate teaching of the Church, preferably citing papal authority, and thereby washed our hands of guilt. It wasn't what we as the living, tangible, visible Church *did* that counted; it was what the idealized, abstracted, personless Church *taught* that mattered. This ploy was used less than two years ago in a major American city to indicate that Catholics need not be disturbed by racial inequalities and the evils of segregation.

Henceforth, authentic Catholic education will keep alive a keen sense of responsibility for the fate of the present generation and the state of the contemporary world. The cold war with modernity almost exhausted Catholicism right up to the time of Pope John. Now it has been called off, and by none less than the last two popes and the Fathers of Vatican II.

We are now, finally, ready to recognize ourselves as a part of our own time and place—sharing the guilt of our generation, as responsible for its sins as the next man, required to meet its moral challenges head on, able to rejoice in its triumphs. Our young people should be taught to realize this. And if some of them undertake to do something about it, hooray—even if they aren't always the soul of tact. I'd rather see them picketing than pouting. I'd rather see young Catholic demonstrators than young Catholic dropouts.

A third example of the mentality that must go before the spirit of the Council can take over has been classically summed up as the siege mentality.

If anything, this took the military metaphors associated with Christianity too literally. Life was indeed regarded as a battleground. The enemy was not principalities and powers, however, but all who did not see what we saw when they turned their gaze to the Catholic Church.

The trouble with Catholic militancy in the past was that it was too often turned against the wrong targets. It was turned not against our own self-satisfaction, our frequent self-righteousness, our own glaring social faults and sins but almost exclusively against others. It was always more comfortable to denounce the divorcee beyond the pale than the racist in our midst, to castigate the atheistic Communist rather than the church-going slum landlord.

But with the new spirit, the Catholic school, hopefully, will engage the young in a sense of responsibility for the world, not only within but beyond the parish.

For in keeping with the Council, the Church these days is much less interested in denouncing other people's errors than in becoming truly engaged itself in the world. There is less interest in condemning others and more in establishing our own genuine commitments.

We Catholics, thank God, have burned our last heretic. Let us hope the time is not far off when we will have also excommunicated our last sinner, anathematized our last dissenter, and perhaps even suspended our last rebellious priest.

The Council was not merely a convocation of ecclesiastics called together to reverse a canonical ruling here and there, to cut back on designated fasts or days of abstinence, to change the hours when the celebration of Mass is permissible, or to authorize vernacular in the liturgy.

Its purpose, rather, was to reform and renew the Church, to do in the twentieth century that which, had it been done in the fifteenth, might have averted the tragedy of Christian disunity.

Reform and renewal of this kind are ineffective unless they permeate every part of the Church and reach to every major action of the Church.

In short, a Catholic enterprise not carried out in the spirit of the Second Vatican Council is no longer authentically Catholic; it must be regarded as an aberration. That generalization now applies all across the board—from the affairs of a local Holy Name Society to the management of a great archdiocese.

So the answer to what can be said about Catholic education after the Council may be reduced to a simple statement: Catholic education now, in order to be authentically Catholic, must at every level reflect the spirit of the Second Vatican Council.

With the new spirit of Catholicism, Catholic education will in effect have a new purpose, a new *raison d'etre.*

It is no dishonor to those who preceded us in time to recognize that the Catholic educational system they founded in the United States was conceived in insecurity and brought forth in religious isolation and theological defensiveness.

The Church's educational establishment inevitably reflected the view of the Catholic vocation held by the generation that founded it and of those who sustained it, up to its present eminence.

This was not, however, the spirit that predominated in the Vatican Council. The old spirit was suspicious of the world, chary of modernity, defensive in its stance. It was standoffish toward other Christian churches, indifferent at best to other religions, and condemnatory in its view of the world.

The role of the laity in the Church was minimal, barely recognized even in the liturgy. The Catholic educational enterprise, like all the Church's major undertakings, was sustained in a spirit of clerical paternalism and general lay obsequence. The specifically Christian vocation of the layman was, to say the least, not prominently emphasized; the freedom of laymen, like the freedom of simple priests, was hardly a primary concern in the classroom.

All that was a product of many forces. It had its virtues as well as its faults; it rendered heroic service as well as insufferable arrogance. I am not here, however, either to praise or to blame it but to bury it. For it is dead. The funeral services were conducted at St. Peter's Basilica, with the Pope and 2,300 bishops presiding.

Today, with the spirit of Vatican II, the Catholic educational effort must put defensiveness and isolation behind it; it must reach out to the community beyond—

to other churches, to non-Christians, to non-believers. Catholic education must be education for ecumenism.

Today our educational effort must also reach out with compassion to the world, with all its complexities and difficulties, its glaring vices and frequently secret virtues, for none hides his virtues as successfully as the worldling. Catholic education must now be education for the secular calling, the lay vocation, the service of the world. It must be *secular* education in a very meaningful sense.

Complacency, we must have collectively learned by now, is death to the spirit. If I may put it this way, post-conciliar Catholic education, then, must be education for honesty and candor beyond the shadow of suspicion.

Actually the greatest days of American Catholic education stretch ahead of us. The revolution set off by Vatican II is not, one wants to assure the timid, something to be feared, a mass of terrible possibilities. There will, of course, be excesses of revolutionary zeal just as we have already seen excesses of counterrevolutionary reaction, but we can survive both extremes.

In the wake of Vatican II, Catholic education must be education for a religious renewal that is based on awareness of what it means to achieve Christian maturity. It must be education for intellectual freedom.

The spirit of Vatican II was the spirit of reform and renewal—reform and renewal not of anything less than the Christian enterprise. All the world listened when the Church finally spoke and acknowledged its faults—listened even when the Church faltered. Its honest inadequacies were forgiven much faster than arrogance would have been.

It is no small thing to ask that the Catholic schools, colleges, seminaries, and universities in this country be saturated with the spirit of the Second Vatican Council. It is really to ask for one more revolution.

NEWSPAPER ACCOUNT OF CRISIS IN CATHOLIC EDUCATION
(**1971**)   From *Los Angeles Times,* March 21, 1971.

Roman Catholic school systems throughout the country are in severe financial trouble and their supporters say they must have public funds to bail them out.

Proponents of aid warn that without substantial help—primarily from states—the church may be forced to close its schools, throwing millions of Catholic students onto public education rolls. This spill into public schools already has begun.

Opponents charge that such warnings are bluff and claim public aid to denominational schools threatens public education and the concept of separation of church and state.

Many arguments challenging use of taxes for parochial school aid already are before the U.S. Supreme Court or working their way through lower courts toward Supreme Court rulings. It may be that eventually the Supreme Court will render a blanket decision on what aid to parochial schools is constitutional—or unconstitutional.

To discover the facts behind the rhetoric of controversy, UPI conducted a national survey over the last few weeks on the state of Roman Catholic elementary and high school education in the United States.

Other denominations also operate schools, but Catholic schools comprise nine-tenths of all private school education in this country. It is the size of the Catholic school system that makes its health a matter of pressing national concern.

Total public school enrollment in the United States for 1969–70 was 45.6 million, according to the U.S. Office of Education. Catholic school enrollment for the same period was 4.6 million, according to a report issued by the National Catholic Educational Assn.

There were 15 states in which Catholic schools educated more than 10% of the school children last year, and others such as California and Michigan where the percentage is lower but where Catholic students number in the hundreds of thousands. Here is the situation in some of them, indicative of what is happening in all:

—Connecticut (12.2% of school population in Catholic schools): Three elementary schools have closed for economic reasons in the archdiocese of Hartford according to its superintendent of schools, the Rt. Rev. James A. Connolly, whose schools educate about half the Catholic school students in the state. He says the "handwriting is on the wall for the others and it's only a matter of time before the church catches up with the diocesan high schools."

—Illinois (15.2% in Catholic schools): The archbishop of Chicago, where one in three children attends Catholic school, had threatened to close the Chicago parochial school system if the 1970 state legislature did not pass substantial parochial school aid. It did not and he did not, but the schools are in trouble.

—Louisiana (12.2%): A $10 million aid-to-private-schools appropriation was found unconstitutional by the state supreme court. Archbishop Philip M. Hannan of New Orleans says, "I don't know how long it will take to revise the (state) constitution, but we do know we have a crisis right now."

—Massachusetts (14.2%): More than 20 Catholic schools have closed in Boston alone. The state Department of Education to aid public schools in areas where parochial schools close, assuming many more will shut within five years.

—Missouri (10.5%): A number of elementary schools and 52 high schools have closed in the last decade, mainly for lack of funds.

—Missouri (10.5%): Lack of funds closed 55 elementary and 17 high schools since 1957 and more may follow suit.

—New Jersey (16.5%): Last November a law was passed authorizing $9.5 million to help private schools teach secular subjects. It is under constitutional attack.

—New York (16.3%): In New York City, the Brooklyn diocese has threatened to close schools educating 200,000 pupils "simultaneously and soon" unless more aid is forthcoming. In Rochester, diocesan schools superintendent, the Rev. Daniel Brent, warned: "A study made last winter revealed that if costs go up 7% and income remains constant we will have to close 46 of the 60 elementary schools in Rochester by 1975. Last year costs increased by 13% and income has remained stable for the last two years."

Gov. Nelson A. Rockefeller believes parochial schools face a "greater crisis" than public schools and has promised aid.

—Ohio (12%): "Indeed our schools are in financial trouble," says the Rev. Kenneth F. Grimes, assistant superintendent of Catholic schools for the Columbus diocese. And this despite state aid, which Father Grimes says "must be increased."

—Pennsylvania (17.2%): Philadelphia Catholic school officials want the present $5 million in state aid doubled. William Valente, president, archdiocese board of education, said a decade ago some Catholics opposed state aid for fear of state control. "But now," he said, "it's a question of survival."

—Rhode Island (16.8%): Ten elementary and one high school have closed already, and two more high schools and a grade school have announced plans to close after this term.

—Wisconsin (14.2%): Archie Buchmiller, state deputy superintendent of public instruction, said parochial school closings have been gradual enough for the state to absorb their students, but warned that in Milwaukee, where 20% of all students attend parochial schools, hardships could develop.

In Michigan, where the percentage is lower but the Catholic school population high, Detroit's John Cardinal Dearden said—after voters and a court decision eliminated aid to parochial schools—that his 328 diocesan schools might be forced to close, throwing the bulk of their 150,000 students into public schools.

California has 300,000 youngsters in Catholic schools and in the last six years 51 schools have closed, with another 38 expected to go under next year. "We're being forced out of the game," says Joseph P. McElligott, education director of the California Catholic Conference.

Two factors are most commonly blamed for the plight of Catholic schools—inflation ("the high cost of everything," one prelate said) and the decrease in available teaching brothers and nuns.

Kansas provides a good example of the inflation problem. Catholic officials there estimate the average cost per pupil has risen from 80 to 100% in the last five years. In 1967-68, the average was $172 per elementary school pupil, compared to $222 for 1969-70. For high schoolers, it went from an average $390 two years ago to $431 last year.

Paying lay teachers rather than teaching nuns has proved a big expense. At one Detroit Catholic school nuns are paid $275 per month—and that represents a tripling of their pay in the last five years. But a beginning lay teacher at the same school earns $8,000 per year.

The National Catholic Educational Assn. says the annual price tag on Catholic education has risen $200 million to $1.4 billion since 1967-68, while the number of schools has decreased 7% and enrollments fallen off 10%.

The financial squeeze faces not only the parochial schools and systems themselves, but the parents now sending their children to such schools. These costs have risen steadily—and in some cases enormously—in recent years.

Charges for elementary schools run from the generally tuition-free grade schools of states such as Nebraska and Minnesota to an annual $360 in some Mississippi schools. In high schools, the range is from a low of $220 in Arkansas to $900 in some Boston schools.

Catholic schools already are receiving some federal assistance and in 36 states provisions have been made in one form or another for at least a minimum of state aid to private schools. Often these are under legal attack.

The first legal consideration is the First Amendment to the U.S. Constitution, which includes these words: "Congress shall make no law respecting an establishment of religion, or prohibiting the free exercise thereof." It often is called "the separation of church and state" clause.

The Supreme Court now has several cases before it on this issue and others are working their way up through the court system. It found in past decisions that it was not a constitutional violation to reimburse parents for bus fare to parochial schools, nor a violation for the state to loan secular school textbooks to parochial students.

Among the types of laws now enacted or seriously proposed to ease the parochial school crisis are these:

—The Pennsylvania law, also adopted with variations in other states, under which the state purchases specified education services from nonpublic schools, reimbursing parochial schools for textbooks, instructional materials and teachers' salaries involved in mathematics, modern foreign languages, physical science and physical education.

—The Ohio law, passed last year, providing Catholic schools with $38 million for lay teacher salary subsidies and for such equipment as visual aids. A similar law is under attack in New Jersey and is proposed elsewhere.

—A bill is before the California legislature to establish a voucher system whereby each child would be entitled to $120 a year to be used to attend the school of his choice, providing it met state standards. Gov. Reagan favors the plan on an experimental basis and the new state superintendent of public instruction, Wilson C. Riles, says he goes along with a "limited, controlled" experiment but considers wider application "too dangerous at this point."

—In Nevada Bishop Joseph Green of the Reno diocese believes legislation allowing property owners to designate their share of school taxes to a particular private school might not violate the state constitutional ban on public funds for sectarian use.

—Oregon favors a "shared time" policy. In Milwaukie, a Portland suburb, for instance, 7th and 8th grade parochial students attend public school classes within their Catholic school in four subjects—science, math, language and social studies. The public school district leases four classrooms from a parochial school and provides textbooks, teaching supplies and teachers in these subjects.

There are cases in the courts now attacking as unconstitutional all of these forms of aid—paying lay teachers of secular subjects, the tuition voucher system, redirection of school tax money and shared time.

The traditional argument in favor of aid to church-run schools is that families who send their children to such schools also pay taxes to support public education— they pay twice. Opponents counter that taxes are not paid on a use basis—childless people, for instance, also pay taxes used for education.

Another argument for "parochiaid," as aid to parochial schools is being dubbed, comes from the Rev. Don Clark of Washington state, who says, "Money is not the issue. Education needs diversity. Diversity is good for education just as it is good for business."

Money certainly is the issue, rebuts Dr. Arthur Rice, associate executive director of the Michigan Education Assn., who said: "Our first concern is to provide equal educational opportunity for each child. I don't think the state can afford to support a multiplicity of school systems and provide a quality education for each child."

In some areas those who opposed parochiaid seem to be backing off. Ohio State Rep. John A. Galbraith opposed his state's law on constitutional grounds, but says now, "I think my views are not as fixed as they used to be. I'm rapidly approaching a state of neutrality on the issue."

The National Catholic Educational Assn. estimates it would add $3.5 billion a year to public school operating budgets if all Catholic schools were to close. On the other side, William Haddad, a leader of New York's PEARL (Public Education and Religious Liberty), calls the threat of closings "bluff."

Jews

A HEBREW SCHOOL (1897)   From "A School for Hebrew," *New York Evening Post*, September 25, 1897

One of the schools of New York which is unknown beyond the Russian district has recently been enlarged and improved, and the building which it occupies, Nos. 225 and 227 East Broadway, has been changed into one of the most attractive structures in that part of the city. Many educational and charitable institutions in that neighborhood receive contributions from members of the Jewish community living in the upper part of the city, and some of these institutions could not exist without the support desired from that quarter. But the Machzikay Talmud Torah School depends for funds entirely on the Russian-Jewish population. This seems only natural when one knows that the school is maintained for the purpose of teaching the Hebrew language and Hebrew literature.

"The Reform Jews who live uptown," said a patriach of the East Side, "know nothing about the Hebrew in their service. They still have a few words of the old language, but the young men and women who read and chant them, and even many of the older people, don't know their meaning unless they look at the printed translation. Another generation, and the little that they have now will pass away and the Hebrew will be forgotten. The beautiful poems in the holy books and the great writings of the Jewish philosophers cannot be translated, and we maintain this school so that our children may not grow up in ignorance of the language in which our fathers wrote."

The school was established about fifteen years ago, and has grown with the Jewish population from one class of twenty-five pupils to twenty-two classes having about eleven hundred pupils ranging in age from six to fifteen years. There are no charges for instruction, and besides being a free school in all that the term implies, needy children who attend are supplied with shoes and clothing. The money for maintaining the institution comes from the annual dues of the members, of whom there are about two thousand, and from contributions from Russian Jews who wish to pay more than the stipulated $3 a year. There is probably no schoolhouse in New York in which less money has been expended for interior decoration than this Hebrew school. The rooms are absolutely bare except for the plain benches and chairs and the desks of the instructors. The pupils are for the most part children of poor parents, and as a class would not bear close inspection for neatness, but they display an earnestness in their work which shows that they share, even in a childish way, the sentiments of their parents and regard the tasks set before them as more than ordinary school work. In order that the work required of them in the Hebrew school may not interfere with their regular school duties, the sessions are from four to seven o'clock on weekdays and from nine to one o'clock on Sunday. "We take no pupils," said Mr. Robison, the head of the school, "who do not attend the public schools, and the translations which the children make are from Hebrew into English."

On entering the building during the school session the stranger is likely to think that he has entered a place where boys are being instructed in chanting queer melodies. From all sides come wailing strains, sometimes uttered by a single voice and again in chorus. In the classroom the teacher stands at one end, directing not only the proper pronunciation of the words, but the intonation, and when a pupil has recited a line or passage, the rest of the class repeats it in concert. All sit with their hats or caps on, because according to the Jewish law—a relic of the Orient—no man may appear before God with his head uncovered. In the upper classes the Bible is the textbook, and the lessons are selected in keeping with the season of the year or the proximity of a holiday. In these classes the boys are also drilled in translation. In the lower classes the rudiments of the language and short words are taught, but even there the boys acquire the sing-song mode of recitation which seems to be a part of Hebrew. In speaking of this characteristic, one of the supporters of the school said: "The Hebrew prayers are chanted in a certain way. The sing-song which you consider queer and which our boys are learning is the same as has been used for thousands of years—not a note has been changed or modified. The music is not written, but it has outlived many compositions which were carefully put on paper. Our boys learn these chants here as we learned them from our fathers, and they will in turn hand them down to their children as we do.

"This all sounds queer to you, and so it does to the Reform Jews, but we hope to see it survive through many generations. That is why a school like this one is necessary. The boys learn to sing patriotic songs in the public schools, and then they come here to learn the sacred music." Some of the boys who are graduated from the Hebrew school go from there to the theological seminary and become rabbis, but that is only a small minority. Many of the graduates become East Side merchants, with the usual ambition toward a Broadway store and an uptown home. A fair percentage of the graduates have become practicing physicians and lawyers. Thirty of the graduates are now teachers in the public schools of New York.

"Why are there no girls in the school?" the visitor asked one of the teachers.

"The girls may learn at home," he answered, "and they do, but we have no place for them here."

This is also a remnant of Orientalism, like the custom by which these people compel the women to occupy a place apart from the men in the houses of worship.

PROBLEMS OF ASSIMILATION ON NEW YORK'S EAST SIDE (1900) From
New York Tribune, September 30, 1900.

A careful student of East Side conditions, a Hebrew himself, recently declared that not more than 40 per cent of American-born Jews observed the dietary laws and religious ceremonies prescribed by the Mosaic law.

"Convenience," said this Jewish student of his race, "convenience and the customs of the society about him—write that down as the explanation of the irreligion of the American-born Jew. No intellectual protest against the traditions of his race moves this class of apostate. The public school; the business world, adjusted to the observation of the Christian, not the Jewish Sabbath; the Saturday night dance; and the complete ignoring of all Jewish holidays by the mass of people surrounding him—these, and a score of similar reasons, explain the situation. The Jew of the second generation does not become a Christian. He is as far from any such conversion as his father, but he finds that to live in a business world adjusted to a Christian calendar is hopelessly inconvenient, if not practically impossible, if he clings to his racial religious observances.

"So long as the boy is in school and lives with his parents, he more or less willingly submits to the parental training, but when he goes out to work and becomes self-supporting, then conditions change. He finds that to keep his job he must work on Saturday, the Jewish Sabbath, and rest on Sunday, the Christian holiday. Similarly, he learns to surrender his celebration of other religious days for business reasons. Thus, little by little, the Jewish boy is transformed into a workaday member of the American business community. Natural as such a result is, it brings with it endless unhappiness to Jewish homes on the East Side. The father, with bewildered sorrow, sees his child steadily becoming estranged from him, not merely in education and in the ordinary things of American life, but even in the observance of rites and laws peculiar to his race through countless centuries. Moreover, since every Jewish ceremony is more or less patriarchal in character and comprehends the whole family in its festivities, sacred days, such as the approaching Day of Atonement, are fraught with extreme sadness, because, from their observation, the second generation will in countless instances be absent. Even in homes where both generations are together, the chasm between Asia and America will not infrequently separate father and son sitting at the same table."

Apart from matters of religion the gulf between father and son on the East Side is broad. Students of local conditions have declared that the vast majority of Jewish immigrants live and die obeying the laws and following the customs of their native land. American language and ways alike remain unintelligible to them, and they depend with almost pathetic helplessness on their children for association with the world about them.

"He is an American—born American—not a 'greenhorn' like me." This is the fashion in which the average Jewish immigrant describes his child. From the very start, this child unconsciously acquires a contempt for the un-American habits and characteristics of his father. The American public school and associations with business life do the rest. The average Jewish boy of fifteen lives the life of New York, contemporaneous to the minute; his father still slumbers in the existence of Kishinev, Lemberg, or Jassy. The separation in habits of religion follows as a natural sequence that earlier separation in all the common phases of life. The laissez-faire spirit of our national life seems in many cases to accomplish what the persecution of ages has failed to bring about—namely, the alienating of the Jewish child from the strict observance of his racial religious rites.

THE JEWISH BOY AT "CHAIDER" (1909)   From Hutchins Hapgood, *The Spirit of the Ghetto* (New York, 1909), pp. 23-28.

With his entrance into the public school the little fellow runs . . . against a system of education and a set of influences which are at total variance with those traditional to his race and with his home life. The religious element is entirely lacking. The educational system of the public schools is heterogeneous and worldly. The boy becomes acquainted in the school reader with fragments of writings on all subjects, with a little mathematics, a little history. His instruction, in the interests of a liberal nonsectarianism, is entirely secular. English becomes his most familiar language. He achieves a growing comprehension and sympathy with the independent, free, rather sceptical spirit of the American boy; he rapidly imbibes ideas about social equality and contempt for authority, and tends to prefer Sherlock Holmes to Abraham as a hero.

The orthodox Jewish influences, still at work upon him, are rapidly weakened. He grows to look upon the ceremonial life at home as rather ridiculous. His old parents, who speak no English, he regards as "greenhorns." English becomes his habitual tongue, even at home, and Yiddish he begins to forget. He still goes to "chaider," but under conditions exceedingly different from those obtaining in Russia, where there are no public schools, and where the boy is consequently shut up within the confines of Hebraic education. In America, the "chaider" assumes a position entirely subordinate. Compelled by law to go to the American public school, the boy can attend "chaider" only before the public school opens in the morning or after it closes in the afternoon. At such times the Hebrew teacher, who dresses in a long black coat, outlandish tall hat, and commonly speaks no English, visits the boy at home, or the boy goes to a neighboring "chaider."

Contempt for the "chaider's" teaching comes the more easily because the boy rarely understands his Hebrew lessons to the full. His real language is English, the teacher's is commonly the Yiddish jargon, and the language to be learned is Hebrew. The problem before him is consequently the strangely difficult one of learning Hebrew, a tongue unknown to him, through a translation into Yiddish, a language of growing unfamiliarity, which, on account of its poor dialectic character, is an inadequate vehicle of thought.

The orthodox parents begin to see that the boy, in order to "get along" in the New World, must receive a Gentile training. Instead of hoping to make a rabbi of him, they reluctantly consent to his becoming an American business man, or, still better, an American doctor or lawyer. The Hebrew teacher, less convinced of the usefulness and importance of his work, is in this country more simply commercial and less disinterested than abroad; a man generally, too, of less scholarship as well as of less devotion.

The growing sense of superiority on the part of the boy to the Hebraic part of his environment extends itself soon to the home. He learns to feel that his parents, too, are "greenhorns." In the struggle between the two sets of influences that of the home becomes less and less effective. He runs away from the supper table to join his gang on the Bowery, where he is quick to pick up the very latest slang; where his talent for caricature is developed often at the expense of his parents, his race, and all "foreigners"; for he is an American, he is "the people," and like his glorious countrymen in general, he is quick to ridicule the stranger. He laughs at the foreign Jew with as much heartiness as at the "dago"; for he feels that he himself is almost as remote from the one as from the other.

"Why don't you say your evening prayer, my son?" asks his mother in Yiddish.

"Ah, what yer givin' us!" replies, in English, the little American-Israelite as he makes a bee-line for the street.

The boys not only talk together of picnics, of the crimes of which they read in the English newspapers, of prize-fights, of budding business propositions, but they gradually quit going to synagogue, give up "chaider" promptly when they are thirteen years old, avoid the Yiddish theatres, seek the up-town places of amusement, dress in the latest American fashion, and have a keen eye for the right thing in neckties. They even refuse sometimes to be present at supper on Friday evenings. Then, indeed, the sway of the old people is broken.

✳   ✳   ✳

A SURVEY OF JEWISH EDUCATION IN NEW YORK CITY (1909)   From Mordecai M. Kaplan and Bernard Cronson, "Report of Committee on Jewish Education of the Kehillah . . . New York, February 27, 1910," in *Jewish Education*, vol. XX, pp. 113–16.

There are at present six different agencies which afford Jewish education to the children of this city:

(a) Talmud Torah Schools

(b) Institutional Schools

(c) Congregational Schools

(d) Sunday Schools

(e) Chedorim

(f) Private Tutors

There are hardly any two schools of the first type which are alike. The description, therefore, which we propose to give in each case is not a description of any one particular school, but of the type as a whole. . . .

(a) A Talmud Torah school is a school established for the purpose of giving Jewish instruction to children, mainly to boys. It is only of late that girls' classes have begun to appear. The schools are located in congested Jewish neighborhoods, and are attended mostly by the children of the poor. In many instances, the children are given shoes and clothing, and in a few cases even meals. On the whole, about 50 per cent of the pupils pay each from forty to fifty cents a month. Membership fees and contributions, however, from those more fortunately situated, constitute the main source of support.

A Talmud Torah school occupies the whole or the greater part of some building, and has at its disposal a number of classrooms ranging from four to twenty. With few exceptions, the cleanliness, ventilation and light of the classrooms are far from what they ought to be. The equipment is very poor. The desks are old and the textbooks thumbworn. Instruction is given daily from 4 p.m. to 8 p.m., in two sessions, to two different groups of children, and on Sundays from 9 a.m. to 3 p.m. The aim of the school authorities is to instil into the children a knowledge of Judaism, by means of as much of the original content as possible, chiefly, the prayer book and the Bible in Hebrew. The curriculum, which is worked out by the principal and the school board, provides for specific teaching of history and religion. But neither the aim nor the curriculum is carried out in practice. . . .

The teachers are either immigrants who have acquired a fair amount of English, though not enough to enable them to use it flexibly and to adapt it to the needs of the children; or young men preparing for some profession, who teach, in order to be able to make their way through college. The salaries are from $25 to $40 a month, only in rare instances exceeding the latter figure. In either case, the teaching is found to be very poor, even though most of the instruction is carried on in English. In this regard, there is a marked improvement in those schools where the Ibrith B'Ibrith method is employed. Seldom, if ever, are any English textbooks made use of; home work is never allotted; the discipline is poor; the attendance is very irregular, and seldom kept up for any length of time. This last is due to the fact that the Jewish population of the poor is constantly shifting from place to place, which circumstance presents another obstacle to the progress that ought to be made in the studies, considering the number of hours devoted to them. A noteworthy fact in these schools is the overcrowded condition of the lower classes and the meagre attendance in the upper classes. The number simply tapers out, and there is no need for any formal graduation. In spite of all these defects, the Talmud Torah schools instil more Jewishness into the lives of the children than any of the agencies following.

(b) The Institution schools are of two types, (1) those that belong to orphan asylums, and (2) those that form part of institutions which do social work.

The Institutional schools of the orphan asylum type have almost ideal equipments and every facility to render them effective religious schools. What is more, they have the opportunity of having the kind of environment, that could easily emphasize in practice the religious lessons that they are taught in the classroom. Unfortunately, little has been done to take advantage of all this to bring about model teaching, that would imbue the inmates with enthusiasm for the Jewish life. Of late there have been evident in some quarters signs of taking the matter of Jewish instruction more seriously. In the meantime, the instruction is not carried on with any serious or definite aim, and with little or no record kept of the work.

The Institutional school of the second type is a marked improvement upon the first. It takes advantage of all the superior equipment it possesses to bring about all of the method and system which is characteristic of the public school. Its aim is to impart a knowledge of religion, in which the knowledge of Hebrew is only of secondary importance. It works for that aim consciously and systematically. It has proper grading, teachers that are acquainted with rules of pedagogy, and a record of all the work done. The attendance is better than in any other kind of Jewish school. The aim, however, is one which does not have the sympathy of Jewish population where these institutional schools exist, because they do not regard it as Jewish enough insofar as it makes Hebrew only secondary. That this is their attitude is proved by the fact that they send mostly their girls to these schools and their boys to the Chedorim. On the other hand, if these schools were to put more stress upon the study of Hebrew, they would not get the teachers that could conduct them on a modern basis.

(c) A Congregational school is one which is connected with a congregation, but which we do not designate as a Sunday school because it holds sessions three or more times a week. The congregations to which their schools belong are generally conservative or orthodox. As they meet in the vestry rooms, the light and ventilation in the classrooms are very seldom of the best. Though the children of the members do not have to pay any tuition fee, they form a very small per cent of the school, because their parents prefer to give them private teachers in their own homes. The school is maintained from the fees collected from children of outsiders who pay from one to two dollars a month. The deficit is supplied from the treasury of the congregation. About one-third of the children are free. Here the proportion of boys to girls is about two to one.

The teachers, who are usually American young men, with here and there some women, possess a fair knowledge of things Jewish. In the case of the majority of the teachers, the salaries, which range from $25 to $35 a month, the former for three times a week, the latter for five times, are merely a means of sustaining them during their student days. Nevertheless, there is more interest displayed in the work, by reason of the lesser number of hours they are obliged to teach than in the Talmud Torah schools. The rabbi of the congregation is usually the superintendent, and he is assisted or hindered in his work by a school committee.

Instruction is given from three to five times a week, afternoons from 4 to 6 p.m., and on Sunday morning from 9 to 12 a.m. A regular curriculum is followed. The work covered is not very extensive, and is usually confined to the reading and translation of the prayers, and of a few passages in the Bible, with a smattering of a few rules of grammar. The instruction is carried on in English, and English textbooks, such as they are, are widely made use of, for History and Religion. In very few cases, the children are given work to do at home. The attendance is very irregular and seldom is of long duration for the same reason as in the Talmud Torah schools. The discipline is inferior to that of the institutional schools, although prizes are offered and graduation held at the end of each year.

(d) A Sunday school is usually a congregational school which meets only once a week, on Sunday mornings. This school is attended for the most part by children of the parents who belong to the congregation. A small per cent of outside children are admitted free. There is another type of Sunday school, known as a Mission school, which is supported by some wealthy congregation, and which meets in some settlement building in a congested section of the city. In both of these schools, the teachers are mostly women, who are also public school teachers, and many of whom volunteer their services gratis; of those who are paid, the salaries average from $10 to $12 a month. The teachers, usually, have the training but not the knowledge necessary for a Jewish school. A vague kind of curriculum is carried out, and the work, such as it is, is supervised by the rabbi and the committee. The teaching is only in English, and extensive use is made of textbooks and illustration material. Homework is given out. The attendance is good, and discipline is fair. An integral part of the Sunday school work is an elaborate system of prizes, graduation and confirmation.

(e) A Cheder is a school conducted by one, two or three men, for the sole purpose of eking out some kind of a livelihood which they failed to obtain by any other means. It generally meets in a room or two, in the basement or upper floor of some old dilapidated building where the rent is at a minimum. It is thus, usually, to be found in the environment of crowded tenement houses, shops, saloons, and dancing halls. The main consideration with the teacher being, to have the outlay at as low a figure as possible, the Cheder is usually filthy, the light dim, and air stuffy. The long table or the rickety desks have seen a better day. The fees of the children, which average from seventy-five cents to a dollar a month, minus the expense involved in the outlay upon the paraphernalia named, constitute the teachers' net earnings. The Cheder is attended mainly by boys and in a few cases also by girls.

The instruction, which seldom goes beyond the reading of the prayer book, and the teaching of a few blessings by rote, is carried on only in Yiddish. The method of instruction is quite unique. It consists of about fifteen minutes of individual instruction, with seldom or never any class work. Each pupil, not knowing when he is needed, straggles in at random, and waits for his turn to come, in the meantime entertaining himself with all sorts of mischief. When his turn comes and the teacher has given him the fifteen minutes, he runs off. There is hardly an ideal aim in the mind of the teacher, except in some cases it is the training for the Bar-Mitzvah feat of reading the Haftorah. The pupils seldom stay with the teacher more than six or eight months, when they go to try another one in the neighborhood.

A variation from this type of Cheder is what I would designate, the modern Cheder, the variation being due to the personality of the one conducting it. Like the Cheder, it is established primarily as a business undertaking. But the teachers interested in it are of Jewish nationalistic tendencies, are well versed in Hebrew and appreciative of modern pedagogic methods. They obtain light, room [sic] quarters, though regardless of the environment. These they manage to keep clean, and to furnish with modern school furniture. Some part of the time is given to instruction of girls as well as boys. The fees range as high as $3 per month.

The school is divided into grades, a curriculum is followed, and the aim is made very definite and limited. The wants of parents are sought to be met with as well as the ideals of the organizers. The discipline is good, and the results accomplished are quite tangible. The good work that could have been done, is of course, vitiated by the business end of it. There are two few of this type, however, to regard them as an important factor in the Jewish education of this city.

(f) The sixth agency, namely, the private tutors, is not amenable to the process of investigation, and we have to satisfy ourselves with a rough estimate of their numbers.

✻   ✻   ✻

THE AIMS OF JEWISH EDUCATION (1912) From "A Brief Summary of the Decisions Arrived at by the Thirty-one Conferences Held by Talmud Torah Principals in New York, 1912," as quoted in Nathan H. Winter, *Jewish Education in a Pluralist Society: Samson Benderly and Jewish Education in the United States* (New York, 1966), pp. 212–16.

1. The aim of Jewish education is the preservation of the Jews as a distinct people, existing and developing in the spirit of the Jewish religion.

2. The Hebrew School is, under present circumstances, the best means of reaching that aim, to instill the religious and ethical truths of Judaism into the hearts of the children at the schools whenever the opportunity presents itself.

3. As the isolation of our children in parochial schools, though undoubtedly effective from a purely Jewish point of view, might injuriously effect our political and social status in this country and would, in addition, demand financial sacrifices at present beyond our reach, and as, on the other hand, the giving of religious instruction at the Public Schools would contradict the basic American principle of eliminating religion from our State institutions, it follows that the present system of teaching our children in Hebrew Schools after Public School hours is the most desirable under existing circumstances. By way of preparing the children for Jewish religious observances, they ought to be familiarized with the meaning of the Jewish festivals and the ceremonies connected with them, and should be made to learn by heart the customary Jewish benedictions and such short prayers as are fit for children. The children should become acquainted with the Jewish prayers in traditional form, without any alteration. Care should be taken that the child shall not merely recite the prayers mechanically, but shall understand the contents of what it prays. In order to acquaint the children with the Jewish ceremonies, which are often neglected in the home, it is greatly advisable that certain ceremonies, such as the building of a Succah, the use of the Lulov and Esrog, etc., should be practiced in the school itself.

4. The curriculum of a Hebrew School should extend over a period of seven years, and should pursue the following subjects: A sufficient knowledge of Hebrew, which should enable the children to understand the prayers, the Pentateuch, the historical portions of the Bible, selections from the Prophets and Hagiographa, selections from the Mishnah, the easier Midrashim, some portions of the Talmud, and some specimens of mediaeval Jewish poetry; Jewish history, ancient and modern, and an acquaintance with Jewish religious observances.

Inasmuch as the first two years of instruction, though of fundamental importance, are necessarily of an introductory character, preparing the children for the studies to follow, stress should be laid on teaching the children during that period to read Hebrew correctly, and to make them sufficiently acquainted with the language to enable them to read and to understand the prayers, and the Pentateuch. In order to make the subject both more intelligible and more attractive to the mind of the child, it should be of a more informal character, and should centre around the lives of our great men, while extensive use should be made of the stereopticon and other means of illustration.

5. The Bible necessarily forms the most important subject of instruction in the Hebrew school. In order to bring the Bible nearer to the mind of American children, it is necessary to acquaint them with the conditions which form the background of the Bible, such as the geography of Palestine and the manners and customs of the

Biblical period. As for the teaching of Jewish history, its main object should be to inspire the children with a love for their People. Jewish history should be taught in close connection with Jewish literature. Thus, in Biblical history, the readings from the Prophets should be used to illustrate the historical events of that period, while the historical events should be so explained as to form the background of the Prophetical readings.

6. The Bible should therefore occupy almost all of the intermediary three years of the curriculum (from the age of eight to eleven). The first year of this intermediary period should be devoted to the study of the Pentateuch; the second year to the historical portions of the Bible, the so-called "earlier Prophets," and the last year of that period, to selected readings from the prophetical writings and the Hagiographa. For this purpose extensive use should be made of the stereopticon and other means of illustration. It is necessary to bring home to the children the grandeur of Jewish history, the heroic struggle and the unparalleled martyrdom of the Jewish People for the sake of its ideals, to arouse their pride in our great past, and to stir their enthusiasm for the endeavors marking the Jewish revival of our own days.

7. The national American holidays which are purely secular in character, such as the Fourth of July, Decoration Day, and Thanksgiving Day, should be celebrated in the Jewish schools by gathering the children together for that purpose. Instead of the regular instruction which should be discontinued, the patriotic significance of these holidays should be brought out, and whenever possible the relation of these holidays to similar events in Jewish history should be pointed out. In the same way, in Post-Biblical history the readings from Post-Biblical literature and the exposition of the historical events should be made to bear upon one another. To attain this end, it is advisable to draw upon the large mass of legends, appealing with particular force to the childish imagination, which cluster around the great events in Post-Biblical history, and to make use of tableaux and dramatizations arranged by the children themselves. It is also advisable that, at the end of the curriculum, when the whole subject is reviewed, the facts of Jewish history should be brought out in connection with those events of general history which stand in direct relation to them, or are able to illustrate them.

8. It is also advisable to arrange special children's services in connection with the schools on the Sabbath and holidays. These services, which shall not exceed one hour for the younger and two hours for the older children, should include a short sermon, and congregational singing by the children should be encouraged in every possible way. On the Great Holidays, however, it seems more advisable that the children should accompany their parents to the synagogue and should in this way be brought in touch with the Congregation of Israel. During the last two years of the curriculum, the Jewish observances should be reviewed from a brief manual of Jewish ritual, special hours to be set apart for that purpose.

9. The selections from the writing of Post-Biblical literature, should, as pointed out above, be read in connection with Jewish history, and be used as far as possible to illustrate the events of the period or the lives of the great men upon which they bear.

During the last year of the curriculum, or during an additional year if it be found possible to keep some of the children longer in school, an elementary course in Talmud should be arranged to give the children an idea of the method of the Talmud.

10. Experience has shown that abstract religious or moral instruction, given as a separate subject, does not appeal to children, and remains ineffective. Systematic

religious instruction shall, as indicated above, be given during the last two years not in an abstract form, but for the purpose of reviewing the Jewish laws and practices with which the children had previously become acquainted.

11. From the fact that, under the stress of modern economic conditions, it is the mother who is bound to play a decisive role in the religious upbringing of the family, it follows that the programme outlined above must and should be applied to girls no less than to boys, with this difference, that, during the last year of the curriculum, instead of selections from the Talmud to be studied by the boys, the girls ought to be taught the religious laws pertaining to the Jewish woman.

12. To prevent physical harm to the children from the additional burden of the Jewish School, it is necessary to introduce such improvements as will make it possible to shorten the time of instruction without minimizing the efficiency of the teaching. Such improvements include smaller classes (maximum thirty children), a better system of admission, the reorganization of the present exceedingly cumbersome and degrading method of collecting the tuition fees during school hours, and a judicious distribution of vacation days.

13. The question of Jewish teachers is undoubtedly the cornerstone of the whole problem of Jewish education. Without well-qualified teachers, any attempt to evolve a system of Jewish education is bound to be a miserable failure. The proper requirements of a successful Jewish teacher in a Jewish school should be a moral and religious conduct of life, a thorough knowledge of the Hebrew language, and an intimate acquaintance with Jewish literature, supplemented by a knowledge of English and an acquaintance with those disciplines which bear on the activity of the teacher, particularly pedagogy and psychology. In view of the fact that the vast majority of teachers at present engaged in Jewish instruction are adequately equipped only in Hebrew or in English, and that there is a lamentable lack of teachers possessing all the requirements indicated above, the Bureau of Education is to be requested to take the necessary steps for the purpose of establishing a Teachers' Training School, to be open in the morning between the hours of nine and one, at a time when most of the teachers are free, in order that they may perfect themselves in those studies in which they are deficient.

In addition to this, the Bureau is to be requested to devise ways and means so to improve the financial condition of the Jewish teachers, that they be no more compelled to engage in outside work for the purpose of making a living, and that they be thus enabled to devote their leisure hours to perfect themselves in their profession.

ABRAHAM HESCHEL ON THE MEANING OF JEWISH EDUCATION

(1953)   From Abraham J. Heschel, *The Insecurity of Freedom: Essays on Human Existence* (New York, 1966), pp. 234–37.

Recognizing the vital importance of Jewish education, we should worry less about technique and more about content. We should concern ourselves not only with sociological surveys of education but also with the religious and spiritual aspects of Jewish education. Are we not in need of a survey of its spiritual aspects? I would like to suggest as a goal of Jewish education that every Jew become a representative of the Jewish spirit, that every Jew become aware that Judaism is an answer to the ultimate problems of human existence and not merely a way of handling observances. The philosophy of Jewish education ought to formulate what insights to set forth from and about our tradition. It should also help us technically by showing us how to adjust and express these insights so that they may become a part of the personality of every pupil.

At all religious schools, pupils are taught the benediction to be said before drinking a beverage. It is taught as a custom, as a practice. But how many teachers attempt to convey the grand mystery and spiritual profundity contained in these three Hebrew words—"Everything came into being by His word"? It is unfair and unfortunate that we ignore, withhold, or fail to communicate the spiritual substance of our tradition.

A reorientation in our educational work both in the schools and on the adult level will have to take place. Our goal must be to teach Judaism as a subject of ultimate personal significance. But do we teach it in this way? I taught a class once whose students, young men of about twenty, had studied for many years at Hebrew schools. In this class the problem came up, whether from the point of view of Judaism it is allowed to take revenge. "Of course, it is allowed," they said. In spite of their having gone to Hebrew schools for almost fifteen years, my students had simply never heard of the injunction, "Thou shalt not take vengeance or bear any grudge," words which are a part of the same verse as the words "love your neighbor as yourself." . . .

. . . The attitudes recorded in some of the Psalms are no less important, we might assume, than the events recorded in the Book of Judges. Yet how few Psalms are taught in our schools while the Books of Judges and Samuel are always taught. "Christianity is a wonderful religion," a Jewish woman active in a Temple remarked. "Why does not Judaism have a Book of Psalms?" We say that we have given the Bible to the world. Have we not given it away?

I have asked mature students what the thirteen *middoth* are. Some of them have heard of the thirteen *middoth* of Rabbi Ishmael, the thirteen principles of interpretation. They had never heard, never been moved by one of the central insights of Moses which became the heart of the liturgy on the Day of Atonement: "The Lord, the Lord, a God merciful and gracious. . . ." The most popular Hebrew text taught in America is the berachoth that a Jew is supposed to say when he has an Aliyah. It is something which every Bar Mitzvah boy must know. I have often asked those who teach these berachoth to the boys who are to become Bar Mitzvah whether they pay attention to the meaning of the term *hayye'olam* and the profound message contained in the phrase "He has implanted in us eternal life." What do we teach the Bar Mitzvah boys? Generalities and externalities. Why not try to teach them the lofty claim of the Jewish spirit? Judaism is a way of action, but it is also a way of inner living. Is it not important to teach our students a verse such as this: "For thus says the high and lofty one who inhabits eternity whose name is holy, 'I dwell in the high and holy place and also with him who is of a contrite and humble spirit'?" (Isaiah 57:15.)

Teaching a child is in a sense preparing him for adolescence. We have to teach him ideas which he can carry over to his maturity. Some of our schools teach subjects which are very entertaining and have their place in the curriculum, but I wonder whether in the later crises of life they will prove to be very helpful. Will they remain alive in his years of maturity, in his bitter trials, disappointments, and frustrations? All our lives we draw upon the inspiration we received in childhood.

We have to remember *that* when we face our pupils, when we ask ourselves what we should teach them. I am committing a heresy, I know, if I suggest that we ought to teach them a phrase such as, "Ye shall be holy," the vision of a *neshamah yetherah*, the meaning of *Schechinah*, rather than words such as *kaddur basis*, but heretical I must be. For difficult as it is to teach these matters, it is not impossible. If it is so easy for the scoffers and cynics to teach successfully in an attitude of contempt, the art of being supercilious, why should we completely fail in teaching how to revere? Indeed, if teaching spiritual attitudes is an impossibility, then all of Judaism is a mistake.

The Hebrew term for education means not only to train but also to dedicate, to consecrate. And to consecrate the child must be our goal, difficult as it may be. The survival of the Jewish people is our basic concern. But what kind of survival, we must continually ask, and for what purpose? Many questions come to mind when one analyzes the ideology underlying the content and composition of contemporary textbooks. Is not the Ba'al Shem as relevant as Bar Kochba? Why are there so few studies in the teaching of the Prayer Book? We are divided among ourselves as to ritual observance, it is true. But we must not be divided when it comes to teaching the spiritual attitudes of Judaism. Let us remember that it is not enough to impart *information*. We must strive to awaken *appreciation* as well.

Our goal must be to enable the pupil to participate and share in the spiritual experience of Jewish living; to explain to him what it means to live as a likeness of God. For what is involved in being a Jew? Duties of the heart, not only external performance; the ability to experience the suffering of others, compassion and acts of kindness; sanctification of time, not the mere observance of customs and ceremonies; the joy of discipline, not the pleasures of conceit; sacrifice not casual celebrations; contrition rather than national pride.

A SURVEY OF JEWISH EDUCATION IN THE UNITED STATES

(1959)   From Alexander M. Dushkin and Uriah Z. Engelman, *Jewish Education in the United States* (New York, 1959), pp. 224–28, 237, 245–49.

III-IV—Is Jewish Education Wanted—How Much and What Kind?

A—EVIDENCE FROM SCHOOL CENSUS AND INVENTORY

*   *   *

7—In 1958 there were 553,600 Jewish children and youth (age 5 through 17) enrolled in Jewish schools. The proportion of pupils to the total population was 10.5% for Jewish schools as compared to 22.4% in the general schools (public and non public). *We estimated that 40–45% of Jewish children were enrolled in Jewish schools in 1958* (36.5% in New York City, 51% in the rest of the country). Since these figures refer to children found in the Jewish schools at *one particular time*, and the majority of them attend only 3 or 4 years out of their eight years of elementary school age, *we estimated that well over 80% of Jewish children receive some Jewish schooling at some time during school age.* Quantitatively speaking, it is clear that the great majority of parents do want and do provide some sort of Jewish schooling for their children.

Evidently, Jewish educators are right in insisting that *our problem is no longer that of getting our children to Jewish school, but rather of having them stay in the schools long enough to make that education valuable.*

8—*During the past decade (1948–1958) the total school enrollment increased by 131.2%;* very much more than any assumed increase in the total Jewish population. Sociological and historic developments must have influenced groups and strata of Jewish parents who had hitherto not been concerned with Jewish education to send their children for some Jewish schooling.

9—The enrollment in 1958 was distributed: 47.1% in Weekday Afternoon schools, 45.1% One-day Sunday schools, and 7.8% Day schools. The distribution in New York City was different from the rest of the country: fewer in the One-day schools (35.0%) and more in the Day schools (21.4%). During the past decade the largest enrollment increase was in Weekday afternoon schools (161.2%), then in Day schools (131.2%), and least in the One-day schools (106.7%).

There seems to be a rather constant general trend toward more intensive Jewish education for an increasing number of children.

10—There has been a steady growth of congregational schools as the prevailing type of Jewish schooling. In 1918, only 23.6% of Jewish pupils in New York were taught in congregational schools. In 1948, 82.7% of all pupils in the United States were in congregational schools, and in 1958 this proportion grew further to 88.5%.

Because of the prevalence of the congregational school as the dominant type of Jewish schooling, *it is incumbent on leaders of the congregational organizations to reconsider the relation of these schools to the community, with a view to clarifying their functions and increasing their effectiveness.*

11—Comparison with the Jewish educational situation half a century ago brings out the fact that the *Hadarim* and *Melamdim* who then taught 36–38% of Jewish children, have now practically disappeared; in their place there is an increase in the proportion attending One-day school at one end, and Day schools at the other. Evidently, despite many shortcomings and basic difficulties, *the over-all pattern of American Jewish education has changed for the better during the past forty years.*

12—During the past decade the enrollment increase was twice as large in the Jewish schools (131.2%) as in the non-Jewish religious schools (57–61%). This is significant in pointing out that *the general American "upsurge of religious sentiment" can account for only a minor part of the increase in Jewish schooling,* which apparently resulted from a maturation of Jewish attitudes from within.

13—Jewish education is still wanted more for boys than for girls. While the proportions are about equal in the One-day schools, there are 62 boys to 38 girls in the Day schools, and 71 boys to only 29 girls in the Weekday Afternoon schools. Further investigation of the causes of this inequality is necessary; tradition seems to be but one factor.

14—There is too great a concentration of enrollment (82%) of children 8 through 13 years old, as compared to the public school enrollment for those ages (47%), and consequently insufficient enrollment (10.3%) at the primary level (ages 4–7) and at the high school level (7.7%). Our children begin their schooling too late and leave it too early. Moreover in the Weekday schools there is a marked and sudden drop in the enrollment of boys 12-13 years old (17.7%) and those over 13 years (3.8%). Among girl pupils the drop does not occur until a year later and is not so marked.

In the One-day schools, too, the drop-out during those ages is considerably greater for boys (from 8.9% to 4.5%) than for girls (from 8.4% to 6.7%).

This finding is quantitative verification of the well known fact that for many boys Bar Mitzvah is the terminal point of their education. *Efforts must be made to counteract the terminal character of the Bar Mitzvah ceremony,* possibly by changing the framework of the education given during those years, along lines indicated elsewhere. . . .

18—During the past 15 years Jewish Day schools increased from 33 schools, of which 26 were in New York, to 214 schools, 136 of them in New York. In 1958 there were 78 Day schools outside of New York. The great majority of the Day schools (77%) are non-congregational. Of all American children attending non-public schools in which both general and religious studies are taught, 91% are Catholic, 8% Protestant, 1% Jewish. The Jewish Day schools resemble in auspices the "parent-society" type of school rather than the "parochial."

The dramatic increase of Jewish Day schools indicates that they have met a deeply felt need for more intensive Jewish education by groups in the community.

19—The daily attendance in the Jewish schools is good; somewhat better in the Weekday schools (85–90%) than in the Sunday schools (80–85%). The fact that attendance is better in the Weekday schools despite the greater demands on the child's time, may be an indication of a more serious attitude to the school by children and parents.

20—However, the holding power of the schools through the years of schooling is not good. Such records as are available indicate (a) that *the average American Jewish child attends about three years in a Weekday Afternoon school, or about four years in a Sunday school,* and (b) that the retention power, as indicated by length of stays in years, varies from school to school, partly in accordance with the length of years required in the school program.

It is clearly necessary to keep in mind that increasing time devoted to Jewish education is to be conceived not only in terms of the number of sessions per week but also in the number of years of schooling.

21—It is very difficult to study the reasons why children leave school, because records are poorly kept and real causes are hard to determine. Such records as are available indicate that besides Bar Mitzvah, the main reasons given are: loss of interest by children, the indifference of parents, and the lack of a transfer system among schools which would enable the child to continue his schooling uninterruptedly when moving into a new neighborhood.

✼   ✼   ✼

B—SCHOOL PERSONNEL

47—In the Jewish schools of the United States there are estimated to be 17,483 teachers, of whom 7,924 teach in Weekday Afternoon and Day schools and 9,559 in One-day schools. The average Weekday school has a staff of four teachers and the average Sunday school about seven teachers. The average teacher in the Weekday schools teaches about 40 pupils divided into two or three classes of about 16 pupils per class (most classes ranging 11 to 21). The One-day school teacher usually teaches one class of about 21 pupils (most classes 15 to 27). As for the teachers in the Jewish Day Schools the indications are that the average teacher teaches one class of about 20 pupils (23 in New York, 18 outside New York). The Study presents summary descriptions of the typical Jewish teachers in the various types of Jewish school.

48—*Jewish teaching is a part time occupation, not only in the One-day schools but to a large extent also in the Weekday schools.* Of the teachers in the Weekday schools 38% stated that they do not consider Jewish teaching their main occupation. Only 25% earn their livelihood by teaching in one school; the others need to teach in more than one Jewish school or to supplement with income from other occupations. *Less than one-half of the teachers in the Hebrew Weekday schools devote their full professional time and energy to Jewish education.* Involved in this is, of course, the fact that the amount of time available to the child after public school hours is limited, and consequently the teacher's possible class teaching hours are also limited. Thus of the Weekday school teachers in the country, only 20% teach 20 hours or more per week, which is considered a full time schedule.

This question is not merely administrative. It goes to the roots of the relation of the teacher to his work. Few people can be expected to have as serious a commitment to part time "extra" occupations as to their job in life. The sense of primary commitment, or the lack of it, is transmitted from teacher to pupil. Therefore, some of the most difficult social-psychological problems in American Jewish education arise from the fact that so many teachers do not consider Jewish teaching seriously enough; it does not "occupy them", except in their marginal time.

*   *   *

VIII—*What Do We Teach Our Children?*
I—THE CURRICULUM OF STUDIES

A—65—The composite curriculum presented in the Study indicates the subjects of instruction, the time allotment and the programmed years of study in Weekday schools, Day schools, One-day schools and Yiddish schools. The curricula of Orthodox and Conservative Weekday schools resemble each other quite closely at the elementary levels. Most Weekday school programs are planned for 4–5 years for ages 8–13; however, 27% of the schools provide for only 2–3 years of curriculum. The Yiddish elementary program is for four years. The Day school elementary program is for a full eight years; likewise that of the One-day school.

The varieties of conception and scope make analysis of subject matter and methodology difficult on a national scale. However, some general comments regarding the subjects of instruction are pertinent:

B—SUBJECTS OF INSTRUCTION

66—Hebrew language instruction is considered in all official curricula as basic, valuable in itself and the key to other studies. However, its teaching suffers from two shortcomings—lack of time and confusion of purpose, particularly in the Weekday schools. The average Weekday school teaches Hebrew somewhat less than 4 years (3.8%) for 36–38 weeks per year 1 1/2 hours per week, or an aggregate of about 220 hours. This would be *the time equivalent of only 1 1/2 years of foreign language instruction* in the public schools. There seems to be very little reasoned choice of graded Hebrew text materials. The situation is aggravated by improper teaching of Hebrew prayers and by beginning the study of Bible-Humash without sufficient preparation.

67—*Prayer and Worship:* There is general consensus that emphasis on individual mechanical reading of Hebrew prayer is wasteful and ineffective. Some schools spend 4–5 hours weekly in teaching mechanical reading. A good deal more could be achieved in less time through functional socialized-rote methods.

68—*Bible:* About *one-half the Afternoon Hebrew schools do not succeed in preparing their pupils for the study of Bible at all.* In most of the schools where it is taught, it is usually begun some time during the second year, with the children decidedly unprepared linguistically. The "Book of Books" becomes for them laborious "dictionary" exercises. Under these conditions they study Humash 2 1/2 years 36–38 weeks per year, 1 3/4 hours per week, or an aggregate of 165 hours. This would be *the time equivalent of only one year of study of literature* in the public schools. Only 30% of the One-day schools provide for study of Bible text in English.

Excluding the Day schools, but including all other schools (Weekday and One-day), *probably no more than 25% of our children learn enough Hebrew to be able to begin the study of the Hebrew Bible, even in simplified texts; and probably less than half of these, 10–15%, can read the simplest Hebrew Bible text without considerable assistance.* Since most Sunday schools do not teach Bible text in English, the likelihood is that the *vast majority of our children* grow up without any knowledge of Bible text, either in Hebrew or in English.

✳   ✳   ✳

71—*Customs and Ceremonies* is a popular study in all schools. Usually taught in connection with the holidays, it is frequently as repetitious as a "twice told tale," unless care is taken to make the holiday projects also occasions for increasing and deepening knowledge.

72—*Israel and Current Events:* Surprisingly little time is set aside for teaching about modern Israel. Further analysis is needed to find out how much and in what manner Israel and general current events are now taught, specifically or in connection with other studies. *Self study techniques should be developed for stimulating and guiding the reading of children about Israel and current events.*

C—73—A considerable variety of *teaching aids* were reported as used by teachers in the various subjects of instruction. . . . Most schools (70%) also report having a school library. However, only 34% have school library rooms, only 40% have librarians (full or part time) and only 25% provide regular budgets for acquiring books. This is another indication of the "thinness" and parsimoniousness of many Jewish schools, *Jewish librarians should be encouraged to engage in organized promotion of Jewish school libraries.*

D—74—*Pupil activities* are encouraged in most schools. These may be "extra-curricular," additional to classroom instruction, or "co-curricular," linked with the studies. Pupil activities in order of frequency are: festival and school assemblies, music (song), junior synagogue, Keren Ami and other children's funds, trips, arts and crafts, dramatics, dance, student government and general clubs. The schools *arts* are extensively used in connection with festival assemblies and other activities.

II—RESULTS OF TEACHING

75—It was not possible to judge the results of teaching on a national scale directly and objectively, because no standardized achievement tests were available.

Recently the American Association for Jewish Education has begun to develop such tests in Hebrew fundamentals and in Jewish history.

76—The results of indefinite data from unstandardized achievement tests indicate that:

    a) in the Fundamentals of Hebrew Language:

        (1) There is no clear progression of knowledge as the child grows in years; the 13 year olds do not score better than the 9 year olds.

        (2) The Hebrew language as such seems to be taught better in the lower grades than in the higher ones.

        (3) In the Weekday schools teaching 8–10 hours per week the total achievement score is better than in those teaching less hours, particularly in the noncongregational schools.

        (4) The pupils in Day schools score very much better than those in other types of schooling; but the pupils in good noncongregational Afternoon schools score as well in Hebrew fundamentals as the corresponding pupils in the Day schools.

        (5) Girls score better than boys.

    b) in Jewish History:

        (1) There is general progression of knowledge through the grades.

        (2) The One-day school pupils score lowest, despite the fact that history is their central study.

    c) in Holidays and Customs:

        (1) There is more regular progression of achievement score than in the other subjects, possibly because in this subject children are aided by their experiences outside the school.

        (2) In this subject, too, the pupils of the Day school score best (the 9 year olds doing better than the 13 year olds in other schools).

        (3) In the One-day schools there is considerable lowering of achievement score at the 13 year old level.

        (4) Girls score better than boys.

77—In attempting to evaluate the "sense of achievement" felt by Jewish school pupils and their parents, the Study found that *only about 35% of the parents are "satisfied" with school achievement,* with or without reservations (pp. 213–215). As for the children, the majority "enjoy or like": Bar Mitzvah preparation, holiday celebrations and Jewish history; but only half of the pupils or less express a sense of achievement in (liking or enjoying) any other of the school subjects or activities. . . .

Chicanos

A PLEA FOR UNDERSTANDING MEXICAN IMMIGRANTS (1920) From Ernestine Alvarado, "Mexican Immigration To The United States," in *Proceedings of the National Conference of Social Work*, (Chicago, 1920), pp. 479–80.

The Mexicans who come to the United States are of three types, namely, the aristocracy or leisure class, who come for political, educational, or business reasons; the middle class, who come for political reasons, but more often for study, business opportunities, and professional advancement; and the peon or laboring class who come for economic betterment. I shall confine my paper to the Mexicans of this third class.

The Mexicans of the lower class who constitute the greater part of the immigration element to this country, respond generously when rightly treated. They are intelligent and indefatigable workers when they are put in the right place. They are reliable, serious, of quick comprehension, and at the same time calm and reflective. In our country, and owing to causes against which the revolution is still fighting, those men have received almost no education; many of them do not know how to read and write. It is imperative that they be educated by you. You can make of them a very useful element in your social life and in the prosperity of the nation.

They come from Mexico in search of new horizons. They have been told about the prosperity of this country, of the liberty that they may enjoy here, of the big salaries they may obtain, of the practicability and value of your methods, of the low cost of living, and thousands of other things which are growing obsolete. They come seeking that wonderful country wherein they hope to find greater liberty than in their own. The "enganchaores," men who come down to Mexico in order to bring labor, make golden promises, so beautiful and bright that they are the more deceived; and although the Mexican government does its utmost to enlighten them, warning them against false offers, they have inherited wandering habits from Aztecs and Castillians, and they go out in search of the golden treasure like mythological argonauts. This bold spirit, this adventurous impulse toward the unknown, implies a greatness of soul, an aspiration toward betterment, a character, which must be taken into account, and it is "up to you," citizens of the United States, to take care of these bold dreamers in order that they may find in your country, if anywhere, at least something of what they have dreamed.

Up to the present the majority of these men have returned to Mexico taking with them disappointment instead of fortune. They have complained of being treated like cattle; that no one knew how to understand their personality, their individuality; that they have fallen into hands that intended only to exploit their physical resistance, frugality, and unselfishness. They have rarely found anyone who has wisely opened to them the path of education, a course which would have been a thousand times more profitable and more human.

The Mexican has a sentiment of patriotism set in his innermost soul. Its roots are deeply embedded in tradition. Unfortunately, our country is misrepresented and abused nearly everywhere in the United States, in theaters, moving pictures, newspapers, books, and private conversations. Perhaps (I would prefer to believe it so), it is done without ill intention, probably thoughtlessly, but it is done. Mexicans find an antagonistic atmosphere for everything that is Mexican, and this fact necessarily tends to make difficult their uniting with you. You could hardly become friends with one who begins by insulting your mother; and for us Mexicans love for our country is not less than love for our mothers.

The best way to attract Mexican immigrants is by educational advantages, not only the education of the immigrants themselves, but also the education of those who are going to be in contact with them. I mean the American people, especially the American workmen. Both American and Mexican workers have a lot to learn from each other. When the time comes that you understand our country, as great as it is unfortunate, you will respect and love those good Mexicans who come to you full of hopes, and then you will know how to treat them in order that those hopes may not be in vain.

To found really friendly relations between our two countries, closer contact between American and Mexican labor must be established. But, unfortunately, the Mexican worker finds very often that it is impossible ffor him to join your workers' organizations. Mexicans go back to Mexico and carry with them the recollection of the animosity they found here. If ever the American worker has found any animosity in Mexico it has been because of the sentiment brought there by Mexicans returning from the United States. All this also will have to disappear when education has taught your laborers that the Mexican laborer does not belong to an inferior race, and should by no means be discriminated against. Fraternity is an international obligation, a duty of humanity. In order that the United States may make effective the high ideals of democracy and liberty, it is necessary for the American laboring man to learn to treat his less fortunate Mexican brother with sympathy and justice.

A CALL FOR THE AMERICANIZATION OF MEXICAN-AMERICAN CHILDREN (1928) From Merton E. Hill, *The Development of An Americanization Program* (Ontario, California, 1928), pp. 98–110.

In the five preceding chapters it has been shown that:

1. Mexican children constitute one-fourth of the elementary pupil population of San Bernardino County, and nearly one-fourth of the pupil population of the elementary schools of the Chaffey Union High School District.

2. The Mexican population in San Bernardino County is on the increase, for three-eighths of the babies of San Bernardino County are Mexican.

3. The children of the thirty races other than American and Mexican composing

the pupil population of San Bernardino County constitute no serious problem in educational administration.

4. The Mexican children are actually making only 42% as satisfactory progress through the schools as are the children of other races.

5. The Mexican pupils have only 58% as good ability to do the work of the schools as have the American pupils; yet they have 90% as good ability as have American pupils to do manual work, they show equal capacity in penmanship.

6. The Mexican adult peons are illiterate and ignorant; 42% of the men and 48% of the women have had no schooling; less than one-fifth of the adults can write English; less than one-fourth of the adults can read English; while less than one-fourth of the adults can speak English.

7. The economic status of the Mexican adults is low; there is a high infant death rate among Mexicans; the homes are unsanitary, crowded, and possess little or no furniture, books, or magazines; unemployment exists to a marked degree; while the average income of the Mexican parents is not sufficient to provide a satisfactory educational background for the children. . . .

The program here suggested will largely solve the Americanization problems by accomplishing the following:

1. The problems involved in Americanization will be recognized.

2. Separate courses of study will be developed for the education of Mexicans.

3. Equipment and buildings will be secured that will make possible carrying out the program.

4. Consistent effort will be made to enroll all Mexican adolescents and adults in classes that will be conducted to meet their actual needs and assure their educational and economic advancement. . . .

The comparative few [Mexican] adults should be enrolled in classes where English is taught when needed. Then there should be provided naturalization classes where American geography, the principles of American government, and American ideals are taught. The ultimate objective of these classes is full citizenship in the United States. Such classes have been maintained in the Chaffey Union High School for many years; the class work culminates each year in the awarding of citizenship certificates to those who are ready for their final papers at the annual commencement exercises of the Chaffey Union High School.

Problems

The greatest problem confronting Southern California today is that of dealing with the Mexican element that is forming year by year a larger proportion of the population. According to present tendencies the time is not far distant when every other child in the elementary schools will be Mexican. The Mexican families live in segregated districts of city and rural districts and import their native standards of living. How shall this element be taken care of? Can the Mexican be raised to the American standards of life? Can American schooling figure in the upbringing of a race? What lessons should be taught and how much should be taught? What skills should be developed? Can the English language replace the Spanish as a medium of current use? Can the high infant death rate be overcome? Can sanitary methods be adopted to replace the less desirable methods that now prevail? Can Mexican adults be led to seek and secure naturalization? And finally, can the Mexican peon be assimilated into the American population as have the races of Europe? These are

THE
MINORITIES

2931

the problems involved everywhere, and an effective Americanization program must take them into account. The considerations involved are:

1. Mexican children can acquire both information and skill.

2. Mexican adults can learn the English language, can acquire useful information about our government, and can learn methods of sanitation.

3. Mexican parents should be taught as well as their children; teach both and prevent rifts in the home.

4. The regular course of study is developed to meet the needs of normal American children and does not meet the needs of Mexican children.

5. Mexican adults will not go to afternoon or evening schools very far from their homes; the school must be taken to them.

6. A new course of study must be created to meet the needs of the Mexican elementary pupils.

7. Separate courses must be set up for Mexican adolescents.

8. Courses must be developed for Mexican adults that will be based upon the actual needs and experiences of those adults.

9. An Americanization program will be justified from an economic standpoint.

10. Every inhabitant or dweller within the territory of the United States has an effect upon the success or failure of the American people; any racial group that numbers from one-fifth to one-fourth of our population has a tremendous effect upon the destiny of our country.

11. Raising the standards educationally, economically, and spiritually should be the aim of any system of education.

From these considerations it seems perfectly clear that there must be set up an Americanization program to take care of the foreign element of any community; it will be the purpose of this chapter to present an educational program for a typical union high school.

Lesson Plans

The educators who are concerned with an Americanization program must set up clearly defined objectives as to what ought to be taught the Mexican peons. The latter will be required to use the English language. To meet this need language lessons should be developed by teachers and by boards of education to be adaptable to children, to adolescents, and to adults. Word or vocabulary lists should be worked out and developed into lesson units. Constant use of these words should be required in class work to accustom the Mexicans to their use. Simple arithmetic lessons leading to a mastery of the four fundamental processes should be developed. This should be done for the mere protection of the adults in their small business relations. Penmanship lessons should be developed, and the Mexican pupils and adults given an opportunity to learn our written language, for they appear to be adept in a certain manual dexterity that leads to proficiency in penmanship. Lessons in hygiene and health should be developed, together with lessons on pre-natal care and that of infants, that the high mortality amongst Mexican babies may be arrested. As the Mexicans are lovers of music and art, lessons should be developed so that they may become trained along these lines wherein they show great proficiency. As the average Mexican adult has had no training in the "home-owning virtues," it will be necessary to develop lessons regarding thrift, saving, and the value of keeping the money in the banks. As the Mexicans show considerable aptitude for handwork of any kind, courses should be developed that will aid them in becoming skilled workers with their hands. Girls should be trained to become domestic servants, and to do various kinds of handwork for which they can be paid adequately after they leave school.

Teaching Procedures

Such illustrative teaching procedures as the following have been determined by experience and through study of the problem:

1. Teach to all only the fundamental processes in arithmetic. Intensive drill in making change.

2. Make use of intensive drill in penmanship. Use old copybook methods. Teach thrift through successive copying of Poor Richard's sayings; teach both men and women to spend less than they earn.

3. Teach reading. Include such things as road signs, railroad signs and advertisements; the buying and selling language of the stores; our best patriotic utterances. Teach the use of the newspaper, the magazine, and the Americanization text-books.

4. Teach every mother during the pre-natal period the care of babies; the preparation and use of clothing; the selection and preparation of wholesome food— food that will raise the energy index of the race.

5. Teach every boy how to make inexpensive furniture for the home. Plans should be drawn for cheap but strong chairs, tables, shelves and cabinets that will be taken and installed in the home. Boys should be taught to make use of discarded tin cans in the development of useful kitchen utensils.

6. Girls should be trained to become neat and efficient house servants.

7. The outstanding students, boys and girls alike, should be trained in leadership. To this end groups will be organized under their own leadership; the industrial high school will have its class officers and its student body officers. All will be trained in voting.

8. Teach boys and girls, men and women how to enjoy wholesome amusements; provide an extensive physical education program that will include health education; train the adolescents of both sexes in self-control. Above all, set up a program such that every Mexican boy and girl within the compulsory age limits, and every Mexican adult shall be organized into classes, arranged by groups according to their abilities and needs, and in spite of handicaps, taught and re-taught until they show the required proficiency to meet the ordinary needs of community life. . . .

*　　*　　*

There should be developed wherever numbers shall warrant a segregation of pupils on an ability basis. Pupils should not be put in Mexican classes because they are Mexicans; they should be put there because they can profit most by the instruction offered in such classes. There should always filter into all schools those Mexicans who can profit by the regular course of study. . . .

What should be done in each individual district where the numbers warrant may be illustrated by the program being worked out in the Chaffey Union High School District. There has been established a new department to be known as the Department of Mexican Education. This step was taken because the survey of the district has shown fifteen hundred Mexicans in the schools in addition to the numbers of adults enrolled in the Americanization classes. This department numbers more than thirty teachers who have volunteered to do what they can to advance the cause of Mexican education. The purpose of this department is to make a scientific study of the Mexican. This study should trace the ethnological evolution of the modern Mexican; it should involve a study of the history of the Mexican people, and finally, it should involve a study of the racial extraction of the Mexican element of the population of San Bernardino County. The Department of Mexican Education should make a further study of the temperament of the race for this should be thoroughly understood in dealing with the people. There should be studied most carefully those qualities and abilities that are recognized as peculiar to the Mexican people, that educational effort in behalf of the Mexican may be applied to the maximum advantage. There should be studied the peculiar aptitudes of these good-natured and kindly people that they may be developed along the best possible lines. . . .

DESCRIPTION OF SEGREGATION OF SCHOOL CHILDREN IN CALIFORNIA (1948)   From W. Henry Cooke, ''The Segregation of Mexican-American School Children in Southern California,'' *School and Society,* vol. LXVII, pp. 417–19.

Schools for "Mexicans" and schools for "Americans" have been the custom in many a Southern California city. It mattered not that the "Mexicans" were born in the United States and that great numbers of them were sons and daughters of United States citizens. It has been the custom that they be segregated at least until they could use English well enough to keep up with English-speaking children. Neither did it matter that many of them had a command of English nor that there was no legal basis for their segregation. Under a law, enacted in 1885 and amended in 1893, it has been possible to segregate Indians and Mongolians in California's public schools. To many an administrator this included "Mexicans." This pattern was followed principally because the majority groups in the local communities wanted it done that way. Since the spring of 1947, a new legal situation has maintained: it is not now legal in California to segregate any ethnic group. And yet the practice still continues in many cities. This fact needs explanation. But first, just what is meant by "racial segregation" as applied to schools?

Segregation as a school policy does not come about by accident. If it exists, there must be intent to separate children between schools or into school groups on the basis of race, national origin, or religion. This sometimes takes the form of an action by a school board providing that all students of a named ethnic group be registered in a given school. In other instances a school board approves the drawing of zone boundaries in such a way as to throw all families of a certain ethnic group into homogeneous areas. When neither of these two methods seems feasible, a policy of transfer of students from zone to zone brings about the same result. Few, if any, cases of segregation of Mexican-Americans have been absolute in nature, for the parents who have had sufficient influence could usually have an exception made for their children. Once made for an elder child, it usually held for all of the succeeding children of the family. Thus it is that the question of privilege raised its head—privilege as between Mexican and Mexican, as well as between Mexican and "Anglo.". . .

The Mexican people came to the United States as agricultural laborers, their wages were traditionally low as compared with American standards, although not with Mexican levels. They found habitat in the edges of California towns where land was cheap, and they built simple and inadequate buildings. Often there would be no sewers in the section they chose and few taps for running water were opened. Many people lived upon small pieces of property that should have housed but one family each. Two decades ago they were hesitant about investing more of their earnings in residences because they harbored the idea that they would soon go back across the border. The fact is that they have stayed in very large numbers, and relatively few of them have left their "colonies" to live in better conditions, although the numbers have been increasing in recent years.

The characteristics of all Mexican-Americans have been set in the minds of most citizens by the descriptions of these early peasants who spoke a foreign tongue and lived unto themselves in ways that seemed uninviting or even squalid. It did not look like discrimination twenty-five years ago to furnish these people with a school and a teacher or two. The building did not have to be much to be better than their homes. The teacher might have been just anybody who would go "down there"; no results were to be expected. Mexican people were roving workers who were a charge upon any school district.

Today these conditions have changed in that the Mexican-Americans have become established as permanent residents in very large numbers. A third generation is now growing up in the once temporary shacks. New houses have been built that would do credit to any worker family. A sizable percentage of Mexican-American young people have become educated, have been around the world with the American armed forces, and want to be accepted in the larger community. Many of the first-generation people and virtually all of the second and third generation speak English. Organizations for their own improvement and integration exist among them. They are now in large numbers "Americans" in every sense of the word. In addition, the whole country is awakening to the injustices under which many backward and colonial peoples have lived. We are more conscious of civil rights for all members of society than we once were. What was once winked at in California can now justly be called discrimination.

That an "Anglo" who was young and intelligent as a business man should be driven out of his new home in a Southern California city because his wife was of Mexican ancestry, although born in that same city and educated in its high school, is an evidence of discrimination. The neighbors waited upon him and he had to sell his home. That a schoolteacher who took her class to a motion picture theater had to divide them so that the "whites" sat in their proper sections and the "Mexicans" in theirs, is evidence of discrimination. When a probation officer finds on his hands a Mexican-American boy who is so brilliant that he gets ahead of his classes and gets into trouble and when this officer tries to place the boy in employment and finds the jobs that are suited to his caliber closed to him because he is a Mexican, there is evidence of discrimination. When a vice-principal of a high school admits that he does not urge Mexican boys to seek varied employment as other boys do because he knows that they cannot do anything more than work in the groves, there is discrimination. When a city council refuses to let Mexican-American boys and girls swim in the public plunge and when it places at the entrance of the bathhouse a red sign reading FOR WHITE RACE ONLY and when it admits through its city clerk that this is for the purpose of keeping out "Mexican" children, it is both ignorance and discrimination.

Many instances of this kind could be cited from California. And yet this state is better than some of its neighbors in that it has adequate laws that prohibit these practices. They continue because communities demand them. The point of this article is not to review the whole field of discrimination, but to study this phenomenon within the public schools—the place above all others where it should not exist.

On the brighter side of the picture several facts can be set forth. The large city school systems of the state have all abolished the segregation of Mexican-Americans and, with the exception of a few vestiges of segregation by zoning or transfer, the segregation of all ethnic groups. Some of these cities have staff members detailed to work upon a better integration and understanding throughout all their schools. This does not mean that all teachers are yet convinced of the values of mixing all students in the schools, but it does reveal an administrative policy that will in time have its effect. In these cities teachers of Negro, Mexican, or Chinese backgrounds are finding their places upon teaching staffs. One large city has five Negro building principals and another has a director of intercultural education. Other cities have committees working on intergroup relationships. In a number of smaller cities where the segregation of Mexican-Americans has been a tradition, the school boards have definitely abolished the policy and practice. In most cases they aroused a clamor of opposition from parents of the majority group, but by tactful handling this has subsided. Some parents sent their children outside of these progressive districts for their schooling in order to avoid having their children sent to the "Mexican school" or to avoid intermingling of their offspring with Mexican-Americans. A number of these changes came about because the administrators realized that segregation was good for neither the English- nor the Spanish-speaking children and that the best type of community could come from having all students learn and play together. Other administrators persuaded their school boards to change to integration because of the danger of lawsuits against them such as four districts in Orange County had had to fight. Certain county superintendents of schools have been working to educate school boards in their jurisdiction to the values of integration and to the dangers of continued segregation. The work of supervisors and the influence of county meetings and institutes have begun to show results in counties that could be named. In other counties changes are overdue.

BLOWOUT IN LOS ANGELES (1968)   From Johns Harrington, "L.A.'s Student Blowout," *Phi Delta Kappan* (Oct. 1968), pp. 74–5, 77–8.

A new kind of monster raised its head in Los Angeles last spring when the city school district faced its first student walkouts in a 113-year history. Whatever happens to the 13 grand jury indictments for conspiracy that are still pending as this is written, the repercussions of the events during the week of March 5 are likely to produce shock waves that will affect schools and minority groups in urban areas throughout the country. Certainly there are lessons to be learned from the "student blowout" that should be helpful to public school teachers and administrators elsewhere.

Five Mexican-American high schools on the east side were involved, but the primarily Negro Jefferson High School also closed its doors for three days. In two predominantly Negro junior high schools as well, pupils left classes for a time. Some set fires in trash cans and broke windows. As a side effect, 800 white students and non-students clashed with police in Venice some 18 miles across the city on the west side.

In addition to its large Negro population, Los Angeles is unique in that it has 800,000 citizens of Mexican descent—the greatest concentration outside Mexico itself. The city is also the most popular "port of entry" in the southwestern United States for immigrants from Mexico.

The extent of participation in the blowout is difficult, if not impossible, to measure accurately. Estimates vary with the point of view and knowledge of the observer. School spokesmen report that some 2,500 students joined in the walkouts, and another 1,000 stayed away from classes because of apparent fear of violence. In the main, however, demonstrations were nonviolent. Demands of demonstrators, agitators, and the few teachers who joined with them ranged from sweeping educational changes to abolishment of corporal punishment and permission to wear miniskirts.

Although the district staff said that newspapers exaggerated the extent of the disorders, an indication of events during the week-long demonstration can be gleaned from such reports as the following:

"Police and school authorities today are probing possible underground agitation as the cause of disorders Tuesday and Wednesday at four Los Angeles high schools. . . .

"One school official attributed the walkouts and rock-throwing, bottle-throwing demonstrations to editorials in an 'underground magazine' which urged students to 'rise up' and protest any conditions they did not like. Two policemen dispersing students at Roosevelt High were hit by flying bottles yesterday. One was hospital-ized for treatment of an eye cut. . . . At Lincoln High about 400 young persons refused to attend classes. They were urged, a school official said, to attend a rally at a nearby park by a bearded youth who wore the uniform of the 'Brown Berets,' a militant Mexican-American group. . . ." (Los Angeles Herald-Examiner, March 7)

"Police Chief Tom Reddin warned today that 'professional agitators' are in for trouble for inciting school walkouts like the one at Belmont High School yesterday, where fires were set, police cars stoned, and six persons arrested." (Los Angeles Herald-Examiner, March 8)

"Two hundred young persons broke up a meeting of the City Board of Education and sent most board members fleeing out a rear door Thursday as a climax to a day of boycotts, arson, and the stoning of police cars at schools attended by minority groups.

"Mrs. Georgiana Hardy, board president, pounded her gavel and adjourned the meeting as a bearded member of the Brown Berets strode down the aisle and took over the guest speaker's microphone.

" 'If you walk out today, we will walk out tomorrow,' shouted the youth." (Los Angeles Times, March 8)

In a statement to the press issued March 8, Jack Crowther, city schools superintendent, declared:

"Every effort is being made to maintain an orderly and normal education process in the Los Angeles city schools. Representatives of the Board of Education and Secondary Division staff are meeting today with student representatives of protest groups to discuss grievances which have been raised regarding some of the high schools.

"It is important to note that, despite the many disturbances at these schools in the last few days, the overwhelming majority of students have remained in class and continued their studies. . . ."

On the following Monday, Crowther addressed a letter to teachers in the schools concerned and asked that they read a message to students. It included:

"Let me emphasize that all of us agree with the desperate need to improve the educational program, buildings, and equipment in your schools. These are the very things which we are fighting for—and indeed on the very day that classes were being disrupted, I and members of the Board of Education were in Sacramento making a desperate plea to the State Legislature for more money to improve our schools.

"I think we can all agree that your viewpoint has been heard—and has been made known dramatically during the last four days of last week. Today your representatives will present their views to the Board of Education.

"Therefore, I am asking each one of you from this moment on to remain in school and continue your class work. Nothing further can be gained by leaving your classes, and the only result of such action will be further harm to your education. Time lost from classes is gone forever and cannot be regained. We know that your parents are anxious and eager for school to continue without further interruption."

Shortly after the first walkouts, the Board of Education took the following actions:

1. Agreed to hold a special meeting at Lincoln High School to discuss educational problems in the East Los Angeles area.

2. Granted amnesty to the students who boycotted classes since March 7.

3. Appointed a Negro principal, vice principal, and head counselor at Jefferson High School. (These assignments were already in process, however, when the demonstrations at Jefferson took place.)

But the board refused to order removal of police from the high school campuses or to ask for release of students who had been arrested during the demonstrations.

The demands and recommendations with which the board and staff were deluged both for and against the walkouts came from a wide variety of sources, including the Educational Issues Committee, a community group in East Los Angeles; the California Association of Educators of Mexican Descent; the East Los Angeles Coordinating Council; the Broadway-Central Coordinating Council; the Citizens' Compensatory Education Advisory Committee; the Los Angeles Teachers Association and the American Federation of Teachers; faculty and student groups, both official and unofficial; the community press; and "underground" newspapers.

The demands themselves covered almost the entire spectrum of the educational program, including:

- Free press
- Free speech
- Bilingual school personnel
- Bilingual instruction
- School buildings
- Cafeteria service
- Community relations
- Corporal punishment
- Counseling ratio
- Electives

- Fences around campuses
- Reading
- Reallocation of R.O.T.C. funds
- Suspension policies
- "Community parents" as teacher aides
- Dress and grooming
- Homogeneous grouping
- Mexican-American contributions to U.S. society
- Administrators of Mexican-American descent
- Nonacademic assemblies
- I. Q. tests
- Library facilities
- Academic courses
- Prejudice of school personnel
- Open restrooms
- Eligibility for student body office
- Swimming pools
- Dismissal or transfer of teachers because of political or philosophical views.

Ironically, some of the demands were direct quotations from statements by Crowther or Stuart Stengel, associate superintendent, Division of Secondary Education, regarding improvements in the educational program that they were seeking. Objectives that have been emphasized by Stengel as "imperative" include:

1. Development of practical testing instruments which will measure the disadvantaged pupil's true potential

2. More counseling services to provide continuous encouragement of pupils to fulfill their potential

3. Full elective programs available in all schools or within a reasonable geographic area, despite comparatively low enrollments in such electives

4. An expanded program for educable mentally retarded pupils

5. Improvement of vocational education programs which will train non-college-bound pupils for gainful employment and the increased development of placement services

6. Improvement of textual and supplementary additional materials which are at both the pupil's ability level and the pupil's interest level

7. An expanded program of English as a second language

8. Provision for experimental classes taught in Spanish in various subject fields

9. Provision of sound human relations training for teachers and administrators

10. Provision for continuous follow-up studies to determine what's happening to the high school graduate.

"It is my belief that the staffs of East Los Angeles secondary schools are doing an outstanding job, within the limitations of what is financially feasible," Stengel said. "I think that our program constantly improves, although not as rapidly, of course, as school personnel and community would like it to ideally."

Since the student blowout, the Board of Education and Staff have been working on responses to the 36 major demands that were presented. As a barrage of scathing criticism from militant groups continued, Crowther told the board:

"It needs to be emphasized that, in the main, many of the items [demanded] are essentially the same as projects which staff has, from time to time, presented to the board for its consideration. The list of demands has created two erroneous implications: 1) that little, if anything, has been attempted by the board and the district in trying to carry out educational improvements demanded by the students and community; and 2) that improvements have been carried out in other schools throughout the district, particularly in more affluent areas, at the expense of East Los Angeles schools.

"One other impression also needs to be clarified: that funds are available to carry out the list of demands. The fact is that no such funds are available without cutting elsewhere. The facts are that a major share of funds is already being allocated to minority area schools (an average of $53 more annually per student than in so-called advantaged areas) . . . .

When the Board of Education granted amnesty to students and appointed Negro administrators at Jefferson High School, the actions were criticized by demonstrators as not going far enough and also by some teacher and other groups for yielding to pressure.

A statement signed by 101 teachers from Roosevelt High School read in part:

"Let it be clearly understood that no teacher whose name appears on this petition wishes to leave Roosevelt. On the contrary, this petition is intended to reflect our loyalty to our school and our deep concern for our students.

"Under the present circumstances, however, we feel that, by submitting to the intimidation of a small militant faction, the Board of Education has acted in error.

"The board's lack of firm action, its display of divided authority, and its nonsupport of local administrators and teachers in their efforts to uphold the provisions of the Education Code and the Administrative Guide of the State of California have made teaching virtually impossible.

"Because of the board's vacillation, teacher morale is depressed, student attitude is confused, and administrative authority is undermined."

Despite the crisis and conflicts of views, however, within a week after the boycott school programs were resumed as Superintendent Crowther and his staff continued to seek additional funds to strengthen the educational program and made both immediate and long-range plans to heal the wounds.

Observers within and without the school system attributed the walkouts to a wide range of causes. Obviously, some were related to recent incidents, such as dissatisfaction with local policies, cancellation of a local high school play, and unrest on college campuses. Others, however, concerned problems that have been growing in intensity for years. Although all agreed that additional help is needed for pupils in East Los Angeles—as in many other urban areas throughout the nation where students should have better educational opportunities and there has been an influx of new residents—some have claimed that the blowout was spontaneous while others have contended that the "rabble-rousers always present" somehow had managed to gain enough momentum to enlist widespread student and community support. Another version was that political opportunists saw a power vacuum and seized the opportunity to cut a niche for themselves. In referring to the blowout in the Los Angeles Times for March 17, 1968, Dial Torgerson wrote, "It was, some say, the beginning of a revolution—the Mexican-American revolution of 1968."

Whatever the cause, or combination of causes, there were many advance indications that storm clouds were reaching threatening proportions. In its February 11 issue—nearly a month before the crisis—the East Los Angeles Gazette carried a banner on page one which read, "Walkout by Students Threatened at Garfield, Five Other Schools."

*   *   *

Since the educational blowout, many steps have been taken to help meet the needs it dramatized. Most of the measures, however, were already on the drawing boards before the shrill voice of dissent shattered the educational calm. Among innovations have been:

1. Appointment of James Taylor, a Negro, to the newly created post of assistant deputy superintendent of instruction (with the rank of an assistant superintendent).
2. Assignment of John Leon, a Mexican-American, as head of a new instructional planning center in East Los Angeles.
3. Authorization by the Board of Education of two highly "innovative" educational "complexes," to be located in East Los Angeles and the Watts area. (Plans for the complexes were initiated long before the blowout.)

"This project is an approach to provide a real breakthrough in the education of minority-group young people by doing an all-out job of providing a variety of services and programs in a concentrated area and by using the newest ideas to put them into effect," Crowther commented. "A flexible, specific program for each school in the complexes will be developed. Our plan is to have ideas come from the school community—by involving parents, other community members, teachers, and administrators."

4. Appointment of Edward Moreno as supervisor of bilingual education in the Instructional Planning Branch and issuance of a study report on what has been done, is being done, and is planned in the Elementary Curriculum Bilingual-Bicultural Program.
5. Conduct of the largest summer school in the history of the Los Angeles city schools, involving 149,000 pupils at 259 locations.

Both elementary and secondary schools offered special classes of various types. One program included five educational enrichment centers for elementary school pupils of varying socioeconomic backgrounds.

6. Teaching of conversational Spanish to 210 teachers in summer workshops.
7. Establishment of the Eastside Bilingual Study Center for approximately 1,800 adults at Salesian High School.
8. Employment of 88 bilingual clerks.
9. Provision of workshops for school personnel to develop greater understanding of the Mexican-American culture and community.
10. Establishment of a classified personnel office for the school system on the east side.

Although instructional materials had already been designed especially to help minority group students, more have been developed and others are on the way. An instructional guide on Mexico was published in 1959, and Angelenos—Then and Now, Californians—Then and Now, and Americans—Then and Now were issued in 1966. The latter series consists of pupil materials for elementary schools which describe the contributions and achievements of members of minority groups. Spanish editions of various pupil materials have been printed or are now being translated. A leaflet called "Blending of Two Cultures" focused on services for Mexican-American pupils.

Reference lists for teachers and pupils include "A Selected List of Books on American Ethnic Groups for Secondary School Libraries," "Recommended Books on American Cultural Minority Groups for Elementary School Libraries," and "Bibliography of Books in Spanish Compiled from Recommended Titles for Secondary Libraries."

Although it is too early to say whether L.A.'s student blowout has been properly patched up or what organizers may think of next, it must be evident to most observers that a heavy thrust is being made by the Los Angeles city schools to provide the kind of education that all pupils need. Many would agree with John Leon, director of the new instructional planning center in Los Angeles, when he recently said:

> It seems to me that in American education we have three major phases. In the first, the schools blame the homes for the failures of children. In the second, the parents and other citizens blame the schools. Now we must enter the third phase, in which schools and homes share the blame for educational problems and work together toward their solution.

Unlike a Grade B movie, however, the story does not necessarily have a happy ending. In fact, for the time being, at least, there seems to be no ending at all. An article in the Los Angeles Times for August 4 reported that the Educational Issues Coordinating Committee of East Los Angeles had "rejected" the Board of Education's handling of the 36 "student" demands for educational reforms. The coordinating committee also has requested status independent of the board and asks that the committee and the district staff choose an independent group of educators to investigate East Los Angeles problems.

"We are not going to be put off," the Times quoted the Rev. Vahac Mardirosian, chairman of the committee, as saying. "We are not going to go away."

The student blowout and its aftermath in Los Angeles have dramatically illustrated the need for better communications between schools and community, more financial help, and greater emphasis on minority group culture. Perhaps the most important lesson, however, is the urgency of decentralization in urban areas to encourage local participation and to assure provision of an educational program that meets local needs. In the future, community influences undoubtedly will have a greater impact on curricular offerings and other aspects of individual school programs.

DESCRIPTION OF THE EDUCATION OF MEXICAN-AMERICANS IN LOS ANGELES (1968)
From "Education and the Mexican-American Community in Los Angeles County," U.S. Civil Rights Commission, *Report of the California State Advisory Committee to the U.S. Commission on Civil Rights* (Washington, D.C., 1968), pp. 1–4.

"Civil rights," as generally defined and interpreted in the United States, is a phrase of vague implications to the Mexican-American who is aware that the Nation offers less of its prosperity to him than it does to others. But he is inclined to blame himself for any failure to gain an equal share of that prosperity.

His experience in this country does not provide the basis for the belief that he can attain first-class citizenship. His tradition stresses one's intrinsic worth, as opposed to the esteem one must fight to obtain from others.

This attitude, however, does not change the reality. There are 5,000,000 Mexican-Americans in the Southwest who have problems with education and employment, more serious in some cases than those suffered by Negroes. It is evident that various forms of discrimination are major causes of these problems.

In recent years, many Mexican-Americans have become more vocal in defining the problems and demanding that society act responsibly toward all its citizens. Understandably, much of the current discussion about Mexican-American problems emanates from metropolitan Los Angeles where the largest concentration of Mexican-Americans within the United States resides.

The 1960 census reported that more than 6,000,000 persons lived in Los Angeles County and at that time the Spanish surname population was the largest minority group with about 10 percent of the total. In East Los Angeles, the Spanish surname population was 70,802 or 67.1 percent. This group has continued to grow as shown by the Special Census in 1965: In East Los Angeles 76 of every 100 residents in 1965 were Mexican-American. The Mexican-American population of East Los Angeles advanced by 6 percent between 1960 and 1965, while the area's total population declined by 8 percent.

Approximately one-fourth to one-third of the total population is Mexican-American in 11 areas outside East Los Angeles: San Fernando, Pacoima, Wilmington, University, Wholesale, Elysian Park, Mount Washington, La Puente, Pico Rivera, Montebello, and Terminal Island. Seven of these areas are close to the East Los Angeles region. In spite of these concentrations, the Mexican-American population is widely distributed throughout the county; in 23 areas surveyed in the county, the Spanish surname population accounts for 10 to 20 percent of the total. In 29 additional areas it is 5 to 9 percent of the total. There is no area from which Spanish surname people are completely absent and only 12 areas where they account for less than 2 percent of the total.

According to the 1960 census, the Spanish surname population ranked below the county averages in many socioeconomic characteristics, such as income, employment, housing, and education. Median family income was $5,762 as compared to $7,287 for other whites. Twenty-five percent of all families had an annual income below $4,000; slightly less than 10 percent had incomes below $2,000 a year. The 1965 unemployment rate for males was 7.6 percent, about 2 percentage points higher than the county average. Fewer than half of all Spanish surname families owned their own homes in 1960. Median value of these owner-occupied homes was $13,000, $2,900 below the county average of $15,900. More than half, 54.6 percent, of all units occupied by Spanish surname families and individuals were built before 1950 and one-fifth were classified as dilapidated or deteriorated.

The 1960 census also reported comparative scholastic achievement for persons over 25 years old. In California, the median school years completed for Spanish surname persons was 8.6; the comparative figure for Anglo-Americans was 12.1 and for nonwhites, 10.5.

According to California's first public school racial census, released in March 1967 by the State Department of Education, 57 percent of the Spanish surname students in districts with more than 50,000 enrollment attended "minority schools." The Department defined a minority school as one which fails to come within 15 percent of matching the proportion of minority students in the school district as a whole. For example, if a school district has a total minority student enrollment of 35 percent, a school in that district with more than 50 percent minority students would be considered a "minority school."

In East Los Angeles where more than 76 percent of the population is Mexican-American, approximately 7 percent, according to the 1960 census, had no schooling at all and less than 9 percent had completed even one year of college.

According to a 1965–66 survey undertaken by the Los Angeles City School System, the two high schools with the highest dropout rates were the predominantly Mexican-American schools, Garfield, where the dropout rate was 53.8 percent, and

Roosevelt, with a 47.5 percent dropout rate. In contrast, two Westside schools, Palisades and Monroe, had dropout rates of 3.1 percent and 2.6 percent respectively.

Mexican-American enrollment in California colleges is extremely low. At the University of California at Los Angeles there were fewer Mexican Americans enrolled in 1967—less than 70—than there were 10 years before despite the huge enrollment increase. At the University of California at Berkeley there were approximately 70 Mexican-American students in a student body of more than 25,000. Even at California State College at Los Angeles, in the heart of the Nation's largest Mexican-American community, there were only 200 Spanish-speaking students out of a student population of 22,000. While Mexican-American students comprise 13.6 percent of California's public school population, they comprise less than one percent of its college student population.

DESCRIPTION OF THE CHICANO MOVEMENT (1970) From Ysidro Ramon
Macias, "The Chicano Movement" *Wilson Library Bulletin,* vol. XLIV, pp. 731–35.

Although no one has categorically determined how the term "Chicano" was born, it is generally accepted that the word came from northern Mexico. It is here that burritos originated, where menudo, mole, pozole, and many other foods prepared by Chicanos are made in a manner distinct from that of greater southern Mexico.

It is also in northern Mexico, because of its proximity to the United States, that the language academically called "Calo" and locally named "Pocho" came into being. Perhaps the citizens of Chihuahua, a city and state of northern Mexico, took the "Chi" from Chihuahua and added the "cano" from Mexicano to arrive at Chicano.

Common in the United States from about the 1930s, the term was used by the Mexicans long before "Mexican-American" and was generally understood to be an intimate name recognizing a particular status not entirely Mexican nor entirely U.S. American.

The term is nothing new, as is popularly supposed. In fact, it commanded significant national attention during the so-called "zoot suit riots" in Los Angeles in the early 1940s. Its use was revived about 1965 at the beginning of the Delano strike and continues to increase, helping to build a definite civil rights movement and philosophy. Actually, the concept behind the Chicano movement goes farther than that of civil rights, since many Chicanos want either a complete revision of the United States political and economic system or separation from it.

Among the salient characteristics of the Chicano are his self-awareness and self-respect, and a language at least the equal if not superior to the Anglo's. He rejects the notion that he must subjugate his heritage in order to rise within American society. Instead he presents the Anglo with the alternative to accept him as an equal. If the Anglo refuses to allow him his self-respect, as is often the case, the Chicano now seeks to establish political and economic hegemony over his communities in order to control them and perpetuate his existence as a distinct entity.

The Chicano is becoming more isolated from Anglo society than ever before because of the Anglo's refusal to accept him. The Chicano asks himself: "Why should I try to prove myself to the Anglos? I will be my own man, respecting my heritage. If accepted as such, it's well; if not, that's all right too."

The Chicano is aware of the history of Mexican peoples in this country. He recognizes that Mexicans fought against Santa Ana at the Alamo; that twenty percent of the G.I.s on the front lines in Vietnam are Chicanos, who comprise but three percent of the total population of this country; that educationally, politically, and socially, gross injustices have been perpetrated against Chicano communities by the dominant Anglo society.

The spirit of "compadrazgo" [social ties between parents and godparents] is part of the Mexican heritage. This sense of personal responsibility or personal commitment is another characteristic that distinguishes the Chicano. Rejecting the Puritan ethic of self-improvement above all else, the Chicano believes that just because he "makes" it, it does not make the system valid to all Chicanos. He recognizes that he is part of a brotherhood, that he has an obligation to work for the betterment of his people in whatever way he can. Accordingly, he automatically devotes a portion of his lifetime energies to work exclusively for the Chicano communities.

The concept of "Chicanismo" has not yet been precisely defined, but it is based on self-awareness and compadrazgo, enriched by the peculiar qualities of the Chicano, or Mexican, heritage. Chicanos point out that they are heirs to a great mixture of cultures, the Indian and the Spanish; and added to this Mexican culture is the experience of living in an English-speaking country, which is continuously endeavoring to erase the Mexican heritage.

Chicanos now accept their unique character as positive and beautiful, no longer as inferior and vulgar forms of expression and behavior. Further, no longer does the color of a Chicano's skin determine his status within his community in the same manner as before. The lighter-skinned Mexican is no longer the favored son; quite the contrary, the darker Indian type is now idealized as are other characteristics and customs which derive from our Indian heritage.

The Chicano movement seeks to play educational roles in three areas: educating the people (Chicanos) regarding their political and economic status; educating Chicanos in their heritage, history, and customs, thereby increasing their self-awareness, pride, and effectiveness as individuals; and promoting institutionalized education within the communities, where little enthusiasm for education existed before.

Two further educational objectives of the movement should be mentioned in this context. The first is to promote the use of "Pocho" (a mixture of Spanish, English, and some unique elements) in literary circles. Chicano and Latino artists have now recognized Pocho, with its Pochismos (idioms of Pocho), as a truly artistic and expressive bastard tongue. Moreover, it expresses the Chicanos better than either Spanish or English and should be preserved and expanded. Accordingly, throughout the great Aztlan (U.S. Southwest), Chicanos express themselves daily in their native tongue, Pocho, and continually seek new ways of reviving, maintaining, and enriching the Chicano culture.

The second goal is that of actively seeking greater recognition for our Mexican culture, language, and traditions, and working for their preservation. This aim is most fundamental; within it one may find the basis for our actions, outlook on life, familial and societal relationships—everything that goes into making us what we are. It is our blood that makes us what we are, and any attempt to apply a tourniquet would be suicidal.

The problems that beset the Chicano community in education are enormous. With the exception of the native American, perhaps no other ethnic group has had such a poor record of achieving normal educational levels. Part of the difficulty may be that, among Mexicans, there appears to have been a general lack of family motivation toward education, especially higher education. When one learns that due to his economic condition the Chicano is not apt to think about education, but is concerned primarily with existing for the moment, and that his lineage from Mexico is predominantly from peasant stock with little or no education itself, it is not difficult to understand why the Chicano communities were not preoccupied with education. Fortunately, the movement has provided tremendous impetus for Chicanos to secure better and higher levels of education.

The language barrier has been and continues to be a nagging educational dilemma. As stated before, many Chicanos are comfortable when speaking Pocho. This tongue serves to identify the Chicano from the Anglo and the Mexican national. When the Pocho-speaking Chicano confronts the English-speaking situation in the schools, however, the result is usually anxiety, frustration, anger. One positive step in the direction of alleviating this condition is teaching English as a second language at the elementary level. Remedies of this kind will, in time, reduce the serious and unjust disparities in levels of education that persist. To cite one example, educational attainment in California for Chicanos is eight years of schooling, compared with ten years for Blacks and twelve years for Anglos.

Greater mobility upward into higher education is sorely needed by Chicanos and is definitely being sought by the movement. Although the means that our own and other Third World communities are employing to reach that end are not generally approved by white America, such mobility is being grudgingly yielded in an increasing number of instances. In order for Chicanos to attain this greater mobility, two basic needs must be satisfied; first, more funds to insure that our qualified brothers and sisters will be able to enroll in the schools in which they are accepted. The reactionary onslaughts launched by Reagan, Rafferty, and Co. in California, plus the decision to discontinue the Educational Opportunity Program, have created a critical situation with regard to the ability of our communities to support Chicano students. The second need is for a more valid and just method of determining intelligence, for the currently used IQ tests are geared to people of white middle-class backgrounds.

It is truly depressing and frustrating for the Chicano that low quality education, including inferior teachers, counselors, schools, and books, all find homes in the "barrio," the Latin neighborhood. These second-rate educational vehicles and personnel continue to strangle and hold back the Chicano communities.

A typical example of racism and segregation is the tracking system employed in California's high schools. Under this system—which features two levels: college preparatory and general curriculum—Chicanos and other minority students are usually placed in general curriculum, regardless of their grades. This program basically prepares the student to graduate from high school and secure manual employment. He is almost thoroughly discouraged from pursuing his studies at a college; instead he is told that he has "vocational aptitude."

In this manner, educational institutions and their curricula perpetuate the Anglo superiority myth; they program Chicanos into mediocre jobs or into dropping out before graduation and discourage college or other forms of higher education for them. Such schools do not deal effectively with the cultural differences of Chicanos, but instead insist on adoption of Anglo-Saxon mores and idiom.

There is certainly great need for a better understanding and consideration of our cultural differences by the dominant Anglo system. For too long it has been 'chic' in the United States to speak a different language or to display differing cultural patterns as long as neither the language nor the culture is Spanish or Spanish-derived. This racist and arrogant view must be eliminated.

In order to correct these injustices and shortcomings, some basic social changes are essential. The Chicano movement, in the manner of other minority movements in the United States, is forcing education to look closer at itself, to make important changes in the social sciences in order to relate more realistically and comprehensively to contemporary society. For too long the archaic, ivory-tower social sciences have been turning out "professionals" who in reality are nothing more than bookish robots with little or no understanding of minority community problems. Now, through political and social pressure, often producing either ethnic studies courses or changes in existing curricula, the social sciences are beginning to change for the better.

Chicano or La Raza Studies may appear in many forms ranging from high school to university levels. In addition to enabling, in fact compelling, the social sciences to relate to the minority communities, Chicano Studies perform an even more important function: teaching the Chicano student the story of Mexico and Mexicans in its true historical context, not as viewed through the eyes of a biased and racist Anglo historian, author, or teacher.

The movement has also given rise to Chicano newspapers, magazines, literature, and textbooks. It has endeavored to reach all levels of the community, including the non-English speaking, the *pintos* (convicts or ex-cons), *tecatos* (drug users, usually of hard drugs), and the *Vatos locos* ("street" persons).

Chicano student groups have initiated various programs in the barrios designed to bring the schools and the community closer together, such as courses in political science taught to the younger Chicanos. Probably the most important function of the Chicano student groups up to this time, however, has been simply to involve the community in meetings, programs and action.

As an educational vehicle, libraries are almost non-functional in our Chicano communities. At best, the barrio is served by a branch library which is almost always poorly stocked in books, magazines, and reference materials, and is unimaginative in general decor. Furthermore, these libraries are staffed by Anglo women, who may want to understand the needs of the barrio youth but cannot evoke any trust from them. Libraries are generally viewed by our communities as extensions of the local schools, and since the schools are a negative and uncomfortable experience, the same feeling is transferred to the library.

Branch libraries, in order to begin to be more effective, should employ Latino librarians and supporting staff. There should certainly be a good stock of books available on ethnic subjects. Without these two requirements, branch libraries located in the barrio will continue to be little used, if at all.

A final word must be said about the sacred cow, the IQ. Countless numbers of Chicanos have received inferior educations based on scores achieved in some IQ test taken when they were about eight years old, barely spoke English, and hardly knew "American" mannerisms. Such "intelligence" tests are biased and invalid. They channel Chicanos into special education classes or seriously undermine a youth's confidence when he is refused participation in classes or experiences because his IQ is not high enough.

Schools and school districts have also been suspected of consciously employing these farcical IQ tests in order to gain benefits for themselves. Currently, in one Southern California city, almost two-thirds of all the children in "mentally retarded" or special education classes are Chicanos. The federal government gives $5,000 to a school district for every child in a "mentally retarded" status. It is common knowledge that this particular school district is not using the $5,000 per child to improve the education of these so-called "mentally retarded" children but rather is channeling these funds to improve the predominantly white schools.

Recently, the Rural Legal Assistance Foundation filed suit in the San Francisco U.S. District Court on behalf of nine school children of Mexican background in Monterey County, charging that these youngsters are "wrongfully placed in classes for the educable mentally retarded because they get low scores in IQ tests given in English, a language they don't know well."

The suit charges that when given the IQ tests in English, the children, ranging from eight to thirteen years, failed. But when they were retested by a bilingual tester in both English and Spanish, they scored an average gain on the test of fifteen points. The school district, the suit stated, refuses to accept the results of the second tests and refuses to re-test the children themselves.

"Placement in classes for the mentally retarded, "the suit adds," is 'tantamount to a life sentence of illiteracy and public dependency.' "

It is for reasons such as these that the Chicano movement is educating its own and others—educating them to effect a change in the entire system, a change that can come only through revolution!

Indians

EDUCATION OF A HOPI BOY (c. 1899)   From Leo W. Simmons, ed., *Sun Chief: The Autobiography of A Hopi Indian* (New Haven, 1942), pp. 88–91, 94–102.

I grew up believing that Whites are wicked, deceitful people. It seemed that most of them were soldiers, government agents, or missionaries, and that quite a few were Two-Hearts. The old people said that the Whites were tough, possessed dangerous weapons, and were better protected than we were from evil spirits and poison arrows. They were known to be big liars too. They sent Negro soldiers againt us with cannons, tricked our war chiefs to surrender without fighting, and then broke their promises. Like Navahos, they were proud and domineering—and needed to be reminded daily to tell the truth. I was taught to mistrust them and to give warning whenever I saw one coming.

✻   ✻   ✻

A few years before my birth the United States Government had built a boarding school at the Keams Canyon Agency. At first our chief, Lolulomai, had not wanted to send Oraibi children, but chiefs from other villages came and persuaded him to accept clothes, tools, and other supplies, and to let them go. Most of the people disliked this and refused to cooperate. Troops came to Oraibi several times to take the children by force and carry them off in wagons. The people said that it was a terrible sight to see Negro soldiers come and tear children from their parents. Some boys later escaped from Keams Canyon and returned home on foot, a distance of forty miles.

Some years later a day school was opened at the foot of the mesa in New Oraibi, where there were a trading post, a post office, and a few governmental buildings. Some parents were permitted to send their children to this school. When my sister started, the teacher cut her hair, burned all her clothes, and gave her a new outfit and a new name, Nellie. She did not like school, stopped going after a few weeks, and tried to keep out of sight of the Whites who might force her to return. About a year later she was sent to the New Oraibi spring to fetch water in a ceremonial gourd for the Ooqol society and was captured by the school principal who permitted her to take the water up to the village, but compelled her to return to school after the ceremony was over. The teachers had then forgotten her old name, Nellie, and called her Gladys. Although my brother was two years older than I, he had managed to keep out of school until about a year after I started, but he had to be careful not to be seen by Whites. When finally he did enter the day school at New Oraibi, they cut his hair, burned his clothes, and named him Ira. .

In 1899 it was decided that I should go to school. I was willing to try it but I did not want a policeman to come for me and I did not want my shirt taken from my back and burned. So one morning in September I left it off, wrapped myself in my Navaho blanket, the one my grandfather had given me, and went down the mesa barefoot and bareheaded.

I reached the school late and entered a room where boys had bathed in tubs of dirty water. Laying aside my blanket, I stepped into a tub and began scrubbing myself. Suddenly a white woman entered the room, threw up her hands, and exclaimed, "On my life!" I jumped out of the tub, grabbed my blanket, darted through the door, and started back up the mesa at full speed. But I was never a swift runner. Boys were sent to catch me and take me back. They told me that the woman was not angry and that "On my life!" meant that she was surprised. They returned with me to the building, where the same woman met me with kind words which I could not understand. Sam Poweka, the Hopi cook, came and explained that the woman was praising me for coming to school without a policeman. She scrubbed my back with soap and water, patted me on the shoulder, and said, "Bright boy." She dried me and dressed me in a shirt, underwear, and very baggy overalls. Then she cut my hair, measured me for a better-fitting suit, called me Max, and told me through an interpreter to leave my blanket and go out to play with the other boys.

The first thing I learned in school was "nail," a hard word to remember. Every day when we entered the classroom a nail lay on the desk. The teacher would take it up and say, "What is this?" Finally I answered "nail" ahead of the other boys and was called "bright."

At first I went to school every day, not knowing that Saturday and Sunday were rest days. I often cut wood in order to get candy and to be called a "smart boy." I was also praised again and again for coming to school without a policeman.

At Christmas we had two celebrations, one in the school and another in the Mission Church. Ralph of the Masau'u Clan and I each received a little painted wagon as a reward for good attendance. Mine was about fifteen inches long with two shafts and a beautiful little gray horse.

I learned little at school the first year, except "bright boy," "smart boy," "yes," and "no," "nail," and "candy." Just before Christmas we heard that a disease, smallpox, was coming west from First Mesa. Within a few weeks news came to us that on Second Mesa the people were dying so fast that the Hopi did not have time to bury them, but just pitched their bodies over the cliff. The government employees and some of the school-teachers fled from Oraibi, leaving only the principal and missionaries, who said that they would stay. About this time my mother had a new baby, named Perry much later.

✳   ✳   ✳.

That autumn some of the people took their children to Keams Canyon to attend the boarding school. Partly because I was tired of working and herding sheep and partly because my father was poor and I could not dress like some of the other boys, I was persuaded to go to the Agency school to learn to read and cipher—and to get clothes. My mother and father took three burros and accompanied me to Keams Canyon. When we arrived at the end of two days, the matron, Mrs. Weans, took me into the building and gave me a bath, clipped my hair, and dressed me in clean clothes.

I ate my supper in the dining room with the other children. My father and mother ate outside in a camp. That night I slept in the dormitory on a bed. This was something new for me and felt pretty good. I was eleven, and the biggest boy in that dormitory; I did not cry. The next morning I had breakfast with the other children. My father and mother went to the kitchen, where the cook fed them. For breakfast we had coffee, oatmeal, fried bacon, fried potatoes, and syrup. The bacon was too salty and the oatmeal too sloppy.

After breakfast we were all told to go to the office and see the superintendent of the Reservation, Mr. Burton, for whom my parents would have to sign their names, or make their marks, before going home. There were a great many of us and we had to stand in line. The agent shook hands with us and patted us on the head, telling us through an interpreter that we had come to be educated. Then he told us to pass into another room where we would receive some gifts. They gave my mother fifteen yards of dress cloth and presented an axe, a claw hammer, and a small brass lamp to my father. Then they asked him to choose between a shovel and a grubbing hoe. He took the hoe.

We did not go to school that day. We returned to the kitchen, where the cook gave my parents two loaves of bread and some bacon, syrup, and meat. Then we went to the camp, where my father saddled a burro and told my mother to mount. "Well, son," they advised me, "don't ever try to run away from here. You are not a good runner, and you might get lost and starve to death. We would not know where to find you, and the coyotes would eat you." I promised. My father climbed on a burro and they started off. I kept my eyes upon them until finally they disappeared in the direction of Oraibi. I moaned and began to cry, fearing that I should never see them again. A Hopi boy named Nash, whom I did not know, spoke to me and told me to stop crying. My parents would come back again, he reassured me, and they might bring me back some good Hopi food. He took me through the Canyon to the other end, where the school building stood. There we gathered some wild roseberries and began eating them until I discovered that they were full of worms.

At noon we all lined up, with the smallest boys in the lead. I was the tallest and the last boy for our dining room. At the table somebody spoke a few words to God, but failed to offer him any of the food. It was very good.

After lunch we smaller boys were given a job cleaning up trash in the yard. When we had finished, Nash and I took a walk up the southeast mesa to the highest point. As we reached the top, Nash turned and said, "Look over to the west." I looked and saw the top of Mount Beautiful, just beyond Oraibi. It seemed far away and I cried a little, wondering whether I would ever get home again. Nash told me not to worry, because I was put there to learn the white people's way of life. He said that when he first came he was homesick, too, but that now he was in the third grade and satisfied. He promised me that when his relatives brought some good Hopi food he would share it with me. His talk encouraged me. As we climbed down the mesa, we heard the supper bell ringing and ran but arrived late. The disciplinarian stepped up to us and struck Nash twice on the buttocks saying, "You are late." Since I was a new boy, he did not put his hands on me—I was lucky.

We went to the dining room and ate bread and a thing called hash, which I did not like. It contained different kinds of food mixed together; some were good and some were bad, but the bad outdid the good. We also had prunes, rice, and tea. I had never tasted tea. The smell of it made me feel so sick that I thought I would vomit. We ate our supper but it did not satisfy me. I thought I would never like hash.

I had trouble defecating, too. A person had to be very careful where he sat. Little houses called privies were provided—one for boys and another for girls. I went into one of them but was afraid to sit down. I thought something might seize me or push me from below and was uneasy about this for several days.

After supper we played a little. Some of the older boys, who had been in school before, wrestled with me. I had been a big, brave lad at home, but now I was timid and afraid. It seemed that I was a little nobody and that any boy could beat me. When it came time for bed the matron took us to the small boys' dormitory, where she made us undress except for our underwear, kneel, and put our elbows on the bed. She taught us to ask Jesus to watch over us while we slept. I had tried praying to Jesus for oranges and candy without success, but I tried it again anyway.

The next day we had to go to school. The little boys went both morning and afternoon. I had to commence at the very bottom in the kindergarten class. When we had entered the classroom and taken our seats, the teacher asked me my name. I did not like my name, Max, so I kept quiet. "Well," said the teacher, "your name shall be Don," and wrote it down in a little book.

The teacher used to pick up a stick, turn the leaves of a chart, and tell us to read. Some of the little boys from First Mesa, who had been there before, could read right along. Although I was the biggest boy in the class, I could not read at all. I felt uncomfortable, especially since they had dressed me in little brown knee pants which I did not like. The first things to learn were "A hat," "A cat," "A horse," "A cow," "An eagle," etc. Then came such things as "A cow has four feet," and "The man had two feet." Another step was, "Put a ball on the box," "Count up to ten." After several days I finally began to understand the words. Soon we were reading long sentences like " 'A rat, a rat,' cried Mae."

I grew tired of school and thought of running away. But one of my father's nephews, Harry Kopi, was watching me and noticed that my face was growing sorrowful. One afternoon, as I was sitting still and sad in the building, he came to me and said, "Come out with me to the place where the pigs live." As we walked along he asked me if I were lonesome, and I almost cried. "I have brought you out here to see the pigs," he said. "When I used to get homesick I would come here and look at them; they made me laugh and feel better." There were about twenty pigs in the pen, all of different sizes. They were funny animals—like dogs with hooves. They looked horrible with their little eyes, sharp mouths, and dirty faces. "Let's go into the pen and ride a pig," said Harry. He caught one by the tail and I clambered on its back and rode it about the pen. It was great fun. I felt better when I got off, and thought to myself that if my homesickness returned I would ride a pig again.

Every Sunday we were taken to the chapel, where we sang, prayed, and had a lesson about Jesus Christ. On those days we were supposed to wear clean clothes and have our faces washed and our hair combed. At Christmas we had parties and a tree and received many gifts.

*   *   *

A few weeks later we had some excitement at school. The assistant disciplinarian, an Oraibi man named Edwin, who had been educated at Grand Junction, climbed through a window into the girls' dormitory one night to sleep with his sweetheart. Soon some of the larger boys tried this with other girls. One night the matron caught Jerry, a Second Mesa boy, in a girl's room. She locked him in another room and kept him there all night without any clothes except his underwear. The next morning she questioned him as to whether he was the only boy involved. Finally he broke down and gave her a long list of names, which she turned over to Mr. Burton, the superintendent.

As we lined up to go to breakfast on the following day, which was the Sabbath, Mr. Burton came with a paper in his hand. "Well, boys," he said, "when I read off your names please step out of line." He started with Edwin and called names slowly until there were thirty boys out of line. Of the larger boys only one was left—Louis, the older clan brother of Nash. When the list was completed the superintendent said, "Will the boys who are left please close up the line and march in to breakfast?" Looking very angry, he led the guilty boys to a large room where he locked them up without any food.

We small boys went into the dining room, where we found that two of the kitchen boys had been summoned to remove their aprons and join the party to be punished. We noticed that many of the girls were absent too. We felt like a flock of sheep huddled together in a corner of a big corral after the wolves have been among them. Mr. Boss, the disciplinarian, said grace quickly and announced, "Eat all you want, children; there will be plenty today." After breakfast, Sunday School was called off. People seemed worried and unfit for prayer.

We stood around in the yard waiting to see what would happen. Mr. Burton and Mr. Boss unlocked the closed room, lined up the boys, and marched them to the girls' dormitory. When they arrived, they were seated in a large room where the girls had already assembled. Mr. Burton gave the culprits a long, stiff talk. Then they were taken to a room upstairs, while we remained in the yard and listened. Soon we heard strapping. Each boy received from fifteen to thirty lashes with a rawhide, the number depending on his age. They were whipped in the presence of the girls, but no boy cried out. Then the girls were taken to another room and paddled, but not before the boys. Some of them cried. After giving the boys another lecture, Mr. Burton marched them through the yard to the toilet, where every boy seemed anxious to go. They were then taken back to the room and locked in again.

At noon we formed a short line and marched back to eat. Later in the day a small boy named Hicks, of the Tewa tribe at First Mesa, went up to a window of the locked room, and the prisoners asked him to bring them some food. He ran to the small boys' building and returned with several rolls of piki. As he was pushing these through a broken pane in the window, the disciplinarian slipped up behind him and caught him. He scolded the boy, laughed and told him to beat it or he would put him in with the prisoners. I stood around all afternoon and watched. For supper the boys were given bread and water and were then released.

In May we had a Decoration Day celebration. We stuck little flags in our caps, took bunches of flowers, and marched out to the graves of two soldiers who had come out here to fight the Hopi and had died.

On June the fourteenth my father came for me and we returned home, riding burros and bringing presents of calico, lamps, shovels, axes, and other tools. It was a joy to get home again, to see all my folks, and to tell about my experiences at school. I had learned many English words and could recite part of the Ten Commandments. I knew how to sleep on a bed, pray to Jesus, comb my hair, eat with a knife and fork, and use a toilet. I had learned that the world is round instead of flat, that it is indecent to go naked in the presence of girls, and to eat the testes of sheep or goats. I had also learned that a person thinks with his head instead of his heart.

✳   ✳   ✳

By the end of summer I had had enough of hoeing weeds and tending sheep. Helping my father was hard work and I thought it was better to be educated. My grandfather agreed that it was useful to know something of the white man's ways, but said that he feared I might neglect the Hopi rules which were more important. He cautioned me that if I had bad dreams while at school, I should spit four times in order to drive them from my mind and counteract their evil influences.

Before sunrise on the tenth of September the police came to Oraibi and surrounded the village, with the intention of capturing the children of the Hostile families and taking them to school by force. They herded us all together at the east edge of the mesa. Although I had planned to go later, they put me with the others. The people were excited, the children and the mothers were crying, and the men wanted to fight. I was not much afraid because I had learned a little about education and knew that the police had not come without orders.

✳   ✳   ✳

The children already at the school were eating their supper when we arrived. Rex and I went to the kitchen and asked for food. We each got a loaf of bread and ate it with some syrup. The cook asked me if I would like some hash. I said, "No." We ate our food at the door and told the people in the kitchen that the children were coming in wagons. Then we went to the dormitory and rested. The next morning we took a bath, had our hair clipped, put on new clothes, and were schoolboys again.

✳   ✳   ✳

The next day I had three surprises. They put me in the dormitory with the big boys, gave me some long khaki pants, and promoted me to the second grade. I was twelve and felt like a man. After a few weeks I was taken off the yard work and given a job with four other boys cleaning the dormitory, making beds, and tidying up the sitting room.

The teacher for the second grade was late in coming from Chicago. Mr. Boss, the disciplinarian, taught us until she arrived in the middle of October. She was a good-looking blond about forty-five, named Mrs. DeVee. She taught us the sounds of the letters showing us how to hold our mouths to pronounce them correctly. I had to work hard to keep up with the class.

I was punished twice within a short time. One day I struck a boy who hit me first; but the teacher looked up only in time to see my blow and made me stand in the corner with my left arm raised high above my head for a full half-hour. This was hard to do. On another occasion I talked too much with a deskmate and Mrs. DeVee made each of us chew a piece of laundry soap until foam came out of our mouths. She said our mouths were dirty. The soap was strong and made our mouths so sore that it pained us to eat for two or three days. When the teacher got sick and had to leave the school I was glad.

I kept close watch on Archie, who was not getting along very well and showed sorrow in his face. It made me remember my first days at school. At last I thought of the pigs and took him over to the pen. He looked at them and laughed. I helped him get on a pig and take a ride. When he became interested, I slipped off my pig and climbed to the edge of the mesa where I sat down and watched. I felt grown up as I sat there in my long pants, looking down at him. We returned to the building before the bell rang.

I got along very well at school that year and heard my name praised highly. In May my father came for me. I returned home and spent the summer working in the fields and herding.

A CRITIQUE OF INDIAN BOARDING SCHOOLS (1910)   From Francis E. Leupp, *The Indian and His Problem* (New York, 1910), pp. 125–27, 129–31.

For reasons plain to any one familiar with the disparity of local conditions, the Indian day-school in the most primitive part of the frontier differs widely from the white day-school anywhere; and, in spite of my desire to assimilate the races as far as practicable in all their activities, I have tried to accentuate this contrast in one or two respects. To me the most pathetic sight in the world is a score of little red children of nature corralled in a close room, and required to recite lessons in concert and go through the conventional daily programme of one of our graded common schools. The white child, born into a home that has a permanent building for its axis, passing most of its time within four solid walls, and breathing from its cradle days the atmosphere of wholesale discipline, is in a way prepared for the confinement and the mechanical processes of our system of juvenile instruction. The little Indian, on the other hand, is descended from a long line of ancestors who have always lived in the open and have never done anything in mass routine; and what sort of antecedents are these to fit him for the bodily restraints and the cut-and-dried mental exercises of his period of pupilage? Our ways are hard enough for him when he is pretty well grown; but in his comparative babyhood—usually his condition when first captured for school purposes—I can conceive of nothing more trying.

My heart warmed toward an eminent educator who once told me that if he could have the training of our Indian children he would make his teachers spend the first two years lying on the ground in the midst of the little ones, and, making a play of study, convey to them from the natural objects right at hand certain fundamental principles of all knowledge. I dare say that this plan, just as stated, would be impracticable under the auspices of a Government whose purse-strings are slow to respond to the pull of any innovation. But I should like to see the younger classes in all the schools hold their exercises in the open air whenever the weather permits. Indeed, during the last year of my administration I established a few experimental school-houses, in regions where the climate did not present too serious obstacles, which had no side-walls except fly-screen nailed to studding, with flaps to let down on the windward sides in stormy weather.

I do not mean that I regard the difference between in-door and out-door instruction as vital in the scheme of Indian schools; but this item serves as well as any other to exemplify the general principle that we shall succeed best by beginning the new life as nearly as possible where the old life left off. We should not make the separation any more violent than necessary; and it is pleasant to note that the more intelligent teachers in the Indian Service are ignoring books as far as they can in the earlier stages of their work. They are teaching elementary mathematics with feathers, or pebbles, or grains of corn; then the relations of numbers to certain symbols on the blackboard are made clear, and thus the pupils are led along almost unconsciously from point to point.

*   *   *

The design kept in view by the advocates of the non-reservation boarding-schools, in carrying the children hundreds of miles away from home and trying to teach them to sever all their domestic ties and forget or despise everything Indian, is to surround them with white people and institutions for the whole formative period of their lives, and thus induce them to settle down among the whites and carve out careers for themselves as the young people of other races do.

This theory has always had its attractions for a certain class of minds, but in practice it has not worked out as expected. Its most ambitious exponent is the Carlisle Indian School, set in the midst of a thrifty farming country. If any experiment in that line could hope to succeed, this one ought to have succeeded. It has been followed by more than a score of similar ventures in the West. A few of these schools were undoubtedly established, as Carlisle was, in response to what their authors believed to be a real demand of the cause of Indian civilization; but in course of time the establishment of new non-reservation schools became a mere meaningless habit. Some Senator or Representative in Congress would take a fancy to adorn his home town with a Government institution, and, if the supply of custom-houses and pension agencies and agricultural experiment stations happened for the moment to be running short, he would stir about to secure votes for an Indian school. Any educational project can count on a certain amount of legislative support on the strength of its name; and, once established, of course a school has to be kept up with goodly annual appropriations. What matter if the Indians do not care to send their children to it? Then the thing to do is to coax, urge, beg, till they give way. If opportunity to obtain an education free of cost does not offer enough attractions in itself, organize a brass band and a football eleven for the boys, and a mandolin club and a basket-ball team for the girls, circulate pictorial pamphlets showing the young players in all their brave regalia, and trust the stay-at-home children to wheedle their parents into consenting!

Nay, until a year or two ago it was the custom, when all mere material devices failed, to give one of the most wide-awake school employees a long leave of absence on full pay, in consideration of his going to this or that reservation and bringing back twenty children. Never mind how he got them—the one point was to get them, good or bad, sound or weakly, anything that would pass a very perfunctory scrutiny and add one name to the school roll. And when two or three such canvassers, representing rival schools, came into collision on the same reservation, resorted to every trick to outwit each other, and competed with bigger and bigger bids for the favor of parents of eligible children, what was the Indian to think? Is it wonderful that a certain old-fashioned Sioux asked a missionary teacher: "How much will you give me if I let my boy go to your school? That other teacher says he will give me an overcoat!"

LEWIS MERIAM ON THE NEED FOR A NEW INDIAN EDUCATION

(1928) From Lewis Meriam, et al., *The Problem of Indian Administration* (Baltimore, 1928), pp. 32–37.

S*chool System.* The first and foremost need in Indian education is a change in point of view. Whatever may have been the official governmental attitude, education for the Indian in the past has proceeded largely on the theory that it is necessary to remove the Indian child as far as possible from his home environment; whereas the modern point of view in education and social work lays stress on upbringing in the natural setting of home and family life. The Indian educational enterprise is peculiarly in need of the kind of approach that recognizes this principle; that is less concerned with a conventional school system and more with the understanding of human beings.

The methods must be adapted to individual abilities, interests, and needs. Indian tribes and individual Indians within the tribes vary so greatly that a standard content and method of education, no matter how carefully they might be prepared, would be worse than futile.

Routinization must be eliminated. The whole machinery of routinized boarding school and agency life works against that development of initiative and independence which should be the chief concern of Indian education in and out of school. The routinization characteristic of the boarding schools, with everything scheduled, no time left to be used at the child's own initiative, every moment determined by a signal or an order, leads just the other way.

For the effort to bring Indian schools up to standard by prescribing from Washington a uniform course of study for all Indian schools and by sending out from Washington uniform examination questions, must be substituted the only method of fixing standards that has been found effective in other school systems, namely, that of establishing reasonably high minimum standards for entrance into positions in the Indian school system. Only thus can the Service get first class teachers and supervisors who are competent to adapt the educational system to the needs of the pupils they are to teach, with due consideration of the economic and social conditions of the Indians in their jurisdiction and of the nature and abilities of the individual child.

The curriculum must not be uniform and standardized. The text books must not be prescribed. The teacher must be free to gather material from the life of the Indians about her, so that the little children may proceed from the known to the unknown and not be plunged at once into a world where all is unknown and unfamiliar. The little desert Indian in an early grade who is required to read in English from a standard school reader about the ship that sails the sea has no mental background to understand what it is all about and the task of the teacher is rendered almost impossible. The material, particularly the early material, must come from local Indian life, or at least be within the scope of the child's experience.

To get teachers and school supervisors who are competent to fit the school to the needs of the children, the Indian Service must raise its entrance requirements and increase its salary scale. The need is not so much for a great increase in entrance salaries as for an increase in the salary range which will permit of rewarding efficient teachers and offering them an inducement to remain in the Indian Service. To offer considerable opportunity for advancement in salary with increasing length of satisfactory service, is now the common practice of the better

THE MINORITIES

school systems of the country, and the government must adopt the same system if it expects to draw into its service some of the best of the new teachers. The Indian schools as a matter of fact require better teachers than do the city school systems for white children. The teacher in the Indian schools has the harder task and cannot secure so much assistance from supervisory officers.

The boarding schools demand special consideration. Under the section on health the recommendations have been summarized that relate to the health of the child, better diet, less over-crowding, less heavy productive work, more thorough physical examinations, and better correlation of remediable defects. These factors have an important bearing on education itself that need not be discussed in this brief summary. It should, however, be said specifically that the half-day plan, with its large amount of non-educational productive labor, tends materially to reduce the efficiency of the boarding schools as educational institutions.

The objection to the heavy assignments of purely productive labor must not be construed as a recommendation against industrial education. On the contrary it is specifically recommended that the industrial education be materially improved. The industrial teachers must be free to plan the industrial teaching from the educational standpoint, largely unhampered by the demands for production to support the schools or the Service. The work must be an educational enterprise, not a production enterprise. The persons selected for industrial teachers must be chosen because of their capacity to teach and not because of their capacity to do the work themselves with the aid of the pupils as helpers. The industries taught must be selected not because they supply the needs of the institution but because they train the pupil for work which he may get at home on the reservation or in some white community to which there is some possibility of his going.

The industrial training must be subjected to the tests of practical use. The Indian Service must attempt to place the Indians who leave the school and help them to become established in productive enterprise either on the reservations or in white communities. It must be prepared to enter into cooperative arrangements with employers so that boys and girls shall have opportunity to gain experience in commercial employment while still having some official connection with the school. In this way the school can place its emphasis on helping the pupil to acquire the necessary fundamental skill and then getting him a job where he can apply this skill in an occupation for which there is a local demand. The schools cannot train for all occupations, but they can aid the boy or girl in acquiring those types of skill that are common to many occupations. The Service should make a survey of the economic opportunities for its pupils and plan its industrial training to meet these ends.

In the discussion of health it has been recommended that the over-crowding of boarding schools be corrected through the maximum possible elimination of young children from these schools. From the educational standpoint the young child does not belong in a boarding school. For normal healthy development he needs his family and his family needs him. Young children, at least up to the sixth grade, should normally be provided for either in Indian Service day schools or in public schools. Not until they have reached adolescence and finished the local schools should they normally be sent to a boarding school.

The survey staff appreciates that it is not practicable instantly to provide day school or public school facilities for every young Indian child and that in some instances the boarding school is the only practicable solution, but the movement away from the boarding school already under way should be accelerated in every practicable manner. One of the definite objectives of the Service, vigorously pressed, should be the elimination of pre-adolescent children from boarding schools.

Because of the nature of the Indian country, the boarding school will for many years to come be essential to provide secondary education of a type adapted to the needs of Indian youth. It can stress provision for their special needs in a way that the typical high school designed for white children already adjusted to the prevailing economic and social system could not do. It must emphasize training in health, in family and community life, in productive efficiency, and in the management and use of property and income to a degree probably unnecessary in general public schools.

Although the boarding school must be distinctive in the emphasis on the special needs of the Indians, it should not be so distinctive that it will not dovetail into the general educational system of the country. The promising Indian boy or girl who has attended an Indian boarding school and who desires to go on with his education should not encounter any educational barrier because of the limitations of the Indian boarding schools. The faculties and their courses of study should be such that they can meet the standards set for accredited high schools. It may prove necessary for the Indian youth who wishes to go on to higher institutions to spend a little longer time in the boarding school than he would have spent in an accredited high school, but the way should exist and should be plainly marked.

The Indian Service should encourage promising Indian youths to continue their education beyond the boarding schools and to fit themselves for professional, scientific, and technical callings. Not only should the educational facilities of the boarding schools provide definitely for fitting them for college entrance, but the Service should aid them in meeting the costs. Scholarships and student loan funds might well be established by the government and by organizations interested in the Indians. State universities in states with a considerable Indian population might be willing to offer special scholarships for the leading graduates of Indian schools. The vocational guidance service should be thoroughly informed regarding the entrance requirements of the leading institutions and their arrangements in respect to scholarships and student aid. The Indian Service itself offers an excellent field for Indians with scientific, professional training in such fields as teaching, nursing, medicine, dentistry, social work, agriculture, engineering, and forestry.

The survey staff is inclined to question the advisability of attempting to establish in the boarding schools, courses to train persons for professions and callings where the more common general standards require high school graduation as preliminary to the special training. The object should be rather to give them in the boarding schools the required high school training and then aid them in going on into well organized schools where they can get the necessary professional training, and graduate equipped to meet the standard requirements.

The practice of conducting normal school training classes for Indian youth who have not the equivalent of an accredited high school course, and then giving these graduates preference for appointment in the Indian Service should, it is believed, be discontinued, because the training is sub-standard. The Indians who wish to teach should be given a sound high school education and then be sent to a recognized school so that when they finish they can secure teaching certificates which will open to them the general teaching field. In the long run this course will be best both for the Indian teachers and for the Indian schools.

The present policy of placing Indian children in public schools near their homes instead of in boarding schools or even in Indian Service day schools is, on the whole, to be commended. It is a movement in the direction of the normal transition, it results as a rule in good race contacts, and the Indians like it. The fact must be recognized, however, that often Indian children and Indian families need more service than is ordinarily rendered by public schools, as has just been elaborated in the discussion of boarding schools. The Indian Service must, therefore, supplement the public school work by giving special attention to health, industrial and social training, and the relationship between home and school. The transition must not be pushed too fast. The public schools must be really ready to receive the Indians, and for some years the government must exercise some supervision to see that the Indian children are really getting the advantage offered by the public school system. The policy of having a federal employee perform the duties of attendance officer is sound, but more emphasis should be placed on work with families in this connection, in an effort not so much to force attendance as to remove the causes of non-attendance.

The Indian day schools should be increased in number and improved in quality and should carry children at least through the sixth grade. The Hopi day schools are perhaps the most encouraging feature of the Indian school system. More can perhaps be done in providing transportation to day schools. Where Indians come in to camp near the day schools, special activities should be undertaken for them. In general the day schools should be made community centers for reaching adult Indians in the vicinity as well as children, and they should be tied into the whole program adopted for the jurisdiction.

A SURVEY OF INDIAN EDUCATION (1943)   From Willard W. Beatty, "Indian Education in the United States," as quoted in C. T. Loram, ed., *The North American Indian Today* (Toronto, 1943), pp. 275–82.

The United States government is obligated to provide education for its Indian citizens by virtue of almost every treaty which it consummated with the Indian tribes since colonial times. This obligation has not always been fulfilled promptly nor consistently, and we owe a great deal to the Christian missions which were the first to fulfil these pledges, and which continue to this day concerned with Indian education, whether or not they are actually operating schools.

The trend in the United States has been increasingly toward public responsibility for the schooling of Indians, either through schools operated by the federal government itself, or by arrangements which have transferred the responsibility to the public schools of the states. At the present time, the federal government is directly responsible for the education of 23,978 Indian children, and contracts with state or local school authorities for the education of approximately 30,000 more, all of whom are of one-fourth or more Indian blood. Our records show an additional 2,039 enrolled in mission or private day schools, and 4,936 in mission, state, or private boarding schools. It is estimated that there are still approximately 10,000 Indian children between the ages of six and eighteen who are not in any school. Many of these are dropouts, many live in remote areas not served by federal or public schools and whose parents are averse to their attending boarding schools, and by far the larger number are on the Navajo Reservation.

Our Navajo schools are not yet adequate in number to care for all of the eligible children, but on the other hand not all the space now provided has been occupied by children. There are several contributing factors to account for this: general unsettled economic conditions on the reservation, lack of understanding of the day-school programme, criticism and opposition by missionaries and traders who thought the decrease in emphasis on the boarding school threatened "vested" interests of one kind or another, and lastly the substitution of a programme of educating the adults to the desirability of schooling for their children, for the old coerced compulsory education.

Of the children in federal schools, 13,797 are in day schools, almost a three-fold increase in ten years. Four thousand seven hundred and sixty-nine are in reservation boarding schools, and 5,412 in non-reservation boarding schools, a substantial decrease in both cases. The Indian Service operates approximately 300 schools in the continental United States, and 120 in Alaska. These figures vary from year to year as schools pass from federal to state operation (or *vice versa*), are closed, consolidated, or newly re-opened as new colonization projects demand new schools.

Fifty-one of our residential schools are in the continental United States, two are in Alaska. The education division also co-operates with the Medical Division in the operation of school units in tuberculosis sanitaria. Twenty of our boarding schools are non-reservation schools, in the sense that they are usually located in or near cities, enrol members of many different tribes, operate a diverse vocational programme, and are not concerned with the development of a reservation economic programme. Thirty-one reservation central schools operate residential divisions caring for from twenty-five to five hundred pupils. Twenty of these schools have substantial day-school enrolment.

Six of the non-reservation schools are junior-senior high schools, three operate twelve grades, and the remaining eleven embrace the first through the ninth grades. These latter enrol only orphans, half-orphans, children from broken homes, or from areas remote from federal or public day schools. Our high schools also accept pupils from areas where the local high school does not furnish adequate vocational instruction.

In six of the reservation schools, the boarding unit cares only for high-school students who have received their elementary education in outlying public or federal day schools of six to nine grades. Twenty-five reservation boarding schools contain elementary grades, and thirteen of these offer all twelve grades of instruction. Including the two Alaska schools, which offer seven through twelve grades, the Indian Service operates thirty senior high schools with boarding units, and seven others wholly on a day basis. This is almost a hundred per cent increase in high-school instruction in ten years.

We also operate twenty consolidated day schools which include elementary and junior high grades. The rest of the day schools stop at the sixth grade, and transfer pupils to the central schools for advanced instruction.

The trend for the last ten years has been toward day schools. While the emphasis has fluctuated at times in the past, we may hope that this trend will continue, for I believe that the community day schools mark a new development in rural education which will be of significance to white as well as Indian education. In the last decade the federal government has built approximately one hundred new day-school buildings (some of these have been replacements) which by their very design are planned for this new type of community programme. The further extension of the day-school programme is now dependent on road building, for bus service is often necessary in order to bring the children into the school centre. The delay in road building partly accounts for the slowness with which many of the Navajo schools have been filled.

For several years, consolidations of some of the smaller day schools was attempted, but we are far from sure that this is a desirable move. There is a definite limit to the number of communities which may be persuaded to work together in the larger schools. Active parent groups in the one-room schools have often failed to maintain activity in the larger school.

We now try to restrict the attendance at boarding schools to children of "institutional" type, or to those who cannot get vocational training where they live. Gradually the mission boarding schools are adopting similar criteria for admission. It is generally accepted that nothing is permanently gained by removing children from their own homes so long as these can be preserved, and that the day schools are exerting greater influence toward the acculturation of both adults and children than was possible while the children were removed from the community—only to be returned after a complete loss of identity with the Indian group, to find their way into a new and difficult acceptance.

Despite the values of the day school, and its definite economy (we can operate a day school for only twelve pupils, at the cost of caring for these in a boarding school—any enrolment over that is money saved), it is probable that most of our remaining boarding schools will be needed for some time to come. This is especially true of the secondary schools, where the expense of duplicating vocational equipment for a number of small day high school units at several points on the reservation, would be prohibitive.

The new Indian high school is definitely vocational in character. Chilocco in Oklahoma, for example, teaches agriculture by offering students the experience of actually operating an eight-thousand acre farm. The Oglala Community High School at Pine Ridge, South Dakota, has a beef cattle herd of eight hundred head as a basis for its instruction in the livestock industry, and makes it possible for boys to earn cattle during their school course, so as to be able to enter one of the reservation cattle co-operatives upon graduation. Many other practical instances might be cited. However, encouragement is given a limited number of Indian students to pursue advanced vocational or collegiate education through the medium of a federal loan fund which amounts to about $150,000 per year.

While the earlier Indian schools were operated by the missions under contract with the federal government, this arrangement was terminated early in the twentieth century. Removal of this basis of support left many mission schools without operating funds, and in a number of instances, the Indian tribes which were being served were persuaded to apply tribal funds to the continued support of the schools. The legality of this arrangement was tested and sustained in the courts. As tribal funds became exhausted, the contracts were taken over by the federal government and included in the "gratuity" appropriations. The policy adhered to in this regard has been to pay only for subsistence, not for instruction. At the present time the total of gratuity appropriations for mission subsistence is about $200,000 out of a total education budget of approximately $10,400,000. Recently our contracts with the missions have included a clause permitting federal supervisors to inspect their schools, which has not heretofore been customary. At the request of the Bureau of Catholic Missions I have assigned this fall one of our abler supervisors to visit and advise in the Catholic mission schools of the northern states. I believe that there will logically follow a considerable expansion of this service.

Congress, under the Johnson-O'Malley Act, authorized the Indian Service to contract with states, districts, and private organizations for educational, medical, and social services for Indians. We now have contracts with the states of California, Minnesota, and Washington for the education of all Indian children in the public schools of those states. The federal government has retained the operation of one residential school in each of the first two states. I regret that Mr. Rockwell, or his associate, Mr. Sande, are not to fulfil their place on tomorrow's programme, for Minnesota has made a most helpful and intelligent attack upon the problem of educating its Indian citizens, and I am sure that their report would have been of great interest and value. In a fourth state, Arizona, we have a contract for the education of those children in public schools who live either on the fringes of the reservations near public schools, or who are not resident on the reservations. We also have a contract with the State of Wisconsin Division of Social Welfare, and with the Michigan Children's Aid Society for the services of welfare workers.

It is the contribution of the new community day school which we believe to be the most significant of our present education programme. Here we are not only educating children at home in their own communities, but are involving adult participation in the programme in a growing degree. We expect an enrolment of at least twenty children, when inaugurating a day school. In areas where the population is scattered it is often necessary to operate a bus to bring this many together. We consider thirty pupils per teacher a good average, and when the number enrolled exceeds forty we add another teacher. Schools of one, two, and three rooms usually offer the first six grades of instruction. Larger schools extend to the ninth grade, and have an extra teacher to handle vocational instruction, and one of the women teachers is chosen because of her training in home economics. In addition most of our day schools employ an Indian woman for housekeeper, who prepares a noon meal for the children, offers some simple instruction in home-making to the girls, and assists the adults who come to the school to participate in its activities. The bus driver often helps with shop work for both boys and men.

The new school buildings reflect the new spirit. They are designed with a classroom for each unit of thirty children, and supply quarters for the teachers and housekeepers. While these are not elaborate we attempt to make them modern and convenient, so as to compensate in some degree for the isolation of many of the posts. Unfortunately such accommodations vary considerably in quality. There is also a kitchen for preparing a noon meal for the children, which in most Indian schools is supplied by the government. Some buildings have a dining room, which is used as a community workroom by the adults during the remainder of the day. Toilet, bathing, and laundry facilities are included, which are used by adults and children alike. Many times our school well is the basic dependable water supply for the community, and Indians come with barrels to obtain their domestic water supply. In the pueblos and in Alaska where the natives live in villages, the school usually does not furnish a noon lunch. There is usually a garage, for both the bus and the teacher's private car, and this structure may also be used as a shop when the bus is outside. Tools are available for use by the men of the community, and horse-shoeing, building of furniture, repair of farm machinery, and many other personal needs are met here. We have suffered surprisingly little from loss of tools. The larger schools are equipped with a library which is opened at night for use by adults. Classes in adult education, varying from instruction in English to discussions of the new civic responsibilities under the reorganization Act, or new ways of inoculating cattle are carried on in most of these schools. In many instances, a clinic is included, and at some posts, quarters are also furnished for a community public health nurse.

I have spoken of the vocational nature of the high-school programme. You may ask what we mean by "vocational." It is a word whose meaning has changed greatly with us in the last few years. We are now keenly interested in finding out what our young people need to know. Some years ago when the Oglala High School in the Sioux country was opened, we offered carpentry, auto mechanics, shoemaking, and similar subjects for the boys. Recently we have completed the first of our continuing vocational surveys at this school and in the area which it serves. It revealed that 98 per cent of the graduates and former students of this school for the last four years were now living on the reservation. Most had never left. At no place on the reservation or in the neighbouring white communities could Indian boys find employment as carpenters, mechanics, or shoemakers. Nobody on the reservation purchased such services, and in the adjoining communities, no white man was able to make a living at them. While many of the boys were employed (about one-half), 84 per cent of those employed were working either for the government or for a mission school—both agencies whose tenure might be thought of as temporary, in that their presence on the reservation has as its main objective making the Indians economically self-sufficient. We would appear to be defeating our own purpose if we do not train children who can make a living independent of such employment. A change in our curriculum inaugurated about two tears ago, by which emphasis has been shifted to cattle-raising and subsistence gardening and irrigated farming already gives promise of more functional service. This vocational survey has been extended to other schools, and has been similarly revealing. It will undoubtedly bring about fundamental changes in many of our high-school programmes.

While this touches upon only the highlights of our educational programme, it is probably sufficient to indicate the trend of Indian education in the United States.

Office of Indian Affairs,
Washington.

A CONGRESSIONAL COMMITTEE RECOMMENDS END TO SEGREGATION OF INDIANS (1952) From *House Report no. 2680,* 83d Cong., 2d Sess, (1954), p. v.

In its report (H. Rept. No. 2503) to the House in the 82d Congress the Interior and Insular Affairs Committee made the following statement: It is the belief of the committee that all legislation dealing with Indian affairs should be directed to the ending of a segregated race set aside from other citizens. It is the recommended policy of this committee that the Indians be assimilated into the Nation's social and economic life. The objectives, in bringing about the ending of the Indian segregation to which this committee has worked and recommends are (1) the end of wardship or trust status as not acceptable to our American way of life, and (2) the assumption by individual Indians of all the duties, obligations, and privileges of free citizens. The committee realizes that these objectives cannot be accomplished overnight, but recommends a constant effort in that direction, with careful and earnest consideration always given to the rights of the Indians.

A NEW APPROACH TO INDIAN EDUCATION (1967) From Paul Conklin,
"Good Day at Rough Rock,"*American Education*, vol. III, pp. 4–9.

On the northern flank of Arizona's Black Mountain, an experiment has been started that could change the entire structure and philosophy of Indian education in America. Here, in a bleak setting of desert, rock, and sagebrush, near the center of the country's largest reservation—25,000 square miles—that is home to 105,000 Navajos, Robert A. Roessel, Jr., director of the Rough Rock Demonstration School, is applying a community control approach that could hold promise for poor, uneducated people everywhere. His method—to work with the Indians, not on them. His thesis—that Indians ought to be able to be Americans and Indians, too. "Education as the Indian knows it on the reservation can best be characterized as the Either-Or type," says Dr. Roessel, a vigorous man with an unruly, greying thatch of hair. "One is either an Indian or a white man, and the way we have traditionally weighted things, the good way is always the non-Indian way and the bad is always the Indian. We tell Indian children they are superstitious and primitive and that their hogans are dirty. We try to impose our values and tell them they should eat green, leafy vegetables and sleep on a bed and brush their teeth. In short, we try to make white men out of Indians. The Indian child listens and looks at himself and sees that he doesn't measure up. In his own eyes he is a failure. Education can be a shattering experience when one is taught nothing but negative things about himself for 12 years."

As he talks, Roessel occasionally squints through the window of his comfortable living room which, in keeping with his educational beliefs, is furnished in modern and Navajo. Outside, the wind blows incessantly, swirling sand against the panes and wearing away at the light-colored buildings that blend with the monochromatic landscape. In the far distance can be seen the looming red sandstone monoliths of Monument Valley.

"Now Indians have begun to question whether it is necessary for them to lose their heritage in order to become citizens of the United States," he continues. "And so the Both-And—both white and Indian—approach to Indian education was born."

Rough Rock Demonstration School is a self-contained community within a scattered population of about 600. It has to be. The nearest paved road is 16 miles away and the nearest sizable town, Gallup, N. Mex., 120 miles. The school has its own water system and fire engine, a spacious classroom-office building with a gymnasium, a separate kitchen-dining room, and a boys' dormitory and a girls' dormitory, each with a capacity of 165 children. The staff are quartered in 36 houses and 8 apartments. Roessel's expectations and hopes for the experiment come through clearly as he speaks of the school.

"Rough Rock is the first school to have the tools and resources to see whether this new approach can be effective. We want to instill in our youngsters a sense of pride in being Indian. We want to show them that they can be Indian and American at the same time, that they can take the best from each way of life and combine it into something viable. When I first came on the reservation as a teacher, I told children they had two legs, one being their Navajo heritage and the other the best part of the white world. They couldn't get along with just one leg, but needed both to be secure and whole."

The Rough Rock staff includes ten full-time classroom teachers, a remedial reading specialist, a speech therapist, an art teacher, a librarian, two TESL (Teaching English as a Second Language) specialists, and two recreation leaders. Fifteen members of the Volunteers in Service to America (VISTA) also work at the school. Of the 91 full-time people on the payroll, 46 are Indians, 35 of them from Rough Rock, a fact that illustrates a vital part of the Roessel philosophy—involving the local community in school life as much as possible.

The school laundry is a good example. Bureau of Indian Affairs schools typically contract their laundry out to private firms, which are usually located in towns many miles away. In the Rough Rock budget $5,000 was set aside for this purpose. Roessel spent $2,000 on washing machines and used the rest to hire two local women to operate them.

No opportunities are missed at the school to help the children understand themselves as Indians. Navajo motifs are freely mixed in with other classroom decorations. The library has a Navajo corner. Recordings of the Navajo music and rituals are played during the school day.

In the evening old men, the historians and medicine men of the tribe, come to the dormitories and tell Navajo folk tales and legends. The staff is preparing biographies of successful Navajos to give the students something on which to pattern their own lives.

Each day, 35 minutes of class time are set aside in the preschool sections and lower three grades, and 45 minutes in grades three through six for "cultural identification" lessons. During the first six weeks the lessons cover the Navajo hogan—its history, how it is built, the ceremonies that surround it, and how life is conducted in it. The second six weeks cover farming and caring for livestock. The third period deals with reservation facilities, the land and climate, Navajo history and tribal government.

A crucial part of "cultural identification" at Rough Rock is the adult arts and crafts program, which has a twofold purpose: to revive dying Navajo handicrafts so that the children of the school can observe the process, and to produce more local wage-earners.

This is the domain of Dr. Roessel's wife, Ruth, who is Navajo. A graduate of Arizona State University and a member of the Governor's Advisory Committee on Indian Education, Ruth is one of the reservation's most skilled weavers. She has also proved herself an able recruiter. Ambrose Roanhorse, renowned as the reservation's most skillful silversmith, came to Rough Rock at her invitation. His first apprentices have already reached the stage where they are ready to market their jewelry.

Sharing the school's arts and crafts center with the silversmiths are a weaver and a moccasin maker. They will soon be joined by basketmakers, potters, leather craftsmen, and rawhide workers.

"This is not art for art's sake, although the Navajo puts great store in creating beautiful things. These skills are extremely marketable and we are training people who otherwise would have no income," Roessel explains. The Indians now eke out a precarious existence herding sheep.

At one time in most Indian schools the children were punished if they spoke Navajo. At Rough Rock they are encouraged and even forced to use their own language. Navajo is taught in the fourth, fifth, and sixth grades for one hour three days a week. Also, for the first time on the reservation, portions of regular classes, such as arithmetic and social studies, are held in Navajo. The purpose is to see whether students find it easier to retain subject matter when taught in their native language, as research has suggested may be the case.

Roessel provides evening tutoring lessons in Navajo for his staff members who do not speak the language. They find it tough going, since Navajo—a harsh, gutt[u]ral tongue—is classified by linguists as the world's second most difficult language.

Because of the importance the Both-And philosophy places on mastery of both English and Navajo, Rough Rock's TESL department is highly active at the school. English is taught formally twice a day, informally at all times. For example, as the children pass through the cafeteria line at noon they must ask for their food in English.

A teaching aid which TESL director Virginia Hoffman has found invaluable is the school's closed-circuit TV system. Once a month she writes a simple play, using staff members and VISTA personnel in the cast. A recent drama, "The Zegaffer-elebra," took place in a painted jungle. The message, spoken by animals with papier-maché heads, dealt with correct intonation and the lengthening of vowels. Future productions will be concerned with gender, number, tense, "to be," and "is going to."

The idea for the Rough Rock experiment began to take shape at Arizona State University in 1959 and 1960 while Roessel studied for a doctor's degree. To gather raw material for his thesis, he visited over 100 Indian communities, talking to the elders about their needs and aspirations.

Much of what Roessel learned during that period was incorporated in a proposal which he and a number of Indian leaders later presented to the Office of Economic Opportunity (OEO) for the establishment of a different kind of Indian school. The result, in 1965, was the Lukachukai Navajo Demonstration School, which foundered after only one year, primarily because of an awkward administrative set-up. The school was funded by OEO, which superimposed a staff of academic and community development specialists on the existing staff of the Bureau of Indian Affairs (BIA) boarding school at Lukachukai, a hamlet not far from Rough Rock. The administrative dichotomy proved too much, and OEO reluctantly withdrew its support.

BIA and OEO, still mindful of the need for a new approach to Indian education and wary of repeating their mistakes at Lukachukai, put up money for another demonstration school that would be independent of them both. The funds, $335,000 from OEO and $307,000 from BIA, were awarded to a private, nonprofit corporation called Demonstration in Navajo Education, Inc.—whose Navajo acronym DINE means the Navajos, or "the people." Roessel was recruited as director and BIA turned over a brand new $3.5 million school which it had just built in Rough Rock.

At the time, Roessel was director of Arizona State University's Indian Community Action Center, one of three such centers established by OEO to provide technical assistance and training to reservation Indians under its Community Action Program.

His decision to go to Rough Rock was not easily made. "I was happy at Tempe, and felt important. I had real influence in the OEO Indian program and went to Washington every week. It wasn't easy to come out here where the roads are terrible and the phones never work. But I had been writing articles too long saying what was wrong with Indian education and Indian programs. Here was a chance to put into practice what I believed, or shut up."

Soon after Roessel's arrival, the people of Rough Rock elected one woman and four men to the school board. All were middle-aged Navajos and only one had ever had as much as a day of formal education. In a move that must have raised eyebrows in many quarters, control of the demonstration school was immediately passed over to the board.

"At least 50 schools on the reservation have their own boards, so in this respect Rough Rock is not unique," Roessel points out. "But the traditional Indian board has a housekeeping function: it builds roads, maintains buildings, and acts as a truant officer. It has no authority or decision-making power, and the superintendent really calls the shots. What we have here is local control in the true sense for the first time.

"The greatest need of Indian education today," he continues, "is to involve Indians. The belief persists that Indians have neither the desire nor the ability to manage their own affairs. It's the old 'father-knows-best' approach that says it's up to me, an expert sitting behind my desk, to make policy for them. But the Both-And philosophy says that Indians are eager for responsibility and, if given a chance, they'll act creatively and assume leadership."

Roessel takes the principle of local control seriously. Once a week he and a few of his senior staff discuss a part of the master program with the school board, explaining the reasons the staff consider it important. In each instance the board has accepted the proposal, modifying it, however, and adding a Navajo cast to it. Roessel sees the modifications as strengthening the demonstration program. So strong is his faith in the board members that he is willing to scrap completely any part that they oppose.

It is not simply rhetoric when Roessel says of Rough Rock, "This is a community-oriented school, rather than child-oriented. In the past, Indian schools have taken little interest in their communities, but here we want to involve adults and teenagers, dropouts, people who have never been to school."

Rough Rock's school facilities—gym, kitchen, dormitories, shower rooms, library—are open to anybody who wants to use them. School fairs, movies, basketball games, talent nights have drawn crowds that increase steadily.

Rough Rock parents are encouraged to come to the school for board meetings, to spend time in the classrooms, to eat in the cafeteria, and to stay overnight in the dormitories. They sometimes come in team-drawn wagons, the men with stiff-brimmed hats and, if they are of the old generation, their hair drawn into tight knots at the back. The women wear long velveteen skirts, silver jewelry, and strings of turquoise and coral. Quiet and grave, they flit shyly about the school like old-fashioned ghosts.

"Our school board has told the parents of this district that they can't use the school as a dumping ground where they can leave their children and forget them. We believe the kids belong to their parents and not to the school. Instead of limiting the child to two or three visits home a year, as is the case in most schools, we let parents take their children home any weekend they want," Roessel says.

To make the dormitories more homelike and to avoid the usual ratio in dormitory staffing of one adult for every 60 children, Roessel employs eight parents to mend clothes, tell stories, help with the twice-a-week shower, and do a variety of other chores that parents know how to do best. For this they receive a dollar an hour. The parents change every six weeks; the school board handles recruiting. With help from instructional aides, parents, and VISTA workers, the Rough Rock adult-child ratio has dropped to 1 to 15.

Just as most Navajo parents know virtually nothing about the way reservation schools are operated, so, too, is it rare to find a teacher in the system who has any first-hand knowledge about how life is lived in the Navajo hogan. In a study conducted in 1963, the Indian Education Center at Arizona State University found that only 15 of 100 reservation teachers had ever visited an Indian home.

One of the reasons for this failure was that the heavy daily routine makes escape from the classroom almost impossible for the teacher. And often the teacher is afraid he will be unwelcome in the hogan. Rough Rock teachers visit the homes of all their students at least twice a year. They are accompanied by the child, and an interpreter when necessary, and tell the parents about their children's progress.

Roessel would also like each of his non-Indian teachers to live in a Navajo hogan for a week. "I want them to see what it means to haul water five miles, to chop wood for heat, to go to bed at dark because there is no light, to eat bread and coffee for a meal," he says.

By giving his staff an awareness of the peculiar texture of Navajo life, Roessel hopes to avert a repetition of the small-scale tragedy that resulted from a teacher's inexperience at another reservation school. The teacher was from the East. Her credentials were excellent, but she had never taught Navajo children before. She noticed one morning that the face and arms of one of her third grade boys were covered by something that looked like soot. In his hair was a substance that resembled grease. With a normal respect for cleanliness, the teacher asked the boy to wash himself. When he refused she took him to the bathroom and washed him.

The boy never returned to school. It turned out that his family had conducted an important healing ceremony on his sick sister, the "soot" and "grease" being part of the ceremonial painting. With her soap and water the teacher destroyed the healing powers of the ceremony. The girl died and the parents could not be shaken in their belief that it was the teacher's fault. No member of the family has set foot in a school since.

Programs for adults have claimed only the peripheral attention of Indian education officials in the past. Through a canvass of the 600 Navajos who live in the area of Rough Rock, it was learned that the men are most interested in auto mechanics instruction. Women want classes in cooking and nutrition. Both are interested in classes in basic literacy. They want to gain a rudimentary knowledge of money and how to make change so they will not be cheated when they buy at the store. They want to acquire a basic English vocabulary of about 50 words that can carry them through their trips to the local trading post and to the outside world.

"It is here in our work with adults that the most significant thrust is being made at Rough Rock. It is an area to which other demonstrations have not been directed, an area of little prior activity," Roessel says. "At Rough Rock the BIA and OEO have said to the Indians in effect, 'This is your school. Make of it what you want. Develop a curriculum that will reflect what you think is important.' This is an isolated, illiterate community where 95 per cent of the people are uneducated, but I am convinced that they have the necessary vision and concern for their future."

It would be hard to find a more disadvantaged community than Rough Rock, where the average family of six makes $500 a year and where cultural life is utterly threadbare. Roessel believes that if Rough Rock can succeed—if these uneducated people can determine the educational needs of their children and their community, then it cannot be said that impoverished, uneducated people any place are unable to provide self-leadership.

"This is why Rough Rock is the most exciting thing going on in Indian education anywhere in the country," says Roessel. "This is why our program has ramifications far outside the Indian world."

Japanese

RESOLUTION OF THE SAN FRANCISCO SCHOOL BOARD (1905)   As quoted in *Proceedings of the Asiatic Exclusion League* (San Francisco, 1908), pp. 8–9.

"Whereas, The attention of the Board of Education of this City, in its visits of inspection to the different schools, has been repeatedly directed toward the attendance of children of Japanese descent as pupils, and to the evil consequences liable to result therefrom through the indiscriminate association of our children with those of the Mongolian race; and

Whereas, Section 1662 of the State Political Code of California vests City Boards of Education with the power to establish separate schools for the accommodation of children of Indian, Mongolian or Chinese descent, and further provides that when such separate schools are established that Indian, Chinese or Mongolian children must not be admitted to other schools of our public school system; and

Whereas, It is the sense of the members of the Board of Education that the admission of children of Japanese or Mongolian descent as pupils to our common schools is contrary to the spirit and the letter of the law and that the co-mingling of such pupils with Caucasian children is baneful and demoralizing in the extreme, the ideas entertained and practiced by people of Mongolian or Japanese affiliations being widely divergent from those of Americans; and

Whereas, The school situation has become serious through the great number of Japanese in our midst, many of our children being excluded from our schools by Japanese children through the right of prior admission incidental to the lack of adequate accommodations and room, through no fault or neglect of this department, attributal to the insufficiency of funds; therefore be it

Resolved, That the Board of Education is determined in its efforts to effect the establishment of separate schools for Chinese and Japanese pupils, not only for the purpose of relieving the congestion at present prevailing in our schools, but also for the higher end that our children should not be placed in any position where their youthful impressions may be affected by association with pupils of the Mongolian race."

THE SAN FRANCISCO CHRONICLE ON SEGREGATION OF JAPANESE SCHOOL CHILDREN (1906)

From editorial, November 6, 1906, as quoted in Senate document no. 147, 59th Cong., 2d Sess. (1906), p. 30.

The most prominent objection to the presence of Japanese in our public schools is their habit of sending young men to the primary grades, where they sit side by side with very young children, because in those grades only are the beginnings of English taught. That creates situations which often become painfully embarrassing. They are, in fact, unendurable.

There is also the objection to taking the time of the teachers to teach the English language to pupils, old or young, who do not understand it. It is a reasonable requirement that all pupils entering the schools shall be familiar with the language in which instruction is conducted. We deny either the legal or moral obligation to teach any foreigner to read or speak the English language. And if we choose to do that for one nationality, as a matter of grace, and not to do the same for another nationality, that is our privilege.

We do not know that the Japanese children are personally objectionable in grades composed of pupils of their own age. We do not know whether they are or not. There is, however, a deep and settled conviction among our people that the only hope of maintaining peace between Japan and the United States is to keep the two races apart. Whatever the status of the Japanese children while still young and uncontaminated, as they grow older they acquire the distinctive character, habits, and moral standards of their race, which are abhorrent to our people. We object to them in the familiar intercourse of common school life as we would object to any other moral poison.

While we deny any moral or legal obligation to give, at public expense, any education whatever to any alien, and consequently if we choose to give as a matter of grace to one and deny it to another, we have also as a matter of grace provided separate schools for the Japanese. In all the Southern States separate schools are provided for white and colored children. To say that we may exclude our own colored citizens from the schools attended by white children, but shall not exclude the children of aliens from such schools, is not only absurd but monstrous.

We deny that the Federal Government has any control whatever over the schools of this State, or any authority whatever to officially deal with them. The tenth amendment to the Constitution declares that "the powers not delegated to the United States by the Constitution, not prohibited by it to the States, are reserved to the States, respectively, or to the people." If the control of public education is not one of the powers by that clause expressly withheld from the Federal jurisdiction, then there is no such power thus withheld, and there is nothing in which the jurisdiction of Congress is not supreme. Secretary Metcalf, now here, is not, as a United States official, entitled to any information whatever in regard to our schools. What is given is given as a matter of courtesy.

Section 2 of Article VI of the Constitution of the United States says: "This Constitution, and the laws of the United States made in pursuance thereof, and all treaties made, or which shall be made, under the authority of the United States, shall be the supreme law of the land." Obviously no treaty can be made by the United States except under its "authority." Any treaty made in excess of that authority is void in that particular. If the United States has no "authority" over the schools of California it can not be clothed with such authority by any contract of its own with a foreign nation. To suppose otherwise would be to suppose that the President and Senate alone could, under guise of a treaty with a foreign nation, usurp every power now held by any State government, and even abolish those governments. If the power of the President and Senate to enact by treaty that which Congress and the President can not enact by law exists, it has no limit. It does not exist. Therefore, whatever engagements the Federal Government may have made with Japan with respect to our schools—if it has made any—are utterly void.

REPORT OF PRESIDENT THEODORE ROOSEVELT ON THE JAPANESE IN SAN FRANCISCO (1906)   From Senate Document no. 147, 59th Cong., 2d Sess. (1906), pp. 1-2.

To the Senate and House of Representatives:

I enclose herewith for your information the final report made to me personally by Secretary Metcalf on the situation affecting the Japanese in San Francisco. The report deals with three matters of controversy—first, the exclusion of the Japanese children from the San Francisco schools; second, the boycotting of Japanese restaurants, and third, acts of violence committed against the Japanese.

As to the first matter, I call your especial attention to the very small number of Japanese children who attend school, to the testimony as to the brightness, cleanliness, and good behavior of these Japanese children in the schools, and to the fact that, owing to their being scattered throughout the city, the requirement for them all to go to one special school is impossible of fulfilment and means that they can not have school facilities. Let me point out further that there would be no objection whatever to excluding from the schools any Japanese on the score of age. It is obviously not desirable that young men should go to school with children. The only point is the exclusion of the children themselves. The number of Japanese children attending the public schools in San Francisco was very small. The Government has already directed that suit be brought to test the constitutionality of the act in question; but my very earnest hope is that such suit will not be necessary, and that as a matter of comity the citizens of San Francisco will refuse to deprive these young Japanese children of education and will permit them to go to the schools.

The question as to the violence against the Japanese is most admirably put by Secretary Metcalf, and I have nothing to add to his statement. I am entirely confident that, as Secretary Metcalf says, the overwhelming sentiment of the State of California is for law and order and for the protection of the Japanese in their persons and property. Both the chief of police and the acting mayor of San Francisco assured Secretary Metcalf that everything possible would be done to protect the Japanese in the city. I authorized and directed Secretary Metcalf to state that if there was failure to protect persons and property, the entire power of the Federal Government within the limits of the Constitution would be used promptly and vigorously to enforce the observance of our treaty, the Supreme law of the land, which treaty guaranteed to Japanese residents everywhere in the Union full and perfect protection for their persons and property; and to this end everything in my power would be done, and all the forces of the United States, both civil and military, which I could lawfully employ, would be employed. I call especial attention to the concluding sentence of Secretary Metcalf's report of November 26, 1906.

THEODORE ROOSEVELT
The White House
December 18, 1906

JAPANESE LANGUAGE SCHOOLS IN CALIFORNIA (1935) From Robert Bell, "Public School Education of Second Generation Japanese In California," in Stanford University Publications, *Education-Psychology*, vol. I, pp. 20–23.

The Japanese-language schools have gone through much the same development in California as in the Islands. The Immigration Commission reported one such school in San Francisco in 1911;[1] the Central Japanese Association of Southern California reported 80 such schools in the United States in 1918, with 2,442 pupils, and 47 kindergartens with 1,023 children;[2] and the writer found 118 language schools ranging from kindergarten through high school in California alone in his inquiry in 1928.[3] In 1933 the number reported officially by the three California language-school associations was 220.

Just as in Hawaii, the language schools in California became, in the immediate post-war years, one of the focal points of criticism for outspoken patriotic groups interested in Americanization. As a result, and without strong opposition from the Japanese—the Japanese Consul-General was reported by the *San Francisco Chronicle* to be in favor of the bill[4]—California added to her school law under Section 1534 of the Political Code[5] a section dealing with the foreign-language schools. The section was closely modeled on the Hawaiian law, and on May 4, 1927, two and a half months after the Supreme Court decision which declared the Hawaiian law non-enforceable, Attorney-General Webb of California ruled the California law invalid in the light of the Supreme Court decision.

Recent inquiry of the State Superintendent of Public Instruction of California as to the present relation of the language schools to the State Department elicited the following reply from the deputy superintendent:

The foreign language schools, which include the Japanese language schools, under the decision in the United States Supreme Court, bear no relationship whatever to the state department of education. The textbooks used in these schools do not have to receive the

---

[1] *United States Immigration Commission Reports* (Washington, D.C., 1911), XXIII,152.

[2] *Japanese Immigration Hearings*, Part III, p. 1049.

[3] Reginald Bell, "A Study of Certain Aspects of the Education of Japanese in Central California" (unpublished A.M. thesis in Stanford University Library, 1928), p. 40.

[4] *Japanese Immigration Hearings*, Part II, p. 546.

[5] *School Law of California* (Sacramento, California, 1925), pp. 50–52.

approval of this department. The schools are no longer subject to our inspection. The hours regulating these schools are such as the schools themselves may establish.[6]

The Japanese-American organizations that have been interested in developing the schools have not been unaware of the social and educational responsibility that is theirs. As early as 1913 the Japanese Educational Association of America, closely affiliated with the Japanese Association of America, gave its attention to the part it was to play not in Japanizing the American-born Japanese child but in fitting him for the American scheme of things. In that year, it adopted the following resolution:

> The goal to be attained in our education is to bring up children who will live and die in America, and as such, the whole educational system must be founded upon the spirit of the public instruction of America.[7]

Commenting on this resolution, the general secretary of the Japanese Association in America said:

> Indeed, from the point of view of the Japanese immigrant they desire that their children shall become not only good citizens of American birth, but also that, being born of Japanese parentage, they shall make a distinct contribution to their American national life by means of some of the finer qualities of their parentage.[8]

It is this hope, and the conviction that it is absolutely necessary from the standpoint of social efficiency and family organization for the children of the second generation to be taught the language of their parents, that lies behind the maintenance of the Japanese-language schools. Again and again, as one reads the testimony before the House Committee on Immigration and Naturalization, this fact is made clear.[9] The children, runs the argument, have no real difficulty in picking up English. But they know little Japanese. Alienation from their parents results, since the parents—particularly the mothers—know relatively little English. This becomes especially disastrous when it comes to interpreting the finer points of moral and social control, and may result in disorganizing the family unit. It may lead to a lack of parental control and to delinquency such as has been marked in other second-generation groups. The Japanese above all things do not want that for their children.[10]

Certain supplemental reasons have been given for the continuance of such schools. In some communities they have served as day nurseries while the parents were both employed. In others, they have served to give pre-school training in English, employing an American teacher to that end, so that the children will enter public school with less of a language handicap. Some commentators contend that the anti-Japanese agitation, throwing the Japanese back upon themselves, strengthening their group consciousness and hence their racial and national solidarity and

[6]Bell, *op. cit.*, p. 40.

[7]*Japanese Immigration Hearings*, Part III, p. 679.

[8]*Ibid.*

[9]*Ibid.*, Part II, p. 696.

[10]The singular success in crime prevention among the second-generation Japanese is described in E. K. Strong, Jr., *et al.*, *Vocational Aptitudes of Second-Generation Japanese in the United States* (Stanford University Publiciations, University Series, Education-Psychology, Vol. I, No. 1, 1933), pp. 155–73.

unsettling them in respect to America, has itself been a strong factor in the growth and development of the language schools.[11] It is noteworthy, however, that they have flourished since the dying down of such agitation. In the opinion of the writer, the reasons cited earlier are more fundamental.

Organization of the Schools

The *raison d'être* of the language schools determined their curriculum and objectives. Obviously if the mother tongue is a necessity, the objectives of these schools are: to speak the language properly; to read it intelligently; and to write simple letters in it. The curriculum has been determined by the objectives: reading, composition, penmanship, memory work, dictation, singing in Japanese, and, because the Japanese are traditionally a people of manners and social discipline, something of instruction in proper conduct and behavior.[12]

Each school is in charge of a local board of Japanese trustees elected at a general meeting of those interested. The boards vary in size, averaging about ten members. The board is responsible for the hiring, paying, and discharging of the teacher, for the general policy of the school, and for its financing.

There are two general plans of support. First, in the larger schools tuition fees charged the parents cover the entire cost. For example, the Fresno Buddhist School, which in 1928 had 225 pupils, charged a fee of $3.00 a month for the first child entered. If there were others in the family attending the charge was $1.75 for each of them. At Reedley, which had 70 children with a lesser grade range and consequently required fewer teachers, $2.00 was charged for the first child, $1.50 for the second, and $1.00 for each child after that.

The second plan of support, necessary in the smaller schools, involves going outside the circle of its patrons for its income. Tuition is charged the parents for each child, and in addition a fee is charged all families in the Japanese community whether or not they have children in school. These fees may vary with the wealth of the patron.

Teachers' salaries vary according to experience, training, time put in on the job, and responsibility. In one of the three California Associations the salaries paid run from $55 to $200 a month. A number of the teachers teach in one school during the regular weekdays of school and in another on Saturday and Sunday.

Qualifications for a permit to teach were fixed by law from 1921 to 1927, but since the Supreme Court decision in the case of *Farrington* v. *Tokushige*, all legal requirements have been waived. The local school boards have in most cases retained the requirement that their teachers must be able to speak both English and Japanese and must be graduates of at least the middle school in Japan. The teachers with whom the writer has come in contact are of a rather high type. Women have not been employed very freely in the schools except as assistants and as kindergarten teachers. American kindergarten teachers have in some cities been employed where

[11] *Japanese Immigration Hearings*, Part II, p. 543.

[12] In 1917 the *Japanese-American Yearbook* reports a limited survey of the curriculum of 28 schools. All of them reported reading; 22, personal conduct; 26, writing or composition; 17, penmanship; 21, singing; 21, spelling; 20, play hours. See *Japanese Immigration Hearings*, Part I, p. 279. The writer in a recent conversation with the director of the Fresno Buddhist School asked for a translation of the report card used in the second grade. The pupils were graded on the following: reading, speaking, dictation, composition, penmanship, personal conduct, attendance, and tardiness.

the public school had not or has not yet put in effective kindergartens. Such was the case at Fresno, at Stockton, and at Florin, to the writer's knowledge.

The Japanese-language schools of the state are formed into three "Japanese Language Associations"—the Central California Association, with headquarters at Fresno; the Southern California Association, with headquarters at Los Angeles; and the Northern California Association, with headquarters at San Francisco.

There are two departments in the Language Associations. One is made up of the teachers of the schools, the other of the trustees. Five directors are elected each year with a one-year tenure, three of the directors from the teacher group, and the other two from the trustees. The associations hold their annual meetings in November and other meetings when one-third of the member schools want them.

The associations, formed for an exchange of opinion in the interest of the schools, are supported from a small fee from the member schools for each pupil enrolled. This provides book funds and research and publication expenses for the associations.

Textbooks have proved a vexing problem. As early as 1912, when the first meeting of the Japanese Educational Association of America was called in San Francisco, this was one of the problems discussed.[13] Subsequently, in the 1915 meeting, a committee on editing adequate textbooks was selected, since only books published in Japan could be obtained. Because these were Japan-centered, they were inadequate, for the children in the United States think in terms of American life, not in terms of Japanese customs and illustrations. These books also failed to aid the Americanization mission undertaken by the language schools.

DESCRIPTION OF EDUCATION IN THE INTERNMENT CAMPS

(1943)   From U.S. Senate, *Miscellaneous Documents, 1–142,* 78th Cong., 1st Sess. (1943), Document no. 96, "Segregation of Loyal and Disloyal Japanese," p. 11.

One-fourth of the evacuee population in the centers is of school age and is in school. This is substantially larger than the proportion of school children in the normal population. Moreover, as has been suggested above, a disproportionately large part of the school population is of high-school age. Virtually all of the school children in the population were born in this country and are citizens. Virtually all were being educated prior to evacuation in American public schools.

It is the policy of the War Relocation Authority to provide elementary and high-school facilities, meeting the minimum standards of the States in which the centers are located and providing education which will permit the students to return to public school outside the centers after the war without loss of credit for the time spent in the centers. Educational programs have been developed and curricula planned in cooperation with the State school authorities of the States in which centers are located. All teaching is in English. No Japanese language schools of the type common on the Pacific coast before evacuation are permitted in the centers.

[13]*Japanese Immigration Hearings,* Part II, p. 698.

Refresher courses in the Japanese language, however, are being given at some of the centers for instructors and interpreters intending to go out in intelligence work.

The entire evacuee population has expressed a keen interest in the educational program. When basic educational plans were being made, the Authority was asked expressly by leaders of the evacuee population to provide as large a proportion as possible of non-Japanese teachers. They felt that prior to evacuation schools had been the biggest single force for Americanization and expressed the hope that their children would continue to have contact with qualified non-Japanese teachers. Because of this fact, and because there are relatively few qualified teachers among the evacuees, original plans called for employment of at least three-fourths of the teaching staff from outside the centers. At the present time, nearly 90 percent of the certified teaching staff is composed of persons who are not of Japanese descent. Evacuees are used extensively as assistant teachers and teacher aides.

Appointed teachers are employed under Civil Service regulations and are paid salaries established under the Classification Act. Because of the administrative necessity of keeping children occupied in the relatively crowded confines of the relocation centers, schools are operated 11 months out of the year. Even on such a basis it will be more than a year before the school time lost during evacuation and relocation is made up.

Schools are now operating in space originally constructed for barracks. Facilities for scientific and vocational work at the high-school level are inadequate. In most centers, living quarters have been crowded to make barrack space available for schools. To relieve this situation, the War Relocation Authority has undertaken to build school buildings of a temporary character similar in construction to the other buildings of the centers. Plans have been completed and priorities secured for the construction of high schools at most centers. Elementary classes, however, will continue to be held in the barracks.

DISCRIMINATORY SCHOOL LEGISLATION IN CALIFORNIA (1943)   From State of California, "Constitution of 1879 as Amended 1943," *Statutes, 55th Legislature, 1943*, p. 470.

Division 4. System of Public Instruction

Chapter 1. Types of Schools
ARTICLE 1. PUBLIC SCHOOLS

8003. The governing board of any school district may establish separate schools for Indian children, excepting children of Indians who are wards of the United States Government and children of all other Indians who are descendants of the original American Indians of the United States, and for children of Chinese, Japanese, or Mongolian parentage.

8004. When separate schools are established for Indian children or children of Chinese, Japanese, or Mongolian parentage, the Indian children or children of

Chinese, Japanese, or Mongolian parentage shall not be admitted into any other school.

REPEAL OF THE DISCRIMINATORY PROVISIONS OF THE CALIFORNIA EDUCATION CODE OF 1943 (1947) From State of California, *Statutes, 59th Legislature, 1947*, p. 1792.

Chapter 737

An act to repeal Sections 8003 and 8004 of the Education Act relating to the establishment of separate schools for the races.

[*Approved by Governor June 14, 1947. Filed with Secretary of State June 14, 1947.*]

The people of the State of California do enact as following:

SECTION 1. Sections 8003 and 8004 of the Education Act are hereby repealed. In effect September 19, 1947.

Blacks

W. E. B. DU BOIS ON THE TRAINING OF NEGROES FOR SOCIAL POWER (1903)   From W. E. B. Du Bois, "The Training of Negroes for Social Power," *Outlook*, vol. LXXV, pp. 409–12.

The responsibility for their own social regeneration ought to be placed largely upon the shoulders of the negro people. But such responsibility must carry with it a grant of power; responsibility without power is a mockery and a farce. If, therefore, the American people are sincerely anxious that the negro shall put forth his best efforts to help himself, they must see to it that he is not deprived of the freedom and power to strive. The responsibility for dispelling their own ignorance implies that the power to overcome ignorance is to be placed in black men's hands; the lessening of poverty calls for the power of effective work; and the responsibility for lessening crime calls for control over social forces which produce crime.

Such social power means, assuredly, the growth of initiative among negroes, the spread of independent thought, the expanding consciousness of manhood; and these things to-day are looked upon by many with apprehension and distrust, and there is systematic and determined effort to avoid this inevitable corollary of the fixing of social responsibility. Men openly declare their design to train these millions as a subject caste, as men to be thought for, but not to think; to be led, but not to lead themselves.

Those who advocate these things forget that such a solution flings them squarely on the other horn of the dilemma: such a subject child-race could never be held accountable for its own misdeeds and shortcomings; its ignorance would be part of the Nation's design, its poverty would arise partly from the direct oppression of the strong and partly from thriftlessness which such oppression breeds; and, above all, its crime would be the legitimate child of that lack of self-respect which caste systems engender. Such a solution of the negro problem is not one which the saner sense of the Nation for a moment contemplates; it is utterly foreign to American institutions, and is unthinkable as a future for any self-respecting race of men. The sound afterthought of the American people must come to realize that the responsibility for dispelling ignorance and poverty and uprooting crime among negroes cannot be put upon their own shoulders unless they are given such independent leadership in intelligence, skill, and morality as will inevitably lead to an independent manhood which cannot and will not rest in bonds.

Let me illustrate my meaning particularly in the matter of educating negro youth.

The negro problem, it has often been said, is largely a problem of ignorance—not simply of illiteracy, but a deeper ignorance of the world and its ways, of the thought and experience of men; an ignorance of self and the possibilities of human souls. This can be gotten rid of only by training; and primarily such training must take the form of that sort of social leadership which we call education. To apply such leadership to themselves, and to profit by it, means that negroes would have among themselves men of careful training and broad culture, as teachers and teachers of teachers. There are always periods of educational evolution when it is deemed quite proper for pupils in the fourth reader to teach those in the third. But such a method, wasteful and ineffective at all times, is peculiarly dangerous when ignorance is widespread and when there are few homes and public institutions to supplement the work of the school. It is, therefore, of crying necessity among negroes that the heads of their educational system—the teachers in the normal schools, the heads of high schools, the principals of public systems, should be unusually well trained men; men trained not simply in common-school branches, not simply in the technique of school management and normal methods, but trained beyond this, broadly and carefully, into the meaning of the age whose civilization it is their peculiar duty to interpret to the youth of a new race, to the minds of untrained people. Such educational leaders should be prepared by long and rigorous courses of study similar to those which the world over have been designed to strengthen the intellectual powers, fortify character, and facilitate the transmission from age to age of the stores of the world's knowledge.

Not all men—indeed, not the majority of men, only the exceptional few among American negroes or among any other people—are adapted to this higher training, as, indeed, only the exceptional few are adapted to higher training in any line; but the significance of such men is not to be measured by their numbers, but rather by the numbers of their pupils and followers who are destined to see the world through their eyes, hear it through their trained ears, and speak to it through the music of their words.

Such men, teachers of teachers and leaders of the untaught, Atlanta University and similar colleges seek to train. We seek to do our work thoroughly and carefully. We have no predilections or prejudices as to particular studies or methods, but we do cling to those time-honored sorts of discipline which the experience of the world has long since proven to be of especial value. We sift as carefully as possible the student material which offers itself, and we try by every conscientious method to give to students who have character and ability such years of discipline as shall make them stronger, keener, and better for their peculiar mission. The history of civilization seems to prove that no group or nation which seeks advancement and true development can despise or neglect the power of well-trained minds; and this power of intellectual leadership must be given to the talented tenth among American negroes before this race can seriously be asked to assume the responsibility of dispelling its own ignorance. Upon the foundation-stone of a few well equipped negro colleges of high and honest standards can be built a proper system of free common schools in the South for the masses of the negro people; any attempt to found a system of public schools on anything less than this—on narrow ideals, limited or merely technical training—is to call blind leaders for the blind.

The very first step toward the settlement of the negro problem is the spread of intelligence. The first step toward wider intelligence is a free public-school system; and the first and most important step toward a public-school system is the equipment and adequate support of a sufficient number of negro colleges. These are first steps, and they involve great movements: first, the best of the existent colleges must not be abandoned to slow atrophy and death, as the tendency is to-day; secondly, systematic attempt must be made to organize secondary education. Below the colleges and connected with them must come the normal and high schools, judiciously distributed and carefully manned. In no essential particular should this system of common and secondary schools differ from educational systems the world over. Their chief function is the quickening and training of human intelligence; they can do much in the teaching of morals and manners incidentally, but they cannot and ought not to replace the home as the chief moral teacher; they can teach valuable lessons as to the meaning of work in the world, but they cannot replace technical schools and apprenticeship in actual life, which are the real schools of work. Manual training can and ought to be used in these schools, but as a means and not as an end—to quicken intelligence and self-knowledge and not to teach carpentry; just as arithmetic is used to train minds and not skilled accountants.

Whence, now, is the money coming for this educational system? For the common schools the support should come from local communities, the State Governments, and the United States government; for secondary education, support should come from local and State Governments and private philanthropy; for the colleges, from private philanthropy and the United States Government. I make no apology for bringing the United States Government in thus conspicuously. The General Government must give aid to Southern education if illiteracy and ignorance are to cease threatening the very foundations of civilization within any reasonable time. Aid to common-school education could be appropriated to the different States on the basis of illiteracy. The fund could be administered by State officials, and the results and needs reported upon by United States educational inspectors under the Bureau of Education. The States could easily distribute the funds so as to encourage local taxation and enterprise and not result in pauperizing the communities. As to higher training, it must be remembered that the cost of a single battle-ship like the Massachusetts would endow all the distinctively college work necessary for negroes during the next half-century; and it is without doubt true that the unpaid balance from bounties withheld from negroes in the Civil War would, with interest, easily supply this sum.

But spread of intelligence alone will not solve the negro problem. If this problem is largely a question of ignorance, it is also scarcely less a problem of poverty. If negroes are to assume the responsibility of raising the standards of living among themselves, the power of intelligent work and leadership toward proper industrial ideals must be placed in their hands. Economic efficiency depends on intelligence, skill, and thrift. The public-school system is designed to furnish the necessary intelligence for the ordinary worker, the secondary school for the more gifted workers, and the college for the exceptional few. Technical knowledge and manual dexterity in learning branches of the world's work are taught by industrial and trade schools, and such schools are of prime importance in the training of colored children. Trade-teaching cannot be effectively combined with the work of the common schools because the primary curriculum is already too crowded, and thorough common-school training should precede trade-teaching. It is, however, quite possible to combine some of the work of the secondary schools with purely technical training, the necessary limitations being matters of time and cost: the question whether the boy can afford to stay in school long enough to add parts of a high-school course to the trade course, and particularly the question whether the school can afford or ought to give trade-training to high-school students who do not intend to become artisans. A system of trade-schools, therefore, supported by State and private aid, should be added to the secondary school system.

An industrial school, however, does not merely teach technique. It is also a school—a center of moral influence and of mental discipline. As such it has peculiar problems in securing the proper teaching force. It demands broadly trained men: the teacher of carpentry must be more than a carpenter, and the teacher of the domestic arts more than a cook; for such teachers must instruct, not simply in manual dexterity, but in mental quickness and moral habits. In other words, they must be teachers as well as artisans. It thus happens that college-bred men and men from other higher schools have always been in demand in technical schools, and it has been the high privilege of Atlanta University to furnish during the thirty-six years of its existence a part of the teaching force of nearly every negro industrial school in the United States, and to-day our graduates are teaching in more than twenty such institutions. The same might be said of Fisk University and other higher schools. If the college graduates were to-day withdrawn from the teaching force of the chief negro industrial schools, nearly every one of them would have to close its doors. These facts are forgotten by such advocates of industrial training as oppose the higher schools. Strong as the argument for industrial schools is—and its strength is undeniable—its cogency simply increases the urgency of the plea for higher training-schools and colleges to furnish broadly educated teachers.

But intelligence and skill alone will not solve the Southern problem of poverty. With these must go that combination of homely habits and virtues which we may loosely call thrift. Something of thrift may be taught in school, more must be taught at home; but both these agencies are helpless when organized economic society denies to workers the just rewards of thrift and efficiency. And this has been true of black laborers in the South from the time of slavery down through the scandal of the Freedmen's Bank to the peonage and crop-lien system of to-day. If the Southern negro is shiftless, it is primarily because over large areas a shiftless negro can get on in the world about as well as an industrious black man. This is not universally true in the South, but it is true to so large an extent as to discourage striving in precisely that class of negroes who most need encouragement. What is the remedy? Intelligence—not simply the ability to read and write or to sew—but the intelligence of a society permeated by that larger vision of life and broader tolerance which are fostered by the college and university. Not that all men must be college-bred, but that some men, black and white, must be, to leaven the ideals of the lump. Can any serious student of the economic South doubt that this to-day is her crying need?

W. E. B. DU BOIS ON BOOKER T. WASHINGTON (1903)   From W. E. B. Du Bois, *The Souls of Black Folk: Essays and Sketches* (Chicago, 1903), pp. 49–59.

Mr. Washington represents in Negro thought the old attitude of adjustment and submission; but adjustments at such a peculiar time as to make his programme unique. This is an age of unusual economic development, and Mr. Washington's programme naturally takes an economic cast, becoming a gospel of Work and Money to such an extent as apparently almost completely to overshadow the higher aims of life. Moreover, this is an age when the more advanced races are coming in closer contact with the less developed races, and the race-feeling is therefore intensified; and Mr. Washington's programme practically accepts the alleged inferiority of the Negro races. Again, in our own land, the reaction from the sentiment of war time has given impetus to race-prejudice against Negroes, and Mr. Washington withdraws many of the high demands of Negroes as men and American citizens. In other periods of intensified prejudice all the Negro's tendency to self-assertion has been called forth; at this period a policy of submission is advocated. In the history of nearly all other races and peoples the doctrine preached at such crises has been that manly self-respect is worth more than lands and houses, and that a people who voluntarily surrender such respect, or cease striving for it, are not worth civilizing.

In answer to this, it has been claimed that the Negro can survive only through submission. Mr. Washington distinctly asks that black people give up, at least for the present, three things,—

First, political power.

Second, insistence on civil rights,

Third, higher education of Negro youth,—

and concentrate all their energies on industrial education, the accumulation of wealth, and the conciliation of the South. This policy has been courageously and insistently advocated for over fifteen years, and has been triumphant for perhaps ten years. As a result of this tender of the palm-branch, what has been the return? In these years there have occurred:

1. The disfranchisement of the Negro.

2. The legal creation of a distinct status of civil inferiority for the Negro.

3. The steady withdrawal of aid from institutions for the higher training of the Negro.

These movements are not, to be sure, direct results of Mr. Washington's teachings; but his propaganda has, without a shadow of doubt, helped their speedier accomplishment. The question then comes: Is it possible, and probable, that nine millions of men can make effective progress in economic lines if they are deprived of political rights, made a servile caste, and allowed only the most meagre chance for developing their exceptional men? If history and reason give any distinct answer to these questions, it is an emphatic *No*. And Mr. Washington thus faces the triple paradox of his career:

1. He is striving nobly to make Negro artisans business men and property-owners; but it is utterly impossible, under modern competitive methods, for workingmen and property-owners to defend their rights and exist without the right of suffrage.

2. He insists on thrift and self-respect, but at the same time counsels a silent submission to civic inferiority such as is bound to sap the manhood of any race in the long run.

3. He advocates common-school and industrial training, and deprecates institutions of higher learning; but neither the Negro common-schools, nor Tuskegee itself, could remain open a day were it not for teachers trained in Negro colleges, or trained by their graduates.

This triple paradox in Mr. Washington's position is the object of criticism by two classes of colored Americans. One class is spiritually descended from Toussaint the Savior, through Gabriel, Vesey, and Turner, and they represent the attitude of revolt and revenge; they hate the white South blindly and distrust the white race generally, and so far as they agree on definite action, think that the Negro's only hope lies in emigration beyond the borders of the United States. And yet, by the irony of fate, nothing has more effectually made this programme seem hopeless than the recent course of the United States toward weaker and darker peoples in the West Indies, Hawaii, and the Philippines,—for where in the world may we go and be safe from lying and brute force?

The other class of Negroes who cannot agree with Mr. Washington has hitherto said little aloud. They deprecate the sight of scattered counsels, of internal disagreement; and especially they dislike making their just criticism of a useful and earnest man an excuse for a general discharge of venom from small-minded opponents. Nevertheless, the questions involved are so fundamental and serious that it is difficult to see how men like the Grimkes, Kelly Miller, J. W. E. Bowen, and other representatives of this group, can much longer be silent. Such men feel in conscience bound to ask of this nation three things:

1. The right to vote.
2. Civic equality.
3. The education of youth according to ability.

They acknowledge Mr. Washington's invaluable service in counseling patience and courtesy in such demands; they do not ask that ignorant black men vote when ignorant whites are debarred, or that any reasonable restrictions in the suffrage should not be applied; they know that the low social level of the mass of the race is responsible for much discrimination against it, but they also know, and the nation knows, that relentless color-prejudice is more often a cause than a result of the Negro's degradation; they seek the abatement of this relic of barbarism, and not its systematic encouragement and pampering by all agencies of social power from the Associated Press to the Church of Christ. They advocate, with Mr. Washington, a broad system of Negro common schools supplemented by thorough industrial training; but they are surprised that a man of Mr. Washington's insight cannot see that no such educational system ever has rested or can rest on any other basis than that of the well-equipped college and university, and they insist that there is a demand for a few such institutions throughout the South to train the best of the Negro youth as teachers, professional men, and leaders.

This group of men honor Mr. Washington for his attitude of conciliation toward the white South; they accept the "Atlanta Compromise" in its broadest interpretation; they recognize, with him, many signs of promise, many men of high purpose and fair judgment, in this section; they know that no easy task has been laid upon a region already tottering under heavy burdens. But, nevertheless, they insist that the way to truth and right lies in straightforward honesty, not in indiscriminate flattery; in praising those of the South who do well and criticising uncompromisingly those who do ill; in taking advantage of the opportunities at hand and urging their fellows to do the same, but at the same time in remembering that only a firm adherence to their higher ideals and aspirations will ever keep those ideals within the realm of possibility. They do not expect that the free right to vote, to enjoy civic rights, and to be educated, will come in a moment; they do not expect to see the bias and prejudices of years disappear at the blast of a trumpet; but they are absolutely certain that the way for a people to gain their reasonable rights is not by voluntarily throwing them away and insisting that they do not want them; that the way for a people to gain respect is not by continually belittling and ridiculing themselves; that, on the contrary, Negroes must insist continually, in season and out of season, that voting is necessary to modern manhood, that color discrimination is barbarism, and that black boys need education as well as white boys.

In failing thus to state plainly and unequivocally the legitimate demands of their people, even at the cost of opposing an honored leader, the thinking classes of American Negroes would shirk a heavy responsibility,—a responsibility to themselves, a responsibility to the struggling masses, a responsibility to the darker races of men whose future depends so largely on this American experiment, but especially a responsibility to this nation,—this common Fatherland. It is wrong to encourage a man or a people in evil-doing; it is wrong to aid and abet a national crime simply because it is unpopular not to do so. The growing spirit of kindliness and reconciliation between the North and South after the frightful differences of a generation ago ought to be a source of deep congratulation to all, and especially to those whose mistreatment caused the war; but if that reconciliation is to be marked by the industrial slavery and civic death of those same black men, with permanent legislation into a position of inferiority, then those black men, if they are really men, are called upon by every consideration of patriotism and loyalty to oppose such a course by all civilized methods, even though such opposition involves disagreement with Mr. Booker T. Washington. We have no right to sit silently by while the inevitable seeds are sown for a harvest of disaster to our children, black and white.

*   *   *

The black men of America have a duty to perform, a duty stern and delicate,—a forward movement to oppose a part of the work of their greatest leader. So far as Mr. Washington preaches Thrift, Patience, and Industrial Training for the masses, we must hold up his hands and strive with him, rejoicing in his honors and glorying in the strength of this Joshua called of God and of man to lead the headless host. But so far as Mr. Washington apologizes for injustice, North or South, does not rightly value the privilege and duty of voting, belittles the emasculating effects of caste distinctions, and opposes the higher training and ambition of our brighter minds,—so far as he, the South, or the Nation, does this,—we must unceasingly and firmly oppose them. By every civilized and peaceful method we must strive for the rights which the world accords to men, clinging unwaveringly to those great words which the sons of the Fathers would fain forget: "We hold these truths to be self-evident: That all men are created equal; that they are endowed by their Creator with certain unalienable rights; that among these are life, liberty, and the pursuit of happiness."

"THE TALENTED TENTH" (1903)   From W. E. B. Du Bois, "The Talented Tenth," in *The Negro Problem* . . . (New York, 1903), pp. 56-75.

The problem of training the Negro is to-day immensely complicated by the fact that the whole question of the efficiency and appropriateness of our present systems of education, for any kind of child, is a matter of active debate, in which final settlement seems still afar off. Consequently it often happens that persons arguing for or against certain systems of education for Negroes, have these controversies in mind and miss the real question at issue. The main question, so far as the Southern Negro is concerned, is: What under the present circumstance, must a system of education do in order to raise the Negro as quickly as possible in the scale of civilization? The answer to this question seems to me clear: It must strengthen the Negro's character, increase his knowledge and teach him to earn a living. Now it goes without saying, that it is hard to do all these things simultaneously or suddenly, and that at the same time it will not do to give all the attention to one and neglect the others; we could give black boys trades, but that alone will not civilize a race of ex-slaves; we might simply increase their knowledge of the world, but this would not necessarily make them wish to use this knowledge honestly; we might seek to strengthen character and purpose, but to what end if this people have nothing to eat or to wear? A system of education is not one thing, nor does it have a single definite object, nor is it a mere matter of schools. Education is that whole system of human training within and without the school house walls, which molds and develops men. If then we start out to train an ignorant and unskilled people with a heritage of bad habits, our system of training must set before itself two great aims—the one dealing with knowledge and character, the other part seeking to give the child the technical knowledge necessary for him to earn a living under the present circumstances. These objects are accomplished in part by the opening of the common schools on the one, and of the industrial schools on the other. But only in part, for there must also be trained those who are to teach these schools—men and women of knowledge and culture and technical skill who understand modern civilization, and have the training and aptitude to impart it to the children under them. There must be teachers, and teachers of teachers, and to attempt to establish any sort of a system of common and industrial school training, without *first* (and I say *first* advisedly) without *first* providing for the higher training of the very best teachers, is simply throwing your money to the winds. School houses do not teach themselves—piles of brick and mortar and machinery do not send out *men*. It is the trained, living human soul, cultivated and strengthened by long study and thought, that breathes the real breath of life into boys and girls and makes them human, whether they be black or white, Greek, Russian or American. Nothing, in these latter days, has so dampened the faith of thinking Negroes in recent educational movements, as the fact that such movements have been accompanied by ridicule and denouncement and decrying of those very institutions of higher training which made the Negro public school possible, and make Negro industrial schools thinkable. It was Fisk, Atlanta, Howard and Straight, those colleges born of the faith and sacrifice of the abolitionists, that placed in the black schools of the South the 30,000 teachers and more, which some, who depreciate the work of these higher schools, are using to teach their own new experiments. If Hampton, Tuskegee and the hundred other industrial schools prove in the future to be as successful as they deserve to be, then their success in training black artisans for the South, will be due primarily to the white colleges of the North and the black colleges of the South, which trained the teachers who to-day conduct these institutions. There was a time when the American people believed pretty devoutly that a log of wood with a boy at one end and Mark Hopkins at the other, represented the highest ideal of human training. But in these eager days it would seem that we have changed all that and think it necessary to add a couple of saw-mills and a hammer to this outfit, and, at a pinch, to dispense with the services of Mark Hopkins.

I would not deny, or for a moment seem to deny, the paramount necessity of teaching the Negro to work, and to work steadily and skillfully; or seem to depreciate in the slightest degree the important part industrial schools must play in the accomplishment of these ends, but I *do* say, and insist upon it, that it is industrialism drunk with its vision of success, to imagine that its own work can be accomplished without providing for the training of broadly cultured men and women to teach its own teachers, and to teach the teachers of the public schools.

*　　*　　*

It is coming to be seen, however, in the education of the Negro, as clearly as it has been in the education of the youths the world over, that it is the *boy* and not the material product, that is the true object of education. Consequently the object of the industrial school came to be the thorough training of boys regardless of the cost of the training, so long as it was thoroughly well done.

Thus, again, in the manning of trade schools we are thrown back upon the higher training as its source and chief support. What is the chief need for the building up of the Negro public school in the South? The Negro race in the South needs teachers to-day above all else. This is the concurrent testimony of all who know the situation. For the supply of this great demand two things are needed—institutions of higher education and money for school houses and salaries. It is usually assumed that a hundred or more institutions for Negro training are to-day turning out so many teachers and college-bred men that the race is threatened with an over-supply. This is sheer nonsense. There are to-day less than 3,000 living Negro college graduates in the United States, and less than 1,000 Negroes in college. Moreover, in the 164 schools for Negroes, 95 per cent of their students are doing elementary and secondary work, work which should be done in the public schools. Over half the remaining 2,157 students are taking high school studies. The mass of so-called "normal" schools for the Negro, are simply doing elementary common school work, or, at most, high school work, with a little instruction in methods. The Negro colleges and the post-graduate courses at other institutions are the only agencies for the broader and more careful training of teachers. The work of these institutions is hampered for lack of funds. It is getting increasingly difficult to get funds for training teachers in the best modern methods, and yet all over the South, from State Superintendents, county officials, city boards and school principals comes the wail, "We need TEACHERS!" and teachers must be trained.

*　　*　　*

There was a time when any aged and wornout carpenter could teach in a trade school. But not so to-day. Indeed the demand for college-bred men by a school like Tuskegee, ought to make Mr. Booker T. Washington the firmest friend of higher training. Here he has as helpers the son of a Negro senator, trained in Greek and the humanities, and graduated at Harvard; the son of a Negro congressman and lawyer, trained in Latin and mathematics, and graduated at Oberlin; he has as his wife, a woman who read Virgil and Homer in the same class room with me; he has as college chaplain, a classical graduate of Atlanta University; as teacher of science, a graduate of Fisk; as teacher of history, a graduate of Smith,—indeed some thirty of his chief teachers are college graduates, and instead of studying French grammars in the midst of weeds, or buying pianos for dirty cabins, they are at Mr. Washington's right hand helping him in a noble work. And yet one of the effects of Mr. Washington's propaganda has been to throw doubt upon the expediency of such training for Negroes, as these persons have had.

Men of America, the problem is plain before you. Here is a race transplanted through the criminal foolishness of your fathers. Whether you like it or not the millions are here, and here they will remain. If you do not lift them up, they will pull you down. Education and work are the levers to uplift a people. Work alone will not do it unless inspired by the right ideals and guided by intelligence. Education must not simply teach work—it must teach Life. The Talented Tenth of the Negro race must be made leaders of thought and missionaries of culture among their people. No others can do this work and Negro colleges must train men for it. The Negro race, like all other races, is going to be saved by its exceptional men.

THE PROGRAM OF THE NIAGARA MOVEMENT (1905) From *The Cleveland Gazette,* July 22, 1905.

We believe that [Negro] American citizens should protest emphatically and continually against the curtailment of their political rights. We believe in manhood suffrage: we believe that no man is so good, intelligent or wealthy as to be entrusted wholly with the welfare of his neighbor.

We believe also in protest against the curtailment of our civil rights. All American citizens have the right to equal treatment in places of public entertainment according to their behavior and deserts.

We especially complain against the denial of equal opportunities to us in economic life; in the rural districts of the south this amounts to peonage and virtual slavery; all over the south it tends to crush labor and small business enterprises: and everywhere American prejudice, helped often by iniquitous laws, is making it more difficult for Negro-Americans to earn a decent living.

Common school education should be free to all American children and compulsory. High school training should be adequately provided for all, and college training should be the monopoly of no class or race in any section of our common country. We believe that in defense of its own institutions, the United States should aid common school education, particularly in the south, and we especially recommend concerted agitation to this end. We urge an increase in public high school facilities in the south, where the Negro-Americans are almost wholly without such provisions. We favor well-equipped trade and technical schools for the training of artisans, and the need of adequate and liberal endowment for a few institutions of higher education must be patent to sincere well-wishers of the race.

We demand upright judges in courts, juries selected without discrimination on account of color and the same measure of punishment, and the same efforts at reformation for black as for white offenders. We need orphanages and farm schools for dependent children, juvenile reformatories for delinquents, and the abolition of the dehumanizing convict-lease system.

*   *   *

We plead for health—for an opportunity to live in decent houses and localities,

for a chance to rear our children in physical and moral cleanliness.

We hold up for public execration the conduct of two opposite classes of men; the practice among employers of importing ignorant Negro-American laborers in emergencies, and then affording them neither protection nor permanent employment; and the practice of labor unions of proscribing and boycotting and oppressing thousands of their fellow-toilers, simply because they are black. These methods have accentuated and will accentuate the war of labor and capital, and they are disgraceful to both sides.

We refuse to allow the impression to remain that the Negro-American assents to inferiority, is submissive under oppression and apologetic before insults. Through helplessness we may submit, but the voice of protest of ten million Americans must never cease to assail the ears of their fellows, so long as America is unjust.

*   *   *

We regret that this nation has never seen fit adequately to reward the black soldiers who in its five wars, have defended their country with their blood, and yet have been systematically denied the promotions which their abilities deserve. And we regard as unjust, the exclusion of black boys from the military and navy training schools.

*   *   *

We repudiate the monstrous doctrine that the oppressor should be the sole authority as to the rights of the oppressed.

The Negro race in America stolen, ravished and degraded, struggling up through difficulties and oppression, needs sympathy and receives criticism; needs help and is given hinderance, needs protection and is given mob-violence, needs justice and is given charity, needs leadership and is given cowardice and apology, needs bread and is given a stone. This nation will never stand justified before God until these things are changed.

Especially are we surprised and astonished at the recent attitude of the church of Christ—on the increase of a desire to bow to racial prejudice, to narrow the bounds of human brotherhood, and to segregate black men in some outer sanctuary. This is wrong, unchristian and disgraceful to the twentieth century civilization.

*   *   *

And while we are demanding, and ought to demand, and will continue to demand the rights enumerated above, God forbid that we should ever forget to urge corresponding duties upon our people.

The duty to vote.

The duty to respect the rights of others.

The duty to work.

The duty to obey the laws.

The duty to be clean and orderly.

The duty to send our children to school.

The duty to respect ourselves, even as we respect others.

DECLARATION OF PRINCIPLES OF THE SOUTHERN EDUCATIONAL

ASSOCIATION (1907)   As quoted in Ray Stannard Baker, *Following the Color Line* (New York, 1908), pp. 284–86.

No higher note has been struck in educational ideals than in the Declaration of Principles adopted last winter (1907) at the meeting of the Southern Educational Association at Lexington, Ky., an exclusively Southern gathering of white men and women. Their resolutions, which for lack of space cannot be here printed in full, should be read by every man and woman in the country who is interested in the future of democratic institutions. I copy here only a few of the declarations:

1. All children, regardless of race, creed, sex, or the social station or economic condition of their parents, have equal right to, and should have equal opportunity for, such education as will develop to the fullest possible degree all that is best in their individual natures, and fit them for the duties of life and citizenship in the age and community in which they live.

2. To secure this right and provide this opportunity to all children is the first and highest duty of the modern democratic state, and the highest economic wisdom of an industrial age and community. Without universal education of the best and highest type, there can be no real democracy, either political or social; nor can agriculture, manufacturers, or commerce ever attain their highest development.

3. Education in all grades and in all legitimate directions, being for the public good, the public should bear the burden of it. The most just taxes levied by the state, or with the authority of the state, by any smaller political division, are those levied for the support of education. No expenditures can possibly produce greater returns and none should be more liberal.

The New South on Negro Education

Concerning Negro education, I am publishing the resolutions in full, because they voice the present thought of the best leadership in the South:

1. We endorse the accepted policy of the states of the South in providing educational facilities for the youth of the Negro race, believing that whatever the ultimate solution of this grievous problem may be, education must be an important factor in that solution.

2. We believe that the education of the Negro in the elementary branches of education should be made thorough, and should include specific instruction in hygiene and home sanitation, for the better protection of both races.

3. We believe that in the secondary education of Negro youth emphasis should be placed upon agriculture and the industrial occupations, including nurse training, domestic science, and home economics.

4. We believe that for practical, economical and psychological reasons Negro teachers should be provided for Negro schools.

5. We advise instruction in normal schools and normal institutions by white teachers, whenever possible, and closer supervision of courses of study and methods of teaching in Negro normal schools by the State Department of Education.

6. We recommend that in urban and rural Negro schools there should be closer and more thorough supervision, not only by city and county superintendents, but also by directors of music, drawing, manual training, and other special topics.

7. We urge upon school authorities everywhere the importance of adequate buildings, comfortable seating, and sanitary accommodations for Negro youth.

8. We deplore the isolation of many Negro schools, established through motives of philanthropy, from the life and the sympathies of the communities in which they are located. We recommend the supervision of all such schools by the state, and urge that their work and their methods be adjusted to the civilisation in which they exist, in order that the maximum good of the race and of the community may be thereby attained.

9. On account of economic and psychological differences in the two races, we believe that there should be a difference in courses of study and methods of teaching, and that there should be such an adjustment of school curricula as shall meet the evident needs of Negro youth.

10. We insist upon such an equitable distribution of the school funds that all the youth of the Negro race shall have at least an opportunity to receive the elementary education provided by the state, and in the administration of state laws, and in the execution of this educational policy, we urge patience, toleration, and justice.

(Signed) G. R. GLENN, P. P. CLAXTON, J. H. PHILLIPS,
C. B. GIBSON, R. N. ROARK, J. H. VAN SICKLE,
Committee.

ACCOUNT OF RACE RELATIONS IN THE PUBLIC SCHOOLS OF CHICAGO (1922) From Chicago Commission on Race Relations, *The Negro in Chicago: A Study of Race Relations and a Race Riot* (Chicago, 1922), pp. 238–41, 246–48.

The public schools furnish one of the most important points of contact between the white and Negro races, because of the actual number of contacts in the daily school life of thousands of Negro and white children, and also because the reactions of young children should indicate whether or not there is instinctive race prejudice.

The Chicago Board of Education makes no distinction between Negro and white children. There are no separate schools for Negroes. None of the records of any teacher or principal shows which children are Negroes and which white. The board does not know how many Negro children there are in any school or in the city at large, nor how many of the teachers are Negroes. It was impossible to obtain from the board, for example, a list of the schools having a large Negro enrolment with which to begin the investigation. An unfortunate but unavoidable incidental effect of the investigation was the focusing of attention of principals and teachers on the Negroes in their schools.

*   *   *

Frequently white teachers in charge of classes with Negro pupils are race conscious and accept the conduct of white children as normal and pay disproportionate attention to the conduct of Negro children as exceptional and distinctive. As a result of the focusing of attention on Negro children, the inquiry, which was intended to get balanced information, developed a disproportionate amount of information concerning their conduct as compared with that of whites. Teachers who considered both races were inclined to believe that Negro children as a group had no special weaknesses that white children as a group did not also exhibit; that some Negro children, like any other children, were good, some were bad, and some indifferent, and that no generalizations about the race could be made from the characteristics or attitude of a few.

It became evident as soon as the investigation started that it was necessary to distinguish between the northern and the southern Negro. The southern Negro is conspicuous the moment one enters the elementary schools. Over-age or retarded children are found in all the lower grades, special classes, and ungraded rooms, and are noticeable all the way to the eighth grade, where seventeen- and nineteen-year-old children are sometimes found. In some schools these children are found in the regular classes; in others there are special rooms for retarded children, and as these groups are often composed almost entirely of Negro children, there is an appearance of segregation which made necessary a study of these retarded children from the South.

The southern child is hampered first of all by lack of educational opportunity in the South. He is usually retarded by two or more years when he enters the northern school because he has never been able to attend school regularly, due to the short term in southern rural schools, distance from school, and inadequacy of teaching force and school equipment. According to a report by the United States Bureau of Education on *Negro Education* 90 per cent of the Negro children between fifteen and twenty years of age attending school in the South are over-age. . . .

*   *   *

Another difficulty was suggested by the principal of a Chicago school (Webster) where 30 per cent of the children are Negroes, who said: "We base our educational ideas on certain backgrounds. The curriculum in Chicago was planned for children who come from families who are educated. It doesn't take children coming from uneducated families into consideration. That isn't fair either to the white or colored children."

The problem of readjustment to life in a northern city also affects the child's school life, and he is self-conscious and inclined to be either too timid or too self-assertive. A Negro teacher in speaking of the difficulties confronting the southern Negro, as well as the whole Negro group, said:

> The southern Negro has pushed the Chicago Negro out of his home, and the Chicago Negro in seeking a new home is opposed by the whites. What is to happen? The whites are prejudiced against the whole Negro group. The Chicago Negro is prejudiced against the southern Negro. Surely it makes a difficult situation for the southern Negro. No wonder he meets a word with a blow. And all this comes into the school more or less.

Another Negro teacher thus analyzes further the adjustment problems which tend to make the Negro newly come from the South unpopular with the Chicago Negro, as well as with the whites:

> These families from the South usually come from the country where there are no close neighbors. . . . Then the family is transplanted to Chicago to an apartment house, and even in with another family. The whole environment is changed and the trouble begins. No sense of property rights, no idea of how to use conveniences, no idea of how to live in

the new home, to keep it up, to live with everybody else so near. On top of that, the father does not fit into his work, and therefore cannot support the family; the mother goes out to work, and what is the result? Poorly kept houses and poorly kept children. . . . A normal home shows itself in the school, and poor home conditions show up still more.

The Negro child born in the North is not found to an unusual extent among the retarded children. He has been able to enter school on time and to attend the full term of nine months; his teachers compare favorably with those in white American and foreign neighborhoods, and his parents as a rule have a better background. Many teachers say that the progress of northern-born Negroes compares very favorably with that of whites. . . . Most kindergarten teachers found the most natural relationship existing between the young Negro and white children. "Neither colored nor whites have any feeling in our kindergarten," said one principal in a school 30 per cent Negro (Webster); "they don't understand the difference between colored and white children." In visiting one school the investigator noticed that the white children who objected to holding hands with the Negro children in the kindergarten and first and second grades were the better-dressed children who undoubtedly reflected the economic class and race consciousness of their parents. The Armour Mission near the school had excluded Negroes from its kindergarten, thereby fostering this spirit among the whites. A teacher in Doolittle (85 per cent) told of a little white girl in another school who cried because she was afraid the color from the Negro children's hands would rub off on hers; in her present school she has known no such instances in the kindergarten. This conduct is paralleled in instances in which Negro children who have never had any contact with white children in the South are afraid of them when they first come North.

Most of the teachers in the higher grades reported that there were no signs of race prejudice in the room. A teacher at Oakland (26 per cent) said that white girls sometimes asked to be moved to another seat when near a very dirty Negro child, but that this often happened when the dirty child was white. This teacher said it was the white mothers from the South, not the children, who wanted their children to be kept away from the Negroes. "The white children don't seem to mind the colored," she said. "I have had three of four mothers come in and ask that their children be kept away from the colored, but they were women from the South and felt race prejudice strongly. But they are the only ones who have complained."

A teacher in a school 90 per cent Negro said that when doubling up in the seats was necessary whites and Negroes frequently chose each other. A teacher at Moseley (70 per cent), when the investigator was present, called upon a white girl to act as hostess to a Negro girl who had just come from the South, and the request was met with pride and pleasure by the white girl. On the same occasion a white boy was asked to help a Negro boy with his arithmetic, and the two doubled up and worked together quite naturally.

"Race makes no difference," declared the principal of a school 92 per cent Negro (Colman). "The other day I had them all digging in the garden, and when they were all ready to go in I kept out one colored boy to help me plant seeds. We could use another boy, so I told Henry to choose anyone out of two rooms and he returned with an Italian. The color makes no difference."

A few instances of jealousy are cited. In one of them resentment ran high because when a loving cup was presented in McKinley (70 per cent) for the best composition, it was awarded by a neutral outside jury to a white girl. The principal of this 70 per cent Negro school, in addition to finding the Negro children jealous, considered their parents insolent and resentful. On the investigator's first visit she said that military discipline was the only kind for children, and that absolute segregation was necessary. At the next interview she said she preferred her school to any other; that there was never any disciplinary difficulty, and that white children who had moved from the district were paying car fare to finish their course at her school.

Discipline

There was considerable variety of opinion among the teachers as to whether Negro children presented any special problems of discipline. The principal of a school 20 per cent Negro (Felsenthal), for example, said that discipline was more difficult in this school than in the branch where 90 per cent were Negroes (Fuller). This principal is an advocate of separate schools. She was contradicted by a teacher in her school who said she had never used different discipline for the Negroes. In schools where the principals were sympathetic and the interracial spirit good the teachers reported that Negro children were much like other children and could be disciplined in the same way. One or two teachers reported that Negro children could not be scolded but must be "jollied along" and the work presented as play. This is interesting in view of the frequent complaint of the children from the South that the teachers in Chicago played with them all the time and did not teach them anything.

Attitude Toward Negro Teachers

Few Negro teachers were found in the schools investigated.

At Doolittle (85 per cent) there were thirty-three teachers, of whom two were Negroes. There was also a Negro cadet. At Raymond (93 per cent) there were six Negro teachers and a Negro cadet in a staff of forty. At Keith (90 per cent) there were six Negro teachers in a staff of twelve. Two of these principals said that their Negro teachers compared favorably with their white teachers and that some of them were excellent. Asked whether there was much antagonism if a Negro teacher was assigned where all the children were white, the principal of a 93 per cent school (Raymond) said there had been one or two such cases. "They are most successful in the foreign districts on the West Side. The European people do not seem to resent the presence of a colored teacher."

Another principal said that this was especially true where the foreign element was Jewish. A Negro teacher in a West Side school, largely Italian, is considered one of the ablest teachers in the school and proved herself highly competent during the war, when she assisted with the work of the draft board in the district.

One or two principals said that they would not have Negro teachers in their schools because the white teachers "could not be intimate with colored teachers," or because Negro teachers were "cocky," or because "the *Defender* preaches propaganda for colored teachers to seek positions in white schools." Sometimes an effort was made to explain the principal's objection to Negro teachers by saying that Negro children had no respect for Negro teachers. One principal whose white teachers were rather below the accepted standard said that the one colored teacher who had been there was obliged to leave because of the children's protest against her. A Negro teacher in a 20 per cent school (Haven) was valued highly by the principal, who advised with her as to what measures could be taken to prevent the appearance of race feeling.

DESCRIPTION OF NEGRO SCHOOLS IN THE SOUTH (1928)   From Lance
G. E. Jones, *Negro Schools in the Southern States* (Oxford, 1928), pp. 102–5, 116–17.

In 1916 it could truthfully be said that public schools for Negroes had
shared comparatively little in the educational advance that had taken place in the
Southern States during the previous fifteen years. Because of this delay private
schools attempted to fill the gap, and since most of them were planned as
institutions for higher education, the whole system of Negro schools (if system it
can be called) became top-heavy. Since 1919, however, there has been a more
sustained attempt to remedy this defect by the provision of public schools of lower
grade.

The new forward movement presents several features by which it is differentiated from similar and earlier developments in the North. True to its traditional
attitude, for example, the South has tended to look first to the improvement of
facilities for higher education—in State Land Grant Colleges, Normal Schools, and
High Schools. There are, it must in justice be pointed out, other reasons for this:
teachers are required for the lower schools, and must, it is urged, be prepared in
College or High School, the larger community which these institutions serve makes
the provision or development of them an easier financial proposition, and the policy
is one which appeals to the Negro and produces spectacular results.

A second characteristic of developments in public education in the Southern
States is that much of the stimulus to greater activity, both on the part of individual
States and local communities, has been provided by the wise administration of
privately controlled funds, notably the Slater Fund, the Jeanes Fund, and the
Rosenwald School Building Fund. Mention should also be made of the Peabody
Fund and the Phelps Stokes Fund, both of which have been responsible in part for
this new interest in Negro education, nor would any enumeration of the kind be
complete without reference to the financial aid rendered to educational enterprises
in the South by the General Education Board, both directly, and also indirectly
through one or other of the above Funds . . . It may be noted that, while the
money in each case has been derived in the first instance from generous Northern
philanthropists, its distribution has been guided mainly by Southerners with
educational experience, and the main purpose in view has been the development of
public schools. It is sometimes suggested that without stimulus from the North the
forward movement in Negro education would not have been initiated, and though a
Southerner might reply that it would be truer to speak of the North co-operating
with a South already alive to its responsibilities, he would be obliged to admit that
the South has been characterized in the past more by apathy than zeal, and that
even the united efforts of Southern zeal and Northern philanthropy have not
succeeded in awakening all the States to a full sense of their responsibility.

This leads to a third observation, namely that taking the South as a whole,
conditions in Negro schools are markedly inferior to those in white schools of
corresponding grade in the same community. There are a few exceptions, such for
example, as Washington, D.C. where, under the Federal Government, conditions
are kept as nearly equal as possible, but these do not invalidate the truth of the
statement. Comparisons reveal that in a community, city or county, which is slack
about the education of its white children—and many such communities exist—there
the Negro fares badly; where zeal for better white schools is shown the Negro

rejoices, for he knows that in the long run his children are likely to fare the better. If therefore we bear this fact in mind, and if we remember also that the South made a late start, and has until recent years progressed but slowly in the provision of educational facilities even for white pupils, we shall realize that conditions in Negro schools vary and are often such as call for prolonged and serious attention on the part of a wealthy and progressive modern nation. It is a curious commentary on the separateness of the races that the majority of white people in the South, and still more in the North, have no real knowledge of the conditions which exist.

Appropriations from public funds for Negro education have increased steadily in recent years, and in a few States the expenditure on public schools for coloured people is as great as the total expenditure on white schools ten years ago. In spite of this increase Negro schools still receive far less than white schools, and comparisons on a per capita basis show that the ratio of expenditure on teachers' salaries, for example, varies from approximate equality in Kentucky to as much as 8 to 1 in South Carolina. The discrepancy is greatest where the percentage of Negro population is highest, a fact due in the first instance to the defensive attitude which the small white group consciously or unconsciously adopts, and in the second place to the local system of administration which places control of school provision in their hands. State appropriations to the counties are made on the basis of population or of school attendance, white and Negro; the county adds a further sum from local taxes, and the County Board of Education, composed of white people, determines the distribution of the whole. In their anxiety to provide adequately for their own children they may assign as much (or more) for the maintenance of a small number of white schools as for a much larger number of Negro schools; and although a far-sighted County Superintendent of Schools can do much to secure a more equitable distribution, the precariousness of his position and the shortness of his tenure of office usually prevent his influence from being continuous. Where a County Superintendent disapproves of Negro education and is unwilling to co-operate in promoting it, he can, and does, hinder its development, even in a progressive State like North Carolina. Indeed among those who are responsible for educational administration there is probably no other single person able so effectively either to promote or retard the educational advancement of the Negro group.

Economic factors may operate either favourably or unfavourably in this matter. Thus fluctuations in the cotton crop have seriously affected the financial position of local communities, and reduced the amount available from local funds, to the disadvantage of both races. The influence of an economic factor of a different kind may be illustrated from events in a Mississippi county, where a few years ago migration to the North was producing a serious shortage of labour. Consultation between white employers and Negro leaders brought to light the fact that the prospect of securing better homes and facilities for education accounted in part for the exodus. As a result of the conference the leaders of both races agreed to co-operate in a programme of school improvement, and the county now possesses a system of Negro schools judged by competent observers to be one of the best organized in the Southern States. The exodus, for the time being, has been arrested.

Conditions in Negro schools as in white schools may vary, therefore, not merely from State to State, but also from county to county, and from community to community: to remedy the variations due to differences in taxable resources of counties the State of North Carolina maintains an Equalization Fund from which it supplements the resources of each county according to its need. Such a recognition of State responsibility is undoubtedly a step in the right direction, and, if more widely adopted in the South, should make ultimately for the equalization of conditions in Negro as well as in white schools.

At the moment the public High School is 'the strategic point of attack' upon the problem of Negro education. In the State of North Carolina for example the number of public High Schools for coloured pupils increased in the four years 1922–6 from 26 to 62, and enrollment has correspondingly increased from 1,448 to 8,237. Progress in other States has not been so rapid, but in all of them an effort is being made to increase facilities for instruction in high-school grades.

＊　　＊　　＊

Many and urgent though the educational needs of the town Negro may be, we must remember that two-thirds of the race still dwell in the rural areas of the South, and their children are cared for in rural schools. The problems to be faced in these schools are many. Six million coloured people are widely, unevenly, and often thinly distributed throughout sixteen States; difficulties attendant upon their distribution have been, and still are, accentuated by the absence of adequate means of communication—many roads being notoriously bad and railroads few; most of them, too, are engaged in agriculture, which in a great part of the South has hitherto meant the growing of cotton; fluctuations in the value of this commodity on the one hand, and the employment of the whole Negro family in its cultivation on the other, have resulted in a low standard of living and health, and in irregular attendance at school. The resources of rural Negro communities are slender, and educationally therefore a great part of the rural South presents a depressing picture of small schools, housed in dilapidated and insanitary wooden buildings, often in churches or the lodge-halls of friendly societies, irregularly attended by boys and girls of all ages who come from distances of from two to seven miles, and stay away whenever the work of home or field appears to require their help, or the weather is at all inclement. Such schools are rarely open for half the year, are often devoid of any furniture but rough plank benches, while the teacher, usually a woman, and little better educated in any real sense than those whom she teaches, endeavours to impart the rudiments of reading, writing and arithmetic with the help of a few ragged and incomplete books, the veriest scraps of paper, and no apparatus beyond what her ingenuity may devise or she may prevail upon the community to buy. The picture is not overdrawn, but fortunately there are many brighter spots, and the movement for better schools is making progress. For this forward movement the Slater and the Rosenwald Funds, aided by the General Education Board, are in a large measure responsible.

ON THE MISEDUCATION OF THE NEGRO (1931)　From Carter G. Woodson, "The Miseducation of the Negro," *Crisis*, vol. XXXVIII, pp. 266–67.

In their own as well as in mixed schools, Negroes are taught to admire the Hebrew, the Greek, the Latin and the Teuton and to despise the African. The thought of the inferiority of the Negro is drilled into him in almost every class he enters. If he happens to leave school after he has mastered the fundamentals, before he has finished high school or reached college, he will naturally escape from some of this bias and may recover in time to be of service to his people.

Practically all of the successful Negroes in this country are those who never learned this prejudice "scientifically" because they entered upon their life's work without formal education. The large majority of the Negroes who have put on the finishing touches of our best colleges, however, are all but worthless in the uplift of their people. If, after leaving school, they have the opportunity to give out to Negroes what traducers of the race have taught them, such persons may earn a living by teaching or preaching to Negroes what someone would like to have them know, but they never become a constructive force in the elevation of those far down. They become estranged from the masses and the gap between them widens as the years go by.

The explanation of this is a simple problem. The schools and colleges of this country are so conducted as to produce this result. For example, an officer of a Negro university, thinking that an additional course on the Negro should be given there, called upon a Negro Doctor of Philosophy of the faculty to offer such work. He promptly informed the officer that he knew nothing about the Negro. He did not go to school to waste his time that way. He went to be educated.

Last year at one of the Negro summer schools, a white instructor gave a course on the Negro, using for his text a work of Jerome Dowd, who teaches that whites are superior to blacks. When asked by one of the students why he used such a textbook, the instructor replied that he wanted them to get Dowd's point of view. If schools for Negroes are places where they must be convinced of their inferiority, they cannot escape from their tormentors and rise to recognition and usefulness.

As another has well said, to handicap a student for life by teaching him that his black face is a curse and that his struggle to change his condition is hopeless is the worst kind of lynching. It kills one's aspirations and dooms him to vagabondage and crime.

In most cases, moreover, when the teachers of Negroes are persons of good intentions, the result is the same. In the school of business administration, for example, Negroes are trained exclusively in the economics and psychology of Wall Street, and are thereby made to despise the opportunities to conduct laundries, repair shoes, run ice wagons, push banana carts, and sell peanuts among their own people.

GUNNAR MYRDAL ON NEGRO EDUCATION (1944)   From Gunnar Myrdal, *An American Dilemma: The Negro Problem and Modern Democracy* (New York, 1944), pp. 879–84, 893–96, 900–05, 907.

EDUCATION
IN THE
UNITED STATES

3000

The trend toward a rising educational level of the Negro population is of tremendous importance for the power relations discussed in this Part of our inquiry. Education means an assimilation of white American culture. It decreases the dissimilarity of the Negroes from other Americans. Since the white culture is permeated by democratic valuations, and since the caste relation is anything but democratic, education is likely to increase dissatisfaction among Negroes. This dissatisfaction strengthens the urge to withdraw from contact with prejudiced whites and causes an intensified isolation between the two groups. Increasing education provides theories and tools for the rising Negro protest against caste status in which Negroes are held. It trains and helps to give an economic livelihood to Negro leaders.

In the Negro community, education is the main factor for the stratification of the Negro people into social classes. The professionals who base their status upon having acquired a higher education form a substantial part of the Negro upper classes. And even in the middle and lower classes, educational levels signify class differences in the Negro community. In addition, education has a symbolic significance in the Negro world: the educated Negro has, in one important respect, become equal to the better class of whites.

These tendencies are most unhampered in the North. There Negroes have practically the entire educational system flung open to them without much discrimination. They are often taught in mixed schools and by white teachers; some of the Negro teachers have white pupils. Little attempt is made to adjust the teaching specifically to the Negroes' existing status and future possibilities. The American Creed permeates instruction, and the Negro as well as the white youths are inculcated with the traditional American virtues of efficiency, thrift and ambition. The American dream of individual success is held out to the Negroes as to the other students. But employment opportunities—and, to a lesser extent, some other good things of life—are so closed to them that severe conflicts in their minds are bound to appear.

Their situation is, however, not entirely unique. Even among the youths from other poor and disadvantaged groups in the North the ideals implanted by the schools do not fit life as they actually experience it. The conflicts are, of course, accentuated in the case of Negroes. Often they become cynical in regard to the official democratic ideals taught by the school. But more fundamentally they will be found to have drunk of them deeply. The American Creed and the American virtues mean much more to Negroes than to whites. They are all turning into the rising Negro protest.

The situation is more complicated in the South. The Negro schools are segregated and the Negro school system is controlled by different groups with different interests and opinions concerning the desirability of preserving or changing the caste status of Negroes. Looked upon as a "movement," Negro education in the South is, like the successful Negro organizations, an interracial endeavor. White liberals in the region and Northern philantropists have given powerful assistance in building up Negro education in the South. They have thereby taken and kept some of the controls. In the main, however, the control over Negro education has been preserved by other whites representing the political power of the region. The salaried officers of the movement—the college presidents, the school principals, the professors, and the teachers—are now practically all Negroes; in the elementary schools and in the high schools they are exclusively Negroes. With this set-up, it is natural and, indeed, necessary that the Negro school adhere rather closely to the accommodating pattern.

Negro teachers on all levels are dependent on white community leaders. This dependence is particularly strong in the case of elementary school teachers in rural districts. Their salaries are low, and their security as to tenure almost nothing. They can be used as disseminators of the whites' expectations and demands on the Negro community. But the extreme dependence and poverty of rural Negro school teachers, and the existence of Negroes who are somewhat better off and more independent than they, practically excluded them from having any status of leadership in the Negro community. In so far as their teaching is concerned, they are, however, more independent than it appears. This is solely because the white superintendent and the white school board ordinarily care little about what goes on in the Negro school. There are still counties where the superintendent has never visited the majority of his Negro schools. As long as Negro stool pigeons do not transfer reports that she puts wrong ideas into the children's heads, the rural Negro school teacher is usually ignored.

In cities the situation is different. Negro elementary and high schools are better; teachers are better trained and better paid. In the Negro community teachers have a higher social status. As individuals they also achieve a measure of independence because they are usually anonymous to the white superintendent and school board. In the cities, the white community as a whole does not follow so closely what happens among the Negroes. The Negro principal in a city school, however, is directly responsible to white officials and watches his teachers more closely than do superintendents of rural schools.

In state colleges the situation is similar, except that the professors have a still higher social status in the Negro community and except that the college tends to become a little closed community of its own, with its own norms, which tends to increase somewhat the independence of the teachers.

In the private colleges there is much more independence from local white opinion within the limits of the campus. A friendly white churchman belonging to the interracial movement recently told the students of Atlanta University, in a commencement address, that the teachers there enjoyed greater academic freedom than their white colleagues at the Georgia state institutions, and this is probably true. The influence exerted by the Northern philanthropists and church bodies who have contributed to the colleges—often exercised through Southern white liberals and interracialists and through outstanding conservative Negro leaders—is, to a great extent, effective as a means of upholding the independence of Negro college presidents and professors.

As conditions are in the South, it is apparent that this influence is indispensable for this purpose. Neither the Negro teachers themselves nor any outside Negro institution could provide a power backing effective enough to keep off local white pressure. This outside white control gives the Negro teachers a considerably greater freedom even to inculcate a protest attitude—if it is cautiously done—than is allowed in publicly supported educational institutions. But it is inherent in the Southern caste situation, and in the traditions of the movement to build up Negro education in the region, that even this control is conservatively directed when compared with Northern standards.

In spite of these controls, strongest at the bottom of the educational system but strong also in the higher institutions, there is no doubt, however, that *the long-range effect of the rising level of education in the Negro people goes in the direction of nourishing and strengthening the Negro protest.* Negro-baiting Senator Vardaman knew this when he said:

> What the North is sending South is not money but dynamite; this education is ruining our Negroes. They're demanding equality.

This would probably hold true of any education, independent of the controls held and the direction given. An increased ability on the part of the Negroes to understand the printed and spoken word cannot avoid opening up contact for them with the wider world, where equalitarian ideas are prevalent. But in the South there is not much supervision of Negro schools. And as we shall see later, Southern whites have been prohibited by their allegiance to the American Creed from making a perfected helot training out of Negro education.

*   *   *

The duty of society to provide for public education was early established in America, and private endowments for educational purposes have been magnificent. America spends more money and provides its youth, on the average, with more schooling than any other country in the world. America has also succeeded in a relatively higher degree than any other country in making real the old democratic principle that the complete educational ladder should be held open to the most intelligent and industrious youths, independent of private means and support from their family. Education has been, and is increasingly becoming, a chief means of climbing the social status scale. It is entirely within this great American tradition when white people, who have wanted to help the Negroes, have concentrated their main efforts on improving Negro education.

*   *   *

As self-improvement through business or social improvement through government appeared so much less possible for them, Negroes have come to affix an even stronger trust in the magic of education. It is true that some Negroes may lately have lost their faith in education, either because the schools available to them—in the South—are so inadequate or—in the North—because they achieve education but not the things they hoped to do with it. This attitude of dissatisfaction is probably part of the explanation why Negro children tend to drop out of high school more than do whites. If both sources of dissatisfaction could be removed, there is reason to believe that American Negroes would revert to their original belief in education. And, aside from such dissatisfaction and even cynicism, the masses of Negroes show even today a naive, almost religious faith in education. To an extent, this faith was misplaced: many Negroes hoped to escape drudgery through education alone. But it is also true that this faith has been justified to a large extent: education is one of the things which has given the Negroes something of a permanent advance in their condition.

*   *   *

The Whites' Attitudes Toward Negro Education

There are apparent conflicts of valuations between whites and Negroes in regard to Negro education. These conflicts, the interests involved, and the theories expressing them determine the forms of Negro education. But the situation is not so simple as just a difference of opinion. In fact, many whites are as eager to improve Negro education as is any Negro, and there are some Negroes who are rather on the other side of the fence, at least for the purpose of an opportunistic accommodation. The situation is complicated by the fact that both whites and Negroes are divided in their own minds. They harbor conflicting valuations within themselves. Only by keeping this constantly in mind can we understand the development of Negro education and correctly evaluate future prospects.

The American Creed definitely prescribes that the Negro child or youth should have just as much educational opportunity as is offered anyone else in the same community. Negroes should be trained to become good and equal citizens in a democracy which places culture high in its hierarchy of values. This equalitarian valuation is strong enough to dominate public policy in the North, in spite of the fact that probably most white people in the North, too, believe the Negroes to be inferior and, anyhow, do not care so much for their potentialities and possibilities as for those of whites. In the South the existing great discrimination in education is an indication that another valuation is dominating white people's actions. But it is a great mistake to believe that the American Creed is not also present and active in the motivations of Southern whites. Behavior is as always a moral compromise. Negroes would not be getting so much education as they are actually getting in the South if the equalitarian Creed were not also active.

By itself, the interest of upholding the caste system would motivate Southern whites to give Negroes practically no education at all or would restrict it to the transmission of only such lowly skills as would make Negroes better servants and farm hands. There is no mistake about this interest; it is real and has economic importance. . . .

"Industrial" *versus* "Classical" Education of Negroes

Quite independent of how the specific value of "vocational" or "industrial" education, as compared with a more liberal education, is viewed, there is no doubt that the popularity among whites, now as earlier, of the former type of Negro education is mainly motivated by the interests of preserving the caste order. "Industrial" education for Negroes is the formula upon which Southern whites have been able to strike a compromise between their belief in education, which stems from the American Creed, and their interests as white Southerners in preserving the caste order of the region.

*   *   *

By and large, *in spite of all the talk about it, no effective industrial training was ever given the Negroes in the Southern public schools,* except training for cooking and menial service. The expensive vocational training, which conflicted so harshly with the interests of the white workers, has never become much more than a slogan. Negro education has mostly remained "academic" and differs only in its low level of expenditure and effectiveness.

Even at the well-endowed centers of Hampton and Tuskegee, the industrial training offered was in demand almost solely because of a need for teachers in the lesser schools, rather than because of the needs of modern industry. This explains why they have been able to realize, in some lines at least, the vocational idea as well as they have, without coming into greater conflict with the interests of white workers. The schools to which those teachers have gone, and are now going, are usually not nearly so well equipped that they could be called "vocational" in any serious meaning of the term. They usually are poor schools, not deserving much of a classification into either "vocational" or "classical." A few exceptional schools excluded, they offer at best some training in domestic service for girls—which, for understandable reasons, meets more encouragement and less fear of competition—of a poor training in the technique of rapidly disappearing handicrafts, sometimes adjusted slightly to modern times by courses in "automobile repair work" or the like.

*   *   *

Negro Attitudes

The attitudes of the whites are of greatest importance for the growth of Negro education, as they have all the power. The Negroes are, however, not without influence, partly because the whites are divided among themselves and divided in their own conscience. The remarkable thing is that the Negroes are split in much the same way and on the same issues.

It is natural, to begin with, that the American Creed interest is more stressed with the Negroes. Deep down in their souls practically all Negroes feel that they have the right to equal opportunities for education. And the sanctity of the American Creed gives them the opportunity to express this opinion and to press the whites for concessions. The stress on education in American culture makes the Negro protest most respectable. But the observer finds also that there are a few upper class Negroes who express about the same opinion as whites, that common Negroes do not need and should not have much education. This is rare, however, and the opinion has to be concealed.

Much more important is the split in the Negro world as to what kind of education is desirable. On the one hand, they sense the caste motivation behind most whites' interest in industrial education for Negroes. They know also that they can hope to win the respect of the whites and take their place as equal citizens in American democracy only if they are educated in the nonvocational cultural values of the broader society. On the other hand, they see the actual caste situation as a reality and know that many lines of work are closed to them. In order to utilize fully the openings left, and in order eventually to open up new roads into industrial employment, they often conclude that Negroes are in particular need of vocational training. They realize also that the great poverty and cultural backwardness of their people motivate a special adaptation of Negro education. On this point there is a possibility of striking a compromise with the liberal white man. In the North most Negroes will not make this concession, and by no means all Negroes, perhaps not even a majority, in the South are prepared to take the stand. Even the ones who do, stress at the same time the necessity of raising educational opportunities and of improving the schools.

THE
MINORITIES

*   *   *

Schrieke, surveying Southern education a few years ago, sums up the situation in the following words:

> . . . although there is some sort and some amount of Negro education everywhere, Negro education still does not have a fixed, legitimate, acknowledged place. It is realized that something must be done in order to keep the Negro satisfied and in order to uphold the American slogan of free schools for every child, but it is rare that a community has any real interest in planning or building a wise system of education for the race. Politically, it is not generally admitted that the Negro has a right to schools or to other public services. . . . The Negro is still not recognized as a citizen despite the Civil War amendments.

This somewhat pessimistic evaluation is warranted by the facts. The educational facilities for Negroes, particularly in many rural regions, are scandalously poor. The white community often blinds itself to the entire matter. But in appraising the situation, it is equally important to recognize that there are dissimilarities in the level of educational facilities offered Negroes, and that there is a definite tendency upward.

This trend is gaining momentum and is pushed not only by Northern philanthropy and the intervention of federal agencies, but also by the growing force of Southern liberalism.

Meanwhile, Southern Negro schools are going to remain inadequate. The North will continue for many decades to get untutored and crude Negro immigrants from the South. These uneducated masses of Southern-born Negroes will be a heavy burden on the social and economic order in the North. It is, therefore, an interest for Northern cities, and not only for the migratory Negroes, that *a program of adult education be instituted to teach the migrating Negro masses the elements of American culture and also, perhaps, elements of vocational skills.*

More significant in the dynamics of Negro education than the low average standards in some regions are the high standards in others, and the general trend toward improvement. The American nation will not have peace with its conscience until inequality is stamped out, and the principle of public education is realized universally.

THE SOUTHERN MANIFESTO (1956) From *The New York Times,* March 12, 1956.

The unwarranted decision of the Supreme Court in the public school cases is now bearing the fruit always produced when men substitute naked power for established law.

The Founding Fathers gave us a Constitution of checks and balances because they realized the inescapable lesson of history that no man or group of men can be safely entrusted with unlimited power. They framed this Constitution with its provisions for change by amendment in order to secure the fundamentals of government against the dangers of temporary popular passion or the personal predilections of public officeholders.

We regard the decision of the Supreme Court in the school cases as a clear abuse of judicial power. It climaxes a trend in the Federal Judiciary undertaking to legislate, in derogation of the authority of Congress, and to encroach upon the reserved rights of the States and the people.

The original Constitution does not mention education. Neither does the 14th amendment nor any other amendment. The debates preceding the submission of the 14th amendment clearly show that there was no intent that it should affect the system of education maintained by the States.

The very Congress which proposed the amendment subsequently provided for segregated schools in the District of Columbia.

When the amendment was adopted in 1868, there were 37 States of the Union. Every one of the 26 States that had any substantial racial differences among its people, either approved the operation of segregated schools already in existence or subsequently established such schools by action of the same law-making body which considered the 14th amendment.

As admitted by the Supreme Court in the public school case (*Brown* v. *Board of Education*), the doctrine of separate but equal schools "apparently originated in *Roberts* v. *City of Boston* (1849), upholding school segregation against attack as being violative of a State constitutional guarantee of equality." This constitutional doctrine began in the North, not in the South, and it was followed not only in Massachusetts, but in Connecticut, New York, Illinois, Indiana, Michigan, Minnesota, New Jersey, Ohio, Pennsylvania and other northern States until they, exercising their rights as States through the constitutional processes of local self-government, changed their school systems.

In the case of *Plessy* v. *Ferguson* in 1896 the Supreme Court expressly declared that under the 14th amendment no person was denied any of his rights if the States provided separate but equal public facilities. This decision has been followed in many other cases. It is notable that the Supreme Court, speaking through Chief Justice Taft, a former President of the United States, unanimously declared in 1927 in *Lum* v. *Rice* that the "separate but equal" principle is "within the discretion of the State in regulating its public schools and does not conflict with the 14th amendment."

This interpretation, restated time and again, became a part of the life of the people of many of the States and confirmed their habits, customs, traditions, and way of life. It is founded on elemental humanity and common sense, for parents should not be deprived by Government of the right to direct the lives and education of their own children.

Though there has been no constitutional amendment or act of Congress changing this established legal principle almost a century old, the Supreme Court of the United States, with no legal basis for such action, undertook to exercise their naked judicial power and substituted their personal political and social ideas for the established law of the land.

This unwarranted exercise of power by the Court, contrary to the Constitution, is creating chaos and confusion in the States principally affected. It is destroying the amicable relations between the white and Negro races that have been created through 90 years of patient effort by the good people of both races. It has planted hatred and suspicion where there has been heretofore friendship and understanding.

Without regard to the consent of the governed, outside agitators are threatening immediate and revolutionary changes in our public-school systems. If done, this is certain to destroy the system of public education is some of the States.

With the gravest concern for the explosive and dangerous condition created by this decision and inflamed by outside meddlers:

We reaffirm our reliance on the Constitution as the fundamental law of the land.

We decry the Supreme Court's encroachments on rights reserved to the States and to the people, contrary to established law, and to the Constitution.

We commend the motives of those States which have declared the intention to resist forced integration by any lawful means.

We appeal to the States and people who are not directly affected by these decisions to consider the constitutional principles involved against the time when they too, on issues vital to them, may be the victims of judicial encroachment.

Even though we constitute a minority in the present Congress, we have full faith that a majority of the American people believe in the dual system of government which has enabled us to achieve our greatness and will in time demand that the reserved rights of the States and of the people be made secure against judicial usurpation.

We pledge ourselves to use all lawful means to bring about a reversal of this decision which is contrary to the Constitution and to prevent the use of force in its implementation.

In this trying period, as we all seek to right this wrong, we appeal to our people not to be provoked by the agitators and troublemakers invading our States and to scrupulously refrain from disorder and lawless acts.

Signed by:

MEMBERS OF THE UNITED STATES SENATE

Walter F. George, Richard B. Russell, John Stennis, Sam J. Ervin, Jr., Strom Thurmond, Harry F. Byrd, A. Willis Robertson, John L. McClellan, Allen J. Ellender, Russell B. Long, Lister Hill, James O. Eastland, W. Kerr Scott, John Sparkman, Olin D. Johnston, Price Daniel, J. W. Fulbright, George A. Smathers, Spessard L. Holland.

MEMBERS OF THE UNITED STATES HOUSE OF REPRESENTATIVES

Alabama: Frank W. Boykin, George M. Grant, George W. Andrews, Kenneth A. Roberts, Albert Rains, Armistead I. Selden, Jr., Carl Elliott, Robert E. Jones, George Huddleston, Jr.

Arkansas: E. C. Gathings, Wilbur D. Mills, James W. Trimble, Oren Harris, Brooks Hays, W. F. Norrell.

Florida: Charles E. Bennett, Robert L. F. Sikes, A. S. Herlong, Jr., Paul G. Rogers, James A. Haley, D. R. Matthews, William Cramer.

Georgia: Prince H. Preston, John L. Pilcher, E. L. Forrester, John James Flynt, Jr., James C. Davis, Carl Vinson, Henderson Lanham, Iris F. Blitch, Phil M. Landrum, Paul Brown.

Louisiana: F. Edward Hebert, Hale Boggs, Edwin E. Willis, Overton Brooks, Otto E. Passman, James H. Morrison, T. Ashton Thompson, George S. Long.

Mississippi: Thomas G. Abernethy, Jamie L. Whitten, Frank E. Smith, John Bell Williams, Arthur Winstead, William M. Colmer.

North Carolina; Herbert C. Bonner, L. H. Fountain, Graham A. Barden, Carl T.

Durham, F. Ertel Carlyle, Hugh Q. Alexander, Woodrow W. Jones, George A. Shuford, Charles R. Jonas.

South Carolina: L. Mendel Rivers, John J. Riley, W. J. Bryan Dorn, Robert T. Ashmore, James P. Richards, John L. McMillan.

Tennessee: James B. Frazier, Jr., Tom Murray, Jere Cooper, Clifford Davis, Ross Bass.

Texas: Wright Patman, John Dowdy, Walter Rogers, O. C. Fisher, Martin Dies.

Virginia: Edward J. Robeson, Jr., Porter Hardy, Jr., J. Vaughan Gary, Watkins M. Abbitt, William M. Tuck, Richard H. Poff, Burr P. Harrison, Howard W. Smith, W. Pat Jennings, Joel T. Broyhill.

CENTRAL HIGH SCHOOL, LITTLE ROCK, SEPTEMBER 23, 1957 From the *Sacramento Bee,* September 23, 1957.

A howling, shrieking crowd of men and women outside Central High School, and disorderly students inside, forced the authorities to withdraw eight Negro students from the school today, three and one half hours after they entered it.

At the stroke of noon, Mayor Woodrow Wilson Mann radioed to police officers on the scene telling them to tell the crowd:

"The Negro students have been withdrawn."

Almost immediately, the three Negro boys and five girls left the school under heavy police escort. The officers took them away in police cars.

Crowds clustered at both ends of the school set up a storm of fierce howling and again surged toward the lines of policemen and state troopers.

Again, they were beaten back.

The explosive climax came after the school had been under siege since 8:45 when the Negroes quietly walked through the doors.

The [city] police, armed with riot guns and tear gas, had the crowd under control.

Inside, meanwhile, students reported seeing Negroes with blood on their clothes. Some whites who came out—in protest against integration—told of wild disorder, with policemen chasing white students through the halls and attacks on Negroes in the building.

The break came shortly before noon.

Superintendent of Schools Virgil Blossom said he asked Gene Smith, assistant chief of police at the scene, if he thought it would be best to pull out the Negroes.

Smith said he did.

Mann's announcement, ordering the police to notify the crowd, came minutes afterward.

Three newspapermen were beaten by the crowd before the sudden turn in the situation.

They are Paul Welch, a reporter, and Gray Villette and Francis Miller, photographers. All are employed by Life magazine.

A man smashed Miller in the face while he was carrying an armful of camera equipment. Miller fell to the ground, bleeding profusely.

All morning, the people had been threatening newsmen. "We ought to wipe up the street with these Yankee reporters," a man said.

Even after the Negroes left the school, the crowds remained.

Teenagers in two automobiles cruised on the outskirts before the withdrawal of the students.

During the hours while the Negroes were in the school, between 30 and 50 white students left.

One girl, Sylvia Jones, said she signed out and when asked her reason, said simply "Integration."

The crowd yelled, cheered and applauded each time a white student left the school. "Don't stay in there with them!" people yelled.

Women were hysterical.

Four Negroes were beaten and some arrests were made before the eight students went into the school.

It was a frightening sight.

The drama packed climax of three weeks of integration struggle in Little Rock came just after the buzzer sounded inside the big 2,000 pupil school at 8:45, signaling the start of classes.

Suddenly, on a street leading toward the school, the crowd spotted four Negro adults, marching in twos down the center of the street.

A man yelled, "Look, here they come!"

They were not the students. One appeared to be a newspaperman. He had a card in his hat and was wearing a camera.

I jumped into a glass windowed telephone booth on the corner. The scene was clearly visible. As the crowd surged toward the four Negroes, they broke and ran.

But they were caught on the lawn of a home nearby. Whites jumped the man with the camera from behind, rode him to the ground, kicking and beating him. They smashed the camera to bits.

This, obviously was a planned diversionary movement to draw the crowd's attention away from the school.

While I was dictating what I saw, someone yelled:

"Look, they're going into the school!"

At that instant, the eight Negroes—three boys and five girls—were crossing the schoolyard toward a side door at the south end of the school.

The girls were in bobby sox and the boys were dressed in open shirts. All were carrying books.

They were not running, not even walking fast. They simply strolled toward the steps, went up, and were inside before all but a few of the 200 people at that end of the street knew it.

Some did see the Negroes, however.

"They've gone in!" A man roared, "Oh, God, they're in the school!"

A woman screamed. "Did they get in? Did you see them go in?"

"They're in now!" some other men yelled.

"Oh, my God!" the woman screamed. She burst into tears and tore at her hair.

Hysteria swept the crowd. Other women began weeping and screaming.

At that moment, a tall, gray-haired man in a brown hunting shirt jumped on the barricade with others holding him. He yelled, waving his arms:

"Who's going through?"

"We all are!" the people shouted.

They broke over and around the wooden barricades, rushing the policemen.

About a dozen policemen were in that corner of the street.

They raised their billy clubs. Some grabbed men and women and hurled them back. Two chased a dark haired man who slipped through their line like a football player. They caught him on the schoolyard, whipped his coat down his arms, pinning them, and hustled him out of the yard.

The weeping and screaming went on among the women.

A man said, "I'm going in there and get my kid out."

An officer gritted, "You're not going anywhere."

Two ambulances rolled up. Nobody was in them.

Suddenly, another roar—and cheering and clapping—came from the crowd. A white student, carrying his books came down the front steps.

He was followed by two bobby sox girls. In the next few minutes, other students came out.

"There's not much education goin' on inside there now," one of the boys who came out told reporters.

A moment later, two policemen suddenly raced into the building through the north door. When they came out, they were holding a girl by both arms, rushing her forcibly toward a police prisoner's wagon.

For an instant, it looked as though the crowd would try to break the police lines again to rescue her.

But they put her in the car and drove swiftly down the street, past the barricade at the south end.

Screams, catcalls and more yelling broke out as the car, whipping dangerously close to the people and the barricades, raced down the street.

A man, distraught, came sprinting after it. "That's my kid in there," he yelled. "Help me get my kid out."

But the car was gone.

The eight Negro students slipped into the school this morning while a group of Negro adults fought the angry crowd of whites to divert their attention.

Reporters who caught just a glimpse of the students as they were rushed into the building through a side door said nine had entered but the school office said the number was eight.

The well executed plan of diversion held the crowd's attention long enough for the Negro students to be driven onto the campus and whisked through the side door. . . .

PRESIDENT EISENHOWER'S ADDRESS TO THE NATION ON THE
LITTLE ROCK CRISIS, (1957)   From *U.S. News & World Report*, October 4, 1957, pp. 64–65.

For a few minutes this evening I should like to speak to you about the serious situation that has arisen in Little Rock. To make this talk I have come to the President's office in the White House. I could have spoken from Rhode Island, where I have been staying recently, but I felt that, in speaking from the house of Lincoln, of Jackson and of Wilson, my words would better convey both the sadness I feel in the action I was compelled today to take and the firmness with which I intend to pursue this course until the orders of the federal court at Little Rock can be executed without unlawful interference.

In that city, under the leadership of demagogic extremists, disorderly mobs have deliberately prevented the carrying out of proper orders from a federal court. Local authorities have not eliminated that violent opposition and, under the law, I yesterday issued a proclamation calling upon the mob to disperse.

This morning the mob again gathered in front of the Central High School of Little Rock, obviously for the purpose of again preventing the carrying out of the court's order relating to the admission of Negro children to that school.

Whenever normal agencies prove inadequate to the task and it becomes necessary for the executive branch of the Federal Government to use its powers and authority to uphold federal courts, the President's responsibility is inescapable.

In accordance with that responsibility, I have today issued an executive order directing the use of troops under federal authority to aid in the execution of federal law at Little Rock, Ark. This became necessary when my proclamation of yesterday was not observed, and the obstruction of justice still continues. . . .

Our personal opinions about the decision have no bearing on the matter of enforcement; the responsibility and authority of the Supreme Court to interpret the Constitution are very clear. . . .

It was my hope that this localized situation would be brought under control by city and State authorities. If the use of local police powers had been sufficient, our traditional method of leaving the problem in those hands would have been pursued. But when large gatherings of obstructionists made it impossible for the decrees of the court to be carried out, both the law and the national interest demanded that the President take action. . . .

The very basis of our individual rights and freedom rests upon the certainty that the President and the executive branch of Government will support and insure the carrying out of the decisions of the federal courts even, when necessary, with all the means at the President's command.

Unless the President did so, anarchy would result.

There would be no security for any except that which each one of us could provide for himself.

The interest of the nation in the proper fulfillment of the law's requirements cannot yield to opposition and demonstrations by some few persons.

Mob rule cannot be allowed to override the decisions of our courts.

Now, let me make it very clear that federal troops are not being used to relieve local and State authorities of their primary duty to preserve the peace and order of the community. Nor are the troops there for the purpose of taking over the responsibility of the school board and the other responsible local officials in running Central High School. The running of our school system and the maintenance of peace and order in each of our States are strictly local affairs, and the Federal Government does not interfere, except in very special cases and when requested by one of the several States. In the present case, the troops are there, pursuant to law, solely for the purpose of preventing interference with the orders of the court.

The proper use of the powers of the executive branch to enforce the orders of a federal court is limited to extraordinary and compelling circumstances. Manifestly, such an extreme situation has been created in Little Rock. This challenge must be met and with such measures as will preserve to the people as a whole their lawfully protected rights in a climate permitting their free and fair exercise. . . .

The decision of the Supreme Court concerning school integration, of course, affects the South more seriously than it does other sections of the country. In that region I have many warm friends, some of them in the city of Little Rock. I have deemed it a great personal privilege to spend in our Southland tours of duty while in the military service and enjoyable recreational periods since that time.

So, from intimate personal knowledge, I know that the overwhelming majority of the people in the South—including those of Arkansas and of Little Rock—are of good will, united in their efforts to preserve and respect the law even when they disagree with it.

They do not sympathize with mob rule. They, like the rest of our nation, have proved in two great wars their readiness to sacrifice for America.

And the foundation of the American way of life is our national respect for the law.

In the South, as elsewhere, citizens are keenly aware of the tremendous disservice that has been done to the people of Arkansas in the eyes of the nation, and that has been done to the nation in the eyes of the world.

At a time when we face grave situations abroad because of the hatred that Communism bears toward a system of government based on human rights, it would be difficult to exaggerate the harm that is being done to the prestige and influence—and, indeed, to the safety—of our nation and the world.

Our enemies are gloating over this incident and using it everywhere to misrepresent our whole nation. We are portrayed as a violator of those standards of conduct which the peoples of the world united to proclaim in the Charter of the United Nations. There they affirmed "faith in fundamental human rights and in the dignity and worth of the human person," and they did so "without distinction as to race, sex, language or religion."

And so, with deep confidence, I call upon the citizens of the State of Arkansas to assist in bringing to an immediate end all interference with the law and its processes. If resistance to the federal court order ceases at once, the further presence of federal troops will be unnecessary and the city of Little Rock will return to its normal habits of peace and order—and a blot upon the fair name and high honor of our nation in the world will be removed.

Thus will be restored the image of America and of all its parts as one nation, indivisible, with liberty and justice for all.

Good night and thank you very much.

MAGAZINE ACCOUNT OF THE LITTLE ROCK SCHOOL CRISIS

(**1957**) From *U.S. News & World Report,* October 4, 1957, pp. 37–41.

To the people of Little Rock, the quiet tree-shaded corner has been known for years as "Fourteenth and Schiller."

The intersection, surrounded by neat homes and tidy lawns, has its counterpart in the residential neighborhoods of every city in America. As long as they can remember, people have been crossing it daily without giving it a second thought.

To the U.S. Army's 101st Airborne Division, "Fourteenth and Schiller" became "Roadblock Alpha." It bristled with bayonets. The only way you could get through—unless you had business in the area—would be to fight some of the toughest men ever to wear an American uniform.

On that first day, Sept. 25, 1957, nobody tried it.

A small crowd of curious people gathered at "Roadblock Alpha" the first thing in the morning—most of them just to see what was going on.

Lieut. William Ness stared at the crowd, and said: "Either you move or we'll move you."

They moved.

Throughout the day, all along Fourteenth Street and all along Schiller, little knots of citizens formed to talk things over. Passing by, you could overhear such remarks as these:

A man in shirt sleeves: "They're trying to cram this thing down our throats."

A woman: "The South has been occupied again."

Another man: "What are they trying to do to us? Bayonets ain't the way to do it."

These troopers meant business. With bayonets ready, they kept people on the move. To resist meant trouble, and nobody doubted it.

Sometime during the morning, a squad of troops moved down the street with a crowd dispersing rapidly in front of them. One man moved out ahead, and soldiers ran after him. Swirling out of the crowd came a teen-age girl, shrieking at the top of her voice:

"You leave my daddy alone! That man's my daddy! You leave him alone!"

She was 15-year-old Luanne Montgomery, a sophomore at Central High School, who had walked out of class because she didn't want to go to school with Negroes. The troopers had ordered her father to move, and pressed him because he wasn't moving fast enough. He wasn't arrested. But his daughter was almost hysterical.

Halfway down the block from Schiller, on Fourteenth Street, Paul Downs, of Springdale, Ark., stood in front of a house, clutching a bandaged arm. He said the bandage covered a bayonet wound. Here is his story:

"I was standing on the corner with other people when the troops came up and told us to move away. Well, I didn't move right away. 'I'm from the South,' I said, 'and I don't move very fast.'

"Before I knew it, the bayonet went into my arm right to the bone. So I got out of there fast. The doc put four stitches in my arm, and here I am back again."

Mr. Downs, 35, is a salesman who spent 13 years in the Army and saw service both in World War II and in Korea.

"All I ask," he said, "is that these troops use some discretion in this thing."

As he talked, a crowd began to gather. Behind the crowd came the troops. They took Mr. Downs away, and his listeners moved on.

Apparently C. E. Blake, a railroad man from North Little Rock, didn't move quite fast enough, either.

At one point, a crowd started forming near "Roadblock Alpha." Troops moved in and grabbed several young men, obviously the leaders. They were marched off to a detention compound.

A short time later, the crowd started jeering. Paratroopers moved forward with fixed bayonets. Mr. Blake, in the crowd stood stock still. The troopers advanced. The tip of a bayonet pricked Mr. Blake's shirt. He grabbed at the rifle, as if to push it away, and a scuffle developed.

Suddenly the butt of a M-1 rifle smashed against Mr. Blake's forehead. He went down, blood flowing from a gash just above his left eye. His wife stood over him, screaming. The troopers moved on. A friend took Mr. Blake to a hospital.

Through most of the day, Little Rock was a city of tense and jumpy people. Nerves were tightest in the school neighborhood. For example—

• A group of people stood near an intersection, silently watching troops hurry past "on the double." Suddenly, from the rear came the sharp clang of metal striking metal. A wave of apprehension swept the crowd. Everybody turned to see what was going on.

It was just two workmen putting up a "No Parking" sign.

• Several teen-agers with "ducktail" haircuts and long sideburns lined a curb making wisecracks at a detachment of troopers. The officer in charge snapped a command. A squad formed, bayonets ready, took one step forward and, in unison, yelled "Hah!" The youngsters scattered like startled rabbits.

• A reporter knocked at a door near Central High School and asked the woman who answered if he could use the telephone.

"Look at the blood on my steps," she said. "Just look there at the blood. The Yankee soldiers did that. Who are you for, anyway? If you're for Eisenhower, you can't use this phone."

Just a few minutes before, a man had been clubbed with a rifle butt while standing in her front yard.

At times, it was a city of wild rumors, too—

Somebody said a man had been bayoneted in the head while he stood on the porch of his own house. Nobody ever located him.

Somebody said fighting had broken out between white boys and Negro workers at a construction site in another part of town. It hadn't.

Somebody said that, inside the school, squads of armed troopers accompanied each Negro child to all classes. Others said they didn't. Troops were stationed inside the school throughout the day, though.

And it was a city beset with moods that ranged from apprehension to cold anger—

• A woman stood in a doorway, looking at Central High. "This is the grimmest day of my life," she said. "I didn't sleep a wink last night."

• Once a crowd, fleeing before the bayonets, dashed to the porch of a private home. A woman, trying to shoo them away, pleaded: "Don't get me in trouble! We want no trouble!"

• A young man glared at the troopers—from a safe distance—and said: "If they'd put their guns down and come across the street, we'd show 'em who's tough around here."

Something happens to you when you find yourself in close company with a bayonet. This happened to a member of the Board of Editors of "U.S. News & World Report":

"I was near the edge of a skirmish line of troops moving down the street with fixed bayonets. One of the paratroopers swerved toward me, apparently bound to clear me out of the neighborhood.

"It happened in an instant. Somebody yelled: 'Hey, he's all right. He's one of the newsmen!' The soldier swerved aside, missing me by a couple of inches.

"For a couple of seconds I was staring at the business end of a 101st Airborne bayonet, and it wasn't a very pretty sight."

It was 9:22 A.M.—40 minutes after the final bell had rung to start the day's classes at Central High.

Racing along Park Street came an olive-drab car—big enough to hold the nine Negro students the U.S. Army was taking to school. Jeeps filled with paratroopers escorted the car.

The cavalcade braked to a stop at the long walk leading up the concrete steps to the main entrance of the school. Three hundred fifty soldiers surrounding the school came to attention.

Paratroopers in full battle dress formed a tight guard around the staff car. The Negro students filed out of the car and started up the walk.

Across the street a group of white students chanted: "Two, four, six, eight—we ain't gonna integrate."

At 9:24 A.M. the Negroes crossed the threshold of the school. With military precision, it had taken the 101st Airborne Division two minutes to integrate Central High.

*   *   *

At 3 o'clock the school day was over.

Probably never before in U.S. history has a school let out amid such a scene as that at Central High. Three hundred and fifty soldiers in full battle gear surrounded the school and its neighborhood, ready for action. Jeeps rolled along the streets. Walkie-talkie radios cracked with military messages. A helicopter roared back and forth at an altitude of only 200 feet as the children trooped out.

But nothing happened. The white students poured out of the school much as they would on any school day—chatting, laughing, outwardly unconcerned. The Negro students were taken out through a side door and left in Army vehicles.

What did the white students think of their first day in mixed classes?

One boy said: "I don't like this integration stuff, but I'm not going to fight about it."

Said another: "We're against it, but there's nothing we can do about it."

A sophomore girl said: "Everything went off fine. At lunch some white boys and girls asked the colored students to eat with them, and they did."

Another girl: "I don't care if they come to school if I don't have to eat with them and undress with them in the locker room."

One boy shrugged his shoulders: "The school year is ruined."

What sort of school day had it been? This came from sophomore Bobby Rhoads as he walked down Park Street on his way home:

"I think all this troop business is stupid. I don't want this integration any more than anyone else, but it looks like it's bound to come.

"It was pretty hard to get anything done in school with everything else that was going on. That helicopter kept buzzing around over the roof all the time and it was hard for us to pay attention."

By nightfall, Little Rock's streets were quiet. The crowd that had formed and disbanded at "Roadblock Alpha" off and on through the day finally thinned to nothing. Only the troops remained.

Somebody asked an officer how long he thought the troops of the U.S. Army would be on duty at Central High.

"Indefinitely," he replied. "We stayed in Germany 15 years."

JAMES MEREDITH ON HIS EXPERIENCES IN MISSISSIPPI (1962) From
James H. Meredith, "I'll Know Victory or Defeat," *Saturday Evening Post,* November 10, 1962, pp. 15–17.

In 1955 I reenlisted. I always had it in mind to come back to Mississippi and study law, but I didn't think I was ready then for the responsibilities I would have to face, so I reenlisted. I was in Japan from 1957 till 1960, and there isn't any doubt that this was the settling-down point for me. I decided not only what I wanted to do, which I have known for a long time in a vague way, but how to go about doing it.

Being in Japan was an amazing experience. Negroes say, "When you're in Japan you have to look in a mirror to remember you're a Negro," and it's true. Japan is the only place where I have not felt the "air of difference."

I was surprised that the Japanese people were so aware of the racial situation in America. For instance, I met a boy—I don't suppose he was more than 12 or 13—and he knew more about Little Rock than most American kids that age. He was amazed when I told him I was from Mississippi and that I intended to go back. This kind of reaction further convinced me that I would go back to Mississippi and try to improve these conditions. I was discharged in July, 1960, and by the end of the month I was back in Kosciusko.

I entered Jackson State College, a Negro school in Jackson, and quickly met other students who felt as I did—that Negroes in Mississippi did not have the rights of full citizens, including the right to the best education the state offered. Someone had to seek admission to the University of Mississippi, and I decided to do it. But there were many of us involved. Although the lawsuit was mine, the others were with me, and I sought their advice on every move I made.

As soon as I filed application for admission, I contacted Medgar Evers, Mississippi field secretary for the N.A.A.C.P., and through him I asked for N.A.A.C.P. legal aid. Mrs. Constance Motley, associate counsel of the N.A.A.C.P. Legal Defense Fund, came to my assistance. The N.A.A.C.P. was prompt and efficient, and that was of prime importance. There was a great morale factor here, and every time we called them, they were there.

The court fight was long, and there were times when I wondered if it would be successful. I kept winning in court, but I didn't get any nearer to the university. Finally, after the Fifth Circuit Court of Appeals had said I should be registered, I felt the responsibility was the Federal Government's; it was out of my hands to do anything.

People have asked me if I wasn't terribly afraid the night we went to Oxford. No, my apprehensions came a long time before that. The hardest thing in human nature is to decide to act. I was doing all right in the Air Force. I got married in 1956, and my wife was able to work as a civil servant on the same bases where I was stationed. I had to give this up, this established way of things, this status, and try something new and unknown. That's where the big decision was—not here, last month, but there, a couple of years ago. Once I made that decision, things just had to happen the way they happened.

*   *   *

Through all that has happened I have tried to remain detached and objective. I have had all sorts of reactions to things that have happened, but mostly they have been personal reactions and realistic reactions, both at the same time. When I was in the middle of the force of marshals being gathered to take me to Oxford I thought, personally, how utterly ridiculous this was, what a terrible waste of time and money and energy, to iron out some rough spots in our civilization. But realistically I knew that these changes were necessary. I knew change was a threat to people and that they would fight it and that this was the only way it could be accomplished.

I have tried to be detached and realistic. When we were turned away the first time I tried to register at the university, and especially the second time, at the State Capitol in Jackson, I saw the mobs and heard them jeering, "Go home, nigger" and that stuff, but I never recognized them as individuals at all, even those who showed the greatest contempt for me. I felt they were not personally attacking me but that they were protesting a change and this was something they felt they must do. I thought it was impersonal. Some of them were crying, and their crying indicated to me even more the pain of change and the fear of things they did not know. I feel the people were keyed up by the actions of their leaders. With Gov. Ross Barnett taking the position he did, the people were bound to act that way, and it didn't really have anything to do with me personally. That's the way I saw it.

I might add that I thought the governor put on a pretty good performance. The first time, when he turned us away at the university, he reminded me of Charlton Heston, I believe it was, in a movie about Andrew Jackson. Very dramatic.

I don't think I have had a real low point in recent weeks. It always seemed to me it was the Government's job to carry out the court order and it would be done. The most annoying time was when there was so much talk about a possible deal between the Federal Government and Governor Barnett. But when the Federal officers told me we were going that Sunday, just a few minutes before we took off for Oxford, the annoyance disappeared.

When we landed in Oxford it was almost dark. We got in a car and I remember seeing a truckload of marshals in front of us and one behind. I went straight to the university and was taken to my rooms—an apartment, I guess you could call it. Since they knew some Government men would be staying with me, I had two bedrooms and a living room and a bathroom. The first thing I did was make my bed. When the trouble started, I couldn't see or hear very much of it. Most of it was at the other end of the campus, and besides I didn't look out of the window. I think I read a newspaper and went to bed around 10 o'clock. I was awakened several times in the night by the noise and shooting outside, but it wasn't near me, and I had no way of knowing what was going on. Some of the students in my dormitory banged their doors for a while and threw some bottles in the halls, but I slept pretty well all night.

I woke up about six-thirty in the morning and looked out and saw the troops. There was a slight smell of tear gas in my room, but I still didn't know what had gone on during the night, and I didn't find out until some marshals came and told me how many people were hurt and killed. I had gotten to know these marshals pretty well in recent weeks, and I was so sorry about this. Some supposedly responsible newspapermen asked me if I thought attending the university was worth all this death and destruction. That really annoyed me. Of course I was sorry! I didn't want that sort of thing. I believe it could have been prevented by responsible political leaders. I understand the President and the attorney general were up most of the night. They had all the intelligence at their disposal, and I believe they handled it to the best of their knowledge and ability. I think it would have been much worse if we had waited any longer. Social change is a painful thing, but it depends on the people at the top. Here they were totally opposed—the state against the Federal Government. There was bound to be trouble, and there was trouble.

Monday morning at eight o'clock I registered, and at nine I went to a class in Colonial American History. I was a few minutes late, and I took a seat at the back of the room. The professor was lecturing on the background in England, conditions there at the time of the colonization of America, and he paid no special attention when I entered. I think there were about a dozen students in the class. One said hello to me, and the others were silent. I remember a girl—the only girl there, I think—and she was crying, but it might have been from the tear gas in the room. I was crying from it myself.

I had three classes scheduled that day. I went to two, and the third didn't meet because there was too much gas in the room. No marshals were in the classrooms with me, nor were they all week.

I have received hundreds of telegrams and more than 1,000 letters, most of them expressions of support. One guy sent me a piece of singed rope, and another sent a poem, I guess you'd have to call it:

Roses are red, violets are blue;
I've killed one nigger and might as well make
     it two.

But most of the letters and telegrams have supported me, and some of them have been really touching—letters from 10- and 11-year-olds who think I'm right and offer me their help and that sort of thing.

As far as my relations with the students go, I make it a practice to be courteous. I don't force myself on them, but that's not my nature anyway. Many of them—most, I'd say—have been courteous, and the faculty members certainly have been. When I hear the jeers and the catcalls—"We'll get you nigger" and all that—I don't consider it personal. I get the idea people are just having a little fun. I think it's tragic that they have to have this kind of fun about me, but many of them are children of the men who lead Mississippi today, and I wouldn't expect them to act any other way. They have to act the way they do. I think I understand human nature enough to understand that.

It hasn't been all bad. Many students have spoken to me very pleasantly. They have stopped banging doors and throwing bottles into my dormitory now.

One day a fellow from my home town sat down at my table in the cafeteria. "If you're here to get an education, I'm for you," he said. "If you're here to cause trouble, I'm against you." That seemed fair enough to me.

*   *   *

I am taking five courses—Colonial American History; a political science course called American Political Parties, Theories and Pressure Groups; French literature; English literature; and algebra. I expect to be able to get my B.A. in history, with a minor in political science, in two semesters and one summer, if everything goes right.

I'm not sure what I will do in the future. A lot depends on how things go at the university. We are just at the beginning of a process of change in Mississippi. I would like to help that process along, and that probably would mean some kind of job in public life. Whether this will be possible in Mississippi or not we'll just have to wait to see. I do know this: If I can't live in Mississippi, I very definitely will leave the country.

If the decision is made to keep the marshals and troops on the campus until I complete my course, it is all right with me, but certainly I hope that won't be necessary. I think the marshals have been superb. They have had an image of America—that the law must be obeyed, no matter what they may think of it or what anybody else may think of it—but they are certainly a distraction on the campus. The thing that grieves me most about all this is that the students are not getting the best college results because they're spending too much time looking on at these various events involving me. I didn't get much studying done that first week, and I don't think anybody else did.

Personally the year will be a hardship for me. My wife will be in college in Jackson. Our son John Howard, who will be three in January, is living with my parents in Kosciusko. I expect to see them both very often, but I don't think families should live apart. On the other hand, this is nothing new to my wife. We spent most of our courtship discussing my plan to come back to Mississippi some day, and I guess you could say her understanding that I would try to do this sometime was almost part of the marriage contract. She has been truly marvelous through all of it. I called her three nights after the trouble, and she picked up the phone and was so calm you'd have thought we just finished a game of 500 rummy and she won. She's a remarkable woman.

I don't think this has had any effect on my family in Kosciusko. I have talked to my father. He asks me how I am, and I ask him how he is. He knows what I mean by the question, and I know what he means by the answer. That's the way it is in our family.

I don't pretend that all the problems are over. But, whatever the problems are, I don't expect them to be too much for me. Nobody really knows where his breaking point is, and I can't say I know where mine is. But I know one thing—in the past the Negro has not been allowed to receive the education he needs. If this is the way it must be accomplished, and I believe it is, then it is not too high a price to pay.

A VIEW OF SEGREGATION IN THE NORTH (1964) From Peggy Streit, "Why They Fight for P.A.T.," *The New York Times Magazine*, September 20, 1964, pp. 20–21, 122–23.

"The way I see it, it's like this," said the taxi driver. "If I had kids of school age I'd join P.A.T. [Parents and Taxpayers]. And I'd keep the kids out of school just as long as we white people didn't get our rights. Now don't get me wrong. I ain't got nothing against colored people. If they want good schools, they ought to have good schools. But they ought to go to schools in *their* neighborhood—just like white kids ought to go to school in *their* neighborhood."

The taxi stopped at a red light. The traffic on Van Wyck Boulevard rumbled by the drab, squat commercial buildings—a bar, a hardware store, a beauty parlor, a real-estate office advertising a six-room two-story, one-family house for $15,000.

"You know Queens?" he asked. "South Richmond Hill? South Ozone Park? NO? I was born and raised here," he said proudly. "Just like my folks. There's a lot of second- and third-generation families out here. It's a real neighborly place—not like New York City where nobody cares who lives next door and nobody owns their own home."

Leaving behind the pounding commercial traffic, the taxi turned off abruptly into a more tranquil world of narrow residential streets lined by modest homes— house after identical house, like rows of ditto marks. But they shared the sedate dignity of a clean, orderly neighborhood, their aging, ungracious architecture softened by the sycamore trees.

"Like I was saying," continued the taxi driver, "you buy a house because you want your kid to go to a school nearby and the church is just around the corner. And then, here comes the government or school board and what do they say? They say, 'Mister, you can't send your kid to school near you. You got to bus him to school in a Negro neighborhood, 20 blocks away, that's been—what do they call it— *paired* with a white school because of racial imbalance.' Now I ask you, is that right? And I say to you, no—that ain't right. We're losing our freedoms in this country. Next thing you know, they'll be telling you where to go to church."

The taxi slowed to a halt outside the home of P.A.T. official June Reynolds. "I'm sure glad I'm not that school-board guy, Gross," he chuckled, with wry satisfaction. "You know how women's voices go up when they get mad? Tell the ladies: 'God bless them.' "

"Now," said Mrs. Reynolds, "what would you like to know about our group?" Her cluttered desk was the only disorder in a living room like countless others in the neighborhood—wall-to-wall carpets, meticulously vacuumed; modern furniture gleaming with polish; earthenware lamps, their orange shades still protected by plastic wrappers; a large-screen television set; reproductions of oriental art on the walls . . . a picture of modest but proud possession.

Size? "There are about 2,700 of us," she replied, "with 300 hard-core members doing most of the work—the executive board, the telephone girls who call about P.A.T. meetings and poll members, and the block captains who ring doorbells for new members."

Membership? "Mostly parents with elementary-school kids, of course, but some people without children. This is a moral issue, too, not just an educational one."

Purpose? "To protect our children, preserve our neighborhood-school system, and keep our children from being bused into strange districts."

Activities? "Well, we organize protests against pairing and busing, and we've been urging members to write to their newspapers and councilmen. Things like that."

The racial issue? She paused irresolutely. "The racial issue doesn't have anything to do with what we want," she said. "We believe in open enrollment. If Negroes want to go to white schools where there's room, they should be allowed to. And we believe in the improvement of Negro schools. It's not true what people say—that we don't like Negroes and we don't want them in our schools. If they live in our neighborhood they have a right here. But nobody has a right to send our children *away* from our neighborhood."

The telephone jangled again and she turned her young, earnest face back to business. "Membership meeting this evening," she said to the caller with urgency. "Try to make it. This is a battle we're fighting, and without your support we'll lose it. Yes, everybody will be there."

That night, everybody included a trim, distinguished-looking man graying at the temples, who stated the central position of the group, again claiming that the P.A.T. stand has nothing to do with race.

"I'm sick of hearing us all called bigots," he said with exasperation. "What we want is the best possible deal for our children. My wife and I bought a house where we did because we like the neighborhood and the schools close by. Now we think our kids may be offered second best and we'd be rotten parents if we didn't oppose that. Why do people think that all opposition to pairing has to be equated with bigotry? Please believe me when I tell you that there isn't a person out here who would willingly hurt anyone."

Stanley Smigiel, president of the South Richmond Hill-South Ozone Park P.A.T. and a grease monkey by trade, was also there. A man of hefty body and voice, he was faintly nervous in his new role as civil leader, mopping his streaming brow with a handkerchief.

"When they told me, 'You got to do this and you got to do that,' that's when my dandruff went up," he said. "I lived in South Jamaica in a Negro area for 30 years. I don't have nothing against Negroes, but the only thing I care about is this: I don't want my child traveling no further than he has to school. What if the bus breaks down? What about snowy days? What if he gets sick and it's an emergency and my wife can't get to him? And furthermore, I don't like him going into classes with a lot of slow readers who will pull down his I. Q. I was a dropout in school and I learned my lesson. I don't want nothing going wrong with my son's education."

June Reynolds, a young, fresh-faced, bright-eyed dedicated dynamo, doesn't have anything against Negroes either. "I went to a school with Negroes when I was a girl," she said. "If I were a Negro, how would I see to it that my kids got a better education and a chance in the world?" She answered herself without hesitation. "I wouldn't live in Harlem for anything in the world. I'd scrub floors. I'd take in laundry. I'd get any kind of job to get out of Harlem—and I know I'd succeed because I believe that in the United States anybody can do anything if he tries hard enough.

"Look at my father. Negroes can at least speak English, but when my father came here from Italy he had to learn the language, so he went to night school. Then he got a job as a wrapper in a bakery. He worked there 47 years and was a supervisor when he retired. The way I see it," she added with finality, "if a Negro lives in Harlem, it's because he likes it there and because he doesn't want to work hard enough to get out of that environment."

Hannah Edell, a round, small, blond woman with soft pink cheeks and a troubled voice, was a little less dogmatic.

"Yes, I think the Negro has been discriminated against," she said, "and I think they should be helped along. But I don't think their problem is educational. It's social. I know that some Negroes think, 'Why should I bother to get an education if I can't get a job afterwards?'—and that's what I mean by a social problem. It's up to large corporations to give them jobs."

She acknowledged the obvious question with a long, hard sigh. "Yes, I know," she said. "Why *shouldn't* large corporations give their jobs to the best-educated— and they are usually white."

She paused then reflected sadly: "It's a vicious circle, isn't it? One hardly knows where to begin. But one thing I do know," she went on, gaining assurance. "They shouldn't begin with our children. Integration isn't a problem for children to solve— or their parents. It's up to the politicians, big corporations—other people. And the Board of Education. This problem has existed for a long time. Why didn't the board do something to improve Negro education a long time ago, so things wouldn't have got to this state?''

*   *   *

Liberty Avenue is a crawling, congested business artery of Richmond Hill flanked by two-story buildings and dotted with the red and purple patterns of tomatoes and egg plants on the fruit stands. It has the vibrant air of a not-too-distant Italy or Germany or Ireland or Israel. The elevated trains roar and rattle overhead, quaking the buildings that border on the tracks.

In a two-flight walk up, John and Felicia Petosa live in six cramped but immaculate rooms. There was a miniature organ against one wall of the living room and a television set, to which a small boy was glued, against another. A narrow hall led to small bedrooms miraculously clean despite the gray elevated, an arm's reach beyond the windows.

Felicia Petosa, married to a cook, is a warm, ardent woman. Her breathless commentary on the world and its problems was stalled only occasionally by the need for a fresh breath. She has two children, the eldest of whom spent his first years in a school in East Brooklyn—an area 70 per cent Negro and Puerto Rican.

"Pathetic," began Mrs. Petosa, taking a deep breath. "The school had no hallway. You got to the second classroom by walking through the first, and the third by walking through the first two. P.T.A. meetings were held next to the boiler room. I could never get interested. Fights all day. When the kids finished fighting at school they fought at home. Just on our block there were over 75 kids. The Puerto Rican lady who lived next door had five and 15 people lived in four rooms. We paid our own exterminator bills, but finally the man said he wouldn't do our place no more because it wouldn't do no good unless the whole block got done. We lived upstairs and the landlord lived down and every day he'd complain about the noise my kids made and I'd say to him, 'Excuse me, I'll go put them in a freezer and take them out for supper.'

"Finally, my husband was getting along better in his business and we moved, and the first day my little boy went to school here his conduct so much improved I took his temperature. I don't have anything against Negroes," added Mrs. Petosa, "but I believe in the neighborhood-school system. Why do our children have to be inconvenienced, just to satisfy the Negroes' whims?"

THE (JOHN A.) McCONE REPORT DESCRIBES THE EDUCATION OF MINORITIES IN LOS ANGELES (1965)   From State of California, Governors Commission On the Los Angeles Riots, *Violence In The City—An End or A Beginning?*, Los Angeles, 1965, pp. 49, 53, 56–61.

Education is the keystone of democracy. It provides communication between the diverse elements of our complex society and aids in the elimination of barriers of race and religion. It holds the greatest promise for breaking the cycle of failure which is at the core of the problems of the disadvantaged area. Hope centers on education.

Having recognized this early in our investigation, we launched an in-depth study to determine the quality of education offered in the public schools in the riot area and in other areas of the city. A comparison was made between schools in the riot area (and other disadvantaged areas of the city) and schools in other sections of the city (citywide, and in an advantaged area). Five study areas were selected within the Los Angeles City Unified School District. Four of these are disadvantaged areas: Watts and Avalon (predominantly Negro and within the riot area), and Boyle Heights and East Los Angeles (predominantly Mexican-American and outside the riot area). The other study area included Pacific Palisades, Westwood, and Brentwood, which are, by comparison, advantaged areas. Citywide data were also compiled.

. . . Are the schools discriminating against children in disadvantaged areas? How do educational services in disadvantaged areas compare with the services in schools in other areas? Are there environmental factors outside the schools that are related to low achievement? These are the fundamental questions, and the Commission investigated each.

*   *   *

In summary, it appears that inequalities exist with respect to incidence of double sessions, cafeterias, libraries, and course offerings for academically talented students. These differences can and should be eliminated. However, the Commission does not feel that these inequalities or the differences in teacher experience or status fully explain the lower achievement of students in disadvantaged areas.

Environmental Factors

There is increasing evidence to indicate that children who live in disadvantaged areas begin school with a deficiency in environmental experiences which are essential for learning. Several factors outside the school itself appear to relate to low achievement in school, such as the level of education of adults in disadvantaged area communities, mobility, and disciplinary and law enforcement problems.

The educational level of any community and of parents substantially influences the achievement of children in school. There is a serious educational deficit in the adult population in disadvantaged areas. According to the 1960 census, about two-thirds of the adults in the disadvantaged areas had failed to graduate from high school. In addition, a high percentage (almost 14%) of the adults living in the four study areas were classified as functional illiterates (defined as completing less than five years of school). Adding to the problem of education has been the tremendous immigration of Negroes from the South where educational opportunities are limited.

Rapidly increasing school enrollment and high population mobility also characterize the disadvantaged areas. The lack of stability in these communities is reflected in extremely high student transiency, that can impair both the learning ability of students and the effectiveness of teachers. In addition, many schools in the disadvantaged area are faced with serious disciplinary problems and with disturbing conditions in the neighborhood that can also affect the educational achievement of students. These conditions include loiterers and distracting and unsavory elements near school sites. The personal security of both teachers and students is often threatened. We believe that adequate school personnel should be provided to deal with disciplinary problems in schools and adequate law enforcement personnel should be provided at or near schools where necessary.

Children in disadvantaged areas are often deprived in their pre-school years of the necessary foundations for learning. They have not had the full range of experiences so necessary to the development of language in the pre-school years, and hence they are poorly prepared to learn when they enter school. Their behavior, their vocabulary, their verbal abilities, their experience with ideas, their view of adults, of society, of books, of learning, of schools, and of teachers are such as to have a negative impact on their school experience. Thus, the disadvantaged child enters school with a serious educational handicap, and because he gets a poor start in school, he drops further behind as he continues through the grades. His course toward academic failure is already set before he enters school; it is rooted in his earliest childhood experiences. The Commission concludes that this is the basic reason for low achievement in the disadvantaged areas.

The schools in the disadvantaged areas do not provide a program that meets the unique educational needs of culturally disadvantaged children. Although special remedial programs are offered in an attempt to compensate for deficiencies in learning, the *basic* organization and orientation of schools is the same in advantaged and disadvantaged areas. The same educational program for children of unequal background does not provide an equal opportunity for children to learn.

Overcoming Low Achievement

We propose that the programs for the schools in disadvantaged areas be vastly reorganized and strengthened so as to strike at the heart of low achievement and break the cycle of failure. We advocate a new, massive, expensive, and frankly experimental onslaught on the problem of illiteracy. We propose that it be attacked at the time and place where there is an exciting prospect of success.

The program for education which we recommend is designed to raise the scholastic achievement of the average Negro child up or to perhaps above the present average achievement level in the City. We have no hard evidence to prove conclusively that the program advocated in this report will accomplish this purpose. We emphasize that the proposed program is designed to raise the level of educational achievement of many who are far below average and the success of such an effort must be proven and this proof can come only from the results of the program itself. Nevertheless, we believe the objectives so essential to our society that funds, teachers, specialists and supervision should be provided as proposed.

First, school services in disadvantaged areas must be extended down to the ages of three and four, in order to give these children the background and reinforcements, particularly in language skills, that they have not received in their "informal" education prior to school. These programs for disadvantaged three and four-year-old children must be provided throughout the regular school year and they must be permanently maintained. Classes must be more than child-care or baby-sitting services; they must be carefully programmed to provide the background these children need to develop verbal and language abilities.

Second, class size must be significantly reduced for children now in elementary and junior high schools in disadvantaged areas. In order to maximize opportunity for effective teaching, class size in these schools should be reduced to a maximum of 22; a less drastic reduction from the present average class of 33 would still be expensive but would offer much less promise of success. These programs would have to be continued for a minimum of three years in the junior high schools and six years in the elementary schools.

Third, additional personnel to cope with disturbed and retarded children, and special problems of the disadvantaged child should be made available in these schools. The energies and services of the teacher can be dissipated if she has to work with a myriad of special problems that are much greater in number and extent than they are in the more advantaged areas. To be effective, the teacher in disadvantaged areas needs much more immediately available help with guidance, welfare, health, and social and emotional problems than do teachers in advantaged areas. While all of these services are presently available, the need for such services is far greater in these disadvantaged areas.

A sharp reduction in class size, together with provision for special supporting services and materials, would offer teachers a more professionally rewarding assignment and would be likely to attract dedicated teachers to seek positions in schools in disadvantaged areas. The Commission's study as well as experience elsewhere support this conclusion.

If we can provide the most effective possible learning situation for the student and attract able teachers to teach in these areas, we will have made the most important step toward solving the problem of low educational achievement. It is clear that the proposed programs will be costly, but not as costly, however, as failure, delinquency, loss of productive manpower, and social dependency. Our society cannot afford this great waste of valuable human resources.

It is our belief that raising the level of scholastic achievement will lessen the trend towards de facto segregation in the schools in the areas into which the Negroes are expanding and, indeed, will tend to reduce all de facto segregation. It is our conclusion that the very low level of scholastic achievement we observe in the predominately Negro schools contributes to de facto segregation in the schools. In turn school segregation apparently contributes importantly to all de facto segregation. We reason, therefore, that raising the scholastic achievement might reverse the entire trend of de facto segregation. There is no proof of this and therefore we cannot demonstrate by specific example that success of the school program we propose will have the effect on de facto segregation within the schools or elsewhere we indicate as a possibility.

Accordingly, our major recommendations are:

1. Elementary and junior high schools in the disadvantaged areas which have achievement levels substantially below the city average should be designated as "Emergency Schools." In each of these schools, an "Emergency Literacy Program" should be established consisting of a drastic reduction in class size to a maximum of 22 students and additional supportive personnel to provide special services. It is estimated that this program will cost at least $250 per year per student in addition to present per student costs and exclusive of capital expenditures, and that it must be continued for a minimum of six years for the elementary schools and three years for the junior high schools.

2. A permanent pre-school program should be established throughout the school year to provide education beginning at age three. Efforts should be focused on the development of language skills essential to prepare children to learn to read and write.

THE COLEMAN REPORT (1966) From U.S. Department of Health, Education, and Welfare, Office of Education, *Equality of Educational Opportunity: Summary Report* (Washington, D.C., 1966), pp. 3, 8–9, 14, 20–22.

Segregation in the Public Schools

The great majority of American children attend schools that are largely segregated—that is, where almost all of their fellow students are of the same racial background as they are. Among minority groups, Negroes are by far the most segregated. Taking all groups, however, white children are most segregated. Almost 80 percent of all white pupils in 1st grade and 12th grade attend schools that are from 90 percent to 100 percent white. And 97 percent at grade 1, and 99 percent at grade 12, attend schools that are 50 percent or more white.

For Negro pupils, segregation is more nearly complete in the South (as it is for whites also), but it is extensive also in all the other regions where the Negro population is concentrated: the urban North, Midwest, and West.

More than 65 percent of all Negro pupils in the 1st grade attend schools that are between 90 and 100 percent Negro. And 87 percent at grade 1, and 66 percent at grade 12, attend schools that are 50 percent or more Negro. In the South, most students attend schools that are 100 percent white or Negro.

The same pattern of segregation holds, though not quite so strongly, for the teachers of Negro and white students. For the Nation as a whole the average Negro elementary pupil attends a school in which 65 percent of the teachers are Negro; the average white elementary pupil attends a school in which 97 percent of the teachers are white. White teachers are more predominant at the secondary level, where the corresponding figures are 59 and 97 percent. The racial matching of teachers is most pronounced in the South, where by tradition it has been complete. On a nationwide basis, in cases where the races of pupils and teachers are not matched, the trend is all in one direction: white teachers teach Negro children but Negro teachers seldom teach white children; just as, in the schools, integration consists primarily of a minority of Negro pupils in predominantly white schools but almost never of a few whites in largely Negro schools.

In its desegregation decision of 1954, the Supreme Court held that separate schools for Negro and white children are inherently unequal. This survey finds that, when measured by that yardstick, American public education remains largely unequal in most regions of the country, including all those where Negroes form any significant proportion of the population. Obviously, however, that is not the only yardstick. The next section of the summary describes other characteristics by means of which equality of educational opportunity may be appraised.

The Schools and Their Characteristics

The school environment of a child consists of many elements, ranging from the desk he sits at to the child who sits next to him, and including the teacher who stands at the front of his class. A statistical survey can give only fragmentary evidence of this environment.

Great collections of numbers such as are found in these pages—totals and averages and percentages—blur and obscure rather than sharpen and illuminate the range of variation they represent. If one reads, for example, that the average annual income per person in the State of Maryland is $3,000, there is a tendency to picture an average person living in moderate circumstances in a middle-class neighborhood holding an ordinary job. But that number represents at the upper end millionaires, and at the lower end the unemployed, the pensioners, the charwomen. Thus the $3,000 average income should somehow bring to mind the tycoon and the tramp, the showcase and the shack, as well as the average man in the average house.

So, too, in reading these statistics on education, one must picture the child whose school has every conceivable facility that is believed to enhance the educational process, whose teachers may be particularly gifted and well educated, and whose home and total neighborhood are themselves powerful contributors to his education and growth. And one must picture the child in a dismal tenement area who may come hungry to an ancient, dirty building that is badly ventilated, poorly lighted, overcrowded, understaffed, and without sufficient textbooks.

Statistics, too, must deal with one thing at a time, and cumulative effects tend to be lost in them. Having a teacher without a college degree indicates an element of disadvantage, but in the concrete situation, a child may be taught by a teacher who is not only without a degree but who has grown up and received his schooling in the local community, who has never been out of the State, who has a 10th grade vocabulary, and who shares the local community's attitudes.

One must also be aware of the relative importance of a certain kind of thing to a certain kind of person. Just as a loaf of bread means more to a starving man than to a sated one, so one very fine textbook or, better, one very able teacher, may mean far more to a deprived child than to one who already has several of both.

Finally, it should be borne in mind that in cases where Negroes in the South receive unequal treatment, the significance in terms of actual numbers of individuals involved is very great, since 54 percent of the Negro population of schoolgoing age, or approximately 3,200,000 children, live in that region.

* * *

It is thus apparent that the tables must be studied carefully, with special attention paid to the regional breakdowns, which often provide more meaningful information than do the nation-wide averages. Such careful study will reveal that there is not a wholly consistent pattern—that is, minorities are not at a disadvantage in every item listed—but that there are nevertheless some definite and systematic directions of differences. Nationally, Negro pupils have fewer of some of the facilities that seem most related to academic achievement: they have less access to physics, chemistry, and language laboratories; there are fewer books per pupil in their libraries; their textbooks are less often in sufficient supply. To the extent that physical facilities are important to learning, such items appear to be more relevant than some others, such as cafeterias, in which minority groups are at an advantage.

* * *

Just as minority groups tend to have less access to physical facilities that seem to be related to academic achievement, so too they have less access to curricular and extracurricular programs that would seem to have such a relationship.

Secondary school Negro students are less likely to attend schools that are regionally accredited; this is particularly pronounced in the South. Negro and

Puerto Rican pupils have less access to college preparatory curriculums and to accelerated curriculums; Puerto Ricans have less access to vocational curriculums as well. Less intelligence testing is done in the schools attended by Negroes and Puerto Ricans. Finally, white students in general have more access to a more fully developed program of extracurricular activities, in particular those which might be related to academic matters (debate teams, for example, and student newspapers).

Again, regional differences are striking. For example, 100 percent of Negro high school students and 97 percent of whites in the metropolitan Far West attend schools having a remedial reading teacher (this does not mean, of course, that every student uses the services of that teacher, but simply that he has access to them) compared with 46 and 65 percent, respectively, in the metropolitan South—and 4 and 9 percent in the nonmetropolitan Southwest.

*   *   *

STUDENT BODY CHARACTERISTICS

. . . The average white high school student attends a school in which 82 percent of his classmates report that there are encyclopedias in their homes. This does not mean that 82 percent of all white pupils have encyclopedias at home, although obviously that would be approximately true. In short, these tables attempt to describe the characteristics of the student bodies with which the "average" white or minority student goes to school.

Clear differences are found on these items. The average Negro has fewer classmates whose mothers graduated from high school; his classmates more frequently are members of large rather than small families, they are less often enrolled in a college preparatory curriculum, they have taken a smaller number of courses in English, mathematics, foreign language, and science.

On most items, the other minority groups fall between Negroes and whites, but closer to whites, in the extent to which each characteristic is typical of their classmates.

Again, there are substantial variations in the magnitude of the differences, with the difference usually being greater in the Southern States.

Achievement in the Public Schools

The schools bear many responsibilities. Among the most important is the teaching of certain intellectual skills such as reading, writing, calculating, and problem-solving. One way of assessing the educational opportunity offered by the schools is to measure how well they perform this task.

*   *   *

Standard achievement tests are available to measure these skills, and several such tests were administered in this survey to pupils at grades 1, 3, 6, 9, and 12.

These tests do not measure intelligence, nor attitudes, nor qualities of character. Furthermore, they are not, nor are they intended to be, "culture-free." Quite the reverse: they are culture-bound. What they measure are the skills which are among the most important in our society for getting a good job and moving up to a better one, and for full participation in an increasingly technical world. Consequently, a

THE
MINORITIES

3029

pupil's test results at the end of public school provide a good measure of the range of opportunities open to him as he finishes school—a wide range of choice of jobs or colleges if these skills are very high; a very narrow range that includes only the most menial jobs if these skills are very low.

*   *   *

With some exceptions—notably Oriental Americans—the average minority pupil scores distinctly lower on these tests at every level than the average white pupil. The minority pupils' scores are as much as one standard deviation below the majority pupils' scores in the first grade. At the 12th grade, results of tests in the same verbal and nonverbal skills show that, in every case, the minority scores are *farther below* the majority than are the 1st graders. For some groups, the relative decline is negligible; for others, it is large.

Furthermore, a constant difference in standard deviations over the various grades represents an increasing difference in grade level gap. For example, Negroes in the metropolitan Northeast are about 1.1 standard deviations below whites in the same region at grades 6, 9, and 12. But at grade 6 this represents 1.6 years behind, at grade 9, 2.4 years, and at grade 12, 3.3 years. Thus, by this measure, the deficiency in achievement is progressively greater for the minority pupils at progressively higher grade levels.

For most minority groups, then, and most particularly the Negro, schools provide no opportunity at all for them to overcome this initial deficiency; in fact, they fall farther behind the white majority in the development of several skills which are critical to making a living and participating fully in modern society. Whatever may be the combination of nonschool factors—poverty, community attitudes, low educational level of parents—which put minority children at a disadvantage in verbal and nonverbal skills when they enter the first grade, the fact is the schools have not overcome it.

Some points should be borne in mind in reading the table. First, the differences shown should not obscure the fact that some minority children perform better than many white children. A difference of one standard deviation in median scores means that about 84 percent of the children in the lower group are below the median of the majority students—but 50 percent of the white children are themselves below that median as well.

A second point of qualification concerns regional differences. By grade 12, both white and Negro students in the South score below their counterparts—white and Negro—in the North. In addition, Southern Negroes score farther below Southern whites than Northern Negroes score below Northern whites. The consequences of this pattern can be illustrated by the fact that the 12th grade Negro in the nonmetropolitan South is 0.8 standard deviation below—or in terms of years, 1.9 years behind—the Negro in the metropolitan Northeast, though at grade 1 there is no such regional difference.

Finally, the test scores at grade 12 obviously do not take account of those pupils who have left school before reaching the senior year. In the metropolitan North and West, 20 percent of the Negroes of ages 16 and 17 are not enrolled in school, a higher dropout percentage than in either the metropolitan or nonmetropolitan South. If it is the case that some or many of the Northern dropouts performed poorly when they were in school, the Negro achievement in the North may be artificially elevated because some of those who achieved more poorly have left school.

Relation of Achievement to School Characteristics

If 100 students within a school take a certain test, there is likely to be great variation in their scores. One student may score 97 percent, another 13; several may score 78 percent. This represents variability in achievement *within* the particular school.

It is possible, however, to compute the average of the scores made by the students within that school and to compare it with the average score, or achievement, of pupils within another school, or many other schools. These comparisons then represent variations *between schools.*

When one sees that the average score on a verbal achievement test in School X is 55 and in School Y is 72, the natural question to ask is: What accounts for the difference?

There are many factors that in combination account for the difference. This analysis concentrates on one cluster of those factors. It attempts to describe what relationship the school's characteristics themselves (libraries, for example, and teachers and laboratories and so on) seem to have to the achievement of majority and minority groups (separately for each group on a nationwide basis, and also for Negro and white pupils in the North and South).

The first finding is that the schools are remarkably similar in the effect they have on the achievement of their pupils when the socioeconomic background of the students is taken into account. It is known that socioeconomic factors bear a strong relation to academic achievement. When these factors are statistically controlled, however, it appears that differences between schools account for only a small fraction of differences in pupil achievement.

The schools *do* differ, however, in the degree of impact they have on the various racial and ethnic groups. The average white student's achievement is less affected by the strength or weakness of his school's facilities, curricula, and teachers than is the average minority pupil's. To put it another way, the achievement of minority pupils depends more on the schools they attend than does the achievement of majority pupils. Thus, 20 percent of the achievement of Negroes in the South is associated with the particular schools they go to, whereas only 10 percent of the achievement of whites in the South is. Except for Oriental Americans, this general result is found for all minorities.

The conclusion can then be drawn that improving the school of a minority pupil will increase his achievement more than will improving the school of a white child increase his. Similarly, the average minority pupil's achievement will suffer more in a school of low quality than will the average white pupil's. In short, whites, and to a lesser extent Oriental Americans, are less affected one way or the other by the quality of their schools than are minority pupils. This indicates that it is for the most disadvantaged children that improvements in school quality will make the most difference in achievement.

All of these results suggest the next question: What are the school characteristics that account for most variation in achievement? In other words, what factors in the school are most important in affecting achievement?

It appears that variations in the facilities and curriculums of the schools account for relatively little variation in pupil achievement insofar as this is measured by standard tests. Again, it is for majority whites that the variations make the least difference; for minorities, they make somewhat more difference. Among the facilities that show some relationship to achievement are several for which minority pupils' schools are less well equipped relative to whites. For example, the existence of science laboratories showed a small but consistent relationship to achievement, and table 2 shows that minorities, especially Negroes, are in schools with fewer of these laboratories.

The quality of teachers shows a stronger relationship to pupil achievement. Furthermore, it is progressively greater at higher grades, indicating a cumulative impact of the qualities of teachers in a school on the pupils' achievement. Again, teacher quality is more important for minority pupil achievement than for that of the majority.

It should be noted that many characteristics of teachers were not measured in this survey; therefore, the results are not at all conclusive regarding the specific characteristics of teachers that are most important. Among those measured in the survey, however, those that bear the highest relationship to pupil achievement are first, the teacher's score on the verbal skills test, and then his educational background—both his own level of education and that of his parents. On both of these measures, the level of teachers of minority students, especially Negroes, is lower.

Finally, it appears that a pupil's achievement is strongly related to the educational backgrounds and aspirations of the other students in the school. Only crude measures of these variables were used (principally the proportion of pupils with encyclopedias in the home and the proportion planning to go to college). Analysis indicates, however, that children from a given family background, when put in schools of different social composition, will achieve at quite different levels. This effect is again less for white pupils than for any minority group other than Orientals. Thus, if a white pupil from a home that is strongly and effectively supportive of education is put in a school where most pupils do not come from such homes, his achievement will be little different than if he were in a school composed of others like himself. But if a minority pupil from a home without much educational strength is put with schoolmates with strong educational backgrounds, his achievement is likely to increase.

This general result, taken together with the earlier examinations of school differences, has important implications for equality of educational opportunity. For the earlier tables show that the principal way in which the school environments of Negroes and whites differ is in the composition of their student bodies, and it turns out that the composition of the student bodies has a strong relationship to the achievement of Negro and other minority pupils.

This analysis has concentrated on the educational opportunities offered by the schools in terms of their student body composition, facilities, curriculums, and teachers. This emphasis, while entirely appropriate as a response to the legislation calling for the survey, nevertheless neglects important factors in the variability between individual pupils within the same school; this variability is roughly four times as large as the variability between schools. For example, a pupil attitude factor, which appears to have a stronger relationship to achievement than do all the "school" factors together, is the extent to which an individual feels that he has some control over his own destiny. Data on items related to this attitude are shown in table 10 along with data on other attitudes and aspirations. The responses of pupils to questions in the survey show that minority pupils, except for Orientals, have far less conviction than whites that they can affect their own environments and futures. When they do, however, their achievement is higher than that of whites who lack that conviction.

Furthermore, while this characteristic shows little relationship to most school factors, it is related, for Negroes, to the proportion of whites in the schools. Those Negroes in schools with a higher proportion of whites have a greater sense of control. Thus such attitudes, which are largely a consequence of a person's experience in the larger society, are not independent of his experience in school.

RACIAL ISOLATION IN THE PUBLIC SCHOOLS (1967)   From *Racial Isolation in the Public Schools: Summary of a Report by the U.S. Commission on Civil Rights*, CCR Clearinghouse Publication No. 7 (Washington, D.C., 1967), pp. 1–5, 11, 16–19.

Introduction

In November 1965, President Johnson asked the U.S. Commission on Civil Rights to "turn its careful attention to the problems of race and education in all parts of the country . . . [and] . . . to develop a firm foundation of facts on which local and State Governments can build a school system that is color-blind."

In asking the Commission to "gather the facts" regarding racial isolation in the schools and "make them available to the Nation as rapidly as possible," President Johnson said:

> Although we have made substantial progress in ending formal segregation of the schools, racial isolation in the schools persists—both in the North and the South—because of housing patterns, school districting, economic stratification and population movements. It has become apparent that such isolation presents serious barriers to quality education. The problems are more subtle and complex than those presented by segregation imposed by law. The remedies may be difficult. But as a first and vital step, the Nation needs to know the facts.

The Commission's study sought to:
   Determine the extent of racial isolation in the public schools;
   Identify the factors that cause and perpetuate the separation of Negroes and whites in the schools;
   Examine the impact of racial isolation upon the educational, economic, and social achievement of Negroes and determine the effects of such isolation upon whites and Negroes;
   Assess the effectiveness of programs designed to eliminate racial isolation in the schools and remedy existing educational disparities.

The Commission's report drew upon existing knowledge, extensive staff investigations, public hearings, and new research performed by contractors and consultants. In the hearings and special conferences, the Commission heard the views of school administrators, teachers, parents, and school children. The Commission also had the advice and assistance of an Advisory Committee of educators, economists, social scientists, and lawyers.

THE
MINORITIES

3033

Four major findings of fact emerge from the report:

Racial isolation in the public schools, whatever its origin, inflicts harm upon Negro students.

Racial isolation in the public schools is intense and is growing worse.

Compensatory efforts to improve education for children within racially and socially isolated schools have not been markedly successful.

School desegregation remedies have been devised which will improve the quality of education for all children.

*　　*　　*

Racial isolation in city schools is caused by many factors. Isolation is rooted in racial discrimination that has been sanctioned and even encouraged by government at all levels. It is perpetuated by the effects of past segregation; reinforced by demographic, fiscal, and educational changes taking place in urban areas; and it is compounded by the policies and practices of urban school systems.

The racial contrasts between city and suburb are paralleled by contrasts in economic and social status. Suburban school districts are acquiring increasing numbers of children from well-educated and relatively affluent families. Almost all of them are white. Children—many of them Negro—from families of relatively low income and educational attainment are left behind in the city.

Housing

The discriminatory practices of the housing industry have been key factors in confining the poor and nonwhite to the cities. The practices and policies of government at all levels have contributed to the separation of racial and economic groups in cities and suburbs. For years, the Federal Government's housing policy was openly discriminatory and largely attuned to the suburban housing needs of relatively affluent, white Americans. Even now, Federal housing policy is inadequate to reverse the trend toward racial isolation in metropolitan areas.

The authority of local governments to decide on building permits, inspection standards, and the location of sewer and water facilities has been used in some instances to discourage private builders from providing housing on a nondiscriminatory basis. The power of eminent domain and suburban zoning and land-use requirements have been devices used to keep Negroes from settling in all-white communities.

Racial zoning ordinances, although declared unconstitutional in 1917, were enforced in some communities as late as the 1950s. Although racially restrictive covenants have not been judicially enforceable since 1948, they still are used, and the housing patterns they helped create continue to exist.

Fiscal Disparities

Increasing disparities in wealth have reinforced the separation between city and suburban populations. Because education is supported primarily by local property taxes, the adequacy of educational services has depended upon the ability of individual communities to raise tax money for education.

Cities are facing increasing financial burdens and demands for social services. Cities which formerly surpassed suburbs in educational expenditures are losing fiscal capacity. Suburban communities surrounding many central cities are spending more per pupil than the core cities. This widening gap between educational services in the suburbs and cities helps induce middle-class white families to settle in the suburbs.

State education aid often fails to equalize the disparity between suburban and central city public schools, and recently enacted Federal aid programs also are often insufficient to reverse the trend. The Elementary and Secondary Education Act of 1965 has helped close the gap but has not eliminated it.

Racial Isolation in Central City Schools

Because of the high degree of residential segregation, Negro and white children typically attend separate schools in the central cities.

Residential segregation in the central cities has resulted in part from past actions of State and local governments such as the enactment of racial zoning ordinances and the judicial enforcement of racially restrictive covenants and from past and present practices of the housing industry. Federal housing programs aimed at meeting the needs of lower income families have been confined to central cities and typically have intensified and perpetuated residential segregation.

Private and parochial school enrollments are an additional factor in the increasing racial isolation in city school systems. Far more children in the cities than in the suburbs attend private schools, and almost all of them are white. This situation intensifies the concentration of Negro children in city public schools.

Educational Policies and Practices

Although school segregation was sanctioned by law and official policy in Southern cities until 1954, there is a legacy of governmentally sanctioned school segregation in the North as well. State statutes authorizing racially separate public schools were on the books in New York until 1938, in Indiana until 1949, and in New Mexico and Wyoming until 1954. Although not sanctioned by law in other States, separate schools were maintained for Negroes in some communities in New Jersey, Illinois, and Ohio, as late as the 1940s and 1950s. In some cities such as New Rochelle, N.Y., and Hillsboro, Ohio, the courts found that school district lines have been gerrymandered for the purpose of racial segregation.

Geographical zoning is the common method of determining school attendance and the neighborhood school is the predominant attendance unit. When these are imposed upon the existing pattern of residential segregation, racial isolation in the schools is the inevitable result. In addition, the day-to-day operating decisions and the policies of local school boards—in matters involving the location of new school facilities, transfer policies, methods of relieving overcrowded schools, and the determination of the boundary lines of attendance areas—often have reinforced racial separation. In many instances there were alternatives that would have reduced racial concentrations.

Results of Racially Isolated Education

The results of education for all students are influenced by a number of factors, including the students' home backgrounds, the quality of education provided in the schools they attend, and the social class background of their classmates. For Negro students, the racial composition of the schools also is important. Racially isolated schools tend to lower Negro students' achievement and restrict their aspirations. By contrast, Negro children who attend predominantly white schools more often score higher on achievement tests, and develop higher aspirations.

The educational and economic circumstances of a child's family long have been recognized as factors which determine the benefits he derives from his education. Differences in children's social and economic backgrounds are strongly related to their achievement in school. The elementary student from a disadvantaged home typically has a lower verbal achievement level than that of a more advantaged student.

The social class level of a student's classmates is another factor that determines the benefits he derives from education. From the early grades through high school, a student is directly influenced by his schoolmates. A disadvantaged student in school with a majority of more advantaged students performs at a higher level than a disadvantaged student in school with a majority of disadvantaged students.

This has a special significance for Negro students. Since there are fewer middle-class Negroes, any remedy for social class isolation would entail substantial racial desegregation.

There also is a strong relationship between the attitudes and achievement of Negro students and the racial composition of the schools which they attend. Relatively disadvantaged Negro students perform better when they are in class with a majority of similarly disadvantaged white students than when they are in a class with a majority of equally disadvantaged Negroes. When more advantaged Negro students are in school with similarly advantaged whites they achieve better than those in school with similarly advantaged Negroes. When disadvantaged Negro students are in class with more advantaged whites, their average performance is improved by as much as two grade levels.

There are differences in the quality of education available to Negro and white students in the Nation's metropolitan areas. For example, schools attended by white children often have more library volumes per student, advanced courses, and fewer pupils per teacher than schools attended by Negro children.

Negro students are more likely than whites to have teachers with lower verbal achievement levels, to have substitute teachers, and to have teachers who are dissatisfied with their school assignment. Do these differences in school qualities account for the apparent effect of racial isolation?

The quality of teaching has an important influence on students' achievement. Yet, Negro students in majority-white schools with poorer teachers generally achieve better than similar Negro students in majority-Negro schools with better teachers.

Racially isolated schools are regarded by the community as inferior institutions. Teachers and students in racially isolated schools recognize the stigma of inferiority which is attached to their schools and this has a negative effect on their attitudes and achievement.

The time spent in a given kind of classroom setting has an impact on student attitudes and achievement. The longer Negro students are in racially isolated schools, the greater the negative impact. The longer Negro students are in desegregated schools, the higher their performance.

The cumulative effects of education extend to adult life and account in part for differences in income and occupation. Negro adults who attended desegregated schools are more likely to be holding white collar jobs and to be earning more than otherwise similarly situated Negroes who attended racially isolated schools.

Racial isolation in the schools also fosters attitudes and behavior that perpetuate isolation in other areas of American life. Negro adults who attended racially isolated schools are more likely to develop attitudes that further alienate them from whites. Negro adults who attended racially isolated schools are more likely to have lower self-esteem and to accept the assignment of inferior status.

Attendance by whites at racially isolated schools also tends to reinforce the very attitudes that assign inferior status to Negroes. White adults who attended all-white schools are more apt than other whites to regard Negro institutions as inferior and to resist measures designed to overcome discrimination against Negroes.

Remedy

There is no general agreement among educators and concerned citizens on the best way to remedy the academic disadvantage of Negro school-children. School systems generally have taken one of two basic approaches: the institution of compensatory education programs in majority-Negro schools, or school desegregation. There has been controversy and disagreement over both approaches.

Conclusion

The central truth which emerges from this report and from all of the Commission's investigations is simply this: Negro children suffer serious harm when their education takes place in public schools which are racially segregated, whatever the source of such segregation may be.

Negro children who attend predominantly Negro schools do not achieve as well as other children, Negro and white. Their aspirations are more restricted than those of other children and they do not have as much confidence that they can influence their own futures. When they become adults, they are less likely to participate in the mainstream of American society, and more likely to fear, dislike, and avoid white Americans. The conclusion drawn by the U.S. Supreme Court about the impact upon children of segregation compelled by law—that it "affects their hearts and minds in ways unlikely ever to be undone"—applies to segregation not compelled by law.

The major source of harm which racial isolation inflicts upon Negro children is not difficult to discover. It lies in the attitudes which such segregation generates in children and the effect these attitudes have upon motivation to learn and achievement. Negro children believe that their schools are stigmatized and regarded as inferior by the community as a whole. Their belief is shared by their parents and by their teachers. And their belief is founded in fact.

Isolation of Negroes in the schools has a significance different from the meaning that religious or ethnic separation may have had for other minority groups because the history of Negroes in the United States has been different from the history of all other minority groups. Negroes in this country were first enslaved, later segregated by law, and now are segregated and discriminated against by a combination of governmental and private action. They do not reside today in ghettos as the result of an exercise of free choice and the attendance of their children in racially isolated schools is not an accident of fate wholly unconnected with deliberate segregation and other forms of discrimination. In the light of this history, the feelings of stigma generated in Negro children by attendance at racially isolated schools are realistic and cannot easily be overcome.

Recommendations

This report describes conditions that result in injustices to children and require immediate attention and action. The responsibility for corrective action rests with government at all levels and with citizens and organizations throughout the Nation. We must commit ourselves as a Nation to the establishment of equal educational opportunity of high quality for all children. As an important means of fulfilling this national goal, the Commission recommends that the President and the Congress give immediate and urgent consideration to new legislation for the purpose of removing present racial imbalances from our public schools, thus to eliminate the dire effects of racial isolation which this report describes, and at long last, providing real equality of educational opportunity by integrating presently deprived American children of all races into a totally improved public educational system.

Without attempting to outline needed legislation in great detail, our study of the problem convinces the Commission that new legislation must embody the following essential principles:

1. Congress should establish a uniform standard providing for the elimination of racial isolation in the schools.

Since large numbers of Negro children suffer harmful effects that are attributable in part to the racial composition of schools they attend, legislation should provide for the elimination of schools in which such harm generally occurs. No standard of general applicability will fit every case precisely; some schools with a large proportion of Negro students may not in fact produce harmful effects while others with a smaller proportion may be schools in which students are disadvantaged because of their race. But the alternative to establishing such a standard is to require a time-consuming and ineffective effort to determine on a case-by-case basis the schools in which harm occurs. As it has in analogous situations, Congress should deal with this problem by establishing reasonable and practical standards which will correct the injustice without intruding unnecessarily into areas where no corrective action is needed.

In prescribing a reasonable standard, there is much to commend the criterion already adopted by the legislature in Massachusetts and the Commissioner of Education of New York, defining as racially imbalanced, schools in which Negro pupils constitute more than 50 percent of the total enrollment. It was found in the report that when Negro students in schools with more than 50 percent Negro enrollment were compared with similarly situated Negro students in schools with a majority-white enrollment, there were significant differences in attitude and performance. It is the schools that have a majority-Negro enrollment that tend to be regarded and treated by the community as segregated and inferior schools. Although there are many factors involved, the racial composition of schools that are majority-Negro in enrollment tends to be less stable than that of majority-white schools and to be subject to more rapid change.

Similar arguments might be advanced for a standard which would deviate slightly from a 50 percent criterion, but a standard set significantly higher would not be adequate to deal with the problem and probably would not result in lasting solutions.

2. Congress should vest in each of the 50 states responsibility for meeting the standard it establishes and should allow the States maximum flexibility in devising appropriate remedies. It also should provide financial and technical assistance to the States in planning such remedies.

It would be unwise for the Federal Government to attempt to prescribe any single solution or set of solutions for the entire Nation. There is a broad range of techniques which are capable of achieving education of high quality in integrated public schools. Each State should be free to adopt solutions best suited to the particular needs of its individual communities.

At the same time it is clear that the responsibility should be placed upon the States rather than the individual school districts. The States, and not individual communities alone, have the capacity to develop and implement plans adequate to the objective. The States have assumed the responsibility for providing public education for all of their citizens and for establishing the basic conditions under which it is offered. Responsibility for achieving the goal of high-quality integrated education can and should be placed upon the States under terms which afford broad scope for local initiative. But in many jurisdictions, particularly the major cities, solutions are not possible without the cooperation of neighboring communities. The States possess the authority and the means for securing cooperation, by consolidating or reorganizing school districts or by providing for appropriate joint arrangements between school districts.

To help the States in devising appropriate remedies, the Federal Government should provide technical and financial assistance.

3. The legislation should include programs of substantial financial assistance to provide for construction of new facilities and improvement in the quality of education in all schools.

In many cases, particularly in the major cities, integrating the public schools will require the construction of new facilities designed both to serve a larger student population and to be accessible to all children in the area to be served. Substantial Federal assistance is needed to supplement the resources of States and localities in building new schools of this kind and providing higher quality education for all children. Federal assistance also can be helpful in encouraging cooperative arrangements between States which provide education services to the same metropolitan area and between separate school districts in a metropolitan area. In addition, Federal financial assistance now available under programs such as said for mass transportation and community facilities should be utilized in ways which will advance the goal of integration.

Regardless of whether the achievement of integration requires new facilities, Federal financial assistance is needed for programs to improve the quality of education. States and localities should have broad discretion to develop programs best suited to their needs. Programs that are among the most promising involve steps—such as the reduction of pupil-teacher ratios, the establishment of upgraded classes and team teaching, and the introduction of specialized remedial instruction—which enable teachers to give more attention to the individual needs of children. Funds also could be used for purposes such as assisting the training of teachers, developing new educational techniques, and improving curriculum.

4. Congress should provide for adequate time in which to accomplish the objectives of the legislation.

It is clear that equal opportunity in education cannot be achieved overnight. Particularly in the large cities where problems of providing equal educational opportunity have seemed so intractable, time will be necessary for such matters as educational and physical planning, assembling and acquiring land, and building new facilities. However, since the problem is urgent a prompt start must be made toward finding solutions, progress must be continuous and substantial, and there must be some assurance that the job will be completed as quickly as possible. The time has come to put less emphasis on "deliberate" and more on "speed."

* * *

The goals of equal educational opportunity and equal housing opportunity are inseparable. Progress toward the achievement of one goal necessarily will facilitate achievement of the other. Failure to make progress toward the achievement of either goal will handicap efforts to achieve the other. The Commission recommends, therefore, that the President and Congress give consideration to legislation which will;

5. Prohibit discrimination in the sale or rental of housing, and

6. Expand programs of Federal assistance designed to increase the supply of housing throughout metropolitan areas within the means of low- and moderate-income families.

Additional funds should be provided for programs such as the rent supplement program and FHA 221(d)(3), and these two programs should be amended to permit private enterprise to participate in them free from the special veto power now held by local governments under present Federal statutes.

In addition, the Commission recommends that the Department of Housing and Urban Development:

7. Require as a condition for approval of applications for low- and moderate-income housing projects that the sites will be selected and the projects planned in a nondiscriminatory manner that will contribute to reducing residential racial concentrations and eliminating racial isolation in the schools.

8. Require as a condition for approval of urban renewal projects that relocation will be planned in a nondiscriminatory manner that will contribute to reducing residential racial concentrations and eliminating racial isolation in the schools.

REPORT ON INNER-CITY SCHOOLS (1968)   From U.S. Riot Commission, *Report of the National Advisory Commission on Civil Disorder* (New York, 1968), pp. 25, 426–36.

Segregation

The vast majority of inner-city schools are rigidly segregated. In 75 major central cities surveyed by the U.S. Commission on Civil Rights in its study, "Racial Isolation in the Public Schools," 75 percent of all Negro students in elementary grades attended schools with enrollments that were 90 percent or more Negro. Almost 90 percent of all Negro students attended schools which had a majority of Negro students. In the same cities, 83 percent of all white students in those grades attended schools with 90 to 100 percent white enrollments.

Racial isolation in the urban public schools is the result principally of residential segregation and widespread employment of the "neighborhood school" policy, which transfers segregation from housing to education. The effect of these conditions is magnified by the fact that a much greater proportion of white than Negro students attend private schools. Studies indicate that in America's twenty largest cities approximately four out of ten white students are enrolled in nonpublic schools, as compared with only one out of ten Negro pupils. The differential appears to be increasing.

Segregation in urban schools is growing. In a sample of 15 large Northern cities, the Civil Rights Commission found that the degree of segregation rose sharply from 1950 to 1965. As Negro enrollments in these 15 cities grew, 97 percent of the increase was absorbed by schools already over 50 percent Negro and 84 percent by schools more than 90 percent Negro. By 1975, it is estimated that, if current policies and trends persist, 80 percent of all Negro pupils in the twenty largest cities, comprising nearly one-half of the nation's Negro population, will be attending 90 to 100 percent Negro schools.

Segregation has several major effects that have acted to reduce the quality of education provided in schools serving disadvantaged Negro neighborhoods.

Most of the residents of these areas are poor. Many of the adults, the product of the inadequate, rural school systems of the South, have low levels of educational attainment. Their children have smaller vocabularies, and are not as well equipped to learn rapidly in school—particularly with respect to basic literary skills—as children from more advantaged homes.

When disadvantaged children are racially isolated in the schools, they are deprived of one of the more significant ingredients of quality education: exposure to other children with strong educational backgrounds. The Coleman Report and the Report of the Civil Rights Commission establish that the predominant socio-economic background of the students in a school exerts a powerful impact upon achievement. Further, the Coleman Report found that "if a minority pupil from a home without much educational strength is put with schoolmates with strong educational backgrounds, his achievement is likely to increase."

Another strong influence on achievement derives from the tendency of school administrators, teachers, parents and the students themselves to regard ghetto schools as inferior. Reflecting this attitude, students attending such schools lose confidence in their ability to shape their future. The Coleman Report found this factor—destiny control—"to have a stronger relationship to achievement than . . . all the [other] 'school' factors together" and to be "related, for Negroes, to the proportion of whites in the schools."

In other words, both class and race factors have a strong bearing on educational achievement; the ghetto student labors under a double burden.

Teachers

The schools attended by disadvantaged Negro children commonly are staffed by teachers with less experience and lower qualifications than those attended by middle-class whites. For example, a 1963 study ranking Chicago's public high schools by the socio-economic status of surrounding neighborhoods found that in the 10 lowest-ranking schools only 63.2 percent of all teachers were fully certified and the median level of teaching experience was 3.9 years. In three of these schools, the median level was one year. Four of these lowest ranking schools were 100 percent Negro in enrollment and three were over 90 percent Negro. By contrast, eight of the ten highest ranking schools had nearly total white enrollments, and the other two were more than 75 percent white. In these schools, 90.3 percent of the teachers were fully certified and the median level of teaching experience was 12.3 years.

Testifying before the Commission, Dr. Paul Daniel Dodson, Director of the New York University Center for Human Relations and Community Services, stated that:

> "Inner-city schools have not been able to hold teaching staff. Between 1952 and 1962 almost half the licensed teachers of New York City left the system. Almost two out of every five of the 50,000 teaching personnel of New York City do not hold regular permanent licenses for the assignments they have.
>
> "In another school system in one of the large cities, it was reported of one inner-city school that of 84 staff members, 41 were temporary teachers, 25 were probationaries and 18 [were] tenure teachers. However, only one of the tenure teachers was licensed in academic subjects."

U.S. Commissioner of Education, Harold Howe, testified that many teachers are unprepared for teaching in schools serving disadvantaged children, "have what is a traumatic experience there and don't last." Moreover, the more experienced teachers normally select the more attractive schools in white neighborhoods, thereby relegating the least experienced teachers to the disadvantaged schools. This process reinforces the view of ghetto schools as inferior.

As a result, teachers assigned to these schools often begin with negative attitudes toward the students, and their ability and willingness to learn. These attitudes are aggravated by serious discipline problems, by the high crime rates in areas surrounding the schools, and by the greater difficulties of teaching students from disadvantaged backgrounds. These conditions are reflected in the Coleman Report's finding that a higher proportion of teachers in schools serving disadvantaged areas are dissatisfied with their present assignments and with their students than are their counterparts in other schools.

Studies have shown that the attitudes of teachers toward their students have very powerful impacts upon educational attainment. The more teachers expect from their students—however disadvantaged those students may be—the better the students perform. Conversely, negative teacher attitudes act as self-fulfilling prophecies: the teachers expect little from their students; the students fulfill the expectation. As Dr. Kenneth Clark observed, "Children who are treated as if they are uneducable invariably become uneducable."

In disadvantaged areas, the neighborhood school concept tends to concentrate a relatively high proportion of emotionally disturbed and other problem children in the schools. Disadvantaged neighborhoods have the greatest need for health personnel, supplementary instructors and counsellors to assist with family problems, provide extra instruction to lagging students and deal with the many serious mental and physical health deficiencies that occur so often in poverty areas.

These conditions, which make effective teaching vastly more difficult, reinforce negative teacher attitudes. A 1963 survey of Chicago public schools showed that the condition creating the highest amount of dissatisfaction among teachers was lack of adequate provision for the treatment of maladjusted, retarded and disturbed pupils. About 79 percent of elementary school teachers and 67 percent of high school teachers named this item as a key factor. The need for professional support for teachers in dealing with these extraordinary problems is seldom, if ever, met.

Although special schools or classes are available for emotionally disturbed and mentally handicapped children, many pupils requiring such help remain in regular classes because of negligence, red tape or unavailability of clinical staff. An example is provided by a National Education Association Study of Detroit:

> Before a disturbed child can receive psychological assistance, he must receive diagnostic testing. But before this happens, the teacher must fill in a form . . . to be submitted . . . to a central office committee. . . . If the committee decides that psychological testing is in order, the teacher must fill out a second form . . . to be submitted to the psychological clinic. The child may then be placed on the waiting list for psychological testing. The waiting period may last for several weeks, several months, or several years. And while he waits, he 'sits in' the regular classroom. . . . Since visiting teachers are scarce and special classes insufficient in number, the child who has been tested is usually returned to the regular classroom to serve more time as a 'sit-in.'

Teaching in disadvantaged areas is made more difficult by the high rate of student turnover. In New York City during 1963–1964, seven of ten students in the average, segregated Negro-Puerto Rican elementary school either entered or left during the year. Similar conditions are common to other inner-city schools. Continuity of education becomes exceedingly difficult—the more so because many of the students entering ghetto schools during the school year come from rural southern schools and are thus behind even the minimum levels of achievement attained by their fellow northern-born students.

Enrollments

In virtually every large American city, the inner city schools attended by Negroes are the most overcrowded. We have cited the vast population exchange—relatively affluent whites leaving the city to be replaced by Negroes—which has taken place over the last decade. The impact on public education facilities has been severe.

Despite an overall decrease in the population of many cities, school enrollment has increased. Over the last 15 years, Detroit has *lost* approximately 20,000 to 30,000 families. Yet during that same period the public school system *gained* approximately 50,000 to 60,000 children. Between 1961 and 1965, Detroit's Negro public school enrollment increased by 31,108, while white enrollment dropped 23,748. In Cleveland between 1950 and 1965, a population loss of 130,000 coincided with a school enrollment increase of 50,000. Enrollment gains in New York City and Chicago were even larger.

Although of lesser magnitude, similar changes have occurred in the public school systems of many other large cities. As white students withdraw from a public school, they are replaced by a greater number of Negro students. This reflects the fact that the Negro population is relatively younger, has more children of school age, makes less use of private schools, and is more densely concentrated than the white population.

As a result, Negro school enrollments have increased even more rapidly than the total Negro population in central cities. In Cincinnati, for example, between 1960 and 1965 the Negro population grew 16 percent, while Negro public school enrollment increased 26 percent. The following data for four other cities illustrate how the proportion of Negroes in public schools has outgrown the Negro proportion of the total city population.

Negro Population and Public School Enrollment

		Negro % of Population			Negro % of Public School Enrollment	
	1950	1965	Change	1950	1965	Change
Atlanta	36.6	43.5	+ 6.9	39.1	53.7	+14.6
Milwaukee	3.5	10.8	+ 7.3	6.6	22.9	+16.3
Oakland	12.4	30.0	+17.6	14.0	45.0	+31.0
Washington	35.0	55.0	+20.0	50.1	89.4	+39.3

Negroes now comprise a majority or near majority of public school students in seven of the ten largest American cities, as well as in many other cities. The following table illustrates the percentage of Negro students for the period 1965–1966 in the public elementary schools of 42 cities, including the 28 largest, 17 of which have Negro majorities:

Proportion of Negro Students in Total Public Elementary School Enrollment, 1965-1966

City	Percent Negro
Washington, D.C.	90.9%
Chester, Pa.	69.3
Wilmington, Del.	69.3
Newark	69.1
New Orleans	65.5
Richmond	64.7
Baltimore	64.3
East St. Louis	63.4
St. Louis	63.3
Gary	59.5
Philadelphia	58.6
Detroit	55.3
Atlanta	54.7
Cleveland	53.9

Memphis	53.2
Chicago	52.8
Oakland	52.1
Harrisburg	45.7
New Haven	45.6
Hartford	43.1
Kansas City	42.4
Cincinnati	40.3
Pittsburgh	39.4
Buffalo	34.6
Houston	33.9
Flint	33.1
Indianapolis	30.8
New York City	30.1
Boston	28.9
San Francisco	28.8
Dallas	27.5
Miami	26.8
Milwaukee	26.5
Columbus	26.1
Los Angeles	23.4
Oklahoma City	21.2
Syracuse	19.0
San Antonio	14.2
Denver	14.0
San Diego	11.6
Seattle	10.5
Minneapolis	7.2

Source: U.S. Commission on Civil Rights,
"Racial Isolation in the Public Schools."

Because this rapid expansion of Negro population has been concentrated in segregated neighborhoods, ghetto schools have experienced acute overcrowding. Shortages of textbooks and supplies have developed. Double shifts are common; hallways and other non-classroom space have been adapted for class instruction; and mobile classroom units are used. Even programs for massive construction of new schools in Negro neighborhoods cannot always keep up with increased overcrowding.

From 1951 to 1963, the Chicago Board of Education built 266 new schools or additions, mainly in all-Negro areas. Yet a special committee studying the schools in 1964 reported that 40 percent of the Negro elementary schools had more than 35 students per available classroom, as compared to 12 percent of the primarily white elementary schools. Of the eight Negro high schools, five had enrollments over 50 percent above designed capacity. Four of the 10 integrated high schools, but only four of the 26 predominantly white high schools, were similarly overcrowded. Comparable conditions prevail in many other large cities.

The Civil Rights Commission found that two-thirds of the predominantly Negro elementary schools in Atlanta were overcrowded. This compared with 47 percent of the white schools. In 1965, all Atlanta Negro high schools were operating beyond their designed capacity; only one of three all-white high schools, and six of eight predominantly white schools were similarly overcrowded.

Washington, D. C. elementary schools with 85–100 percent Negro enrollments operated at a median of 115 percent of capacity. The one predominantly white high school operated at 92.3 percent, an integrated high school at 101.1 percent, and the remaining schools—all predominantly Negro—at 108.4 percent to 127.1 percent of capacity.

Overcrowded and inadequately supplied schools have severe effects upon the quality of education, the most important of which is that teachers are forced to concentrate on maintaining classroom discipline, and thus have little time and energy to perform their primary function—educating the students.

Facilities and Curricula

Inner-city schools are not only overcrowded, they also tend to be the oldest and most poorly equipped.

In Detroit, 30 of the school buildings still in use in these areas were dedicated during the administration of President Grant. In Cincinnati, although from 1950 to 1965 Negro student population expanded at a faster pace than white, most additional school capacity planned and constructed was in predominantly white areas. According to a Civil Rights Commission report on Cincinnati, the added Negro pupil population was housed, for the most part, in the same central-city schools vacated by the whites.

With respect to equipment, the Coleman Report states that "Negro pupils have fewer of some of the facilities that seem most related to achievement: They have less access to physics, chemistry, and language laboratories; there are fewer books per pupil in their libraries; their textbooks are less often in sufficient supply."

The quality of education offered by ghetto schools is diminished further by use of curricula and materials poorly adapted to the life-experiences of their students. Designed to serve a middle-class culture, much educational material appears irrelevant to the youth of the racial and economic ghetto. Until recently, few texts featured any Negro personalities. Few books used or courses offered reflected the harsh realities of life in the ghetto, or the contribution of Negroes to the country's culture and history. This failure to include materials relevant to their own environment has made students skeptical about the utility of what they are being taught. Reduced motivation to learn results.

Funds

Despite the overwhelming need, our society spends less money educating ghetto children than children of suburban families. Comparing the per capita education costs for ghetto schools with suburban, one educator, in testimony before this Commission, said:

If the most educated parents with the highest motivated children find in their wisdom that it costs $1,500 per child per year to educate their children in the suburbs, isn't it logical that it would cost an equal amount to educate the less well motivated, low-income family child in the inner city? Such cost would just about double the budget of the average inner-city school system.

Twenty-five school boards in communities surrounding Detroit spent up to $500 more per pupil per year to educate their children than the city. Merely to bring the teacher/pupil ratio in Detroit in line with the state average would require an additional 16,650 teachers at an annual cost of approximately $130 million.

There is evidence that the disparity in educational expenditures for suburban and inner-city schools has developed in parallel with population shifts. In a study of twelve metropolitan areas, the Civil Rights Commission found that, in 1950, 10 of the 12 central cities spent more per pupil than the surrounding suburbs; by 1964, in seven of the 12 the average suburb spent more per pupil than the central city in seven.

This reversal reflects the declining or stagnant city tax base, and increasing competition from nonschool needs (police, welfare, fire) for a share of the municipal tax dollar. The suburbs, where nonschool needs are less demanding, allocate almost twice the proportion of their total budgets to education as the cities.

State contributions to city school systems have not had consistent equalizing effects. The Civil Rights Commission found that, although state aid to city schools has increased at a rate proportionately greater than for suburban schools, states continue to contribute more per pupil to suburban schools in seven of the twelve metropolitan areas studied. The following table illustrates the findings:

Revenues per Pupil from State sources

Place	Amount Per Pupil		Percent Increase
	1950	1964	1950-64
Baltimore City	$ 71	$171	140.8
Suburbs	90	199	121.1
Birmingham City	90	201	123.3
Suburbs	54	150	177.7
Boston City	19	52	173.7
Suburbs	30	75	150.0
Buffalo City	135	284	110.4
Suburbs	165	270	63.6
Chattanooga City	62	136	119.4
Suburbs	141	152	7.8
Chicago City	42	154	266.6
Suburbs	32	110	243.8
Cincinnati City	51	91	78.4
Suburbs	78	91	16.7
Cleveland City	50	88	76.0
Suburbs	39	88	125.6
Detroit City	135	189	40.0
Suburbs	149	240	61.1
New Orleans City	152	239	57.2
Suburbs	117	259	121.4
St. Louis City	70	131	87.1
Suburbs	61	143	134.4
San Francisco City	122	163	33.6
Suburbs	160	261	63.1

Source: "U.S. Commission on Civil Rights, Racial
Isolation in the Public Schools."

Federal assistance, while focused on the innercity schools, has not been at a scale sufficient to remove the disparity. In the 1965–1966 school year, federal aid accounted for less than 8 percent of total educational expenditures. Our survey of federal programs in Detroit, Newark and New Haven during the school year 1967–1968 found that a median of approximately half the eligible school population is receiving assistance under Title I of the Elementary and Secondary Education Act (ESEA).

Community-School Relations

Teachers of the poor rarely live in the community where they work and sometimes have little sympathy for the life styles of their students. Moreover, the growth and complexity of the administration of large urban school systems has compromised the accountability of the local schools to the communities which they serve, and reduced the ability of parents to influence decisions affecting the education of their children. Ghetto schools often appear to be unresponsive to the community, communication has broken down, and parents are distrustful of officials responsible for formulating educational policy.

The consequences for the education of students attending these schools are serious. Parental hostility to the schools is reflected in the attitudes of their children. Since the needs and concerns of the ghetto community are rarely reflected in educational policy formulated on a citywide basis, the schools are often seen by ghetto youth as being irrelevant.

On the basis of interviews of riot area residents in Detroit, Dr. Charles Smith, of the U.S. Office of Education's comprehensive elementary and secondary education program, testified that "one of the things that came through very clearly to us is the fact that there is an attitude which prevails in the inner city that says in substance we think education is irrelevant."

Dr. Dodson explained this phenomenon as follows:

"This divergence of goals [between the dominant class and ghetto youth] makes schools irrelevant for the youth of the slum. It removes knowledge as a tool for groups who are deviant to the ethos of the dominant society. It tends to destroy the sense of self-worth of minority background children. It breeds apathy, powerlessness and low self-esteem. The majority of ghetto youth would prefer to forego the acquisition of knowledge if it is at that cost. One cannot understand the alienation of modern ghetto youth except in the context of this conflict of goals."

The absence of effective community-school relations has deprived the public education system of the communication required to overcome this divergence of goals. In the schools, as in the larger society, the isolation of ghetto residents from the policy-making institutions of local government is adding to the polarization of the community and depriving the system of its self-rectifying potential.

Ghetto Environment

All of the foregoing factors contribute substantially to the poor performance of ghetto schools. Inadequate and inefficient as these schools are, the failure of the public education system with respect to Negro students cannot fully be appraised apart from the constant and oppressive ghetto environment.

*   *   *

Education in a democratic society must equip children to develop their potential and to participate fully in American life. For the community at large, the schools have discharged this responsibility well. But for many minorities, and particularly for the children of the ghetto, the schools have failed to provide the educational experience which could overcome the effects of discrimination and deprivation.

This failure is one of the persistent sources of grievance and resentment within the Negro community. The hostility of Negro parents and students toward the school system is generating increasing conflict and causing disruption within many city school districts. But the most dramatic evidence of the relationship between educational practices and civil disorders lies in the high incidence of riot participation by ghetto youth who have not completed high school.

The bleak record of public education for ghetto children is growing worse. In the critical skills—verbal and reading ability—Negro students are falling further behind whites with each year of school completed. The high unemployment and underemployment rate for Negro youth is evidence, in part, of the growing educational crisis.

We support integration as the priority education strategy; it is essential to the future of American society. In this last summer's disorders we have seen the consequences of racial isolation at all levels, and of attitudes toward race, on both sides, produced by three centuries of myth, ignorance and bias. It is indispensable that opportunities for interaction between the races be expanded.

We recognize that the growing dominance of pupils from disadvantaged minorities in city school populations will not soon be reversed. No matter how great the effort toward desegregation, many children of the ghetto will not, within their school careers, attend integrated schools.

If existing disadvantages are not to be perpetuated, we must drastically improve the quality of ghetto education. Equality of results with all-white schools must be the goal.

To implement these strategies, the Commission recommends:

● Sharply increased efforts to eliminate de facto segregation in our schools through substantial federal aid to school systems seeking to desegregate either within the system or in cooperation with neighboring school systems.

● Elimination of racial discrimination in Northern as well as Southern schools by vigorous application of Title VI of the Civil Rights Act of 1964.

● Extension of quality early childhood education to every disadvantaged child in the country.

● Efforts to improve dramatically schools serving disadvantaged children through substantial federal funding of year-round compensatory education programs, improved teaching, and expanded experimentation and research.

● Elimination of illiteracy through greater federal support for adult basic education.

● Enlarged opportunities for parent and community participation in the public schools.

- Reoriented vocational education emphasizing work-experience training and the involvement of business and industry.
- Expanded opportunities for higher education through increased federal assistance to disadvantaged students.
- Revision of state aid formulas to assure more per-student aid to districts having a high proportion of disadvantaged school-age children.

The Supreme Court as National School Board—The Religious Issue

---

DECISION ON THE CONSTITUTIONAL RIGHT TO OPERATE A RELIGIOUS SCHOOL (1925) From *Pierce et al.* v. *Society of Sisters*, 268 U.S. 510 (1925).

Appeals from the District Court of the U.S. for the District of Oregon.

MR. JUSTICE McREYNOLDS DELIVERED THE OPINION OF A UNANIMOUS COURT.

✳   ✳   ✳

The challenged Act, effective September 1, 1926, requires every parent, guardian or other person having control or charge or custody of a child between eight and sixteen years to send him to "a public school for the period of time a public school shall be held during the current year" in the district where the child resides; and failure so to do is declared a misdemeanor. There are exemptions—not specially important here—for children who are not normal, or who have completed the eighth grade, or who reside at considerable distances from any public school, or whose parents or guardians hold special permits from the County Superintendent. The manifest purpose is to compel general attendance at public schools by normal children, between eight and sixteen, who have not completed the eighth grade. And without doubt enforcement of the statute would seriously impair, perhaps destroy, the profitable features of appellees' business and greatly diminish the value of their property.

Appellee, the Society of Sisters, is an Oregon corporation, organized in 1880, with power to care for orphans, educate and instruct the youth, establish and maintain academies or schools, and acquire necessary real and personal property. It has long devoted its property and effort to the secular and religious education and care of children, and has acquired the valuable good will of many parents and guardians. It conducts interdependent primary and high schools and junior colleges, and maintains orphanages for the custody and control of children between eight and sixteen. In its primary schools many children between those ages are taught the subjects usually pursued in Oregon public schools during the first eight years. Systematic religious instruction and moral training according to the tenets of the Roman Catholic Church are also regularly provided.

✳   ✳   ✳

No question is raised concerning the power of the State reasonably to regulate all schools, to inspect, supervise and examine them, their teachers and pupils; to require that all children of proper age attend some school, that teachers shall be of good moral character and patriotic disposition, that certain studies plainly essential to good citizenship must be taught, and that nothing be taught which is manifestly inimical to the public welfare.

The inevitable practical result of enforcing the Act under consideration would be destruction of appellees' primary schools, and perhaps all other private primary schools for normal children within the State of Oregon. These parties are engaged in a kind of undertaking not inherently harmful, but long regarded as useful and meritorious. Certainly there is nothing in the present records to indicate that they have failed to discharge their obligations to patrons, students or the State. And there are no peculiar circumstances or present emergencies which demand extraordinary measures relative to primary education.

Under the doctrine of *Meyer* v. *Nebraska*, 262 U.S. 390, we think it entirely plain that the Act of 1922 unreasonably interferes with the liberty of parents and guardians to direct the upbringing and education of children under their control. As often heretofore pointed out, rights guaranteed by the Constitution may not be abridged by legislation which has no reasonable relation to some purpose within the competency of the State. The fundamental theory of liberty upon which all governments in this Union repose excludes any general power of the State to standardize its children by forcing them to accept instruction from public teachers only. The child is not the mere creature of the State; those who nurture him and direct his destiny have the right, coupled with the high duty, to recognize and prepare him for additional obligations.

* * *

The decrees below are *affirmed.*

DECISION ON TEXTBOOKS AND RELIGIOUS SCHOOLS (1930) From
Cochran v. *Louisiana State Board of Education,* 281 U.S. 370 (1930).

The appellants, as citizens and taxpayers of the State of Louisiana, brought this suit to restrain the state board of education and other state officials from expending any part of the severance tax fund in purchasing school books and in supplying them free of cost to the school children of the state, under Acts No. 100 and No. 143 of 1928, upon the ground that the legislation violated specific provisions of the constitution of the state and also Section 4 of Article IV and the Fourteenth Amendment of the Federal Constitution. The supreme court of the state affirmed the judgment of the trial court, which refused to issue an injunction. 168 La. 1030.

Act No. 100 of 1928 provided that the severance tax fund of the state, after allowing funds and appropriations as required by the state constitution, should be devoted "first, to supplying school books to the school children of the state." The board of education was directed to provide school books for school children free of cost to such children." Act No. 143 of 1928 made appropriations in accordance with the above provisions. The supreme court of the state, following its decision in *Borden v. Louisiana State Board of Education*, 168 La. 1005, held that these acts were not repugnant to either the state or the Federal Constitution.

✻　　✻　　✻

The contention of the appellant under the Fourteenth Amendment is that taxation for the purchase of school books constituted a taking of public property for a private purpose. . . . The purpose is said to be to aid private, religious, sectarian, and other schools not embraced in the public educational system of the state by furnishing textbooks free to the children attending such private schools. The operation and effect of the legislation in question were described by the supreme court of the state as follows. . . .

"One may scan the acts in vain to ascertain where any money is appropriated for the purchase of school books for the use of any church, private, sectarian, or even public school. The appropriations were made for the specific purpose of purchasing school books for the use of the school children of the state free of cost to them. It was for their benefit and the resulting benefit to the state that the appropriations were made. True, these children attend some school; public or private, the latter, sectarian or nonsectarian, and that the books are to be furnished them for their use, free of cost, whichever they attend. The schools, however, are not the beneficiaries of these appropriations. They obtain nothing from them, nor are they relieved of a single obligation because of them. The school children and the state alone are the beneficiaries. It is also true that the sectarian schools, which some of the children attend, instruct their pupils in religion, and books are used for that purpose, but one may search diligently the acts, though without result, in an effort to find anything to the effect that it is the purpose of the state to furnish religious books for the use of such children. . . . What the statutes contemplate is that the same books that are furnished children attending public schools shall be furnished children attending private schools. This is the only practical way of interpreting and executing the statutes, and this is what the state board of education is doing. Among these books, naturally, none is to be expected, adapted to religious instruction." The court also stated, although the point is not of importance in relation to the federal question, that it was "only the use of the books that is granted to the children or, in other words, the books are lent to them."

Viewing the statute as having the effect thus attributed to it, we cannot doubt that the taxing power of the state is exerted for a public purpose. The legislation does not segregate private schools, or their pupils, as its beneficiaries or attempt to interfere with any matters of exclusively private concern. Its interest is education, broadly; its method, comprehensive.

DECISION ON MANDATORY SALUTING OF THE FLAG (1940) From
Minersville School District v. *Gobitis,* 310 U.S. 586 (1940).

On Writ of Certiorari to the United States Circuit Court of Appeals for the Third Circuit.

Frankfurter, J. A grave responsibility confronts this Court whenever in course of litigation it must reconcile the conflicting claims of liberty and authority. But when the liberty invoked is liberty of conscience, and the authority is authority to safeguard the nation's fellowship, judicial conscience is put to its severest test. Of such a nature is the present controversy.

Lillian Gobitis, aged twelve, and her brother William, aged ten, were expelled from the public schools of Minersville, Pennsylvania, for refusing to salute the national flag as part of a daily school exercise. The local Board of Education required both teachers and pupils to participate in this ceremony. The ceremony is a familiar one. The right hand is placed on the breast and the following pledge recited in unison: "I pledge allegiance to my flag, and to the Republic for which it stands; one nation indivisible, with liberty and justice for all." While the words are spoken, teachers and pupils extend their right hands in salute to the flag. The Gobitis family are affiliated with "Jehovah's Witnesses," for whom the Bible as the Word of God is the supreme authority. The children had been brought up conscientiously to believe that such a gesture of respect for the flag was forbidden by command of scripture.

The Gobitis children were of an age for which Pennsylvania makes school attendance compulsory. Thus they were denied a free education and their parents had to put them into private schools. To be relieved of the financial burden thereby entailed, their father, on behalf of the children and in his own behalf, brought this suit. He sought to enjoin the authorities from continuing to exact participation in the flag-salute ceremony as a condition of his children's attendance at the Minersville school. After trial of the issues, Judge Maris gave relief in the District Court on the basis of a thoughtful opinion; his decree was affirmed by the Circuit Court of Appeals. Since this decision ran counter to several per curiam dispositions of this Court, we granted certiorari to give the matter full reconsideration. By their able submissions, the Committee on the Bill of Rights of the American Bar Association and the American Civil Liberties Union, as friends of the Court, have helped us to our conclusion.

We must decide whether the requirement of participation in such a ceremony, exacted from a child who refuses upon sincere religious grounds, infringes without due process of law the liberty guaranteed by the Fourteenth Amendment.

Centuries of strife over the erection of particular dogmas as exclusive or all-comprehending faiths led to the inclusion of a guarantee for religious freedom in the Bill of Rights. The First Amendment, and the Fourteenth through its absorption of the First, sought to guard against repetition of those bitter religious struggles by prohibiting the establishment of a state religion and by securing to every sect the free exercise of its faith. So pervasive is the acceptance of this precious right that its scope is brought into question, as here, only when the conscience of individuals collides with the felt necessities of society.

Certainly the affirmative pursuit of one's convictions about the ultimate mystery of the universe and man's relation to it is placed beyond the reach of law.

Government may not interfere with organized or individual expression of belief or disbelief. Propagation of belief—or even of disbelief in the supernatural—is protected, whether in church or chapel, mosque or synagogue, tabernacle or meetinghouse. Likewise the Constitution assures generous immunity to the individual from imposition of penalties for offending, in the course of his own religious activities, the religious views of others, be they a minority or those who are dominant in government.

But the manifold character of man's relations may bring his conception of religious duty into conflict with the secular interests of his fellow-men. When does the constitutional guarantee compel exemption from doing what society thinks necessary for the promotion of some great common end, or from a penalty for conduct which appears dangerous to the general good? To state the problem is to recall the truth that no single principle can answer all of life's complexities. The right to freedom of religious belief, however dissident and however obnoxious to the cherished beliefs of others—even of a majority—is itself the denial of an absolute. But to affirm that the freedom to follow conscience has itself no limits in the life of a society would deny that very plurality of principles which, as a matter of history, underlies protection of religious toleration. Compare Mr. Justice Holmes in Hudson County Water Co. v. McCarter, 209 U.S. 349, 355. Our present task then, as so often the case with courts, is to reconcile two rights in order to prevent either from destroying the other. But, because in safeguarding conscience we are dealing with interests so subtle and so dear, every possible leeway should be given to the claims of religious faith.

In the judicial enforcement of religious freedom we are concerned with a historic concept. See Mr. Justice Cardozo in Hamilton v. Regents, 293 U.S. 245, at page 265. The religious liberty which the Constitution protects has never excluded legislation of general scope not directed against doctrinal loyalties of particular sects. Judicial nullification of legislation cannot be justified by attributing to the framers of the Bill of Rights views for which there is no historic warrant. Conscientious scruples have not, in the course of the long struggle for religious toleration, relieved the individual from obedience to a general law not aimed at the promotion or restriction of religious beliefs. The mere possession of religious convictions which contradict the relevant concerns of a political society does not relieve the citizen from the discharge of political responsbilities. The necessity for this adjustment has again and again been recognized. In a number of situations the exertion of political authority has been sustained, while basic considerations of religious freedom have been left inviolate. Reynolds v. United States, 98 U.S. 145; Davis v. Beason, 133 U.S. 333; Selective Draft Law Cases, 245 U.S. 366; Hamilton v. Regents, 293 U.S. 245. In all these cases the general laws in question, upheld in their application to those who refused obedience from religious conviction, were manifestations of specific powers of government deemed by the legislature essential to secure and maintain that orderly, tranquil, and free society without which religious toleration itself is unattainable. Nor does the freedom of speech assured by Due Process move in a more absolute circle of immunity than that enjoyed by religious freedom. Even if it were assumed that freedom of speech goes beyond the historic concept of full opportunity to utter and to disseminate views, however heretical or offensive to dominant opinion, and includes freedom from conveying what may be deemed an implied but rejected affirmation, the question remains whether school children, like the Gobitis children, must be excused from conduct required of all the other children in the promotion of national cohesion. We are dealing with an interest inferior to none in the hierarchy of legal values. National unity is the basis of national security. To deny the legislature the right to select appropriate means for its attainment presents a totally different order of problem from that of the propriety of subordinating the possible ugliness of littered streets to the free expression of opinion through distribution of handbills. Compare Schneider v. State of New Jersey, 308 U.S. 147.

Situations like the present are phases of the profoundest problem confronting a democracy—the problem which Lincoln cast in memorable dilemma: "Must a government of necessity be too strong for the liberties of its people, or too weak to maintain its own existence?" No mere textual reading or logical talisman can solve the dilemma. And when the issue demands judicial determination, it is not the personal notion of judges of what wise adjustment requires which must prevail.

Unlike the instances we have cited, the case before us is not concerned with an exertion of legislative power for the promotion of some specific need or interest of secular society—the protection of the family, the promotion of the family, the promotion of health, the common defense, the raising of public revenues to defray the cost of government. But all these specific activities of government presuppose the existence of an organized political society. The ultimate foundation of a free society is the binding tie of cohesive sentiment. Such a sentiment is fostered by all those agencies of the mind and spirit which may serve to gather up the traditions of a people, transmit them from generation to generation, and thereby create that continuity of a treasured common life which constitutes a civilization. "We live by symbols." The flag is a symbol of our national unity, transcending all internal differences, however large, within the framework of the Constitution. This Court has had occasion to say that ". . . the flag is the symbol of the nation's power,—the emblem of freedom in its truest, best sense. . . . it signifies government resting on the consent of the governed; liberty regulated by law; the protection of the weak against the strong; security against the exercise of arbitrary power; and absolute safety for free institutions against foreign aggression." Halter v. Nebraska, 205 U.S. 34.

The case before us must be viewed as though the legislature of Pennsylvania had itself formally directed the flag-salute for the children of Minersville; had made no exemption for children whose parents were possessed of conscientious scruples like those of the Gobitis family; and had indicated its belief in the desirable ends to be secured by having its public school children share a common experience at those periods of development when their minds are supposedly receptive to its assimilation, by an exercise appropriate in time and place and setting, and one designed to evoke in them appreciation of the nation's hopes and dreams, its sufferings and sacrifices. The precise issue, then, for us to decide is whether the legislatures of the various states and the authorities in a thousand counties and school districts of this country are barred from determining the appropriateness of various means to evoke that unifying sentiment without which there can ultimately be no liberties, civil or religious. To stigmatize legislative judgment in providing for this universal gesture of respect for the symbol of our national life in the setting of the common school as a lawless inroad on that freedom of conscience which the Constitution protects, would amount to no less than the pronouncement of pedagogical and psychological dogma in a field where courts possess no marked and certainly no controlling competence. The influences which help toward a common feeling for the common country are manifold. Some may seem harsh and others no doubt are foolish. Surely, however, the end is legitimate. And the effective means for its attainment are still so uncertain and so unauthenticated by science as to preclude us from putting the widely prevalent belief in flag-saluting beyond the pale of legislative power. It mocks reason and denies our whole history to find in the allowance of a requirement to salute our flag on fitting occasions the seeds of sanction for obeisance to a leader.

The wisdom of training children in patriotic impulses by those compulsions which necessarily pervade so much of the educational process is not for our independent judgment. Even were we convinced of the folly of such a measure, such belief would be no proof of its unconstitutionality. For ourselves, we might be tempted to say that the deepest patriotism is best engendered by giving unfettered scope to the most crochety beliefs. Perhaps it is best, even from the standpoint of those interests which ordinances like the one under review seek to promote, to give to the least popular sect leave from conformities like those here in issue. But the court-room is not the arena for debating issues of educational policy. It is not our province to choose among competing considerations in the subtle process of securing effective loyalty to the traditional ideals of democracy, while respecting at the same time individual idiosyncracies among a people so diversified in racial origins and religious allegiances. So to hold would in effect make us the school board for the country. That authority has not been given to this Court, nor should we assume it.

We are dealing here with the formative period in the development of citizenship. Great diversity of psychological and ethical opinion exists among us concerning the best way to train children for their place in society. Because of these differences and because of reluctance to permit a single, ironcast system of education to be imposed upon a nation compounded of so many strains, we have held that, even though public education is one of our most cherished democratic institutions, the Bill of Rights bars a state from compelling all children to attend the public schools. Pierce v. Society of the Sisters of the Holy Names of Jesus and Mary, 268 U.S. 510. But it is a very different thing for this Court to exercise censorship over the conviction of legislatures that a particular program or exercise will best promote in the minds of children who attend the common schools an attachment to the institutions of their country.

What the school authorities are really asserting is the right to awaken in the child's mind considerations as to the significance of the flag contrary to those implanted by the parent. In such an attempt the state is normally at a disadvantage in competing with the parent's authority, so long—and this is the vital aspect of religious toleration—as parents are unmolested in their right to counteract by their own persuasiveness the wisdom and rightness of those loyalties which the state's educational system is seeking to promote. Except where the transgression of constitutional liberty is too plain for argument, personal freedom is best maintained—so long as the remedial channels of the democratic process remain open and unobstructed—when it is ingrained in a people's habits and not enforced against popular policy by the coercion of adjudicated law. That the flag-salute is an allowable portion of a school program for those who do not invoke conscientious scruples is surely not debatable. But for us to insist that, though the ceremony may be required, exceptional immunity must be given to dissidents, is to maintain that there is no basis for a legislative judgment that such an exemption might introduce elements of difficulty into the school discipline, might cast doubts in the minds of the other children which would themselves weaken the effect of the exercise.

The preciousness of the family relation, the authority and independence which give dignity to parenthood, indeed the enjoyment of all freedom, presuppose the kind of ordered society which is summarized by our flag. A society which is dedicated to the preservation of these ultimate values of civilization may in self-protection utilize the educational process for inculcating those almost unconscious feelings which bind men together in a comprehending loyalty, whatever may be their lesser differences and difficulties. That is to say, the process may be utilized so long as men's right to believe as they please, to win others to their way of belief, and their right to assemble in their chosen places of worship for the devotional ceremonies of their faith, are all fully respected.

Judicial review, itself a limitation on popular government, is a fundamental part of our constitutional scheme. But to the legislature no less than to courts is committed the guardianship of deeply-cherished liberties. Where all the effective means of inducing political changes are left free from interference, education in the abandonment of foolish legislation is itself a training in liberty. To fight out the wise use of legislative authority in the forum of public opinion and before legislative assemblies rather than to transfer such a contest to the judicial arena, serves to vindicate the self-confidence of a free people.

Reversed.

DECISION ON MANDATORY SALUTING OF THE FLAG (1943)   From *West Virginia State Board of Education* v. *Barnette,* 319 U.S. 624 (1943).

Appeal from the U.S. District Court for the Southern District of West Virginia.

MR. JUSTICE JACKSON DELIVERED THE OPINION OF THE COURT.

Following the decision by this Court on June 3, 1940, in *Minersville School District* v. *Gobitis,* 310 U.S. 586, the West Virginia legislature amended its statutes to require all schools therein to conduct courses of instruction in history, civics, and in the Constitutions of the United States and of the State "for the purpose of teaching, fostering and perpetuating the ideals, principles and spirit of Americanism, and increasing the knowledge of the organization and machinery of the government." Appellant Board of Education was directed, with advice of the State Superintendent of Schools, to "prescribe the courses of study covering these subjects" for public schools. The Act made it the duty of private, parochial and denominational schools to prescribe courses of study "similar to those required for the public schools."

The Board of Education on January 9, 1942, adopted a resolution containing recitals taken largely from the Court's *Gobitis* opinion and ordering that the salute to the flag become "a regular part of the program of activities in the public schools," that all teachers and pupils "shall be required to participate in the salute honoring the Nation represented by the Flag; provided, however, that refusal to salute the Flag be regarded as an act of insubordination, and shall be dealt with accordingly."

The resolution originally required the "commonly accepted salute to the Flag" which it defined. Objections to the salute as "being too much like Hitler's were raised by the Parent and Teachers Association, the Boy and Girl Scouts, the Red Cross, and the Federation of Women's Clubs. Some modification appears to have been made in deference to these objections, but no concession was made to

Jehovah's Witnesses. What is now required is the "stiff-arm" salute, the saluter to keep the right hand raised with palm turned up while the following is repeated: "I pledge allegiance to the Flag of the United States of America and to the Republic for which it stands; one Nation, indivisible, with liberty and justice for all."

Failure to conform is "insubordination" dealt with by expulsion. Readmission is denied by statute until compliance. Meanwhile the expelled child is "unlawfully absent" and may be proceeded against as a delinquent. His parents or guardians are liable to prosecution, and if convicted are subject to fine not exceeding $50 and jail term not exceeding thirty days.

Appellees, citizens of the United States and of West Virginia, brought suit in the United States District Court for themselves and others similarly situated asking its injunction to restrain enforcement of these laws and regulations against Jehovah's Witnesses. The Witnesses are an unincorporated body teaching that the obligation imposed by the law of God is superior to that of laws enacted by temporal government. Their religious beliefs include a literal version of Exodus, Chapter 20, verses 4 and 5, which says: "Thou shalt not make unto thee any graven image, or any likeness of anything that is in heaven above, or that is in the earth beneath, or that is in the water under the earth; thou shalt not bow down thyself to them nor serve them." They consider that the flag is an "image" within this command. For this reason they refuse to salute it.

Children of this faith have been expelled from school and are threatened with exclusion for no other cause. Officials threaten to send them to reformatories maintained for criminally inclined juveniles. Parents of such children have been prosecuted and are threatened with prosecutions for causing delinquency.

The Board of Education moved to dismiss the complaint setting forth these facts and alleging that the law and regulations are an unconstitutional denial of religious freedom, and of freedom of speech, and are invalid under the "due process" and "equal protection" clauses of the Fourteenth Amendment to the Federal Constitution. The cause was submitted on the pleadings to a District Court of three judges. It restrained enforcement as to the plaintiffs and those of that class. The Board of Education brought the case here by direct appeal.

This case calls upon us to reconsider a precedent decision, as the Court throughout its history often has been required to do. Before turning to the *Gobitis* case, however, it is desirable to notice certain characteristics by which this controversy is distinguished.

The freedom asserted by these appellees does not bring them into collision with rights asserted by any other individual. It is such conflicts which most frequently require intervention of the State to determine where the rights of one end and those of another begin. But the refusal of these persons to participate in the ceremony does not interfere with or deny rights of others to do so. Nor is there any question in this case that their behavior is peaceable and orderly. The sole conflict is between authority and rights of the individual.

✻   ✻   ✻

There is no doubt that, in connection with the pledges, the flag salute is a form of utterance. Symbolism is a primitive but effective way of communicating ideas. The use of an emblem or flag to symbolize some system, idea, institution, or personality, is a short cut from mind to mind. Causes and nations, political parties, lodges and ecclesiastical groups seek to knit the loyalty of their followings to a flag or banner, a color or design.

*   *   *

It is also to be noted that the compulsory flag salute and pledge requires affirmation of a belief and an attitude of mind. It is not clear whether the regulation contemplates that pupils forego any contrary convictions of their own and become unwilling converts to the prescribed ceremony or whether it will be acceptable if they simulate assent by words without belief and by a gesture barren of meaning. It is now a commonplace that censorship or suppression of expression of opinion is tolerated by our Constitution only when the expression presents a clear and present danger of action of a kind the State is empowered to prevent and punish. It would seem that involuntary affirmation could be commanded only on even more immediate and urgent grounds than silence. But here the power of compulsion is invoked without any allegation that remaining passive during a flag salute ritual creates a clear and present danger that would justify an effort even to muffle expression. To sustain the compulsory flag salute we are required to say that a Bill of Rights which guards the individual's right to speak his own mind, left it open to public authorities to compel him to utter what is not in his mind.

Whether the First Amendment to the Constitution will permit officials to order observance of ritual of this nature does not depend upon whether as a voluntary exercise we would think it to be good, bad or merely innocuous. Any credo of nationalism is likely to include what some disapprove or to omit what others think essential, and to give off different overtones as it takes on different accents or interpretations. If official power exists to coerce acceptance of any patriotic creed, what it shall contain cannot be decided by courts, but must be largely discretionary with the ordaining authority, whose power to prescribe would no doubt include power to amend. Hence validity of the asserted power to force an American citizen publicly to profess any statement of belief or to engage in any ceremony of assent to one, presents questions of power that must be considered independently of any idea we may have as to the utility of the ceremony in question.

Nor does the issue as we see it turn on one's possession of particular religious views or the sincerity with which they are held. While religion supplies appellees' motive for enduring the discomforts of making the issue in this case, many citizens who do not share these religious views hold such a compulsory rite to infringe constitutional liberty of the individual. It is not necessary to inquire whether nonconformist beliefs will exempt from the duty to salute unless we first find power to make the salute a legal duty.

The *Gobitis* decision, however, *assumed,* as did the argument in that case and in this, that power exists in the State to impose the flag salute discipline upon school children in general. The Court only examined and rejected a claim based on religious beliefs of immunity from an unquestioned general rule. The question which underlies the flag salute controversy is whether such a ceremony so touching matters of opinion and political attitude may be imposed upon the individual by official authority under powers committed to any political organization under our Constitution. We examine rather than assume existence of this power and, against this broader definition of issues in this case, reexamine specific grounds assigned for the *Gobitis* decision.

1. It was said that the flag-salute controversy confronted the Court with "the

problem which Lincoln cast in memorable dilemma: 'Must a government of necessity be too *strong* for the liberties of its people, or too *weak* to maintain its own existence?' " and that the answer must be in favor of strength. . . .

We think these issues may be examined free of pressure or restraint growing out of such considerations.

It may be doubted whether Mr. Lincoln would have thought that the strength of government to maintain itself would be impressively vindicated by our confirming power of the State to expel a handful of children from school. Such oversimplification, so handy in political debate, often lacks the precision necessary to postulates of judicial reasoning. If validly applied to this problem, the utterance cited would resolve every issue of power in favor of those in authority and would require us to override every liberty thought to weaken or delay execution of their policies.

Government of limited power need not be anemic government. Assurance that rights are secure tends to diminish fear and jealousy of strong government, and by making us feel safe to live under it makes for its better support. Without promise of a limiting Bill of Rights it is doubtful if our Constitution could have mustered enough strength to enable its ratification. To enforce those rights today is not to choose weak government over strong government. It is only to adhere as a means of strength to individual freedom of mind in preference to officially disciplined uniformity for which history indicates a disappointing and disastrous end.

The subject now before us exemplifies this principle. Free public education, if faithful to the ideal of secular instruction and political neutrality, will not be partisan or enemy of any class, creed, party, or faction. If it is to impose any ideological discipline, however, each party or denomination must seek to control, or failing that, to weaken the influence of the educational system. Observance of the limitations of the Constitution will not weaken government in the field appropriate for its exercise.

2. It was also considered in the *Gobitis* case that functions of educational officers in States, counties and school districts were such that to interfere with their authority "would in effect make us the school board for the country."

The Fourteenth Amendment, as now applied to the States, protects the citizen against the State itself and all of its creatures—Boards of Education not excepted. These have, of course, important, delicate, and highly discretionary functions, but none that they may not perform within the limits of the Bill of Rights. That they are educating the young for citizenship is reason for scrupulous protection of Constitutional freedoms of the individual, if we are not to strangle the free mind at its source and teach youth to discount important principles of our government as mere platitudes.

Such Boards are numerous and their territorial jurisdiction often small. But small and local authority may feel less sense of responsibility to the Constitution, and agencies of publicity may be less vigilant in calling it to account. The action of Congress in making flag observance voluntary and respecting the conscience of the objector in a matter so vital as raising the Army contrasts sharply with these local regulations in matters relatively trivial to the welfare of the nation. There are village tyrants as well as village Hampdens, but none who acts under color of law is beyond reach of the Constitution.

3. The *Gobitis* opinion reasoned that this is a field "where courts possess no marked and certainly no controlling competence," that it is committed to the legislatures as well as the courts to guard cherished liberties and that it is constitutionally appropriate to "fight out the wise use of legislative authority in the forum of public opinion and before legislative assemblies rather than to transfer

such a contest to the judicial arena," since all the "effective means of inducing political changes are left free."

The very purpose of a Bill of Rights was to withdraw certain subjects from the vicissitudes of political controversy, to place them beyond the reach of majorities and officials and to establish them as legal principles to be applied by the courts. One's right to life, liberty, and property, to free speech, a free press, freedom of worship and assembly, and other fundamental rights may not be submitted to vote; they depend on the outcome of no elections.

In weighing arguments of the parties it is important to distinguish between the due process clause of the Fourteenth Amendment as an instrument for transmitting the principles of the First Amendment and those cases in which it is applied for its own sake. The test of legislation which collides with the Fourteenth Amendment, because it also collides with the principles of the First, is much more definite than the test when only the Fourteenth is involved. Much of the vagueness of the due process clause disappears when the specific prohibitions of the First become its standard. The right of a State to regulate, for example, a public utility may well include, so far as the due process test is concerned, power to impose all of the restrictions which a legislature may have a "rational basis" for adopting. But freedoms of speech and of press, of assembly, and of worship may not be infringed on such slender grounds. They are susceptible of restriction only to prevent grave and immediate danger to interests which the State may lawfully protect. It is important to note that while it is the Fourteenth Amendment which bears directly upon the State it is the more specific limiting principles of the First Amendment that finally govern this case.

Nor does our duty to apply the Bill of Rights to assertions of official authority depend upon our possession of marked competence in the field where the invasion of rights occurs. True, the task of translating the majestic generalities of the Bill of Rights, conceived as part of the pattern of liberal government in the eighteenth century, into concrete restraints on officials dealing with the problems of the twentieth century, is one to disturb self-confidence. These principles grew in soil which also produced a philosophy that the individual was the center of society, that his liberty was attainable through mere absence of governmental restraints, and that government should be entrusted with few controls and only the mildest supervision over men's affairs. We must transplant these rights to a soil in which the *laissez-faire* concept or principle of noninterference has withered at least as to economic affairs, and social advancements are increasingly sought through closer integration of society and through expanded and strengthened governmental controls. These changed conditions often deprive precedents of reliability and cast us more than we would choose upon our own judgment. But we act in these matters not by authority of our competence but by force of our commissions. We cannot, because of modest estimates of our competence in such specialties as public education, withhold the judgment that history authenticates as the function of this Court when liberty is infringed.

4. Lastly, and this is the very heart of the *Gobitis* opinion, it reasons that "National unity is the basis of national security," that the authorities have "the right to select appropriate means for its attainment," and hence reaches the conclusion that such compulsory measures toward "national unity" are constitutional. Upon the verity of this assumption depends our answer in this case.

National unity as an end which officials may foster by persuasion and example is not in question. The problem is whether under our Constitution compulsion as here employed is a permissible means for its achievement.

Struggles to coerce uniformity of sentiment in support of some end thought essential to their time and country have been waged by many good as well as by evil men. Nationalism is a relatively recent phenomenon but at other times and places the ends have been racial or territorial security, support of a dynasty or regime, and particular plans for saving souls. As first and moderate methods to attain unity have failed, those bent on its accomplishment must resort to an ever-increasing severity. As governmental pressure toward unity becomes greater, so strife becomes more bitter as to whose unity it shall be. Probably no deeper division of our people could proceed from any provocation than from finding it necessary to choose what doctrine and whose program public educational officials shall compel youth to unite in embracing. Ultimate futility of such attempts to compel coherence is the lesson of every such effort from the Roman drive to stamp out Christianity as a disturber of its pagan unity, the Inquisition, as a means to religious and dynastic unity, the Siberian exiles as a means to Russian unity, down to the last failing efforts of our present totalitarian enemies. Those who begin coercive elimination of dissent soon find themselves exterminating dissenters. Compulsory unification of opinion achieves only the unanimity of the graveyard.

It seems trite but necessary to say that the First Amendment to our Constitution was designed to avoid these ends by avoiding these beginnings. There is no mysticism in the American concept of the State or of the nature or origin of its authority. We set up government by consent of the governed, and the Bill of Rights denies those in power any legal opportunity to coerce that consent. Authority here is to be controlled by public opinion, not public opinion by authority.

The case is made difficult not because the principles of its decision are obscure but because the flag involved is our own. Nevertheless, we apply the limitations of the Constitution with no fear that freedom to be intellectually and spiritually diverse or even contrary will disintegrate the social organization. To believe that patriotism will not flourish if patriotic ceremonies are voluntary and spontaneous instead of a compulsory routine is to make an unflattering estimate of the appeal of our institutions to free minds. We can have intellectual individualism and the rich cultural diversities that we owe to exceptional minds only at the price of occasional eccentricity and abnormal attitudes. When they are so harmless to others or to the State as those we deal with here, the price is not too great. But freedom to differ is not limited to things that do not matter much. That would be a mere shadow of freedom. The test of its substance is the right to differ as to things that touch the heart of the existing order.

If there is any fixed star in our constitutional constellation, it is that no official, high or petty, can prescribe what shall be orthodox in politics, nationalism, religion, or other matters of opinion or force citizens to confess by word or act their faith therein. If there are any circumstances which permit an exception, they do not now occur to us. . . .

The decision of this Court in *Minersville School District* v. *Gobitis* and the holdings of those few *per curiam* decisions which preceded and foreshadowed it are overruled, and the judgment enjoining enforcement of the West Virginia Regulation is *affirmed*.

*   *   *

One who belongs to the most vilified and persecuted minority in history is not likely to be insensible to the freedoms guaranteed by our Constitution. Were my purely personal attitude relevant I should wholeheartedly associate myself with the general libertarian views in the Court's opinion, representing as they do the thought and action of a lifetime. But as judges we are neither Jew nor Gentile, neither Catholic nor agnostic. We owe equal attachment to the Constitution and are equally bound by our judicial obligations whether we derive our citizenship from the earliest or the latest immigrants to these shores. As a member of this Court I am not justified in writing my private notions of policy into the Constitution, no matter how deeply I may cherish them or how mischievous I may deem their disregard.

DECISION ON BUSING OF CHILDREN TO RELIGIOUS SCHOOLS AT PUBLIC EXPENSE (1947)   From *Everson* v. *Board of Education,* 330 U.S. 1 (1947).

Appeal from the Court of Errors and Appeals of New Jersey.

MR. JUSTICE BLACK DELIVERED THE OPINION OF THE COURT.

A New Jersey statute authorizes its local school districts to make rules and contracts for the transportation of children to and from schools. The appellee, a township board of education, acting pursuant to this statute, authorized reimbursement to parents of money expended by them for the bus transportation of their children on regular busses operated by the public transportation system. Part of this money was for the payment of transportation of some children in the community to Catholic parochial schools. These church schools give their students, in addition to secular education, regular religious instruction conforming to the religious tenets and modes of worship of the Catholic Faith. The superintendent of these schools is a Catholic priest.

The appellant, in his capacity as a district taxpayer, filed suit in a state court challenging the right of the Board to reimburse parents of parochial school students. He contended that the statute and the resolution passed pursuant to it violated both the State and the Federal Constitutions. That court held that the legislature was without power to authorize such payment under the state constitution. . . . The New Jersey Court of Errors and Appeals reversed, holding that neither the statute nor the resolution passed pursuant to it was in conflict with the State constitution or the provisions of the Federal Constitution in issue. . . .

Since there has been no attack on the statute on the ground that a part of its language excludes children attending private schools operated for profit from enjoying State payment for their transportation, we need not consider this exclusionary language; it has no relevancy to any constitutional question here presented. Furthermore, if the exclusion clause had been properly challenged, we do not know whether New Jersey's highest court would construe its statutes as precluding payment of the school transportation of any group of pupils, even those of a private school run for profit. Consequently, we put to one side the question as to the validity of the statute against the claim that it does not authorize payment for the transportation generally of school children in New Jersey.

The only contention here is that the state statute and the resolution, insofar as they authorized reimbursement to parents of children attending parochial schools, violate the Federal Constitution in these two respects, which to some extent overlap. *First.* They authorize the State to take by taxation the private property of some and bestow it upon others, to be used for their own private purposes. This, it is alleged, violates the due process clause of the Fourteenth Amendment. *Second.* The statute and the resolution forced inhabitants to pay taxes to help support and maintain schools which are dedicated to, and which regularly teach, the Catholic Faith. This is alleged to be a use of state power to support church schools contrary to the prohibition of the First Amendment which the Fourteenth Amendment made applicable to the states.

First. The due process argument that the state law taxes some people to help others carry out their private purposes is framed in two phases. The first phase is that a state cannot tax A to reimburse B for the cost of transporting his children to church schools. This is said to violate the due process clause because the children are sent to these church schools to satisfy the personal desires of their parents, rather than the public's interest in the general education of all children. This argument, if valid, would apply equally to prohibit state payment for the transportation of children to any nonpublic school, whether operated by a church or any other nongovernment individual or group. But, the New Jersey legislature has decided that a public purpose will be served by using tax-raised funds to pay the bus fares of all school children, including those who attend parochial schools. The New Jersey Court of Errors and Appeals has reached the same conclusion. The fact that a state law, passed to satisfy a public need, coincides with the personal desires of the individuals most directly affected is certainly an inadequate reason for us to say that a legislature has erroneously appraised the public need. . . .

*　*　*

It is much too late to argue that legislation intended to facilitate the opportunity of children to get a secular education serves no public purpose. . . . The same thing is no less true of legislation to reimburse needy parents, or all parents, for payment of the fares of their children so that they can ride in public busses to and from schools rather than run the risk of traffic and other hazards incident to walking or "hitchhiking." . . . Nor does it follow that a law has a private rather than a public purpose because it provides that tax-raised funds will be paid to reimburse individuals on account of money spent by them in a way which furthers a public program. . . . Subsidies and loans to individuals such as farmers and home-owners, and to privately owned transportation systems, as well as many other kinds of businesses, have been commonplace practices in our state and national history.

Insofar as the second phase of the due process argument may differ from the first, it is by suggesting that taxation for transportation of children to church schools constitutes support of a religion by the State. But if the law is invalid for this reason, it is because it violates the First Amendment's prohibition against the establishment of religion by law. This is the exact question raised by appellant's second contention, to consideration of which we now turn.

Second. The New Jersey statute is challenged as a "law respecting an establishment of religion." The First Amendment, as made applicable to the states by the Fourteenth, *Murdock* v. *Pennsylvania*, 319 U.S. 105, commands that a state "shall make no law respecting an establishment of religion, or prohibiting the free exercise thereof." These words of the First Amendment reflected in the minds of early Americans a vivid mental picture of conditions and practices which they fervently wished to stamp out in order to preserve liberty for themselves and for their posterity. Doubtless their goal has not been entirely reached; but so far has the Nation moved toward it that the expression "law respecting an establishment of religion," probably does not so vividly remind present-day Americans of the evils, fears, and political problems that caused that expression to be written into our Bill of Rights. Whether this New Jersey law is one respecting an "establishment of religion" requires an understanding of the meaning of that language, particularly with respect to the imposition of taxes. Once again, therefore, it is not inappropriate briefly to review the background and environment of the period in which that constitutional language was fashioned and adopted. . . .

✳   ✳   ✳

The "establishment of religion" clause of the First Amendment means at least this: Neither a state nor the Federal Government can set up a church. Neither can pass laws which aid one religion, aid all religions, or prefer one religion over another. Neither can force nor influence a person to go to or to remain away from church against his will or force him to profess a belief or disbelief in any religion. No person can be punished for entertaining or professing religious beliefs or disbeliefs, for church attendance or non-attendance. No tax in any amount, large or small, can be levied to support any religious activities or institutions, whatever they may be called, or whatever form they may adopt to teach or practice religion. Neither a state nor the Federal Government can, openly or secretly, participate in the affairs of any religious organizations or groups and *vice versa*. In the words of Jefferson, the clause against establishment of religion by law was intended to erect "a wall of separation between church and State." . . .

We must consider the New Jersey statute in accordance with the foregoing limitations imposed by the First Amendment. But we must not strike that state statute down if it is within the State's constitutional power even though it approaches the verge of that power. . . . New Jersey cannot consistently with the "establishment of religion" clause of the First Amendment contribute tax-raised funds to the support of an institution which teaches the tenets and faith of any church. On the other hand, other language of the amendment commands that New Jersey cannot hamper its citizens in the free exercise of their own religion. Consequently, it cannot exclude individual Catholics, Lutherans, Mohammedans, Baptists, Jews, Methodists, Non-believers, Presbyterians, or the members of any other faith, *because of their faith, or lack of it,* from receiving the benefits of public welfare legislation. While we do not mean to intimate that a state could not provide transportation only to children attending public schools, we must be careful, in protecting the citizens of New Jersey against state-established churches, to be sure that we do not inadvertently prohibit New Jersey from extending its general state law benefits to all its citizens without regard to their religious belief.

Measured by these standards, we cannot say that the First Amendment prohibits New Jersey from spending tax-raised funds to pay the bus fares of parochial school pupils as a part of a general program under which it pays the fares of pupils attending public and other schools. It is undoubtedly true that children are helped to get to church schools. There is even a possibility that some of the children might not be sent to the church schools if the parents were compelled to pay their children's bus fares out of their own pockets when transportation to a public school would have been paid for by the State. The same possibility exists where the state requires a local transit company to provide reduced fares to school children including those attending parochial schools, or where a municipally owned transportation system undertakes to carry all school children free of charge. Moreover, state-paid policemen, detailed to protect children going to and from church schools from the very real hazards of traffic, would serve much the same purpose and accomplish much the same result as state provisions intended to guarantee free transportation of a kind which the state deems to be best for the school children's welfare. And parents might refuse to risk their children to the serious danger of traffic accidents going to and from parochial schools, the approaches to which were not protected by policemen. Similarly, parents might be reluctant to permit their children to attend schools which the state had cut off from such general government services as ordinary police and fire protection, connections for sewage disposal, public highways and sidewalks. Of course, cutting off church schools from these services, so separate and so indisputably marked off from the religious function, would make it far more difficult for the schools to operate. But such is obviously not the purpose of the First Amendment. That Amendment requires the state to be a neutral in its relations with groups of religious believers and nonbelievers; it does not require the state to be their adversary. State power is no more to be used so as to handicap religions than it is to favor them. . . .

The First Amendment has erected a wall between church and state. That wall must be kept high and impregnable. We could not approve the slightest breach. New Jersey has not breached it here.

Affirmed.

DECISION ON RELEASED TIME FOR RELIGIOUS INSTRUCTION ON SCHOOL PREMISES (1948)   From *Illinois ex rel. McCollum* v. *Board of Education,* 333 U.S. 203 (1948).

Appeal from the Supreme Court of Illinois.

MR. JUSTICE BLACK DELIVERED THE OPINION OF THE COURT.

This case relates to the power of a state to utilize its tax-supported public school system in aid of religious instruction insofar as that power may be restricted by the First and Fourteenth Amendments to the Federal Constitution.

The appellant, Vashti McCollum, began this action for mandamus against the Champaign Board of Education in the Circuit Court of Champaign County, Illinois. Her asserted interest was that of a resident and taxpayer of Champaign and of a parent whose child was then enrolled in the Champaign public schools. Illinois has a compulsory education law which, with exceptions, requires parents to send their children, aged seven to sixteen, to its tax-supported public schools where the children are to remain in attendance during the hours when the schools are regularly in session. Parents who violate this law commit a misdemeanor punishable by fine unless the children attend private or parochial schools which meet educational standards fixed by the State. District boards of education are given general supervisory powers over the use of the public school buildings within the school districts. . . .

Appellant's petition for mandamus alleged that religious teachers, employed by private religious groups, were permitted to come weekly into the school buildings during the regular hours set apart for secular teaching, and then and there for a period of thirty minutes substitute their religious teaching for the secular education provided under the compulsory education law. The petitioner charged that this joint public-school religious-group program violated the First and Fourteenth Amendments to the United States Constitution. . . .

Although there are disputes between the parties as to various inferences that may or may not properly be drawn from the evidence concerning the religious program, the following facts are shown by the record without dispute. In 1940 interested members of the Jewish, Roman Catholic, and a few of the Protestant faiths formed a voluntary association called the Champaign Council on Religious Education. They obtained permission from the Board of Education to offer classes in religious instruction to public school pupils in grades four to nine inclusive. Classes were made up of pupils whose parents signed printed cards requesting that their children be permitted to attend; they were held weekly, thirty minutes for the lower grades, forty-five minutes for the higher. The council employed the religious teachers at no expense to the school authorities, but the instructors were subject to the approval and supervision of the superintendent of schools. The classes were taught in three separate religious groups by Protestant teachers, Catholic priests, and a Jewish rabbi, although for the past several years there have apparently been no classes instructed in the Jewish religion. Classes were conducted in the regular classrooms of the school building. Students who did not choose to take the religious instruction were not released from public school duties; they were required to leave their classrooms and go to some other place in the school building for pursuit of their secular studies. On the other hand, students who were released from secular study for the religious instructions were required to be present at the religious classes. Reports of their presence or absence were to be made to their secular teachers.

The foregoing facts, without reference to others that appear in the record, show the use of tax-supported property for religious instruction and the close cooperation between the school authorities and the religious council in promoting religious education. The operation of the State's compulsory education system thus assists and is integrated with the program of religious instruction carried on by separate religious sects. Pupils compelled by law to go to school for secular education are released in part from their legal duty upon the condition that they attend the religious classes. This is beyond all question a utilization of the tax-established and tax-supported public school system to aid religious groups to spread their faith. And it falls squarely under the ban of the First Amendment (made applicable to the States by the Fourteenth) as we interpreted it in *Everson* v. *Board of Education*, 330 U.S. 1.

✻   ✻   ✻

Recognizing that the Illinois program is barred by the First and Fourteenth Amendments if we adhere to the views expressed both by the majority and the minority in the *Everson* case, counsel for the respondents challenge those views as dicta and urge that we reconsider and repudiate them. They argue that historically the First Amendment was intended to forbid only government preference of one religion over another, not an impartial governmental assistance of all religions. In addition they ask that we distinguish or overrule our holding in the *Everson* case that the Fourteenth Amendment made the "establishment of religion" clause of the First Amendment applicable as a prohibition against the States. After giving full consideration to the arguments presented we are unable to accept either of these contentions.

To hold that a state cannot consistently with the First and Fourteenth Amendments utilize its public school system to aid any or all religious faiths or sects in the dissemination of their doctrines and ideals does not, as counsel urge, manifest a governmental hostility to religion or religious teachings. A manifestation of such hostility would be at war with our national tradition as embodied in the First Amendment's guaranty of the free exercise of religion. For the First Amendment rests upon the premise that both religion and government can best work to achieve their lofty aims if each is left free from the other within its respective sphere. Or, as we said in the *Everson* case, the First Amendment has erected a wall between Church and State which must be kept high and impregnable.

Here not only are the State's tax-supported public school buildings used for the dissemination of religious doctrines. The State also affords sectarian groups an invaluable aid in that it helps to provide pupils for their religious classes through use of the State's compulsory public school machinery. This is not separation of Church and State.

The cause is reversed and remanded to the State Supreme Court for proceedings not inconsistent with this opinion.

Reversed and remanded.

MR. JUSTICE FRANKFURTER DELIVERED THE FOLLOWING OPINION, IN WHICH MR. JUSTICE JACKSON, MR. JUSTICE RUTLEDGE, AND MR. JUSTICE BURTON JOIN.

We dissented in *Everson* v. *Board of Education*, 330 U.S. 1, because in our view the Constitutional principle requiring separation of Church and State compelled invalidation of the ordinance sustained by the majority. Illinois has here authorized the commingling of sectarian with secular instruction in the public schools. The Constitution of the United States forbids this.

This case, in the light of the *Everson* decision, demonstrates anew that the mere formulation of a relevant Constitutional principle is the beginning of the solution of a problem, not its answer. This is so because the meaning of a spacious conception like that of the separation of Church from State is unfolded as appeal is made to the principle from case to case. We are all agreed that the First and the Fourteenth Amendments have a secular reach far more penetrating in the conduct of Government than merely to forbid an "established church." But agreement, in the abstract, that the First Amendment was designed to erect a "wall of separation between church and State," does not preclude a clash of views as to what the wall separates. Involved is not only the Constitutional principle but the implications of judicial review in its enforcement. Accommodation of legislative freedom and Constitutional limitations upon that freedom cannot be achieved by a mere phrase. We cannot illuminatingly apply the "wall-of-separation" metaphor until we have considered the relevant history of religious education in America, the place of the "released time" movement in that history, and its precise manifestation in the case before us.

To understand the particular program now before us as a conscientious attempt to accommodate the allowable functions of Government and the special concerns of the Church within the framework of our Constitution and with due regard to the kind of society for which it was designed, we must put this Champaign program of 1940 in its historic setting. Traditionally, organized education in the Western world was Church education. It could hardly be otherwise when the education of children was primarily study of the Word and the ways of God. Even in the Protestant countries, where there was a less close identification of Church and State, the basis of education was largely the Bible, and its chief purpose inculcation of piety. To the extent that the State intervened, it used its authority to further aims of the Church.

The emigrants who came to these shores brought this view of education with them. Colonial schools certainly started with a religious orientation. When the common problems of the early settlers of the Massachusetts Bay Colony revealed the need for common schools, the object was the defeat of "one chief project of that old deluder, Satan, to keep men from the knowledge of the Scriptures." The Laws and Liberties of Massachusetts, 1648 edition (Cambridge 1929) 47.

The evolution of colonial education, largely in the service of religion, into the public school system of today is the story of changing conceptions regarding the American democratic society, of the functions of State-maintained education in such a society, and of the role therein of the free exercise of religion by the people. The modern public school derived from a philosophy of freedom reflected in the First Amendment. . . .

Separation in the field of education, then, was not imposed upon unwilling States by force of superior law. In this respect the Fourteenth Amendment merely reflected a principle then dominant in our national life. To the extent that the Constitution thus made it binding upon the States, the basis of the restriction is the whole experience of our people. Zealous watchfulness against fusion of secular and religious activities by Government itself, through any of its instruments but especially through its educational agencies, was the democratic response of the American community to the particular needs of a young and growing nation, unique in the composition of its people. . . .

It is pertinent to remind that the establishment of this principle of Separation in the field of education was not due to any decline in the religious beliefs of the people. Horace Mann was a devout Christian, and the deep religious feeling of James Madison is stamped upon the Remonstrance. The secular public school did not imply indifference to the basic role of religion in the life of the people, nor rejection of religious education as a means of fostering it. The claims of religion were not minimized by refusing to make the public schools agencies for their assertion. The nonsectarian or secular public school was the means of reconciling freedom in general with religious freedom. The sharp confinement of the public schools to secular education was a recognition of the need of a democratic society to educate its children, insofar as the State undertook to do so, in an atmosphere free from pressures in a realm in which pressures are most resisted and where conflicts are most easily and most bitterly engendered. Designed to serve as perhaps the most powerful agency for promoting cohesion among a heterogeneous democratic people, the public school must keep scrupulously free from entanglement in the strife of sects. The preservation of the community from divisive conflicts, of Government from irreconcilable pressures by religious groups, of religion from censorship and coercion however subtly exercised, requires strict confinement of the State to instruction other than religious, leaving to the individual's church and home, indoctrination in the faith of his choice. . . .

MR. JUSTICE JACKSON, *concurring.*

DECISION ON RELEASED TIME FOR RELIGIOUS INSTRUCTION OFF SCHOOL PREMISES (1952) From *Zorach* v. *Clauson,* 343 U.S. 306 (1952).

Appeal from the Court of Appeals of New York.

MR. JUSTICE DOUGLAS DELIVERED THE OPINION OF THE COURT.

New York City has a program which permits its public schools to release students during the school day so that they may leave the school buildings and school grounds and go to religious centers for religious instruction or devotional exercises. A student is released on written request of his parents. Those not released stay in the classroom. The churches make weekly reports to the schools, sending a list of children who have been released from public school but who have not reported for religious instruction.

This "released time" program involves neither religious instruction in public school classrooms nor the expenditure of public funds. All costs, including the application blanks, are paid by the religious organizations. The case is therefore unlike *McCollum* v. *Board of Education,* 333 U.S. 203, which involved a "released time" program from Illinois. In that case the classrooms were turned over to religious instructors. We accordingly held that the program violated the First Amendment which (by reason of the Fourteenth Amendment) prohibits the states from establishing religion or prohibiting its free exercise.

Appellants, who are taxpayers and residents of New York City and whose children attend its public schools, challenge the present law, contending it is in essence not different from the one involved in the *McCollum* case. Their argument, stated elaborately in various ways, reduces itself to this: the weight and influence of the school is put behind a program for religious instruction; public school teachers police it, keeping tab on students who are released; the classroom activities come to a halt while the students who are released for religious instruction are on leave; the school is a crutch on which the churches are leaning for support in their religious training; without the cooperation of the schools this "released time" program, like the one in the *McCollum* case, would be futile and ineffective. The New York Court of Appeals sustained the law against this claim of unconstitutionality. . . .

The briefs and arguments are replete with data bearing on the merits of this type of "released time" program. Views *pro* and *con* are expressed, based on practical experience with these programs and with their implications. We do not stop to summarize these materials nor to burden the opinion with an analysis of them. For they involve considerations not germane to the narrow constitutional issue presented. They largely concern the wisdom of the system, its efficiency from an educational point of view, and the political considerations which have motivated its adoption or rejection in some communities. Those matters are of no concern here, since our problem reduces itself to whether New York by this system has either prohibited the "free exercise" of religion or has made a law "respecting an establishment of religion" within the meaning of the First Amendment.

It takes obtuse reasoning to inject any issue of the "free exercise" of religion into the present case. No one is forced to go to the religious classroom and no religious exercise or instruction is brought to the classrooms of the public schools. A student need not take religious instruction. He is left to his own desires as to the manner or time of his religious devotions, if any.

There is a suggestion that the system involves the use of coercion to get public school students into religious classrooms. There is no evidence in the record before us that supports that conclusion. The present record indeed tells us that the school authorities are neutral in this regard and do no more than release students whose parents so request. If in fact coercion were used, if it were established that any one or more teachers were using their office to persuade or force students to take the religious instruction, a wholly different case would be presented. Hence we put aside that claim of coercion both as respects the "free exercise" of religion and "an establishment of religion" within the meaning of the First Amendment.

Moreover, apart from that claim of coercion, we do not see how New York by this type of "released time" program has made a law respecting an establishment of religion within the meaning of the First Amendment. There is much talk of the separation of Church and State in the history of the Bill of Rights and in the decisions clustering around the First Amendment. . . . There cannot be the slightest doubt that the First Amendment reflects the philosophy that Church and State should be separated. And so far as interference with the "free exercise" of religion and "establishment" of religion are concerned, the separation must be complete and unequivocal. The First Amendment within the scope of its coverage permits no exception; the prohibition is absolute. The First Amendment, however, does not say that in every and all respects there shall be a separation of Church and State. Rather, it studiously defines the manner, the specific ways, in which there shall be no concert or union or dependency one on the other. That is the common sense of the matter. Otherwise the state and religion would be aliens to each other—hostile, suspicious, and even unfriendly. Churches could not be required to pay even property taxes. Municipalities would not be permitted to render police or fire protection to religious groups. Policemen who helped parishioners into their places of worship would violate the Constitution. Prayers in our legislative halls; the appeals to the Almighty in the messages of the Chief Executive; the proclamations making Thanksgiving Day a holiday; "so help me God" in our courtroom oaths—these and all other references to the Almighty that run through our laws, our public rituals, our ceremonies would be flouting the First Amendment. A fastidious atheist or agnostic could even object to the supplication with which the Court opens each session: "God save the United States and this Honorable Court."

We would have to press the concept of separation of Church and State to these extremes to condemn the present law on constitutional grounds. The nullification of this law would have wide and profound effects. A Catholic student applies to his teacher for permission to leave the school during hours on a Holy Day of Obligation to attend a mass. A Jewish student asks his teacher for permission to be excused for Yom Kippur. A Protestant wants the afternoon off for a family baptismal ceremony.

In each case the teacher requires parental consent in writing. In each case the teacher, in order to make sure the student is not a truant, goes further and requires a report from the priest, the rabbi, or the minister. The teacher in other words cooperates in a religious program to the extent of making it possible for her students to participate in it. Whether she does it occasionally for a few students, regularly for one, or pursuant to a systematized program designed to further the religious needs of all the students does not alter the character of the act.

We are a religious people whose institutions presuppose a Supreme Being. We guarantee the freedom to worship as one chooses. We make room for as wide a variety of beliefs and creeds as the spiritual needs of man deem necessary. We sponsor an attitude on the part of government that shows no partiality to any one group and that lets each flourish according to the zeal of its adherents and the appeal of its dogma. When the state encourages religious instruction or cooperates with religious authorities by adjusting the schedule of public events to sectarian needs, it follows the best of our traditions. For it then respects the religious nature of our people and accommodates the public service to their spiritual needs. To hold that it may not would be to find in the Constitution a requirement that the government show a callous indifference to religious groups. That would be preferring those who believe in no religion over those who do believe. Government may not finance religious groups nor undertake religious instruction nor blend secular and sectarian education nor use secular institutions to force one or some religion on any person. But we find no constitutional requirement which makes it necessary for government to be hostile to religion and to throw its weight against efforts to widen the effective scope of religious influence. The government must be neutral when it comes to competition between sects. It may not thrust any sect on any person. It may not make a religious observance compulsory. It may not coerce anyone to attend church, to observe a religious holiday, or to take religious instruction. But it can close its doors or suspend its operations as to those who want to repair to their religious sanctuary for worship or instruction. No more than that is undertaken here.

This program may be unwise and improvident from an educational or a community viewpoint. . . . Our individual preferences, however, are not the constitutional standard. The constitutional standard is the separation of Church and State. The problem, like many problems in constitutional law, is one of degree. . . .

Affirmed.

MR. JUSTICE BLACK, DISSENTING.

I see no significant difference between the invalid Illinois system and that of New York here sustained. Except for the use of the school buildings in Illinois, there is no difference between the systems which I consider even worthy of mention. In the New York program, as in that of Illinois, the school authorities release some of the children on the condition that they attend the religious classes, get reports on whether they attend, and hold the other children in the school building until the religious hour is over. As we attempted to make categorically clear, the *McCollum* decision would have been the same if the religious classes had not been held in the school buildings. . . .

*   *   *

Of course, a State may provide that the classes in its schools shall be dismissed, for any reason, or no reason, on fixed days, or for special occasions. The essence of this case is that the school system did not "close its doors" and did not "suspend its operations." There is all the difference in the world between letting the children out of school and letting some of them out of school into religious classes. If every one is free to make what use he will of time wholly unconnected from schooling required by law—those who wish sectarian instruction devoting it to that purpose, those who have ethical instruction at home, to that, those who study music, to that—then of course there is no conflict with the Fourteenth Amendment.

The pith of the case is that formalized religious instruction is substituted for other school activity which those who do not participate in the released-time program are compelled to attend. The school system is very much in operation during this kind of released time. If its doors are closed, they are closed upon those students who do not attend the religious instruction, in order to keep them within the school. That is the very thing which raises the constitutional issue. It is not met by disregarding it. Failure to discuss this issue does not take it out of the case. . . .

The deeply divisive controversy aroused by the attempts to secure public school pupils for sectarian instruction would promptly end if the advocates of such instruction were content to have the school "close its doors or suspend its operations"—that is, dismiss classes in their entirety, without discrimination—instead of seeking to use the public schools as the instrument for securing attendence at denominational classes. The unwillingness of the promoters of this movement to dispense with such use of the public schools betrays a surprising want of confidence in the inherent power of the various faiths to draw children to outside sectarian classes—an attitude that hardly reflects the faith of the greatest religious spirits.

MR. JUSTICE JACKSON, DISSENTING.

This released time program is founded upon a use of the State's power of coercion, which, for me, determines its unconstitutionality. . . .

If public education were taking so much of the pupils' time as to injure the public or the students' welfare by encroaching upon their religious opportunity, simply shortening everyone's school day would facilitate voluntary and optional attendance at Church classes. But that suggestion is rejected upon the ground that if they are made free many students will not go to the Church. Hence, they must be deprived of freedom for this period, with Church attendance put to them as one of the two permissible ways of using it.

The greater effectiveness of this system over voluntary attendance after school hours is due to the truant officer who, if the youngster fails to go to the Church school, dogs him back to the public schoolroom. Here schooling is more or less suspended during the "released time" so that nonreligious attendants will not forge ahead of the churchgoing absentees. But it serves as a temporary jail for a pupil who will not go to Church. It takes more subtlety of mind than I possess to deny that this is governmental constraint in support of religion. It is as unconstitutional, in my view, when exerted by indirection as when exercised forthrightly.

As one whose children, as a matter of free choice, have been sent to privately supported Church schools, I may challenge the Court's suggestion that opposition to this plan can only be antireligious, atheistic, or agnostic. My evangelistic brethren confuse an objection to compulsion with an objection to religion. It is possible to hold a faith with enough confidence to believe that what should be rendered to God does not need to be decided and collected by Caesar.

The day that this country ceases to be free for irreligion it will cease to be free for religion—except for the sect that can win political power. The same epithetical jurisprudence used by the Court today to beat down those who oppose pressuring children into some religion can devise as good epithets tomorrow against those who object to pressuring them into a favored religion. And, after all, if we concede to the State power and wisdom to single out "duly constituted religious" bodies as exclusive alternatives for compulsory secular instruction, it would be logical to also uphold the power and wisdom to choose the true faith among those "duly constituted." We start down a rough road when we begin to mix compulsory public education with compulsory godliness. . . .

The wall which the Court was professing to erect between Church and State has become even more warped and twisted than I expected. Today's judgment will be more interesting to students of psychology and of the judicial processes than to students of constitutional law.

DECISION ON RECITATION OF PRAYERS IN PUBLIC SCHOOLS
(**1962**) From *Engel* v. *Vitale*, 370 U.S. 421 (1962).

Certiorari to the Court of Appeals of New York.

MR. JUSTICE BLACK DELIVERED THE OPINION OF THE COURT.

We think that by using its public school system to encourage recitation of the Regents' prayer, the State of New York has adopted a practice wholly inconsistent with the Establishment Clause. There can, of course, be no doubt that New York's program of daily classroom invocation of God's blessings as prescribed in the Regents' prayer is a religious activity. It is a solemn avowal of divine faith and supplication for the blessings of the Almighty. The nature of such a prayer has always been religious, none of the respondents has denied this and the trial court expressly so found. . . .

The petitioners contend among other things that the state laws requiring or permitting use of the Regents' prayer must be struck down as a violation of the Establishment Clause because that prayer was composed by governmental officials as a part of a governmental program to further religious beliefs. For this reason, petitioners argue, the State's use of the Regents' prayer in its public school system breaches the constitutional wall of separation between Church and State. We agree with that contention since we think that the constitutional prohibition against laws respecting an establishment of religion must at least mean that in this country it is no part of the business of government to compose official prayers for any group of the American people to recite as a part of a religious program carried on by government.

It is a matter of history that this very practice of establishing governmentally composed prayers for religious services was one of the reasons which caused many

THE
MINORITIES

3075

of our early colonists to leave England and seek religious freedom in America. The Book of Common Prayer, which was created under governmental direction and which was approved by Acts of Parliament in 1548 and 1549, set out in minute detail the accepted form and content of prayer and other religious ceremonies to be used in the established, tax-supported Church of England. The controversies over the Book and what should be its content repeatedly threatened to disrupt the peace of that country as the accepted forms of prayer in the established church changed with the views of the particular ruler that happened to be in control at the time. Powerful groups representing some of the varying religious views of the people struggled among themselves to impress their particular views upon the Government and obtain amendments of the Book more suitable to their respective notions of how religious services should be conducted in order that the official religious establishment would advance their particular religious beliefs. Other groups, lacking the necessary political power to influence the Government on the matter, decided to leave England and its established church and seek freedom in America from England's governmentally ordained and supported religion.

It is an unfortunate fact of history that when some of the very groups which had most strenuously opposed the established Church of England found themselves sufficiently in control of colonial governments in this country to write their own prayers into law, they passed laws making their own religion the official religion of their respective colonies. Indeed, as late as the time of the Revolutionary War, there were established churches in at least eight of the thirteen former colonies and established religions in at least four of the other five. But the successful Revolution against English political domination was shortly followed by intense opposition to the practice of establishing religion by law. This opposition crystallized rapidly into an effective political force in Virginia where the minority religious groups such as Presbyterians, Lutherans, Quakers and Baptists had gained such strength that the adherents to the established Episcopal Church were actually a minority themselves. In 1785–1786, those opposed to the established Church, led by James Madison and Thomas Jefferson, who, though themselves not members of any of these dissenting religious groups, opposed all religious establishments by law on grounds of principle, obtained the enactment of the famous "Virginia Bill for Religious Liberty" by which all religious groups were placed on an equal footing so far as the State was concerned. Similar though less far-reaching legislation was being considered and passed in other States.

By the time of the adoption of the Constitution, our history shows that there was a widespread awareness among many Americans of the dangers of a union of Church and State. These people knew, some of them from bitter personal experience, that one of the greatest dangers to the freedom of the individual to worship in his own way lay in the Government's placing its official stamp of approval upon one particular kind of prayer or one particular form of religious services. They knew the anguish, hardship and bitter strife that could come when zealous religious groups struggled with one another to obtain the Government's stamp of approval from each King, Queen, or Protector that came to temporary power. The Constitution was intended to avert a part of this danger by leaving the government of this country in the hands of the people rather than in the hands of any monarch. But this safeguard was not enough. Our Founders were no more willing to let the content of their prayers and their privilege of praying whenever they pleased be influenced by the ballot box than they were to let these vital matters of personal conscience depend upon the succession of monarchs. The First Amendment was added to the Constitution to stand as a guarantee that neither the power nor the prestige of the Federal Government would be used to control, support or influence the kinds of prayer the American people can say—that the people's religions must not be subjected to the pressures of government for change each time a new political administration is elected to office. Under that Amendment's prohibition against governmental establishment of religion, as reinforced by the provisions of the Fourteenth Amendment, government in this country, be it state or federal, is without power to prescribe by law any particular form of prayer which is to be used as an official prayer in carrying on any program of governmentally sponsored religious activity.

There can be no doubt that New York's state prayer program officially establishes the religious beliefs embodied in the Regents' prayer. The respondents' argument to the contrary, which is largely based upon the contention that the Regents' prayer is "non-denominational" and the fact that the program, as modified and approved by state courts, does not require all pupils to recite the prayer but permits those who wish to do so to remain silent or be excused from the room, ignores the essential nature of the program's constitutional defects. Neither the fact that the prayer may be denominationally neutral nor the fact that its observance on the part of the students is voluntary can serve to free it from the limitations of the Establishment Clause, as it might from the Free Exercise Clause, of the First Amendment, both of which are operative against the States by virtue of the Fourteenth Amendment. Although these two clauses may in certain instances overlap, they forbid two quite different kinds of governmental encroachment upon religious freedom. The Establishment Clause, unlike the Free Exercise Clause, does not depend upon any showing of direct governmental compulsion and is violated by the enactment of laws which establish an official religion whether those laws operate directly to coerce nonobserving individuals or not. This is not to say, of course, that laws officially prescribing a particular form of religious worship do not involve coercion of such individuals. When the power, prestige and financial support of government is placed behind a particular religious belief, the indirect coercive pressure upon religious minorities to conform to the prevailing officially approved religion is plain. But the purposes underlying the Establishment Clause go much further than that. Its first and most immediate purpose rested on the belief that a union of government and religion tends to destroy government and to degrade religion. The history of governmentally established religion, both in England and in this country, showed that whenever government had allied itself with one particular form of religion, the inevitable result had been that it had incurred the hatred, disrespect and even contempt of those who held contrary beliefs. That same history showed that many people had lost their respect for any religion that had relied upon the support of government to spread its faith. The Establishment Clause thus stands as an expression of principle on the part of the Founders of our Constitution that religion is too personal, too sacred, too holy, to permit its "unhallowed perversion" by a civil magistrate. Another purpose of the Establishment Clause rested upon an awareness of the historical fact that governmentally established religions and religious persecutions go hand in hand. The Founders knew that only a few years after the Book of Common Prayer became the only accepted form of religious services in the established Church of England, an Act of Uniformity was passed to compel all Englishmen to attend those services and to make it a criminal offense to conduct or attend religious gatherings of any other kind—a law which was consistently flouted by dissenting religious groups in England and which contributed to widespread persecutions of people like John Bunyan who persisted in holding "unlawful [religious] meetings . . . to the great disturbance and distraction of the good subjects of this kingdom. . . ." And they knew that similar persecutions had received the sanction of law in several of the colonies in this country soon after the establishment of official religions in those colonies. It was in large part to get completely away from this sort of systematic religious persecution that the Founders brought into being our Nation, our Constitution, and our Bill of Rights with its prohibition against any governmental establishment of religion. The New York laws officially prescribing the Regents' prayer are inconsistent with both the purposes of the Establishment Clause and with the Establishment Clause itself.

It has been argued that to apply the Constitution in such a way as to prohibit state laws respecting an establishment of religious services in public schools is to indicate a hostility toward religion or toward prayer. Nothing, of course, could be more wrong. The history of man is inseparable from the history of religion. And perhaps it is not too much to say that since the beginning of that history many people have devoutly believed that "More things are wrought by prayer than this world dreams of." It was doubtless largely due to men who believed this that there grew up a sentiment that caused men to leave the cross-currents of officially established state religions and religious persecution in Europe and come to this country filled with the hope that they could find a place in which they could pray when they pleased to the God of their faith in the language they chose. And there were men of this same faith in the power of prayer who led the fight for adoption of our Constitution and also for our Bill of Rights with the very guarantees of religious freedom that forbid the sort of governmental activity which New York has attempted here. These men knew that the First Amendment, which tried to put an end to governmental control of religion and of prayer, was not written to destroy either. They knew rather that it was written to quiet well-justified fears which nearly all of them felt arising out of an awareness that governments of the past had shackled men's tongues to make them speak only the religious thoughts that government wanted them to speak and to pray only to the God that government wanted them to pray to. It is neither sacrilegious nor antireligious to say that each separate government in this country should stay out of the business of writing or sanctioning official prayers and leave that purely religious function to the people themselves and to those the people choose to look to for religious guidance.

Reversed and remanded.

Mr. Justice Frankfurter took no part in the decision of this case.

Mr. Justice White took no part in the consideration or decision of this case.

Mr. Justice Douglas, concurring.

MR. JUSTICE STEWART, DISSENTING.

With all respect, I think the Court has misapplied a great constitutional principle. I cannot see how an "official religion" is established by letting those who want to say a prayer say it. On the contrary, I think that to deny the wish of these school children to join in reciting this prayer is to deny them the opportunity of sharing in the spiritual heritage of our Nation.

The Court's historical review of the quarrels over the Book of Common Prayer in England throws no light for me on the issue before us in this case. England had then and has now an established church. Equally unenlightening, I think, is the history of the early establishment and later rejection of an official church in our own States. For we deal here not with the establishment of a state church, which would, of course, be constitutionally impermissible, but with whether school children who want to begin their day by joining in prayer must be prohibited from doing so. Moreover, I think that the Court's task, in this as in all areas of constitutional adjudication, is not responsibly aided by the uncritical invocation of metaphors like the "wall of separation," a phrase nowhere to be found in the Constitution. What is relevant to the issue here is not the history of an established church in sixteenth century England or in eighteenth century America, but the history of the religious traditions of our people, reflected in countless practices of the institutions and officials of our government.

At the opening of each day's Session of this Court we stand, while one of our officials invokes the protection of God. Since the days of John Marshall our Crier has said, "God save the United States and this Honorable Court." Both the Senate and the House of Representatives open their daily Sessions with prayer. Each of our Presidents, from George Washington to John F. Kennedy, has upon assuming his Office asked the protection and help of God.

The Court today says that the state and federal governments are without constitutional power to prescribe any particular form of words to be recited by any group of the American people on any subject touching religion. The third stanza of "The Star-Spangled Banner," made our National Anthem by Act of Congress in 1931, contains these verses:

> "Blest with victory and peace, may the heav'n rescued land
> Praise the Pow'r that hath made and preserved us a nation!
> Then conquer we must, when our cause it is just,
> And this be our motto 'In God is our Trust.' "

In 1954 Congress added a phrase to the Pledge of Allegiance to the Flag so that it now contains the words "one Nation *under God,* indivisible, with liberty and justice for all." In 1952 Congress enacted legislation calling upon the President each year to proclaim a National Day of Prayer. Since 1865 the words "IN GOD WE TRUST" have been impressed on our coins.

Countless similar examples could be listed, but there is no need to belabor the obvious. . . .

I do not believe that this Court, or the Congress, or the President has by the actions and practices I have mentioned established an "official religion" in violation of the Constitution. And I do not believe the State of New York has done so in this case. What each has done has been to recognize and to follow the deeply entrenched and highly cherished spiritual traditions of our Nation—traditions which come down to us from those who almost two hundred years ago avowed their "firm reliance on the Protection of divine Providence" when they proclaimed the freedom and independence of this brave new world.

I dissent.

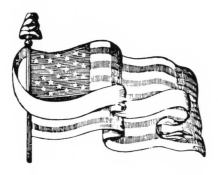

DECISION ON BIBLE READING IN THE PUBLIC SCHOOLS (1963) From
Abington School District v. Schempp, 374 U.S. 203 (1963).

Appeal from U.S. District Court for the Eastern District of Pennsylvania.

MR. JUSTICE CLARK DELIVERED THE OPINION OF THE COURT.

First, this Court has decisively settled that the First Amendment's mandate that "Congress shall make no law respecting an establishment of religion, or prohibiting the free exercise thereof" has been made wholly applicable to the States by the Fourteenth Amendment. . . .

Second, this Court has rejected unequivocally the contention that the Establishment Clause forbids only governmental preference of one religion over another. Almost 20 years ago in *Everson* . . . the Court said that "[n]either a state nor the Federal Government can set up a church. Neither can pass laws which aid one religion, aid all religions, or prefer one religion over another. . . ."

While none of the parties to either of these cases has questioned these basic conclusions of the Court, both of which have been long established, recognized and consistently reaffirmed, others continue to question their history, logic and efficacy. Such contentions, in the light of the consistent interpretation in cases of this Court, seem entirely untenable and of value only as academic exercises. . . .

The wholesome "neutrality" of which this Court's cases speak thus stems from a recognition of the teachings of history that powerful sects or groups might bring about a fusion of governmental and religious functions or a concert or dependency of one upon the other to the end that official support of the State or Federal Government would be placed behind the tenets of one or of all orthodoxies. This the Establishment Clause prohibits. And a further reason for neutrality is found in the Free Exercise Clause, which recognizes the value of religious training, teaching and observance and, more particularly, the right of every person to freely choose his own course with reference thereto, free of any compulsion from the state. This the Free Exercise Clause guarantees. Thus, as we have seen, the two clauses may overlap. As we have indicated, the Establishment Clause has been directly considered by this Court eight times in the past score of years and, with only one Justice dissenting on the point, it has consistently held that the clause withdrew all legislative power respecting religious belief or the expression thereof. The test may be stated as follows: what are the purpose and the primary effect of the enactment? If either is the advancement or inhibition of religion then the enactment exceeds the scope of legislative power as circumscribed by the Constitution. That is to say that to withstand the strictures of the Establishment Clause there must be a secular legislative purpose and a primary effect that neither advances nor inhibits religion. . . . The Free Exercise Clause, likewise considered many times here, withdraws from legislative power, state and federal, the exertion of any restraint on the free exercise of religion. Its purpose is to secure religious liberty in the individual by prohibiting any invasions thereof by civil authority. Hence it is necessary in a free exercise case for one to show the coercive effect of the enactment as it operates against him in the practice of his religion. The distinction between the two clauses is apparent—a violation of the Free Exercise Clause is predicated on coercion while the Establishment Clause violation need not be so attended. . . .

. . . In both cases the laws require religious exercises and such exercises are being conducted in direct violation of the rights of the appellees and petitioners. Nor are these required exercises mitigated by the fact that individual students may absent themselves upon parental request, for that fact furnishes no defense to a claim of unconstitutionality under the Establishment Clause. . . . Further, it is no defense to urge that the religious practices here may be relatively minor encroachments on the First Amendment. The breach of neutrality that is today a trickling stream may all too soon become a raging torrent and, in the words of Madison, "it is proper to take alarm at the first experiment on our liberties." . . .

It is insisted that unless these religious exercises are permitted a "religion of secularism" is established in the schools. We agree of course that the State may not establish a "religion of secularism" in the sense of affirmatively opposing or showing hostility to religion, thus "preferring those who believe in no religion over those who do believe." . . . We do not agree, however, that this decision in any sense has that effect. In addition, it might well be said that one's education is not complete without a study of comparative religion or the history of religion and its relationship to the advancement of civilization. It certainly may be said that the Bible is worthy of study for its literary and historic qualities. Nothing we have said here indicates that such study of the Bible or of religion, when presented objectively as part of a secular program of education, may not be effected consistently with the First Amendment. But the exercises here do not fall into those categories. They are religious exercises, required by the States in violation of the command of the First Amendment that the Government maintain strict neutrality, neither aiding nor opposing religion.

Finally, we cannot accept that the concept of neutrality, which does not permit a State to require a religious exercise even with the consent of the majority of those affected, collides with the majority's right to free exercise of religion. While the Free Exercise Clause clearly prohibits the use of state action to deny the rights of free exercise to *anyone*, it has never meant that a majority could use the machinery of the State to practice its beliefs. Such a contention was effectively answered by MR. JUSTICE JACKSON for the Court in *West Virginia State Board of Education* v. *Barnette*. . . .

"The very purpose of the Bill of Rights was to withdraw certain subjects from the vicissitudes of political controversy, to place them beyond the reach of majorities and officials and to establish them as legal principles to be applied by the courts. One's right to . . . freedom of worship . . . and other fundamental rights may not be submitted to vote; they depend on the outcome of no elections."

The place of religion in our society is an exalted one, achieved through a long tradition of reliance on the home, the church and the inviolable citadel of the individual heart and mind. We have come to recognize through bitter experience that it is not within the power of government to invade that citadel, whether its purpose or effect be to aid or oppose, to advance or retard. In the relationship between man and religion, the State is firmly committed to a position of neutrality. Though the application of that rule requires interpretation of a delicate sort, the rule itself is clearly and concisely stated in the words of the First Amendment. . . .

DECISION ON DISTRIBUTION OF TEXTBOOKS TO RELIGIOUS SCHOOLS AT PUBLIC EXPENSE (1968) From *Board of Education of Central School District* v. *Allen,* 392 U.S. 236 (1968).

Appeal from the Court of Appeals of New York.

MR. JUSTICE WHITE DELIVERED THE OPINION OF THE COURT.

A law of the State of New York requires local public school authorities to lend textbooks free of charge to all students in grades seven through 12; students attending private schools are included. This case presents the question whether this statute is a "law respecting the establishment of religion or prohibiting the free exercise thereof," and so in conflict with the First and Fourteenth Amendments to the Constitution, because it authorizes the loan of textbooks to students attending parochial schools. We hold that the law is not in violation of the Constitution.

Until 1965, § 701 of the Educational Law of the State of New York authorized public school boards to designate textbooks for use in the public schools, to purchase such books with public funds, and to rent or sell the books to public school students. In 1965 the Legislature amended § 701, basing the amendments on findings that the "public welfare and safety require that the state and local communities give assistance to educational programs which are important to our national defense and the general welfare of the state." Beginning with the 1966–1967 school year, local school boards were required to purchase textbooks and lend them without charge "to all children residing in such district who are enrolled in grades seven to twelve of a public or private school which complies with the compulsory education law." The books now loaned are "text-books which are designated for use in any public, elementary or secondary schools of the state or are approved by any boards of education," and which—according to a 1966 amendment—"a pupil is required to use as a text for a semester or more in a particular class in the school he legally attends." . . .

On appeal, the New York Court of Appeals . . . by a . . . 4-3 vote held that §701 was not in violation of either the State or the Federal Constitution. . . . The Court of Appeals said that the law's purpose was to benefit all school children, regardless of the type of school they attended, and that only textbooks approved by public school authorities could be loaned. It therefore considered § 701 "completely neutral with respect to religion, merely making available secular textbooks at the request of the individual student and asking no question about what school he attends." Section 701, the Court of Appeals concluded, is not a law which "establishes a religion or constitutes the use of public funds to aid religious schools." . . .

Everson and later cases have shown that the line between state neutrality to religion and state support of religion is not easy to locate. . . . The statute upheld in *Everson* would be considered a law having "a secular legislative purpose and a primary effect that neither advances nor inhibits religion." We reach the same result with respect to the New York law requiring school books to be loaned free of charge to all students in specified grades. The express purpose of § 701 was stated by the New York Legislature to be furtherance of the educational opportunities available to the young. Appellants have shown us nothing about the necessary effects of the statute that is contrary to its stated purpose. The law merely makes available to all children the benefits of a general program to lend school books free of charge. Books are furnished at the request of the pupil and ownership remains, at least technically, in the State. Thus no funds or books are furnished to parochial schools, and the financial benefit is to parents and children, not to schools. Perhaps free books make it more likely that some children choose to attend a sectarian school, but that was true of the state-paid bus fares in *Everson* and does not alone demonstrate an unconstitutional degree of support for a religious institution.

Of course books are different from buses. Most bus rides have no inherent religious significance, while religious books are common. However, the language of § 701 does not authorize the loan of religious books, and the State claims no right to distribute religious literature. Although the books loaned are those required by the parochial school for use in specific courses, each book loaned must be approved by the public school authorities; only secular books may receive approval. The law was construed by the Court of Appeals of New York as "merely making available secular textbooks at the request of the individual student," . . . and the record contains no suggestion that religious books have been loaned. Absent evidence, we cannot assume that school authorities, who constantly face the same problem in selecting textbooks for use in the public schools, are unable to distinguish between secular and religious books or that they will not honestly discharge their duties under the law. In judging the validity of the statute on this record we must proceed on the assumption that books loaned to students are books that are not unsuitable for use in the public schools because of religious content.

The major reason offered by appellants of distinguishing free textbooks from free bus fares is that books, but not buses, are critical to the teaching process, and in a sectarian school that process is employed to teach religion. However, this Court has long recognized that religious schools pursue two goals, religious instruction and secular education. In the leading case of *Pierce* v. *Society of Sisters*, 268 U.S. 510 (1925), the Court held that although it would not question Oregon's power to compel school attendance or require that the attendance be at an institution meeting State-imposed requirements as to quality and nature of curriculum, Oregon had not shown that its interest in secular education required that all children attend publicly operated schools. A premise of this holding was the view that the State's interest in education would be served sufficiently by reliance on the secular teaching that accompanied religious training in the schools maintained by the Society of Sisters. Since *Pierce*, a substantial body of case law has confirmed the power of the States to insist that attendance at private schools, if it is to satisfy state compulsory-attendance laws, be at institutions which provide minimum hours of instruction, employ teachers of specified training, and cover prescribed subjects of instruction. Indeed, the State's interest in assuring that these standards are being met has been considered a sufficient reason for refusing to accept instruction at home as compliance with compulsory education statutes. These cases were a sensible corollary of *Pierce* v. *Society of Sisters:* if the State must satisfy its interest in secular education through the instrument of private schools, it has a proper interest in the manner in which those schools perform their secular educational function. Another corollary was *Cochran* v. *Louisiana State Board of Education*, 281 U.S. 370 (1930), where appellants said that a statute requiring school books to be furnished without charge to all students, whether they attended public or private schools, did not serve a "public purpose," and so offended the Fourteenth Amendment. Speaking through Chief Justice Hughes, the Court summarized as follows its conclusion that Louisiana's interest in the secular education being provided by private schools made provision of textbooks to students in those schools a properly public concern: "[The State's] interest is education, broadly; its method, comprehensive. Individual interests are aided only as the common interest is safeguarded." . . .

Underlying these cases, and underlying also the legislative judgments that have preceded the court decisions, has been a recognition that private education has played and is playing a significant and valuable role in raising national levels of knowledge, competence, and experience. Americans care about the quality of the secular education available to their children. They have considered high quality education to be an indispensable ingredient for achieving the kind of nation, and the kind of citizenry, that they have desired to create. Considering this attitude, the continued willingness to rely on private school systems, including parochial systems, strongly suggests that a wide segment of informed opinion, legislative and otherwise, has found that those schools do an acceptable job of providing secular education to their students. This judgment is further evidence that parochial schools are performing, in addition to their sectarian function, the task of secular education.

Against this background of judgment and experience, unchallenged in the meager record before us in this case, we cannot agree with appellants either that all teaching in a sectarian school is religious or that the processes of secular and religious training are so intertwined that secular textbooks furnished to students by the public are in fact instrumental in the teaching of religion. This case comes to us after summary judgment entered on the pleadings. Nothing in this record supports the proposition that all textbooks, whether they deal with mathematics, physics, foreign languages, history, or literature, are used by the parochial schools to teach religion. No evidence has been offered about particular schools, particular courses, particular teachers, or particular books. We are unable to hold, based solely on judicial notice, that this statute results in unconstitutional involvement of the State with religious instruction or that §701, for this or the other reasons urged, is a law respecting the establishment of religion within the meaning of the First Amendment. . . .

The judgment is affirmed.

MR. JUSTICE BLACK, DISSENTING.

I believe the New York law held valid is a flat, flagrant, open violation of the First and Fourteenth Amendments which together forbid Congress or state legislatures to enact any law "respecting an establishment of religion." For that reason I would reverse the New York Court of Appeals' judgments. . . .

It is true, of course, that the New York law does not as yet formally adopt or establish a state religion. But it takes a great stride in that direction and coming events cast their shadows before them. The same powerful sectarian religious propagandists who have succeeded in securing passage of the present law to help religious schools carry on their sectarian religious purposes can and doubtless will continue their propaganda, looking toward complete domination and supremacy of their particular brand of religion. And it nearly always is by insidious approaches that the citadels of liberty are most successfully attacked. . . .

The First Amendment's bar to establishment of religion must preclude a State from using funds levied from all of its citizens to purchase books for use by sectarian schools, which, although "secular," realistically will in some way inevitably tend to propagate the religious views of the favored sect. Books are the most essential tool of education since they contain the resources of knowledge which the educational process is designed to exploit. In this sense it is not difficult to distinguish books, which are the heart of any school, from bus fares, which provide a convenient and helpful general public transportation service. With respect to the former, state financial support actively and directly assists the teaching and propagation of sectarian religious viewpoints in clear conflict with the First Amendment's establishment bar; with respect to the latter, the State merely provides a general and nondiscriminatory transportation service in no way related to substantive religious views and beliefs.

This New York law, it may be said by some, makes but a small inroad and does not amount to complete state establishment of religion. But that is no excuse for upholding it. It requires no prophet to foresee that on the argument used to support this law others could be upheld providing for state or federal government funds to buy property on which to erect religious school buildings or to erect the buildings themselves, to pay the salaries of the religious school teachers, and finally to have the sectarian religious groups cease to rely on voluntary contributions of members of their sects while waiting for the Government to pick up all the bills for the religious schools. . . .

I still subscribe to the belief that tax-raised funds cannot constitutionally be used to support religious schools, buy their school books, erect their buildings, pay their teachers, or pay any other other of their maintenance expenses, even to the extent of one penny. The First Amendment's prohibition against governmental establishment of religion was written on the assumption that state aid to religion and religious schools generates discord, disharmony, hatred, and strife among our people, and that any government that supplies such aids is to that extent a tyranny. And I still believe that the only way to protect minority religious groups from majority groups in this country is to keep the wall of separation between church and state high and impregnable as the First and Fourteenth Amendments provide. The Court's affirmance here bodes nothing but evil to religious peace in this country.

MR. JUSTICE DOUGLAS, *dissenting.*

The Supreme Court as National School Board—The Racial Issue

PLESSY v. FERGUSON (1896)   163 U.S. 537.

MR. JUSTICE BROWN, AFTER STATING THE CASE, DELIVERED THE OPINION OF THE COURT.

This case turns upon the constitutionality of an act of the General Assembly of the State of Louisiana, passed in 1890, providing for separate railway carriages for the white and colored races. . . .

The information filed in the criminal District Court charged in substance that Plessy, being a passenger between two stations within the State of Louisiana, was assigned by officers of the company to the coach used for the race to which he belonged, but he insisted upon going into a coach used by the race to which he did not belong. Neither in the information nor plea was his particular race or color averred.

The petition for the writ of prohibition averred that petitioneer was seven eighths Caucasian and one eighth African blood; that the mixture of colored blood was not discernible in him, and that he was entitled to every right, privilege and immunity secured to citizens of the United States of the white race; and that, upon such theory, he took possession of a vacant seat in a coach where passengers of the white race were accommodated, and was ordered by the conductor to vacate said coach and take a seat in another assigned to persons of the colored race, and having refused to comply with such demand he was forcibly ejected with the aid of a police officer, and imprisoned in the parish jail to answer a charge of having violated the above act.

The constitutionality of this act is attacked upon the ground that it conflicts both with the Thirteenth Amendment of the Constitution, abolishing slavery, and the Fourteenth Amendment, which prohibits certain restrictive legislation on the part of the States. . . .

A statute which implies merely a legal distinction between the white and colored races—a distinction which is founded in the color of the two races, and which must always exist so long as white men are distinguished from the other race by color—has no tendency to destroy the legal equality of the two races, or reestablish a state of involuntary servitude. Indeed, we do not understand that the Thirteenth Amendment is strenuously relied upon by the plaintiff in error in this connection. . . .

The object of the [Fourteenth] amendment was undoubtedly to enforce the absolute equality of the two races before the law, but in the nature of things it could not have been intended to abolish distinctions based upon color, or to enforce social, as distinguished from political equality, or a commingling of the two races upon terms unsatisfactory to either. Laws permitting, and even requiring, their separation in places where they are liable to be brought into contact do not necessarily imply the inferiority of either race to the other, and have been generally, if not universally, recognized as within the competency of the state legislatures in the exercise of their police power. The most common instance of this is connected with the establishment of separate schools for white and colored children, which has been held to be a valid exercise of the legislative power even by courts of States where the political rights of the colored race have been longest and most earnestly enforced.

*   *   *

It is claimed by the plaintiff in error that, in any mixed community, the reputation of belonging to the dominant race, in this instance the white race, is *property,* in the same sense that a right of action, or of inheritance, is property. Conceding this to be so, for the purposes of this case, we are unable to see how this statute deprives him of, or in any way affects his right to, such property. If he be a white man and assigned to a colored coach, he may have his action for damages against the company for being deprived of his so called property. Upon the other hand, if he be a colored man and be so assigned, he has been deprived of no property, since he is not lawfully entitled to the reputation of being a white man.

In this connection, it is also suggested by the learned counsel for the plaintiff in error that the same argument that will justify the state legislature in requiring railways to provide separate accommodations for the two races will also authorize them to require separate cars to be provided for people whose hair is of a certain color, or who are aliens, or who belong to certain nationalities, or to enact laws requiring colored people to walk upon one side of the street, and white people upon the other, or requiring white men's houses to be painted white, and colored men's black, or their vehicles or business signs to be of different colors, upon the theory that one side of the street is as good as the other, or that a house or vehicle of one color is as good as one of another color. The reply to all this is that every exercise of the police power must be reasonable, and extend only to such laws as are enacted in good faith for the promotion for the public good, and not for the annoyance or oppression of a particular class. . . .

So far, then, as a conflict with the Fourteenth Amendment is concerned, the case reduces itself to the question whether the statute of Louisiana is a reasonable regulation, and with respect to this there must necessarily be a large discretion on the part of the legislature. In determining the question of reasonableness it is at liberty to act with reference to the established usages, customs and traditions of the people, and with a view to the promotion of their comfort, and the preservation of the public peace and good order. Gauged by this standard, we cannot say that a law which authorizes or even requires the separation of the two races in public conveyances is unreasonable, or more obnoxious to the Fourteenth Amendment than the acts of Congress requiring separate schools for colored children in the District of Columbia, the constitutionality of which does not seem to have been questioned, or the corresponding acts of state legislatures.

We consider the underlying fallacy of the plaintiff's argument to consist in the assumption that the enforced separation of the two races stamps the colored race with a badge of inferiority. If this be so, it is not by reason of anything found in the act, but solely because the colored race chooses to put that construction upon it. The argument necessarily assumes that if, as has been more than once the case, and is not unlikely to be so again, the colored race should become the dominant power in the state legislature, and should enact a law in precisely 'similar terms, it would thereby relegate the white race to an inferior position. We imagine that the white race, at least, would not acquiesce in this assumption. The argument also assumes that social prejudices may be overcome by legislation, and that equal rights cannot be secured to the negro except by an enforced commingling of the two races. We cannot accept this proposition. If the two races are to meet upon terms of social equality, it must be the result of natural affinities, a mutual appreciation of each other's merits and a voluntary consent of individuals. As was said by the Court of Appeals of New York in *People* v. *Gallagher,* 93 N.Y. 438, 448, "this end can neither be accomplished nor promoted by laws which conflict with the general sentiment of the community upon whom they are designed to operate. When the government, therefore, has secured to each of its citizens equal rights before the law and equal opportunities for improvement and progress, it has accomplished the end for which it was organized and performed all of the functions respecting social advantages with which it is endowed." Legislation is powerless to eradicate racial instincts or to abolish distinctions based upon physical differences, and the attempt to do so can only result in accentuating the difficulties of the present situation. If the civil and political rights of both races be equal one cannot be inferior to the other civilly or politically. If one race be inferior to the other socially, the Constitution of the United States cannot put them upon the same plane.

Affirmed.

MR. JUSTICE HARLAN, DISSENTING.

The white race deems itself to be the dominant race in this country. And so it is, in prestige, in achievements, in education, in wealth and in power. So, I doubt not, it will continue to be for all time, if it remains true to its great heritage and holds fast to the principles of constitutional liberty. But in view of the Constitution, in the eye of the law, there is in this country no superior, dominant, ruling class of citizens. There is no caste here. Our Constitution is color-blind, and neither knows nor tolerates classes among citizens. In respect of civil rights, all citizens are equal before the law. The humblest is the peer of the most powerful. The law regards man as man, and takes no account of his surroundings or of his color when his civil rights as guaranteed by the supreme law of the land are involved. It is, therefore, to be regretted that this high tribunal, the final expositor of the fundamental law of the land, has reached the conclusion that it is competent for a State to regulate the enjoyment by citizens of their civil rights solely upon the basis of race.

In my opinion, the judgment this day rendered will, in time, prove to be quite as pernicious as the decision made by this tribunal in the *Dred Scott case.* It was adjudged in that case that the descendants of Africans who were imported into this country and sold as slaves were not included nor intended to be included under the word "citizens" in the Constitution, and could not claim any of the rights and privileges which that instrument provided for and secured to citizens of the United States; that at the time of the adoption of the Constitution they were "considered as a subordinate and inferior class of beings, who had been subjugated by the dominant race, and, whether emancipated or not, yet remained subject to their authority, and had no rights or privileges but such as those who held the power and the government might choose to grant them." 19 How. 393, 404. The recent amendments of the Constitution, it was supposed, had eradicated these principles from our institutions. But it seems that we have yet, in some of the States, a dominant race—a superior class of citizens, which assumes to regulate the enjoyment of civil rights, common to all citizens, upon the basis of race. The present decision, it may well be apprehended, will not only stimulate aggressions, more or less brutal and irritating, upon the admitted rights of colored citizens, but will encourage the belief that it is possible, by means of state enactments, to defeat the beneficient purposes which the people of the United States had in view when they adopted the recent amendments of the Constitution, by one of which the blacks of this country were made citizens of the United States and of the States in which they respectively reside, and whose privileges and immunities, as citizens, the States are forbidden to abridge. Sixty millions of whites are in no danger from the presence here of eight millions of blacks. The destinies of the two races, in this country, are indissolubly linked together, and the interests of both require that the common government of all shall not permit the seeds of race hate to be planted under the sanction of law. What can more certainly arouse race hate, what more certainly create and perpetuate a feeling of distrust between these races, than state enactments, which, in fact, proceed on the ground that colored citizens are so inferior and degraded that they cannot be allowed to sit in public coaches occupied by white citizens? That, as all will admit, is the real meaning of such legislation as was enacted in Louisiana. . . .

I am of opinion that the statute of Louisiana is inconsistent with the personal liberty of citizens, white and black, in that State, and hostile to both the spirit and letter of the Constitution of the United States. If laws of like character should be enacted in the several States of the Union, the effect would be in the highest degree mischievous. Slavery, as an institution tolerated by law would, it is true, have disappeared from our country, but there would remain a power in the States, by sinister legislation, to interfere with the full enjoyment of the blessings of freedom; to regulate civil rights, common to all citizens, upon the basis of race; and to place in a condition of legal inferiority a large body of American citizens, now constituting a part of the political community called the People of the United States, for whom, and by whom through representatives, our government is administered. Such a system is inconsistent with the guarantee given by the Constitution to each State of a republican form of government, and may be stricken down by Congressional action, or by the courts in the discharge of their solemn duty to maintain the supreme law of the land, anything in the constitution or laws of any State to the contrary notwithstanding.

For the reasons stated, I am constrained to withhold my assent from the opinion and judgment of the majority.

A STATE MAY PROHIBIT MIXING OF RACES IN THE SCHOOLS

(1908) From *Berea College* v. *Commonwealth of Kentucky,* 211 U.S. 45 (1908).

MR. JUSTICE BREWER DELIVERED THE OPINION OF THE COURT

There is no dispute as to the facts. That the act does not violate the constitution of Kentucky is settled by the decision of its highest court, and the single question for our consideration is whether it conflicts with the Federal Constitution. The Court of Appeals discussed at some length the general power of the State in respect to the separation of the two races. It also ruled that "the right to teach white and negro children in a private school at the same time and place is not a property right. Besides, appellant as a corporation created by this State has no natural right to teach at all. Its right to teach is such as the State sees fit to give to it. The State may withhold it altogether, or qualify it." *Allgeyer* v. *Louisiana,* 165 U.S. 578.

* * *

Again, the decision by a state court of the extent and limitation of the powers conferred by the State upon one of its own corporations is of a purely local nature. In creating a corporation a State may withhold powers which may be exercised by and cannot be denied to an individual. It is under no obligation to treat both alike. In granting corporate powers the legislature may deem that the best interests of the State would be subserved by some restriction, and the corporation may not plead that in spite of the restriction it has more or greater powers because the citizen has. "The granting of such right or privilege [right or privilege to be a corporation] rests entirely in the discretion of the State, and, of course, when granted, may be accompanied with such conditions as its legislature may judge most befitting to its interests and policy." *Home Ins. Co.* v. *New York,* 134 U.S. 594, 600; *Perine* v. *Chesapeake & Delaware Canal Co.,* 9 How. 172, 184; *Horn Silver Mining Co.* v. *New York,* 143 U.S. 305-312. The act of 1904 forbids "any person, corporation or association of persons to maintain or operate any college," etc. Such a statute may conflict with the Federal Constitution in denying to individuals powers which they may rightfully exercise, and yet, at the same time, be valid as to a corporation created by the State.

It may be said that the Court of Appeals sustained the validity of this section of the statute, both against individuals and corporations. It ruled that the legislation was within the power of the State, and that the State might rightfully thus restrain all individuals, corporations and associations. But it is unnecessary for us to consider anything more than the question of its validity as applied to corporations.

The statute is clearly separable and may be valid as to one class while invalid as to another. Even if it were conceded that its assertion of power over individuals cannot be sustained, still it must be upheld so far as it restrains corporations.

There is no force in the suggestion that the statute, although clearly separable, must stand or fall as an entirety on the ground the legislature would not have enacted one part unless it could reach all. That the legislature of Kentucky desired to separate the teaching of white and colored children may be conceded, but it by no means follows that it would not have enforced the separation so far as it could do so, even though it could not make it effective under all circumstances. In other

THE
MINORITIES

3091

words, it is not at all unreasonable to believe that the legislature, although advised beforehand of the constitutional question, might have prohibited all organizations and corporations under its control from teaching white and colored children together, and thus made at least uniform official action. The rule of construction in questions of this nature is stated by Chief Justice Shaw in *Warren* v. *Mayor of Charlestown*, 2 Gray 84, quoted approvingly by this court in *Allen* v. *Louisiana*, 103 U.S. 80–84.

"But if they are so mutually connected with and dependent on each other, as conditions, considerations or compensations for each other as to warrant a belief that the legislature intended them as a whole, and that if all could not be carried into effect, the legislature would not pass the residue independently, and some parts are unconstitutional, all the provisions which are thus dependent, conditional or connected, must fall with them."

See also *Loeb* v. *Township Trustees*, 179 U.S. 472, 490, in which this court said:

"As one section of a statute may be repugnant to the Constitution without rendering the whole act void, so, one provision of a section may be invalid by reason of its not conforming to the Constitution, while all the other provisions may be subject to no constitutional infirmity. One part may stand, while another will fall, unless the two are so connected or dependent on each other in subject-matter, meaning or purpose, that the good cannot remain without the bad. The point is, not whether the parts are contained in the same section, for, the distribution into sections is purely artificial; but whether they are essentially and inseparably connected in substance—whether the provisions are so interdependent that one cannot operate without the other."

Further, insamuch as the Courts of Appeals considered the act separable, and while sustaining it as an entirety gave an independent reason which applies only to corporations, it is obvious that it recognized the force of the suggestions we have made. And when a state statute is so interpreted this court should hesitate before it holds that the Supreme Court of the State did not know what was the thought of the legislature in its enactment. *Missouri, Kansas & Texas Railway* v. *McCann*, 174 U.S. 580, 586; *Tullis* v. *Lake Erie & Western Railroad*, 175 U.S. 348, 353.

While the terms of the present charter are not given in the record, yet it was admitted on the trial that the defendant was a corporation organized and incorporated under the general statutes of the State of Kentucky, and of course the state courts, as well as this court on appeal, take judicial notice of those statutes. Further, in the brief of counsel for the defendant is given a history of the incorporation proceedings, together with the charters. from that it appears that Berea College was organized under the authority of an act for the incorporation of voluntary associations, approved March 9, 1854 (2 Stanton Rev. Stat. Ky. 553), which act was amended by an act of March 10, 1856 (2 Stanton, 555), and which in terms reserved to the General Assembly "the right to alter or repeal the act to which this act is an amendment, at any time hereafter." After the constitution of 1891 was adopted by the State of Kentucky and on June 10, 1899, the college was reincorporated under the provisions of chap. 32, art. 8, Ky. Stat. (Carroll's Ky. Stat. 1903, p. 459), the charter defining its business in these words: "Its object is the education of all persons who may attend its institution of learning at Berea, and, in the language of the original articles, 'to promote the cause of Christ.'" The constitution of 1891 provided in § 3 of the bill of rights that "Every grant of a franchise, privilege or exemption shall remain, subject to revocation, alteration or amendment." Carroll's Ky. Stat. 1903, p. 86. So that the full power of amendment was reserved to the legislature.

*   *   *

Again, it is insisted that the Court of Appeals did not regard the legislation as making an amendment, because another prosecution instituted against the same corporation under the fourth section of the act, which makes it a misdemeanor to teach pupils of the two races in the same institutions, even although one race is taught in one branch and another in another branch, provided the two branches are within twenty-five miles of each other, was held could not be sustained, the court saying: "This last section, we think, violates the limitations upon the police power: It is unreasonable and oppressive." But while so ruling it also held that this section could be ignored and that the remainder of the act was complete not withstanding. Whether the reasoning of the court concerning the fourth section be satisfactory or not is immaterial, for no question of its validity is presented, and the Court of Appeals, while striking it down, sustained the balance of the act. We need concern ourselves only with the inquiry whether the first section can be upheld as coming within the power of a State over its own corporate creatures.

We are of opinion, for reasons stated, that it does come within that power, and on this ground the judgment of the Court of Appeals of Kentucky is

Affirmed.

MR. JUSTICE HARLAN, dissenting.

DECISION ON A CHINESE CHILD ASSIGNED TO A BLACK SCHOOL
(1927)   From *Gong Lum* v. *Rice,* 275 U.S. 78 (1927).

MR. CHIEF JUSTICE TAFT DELIVERED THE OPINION OF THE COURT.

This was a petition for mandamus filed in the state Circuit Court of Mississippi for the First Judicial District of Bolivar County.

Gong Lum is a resident of Mississippi, resides in the Rosedale Consolidated High School District, and is the father of Martha Lum. He is engaged in the mercantile business. Neither he nor she was connected with the consular service or any other service of the government of China, or any other government, at the time of her birth. She was nine years old when the petition was filed, having been born January 2l, 1915, and she sued by her next friend, Chew How, who is a native born citizen of the United States and the State of Mississippi. The petition alleged that she was of good moral character and between the ages of five and twenty-one years, and that, as she was such a citizen and an educable child, it became her father's duty under the law to send her to school; that she desired to attend the Rosedale Consolidated High School; that at the opening of the school she appeared as a pupil, but at the noon recess she was notified by the superintendent that she would not be allowed to return to school; that an order had been issued by the Board of Trustees, who are made defendants, excluding her from attending the school solely on the ground that she was of Chinese descent and not a member of the white or Caucasian race, and that their order had been made in pursuance to instructions from the State Superintendent of Education of Mississippi, who is also made a defendant.

The petitioners further show that there is no school maintained in the District for the education of children of Chinese descent, and none established in Bolivar County where she could attend.

The Constitution of Mississippi requires that there shall be a county common school fund, made up of poll taxes from the various counties, to be retained in the counties where the same is collected, and a state common school fund to be taken from the general fund in the state treasury, which together shall be sufficient to maintain a common school for a term of four months in each scholastic year, but that any county or separate school district may levy an additional tax to maintain schools for a longer time than a term of four months, and that the said common school fund shall be distributed among the several counties and separate school districts in proportion to the number of educable children in each, to be collected from the data in the office of the State Superintendent of Education in the manner prescribed by law; that the legislature encourage by all suitable means the promotion of intellectual, scientific, moral and agricultural improvement, by the establishment of a uniform system of free public schools by taxation or otherwise, for all children between the ages of five and twenty-one years, and, as soon as practicable, establish schools of higher grade.

The petition alleged that, in obedience to this mandate of the Constitution, the legislature has provided for the establishment and for the payment of the expenses of the Rosedale Consolidated High School, and that the plaintiff, Gong Lum, the petitioner's father, is a taxpayer and helps to support and maintain the school; that Martha Lum is an educable child, is entitled to attend the school as a pupil, and that this is the only school conducted in the District available for her as a pupil; that the right to attend it is a valuable right; that she is not a member of the colored race nor is she of mixed blood, but that she is pure Chinese; that she is by the action of the Board of Trustees and the State Superintendent discriminated against directly and denied her right to be a member of the Rosedale School; that the school authorities have no discretion under the law as to her admission as a pupil in the school, but that they continue without authority of law to deny her the right to attend it as a pupil. For these reasons the writ of mandamus is prayed for against the defendants commanding them and each of them to desist from discriminating against her on account of her race or ancestry and to give her the same rights and privileges that other educable children between the ages of five and twenty-one are granted in the Rosedale Consolidated High School.

The petition was demurred to by the defendants on the ground, among others, that the bill showed on its face that plaintiff is a member of the Mongolian or yellow race, and therefore not entitled to attend the schools provided by law in the State of Mississippi for children of the white or Caucasian race.

The trial court overruled the demurrer and ordered that a writ of mandamus issue to the defendants as prayed in the petition.

The defendants then appealed to the Supreme Court of Mississippi, which heard the case. In its opinion, it directed its attention to the proper construction of §207 of the State Constitution of 1890, which provides:

"Separate schools shall be maintained for children of the white and colored races."

The Court held that this provision of the Constitution divided the educable children into those of the pure white or Caucasian race, on the one hand, and the brown, yellow and black races, on the other, and therefore that Martha Lum of the Mongolian or yellow race could not insist on being classed with the whites under this constitutional division. The Court said:

"The legislature is not compelled to provide separate schools for each of the colored races, and, unless and until it does provide such schools and provide for segregation of the other races, such races are entitled to have the benefit of the colored public schools. Under our statutes a colored public school exists in every county and in some convenient district in which every colored child is entitled to obtain an education. These schools are within the reach of all the children of the state, and the plaintiff does not show by her petition that she applied for admission to such schools. On the contrary the petitioner takes the position that because there are no separate public schools for Mongolians that she is entitled to enter the white public schools in preference to the colored public schools. A consolidated school in this state is simply a common school conducted as other common schools are conducted; the only distinction being that two or more school districts have been consolidated into one school. Such consolidation is entirely discretionary with the county school board having reference to the condition existing in the particular territory. Where a school district has an unusual amount of territory, with an unusual valuation of property therein, it may levy additional taxes. But the other common schools under similar statutes have the same power.

"If the plaintiff desires, she may attend the colored public schools of her district, or, if she does not so desire, she may go to a private school. The compulsory school law of this state does not require the attendance at a public school, and a parent under the decisions of the Supreme Court of the United States has a right to educate his child in a private school if he so desires. But plaintiff is not entitled to attend a white public school."

As we have seen, the plaintiffs aver that the Rosedale Consolidated High School is the only school conducted in that district available for Martha Lum as a pupil. They also aver that there is no school maintained in the district of Bolivar County for the education of Chinese children and none in the county. How are these averments to be reconciled with the statement of the State Supreme Court that colored schools are maintained in every county by virtue of the Constitution? This seems to be explained, in the language of the State Supreme Court, as follows:

"By statute it is provided that all the territory of each county of the state shall be divided into school districts separately for the white and colored races; that is to say, the whole territory is to be divided into white school districts, and then a new division of the county for colored school districts. In other words, the statutory scheme is to make the districts outside of the separate school districts, districts for the particular race, white or colored, so that the territorial limits of the school districts need not be the same, but the territory embraced in a school district for the colored race may not be the same territory embraced in the school district for the white race, and *vice versa*, which system of creating the common school districts for the two races, white and colored, does not require schools for each race as such to be maintained in each district, but each child, no matter from what territory, is assigned to some school district, the school buildings being separately located and separately controlled, but each having the same curriculum, and each having the same number of months of school term, if the attendance is maintained for the said statutory period, which school district of the common or public schools has certain privileges, among which is to maintain a public school by local taxation for a longer period of time than the said term of four months under named conditions which apply alike to the common schools for the white and colored races."

We must assume then that there are school districts for colored children in Bolivar County, but that no colored school is within the limits of the Rosedale Consolidated High School District. This is not inconsistent with there being, at a place outside of that district and in a different district, a colored school which the plaintiff Martha Lum, may conveniently attend. If so, she is not denied, under the existing school system, the right to attend and enjoy the privileges of a common school education in a colored school. If it were otherwise, the petition should have contained an allegation showing it. Had the petition alleged specifically that there was no colored school in Martha Lum's neighborhood to which she could conveniently go, a different question would have been presented, and this, without regard to the State Supreme Court's construction of the State Constitution as limiting the white schools provided for the education of children of the white or Caucasian race. But we do not find the petition to present such a situation.

The case then reduces itself to the question whether a state can be said to afford to a child of Chinese ancestry born in this country, and a citizen of the United States, equal protection of the laws by giving her the opportunity for a common school education in a school which receives only colored children of the brown, yellow or black races.

The right and power of the state to regulate the method of providing for the education of its youth at public expense is clear. In *Cumming v. Richmond County Board of Education* persons of color sued the Board of Education to enjoin it from maintaining a high school for white children without providing a similar school for colored children which had existed and had been discontinued. Mr. Justice Harlan, in delivering the opinion of the Court, said:

"Under the circumstances disclosed, we cannot say that this action of the state court, was within the meaning of the Fourteenth Amendment, a denial by the State to the plaintiffs and to those associated with them of the equal protection of the laws, or of any privileges belonging to them as citizens of the United States. We may add that while all admit that the benefits and burdens of public taxation must be shared by citizens without discrimination against any class on account of their race, the education of the people in schools maintained by state taxation is a matter belonging to the respective States, and any interference on the part of Federal authority with the management of such schools can not be justified except in the case of a clear and unmistakable disregard of the rights secured by the supreme law of the land."

The question here is whether a Chinese citizen of the United States is denied equal protection of the laws when he is classed among the colored races and furnished facilities for education equal to that offered to all, whether white, brown, yellow or black. Were this a new question, it would call for very full argument and consideration, but we think that it is the same question which has been many times decided to be within the constitutional power of the state legislature to settle without intervention of the federal courts under the Federal Constitution.

In *Plessy v. Ferguson*, in upholding the validity under the Fourteenth Amendment of a statute of Louisiana requiring the separation of the white and colored races in railway coaches, a more difficult question than this, this Court, speaking of permitted race separation, said:

"The most common instances of this is connected with the establishment of separate schools for white and colored children, which has been held to be a valid exercise of the legislative power even by courts of States where the political rights of the colored race have been longest and most earnestly enforced."

The case of *Roberts v. City of Boston* in which Chief Justice Shaw of the Supreme Judicial Court of Massachusetts, announced the opinion of that court upholding the separation of colored and white schools under a state constitutional injunction of equal protection, the same as the Fourteenth Amendment, was then referred to, and this Court continued:

"Similar laws have been enacted by Congress under its general power of legislation over the District of Columbia as well as by the legislatures of many of the States, and have been generally, if not uniformly, sustained by the Courts," citing many of the cases above named.

Most of the cases cited arose, it is true, over the establishment of separate schools as between white pupils and black pupils, but we can not think that the question is any different or that any different result can be reached, assuming the cases above cited to be rightly decided, where the issue is as between white pupils and the pupils of the yellow races. The decision is within the discretion of the state in regulating its public schools and does not conflict with the Fourteenth Amendment. The judgment of the Supreme Court of Mississippi is

Affirmed.

EQUAL OPPORTUNITY FOR LEGAL EDUCATION MUST BE PROVIDED WITHIN A STATE'S OWN BORDERS (1938) From *Missouri Ex/ Rel Gaines* v. *Canada*, 306 U.S. 337.

CHIEF JUSTICE HUGHES DELIVERED THE OPINION OF THE COURT

. . . We must regard the question whether the provision for the legal education in other states of negroes resident in Missouri is sufficient to satisfy the constitutional requirement of equal protection, as the pivot upon which this case turns.

The state court stresses the advantages that are afforded by the law schools of the adjacent states, Kansas, Nebraska, Iowa and Illinois, which admit non-resident negroes. . . .

We think that these matters are beside the point. The basic consideration is not as to what sort of opportunities other states provide, or whether they are as good as those in Missouri, but as to what opportunities Missouri itself furnishes to white students and denies to negroes solely upon the ground of color. The admissibility of laws separating the races in the enjoyment of privileges afforded by the state rests wholly upon the quality of the privileges which the laws give to the separated groups within the state. The question here is not of a duty of the state to supply legal training, or of the quality of the training which it does supply, but of its duty when it provides such training to furnish it to the residents of the state upon the basis of an equality of right. By the operation of the laws of Missouri a privilege has been created for white law students which is denied to negroes by reason of their race. The white resident is afforded legal education within the state; the negro resident having the same qualifications is refused it there and must go outside the state to obtain it. That is a denial of the equality of legal right to the enjoyment of the privilege which the state has set up, and the provision for the payment of tuition fees in another state does not remove the discrimination.

The equal protection of the laws is "a pledge of the protection of equal laws" . . . Manifestly, the obligation of the state to give the protection of equal laws can be performed only where its laws operate, that is, within its own jurisdiction. It is there that the equality of legal right must be maintained. . . . We find it impossible to conclude that what otherwise would be an unconstitutional discrimination, with respect to the legal right to the enjoyment of opportunities within the state, can be justified by requiring resort to opportunities elsewhere. That resort may mitigate the inconvenience of the discrimination but cannot serve to validate it.

Nor can we regard the fact that there is but a limited demand in Missouri for the legal education of negroes as excusing the discrimination in favor of whites. - . . .

Here, petitioner's right was a personal one. It was as an individual that he was entitled to the equal protection of the laws, and the state was bound to furnish him within its borders facilities for legal education substantially equal to those which the state there afforded for persons of the white race, whether or not other negroes sought the same opportunity.

It is urged, however, that the provision for tuition outside the state is a temporary one,—that it is intended to operate merely pending the establishment of a law department for negroes at Lincoln University. While in that sense the discrimination may be termed temporary, it may nevertheless continue for an indefinite period by reason of the discretion given to the curators of Lincoln University and the alternative of arranging for tuition in other states, as permitted by the state law as construed by the state court, so long as the curators find it unnecessary and impracticable to provide facilities for the legal instruction of negroes within the state. In that view, we cannot regard the discrimination as excused by what is called its temporary character. . . .

. . . We are of the opinion that . . . petitioner was entitled to be admitted to the law school of the state university in the absence of other and proper provision for his legal training within the state. . . .

SEGREGATION OF A GRADUATE STUDENT IN A STATE UNIVERSITY RULED UNCONSTITUTIONAL (1950)   From *McLaurin* v. *Oklahoma State Regents,* 339 U.S. 637.

CHIEF JUSTICE VINSON DELIVERED THE OPINION OF THE COURT

. . . Thus he (McLaurin) was required to sit apart at a designated desk in an anteroom adjoining the classroom; to sit at a designated desk on the mezzanine floor of the library, but not to use the desks in the regular reading room; and to sit at a designated table and to eat at a different time from the other students in the school cafeteria.

To remove these conditions, appellant filed a motion to modify the order and judgment of the District Court. That court held that such treatment did not violate the provisions of the Fourteenth Amendment and denied the motion. This appeal followed.

In the interval between the decision of the court below and the hearing in this Court, the treatment afforded appellant was altered. For some time, the section of the classroom in which appellant sat was surrounded by a rail on which there was a sign stating, "Reserved For Colored", but these have been removed. He is now assigned to a seat in the classroom in a row specified for colored students; he is assigned to a table in the library on the main floor; and he is permitted to eat at the same time in the cafeteria as other students although here again he is assigned to a special table.

It is said that the separations imposed by the State in his case are in form merely nominal. McLaurin uses the same classroom, library and cafeteria as students of other races; there is no indication that the seats to which he is assigned in these rooms have any disadvantage of location. He may wait in line in the cafeteria and there stand and talk with his fellow students, but while he eats he must remain apart.

These restrictions were obviously imposed in order to comply, as nearly as could be, with the statutory requirements of Oklahoma. But they signify that the State, in administering the facilities it affords for professional and graduate study, sets McLaurin apart from the other students. The result is that appellant is handicapped in his pursuit of effective graduate instruction. Such restrictions impair and inhibit his ability to study, to engage in discussions and exchange views with other students, and, in general, to learn his profession.

Our society grows increasingly complex, and our need for trained leaders increases correspondingly. Appellant's case represents, perhaps, the epitome of that need, for he is attempting to obtain an advanced degree in education, to become, by definition, a leader and trainer of others. Those who will come under his guidance and influence must be directly affected by the education he receives. Their own education and development will necessarily suffer to the extent that his training is unequal to that of his classmates. State-imposed restrictions which produce such inequalities cannot be sustained.

It may be argued that appellant will be in no better position when these restrictions are removed, for he may still be set apart by his fellow students. This we think irrelevant. There is a vast difference—a Constitutional difference—between restrictions imposed by the state which prohibit the intellectual commingling of students, and the refusal of individuals to commingle where the state presents no such bar. . . .

The removal of the state restrictions will not necessarily abate individual and group predilections, prejudices and choices. But at the very least, the state will not be depriving appellant of the opportunity to secure acceptance by his fellow students on his own merits.

We conclude that the conditions under which this appellant is required to receive his education deprive him of his personal and present right to the equal protection of the laws. See *Sweatt* v. *Painter*, 339 U.S. We hold that under these circumstances the Fourteenth Amendment precludes differences in treatment by the state based upon race. Appellant, having been admitted to a state-supported graduate school, must receive the same treatment at the hands of the state as students of other races. . . .

DECISION ON A SEPARATE SCHOOL OF LAW FOR NEGROES IN TEXAS

(1950)   From *Sweatt v. Painter,* 339 U.S. 629.

Certiorari to the Supreme Court of Texas.

MR. CHIEF JUSTICE VINSON DELIVERED THE OPINION OF A UNANIMOUS COURT.

This case and *McLaurin v. Oklahoma State Regents,* . . . present differing aspects of this general question: To what extent does the Equal Protection Clause of the Fourteenth Amendment limit the power of a state to distinguish between students of different races in professional and graduate education in a state university? Broader issues have been urged for our consideration, but we adhere to the principle of deciding constitutional questions only in the context of the particular case before the Court. We have frequently reiterated that this Court will decide constitutional questions only when necessary to the disposition of the case at hand, and that such decisions will be drawn as narrowly as possible. . . . Because of this traditional reluctance to extend constitutional interpretations to situations or facts which are not before the Court, much of the excellent research and detailed argument presented in these cases is unnecessary to their disposition.

In the instant case, petitioner filed an application for admission to the University of Texas Law School for the February, 1946 term. His application was rejected solely because he is a Negro. Petitioner thereupon brought this suit for mandamus against the appropriate school officials, respondents here, to compel his admission. At that time, there was no law school in Texas which admitted Negroes.

The State trial court recognized that the action of the State in denying petitioner the opportunity to gain a legal education while granting it to others deprived him of the equal protection of the laws guaranteed by the Fourteenth Amendment. The court did not grant the relief requested, however, but continued the case for six months to allow the State to supply substantially equal facilities. At the expiration of the six months, in December, 1946, the court denied the writ on the showing that the authorized university officials had adopted an order calling for the opening of a law school for Negroes the following February. While petitioner's appeal was pending, such a school was made available, but petitioner refused to register therein. The Texas Court of Civil Appeals set aside the trial court's judgment and ordered the cause "remanded generally to the trial court for further proceedings without prejudice to the rights of any party to this suit."

On remand, a hearing was held on the issue of the equality of the educational facilities at the newly established school as compared with the University of Texas Law School. Finding that the new school offered petitioner "privileges, advantages, and opportunities for the study of law substantially equivalent to those offered by the State to white students at the University of Texas," the trial court denied mandamus. The Court of Civil Appeals affirmed. . . .

The University of Texas Law School, from which petitioner was excluded, was staffed by a faculty of sixteen full-time and three part-time professors, some of whom are nationally recognized authorities in their field. Its student body numbered 850. The library contained over 65,000 volumes. Among the other facilities available to the students were a law review, moot court facilities, scholarship funds, and Order of the Coif affiliation. The school's alumni occupy the most distinguished positions in the private practice of the law and in the public life of the State. It may properly be considered one of the nation's ranking law schools.

The law school for Negroes which was to have opened in February, 1947, would have had no independent faculty or library. The teaching was to be carried on by four members of the University of Texas Law School faculty, who were to maintain their offices at the University of Texas while teaching at both institutions. Few of the 10,000 volumes ordered for the library had arrived; nor was there any full-time librarian. The school lacked accreditation.

Since the trial of this case, respondents report the opening of a law school at the Texas State University for Negroes. It is apparently on the road to full accreditation. It has a faculty of five full-time professors; a student body of 23; a library of some 16,500 volumes serviced by a full-time staff; a practice court and legal aid association; and one alumnus who has become a member of the Texas Bar.

Whether the University of Texas Law School is compared with the original or the new law school for Negroes, we cannot find substantial equality in the educational opportunities offered white and Negro law students by the State. In terms of number of the faculty, variety of courses and opportunity for specialization, size of the student body, scope of the library, availability of law review and similar activities, the University of Texas Law School is superior. What is more important, the University of Texas Law School possesses to a far greater degree those qualities which are incapable of objective measurement but which make for greatness in a law school. Such qualities, to name but a few, include reputation of the faculty, experience of the administration, position and influence of the alumni, standing in the community, traditions and prestige. It is difficult to believe that one who had a free choice between these law schools would consider the question closed.

Moreover, although the law is a highly learned profession, we are well aware that it is an intensely practical one. The law school, the proving ground for legal learning and practice, cannot be effective in isolation from the individuals and institutions with which the law interacts. Few students and no one who has practiced law would choose to study in an academic vacuum, removed from the interplay of ideas and the exchange of views with which the law is concerned. The law school to which Texas is willing to admit petitioner excludes from its student body members of the racial groups which number 85% of the population of the State and include most of the lawyers, witnesses, jurors, judges, and other officials with whom petitioner will inevitably be dealing when he becomes a member of the Texas Bar. With such a substantial and significant segment of society excluded, we cannot conclude that the education offered petitioner is substantially equal to that which he would receive if admitted to the University of Texas Law School.

It may be argued that excluding petitioner from that school is no different from excluding white students from the new law school. This contention overlooks realities. It is unlikely that a member of a group so decisively in the majority, attending a school with rich traditions and prestige which only a history of consistently maintained excellence could command, would claim that the opportunities afforded him for legal education were unequal to those held open to petitioner. That such a claim, if made, would be dishonored by the State, is no answer. "Equal protection of the laws is not achieved through indiscriminate imposition of inequalities." *Shelley* v. *Kraemer*, 334 U.S. 1, 22 (1948).

It is fundamental that these cases concern rights which are personal and present. This Court has stated unanimously that "The State must provide [legal education] for [petitioner] in conformity with the equal protection clause of the Fourteenth

Amendment and provide it as soon as it does for applicants of any other group." *Sipuel* v. *Board of Regents*, 332 U.S. 631, 633 (1948). That case "did not present the issue whether a state might not satisfy the equal protection clause of the Fourteenth Amendment by establishing a separate law school for Negroes." *Fisher* v. *Hurst*, 333 U.S. 147, 150 (1948). In *Missouri ex rel. Gaines* v. *Canada*, 305 U.S. 337, 351 (1938), the Court, speaking through CHIEF JUSTICE HUGHES, declared that "petitioner's right was a personal one. It was as an individual that he was entitled to the equal protection of the laws, and the State was bound to furnish him within its borders facilities for legal education substantially equal to those which the State there afforded for persons of the white race, whether or not other Negroes sought the same opportunity." These are the only cases in this Court which present the issue of the constitutional validity of race distinctions in state-supported graduate and professional education.

In accordance with these cases, petitioner may claim his full constitutional right: legal education equivalent to that offered by the State to students of other races. Such education is not available to him in a separate law school as offered by the State. We cannot, therefore, agree with respondents that the doctrine of *Plessy* v. *Ferguson*, 163 U.S. 537 (1896) requires affirmance of the judgment below. Nor need we reach petitioner's contention that *Plessy* v. *Ferguson* should be reexamined in the light of contemporary knowledge respecting the purposes of the Fourteenth Amendment and the effects of racial segregation. . . .

We hold that the Equal Protection Clause of the Fourteenth Amendment requires that petitioner be admitted to the University of Texas Law School. The judgment is reversed and the cause is remanded for proceedings not inconsistent with this opinion.

Reversed.

BROWN v. BOARD OF EDUCATION (1954)   From *Brown et al.* v. *Board of Education of Topeka et al.,* 347 U.S. 483 (1954).

MR. CHIEF JUSTICE WARREN DELIVERED THE OPINION OF THE COURT.

These cases come to us from the States of Kansas, South Carolina, Virginia, and Delaware. They are premised on different facts and different local conditions, but a common legal question justifies their consideration together in this consolidated opinion.[1]

---

[1]In the Kansas case, *Brown* v. *Board of Education*, the plaintiffs are Negro children of elementary school age residing in Topeka. They brought this action in the United States District Court for the District of Kansas to enjoin enforcement of a Kansas statute which permits, but does not require, cities of more than 15,000 population to maintain separate school facilities for Negro and white students. Kan. Gen. Stat. § 72-1724 (1949). Pursuant to that authority, the Topeka Board of Education elected to establish segregated elementary schools. Other public schools in the community, however, are operated on a nonsegregated basis. The three-judge District Court, convened under 28 U.S.C. § 2281 and 2284, found that segregation in public education has a detrimental effect upon Negro children, but denied relief on the ground that the Negro and white schools were substantially equal with respect to buildings, transportation, curricula, and educational qualifications of teachers. 98 F. Supp. 797. The case is here on direct appeal under 28 U.S.C. §1253.

In the South Carolina case, *Briggs* v. *Elliott*, the plaintiffs are Negro children of both elementary and high school age residing in Clarendon County. They brought this action in the United States District Court for the Eastern District of South Carolina to enjoin enforcement

In each of the cases, minors of the Negro race, through their legal representatives, seek the aid of the courts in obtaining admission to the public schools of their community on a nonsegregated basis. In each instance, they had been denied admission to schools attended by white children under laws requiring or permitting segregation according to race. This segregation was alleged to deprive the plaintiffs of the equal protection of the laws under the Fourteenth Amendment. In each of the cases other than the Delaware case, a three-judge federal district court denied relief to the plaintiffs on the so-called "separate but equal" doctrine announced by this Court in *Plessy* v. *Ferguson*, 163 U.S. 537. Under that doctrine, equality of treatment is accorded when the races are provided substantially equal facilities, even though these facilities be separate. In the Delaware case, the Supreme Court of Delaware adhered to that doctrine, but ordered that the plaintiffs be admitted to the white schools because of their superiority to the Negro schools.

The plaintiffs contend that segregated public schools are not "equal" and cannot be made "equal," and that hence they are deprived of the equal protection of the laws. Because of the obvious importance of the question presented, the Court took

of provisions in the state constitution and statutory code which require the segregation of Negroes and whites in public schools. S. C. Const., Art. XI, § 7; S. C. Code § 5377 (1942). The three-judge District Court, convened under 28 U. S. C. § 2281 and 2284, denied the requested relief. The court found that the Negro schools were inferior to the white schools and ordered the defendants to begin immediately to equalize the facilities. But the court sustained the validity of the contested provisions and denied the plaintiffs admission to the white schools during the equalization program. 98 F. Supp. 529. This Court vacated the District Court's judgement and remanded the case for the purpose of obtaining the court's views on a report filed by the defendants concerning the progress made in the equalization program. 342 U.S. 350. On remand, the District Court found that substantial equality had been achieved except for buildings and that the defendants were proceeding to rectify this inequality as well. 103 F. Supp. 920. The case is again here on direct appeal under 28 U.S.C. § 1253.

In the Virginia case, *Davis* v. *County School Board*, the plaintiffs are Negro children of high school age residing in Prince Edward County. They brought this action in the United States District Court for the Eastern District of Virginia to enjoin enforcement of provisions in the state constitution and statutory code which require the segregation of Negroes and whites in public schools. Va. Const., § 140; Va. Code § 22-221 (1950). The three-judge District Court, convened under 28 U.S.C.§ 2281 and 2284, denied the requested relief. The court found the Negro school inferior in physical plant, curricula, and transportation, and ordered the defendants forthwith to provide substantially equal curricula and transportation and to "proceed with all reasonable diligence and dispatch to remove" the inequality in physical plant. But, as in the South Carolina case, the court sustained the validity of the contested provisions and denied the plaintiffs admission to the white schools during the equalization program. 103 F. Supp. 337. The case is here on direct appeal under 28 U.S.C. § 1253.

In the Delaware case, *Gebhart* v. *Belton*, the plantiffs are Negro children of both elementary and high school age residing in New Castle County. They brought this action in the Delaware Court of Chancery to enjoin enforcement of provisions in the state constitution and statutory code which require the segregation of Negroes and whites in public schools. Del. Const., Art. X, § 2; Del. Rev. Code § 2631 (1935). The Chancellor gave judgment for the plaintiffs and ordered their immediate admission to schools previously attended only by white children, on the ground that the Negro schools were inferior with respect to teacher training, pupil-teacher ratio, extracurricular activities, physical plant, and time and distance involved in travel. 87 A. 2d 862. The Chancellor also found that segregation itself results in an inferior education for Negro children (see note 10, *infra*), but did not rest his decision on that ground. *Id.*, at 865. The Chancellor's decree was affirmed by the Supreme Court of Delaware, which intimated, however, that the defendants might be able to obtain a modification of the decree after equalization of the Negro and white schools had been accomplished. 91 A. 2d 137, 152. The defendants, contending only that the Delaware courts had erred in ordering the immediate admission of the Negro plaintiffs to the white schools, applied to this Court for certiorari. The writ was granted, 344 U.S. 891. The plaintiffs, who were successful below, did not submit a cross-petition.

jurisdiction. Argument was heard in the 1952 Term and reargument was heard this Term on certain questions propounded by the Court.

Reargument was largely devoted to the circumstances surrounding the adoption of the Fourteenth Amendment in 1868. It covered exhaustively consideration of the Amendment in Congress, ratification by the states, then-existing practices in racial segregation, and the views of proponents and opponents of the Amendment. This discussion and our own investigation convince us that, although these sources cast some light, it is not enough to resolve the problem with which we are faced. At best, they are inconclusive. The most avid proponents of the post-War Amendments undoubtedly intended them to remove all legal distinctions among "all persons born or naturalized in the United States." Their opponents, just as certainly, were antagonistic to both the letter and the spirit of the Amendments and wished them to have the most limited effect. What others in Congress and the state legislatures had in mind cannot be determined with any degree of certainty.

An additional reason for the inconclusive nature of the Amendment's history, with respect to segregated schools, is the status of public education at that time. In the South, the movement toward free common schools, supported by general taxation, had not yet taken hold. Education of white children was largely in the hands of private groups. Education of Negroes was almost nonexistent, and practically all of the race were illiterate. In fact, any education of Negroes was forbidden by law in some states. Today, in contrast, many Negroes have achieved outstanding success in the arts and sciences as well as in the business and professional world. It is true that public school education at the time of the Amendment had advanced further in the North, but the effect of the Amendment on Northern States was generally ignored in the congressional debates. Even in the North, the conditions of public education did not approximate those existing today. The curriculum was usually rudimentary; ungraded schools were common in rural areas; the school term was but three months a year in many states; and compulsory school attendance was virtually unknown. As a consequence, it is not surprising that there should be so little in the history of the Fourteenth Amendment relating to its intended effect on public education.

In the first cases in this Court construing the Fourteenth Amendment, decided shortly after its adoption, the Court interpreted it as proscribing all state-imposed discriminations against the Negro race. The doctrine of "separate but equal" did not make its appearance in this Court until 1896 in the case of *Plessy* v. *Ferguson, supra*, involving not education but transportation. American courts have since labored with the doctrine for over half a century. In this Court, there have been six cases involving the "separate but equal" doctrine in the field of public education. In *Cumming* v. *County Board of Education*, 175 U.S. 528, and *Gong Lum* v. *Rice*, 275 U.S. 78, the validity of the doctrine itself was not challenged. In more recent cases, all on the graduate school level, inequality was found in that specific benefits enjoyed by white students were denied to Negro students of the same educational qualifications. *Missouri ex rel. Gaines* v. *Canada*, 305 U.S. 337; *Sipuel* v. *Oklahoma*, 332 U.S. 631; *Sweatt* v. *Painter*, 339 U.S. 629; *McLaurin* v. *Oklahoma State Regents*, 339 U.S. 637. In none of these cases was it necessary to re-examine the doctrine to grant relief to the Negro plaintiff. And in *Sweatt* v. *Painter, supra*, the Court expressly reserved decision on the question whether *Plessy* v. *Ferguson* should be held inapplicable to public education.

In the instant cases, that question is directly presented. Here, unlike *Sweatt* v. *Painter*, there are findings below that the Negro and white schools involved have been equalized, or are being equalized, with respect to buildings, curricula, qualifications and salaries of teachers, and other "tangible" factors. Our decision, therefore, cannot turn on merely a comparison of these tangible factors in the Negro and white schools involved in each of the cases. We must look instead to the effect of segregation itself on public education.

In approaching this problem, we cannot turn the clock back to 1868 when the Amendment was adopted, or even to 1896 when *Plessy* v. *Ferguson* was written. We must consider public education in the light of its full development and its present place in American life throughout the Nation. Only in this way can it be determined if segregation in public schools deprives these plaintiffs of the equal protection of the laws.

Today, education is perhaps the most important function of state and local governments. Compulsory school attendance laws and the great expenditures for education both demonstrate our recognition of the importance of education to our democratic society. It is required in the performance of our most basic public responsibilities, even service in the armed forces. It is the very foundation of good citizenship. Today it is a principal instrument in awakening the child to cultural values, in preparing him for later professional training, and in helping him to adjust normally to his environment. In these days, it is doubtful that any child may reasonably be expected to succeed in life if he is denied the opportunity of an education. Such an opportunity, where the state has undertaken to provide it, is a right which must be made available to all on equal terms.

We come then to the question presented: Does segregation of children in public schools solely on the basis of race, even though the physical facilities and other "tangible" factors may be equal, deprive the children of the minority group of equal educational opportunities? We believe that it does.

In *Sweatt* v. *Painter,supra*, in finding that a segregated law school for Negroes could not provide them equal educational opportunities, this Court relied in large part on "those qualities which are incapable of objective measurement but which make for greatness in a law school." In *McLaurin* v. *Oklahoma State Regents, supra*, the Court, in requiring that a Negro admitted to a white graduate school be treated like all other students, again resorted to intangible considerations: ". . . his ability to study, to engage in discussions and exchange views with other students, and, in general, to learn his profession." Such considerations apply with added force to children in grade and high schools. To separate them from others of similar age and qualifications solely because of their race generates a feeling of inferiority as to their status in the community that may affect their hearts and minds in a way unlikely ever to be undone. The effect of this separation on their educational opportunities was well stated by a finding in the Kansas case by a court which nevertheless felt compelled to rule against the Negro plaintiffs:

> Segregation of white and colored children in public schools has a detrimental effect upon the colored children. The impact is greater when it has the sanction of the law; for the policy of separating the races is usually interpreted as denoting the inferiority of the negro group. A sense of inferiority affects the motivation of a child to learn. Segregation with the sanction of law, therefore, has a tendency to [retard] the educational and mental development of negro children and to deprive them of some of the benefits they would receive in a racial[ly] integrated school system.

THE
MINORITIES

Whatever may have been the extent of psychological knowledge at the time of

Plessy v. *Ferguson*, this finding is amply supported by modern authority.[2] Any language in *Plessy* v. *Ferguson* contrary to this finding is rejected.

We conclude that in the field of public education the doctrine of "separate but equal" has no place. Separate educational facilities are inherently unequal. Therefore, we hold that the plaintiffs and others similarly situated for whom the actions have been brought are, by reason of the segregation complained of, deprived of the equal protection of the laws guaranteed by the Fourteenth Amendment. This disposition makes unnecessary any discussion whether such segregation also violates the Due Process Clause of the Fourteenth Amendment.

Because these are class actions, because of the wide applicability of this decision, and because of the great variety of local conditions, the formulation of decrees in these cases presents problems of considerable complexity. On reargument, the consideration of appropriate relief was necessarily subordinated to the primary question—the constitutionality of segregation in public education. We have now announced that such segregation is a denial of the equal protection of the laws. In order that we may have the full assistance of the parties in formulating decrees, the cases will be restored to the docket, and the parties are requested to present further argument on Questions 4 and 5 previously propounded by the Court for the reargument this Term. The Attorney General of the United States is again invited to participate. The Attorneys General of the states requiring or permitting segregation in public education will also be permitted to appear as *amici curiae* upon request to do so by September 15, 1954, and submission of briefs by October 1, 1954.

It is so ordered.

"WITH ALL DELIBERATE SPEED" (1955)   From *Brown* v. *Board of Education*, 349 U.S. 294.

MR. CHIEF JUSTICE WARREN DELIVERED THE OPINION OF THE COURT.

These cases were decided on May 17, 1954. The opinions of that date, declaring the fundamental principle that racial discrimination in public education is unconstitutional, are incorporated herein by reference. All provisions of federal, state, or local law requiring or permitting such discrimination must yield to this principle. There remains for consideration the manner in which relief is to be accorded.

Because these cases arose under different local conditions and their disposition will involve a variety of local problems, we requested further argument on the question of relief. In view of the nationwide importance of the decision, we invited the Attorney General of the United States and the Attorneys General of all states requiring or permitting racial discrimination in public education to present their

---

[2]K. B. Clark, Effect of Prejudice and Discrimination on Personality Development (Midcentury White House Conference on Children and Youth, 1950); Witmer and Kotinsky, Personality in the Making (1952), c. VI; Deutscher and Chein, The Psychological Effects of Enforced Segregation: A Survey of Social Science Opinion, 26 J. Psychol. 259 (1948); Chein, What are the Psychological Effects of Segregation Under Conditions of Equal Facilities?, 3 Int. J. Opinion and Attitude Res. 229 (1949); Brameld, Educational Costs, in Discrimination and National Welfare (MacIver, ed., 1949), 44–48; Frazier, The Negro in the United States (1949), 674–681. And see generally Myrdal, An American Dilemma (1944).

views on that question. The parties, the United States, and the States of Florida, North Carolina, Arkansas, Oklahoma, Maryland, and Texas filed briefs and participated in the oral argument.

These presentations were informative and helpful to the Court in its consideration of the complexities arising from the transition to a system of public education freed of racial discrimination. The presentations also demonstrated that substantial steps to eliminate racial discrimination in public schools have already been taken, not only in some of the communities in which these cases arose, but in some of the states appearing as *amici curiae*, and in other states as well. Substantial progress has been made in the District of Columbia and in the communities in Kansas and Delaware involved in this litigation. The defendants in the cases coming to us from South Carolina and Virginia are awaiting the decision of this Court concerning relief.

Full implementation of these constitutional principles may require solution of varied local school problems. School authorities have the primary responsibility for elucidating, assessing, and solving these problems; courts will have to consider whether the action of school authorities constitutes good faith implementation of the governing constitutional principles. Because of their proximity to local conditions and the possible need for further hearings, the courts which originally heard these cases can best perform this judicial appraisal. Accordingly, we believe it appropriate to remand the cases to those courts.

In fashioning and effectuating the decrees, the courts will be guided by equitable principles. Traditionally, equity has been characterized by a practical flexibility in shaping its remedies and by a facility for adjusting and reconciling public and private needs. These cases call for the exercise of these traditional attributes of equity power. At stake is the personal interest of the plaintiffs in admission to public schools as soon as practicable on a nondiscriminatory basis. To effectuate this interest may call for elimination of a variety of obstacles in making the transition to school systems operated in accordance with the constitutional principles set forth in our May 17, 1954, decision. Courts of equity may properly take into account the public interest in the elimination of such obstacles in a systematic and effective manner. But it should go without saying that the vitality of these constitutional principles cannot be allowed to yield simply because of disagreement with them.

While giving weight to these public and private considerations, the courts will require that the defendants make a prompt and reasonable start toward full compliance with our May 17, 1954, ruling. Once such a start has been made, the courts may find that additional time is necessary to carry out the ruling in an effective manner. The burden rests upon the defendants to establish that such time is necessary in the public interest and is consistent with good faith compliance at the earliest practicable date. To that end, the courts may consider problems related to administration, arising from the physical condition of the school plant, the school transportation system, personnel, revision of school districts and attendance areas into compact units to achieve a system of determining admission to the public schools on a nonracial basis, and revision of local laws and regulations which may be necessary in solving the foregoing problems. They will also consider the adequacy of any plans the defendants may propose to meet these problems and to effectuate a transition to a racially nondiscriminatory school system. During this period of transition, the courts will retain jurisdiction of these cases.

The judgments below, except that in the Delaware case, are accordingly reversed and the cases are remanded to the District Courts to take such proceedings and enter such orders and decrees consistent with this opinion as are necessary and proper to admit to public schools on a racially nondiscriminatory basis with all deliberate speed the parties to these cases. The judgment in the Delaware case—ordering the immediate admission of the plaintiffs to schools previously attended only by white children—is affirmed on the basis of the principles stated in our May 17, 1954, opinion, but the case is remanded to the Supreme Court of Delaware for such further proceedings as that Court may deem necessary in light of this opinion.

It is so ordered.

DECISION ON STATES' RIGHT TO DELIBERATE BUT NOT OBSTRUCT DESEGREGATION OF SCHOOLS (1958) From *Cooper* v. *Aaron,* 358 U.S. 1 (1958).

Certiorari to the United States Court of Appeals for the Eighth Circuit.

OPINION OF THE COURT BY THE CHIEF JUSTICE, MR. JUSTICE BLACK,
MR. JUSTICE FRANKFURTER, MR. JUSTICE DOUGLAS, MR. JUSTICE BURTON, MR. JUSTICE CLARK,
MR. JUSTICE HARLAN, MR. JUSTICE BRENNAN, AND MR. JUSTICE WHITTAKER.

As this case reaches us it raises questions of the highest importance to the maintenance of our federal system of government. It necessarily involves a claim by the Governor and Legislature of a State that there is no duty on state officials to obey federal court orders resting on this Court's considered interpretation of the United States Constitution. Specifically it involves actions by the Governor and Legislature of Arkansas upon the premise that they are not bound by our holding in *Brown* v. *Board of Education*, 347 U.S. 483. That holding was that the Fourteenth Amendment forbids States to use their governmental powers to bar children on racial grounds from attending schools where there is state participation through any arrangement, management, funds or property. We are urged to uphold a suspension of the Little Rock School Board's plan to do away with segregated public schools in Little Rock until state laws and efforts to upset and nullify our holding in *Brown* v. *Board of Education* have been further challenged and tested in the courts. We reject these contentions.

The case was argued before us on September 11, 1958. On the following day we unanimously affirmed the judgment of the Court of Appeals for the Eighth Circuit, which had reversed a judgment of the District Court for the Eastern District of Arkansas. The District Court had granted the application of the petitioners, the Little Rock School Board and School Superintendent, to suspend for two and one-half years the operation of the School Board's court-approved desegregation program. In order that the School Board might know, without doubt, its duty in this regard before the opening of school, which had been set for the following Monday, September 15, 1958, we immediately issued the judgment, reserving the expression of our supporting views to a later date. This opinion of all the members of the Court embodies those views.

The following are the facts and circumstances so far as necessary to show how the legal questions are presented. . . .

                    ✳   ✳   ✳

On May 20, 1954, three days after the first *Brown* opinion, the Little Rock District School Board adopted, and on May 23, 1954, made public, a statement of policy entitled "Supreme Court Decision—Segregation in Public Schools." In this statement the Board recognized that "It is our responsibility to comply with Federal Constitutional Requirements and we intend to do so when the Supreme Court of the United States outlines the method to be followed."

Thereafter the Board undertook studies of the administrative problems confronting the transition to a desegregated public school system at Little Rock. It instructed the Superintendent of Schools to prepare a plan for desegregation, and approved such a plan on May 24, 1955, seven days before the second *Brown* opinion. The plan provided for desegregation at the senior high school level (grades 10 through 12) as the first stage. Desegregation at the junior high and elementary levels was to follow. It was contemplated that desegregation at the high school level would commence in the fall of 1957, and the expectation was that complete desegregation of the school system would be accomplished by 1963. Following the adoption of this plan, the Superintendent of Schools discussed it with a large number of citizen groups in the city. As a result of these discussions, the Board reached the conclusion that "a large majority of the residents" of Little Rock were of "the belief . . . that the Plan, although objectionable in principle," from the point of view of those supporting segregated schools, "was still the best for the interests of all pupils in the District."

Upon challenge by a group of Negro plaintiffs desiring more rapid completion of the desegregation process, the District Court upheld the School Board's plan, *Aaron* v. *Cooper,* 143 F. Supp. 855, The Court of Appeals affirmed. 243 F2d 361. Review of that judgment was not sought here.

While the School Board was thus going forward with its preparation for desegregating the Little Rock school system, other state authorities, in contrast, were actively pursuing a program designed to perpetuate in Arkansas the system of racial segregation which this Court had held violated the Fourteenth Amendment. First came, in November 1956, an amendment to the State Constitution flatly commanding the Arkansas General Assembly to oppose "in every Constitutional manner the Un-constitutional desegregation decisions of May 17, 1954 and May 31, 1955 of the United States Supreme Court," . . . and, through the initiative, a pupil assignment law. . . . Pursuant to this state constitutional command, a law relieving school children from compulsory attendance at racially mixed schools. . . . and a law establishing a State Sovereignty Commission, . . . were enacted by the General Assembly in February 1957.

The School Board and the Superintendent of Schools nevertheless continued with preparations to carry out the first stage of the desegregation program. Nine Negro children were scheduled for admission in September 1957 to Central High School, which has more than two thousand students. Various administrative measures, designed to assure the smooth transition of this first stage of desegregation, were undertaken.

On September 2, 1957, the day before these Negro students were to enter Central High, the school authorities were met with drastic opposing action on the part of the Governor of Arkansas who dispatched units of the Arkansas National Guard to the Central High School grounds, and placed the school "off limits" to colored students. As found by the District Court in subsequent proceedings, the

Governor's action had not been requested by the school authorities, and was entirely unheralded. . . .

The next day, September 3, 1957, the Board petitioned the District Court for instructions, and the court, after a hearing, found that the Board's request of the Negro students to stay away from the high school had been made because of the stationing of the military guards by the state authorities. The court determined that this was not a reason for departing from the approved plan, and ordered the School Board and Superintendent to proceed with it.

On the morning of the next day, September 4, 1957, the Negro children attempted to enter the high school but, as the District Court later found, units of the Arkansas National Guard "acting pursuant to the Governor's order, stood shoulder to shoulder at the school grounds and thereby forcibly prevented the 9 Negro students . . . from entering," as they continued to do every school day during the following three weeks. . . .

That same day, September 4, 1957, the United States Attorney for the Eastern District of Arkansas was requested by the District Court to begin an immediate investigation in order to fix responsibility for the interference with the orderly implementation of the District Court's direction to carry out the desegregation program. Three days later, September 7, the District Court denied a petition of the School Board and the Superintendent of Schools for an order temporarily suspending continuance of the program.

Upon completion of the United States Attorney's investigation, he and the Attorney General of the United States, at the District Court's request, entered the proceedings and filed a petition on behalf of the United States, as *amicus curiae*, to enjoin the Governor of Arkansas and officers of the Arkansas National Guard from further attempts to prevent obedience to the court's order. After hearings on the petition, the District Court found that the School Board's plan had been obstructed by the Governor through the use of the National Guard troops, and granted a preliminary injunction on September 20, 1957, enjoining the Governor and the officers of the Guard from preventing the attendance of Negro children at Central High School, and from otherwise obstructing or interfering with the orders of the court in connection with the plan. . . . The National Guard was then withdrawn from the school.

The next school day was Monday, September 23, 1957. The Negro children entered the high school that morning under the protection of the Little Rock Police Department and members of the Arkansas State Police. But the officers caused the children to be removed from the school during the morning because they had difficulty controlling a large and demonstrating crowd which had gathered at the high school. . . . On September 25, however, the President of the United States dispatched federal troops to Central High School and admission of the Negro students to the school was thereby effected. Regular army troops continued at the high school until November 27, 1957. They were then replaced by federalized National Guardsmen who remained throughout the balance of the school year. Eight of the Negro students remained in attendance at the school throughout the school year.

We come now to the aspect of the proceedings presently before us. On February 20, 1958, the School Board and the Superintendent of Schools filed a petition in the District Court seeking a postponement of their program for desegregation. Their position in essence was that because of extreme public hostility, which they stated had been engendered largely by the official attitudes and actions of the Governor and the Legislature, the maintenance of a sound educational program at Central

High School, with the Negro students in attendance, would be impossible. The Board therefore proposed that the Negro students already admitted to the school be withdrawn and sent to segregated schools, and that all further steps to carry out the Board's desegregation program be postponed for a period later suggested by the Board to be two and one-half years.

After a hearing the District Court granted the relief requested by the Board. . . .

In affirming the judgment of the Court of Appeals which reversed the District Court we have accepted without reservation the position of the School Board, the Superintendent of Schools, and their counsel that they displayed entire good faith in the conduct of these proceedings and in dealing with the unfortunate and distressing sequence of events which has been outlined. We likewise have accepted the findings of the District Court as to the conditions at Central High School during the 1957–1958 school year, and also the findings that the educational progress of all the students, white and colored, of that school has suffered and will continue to suffer if the conditions which prevailed last year are permitted to continue.

The significance of these findings, however, is to be considered in light of the fact, indisputably revealed by the record before us, that the conditions they depict are directly traceable to the actions of legislators and executive officials of the State of Arkansas, taken in their official capacities, which reflect their own determination to resist this Court's decision in the *Brown* case and which have brought about violent resistance to that decision in Arkansas. In its petition for certiorari filed in this Court, the School Board itself describes the situation in this language: "The legislative, executive, and judicial departments of the state government opposed the desegregation of Little Rock schools by enacting laws, calling out troops, making statements villifying [sic] federal law and federal courts, and failing to utilize state law enforcement agencies and judicial processes to maintain public peace."

One may well sympathize with the position of the Board in the face of the frustrating conditions which have confronted it, but, regardless of the Board's good faith, the actions of the other state agencies responsible for those conditions compel us to reject the Board's legal position. Had Central High School been under the direct management of the State itself, it could hardly be suggested that those immediately in charge of the school should be heard to assert their own good faith as a legal excuse for delay in implementing the constitutional rights of these respondents, when vindication of those rights was rendered difficult or impossible by the actions of other state officials. The situation here is in no different posture because the members of the School Board and the Superintendent of Schools are local officials; from the point of view of the Fourteenth Amendment, they stand in this litigation as the agents of the State.

The constitutional rights of respondents are not to be sacrificed or yielded to the violence and disorder which have followed upon the actions of the Governor and Legislature. As this Court said some forty-one years ago in a unanimous opinion in a case involving another aspect of racial segregation: "It is urged that this proposed segregation will promote the public peace by preventing race conflicts. Desirable as this is, and important as is the preservation of the public peace, this aim cannot be accomplished by laws or ordinances which deny rights created or protected by the Federal Constitution." *Buchanan* v. *Warley*, 245 U.S. 60, 81. Thus law and order are not here to be preserved by depriving the Negro children of their constitutional rights. The record before us clearly establishes that the growth of the Board's difficulties to a magnitude beyond its unaided power to control is the product of state action. Those difficulties, as counsel for the Board forthrightly conceded on the oral argument in this Court, can also be brought under control by state action.

The controlling legal principles are plain. The command of the Fourteenth Amendment is that no "State" shall deny to any person within its jurisdiction the equal protection of the laws. "A State acts by its legislative, its executive, or its judicial authorities. It can act in no other way. The constitutional provision, therefore, must mean that no agency of the State, or of the officers or agents by whom its powers are exerted, shall deny to any person within its jurisdiction the equal protection of the laws. Whoever, by virtue of public position under a State government, . . . denies or takes away the equal protection of the laws, violates the constitutional inhibition; and as he acts in the name and for the State, and is clothed with the State's power, his act is that of the State. This must be so, or the constitutional prohibition has no meaning." *Ex parte Virginia*, 100 U.S. 339, 347. Thus the prohibitions of the Fourteenth Amendment extend to all action of the State denying equal protection of the laws; whatever the agency of the State taking the action, . . . or whatever the guise in which it is taken. . . . In short, the constitutional rights of children not to be discriminated against in school admission on grounds of race or color declared by this Court in the *Brown* case can neither be nullified openly and directly by state legislators or state executive or judicial officers, nor nullified indirectly by them through evasive schemes for segregation whether attempted "ingeniously or ingenuously." . . .

What has been said, in the light of the facts developed, is enough to dispose of the case. However, we should answer the premise of the actions of the Governor and Legislature that they are not bound by our holding in the *Brown* case. It is necessary only to recall some basic constitutional propositions which are settled doctrine.

Article VI of the Constitution makes the Constitution the "supreme Law of the Land." In 1803, CHIEF JUSTICE MARSHALL, speaking for a unanimous Court, referring to the Constitution as "the fundamental and paramount law of the nation," declared in the notable case of *Marbury* v. *Madison*, 1 Cranch 137, 177, that "It is emphatically the province and duty of the judicial department to say what the law is." This decision declared the basic principle that the federal judiciary is supreme in the exposition of the law of the Constitution, and that principle has ever since been respected by this Court and the Country as a permanent and indispensable feature of our constitutional system. It follows that the interpretation of the Fourteenth Amendment enunciated by this Court in the *Brown* case is the supreme law of the land, and Art. VI of the Constitution makes it of binding effect on the States "any Thing in the Constitution or Laws of any State to the Contrary notwithstanding." Every state legislator and executive and judicial officer is solemnly committed by oath taken pursuant to Art. VI, cl, "to support this Constitution." CHIEF JUSTICE TANEY, speaking for a unanimous Court in 1859, said that this requirement reflected the framers' "anxiety to preserve it [the Constitution] in full force, in all its powers, and to guard against resistance to or evasion of its authority, on the part of a State. . . ." *Ableman* v. *Booth*, 21 How. 506, 524.

No state legislator or executive or judicial officer can war against the Constitution without violating his undertaking to support it. CHIEF JUSTICE MARSHALL spoke for a unanimous Court in saying that: "If the legislatures of the several states may, at will, annul the judgments of the courts of the United States, and destroy the rights acquired under those judgments, the constitution itself becomes a solemn mockery. . . ." *United States* v. *Peters*, 5 Cranch 115, 136. A Governor who asserts a power to nullify a federal court order is similarly restrained. If he had such power, said Chief Justice Hughes, in 1932, also for a unanimous Court, it is manifest that the fiat of a state Governor, and not the Constitution of the United States, would be the supreme law of the land; that the restrictions of the Federal Constitution upon the exercise of state power would be but impotent phrases." *Sterling* v. *Constantin,* 287 U.S. 378, 397–398.

It is, of course, quite true that the responsibility for public education is primarily the concern of the States, but it is equally true that such responsibilities, like all other state activity, must be exercised consistently with federal constitutional requirements as they apply to state action. The Constitution created a government dedicated to equal justice under the law. The Fourteenth Amendment embodied and emphasized that ideal. State support of segregated schools through any arrangement, management, funds, or property cannot be squared with the Amendment's command that no State shall deny to any person within its jurisdiction the equal protection of the laws. The right of a student not to be segregated on racial grounds in schools so maintained is indeed so fundamental and pervasive that it is embraced in the concept of due process of law. *Bolling* v. *Sharpe,* 347 U.S. 497. The basic decision in *Brown* was unanimously reached by this Court only after the case had been briefed and twice argued and the issues had been given the most serious consideration. Since the first *Brown* opinion three new Justices have come to the Court. They are at one with the Justices still on the Court who participated in that basic decision as to its correctness, and that decision is now unanimously reaffirmed. The principles announced in that decision and the obedience of the States to them, according to the command of the Constitution, are indispensable for the protection of the freedoms guaranteed by our fundamental charter for all of us. Our constitutional idea of equal justice under law is thus made a living truth.

DECISION ON PUBLIC TAX MONIES USED FOR SUPPORT OF RACIALLY SEGREGATED PRIVATE SCHOOLS (1964)   From *Griffin* v. *County School Board of Prince Edward,* 377 U.S. 218 (1964).

Certiorari to the United States Court of Appeals for the Fourth Circuit.

MR. JUSTICE BLACK DELIVERED THE OPINION OF THE COURT.

This litigation began in 1951 when a group of Negro school children living in Prince Edward County, Virginia, filed a complaint in the United States District Court for the Eastern District of Virginia alleging that they had been denied admission to public schools attended by white children and charging that Virginia laws requiring such school segregation denied complainants the equal protection of the laws in violation of the Fourteenth Amendment. On May 17, 1954, ten years ago, we held that the Virginia segregation laws did deny equal protection. *Brown* v. *Board of Education,* 347 U.S. 483. . . . On May 31, 1955, after reargument on the nature of relief, we remanded this case, along with others heard with it, to the District Courts to enter such orders as "necessary and proper to admit [complainants] to public schools on a racially nondiscriminatory basis with all deliberate speed. . . ." *Brown* v. *Board of Education*, 349 U.S. 294. . . .

Efforts to desegregate Prince Edward County's schools met with resistance. In 1956 Section 141 of the Virginia Constitution was amended to authorize the General Assembly and local governing bodies to appropriate funds to assist students to go to public or to nonsectarian private schools, in addition to those owned by the State or by the locality. The General Assembly met in special session and enacted legislation to close any public schools where white and colored children were enrolled together, to cut off state funds to such schools, to pay tuition grants to children in nonsectarian private schools, and to extend state retirement benefits to teachers in newly created private schools. The legislation closing mixed schools and cutting off state funds was later invalidated by the Supreme Court of Appeals of Virginia, which held that these laws violated the Virginia Constitution. . . . In April 1959 the General Assembly abandoned "massive resistance" to desegregation and turned instead to what was called a "freedom of choice" program. The Assembly repealed the rest of the 1956 legislation, as well as a tuition grant law of January 1959, and enacted a new tuition grant program. At the same time the Assembly repealed Virginia's compulsory attendance laws and instead made school attendance a matter of local option.

In June 1959, the United States Court of Appeals for the Fourth Circuit directed the Federal District Court (1) to enjoin discriminatory practices in Prince Edward County schools, (2) to require the County School Board to take "immediate steps" toward admitting students without regard to race to the white high school "in the school term beginning September 1959," and (3) to require the Board to make plans for admissions to elementary schools without regard to race. . . . Having as early as 1956 resolved that they would not operate public schools "wherein white and colored children are taught together," the Supervisors of Prince Edward County refused to levy any school taxes for the 1959–1960 school year, explaining that they were "confronted with a court decree which requires the admission of white and colored children to all the schools of the county without regard to race or color." As a result, the county's public schools did not reopen in the fall of 1959 and have remained closed ever since, although the public schools of every other county in Virginia have continued to operate under laws governing the State's public school system and to draw funds provided by the State for that purpose. A private group, the Prince Edward School Foundation, was formed to operate private schools for white children in Prince Edward County and, having built its own school plant, has been in operation ever since the closing of the public schools. An offer to set up private schools for colored children in the county was rejected, the Negroes of Prince Edward preferring to continue the legal battle for desegregated public schools, and colored children were without formal education from 1959 to 1963, when federal, state, and county authorities cooperated to have classes conducted for Negroes and whites in school buildings owned by the county. During the 1959–1960 school year the Foundation's schools for white children were supported entirely by private contributions, but in 1960 the General Assembly adopted a new tuition grant program making every child, regardless of race, eligible for tuition grants of $125 or $150 to attend a nonsectarian private school or a public school outside his locality, and also authorizing localities to provide their own grants. The Prince Edward Board of Supervisors then passed an ordinance providing tuition grants of $100, so that each child attending the Prince Edward School Foundation's schools received a total of $225 if in elementary school or $250 if in high school. In the 1960–1961 session the major source of financial support for the Foundation was in the indirect form of these state and county tuition grants, paid to children attending Foundation's schools. At the same time, the County Board of Supervisors passed an ordinance allowing property tax credits up to 25% for contributions to any "nonprofit, nonsectarian private school" in the county.

In 1961 petitioners here filed a supplemental complaint, adding new parties and seeking to enjoin the respondents from refusing to operate an efficient system of public free schools in Prince Edward County and to enjoin payment of public funds to help support private schools which excluded students on account of race. . . . For reasons to be stated, we agree with the District Court that, under the circumstances here, closing the Prince Edward County schools while public schools in all the other counties of Virginia were being maintained denied the petitioners and the class of Negro students they represent the equal protection of the laws guaranteed by the Fourteenth Amendment. . . .

In *County School Board of Prince Edward County* v. *Griffin*, 204 Va. 650, 133 S.E.2d 565 (1963), the Supreme Court of Appeals of Virginia upheld as valid under state law the closing of the Prince Edward County public schools, the state and county tuition grants for children who attend private schools, and the county's tax concessions for those who make contributions to private schools. The same opinion also held that each county had "an option to operate or not to operate public schools." . . .

Virginia law, as here applied, unquestionably treats the school children of Prince Edward differently from the way it treats the school children of all other Virginia counties. Prince Edward children must go to a private school or none at all; all other Virginia children can go to public schools. Closing Prince Edward's schools bears more heavily on Negro children in Prince Edward County since white children there have accredited private schools which they can attend, while colored children until very recently have had no available private schools, and even the school they now attend is a temporary expedient. Apart from this expedient, the result is that Prince Edward County school children, if they go to school in their own county, must go to racially segregated schools which, although designated as private, are beneficiaries of county and state support.

A State, of course, has a wide discretion in deciding whether laws shall operate statewide or shall operate only in certain counties, the legislature "having in mind the needs and desires of each." . . . But the record in the present case could not be clearer that Prince Edward's public schools were closed and private schools operated in their place with state and county assistance, for one reason, and one reason only: to ensure, through measures taken by the county and the State, that white and colored children in Prince Edward County would not, under any circumstances, go to the same school. Whatever non-racial grounds might support a State's allowing a county to abandon public schools, the object must be a constitutional one, and grounds of race and opposition to desegregation do not qualify as constitutional.

In *Hall* v. *St. Helena Parish School Board*, 197 F. Supp. 649 (D.C.E.D. La. 1961), a three-judge District Court invalidated a Louisiana statute which provided "a means by which public schools under desegregation orders may be changed to 'private' schools operated in the same way, in the same buildings, with the same furnishings, with the same money, and under the same supervision as the public schools." . . . In addition, that statute also provided that where the public schools were "closed," the school board was "charged with responsibility for furnishing free lunches, transportation, and grants-in-aid to the children attending the 'private' schools." *Ibid.* We affirmed the District Court's judgment invalidating the Louisiana

THE
MINORITIES

3115

statute as a denial of equal protection. 368 U.S. 515 (1962). While the Louisiana plan and the Virginia plan worked in different ways, it is plain that both were created to accomplish the same thing: the perpetuation of racial segregation by closing public schools and operating only segregated schools supported directly or indirectly by state or county funds. . . . Either plan works to deny colored students equal protection of the laws. Accordingly, we agree with the District Court that closing the Prince Edward schools and meanwhile contributing to the support of the private segregated white schools that took their place denied petitioners the equal protection of the laws.

We come now to the question of the kind of decree necessary and appropriate to put an end to the racial discrimination practiced against these petitioners under authority of the Virginia laws. That relief needs to be quick and effective. The parties defendant are the Board of Supervisors, School Board, Treasurer, and Division Superintendent of Schools of Prince Edward County, and the State Board of Education and the State Superintendent of Education. All of these have duties which relate directly or indirectly to the financing, supervision, or operation of the schools in Prince Edward County. The Board of Supervisors has the special responsibility to levy local taxes to operate public schools or to aid children attending the private schools now functioning there for white children. The District Court enjoined the county officials from paying county tuition grants or giving tax exemptions and from processing applications for state tuition grants so long as the county's public schools remained closed. We have no doubt of the power of the court to give this relief to enforce the discontinuance of the county's racially discriminatory practices. . . . The injunction against paying tuition grants and giving tax credits while public schools remain closed is appropriate and necessary since those grants and tax credits have been essential parts of the county's program, successful thus far, to deprive petitioners of the same advantages of a public school education enjoyed by children in every other part of Virginia. For the same reasons the District Court may, if necessary to prevent further racial discrimination, require the Supervisors to exercise the power that is theirs to levy taxes to raise funds adequate to reopen, operate, and maintain without racial discrimination a public school system in Prince Edward County like that operated in other counties in Virginia.

The District Court held that "the public schools of Prince Edward County may not be closed to avoid the effect of the law of the land as interpreted by the Supreme Court, while the Commonwealth of Virginia permits other public schools to remain open at the expense of the taxpayers." . . . At the same time the court gave notice that it would later consider an order to accomplish this purpose if the public schools were not reopened by September 7, 1962. That day has long passed, and the schools are still closed. On remand, therefore, the court may find it necessary to consider further such an order. An order of this kind is within the court's power if required to assure these petitioners that their constitutional rights will no longer be denied them. The time for mere "deliberate speed" has run out, and that phrase can no longer justify denying these Prince Edward County school children their constitutional rights to an education equal to that afforded by the public schools in the other parts of Virginia.

The judgment of the Court of Appeals is reversed, the judgment of the District Court is affirmed, and the cause is remanded to the District Court with directions to enter a decree which will guarantee that these petitioners will get the kind of education that is given in the State's public schools.

MR. JUSTICE BRENNAN DELIVERED THE OPINION OF A UNANIMOUS COURT.

Petitioners brought this action in March 1965 seeking injunctive relief against respondent's continued maintenance of an alleged racially segregated school system. New Kent County is a rural county in Eastern Virginia. About one-half of its population of some 4,500 are Negroes. There is no residential segregation in the county; persons of both races reside throughout. The school system has only two schools, the New Kent school on the east side of the county and the George W. Watkins school on the west side. In a memorandum filed May 17, 1966, the District Court found that the "school system serves approximately 1,300 pupils, of which 740 are Negro and 550 are White. The School Board operates one white combined elementary and high school [New Kent], and one Negro combined elementary and high school [George W. Watkins]. There are no attendance zones. Each school serves the entire county." The record indicates that 21 school buses—11 serving the Watkins school and 10 serving the New Kent school—travel overlapping routes throughout the county to transport pupils to and from the two schools.

The segregated system was initially established and maintained under the compulsion of Virginia constitutional and statutory provisions mandating racial segregation in public education. . . . The respondent School Board continued the segregated operation of the system after the *Brown* decisions, presumably on the authority of several statutes enacted by Virginia in resistance to those decisions. Some of these statutes were held to be unconstitutional on their face or as applied. One statute, the Pupil Placement Act (1964), not repealed until 1966, divested local boards of authority to assign children to particular schools and placed that authority in a State Pupil Placement Board. Under that Act children were each year automatically reassigned to the school previously attended unless upon their application the State Board assigned them to another school; students seeking enrollment for the first time were also assigned at the discretion of the State Board. To September 1964, no Negro pupil had applied for admission to the New Kent school under this statute and no white pupil had applied for admission to the Watkins school.

The School Board initially sought dismissal of this suit on the ground that petitioners had failed to apply to the State Board for assignment to New Kent school. However, on August 2, 1965, five months after the suit was brought, respondent School Board, in order to remain eligible for federal financial aid, adopted a "freedom-of-choice" plan for desegregating the schools. Under that plan, each pupil except those entering the first and eighth grades, may annually choose between the New Kent and Watkins schools and pupils not making a choice are assigned to the school previously attended; first and eighth grade pupils must affirmatively choose a school. . . .

The pattern of separate "white" and "Negro" schools in the New Kent County school system established under compulsion of state laws is precisely the pattern of segregation to which *Brown I* and *Brown II* were particularly addressed, and which *Brown I* declared unconstitutionally denied Negro school children equal protection of the laws. Racial identification of the system's schools was complete, extending not just to the composition of student bodies at the two schools but to every facet

THE
MINORITIES

3117

of school operations—faculty, staff, transportation, extra-curricular activities and facilities. In short, the State, acting through the local school board and school officials, organized and operated a dual system, part "white" and part "Negro."

It was such dual systems that 14 years ago *Brown I* held unconstitutional and a year later *Brown II* held must be abolished; school boards operating such school systems were *required* by *Brown II* "to effectuate a transition to a racially nondiscriminatory school system. . . ." It is of course true that for the time immediately after *Brown II* the concern was with making an initial break in a long-established pattern of excluding Negro children from schools attended by white children. The principal focus was on obtaining for those Negro children courageous enough to break with tradition a place in the "white" schools. . . . Under *Brown II* that immediate goal was only the first step, however. The transition to a unitary, nonracial system of public education was and is the ultimate end to be brought about; it was because of the "complexities arising from the transition to a system of public education freed of racial discrimination" that we provided for "all deliberate speed" in the implementation of the principles of *Brown I*.

*   *   *

It is against this background that 13 years after *Brown II* commanded the abolition of dual systems we must measure the effectiveness of respondent School Board's "freedom-of-choice" plan to achieve that end. The School Board contends that it has fully discharged its obligation by adopting a plan by which every student, regardless of race, may "freely" choose the school he will attend. The Board attempts to cast the issue in its broadest form by arguing that its "freedom-of-choice" plan may be faulted only by reading the Fourteenth Amendment as universally requiring "compulsory integration," a reading it insists the wording of the Amendment will not support. But the argument ignores the thrust of *Brown II*. In the light of the command of that case, what is involved here is the question whether the Board has achieved the "racially nondiscriminatory school system" *Brown II* held must be effectuated in order to remedy the established unconstitutional deficiencies of its segregated system. In the context of the state-imposed segregated pattern of long standing, the fact that in 1965 the Board opened the doors of the former "white" school to Negro children and of the "Negro" school to white children merely begins, not ends, our inquiry whether the Board has taken steps adequate to abolish its dual, segregated system. *Brown II* was a call for the dismantling of well-entrenched dual systems tempered by an awareness that complex and multifaceted problems would arise which would require time and flexibility for a successful resolution. School boards such as the respondent then operating state-compelled dual systems were nevertheless clearly charged with the affirmative duty to take whatever steps might be necessary to convert to a unitary system in which racial discrimination would be eliminated root and branch. . . . The constitutional rights of Negro school children articulated in *Brown I* permit no less than this; and it was to this end that *Brown II* commanded school boards to bend their efforts.

In determining whether respondent School Board met that command by adopting its "freedom-of-choice" plan, it is relevant that this first step did not come until some 11 years after *Brown I* was decided and 10 years after *Brown II* directed the making of a "prompt and reasonable start." This deliberate perpetuation of the unconstitutional dual system can only have compounded the harm of such a system.

Such delays are no longer tolerable, for "the governing constitutional principles no longer bear the imprint of newly enunciated doctrine." . . . Moreover, a plan that at this late date fails to provide meaningful assurance of prompt and effective disestablishment of a dual system is also intolerable. "The time for mere 'deliberate speed' has run out;" . . . "the context in which we must interpret and apply this language [of *Brown II*] to plans for desegregation has been significantly altered." . . . The burden on a school board today is to come forward with a plan that promises realistically to work, and promises realistically to work *now*.

The obligation of the district courts, as it always has been, is to assess the effectiveness of a proposed plan in achieving desegregation. There is no universal answer to complex problems of desegregation; there is obviously no one plan that will do the job in every case. The matter must be assessed in light of the circumstances present and the options available in each instance. It is incumbent upon the school board to establish that its proposed plan promises meaningful and immediate progress toward disestablishing state-imposed segregation. It is incumbent upon the district court to weigh that claim in light of the facts at hand and in light of any alternatives which may be shown as feasible and more promising in their effectiveness. Where the court finds the board to be acting in good faith and the proposed plan to have real prospects for dismantling the state-imposed dual system "at the earliest practicable date," then the plan may be said to provide effective relief. Of course, the availability to the board of other more promising courses of action may indicate a lack of good faith; and at the least it places a heavy burden upon the board to explain its preference for an apparently less effective method. Moreover, whatever plan is adopted will require evaluation in practice, and the court should retain jurisdiction until it is clear that state-imposed segregation has been completely removed. . . .

We do not hold that "freedom of choice" can have no place in such a plan. We do not hold that a "freedom-of-choice" plan might of itself be unconstitutional, although that argument has been urged upon us. Rather, all we decide today is that in desegregating a dual system a plan utilizing "freedom of choice" is not an end in itself. . . .

Although the general experience under "freedom of choice" to date has been such as to indicate its ineffectiveness as a tool of desegregation, there may well be instances in which it can serve as an effective device. Where it offers real promise of aiding a desegregation program to effectuate conversion of a state-imposed dual system to a unitary, nonracial system there might be no objection to allowing such a device to prove itself in operation. On the other hand, if there are reasonably available other ways, such for illustration as zoning, promising speedier and more effective conversion to a unitary, nonracial school system, "freedom of choice" must be held unacceptable.

The New Kent School Board's "freedom-of-choice" plan cannot be accepted as a sufficient step to "effectuate a transition" to a unitary system. In three years of operation not a single white child has chosen to attend Watkins school and although 115 Negro children enrolled in New Kent school in 1967 (up from 35 in 1965 and 111 in 1966) 85% of the Negro children in the system still attend the all-Negro Watkins school. In other words, the school system remains a dual system. Rather than further the dismantling of the dual system, the plan has operated simply to burden children and their parents with a responsibility which *Brown II* placed squarely on the School Board. The Board must be required to formulate a new plan and, in light of other courses which appear open to the Board, such as zoning, fashion steps which promise realistically to convert promptly to a system without a "white" school and a "Negro" school, but just schools.

. . . The case is remanded to the District Court for further proceedings consistent with this opinion.

23

RE-APPRAISAL,
1951–1973

The Critics

ALBERT LYND CRITICISES THE EDUCATIONAL ESTABLISHMENT
(1950)   From Albert Lynd, "Quackery In The Public Schools," *The Atlantic,* vol. CLXXV,
pp. 33–35, 37–38.

Next to the minister, the high school principal of thirty years ago was the
most learned fellow in town. Today you may find your local high school in charge of
a brisk Kiwanian whose "professional" training has been free of the elements of
traditional culture. His teaching experience may have had nothing to do with letters
or science; it may have been in auto driving or basketball or pattern-making or
"guidance"; no matter in any case, because what counts in the advancement of his
career is his accumulation of courses in "administration." He may even wear the
splendid title of Doctor, earned through researches into the theory and function of a
school cafeteria. He may not be able to decipher the Latin date on the cornerstone
of his own school building, or to read a single word in any other foreign language,
living or dead, or even to write a decently turned paragraph in English, but he can
lead an enraptured class discussion in A Democratic Solution of Our Traffic
Problem.

Who or what is responsible for the change? As a parent required by law to
submit your youngster to the ministrations of the local school and to pay taxes for
its support, it may occur to you that the question of who gave whom the authority
to make all such changes may be even more disturbing than the reforms themselves.
It occurred to me after some experience on a suburban school board.

The traditional educational system tried to improve the student's private
universe by pumping into him as much as he could hold of objective information.
The elementary steps were rigid drillings in reading, writing, and arithmetic; the
youngster who could not handle these was pilloried as a dunce. The new
dispensation seeks rather to educe "skills" for "socially useful" results, although it is
not very clear who the umpires of these results are supposed to be. The elementary
approach is subjective; the student's interest is teased through painless projects
appealing to his natural inclinations. The dunce is abolished as psychologically
reprehensible.

Wherever the newer rite has strongly prevailed, there have been some parental
complaints that children today seem not to be able to read, write, and calculate as
well as they once could at the same age. As a parent I have found the explanation
contradictory when cleared of the usual pedagogical jargon. I have been assured first
that the schools do not really neglect these traditional accomplishments, and next,
that when they do so it is in the interest of more socially useful objectives.

RE-APPRAISAL
1951–1973

It is rather late in the day for the parent-taxpayer to make up his mind on the general case for the new pedagogy, because in some measure it has become established nearly everywhere. In brooding about this, however, a curious citizen may be struck by a conclusion so obvious and so important that he will marvel at its rare mention in all the bales of printed argument about the new education. Although he, the taxpayer, owns the schools, pays the teachers, builds the buildings, buys the equipment, and submits to frequent professional rebuke for not paying, building, and buying more, an educational revolution is being put over within his schools on which he has been neither consulted nor candidly informed.

It is true that our citizen's grandfather was not consulted, either, on the merits of traditional schooling. But good or bad, that system in its day enjoyed the measure of passive acceptance which political scientists call general consent, because it was considered by laymen to be as obvious and inevitable as the procession of the equinoxes.

Whatever the shining merits of the new pedagogy, its measure and content are now determined for the schools in your town and mine by persons whom the school-owning citizens have neither elected nor approved, directly or indirectly. The local school board, unless it is unusual to an extraordinary degree, fusses over budgets and plumbing and bus routes but merely rubber-stamps the edicts of remote and self-constituted authorities on the proper educational diet for your children. With respect to the inner mysteries of the pedagogical cult, the average board member behaves like a humble lay brother in the presence of an infallible priesthood.

The superprofessionals who determine the kind of education to which your child must submit and for which you must pay taxes are the professors of "education" in the larger universities and teachers' colleges. Some of the most influential of these institutions are privately endowed, but even in the state-owned colleges the decisions of the educational panjandrums are not even remotely subject to the scrutiny of the citizen who picks up the check for the local schools. And these decisions are subject to change whenever the gift of tongues may descend upon a new prophet of pedagogy.

By patient lobbying over many years, the superpedagogues have so influenced state and local laws that their training courses in teaching theory and method are virtually essential to the eligibility of any candidate for a job in your schools. In most states this is accomplished by "certification" laws. These have been obtained from upcountry legislators who are awed by professorial millinery. Eager to show a proper zeal for Our Schools, they have been easily persuaded that an educated teacher is necessarily one who has had a certain amount of head-rubbing by a professor of education.

No matter whether their motives be the highest in the universe, it seems apparent to any observant member of a school board that these boys in the educational back room have traded on the apathy or awe of the laymen in nominal control to build a tight educational bureaucracy, to which every working teacher or administrator must defer if he dares dream of advancement. The average superintendent of schools is usually a man of unquestioned personal integrity, but given his usual training it is almost impossible for him to be in his inner professional heart the executive agent of the local school board. He is rather the ranking local lobbyist and front man for some professional ideology of curriculum, discipline, and teacher status. He has some choice among these, but is it not usually determined by the sentiments of local parents and taxpayers; it is more likely to be guided by the cerebrations of those university professors of education who helped him to get his job by their recommendations to the docile local board. His advancement is not a matter within the control of the board, whose top appointment he already holds; it may depend upon future recommendations of the superprofessionals to the awed laymen of some larger town.

In the same manner down the line, your child's teacher is conditioned to perform according to theories and policies which derive their sanction from neither local parents nor their elected representatives. In many jurisdictions she cannot even get a raise in pay unless she devotes her summers to getting herself still more thoroughly indoctrinated by the distant arbiters of your school methods.

All this you may discover for yourself if you are curious enough and stubborn enough to risk the ruffled dignity, the hurt look, or the patient smile used by pedagogues on a tiresome child who asks too many questions. These you will get if you take too literally the standing invitation to "know your schools"—that is, if you poke around for information less superficial than the hosannas of the P.T.A. The power of the educational bureaucracy over your school system is least if yours is a very large city, because in a great metropolis even these talented strategists find it difficult to compete for authority with the resident school politicians. It is small, too, in remote and "backward" rural schools. But in the white-collar suburb with "good" schools, it flourishes on a scale which may remind you of Lord Acton's classic warning about the corrupting effects of all power.

*　　*　　*

What can you do about this politically irresponsible control of your local schools? If you are interested you can make your own investigation. You will find that your school system is esteemed "good" by the professionals to the extent that your board gives lamblike assent to their edicts. (For example, to the completely unqualified planks IV C–3 and IV C–4 in the 1949 Platform of the National Education Association: "Lay boards should be guided by the recommendations of professional educators" and "School budgets should be prepared by the school superintendent and adopted by the board of education." In this instinctive professional denial of any lay discretion, these lines could have been written seven centuries ago by old Pope Boniface VIII in his famous *Clericis Laicos!*) But I can simplify your investigation of professional opinion on your schools; it is derived from the equation that more money automatically means better schooling.

If you find, next, that your child cannot read or calculate half as well as you could at his age, you can complain that the older education, whatever its faults, had to prove its achievements by these objective tests. I can spare you this effort, too, by telling you the reply you will get: "In the new education we pay adequate attention to those skills but our aim is upon more important social objectives." They have you there, because you won't live long enough to test them. You cannot put your calipers upon a whole social unit a few generations hence, even if you could discover what you should measure.

Next, you can dedicate yourself to the useful career of a school crank. You can vest the professionals in that salutary hair-shirt that most of us have to wear in other professions and businesses: the objective scrutiny of persons free of our own occupational bias toward self-congratulation.

Finally, you can attempt to cure the frustrations developed in these activities by getting yourself elected to your local school board. There you can make it clear to your colleagues and your professional associates that you are a representative of the children, the parents, and the taxpayers of your town, not of a professional camarilla vis-à-vis the town. This will make a satisfying noise which will have a certain therapeutic effect on your blood pressure. But it will have no other practical effect. When this becomes clear to you, you can do what other worried parents have done: mortgage your house and put your youngster in one of the good private schools, where the best teaching today is being done by high-quality liberal arts graduates for whom the professors of education are only an inspiration for humor in the Masters' Common Room.

Of course you must then contribute to the support of two school establishments. As you do this, you can reflect on the meaning of an educational "democracy" which, by filling the public schools with hocus-pocus, limits the opportunity for the cultivated development of intelligent children to those whose parents can afford private schooling. But you may draw some comfort from the knowledge that the greatness of this nation lies in its infinite capacity for surviving hocus-pocus!

THE PASADENA CASE: A WARNING TO EDUCATORS (1951) From Frank Chodorov, "Educators Should Be Warned by the Pasadena Revolt," *Saturday Evening Post,* July 14, 1951, p. 10.

Are parents, as parents, relieved of all obligation for the education of their school-age children? Do parents, as taxpayers, have any right to express an opinion on the curriculum or teaching methods in the public schools?

These are the questions that have emerged from the now-famous "Pasadena Case." They are, of course, fundamental, and transcend the particular issues involved in the controversy, and the attendant passions. To see how they have come to the surface calls for a brief summary of the main events in this highly publicized controversy.

A superintendent of schools—one with a national reputation—was hired by this education-conscious California city. Immediately he began introducing changes in subject matter and teaching technique, toward the end that Pasadena might have the "best" and "most modern." Taken as a whole, the reforms followed the lines of what is called "progressive" education, which emphasizes the adjustment of the child to the group, rather than his development as an individual. The acquisition of knowledge, this philosophy of education holds, is of little or no importance, while the molding of the child to the social order is the principal business of modern schooling.

These ideas did not set too well with many Pasadena parents; they held to the notion that schools were for the teaching of the three *R*'s and some other subjects which their children might find helpful. Their dissatisfaction with the innovations came to the boiling point when the superintendent asked for a considerable boost in school taxes to meet the higher cost of "progressivism." The election campaign let loose all their pent-up dissidence. The charges of "socialism" and "communism" were freely hurled at the new system, and the superintendent was excoriated for being a traitor to American tradition. The passions aroused did not subside with the overwhelming defeat of the tax proposal, but found expression in a popular demand for the removal of the superintendent.

With the resignation of the superintendent, the "case" should have been closed. The fact is, it seems to have started with that event, for the advocates of "progressive" education have taken the dismissal as a challenge to their ideas. A book-length story of the incident, in which the author gives the superintendent's side the better of it, has received laudatory reviews from highly placed educators, and pamphleteers have taken up the cudgels for the superintendent and his philosophy, and against the people who deposed him. Perhaps all this agitation is due to the fear that the ousting of the superintendent, who stands high in the "progressive" movement, portends further setbacks in other cities where an aroused citizenry are on the march.

Putting aside the arguments for and against "progressivism," the implications of the general position taken by these protagonists are: (a) parents have no competence in the field of education and therefore ought not to interfere with the "experts"; (b) as taxpayers they have no more right to express an opinion on how their children should be educated than a patient has a right to dictate the doctor's prescription.

Whether or not "progressive" education is a tool of socialism, as charged, there is no question about the socialistic character of that position. It very definitely holds that the individualistic relationship between parent and child terminates when the latter enters the public school. At that moment, it says, the child becomes a ward of the community, as far as its education is concerned, and the community, operating through its "experts," must not be interfered with in the exercise of its guardianship. This is not far removed from the Spartan doctrine that the child belongs to the state and should be trained exclusively for its service.

Thus the "Pasadena Case" has blossomed out into a fundamental moral and social question. Even if "progressivism" were to go back to teaching the three R's, and were to revert to the idea that the purpose of education is to prepare the child for a happy and fruitful individual life, rather than to turn out a cog for the social machine; even if there were no quarrel with what or how the teachers taught, could we, should we, accept the idea of alienation from home ties? Is it consistent with the nature of things for the mother to rid herself of all concern in the intellectual development of her offspring? Finally, is it consonant with democracy to say that the taxpayer has no voice in how his money shall be spent?

JOHN DEWEY'S CRITIQUE OF PROGRESSIVE EDUCATION (1952)   From John Dewey, Introduction to Elsie Ripley Clapp, *The Use of Resources in Education* (New York, 1952), pp. vii–xi.

The invitation of the John Dewey Society to write something by way of introduction to Miss Clapp's account of two important educational experiments is an honor and also something of an embarrassment. It is an honor to become associated, however indirectly, with the ground-breaking educational undertakings which are here reported by the one who was largely responsible for initiating them. The invitation is an embarrassment because Miss Clapp has not only given a full, vivid and convincing description of the practical phases of the work, what was done and how; she has also given a clear and illuminating interpretation of its theoretical content and meaning: the purposes that inspired it, the leading principles that guided it, the educational philosophy of which it is an expression and embodiment. It would be to engage in a wholly superfluous performance if I were to detain the reader with any restatement of the basic ideas Miss Clapp has so effectively stated in the context of describing the educational work actually done, where the ideas take on life and their consequences become manifest.

But it may not be altogether superfluous for me to say something about the whole educational movement of which the work here described and interpreted is a part. This seems to me all the more appropriate to do because the work which is the occasion for my remarks concretely exemplifies, in my judgment, what is most valuable in the movement.

In the course of more than half a century of participation in the theory and practice of education, I have witnessed many successes and many failures in what is most popularly known as "progressive education," but is also known as "the new education," "modern education," and so on. These designations are singular but they cover a plurality of different movements which have in common the general objective of improving the educational system but which differ from one another in many specific respects—ideas, principles, policies and programs. The confusion in public discussion of educational problems does not arise from using the term "progressive education" instead of "new education" or vice versa. It arises from using these designations as if they were proper names, denoting a singular entity. This is hardly the place to enter into terminological problems; however, it is in place to point out that I shall use the designations "progressive education" and "the progressive education movement" as common names, that is, as convenient linguistic means of referring to the whole complex of diversified movements and efforts to improve the practice and theory of education.

During the past few years, organized attacks on the achievements of progressive education have become more extensive and virulent than ever before. The current effort to turn the clock back in education is a real cause for alarm but not for surprise. The educational system is part of the common life and cannot escape suffering the consequences that flow from the conditions prevailing outside the school building. When repressive and reactionary forces are increasing in strength in all our other institutions—economic, social and political—it would be folly to expect the school to get off free.

For the same reason, it is folly to think that the progressive education movement was something thought up and put over by the teachers all by themselves. On the intellectual side, it was part of the wider movement of thought, the inquiries into the nature and problems of growth which constitute the great contribution of the second half of the nineteenth century to the advancement of human knowledge in the biological, psychological and sociological sciences. On the social side, it was part of the widespread effort to liberate individuals and institutions from bondage to repressive modes of life. Without the support of the progressive and enlightening forces in the community, intellectual and social, the teachers of new vision would have been at best like Arnold's Shelley, ineffectual angels, born out of their time, and all their best plans and ideas would have had little or no effect on the educational system.

The most widespread and marked success of the progressive education movement has been in bringing about a significant change in the life-conditions in the classroom. There is a greater awareness of the needs of the growing human being, and the personal relations between teachers and students have been to a noticeable extent humanized and democratized. But the success in these respects is as yet limited; it is largely atmospheric; it hasn't yet really penetrated and permeated the foundations of the educational institution. The older gross manifestations of the method of education by fear and repression—physical, social and intellectual—which was the established norm for the educational system before the progressive education movement began have, generally speaking, been eliminated. But the basic attitudes underlying the gross manifestations have in many areas still to be rooted out. The fundamental authoritarianism of the old education persists in various modified forms. There is a great deal of talk about education being a cooperative enterprise in which teachers and students participate democratically, but there is far more talk about it than the doing of it. To be sure, many teachers, particularly in the kindergarten and elementary schools, take the children into sharing with them to an extent impossible and inconceivable under the old system whose supreme achievement of educational wisdom is enshrined in its maxim: spare the rod and spoil the child.

In the secondary schools and colleges, however, there isn't much sharing on the part of teachers in the needs and concerns of those whom they teach. Of course, the conditions still too largely prevailing in the school—the size of the classes, the load of work, and so on—make it difficult to carry on the educative process in any genuinely cooperative, democratic way. These conditions, however, are not the sole causes for the failures in educational democracy, as is evident from the fact that in "progressive" schools where these deplorable conditions do not exist education as thoroughgoing sharing is often rather more a theme of discourse in various courses in the curriculum than a practice observable in the conduct of the school. What it really means to make the educative process a genuine sharing, a truly cooperative transaction in which both teachers and students engage as equals and learners is demonstrated in the cases Miss Clapp describes. Nothing I can say in amplification of that point would add to what the reader will find abundantly illustrated in this work.

It should be a commonplace, but unfortunately it is not, that no education—or anything else for that matter—is progressive unless it is making progress. Nothing is more reactionary in its consequences than the effort to live according to the ideas, principles, customs, habits or institutions which at some time in the past represented a change for the better but which in the present constitute factors in the problems confronting us. The fact that a given change was made in order to realize a desirable end in view signifies that the life-conditions before and after are different. In the process of attaining that good, a new situation was created. A new complex of life-conditions was brought into existence presenting its own distinctive characteristics and problems. Blind attachment to what was good for a state of affairs that no longer exists prevents recognition of the needs of the present and blots out of view the desirable ends that those needs should generate. As Emerson puts it, the attained good tends to become the enemy of the better.

New problems cannot be met intelligently by routine application of ideas and principles which were developed in solving different problems. New problems demand for their intelligent solution the projection of new purposes, new ends in view; and new ends necessitate the development of new means and methods. Of course, the "new" is, in all cases, relatively, not absolutely, new. Even though something absolutely new may be desirable, and some may delude themselves into thinking they have something absolutely new, the continuities in culture and experience exclude the possibility of anything having in fact this absolute character.

RE-APPRAISAL
1951–1973

3129

The danger of cutting through all relations and connections inherited from the past is purely chimerical. The real danger is in perpetuating the past under forms that claim to be new but are only disguises of the old.

What has just been said is illustrated in the history of the progressive education movement—as in every other area of human effort and advance. It accounts for the failure in the movement which can no more be attributed to the teachers alone than can its successes. To change long-established habits in the individual is a slow, difficult and complicated process. To change long-established institutions—which are social habits organized in the structure of the common life—is a much slower, more difficult and far more complicated process. The drive of established institutions is to assimilate and distort the new into conformity with themselves. This drive or tendency in the educational institution is perhaps most glaringly evident in the way the ideas and principles of the educational philosophy I have had a share in developing are still for the most part taught, more than half a century after they began to find their way in various parts of the school. In teachers colleges and elsewhere the ideas and principles have been converted into a fixed subject matter of ready-made rules, to be taught and memorized according to certain standardized procedures and, when occasion arises, to be applied to educational problems externally, the way mustard plasters, for example, are applied.

In other words, habits of "learning" institutionalized and perpetuated for centuries seek to transform into their own image ideas and principles which explicitly emphasize that learning is a method of growth and that the educative process does not consist in acquiring a kit of tools but is a process of learning means and methods of human growth which can never be fixed but must be constantly developed for the intelligent solution of new problems or more adequate solution of old problems partially solved. Considered from the most general philosophical point of view, this conversion—or perversion—of means and methods into a fixed, self-sufficient subject matter is due to the persistence and power of the traditional notion that the qualities of ideas are inherent, eternal and immutable essences. On this theory, the principles of progressive education (of whatever sort they may be) are "inherently progressive" and anyone who can recite them is *ipso facto* a "progressive" teacher.

It may perhaps be said that to train teachers in the right principles the wrong way is an improvement over teacher-training that is wrong in both respects. But it is not much of an improvement. For the *method* of training—inside or outside the school—forms character. The *method* of teacher-training in teachers colleges is not of course the sole determinant of the characters of the future teachers; but in so far as the method of training is successful it forms their character *as teachers*, and hence is a significant determinant of their moral development. Training in the right principles the wrong way means in effect to create a split between the moral and intellectual training of teachers. The principles they learn to recite acquire the function of a verbal veneer. To the extent that their training is effective and until it is modified (for better or worse) by post-training experiences, they will teach as they were taught in fact, not as they were taught *about* teaching as a subject of éducational theory.

Speaking again from the most general philosophical standpoint, this authoritarian principle in education and the consequences that flow from it in the conduct of the school will never be effectively eradicated as long as the traditional notion prevails that the qualities of ideas are inherent essences. For it follows from this notion or doctrine that the education of teachers consists in transmitting to them certain collections of fixed, immutable subject matter which they in turn are to transmit to the students under them. The educational regimen thus consists of authorities at the upper end handing down to the receivers at the lower end what they must accept. This is not education but indoctrination, propaganda. It is a type of "education" fit for the foundations of a totalitarian society and, for the same reason, fit to subvert, pervert and destroy the foundations of a democratic society.

For the creation of a democratic society we need an educational system where the processs of moral-intellectual development is in practice as well as in theory a cooperative transaction of inquiry engaged in by free, independent human beings who treat ideas and the heritage of the past as means and methods for the further enrichment of life, quantitatively and qualitatively, who use the good attained for the discovery and establishment of something better.

But I fear I have already detained the reader too long from making first-hand acquaintance with Miss Clapp's stimulating and illuminating account of practical demonstrations of the good that has been attained by the progressive education movement and of the better that is to come.

ARTHUR BESTOR ON THE INTERLOCKING DIRECTORATE OF PROFESSIONAL EDUCATORS (1953) From Arthur Bestor, *Educational Wastelands: The Retreat from Learning . . .* (Urbana, Ill., 1953), pp. 106–14.

University and graduate departments of education began as agencies of genuine interdisciplinary investigation and teaching. When, however, they began to recruit their faculties from young men trained by themselves, they gradually lost their original character. Several academic generations have now passed, and the overwhelming majority of present-day professors of education have received virtually all their advanced training in departments of education. Their knowledge of the disciplines that are required to solve pedagogical problems is for the most part elementary and secondhand. And this knowledge is being passed on, increasingly diluted and increasingly out-of-date, to new generations of professional educationists. John Dewey was himself a philosopher, and he brought philosophy to bear upon educational problems. Today, however, the so-called "philosophy of education" offered in most departments of pedagogy has lost touch with living philosophical thought, for it is taught mainly by men trained not in philosophy itself but merely in their predecessors' courses in the philosophy of education. What began as the free and creative speculation of philosophic minds upon educational questions has congealed into educational dogma passed on from generation to generation by men who no longer speculate but merely expound.

This has happened to each of the great disciplines that ought to be contributing to vital educational thinking. Educational psychologists maintain closer connections with the parent discipline than other educationists, perhaps, but the gap is wide and growing wider. The history of education and educational sociology are rarely taught by men trained as historians or sociologists. Professors of educational administration have practically nothing to do with the experts who study and teach public administration in general in departments of political science. Even the courses in the teaching of specific subjects—mathematics, history, English, and the like—are mainly in the hands of educationists, not mathematicians or historians or scholars in the field of English language and literature.

Cross-fertilization, the original purpose of departments of education, has ceased, and we are up against the fact that the products of cross-fertilization—the hybrids—are frequently sterile.

The quality of purpose has declined with the decline in the quality of staff. University and graduate departments of education were founded with the idea of raising school-teaching from a vocation to a profession. This was to be accomplished—it could only be accomplished—by requiring a thorough training in the liberal arts before permitting a student to embark upon specialized training in pedagogy. But the founders of advanced departments of education failed to reckon with the fact that a large number of institutions and instructors had a vested interest in a lower and narrower type of pedagogical training. Normal schools were reluctant to give up what they had been doing. They expanded into colleges, but rarely sloughed off completely their narrow vocational approach to the problem of training teachers. The old-time specialists in normal-school pedagogy were insistent that they be recognized as full-fledged professors of education, and they began to migrate to the new university departments. As a result there occurred a rapid debasement of the original ideal. Instead of a new and genuinely professional approach to education there was a mere upgrading in the numbering of the old courses in pedagogical method. For most students these courses were apt to be piled, layers thick, upon an undergraduate major in pedagogy, not upon a major in one of the liberal arts. In the end, so-called graduate work in education tended to become merely a prolonged and attenuated program of vocational training.

Another unforeseen factor leading to the deterioration of university departments of education was the tremendous influence that came to be exerted upon them by the administrative bureaucracy of the public schools. It was peculiarly necessary for professors of education to maintain their independence from such pressures, since one of their major responsibilities was to examine, criticize, and judge with scholarly impartiality the programs that school administrators were carrying out. Their duty was to transmit to superintendents, principals, and teachers in the field the considered judgment on educational matters of the academic world. Such a pattern, however, never came into being. Instead, public school administrators and university departments of education drew together in a community of interest that was far stronger than any which developed between the department of education and the other faculties of the university. The direct consequence was that professors of education abandoned any pretence of being independent, academic critics of public school development, and became hard-and-fast partners of the administrative bureaucracy in the making of public school policy. Their role thereafter could only be that of apologists, and rather indiscriminate apologists, for every new program introduced into the public schools.

To the scholar from an established discipline, one of the most shocking facts about the field of education is the almost complete absence of rigorous criticism from within. Among scientists and scholars, criticism of one another's findings is regarded as a normal and necessary part of the process of advancing knowledge. But full and frank criticism of new educational proposals rarely comes from other professional educationists. The educational journals are almost devoid of critical reviews, which form an essential part of similar publications in other fields. The paean of praise that greets every novel program, the closing of ranks that occurs whenever a word of criticism is spoken from outside, is a symptom of the fact that independence of thought has ceased to be a virtue among professional educationists. This monolithic resistance to criticism reveals the existence and influence of what can only be described as an educational party-line—a party-line that protects the vested interests of both school administrators and professors of education. Even in Parent-Teacher Associations—admirable bodies in many respects—free discussion of the basic educational philosophy of the public schools is tightly controlled through frequent invocation and strict interpretation of a national by-law which provides that the organization "shall not seek to direct the administrative activities of the schools or to control their policies." Communication thus becomes a one-way affair. The theories of professional educationists may be freely expounded in P.T.A. meetings. But program committees are often given to understand that they may not schedule speakers of opposite views, for this would constitute an attempt to interfere with the policies of the schools.

The extreme unwillingness of professional educationists to submit their proposals to free public discussion and honest criticism frequently assumes the even uglier form of showering critics, no matter how upright and well-informed, with vituperation and personal abuse. A scientist or scholar who publishes a criticism of educational trends, even in a scientific journal, is liable to be denounced by professional educationists in responsible positions who do not think it beneath their dignity to hurl at him such epithets as these: "a peripatetic hatchet man," "a demagogue rather than a scholar," and "a master of the pointed phrase rather than the finished thought." Other educationists shamelessly employ the doctrine of "guilt by association" and try to show that because certain criticisms made by responsible scholars have been utilized in the propaganda of reactionary opponents of public education, all alike are to be regarded as "enemies" of the public schools.

Implicit in this kind of statement is the idea that no person can have an informed opinion on school matters save one who has been trained in pedagogy. A lifetime of teaching apparently cannot make a scholar or scientist anything but a meddlesome amateur when public educational policy is up for discussion. Such notions tend to inspire among the lesser lights of the educationist world an arrogance such as one meets in no other profession and which occasionally erupts in an attempt even to suppress freedom of discussion on public educational questions.

This hushing up of criticism is an attitude that belongs, not to a company of independent scholars, but to a bureaucracy, a party, a body united in defense of a vested interest. Professors of education are too deeply involved in the current public school situation to be reliable and fearless critics of it. They have aided the educational administrators in freeing the schools from their rightful responsibility to science and scholarship. In return, the educational bureaucracy has aided the professors of education in gaining within the universities a position of power which has enabled them to defy the academic standards of other departments of the institution. The structure of power within the educationist profession has much more to do with the present state of the public schools and the teaching profession in America than citizens are apt to realize.

The existence of what amounts to an interlocking directorate involving professors of education and school administrators is most clearly revealed in the policies governing the training of teachers. State educational officials exert control over such programs by the requirements they lay down for the certification of teachers, and these universally include substantial course work in pedagogy. Public school superintendents and principals reinforce this emphasis by the criteria they use in employing and promoting teachers. The beneficiaries are the professors of education, who are thus assured of a steady flow of students through their courses. This elaborate and rigorous prescription of pedagogical courses is rather curiously at variance with the principles which educationists profess in other matters. They wish as little as possible of the secondary school curriculum to be prescribed by outside authorities, and they vehemently assert that the colleges need not and should not insist upon any particular set of courses as a prerequisite for admission. But educationists are quite ready to invoke the coercive power of the state to compel every prospective teacher to take a specified number of courses in pedagogy.

Another inconsistency is involved. If an historian asserts that a knowledge of history can contribute to intelligent citizenship, the educationist is apt to condemn him for believing in "transfer of training" and to insist that history must prove its right to a place in the curriculum by incontrovertible experimental evidence that its study does produce better citizens. But the educationist demands a state-imposed requirement in pedagogy without presenting any experimental evidence whàtsoever that such course work produces better teachers. A professor of education informs me that nowhere in the literature of the "science" of education "can be found a single study, or controlled experiment, that establishes that a person is any better teacher by virtue of professional courses in Education. Surely this is a primary question into which their research organizations ought to inquire, and the worth of courses in Education could be established easily by the use of control and experimental groups equated as to initial ability, if there is any worth there. Is it not a little curious that such elemental research has been avoided by them?" I have called the statement to the attention of a number of educationists, and none has been able to point out a single study that would invalidate the generalization.

Justifiable or not, the state-enforced requirement in pedagogy is the taproot of the great educationist upas tree. The one inescapable prerequisite to a career in public school teaching and administration is course work in a department of education. Consequently this is the one department in which every student must enroll who wishes to teach or to be eligible to teach. The typical department of education knows very well how to extort every possible advantage from this strategic position. In most institutions it has managed to seize effective control over the placement of teachers. It frequently undertakes to plan all teachers' programs for them, regardless of their academic interests. It institutes programs of its own leading to a major or even a separate degree in education. It encourages its students to pile up course work in pedagogy far beyond the legal minimum. It frequently creates among its students the impression that they will be suitably rewarded for strict adherence in class to the educationist party line, and that too-vocal dissent will hurt their chances of future employment.

Protected behind state requirements which no department but itself can satisfy, the department is able to defy, or even to wage aggressive warfare against, the academic standards of the university. It exerts almost continuous pressure to break down admissions requirements, particularly those that might affect the work of the high schools. It frequently works to eliminate general graduation requirements that specify work in foreign languages and mathematics. The department of education typically refuses to look upon the university as a community of scholars working to a common end, and attempts to arrogate to itself control over all course offerings relating to educational problems. It sets up courses of its own in the teaching of the various school subjects, and gradually withdraws all future teachers from courses of this kind offered by the subject-matter departments. It generally refuses to entrust the teaching of educational psychology to independent departments of psychology, or the philosophy of education to departments of philosophy. In its relationship with the university of which it is a part, the typical department of education shows no real interest in interdisciplinary co-operation and no sense of academic partnership. Instead its faculty manifest a desire to insulate the schools and their teachers from every possible contact with recognized academic disciplines.

The abuse is even more appalling at the graduate level. The argument that pedagogical courses are necessary to prepare a novice for an unfamiliar vocation no longer has the slightest relevance, for graduate students in education are, as a rule, teachers with considerable experience. But administrators and teachers have been so thoroughly indoctrinated with the view that course work in pedagogy is the one thing of supreme importance, that experienced teachers return year after year, or summer session after summer session, to thresh old straw in departments of education, completely overlooking the glaring inadequacies of their training in the disciplines they profess to teach. Such inadequacies are unavoidable in a beginning teacher, for he cannot well know in advance what courses he may be assigned to handle outside the field of his major interest. If teacher certification requirements were designed for the benefit of the schools, however, instead of the benefit of professors of education, they would be phrased in such a way as to compel a teacher to bring his training in every subject he teaches up to a respectable minimum before embarking on additional courses in mere pedagogy.

On every hand there is evidence of the debasement which the teaching profession is undergoing at the hands of the interlocking directorate of professional educationists. Forced to undergo the humiliation of piling up credits in sterile courses in pedagogy, virtually forbidden to align himself with scholars and scientists in his chosen field, ceaselessly indoctrinated in an "official" educational philosophy, subjected to minute control and supervision by a professional educational hierarchy, the public school teacher cannot hope to resist administrative dictation or to secure a real voice in the formulation of educational policy. Though large numbers of able teachers oppose the anti-intellectual trend in education that is so obvious today, they are powerless to do anything about it. The educational directorate has seen to that. It does the hiring and firing, and it knows how to check thereby the expression of critical opinions. The organs by which teachers might bring their views to public attention—the educational associations and the journals—are under the throttling control of the directorate. The public has been led to believe that the educational philosophy now guiding the public schools is a philosophy to which the teachers and the scholars of the nation willingly subscribe. Actually, however, the voice which the citizen hears in favor of programs like "life-adjustment" education is the voice neither of the classroom teacher nor of the scholar. It is the voice of the professor of education or one of his allies in the public school directorate.

Across the educational world today stretches an iron curtain which the professional educationists are busily fashioning. Behind it, in slave-labor camps, are the classroom teachers, whose only hope of rescue is from without. On the hither side lies the free world of science and learning, menaced but not yet conquered. A division into two educational worlds is the great danger that faces us today. American intellectual life is threatened because the first twelve years of formal schooling in the United States are falling more and more completely under the policy-making control of a new breed of educator who has no real place in—who does not respect and who is not respected by—the world of scientists, scholars, and professional men.

"JOHNNY CAN'T READ" (1955)   From Rudolph Flesch, *Why Johnny Can't Read—and What You Can Do About It* (New York, 1955), pp. 1–5.

Dear Mary:

I have decided to start this book with a letter to you. You know that the idea came to me when I offered to help Johnny with his reading. It's really his book—or yours. So the only proper way to start it is with the words "Dear Mary."

You remember when I began to work with Johnny half a year ago. That was when he was twelve and they put him back into sixth grade because he was unable to read and couldn't possibly keep up with the work in junior high. So I told you that I knew of a way to teach reading that was altogether different from what they do in schools or in remedial reading courses or anywhere else. Well, you trusted me, and you know what has happened since. Today Johnny can read—not perfectly, to be sure, but anyone can see that in a few more months he will have caught up with other boys of his age. And he is happy again: You and I and everyone else can see that he is a changed person.

I think Johnny will go to college. He has a very good mind, as you know, and I don't see why he shouldn't become a doctor or a lawyer or an engineer. There is a lot in Johnny that has never come to the surface because of this reading trouble.

Since I started to work with Johnny, I have looked into this whole reading business. I worked my way through a mountain of books and articles on the subject, I talked to dozens of people, and I spent many hours in classrooms, watching what was going on.

What I found is absolutely fantastic. The teaching of reading—all over the United States, in all the schools, in all the textbooks—is totally wrong and flies in the face of all logic and common sense. Johnny couldn't read until half a year ago for the simple reason that nobody ever showed him how. Johnny's only problem was that he was unfortunately exposed to an ordinary American school.

You know that I was born and raised in Austria. Do you know that there are no remedial reading cases in Austrian schools? Do you know that there are no remedial reading cases in Germany, in France, in Italy, in Norway, in Spain—practically anywhere in the world except in the United States? Do you know that there was no such thing as remedial reading in this country either until about thirty years ago? Do you know that the teaching of reading never was a problem anywhere in the world until the United States switched to the present method around about 1925?

This sounds incredible, but it is true. One of the articles on reading that I found was by a Dr. Ralph C. Preston, of the University of Pennsylvania, who reported on his experiences on a trip through Western Germany in the April, 1953, *Elementary School Journal.* Dr. Preston visited a number of classrooms in Hamburg and Munich. "After the experience of hearing these German children read aloud," he says, "I began to attach some credence to a generally expressed opinion of German teachers that before the end of Grade 2 almost any child can read orally (without regard to degree of comprehension) almost anything in print!"

Of course, Dr. Preston, being an American educator, didn't draw the obvious conclusion from what he saw. The explanation is simply that the method used over there works, and the method used in our schools does not. We too could have perfect readers in all schools at the end of second grade if we taught our children by the system used in Germany.

Now, what is this system? It's very simple. Reading means getting meaning from certain combinations of letters. Teach the child what each letter stands for and he can read.

Ah no, you say, it can't be that simple. But it is. Let me give you an illustration.

I don't know whether you know any shorthand. Let's suppose you don't. Let's suppose you decide to learn how to read English shorthand.

Right away you say that nobody learns how to *read* shorthand. People who want to know shorthand learn how to *write* it; the reading of it comes by the way.

Exactly. That's why shorthand is such a good illustration of this whole thing. It's just a system of getting words on paper. Ordinary writing is another such system. Morse code is a third. Braille is a fourth. And so it goes. There are all sorts of systems of translating spoken words into a series of symbols so that they can be written down and read back.

Now the way to learn any such system is to learn to write and to read it at the same time. And how do you do that? The obvious answer is, By taking up one symbol after another and learning how to write it and how to recognize it. Once you are through the whole list of symbols, you can read and write; the rest is simply practice—learning to do it more and more automatically.

Since the dawn of time people have learned mechanical means of communication in this way—smoke signals and drums in the jungle and flag language and I don't know what all. You take up one item after another, learn what it stands for, learn how to reproduce it and how to recognize it, and there you are.

Shorthand, as I said, is an excellent example. I don't know any English shorthand myself, but I went to a library and looked up the most widely used manual of the Gregg system, the *Functional Method* by L. A. Leslie. Sure enough, it tells you about the symbols one after the other, starting out with the loop that stands for the long *a* in *ache, make,* and *cake.* After a few lessons, you are supposed to know the shape of all the shorthand "letters," and from there on it's just a matter of practice and picking up speed.

Our system of writing—the alphabet—was invented by the Egyptians and the Phoenicians somewhere around 1500 B.C. Before the invention of the alphabet there was only picture writing—a picture of an ox meant "ox," a picture of a house meant "house," and so on. (The Chinese to this day have a system of writing with symbols that stand for whole words.) As soon as people had an alphabet, the job of reading and writing was tremendously simplified. Before that, you had to have a symbol for every word in the language—10,000, 20,000 or whatever the vocabulary range was. Now, with the alphabet, all you had to learn was the letters. Each letter stood for a certain sound, and that was that. To write a word—any word—all you had to do was break it down into its sounds and put the corresponding letters on paper.

So, ever since 1500 B.C. people all over the world—wherever an alphabetic system of writing was used—learned how to read and write by the simple process of memorizing the sound of each letter in the alphabet. When a schoolboy in ancient Rome learned to read, he didn't learn that the written word *mensa* meant a table, that is, a certain piece of furniture with a flat top and legs. Instead, he began by learning that the letter *m* stands for the sound you make when you put your lips together, that *e* means the sound that comes out when you open your mouth about halfway, that *n* is like *m* but with the lips open and the teeth together, that *s* has a hissing sound, and that *a* means the sound made by opening your mouth wide. Therefore, when he saw the written word *mensa* for the first time, he could read it right off and learn, with a feeling of happy discovery, that this collection of letters meant a table. Not only that, he could also write the word down from dictation without ever having seen it before. And not only *that*, he could do this with practically every word in the language.

This is not miraculous, it's the only natural system of learning how to read. As I said, the ancient Egyptians learned that way, and the Greeks and the Romans, and the French and the Germans, and the Dutch and the Portuguese, and the Turks and the Bulgarians and the Esthonians and the Icelanders and the Abyssinians—every single nation throughout history that used an alphabetic system of writing.

Except, as I said before, twentieth-century Americans—and other nations in so far as they have followed our example. And what do we use instead? Why, the only other possible system of course—the system that was in use before the invention of the alphabet in 1500 B.C. We have decided to forget that we write with letters and learn to read English as if it were Chinese. One word after another after another after another. If we want to read materials with a vocabulary of 10,000 words, then we have to memorize 10,000 words; it we want to go to the 20,000 word range, we have to learn, one by one, 20,000 words; and so on. We have thrown 3,500 years of civilization out the window and have gone back to the Age of Hammurabi.

You don't believe me? I assure you what I saying is literally true. Go to your school tomorrow morning—or if Johnny has brought home one of his readers, look at it. You will immediately see that all the words in it are learned by endless repetition. Not a sign anywhere that letters correspond to sounds and that words can be worked out by pronouncing the letters. No. The child is told what each word means and then they are mechanically, brutally hammered into his brain.

VLADIMIR NABOKOV CARICATURES A PROGRESSIVE SCHOOL FOR GIRLS (1955) From *Lolita* (Greenwich, Conn., 1955), pp. 161–63.

I had hoped Beardsley School for girls, an expensive day school, with lunch thrown in and a glamorous gymnasium, would, while cultivating all those young bodies, provide some formal education for their minds as well. Gaston Godin, who was seldom right in his judgment of American habitus, had warned me that the institution might turn out to be one of those where girls are taught, as he put it with a foreigner's love for such things: "not to spell very well, but to smell very well." I don't think they achieved even that.

At my first interview with headmistress Pratt, she approved of my child's "nice blue eyes" (blue! Lolita!) and of my own friendship with that "French genius" (a genius! Gaston!)—and then, having turned Dolly over to a Miss Cormorant, she wrinkled her brow in a kind of [*recueillement*] and said:

"We are not so much concerned, Mr. Humbird, with having our students become bookworms or be able to reel off all the capitals of Europe which nobody knows anyway, or learn by heart the dates of forgotten battles. What we are concerned with is the adjustment of the child to group life. This is why we stress the four D's: Dramatics, Dance, Debating and Dating. We are confronted by certain facts. Your delightful Dolly will presently enter an age group where dates, dating, date dress, date book, date etiquette, mean as much to her as say, business, business connections, business success, mean to you, or as much as [smiling] the happiness of my girls means to me. Dorothy Humbird is already involved in a whole system of social life which consists, whether we like it or not, of hot-dog stands, corner drugstores, malts and cokes, movies, square-dancing, blanket parties on beaches, and even hair-fixing parties! Naturally at Beardsley School we disapprove of some of these activities; and we rechannel others into more constructive directions. But we do try to turn our backs on the fog and squarely face the sunshine. To put it briefly, while adopting certain teaching techniques, we are more interested in communication than in composition. That is, with due respect to Shakespeare and others, we want our girls to communicate freely with the live world around them rather than plunge into musty old books. We are still groping perhaps, but we grope intelligently, like a gynecologist feeling a tumor. We think, Dr. Humburg, in organismal and organizational terms. We have done away with the mass of irrelevant topics that have traditionally been presented to young girls, leaving no place, in former days, for the knowledges and the skills, and the attitudes they will need in managing their lives and—as the cynic might add—the lives of their husbands. Mr. Humberson, let us put it this way: the position of a star is important, but the most practical spot for an icebox in the kitchen may be even more important to the budding housewife. You say that all you expect a child to obtain from school is a sound education. But what do we mean by education? In the old days it was in the main a verbal phenomenon; I mean, you could have a child learn by heart a good encyclopedia and he or she would know as much as or more than a school could offer. Dr. Hummer, do you realize that for the modern pre-adolescent child, medieval dates are of less vital value than weekend ones [twinkle]?—to repeat a pun that I heard the Beardsley college psychoanalyst permit herself the other day. We live not only in a world of thoughts, but also in a world of things. Words without experience are meaningless. What on earth can Dorothy Hummerson care for Greece and the Orient with their harems and slaves?"

THE ORGANIZATION CHILDREN (1956)   From William H. Whyte, *The Organization Man* (New York, 1956), pp. 423–30.

The organization man's emphasis on the group, I have been maintaining, is not a temporary phenomenon dictated by external necessity; it is a response to what he feels is a moral imperative, and more and more he is openly articulating it. I have looked at the church in this perspective; now I would like to turn to the schools. Like the churches they had to be build from scratch, and in building them the young parents had to declare themselves. Their children will be transients too, and the pressures of the organization life ahead for them will be, if anything, more intense. What, then, should be emphasized? In helping shape the curriculum, parents are at once giving a guide and revealing themselves.

The Park Foresters threw themselves into the job of creating a school system with tremendous energy. With few precedents to go on and virtually no industrial tax base, they have developed a system which includes a spankingly attractive high school, six cheerful elementary schools, and several more a-building. Educators all over the country have been lavish in their praise. In 1954 the high school was selected as one of the five winners in the "All-America Schools" contest of the National Municipal League, and other awards for the school have been streaming in.

They have both profited and suffered from an unusual turnover problem. The leadership of the school boards, for example, is constantly turning over. The first elementary-school superintendent, Robert Anderson, and the young chemist who headed the school board could never be sure from one month to the next just who would be working with them. While they were there, board members worked devotedly. Just about the time one became saturated in the school problems, it seemed, his company would transfer him, and the break in continuity persists to this day.

Teachers have also been a worry. There is a high turnover of younger teachers in any community, but Park Forest is at an especial disadvantage in this matter. There aren't any bachelors around. (Of some 5,000 males in 1954 only one was unmarried, and he has since left.) Several court units have been set aside for unmarried girl teachers, but this kind of sorority life doesn't jibe with the community, or with the girls, and the rate of departure has been heavy.

More important, the children move too. The impact is as severe on the teachers as on the children themselves, for the teachers are thereby robbed of a good bit of the feeling of achievement they get from watching the children develop. As Anderson put it: "In any school you have to put a six-months' investment in a child before the two of you can start functioning right—you have to test them, get the parents involved, get the kids settled down in a group. We do this all right—but then what happens? They move, and you have to start all over again."

The children, however, have proved to be highly adaptable material, and the teachers who have had experience in traditional communities are quick to note how much more socially responsive the children of transients are than others. "Social maturity comes faster here for children like this," explains one teacher. "The adjustment to the group doesn't seem to involve so many problems for them. I have noticed that they seem to get the feeling that nobody is the boss—there is a feeling of complete co-operation. Partly this comes from early exposure to court play."

Like their parents, in short, the children already have a high degree of social skill, and the environment itself will further intensify this in them. This being the case, it could be argued, there is no necessity for the school to duplicate, and thus they are all the more free to concentrate on the other, more inward, aspects. But neither the parents nor the schools feel this way. From the beginning the curriculum has borne down very heavily on the pragmatic and the social, and the concept of adjustment has been dominant.

The first superintendent left, with a well-earned sigh of relief, to be a professor at the Harvard Graduate School of Education. What curriculum changes have ensued, however, have not been major. Anderson's successor, Superintendent Gerald Smith, has talked of introducing the "Fourth R, Responsibility," but this seems largely another way of describing the established policy. The disciplining vehicle, Smith explains, is the group. The teacher strives not to discipline the child directly but to influence all the children's attitudes so that as a group they recognize correct behavior. If a child falls out of line, he does not have to be subjected to authoritarian strictures of elders; he senses the disapproval of the group and, in that way, the school believes, learns to discipline himself as much as possible.

The child who tends to be withdrawn is given special attention. "Johnny wasn't doing so well at school," one mother told me. "The teacher explained to me that he was doing fine on his lessons but that his social adjustment was not as good as it might be. He would pick just one or two friends to play with, and sometimes he was happy to remain by himself." There are many such instances, and, save for a few odd parents, most are grateful that the schools work so hard to offset tendencies to introversion and other suburban abnormalities.

Park Forest schools are not extreme in this respect, and most Park Foresters are anxious that the curriculum be recognized as middle of the road. But they do agree that there is a noticeably permissive atmosphere. They point out, for example, that the schools follow a method by which the student group is encouraged to take a strong hand in the planning of what they are to be taught. The children are not exactly put in charge, but the teacher makes a point of asking them what it is they would like to know about a particular subject, rather than unilaterally giving them what she thinks they ought to learn. As Superintendent Smith explained it: "If the topic under discussion is India, the children are asked what they would like to know about that country. Queries might range from elephants to the mysteries of bathing in the Ganges. By the time juvenile curiosities are satisfied, the children have a reasonable knowledge of India's terrain, vegetation, animal life, religions, caste systems, and politics."

The schools are similarly flexible in grading. To use fixed standards of performance, the authorities feel, would straitjacket the child. As a consequence, the primaries, as in many other schools, are ungraded, and in later classes formal reports of the A-B-C-D-F or percentage type have been discarded. "It is obviously impossible," curriculum consultant Lucille Thimblin explains, "for a teacher to reduce the many-sided aspects of a pupil's development to an accurate numerical value." Under the old method, she says, a bright pupil who has made little effort might get the highest mark while another child who works hard might fail to get a respectable mark. The school could get around this by simply using the two terms "satisfactory" and "unsatisfactory" and this would be helpful, Mrs. Thimblin points out, in that "this type of report does reduce the competition for scholastic leadership." Unfortunately, however, while it would make for better adjustment, "it it very likely also to reduce some pupils' incentive to do better work." The solution: a check list to supplement parent-teacher conferences. In this the student's academic progress is rated on the basis of his individual capabilities rather than against an arbitrary norm. He is also rated in terms of his social group and whether or not he meets the standards attainable for every member of the group.

There are a few parental misgivings about the elementary schools. As far as discipline is concerned, parents sometimes wonder if perhaps the school isn't a bit too permissive. Occasionally parents talk of sending their children to Park Forest's parochial school so they would "get some discipline"; they rarely get around to trying, but they still sigh aloud over the elementary schools' laxness. Even parents who are satisfied with the children's behavior are sometimes critical, for though not many may think their own children lack discipline, they are very sure that everybody else's children do. Habitual is the complaint of their "freshness." ("The kids here call everybody by their first names. If one of my neighbors' children ever came up and called me Mrs. George, I think I would drop dead from surprise.") As a few Park Foresters take pains to note, however, parents are somewhat unreasonable about this; whatever their faults, harsh parental discipline is not one of them, and they cannot fairly ask the schools to do what they won't.

There is always a controversy of some kind going on over the elementary schools, but it is more on administration and taxes than matters scholastic. On the whole, it seems clear, the parents are very well satisfied with the curriculum. At

3141

Park Forest, a PTA committee proudly agreed, learning is a "painless process." "The teacher and the pupils plan together," the committee's report went on, "and everyone has a conscious feeling of belonging—as an individual and as a group participant. . . . Everything they learn is related to something they've experienced in their everyday life or through TV, radio, movies, or on the playground." A few parents are still not altogether adjusted to the absence of primary grades, but this criticism usually comes from people who arrived from a town with a more traditional school, and in time evaporates. Similarly, though some feel there is a slighting of fundamentals, all are impressed with the reports from Park Forest alumni that their children are doing very well academically in their new communities because of their Park Forest schooling. If they had to choose, furthermore, most Park Foresters would hate to see the schools discard the emphasis on practical, contemporary problems. "Janet is studying marketing," one parent told me, "and she's only in the sixth grade. She's studying ads and discounts—things I didn't get until college. These kids are certainly getting a broad view of things."

It is in the high school, however, that the new suburbia's philosophy gets its most significant expression. The philosophy is by no means unique to Park Forest. High-school superintendent Eric Baber speaks very much like many superintendents elsewhere, and his writings do not show unorthodoxy but, rather, a deep grasp of contemporary educational literature. What makes Park Forest's high school unique is that, where in traditional communities what has been called the "life adjustment" curriculum has been introduced a bit at a time, at Park Forest it has been the foundation. The new $1,600,000 "learning laboratory" is not only one of the most modern in the country, in spirit as well as brick it is the embodiment of the suburban temper.

Five years ago, when the school was still in the planning stage, Baber told parents that the trouble with U.S. education is that it is concentrated far too much on the intellectual aspect of education. Even teachers' colleges, he observed sadly, still require plane geometry for admission. Except for a small coterie, he asked, of what value to most people are the traditional academic disciplines? "The so-called 'bright student' is often one of the dumbest or least apt when he gets away from his textbooks and memory work," Baber told a teachers' workshop. "This is evidenced by the fact that many $20,000-to-$100,000-a-year jobs in business, sales, sports, radio . . . are held by persons with I.Q.s of less than ninety."

Baber is not actually against intelligence. He believes it should be channeled toward real-life, vocational needs more than to the academic requirements of the colleges. Since Park Forest, unlike many towns, is predominantly college-educated, most students will be going on to college anyway; thus the "two-school," vocational versus academic problems might not seem particularly pertinent. A large share of the school plant nevertheless was designed with great attention to the vocational, and so was the curriculum.

Of the total of seventy subjects originally offered, only one half were in traditional academic subjects—and the latter, furthermore, were by no means ivory tower. Of seven offerings in English available to juniors and seniors, the one devoted to grammar, rhetoric, and composition was a one-semester "refresher course . . . for students who feel the need for additional preparation." Of more appeal to teenagers would be the full-year courses in journalism and in speech (for which, in the "communication laboratory," facilities are available for practical things like radio and TV debating).

The seventy formal subject offerings by no means exhausted the life-adjustment curriculum. Baber felt that the schools must assume more responsibility for the *total* growth of the child. Conceivably, this could be left to other agencies—to the family, or the church, or society itself, for example. Nevertheless, through such media as courses in family group living (twelfth-grade elective) and "doing" sessions in actual situations, the school tackled it. "Ours is an age of group action," Baber says.[1]

DAVID RIESMAN ON THE TEACHER'S ROLE IN PROGRESSIVE EDUCATION From David Riesman, *The Lonely Crowd* (New York, 1956), pp. 79–85.

Progressive education began as a movement to liberate children from the crushing of talent and breaking of will that was the fate of many, even of those whose inner-direction might have seemed to them and to the observer stable and sound enough. Its aim, and to a very considerable degree, its achievement, was to develop the individuality of the child; and its method was to focus the teacher's attention on more facets of the child than his intellectual abilities. Today, however, progressive education is often no longer progressive; as people have become more other-directed, educational methods that were once liberating may even tend to thwart individuality rather than advance and protect it. The story can be quickly told.

Progressive schools have helped lower the age of school entry; the two- to five-year-old groups learn to associate school not with forbidding adults and dreary subjects but with play and understanding adults. The latter are, increasingly, young college graduates who have been taught to be more concerned with the child's social and psychological adjustment than with his academic progress—indeed, to scan the intellectual performance for signs of social maladjustment. These new teachers are more specialized. They don't claim to "understand children" but to have studied Gesell on the "fives" or the "nines"; and this greater knowledge not only prevents the children from uniting in a wall of distrust or conspiracy against the school but also permits the teacher to take a greater hand in the socialization of spheres—consumption, friendship, fantasy—which the older-type teacher, whatever her personal desires, could not touch. Our wealthier society can afford this amount of individuation and "unnecessary" schooling.

Physical arrangements, too—in seating, age-grading, decoration—symbolize the changes in the teacher's function. The sexes are mixed. Seating is arranged "informally." That is, *alphabetic* forms disappear, often to be replaced by *sociometric* forms that bring together compeers. This often means that where to sit becomes problematical—a clue to one's location on the friendship chart. Gesell

[1] Lest I seem to be applying the word *vocational* unfairly, let me note that Dr. Baber is equable about it. From a letter to the writer from Dr. Baber: "In general, I believe you have given a reasonably accurate description of the high-school situation. The frequent use of the word *vocational* as applied to our educational program is acceptable if broadly defined as useful or functional. . . . We emphasize *general education* and the development of understandings, skills, and critical thinking directly related to current problems of social living. If I were to attempt to define the bases of our educational program I believe it would be in terms of three fundamental concepts: (1) the philosophy of experimentalism, compromised somewhat by the pressures of tradition, (2) an organismic (or Gestalt) psychology, and (3) democratic educational leadership."

grading is as severe as intellectual grading was in the earlier era; whatever their intellectual gifts, children stay with their presumed social peers.[1] The desks change their form, too; they are more apt to be movable tables with open shelves than places where one may hide things. The teacher no longer sits on a dais or struts before a blackboard but joins the family circle.

Above all, the walls change their look. The walls of the modern grade school are decorated with the paintings of the children or their montages from the class in social studies. Thus the competitive and contemporary problems of the children look down on them from walls which, like the teacher herself, are no longer impersonal. This looks progressive, looks like a salute to creativeness and individuality; but again we meet paradox. While the school deemphasizes grades and report cards, the displays seem almost to ask the children: "Mirror, mirror on the wall, who is fairest of us all?"[2]

While the children's paintings and montages show considerable imaginative gift in the pre-adolescent period, the school itself is nevertheless still one of the agencies for the destruction of fantasy, as it was in the preceding era. Imagination withers in most of the children by adolescence. What survives is neither artistic craft nor artistic fantasy but the socialization of taste and interest that can already be seen in process in the stylization of perception in the children's paintings and stories. The stories of the later progressive grades are apt to be characterized by "realism." This realism is subtly influenced by the ideals of progressive movement. Caesar and Pompeii are replaced by visits to stores and dairies, by maps from *Life,* and by *The Weekly Reader;* and fairy tales are replaced by stories about trains, telephones, and grocery stores, and, later, by material on race relations or the United Nations or "our Latin American neighbors."

These changes in arrangement and topic assist the breakdown of walls between teacher and pupil; and this in turn helps to break down walls between student and

---

[1] Howard C. Becker ("Role and Career Problems of the Chicago Public School Teacher," unpublished Ph.D. dissertation, University of Chicago, 1951) has been observing the classroom consequences of the decline of the practice both of skipping grades and of holding children back who must repeat the grade. The teachers, faced with a group of identical age but vastly different capacities and willingnesses, meet the situation by dividing the class into two or three like-minded groups. Mobility between groups is discouraged, and children are encouraged to imitate their groupmates. The teacher herself, in the public schools, is probably inner-directed, but she is forced by her situation to promote other-direction among her charges.

The following quotation from Mr. Becker's interviews is a poignant example of how a teacher will promote other-direction in her efforts to get the children to have more interesting weekends: "Every class I have I start out the year by making a survey. I have each child get up and tell what he did over the weekend. These last few years I've noticed that more and more children get up and say, 'Saturday I went to the show, Sunday I went to the show' . . . I've been teaching twenty-five years, and it never used to be like that. Children used to do more interesting things, they would go places instead of 'Saturday I went to the show, Sunday I went to the show' . . . What I do is to give a talk on all the interesting things that could be done—like going to museums and things like that. And also things like playing baseball and going on bike rides. By the end of the term a child is ashamed if he has to get up and say, 'Saturday I went to the show, Sunday I went to the show.' All the rest of the children laugh at him. So they really try to do some interesting things."

[2] Still more paradoxically, it often happens that those schools that insist most strongly that the child be original and creative by this very demand make it difficult for him to be so. He dare not imitate an established master nor, in some cases, even imitate his own earlier work. Though the introduction of the arts into the school opens up the whole art world to many children, who would have no time or stimulation outside, other children are forced to socialize performances that would earlier have gone unnoticed by peers and adults.

student, permitting that rapid circulation of tastes which is a prelude to other-directed socialization. Whereas the inner-directed school child might well have hidden his stories and paintings under his bed—like the adult who, as we saw, often kept a diary—the other-directed child reads his stories to the group and puts his paintings on the wall. Play, which in the earlier epoch is often an extracurricular and private hobby, shared at most with a small group, now becomes part of the school enterprise itself, serving a "realistic" purpose.

The teacher's role in this situation is often that of opinion leader. She is the one who spreads the messages concerning taste that come from the progressive urban centers. She conveys to the children that what matters is not their industry or learning as such but their adjustment in the group, their cooperation, their (carefully stylized and limited) initiative and leadership.

Especially important is the fact that the cooperation and leadership that are inculcated in and expected of the children are frequently contentless. In nursery school it is not important whether Johnny plays with a truck or in the sandbox, but it matters very much whether he involves himself with Bill—via any object at all. To be sure, there are a few, a very few, truly progressive schools where the children operating on the Dalton plan and similar plans exercise genuine choice of their program, move at their own pace, and use the teacher as a friendly reference library; here cooperation is necessary and meaningful in actual work on serious projects. Far more frequently, however, the teacher continues to hold the reins of authority in her hands, hiding her authority, like her compeer, the other-directed parent, under the cloak of "reasoning" and manipulation. She determines the program and its pace—indeed, often holding the children back because she fails to realize that children, left to themselves, are capable of curiosity about highly abstract matters. She may delay them by making arithmetic "realistic" and languages fun—as well as by substituting social studies for history. In extreme forms of this situation there is nothing on which the children have to cooperate in order to get it done. The teacher will do it for them anyway. Hence when she asks that they be cooperative she is really asking simply that they be nice.

However, though the request seems simple, it is not casually made: the teacher is very tense about it. Deprived of older methods of discipline, she is, if anything, even more helpless than the parents who can always fall back on those methods in a pinch, though guiltily and rather ineffectively. The teacher neither dares to nor cares to; she has been taught that bad behavior on the children's part implies poor management on her part. Moreover, she herself is not interested in the intellectual content of what is taught, nor is this content apt to come up in a staff meeting or PTA discussion. These adult groups are often concerned with teaching tolerance, both ethnic and economic; and the emphasis on social studies that results means that intellectual content and skill become still more attenuated. Consequently, the teacher's emotional energies are channeled into the area of group relations. Her social skills develop; she may be sensitive to cliques based on "mere friendship" and seek to break them up lest any be left out. Correspondingly, her love for certain specific children may be trained out of her. All the more, she needs the general cooperation of all the children to assure herself that she is doing her job. Her surface amiability and friendliness, coupled with this underlying anxiety concerning the children's response, must be very confusing to the children who will probably conclude that to be uncooperative is about the worst thing one can be.

Of course the teacher will see to it that the children practice cooperation in small matters: in deciding whether to study the Peruvians or the Colombians, in nominating class officers for early practice in the great contemporary rituals of electioneering and parliamenteering, and in organizing contributions for the Red Cross or a Tag Day. Thus the children are supposed to learn democracy by underplaying the skills of intellect and overplaying the skills of gregariousness and amiability—skill democracy, in fact, based on respect for ability to do something, tends to survive only in athletics.

There is, therefore, a curious resemblance between the role of the teacher in the small-class modern school—a role that has spread from the progressive private schools to a good number of the public schools—and the role of the industrial relations department in a modern factory. The latter is also increasingly concerned with cooperation between men and men and between men and management, as technical skill becomes less and less of a major concern. In a few of the more advanced plants there is even a pattern of democratic decision on moot matters— occasionally important because it affects piecework rates and seniority rules, but usually as trivial as the similar decisions of grammar-school government. Thus the other-directed child is taught at school to take his place in the society where the concern of the group is less with what it produces than with its internal group relations, its morale.

ESTABLISHMENT OF THE COUNCIL FOR BASIC EDUCATION (1956)
From Mortimer Smith, *A Citizen's Manual for Public Schools* (Boston, 1959), p. 1.

The Council for Basic Education, 725 Fifteenth Street, N.W., Washington, D.C. 20005, which sponsors this manual, is a non-profit, lay-oriented group devoted to the maintenance of quality in American education; it is financed by foundation grants and by the dues and payments of its members and subscribers. As explained in its original statement of purpose in 1956:

> The Council for Basic Education was established in the belief that the purpose of education is the harmonious development of the mind, the will, and the conscience of each individual so that he may use to the full his intrinsic powers and shoulder the responsibilities of citizenship. It believes in the principle of universal education and in the tax-supported public school system. It insists that only by the maintenance of high academic standards can the ideal of democratic education be realized—the ideal of offering to all the children of all the people of the United States not merely an opportunity to attend school, but the privilege of receiving there the soundest education that is offered any place in the world.

RE-APPRAISAL
1951–1973

3146

Among the Council's regular activities in support of these ideals is the publication of a monthly newsletter, the *CBE Bulletin*, and the organization of research and publication projects of special significance to the strengthening of basic education.

THE COUNCIL FOR BASIC EDUCATION'S PROGRAM (1959) From
Mortimer Smith, *A Citizen's Manual For Public Schools* (Boston, 1959), pp. 6–8, 10–12.

To revert to the question of what basic education in the schools means: the first necessity is to decide what the primary purpose of schools is. The school has, of course, many subsidiary purposes, but the Council for Basic Education believes that its primary purpose is fourfold: (1) to teach young people how to read and write and figure; (2) to transmit the facts about the heritage and culture of the race; (3) in the process of (1) and (2) to train the intelligence and to stimulate the pleasures of thought; and (4) to provide that atmosphere of moral affirmation without which education is merely animal training. In the words of the educator I. L. Kandel, the school is the place for "making the child literate in the essential fields of human knowledge."

Granted the above as a valid definition of the purpose of schools, what should be a curriculum for carrying out this purpose? When Professor Kandel speaks of the essential fields of human knowledge he is obviously not talking about education in the large, about the sum total of experiences, information, and skills the individual acquires along the way, but about the necessarily limited experiences which take place in the formal institution of the school. The school can't be all things to all men—or all children. If it works at making them literate in language, mathematics, science, and history (an admittedly large task), can it also be expected to teach them how to drive automobiles, how to act on dates, how to be well groomed, and how to have attractive personalities?

The early years of formal education are pre-eminently the time for providing those sets of symbols and sets of facts which are indispensable before understanding can come alive, just as a long preparation in mechanical practice is necessary before the pianist can interpret music. One cannot argue that these facts and symbols must be soft-pedaled or postponed for fear a child will not always see the "why" of learning some of them.

The current notions of "readiness" and "child development" and "individual differences" often have the effect of dulling the eagerness of small children to learn. The insights about how learning takes place and about rates of growth, which have been among the valuable contributions of psychology to education, tend in some quarters to become dogmas, sometimes seeming to assure the teacher that subject matter and standards are unimportant because pupils will learn when they are "ready," according to some personal law of growth. Perhaps most normal children are more anxious to read and spell and do their sums than theorists give them credit for; and for this reason it is not asking too much that drill in the basic subjects should begin earlier than it does now, and be on a more intensive scale. (It is not unusual for some schools to delay teaching arithmetic until the third grade—and some have been known to begin it as late as the *sixth* grade! One authoritative body, the National Council of Teachers of English, has suggested that grammar is taught too early in American schools, that it need not be taught prior to the seventh grade and then should "be confined to establishing the fundamental concepts of subject and predicate only," and "to some students it may not be taught at all."[1]

[1] *The English Language Arts in the Secondary School,* prepared by the Commission on the English Curriculum of the National Council of Teachers of English. Appleton-Century-Crofts, Inc., New York, 1956, p. 364.

In any sound program of basic education, children will be given an ordered picture of the physical world, including knowledge of the location of states, countries, and cities. This involves memorizing, which some educators like to call parroting, but perhaps it is better to have some parroting of facts about the world than parroting of adults' opinions about the United Nations or about vast and complex social problems. What is being talked about here, of course, is geography, which, like history, has long since become the victim of that Hydra-headed monster, the social studies. In our efforts to integrate such subjects as history, geography, and civics and to bring them into relationship with each other—worthy enough aims—we have often diluted their content and been left with weak substitutes for the genuine article. Historical and geographical knowledge among young people—the lack of which is almost universally recognized—will probably not improve until history and geography are restored as separate subjects, but in view of the strongly entrenched position of social studies, the prospects for reform are not bright.

Education in any degree involves the ability to grasp and express ideas, and this in turn calls for a knowledge of formal English, a sense of good usage and style, precision in expression. English is the one subject which must run like a golden thread through the whole fabric of our educational system, from kindergarten to college. The decline in decent use of our native tongue in recent years is the result in part of the decline in respect for English among educators, many of whom contend frankly that correctness in speech and writing is determined solely by current usage. They do not make clear whose usage, but if contemporary fashion is to be the criterion let us emulate Winston Churchill rather than Harry Truman, Walter Lippmann rather than Walter Winchell, Robert Frost rather than Mickey Spillane.

To sum up, this should be the *bare minimum* expected of a normal child finishing the elementary school: He should be able to read and write with some fluency, and spell, add, subtract, multiply, and divide with accuracy; he should know the basic geographical facts of his country and the world; have a knowledge of elementary science; know something of the culture and history of other peoples and much of his own. And above all, his schooling should have taught him the difference between aimless mental activity and orderly thought.

The subjects which serve to develop these matters constitute the basic curriculum of the lower school, but there are, of course, other matters which are the proper concern of the school: physical education, for example (in due subordination to the academic disciplines), and music and art. These last two subjects should probably be approached with the emphasis on appreciation rather than performance, although where performing ability is present it should be developed. For most pupils, however, it is probably better to develop in them an appreciation of good music than to teach them to play mediocre music badly.

And what about the high school and its relation to basic education? Perhaps the first thing that needs to be said here is that it is misguided sentimentalism which insists that all students should be urged to stay in high school beyond the legal leaving age. By the time the student has reached sixteen (the leaving age in most states) his talent for absorbing education and his attitude toward work are usually established with a high degree of reliability. If he is one of that small minority who cannot or will not learn, or make a decent effort to learn, the school should not attempt to increase its "holding power" by substituting for education a program in social therapeutics. It is doubtful if he will be the better for the attempt, and it is certain that the school will be the worse for the dilution of its purpose.

While the high school student is naturally capable of more judgment than a pupil in the elementary school and should be interested not only in the appearance of things but in their significance as well, the general principle holds here, too, that the school's task is primarily transmission of factual knowledge in the basic subjects. As Aristotle pointed out a long time ago, a boy can be a mathematician but he cannot be a philosopher, mathematics dealing with abstractions which can be understood by the immature but philosophy being derived from experience which the boy does not have.

Speaking again in terms of a bare minimum, this should probably be a program not only for the above average but for the average student as well: English (literature, composition, grammar) throughout the four years; at the very least, two years of history; a year of plane geometry and one of elementary algebra,[1] an opportunity to select advanced math; a year of biology, and one of a physical science; some foreign languages for all, much for the college bound; music and art as electives; and physical education properly subordinated to the academic program. This, or a similar program, should be the basic curriculum in any high school—academic, business, or vocational.

In the agonizing reappraisal of American education which has been going on since Sputnik, more and more parents and educators are coming to accept the necessity for a stronger academic program in the elementary and high schools— although it is easy to be skeptical about the genuineness of the conversion of some educators. One suspects that many of them are paying only lip service to a strong academic program and are apt in private to agree with those educators who drew up, sixteen years ago (only applying it to secondary schools), a report of the President's Commission on Higher Education, in which it was stated that "we shall be denying educational opportunity to many young people as long as we maintain the present orientation of higher education toward verbal skills and intellectual interest."

There is a strange quirk in modern educational thinking which produces pessimism about the school's ability to teach such tangibles as geography, spelling, and reading, but optimism about the ability of the school to teach such intangibles as good citizenship and wise use of leisure time and to produce tolerant, well-rounded personalities. This quirk was illustrated in a report issued a few years ago by an important group of professional educators which, after stating that the school can and should be teaching a great variety of non-academic matter, then pointed out that about all the school can do in the field of English for over half of the students in secondary schools is to teach them to read newspapers and magazines "reasonably well."

---

[1] As pointed out in *Teaching the Third R: A Comparative Study of American and European Textbooks in Arithmetic* by Charles H. Schutter and Richard L. Spreckelmeyer (Washington: Council for Basic Education, 1959), in Europe the areas familiar in America as Algebra I and Plane Geometry have been essentially completed by many students at the end of the eighth year. The authors advocate a similar early introduction of these subjects in American schools.

EDUCATION WITHOUT INSTRUCTION (1959)   From Jacques Barzun, *The House of Intellect* (New York, 1959), pp. 88–91, 102–04.

Clearly, the blame for much that is lacking or painful in our manners can be laid upon our education, individual and collective. The same cause will also explain what is wrong with our politics and ways of business, with our press and public opinion. Indeed, whatever is wrong is the fault of the schools, for is it not there that we learn to become what we are? This common indictment overlooks but one point, which is that the schools are run by adults—and run to suit other adults in political, intellectual, or business life. The schools are thus as fully the product of our politics, business, and public opinion as these are the products of our schools. It is because the link is so close that the schools are so hard to change.

They are, for the same reason, hard to describe, showing as they do the diversity and elusiveness of culture itself. Because it is thought of as a sheltered place invaded by worldlings, the school is often forgiven for resembling the world; it is always possible to say, "That is society's doing, not the school's." But this only proves that the best of schools can be no more than half-innocent. They work with spoiled materials: teachers marred by the ugly world and children already stamped with the defects that their parents condone by habit or foster on principle.

From these facts one great truth emerges: there is, there can be, no such thing as a good school.

The conclusion is repellent to our desire of perfection, but it is inescapable. It does not mean that all schools are bad: some are better than others, but none will do what in our naive fancy we liken to the work of an instrument of precision functioning independently of its makers. Any school has a system, and its action is therefore that of a cookie cutter carelessly handled. Schools that repudiate system as harsh and unjust turn out anarchical and more unjust. That is why the profoundest theorist of modern education, Rousseau, limited his scheme to one child and a tutor. Rousseau begins by pointing out that the story of Emile is not a model, but an ideal case that suggests new intentions rather than new practices. It is not imitable, if only because the tutor is a genius who devotes all his time and thought to a pupil who is unnaturally responsive.

Today, the Western world is at the other extreme from this situation. It is headed toward mass schooling, the European half of that world making the attempt some sixty years after the United States. Our current discussion of education in America is thus of peculiar interest, because we, dissatisfied with our handiwork, are seeking to change just at the time when England, France, and Germany are courageously starting to repeat our mistakes. Our words and acts are doubly important because we are the pioneers others copy or listen to.

Ours is surely the most remarkable of educational systems in that it is the only one to deal with anything like the same numbers with so much liberality and persistence. We offer education from infancy to—I was about to say 'the grave.' Education in the United States is a passion and a paradox. Millions want it and commend it, and are busy about it, at the same time as they are willing to degrade it by trying to get it free of charge and free of work. Education with us has managed to reconcile the contradictory extremes of being a duty and a diversion, and to elude intellectual control so completely that it can become an empty ritual without arousing protest.

Not that we have ever been satisfied with our schools. Long before the postwar self-searching, thousands of meetings and millions of words were being spent each year in debating improvements. But our characteristic softness then and now invests the whole attempt and reduces it for the most part to abstract worry and repetitious piety. The *doyen* of educational theorists in this country,[1] addressing in 1955 the Middle Atlantic States Philosophy of Education Association, opened his remarks with the words: There is urgent current need for a broader and more effective education.' Last year, another critic, whose words make him representative of many others, expressed alarm at the insufficiency of present-day teaching in science. Did he suggest something to do, now or as soon as possible? No. He asked for a 'broad concept.' A third lecturer, a well-known businessman, who knows the general resistance to intellectual subjects, wants to turn the present outcry to use by strengthening the universities' public position. Excellent. But what does he, an expert in 'public relations,' set forth as his main point? Defining goals: 'The broad role of the institution must be defined.' He does after a bit speak of curriculum, higher faculty salaries, and new buildings; but he soon relapses into 'broad' ideas: 'Creative thinking and creative teachers must, it seems to me, be given primary importance in defining the goals of any institution. Read any segment of the press, lay or learned, and you will find that the angry protests and anxious injunctions swing between what is broad and what is creative. A visitor from outer space would conclude that we had lost, or perhaps never formed, any communicable idea of the purpose of schools.

We did have such an idea until about 1900, when it began to yield to the indefiniteness of mass education. But that phrase alone is enough to quell our impatience. We can never forget the magnitude of the difficulties in what we then undertook. The worst faults of the schooling we now give are due to the large numbers of pupils relatively to the natural supply of true teachers. And most of the other faults are due to the unending task of acclimating the alien and native millions to increasingly complicated modes of life. If the high schools make dating and 'driver education' part of the curriculum in place of Latin and trigonometry, it is because 'preparing for life' means giving information that is of everyday use, fraught with social consequence, and that no one else will impart.

But what of Intellect and its ancient nursery, the classical curriculum? The answer is soon given. Who would teach it? How many parents would approve of it? How would children respond to it? Suppose it magically restored, what gaps and failures in the common mind would immediately be deplored, unrelieved by scattered intellectual accomplishments that millions of citizens would rightly deem useless?

It is a proof of the low state of our Intellect that the present debate on education refers to 'our schools' at large, without marking off kinds and grades. People argue for 'more science' or 'the liberal arts' or 'better English' or 'a longer siege of American history,' without considering the conditions of teaching and study that now obtain. Nor is due attention given to the country's beliefs and acts regarding Intellect and its employment. No doubt the continual comparisons with 'Soviet education,' of which very few know anything reliable, have upset us; and so has the image of the 'tidal wave' of youth expected by 1970. This prospect in turn leads to agitation about the educational use of television and other machinery, again in the belief that multiplying voices, rooms, and seats to the right number will bring

[1] William H. Kilpatrick, Professor Emeritus of Education in Teachers College.

'education' to the newcomers. Whether the educating that now goes on face to face will remain the same when put on the screen is a question seldom raised. Hardly anyone knows what does go on, nor is there agreement about what should go on and does not.

The notion of helping a child has in the United States displaced that of teaching him. Anyone who tries to preserve the distinction is obviously unhelpful, and is at once known for a declared enemy of youth. The truth is that even apart from its hostility to Intellect, systematic coddling is as dangerous as it is impertinent.

The first possibility is that the maternalistic teacher does not know what he is doing. It is worth noting that when the schools of Portland, Oregon, put bright pupils in fast classes under the best teachers, some of the problem children became good citizens. It is a likely supposition that they had simply been bored. For boredom is not the trivial, harmless experience that common speech assumes: it is a violent assault on the self which it cannot or dare not resist. In bored children the animal spirits seek and usually find an indirect revenge. Other children, it may also be supposed, are already fairly 'free and strong individuals' at ten or twelve and they resent being interrupted every fifteen minutes for 'contact' when they want to 'focus on the matter at hand.' Conversation with the young shows that they often regard the mental and bodily agitation of the modern school as coercive and unjust, for all its assured love. Meanwhile their fidgets have been cultivated upon theory. As for 'fantasy' (which is always being subdued to 'reality,' as if it were easy to tell which is which), the true guardians of art, who know that fantasy is the food from which genius *makes* reality, should swear out a warrant against its blithe interrupters.

We see here the final inversion of purpose characteristic of the self-conscious curriculum: it assumes in each pupil the supremely gifted mind, which must not be tampered with, and the defective personality, which the school must remodel. Its incessant desire is to round off edges, to work to moral specifications—in short, to manipulate the young into a semblance of the harmonious committee, in accordance with the statistics of child development. This is the wickedness of the philanthropists, that they invoke the force of the group, on top of their own, to achieve something that no one has given them license to attempt. One may say that their tampering with the child's personality is saved from guilt because their goal remains vague and their effort largely unsuccessful. But imagine an explicit program, political or religious, and a corps of teachers more than gushingly dedicated to it, and you would have an irresistible machine for warping both mind and character.

It would of course take genuine intellectuals to organize the work while concealing their hand. At present, our 'liberal' teachers' college products show but the bare makings of a totalitarian force—the zeal for inducing 'the right attitude'; a thick-skinned intolerance toward all who doubt or criticize so much goodness; and a special language, a flatulent Newspeak, which combines self-righteousness with permanent fog, so that its users are invulnerable—others abide our question, they are free.

The politics of the adjustment curriculum, at any rate, are clear: it is manipulation by sentiment and dubious authority, exercised by the least educated and the most vapid minds of the nation. The manipulators view themselves as a vanguard of liberal thought, and after thirty years of supremacy still believe that they are bold. The historic position of liberalism is in fact one with which they have no sympathy, for it is intellectual. It gives freedom of opinion—subject to keeping the peace—and thereby licenses, not playing with souls, but playing with ideas—

debate and contradiction, the very opposite of that moralistic putting into Coventry which is the regular tactics of the educationist against criticism or heresy. The contrast was restated not long ago by a teacher of philosophy, in words so happily uncommon as to be unmistakable:

'Our concern as a profession is with the liquidation of ignorance. . . . If, as pedagogue, I allow myself to become professionally involved in the fact that persons are diseasable, or capable of bad will, or mortal, I am soon . . . beyond my depth. My business is with the liquidation of ignorance, not the liquidation of those other matters. I have an interest in them, to be sure; but this interest does not define me professionally.'

That interest in 'those other matters' is the interest of anyone who finds obstacles in his path and tries to remove them. The teacher of the very young child, like his parents, does what he can to prevent interference with the child's natural desire to learn, while seeing to it that the child is not overtaxed or maltreated. But this solicitude is not an end in itself, however much some teachers prefer its protective glow to the dull task of drilling the alphabet. 'Adjustment' at this stage is purely for the sake of implanting fundamental knowledge and good learning habits. To try to adjust the undeveloped inner self to an equally indefinite outer world is presumption. And to do so at the expense of intellectual subject matter is simply to ignore one's own business as teacher and 'helper.' For Intellect is also a means of adjustment. It is adjustment at any point in life to understand what another is saying, to recognize clearly a complex demand, and to gather one's wits so as to respond to it exactly and promptly.

THE SOVIET UNION: A NATION COMMITTED TO EDUCATION (1959)

From Report of the First Official U.S. Educational Mission to the U.S.S.R., "Soviet Commitment to Education," *Office of Education Bulletin 1959, No. 16* (Washington D. C., 1959), pp. 1–4.

The one fact that most impressed us in the U.S.S.R. was the extent to which the Nation is committed to education as a means of national advancement. In the organization of a planned society in the Soviet Union, education is regarded as one of the chief resources and techniques for achieving social, economic, cultural, and scientific objectives in the national interest. Tremendous responsibilities are therefore placed on Soviet schools, and comprehensive support is provided for them by all segments and agencies of Soviet society.

One of the leading Soviet educators told us: "We believe in a planned society, you in individual initiative. Let time tell." They are convinced that time is on their side and that through education and hard work they can win their way to world acceptance of Communist ideology.

Everywhere we went in the U.S.S.R. we were struck by the zeal and enthusiasm which the people have for education. It is a kind of grand passion with them.

Wherever we turned we heard the slogan: "Reach and over-reach America." And everywhere, the people seem to respond in the conviction that education, in addition to hard work and the postponement of many creature comforts, is the best means of winning world supremacy.

Education reaches far beyond school-age children and youth and is eagerly sought by hundreds of thousands of full-time workers who are also full-time students; hundreds of thousands of others take correspondence courses. Many of these correspondence students also hope to qualify for university entrance. They do this because being well educated is the key to advancement. We are sure that the Soviet people anticipate the day when their present sacrifice for knowledge will bring them many rewards, but right now, as we see it, they regard good schools and universities as the necessities in their race for world supremacy.

And they have been building schools and universities at a rapid pace. Down on the borders of China where only a half-century ago the people were almost 100 percent illiterate, we saw thriving schools, an impressive scientific academy, and other institutions that have reduced illiteracy and advanced knowledge to an astonishing degree. From the shores of the Black Sea to remote Siberia we found the attitude summed up in the expression of a Soviet education official: "A child can be born healthy, but he can't be born educated."

We have the impression that most people in the U.S.S.R. feel that conditions are improving gradually, that they are looking ahead for 5, 10, 15, or 20 years. They appear to be completely confident about achieving a quality of life and a standard of living fully as high as ours but realize that it will take time, sacrifice, and hard work.

There is still a considerable shortage of building resulting in part from tremendous damage during World War II. Very likely few people in the United States are familiar with the extent of the damage to both cities and rural communities in the Soviet Union in World War II—we were shown films of whole cities in ruins. Although whole cities have been rebuilt in less than 15 years, the normal supply of building and housing replacements, always low, has necessarily fallen behind. Housing is scarce, though relatively cheap.

People appear to be well fed and to have ample access to food stores and restaurants. Food is abundant, though not of much variety, and it is expensive. Clothing seemed to us to be very expensive and not readily available. In general, however, people seemed to be neatly, if not stylishly, dressed, by American standards.

There seems to be complete equality between men and women. The relationship between boys and girls in school appears to be characterized by dignity and mutual respect for each other. At each desk there is usually one boy and one girl. A professor at the University of Leningrad said: "With us, boys and girls, men and women, are partners. We are partners in education, partners in love, and partners in work."

A woman is expected to do any job as well as a man. Many women have entered the professions, particularly medicine. We saw women working with electrical crews, repairing telephone equipment, operating streetcars and busses, and working in factories. We noticed that many women specialized in mathematics and physics.

Education has been and is recognized as the source of past accomplishments and as the way to the future. The developments in the organization and practices of education at all levels during the past half century have been impressive both for their speed and for their extent. Wherever we went our hosts described with pride the contrasts between the present conditions and those existing before the revolution. That we returned with our faith renewed in the superiority of the American system for our society does not discount the tremendous efforts the

Soviets are exerting to advance their kind of education to strengthen the Communist system. They tell many dramatic stories of the progress of their education, and all credited education with the improvement in their condition. The story summarized below, which we heard at the Ministry of Education in the Uzbek Republic, is one of the more dramatic but perhaps typical.

This is a highly developed agricultural and industrial region now, but before the revolution it was a colony of Czarist Russia and was much retarded. Agriculture was primitive, crops were small, and the country was under-developed. Only 2 percent of the population was literate; there were no institutions of higher education, and the 160 schools were attended by 17,300 children of privileged families. There were no engineers, doctors, or teachers with higher education.

Opportunity for education came immediately after the revolution, although schools were developed gradually. On December 2, 1920, Lenin decreed the establishment of the University of the Republics of Asia. In 1919 a decree on the elimination of illiteracy was published, and shortly afterward literate people began to teach the illiterate. Now we have an academy of science, an academy of agricultural sciences, 34 higher education establishments, 100 technicums, 50 special technical schools, 5,800 general or 10-year schools, 12 pedagogical institutes to prepare teachers, and 1,400 kindergartens. We have schools for people of each nationality in their own tongue, and we also have inservice education establishments. Altogether 1,300,000 children of all nationalities have an opportunity for education. More than 50 percent of our 80,000 teachers have higher education.

We have many establishments to develop the interests of children. We work out our own courses of study for schools. Each Republic develops curriculums for itself because of differences in language.

We have enough money to expand our education programs and buildings. Our people are rich; they like to work. All our people want peace. *We are sure we are able to meet the problems we face.*

As is indicated earlier, Uzbekistan is not an isolated example; we heard similar stories in other places—the description of similar accomplishments in the Tatar Republic, for example, was equally impressive. Such progress is dramatized for the people of the U.S.S.R. continuously by the State and the Party. In every possible way—particularly through art, music, and literature—the people are reminded of what has been done. Everywhere, in every school we visited, we saw pictures or statues of Lenin, and less frequently, Marx and Stalin, even in kindergartens. From infancy, children are taught that the highest good is to serve the State; school children through their clubs or circles, in classes, and in games are taught to identify all good things with the State; on class excursions and tours of museums, shrines, factories, they are taught the history of the revolution and to honor its heroes, underplaying the pre-revolutionary achievements and emphasizing Soviet progress.

What we observed of Soviet education gave us the impression that the entire operation was being carried out on a systematically planned basis to achieve Communist objectives. To be sure, there were some excellent prerevolutionary foundations, institutions, and traditions of Russian education on which to build the Soviet structure—the academic secondary school of Imperial Russia; the Ballet School in Leningrad, over 200 years old; the great universities, especially in Leningrad and Moscow; the National Academy of Sciences; and the School for the Blind in Moscow that celebrated its 75th anniversary in 1947. These are just a few of the substantial roots from the past, and they should not be overlooked. It was always stressed, however, that education was restricted in prerevolutionary days to a very small proportion of the population of the vast area—one-sixth of the earth's surface—that today is the U.S.S.R.

Today, of course, education is planned, financed, controlled, and administered by the State. Even though education in the U.S.S.R. is controlled by the Government and is therefore standardized and regimented, there is some flexibility of operation. Furthermore decisions on policy, on textbooks, on teacher training, on curriculum, and on similar matters are not always made arbitrarily. We found fairly widespread evidence that before making decisions on education, the Government seeks opinions from specialists at all levels of education, from teachers throughout the country, and information based on research and experience. And it seems to get willing cooperation.

Few nations or people are today more passionately committed to education than the Soviet Union and the Soviet people are. The Soviets see what has already been accomplished and are confident of the future.

EDUCATION: AMERICA'S FIRST LINE OF DEFENSE (1959)   From Hyman G. Rickover, *Education and Freedom* (New York, 1959), pp. 15, 18–24, 37–38.

This book is a collection of speeches made during the last four years. Some have been shortened, others expanded, and some new material has been added to produce an orderly sequence. There is no Aristotelian unity in it but each chapter touches on some aspect of education and freedom. Each, whether or not it deals with education directly, points up the need of better schooling for all our children— education far superior to anything we in this country have ever had or ever needed in the past. Only massive upgrading of the scholastic standards of our schools will guarantee the future prosperity and freedom of the Republic.

*   *   *

For as long as I have worked in the atomic-energy field I have been absorbed in educational problems. Indeed, I found the two so intertwined that I would have had to be most unobservant not to have gotten myself involved with American education. When I started on the work of harnessing the energy of the atom for propulsion of naval ships and generation of electricity in civilian power plants, I had in my group a handful of men with training in nuclear engineering. We knew that our project would present difficult technical problems, particularly since I deemed it necessary to speed the work by telescoping the usual pattern of development which proceeds from theoretical to applied research, to laboratory experimentation, and finally to practical application. We designed and built reactors directly for practical use in ships and power plants, skipping the stage when theory is tried out on laboratory models. To the layman—and alas even more so to the public-relations man—such models always seem to be equivalent to the working, finished product. This is not so. This country has many laboratory reactors—reactors producing some electricity under ideal laboratory conditions, and much is to be learned from them. There is a vast difference, however, between a research or experimental reactor and a reactor which must actually produce useful power for a ship or an electric grid. Whereas laboratory conditions favor the new project, reality is troublesome.

When I set up my reactor group twelve years ago, I put all my energy into finding the right people and wasted no time creating an "ideal" organization. In fact we still have no formal organization. We have excellent people, carefully chosen, thoroughly trained for their job, and strongly motivated because of their intense interest in the work. Such people cannot be fitted into the usual hierarchic organization which exists in most industrial and government complexes. They must be given freedom to work out their own problems and to assume responsibility for what they do. They need an environment that allows them to be venturesome and does not stifle their initiative with routines; in a novel development project there can be no routine.

Our country will not be able to make rapid technological progress unless we reorganize our institutions. These must be pried from their exaggerated veneration for routine and protocol and made to see that provison must be made for both routine work and for new and creative work; for routine workers and for people with specialized knowledge who must be allowed to operate outside routine procedures. We have not yet solved this problem; chiefly, I believe, because it is relatively new, a consequence of two new phenomena—the scientific revolution and organizational growth necessitated by population expansion.

The scientific revolution now engulfs us though not all of us are fully aware of this. We must expect that science will influence our mores in ever increasing degree. There will be some unemployment in the ranks of people whose principal qualification is their ability to get along, to fit into organizational structures, and to adjust. The man of the future on whom we shall depend more and more is the technical expert. Today he is still subservient to nontechnical leaders in government and industry, and his work is hampered and sometimes destroyed by men in whom is vested great power but who cannot understand the realities of the new, artificial, technological age. But the "verbal" men are on the way out; the men who can handle the intricate mysteries of complex scientific and engineering projects are on the way in. That applies all along the line down to the skilled workman on whose judgment, concentrated attention, and responsibility may depend the functioning of some new and gigantic piece of engineering. To put this in military terms: we shall need more technical sergeants and fewer martinets. In our naval nuclear program we have taken cognizance of this demand for a different kind of man and we have set up schools to train the officers and men who will run the new atomic navy.

Another relatively new phenomenon in American life which compels us to find room for creative people in our institutions is the sheer mass of our people. Government and industry must in some manner organize and manage our huge population to prevent chaos and insure safety and efficiency. No other industrial democracy has to cope with a problem of quite such staggering dimensions for none is so populous or grows at such dizzying speed as we do.

Our founding fathers knew that size endangers democratic institutions and they had some misgivings as to whether democracy would function in as populous a country as ours. In the mid-eighteenth century, when plans for an independent America began to ripen, we *had 1.2 million people*—exactly twice the population of the only then existing democracy, Switzerland. All other democracies had been small city-states—Plato's republic was to have had 5,040 citizens! Where Switzerland had quadrupled its population in two hundred years, we *increased more than a hundred-fold*. We can be proud of our record of maintaining democratic processes, even expanding them, despite this enormous increase in population. While we have been highly successful politically, economically there has of necessity been a gradual loss of personal freedom. Each year fewer people are self-employed; more become submerged in huge organizations. In fact, nothing grows faster than organization. Increasing specialization aggravates this trend. Even professional people have been losing independence and increasingly work as members of a team. Without organizations run by competent administrators we simply could not get along. This presents few problems if the work is routine. A capable administrator can learn enough about the techniques of routine production or service to organize it efficiently; he knows how to oil the machinery and dovetail individual work into the whole. The people under him do not know more than he about the essentials of the routine procedures in which they are engaged.

It is entirely different with experts having specialized knowledge. Few administrators know enough about the work of subordinate experts to be competent to administer or manage them efficiently. Most administrators reach their positions in the organizational hierarchy because they understand routine personnel problems, know how to keep people working contentedly, and are always subservient to the wishes of their superiors. The typical administrator is used to "group-think" in committees—whether brainstorming or ordinary—and has limited his own originality so severely that he has no understanding of the freedom essential to the creative worker. His mental processes are the very opposite of those of the expert, especially the scientist or engineer. Men whose minds have been trained to respect intellectual honesty and scientific fact simply cannot submit to the orders of administrative superiors whose intellectual honesty they may not respect and whose "scientific facts" they may regard as fable. *There is no hierarchy in matters of the mind.*

This causes a great deal of friction. What appears to the organization man as an almost criminal insubordination is to the trained professional a vital necessity; unless he is allowed to follow his own judgment in matters pertaining to his specialty, he becomes a hack. His intellectual freedom is so intimate a part of his nature that to yield to a superior lacking technical knowledge is to degrade himself and become unfree. Actually, administrators can contribute very little that is useful to the work of creative people. In fact, nobody can waste as much time as a super-efficient administrator trying to run a group of "eggheads."

I fear that we have gone far toward lowering the output of our brainworkers by overorganizing them. We are drowning in paper work. We are talking ourselves into a standstill in endless committees—those pets of the administrator. We are losing the genius we once had for improvisation. Nowadays nothing can be done without elaborate preparation, organization, and careful rehearsal. We have been diluting responsibility for making decisions by piling layers of supervisory administrative levels, pyramid fashion, upon the people who do the real work. All this delays new developments. To the technical difficulties of creating something new are added the constant frustrations of interference by men who do not understand technical matters. If we are to regain ground lost to the Russians in important developments, we must learn how to run organizations with sufficient flexibility so that routine work may proceed efficiently without interfering with creative work. Somehow every organization must make room for inner-directed, obstreperous, creative people; sworn enemies of routine and the *status quo,* always ready to upset the applecart by thinking up new and better ways of doing things. They are troublesome mavericks, unloved by the administrator who cannot forgive their contempt for conventions. However, unless these people are permitted to lead the way, there will be stagnation.

It was men of independent mind and venturesome spirit that I set out to find for my nuclear propulsion group. From the start it was evident that no experienced men of this type were available. Before we could tackle our work, we therefore had to find young people showing *potentialities* of growth whom we could then ourselves train intensively for work on reactor design. This took time, but in the end it has proved far more satisfactory than the usual custom of raiding the small hoards of already qualified people accumulated by other government agencies or industries. We set up special schools and turned ourselves into teachers, discovering in the process that the fundamentals of a good liberal-arts education had been skimped in the education given these bright young men. The search for and training of promising young people still take up much of my time and that of my leading engineers for we are constantly expanding and there are of course losses through attrition. These, fortunately, are few so that we reap pretty much of a full harvest from our educational efforts.

Among the young engineers we interview we find few who have received thorough training in engineering fundamentals or principles; but most have absorbed quantities of facts—much easier to learn than principles but of little use without application of principles. Once a principle has been acquired it becomes a part of one and is never lost. It can be applied to novel problems and does not become obsolete as do all facts in a changing society. American education in general emphasizes learning factual know-how at the cost of absorbing fundamental principles, just as it stresses conditioning of behavior at the cost of developing the ability to think independently. Most of our schools have lost sight of the fact that a well-trained mind can cope with many unforeseen problems. Instead, they try to foresee every possible future difficulty a young person may encounter and then give a special course in how to deal with it. This is a hopeless endeavor, for in a rapidly changing world no one can foresee what future problems will have to be met.

I have interviewed more than two thousand young men in the last twelve years. My naval-reactor engineering group presently numbers about one hundred fifty. Since the men I interviewed had already passed through a number of previous interviews which weeded out all but the best, it can be seen that those who could not meet the requirements of the nuclear-power project—and hence inferentially of any new development project—vastly outnumbered those who qualified.

This experience made a deep impression on me. It led me directly to a study of why our educational system produces a few men who are qualified to do the work which we must do if we are to progress. Our schools are the greatest "cultural lag" we have today. When I read official publications put out by the men who run our educational system—booklets such as *Life-Adjustment Education for Every Youth* or *Education for All Youth*—I have the strange feeling of reading about another world, a world long since departed if it ever existed at all. I sense the kindly spirit, the desire to make every child happy, the earnest determination to give advice on every problem any young person might ever meet in life—and withal so complete a misunderstanding of the needs of young people in today's world that it frightens me. If I speak out against this mistaken concept of what twentieth-century American education must be, I do so out of no desire to find fault with those who misread the demands of the times but from anxiety for the future of our children. I am worried about the chances which young people, so poorly equipped to deal with modern life, will have when things become more complex and difficult, as they surely will before very long.

I began by wanting to remove obstacles hindering my work. My interest was simply to build nuclear reactors. Reactors of all kinds: for submarines, destroyers, cruisers, aircraft carriers, and for central power stations. Anything that interfered with building them as fast as possible was bad. But, as with Plato when he asked "What is Justice?" my investigations led me from the particular to the general and resulted in this present inquiry into the delays which lengthen our lead time so dangerously. Not only in production of things, but in production of well-qualified professional people as well, we now need more time than does Russia or, for that matter, Europe. I believe we must put first things first. This means, above all else, that we must bring excellence to American education. Let us stop fooling ourselves by counting school desks without considering what the children sitting at these desks are being taught. Many of our children are merely parked in the schools. They merely have a good time there. Few get a twentieth-century education.

Our complicated nuclear reactors are but the forerunners of many more projects of even greater complexity, requiring more people with good education and strong motivation. I speak out only because I must. Because in my work I have had a glimpse of the future. The future belongs to the best-educated nation. Let it be ours.

JAMES CONANT'S CRITIQUE OF THE AMERICAN HIGH SCHOOL

(1959)   From James B. Conant, *The American High School To-Day* (New York, 1959), pp. 22-23, 40.

The question I set out to answer I can now answer in the affirmative. *I found eight schools which, in my judgment, were satisfactorily fulfilling the three main objectives of a comprehensive high school.* They were offering adequate instruction in English and social studies as part of general education required of all. These schools were providing significant nonacademic programs which were elected by a substantial number of students. In these same schools, the academic inventory showed that more than half the academically talented boys had studied at least seven years of mathematics and science as well as seven years of English and social studies. This fact is interesting in view of the recent stress on mathematics and science. (I shall report a few pages later on the quality of instruction.) On the other hand, in no school had a majority of the academically talented girls studied as much as seven years of mathematics and science.

The situation with regard to the study of foreign languages in these eight schools was, in most cases, not satisfactory. In only two schools had a majority of the academically talented boys studied foreign language for as long as three years. In most schools, even the few who had elected to study foreign languages for three or four years had to be content with two years of one language and one or two of another. The academic inventory showed a somewhat better picture so far as the academically talented girls were concerned: in five schools a majority of these girls had studied foreign language for three or more years.

A little arithmetic makes it clear that in those schools in which a majority of the academically talented boys had studied seven years of English and social studies, as well as three years of foreign languages and seven years of mathematics and science, a total of seventeen academic courses with homework had been taken in four years. In only one of the eight schools was this the case for the academically talented boys, and in no school was it the case for the girls.

In all but a few of the schools I have visited, the majority of bright boys and girls were not working hard enough. Academic studies did not cover a wide enough range. Both these deficiencies in the majority of schools on which I have information can be readily corrected by a shift of emphasis on the part of those in charge. Improvement would come about almost automatically in most schools if seven years of English and social studies were required and if, instead of a two-year course in a foreign language, a sequence of four years of at least one foreign language were offered, provided the counselors emphasized the importance of foreign language for the academically talented boys and mathematics and science for the academically talented girls.

*   *   *

Conclusion

I can sum up my conclusions in a few sentences. The number of small high schools must be drastically reduced through district reorganization. *Aside from this important change, I believe no radical alteration in the basic pattern of American education is necessary in order to improve our public high schools.* If all the high schools were functioning as well as some I have visited, the education of all American youth would be satisfactory, except for the study of foreign languages and the guidance of the more able girls. Most of the schools which I found unsatisfactory in one or more respects could become satisfactory by relatively minor changes, though I have no doubt that there are schools even of sufficient size where major improvements in organization and instruction would be in order. If the fifty-five schools I have visited, all of which have a good reputation, are at all representative of American public high schools, I think one general criticism would be in order: *The academically talented student, as a rule, is not being sufficiently challenged, does not work hard enough, and his program of academic subjects is not of sufficient range.* The able boys too often specialize in mathematics and science to the exclusion of foreign languages and to the neglect of English and social studies. The able girls, on the other hand, too often avoid mathematics and science as well as the foreign languages. As I have indicated in the preceding paragraph, a correction of this situation in many instances will depend upon an altered attitude of the community quite as much as upon action by a school board or the school administration.

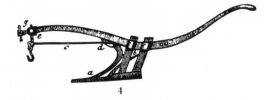

ON THE MIS-EDUCATION OF AMERICAN TEACHERS (1963) From James
D. Koerner, "How Not to Teach Teachers," *Atlantic,* vol. CCXI, pp. 59–63.

Unlike most educational controversies, the training of teachers for the public schools is a subject that generates continuous heat. A kind of rhythm characterizes other issues—why Johnny can't read, or college freshmen can't write, why IQ tests are unreliable, or whether schools should be palaces; such controversies wax and wane. But the problem of how best to prepare teachers, being central to everything else in education, is a war without end. The traditional combatants, professors of academic subjects versus professors of education, have held a series of disarmament conferences in the last few years which, while not producing any substantive results, have eased the tension a bit. Still, the basic quarrel abides, and the cannonading continues from both sides, often rather wide of the right targets.

During the past two years, I have visited, for periods of from a day to a week, sixty-three institutions that train teachers—universities, multi-purpose colleges, liberal arts colleges, and teachers colleges, in all sections of the country and representing all types of programs now in operation. I have looked especially at the preparatory programs for teachers of academic subjects, both the liberal arts and the professional part, and I have examined the graduate programs leading to the numerous masters' and doctors' degrees in education. I have visited about two hundred classes in both academic and professional subjects; have talked with many hundreds of administrators, students, and members of the faculty; have read through a small library of books, reports, monographs, pamphlets, and periodicals; have examined several thousand transcripts of credit for graduates of education programs; have attended innumerable educational meetings, conferences, seminars, and conventions; and in sundry other ways have acquainted myself with the massive industry of professional education.

It has been, I regret to say, a cheerless experience. When all the complexity of the field is recognized and all the necessary qualifications made, the simple fact remains that the education of American teachers, school administrators, and other professionals is more often a failure than a success. This is so because neither the liberal arts nor the professional component of these training programs comes even close to its theoretical goal.

In the first place, the field of professional education, which controls the training programs for teachers and administrators, has become an unwieldy, slow-witted, bureaucratic colossus, standing on a slippery foundation built on sand. It is the most poorly defined, formless field in higher education. It is the most derivative, taking its substance from the academic fields of psychology, history, philosophy, and the social sciences, all of which it has digested badly while adding little that is uniquely its own. Because it has failed to bring a unifying theory into this multifariousness, its training programs continue to be constructed on tenuous and untested hypotheses, or on whatever is expedient in a given instance.

Although education does not yet know how much or what kind of professional preparation is needed by teachers and administrators, it has constructed a plenitude of mandatory training programs on the assumption that it does. These programs, despite a long history of inadequacy, remain frozen into law in state certification requirements. More important, those who run teacher-training programs have become frozen in their own thinking and are now far too busy managing an established business with a rapid growth rate to have much time or inclination for the examination of first principles.

Education has been corrupted by money and power. It is a big business. It turns out a quarter of all the undergraduate degrees awarded by American institutions, and in 1963 will graduate about 150,000 persons eligible to teach in public schools, a good many of whom will not teach, and a good many more of whom will not teach long. It awards half of all masters' degrees, and more doctors' degrees, by a sizable margin, than any other single academic field. To man this giant machine, the field has well over 20,000 full-time faculty, making it second in size only to the field of English. Outside the institutions themselves, there is a constellation of large professional and service organizations that is an integral part of the education machine. All this has happened in an astonishingly short time, and success has seduced the field into arrogance and administrative busywork and away from basic concerns.

Thus, one of the reasons that the education of American teachers is fundamentally a failure is that professional education, which constructs and controls the training programs, has extremely poor credentials as an academic discipline. The fact that it has won recognition as such a discipline, which it has done through the abdication of responsibility by the liberal arts departments, is not a qualification; it merely makes possible the building of more academic empires on sandy foundations.

This general disability, as well as the specific ills that education is heir to, is mostly traceable, as it would be in any other field, to the faculty. It is an indecorous thing to say and is obviously offensive to educationists, but it is the truth, and it should be said: the intellectual caliber of the education faculty is *the* fundamental limitation of the field. Because no educational program can transcend the quality of its faculty, any long-range improvement in teacher training will have to wait upon improvement in those who staff schools and departments of education. Although a good many men of excellent ability are to be found in education, particularly among the younger faculty, their number is minute in relation to the whole.

Yet the preparatory programs for public school teachers are chiefly under the *de facto* supervision of the education faculty. It is here that admission to the training programs is controlled, here that the programs themselves are constructed, here that the future teacher accumulates courses in education and pedagogy, here that he develops whatever professional outlook he has, here that, hopefully, he learns what to do with what, hopefully, he has acquired from his academic courses. Cardinal Newman, who wrote one of the great treatises on liberal education, saw only one reason for courses: "The general principles of any study you may learn by books at home; but the detail, the colour, the tone, the air, the life which makes it live in us, you must catch all these from those in whom it already lives." It does not live in the greatest part of the present education faculty; in this unfortunate fact lies education's greatest problem.

Weak students gravitate to weak faculties. Education students, along with students in agriculture and business administration, fill the lower ranks of the academic ladder. Every major study of the subject, beginning with a classic one in the state of Pennsylvania in 1928–1932 and coming down to very recent ones, has arrived at the same conclusion: education students show up badly, both in achievement and native ability, when compared with students in other fields—a fact that has been known informally throughout higher education for half a century. Teaching attracts poor students for a combination of academic, social, and economic reasons, but the bland acceptance of this condition by the education faculty, its failure to weed out the incompetent and to raise its standards of admission and performance create a circular problem: a weak faculty maintains low standards that attract weak students; together they deter better faculty from entering the field and raising standards that would attract better students into better programs. "All other reforms," as John Dewey once observed, "are conditioned upon reform in the quality and character of those who engage in the teaching profession."

Some headway is being made. A great many teacher-training programs that used to take anyone who appeared at the door have raised admission standards in recent years. A grade average of C or a shade better is becoming a common requirement in these programs. This is helpful, though it may not in itself mean much. Grade averages are most significant when one knows what the quality of the instruction is, what the grading practices are, and what groups a given student is competing against. A C average is not an impressive requirement, especially in teachers colleges and state colleges, if one is trying to educate educators, nor is it commensurate with grade averages for entrance to professional programs in other fields. Still, the grade requirement is on the rise and in time should make some difference in the quality of teacher turned out.

No headway is being made, so far as I can see, on admissions standards at the all-important graduate level. With the exception of students enrolled in the so-called Master of Arts in Teaching programs, who are usually capable persons, candidates for the masters' and doctors' degrees are rarely screened in education as they are in other fields. Ironically, it is often easier for one to be admitted to graduate study in education than to undergraduate programs in the same institution. A bachelor's degree which might be twenty years old and from a third-rate institution is often adequate for admission, especially to those advanced-degree programs that are wholly under the control of the education division. Whatever reasons there may have been historically for taking low-caliber people in the training programs for teachers, there has never been and certainly is not now any reason for taking them in the graduate programs. The ramifying influence of low standards in graduate education is painfully clear: the masters and doctors turned out become administrators who hire teachers, construct curricula, and set standards in public schools; they also staff professional associations, accrediting agencies, and become professors of education.

The education courses themselves deserve their ill repute. Most of them are indeed puerile, repetitious, dull, and ambiguous—incontestably. Two factors make them this way: the limitations of the instructor, and the limitations of subject matter that has been remorselessly fragmented, subdivided, and inflated, and that in many instances was not adequate in its uninflated state. That some teachers and courses in education can be found to equal the best in the academic areas is a happy fact. A course in the history of education, taught by, say, Lawrence Cremin of Columbia Teachers College, or a course in the psychological theories of how young people learn things, taught by Ernest Hilgard of Stanford, or one in the methods of teaching high school English, taught by Edward Gordon of Yale—such courses could be as valuable as any on the campus. But the mere effort needed to identify the intellectual leaders or the outstanding teachers in professional education today testifies to their scarcity.

The principal subjects of the professional curriculum—teaching methods, practice teaching and the educational aspects of history, philosophy, and psychology—are almost never taught and the textbooks almost never written by persons who are themselves trained historians, philosophers, psychologists, or proven experts in teaching. Hence, there is nothing more obvious in the typical education class, apart from the remarkable docility of the students, than the lack of real depth and scholarship on the part of the instructor. Frequently, a strong strain of anti-intellectualism is discernible. Frequently, utilitarianism takes the place of intellectualism, the "tender-minded" approach, as William James called it, takes the place of the "tough-minded," the ritualistic takes the place of the realistic, the uncritical acceptance of shibboleths takes the place of the critical analysis of ideas. There is a universal devotion to the "discussion method," which most often signifies, as it does in public schools, an aimless, generalized bull session. Great use is also made of group dynamics, field trips, panel discussions, student-directed projects, and an infinite variety of movies and other visual aids; these devices no doubt have their uses, one of which seems to be to kill time.

The best students are repelled by all this, the average ones are bored, the poor are pleased. With the exception of practice teaching, which is not really a course, the professional curriculum for teachers is perhaps 50 to 75 percent water. At the graduate level, the dilution is often much higher.

Apart from the question of quality, the quantity of education courses required or permitted in teacher training also deserves the harsh things that are usually said about it. This is one of oldest issues between the academician, who has traditionally inveighed against what he regarded as an excessive number of education courses, and the educationist, who has usually claimed that the number of courses is quite modest and reasonable. Nobody, so far as I could discover in surveying results of educational research, had tried to collect information on the subject from the only reliable source that exists, the transcripts of credit for graduates of the various education programs. I therefore gathered a representative sample of such transcripts from thirty-two institutions and made numerous calculations from them.

The transcripts indicate, among many other things, that the preparing institutions go far beyond state certification requirements in education courses. Elementary school teachers get an average of forty-nine semester hours in education, while the average requirement for state licensure is twenty-four. Secondary school teachers get about twenty-seven semester hours, while the average state requirement is eighteen. Elementary school teachers, that is, spend about 40 percent of their four years of college taking education courses in such subjects as Educational Psychology (usually three or four courses under different names but covering about the same material), Audio-Visual Aids, Personal and Community Hygiene, and Elementary School Curriculum; they also take a seemingly endless series of discrete courses in how to teach each subject of the elementary school at each level of the elementary school. Secondary teachers spend nearly 25 percent of their time taking education courses. These are national averages. If one looks only at the liberal arts colleges, the averages go sharply down in education and up in academic courses; if one looks at schools that are present or erstwhile teachers colleges, which prepare very large numbers of teachers, the averages go sharply up in education and down in academic courses. These figures, of course, do not cover the graduate programs in education, in many of which not a single academic course is taken, and where the time is spent in courses so trivial that they must be seen to be believed.

I submit that this much undergraduate time devoted to education, especially in view of the redundant and intellectually thin nature of the courses and the consistently negative reaction of students to them, is indefensible. And it clearly cannot help but deter the very people most needed in teaching; a really bright student will not suffer such a diet. If educationists are serious about improving teacher training and the quality of students, one of the most effective steps they could take would be to reduce course offerings and requirements by perhaps 50 percent, while insisting that the remainder be taught with some distinction.

The remedies for the faults of professional education are implicit in the discussion. If admission standards are low, they should be raised; if course work is sterile, it needs revitalization; if the faculty is weak, new graduate programs and new faculty hiring policies are indicated. The real question is not what needs doing, but how to get what needs doing done. The forces for change in teacher education are now greater than they have been for a long time. There are more "Young Turks" around, more support for new programs from foundations and college administrations, more interest on the part of academic folk, and more pressure for reform from the public than ever before. But to all these forces there are others that are opposite and often more than equal.

The greatest obstacle to reform is the field of education itself. This is natural. Teaching training is a major industry, the income from which supports not only schools and departments and professors of education but often other branches of the university as well, even entire institutions. Sometimes the income is fairly good, permitting high salaries and fast promotions for the education faculty. Like any vast bureaucracy, education is by nature pretty much dedicated to the status quo and has developed a centripetal circle of power to perpetuate it. At the center are the institutions themselves, while orbiting around them are accrediting associations, the state departments of education, and the administrator-dominated state and national agencies like the NEA. Such a concentration of power naturally looks with a cold eye on suggestions for change, especially those coming from outside. It has a built-in radar that sounds the warning at the approach of any proposal that threatens to diminish the establishment, or that might jeopardize jobs or status.

Thus, the field has a history of opposition, more or less automatic, to most proposals for reform that have been made over the last half century. It held the line for decades against increasing the liberal content of its programs at the expense of the pedagogical; it fought like a tiger to maintain *in statu quo* state certification requirements, that monument to administrative rigidity; it met criticism with fury, denunciation, and diversionary attack. There has always been, for example, enormous opposition to any proposal that would license teachers in a way that would make the most sense to a great many people—through a system of qualifying examinations. Under such a system, people could be qualified to teach when they could demonstrate their ability to do so, which would mean giving them better examinations in subject matter than are yet available, and possibly some sort of probationary internship. It would mean that the main criterion for entrance to teaching would shift from the mechanical counting up of credits and courses, often of dubious pedigree, to performance. In the nature of things, most teachers, whatever system prevails, will continue to come through organized programs in colleges, but they would be required under an examination system to prove their grasp of the subjects they propose to teach as well as their capacity to teach them. The doors to teaching would thus be open to anyone. Einstein might be able to teach third-grade arithmetic, after all; able immigrants might be admitted to the classroom to teach their native languages; and the services of many kinds of persons of genuine intellectual accomplishment might be made available to the public schools. An examinations system, whether administered at the state, regional, or national level, would also be a valuable check against the quality of individual institutions—certainly far better than the ineffectual accreditation programs now in operation.

Professional education, except in isolated instances, presents a monolithic opposition to such a scheme and goes to picturesque lengths to find reasons why mandatory qualifying examinations will not work. The educationists' real objection, however, is to the reduced status of professional education, of course work, and of graduation from organized programs that inheres in the plan. Also, the concept of professionalism, which has preoccupied the field of education for so many years, is violated. Qualifying examinations seem to say that public school teaching is not really a profession (which it probably is not) and that people can perform well in it without professional preparation (which they obviously can). I do not believe that any system of qualifying examinations, beyond the perfunctory ones that now exist in a few places, has any chance of adoption. The conditions of life in the world of professional education preclude it, as they preclude other reforms that are urgently needed.

That being true, what are some of the practical, concrete reforms that could be made now within the existing establishment?

1. The time devoted in teacher-training programs to education courses should be restricted to state requirements, which allow ample time for pedagogical work of any consequence.

2. At least two thirds of the work for all graduate degrees in education (the Master of Arts in Teaching degree excepted, where it might be about half) should be in the liberal arts area, and students in these programs should be required to measure up to the customary graduate standards.

3. The regular four-year undergraduate program should remain the standard preparation for new teachers. The Master of Arts in Teaching programs should by all means be continued and encouraged for liberal arts graduates without previous work in education; but the accelerating movement toward making five years of preparation mandatory for all new teachers is ill advised. It merely takes the pressure off the undergraduate programs to improve themselves, and it inflicts an enormous and unnecessary burden on an already overtaxed system of graduate education. Four years are ample, provided they are wisely used.

4. The remaining teachers colleges in the United States should be shut down or converted to general-purpose institutions, and those that have already been converted in name should move much faster toward conversion in fact. Removal of the word "Teachers" or "Education" from the name of the school, even when done by the state legislature, does not make the school a liberal arts institution. Most of the colleges that have made such changes still have the same faculty teaching the same kind of students in the same kind of programs as they formerly had.

5. Undergraduate majors in education should be eliminated, and all teachers, including elementary teachers and special school personnel, should be required to major in an academic subject. A reasonable reduction in education courses would make this possible, while the time devoted to the student's general education would remain about what it now is.

6. Education courses that are derived directly from academic disciplines, such as those in educational psychology and in the history and philosophy of education, should be taught only by persons fully qualified to teach in the appropriate academic departments of the same institution. This commonsense recommendation would mean that 90 percent of the people now teaching these courses would cease to teach them, and so is a bit utopian, but it is a goal toward which education ought to be moving with all deliberate speed.

7. If competent faculty cannot be secured to teach methods courses—and most such courses are incompetently taught now—formal courses in the subject should be eliminated.

8. Persons whose graduate training has been in education and who have no recognized qualifications in an academic field should not be allowed to teach academic courses, as they now frequently do in teachers colleges and many smaller institutions.

Unfortunately, the political realities of the education field dictate a future built upon the past, which means that modest, short-term gains, a kind of mild meliorism, will probably be the pattern of the future. The key question is whether improvement of this sort can keep up with the problems of exploding enrollments, the advancement of knowledge itself, and the other educational exigencies of the nation. In any event, continued improvement in teacher education, slow or fast, will come only in response to unrelenting pressure from the public, the scholarly and scientific community, and the small minority of educationists who know better than anyone else what is wrong and who want to change it.

The Defenders

ON A NEW POLICY FOR PROGRESSIVE EDUCATION (1947)   From
Theodore Brameld, "A New Policy for A.E.F. (American Education Fellowship)," *Progressive
Education*, vol. XXV, pp. 258–60, 262, 269.

Since 1919 the American Education Fellowship (formerly called the Progressive Education Association) has served a distinctive role in the educational
world. Its record of pioneering is long, its achievements influential. Few, if any,
persons familiar with the last quarter-century of school history would deny this
assertion, even though they may at times criticize some of the methods or outcomes
for which the organization has been responsible. Nor would they deny that, directly
or indirectly, its influence has extended far beyond the United States; throughout the
world—China, India, South America, Australia, Europe—educators have studied and
often adopted theories and practices developed by its own commission, published in
its many pamphlets and volumes, and demonstrated by its members through
projects, research, and school reorganization.

While it is impossible to summarize here in an adequate sense a list of its
accomplishments, the AEF from its inception has stood first of all for a dynamic
conception of education as vital experience in democratic learning and living.
Therefore it has, on the other hand, opposed all forms of school autocracy—whether
in the form of administrative organization which denies genuine participation to
teachers, students, and parents; or in the form of classroom authoritarianism which
places the child in a position of meekness and passivity, and which assumes that
learning is chiefly an absorption of predetermined subject-matters. On the other
hand, the organization has vigorously supported a great variety of efforts to make
the school a living symbol of democracy in the way that superintendents and other
officials share their own responsibilities and decisions with the entire personnel; in
the way that students join in curriculum planning, rule-making, and school
activities; in the way that the whole school radiates its influence through the
community by utilizing resources, by influencing civic policy, by drawing adults
into its program.

Many of these efforts, while they have by no means succeeded in transforming
the entire traditional pattern, are bearing rich educational fruits. Not only have
countless schools been modified. Other organizations of large membership have
increasingly advocated and stimulated educational experimentation of kinds which
were often initiated by the American Education Fellowship. This is not at all to
assert, of course, that the AEF is solely responsible for recent progress toward a
more workable conception of democratic education; what is asserted is that, in

RE-APPRAISAL
1951–1973

addition to its own very considerable responsibility, school leaders everywhere have of late been converging more and more toward the major objective which it first clearly formulated in America. The AEF welcomes this convergence wholeheartedly; it will not only continue to exert its own efforts in behalf of more democratic schools as it has defined them; it will seek to co-operate with all other educational groups dedicated to their establishment.

But the historic role of the AEF as a spearhead organization, is no longer fulfilled sufficiently by these types of effort. The degree of consensus about the criteria of sound public education in a democracy is now sufficiently large, at least in principle, so that many of the experiments which were earlier quite unique, even heretical, are no longer so regarded. Since accordingly we may predict that given enough time and financial support, American education will move forward along the lines earlier advocated, the question arises whether the AEF has completed its pioneering work—whether its membership and resources could not now better be utilized by dissemination among other organizations larger and richer. This is not only an honest question at the present juncture, it is crucial.

It is crucial, however, not merely or even chiefly because upon its answer depends the further existence of the AEF. Organizations of this sort, like others, can in no sense justify themselves merely because they have had an honorable career, or because many loyal members would feel sad if they dissolved. No, the answer is crucial because America and the world have entered a new period in their evolution—a period which creates unprecedented educational tasks because it generates unprecedented problems of great magnitude and danger. In an important sense, indeed, the responsibilities which education faces today and tomorrow are vastly more serious/more compelling, than after the first World War. Whether the schools will assume their responsibility in time remains uncertain. That they have the obligation to do so, is, however, utterly certain. And it is precisely this obligation which provides the imperative for a reconstituted and rededicated organizational frontier.

The American Education Fellowship can and must once more therefore become this kind of organization. It can and must prove to teachers, parents, students, administrators, and to the public, that never in history has civilization itself been in greater jeopardy. At the same time, it can and must demonstrate that the opportunity is available to empower education, as never before, with vision and strength on behalf of a peaceful and humane world for the masses of mankind. Here is the vanguard task of the American Education Fellowship in the quarter-century we are now entering.

*   *   *

II

To examine and specify the main characteristics of this period should be one of the first lines of responsibility of the new AEF. That is, it should assist education on every level to understand how fraught with tension, friction, and overt conflict are both our domestic and international relations. Nothing short of the utmost realism and forthrightness will help citizens—young and old alike—to reorganize the depth, breadth, and obstinacy of contemporary problems. The habit of much education still to gloss over these problems because controversial or complex, still to ignore training in propaganda analysis and other techniques essential to their understanding, is proof enough that here alone the AEF could make a tremendous contribution.

The complexities of the social, political, and economic relations of this period should not, moreover, be an excuse for denying that they gravitate around two fundamental and related facts. The first is the fact of an unstable and precarious economy, with its accomplishment of insecurity, inflation, its cycles of boom-and-bust. The second is the fact of national rivalry and hostility with their potential of atomic war accompanied by the horrors of destruction and death on a scale never before imagined.

Yet despite their indisputability, neither of these factors receives a fraction of the attention that education, ostensibly devoted to freedom and truth, should be giving them. To consider the first a moment further, memories are not so short, of course, as to forget the economic events following World War I—the years of reckless prosperity and high living, of growing corporate power and disparities of wealth, followed by years by devastating depression, hunger and fear. During the "thirties" some American educators became sufficiently concerned to voice their anger at this tragedy through the pages especially of one journal, *The Social Frontier*, and through the volumes especially of the Commission of the Social Studies (American Historical Association). They courageously analyzed the failures of a system which could cause such havoc, and they demanded thoroughgoing changes to eliminate those failures. Yet, as the depression waned and we became preoccupied with winning World War II, even their voices softened to a whisper. It was almost as though those theorists were right who have said that education is always chiefly a reflector of the social order—rather than a critic, leader, and re-creator of social order and culture. At the present moment, it is true that no section of American education is calling attention strongly and clearly to the fact that the prosperity of this decade is, in no essential way, different from that of the "twenties"—that again we are living and spending recklessly, allowing big business free rein, permitting further concentrations of economic power, building a top-heavy profit structure which, if it rises unchecked, will again inevitably crash.

In only one great respect—though a most crucial one—the present decade differs from the "twenties." While America seems to have learned little from its recent economic experience, other parts of the world have learned much. All over the earth powerful movements of the common people are demanding that these absurd and destructive fluctuations of the industrial system should end—that public controls be exerted over economic processes of sufficient strength and rationality to guarantee stability, much greater equalization of wealth, and the securities of a rising standard of living which the proven potentialities of abundance make entirely feasible. America is out of step with the world. Yet her position is of such power and strategic importance that, if and when another and worse depression comes, she will shake and probably undermine many economic institutions elsewhere. Here, too, are facts which education ignores at its own peril and the world's.

The second fact—national rivalry and suspicion—receives, to be sure, a modicum of analysis in the schools. The roots of this terrifying reality, themselves largely economic, are seldom exposed, however, to the sunlight of honest scrutiny, and the solution of international order is too often treated both romantically and superficially. Once more the record of the past quarter century is helpful; in the 'twenties, thousands of schools studied the League of Nations and propagandized in behalf of peace. But they usually failed to show how any League was bound to fail sooner or later so long as national sovereignty remained intact, so long as bitter competition for foreign markets and natural resources was practiced by the same nations which hypocritically paid lip-service to internationalism. Thus when war came again, the disillusionment of millions of young men and women was in no small way the only clear effect of all efforts by the schools on behalf of peace.

And yet today it is important to inquire whether the only important "contribution" they are making is not, again, chiefly a repetition of the past. They may study and endorse the United Nations, to be sure; and that is helpful. But they seldom face the contradiction between high-minded objectives for all nations and the still dominant power of sovereignty of each nation. Students are taught that internationalism is desirable; they are also taught that the United States is supreme in its own right. They are taught that all countries must co-operate; they are also taught that we should keep the secret of atomic energy. They are taught that we should support the efforts of common peoples in other parts of the world to rise in power; they are also taught to be uncritical of a foreign policy which serves to thwart those efforts in countries like Greece, China, and Spain. They are taught the slogans of equality, freedom, and brotherhood; yet millions of them are taught (if in no other way than by failing to study alternatives) that the white race is superior to other races, that Christians are superior to Mohammedans or Jews.

The two great constructive purposes which should now govern the American Education Fellowship follow directly from this brief analysis. They are:

I. To channel the energies of education toward the reconstruction of the economic system—a system which should be geared with the increasing socializations and public controls now developing in England, Sweden, New Zealand, and other countries; a system in which national and international planning of production and distribution replaces the chaotic planlessness of traditional "free enterprise"; a system in which the interests, wants, and needs of the consumer dominate those of the producer; a system in which natural resources, such as coal and iron ore, are owned and controlled by the people; a system in which public corporations replace monopolistic enterprises and privately owned "public" utilities; a system in which federal authority is synchronized with decentralized regional and community administration; a system in which social security and a guaranteed annual wage sufficient to meet scientific standards of nourishment, shelter, clothing, health, recreation, and education, are universalized; a system in which the majority of the people is the sovereign determinant of every basic economy policy.

II. To channel the energies of education toward the establishment of genuine international authority in all crucial issues affecting peace and security; an order therefore in which all weapons of war (including atomic energy, first of all) and police forces are finally under that authority; an order in which international economic planning of trade, resources, labor distribution and standards, is practiced parallel with the best standards of individual nations; an order in which all nationalities, races, and religions receive equal rights in its democratic control; an order in which "world citizenship" thus assumes at least equal status with national citizenship.

*   *   *

V

In making these important recommendations, the American Education Fellowship will continue, it should be reiterated, to support the kind of experimentation for which it is most famous. It will continue to emphasize "learning by doing," "community schools," "the integrated curriculum," "teacher–pupil planning" and other objectives of "progressive education" as these now become more widely accepted.

But such objectives are now subordinate, even while indispensable, to the larger, more audacious and magnetic objectives impelled by a world in crisis. Faced by the alternatives of economic chaos and atomic war, on the one hand, of world-wide plenty and enforceable international order, on the other hand, this organization should become the clearest, most purposeful educational spokesman for the second of these alternatives. Thus, and only thus, can it become even more the great vanguard influence which it has been for nearly three decades—an influence which, as before, is certain to extend far beyond its own membership and even its own country.

To prove that education is not a mere mirror of dominant ideologies, *not* a device for bolstering outmoded economic systems and diseased nationalisms, but rather that education is a penetrating critic, dynamic leader, and imaginative re-creator which anticipates dangers *before* they crystallize into calamities, which helps simultaneously to reshape the culture of America and the world in accordance with the imperatives of our revolutionary age—this is the supreme obligation of the American Education Fellowship in our time. This is its new policy.

ON THE THREAT TO AMERICAN PUBLIC EDUCATION (1951)   From
Ernest O. Melby, "Dishonest and Unjustified," National Education Association *Journal*, vol.
XL, pp. 441–42.

F rom coast to coast the entire nation is pocked with battlefields of war against modern education. Today, education is in danger!

We believe that the type of criticism now being offered is alarming, *not* healthy or constructive. It threatens to weaken the whole fabric of democratic living at a time when we can least afford it. Its successful prosecution will hurl education back to its dark ages and mean the end of the American school system developed and improved since colonial days.

Three Momentous Ideas

These attacks are dishonest and unjustified in that they are aimed at the heart of good education, the very foundations upon which our educational program has been built. These foundations consist of three momentous ideas:

The *first* idea is that *education is rooted in democratic philosophy*. One of the most powerful ideas which came to birth with our nation was that the democratic way of life requires an educated citizenry capable of actively participating in the affairs of state. This requirement is even more essential in 1951 than it was in 1776. Educational processes are needed to solve our problems.

Education is the life-line to our free institutions; if it is destroyed or weakened, so is democracy. Our freedoms must be cherished, and the responsibilities which accompany them must be learned. This is accomplished in the educational program through teaching a "do democracy" rather than a "talk democracy."

The *second* idea is that *good education must be a growing, changing, and dynamic process.* An 1890 program of education will not do in 1951. Along with the established learnings, education must be concerned with new demands and new knowledge. Teaching must take into account, for example, human relationships, mass media of communication, studies in child growth and development, and mental health.

The *third* idea is that *good education is spiritual in nature.* Moral and spiritual values are as much a part of American school tradition as the Three R's. The ways of democracy involving respect for truth and personality, faith in the common man and in human brotherhood are taught in our elementary and secondary schools. It would be good indeed if the adult community gave youth a more favorable environment in which to apply spiritual learnings acquired in school.

Allegations

Say the critics of the public schools, "The Three Rs are being neglected. We must return to teaching the fundamentals. The school is usurping the functions of the home. We want no subjects taught together. Teach history, teach geography, teach sociology—but teach them separately. We want more rigid discipline in our schools. The public schools are godless."

Answers

These allegations do not square with the facts. They do not take into account the vast improvements in the content, materials, and procedures of instruction. They disregard changing conditions, advances of science, contributions of psychology and research, years of child study, expanding knowledge, efforts to relate school living to life situations, and Twentieth-Century needs.

The technics of education, like the teaching of the Three Rs, have not been pulled out of a hat. Much evidence on pupil achievement in the basic skills is available. The remarkable improvements in the mastery of these areas should be better understood by the public. Those who really wish reading, writing, and arithmetic taught as they were taught 20 years ago deny the power of growth to education.

In the school-versus-home bugaboo the critics overlook the wider areas of responsibility thrust upon the school by depression, war, and emergencies. They would do away with extracurriculum activities, music, arts, and courses in homemaking and child care, thus whittling the program down to a college-preparatory course. The result would be that the public schools would no longer be for all the children of all the people.

The issue of teaching subjects together or separately appears to center upon the social studies. It ignores the relatedness of all subjects and the fact that learning is plural, not singular. It implies that schools are slighting American history and tradition. That is another tragic misunderstanding.

History is prominent in social-studies programs. The charge of neglecting history was made in Pasadena, for example, although an examination of the curriculum revealed a direct study of American history and tradition in some form in practically every grade. So intimately is American tradition interwoven with the total program of education that to eliminate it would be to unravel the fabric of the program.

Our educators believe that children will not be misled by bogus promises of other ideologies if they learn the nature of our free society and its promises to all and understand the differences between democratic and communistic philosophy. Communist propaganda cannot be met by ignorance. Only those who have a clear understanding, are in possession of the facts, and know the reasoning processes of both free society and communistic societies can cope with propaganda.

So schools must deal with controversial issues. In doing so they are sometimes accused of leftist leanings by persons who fail to realize that teaching *about* communism is not the same as teaching communism. What the schools are trying to do is to equip boys and girls to deal with the present ideological conflict successfully.

As for the charge that education is too soft today, let us say again that the American educational program is rooted in democratic values. This thinking holds that one really becomes disciplined when he learns to discipline himself. It is expected that he will make mistakes as he learns, but school is the place to learn, a place to make mistakes. In school, guidance is available to help the learner understand the nature of his mistakes and to give him other situations in which to learn.

We believe it is this kind of citizen which a democracy needs. We believe in the development of democratic discipline. It should be remembered that an authoritarian school with a rigid curriculum and arbitrary disciplinary practices tends to destroy individual initiative, to level out the inventive and creative qualities of individual children, and to put a brake upon the creative and productive talents of boys and girls. It is, therefore, clear that many of the critics of public education do not understand that today schools are really seeking to give boys and girls the qualities of mind and heart that are important in a democratic society, those qualities which make large demands upon individual initiative, responsibility, and .self-reliance.

If those who call the schools "godless" mean that the schools are not indoctrinating students in one or another of the religions, they are right. Public schools are meant to serve all the children without sectarian indoctrination.

If they mean that the public schools are failing to teach moral and spiritual values, they are dead wrong. How can one teach citizenship, music, art, literature, drama, without teaching values? Certainly all of these convey the deepest sense of reverence for the sacredness of human personality and the ideals of justice and brotherhood under God.

In continuing to work for good education, it is necessary for us to realize that the entire educational system is under attack. The mood of the times is ripe for scapegoating, and it is easy to blame everything on the school. Be the attacks rooted in fear of methodology or in reluctance to spend an adequate amount of money on public education, scapegoating has had serious effects upon education.

Criticism of educational practice is desirable. When it is sincere and well-founded, it contributes to the improvement of our education. But criticism based upon misinformation and misunderstandings serves only to confuse the public and interferes with the effective discharge of duty by our teachers.

END OF PROGRESSIVE EDUCATION ANNOUNCED (1957)   From *The New York Times*, July 24, 1957.

The end of the Progressive Education magazine was announced yesterday by Dr. H. Gordon Hullfish, Professor of Education at Ohio University. Dr. Hullfish is secretary-treasurer of the John Dewey Society and was the last president of the Progressive Education Association.

"This closes the saga of the P.E.A.," Dr. Hullfish said, somewhat sadly. "We tried to save the magazine for the last two years, but found the job too much for us. We are down to 2,000 subscribers, from our original 10,000."

Among the former progress doctrines now commonly found in the schools are these, as listed by Dr. Hullfish:

● Adoption of the project method in education. Under this method, subjects are grouped together and taught as a single unit.

● Recognition of the function of interest in relationship to study. Education is made "fun" rather than "boring."

● Friendlier attitude in the classroom between teacher and pupils.

● More student activities. Children are encouraged to take part in classroom programs and other school work.

● Greater emphasis on self-discipline. Teachers try to get pupils to behave because they want to, not because they are ordered to.

Problems

LEARNING PROBLEMS OF PUERTO RICAN CHILDREN (1960)   From
Sophie L. Elam, "Acculturation And Learning Problems of Puerto Rican Children," *Teachers College Record*, vol. LXI, pp. 258–64.

$\mathbf{M}$any studies have been made and much has been said about the Puerto Rican child in cities. Although there are characteristics common to Puerto Rican children, these are by no means very different from those of other minority and emigrant children in the lower economic range. Problems of acculturation of emigrant groups are not new in our society, but invariably there is an urgency about them which is reflected in the many problems in the school and the community.

Perhaps as we look back at other migrations and note how these have been assimilated it is possible to reflect that people who, like the Puerto Ricans, have recently come out of a rural peasant cultural pattern of living find acculturation more difficult than those who come from an urban center. It may well be that rural peoples tend to be tradition-oriented while those from metropolitan communities are more other-directed so that they more readily respond to the cues available to them in our culture.

Acculturation is basically a problem of accommodation to a whole new set of patterns and being. It is actually the change-over from one culture to another. Culture is primarily a learning which is begun at birth and which provides the base for living. It permeates all behavior, from the simple fundamentals of eating and dressing and talking to the more complex and involved patterns of communication, use of symbols, and the development of a value system. Culture is also considered to be a determinant of the way one perceives oneself and others. It involves the totality of living from the biological to the social and intellectual. And the greatest complexity of the adjustment lies largely on the social sphere. ". . . under situations of stress or strain, of rapid change and consequent disorientation there is likely to be an increase in manifest ill health."[1]

Despite the vast network of our communications in mass media each emigrant group maintains almost intact its social constructs. For the adult who is already completely oriented to a way of life and whose whole gamut of responses is organized around the expected cues in his culture, the transition is difficult enough. He must select from the new what has resemblance to the familiar and add to this

[1]Margaret Mead, *Cultural Patterns and Technological Change*, New York, Mentor Books, 1955.

repertoire by trial and error the new learnings as they are needed. He tends to remain in his own ethnic and cultural clusters, both in industry and in neighborhood living, as witness the conclaves of Puerto Ricans in our cities.

But for the child who is still in the process of learning his social role and the inherent responses, the transition—often in only a few hours from the known to the unknown; from the simple to the complex environment; from rural areas to the cosmopolitan city—creates an even greater problem. It is the children who manifest the greatest degree of maladjustment.[2]

When the culture process is interrupted or suddenly changed, learning seems to cease. The new setting often destroys the foundations of security. It is, therefore, little wonder that the child who is an emigrant has not completely learned the culture of the land of origin before he is thrust into the new world with a brand-new set of learning conditions to deal with. He is also usually the child of a family that is socially and economically disadvantaged and is therefore heir to all the insecurity, fears, and instabilities of our society to a larger degree than others. Both he and the adults in his family pursue a day-to-day existence with the attendant problems of inadequate housing, clothing, and nourishment. His parents too are caught in the crosscurrents of adjustment: to find jobs though they may be unskilled; to find housing at a cost they can afford when there is little available; to hold onto their own culture in a setting which neither understands nor is able to accept.

The Puerto Rican child is thus caught between the two cultures, that of his people and the one which he must meet every day in the school. Sometimes he must respond to one that contradicts his own. The little girl who has been compliant is now expected to be active and responsive, to take the initiative, to face new people and situations on her own. In the schoolroom she is expected to talk and play with boys and to socialize more freely with her peers. There are rewards in our culture for this, but when she goes home she is forbidden to go out on the street to play. At home there is no reward for enterprising deeds, but rather the awaited and expected punishment. The emigrant child's age and sex roles and his developmental tasks are not the same as ours. If he adjusts to one, he negates the other, and as a result may lose his sense of identity with his family. The rewards we offer for these "disloyalties" are perhaps not as satisfying, nor can they be easily integrated into the patterns of the home and the other cultures. We do, in fact, tend to create "culture conflict"—the battle of the supremacy of cultures in the family and the clash of roles between parents and children.[3]

Parents play the primary role in transmitting culture to the child. This is part of the socialization process. The child identifies with the parent and internalizes the learnings. In the new environment the parent is no longer in tune with the prevalent culture. He cannot command his child's involvement, since the new society does not value his contribution to the socialization of his own child. The dichotomies and dualisms we create tend to whip the dog we taught to eat. Such a situation is evident in the story of Ana, the sixth of eight children in a family.[4] She was eight years old when she came to the mainland. Ana's mother is the strong and managing figure in the family—a traditional Puerto Rican mother who holds her daughters in

[2]*Ibid.*, p. 281.

[3]*Ibid.*, p. 254.

[4]The cases described below are derived from the operation of a training program for undergraduates in Education at the City College of New York. Students serve as leaders for groups of children in a community group work program. The names of all cases described here are fictitious.

rigid control. They are not allowed out on the streets; they must not talk to other people, particularly boys. Even the older girls are kept in this strict regimen. Ana could perhaps have developed some ease in interchange, but the mother's restrictions were so forceful that the girl's only recourse was to deny all contact. As a result, no one was able to reach out to Ana. She went on to junior high school, where she is barely passing. In addition, she has developed even more reticence and isolates herself. She has frequent headaches and stomach upsets, and is absent from school very often.

This is a rather extreme example of the frequently found conflict in social roles particularly in reference to the upbringing of girls. Since the neighborhoods in which these families settle are often socially disorganized, there is a kind of justification for the fears of the parents which further constrict the life of the girls and the younger children. It is important in working with Puerto Rican parents to help them find ways to protect their children without completely depriving them of social interchange. However, the traditions are so firmly imbedded in the structure of their living that this is difficult to achieve. It is equally difficult to help growing children find the channel between outright rebellion and complete submission. Hence they live in an atmosphere of conflict and indecision. It is at this point that they either compliantly submit and lose the ability to relate to their own peer group, or completely leave their families and join the peer group, thereby losing the support which they still need so much.

The language disability which pervades all these problems is very real. It is also a measure of the emotional stability of the person at this time of pressure. The differential rates of language learning are not only the result of age differentials and intelligence levels (the younger child learning more rapidly than the older and the brighter child learning faster than the duller), but also cues to the general level of the individual's emotional adjustment and the resolution of cultural identification and conflicts. Language is one of the tools for learning which the emigrant child lacks. He is left with only the cues he can obtain from nonverbal communication; the expressive gestures which may convey some meaning for him. Here, too, however, a facial expression or a gesture may mean something else to him, since gestures are also a language and are richly colored by each culture with specific meanings. Meanwhile he must manage without the necessary cues for directing his behavior.

As a result of these handicaps the child begins to feel inadequate. He cannot solve all the problems of adjustment to a new land, new language, new living, and new culture. He cannot seek support from his parents since they too are faced with the identical problems and with the added responsibility of founding their families in this new land. Therefore, if the child fails he suffers further indignity. He may reason that it is better not to try. Then one has not failed. Or better still, it is possible to remain so indifferent, uninvolved, and apathetic that one evades all responsibility for functioning in a setting fraught with failure and with many demands that one cannot meet.[5] This kind of "culture shock" is frequently found in great or small degree in many of our children and families.

The school is brought face to face with these problems. There may be some variation in the nature of these difficulties in different families or individuals, but the total problem is present in every child the school works with who has recently

[5]A. Anastasi and F. A. Cordova, "Some Effects of Bilingualism upon the Intelligence Test Performance of Puerto Rican Children in New York City," *Journal of Educational Psychology*, 44, 1-19.

arrived from Puerto Rico. Neither the school nor the teacher has been trained to see behavior in the light of these causes. Rather, they tend to meet each situation separately either as a discipline question or as an education problem. Our training practices in education have dealt chiefly with the child who is native to our land and has no outstanding language problem. The child of the lower economic and social strata is also rarely dealt with in our academic courses. Most of our textbooks are written by middle-class professors for middle-class teachers of middle-class children. We tend to think of education as primarily establishing literacy and the ability to deal with the daily technics of middle-class living in urban centers.

Education, although drawn from many other disciplines, for a long time tended to ignore the findings in anthropology, social psychology, and clinical psychology. Or at least it has not found a way to integrate these findings into the educational and developmental sequence usually taught in the teacher-preparation courses. We tend to divide sharply our disciplines at the college level, thus making it more difficult to provide an inter-disciplinary approach to the problems that the school faces. It seems hardly necessary to point out that if we are to work with a large number of children from a given culture we must, at the very least, learn something of the specifics of that culture, and how it pervades the entire personality and its perceptions in new situations. Learning how Puerto Rican children dance or play ball or count in Spanish will not make the teacher aware of how Puerto Rican children view their inadequacy in learning the fundamentals of arithmetic or how and why it is so difficult for them to retain the fact that three and four are seven or remember that our *j* does not sound like *h*. There needs to be rather the concept of "*fundamental education* to cover the whole of living; to teach not only new ways but the need and the incentive for new ways."

How does it feel to be unable to comprehend the cues in this new setting? How does it feel not to understand what people are saying? How do anxiety and insecurity affect a child's readiness to learn? How do people acquire a new culture without stress and destruction to their sense of well-being? The findings and skills of anthropology, sociology, and social and clinical psychology will help us to interpret this kind of defeat and better still to learn to look for these problems. They will perhaps also sharpen our focus and help us to find the educational methods which are best employed for reaching these children who really so desperately want to achieve. The individual caught in the maelstrom of conflicting cultures and feelings can be helped to move from inadequacy and near panic (as in "culture shock") to independence and courage.

*   *   *

THE PROSPECTS OF SUPERIOR CULTURE IN MASS SOCIETY

(**1960**)   From Edward Shils, "Mass Society And Its Culture," *Daedalus.* vol. LXXXIX, pp. 311–14.

The problems of superior culture in mass society are the same as in any society. These problems are the maintenance of its quality and influence on the rest of the society.

To maintain itself, superior culture must maintain its own traditions and its own internal coherence. The progress of superior culture (and its continued self-renewal and expansion) require that the traditions be sustained, however much they are revised or partially rejected at any time.

Respect for the traditions in one's own field, together with freedom in dealing with those traditions, are the necessary conditions for creative work. The balance between them is difficult to define, and it is no less difficult to discern the conditions under which the balance can be achieved and maintained. Of great importance is the morale (in its broadest sense) of the intellectuals who take on administrative and teaching responsibilities for the maintenance and advancement of high culture. Within this section of the intellectual class, there must be an incessant scrutiny of every institutional innovation, with regard to its possible impact on intellectual morale. An essential element in this internal state is a balance between respect and freedom in relation to the immanent traditions of each field of intellectual work.

Serious intellectuals have never been free from pressure on the part of sectors of society other than their own. The intellectual sector has always been relatively isolated, regardless of the role of intellectuals in economic and political life. The external world is always jealous of the devotion of the intellectuals to their own gods, and of the implicit criticism which that devotion directs against the ruling values of the other spheres. Intellectuals have always been faced with the task of continuing their own tradition, developing it, differentiating it, improving it as best they could. They have always had to contend with church, state, and party, with merchants and soldiers who have sought to enlist them in their service and to restrict and damage them in word and deed if they did not yield to temptations and threats. The present situation has much in common with the past. The responsibilities of intellectuals also remain the same: to serve the standards they discern and develop and to find a way of rendering unto Caesar what is Caesar's without renouncing what belongs to their own proper realm.

There is no doubt in my mind that the main "political" tradition by which most of our literary, artistic, and social-science intellectuals have lived in America is unsatisfactory. The fault does not lie exclusively with the intellectuals. The philistine Puritanism and provincialism of our elites share much of the blame, as does the populism of professionsal and lay politicians. Nonetheless, the intellectuals cannot evade the charge that they have done little to ameliorate the situation. Their own political attitudes have been alienated, they have run off into many directions of frivolity. The most recent of such episodes in the 1930's and 1940's were also the most humiliating, and temporarily the most damaging, to the position of intellectuals in American society.

One of the responsibilities implied by their obligation to maintain good relations with the nonintellectual elite is the "civilization" of political life, i.e., the infusion of the standards and concerns of a serious, intellectually disciplined contemplation of the deeper issues of political life into everyday politics. Our intellectuals have in the main lectured politicians, upbraided them, looked down their noses at them, opposed them, and even suspected those of their fellow intellectuals who have become politicians of moral corruption and intellectual betrayal.

The intellectuals who have taken on themselves the fostering of superior culture are part of the elite in any country; but in the United States they have not felt bound by any invisible affiliation with the political, economic, ecclesiastical, military, and technological elites.[1]

The "civilization" of political life is only one aspect of the "process of civilization," which is the expansion of the culture of the center into the peripheries of society and, in this particular context, the diffusion of superior culture into the areas of society normally consuming mediocre and brutal culture.

Within the limits mentioned earlier in this essay, the prospects for superior culture seemed to be reasonably good. The overlapping at certain points on the part of the producers of superior culture and those of mediocre culture has resulted in an expansion of the elements of superior culture which reaches persons whose usual inclinations do not lead them to seek it out. Popularization brings a better content, but not all of this expansion is popularization; much of it is the presentation (and consumption) of genuinely superior cultural work. An improvement in our educational system at the elementary and secondary levels, which is assuredly practicable and likely, will also further this process of civilization. A better education of taste, which a richer, less scarcity-harassed society can afford, the opening and enrichment of sensitivity, which leisure and a diversified environment can make possible, and a more fruitful use of available intelligence can also push forward the "process of civilization."

Of course, men will remain men, their capacities to understand, create, and experience will vary, and very many are probably destined to find pleasure and salvation at other and lower cultural levels. For the others, the prospect of a more dignified and richer cultural life does not seem out of the question. It would certainly be an impossible one, however, if all intellectuals devoted themselves to education and popularization. In a short time the superior culture which would be transmitted through the "process of civilization" would fade and desiccate.

Thus, if the periphery is not to be polished while the center becomes dusty, the first obligation of the intellectuals is to look after intellectual things, to concentrate their powers on the creation and reproduction and consumption of particular works of philosophy, art, science, literature, or scholarship, to receive traditions in which these works stand with a discriminating readiness to accept, elaborate, or reject. If that is done, there will be nothing to fear from the movement of culture in mass society.

[1]This is not a condition unique to the United States. Only Great Britain has managed to avoid it for most of the period since the French Revolution, yet there, too, the past few years have not provided notable examples of Britain's good fortune in avoiding this separation.

ON TELEVISION AND THE LIVES OF CHILDREN (1961)   From Wilbur
Schramm et al., *Television in the Lives of Our Children* (Stanford, Calif., 1961), pp. 24–27,
29–30.

When Does a Child Begin to Use Television?

The first direct experience with television typically comes at age two.
Chances are, the child will eavesdrop on a program someone else has tuned in. But
he soon begins to explore the world of television and to develop tastes and
preferences of his own. By the age of three he is able to shout for his favorite
programs. The chances are, these are children's programs, by which we mean that
they are billed as children's television, typically have animal heroes or animated
cartoon figures, and all have a high proportion of fantasy and broad action. Thus we
introduce children to television as fantasy. It is interesting to speculate what might
be the influence on their later uses of television, if we let them see the medium very
early as a window on the real rather than the fantasy world.

By the age of three, then, the average child is already making fairly regular use
of television. He sees a number of "children's" programs, soon branches out into
Westerns and similar entertainment.

Magazines have also become important for him. Most often, these are picture
magazines. He does an impressive amount of "picture reading," hurrying over some
pictures, staring a long while at the pictures that interest him. Until he is six or
seven, he knows magazines only as pictures, as sources of the stories his parents
read to him, or as vehicles for his own "pretend" reading. Yet the pictures he sees at
an early age must have a considerable impact on him.

Somewhere between the ages of three and six, he usually becomes acquainted
with radio. He hears it first as a program someone else in the family has tuned in. It
may be popular music, chosen by a teen-age sister or brother; a day show, tuned in
by his mother for entertainment while she does housework; or a news broadcast,
perhaps tuned in by his father. The majority of his radio listening is likely to be
eavesdropping, rather than his own choice, for some time. But he discovers some
programs that please him and probably tries to return to them: lively music, or
radio children's programs.

Some time before the years of going to school, he is probably taken to see
movies. If he goes to the drive-in with his parents, the chances are that his first taste
of movies is an adult show, and he dozes most of the evening in the back seat of the
car. If he is taken to the theater, his first movie is probably a Western or an
animated cartoon, or both of these on the same day. These tend to be his early
favorites in movies; when he has a choice he tries to see a cartoon or a "cowboy"
show.

By the age of six, then, the child ordinarily has been introduced to all the
audiovisual media, has built up strong likings and preference for television
programs, and has met printed media through pictures and through the stories
people find in them to read to him.

His active use of printed media begins, of course, with school time. As he learns
to read, he begins to sound out some of the stories for himself. He reads simple
books, jumping back and forth from text to pictures. He discovers children's
magazines, and begins to translate some of the captions in picture magazines. From
some of his fellows, he has learned about comic books and has begun to look at

them; now he reads them. And last of all, he begins to find the newspaper useful. Here, too, he typically begins with the comic strips (although a few children begin at once with news reading). He is ten or eleven before he reads any great variety of content in the newspaper.

This process of learning to use the mass media, from the time when broadcast sound first blends into the child's environment until he is able to look at a newspaper or magazine and decide, with some assurance and skill, what to read, requires for the average child about ten years. Let us point out some highlights on the map of this period.

For one thing, it is evident that the pattern by which a child is introduced to the media is one of increasing control over the content. At first, radio and television are merely background, entirely out of the child's control. The child does not even, for a long while, decide what bedtime story he will hear. Later, the child himself becomes able to choose favorite programs on television, and favorite stories to be read or told to him; but he is still in bondage to broadcast schedules and parental availability, and, of course, to someone else's sense of pace and emphasis. Looking at pictures gives the child a chance to repeat, to pace himself, to imagine his own stories, but he is still subject to the adult taste which provides the magazine in the first place. His first real control over the media occurs when he becomes able to read. As he becomes more skillful, he has more control over the conditions. He varies the timing, the speed, the repetitions to suit himself. Finally, he becomes master of the process of selection. He knows what can be found in the newspaper, what is available in different kinds of magazines, where to find the books he wants to read. It takes about ten years to win this freedom.

In the second place, it is worth noting that the child is introduced to the mass media almost wholly as fantasy and as audiovisual experiences. This is, of course, in the child's most pliable and impressionable years. The way he begins to use television may well help to explain why the idea that television is *for fantasy* is so deeply ingrained in a child that he often has the greatest difficulty in thinking of *educational* television, let us say, as a proper use of the medium. And similarly, this may help to explain why the printed media, associated with school as they are, seem the proper places to look for informational, as opposed to entertainment, material.

Third, the dominance of television in this first ten years is impressive.

In the Rocky Mountain city where television has been longest available, parents reported 2.8 as the median age at which children began to use television—meaning that half the children had begun to use it by about the age of two years and ten months. In San Francisco, where we made special efforts to distinguish between exploratory use and regular use of the medium, we found that 37 per cent of children were already making fairly regular use of the medium at age three; two-thirds, by age four; over 80 per cent, by age five (kindergarten); and over 90 per cent, by age six when they were in the first grade of elementary school.

✲ ✲ ✲

It is therefore television, more than any other medium, that furnishes a common body of information for the early socialization of children. It is television, more than any other channel, that builds the "set" with which a child approaches the mass media. All other media choices are judged against what he has come to expect of television.

*   *   *

How Much Time Does a Child Spend on Television?

We should warn that this question is not as simple as it seems.

It would be prohibitively expensive to *observe* the television behavior of a large number of children over a long period of time; therefore a researcher must collect someone's *estimate* of time spent on television. But whose estimate? The child's or his mother's? And how is the estimate obtained? By memory, by diary, by checking a list of programs? Each of these things makes a difference in the size of the estimate one obtains.

In Appendix III we have discussed at some length the problem of arriving at an accurate estimate of television viewing time and have given a number of estimates obtained in different ways and by different researchers. In general, we are using figures which are in the middle of several estimates, and which we have reason to think are as accurate as we can obtain. But no reader of this book should think that estimates of a child's television time are as firm, let us say, as measurements of a child's height or weight.

Another warning: some researchers estimate a child's listening time per *average weekday*, others per *Sunday*, others per *average day* (which means weekday or Sunday). In comparing figures from book to book, or study to study, a reader must notice carefully what kind of day is being measured.

A final warning: There are very few average children. Therefore, averages must not be thought of as representing more than they do—a middle point. For example, in one large group of boys in a certain school grade we obtained an average weekday viewing time of just over two and one-half hours a day. But only one-sixth of all the viewing times actually were between two and one-quarter and two and three-quarter hours. Actually, 16 per cent of these boys viewed more than four hours a day; and 5 per cent viewed less than 15 minutes. Therefore, when you read about averages in the following pages, you should not think of the children all necessarily clustering closely around the average, but possibly large groups of them far under or far above the average. In this kind of situation, it is more important to find out why these large differences exist than what the average is, and in the latter part of this book we have given a greal deal of consideration to the problem of why the television behavior of children of the same age is often so different.

Now, having warned you, let us proceed to answer the question.

A child who has begun to use television by age three typically uses it about 45 minutes a weekday (Monday through Friday). By age five, his viewing has increased until, on the average, it is a little over two hours a day. From age six until about the sixth grade, when the child is entering adolescence, viewing time is on a slowly rising plane between two and two and one-half hours. Then viewing time rises rather sharply to a high of a little over three hours a day. This hump usually occurs somewhere between the fifth and eighth grades. Then it enters upon a slowly falling slope until by the twelfth grade (about age seventeen) it is again between two and two and one-half hours. . . .

These are weekday figures. Sunday viewing averages from one-half to one hour longer. . . .

These are conservative figures. They are less than some other studies have found, and, as we shall say in a minute, they are less than we found in some places. But, even so, they are spectacular. They mean that throughout the years of school, a child spends within 5 per cent as much time on television as on school. From ages three through sixteen, he spends *more* total time on television than on school. In these years he devotes about one-sixth of all his waking hours to television. In fact, he is likely to devote more time to television than to any other activity except sleep and perhaps play, depending on how play is defined!

JAMES CONANT ON THE RELATION BETWEEN THE HIGH SCHOOL AND ITS COMMUNITY (1961)   From James B. Conant, *Slums and Suburbs* (New York, 1961), pp. 1–3, 40–41.

This is a book of contrasts. I shall present a picture of two totally different kinds of neighborhoods and the public schools which serve them. I shall discuss city slums and wealthy suburbs. In the large metropolitan areas of New York, Philadelphia, Detroit, Chicago, and St. Louis, one has no difficulty in locating examples of both. In some cases twenty minutes' or half an hour's drive will enable a person to go from one to the other. A visit to the high school serving each community will open the eyes of a visitor to the complexities of American public education. Within the limitation imposed by the budget, the schools in the two totally different neighborhoods may be doing a good job. Yet their basic problems are in many respects quite unlike. And the differences spring from the differences in the nature of the families being served. One lesson to be drawn from visiting and contrasting a well-to-do suburb and a slum is all important for understanding American public education. *The lesson is that to a considerable degree what a school should do and can do is determined by the status and ambitions of the families being served.*

In the suburban high school from which 80 per cent or more of the graduates enter some sort of college, the most important problem from the parents' point of view is to ensure the admission of their children to prestige colleges; consequently there is great concern over good teaching of academic subjects. From the educator's point of view, however, the most vexing problem is to adjust the family's ambitions to the boy's or girl's abilities. In the city slum, where as many as a half of the children drop out of school in grades 9, 10, and 11, the problems are almost the reverse of those facing the principal and guidance officer of the rich suburban school. The task with which the school people in the slum must struggle is, on the one hand, to prepare a student for getting and keeping a job as soon as he leaves school and, on the other hand, to encourage those who have academic talent to aim at a profession through higher education. The task thus stated seems simple. In actual fact the difficulties are appalling. So appalling, indeed, that as I prepared to spell them out in my final report to the Carnegie Corporation, I decided to write a small book devoted largely to their consideration.

I have done so because I am convinced we are allowing social dynamite to accumulate in our large cities. I am not nearly so concerned about the plight of suburban parents whose offspring are having difficulty finding places in prestige colleges as I am about the plight of parents in the slums whose children either drop out or graduate from school without prospects of either further education or employment. In some slum neighborhoods I have no doubt that over a half of the boys between sixteen and twenty-one are out of school and out of work. Leaving aside human tragedies, I submit that a continuation of this situation is a menace to the social and political health of the large cities.

The improvement of slum conditions is only in part a question of improving education. But the role of the schools is of the utmost importance. As I hope to make clear in later pages, the school authorities ought to be given the responsibility for helping out-of-school youth between the ages of sixteen and twenty-one both to further their education and gain employment. Added responsibilities, however, require additional funds. Indeed the whole problem of financing public education in the large cities is a major national concern.

The contrast in money available to the schools in a wealthy suburb and to the schools in a large city jolts one's notions of the meaning of equality of opportunity. The pedagogic tasks which confront the teachers in the slum schools are far more difficult than those which their colleagues in the wealthy suburbs face. Yet the expenditure per pupil in the wealthy suburban school is as high as $1,000 per year. The expenditure in a big city school is less than half that amount. An even more significant contrast is provided by looking at the school facilities and noting the size of the professional staff. In the suburb there is likely to be a spacious modern school staffed by as many as 70 professionals per 1,000 pupils; in the slum one finds a crowded, often dilapidated and unattractive school staffed by 40 or fewer professionals per 1,000 pupils. The contrast challenges any complacency we may have about our method of financing public schools—even within a rich state like New York.

*   *   *

The Role of the Schools

At the outset I must record an educational heresy, or rather support a proposition that many will accept as self-evident but that some professors of the liberal arts will denounce as dangerously heretical. *I submit that in a heavily urbanized and industrialized free society the educational experiences of youth should fit their subsequent employment.* There should be a smooth transition from full-time schooling to a full-time job, whether that transition be after grade 10 or after graduation from high school, college, or university.

This is an ideal situation admittedly, and one which is at present approached only in the learned professions and in a few instances the occupations for which undergraduate courses provide the necessary training. In the case of the learned professions, those in charge of the last stage in the educational journey—the professors of law, of medicine, and those who direct the research of candidates for the Ph.D.—have usually a sense of responsibility for their students based on their own passionate interest in promoting the best interests of their profession. Graduates of some undergraduate professional courses in some institutions are also often assisted in finding employment. Engineering is perhaps the best example. With the present shortage of teachers, professors of education have no difficulty in finding jobs for their students. While the universities or colleges do not accept responsibility for the placement of their graduates, many, if not all, spend time and money in helping the young man or woman to find a job. In many cases the subsequent career is followed with interest, and assistance is provided in re-employment. Sixty years ago the situation was very different. Concern with placement of college and university graduates was a product of the depression years. The change, I believe, has been important and in the best interests of both the individual and society. For the college graduate who has received a general or liberal education without majoring in a professional or semi-professional field, many difficulties of finding a suitable job will remain. Still, by and large, one can say at the college and university level a considerable fraction of the youth involved make a smooth transition from education to a job.

When we examine the situation at the high school level, we find quite a different state of affairs. Although half or more of the graduates of many high schools seek employment immediately on graduation, only in a few cities does one find an effective placement service. I make this statement without intending any reproach to either social agencies, employment offices, or to guidance officers. The obligations of the school should not end when the student either drops out of school or graduates. At that point the cumulative record folder concerning a student's educational career is usually brought to an end. It should not be. To my mind, *guidance officers, especially in the large cities, ought to be given the responsibility for following the post-high school careers of youth from the time they leave school until they are twenty-one years of age.* Since compulsory attendance usually ends at age sixteen, this means responsibility for the guidance of youth ages sixteen to twenty-one who are out of school and either employed or unemployed. This expansion of the school's function will cost money and will mean additional staff—at least a doubling of the guidance staff in most of the large cities. But the expense is necessary, for vocational and educational guidance must be a continuing process to help assure a smooth transition from school to the world of work. The present abrupt break between the two is unfortunate. What I have in mind suggests, of course, a much closer relationship than now exists among the schools, employers, and labor unions, as well as social agencies and employment offices.

PAUL GOODMAN ON THE PROBLEMS OF GROWING UP IN AMERICA
(**1962**)   From *Growing Up Absurd* (New York, 1962), pp. ix–xvi.

In every day's newspaper there are stories about the two subjects that I have brought together in this book, the disgrace of the Organized System of semimonopolies, government, advertisers, etc., and the disaffection of the growing generation. Both are newsworthily scandalous, and for several years now both kinds of stories have come thicker and faster. It is strange that the obvious connections between them are not played up in the newspapers; nor, in the rush of books on the follies, venality, and stifling conformity of the Organization, has there been a book on Youth Problems in the Organized System.

Those of the disaffected youth who are articulate, however—for instance, the Beat or Angry young men—are quite clear about the connection: their main topic is the "system" with which they refuse to co-operate. They will explain that the "good" jobs are frauds and sells, that it is intolerable to have one's style of life dictated by Personnel, that a man is a fool to work to pay installments on a useless refrigerator for his wife, that the movies, TV, and Book-of-the-Month Club are beneath contempt, but the Luce publications make you sick to the stomach; and they will describe with accuracy the cynicism and one-upping of the "typical" junior executive. They consider it the part of reason and honor to wash their hands of all of it.

Naturally, grown-up citizens are concerned about the beatniks and delinquents. The school system has been subjected to criticism. And there is a lot of official talk about the need to conserve our human resources lest Russia get ahead of us. The question is why the grownups do not, more soberly, draw the same connections as the youth. Or, since no doubt many people *are* quite clear about the connection that the structure of society that has become increasingly dominant in our country is disastrous to the growth of excellence and manliness, why don't more people speak up and say so, and initiate a change? The question is an important one and the answer is, I think, a terrible one: that people are so bemused by the way business and politics are carried on at present, with all their intricate relationships, that they have ceased to be able to imagine alternatives. We seem to have lost our genius for inventing changes to satisfy crying needs.

But this stupor is inevitably the baleful influence of the very kind of organizational network that we have: the system pre-empts the available means and capital; it buys up as much of the intelligence as it can and muffles the voices of dissent; and then it irrefutably proclaims that itself is the only possibility of society, for nothing else is thinkable. Let me give a couple of examples of how this works. Suppose (as is the case) that a group of radio and TV broadcasters, competing in the Pickwickian fashion of semimonopolies, control all the stations and channels in an area, amassing the capital and variously bribing Communications Commissioners in order to get them; and the broadcasters tailor their programs to meet the requirements of their advertisers, of the censorship, of their own slick and clique tastes, and of a broad common denominator of the audience, none of whom may be offended: they will then claim not only that the public wants the drivel that they give them, but indeed that nothing else is being created. Of course it is not! not for *these* media; why should a serious artist bother? Or suppose again (as is not quite the case) that in a group of universities only faculties are chosen that are "safe" to the businessmen trustees or the politically appointed regents, and these faculties give out all the degrees and licenses and union cards to the new generation of students, and only such universities can get Foundation or government money for research, and research is incestuously staffed by the same sponsors and according to the same policy, and they allow no one but those they choose, to have access to either the classroom or expensive apparatus: it will then be claimed that there is no other learning or professional competence; that an inspired teacher is not "solid"; that the official projects are the direction of science; that progressive education is a failure; and finally, indeed—as in Dr. James Conant's report on the high schools— that only 15 per cent of the youth are "academically talented" enough to be taught hard subjects. This pre-empting of the means and the brains by the organization, and the shutting out of those who do not conform, can go so far as to cause delusions, as when recently the president of Merck and Company had the effrontery to warn the Congress that its investigation of profiteering in drugs might hinder the quest of scientific knowledge! as if the spirit of Vesalius and Pasteur depended on the financial arrangements of Merck and Company.

But it is in these circumstances that people put up with a system because "there are no alternatives." And when one cannot think of anything to do, soon one ceases to think at all.

To my mind the worst feature of our present organized system of doing things is its indirectness, its blurring of the object. The idea of directly addressing crying objective public needs, like shelter or education, and using our immense and indeed *surplus* resources to satisfy them, is anathema. For in the great interlocking system of corporations people live not by attending to the job, but by status, role playing, and tenure, and they work to maximize profits, prestige, or votes regardless of utility or even public disutility—e.g., the plethora of cars has now become a public disutility, but automobile companies continue to manufacture them and persuade people to buy them. The indespensable premise of city planning, according to a vice president of Webb and Knapp, is to make a "modest long-term profit on the promoter's investment." (His exact sentence, to a meeting of young planners, was, "What we're going to have built will be built only if some developer is going to make a profit from it."!) Obviously he is not directly interested in housing people or in city convenience and beauty; he is directly interested in being a good vice president of Webb and Knapp. That is his privilege, but it is not a useful goal, and an idealistic young fellow would not want to be such a man. Another example: Some earnest liberal Congressmen are baffled "how to give Federal aid to education and not interfere in the curriculum and teaching." But when the teaching *function* is respected and assayed by the teacher's peers-in-skill, no one *can* interfere, no one would dare (just as Harvard tossed out McCarthy). The sole function of administration is to smooth the way, but in this country we have the topsy-turvy situation that a teacher must devote himself to satisfying the administrator and financier rather than to doing his job, and a universally admired teacher is fired for disobeying an administrative order that would hinder teaching. (See Appendix A.) Let me give another example, because I want to make this point very clear: These same Congressmen are concerned "how to discourage low-level programming in private TV stations without censorship." Their question presupposes that in communication the prior thing is the existence of networks and channels, rather than something to communicate that needs diffusing. But the prior thing *is* the program, and the only grounds for the license to the station is its ability to transmit it. Nothing could be more stupid than for the communications commission to give to people who handle the means of broadcasting the inventing of what to broadcast, and then, disturbed at the poor quality, to worry about censorship.

We live increasingly, then, in a system in which little direct attention is paid to the object, the function, the program, the task, the need; but immense attention to the role, procedure, prestige, and profit. We don't get the shelter and education because not enough mind is paid to *those* things. Naturally the system is inefficient; the overhead is high; the task is rarely done with love, style, and excitement, for such beauties emerge only from absorption in real objects; sometimes the task is not done at all; and those who could do it best become either cynical or resigned.

In the light of this criticism, the recent scandalous exposures of the advertisers, the government, and the corporations are heartening rather than dismaying. (I am writing in the winter of 1956–60 and we have been hearing about TV, the FCC, Title I, and the Drug Industry; by the time this is published there will be a new series.) The conditions exposed are not new, but now the public skepticism and disgust are mounting; to my ear there is even a new ring; and the investigations are being pushed further, even further than intended by the investigators. The effect of this must be to destroy for many people the image of inviolability and indispensability of the kind of system I have been discussing, to show its phony workings and inevitable dangers. It is the collapse of "public relations."

When the existing state of things is suddenly measured by people against far higher standards than they have been used to, it is no longer the case that there are no alternatives. People are forced by their better judgment to ask very basic questions: Is it possible, *how* is it possible, to have more meaning and honor in work? to put wealth to some real use? to have a high standard of living of whose quality we are not ashamed? to get social justice for those who have been shamefully left out? to have a use of leisure that is not a dismaying waste of a hundred million adults? The large group of independent people who have been out of the swim, with their old-fashioned virtues, suddenly have something admirable about them; one is surprised that they still exist, and their existence is relevant. And from the members of the Organized System itself come acute books criticizing the shortcomings of the Organized System.

It is my belief that we are going to have a change. And once the Americans can recover from their mesmerized condition and its political apathy, our country will be in a most fortunate situation. For the kinds of radical changes we need are those that are appropriate to a fairly general prosperity. They are practicable. They can be summed up as simply restoring, in J. K. Galbraith's phrase, the "social balance" that we have allowed to become lopsided and runaway in the present abuse of the country's wealth. For instance, since we have a vast surplus productivity, we can turn to finding jobs that will bring out a youth's capacity, and so really conserve human resources. We can find ways to restore to the worker a say in his production, and so really do something for manly independence. Since we have a problem of what to do with leisure, we can begin to think of necessary community enterprises that want doing, and that people can enthusiastically and spontaneously throw themselves into, and be proud of the results (e.g., beautifying our hideous small towns). Since we have the technology, the capital, and the labor, why should we not have livable cities? Should it be hard to bring back into society the 30 per cent who are *still* ill fed and ill housed, and more outcast than ever? What is necessary is directly addressing definite objective needs and using available resources to satisfy them; doing things that are worth while just because they are worth while, since we can. Politically, what we need is government in which a man offers himself as a candidate because he has a new program that he wants to effectuate, and we choose him because we want that good, and judge that he is the best man to effectuate it. Is that outlandish?

The present widespread concern about education is only superficially a part of the Cold War, the need to match the Russian scientists. For in the discussions, pretty soon it becomes clear that people are uneasy about, ashamed of, the world that they have given the children to grow up in. That world is not manly enough, it is not earnest enough; a grownup may be cynical (or resigned) about his own convenient adjustments, but he is by no means willing to see his children robbed of a worth-while society. With regard to the next generation, everybody always has a higher standard than the one he is used to. The standard is ceasing to be one of money and status and is becoming a standard of the worth of life. But worth, like happiness, comes from bona-fide activity and achievement.

My stratagem in this book is a simple one. I assume that the young *really* need a more worth-while world in order to grow up at all, and I confront this real need with the world that they have been getting. This is the source of their problems. *Our* problem is to remedy the disproportion. We can. Our inheritance, our immense productivity, has been pre-empted and parceled out in a kind of domainal system;

but this grandiose and seemingly impregnable feudalism is vulnerable to an earnest attack. One has the persistent thought that if ten thousand people in all walks of life will stand up on their two feet and talk out and insist, we shall get back our country.

PROBLEMS OF MIGRANT EDUCATION (1963)   From George E. Haney, "Problems And Trends In Migrant Education," *School Life,* pp. 5-9.

The most educationally deprived group of children in the Nation—these are the children of our domestic agricultural migratory workers (Hearings before Senate Subcommittee on Migratory Labor, 1961). Most migrant children enter school late, their attendance is poor, their progress is slow, and they drop out early. The result? Most of them are far below the average grade level for their age, their achievement is usually under the fourth grade, and the illiteracy rate among them is high.

The sorry plight of these children has become a critical national problem since illiteracy or lack of an elementary education can condemn them to a life of ignorance, poverty, and dependence on society.

For more than a decade the public has been aware of the plight of these children. In 1951 the President's Commission on Migratory Labor said:

> This Commission wishes to reiterate its conviction that the education of the children of migratory farmworkers (and their parents also) is one of the most urgent and most essential of many steps which the Nation can and should take to improve the lot of migrants who have for so long been deprived of what the rest of us take for granted.

Even though local and State educational agencies have made considerable progress in improving educational programs for these children in the decade since the Commission spoke, recent studies and reports indicate that tens of thousands of migrant children still do not have an opportunity for education equal to that of other American children.

Just how many thousands of migrant children there are is hard to determine because they are on the move so much of the time. In 1954 the U.S. Department of Agriculture estimated that the number under eighteen years old ranged between 175,000 and 225,000. In 1962 in hearings before the Senate subcommittee the number was put at 150,000.

It is not hard to believe that the vast majority of these migrant children are being denied their birthright. There is ample evidence that they are among the most educationally deprived in the country: surveys and studies by Federal and State agencies and local school systems report facts too much alike to be questioned. For example:

A 1960 survey by the U.S. Department of Agriculture found that migratory farmworkers twenty years old and older had completed a median of 6.9 years of school compared with ten years for all Americans in the same age group (*Monthly Labor Review*, vol. 85, p. iii).

A survey paper prepared for the 1960 White House Conference on Children and Youth says that these children are far below grade level and that their average achievement in school generally is under fourth grade—the minimum standard for literacy.

The Department of Labor says that, among 2,301 migrant children found employed on farms in violation of the child-labor provisions of the Fair Labor Standards Act, seventy-two percent were enrolled in grades below the normal level for their ages.

A 1959 study by the Colorado State Department of Education found that sixteen percent of all parents surveyed had no formal education, and less than twenty-five percent had completed only the grades in the first to fourth level.

A 1961 report from New Jersey says "Though complete data are not available, school reports from several States show that possibly as few as one in fifty enters high school and fewer than this graduate. Consequently vocational training courses and school guidance services usually offered in the high school are virtually out of reach of these youngsters." (Curtis Gatlin, 1960).

The States of Ohio, Oregon, Pennsylvania, and Texas and others have made similar studies of the educational achievement of migrant children, and all indicate a high rate of retardation among them. The studies also indicate that they become progressively more retarded, that they fall further behind until they drop out of school in the elementary grades, and that few enroll in high school.

Studies and State surveys have found that migratory pupils are not educationally retarded because they lack intelligence or ability, but because they lack the opportunity to attend school regularly and to receive a continuous program of education.

The schooling of the migrant child is frequently interrupted by movements of his parents from one community to another. Studies indicate that most migrant families do not spend more than five months, or at the most seven months, in any one place. Each time the family moves during the regular school year, the child loses time from school.

Each year these 150,000 children accompany their parents from community to community and from State to State. And each year they confront local and State school authorities with serious educational problems. The high rate of retardation and the low educational attainment of migrant children compound the schools' problems of providing for them. In turn, the inability of some schools to meet these problems contributes to the further retardation of the children.

Problems

Providing for the education of migrant children during the regular school year creates many difficult and complex problems which have many social and economic ramifications. The seasonal impact of migratory children on school systems along the routes creates problems of finance, school transfer records, grade placement of pupils, and provision of teachers and school facilities. There is, in addition, the problem of getting migratory children to enroll and attend school regularly.

SEASONAL IMPACT

In some communities it is not uncommon for the number of school-age children to increase by more than 100 percent during the harvest season. Lack of financial support to provide additional classrooms, teachers, transportation, equipment, textbooks, and supplies often makes them an unacceptable burden. Since the numbers of workers vary greatly from year to year, school officials find it difficult to plan provision for the migratory children who will reside in their community during the harvest season. This presents a most serious problem to officials with restricted budgets. If officials have no assurance of the number, they may decide that expenditures for additional facilities are not economically advisable.

It is not uncommon for migrant children to be told on arriving home from school at the end of the day that they must immediately get ready to move on to the next community. Since school officials have had no advance information about the children leaving or where they are going, they do not send transfer records along. If the children enter school in the next stop on the road, their new teachers may write to former teachers for transfer record cards. Many children, however, do not reenter schools in other communities while they are on the trek. By the time they arrive at their home base in November, some have forgotten the names or addresses of the schools they attended.

Educators say that many migrant children still do not bring transfer records, and that those they present do not contain sufficient information for grade placement. In 1955 the U.S. Office of Education developed a transfer record form for children to carry from school to school. Several districts have used this form, but because of the difficulties of migrant life and State variations in regulations, it has had limited use. Some communities in California and Colorado have agreements with other communities in and out of their own States to send records by mail when children move.

Although more migrants than formerly are presenting transfer records, a survey of seven State programs found that interstate agreements were needed on the type of information to be supplied and the methods of sending records from school to school (Haney, 1963). It has also been suggested that a clearinghouse be established for the school records of migratory children in the east coast stream (U.S. Department of Health, Education and Welfare, 1963).

GRADE PLACEMENT OF PUPILS

One of the serious obstacles to officials in planning a suitable program for a migrant child is their not knowing the level of his academic achievement and the grade in which he should be placed to enable him to progress and benefit the most from his educational experience. When a migrant does not bring a record from the previous schools he has attended an evaluation can be made on the basis of such factors as his chronological age, achievement, reading ability, physical maturity, and social adjustment. Much time is lost in this procedure by both the pupil and the teacher. If migrant children carried their school records with them, schools could plan suitable programs for them and place them without loss of time and effort.

PROVIDING TEACHERS FOR MIGRANT CHILDREN

One of the critical problems in the education of migrant children is to provide teachers who understand their cultural background and their socioeconomic and educational needs. It is difficult for teachers with overcrowded classrooms to adapt the established curriculum to children who enter school late or to initiate a different program of studies for them. This presents a difficult task to the experienced teacher and an almost impossible problem to the unprepared or inexperienced teacher.

When school districts have an unusually large influx of children, providing teachers as well as classrooms for them may seriously handicap the school program.

The children may enter a community in late September or early October, from two to eight weeks after the opening of school. Unless the district has already made plans for them, it may have difficulty in finding qualified teachers to augment the regular staff.

THE SCHOOL ATTENDANCE PROBLEM

It is estimated that a large number of school-age children do not attend school from the time they leave their home-base State early in April until they return in November or December. The Office survey of seven State programs (1961) found that approximately fifty percent of the migrant children who resided in Ohio and Oregon and twenty-five to thirty percent of those who resided in Colorado during the regular school sessions never enrolled in school.

A study in Michigan reports that seventeen percent of 917 children did not attend school during the year 1956–57. Reports from home-base schools in Florida and Texas reveal that most migrant children arrive at school two and three months late and leave as much as six and eight weeks before school closes in the spring, and that most of them do not enter school from the time they leave their home base until they return.

The Office survey also revealed a number of reasons why migrant children do not attend school regularly or never enroll during the regular school year. Among the most important are the following: the parents' lack of education or their attitude toward the importance of education for their children; their need for the children's earnings or for older children to care for their younger brothers and sisters while the mother works in the field; and the language barrier in areas where Spanish-speaking migrants are working. Other reasons reported by the survey, though less important, kept children out of school: The communities' attitude of rejection or indifference toward migrants; attendance laws of some communities, which bar transients; failure of local officials to enforce attendance and child labor laws; lack of school facilities to provide for a large influx of migrants; lack of proper food or clothing for children of school age; lack of school transfer records; lack of financial assistance to provide school supplies and facilities for the migrants.

Some communities along the migrants' routes declare "crop vacations" and close schools during the peak of the harvest season so that children can help gather crops. Local children have an opportunity to make up lost time, but migratory pupils do not. They move on to the next community where schools may also be closed for crop vacations.

NEED FOR EDUCATIONAL CONTINUITY

The variations between school districts and States in textbooks, curriculums, and programs of study make it difficult to provide migrant children with a continuous and sequential educational program. Different teachers, textbooks, methods of study, and achievement standards confuse and shake the self-confidence of children who may enroll in as many as four or five schools each year. This situation encourages dropouts.

In order to provide more continuity and articulation in the educational program of children on the move, some educators have proposed that short-term units in basic skills be developed for use in both regular and summer sessions. With an outline of such units, the children would have a better opportunity to progress from one unit to another in each school where they enroll. The units would provide a guide to a more continous program of study and would help avoid duplications and omissions in their educational programs.

Short units could be developed through experimentation and cooperation among school districts and States along specific migratory routes. Such cooperation would, however, call for interstate agreements, which are hard to obtain. In addition funds would be required for curriculum research and experimentation.

FINANCING SCHOOL PROGRAMS

It is difficult for some school systems to solve financial problems created by children who cross district and State lines. It is especially difficult for rural schools: "The seasonal impact of these children produces an acute fiscal problem for rural educational systems which, in comparison to urban school systems, already face the most serious handicap in our educational system" (Subcommittee hearings, 1961).

The many problems teachers and administrators face in trying to provide for migrant children has made State action and support necessary in some States. In 1962 nine States were providing financial assistance to school districts for the operation of summer schools. Other States were providing financial assistance to local school districts on the basis of average daily attendance of migratory children at the regular school session. For example, Pennsylvania reimburses the school districts one dollar per day per child attending regular sessions, up to forty days.

Summer programs

Since most migrant children attend school six or seven months during the school year and must adjust to several new schools each year, they are seldom able to earn promotion from grade to grade. Local communities and States have made several notable efforts to provide a more continuous program of education for these children.

Several Northern States are supporting summer session programs to provide migrant children with an opportunity to make up time lost from school. These schools were first organized by voluntary and religious groups in the early 1940's, most of them as experimental pilot projects. But as the schools gave evidence of meeting the migrants' urgent need for education, the States began to assume the responsibility for their operation as early as 1947.

During the summer of 1961, seven States (California, Colorado, New Jersey, New York, Ohio, Oregon and Pennsylvania) were providing financial assistance to school districts for the operation of summer schools for migrant children. In 1962 the State of Washington operated a pilot summer school for them, and Wisconsin operated summer sessions for all children to which they were eligible.

In spite of the fact that classes were held during the summer months when children were not forced to attend and when their wages were needed, the enrollments increased and many children returned the following years. Case studies in several of these States reveal that many children have been able to make up one or more grades of schooling. A 1962 report on the summer program in Oregon says that children who attend regularly for three weeks or more made scholastic gains of from two to four months, that two boys advanced a full grade in reading, and that all made some progress.

It has been estimated that 205 summer schools would be needed for the twenty

States using the largest number of migrant workers with children (Subcommittee hearings, 1961).

*　　*　　*

THE SALT LAKE TRIBUNE CRITICIZES TEACHER STRIKES (1964) From
Salt Lake Tribune, May 17, 1964.

Action of the Utah Education Association's House of Delegates calling a two-day "recess" in the public schools of the state can be regarded only with consternation and regret.

A "recess" called unilaterally by an employe group is really a strike. Thus the UEA leadership resorts to the prime weapon of trade unionism, a movement with which the National Education Association is locked in grim conflict.

STRIKES BY TEACHERS fall into the same category as strikes by doctors, hospital employees, police, firemen, sanitation workers and others engaged in necessary public service. Such walkouts make a mockery of the professional status which members claim.

The resolution calling for the strike over Monday and Tuesday ("to be made up") was taken to "protest the refusal" of Governor Clyde to act upon the recommendations of his school study committee, and "to give time for all teachers to meet in Salt Lake City on Tuesday, May 19, to determine, as a body, a further course of action."

The 600-odd member House of Delegates representing local teacher organizations also requested that the National Education Association "immediately impose national sanctions against the state of Utah. . . ."

If the NEA complies, teachers throughout the U.S. will be urged to follow customary union procedures and to refrain from accepting school positions in the state, thus aggravating an already complicated problem.

The group also urged the Governor's School Study Committee, which last week recommended a special legislative appropriation of six million dollars for Utah schools, to complete its final report.

WE CAN ONLY PRAY that cooler heads in the Utah Education Association membership will prevail and that the error in judgment of the House of Delegates will not be compounded. As the Tribune said in 1957 and again in 1963 when teacher strikes were threatened, the high calling of Utah's educators and their expressed concern for the children's welfare face an acid test.

Alternatives suggested by the UEA House of Delegates, to be placed before the 10,000 Utah educators, include "an indefinite extension of this recess," which would mean a strike to the finish; curtailment of summer programs; cutting the school year from 180 to 170 days, "thus concentrating available finances toward quality education during the lesser period," but without cutting pay of personnel.

Another alternative would be mass refusal to sign contracts until either the Legislature is called into special session to make the proposed emergency appropriation or the State Board of Education shortens the school year.

It is hard to see how compressing the school year would save funds of consequence or assure "quality education."

Since a large proportion of school operation budgets goes for salaries, the savings likely would be less than 1 per cent in most districts.

School funds are apportioned according to students in daily classroom attendance. With most Utah schools within a week or two of closing, it is hard to see how lost classroom time can be made up.

IT IS UNDERSTANDABLE that Utah teachers are angry and frustrated because the governor refused to follow the unanimous recommendations of his own study committee. A great deal of public sentiment doubtless swung to the teachers after this action. If the majority of Utah's 10,000 educators now go out on strike, however, it will only register callousness and result in erosion of their reputation.

The UEA membership is aware that Governor Clyde, wrong or right, is adamant. He will never call a special session during the remainder of his term. Even with initiative action, no relief is in sight until January, when a new governor, a completely new House of Representatives and half the Senate members take office. Instead of displaying anger and force with the strike weapon now, the Utah educators and their friends would be better advised to take their case to the people of Utah in the political arena this summer and fall.

During one New York school crisis, Max Lerner, himself a prominent teacher and articulate spokesman for education, wrote in his syndicated column:

"AMIDST THE CHARGES and countercharges, the pulling and pushing, it is the children who are in danger. . . . A bus strike is an inconvenience; a school strike is a disaster!

"The strike as a weapon just doesn't make sense here. There are plenty of opponents of public education across the nation. Any widespread and sustained use of the strike weapon will play directly into their hands."

A strike against the children and the public with attendant publicity and degeneration of Utah's reputation will not win friends and influence people wither at the polls or in the next State Legislature. It could prove to be a disastrous boomerang.

NEWS ACCOUNT OF DRUG USE IN THE PUBLIC SCHOOLS OF PALOS VERDES, CALIFORNIA (1968) From *Los Angeles Times*, August 18, 1968.

A two-way mirror overlooks the restroom of Palos Verdes High School, but school officials don't use it.

The mirror is there to catch students taking drugs, and the disciplinarians aren't watching because they believe the mushrooming drug problem on Palos Verdes Peninsula has a better solution.

But a resourceful and aggressive antidrug effort has failed to keep the area's problem, by no means a unique one, from spreading down to sixth graders.

Control has been hampered in part because the nature of life in the affluent community has given the drug problem some surprising aspects.

For example:

Fourteen-year-olds enforce parental protection of their drug use by threatening to turn themselves in. Parents fear the social ostracism which publicity in the local newspaper would bring, local youth counselors say.

Both high schools and intermediate schools are reluctant to inform parents about their children's drug activities because school officials fear libel suits, say police and counselors.

Peninsula children are so well off that young users give away marijuana and pills rather than selling them. "There's a communal feel to the stuff," says the Rev. Mel Knight, an active counselor. "One kid buys it one time and another the next time."

And the same children have so little sense of the illegality of their actions that they arrange to burglarize each other's houses for sleeping pills from the family medicine cabinets, according to Mr. Knight and others.

* * *

Palos Verdes and Rolling Hills high schools, where drug use surfaced over a year ago, now have a proportion of drug-experienced students which police estimate at 50% and counselors put at 75%. An estimated third of the total are habitual or "hard" users.

Last winter drug use spread to Margate Intermediate School (sixth through eighth grades) and was exposed in March when the Palos Verdes Peninsula News, a local paper, reported a marijuana party involving 35 Margate students.

Students without drug experience and counselors who have worked with users at Margate estimate that 300 of Margate's 1000 boys and girls have experimented with drugs since the beginning of the year, and approximately 50 are hard, even daily, users.

Most of the drugs which the 13- and 14-year-olds use are barbiturates—Nembutal, Seconal and Tuinal. Some, say counselors and police, inject methedrine into their veins with hypodermics, most often in the underside of their tongues to avoid detectable needle marks.

One group smoked marijuana in the morning while waiting for the school bus in order to arrive at school "already high," a participant reported.

Peninsula organizations reacted quickly when drug use in the area became public in 1967.

Four local churches quickly organized a "hot line." The line, designed for anyone in drug trouble, is a 24-hour answering service whose staffers listen to problems and refer callers to psychiatrists, ministers, or others for consultation depending on individual needs.

In urgent cases, help is dispatched immediately.

The Peninsula Council for Youth, which funds the hot line, also began a series of seminars for parents and students on drug abuse. Similar programs were set up informally by high school counselors.

News of the Margate drug problem, though it shocked parents, surprised neither the school nor the police.

When drugs first came onto the intermediate school campus, one science teacher who enjoyed the confidence of his pupils immediately discovered their involvement and began informal counseling, with the knowledge of the principal. Since then he has spent a great deal of his own time talking with users or potential users and visiting parents to tell them about their children's drug activities.

The school also held a parents' meeting, attended by 700, to inform parents of the extent of drug use at Margate.

Meanwhile, police were busy.

Palos Verdes police had heard rumors of drugs being sold by high school students to Margate youngsters as early as last November, according to Det. Sgt. Monte Newman, one of two PV narcotics detectives. The difficulty of gathering evidence by legal means and a hesitancy to arrest 13-year-olds restricted action, however.

"I can't grab (a suspect) and search him or I'll get sued," Newman said.

Police also cooperated with school and hotline counselors by arresting young users to frighten them but not filing charges. Since May the arrests of key pushers on the peninsula has effectively curtailed drug use among the youngest offenders, Newman said, since they are not old enough to drive and depend on local contacts for supply.

Doctors and knowledgeable counselors are particularly worried that the drug problem has reached 13- and 14-year-olds.

"Drugs at this adolescent stage are a hell of a danger," says Dr. Alan Schneiderman, a San Pedro physician who treated one young user. Drug use becomes "like a new club," he says, "an additional center of antagonism" against parents and school authorities.

In the case he treated, Schneiderman said barbiturates and Dexedrine "magnified" the resentments and assertions of independence normal to adolescent development, creating an unbridgeable gap between child and parents. He also said his subject was constantly depressed except while under the influence of drugs.

Police, school officials and counselors agree that parents are their major obstacle. They cite parental laxity and neglect as major reasons for the spread of drug use into the younger classes.

"Parents in this community are delinquent," Mr. Knight puts it bluntly.

He argues that, at the intermediate school level, only parents have sufficient authority to control their children, since the jurisdiction of both school and police is limited.

Hyperactive as well as inactive parents create difficulties, however.

Counselors say a few parents get so angry at their children for using drugs that they make rehabilitation impossible, isolating the offenders from expert help as well as suspect classmates. One parent of a 14-year-old girl who found herself in serious trouble with barbiturates and Dexedrine (a stimulant) removed her from school before her graduation and threatened to make spot checks on her at school next fall.

The same parents made counseling efforts at school more difficult by demanding rigid policing and searches on school grounds, officials say. One similar parent proposed two-way mirrors at Margate.

*　　*　　*

"We're trying to keep from driving this underground," says Gerald Evans, the principal of Margate. He and most other peninsula counselors advocate education and rebuilding of parental authority as the best means of treating the roots of the problem. They say parents demonstrate ignorance about drugs in general and their children's activities in particular.

Counselors and physicians identify massive social pressure as a reason many of the Margate youngsters start taking drugs, but the students themselves disagree. One

8th grader who said he had never taken drugs said he had never been pressured to do so. "The kids that take drugs keep them to themselves," he said.

Every Margate student interviewed, however, knew that some of his classmates took drugs, and most knew which classmates and which drugs.

"We'd never tell," one said. "We'd get beat up."

Drugs are such a common topic that, as a joke, students in class occasionally make counterfeit Dexedrine pills from chalk and pass them around.

Although only about 50 of the Margate youngsters and perhaps a third of the high school students take drugs regularly, the users seem to be those who used to indulge in other forbidden activities. Sgt. Newman said trouble with under-age drinking on the peninsula has almost disappeared since the advent of drugs there.

*   *   *

Counselors say Margate is not the only intermediate school with drugs.

They agree with police and Margate officials that the major source for the young users is older siblings who attend the two local high schools. One counselor says there is "a new hero ethic" which the high schools have passed down to the intermediates in which straight (non-user) students are referred to as "lame."

Hotline representatives say they have counseled young drug users from four separate intermediate schools on the peninsula, including Margate.

Margate, they say, is unusual not for the extent of its problem but for its admission of the difficulty and its attempts to deal with it. Police and all agencies working on the drug problem in Palos Verdes uniformly commend the school for its cooperation and desire to clear up its trouble, despite unfavorable exposure and harsh parental criticism.

LETTER FROM A PRINCIPAL OF AN INNER-CITY SCHOOL (1969)   From *The Washington Monthly*, vol. I (Oct. 1969), p. 32.

Paul Junior High School
Washington, D.C.
September 9, 1969

DEAR PARENTS:

I want you to know that we here at Paul are deeply concerned about the safety of your children.

Several things have been done to assure us that every person in the building is given greater protection. They are as indicated below:

1. Self-locking doors with panic bars have been installed on all entrances.
2. All gates to the playground are locked at 9:30 A.M. so that entrance to the building can be gained through the main entrance only.
3. Increased staff surveillance of buildings and grounds.

We have further requested that the Juvenile Court handle criminal attacks as criminal attacks and not as the mere exuberance of youth.

We have also urged that the following measures be taken immediately:

RE-APPRAISAL
1951–1973

3201

By the Superintendent of Personnel:

1. Provide two additional custodians to monitor entrances.
2. Provide a night watchman.

By the Chief of Police:

1. Establish short beats in the immediate area (to include building and playground) of all schools.

By the Teachers:

1. Limit hall passes to the absolute minimum.
2. Inform students that the punishment for threats and/or violence is immediate suspension and possible expulsion or incarceration.
3. Inform students of the seriousness of jeopardizing building security by opening latched outside doors, the penalty for which is immediate suspension.

Very sincerely yours,

/s/EDWARD ARMSTEAD, JR.

Principal

ARTHUR R. JENSEN ON INTELLIGENCE AND SCHOLASTIC ACHIEVEMENT (1969) From "How Much Can We Boost I.Q. and Scholastic Achievement?," *Harvard Educational Review*, vol. XXXIX, pp. 2-5, 78-82, 103-04, 115-17.

The Failure of Compensatory Education

Compensatory education has been tried and it apparently has failed.

Compensatory education has been practiced on a massive scale for several years in many cities across the nation. It began with auspicious enthusiasm and high hopes of educators. It had unprecedented support from Federal funds. It had theoretical sanction from social scientists espousing the major underpinning of its rationale: the "deprivation hypothesis," according to which academic lag is mainly the result of social, economic, and educational deprivation and discrimination—an hypothesis that has met with wide, uncritical acceptance in the atmosphere of society's growing concern about the plight of minority groups and the economically disadvantaged.

*   *   *

Why has there been such uniform failure of compensatory programs wherever they have been tried? What has gone wrong? In other fields, when bridges do not stand, when aircraft do not fly, when machines do not work, when treatments do not cure, despite all conscientious efforts on the part of many persons to make them do so, one begins to question the basic assumptions, principles, theories, and hypotheses that guide one's efforts. Is it time to follow suit in education?

The theory that has guided most of these compensatory education programs, sometimes explicitly, sometimes implicitly, has two main complementary facets: one might be called the "average children concept," the other the "social deprivation hypothesis."

The "average children" concept is essentially the belief that all children, except for a rare few born with severe neurological defects, are basically very much alike in their mental development and capabilities, and that their apparent differences in these characteristics as manifested in school are due to rather superficial differences in children's upbringing at home, their preschool and out-of-school experiences, motivations and interests, and the educational influences of their family background. All children are viewed as basically more or less homogeneous, but are seen to differ in school performance because when they are out of school they learn or fail to learn certain things that may either help them or hinder them in their school work. If all children could be treated more alike early enough, long before they come to school, then they could all learn from the teacher's instruction at about the same pace and would all achieve at much the same level, presumably at the "average" or above on the usual grade norms.

The "social deprivation hypothesis" is the allied belief that those children of ethnic minorities and the economically poor who achieve "below average" in school do so mainly because they begin school lacking certain crucial experiences which are prerequisites for school learning—perceptual, attentional, and verbal skills, as well as the self-confidence, self-direction, and teacher-oriented attitudes conducive to achievement in the classroom. And they lack the parental help and encouragement needed to promote academic achievement throughout their schooling. The chief aim of preschool and compensatory programs, therefore, is to make up for these environmental lacks as quickly and intensively as possible by providing the assumedly appropriate experiences, cultural enrichment, and training in basic skills of the kind presumably possessed by middle-class "majority" children of the same age.

The success of the effort is usually assessed in one or both of two ways: by gains in IQ and in scholastic achievement. The common emphasis on gains in IQ is probably attributable to the fact that it can be more efficiently "measured" than scholastic achievement, especially if there is no specific "achievement" to begin with. The IQ test can be used at the very beginning of Headstart, kindergarten, or first grade as a "pre-test" against which to assess "post-test" gains. IQ gains, if they occur at all, usually occur rapidly, while achievement is a long-term affair. And probably most important, the IQ is commonly interpreted as indicative of a more general kind of intellectual ability than is reflected by the acquisition of specific scholastic knowledge and skills. Since the IQ is known to predict scholastic performance better than any other single measurable attribute of the child, it is believed, whether rightly or wrongly, that if the child's IQ can be appreciably raised, academic achievement by and large will take care of itself, given normal motivation and standard instruction. Children with average or above-average IQs generally do well in school without much special attention. So the remedy deemed logical for children who would do poorly in school is to boost their IQs up to where they can perform like the majority—in short to make them all at least "average children." Stated so bluntly, the remedy may sound rather grim, but this is in fact essentially what we are attempting in our special programs of pre-school enrichment and compensatory education. This simple theme, with only slight embellishments, can be found repeated over and over again in the vast recent literature on the psychology and education of children called culturally disadvantaged.

So here is where our diagnosis should begin—with the concept of the IQ: how it came to be what it is; what it "really" is; what makes it vary from one individual to another; what can change it, and by what amount.

*   *   *

RACE DIFFERENCES

The important distinction between the individual and population must always be kept clearly in mind in any discussion of racial differences in mental abilities or any other behavioral characteristics. Whenever we select a person for some special educational purpose, whether for special instruction in a grade-school class for children with learning problems, or for a "gifted" class with an advanced curriculum, or for college attendance, or for admission to graduate training or a professional school, we are selecting an individual, and we are selecting him and dealing with him as an individual for reasons of his individuality. Similarly, when we employ someone, or promote someone in his occupation, or give some special award or honor to someone for his accomplishments, we are doing this to an individual. The variables of social class, race, and national origin are correlated so imperfectly with any of the valid criteria on which the above decisions should depend, or, for that matter, with any behavioral characteristic, that these background factors are irrelevant as a basis for dealing with individuals—as students, as employees, as neighbors. Furthermore, since, as far as we know, the full range of human talents is represented in all the major races of man and in all socioeconomic levels, it is unjust to allow the mere fact of an individual's racial or social background to affect the treatment accorded to him. All persons rightfully must be regarded on the basis of their individual qualities and merits, and all social, educational, and economic institutions must have built into them the mechanisms for insuring and maximizing the treatment of persons according to their individual behavior.

If a society completely believed and practiced the ideal of treating every person as an individual, it would be hard to see why there should be any problems about "race" per se. There might still be problems concerning poverty, unemployment, crime, and other social ills, and, given the will, they could be tackled just as any other problems that require rational methods for solution. But if this philosophy prevailed in practice, there would not need to be a "race problem."

The question of race differences in intelligence comes up not when we deal with individuals as individuals, but when certain identifiable groups or subcultures within the society are brought into comparison with one another as groups or populations. It is only when the groups are disproportionately represented in what are commonly perceived as the most desirable and the least desirable social and occupational roles in a society that the question arises concerning average differences among groups. Since much of the current thinking behind civil rights, fair employment, and equality of educational opportunity appeals to the fact that there is a disproportionate representation of different racial groups in the various levels of the educational, occupational, and socioeconomic hierarchy, we are forced to examine all the possible reasons for this inequality among racial groups in the attainments and rewards generally valued by all groups within our society. To what extent can such inequalities be attributed to unfairness in society's multiple selection processes? ("Unfair" meaning that selection is influenced by intrinsically irrelevant criteria, such as skin color, racial or national origin, etc.) And to what extent are these inequalities attributable to really relevant selection criteria which apply equally to all individuals but at the same time select disproportionately between some racial groups because there exist, in fact, real average differences among the groups—differences in the population distributions of those characteristics which are indisputably relevant to educational and occupational performance? This is certainly one of the most important questions confronting our nation today. The answer, which can be found only through unfettered research, has enormous consequences for the welfare of all, particularly of minorities whose plight is now in the foreground of public attention. A preordained, doctrinaire stance with regard to this issue hinders the achievement of a scientific understanding of the problem. To rule out of court, so to speak, any reasonable hypotheses on purely ideological grounds is to argue that static ignorance is preferable to increasing our knowledge of reality. I strongly disagree with those who believe in searching for the truth by scientific means only under certain circumstances and eschew this course in favor of ignorance under other circumstances, or who believe that the results of inquiry on some subjects cannot be entrusted to the public but should be kept the guarded possession of a scientific elite. Such attitudes, in my opinion, represent a danger to free inquiry and, consequently, in the long run, work to the disadvantage of society's general welfare. "No holds barred" is the best formula for scientific inquiry. One does not decree beforehand which phenomena cannot be studied or which questions cannot be answered.

GENETIC ASPECTS OF RACIAL DIFFERENCES.

No one, to my knowledge, questions the role of environmental factors, including influences from past history, in determining at least some of the variance between racial groups in standard measures of intelligence, school performance, and occupational status. The current literature on the culturally disadvantaged abounds with discussion—some of it factual, some of it fanciful—of how a host of environmental factors depresses cognitive development and performance. I recently co-edited a book which is largely concerned with the environmental aspects of disadvantaged minorities. . . . But the possible importance of genetic factors in racial behavioral differences has been greatly ignored, almost to the point of being a tabooed subject, just as were the topics of venereal disease and birth control a generation or so ago.

My discussions with a number of geneticists concerning the questions of a genetic basic of differences among races in mental abilities have revealed to me a number of rather consistently agreed-upon points which can be summarized in general terms as follows: Any groups which have been geographically or socially isolated from one another for many generations are practically certain to differ in their gene pools, and consequently are likely to show differences in any pheno-typic characteristics having high heritability. This is practically axiomatic, according to the geneticists with whom I have spoken. Races are said to be "breeding populations," which is to say that matings within the group have a much higher probability than matings outside the group. Races are more technically viewed by geneticists as populations having different distributions of gene frequencies. These genetic differences are manifested in virtually every anatomical, physiological, and biochemical comparison one can make between representative samples of identifiable racial groups. . . . There is no reason to suppose that the brain should be exempt from this generalization. (Racial differences in the relative frequencies of various blood constituents have probably been the most thoroughly studied so far.)

But what about behavior? If it can be measured and shown to have a genetic component, it would be regarded, from a genetic standpoint, as no different from other human characteristics. There seems to be little question that racial differences in genetically conditional behavioral characteristics, such as mental abilities, should exist, just as physical differences. The real questions, geneticists tell me, are not whether there are or are not genetic racial differences that affect behavior, because there undoubtedly are. The proper questions to ask, from a scientific standpoint, are: What is the direction of the difference? What is the magnitude of the difference? And what is the significance of the difference—medically, socially, educationally, or from whatever standpoint that may be relevant to the characteristic in question? A difference is important only within a specific context. For example, one's blood type in the ABO system is unimportant until one needs a transfusion. And some genetic differences are apparently of no importance with respect to any context as far as anyone has been able to discover—for example, differences in the size and shape of ear lobes. The idea that all genetic differences have arisen or persisted only as a result of natural selection, by conferring some survival or adaptive benefit on their possessors, is no longer generally held. There appear to be many genetic differences, or polymorphisms, which confer no discernible advantages to survival.

NEGRO INTELLIGENCE AND SCHOLASTIC PERFORMANCE.

Negroes in the United States are disproportionately represented among groups identified as culturally or educationally disadvantaged. This, plus the fact that Negroes constitute by far the largest racial minority in the United States, has for many years focused attention on Negro intelligence.

. . . The basic data are well known: on the average, Negroes test about 1 standard deviation (15 IQ points) below the average of the white population in IQ, and this finding is fairly uniform across the 81 different tests of intellectual ability used in the studies reviewed by Shuey. This magnitude of difference gives a median overlap of 15 percent, meaning that 15 percent of the Negro population exceeds the white average. In terms of proportions of variance, if the numbers of Negroes and whites were equal, the differences between racial groups would account for 23 percent of the total variance, but—an important point—the differences within groups would account for 77 percent of the total variance. When gross socioeconomic level is controlled, the average difference reduces to about 11 IQ points . . . which, it should be recalled, is about the same spread as the average difference between siblings in the same family. So-called "culture-free" or "culture-fair" tests tend to give Negroes slightly lower scores, on the average, than more conventional IQ tests such as the Stanford-Binet and Wechsler scales. Also, as a group, Negroes perform somewhat more poorly on those subtests which tap abstract abilities. The majority of studies show that Negroes perform relatively better on verbal than on non-verbal intelligence tests.

In tests of scholastic achievement, also judging from the massive data of the Coleman study . . . Negroes score about 1 standard deviation (SD) below the average for whites and Orientals and considerably less than 1 SD below other disadvantaged minorities tested in the Coleman study—Puerto Rican, Mexican-American, and American Indian. The 1 SD decrement in Negro performance is fairly constant throughout the period from grades 1 through 12.

Another aspect of the distribution of IQs in the Negro population is their lesser variance in comparison to the white distribution. This shows up in most of the studies reviewed by Shuey. The best single estimate is probably the estimate based on a large normative study of Stanford-Binet IQs of Negro school children in five Southeastern states, by Kennedy, Van De Riet, and White (1963). They found the SD of Negro children's IQs to be 12.4, as compared with 16.4 in the white normative sample. The Negro distribution thus has only about 60 percent as much variance (i.e., SD^2) as the white distribution.

There is an increasing realization among students of the psychology of the disadvantaged that the discrepancy in their average performance cannot be completely or directly attributed to discrimination or inequalities in education. It seems not unreasonable, in view of the fact that intelligence variation has a large genetic component, to hypothesize that genetic factors may play a part in this picture. But such an hypothesis is anathema to many social scientists. The idea that the lower average intelligence and scholastic performance of Negroes could involve, not only environmental, but also genetic, factors has indeed been strongly denounced. . . . But it has been neither contradicted nor discredited by evidence.

The fact that a reasonable hypothesis has not been rigorously proved does not mean that it should be summarily dismissed. It only means that we need more appropriate research for putting it to the test. I believe such definitive research is entirely possible but has not yet been done. So all we are left with are various lines of evidence, no one of which is definitive alone, but which, viewed all together, make it a not unreasonable hypothesis that genetic factors are strongly implicated in the average Negro-white intelligence difference. The preponderance of the evidence is, in my opinion, less consistent with a strictly environmental hypothesis than with a genetic hypothesis, which, of course, does not exclude the influence of environment or its interaction with genetic factors.

We can be accused of superficiality in our thinking about this issue, I believe, if we simply dismiss a genetic hypothesis without having seriously thought about the relevance of typical findings such as the following:

FAILURE TO EQUATE NEGROES AND WHITES IN IQ AND SCHOLASTIC ABILITY

No one has yet produced any evidence based on a properly controlled study to show that representative samples of Negro and White children can be equalized in intellectual ability through statistical control of environment and education.

HOTHOUSE OR FERTILIZER?

There seems to be little doubt that a deprived environment can stunt intellectual development and that immersion in a good environment in early childhood can largely overcome the effects of deprivation, permitting the individual's genetic potential to be reflected in his performance. But can special enrichment and instructional procedures go beyond the prevention or amelioration of stunting? As Vandenberg . . . has asked, does enrichment act in a manner similar to a hothouse, forcing an early bloom which is nevertheless no different from a normal bloom, or does it act more like a fertilizer, producing bigger and better yields? There can be little question about the hothouse aspect of early stimulation and instruction. Within limits, children can learn many things at an earlier age than that at which they are normally taught in school. This is especially true of forms of associative learning which are mainly a function of time spent in the learning activity rather than of the development of more complex cognitive structures. While most children, for example, do not learn the alphabet until 5 or 6 years of age, they are fully capable of doing so at about 3, but it simply requires more time spent in learning. The cognitive structures involved are relatively simple as compared with, say, learning to copy a triangle or a diamond. Teaching a 3-year-old to copy a diamond is practically impossible; at five it is extremely difficult; at seven the child apparently needs no "teaching"—he copies the diamond easily. And the child of five who has been taught to copy the diamond seems to have learned something different from what the seven-year-old "knows" who can do it without being "taught." Though the final performance of the five-year-old and the seven-year-old may look alike, we know that the cognitive structures underlying their performance are different. Certain basic skills can be acquired either associatively by rote learning or cognitively by conceptual learning, and what superficially may appear to be the same performance may be acquired in preschoolers at an associative level, while at a conceptual level in older children. Both the four-year-old and the six-year-old may know that 2 + 2 = 4, but this knowledge can be associative or cognitive. Insufficient attention has been given in preschool programs so far to the shift from associative to cognitive learning. The preschooler's capacity for associative learning is already quite well developed, but his cognitive or conceptual capacities are as yet rudimentary and will undergo their period of most rapid change between about five and seven years of age (White, 1965). We need to know more about what children can learn before age five that will transfer positively to later learning. Does learning something on an associative level facilitate or hinder learning the same content on a conceptual level?

While some preschool and compensatory programs have demonstrated earlier than normal learning of certain skills, the evidence for accelerating cognitive development or the speed of learning is practically nil. But usually this distinction is not made between sheer performance and the nature of the cognitive structures which support the gains in performance, and so the research leaves the issue in doubt. The answer to such questions is to be found in the study of the kinds and amount of transfer that result from some specific learning. The capacity for transfer of training is one of the essential aspects of what we mean by intelligence. The IQ gains reported in enrichment studies appear to be gains more in what Cattell called 'crystallized,' in contrast to "fluid," intelligence. This is not to say that gains of this type are not highly worthwhile. But having a clearer conception of just what the gains consist of will give us a better idea of how they can be most effectively followed up and of what can be expected of their effects on later learning and achievement.

* * *

Thus, ordinary IQ tests are not seen as being "unfair" in the sense of yielding inaccurate or invalid measures for the many disadvantaged children who obtain low scores. If they are unfair, it is because they tap only one part of the total spectrum of mental abilities and do not reveal that aspect of mental ability which may be the disadvantaged child's strongest point—the ability for associative learning.

Since traditional methods of classroom instruction were evolved in populations having a predominantly middle-class pattern of abilities, they put great emphasis on cognitive learning rather than associate learning. And in the post-Sputnik era, education has seen an increased emphasis on cognitive and conceptual learning, much to the disadvantage of many children whose mode of learning is predominantly associative. Many of the basic skills can be learned by various means, and an educational system that puts inordinate emphasis on only one mode or style of learning will obtain meager results from the children who do not fit this pattern. At present, I believe that the educational system—even as it falteringly attempts to help the disadvantaged—operates in such a way as to maximize the importance of Level II (i.e., intelligence or g) as a source of variance in scholastic performance. Too often, if a child does not learn the school subject matter when taught in a way that depends largely on being average or above average on g, he does not learn at all, so that we find high school students who have failed to learn basic skills which they could easily have learned many years earlier by means that do not depend much on g. It may well be true that many children today are confronted in our schools with an educational philosophy and methodology which were mainly shaped in the past, entirely without any roots in these children's genetic and cultural heritage. The educational system was never allowed to evolve in such a way as to maximize the actual potential for learning that is latent in these children's patterns of abilities. If a child cannot show that he "understands" the meaning of $1 + 1 = 2$ in some abstract, verbal, cognitive sense, he is, in effect, not allowed to go on to learn $2 + 2 = 4$. I am reasonably convinced that all the basic scholastic skills can be learned by children with normal Level I learning ability, provided the instructional techniques do not make g (i.e., Level II) the *sine qua non* of being able to learn. Educational researchers must discover and devise teaching methods that capitalize on existing abilities for the acquisition of those basic skills which students will need in order to get good jobs when they leave school. I believe there will be greater rewards for all concerned if we further explore different types of abilities and modes of learning, and seek to discover how these various abilities can serve the aims of education. This seems more promising than acting as though only one pattern of abilities, emphasizing g, can succeed educationally, and therefore trying to inculcate this one ability pattern in all children.

If the theories I have briefly outlined here become fully substantiated, the next step will be to develop the techniques by which school learning can be most effectively achieved in accordance with different patterns of ability. By all means, schools must discover g wherever it exists and see to it that its educational correlates are fully encouraged and cultivated. There can be little doubt that certain educational and occupational attainments depend more upon g than upon any other single ability. But schools must also be able to find ways of utilizing other strengths in children whose major strength is not of the cognitive variety. One of the great and relatively untapped reservoirs of mental ability in the disadvantaged, it appears from our research, is the basic ability to learn. We can do more to marshal this strength for educational purposes.

If diversity of mental abilities, as of most other human characteristics, is a basic fact of nature, as the evidence indicates, and if the ideal of universal education is to be successfully pursued, it seems a reasonable conclusion that schools and society must provide a range and diversity of educational methods, programs, and goals, and of occupational opportunities, just as wide as the range of human abilities. Accordingly, the ideal of equality of educational opportunity should not be interpreted as uniformity of facilities, instructional techniques, and educational aims for all children. Diversity rather than uniformity of approaches and aims would seem to be the key to making education rewarding for children of different patterns of ability. The reality of individual differences thus need not mean educational rewards for some children and frustration and defeat for others.

AN ANSWER TO ARTHUR R. JENSEN (1969)

From William F. Brazziel, "A Letter From The South," *Harvard Educational Review*, vol. XXXIX, pp. 348–50, 353–56.

Sirs:

Thirteen years ago plaintiffs brought suit in Federal District Court to integrate the Louisiana public schools. The main argument of the defense attorneys and the superintendent of public instruction was that "white teachers could not understand the Nigra mind" and, therefore, would not be able to teach them effectively in integrated classrooms. The defense quoted heavily from the theories of white intellectual supremacy as expounded by Henry Garrett and Audrey Shuey.

Last week, a scant five days after Arthur Jensen made headlines in Virginia papers regarding inferiority of black people as measured by IQ tests, defense attorneys and their expert witnesses fought a suit in Federal District Court to integrate Greensville and Caroline County schools. Their main argument was that "white teachers could not understand the Nigra mind" and that the Nigra children should be admitted to the white schools on the basic of standardized tests. Those who failed to make a certain score would be assigned to all black remedial schools where "teachers who understood them could work with them." The defense in this case quoted heavily from the theories of white intellectual supremacy as expounded by Arthur Jensen.

It will help not one bit for Jensen or the HER editorial board to protest that they did not intend for Jensen's article to be used in this way. For in addition to superiority in performing conceptual cluster tricks on test sheets, the hard line segregationist is also vastly superior in his ability to bury qualifying phrases and demurrers and in his ability to distort and slant facts and batter his undereducated clientele into a complete state of hysteria where race is concerned.

Jensen and the HER editorial board will modestly admit that they have superior intellects and I am sure they realized the consequences of their actions. Questions now arise as to why they decided to raise this issue, in this way, and at this time.

Fortunately, doubts about the ability of black and yellow people to master war, finance, science and technology are waning rapidly in both white and black minds. The imprecision of standardized testing is now clear to most literate people and the criminal use to which they are put in schools is also becoming clearer. Black history has made people aware that white people did *not* give America such things as the stoplight, the shoe last, heart operations and sugar refining but that black people did this. That John Smith did not develop corn and tobacco but learned to grow these crops from the Indians. And the beat goes on. People are now witnessing with their very eyes the fact of black youth finally given a half of a chance at education and jobs and being able to make exotic formulas for bombs and napalm as well as anyone else. As a result of all of this, I think the present set-to might be the last go-round for white supremacy psychological theory.

I would hope the Jensenites could alter their stance and approach and try to bring some good out of this situation after all. They might work their way out of ethnic learning styles by broadening their research to include all ethnic groups. We have some rather learned men in our area who believe that English-Americans are atop the pyramid of abstract learning abilities with Welsh, German, French, Belgian, Norwegian, Swiss, Finnish, Danish and Swedish occupying the next nine rungs in the order listed. After the top ten have been given their just due, these gentlemen give a smattering of attention to the rest of Europe and proceed to ignore the rest of the world. The Jensenites might try to clear this up in some way. They might even look into intra-group differences within the top ten. I would suspect that many would be found and that it would be healthy to make this known at professional meetings, in the journals and in the news media.

We also have a religious wing in this group who suspect that English-American children who are brought up in Southern Baptist churches perceive things differently and might really deserve the top spot upon the pyramid. Southern-English-American-Episcopalians regard these assertions with a great deal of amusement. But who really knows? We all will if the ethnic learning line of research is extended logically to include every possible ethnic, regional and religious stock.

Also in the status research vein, we need research on the effects of racism and caste status on learning. The Jensenites can provide this by following Robert Coles and others around in Mississippi and South Carolina to study the parasitic worm and starvation situation among black children. Autopsies of a few who died might yield valuable evidence on the brain damages wrought by malnourishment. The team could change themselves into black people ala John Griffin and run the hostility gauntlet as they tried to find some information in the local library. Or the hilarity gauntlet as they made application for a professional or skilled job. They could fly as black men to Boston or Oakland and make the same applications to the craft union nearest the airport. Or they could try to get a tenured appointment in the Harvard Graduate School of Education, or a spot on the HER editorial board, or simply a rank higher than assistant professor among the 7,000 member Harvard faculty.

The Jensenites could give the same black injections to their children, enroll them in a different school and record what happens to them. Children learn efficiently if listening, reading, discussion, peer-group interaction, library resources and teacher-pupil interaction are all used efficiently. The investigators might be very interested in the change in quality in the last four areas for their now black off-spring and to see who is to blame and how the situation can be improved. To add a spicy dimension, low IQ scores could be substituted in the transfer folders.

Creation of multi-ethnic and multi-racial tests would also be a method of bringing some good out of the situation. If the only way to make exactly the same score on test items is to be of the same race, economic class, ethnic stock, and religious persuasion as the committee that developed the instrument, then we either must make intensive efforts to inter-marry, re-distribute income and institute religious purges and programs in this country or we must try to integrate more multi-racial and multi-ethnic material into the instruments. Said in the words of Dr. Nathan Wright, the Newark black power theorist, we must try to "dehonkify" the instruments.

Jensen's major error, I believe, was his inconsistency in following a definite line of reasoning regarding the separation of gene linkage and pre-postnatal ravages of protein malnutrition. The latter is the most intensively researched thesis these days with NIH teams leading the way. Jensen did not even mention this line of research which (together with research in infant stimulation) I believe has answers for 42% mental retardation found in low-low (Jensen's level V) income black children and a lot of the other differences. In a half-starved brain like these kids have, how are we to really know if high or low IQ genes were linked? Jensen did not tell us how.

Jensen calls compensatory education a failure. So did reporters of the *Washington Post* who in turn received and printed a report by the ESEA staff of the Virginia

Department of Education calling their allegations inaccurate and stating that they had hard data to back their claims. In response to a request for same, I received tables for statewide pre-post testing of 10,200 pupils in 15 school districts for 1967–68. The data show average month's increase in grade equivalency per month of 1.06 of instruction or an average overgain in achievement of more than half a year per pupil as a result of compensatory education. Children scoring in the lowest decile had decreased from 41% to 28%. In the second quartile the number jumped from 8% to 16% and the drop-rate had decreased by 63%. The officials noted that age-grade decrement had been scotched and that they believe that they had convincing evidence that their Title I program was a success. And this from one of the more conservative states in the Union and one with a record of slow starts in educational innovations. School people, it seems, are just now learning how to run compensatory programs. Or really try to. The first report to the President of the National Advisory Council on Disadvantaged Children noted this reluctance to really plan and implement on the part of many school systems. They quoted one superintendent who stated flatly that "it was useless and a waste of money to teach those jigs anything." Let us all hope he has since initiated a good program and that he doesn't read Jensen's article.

In drawing conclusions from 200-300 comparative studies of black-white IQ, Jensen failed to consider that all of the pre-1948 studies and most of the post-'48 studies failed to give attention to the deprivation axioms made popular by the University of Chicago group (Davis, Eels, et al) and until recently almost no psychometrists gave attention to the fact that white examiners in a black classroom are, in many, many cases, getting an invalid test performance. Their color, voice, manner, gestures turn many kids off, and they refuse to try. This phenomenon is growing in intensity and must be dealt with. How are you going to have a valid test session with kids who read in black papers and magazines that white researchers are sending their kids to Harvard by over-studying the black communities with federal grants? Or with kids who received a leaflet from a community group blasting tests as an "unfair tool of colonialists who control the black community"?

I believe that Jensen is wrong and I hope he does not do too much damage. I believe the HER editorial board should publish the rebuttals in the same issue with future attacks on the Negro. Rumors abound that attacks on the Negro church are planned. This will scotch the sensationalism of the press caused by the lag in time between issues. Indeed, the rebuttals will never be read by reporters, much less printed.

Jensen failed to take into consideration the black infant mortality rate as a factor in black infant supremacy on the motoric area of the Bayley Scales. This rate is three times that of white infants. Black kids must literally undergo a survival of the fittest test to be born, once conceived, and to stay alive.

Jensen has a serious contradiction in his analysis of tests and studies of black IQ. After offering half dozen or so studies to document his thesis that black kids don't do as well on IQ tests as white kids, Jensen closes his paper by stating that IQ tests fail to measure the full potential of black kids.

Jensen failed to consider the 1969 report of the Research and Evaluation Branch of Project Head Start in writing off Head Start gains as transitory. According to this report of several studies of the maintenance of gains, the investigators concluded that the gains were maintained when the children were enrolled in first grades or kindergartens in middle-class schools. Edmund Gordon of Teachers College and John McDavid of Miami led the team which wrote this report.

Jensen, like other psychologists, is completely incapable of un-raveling what would have to be un-raveled in order to separate genetic from environmental influences where American black and white people are concerned, to wit:

1. If 90% of the black people in America have ancestors that include white people, how can we tell when black genes or white genes make for a wrong mark on a test score sheet?

2. If a large per cent of white people have black ancestors, who are they? Are their samples controlled for this factor? Which genes, black or white, make for right marks on a test score sheet?

3. How can we parse out the effects of brain damage, brain stunting (due to malnutrition) and lack of early stimulation? Which accounts for a wrong mark on the test score sheet?

4. How can we parse and measure the degree of access and welcome of black people to cultural learnings?

5. How can we parse and measure the interest in and acceptance of the white "way of life" by black mothers and children? One can't get good scores on a "way of life" test like IQ unless one lives and accepts this life fully.

6. How can we develop indices which show comparability of school strengths, weaknesses and emphases? The school assessment study by Tyler's group is just getting underway over loud cries from many school people.

Jensen failed to consider the learning styles of black parents and the origins of these learning styles when he made white-black comparisons on associative and problem-solving learning. If you go to many rural schools in the south today, you will find the associative type of learning proceeding as it has for many, many years—for both races. This is the learning heritage of most big city black parents. They pass this style on to the kids early and it shows up in test profiles. If conceptual learning is viewed as a gradual acculturation process and offered early in school careers, these kids can be made to think. Jensen's exhortations to teachers to rely completely on associative learning might preclude this ever becoming a reality, however. Before any more articles are published, I think Jensen should do more work in the area of black history, demography and culture and that he should try to get into the area of racism and isolation and the big role they play in differences. There really is merit in his actually taking the black injections and getting first-hand information. He would only have to be a black man for two months.

Jensen's "g factor," the main basis of his claims for white supremacy, cannot be accepted as the mysterious phenomenon he postulates. Even little children now know from their television science that if something really exists, scientists will isolate it and measure it—especially before making serious conclusions about it.

I believe Jensen made two good points. One is that IQ tests don't show the full learning potential of kids who are poor and black. I was happy to learn that he had invented a test which does a better job. We should all buy it. He should make millions. The other is that intensive instruction rather than "cultural enrichment" is necessary to make these kids learn if they are locked in neighborhood schools. Unlike Jensen, I believe that they can proceed from associative learning to abstract reasoning if the instruction gradually brings them to this point. And even with this, I believe black kids will continue to think and score test items differently until full equality is achieved. Black kids screen out much of the curriculum and perceive the rest differently. Consider perceptions of Tarzan and the British Empire, for examples. Of course some black nationalists feel that it is a blessing that black people don't think like white people. As long as they can handle modern technology, make war, manipulate stocks, etc., I don't guess it really matters.

I believe the most potent strategy in the end will prove to be a combination of early stimulation and imprinting, and integrated schools with teachers who are free of racial and social class prejudices. IQ tests will also be eliminated from the schools. This is the strategy on which Neil Sullivan based his cross-bussing operations for the Berkeley schools. This may account for some of Jensen's concerns and reservations and perhaps, for his article. Pettigrew and others presented evidence in their work for the Civil Rights Commission that the earlier black children were placed in integrated schools, the closer they came to white norms on achievements tests. In turn, the white children came closer to perfection in their social learnings while losing no ground in test proficiency. The black children pick up the mysteries of Jensen's "g-factor" through association, I suppose, while the white children pick up the mysteries of "soul."

DESCRIPTION OF BUREAUCRATIC PATHOLOGY IN NEW YORK CITY
(1969)   From David Rogers, *110 Livingston Street* (New York, 1969), pp. 266–68.

School officials desperately need more explanations for their failures and more suggestions for reversing such failures than they have received thus far. Some are beginning to realize that time is running out on them, and that they had better reform the schools quickly before ghetto unrest leads to rioting, to demands to take over the schools, and the white middle class exodus contributes to the final downfall of big-city public education.

The temptation in diagnosing how the schools have failed is to search for scapegoats. Actually, the entire institution of public education is to blame, as are the present conditions of urban life that it confronts.

Nobody can make the system work if the bureaucratic structure is not radically altered. State education laws, traditions, rules, and interlocking administrative relationships victimize anybody who comes into contact with the system—parents with legitimate complaints, people applying for teaching licenses, city officials developing community renewal programs, publishers struggling to get their textbooks and readers into the classrooms even after the principals and teachers have accepted them, teachers and principals waiting months to receive needed supplies from headquarters, and pupils in the classrooms. To maneuver through the bureaucratic maze of the New York City school system takes more patience and political connections than most people can ever hope to have.

It is almost impossible to innovate in the institution. Policy statements are only the beginning of the process. Those who make the decisions, even if they were more eager for reform, must negotiate with the professional staff to secure compliance with their directives. They must secure efficient coordination of the actions of all units carrying out the plans, and they must provide rewards and punishments that will ensure compliance, institute performance measures, and evaluate how the plans actually worked. Legal and bureaucratic constraints, however, limit the power of the superintendent and the board over the headquarters and field staff, and reforms mandated from above are seldom carried out as they were intended.

Chester Barnard, a distinguished writer and theorist on administration, has noted that an order is never an order unless it is obeyed. Barnard was pointing to a central component of administrative authority, namely, that it exists only when it is regarded as "legitimate" by those in subordinate positions.

A Model of Bureaucratic Pathology

The New York City school system is typical of what social scientists call a "sick" bureaucracy—a term for organizations whose traditions, structure, and operations subvert their stated missions and prevent any flexible accommodation to changing client demands. It has all those characteristics that every large bureaucratic organization has, but they have been instituted and followed to such a degree that they no longer serve their original purpose. Such characteristics as (1) overcentralization, the development of many levels in the chain of command, and an upward orientation of anxious subordinates; (2) vertical and horizontal fragmentation, isolating units from one another and limiting communication and coordination of functions; (3) the consequent development of chauvinism within particular units, reflected in actions to protect and expand their power; (4) the exercise of strong, informal pressure from peers within units to conform to their codes, geared toward political protection and expansion and ignoring the organization's wider goals; (5) compulsive rule following and rule enforcing; (6) the rebellion of lower-level supervisors against headquarters directives, alternating at times with overconformity, as they develop concerns about ratings and promotions; (7) increasing insulation from clients, as internal politics and personal career interests override interests in serving various publics; and (8) the tendency to make decisions in committees, making it difficult to pinpoint responsibility and authority are the institution's main pathologies.

Such characteristics are exaggerations of a number of administrative patterns that may not be bad if they are not carried too far. In the New York City school system, however, they are carried to the point where they paralyze the system in the face of rapid social changes that demand new administrative arrangements and programs.

Though the term "bureaucracy" usually has negative connotations in popular usage, I am using it here in a neutral sense, referring simply to social patterns associated with large scale organizations. There can be "good" and "bad" bureaucracy, and much of my analysis of the New York City school system, using the social science model of bureaucratic pathology, will include examples of "bad" bureaucracy.

THE HIGH SCHOOL REVOLUTIONARIES (1970) From Marc Libarle and Tom

Seligson, *The High School Revolutionaries* (New York, 1970), pp. 4–5, 13–14, 19–20, 29–31.

I Saw America in the Streets

DAVID ROMANO

No matter how good the teacher may be, no matter how many books he may have published (there are many accomplished teachers at Staples: teachers with Ph.D's, teachers who have published, teachers who attended Harvard and Columbia), he is not going to be able to teach anything if his students don't come to class. It's almost impossible to get the kids to come to class now, and once they're in class the situation is so bad that instead of learning anything or even being in a neutral situation they have an adverse reaction to anything that is being taught to them. This student boredom is reflected in the large numbers of Staples' students who cut school and classes regularly. (Out of a school of about nineteen hundred students, approximately three hundred skip the entire day, every day, and the number of students who cut individual classes often totals up to nine hundred, or half the school.) I think this shows that students are not just bored with individual classes, but with school generally. The only students who attend classes consistently are those who are intimidated by their teachers. Staples is probably no better or no worse than most schools in this country.

I think the educational system from top to bottom, from kindergarten to college, is in pretty bad shape. The experience of a Staples Experimental English class is indicative of this. The course, instituted this year and open only to Seniors, allowed the students the option to either come to class or stay away. In class they were allowed to study anything they wanted, anything that interested them. With this freedom, almost all the Senior students, instead of putting it to good use, decided to stay away. After eleven years of stifling classroom experience, these students were unable to take advantage of this freedom. They'd come to class, sign out, and then they'd leave. They'd go down to the school lounge, or they'd smoke cigarettes, or they'd just leave campus. While a few students did put this opportunity to good use, most of them were too brainwashed to do so.

Turn Left at Scarsdale

MICHAEL MARQUSEE

I have lived in Scarsdale for most of my life, and I write from the viewpoint of the affluent student turned radical. This contradiction between my political thinking and economic and social background may seem strange, but it is one of which I am constantly aware; in fact, it is my upbringing in this culture which has directly influenced my radicalization and is in some ways the cause of it.

The Scarsdale community can be described as an upper middle-class community. With the average income over $25,000 and a virtually all-white population, Scarsdale is the ideally insulated town, excluding the poor and the black. It is a community of family units in which the father usually commutes to New York City while the mother stays home to tend the children who attend, for the most part, one of the highly-rated Scarsdale public schools. The jobs that the men in Scarsdale commute to are almost all either in one of the professions or in business. In this community, my friends and myself are all children of desk-sitters. Our fathers work in a 9 to 5, tie-and-jacket world where the guiding principle is usually that of finding the easiest path to the most money.

Obviously, laborers of any kind and low-ranking desk-job holders find no place for themselves in Scarsdale. In fact, for most of us, the only working-class people we ever have contact with are the employees our parents hire to clean house, do the gardening, or repair the washing machines, heaters, cars, stoves, and swimming pools.

Scarsdale prides itself on its cultural and intellectual interests. There are many patrons of Lincoln Center, frequent theater-goers, and supposedly avid book-readers. Most of us live in large, one-family houses, among which there is little variety. The town has a calm, serene mood, with its quiet, uncrowded streets, and absence of night activity. There is a generally restrained and almost unfriendly attitude toward one's neighbors. The mothers of the town engage in various "wifely" activities: watching the kids, directing her staff, chatting on the phone, shopping, playing tennis, or maybe some occasional stuffing letters at a local political office.

Finally, in this catalogue of Scarsdale family elements, there are the children, and we are in many ways the center of family and community attention. Virtually all parents see their child's function within school as the attainment of high grades, or in other words, academic success and a better chance for admission to a highly-rated college. . . .

I return to the subject of school because finally it is the center of all our activity and is the primary tool with which the young of Scarsdale are molded into finished products. The word "process" has repeatedly cropped up here because it is indicative of the nature of existence in my community. Thus, Scarsdale High seeks to produce college graduates who are in turn directed into a field within the professional or business community. This "process" is not so far removed from the pattern whereby black kids in a ghetto school are trained for "niggerly" jobs (or no jobs) or where working-class kids are sent to vocational schools. As has been said, the student is universally a nigger. We are subservient to all authority and our lives are controlled by that authority from the selection of our careers to the development of our values. This is a system which should be abhorrent to all who hold supposedly "human," "progressive" values, yet it is endorsed by almost all in the adult world, for they see it as a necessary preface to that wondrous goal—a career.

Choose anything you want but have a career—a definite, disciplined job or skill that involves a routine of work. In that routine is security, happiness, and normalcy. This is a standard defense of the school system. They preach that this process aids in our attainment of fulfillment. It gives us opportunities. Bullshit. This process, as I and my friends in affluent Scarsdale have discovered, is one of limitation and misdirection. Imagine spending your entire thinking life attending classes which have been planned by someone thirty years older than you who usually has little in common with you; having your daily schedule worked out by someone who probably has never seen you; sitting down in assigned desks at the signal of a bell and standing up again fifty minutes later at the same signal, only to move to another pre-planned class and follow the same routine, all day, every day, in pursuit of a goal someone else has set for you and which, whether you believe in it or not, seems to offer as little excitement as the dreary schedule you now go through. This is the high school student, and that existence is one directed toward limitation, demoralization, and I repeat, manipulation. One of the weapons which the school uses in directing our course is a steady, subtle humiliation which starts the moment we learn in kindergarten that we must raise our hand (an absurd ritual) in order to get permission to go to the bathroom. It is continued in the hundreds of orderly lines we all form to move around elementary school, the disgrace we suffer when we make a wrong answer to an easy question, and the paranoia and tension that accompany the distribution of grades on all levels of education.

For a student, grades can become an obsessive force in life. All our activities in school revolve around our grades. However, few students actually believe they are an accurate measure of someone's intelligence or capabilities. Teachers often say they indicate a student's "performance." They picked the right word. Attaining high grades in school is usually just a matter of performing or acting out the role of dutiful student with a straight face. Given a talent for bullshitting, anybody can pull an A. The difference between one grade or another, even if it's between a B+ and an A, can absorb some students to the point of neurosis. The parents are almost all excessively concerned with their child's grades, and some will punish or reward their kids according to their quarterly standing. All of them encourage and even push their kids into working for a higher grade whether that means learning anything or not. Often, we find ourselves orienting everything toward creating a good impression the last few weeks of each marking period and then dropping it at the beginning of a new one until report-card time comes around again. . . .

Right On

N. K. JAMAL

. . . Most black slum children are facing hard life every day. They walk down hot smelly streets in the summer. They walk down cold, slushy, dirty, dangerous streets during winter. Any season the sidewalks are strewn with uncovered garbage cans, some lying horizontally on the ground, trash falling into the children's paths. They walk past tall, dingy tenements on the way to school. They look up at the little old women who stare at them from three stories up—little women who sit there at the rusty, maybe broken and crumbled window ledge, reminiscing.

Traffic on the corner frightens children as they go to school. They never grow accustomed to the death-dealing automobiles that virtually fly past them in hordes in the early morning. They cross the streets, wary of broken glass that could cut them, possibly causing permanent injury.

On the school block, pimps coax the little girls as they walk past. Prostitutes pucker their lips at the little boys, telling them to come and see them when they grow up. Dope addicts nod, not at the children, not at anyone in particular, just nodding, in their vertical sleeping positions. Dope pushers attempt to sell the children little pieces of candy that are not as innocent as they look.

Further up the block gangs of boys and girls are giving one boy the shakedown. Others are yelling and screaming in fright or glee as two boys fight. Still others yelp as someone throws a bowl of hot, scalding water out of the third floor window of the adjoining tenement.

This is life as the average black student lives it—every day. This is the sharp, focused world of reality. The world of the slum child.

Yet, once the student enters the classroom, this world mysteriously changes. The harsh roughness of existence is erased. The everyday life of Harlem, Watts, Detroit, Newark, or Washington, D.C. fades into the past. Everything that should have been used to determine the nature and direction of the student's education is discarded.

As David himself said, his education and mine have indeed been subtle. Education was not about the subjects of English, Math, and History, which were "taught," but rather about the workings of the system. Hypocritical education under false pretenses. The education we all received was actually about the subtleness of the structure that was educating us, the why of this subtleness, and the useful purposes we might later serve to the system. This was our education. We were awakening. David was awakening. We began to see a set, noted formula. A pattern. Guidelines by which the system knew it could prepare the student for his predetermined place in society.

The method? Soothe the student. Pull the kid out of the hard-hitting realities of life and push him up the path that leads into the soothing world of Mother Goose.

Kill the pessimism of his real life with the optimism of Honest Abe, the self-educated farmboy grown President.

Don't let him become aware of his color. Make him see no color. Let Dick and Jane become his everyday, colorless friends. Avoid questions about why Dick and Jane don't have a darker friend on their whole block.

Talk to him about Spot, and ask him if he has a dog of his own (don't let him trap you with discussion about the stray, rabid dogs roaming ghetto streets).

This was the formula—and if followed correctly, it worked.

The formula was set by the general society. Public education is society's baby. It arises from the need for society to determine what the individual should do with his life, and how he will live it. It arises from society's need to be able to control the individual—he belongs here, and she belongs there. Therefore, educate him to become this, and her to become that.

The formula is still being instituted by the entire school system, with the individual teacher being the most immediate and vulnerable component, the administration, principals, district supervisors, and the Board of Education and its members being the extensions, and total control being in the hands of a select group.

The method of institution of the formula is up to the individual teacher. In a circle of thirty or so teachers, there can be thirty stories about how each teacher managed to pull her student from the facts of his existence, to the bourgeois world of *Our Friends and Neighbors*—from the rugged tenements of Harlem to the clean-swept, mowed-lawn atmosphere of suburbia in a matter of minutes.

Then she will discourse on the success she has had in this transformation with minimal balking from her students during or after the transition. In short, she is proud that she can hide the discrepancy between life and the classroom from the student.

An amazing feat in itself, this process brings to mind the sad realization that the entire education the student receives is merely an escapist barbiturate to soothe and hold the student until he is ready to take his acceptable, preset place in society.

The nature of the education of the student is an incredible story. It would appear from the outset that the student's education should be geared to his environment. But, as has already been pointed out several times in the foregoing pages, the education was only to prepare the child for his "slot" in life (as a data-processing card has its slot in the computer, so has the student his "slot" in society).

The student can be going to school in a Harlem area—in fact, in middle Harlem, on 114th Street, down the block from one of the busiest dope and prostitution traffic corners in the world, and up the street from one of the most crime-ridden apartment buildings in New York City—and yet once he crosses the threshold of his school building and enters the classroom, a fantastic psychedelic illusion of truth, warmth, and everlasting beauty (as interpreted by the system), looms before him, inviting him to come in and be "educated."

He sees young boys and girls moving around in an impossible world of dreams and middle-class aspirations. He watches them, as they float in white shirts and ties that they cannot afford, blue skirts and blouses, doldrum uniforms reflecting the gray attitudes of the school administration.

Their thoughts and dreams aspire beyond reality—they reach for the white middle-class star that shines high above them. They prepare to make the necessary change—to usurp their inherited blackness to become half-white members of the "Negro Middle Class."

This is not their fault. This is their teaching. It is a fact that society's recognized position for these students is in the Negro Middle Class, where they best serve society as prime examples of "those who made it." These are the students who would, in centuries past, have been recognized as the former slave who escaped, got rich, and then decided that he needed a few black slaves of his own, because if "Massa has it, why cain't I . . .?"

Then there are the others. Our student watches a group of kids walk by who do not conform. They don't obey the rules. They don't wear ties. They don't care about society. They fight, they lie, they cheat, and they steal. These are the victims of society. These are the ones most affected by their environment, and yet these are the ones who receive the least benefit from the school system. It is said of these, "They are too hard-headed," "He is uneducable," "She will never learn," and "I tried, but he won't listen." These are the students who must resign themselves to Gym, Shop, and Hygiene classes as their education. These are the ones who have only society's worst to look forward to—jobs as unskilled laborers, welfare, and the Selective Service.

*   *   *

ON SEXUAL DISCRIMINATION IN HIGHER EDUCATION (1970)   From Ann Sutherland Harris, "The Second Sex in Academe," *AAUP Bulletin,* vol. LVI, pp. 283–84.

I am only one of thousands of women who believe that Congress will be increasingly occupied in the 1970's with the legislation necessary to insure that women have equal rights and equal opportunities in the United States. Women are organizing now as they have not since their battle for the right to vote fifty years ago, more and more women having realized that they are treated as second-class citizens. The word "sex" was added to Section 702 of Title VII of the Civil Rights Act as a joke, but equality for women is not a joke. It is a serious issue, although many otherwise fair-minded individuals still refuse to believe that discrimination against women is a serious problem or is a problem that should be taken seriously.

That the overall distribution of women in institutions of higher education is highly suggestive of discriminatory attitudes and practices no one can deny, but research into the problem of discrimination against women in higher education is handicapped at present by the scarcity of studies of individual colleges and universities. This study concentrates therefore on those institutions for which it has been possible to obtain up-to-date statistics. Some of these have just been prepared by senate committees; others have been collected by women's groups in the institutions concerned. There is an urgent need for more statistical data of this kind, especially for such information which extends beyond the areas of faculty distribution, student admission, and fellowships to those of staff and administrative employment, salaries, relative rates of promotion, and distribution by individual subject.

Several remarks by men famous in the academic world reveal all too clearly how women are regarded in academe. When President Nathan Pusey of Harvard realized that the draft was going to reduce the number of men applying to Harvard's graduate school, his reaction was, "We shall be left with the blind, the lame, and the women." Harvard has no tenured women professors, and its excuse for limiting its female undergraduate enrollment to 25 per cent of the total is that there is insufficient accommodation for more women. What this really means is that the institution is reluctant to give a man's place to a woman. At Yale, when the new women undergraduates recently protested the quota on female undergraduates and made the modest demand for an additional fifty women at an alumni dinner, one of the male alumni was cheered when he said, "We are all for women, but Yale must produce a thousand male leaders every year." Those men alumni did not think that women have similar leadership potential, or, as Kingman Brewster put it, "Much of the quality that exists at Yale depends on the support of people who don't believe strongly in coeducation." But Yale is slowly learning that women are fed up with only vicarious participation in aspects of human activity outside the home. Charles de Carlo recently succeeded Esther Rauschenbusch as President of Sarah Lawrence, in one of many recent instances in which women presidents have been succeeded by male presidents. He said, shortly after his appointment, that "feminine instincts are characterized by caring qualities, concern for beauty and form, reverence for life, empathy in human relations, and a demand that men be better than they are." President de Carlo apparently thinks that women are myths—muses, madonnas—but not people with the potential and full range of characteristics ascribed to men.

Sometimes there appears in serious publications what may to the uninitiated seem to be a perfectly reasonable objection to giving women the same opportunities as men. For example:

> Too many young women are casually enrolling in graduate schools across the country without having seriously considered the obligation which they are assuming by requesting that such expenditures be made for them. And they are not alone to blame. Equally at fault are two groups of faculty—undergraduate instructors who encourage their women students to apply to graduate school without also helping them consider the commitment that such an act implies, and graduate admissions counsellors who blithely admit girls with impressive academic records without looking for other evidence that the applicant has made a sincere commitment to graduate study.

That women who go to graduate school do make a serious commitment is proved by studies that have taken into account the degree of education of working women. Such studies show that the amount of education a woman has received is a more important factor with respect to her decision to work than either marriage or children. The higher her level of education, the more likely she is to be working full time. Helen Astin found that of the almost 2,000 women doctorates she surveyed 10 years after they completed their Ph.D.'s, 91 per cent were working, 81 per cent of them full time. The percentage of men who work full time is not, incidentally, 100 per cent, as most of us think, but was, in 1968, 69.4 per cent of all men of working age.

The attitudes of mind reflected in the foregoing quotations are not uncommon. Responses to a questionnaire published by the AAUW (American Association of University Women) in its January *Journal* showed that the majority of the over 3,000 men who replied believed "that woman's first responsibility is to be the feminine companion of men and a mother, that women have less need to achieve in the working world, that they have adequate opportunity to develop their potential, that the job turn-over rate and sick-leave rate of women is higher than that of men, [and] that women have difficulty dealing with males in subordinate positions" (McCune). The majority of the women did not agree with those statements, however, and they were right not to. With women now comprising over a third of the work force, more women of working age are working than are staying at home. It is working women, and not the suburban housewives, who comprise the silent majority. For some time, women have voted with their feet to get out of the home, even though the jobs that they are offered are for the most part menial and poorly paid. Those women, however, who wish to become professors, lawyers, and doctors can hardly have less need to achieve in the working world than men, for they will need far more determination than men need to reach the same status and enjoy the same opportunities and compensations. The sick-leave rate and turn-over rates for women are in fact, according to the latest figures from the Women's Bureau of the Department of Labor, slightly lower than those of men, when those rates are standardized, as they must be, for occupation and income. Shirley McCune remarks, "If males bring this mind-set to employment situations, it undoubtedly affects their behavior towards females." That is an understatement. That men's notions of women's "place" and women's "roles" do affect the way men treat women in employment situations in academe is made abundantly clear by the statistics showing the distribution of women in the academic world, as it has been also by Lawrence Simpson's recent study (discussed later).

The rule is a simple one: the higher, the fewer. Although more women than men finish high school (and this has been true since 1920), fewer women than men go on to college, partly because it is harder for a woman to gain entrance to college with the necessary financial support. Fewer women than men go on to get higher degrees, again largely because graduate departments discriminate against women in admissions policies and in the distribution of fellowships. Once they qualify, the higher-the-fewer rule continues to apply: the higher in terms of rank, salary, prestige, or responsibility, the fewer the number of women to be found. Moreover, their numbers have been declining since 1946, despite the increase in the numbers of M.A.'s and Ph.D.'s going to women in the 1960's. Only 1 per cent of presidents of colleges and universities are lay women and their proportions are declining still.

ALEXANDER M. BICKEL'S EPITAPH FOR DESEGRATION (1970) From

"Desegregation: Where Do We Go From Here?," *The New Republic*, February 7, 1970, pp. 20-22.

It will be sixteen years this May since the Supreme Court decreed in *Brown* v. *Board of Education* that the races may not be segregated by law in the public schools, and six years in July since the doctrine of the *Brown* case was adopted as federal legislative and executive policy in the Civil Rights Act of 1964. Yet here we are, apparently struggling still to desegregate schools in Mississippi, Louisiana and elsewhere in the deep South, and still meeting determined resistance, if no longer much violence or rioting.

The best figures available indicate that only some 23 percent of the nationwide total of more than six million Negro pupils go to integrated public schools. About half the total of more than six million Negro pupils are in the South, and there the percentage of Negroes in school with whites is only 18.

What has gone wrong? The answer is, both less and a great deal more than meets the eye; it is true both that the school desegregation effort has been a considerable success, and that is has not worked.

The measure of the success is simply taken. Sixteen years ago, local law, not only in the 11 Southern states but in border states, in parts of Kansas, in the District of Columbia, forbade the mixing of the races in the schools, and official practice had the same effect in some areas in the North, for example portions of Ohio and New Jersey. Ten years ago, Southern communities were up in arms, often to the point of rioting or closing the public schools altogether, over judicial decrees that ordered the introduction of a dozen or two carefully selected Negro children into a few previously all-white schools. There are counties in the deep South that still must be reckoned as exceptions, but on the whole, the principle of segregation has been effectively denied, those who held it have been made to repudiate it, and the rigid legal structure that embodied it has been destroyed. That is no mean achievement, even though it still needs to be perfected and completed, and it is the achievement of law, which had irresistible moral force, and was able to enlist political energies in its service.

The achievement is essentially Southern. The failure is nationwide. And the failure more than the achievement is coming to the fore in those districts in Mississippi and Louisiana where the Supreme Court and a reluctant Nixon Administration are now enforcing what they still call desegregation on very short deadlines. In brief, the failure is this: To dismantle the official structure of segregation, even with the cooperation in good faith of local authorities, is not to create integrated schools, anymore than integrated schools are produced by the absence of an official structure of school segregation in the North and West. The actual integration of schools on a significant scale is an enormously difficult undertaking, if a possible one at all. Certainly it creates as many problems as it purports to solve, and no one can be sure that even if accomplished, it would yield an educational return.

School desegregation, it will be recalled, began and for more than a decade was carried out under the so-called "deliberate speed" formula. The courts insisted that the principle of segregation and, gradually, all its manifestations in the system of law and administration be abandoned; and they required visible proof of the abandonment, namely, the presence of black children in school with whites. The expectation was that a school district which had been brought to give up the objective of segregation would gradually reorganize itself along other nonracial lines, and end by transforming itself from a dual into a unitary system.

All too often, that expectation was not met. The objective of segregation was not abandoned in good faith. School authorities would accept a limited Negro presence in white schools, and would desist from making overt moves to coerce the separation of the races, but would manage nevertheless to continue operating a dual system consisting of all black schools for the vast majority of Negro children, and of white and a handful of nearly white schools for all the white children. This was sham compliance—tokenism it was contemptuously called, and justly so—and in the past few years, the Supreme Court, and HEW acting under the Civil Rights Act of 1964, determined to tolerate it no longer.

HEW and some lower federal courts first raised the ante of tokenism, requiring stated percentages of black children in school with whites. Finally they demanded that no school in a given system be allowed to retain its previous character as a white or black school. Faculties and administrators had to be shuffled about so that an entirely or almost entirely black or white faculty would no longer characterize a school as black or white. If a formerly all-Negro school was badly substandard, it had to be closed. For the rest, residential zoning, pairing of schools by grades, some busing and majority-to-minority transfers were employed to ensure distribution of both races through the school system. In areas where blacks were in a majority, whites were necessarily assigned to schools in which they would form a minority. All this has by no means happened in every school district in the South, but it constitutes the current practice in desegregation. Thus among the decrees recently enforced in Mississippi, the one applicable in Canton called for drawing an East-West attendance line through the city so that each school became about 70 percent black and 30 percent white. Elsewhere schools were paired to the same end.

It bears repeating that such measures were put into effect because the good faith of school authorities was in doubt, to say the least, and satisfactory evidence that the structure of legally enforced segregation had been eliminated was lacking. But whatever, and however legitimate, the reasons for imposing such requirements, the consequences have been perverse. Integration soon reaches a tipping point. If whites are sent to constitute a minority in a school that is largely black, or if blacks are sent to constitute something near half the population of a school that was formerly white or nearly all-white, the whites flee, and the school becomes all or nearly all-black; resegregation sets in, blacks simply changing places with whites. The whites move, within the city or out of it into suburbs, so that under a system of zoning they are in white schools because the schools reflect residential segregation; or else they flee the public school system altogether, into private and parochial schools.

It is not very fruitful to ask whether the whites behave as they do because they are racists, or because everybody seeks in the schools some sense of social, economic, cultural group identity. Whatever one's answer, the whites do flee, or try to, whether in a Black Belt county where desegregation has been resisted for 16 years in the worst of faith and for the most blatant of racist reasons, or in Atlanta, where in recent years, at any rate, desegregation has been implemented in the best of faith, or in border cities such as Louisville, St. Louis, Baltimore or Washington, DC, where it was implemented in good faith 15 years ago, or in Northern cities where legal segregation has not existed in over half a century. It is feckless to ask whether this should happen. The questions to ask are whether there is any way to prevent the whites' fleeing, or whether there are gains sufficient to offset the flight of the whites in continuing to press the process of integration.

To start with the second question, a negative answer seems obvious. What is the use of a process of racial integration in the schools that very often produces, in absolute numbers, more black and white children attending segregated schools than before the process was put into motion? The credible disestablishment of a legally enforced system of segregation is essential, but it ought to be possible to achieve it without driving school systems past the tipping point of resegregation—and perhaps this, without coming right out and saying so, is what the Nixon Administration has been trying to tell us. Thus in Canton, Mississippi, a different zoning scheme would apparently have left some all-black and all-white schools, but still put about thirty-five percent of black pupils in schools with whites.

We live by principles, and the concrete expression in practice of the principles we live by is crucial. *Brown* v. *Board of Education* held out for us the principle that it is wrong and ultimately evil to classify people invidiously by race. We would have mocked that principle if we had allowed the South to wipe some laws formally off its books, and then continue with segregation as usual, through inertia, custom, and the application of private force. But substantial, concrete changes vindicating the principle of the *Brown* case were attainable in the South without at the same time producing the absurd result of resegregation.

This argument assumes, however, that the first of the two questions posed above is also to be answered in the negative. Is there, in truth, no way to prevent resegregation from occurring? Approaching the problem as one of straight feasibility, with no normative implications, one has to take account of an important variable. It is relatively simple to make flight so difficult as to be just about impossible for relatively poor whites in rural areas in the South. There is little residential segregation in these areas, and there is no place to move to except private schools. State and local governments can be forbidden to aid such private schools with tuition grants paid to individual pupils, and the Supreme Court has so forbidden them. Private schools can also be deprived of federal tax exemption unless they are integrated, and a federal court in the District of Columbia has at least temporarily so deprived them. They can be deprived of state and local tax aid as well. Lacking any state support, however indirect, for private schools, all but well-to-do or Catholic whites in the rural and small-town South will be forced back into the public schools although in the longer run, we may possibly find that what we have really done is to build in an incentive to residential segregation, and even perhaps to substantial population movement into cities.

On a normative level, is it right to require a small, rural and relatively poor segment of the national population to submit to a kind of schooling that is disagreeable to them (for whatever reasons, more or less unworthy), when we do not impose such schooling on people, in cities and in other regions, who would also dislike it (for not dissimilar reasons, more or less equally worthy or unworthy?). This normative issue arises because the feasibility question takes on a very different aspect in the cities. Here movement to residentially segregated neighborhoods or suburbs is possible for all but the poorest whites, and is proceeding at a rapid pace. Pursuit of a policy of integration would require, therefore, pursuit of the whites with busloads of inner-city Negro children, or even perhaps with trainloads or helicopter-loads, as distances lengthen. Very substantial resources would thus be needed. They have so far nowhere been committed, in any city.

One reason they have not is that no one knows whether the enterprise would be educationally useful or harmful to the children, black and white. Even aside from the politics of the matter, which is quite a problem in itself, there is a natural hesitancy, therefore, to gamble major resources on a chase after integration, when it is more than possible that the resources would in every sense be better spent in trying to teach children how to read in place. Moreover, and in the long view more importantly, large-scale efforts at integration would almost certainly be opposed by leading elements in urban Negro communities.

Polls asking abstract questions may show what they will about continued acceptance of the goal of integration, but the vanguard of black opinion, among intellectuals and political activists alike, is oriented more toward the achievement of group identity and some group autonomy than toward the use of public schools as assimilationist agencies. In part this trend of opinion is explained by the ineffectiveness, the sluggishness, the unresponsiveness, often the oppressiveness of large urban public school systems, and in part it bespeaks the feeling shared by so many whites that the schools should, after all, be an extension of the family, and that the family ought to have a sense of class and cultural identity with them. And so, while the courts and HEW are rezoning and pairing Southern schools in the effort to integrate them, Negro leaders in Northern cities are trying to decentralize them, accepting their racial character and attempting to bring them under community control. While the courts and HEW are reassigning faculties in Atlanta to reflect the racial composition of the schools and to bring white teachers to black pupils and black teachers to white ones, Negro leaders in the North are asking for black principals and black teachers for black schools.

Where we have arrived may be signaled by a distorted mirror image that was presented in the Ocean Hill-Brownsville decentralized experimental school district in New York during the teachers' strikes of the fall of 1968. A decade earlier, black children in Little Rock and elsewhere in the South were escorted by armed men through white mobs to be taught by white teachers. In Ocean Hill-Brownsville in 1968, white teachers had to be escorted by armed men through black mobs to teach black children.

Can we any longer fail to acknowledge that the federal government is attempting to create in the rural South conditions that cannot in the foreseeable future be attained in large or medium urban centers in the South or in the rest of the country? The government is thus seen as applying its law unequally and unjustly, and is, therefore, fueling the politics of George Wallace. At the same time, the government is also putting itself on a collision course with the aspirations of an articulate and vigorous segment of national Negro leadership. Even if we succeed at whatever cost, in forcing and maintaining massively integrated school systems in parts of the rural South, may we not find ourselves eventually dismantling them again at the behest of blacks seeking decentralized community control?

There must be a better way to employ the material and political resources of the federal government. The process of disestablishing segregation is not quite finished, and both HEW and the courts must drive it to completion, as they must also continually police the disestablishment. But nothing seems to be gained, and much is risked or lost by driving the process to the tipping point of resegregation. A prudent judgment can distinguish between the requirements of disestablishment and plans that cannot work, or can work only, if at all, in special areas that inevitably feel victimized.

There are black schools all over the country. We don't really know what purpose would be served by trying to do away with them, and many blacks don't want them done away with. Energies and resources ought to go into their improvement and, where appropriate, replacement. Energies and resources ought to go into training teachers, and into all manner of experimental attempts to improve the quality of education. The involvement of cohesive communities of parents with the schools is obviously desired by many leaders of Negro opinion. It may bear educational fruit, and is arguably an inalienable right of parenthood anyway. Even the growth of varieties of private schools, hardly integrated, but also not segregated, and enjoying state support through tuition grants for blacks and whites alike, should not be stifled, but encouraged in the spirit of an unlimited experimental search for more effective education. Massive school integration is not going to be attained in this country very soon, in good part because no one is certain that it is worth the cost. Let us, therefore, try to proceed with education.

EPITAPH FOR DESEGREGATION? (**1970**)   From An Answer By Charles V. Hamilton in *New Republic*, March 7, 1970, pp. 35–36.

Professor Bickel has written a careful and thoughtful article. What has to be understood is that in our laudable quest to do away with a reprehensible policy and practice of legal racial segregation, we must at all times be mindful of other desirable normative goals. Structural desegregation, even where whites do not flee, is not essentially the only goal. We must become much more concerned with the kinds of instructional materials used in those classrooms; we must devote considerably more time and attention to teacher attitudes, lest we find that while the classrooms have white and black children together, they nonetheless will be exposed to the same materials and attitudes that informed a legally segregated system.

Likewise, it may be possible to bus children all over town, but do we seriously believe that this will facilitate parental involvement in the schools? Is it realistic to think that those parents will travel long distances to attend PTA meetings? I believe that education has to be seen as a family-community-centered affair, not simply as a child-oriented venture, and this is particularly true where we are talking about a black society that is striving to develop collectively, and not as individuals. The former goal is a normative value we must keep in mind as we try to devise ways to overcome the despicable policy of legal (or even de facto) segregation.

Let us make sure the law is clear, so there can be no legal impediment to those seeking to implement immediately a free and open society on their own. But let us also be aware of other equally desirable socio-political imperatives at this time, that there is a sound argument to be made for supporting new kinds of educational institutions of development and growth. This frequently gets obscured by the polemical charges of "black racism" and "separatism." But polemics are hardly useful in picking through to solutions of longstanding social problems.

Perhaps government policy could support—through subsidies for example—those parents (black and white) who want to transport their children to desegregated classrooms. I am sure there are such parents who feel it educationally and socially desirable to pursue such goals. And this is not to be confused with the discredited "freedom of choice" plans, which have as their goal the maintenance of segregation. Such support would be perfectly manageable, constitutional and probably not

RE-APPRAISAL
1951–1973

3227

economically prohibitive, and it could insist that the substance of the education be tended to—non-racist materials, etc. It is possible to develop criteria for support quite consistent with Brown v. Board. That is, if the private choices result in perpetuating segregation, they would not be assisted by government support of any kind.

And at the same time, it is possible, as Professor Bickel says, to "proceed with education" by making serious commitments to upgrading the quality of education. The hard fact is that unless we tend to the latter in any case, desegregation will not matter. I have serious doubts about the efficacy of integrating little black children into some of those educationally racist classrooms. Thus, a policy of quality education is not (as so often posed) the antithesis of a desegregation policy. We have to tend to quality whether we never desegregate another classroom. And let it be clearly understood, I am talking about the all-white, as well as the all-black classrooms—a fact frequently overlooked in discussions of this subject. Educationally, this may well be a greater long-term contribution to a viable society than some mechanistic programs of desegregation now being formulated and tried.

Of course, if the society is not prepared to make such a serious commitment—and surely we know this is an open question—then I suspect we are all just playing at school, anyway.

Finally, my notions should not be interpreted as capitulating to segregationists. Those people must be fought at every turn. But in our determination to defeat them, let us not devise plans that are dysfunctional in other serious ways. The principle is a free and open society, and we can pursue several realistic routes to its achievements. Professor Bickel is correct.

Innovations

B. F. SKINNER ON REINFORCEMENT TECHNIQUES IN EDUCATION

(1954)   From B. F. Skinner, "The Science of Learning and the Art of Teaching," *Harvard Educational Review*, vol. XXIV, pp. 86–87, 91–94, 96–97.

Some promising advances have recently been made in the field of learning. Special techniques have been designed to arrange what are called "contingencies of reinforcement"—the relations which prevail between behavior on the one hand and the consequences of that behavior on the other—with the result that a much more effective control of behavior has been achieved. It has long been argued that an organism learns mainly by producing changes in its environment, but it is only recently that these changes have been carefully manipulated. In traditional devices for the study of learning—in the serial maze, for example, or in the T-maze, the problem box, or the familiar discrimination apparatus—the effects produced by the organism's behavior are left to many fluctuating circumstances. There is many a slip between the turn-to-the-right and the food-cup at the end of the alley. It is not surprising that techniques of this sort have yielded only very rough data from which the uniformities demanded by an experimental science can be extracted only by averaging many cases. In none of this work has the behavior of the individual organism been predicted in more than a statistical sense. The learning processes which are the presumed object of such research are reached only through a series of inferences. Current preoccupation with deductive systems reflects this state of the science.

Recent improvements in the conditions which control behavior in the field of learning are of two principal sorts. The Law of Effect has been taken seriously; we have made sure that effects *do* occur and that they occur under conditions which are optimal for producing the changes called learning. Once we have arranged the particular type of consequence called a reinforcement, our techniques permit us to shape up the behavior of an organism almost at will. It has become a routine exercise to demonstrate this in classes in elementary psychology by conditioning such an organism as a pigeon. Simply by presenting food to a hungry pigeon at the right time, it is possible to shape up three or four well-defined responses in a single demonstration period—such responses as turning around, pacing the floor in the pattern of a figure-8, standing still in a corner of the demonstration apparatus, stretching the neck, or stamping the foot. Extremely complex performances may be reached through successive stages in the shaping process, the contingencies of reinforcement being changed progressively in the direction of the required behavior. The results are often quite dramatic. In such a demonstration one can *see* learning take place. A significant change in behavior is often obvious as the result of a single reinforcement.

A second important advance in technique permits us to maintain behavior in given states of strength for long periods of time. Reinforcements continue to be important, of course, long after an organism has learned *how* to do something, long after it has acquired behavior. They are necessary to maintain the behavior in strength. Of special interest is the effect of various schedules of intermittent reinforcement. Charles B. Ferster and the author are currently preparing an extensive report of a five-year research program, sponsored by the Office of Naval Research, in which most of the important types of schedules have been investigated and in which the effects of schedules in general have been reduced to a few principles. On the theoretical side we now have a fairly good idea of why a given schedule produces its appropriate performance. On the practical side we have learned how to maintain any given level of activity for daily periods limited only by the physical exhaustion of the organism and from day to day without substantial change throughout its life. Many of these effects would be traditionally assigned to the field of motivation, although the principal operation is simply the arrangement of contingencies of reinforcement.

*　　*　　*

One of the most dramatic applications of these techniques has recently been made in the Harvard Psychological Laboratories by Floyd Ratliff and Donald S. Blough, who have skillfully used multiple and serial schedules of reinforcement to study complex perceptual processes in the infrahuman organism. They have achieved a sort of psychophysics without verbal instruction. In a recent experiment by Blough, for example, a pigeon draws a detailed dark-adaptation curve showing the characteristic breaks of rod and cone vision. The curve is recorded continuously in a single experimental period and is quite comparable with the curves of human subjects. The pigeon behaves in a way which, in the human case, we would not hesitate to describe by saying that it adjusts a very faint patch of light until it can just be seen.

In all this work, the species of the organism has made surprisingly little difference. It is true that the organisms studied have all been vertebrates, but they still cover a wide range. Comparable results have been obtained with pigeons, rats, togs, monkeys, human children, and most recently, by the author in collaboration with Ogden R. Lindsley, human psychotic subjects. In spite of great phylogenetic differences, all these organisms show amazingly similar properties of the learning process. It should be emphasized that this has been achieved by analyzing the effects of reinforcement and by designing techniques which manipulate reinforcement with considerable precision. Only in this way can the behavior of the individual organism be brought under such precise control. It is also important to note that through a gradual advance to complex interrelations among responses, the same degree of rigor is being extended to behavior which would usually be assigned to such fields as perception, thinking, and personality dynamics.

From this exciting prospect of an advancing science of learning, it is a great shock to turn to that branch of technology which is most directly concerned with the learning process—education. Let us consider, for example, the teaching of arithmetic in the lower grades. The school is concerned with imparting to the child a large number of responses of a special sort. The responses are all verbal. They consist of speaking and writing certain words, figures, and signs which, to put it roughly, refer to numbers and to arithmetic operations. The first task is to shape up these responses—to get the child to pronounce and to write responses correctly, but the principal task is to bring this behavior under many sorts of stimulus control. This is what happens when the child learns to count, to recite tables, to count while ticking off the items in an assemblage of objects, to respond to spoken or written numbers by saying "odd," "even," "prime," and so on. Over and above this elaborate repertoire of numerical behavior, most of which is often dismissed as the product of rote learning, the teaching of arithmetic looks forward to those complex serial arrangements of responses involved in original mathematical thinking. The child must acquire responses of transposing, clearing fractions, and so on, which modify the order or pattern of the original material so that the response called a solution is eventually made possible.

Now, how is this extremely complicated verbal repertoire set up? In the first place, what reinforcements are used? Fifty years ago the answer would have been clear. At that time educational control was still frankly aversive. The child read numbers, copied numbers, memorized tables, and performed operations upon numbers to escape the threat of the birch rod or cane. Some positive reinforcements were perhaps eventually derived from the increased efficiency of the child in the field of arithmetic and in rare cases some automatic reinforcement may have resulted from the sheer manipulation of the medium—from the solution of problems or the discovery of the intricacies of the number system. But for the immediate purposes of education the child acted to avoid or escape punishment. It was part of the reform movement known as progressive education to make the positive consequences more immediately effective, but any one who visits the lower grades of the average school today will observe that a change has been made, not from aversive to positive control, but from one form of aversive stimulation to another. The child at his desk, filling in his workbook, is behaving primarily to escape from the threat of a series of minor aversive events—the teacher's displeasure, the criticism or ridicule of his classmates, an ignominious showing in a competition, low marks, a trip to the office "to be talked to" by the principal, or a word to the parent who may still resort to the birch rod. In this welter of aversive consequences, getting the right answer is in itself an insignificant event, any effect of which is lost amid the anxieties, the boredom, and the aggression which are the inevitable by-products of aversive control.[1]

Secondly, we have to ask how the contingencies of reinforcement are arranged. When is a numerical operation reinforced as "right"? Eventually, of course, the pupil may be able to check his own answers and achieve some sort of automatic reinforcement, but in the early stages the reinforcement of being right is usually accorded by the teacher. The contingencies she provides are far from optimal. It can easily be demonstrated that, unless explicit mediating behavior has been set up, the lapse of only a few seconds between response and reinforcement destroys most of the effect. In a typical classroom, nevertheless, long periods of time customarily elapse. The teacher may walk up and down the aisle, for example, while the class is working on a sheet of problems, pausing here and there to say right or wrong. Many seconds or minutes intervene between the child's response and the teacher's reinforcement. In many cases—for example, when papers are taken home to be corrected—as much as 24 hours may intervene. It is surprising that this system has any effect whatsoever.

[1] Skinner, B. F., *Science and Human Behavior*. New York: Macmillan, 1953.

A third notable shortcoming is the lack of a skillful program which moves forward through a series of progressive approximations to the final complex behavior desired. A long series of contingencies is necessary to bring the organism into the possession of mathematical behavior most efficientsually necessary to reinforce the behavior in blocks of restonses—as in correcting a work sheet or page from a workbook. The responses within such a block must not be interrelated. The answer to one problem must not depend upon the answer to another. The number of stages through which one may progressively approach a complex pattern of behavior is therefore small, and the task so much the more difficult. Even the most modern workbook in beginning arithmetic is far from exemplifying an efficient program for shaping up mathematical behavior.

Perhaps the most serious criticism of the current classroom is the relative infrequency of reinforcement. Since the pupil is usually dependent upon the teacher for being right, and since many pupils are usually dependent upon the same teacher, the total number of contingencies which may be arranged during, say, the first four years, is of the order of only a few thousand. But a very rough estimate suggests that efficient mathematical behavior at this level requires something of the order of 25,000 contingencies. We may suppose that even in the brighter student a given contingency must be arranged several times to place the behavior well in hand. The responses to be set up are not simply the various items in tables of addition, subtraction, multiplication, and division; we have also to consider the alternative forms in which each item may be stated. To the learning of such material we should add hundreds of responses concerned with factoring, identifying primes, memorizing series, using short-cut techniques of calculation, constructing and using geometric representations or number forms, and so on. Over and above all this, the whole mathematical repertoire must be brought under the control of concrete problvety. Perhaps 50,000 contingencies is a more conservative estimate. In this frame of reference the daily assignment in arithmetic seems pitifully meagre.

The result of all this is, of course, well known, Even our best schools are under criticism for their inefficiency in the teaching of drill subjects such as arithmetic. The contition in the average school is a matter of wide-spread national concern. Modern children simply do not learn arithmetic quickly or well. Nor is the result simply incompetence. The very subjects in which modern techniques are weakest are those in which failure is most conspicuous, and in the wake of an ever-growing incompetence come the anxieties, uncertainties, and aggressions which in their turn present other problems to the school. Most pupils soon claim the asylum of not being "ready" for arithmetic at a given level or, eventually, of not having a mathematical mind. Such explanations are readily seized upon by defensive teachers and parents. Few pupils ever reach the stage at which automatic reinforcements follow as the natural consequences of mathematical behavior. On the contrary, the figures and symbols of mathematics have become standard emotional stimuli. The glimpse of a column of figures, not to say an algebraic symbol or an integral sign, is likely to set off—not mathematical behavior—but a reaction of anxiety, guilt, or fear.

*   *   *

There would be no point in urging these objections if improvement were impossible. But the advances which have recently been made in our control of the learning process suggest a thorough revision of classroom practices and, fortunately, they tell us how the revision can be brought about. This is not, of course, the first time that the results of an experimental science have been brought to bear upon the practical problems of education. The modern classroom does not, however, offer much evidence that research in the field of learning has been respected or used. This condition is no doubt partly due to the limitations of earlier research. But it has been encouraged by a too hasty conclusion that the laboratory study of learning is inherently limited because it cannot take into account the realities of the classroom. In the light of our increasing knowledge of the learning process we should, instead, insist upon dealing with those realities and forcing a substantial change in them. Education is perhaps the most important branch of scientific technology. It deeply affects the lives of all of us. We can no longer allow the exigencies of a practical situation to suppress the tremendous improvements which are within reach. The practical situation must be changed.

There are certain questions which have to be answered in turning to the study of any new organism. What behavior is to be set up? What reinforcers are at hand? What responses are available in embarking upon a program of progressive approximation which will lead to the final form of the behavior? How can reinforcements be most efficiently scheduled to maintain the behavior in strength? These questions are all relevant in considering the problem of the child in the lower grades.

In the first place, what reinforcements are available? What does the school have in its possession which will reinforce a child? We may look first to the material to be learned, for it is possible that this will provide considerable automatic reinforcement. Children play for hours with mechanical toys, paints, scissors and paper, noise-makers, puzzles—in short, with almost anything which feeds back significant changes in the environment and is reasonably free of aversive properties. The sheer control of nature is itself reinforcing. This effect is not evident in the modern school because it is masked by the emotional responses generated by aversive control. It is true that automatic reinforcement from the manipulation of the environment is probably only a mild reinforcer and may need to be carefully husbanded, but one of the most striking principles to emerge from recent research is that the *net* amount of reinforcement is of little significance. A very slight reinforcement may be tremendously effective in controlling behavior if it is wisely used.

If the natural reinforcement inherent in the subject matter is not enough, other reinforcers must be employed. Even in school the child is occasionally permitted to do "what he wants to do," and access to reinforcements of many sorts may be made contingent upon the more immediate consequences of the behavior to be established. Those who advocate competition as a useful social motive may wish to use the reinforcements which follow from excelling others, although there is the difficulty that in this case the reinforcement of one child is necessarily aversive to another. Next in order we might place the good will and affection of the teacher, and only when that has failed need we turn to the use of aversive stimulation.

In the second place, how are these reinforcements to be made contingent upon the desired behavior? There are two considerations here—the gradual elaboration of extremely complex patterns of behavior and the maintenance of the behavior in strength at each stage. The whole process of becoming competent in any field must be divided into a very large number of very small steps, and reinforcement must be contingent upon the accomplishment of each step. This solution to the problem of creating a complex repertoire of behavior also solves the problem of maintaining the behavior in strength. We could, of course, resort to the techniques of scheduling already developed in the study of other organisms but in the present state of our knowledge of educational practices, scheduling appears to be most effectively arranged through the design of the material to be learned. By making each successive step as small as possible, the frequency of reinforcement can be raised to a maximum, while the possibly aversive consequences of being wrong are reduced to a minimum. Other ways of designing material would yield other programs of reinforcement. Any supplementary reinforcement would probably have to be scheduled in the more traditional way.

These requirements are not excessive, but they are probably incompatible with the current realities of the classroom. In the experimental study of learning it has been found that the contingencies of reinforcement which are most efficient in controlling the organism cannot be arranged through the personal mediation of the experimenter. An organism is affected by subtle details of contingencies which are beyond the capacity of the human organism to arrange. Mechanical and electrical devices must be used. Mechanical help is also demanded by the sheer number of contingencies which may be used efficiently in a single experimental session. We have recorded many millions of responses from a single organism during thousands of experimental hours. Personal arrangement of the contingencies and personal observation of the results are quite unthinkable. Now, the human organism is, if anything, more sensitive to precise contingencies than the other organisms we have studied. We have every reason to expect, therefore, that the most effective control of human learning will require instrumental aid. The simple fact is that, as a mere reinforcing mechanism, the teacher is out of date. This would be true even if a single teacher devoted all her time to a single child but her inadequacy is multiplied many-fold when she must serve as a reinforcing device to many children at once. If the teacher is to take advantage of recent advances in the study of learning, she must have the help of mechanical devices.

✻   ✻   ✻

Some objections to the use of such devices in the classroom can easily be foreseen. The cry will be raised that the child is being treated as a mere animal and that an essentially human intellectual achievement is being analyzed in unduly mechanistic terms. Mathematical behavior is usually regarded, not as a repertoire of responses involving numbers and numerical operations, but as evidences of mathematical ability or the exercise of the power of reason. It is true that the techniques which are emerging from the experimental study of learning are not designed to "develop the mind" or to further some vague "understanding" of mathematical relationships. They are designed, on the contrary, to establish the very behaviors which are taken to be the evidences of such mental states or processes. This is only a special case of the general change which is under way in the interpretation of human affairs. An advancing science continues to offer more and more convincing alternatives to traditional formulations. The behavior in terms of which human thinking must eventually be defined is worth treating in its own right as the substantial goal of education.

Of course the teacher has a more important function than to say right or wrong. The changes proposed would free her for the effective exercise of that function. Marking a set of papers in arithmetic—"Yes, nine and six *are* fifteen; no, nine and seven *are not* eighteen"—is beneath the dignity of any intelligent individual. There is more important work to be done—in which the teacher's relations to the pupil cannot be duplicated by a mechanical device. Instrumental help would merely improve these relations. One might say that the main trouble with education in the lower grades today is that the child is obviously not competent and *knows it* and that the teacher is unable to do anything about it and *knows that too*. If the advances which have recently been made in our control of behavior can give the child a genuine competence in reading, writing, spelling, and arithmetic, then the teacher may begin to function, not in lieu of a cheap machine, but through intellectual, cultural, and emotional contacts of that distinctive sort which testify to her status as a human being.

Another possible objection is that mechanized instruction will mean technological unemployment. We need not worry about this until there are enough teachers to go around and until the hours and energy demanded of the teacher are comparable to those in other fields of employment. Mechanical devices will eliminate the more tiresome labors of the teacher but they will not necessarily shorten the time during which she remains in contact with the pupil.

A more practical objection: Can we afford to mechanize our schools? The answer is clearly yes. The device I have just described could be produced as cheaply as a small radio or phonograph. There would need to be far fewer devices than pupils, for they could be used in rotation. But even if we suppose that the instrument eventually found to be most effective would cost several hundred dollars and that large numbers of them would be required, our economy should be able to stand the strain. Once we have accepted the possibility and the necessity of mechanical help in the classroom, the economic problem can easily be surmounted. There is no reason why the schoolroom should be any less mechanized than, for example, the kitchen. A country which annually produces millions of refrigerators, dish-washers, automatic washing-machines, automatic clothes-driers, and automatic garbage disposers can certainly afford the equipment necessary to educate its citizens to high standards of competence in the most effective way.

There is a simple job to be done. The task can be stated in concrete terms. The necessary techniques are known. The equipment needed can easily be provided. Nothing stands in the way but cultural inertia. But what is more characteristic of America than an unwillingness to accept the traditional as inevitable? We are on the threshold of an exciting and revolutionary period, in which the scientific study of man will be put to work in man's best interests. Education must play its part. It must accept the fact that a sweeping revision of educational practices is possible and inevitable. When it has done this, we may look forward with confidence to a school system which is aware of the nature of its tasks, secure in its methods, and generously supported by the informed and effective citizens whom education itself will create.

THE NEW MATH (1958)   From Max Beberman, *An Emerging Program of Secondary School Mathematics* (Cambridge, Mass., 1958), pp. 1–6, 21–28, 33–38.

Introduction

In 1952, a few of us at the University of Illinois asked ourselves: Can able mathematicians together with skillful teachers develop materials of instruction and train high school teachers in their use so that the products of the program are enthusiastic students who understand mathematics? An affirmative answer could be justified only by a constructive existence proof, and we set ourselves the task of furnishing such a proof.

We are still at work on this task. The core of the working staff consist of Herbert E. Vaughan of the Department of Mathematics of the University of Illinois, and Gertrude Hendrix, William T. Hale, Eleanor McCoy, and myself of University High School, the laboratory school of the College of Education. A group called the University of Illinois Committee on School Mathematics (UICSM) serves as an advisory board to the staff, and draws its membership from the Colleges of Education, Engineering, and Liberal Arts and Sciences. I serve as administrative head of the project; Hale and I teach some of the newly developed courses at the laboratory school; Vaughan provides the principal mathematical substance of the program; Vaughan and I write the instructional materials, with considerable assistance from the other members of the staff; and Hendrix and McCoy direct the teacher-training phase of the project.

We now have courses for the four high school grades on trial in classrooms in a dozen pilot schools. Some forty teachers and over seventeen hundred students are participating. Some of these students are gifted eighth graders (or highly gifted seventh graders); the rest are students who would ordinarily be enrolled in conventional "college preparatory" or "academic" mathematics courses.

Our courses are still in the process of development. Portions of them have been used for as many as three consecutive years, but other portions are very recent revisions or are entirely new. One result of this experimentation and revision is our recognition of two major principles which we have used as guides in developing courses and in teaching students. For a time, these principles operated at a nonverbal level. It is only recently that we have been able to verbalize them and to identify them as our basic guides. A major portion of this report is devoted to the presentation and illustration of these principles.

The development of a new course of study is not undertaken in a vacuum. One has in mind an image of a student and a catalog of the student's knowledge and misknowledge. A student entering the ninth grade knows something about arithmetic and geometry; he has available to him a battery of algorisms for computing with "unsigned" real numbers, he is aware of some arithmetic generalizations, he has learned quite a few mensuration formulas, and he has solved many "practical" problems which involve applications of arithmetic and geometry. The curriculum developer also has in mind the traditional expectations of what a college-bound high school graduate should know of mathematics. He is expected, among other things, to solve equations (singly and in systems), to use algorisms and formulas in transforming algebraic and trigonometric expressions, to deduce theorems from postulates, to find ordered pairs which belong to relations, to graph relations, and to apply his knowledge to a host of geometric and physical problems.

We think that these objects are sensible and proper, and our curriculum is planned accordingly. But we insist upon an important qualification: the student must understand his mathematics. Now, the word 'understand' and its close relative 'meaningful' have been bandied about in educational circles to a point where just about everyone pledges allegiance to the goal of teaching meaningful and understandable mathematics. We have tried to translate these words into operational terms. We believe that a student will come to understand mathematics when his textbook and teacher use unambiguous language and when he is enabled to discover generalizations by himself. These two desiderata—discovery, and precision in language—are closely connected, for new discoveries are easier to make once previous discoveries are crystallized in precise descriptions (it is easier to discover how to solve equations when you know what an equation and a variable are!), and skill in the precise use of language enables a student to give clear expression to his discoveries. Despite the tie between these two facets of understanding, I shall, for convenience' sake, discuss them separately.

Precision of Language

The procedure through which a child becomes aware of a mathematical entity such as a number or a function is undoubtedly quite complicated and has yet to be described. However, let us assume that there are such things as mathematical entities, that their existence is nonphysical, and that human beings do develop awareness of them. As a child becomes aware of such an entity, he may want to talk about it. In such a case, he needs a name for it. Consider the preschool child who notices that to dress her three dolls she must have three dresses, three hats, three parasols, and three pairs of shoes. Her awareness of the class of sets of three things is an awareness of an entity. The entity is the number three and a name of the entity is the word 'three.' But the existence of the entity does not depend upon the invention of the word 'three', and the fact that a child may be acquainted with the word 'three' cannot be considered a sure sign that he has even the slightest awareness of the number three. To say that a child understands the number three is to say that the child is aware of this class of matching sets. He demonstrates this awareness by asserting correctly (through action or through words) that a given set either belongs or does not belong to this class. If the child is to function as a social being, he needs to communicate his awareness and, therefore, he needs a name (a word, perhaps merely a gesture) to denote the mathematical entity.

The social intercourse which is facilitated by the invention of a name undoubtedly results in a sharpening of the awareness and, therefore, in a "deepening of the understanding" of the entity. But an increasing familiarity with a name should not invest it with the properties of that which it denotes. The name and entity are distinct and must not be confused. It is our contention that in the exposition of elementary and secondary mathematics there is so much confusion of names with their referents that in many cases the student has never discovered that there is a distinction between symbols and their referents. Confusion in exposition is of little consequence to a student who has managed to maintain for himself the distinction between mathematical entities and the symbols which denote them because most of the time, as the cliche goes, "the intention is clear from the context". But, for the student who has not yet become aware of the mathematical entities in question, an exposition which is guilty of this confusion is just about useless. It is even dangerous, for a student can through imitation give behavioral evidence of understanding even though the awareness which is part of understanding is missing.

[1]Although mathematics educators now seem to regard 'meaningful mathematics' as platitudinous, it is greeted with warmth and surprise by most laymen. This lay attitude is surely an indictment of the conventional program.

Discovery

A second major principle which has guided us in developing the UICSM program is that the student will come to understand mathematics if he plays an active part in developing mathematical ideas and procedures. To us this means that after we have selected a body of subject matter to be learned we must design both exposition and exercises in such a way that the student will discover principles and rules.

It may be argued by some that this procedure is too authoritarian, and that the most desirable situation would be to permit the student to proceed without preselection of content and without direction. We concede that this may be a desirable state of affairs in a class which is under the tutelage of a gifted teacher. But we are developing a curriculum for the mass of schools which demand a preselected content and for the mass of teachers who want textbooks. And we maintain that even with preselected content there are opportunities for the expression of individuality on the part of the student. Some of our most fruitful text developments and revisions have come from problems suggested by our students and from leads which they have uncovered and pursued.

In what follows I present several examples of developments in our program which result in discoveries by students. I do this to illustrate our notion of discovery. The illustration is followed by a defense of the "discovery method" of teaching mathematics.

Teachers of the conventional course in beginning algebra recognize the fact that students are very quick in discovering a rule for adding directed numbers. In fact, the usual rule stated in textbooks is a necessarily complicated description of an algorism, and usually contains some confusion of symbol with referent. Any student capable of learning algebra in the first place will have invented this algorism. Any student who is able to interpret the textbook description is also able to carry out the algorism for adding without using the text description. Hence, our earliest opportunity for an important discovery in the UICSM program occurs in connection with the rule for adding directed numbers. All students succeed in this first attempt. On the other hand, the complete algorism for multiplication is seldom discovered under conventional treatments. Moreover, since we regard the positive numbers as different from the nondirected numbers, our students cannot discover that "$(+4) \times (+3) = +12$ because $(+4) \times (+3) = 4 \times 3$". In fact, since we regard a positive number such as $+4$ as different from the number 4, we were compelled to invent a physical interpretation for symbols such as "$(+4) \times (+3)$" and "$(+4) \times (-3)$" just as we invented a physical interpretation for symbols such as "$(+7) + (-8)$" and "$(-3) + (-2)$". (Of course, the algorism must eventually be justified either by a definition of the operation in question and a definition of directed numbers, or from postulates for the directed-number system. But, since we feel that neither the constructive nor the postulational approach is appropriate at the eighth- or ninth-grade levels, we make do with a carefully contrived and reasonable physical interpretation.) Once a student accepts the physical interpretation, he can use it to simplify symbols such as "$(-4) \times (+3)$". He is eager to find a way to get answers without using the physical interpretation. So he hunts for an algorism; when he finds it, he says that he has a short cut. The student who is slow to discover the algorism can continue to use the physical interpretation; the fact that others in the class are getting answers with great speed is usually enough to spur him on toward discovery.

It is important to point out here that it is unnecessary to require a student to verbalize his discovery to determine whether he is aware of a rule. The teacher can use a sequence of questions to determine whether the awareness is present. In fact, immediate verbalization has the obvious disadvantage of giving the game away to other students, as well the more serious disadvantage of compelling the student to make a statement when he may not have the linguistic capacity to do so. This is especially the case when a student does not yet know how to use variables. A premature verbalization is, almost by definition in such a case, imprecise and, thus, not a faithful rendering of what the student actually believes, or is coming to believe. The teacher's acceptance of an imprecise verbalization is a signal to the student that he has completed the process of searching for a generalization. And even a precise verbalization from the student is not a sure sign that he is aware of the class of instances of the generalization, for he may regard the generalization itself as just another "instance". (The preceding sentence is a possible explanation of the phenomenon of the student who has "learned" a rule or has even "discovered" one as evidenced by his stating it, but who misapplies it in subsequent exercises.) This technique of delaying the verbalization of important discoveries is characteristic of the UICSM program, and differentiates our discovery method from other methods which are also called 'discovery methods' but which always involve the immediate verbalization of discoveries.

✳   ✳   ✳

Somewhat related to the notion of discovery in teaching is our insistence that the student become aware of a concept before a name has been assigned to the concept. (This awareness frequently leads to the student's invention of a name, an activity which also involves creativity.) This point of view has enabled us to include in our program certain concepts which observers claim belong to the province of graduate courses in mathematics because of the "abstract" nature of the concepts. Our experience in teaching students that a relation is a set of ordered pairs is an example. To be sure, we take considerably more time in getting our students to àrrive at this notion than can be taken at the graduate course level. (But it may also be the case that the reputation that this notion has of being difficult can be attributed to the fact that not enough time is devoted in graduate courses to building the concept for the student!) Through a series of activities and exercises in which a student becomes quite familiar with graphs of sets of ordered pairs (advancing from finite domains and ranges to infinite ones), the student builds for himself the concept that a set of ordered pairs is an entity and that membership in the set can be expressed by means of a graph, and, in some cases, by means of a simple sentence. Since the sentence also expresses in a vague way a "relation" between the components of a member of the set of ordered pairs, it is natural and convenient to regard the set itself as the relation. By focusing the student's attention on the graphs of relations, it is possible to build considerable geometric intuition about such properties of relations as reflexiveness, irreflexiveness, symmetry, asymmetry, antisymmetry, and transitivity. Our students are comfortable with phrases such as 'equality is a subset of congruence', "is the converse of", and 'proportionality is an equivalence relation'. It is an easy step from the general study of relations to the study of functions as a special class of relations.

JEROME BRUNER ON THE STRUCTURE OF KNOWLEDGE (1960)   From
Jerome S. Bruner, *The Process of Education* (New York, 1960), pp. 5–15, 33, 37–40.

It is interesting that around the turn of the last century the conception of the learning process as depicted by psychology gradually shifted away from an emphasis upon the production of general understanding to an emphasis on the acquisition of specific skills. The study of "transfer" provides the type case—the problem of the gain in mastery of other activities that one achieves from having mastered a particular learning task. Whereas the earlier emphasis had led to research studies on the transfer of formal discipline—the value obtained from the training of such "faculties" as analysis, judgment, memory, and so forth—later work tended to explore the transfer of identical elements or specific skills. In consequence, there was relatively little work by American psychologists during the first four decades of this century on the manner in which the student could be trained to grasp the underlying structure or significance of complex knowledge. Virtually all of the evidence of the last two decades on the nature of learning and transfer has indicated that, while the original theory of formal discipline was poorly stated in terms of the training of faculties, it is indeed a fact that massive general transfer can be achieved by appropriate learning, even to the degree that learning properly under optimum conditions leads one to "learn how to learn." These studies have stimulated a renewed interest in complex learning of a kind that one finds in schools, learning designed to produce general understanding of the structure of a subject matter. Interest in curricular problems at large has, in consequence, been rekindled among psychologists concerned with the learning process.

A word is needed at this point to explain in fuller detail what is meant by the *structure* of a subject, for we shall have occasion to return to this idea often in later pages. Three simple examples—from biology, from mathematics, and from the learning of language—help to make the idea clearer. Take first a set of observations on an inchworm crossing a sheet of graph paper mounted on a board. The board is horizontal; the animal moves in a straight line. We tilt the board so that the inclined plane or upward grade is 30°. We observe that the animal does not go straight up, but travels at an angle of 45° from the line of maximum climb. We now tilt the board to 60°. At what angle does the animal travel with respect to the line of maximum climb? Now, say, he travels along a line of 75° off the straight-up line. From these two measures, we may infer that inchworms "prefer" to travel uphill, if uphill they must go, along an incline of 15°. We have discovered a tropism, as it is called, indeed a geotropism. It is not an isolated fact. We can go on to show that among simple organisms, such phenomena—regulation of locomotion according to a fixed or built-in standard—are the rule. There is a preferred level of illumination toward which lower organisms orient, a preferred level of salinity, of temperature, and so on. Once a student grasps this basic relation between external stimulation and locomotor action, he is well on his way toward being able to handle a good deal of seemingly new but, in fact, highly related information. The swarming of locusts where temperature determines the swarm density in which locusts are forced to travel, the species maintenance of insects at different altitudes on the side of a mountain where crossbreeding is prevented by the tendency of each species to travel in its preferred oxygen zone, and many other phenomena in biology can be understood in the light of tropisms. Grasping the structure of a subject is understanding it in a way that permits many other things to be related to it meaningfully. To learn structure, in short, is to learn how things are related.

Much more briefly, to take an example from mathematics, algebra is a way of arranging knowns and unknowns in equations so that the unknowns are made knowable. The three fundamentals involved in working with these equations are commutation, distribution, and association. Once a student grasps the ideas embodied by these three fundamentals, he is in a position to recognize wherein "new" equations to be solved are not new at all, but variants on a familiar theme. Whether the student knows the formal names of these operations is less important for transfer than whether he is able to use them.

The often unconscious nature of learning structures is perhaps best illustrated in learning one's native language. Having grasped the subtle structure of a sentence, the child very rapidly learns to generate many other sentences based on this model though different in content from the original sentence learned. And having mastered the rules for transforming sentences without altering their meaning—"The dog bit the man" and "The man was bitten by the dog"—the child is able to vary his sentences much more widely. Yet, while young children are able to *use* the structural rules of English, they are certainly not able to say what the rules are.

The scientists constructing curricula in physics and mathematics have been highly mindful of the problem of teaching the structure of their subjects, and it may be that their early successes have been due to this emphasis. Their emphasis upon structure has stimulated students of the learning process. The reader will find the emphasis reflected many times in the pages that follow.

Clearly there are general questions to be faced before one can look at specific problems of courses, sequences, and the like. The moment one begins to ask questions about the value of specific courses, one is asking about the objectives of education. The construction of curricula proceeds in a world where changing social, cultural, and political conditions continually alter the surroundings and the goals of schools and their students. We are concerned with curricula designed for Americans, for their ways and their needs in a complex world. Americans are a changing people; their geographical mobility makes imperative some degree of uniformity among high schools and primary schools. Yet the diversity of American communities and of American life in general makes equally imperative some degree of variety in curricula. And whatever the limits placed on education by the demands of diversity and uniformity, there are also requirements for productivity to be met: are we producing enough scholars, scientists, poets, lawmakers, to meet the demands of out times? Moreover, schools must also contribute to the social and emotional development of the child if they are to fulfill their function of education for life in a democratic community and for fruitful family life. If the emphasis in what follows is principally on the intellectual side of education, it is not that the other objectives of education are less important.

We may take as perhaps the most general objective of education that it cultivate excellence; but it should be clear in what sense this phrase is used. It here refers not only to schooling the better student but also to helping each student achieve his optimum intellectual development.

*   *   *

Four themes are developed in the chapters that follow. The first of these has already been introduced: the role of structure in learning and how it may be made central in teaching. The approach taken is a practical one. Students, perforce, have a limited exposure to the materials they are to learn. How can this exposure be made to count in their thinking for the rest of their lives? The dominant view among men who have been engaged in preparing and teaching new curricula is that the answer to this question lies in giving students an understanding of the fundamental structure of whatever subjects we choose to teach. This is a minimum requirement for using knowledge, for bringing it to bear on problems and events one encounters outside a classroom—or in classrooms one enters later in one's training. The teaching and learning of structure, rather than simply the mastery of facts and techniques, is at the center of the classic problem of transfer. There are many things that go into learning of this kind, not the least of which are supporting habits and skills that make possible the active use of the materials one has come to understand. If earlier learning is to render later learning easier, it must do so by providing a general picture in terms of which the relations between things encountered earlier and later are made as clear as possible.

Given the importance of this theme, much too little is known about how to teach fundamental structure effectively or how to provide learning conditions that foster it. Much of the discussion in the chapter devoted to this topic has to do with ways and means of achieving such teaching and learning and with the kinds of research needed to help in preparing curricula with emphasis on structure.

The second theme has to do with readiness for learning. Experience over the past decade points to the fact that our schools may be wasting precious years by postponing the teaching of many important subjects on the ground that they are too difficult. The reader will find the chapter devoted to this theme introduced by the proposition that the foundations of any subject may be taught to anybody at any age in some form. Though the proposition may seem startling at first, its intent is to underscore an essential point often overlooked in the planning of curricula. It is that the basic ideas that lie at the heart of all science and mathematics and the basic themes that give form to life and literature are as simple as they are powerful. To be in command of these basic ideas, to use them effectively, requires a continual deepening of one's understanding of them that comes from learning to use them in progressively more complex forms. It is only when such basic ideas are put in formalized terms as equations or elaborated verbal concepts that they are out of reach of the young child, if he has not first understood them intuitively and had a chance to try them out on his own. The early teaching of science, mathematics, social studies, and literature should be designed to teach these subjects with scrupulous intellectual honesty, but with an emphasis upon the intuitive grasp of ideas and upon the use of these basic ideas. A curriculum as it develops should revisit these basic ideas repeatedly, building upon them until the student has grasped the full formal apparatus that goes with them. Fourth-grade children can play absorbing games governed by the principles of topology and set theory, even discovering new "moves" or theorems. They can grasp the idea of tragedy and the basic human plights represented in myth. But they cannot put these ideas into formal language or manipulate them as grownups can. There is much still to be learned about the "spiral curriculum" that turns back on itself at higher levels. . . .

The third theme involves the nature of intuition—the intellectual technique of arriving at plausible but tentative formulations without going through the analytic steps by which such formulations would be found to be valid or invalid conclusions. Intuitive thinking, the training of hunches, is a much-neglected and essential feature of productive thinking not only in formal academic disciplines but also in everyday life. The shrewd guess, the fertile hypothesis, the courageous leap to a tentative conclusion—these are the most valuable coin of the thinker at work, whatever his line of work. Can school children be led to master this gift?

The three themes mentioned so far are all premised on a central conviction: that intellectual activity anywhere is the same, whether at the frontier of knowledge or in a third-grade classroom. What a scientist does at his desk or in his laboratory, what a literary critic does in reading a poem, are of the same order as what anybody else does when he is engaged in like activities—if he is to achieve understanding. The difference is in degree, not in kind. The schoolboy learning physics *is* a physicist, and it is easier for him to learn physics behaving like a physicist than doing something else. The "something else" usually involves the task of mastering what came to be called at Woods Hole a "middle language"—classroom discussions and textbooks that talk about the conclusions in a field of intellectual inquiry rather than centering upon the inquiry itself. Approached in that way, high school physics often looks very little like physics, social studies are removed from the issues of life and society as usually discussed, and school mathematics too often has lost contact with what is at the heart of the subject, the idea of order.

The fourth theme relates to the desire to learn and how it may be stimulated. Ideally, interest in the material to be learned is the best stimulus to learning, rather than such external goals as grades or later competitive advantage. While it is surely unrealistic to assume that the pressures of competition can be effectively eliminated or that it is wise to seek their elimination, it is nonetheless worth considering how interest in learning per se can be stimulated. There was much discussion at Woods Hole of how the climate in which school learning occurs can be improved, discussion that ranged over such diverse topics as teacher training, the nature of school examinations, the quality of a curriculum. Chapter 5 is devoted to this set of problems.

While there was considerable discussion at Woods Hole of the apparatus of teaching—films, television, and audio-visual aids, teaching machines, and other devices that a teacher may use in instruction—there was anything but consensus on the subject. Virtually all of the participants agreed that not teaching devices but teachers were the principal agents of instruction, but there was a division of opinion on how the teacher was to be aided. The disagreement, perhaps, can be summarized (though oversimplified in the process) in terms of the relative emphasis placed upon the teacher as such and upon the aids that the teacher might employ. The two extreme positions—stated in exaggerated form—were, first, that the teacher must be the sole and final arbiter of how to present a given subject and what devices to use, and, second, that the teacher should be explicator and commentator for prepared materials made available through films, television, teaching machines, and the like. The implication of the first extreme position is that every effort should be made to educate the teacher to a deep knowledge of his or her subject so that he or she may do as good a job as possible with it, and at the same time the best materials should be made available for the teacher.

*　　*　　*

We begin with the hypothesis that any subject can be taught effectively in some intellectually honest form to any child at any stage of development. It is a bold hypothesis and an essential one in thinking about the nature of a curriculum. No evidence exists to contradict it; considerable evidence is being amassed that supports it.

To make clear what is implied, let us examine three general ideas. The first has to do with the process of intellectual development in children, the second with the act of learning, and the third with the notion of the "spiral curriculum" introduced earlier.

*　　*　　*

The curriculum of a subject should be determined by the most fundamental understanding that can be achieved of the underlying principles that give structure to that subject. Teaching specific topics or skills without making clear their context in the broader fundamental structure of a field of knowledge is uneconomical in several deep senses. In the first place, such teaching makes it exceedingly difficult for the student to generalize from what he has learned to what he will encounter later. In the second place, learning that has fallen short of a grasp of general principles has little reward in terms of intellectual excitement. The best way to create interest in a subject is to render it worth knowing, which means to make the knowledge gained usable in one's thinking beyond the situation in which the learning has occurred. Third, knowledge one has acquired without sufficient structure to tie it together is knowledge that is likely to be forgotten. An unconnected set of facts has a pitiably short half-life in memory. Organizing facts in terms of principles and ideas from which they may be inferred is the only known way of reducing the quick rate of loss of human memory.

Designing curricula in a way that reflects the basic structure of a field of knowledge requires the most fundamental understanding of that field. It is a task that cannot be carried out without the active participation of the ablest scholars and scientists. The experience of the past several years has shown that such scholars and scientists, working in conjunction with experienced teachers and students of child development, can prepare curricula of the sort we have been considering.

*　　*　　*

The "spiral curriculum." If one respects the ways of thought of the growing child, if one is courteous enough to translate material into his logical forms and challenging enough to tempt him to advance, then it is possible to introduce him at an early age to the ideas and styles that in later life make an educated man. We might ask, as a criterion for any subject taught in primary school, whether, when fully developed, it is worth an adult's knowing, and whether having known it as a child makes a person a better adult. If the answer to both questions is negative or ambiguous, then the material is cluttering the curriculum.

If the hypothesis . . . is true—that any subject can be taught to any child in some honest form—then it should follow that a curriculum ought to be built around the great issues, principles, and values that a society deems worthy of the continual concern of its members. Consider two examples—the teaching of literature and of science. If it is granted, for example, that it is desirable to give children an awareness of the meaning of human tragedy and a sense of compassion for it, is it not possible at the earliest appropriate age to teach the literature of tragedy in a manner that illuminates but does not threaten? There are many possible ways to begin: through a retelling of the great myths, through the use of children's classics, through presentation of and commentary on selected films that have proved themselves. Precisely what kinds of materials should be used at what age with what effect is a subject for research—research of several kinds. We may ask first about the child's conception of the tragic, and here one might proceed in much the same way that Piaget and his colleagues have proceeded in studying the child's conception of physical causality, of morality, of number, and the rest. It is only when we are equipped with such knowledge that we will be in a position to know the child will translate whatever we present to him into his own subjective terms. Nor need we wait for all the research findings to be in before proceeding, for a skillful teacher can also experiment by attempting to teach what seems to be intuitively right for children of different ages, correcting as he goes. In time, one goes beyond to more complex versions of the same kind of literature or simply revisits some of the same books used earlier. What matters is that later teaching build upon earlier reactions to literature, that it seek to create an ever more explicit and mature understanding of the literature of tragedy. Any of the great literary forms can be handled in the same way, or any of the great themes—be it the form of comedy or the theme of identity, personal loyalty, or what not.

So too in science. If the understanding of number, measure, and probability is judged crucial in the pursuit of science, then instruction in these subjects should begin as intellectually honestly and as early as possible in a manner consistent with the child's forms of thought. Let the topics be developed and redeveloped in later grades. Thus, if most children are to take a tenth-grade unit in biology, need they approach the subject cold? Is it not possible, with a minimum of formal laboratory work if necessary, to introduce them to some of the major biological ideas earlier, in a spirit perhaps less exact and more intuitive?

Many curricula are originally planned with a guiding idea much like the one set forth here. But as curricula are actually executed, as they grow and change, they often lose their original form and suffer a relapse into a certain shapelessness. It is not amiss to urge that actual curricula be reexamined with an eye to the issues of continuity and development. . . . One cannot predict the exact forms that revision might take; indeed, it is plain that there is now available too little research to provide adequate answers. One can only propose that appropriate research be undertaken with the greatest vigor and as soon as possible.

PRE-SCHOOL ENRICHMENT (1962)   From J. McVicker Hunt, "The Psychological Basis for Using Pre-School Enrichment As An Antidote For Cultural Deprivation," *Merrill-Palmer Quarterly*, vol. X, pp. 237–40.

Although the question of the permanence of the effects of experiental deprivation during infancy is far from answered, such evidence as I have been able to find, and as I have summarized here, would indicate that if the experiental deprivation does not persist too long, it is reversible to a substantial degree. If this be true, the idea of enriching the cognitive fare in day-care centers and in nursery schools for the culturally deprived looks very promising.

RE-APPRAISAL
1951–1973

The fact that cultural deprivation is such a global and undifferentiated conception at present invites at least speculative attempts to construe the nature of the deficit and to see wherein and when the infant of the poor and lower-class parents is most likely to be experientially deprived.

One of the important features of lower-class life in poverty is crowding. Many persons live in little space. Crowding, however, may be no handicap for a human infant during most of his first year of life. Although there is no certainty of this, it is conceivable that being a young infant among a large number of people living within a room may actually serve to provide such wide variations of visual and auditory inputs that it will facilitate development more than will the conditions typical of the culturally privileged during most of the first year.

During the second year, on the other hand, living under crowded conditions could well be highly hampering. As the infant begins to throw things and as he begins to develop his own methods of locomotion, he is likely to find himself getting in the way of adults already made ill-tempered by their own discomforts and by the fact that they are getting in each other's way. Such considerations are dramatized in Lewis's (1961) *The Children of Sanchez,* an anthropological study of life in poverty. In such a crowded atmosphere, the activities in which the child must indulge for the development of his own interests and skills must almost inevitably be sharply curbed.

Beginning in the third year, moreover, imitation of novel patterns should presumably be well-established, and should supply a mechanism for learning vocal language. The variety of linguistic patterns available for imitation in the models provided by lower-class adults is both highly limited and wrong for the standards of later schooling. Furthermore, when the infant has developed a number of pseudo-words and has achieved the "learning set" that "things have names" and beings asking "what's that?", he is all too unlikely to get answers. Or, the answers he gets are all too likely to be so punishing that they inhibit such questioning. The fact that his parents are preoccupied with the problems associated with their poverty and their crowded living conditions leaves them will little capacity to be concerned with what they conceive to be the senseless questions of a prattling infant. With things to play with and room to play in highly limited, the circumstances of the crowded lower-class offer little opportunity for the kinds of environmental encounters required to keep a two-year-old youngster developing at all, and certainly not at an optimal rate and not in the direction demanded for adaptation in a highly technological culture.

If this armchair analysis has any validity, it suggests that the infant developing in the crowded circumstances of lower-class poverty may develop well through the first year; begin to show retardation during the second year; and show even more retardation during the third, fourth, and fifth years. Presumably, that retardation which occurs during the second year, and even that during the third year, can probably be reversed to a considerable degree by supplying proper circumstances in either a nursery school or a day-care center for children of four and five—but I suspect it would be preferable to start with children at three years of age. The analysis made here, which is based largely upon what I have learned from Piaget (1936) and from my own observations of development during the pre-school years, could be tested. You may be interested to know that Dr. Ina Uzgiris and I are attempting to develop a way of using the sensorimotor and early symbolic schemata which Piaget has described for the first two, and hopefully three, years of the child's life, to provide a method of assessing intellectual and motivational development. If our effort is successful, it should provide a tool with which to determine when and how the conditions of development within the crowded circumstances of poverty begin to result in retardation and/or apathy.

Pre-school Enrichment and the Problem of the Match

Our traditional emphasis in education upon arithmetic and language skills can well lead us astray in the attempt to develop a program of pre-school enrichment. If Piaget's . . . observations are correct, spoken language—that is to say the motor side of the language skill—comes only after images, or the central processes representing objects and events, have been developed out of repeated encounters with those objects and events. The fact that chimpanzees show clearly the capacity to dissemble their own purposes even though they lack language . . . lends support from phylogenetic comparisons to this notion of Piaget's. You have undoubtedly heard that O. K. Moore, of Yale, has been teaching pre-school children to read with the aid of an electric typewriter hooked up to an electronic system of storing and retrieving information. The fact that, once children have learned to recognize letters by pressing the proper keys of a typewriter, they are then enabled to discover spontaneously that they can draw these letter with chalk on a blackboard, lends further support to the image-primacy thesis. Moreover, Moore has observed that the muscular control of such four-year-olds as have presumably acquired solid imagery of the letters in the course of their experience with those letters at the electric typewriter corresponds to that typical of seven- or eight-year-olds (personal communication).

What appears to be important for a pre-school enrichment program is an opportunity to encounter circumstances which will foster the development of these semi-autonomous central processes that can serve as imagery representative of objects and events and which can become the referents for the spoken symbols required in the phonemic combinations of spoken or written language. Moore's results also suggest to me that these semiautonomous central processes, if adequately developed, can serve as the basis for motor control. Such considerations suggest that a proper pre-school enrichment program should provide children with an opportunity to encounter a wide variety of objects and circumstances. They suggest that the children should also have an opportunity to imitate a wide variety of models of action and of motor language. The danger of attempting to prescribe materials and models at this stage of knowledge, however, is that the prescriptions may well fail to provide a proper match with what the child already has in his storage. The fact that most teachers have their expectations based on experience with culturally-privileged children makes this problem of the match especially dangerous and vexing in work with the culturally deprived.

PIAGET ON THE STAGES OF COGNITIVE DEVELOPMENT IN

CHILDREN (1962)   From Barbara Inhelder, "Some Aspects of Piaget's Genetic Approach to Cognition," as quoted in William Kessen and Clementine Kuhlman, eds., "Thought in the Young Child." *Monographs of the Society for Research in Child Development,* vol. XXVII, pp. 24–28.

Three operational structures can be distinguished in the cognitive development of the child; each one characterizes the attainment of a major stage of development and, within each one, substages can be distinguished.

Stage I. Sensory-motor operations. The first major stage occupies approximately the first 18 months. It is characterized by the progressive formation of the schema of the permanent object and by the sensory-motor structuration of one's immediate spatial surroundings. The observations and longitudinal studies carried out by Piaget on his own children indicate that this progression originates in the functional exercising of mechanisms that are reflexive in origin, and leads gradually to a system of movements and of displacements. In this way the child's conception of the permanence of objects is brought about. This sensory-motor system is made up of displacements which, although they are not reversible in the mathematical sense, are nonetheless amenable to inversion *(renversables)*. The displacements made in one direction can be made in the inverse direction; the child can return to his starting point; he can attain the same goal by different routes. In the coordination of these movements into a system, the child comes to realize that objects have permanence; they can be found again, whatever their displacements (even if these be out of the field of vision). . . .

Stage II. Concrete thinking operations. The second developmental stage extends from the middle of the second year until the eleventh or twelfth year. It is characterized by a long process of elaboration of mental operations. The process is completed by about the age of 7 and is then followed by an equally long process of structuration. During their elaboration, concrete thought processes are irreversible. We observe how they gradually become reversible. With reversibility, they form a system of concrete operations. For example, we can establish that although a 5-year-old has long since grasped the permanence of objects, he has by no means yet any notion of the elementary physical principle of the conservation of matter.

Let us consider one of the many possible examples: Given two equal balls of plasticine, the child is asked to roll one of them into a long sausage form, to flatten it into a pancake, or to break it into small pieces. He is then asked, in terms adapted to his understanding, whether the quantity of matter has increased, decreased, or remained the same. This experiment and others similar to it have shown that most 5- or 6-year-olds assert without hesitation that each change in form involves a change in the amount of matter. Influenced sometimes by the increase in one dimension, sometimes by the decrease in the other, the child seems uncritically to accept the dictates of whatever aspect of change he happens to perceive. Errors decrease gradually as the older child becomes more and more inclined to relate different aspects or dimensions to one another, until we finally come to a principle of invariance, which may be formulated somewhat as follows: "There must be the same amount of plasticine all the time. You only have to make the sausage into a ball again and you can see right away that nothing is added and nothing is taken away."

After a period of gradual construction, and at about 7 years of age, a thought structure is formed; as a structure, it is not yet separated from its concrete content. In contrast with the sensory-motor actions of the first stage—which were executed only in succession—the various thought operations of the second stage are carried out simultaneously, thus forming systems of operations. These systems, however, are still incomplete. They are characterized by two forms of reversibility: (a) negation, as expressed in the plasticine experiment, in which a perceived change in form is canceled by its corresponding negative thought operation; and (b) reciprocity, as expressed in the child's discovery that "being a foreigner" is a reciprocal relationship, of that left-right, before-behind spatial relationships are relative. At the concrete level, these forms of reversibility are used independently of one another; in formal thought, they will form one unified system of operations.

The gradual formation of this system of reciprocal relations can be observed most easily in an experiment concerning the relativity of points of view in a system of perspectives. The material for such an experiment—conducted by Piaget and Meyer-Taylor—consists of a landscape of three cardboard mountains, and a series of pictures of landscapes drawn from different points of view. The child remains at a given position, while the experimenter moves from one to another. For each position taken by the experimenter, the child is asked to select the picture which represents what the experimenter sees. It is difficult for 5-year-olds to realize that another person may see something different from what he (the child) sees. However, during the following years, the increasingly operational character of the child's thought leads to a definite progress in his choice of pictures, until finally he solves the problem.

Thus, during the course of this second period of development, we can follow the genesis of thought processes which—at about 7 years of age—issues in the elementary logicomathematical thought structures. Nevertheless, it still requires years before these structures are brought to bear on all possible concrete contents. It can be shown, for example, that the principle of invariance (constancy, conservation) is applied to the quantity of matter earlier than to weight, and to volume still later. In every case, as earlier schemas are integrated into later ones, they are altered in the process. Thus, the process seems indeed to be one of genetic construction—a gradual process of equilibration within a limited system of concrete operations. Equilibrium within this system is attained at about 11 or 12 years of age. This operational structure, in turn, forms the basis of the development of the formal thinking operations.

Stage III. Formal thinking operations. The third stage of intellectual development begins, on the average, at about 11 or 12 years of age and is characterized by the development of formal, abstract thought operations. In a rich cultural environment, these operations come to form a stable system of thought structures at about 14 or 15 years of age.

In contrast to the child in stage II, whose thought is still bound to the concrete here and now, the adolescent is capable of forming hypotheses and of deducing possible consequences from them. This hypotheticodeductive level of thought expresses itself in linguistic formulations containing propositions and logical constructions (implication, disjunction etc.). It is also evident in the manner in which experiments are carried out, and proofs provided. The adolescent organizes his experimental procedure in a way that indicates a new sort of thought structure.

The following are two of many possible examples of formal thinking, one concerning combinatorial or formal logic, and the other, proportionality. In the experiment on combinatorial logic, the child is presented with five bottles of colorless liquid. The first, third, and fifth bottles, combined together, will produce a brownish color; the fourth contains a color-reducing solution, and the second bottle is neutral. The child's problem is to find out how to produce a colored solution. The adolescent in this third stage of development gradually discovers the combinatorial method. This method consists in the construction of a table of all the possible combinations and of determining the effectiveness or the ineffectiveness of each factor.

In experiments on proportionality the adolescent is given a candle, a projection screen, and a series of rings of different diameters; each ring is on a stick which can be stuck into a board with evenly spaced holes. The instructions are to place all the rings between the candle and the screen in such a way that they will produce only a single "unbroken" shadow on the screen—the shadow of a "ring". Gradually, the adolescent discovers that "there must be some relationship", and he tries to find out what relationship it is by systematic attempts, until finally he becomes aware that it is a matter of proportionality. As one bright 15-year-old said, "The thing is to keep the same proportion between the size of the ring and the distance from the candle; the absolute distance doesn't matter."

*   *   *

These experimental methods of procedure were not "taught" in our Geneva schools when our subjects were at this age level. Our subjects, at the point of departure for the formal thought structures, discovered these procedures without specific tuition.

In analyzing these thought structures, Piaget found that they come more and more to approximate formal models as the subject's experimental procedures become more and more effective. The combinatorial method, for example, corresponds to a lattice structure and the method of proportionality to the structure of a group. Above all, the formal thought structure, as compared to the concrete, is marked by a higher degree of reversibility. And, in this case, the two forms of reversibility already constituted—negation and reciprocity—are now united in a completely operational system. We can say that the new operational abilities formed during this third period are the abilities that open up unlimited possibilities for the youth to participate constructively in the development of scientific knowledge—provided that his setting offers him a suitable practice-ground and a favorable intellectual atmosphere.

BENJAMIN BLOOM ON THE SIGNIFICANCE OF EARLY ENVIRONMENT

EDUCATION IN THE UNITED STATES

(**1964**)   From Benjamin Bloom, *Stability and Change in Human Characteristics* (New York, 1964), pp. 88–91, 203–5, 209–11, 214–16.

3250   There is little doubt that intelligence development is in part a function of the environment in which the individual lives. The evidence from studies of identical twins reared separately and reared together as well as from longitudinal studies in which the characteristics of the environments are studied in relation to changes in intelligence test scores indicate that the level of measured general intelligence is partially determined by the nature of the environment. The evidence so far available suggests that extreme environments may be described as *abundant* or *deprived* for the development of intelligence in terms of the opportunities for learning verbal and language behavior, opportunities for direct as well as vicarious experience with a complex world, encouragement of problem solving and independent thinking, and the types of expectations and motivations for intellectual growth.

The effects of the environments, especially of the extreme environments, appear to be greatest in the early (and more rapid) periods of intelligence development and least in the later (and less rapid) periods of development. Although there is relatively little evidence of the effects of changing the environment on the changes in intelligence, the evidence so far available suggests that marked changes in the environment in the early years can produce greater changes in intelligence than will equally marked changes in the environment at later periods of development.

Much more research is needed to develop precise descriptions and quantitative measurements of environments as they relate to the development of intelligence. More research is also needed, especially of a longitudinal nature, on the amount of change in intelligence which can be produced by shifting a person from one environment to another. However, a conservative estimate of the effect of extreme environments on intelligence is about 20 I.Q. points. This could mean the difference between a life in an institution for the feeble-minded or a productive life in society. It could mean the difference between a professional career and an occupation which is at the semiskilled or unskilled level. A society which places great emphasis on verbal learning and rational problem solving and which greatly needs highly skilled and well-trained individuals to carry on political-social-economic functions in an increasingly complex world cannot ignore the enormous consequences of deprivation as it affects the development of general intelligence. Increased research is needed to determine the precise consequences of the environment for general intelligence. However, even with the relatively crude data already available, the implications for public education and social policy are fairly clear. Where significantly lower intelligence can be clearly attributed to the effects of environmental deprivations, steps must be taken to ameliorate these conditions as early in the individual's development as education and other social forces can be utilized. . . .

Our attempts to describe the development of intelligence [are] really attempts to describe stability and change in measurements of intelligence. Such measurements are based on particular tests and test problems, and these measurements are undoubtedly affected by the experiences individuals have had both in school and out of school. It seems likely that performance on these tests is responsive to the experiences individuals have had and that change in the general picture of stability and change could be produced by new developments in education and by different child-rearing practices. All this is merely an attempt to alert the reader to the view that our picture of stability and change in measured intelligence is one based on things as they now are, and this includes the particular tests to measure intelligence, the child-rearing practices of families in Western cultures, and educational practices in the schools. It is conceivable that changes in any or all of these could produce a very different picture than the one we have been able to draw. It is to be hoped that we can find ways of prolonging the growth of general intelligence throughout life. It is to be hoped that we can drastically reduce the incidence of low levels of intelligence and increase the proportion of individuals reaching high levels of measured intelligence. There is some evidence that the secular trend in the increase of height over the past 40 years is paralleled by a similar trend in the increase of general intelligence over several decades (Terman and Merrill, 1937).

*   *   *

That the environment does influence change in a characteristic is documented throughout this work. Studies of identical twins reared together and reared apart demonstrate that the nature of the environment will determine the extent to which individuals, with presumably identical genetic characteristics, will develop in similar or very different ways. Also studies of the effect of *changes* in environments further document the extent to which the environment influences the development of particular characteristics. This is not to say that each characteristic is equally influenced by the environment. Thus educational achievement is rather obviously influenced by environmental differences, while height is likely to be influenced by the environment to a lesser degree. Nevertheless, without taking a position on the relative influence of heredity and environment, we cannot imagine any research worker or any research in disagreement with the basic proposition that *the environment is a determiner of the extent and kind of change taking place in a particular characteristic.*

*   *   *

Throughout this work we have attempted to demonstrate the general curve for the development of each characteristic. In most of these curves there appears to be a period of relatively rapid development, usually in the early years, followed by periods of less rapid development. Much of the growth of human characteristics seems to conform to a negatively accelerated curve which may be described as a parabolic curve. We should hasten to add that there are some characteristics which appear to grow at a relatively constant rate. However, a most important generalization supported by our findings is that *growth is generally not in equal units per unit of time.* Admitting, then, that there are some exceptions to the proposition, we have been interested in the varying effects of the environment on a characteristic at different phases in its development. We would venture the proposition that *a characteristic can be more drastically affected by the environment in its most rapid period of growth than in its least rapid period of growth.* This proposition is logically supported by the rather obvious point that once a characteristic has reached its complete *development,* (height at age 20, intelligence or I.Q. at about 20, etc.) variations in the environment could have no further effect on that characteristic. Similarly, in a period of very *little development* of a characteristic, the variations in the environment could have very little effect on the characteristic. Moving then to the more and more rapid periods of development, we would anticipate that the environment would have more and more effect on the characteristic. Thus, to take a simple and rather extreme example, the gain in the height of boys from birth to age 3 is about 24% of mature stature, whereas the gain during the period age 3 to 6 represents about 9% of mature stature. It is likely that the environment could affect the development of stature more during the period of birth to 3 years than during the age period 3 to 6 years.

*   *   *

The prolongation of the period of dependency for youth in the Western cultures has undoubtedly been a factor in desensitizing parents, school workers, and behavioral scientists to the full importance of the very early environmental and experimental influences. Youth are usually required to attend school until at least 16 years of age and the majority live at home and attend school until about age 18.

Another factor which has contributed to our lack of full awareness of the enormous influence of the early environment is the limited evidence on the effects of the early environment. And, even when such evidence is available from longitudinal studies of intelligence and personality, it has most frequently been interpreted as indicating little predictive significance for early measures of these characteristics. There appears to be an implicit assumption running through the culture that change in behavior and personality can take place at any age or stage in development and that the developments at one age or stage are no more significant than those which take place at another.

A central finding in this work is that for selected characteristics there is a negatively accelerated curve of development which reaches its midpoint before age 5. We have reasoned that the environment would have its greatest effect on a characteristic during the period of its most rapid development.

*   *   *

We believe that the early environment is of crucial importance for three reasons. The first is based on the very rapid growth of selected characteristics in the early years and conceives of the variations in the early environment as so important because they shape these characteristics in their most rapid periods of formation. . . .

However, another way of viewing the importance of the early environment has to do with the sequential nature of much of human development. Each characteristic is built on a base of that same characteristic at an earlier time or on the base of other characteristics which precede it in development. Hebb (1949) has pointed out the differences in activity and exploratory behavior of animals reared in very stimulating environments in contrast to those reared under very confining conditions. Such differences in initial behavior are of significance in determining the animal's activity and intelligence at later stages in its development. Erickson (1950) has described stages in the development of human beings and the ways in which the resolution of a developmental conflict at one stage will in turn affect the resolutions of subsequent developmental conflicts. The entire psychoanalytic theory and practice is based on a series of developmental stages (Freud, 1933; Freud, 1937; Horney, 1936; Sullivan, 1953) with the most crucial ones usually taking place before about age 6. The resolution of each stage has consequences for subsequent stages. Similarly, other more eclectic descriptions of development (Havighurst, 1953; Piaget, 1932; Murray, 1938; Gesell, 1945) emphasize the early years as the base for later development. All these theoretical as well as empirical descriptions of development point up the way in which the developments at one period are in part determined by the earlier developments and in turn influence and determine the nature of later developments. For each of these viewpoints, the developments that take place in the early years are crucial for all that follows.

A third reason for the crucial importance of the early environment and early experiences stems from learning theory. It is much easier to learn something new than it is to stamp out one set of learned behaviors and replace them by a new set. The effect of earlier learning on later learning is considered in most learning theories under such terms as habit, inhibition, and restructuring. Although each learning theory may explain the phenomena in different ways, most would agree that the first learning takes place more easily than a later one that is interfered with by an earlier learning. Observation of the difficulties one experiences in learning a new language after the adolescent period and the characteristic mispronunciations which tend to remain throughout life are illustrations of the same phenomena.

A HIERARCHY OF EDUCATIONAL TASKS (1964)   From Frank M. Hewett, "A Hierarchy of Educational Tasks For Children With Learning Disorders," *Exceptional Children,* vol. XXXI, pp. 207–14.

The child who fails to learn in school is communicating vital information about himself. He may be revealing his general intellectual limitations or some specific sensory or preceptual-motor handicap. He may be apprising us of the inadequacy of his previous schooling due to poor teaching methods or sporadic attendance. He also may be communicating an inability to cope with social and emotional stress which is manifest through poor concentration, comprehension, and recall in the classroom.

Seldom is such a child's message clearly understood and seldom is the explanation for his learning problem a simple and specific one. Constitutional, environmental, and psychological factors usually overlap, making it difficult for the educator to properly program the child according to his most basic needs.

In the search for remedial and educational guidelines, teachers have looked to the clinical psychologist, the educational psychologist, and the child psychiatrist for assistance. While these child specialists offer relevant generalizations regarding learning and behavior, their contributions are not always practical in the classroom setting. The battle strategies laid down by the military advisors in the tactical planning room may need alteration and clarification before they are useful to the field general on the front lines.

It is this gap between theory and practice that the concept of a hierarchy of educational tasks for children with learning disorders attempts to narrow. The basic assumption underlying the hierarchy holds that an effective educational program for children with learning disorders depends on the establishment of a point of meaningful contact between the teacher and the child. Such a point of contact is only possible when the child is experiencing gratification in the learning situation and the teacher is in control.

There is a wide range of types of gratification which the child may experience while learning (from a candy reward for each correct response to recognition for academic efforts by a place on the honor roll), and there are many levels of teacher control (from permissiveness in structuring to careful setting of behavioral limits and academic expectations). It is establishing this point of contact while providing appropriate student gratification and teacher control that is a crucial consideration for the teacher of children with learning problems. The normal achiever may be motivated by grades, competition with other students, and a variety of other social and intellectual rewards, but the nonachiever may be deterred from entering into the learning situation by these same factors. While normal classroom procedures may dictate that all students be held for definite academic and behavior standards, the child with a learning problem may have to be viewed within a broader educational frame of reference.

The theoretical framework to be presented in this paper has grown out of three years experience teaching hospitalized emotionally handicapped children and adolescents with learning problems at the Neuropsychiatric Institute School (NPI) at the University of California, Los Angeles. It is the result of a felt need on the part of the staff teachers for a set of working hypotheses with which to formulate realistic goals for their complex and highly variable students.

Meaningful contact and varying degrees of student gratification and teacher control are possible on seven educational task levels. These will be discussed following a brief historical review of the concept of a hierarchy of human development and behavior.

*   *   *

The hierarchy of educational tasks which makes up the subject matter of this paper represents an attempt to organize and formulate psychological principles of development into practical terms for the educator. Each level is concerned with the reciprocal tasks of student and teacher in the formation of a working educational relationship. In an ascending order, the hierarchy of educational tasks consists of primary, acceptance, order, exploratory, relationship, mastery, and achievement task levels.

Primary Task Level

The most primitive level on which teacher and child may interact is the primary task level. Here, the teacher's task is to provide maximum gratification and to establish contact on the student's own terms, thus laying the groundwork for future interactions in which more control and direction may be exercised. This level is generally only applicable in cases of severe learning disability where the student is inaccessible to social controls or totally resistant to learning. The child's task is minimal at the primary level. The teacher may appeal to such basic needs as a desire for candy or money rather than to more complex social needs. It is at this level that operant conditioning work with severely regressed schizophrenics and autitic children is undertaken. Lindsley . . ., Ferster . . ., Isaacs . . . and Weiland . . . have demonstrated that such inaccessible individuals may take note of a teacher or therapist who has a piece of candy, gum or the like, pay attention and begin to learn or relearn appropriate behavior in order to obtain the desired reward.

Related work starting at the primary level has been done by Slack, (in a lecture to NPI Staff, 1963), who has shown how a desire for money may be an effective motivator for getting a school drop out with serious motivation and learning problems to learn to read. Slack approached such individuals and asked them to help him evaluate a teaching machine reading program. For their efforts these boys were given a penny for each frame of the reading program. In the course of acquiring $30 and exposure to a basic reading vocabulary, many of these boys actually learned to read. More important, many manifested a new interest in school and learning and continued their formal education. Similar methods have proven successful with inmates in state prisons.

In the NPI school, a two-year educational program was recently completed with a twelve-year-old autistic boy who had never developed speech . . . The goal of the program was to teach this withdrawn and unsocialized boy to read and write and thus enable him to communicate more appropriately with the environment. Candy gumdrops established the first point of contact between teacher and student. The boy paid attention and engaged in simple reading activities such as picture-word matching in order to obtain an immediate candy reward. Once this contact was established, the boy was given higher level tasks. This is an important characteristic of the hierarchy; while the teacher may initiate contact with the child on the lowest appropriate level, the eventual goal is to engage him in higher level tasks.

Acceptance Task Level

The second task level consists of acceptance tasks for both teacher and child. At this level, the teacher communicates complete acceptance of the child and attempts to establish the beginning of a relationship with him, still primarily on the child's terms. While the child may have perceived the teacher as an undifferentiated means to immediate gratification at the primary level, he now has the task of relating to the teacher as a social object. The child acknowledges the teacher's presence and responds more attentively to verbal interaction. This is only the very early stage of a genuine interpersonal relationship between teacher and child which will be the focus of a later level. At the acceptance level the teacher sets few behavioral limits and usually works on a one-to-one basis with the child. The student competes only with his own record and no grades are given. In addition, academic demands are minimal and the teacher's main goal is to make the child secure and successful in the learning situation. Toward this end a variety of activities such as playing games and taking walks may be utilized.

The child who refuses to get out of his parents' car and come into the classroom may be joined in the back seat by the teacher who initiates contact through reassurance and gradual building of an accepting relationship. At the NPI school, teachers often go on the wards and into the bedrooms of frightened withdrawn children who refuse to get out of bed and come to school. The teacher may sit on the bed next to the child and use a small projector to show him colored slides on the ceiling, or read him stories, or play simple games with him. The teacher who hopes to be successful with children who have serious learning problems and who are threatened by the prospect of further failure should be prepared to settle for the minimal but significant tasks on the acceptance level.

Order Task Level

Once the child feels accepted and is secure enough to form a limited relationship with the teacher, he is ready to be held for order tasks on the next level of the hierarchy. The teacher's task at this level is to increase her control and gradually impose structure, routine, and definite limits in the learning situation. Although academic deficiencies are still completely accepted, the student is now held for more appropriate behavior. He no longer works on his own terms and must accept certain conditions for learning. The work of Cruickshank . . . Haring and Phillips . . . suggests that well structured classroom environments facilitate learning among hyperactive and distractible students with learning problems. The concept of order and routine is basic to an effective learning situation for all children but particularly important for children with learning disorders whose erratic patterns of functioning in the classroom have contributed to their failure to learn. At the order level the teacher carefully judges the child's capacity for choice, presents him with small realistically attainable units of work and removes extraneous stimuli which are distracting in an effort to promote maximum gratification and success in the classroom.

At the NPI school, a resistant, nonconforming child who has failed to learn is often brought into the classroom for periods of ten to fifteen minutes a day. During this short period, the child's task is to function at the order level as a "student"—sit at a desk, follow simple directions and routines, and control his behavior. Longer periods are introduced as the student is able to tolerate them. During this time the child may be given certain order tasks to do such as sorting objects on the basis of size and color, puzzle making, or map coloring and labeling.

Recently a seventeen-year-old boy with a severe physical disability who had never learned to read was provided with an elaborate experiential reading program based solely on his great interest in rockets. The teacher spared no amount of effort in providing the boy with stimulating and interesting material. The boy, however, came to school when he pleased, would only work as long as he wished, and in essence set his own limits in the learning situation. Despite the ingenuity and total dedication of the teacher, the reading program was a complete failure. It was only after a staff conference during which the lack of limits and teacher control in the program were examined that a change was made. The boy was later told than an instructional program in reading was avilable for him but only at certain specific times. If he wanted to learn to read, he had to participate exactly as the teacher directed, otherwise he did not have to come to school. The results were surprising. The boy showed up in class regularly and began to learn to read. He worked diligently and functioned on the teacher's terms. While for some students, an experiential or exploratory program, such as the one first tried with this boy, would be successful, it was necessary in this case to engage the student in tasks at the order level before learning could take place. Exploratory educational activities, to be discussed at the next level, are more likely to be successful once the student is functioning on the order-task level.

The task of maintaining order may be overlearned by the rigid and obsessive-compulsive child with a learning problem. It will be the teacher's task to direct such a child's energies from, rather than toward, more order and routine. This is another characteristic within all levels of the hierarchy. It is the teacher's task to help students who display extreme behavior to achieve a healthier balance.

Exploratory Task Level

Exploratory tasks are found on the next level of the hierarchy. Once the teacher and child have formed a beginning working relationship, they may explore the environment together. Now it is the teacher's task to introduce learning by offering the child a rich variety of multisensory experiences. The child's task is to reach out and explore the real world around him with his eyes, ears, hands, nose, and even his taste buds. It is the appeal that exploratory activities have for the child, not their appropriateness for his chronological age or grade level, that is important.

The teacher assesses the sense of modalities by which the child learns best. Where sensory and perceptual motor problems exist, particular attention is paid to making the child's learning experience as reinforcing as possible. The work of Kephart . . . and others has stressed the importance of readying a child for more complex educational tasks by special emphasis on the basic perceptual motor components of learning; these are undertaken at the exploratory level. Concrete experiences are utilized as a basis for instruction. The stimulus value and impact of all materials is enhanced and immediate feedback is provided the child following each exploratory experience. Exploratory activities such as music, simple games, imaginative play, story telling and arts and crafts, are often useful in reaching a child who is not ready for academic instruction.

The Fernald . . . method of kinesthetic word tracing and experiential story writing as a means of teaching remedial reading and spelling is an example of an educational program organized at the exploratory level. The child is given a highly reinforcing means of word learning which provides him with visual, auditory, and kinesthetic cues. In addition he writes a daily story in class about anything of interest to him. This combination approach which reinforces reading and spelling offers an opportunity written expression and is a highly successful approach with children with learning disorders.

An eleven-year-old catatonic schizophrenic boy in the NPI school was carried to school in a rigidly immobilized state. After several weeks he interacted and cooperated with his teacher for the first time by pushing a lever which turned on a slide projector and exposed a series of colored pictures of prehistoric animal life in front of him. The boy was motivated by a strong personal interest in prehistoric animals. A teacher of sixth grade normal children observed this boy's daily lever pushing interaction with the teacher and remarked that it was "interesting" but expressed concern because no regular sixth grade science curriculum in her school included the study of prehistoric life. Needless to say, the concept of a hierarchy of educational tasks and the necessity for establishing a point of contact with a severely handicapped child was alien to her.

Relationship Task Level

Relationship tasks are found on the next level of the hierarchy. The teacher has the task of increasing her value as a social reinforcer and forming a genuine interpersonal relationship with the child. This implies more than mutual acceptance which was the focus of the acceptance task level for the interpersonal relationship now becomes an important source of motivation. The child is concerned with gaining the teacher's approval and recognition. The teacher expresses more personal interest in the child and uses social approval and disapproval more freely as a means of motivation and control. It is at this level that the child's peer relationships also are of greater concern to the teacher. Students with similar interests and needs may be paired and more group instruction may be utilized.

Since the child who has failed to learn in school has often been subjected to considerable social devaluation, the tasks at this level are of particular importance. The teacher who sets realistic academic goals for the nonachiever and who helps him achieve success resulting in deserved praise and recognition will be shaping positive academic and social attitudes which may have far-reaching implications. A relationship with an adult who objectively deals with one's shortcomings while communicating respect and acceptance may be highly significant to the child with a learning disorder who has had previous faulty relationships with rejected parents and unreasonable teachers.

A bright thirteen-year-old boy in the NPI school who was deficient in all achievement areas, particularly long division, had adopted the position that he was far too intelligent to concern himself with mundane educational matters. He was going to design a computer that would solve all mathematical problems in order to prove his genius. This boy's fear of facing the reality of his educational needs was prompted by achievement-conscious parents who would not settle for anything but an all "A" report card. The teacher devoted almost an entire semester forming a relationship with this boy. The relationship was developed while working on science experiments at the exploratory level. The turning point occurred when the boy completed a simple electrical device with the teacher's help. He found he could diagram and explain its function mathematically. The boy explained to the teacher, "This is the first thing I ever made that worked and that I really understand." From this point on, the boy talked less and less on his grandiose and unrealistic aspirations and began to work on his existing school problems.

The five previously discussed levels are essentially readiness levels for formal academic work. They have been stressed more than will be the remaining two levels because their importance may be overlooked by the teacher who views the child with a learning disorder as primarily in need of remedial academic help. Not until the child has shown the capacity to handle the lower level tasks is he seen as really ready to undertake remedial work solely on the mastery level. While remedial work may be given on any level, the emphasis will not be on academic accomplishment but on more basic educational needs as implied by the hierarchy.

Mastery Task Level

When the child is ready to deal with his academic deficiencies and concentrate on basic curriculum, mastery tasks on the next level of the hierarchy are undertaken.

The teacher's task at the mastery level is to help the student acquire essential information and understanding about the environment and to develop the intellectual and vocational skills necessary for social survival. The students learn reading, writing, and arithmetic since these skills are basic for all learning. The emphasis is on practical application of these skills to daily living. Intelligence and achievement testing are important at the mastery level. The teacher carefully assesses a given child's learning potential as well as his specific academic deficits before formulating a program on the mastery level. In addition, the use of progress tests and grading may be introduced.

Since the emotionally handicapped child with a learning disorder may have a marginal if not faulty reality orientation and limited resources for communication and social interaction, mastery skills are vitally important to him. One of the characteristics of emotionally handicapped children is that they often complete tasks on the hierarchy out of sequence. The schizophrenic child may learn to read, spell, and master number concepts while relating to the teacher on the primary level. Despite these academic gains, such a child may make no progress on the acceptance, order, exploratory, and relationship level. In the broadest sense, despite academic progress, the child is still suffering from a serious learning disorder and the teacher's goals should be set accordingly.

Achievement Task Level

Not a great deal needs to be said about achievement tasks which constitute the higher level on the hierarchy. The child who is consistently self-motivated, achieving up to his intellectual potentials, eager for new learning experiences, and socially well-integrated in the classroom, is functioning on the achievement level. All teachers know the joy of working with such children. These are the children who have successfully completed all the tasks described on the lower levels and who are in a position to devote their energies to learning.

Discussion

The staff teachers of the NPI school have found it useful to describe and program all students within the framework of the educational tasks levels on the hierarchy. The student's observed functioning level is plotted for each task shortly after his enrollment and an educational program is formulated for him. In the charting of these plans, the following considerations are made:

(1) The most significant goals will be set on the lowest task levels where the student is either deficient or given to extremes. The chances that a student will be successful at a given task level are greatly increased if he is adequately functioning at all lower levels.

(2) The educational program may be best instituted on a task level where the student is functioning reasonably well. This initial level may be above or below the level viewed as most in need of emphasis. Therefore, the schizophrenic overachiever may be reached initially on a purely academic and intellectual level with the more important tasks of the relationship and exploratory levels emphasized as soon as possible.

(3) Once contact has been established with a student on a particular level, the teacher attempts to deal with unmet tasks on lower levels, and then to move up the hierarchy as quickly as possible.

(4) Several task levels may be worked on concurrently and seldom will a teacher restrict an educational program to only one level. However, lower, unmet task levels will receive greater emphasis.

(5) From time to time, students may regress in their functioning at a particular task level necessitating a reassessment of goals and a possible alteration of the educational program.

✳   ✳   ✳

It is hoped that this concept of a hierarchy of educational tasks may make psychological principles of development more meaningful to teachers and provide them with a measure of educational economy in understanding and adequately programming for children with learning disorders.

The compulsory system has become a universal trap, and it is no good. Very many of the youth, both poor and middle class, might be better off if the system simply did not exist, even if they then had no formal schooling at all. (I am extremely curious for a philosophic study of Prince Edward County in Virginia, where for some years schooling did not exist for Negro children.)

But what would become of these children? For very many, both poor and middle class, their homes are worse than the schools, and the city streets are worse in another way. Our urban and suburban environments are precisely not cities or communities where adults naturally attend to the young and educate to a viable life. Also, perhaps especially in the case of the overt drop-outs, the state of their body and soul is such that we must give them refuge and remedy, whether it be called school, settlement house, youth worker, or work camp.

There are thinkable alternatives. Throughout this little book, as occasion arises, I shall offer alternative proposals that I as a single individual have heard of or thought up. Here are half a dozen directly relevant to the subject we have been discussing, the system as compulsory trap. In principle, when a law begins to do more harm than good, the best policy is to alleviate it or try doing without it.

i. Have "no school at all" for a few classes. These children should be selected from tolerable, though not necessarily cultured, homes. They should be neighbors and numerous enough to be a society for one another and so that they do not feel merely "different." Will they learn the rudiments anyway? This experiment cannot do the children any academic harm, since there is good evidence that normal children will make up the first seven years school-work with four to seven months of good teaching.

ii. Dispense with the school building for a few classes; provide teachers and use the city itself as the school—its streets, cafeterias, stores, movies, museums, parks, and factories. Where feasible, it certainly makes more sense to teach using the real subject-matter than to bring an abstraction of the subject-matter into the school building as "curriculum." Such a class should probably not exceed 10 children for one pedagogue. The idea—it is the model of Athenian education—is not dissimilar to Youth gang work, but not applied to delinquents and not playing to the gang ideology.

iii. Along the same lines, but both outside and inside the school building, use appropriate *unlicensed* adults of the community—the druggist, the storekeeper, the mechanic—as the proper educators of the young into the grown-up world. By this means we can try to overcome the separation of the young from the grown-up world so characteristic in modern urban life, and to diminish the omnivorous authority of the professional school-people. Certainly it would be a useful and animating experience for the adults. (There is the beginning of such a volunteer program in the New York and some other systems.)

iv. Make class attendance not compulsory, in the manner of A. S. Neill's Summerhill. If the teachers are good, absence would tend to be eliminated; if they are bad, let them know it. The compulsory law is useful to get the children away from the parents, but it must not result in trapping the children. A fine modification of this suggestion is the rule used by Frank Brown in Florida: he permits the children to be absent for a week or a month to engage in any worthwhile enterprise or visit any new environment.

v. Decentralize an urban school (or do not built a new big building) into small units, 20 to 50, in available store-fronts or clubhouses. These tiny schools, equipped with record-player and pin-ball machine, could combine play, socializing, discussion, and formal teaching. For special events, the small units can be brought together into a common auditorium or gymnasium, so as to give the sense of the greater community. Correspondingly, I think it would be worthwhile to give the Little Red Schoolhouse a spin under modern urban conditions, and see how it works out: that is, to combine all the ages in a little room for 25 to 30, rather than to grade by age.

vi. Use a pro rata part of the school money to send children to economically marginal farms for a couple of months of the year, perhaps 6 children from mixed backgrounds to a farmer. The only requirement is that the farmer feed them and not beat them; best, of course, if they take part in the farm-work. This will give the farmer cash, as part of the generally desirable program to redress the urban-rural ratio to something nearer to 70% to 30%. (At present, less than 8% of families are rural.) Conceivably, some of the urban children will take to the other way of life, and we might generate a new kind of rural culture.

I frequently suggest these and similar proposals at teachers colleges, and I am looked at with an eerie look—do I really mean to *diminish* the state-aid grant for each student-day? But mostly the objection is that such proposals entail intolerable administrative difficulties.

Above all, we must apply these or any other proposals to particular individuals and small groups, without the obligation of uniformity. There is a case for uniform standards of achievement, lodged in the Regents, but they *cannot* be reached by uniform techniques. The claim that standardization of procedure is more efficient, less costly, or alone administratively practical, is often false. Particular inventiveness requires thought, but thought does not cost money.

A DIALOGUE BETWEEN MARIO MONTESSORI AND A. S. NEILL

(1964)   From "Mario Montessori and A. S. Neill: A Redbook Dialogue," *Redbook,* (December, 1964), pp. 42, 88–92.

NEILL (*With a characteristic twinkle*): What'll we fight about?

MONTESSORI (*Smiling*): I have no intention of fighting with you. You're probably a very hard fighter. You've been fighting all your life—for your cause, I mean.

NEILL: My dear man, you're dealing with a profoundly ignorant person. I've never read John Dewey. I've been accused of being a follower of Rousseau but I've never read the man. Many years ago I bought the Montessori books. Then I visited a Montessori school in London and got a shock. There was a lady there who— Signorina Maccheroni was her name——

MONTESSORI: That's right. She's still there.

NEILL: We were watching some children, and one boy was building a long stair out of special blocks and he began to use it as a train, puffing across the room, and she got frightfully annoyed and went and took the train away from him. And I said, "What the devil did you do that for?" She says, "He's using the apparatus for the wrong purpose." I said, "Well, if a child can't use his fantasy in play, if that's Montessorianism, I don't like it." Why must you make him stick to the long stair? What's the answer to that? Mind you, it was long ago, fifty years ago. But was she right or wrong?

MONTESSORI: First of all, Mr. Neill, I——

NEILL: Don't call me *Mister* Neill.

MONTESSORI: All right, Neill; first of all, I would like to say that I am much more ignorant than you are. Now, getting to your question, Dr. Montessori started her observations with very poor children. They were very disorderly, you might say, In fact, if it is possible to have gangsters of three and four years of age, they were that kind. Then, through the experience she gave them with certain learning apparatus, their behavior changed. She didn't understand why it changed until many years later, not until she was your age. But in her effort to understand how these destructive elements were replaced by something positive, she tried for a while to perserve the conditions of that first school. That was why, in the beginning, she was quite rigid. Now, when a child is born, he certainly is new to the world, isn't he?

NEILL: What?

MONTESSORI: New to the world. And one of his unconscious tasks is to classify his environment, to be able to recognize different objects—their size, qualities. In other words, he starts to classify. The "long stair" was part of the apparatus to help train a child to recognize different dimensions, and so forth. During a certain sensitive period very early in life he is attracted by nature to building such experience. If the child cannot fulfill his natural urges, he escapes into fantasy. The aim is not to stop him from escaping into fantasy but to try to bring him back—to implement his natural urges toward coordination, self-control, intelligence. As for your criticism of the apparatus, Dr. Montessori used to say, You are free to give the children anything. You can have a train if you want a train. If you want bricks you can have bricks. But if you use a microscope for riding horseback, it's useless to have a microscope. And that was why that distinction was made.

NEILL: The Montessorians talk so much about education. You know, I don't care a darn for education. What do you call education?

MONTESSORI: Well, everybody considers education reading and writing and mathematics. It is absolutely not that. That's one disagreement Dr. Montessori had and I'm having with some schools that call themselves Montessori, particularly in the United States right now. They stress how to teach the children to teach themselves. What Dr. Montessori was interested in was the construction of harmonious personalities in children so that they will not come into conflict with themselves and into conflict with adults.

NEILL: She must have been frightfully handicapped by her parents.

MONTESSORI: By whose parents?

NEILL: By the parents of her pupils. She hadn't any boarding schools, had she? The children must have been under terrific conflict.

MONTESSORI: Quite—quite. The parents were casual workers. Some of them had criminal records. They were dirty, and the mothers never combed their hair. In fact, the slovenliness was such that if you asked a woman after she had married, "Why don't you take care of yourself any more?" she'd say, "After all, I have a husband now; I don't need to." That was the attitude, and it certainly must have influenced the children. But surprisingly, the children then began to transform the parents.

When these children came home all clean and began putting things in order, the mothers seemed ashamed, and they too became more clean and tidy.

NEILL: Yes, yes.

MONTESSORI: Yes, and these mothers, after the children learned how to read and to write, they came to Dr. Montessori and said, "I'm so terribly ashamed. My child knows how to write and I do not. Please teach me." That is a positive influence from children four and five years old.

NEILL: This is beyond me. It's beyond me.

MONTESSORI: Why should this be beyond you?

NEILL: It's beyond me because you're talking about education, the three R's and science, and I'm thinking about the dynamics of life, the dynamic in a child, how we're going to prevent that child from becoming a Gestapo, or becoming a color hater and all these things. The sickness of the world. I'm interested in what we're going to do for children to stop them from being haters to stop them from being antilife. The methods, I don't think—

MONTESSORI: How do you feel that children can be saved from this kind of thing?

NEILL: Well, the first thing is to be loved. I mean, the only child I've ever had in my school I couldn't do very much with was the child who had no love as a baby. [*Pausing.*] There was a terrifying film on the BBC about a year ago about some nursery school in France where the nurses or nuns, or whoever they were, only gave physical attention and no love; and every child in the room was sitting rocking like that—and the journalist gave one a teddy bear and she just looked at it indifferently. They were all dead faces, all dead eyes. It was a terrible picture of what happens when a child doesn't get loved. And so I go from the point of view that the first thing a child wants is to be loved from the very beginning, and I don't care whether they learn reading by look-say or by the phonetic method. In fifty years it won't matter. At Summerhill we don't try to mold children in any way. I mean, we let them live and govern themselves. It's not so easy when they're four or five years old. We don't get them till they're five or six, and then they gradually sit at all the selfgovernment meetings and talk, very often talk sensibly when they're five. Fundamentally, I think, that's the idea of Summerhill anyhow, that the child must be free from the very beginning to be itself without being told how to live. Mind you, it is told how to live by living in the community. It's got to adapt itself.

MONTESSORI: I agree with you absolutely. I will give another example much stronger than you have given me. There was a Dutch doctor, in about 1923 or 1924, who had a nursery for orphans where some working mothers also left children in the day. But many of the orphans died.

NEILL: The orphans what?

MONTESSORI: By the time they were six months the orphans began to perish, die. They had the most perfect hygienic conditions. The nurses treated each child the same, orphan or not. The children of the working mothers were from poor people, who were dirty, who lived in unfavorable conditions, hygienically speaking. Yet these children flourished. The doctor saw that the only difference was that when a mother came, she took the child and began to kiss him and fondle him and things like that, and the orphans, those poor devils, had nothing of this kind. So the doctor told the nurses, do as the mothers do, start making love to the children. And what happened? The phenomenon of the orphans dying disappeared. So the need for love is tremendous in children. The only trouble comes in allowing mothers, as you say, to indoctrinate the children for things which they are not at the age to do. It goes against the guidance of nature, and that's where the trouble comes. You read in Dr. Montessori's first books that she considered adults to be the first enemy of the child, among them the mother and father. They did not understand the natural process of growth, and they saw the child doing something, trying to touch something—"That you cannot touch, this you cannot do, that you cannot do." And therefore there is the conflict that child finds himself in—the conflict between this driving energy that asks him to become a capable person and the parent's or the educator's ideas which tell him, "No, you must not do that, because I think it is not right."

NEILL: Yes, but mind you, in actual practice, you can't avoid a little of that. If a mother's cooking the dinner, she can't allow the child to go up and put his hands on the stove. She's got to say no, you see.

MONTESSORI: Of course, of course. That is common sense.

NEILL That's another matter, yes.

MONTESSORI: But, at the time, for instance, if the child wanted to play with something of his father's, the mother would slap it—"Leave it alone because that's for Papa." And if he tried to get a plate, "Leave it alone because you are going to break it." Then they would give them idle toys and unbreakable things. As soon as the child gets a breakable thing it would smash it down. Naturally. But afterward, as I say, when Dr. Montessori gave them a chance to grow in their own way, all this aggression and destructiveness disappeared. That was what converted Dr. Montessori, this disappearance of hatred and violence.

NEILL: Well, I'm all on the side of any system that minimizes hatred, of course I am. By the way, when I used to treat the children in analysis—I was more or less Freudian in those days—I got one of my staff to make a family of father and mother and brother and sister—dolls with sexual organs and, of course, different clothes—and I just left them lying about in my office. I had to renew the mother every six weeks. She was kicked to death and the father wasn't. It seemed to disprove completely Freud's theory about the father. It was the mother who was hated all the time.

MONTESSORI: What age were the children?

NEILL: Oh, up to twelve.

MONTESSORI: Up to twelve. Well there, at that age, a lot of violence appears. I suppose that if it was at the age of three and four, it would be just the opposite.

NEILL: I'm trying to link up what you say about education and reading and writing with what I think is important—freeing a child from guilt. Freedom from the idea of sin, freedom from the idea that the sexual parts are wicked. That's the sort of thing I'm interested in, freedom from guilt feelings, and I don't see how this is fitting in.

MONTESSORI: Well, it fits in the sense that if children are not permitted to have constructive experiences, they will find less desirable ones. Dr. Montessori had an expression, a little vulgar. She'd say, "If these hands want to do things with objects [*motioning out in the air*] and the hands are forbidden, where do they go? Naturally, they go down here."

NEILL: No, no, no, I think that's wrong. That fits in with the public [British private] school idea that the more you give the boys games, the less they'll masturbate.

MONTESSORI: No, no, no, not games, not games, not games. I find the child, in building himself into a person, has a hunger for certain things, not games. At the age I mean there are certain experiences which he prefers to games, so much so that he leaves toys. If you want to learn to swim, how can you develop your coordination if you're stopped from trying? And if you are not allowed to develop your coordination, you will seek satisfaction elsewhere. In the same way, mentally, if you're stopped from acquiring certain experiences, then you'll find compensation somewhere else. One way a child may go is toward masturbation. But this disappeared, my dear sir, disappeared when the children were permitted to do the things they really wanted and needed to do. It was not a question of repression.

NEILL: I never see it in my school either. I haven't seen one of my children masturbating in forty years, but I wouldn't think it healthy if masturbation disappeared.

MONTESSORI: But you agree with me that it is not something natural? After all, the organs are created, and when they are mature they will develop the inclination to function. But in the premature age, if they are brought into use then, it means there is something lacking.

NEILL: Not so much lacking—a fear of "You mustn't do that." I believe it begins in the cradle, myself, this reacting to adults. I don't agree, by the way, that masturbation is unnatural. Maybe there's too much attempt by the Montessorians to impose adult patterns. I feel that way without the evidence. I don't know enough about it, you see. I just feel there's a sort of adult pattern coming out of it, somehow.

MONTESSORI: Our essence, our central aim, is to serve the child for the sake of life, not for the sake of the three R's. But if society requests that the child learn the three R's for the advancement of the individual, not knowing them will be a handicap. It is not we who teach the child the three R's. We merely put before him the apparatus through which he gets a certain experience which is attractive to him. Working with this appartus, each child gathers his own knowledge of the three R's. Again it is self-creation, not imposition.

NEILL: When it comes to his learning things on his own, I can't think of any boy we've ever had who hasn't learned to use his hands. Some of them make their own furniture. They fantasy a thing and then turn it into something constructive. I think free children are very constructive, in the main.

MONTESSORI: Well, now, would you agree that if the child wants to do something with, let us say, carpentry—a box or anything like that— he would need to know the use of tools? Doesn't he need the self-discipline of learning the proper way to use them?

NEILL: Yes, but I have something to say about that. Some years ago I went to see a big school noted for its handwork, and I saw about twenty-four boys all planing, and I said to the teacher, how many of these boys will carry this on as a hobby when they leave? And he said, not one. And I didn't say it to him, but I think the reason was that they were only learning techniques or learning how to make joints instead of making a thing. I think the opposite way is the right way. In my school, for example, a child wants to make a box. He gets a saw and then he saws wood and nails it together roughly, and then next time he maybe puts screw nails in, and not always, but usually, when he gets older he says I don't like this. How do I make a joint? So then is the time to tell him. When he wants to do it, you see. I think that's where our handwork teaching is all wrong. It begins at the wrong end.

MONTESSORI: Absolutely. Absolutely.

NEILL: I had to drop a theory I've had for years. I've written about it. My theory was, you see, that children won't make a thing unless they can attach a fantasy to it. He makes a boat, he makes an airplane, he makes a sword. I used to have a hobby of hammering copper or brass, making brass bowls or trays. The children used to look at me with a slight superiority—look at old Neill, you see—and they didn't want to hammer brass because you can't attach a fantasy to a brass bowl. You can't fly the world with it. You can't go under the sea with it. But I had to modify my theory because my stepson was trained by the best potter in England. Then my boy started teaching pottery and he's getting some marvelous things out of small pupils.

They're making teapots and things that look practical and professional. And so my theory goes out the window like that. Children will indeed make things without fantasy.

MONTESSORI: Is it your idea that as children grow up among adults, their fantasy is crushed?

NEILL: Oh, the fantasy is destroyed. That's why it's so evil to send missionaries to convert the heathen. It's not right to destroy anybody's fantasy. You've no right to do it. I'd think myself a criminal if I were to go to somebody who's deeply religious and I tried to destroy his religious beliefs; and I think it would be criminal. Of course it would. And the same with a child.

MONTESSORI: Well, you think, then, that it is possible to crush fantasy?

NEILL: You can distort it. That may be one of the bases of the sickness of the world. The arresting of fantasy and the perversion of fantasy. You see, religion has become a fantasy. It's become perverted, and nobody is a Christian today. As Nietzche said, Christ was the first and last Christian. Jesus was real, but today I think our idea of Christianity is pure fantasy. Otherwise all the bishops would be sitting in Trafalgar Square against the H-bomb or something, instead of leaving it to an atheist like Bertrand Russell. Well, I'm wandering a bit. I'm wandering.

MONTESSORI: Well, you were saying that playing games—red Indians or something like that—is fantasy. I used to take children camping with me, a place in a wood where there was a stream. One day when they were playing red Indians they saw me absorbed with a plant which grew bent like that, instead of growing straight up, and I told them this was because the plant was looking for light. They said, "What? The plant looks for light?" Then they became interested, little by little, in other aspects of nature. Soon, in class, they began to do vegtable phsiology in a scientific way. Now, this led them, on their next camping trips, to observe the botanical situation, the geological situation, to recognize the work of a stream—erosion and deposition—things like that. Their outings, instead of being occasions for fantasy, such as playing Indians, became a sort of continuous exploratory journey. One time we had a lunch ready but couldn't get them to lunch because they were so interested in their scientific studies.

NEILL: How does this fit in with trying to guarantee that these children aren't going to beat their children or tell their children lies or try to control their children's lives, their emotions? Because I'm convinced that none of my old pupils will ever beat a child or tell them lies about anything or mold their opinions or characters in any way; and that's all I want. That's all. That satisfies me, and I'm wondering how much this fits in with the other things.

MONTESSORI: Well, when one grows up as I am describing, you don't need to tell lies. You don't tell lies. Dr. Montessori showed that we have hardly begun to discover the possibilities for developing honest, decent, happy human beings.

NEILL: We agree about that. The question is, how are you going to get there?

MONTESSORI: Well, I think she did what you also do—giving children freedom. But she also investigated how children go through sensitive periods.

NEILL: Sensitive periods?

MONTESSORI: Sensitive periods that unconsciously lead the child toward learning experiences and emotional equilibrium. These sensitive periods change from age to age. For instance, who is it that teaches a child to talk? When I studied English, I had books, I had teachers, I had help, I had professors. But I could never acquire the English of a child born in England. That child does it just by himself. There is nobody who teaches him. How is that possible at so young an age? The child starts his first syllables at six months, when there is no organized intelligence, no possibility of instructing him. Yet the child acquires the language so perfectly in its pronunciation and structure that it becomes the mother tongue.

NEILL: Yes, but he acquires balance and walking without any instruction, too.

MONTESSORI: Exactly, exactly. Speech is not the only thing. So in this process, evidently there is tremendous attraction felt by the child for the spoken word, for the way people talk. One will even acquire the subtle patterns of the gestures of the Chinese, and another the gestures of Italians. Dr. Montessori called this the absorbent mind of the child, the photographic mind, which acts not only through the intellect but also the emotions. At a certain stage of development, seeing others write, he starts writing. I think there is where the majority of educators do not consider the real feelings of the child. In most places, despite the child's demonstrated inclinations, it is forbidden by law for a child to learn to read or to write before he is six or seven.

NEILL: Where, in Italy?

MONTESSORI: In many countries. In many countries. In Italy, yes. In Switzerland it is forbidden. In France, the United States and elsewhere children are forbidden to learn until long after they have shown they are ready to do so. But Dr. Montessori had intercommunicating classes of children from three to six, for instance, in one room, and then from six to nine in another, each child working on his own level. Certain children would see older children, for instance, working, with a teacher's guidance, on the decimal system. Who could imagine something like that to be attractive to a child of four? But children of four and a half in her classes had such an intense interest that they actually appropriated the material for learning such things—and their interest lasted! Yet children of seven and eight were only mildly—only briefly interested. If you introduced reading and writing at seven years of age, it became something so terribly boring that the children hated it. Whereas the children of four, four and a half, they explode into writing. We've had the experience in several countries of Europe and Asia and America that a favorable age for learning reading and writing is between four and a half and five. Some people learn before. Three and a half. So in that sense the freedom that Dr. Montessori gave was not the so-called freedom of not having to do these things because they were too young, but to give them the opportunity to do them and see what the result was. That's why Dr. Montessori called it free choice. Whether it was learning to write or learning arithmetic.

NEILL: To hell with arithmetic. . . .

MONTESSORI: Why do you say to hell with arithmetic?

NEILL: That's partly personal. You see, I spent four years at Edinburgh University taking an Honours English degree and then I went to found a school in Germany in 1921, and suddenly I found I had to sit silent and listen to people talking about art and philosophy and music. I didn't learn a thing about them, and it struck me then what a miserably narrow thing any university education is. And it's true, I think, all of that stuff you learn at school, most of it, flies away. I once could read Homer in Greek; I can't now. I once could read Latin. I can't read Latin today. So much of that has gone, so that I discounted it as being relatively unimportant.

MONTESSORI: It is relatively unimportant.

NEILL: I've often had critics say to me, "Is it fair to keep a child away from music? It's not that they have to know music, but look at the joy they get." But look at the millions of good, happy people who don't learn music. Look at the millions who don't know anything about astronomy and things like that. So many things to know. But I find that children simply follow what they can. One boy with not much gray matter has just left our school. He's a carpenter, quite a good one and quite happy.

Four other boys are university professors—or at least lecturers. I had a boy of seventeen who left Summerhill unable to read or write. He's now a very successful engineer.

MONTESSORI: He couldn't read or write at the age of seventeen?

NEILL: No, he couldn't. He learned because he found that without reading he couldn't read engineering plans. That was a complicated case, because he had a grandmother who tried to make him read the Bible at three, I think. My daughter learned to read and write without any teaching at all, really, at five or six.

MONTESSORI: If one is interested, he will go to the effort of reading and writing, no matter at what age. We had one child who absolutely didn't want to read or write. No interest at all. Then he became intensely interested in biology. We had illustrated books in the class. He kept begging a friend to read him bits from them. His friend did it for three or four days, but finally he said, "Look, I have to do my own work. You go away." And then the first boy went to his teacher and said, "Please teach me how to read." And he learned very quickly.

NEILL: One drawback, I think, was the invention of the talkie cinema. In the early days when my children went to the old silents, with the printed words, one kid would ask, "What does that say?" and the other would say, "Oh, shut up. I'm watching." So they had to learn to read for themselves, you see.

MONTESSORI: They're actually doing that for adults in Indonesia now—did you know that? Movies are free, but only for those who know how to read. It seems to be a great success. But the sensitive period means that there is a natural interest for certain things at certain times of life. For instance, the question of square and cube root. These were very difficult in Dr. Montessori's day for children of thirteen and fourteen, just as they are today. But very funnily—she found them an immense joy for children of eight.

NEILL: Well, I believe that that isn't the important thing. The important thing is being yourself.

MONTESSORI: I agree.

NEILL: You hear all this talk about teaching social studies to make good citizens. I don't care about teaching social studies. I'm interested in living social studies. And the only way to do that is to let them govern themselves.

MONTESSORI: How does your self-government work?

NEILL: Well, self-government. You see, we meet every Saturday night and make our own laws. The chairman's always one of the children. And they pass laws and everybody has one vote. Because I'm headmaster it doesn't mean that what I propose is carried. What the group passes becomes law that everybody must observe. No minority rights. But the minority accepts them, as a general rule. They're quite sensible laws, you see. Now, remember we're a residence school. You couldn't very well have self-government in a day school. There's nothing to govern about. In our meetings you don't hear anything about lessons. What's brought up is So-and-so disturbed the community last night by making a row after lights-out time. Somebody rode my bicycle. Somebody swore in public down at the cinema. It's a social thing. Tell me, what happens when a child swears in a Montessori school? Do they swear at Montessori schools?

MONTESSORI: If they want to, yes.

NEILL: With the approval of the teacher?

MONTESSORI: Well, yes, with the approval of the teacher. Look, you must not—you had your experience long ago at a Montessori—

NEILL: I had the wrong experience—

MONTESSORI: But if you want to know what I'm doing in my old age, I'm trying to

3269

destroy the idea that Montessori schools are the perfect answer for all children—a view held by the prefectionist, rigid Montessorians. They have taken a grasp of only certain aspects of Montessorianism and sometimes condemn those who do not agree. They even condemned Dr. Montessori! Once she was trying something new, different from the way it was written in her book, and a teacher objected, "You cannot do that. That way is not Montessori." So if you bring me an example of something bad in a Montessori school, I can bring you much worse examples.

NEILL: Look at Freud and what they do in his name. Look at those American Summerhill schools. I sent a letter to the *Greenwich Village Voice,* in New York, disclaiming any affiliation with any American school that calls itself a Summerhill school. I've heard so many rumors about them. It's one thing to use freedom. Quite another to use license. I haven't visited regular American schools, but more than half the young people now in my school are Americans. There is a difference between American children and English children. The Americans are accustomed more to license than freedom, I think. In America I visited the home of a psychologist, or someone like that, hoping to have a chat with him. But his wife and two kids were in the room. The children monopolized the conversation. In another case visitors came with a new Cadillac. They had a boy of thirteen. The boy was bored with talking, and he said, "Dad, give me the car keys; I'm going for a ride." Dad says, "Okay, Son." A boy of thirteen with a Cadillac! I don't know if that's usual in America, but that's the impression I got. At Summerhill we've had difficulties with American children coming over. They've read my book, you see. They say, "This is a free school; we'll do what we like." And when they find they're up against self-government and they can't do what they like, they object.

MONTESSORI: How would you distinguish between freedom and license?

NEILL: Well, freedom in my school is, do what you like as long as you don't interfer with somebody else. Put it this way. If a child doesn't want to study mathematics, it's nobody's business; its his own. But if he wants to play a trumpet when other people are sleeping, that's everybody's business. That's license.

MONTESSORI: I agree. Absolutely.

COMPENSATORY EDUCATION (1965)   From Benjamin S. Bloom, et. al., *Compensatory Education For Cultural Deprivation* (New York, 1965), pp. 4–11, 13–15, 17–19.

In the present educational system in the U.S. (and elsewhere) we find a substantial group of students who do not make normal progress in their school learning. Predominantly, these are the students whose early experiences in the home, whose motivation for present school learning, and whose goals for the future are such as to handicap them in schoolwork. This group may also be defined as those who do not complete secondary education. As a first estimate, we would include the approximately one-third of the high-school entrants in the nation who do not complete secondary school. This figure is higher in many cities where slum living and educational segregation enlarge the problem.

It is this group with which we are at present concerned. We will refer to this group as culturally disadvantaged or culturally deprived because we believe the roots of their problem may in large part be traced to their experiences in homes which do not transmit the cultural patterns necessary for the types of learning characteristic of the schools and the larger society.

A large proportion of these youth come from homes in which the adults have a minimal level of education. Many of them come from homes where poverty, large family size, broken homes, discrimination, and slum conditions further complicate the picture.

While this group does include such in-migrants to the urban areas as Puerto Ricans, Mexicans, and southern-rural Negroes and whites, it also includes many individuals who were born in the large cities. It also includes many individuals living in small towns and rural areas. The designation of cultural deprivation should not be equated with membership in any ethnic group, but should be defined in terms of characteristics of the individual and/or the characteristics of his environment.

Cultural deprivation should not be equated with race. It is true that a large number of Negro children, especially those from homes with functionally illiterate parents, are likely to be culturally deprived. However, it is likely that as many as one-third of the Negro children in the large cities of the U. S. are at least the equal of the white norms for educational development. It should, however, be recognized that dramatic attention to the problems of cultural deprivation has come from the civil rights movement, as well as from the rearrangement of whites and Negroes in the large cities with regard to place of residence and school attendance.

✳   ✳   ✳

Basic Needs

Section 2. There is almost unanimous agreement that the prior satisfaction of the so-called basic needs is necessary before human beings can become concerned with and perform higher-level functions. With children, the adequate satisfaction of nutritional needs and the need for sleep and rest heightens the probability of their being able to perform competently in school situations. Adequate living conditions, clothing, exercise, and the availability of medical care—all contribute to the heightened probability of increased capability in school situations.

For children of low-income families, public health statistics generally confirm the increased incidence of gross organ deficiencies (for example, dental problems, defective vision, impaired hearing) as well as diseases commonly associated with adverse economic circumstances, such as tuberculosis. In addition, there are a variety of illnesses of debilitating nature that are commonly not treated in this group and sap their energies. Included here are various specific deficiency problems and parasitic invasions.

These deficiencies in basic needs operate to influence learning in a number of ways. Much of the energy and attention of the child is directed to his immediate needs and he is less able to attend to learning and school tasks which must seem to him as less urgent and obviously not very relevant to his present state. Even if the child does become accustomed to a lower level of living and to the rare feeling of well-being, he may have such a low level of energy as to be easily fatigued and to have relatively little endurance for the complex and demanding tasks of learning.

Furthermore, the satisfaction of immediate goals becomes more important to these children and their parents and less energy is available for distinct goals or long-range planning. Present-time orientation becomes far more central in their conception of things than future-time orientation—and much of education and learning is necessarily for some future time.

When children learn that their basic needs cannot be adequately provided for in a dependable way, they too often adopt a fatalistic attitude which generalizes to alter their patterns of living. Their ability to cope with the environment—to see light ahead—is impaired. Such passivity and defeatism (and, possibly, hostility) stemming from need deprivation is learned by the child from both the realities of living and from the parents who, through their daily behavior, communicate a general attitudinal orientation. This general attitude orientation can do much to give the child a self-fulfilling prophecy in which he expects to be frustrated in meeting his basic needs and in turn his expectations determine his views about himself and his environment. This prophecy, which is repeatedly verified, has basic consequences on personality and character.

While we must not confuse biological deprivation with cultural deprivation, there is little doubt that very frequently the two are associated, especially in the more poverty-stricken groups in our society. We do wish to emphasize that meeting these physical needs does not, by itself, lead to better learning. The adequate meeting of the basic needs merely sets the stage for the more direct attack on the problems of learning in this group.

Some Implications for the Schools

We do not regard the schools as having major responsibility for solving problems of poverty, but it is clear that the schools have a responsibility in helping school children meet these basic biological needs and especially so when adequate school learning is partially blocked by these need deficits. In our society parents take pride in "providing for their children" and the permanent "taking over" of such functions by the school or the community can have an adverse effect on the parents' sense of adequacy. Insofar as possible, provision for children should be made by their parents. However, we wish to stress that the physical needs of the children must be met and that no child should be expected to learn under conditions likely to nullify the efforts of the teacher and the school.

We have listened to many anecdotes about "heroic" school principals who provided special services such as dental care, clothing, and food either on their own or in violation of school regulations. While we might applaud such efforts, we are inclined to believe that these are the exceptions and that many children must do without because there is no way in which such basic needs can be met within the present school regulations.

That children should struggle to learn under such handicaps should be regarded as a serious indictment of school regulations and community morality. No child should be permitted or expected to learn under such adverse circumstances as hunger, fatigue, disease, or impaired bodily functions. If it is the school regulations which are at fault, they must be changed. If it is the lack of food and other provisions, action at the community, state, or national level should be quick and adequate.

1. Each child should be assured of an adequate breakfast to help him begin the learning tasks of the day. Each child should also be assured of a mid-day meal. If these meals cannot be provided by the home, they should be provided by the school or the community in such a way that no child feels a sense of shame or special distinction.

2. Each child should be given appropriate and frequent physical examinations by nurses, doctors, and dentists to determine special needs with respect to fatigue, disease, and dental, visual, and hearing problems. If these health services cannot be provided by the parents, it is the responsibility of the school and the community to see that they are taken care of.

3. No child should be subjected to feelings of inadequacy and shame because of lack of necessary clothing. If these needs cannot be provided by the parents, it is the responsibility of the school and community to see that each child is adequately clothed.

Early Experience

Section 3. It is clear that children do not come to school equally prepared for the learning tasks of first grade. This statement will not come as a surprise to elementary-school teachers who have always had to deal with such differences. However, the research of the past decade has been of great value in helping us understand not only how the children may be different in their responsiveness to learning experiences but also how some of these differences come to be.

Until recently, differences in children's I.Q. were attributed largely to native endowment; very little of the variation was attributed to the effects of environment. The more recent research has demonstrated that for children growing up under adverse circumstances the I.Q. may be depressed by a significant amount and that intervention at certain points (and especially in the period from ages three to nine) can raise the I.Q. by as much as ten to fifteen points. Such effects have been most clearly demonstrated for children with initial I.Q.'s of less than 110. While there is nothing sacred about the I.Q., it has been a useful indicator of general learning capability in the schools. A change in I.Q. is symptomatic of a change in general learning capability and this is likely to be verified by more direct measures of school learning. Furthermore, the measurement of the culturally deprived child's intelligence at one point does not determine the upper limits of what he might be able to learn in the schools if more favorable conditions are subsequently provided in the home and/or in the school.

Research reveals the aspects of the home environment which seem to be most significant in affecting the level of measured intelligence of the child as well as his school learning. In most general terms these may be described as involving provisions for general learning, models and help in language development, and parental stimulation and concern for achievement and learning on the part of the child. For the most part, it is the adults in the home who serve to stimulate the child's intellectual development. Other research reveals the very early development of the child's language and cognition and the extent to which further growth takes place each year.

RE-APPRAISAL
1951–1973

* * *

As the child attempts to communicate with others, and especially with his parents, he uses a relatively crude and limited language. In many middle-class homes, the child's language is extended by the parent's responses to his statements and questions. In culturally deprived homes, the parent is more likely to respond to the child with a monosyllable or to nod the head without using any words. The point of this is that one major difference between culturally deprived and more advantaged homes is the extension and development of the speech of children. Such differences have become very evident as a result of the studies done in various homes where parents are observed interacting with their children.

*   *   *

Put in other terms, the child in many middle-class homes is given a great deal of instruction about the world in which he lives, to use language to fix aspects of this world in his memory, and to think about similarities, differences, and relationships in this very complex enviroment. Such instruction is individual and is timed in relation to the experiences, actions, and questions of the child. Parents make great efforts to motivate the child, to reward him, and to reinforce desired responses. The child is read to, spoken to, and is constantly subjected to a stimulation set of experiences in a very complex environment. In short, he "learns to learn" very early. He comes to view the world as something he can master through a relatively enjoyable type of activity, a sort of game, which is learning. In fact, much of the approval he gets is because of his rapid and accurate response to this informal instruction in the home.

"Learning to learn" should not be confused with the early teaching of the child to read, to spell, and even to do simple arithmetic. Such coaching in the home is merely trying to do the school's task before the child enters public education. "Learning to learn" is a far more basic type of learning than coaching the child on school learning. It includes motivating the child to find pleasure in learning. It involves developing the child's ability to attend to others and to engage in purposive action. It includes training the child to delay the gratification of his desires and wishes and to work for rewards and goals which are more distant. It includes developing the child's view of adults as sources of information, and ideas, and also as sources of approval and reward. Through such development the child changes his self-expectations and his expectations of others.

While all of this is not absent in the culturally deprived home, it does not play such a central role in child rearing in such homes. The size of the family, the concern of the parents with the basic necessities of life, the low level of educational development of the parents, the frequent absence of a male parent, and the lack of a great deal of interaction between children and adults all conspire to reduce the stimulation, language development, and intellectual development of such children.

*   *   *

Implications for the Schools

Ideally, the early intellectual development of the child should take place in the home. Some efforts have been made to help parents learn how to teach their children. Under some conditions this is likely to be fruitful. But we must express pessimism about such possibilities when the total syndrome of poverty, broken homes, slum living, large families, and illiteracy all conspire against the intellectual development of the child. To point out the small number of exceptional children who are able to overcome these handicaps is not to prove that these conditions have no effect: it is to demonstrate the rarity of the exceptions to the general effects of cultural deprivation.

All later learning is likely to be influenced by the very basic learning which has taken place by the age of five or six. If adequate basic learning cannot be provided in the home, it is the responsibility of the schools to insure that the culturally deprived children have as good a set of initial skills and intellectual development as children from more culturally advantaged homes. This position may te taken in the interest of the individual child. But also, this position may be taken to insure that the work of the schools for the next ten years will not be largely wasted because of what has taken place in the previous two or three years. Careful studies in the U. S. and other countries demonstrate that it is possible to bring culturally deprived children up to satisfactory stages of readiness for the regular school learning. If this can be done on a broader base, then the regular learning procedures of the schools which are now quite effective for the advantaged children are also likely to be effective for the culturally disadvantaged children.

While we would advocate that the intellective training of the child be done in the home and by the parents, if they cannot do it adequately, the school is the logical social agency to do it.

Recommendations

1. Nursery schools and kindergartens should be organized to provide culturally deprived children with the conditions for their intellectual development and the learning-to-learn stimulation which is found in the most favorable home environments.

Such nursery schools and kindergartens should be very different from the nursery schools and kindergartens commonly used for middle-class children. These nursery schools and kindergartens must systematically provide for the intellectual development of the child. Much learning can take place through games, concrete materials (blocks, toys, objects), and dramatic play. The adult teachers must provide a supportive structured environment in which being read to, music, and art are enjoyable social experiences for the children. Specifically, the primary task of these nursery schools and kindergartens should be to provide for:

a. Stimulation of children to perceive aspects of the world about them and to fix these aspects by the use of language.

b. Development of more extended and accurate language.

c. Development of a sense of mastery over aspects of the immediate environment and an enthusiasm for learning for its own sake.

d. Development of thinking and reasoning and the ability to make new insights and discoveries for oneself.

e. Development of purposive learning activity and the ability to attend for longer periods of time.

2. A national commission composed of teachers and other specialists should be created to co-ordinate and to develop curricular guidelines, materials, and methods for this special type of nursery school-kindergarten.

This commission should be charged with responsibility for experimenting with alternative approaches to these problems and for evaluating the effectiveness of such curricula with different groups of children.

3. The teachers for this new type of nursery school-kindergarten should be carefully trained for the very specific set of tasks they must assume. Essentially, these teachers should be trained to do for many children what very good parents can do for a small number of their own children.

There is an urgency about this problem and it is likely that some of the training will have to be done while the teachers are actually in the schools. Volunteer workers (including parents) and adolescent assistants could do much to provide the necessary conditions for learning in these nursery school-kindergartens.

4. The parents must be sufficiently involved in the nursery school-kindergarten to understand its importance for their child and to give support and reinforcement to the tasks of these special schools. The parents should be so committed to this type of school that they are willing to do everything possible to insure the continuity of the child's school experiences.

Ideally, the parents should learn the appropriate communication patterns so that they can do much of this on their own with their own children. One might foresee the time when most parents can provide such stimulating home environments for the development of their children that special nursery school-kindergartens will not be widely needed. To this end, every effort should be made to have parents serve as part-time assistants and observers in these schools.

TUITION GRANTS AND THE PRIVATE SCHOOL ALTERNATIVE

(1965)   From Christopher Jencks, "Is The Public School Obsolete?," *The Public Interest* (Winter, 1966), pp. 18–27.

As a rule of thumb, America spends about half as much educating the children of the poor as the children of the rich. The difference derives from two factors. First, the annual expenditure per pupil in a prosperous suburb is usually at least fifty percent more than in a slum in the same metropolitan area. Second, this additional expenditure, in combination with better family and neighborhood conditions, encourages suburban children to stay in school half again as long as slum children (from kindergarten through college, instead of from first through tenth or eleventh grade). The cumulative result, in round figures, is that the taxpayers typically spend less than $5,000 for the formal education of most slum children compared to more than $10,000 for many suburban children.

*   *   *

It would be politically difficult to equalize opportunity between the slums and the suburbans under the best of circumstances. But not even the better financed slum schools (e.g. those in Harlem, on which more money is spent than in most suburbs outside the New York area) achieve results comparable to suburban systems. This in turn makes it even more difficult to raise the necessary money than it would otherwise be. If an extra $20 billion a year would bring slum children up to the academic level of their suburban rivals, some legislators would support the expenditure out of idealism. But many legislators feel—and not without reason—that even if they gave the schools an unlimited budget, the children of the slums would continue to grow up both personally and academically cripled.

These fears may be exaggerated. They certainly ought to be tested empirically before being accepted at face value. The Ford Foundation, for example, instead of sprinkling money around in dozens of different projects and places, ought to try raising school expenditures in one slum area to, say, double the level in nearby suburbs—just to see what would happen. It would, of course, take many years to tell. Children who were more than two or three when the experiment began would already have been scarred, often hopelessly, by the existing system. It would be a generation before the impact of the extra money on today's infants could be fully weighed. But if it turned out that an extra $100 million a year made a dramatic difference in, say, the slums of Washington, D.C., it would become very much easier to get comparable sums from taxpayers on other areas.

Unfortunately, an extra $100 million might not make a dramatic difference in Washington—or in most other places either. Much that has been said and wirtten about slum schools, not only in Washington but in places where race is not an issue, suggests that inadequate funds are only part of their problem. They also have the wrong motives and objectives. Some slum schools seem to be less educational than penal institutions. Their function is more to pacify the young than to teach them. They are ruled by fear, not love, infected by boredom, not curiosity. Such schools should not be given more money; they should be closed.

The roots of the problem go very deep. At times the problem seems to be public control itself. Because the slum school is public, it is accountable to the taxpayer. As in every other public enterprise, this kind of minute accountability to publicity-hungry elected officials leads to timidity among the employees. Public control puts a premium not on achieving a few spectacular successes but on avoiding any spectacular failures. In this respect there is not much difference between education and other fields of public endeavor. Nevertheless, public control over education has achieved a sanctity and respectability which public control over other enterprises has never mustered. Conversely, the ideologists of private enterprise have, with the conspicuous exception of Milton Friedman, been comparatively slow to apply their arguments in behalf of private schools.

Yet public control is not a sufficient explanation of the problems of the slum school, for public control seems to have worked quite well in some suburbs and small towns. The problem seems to be tuat in the slums public control has been linked to inadequate funds for performing the job assigned. Slum schools have found it difficult to get extra money even when there was reason to believe that the marginal return on this money would be very good. Educators might argue, for example, that doubling expenditures in the slums would treble results. But since we have no good way to measure this, skeptical legislators have been slow to provide extra money. As a result, pay scales in big city school systems have been too low to compete with most other jobs requiring equivalent training, skill, and masochism.

And so, in turn, many slum teachers and administrators have comparatively little competence, confidence or committment.

In city after city this has led to the creation of a system of education whose first axiom is that *everyone*, on every level, is incompetent and irresponsible. From this axiom comes the corollary that everyone must be carefully watched by a superior. The school board has no faith in the central administration, the central administration has no faith in the principals, the principals have no faith in the teachers, and the teachers have no faith in the students. Decision-making is constantly centralized into as few hands as possible rather than being decentralized into as many hands as possible, in the hope of reducing errors to a minimum. Of course such a system also reduces individual initiative to a minimum, but that is a price which a publicly controlled bureaucracy, whose aim is not profits but survival, usually seems willing to pay. In such a system it seems natural not to give the principal of a school control over his budget, not to give teachers control over their syllabus, and not to give the students control over anything. Distrust is the order of the day, symbolized by the elaborate accounting system, the endless forms to be filled out for the central office, the time clocks and the two-way radios for monitoring classrooms from the front office, the constant tests and elaborate regulations for students.

In such a system everyone gets along by going along with the man over him. Most come to see themselves as play actors. The student tries to dope out what the teacher wants, and gives it to him. Usually all he wants is a reasonable amount of quiet in class and some appearance of docility in doing assignments. The teachers, in turn, try to figure out what the principal wants. That usually means filing grades and attendance records promptly, keeping trouble over discipline to a minimum, and avoiding complaints from parents or students. The principal, in turn, tries to keep the central administration happy (and the administration tries to keep the school board happy) by not sticking his neck out and by damping down "trouble" before it gets "out of hand."

Organizational sclerosis of this kind is extremely difficult to cure. For obvious reasons innovation from the bottom up becomes impossible and unthinkable. But even innovation from the top down is difficult. It is easy to get people to go through the *forms* of change, but it is almost impossible to get them to *really* change, because they are frozen into defensive postures based on years of standpattism. If the principal tells the teachers he wants them to revamp the curriculum, they immediately begin looking to him—not to their students in the classroom—for cues and clues about what kinds of changes to propose. If the teachers tell the students to think for themselves, the students interpret this as just another move by the teacher to complicate "the game," another frustration in their efforts to "give the teacher what he wants." If the school board tries raising salaries in order to attract new kinds of teachers, it must still assign them to the same old schools, where they are still treated like filing clerks. So the more imaginative and dedicated teachers leave after a year or two for other schools—often in suburbia—which treat them better. In such circumstances more money may just mean more of the same.

A business which becomes afflicted with this kind of disease either goes bankrupt or else creates a monopoly or cartel to protect itself from more dynamic competition. The same is true of school systems. Were it not for their monopoly on educational opportunities for the poor, most big city school systems would probably go out of business. If, for example, the poor were simply given the money that is now spent on their children's education in public schools, and were told they could spend this money in private institutions, private schools would begin to spring up to serve slum children. In due course such schools would probably enroll the great majority of these children. The case of the parochial schools illustrates this point. These schools are seldom really free, but many parents, including some non-Catholics, make considerable sacrifices to send their children to them. In some cases, of course, this is a matter of religious faith. But if one asks parents why they prefer the parochial schools, the answer is often that they think the schooling itself is better than what the public schools in their area offer. Evidence collected by Peter Rossi and Andrew Greeley of the National Opinion Research Center suggests that the parochial schools usually *do* do more for their students than their public competitors, at least judging by the records of their alumni. This seems to be so despite the fact that they have less money, pay lower salaries to lay teachers, have larger classes, older buildings, and fewer amenities of every sort.

There is, of course, considerable reluctance among non-Catholics (and also among anti-clerical Catholics) to admit that the parochial schools might be doing something of value. Most non-Catholics, including myself, have an instinctive distrust of the Church. We have readily accepted the proposition that its schools were "divisive," despite research evidence which shows that aside from their religious practices parochial school graduates have about the same habits and values as Catholics who attend public schools. A similar prejudice clouds efforts to discuss what have traditionally been called "private" schools. Educators have taught us to use "public" as a synonym for "democratic" or just plain "good," and to associate "private" with "elitist" and "inequality." In part this is because when we think of a "public" school we conjure up a small-town or suburban school which is responsible and responsive to those whom it serves; a "private" school, on the other hand, is imagined as a posh country club for the sons of the rich. Yet using this kind of language to describe the "public" schools of Harlem surely obscures as much as it reveals. The Harlem schools are hardly more responsible or responsive to those whom they nominally serve than the typical "private" school. They are "public" only in the legal sense that the Post Office, for example, is "public," i.e., they are tax supported, open to all, ultimately answerable to public officials who have almost no interest in them. Conversely, while it is true that "private" schools have in the past catered mainly to the well-off, this seems to reflect economic necessity more than social prejudice. If the poor were given as much money to spend on education as the rich, there is every reason to assume that the private sector would expand to accommodate them. Indeed, if we were to judge schools by their willingness to subsidize the poor, we would have to say that private schools have shown *more* interest in the poor than public ones. Has any suburban board of education used its own money to provide scholarships for slum children? Most refuse to admit such children even if their way is paid. Many private boards of trustees, on the other hand, have made such efforts, albeit on a small scale.

Private control has several advantages in a school which serves slum children. To begin with, it makes it possible to attack the problem in manageable bites. It is inconceivable that a big city school system can be reformed all at once. Failing that, however, it may be impossible to reform it at all. If, for example, the system is geared to docile teachers who do not want and cannot handle responsibility, how is it to accomodate the enterprising minority who have ideas of their own and want freedom to try them out? The superintendent cannot alter the whole system to deal with a handful of such teachers, even if he wants to. But if he does not alter the system, the better teachers will usually leave—or not come in the first place. Somehow the system must be broken up so that its parts can develop at different paces, in different styles, and even in different directions. Little cells of excellence must be nourished, gradually adding to their own number and excitement. Unusual talent must not be spread so thin over the whole system that no single place achieves the critical mass needed to sustain a chain reaction. Yet this is just what a conventional, centrally controlled system tends to do, for in such a system "special treatment" for a particular school is quickly defined as "favoritism." (This attitude is illustrated in the response of big cities to the offer of federal funds under the new Elementary and Secondary Education Act. Almost nobody wants to concentrate this money in a few places to create really good schools; everyone wants to spread it across the whole system.)

A second virtue of private schools is that they get away from the increasingly irrelevant tradition of neighborhood schools. Every psychologist and sociologist now recognizes that what children learn formally from their teachers is only a small fraction of their overall education. What they learn informally from their classmates is equally or more important. For this reason it is extremely important to expose slum children to classmates who teach them things which will be an asset rather than a liability as they grow older. A school which draws only from the slum itself will not provide this kind of stimulus. Instead, ways must be found to mix slum children with racially and economically different classmates.

In principle, of course, this kind of ethnic and economic mixing ought to be easier within a public system than a private one. But this may not be so in practice. In a publicly controlled system every school is required to follow essentially the same educational policies and practices as every other one. This means that the differences between schools derive largely if not exclusively from the differences in their student bodies. (Ability to hold good administrators and teachers seems to depend largely on this, for example.) So long as the student "mix" is decisive, middle-class parents are understandably reluctant to send their children to school with substantial numbers of lower-class children. White parents feel the same way about schools with large numbers of Negro children. But if the traditions and distinctive identity of a school depend not on the character of the student body but on the special objectives and methods of the staff, middle-class parents who approve of these objectives and methods will often send their children despite the presence of poorer classmates. This is clearest, perhaps, in the parochial schools. It might also be possible in non-sectarian private schools, if these had the money to give poor children scholarships, or if outside groups provided such scholarships to large numbers of children.

Getting rid of the neighborhood school, whether by creating citywide public schools are private ones, could also have the virtue of providing the poor with a real choice about the kinds of schools their children attend. At present, the neighborhood school must try to be all things to all people in its area. Anything daring is bound to displease somebody, and so must be avoided. But if schools could simply tell those who disliked their methods to look elsewhere, and could look all over a large city for a clientele which wanted a particular brand of education, there would be a better chance both for innovation in the schools and for satisfying the diverse needs of different students. It should be possible, for example, for poor people to send their children to a school which segregates the sexes, or employs the Montessori method, or teaches reading phonetically, or emulates the Summerhill approach. Not everyone wants such things, but *some* do, and they should be able to get them. Given the present outlook of the men who control big city public schools, the only way to make these choices available is probably in the private sector.

In principle there are two ways to develop a larger measure of private initiative and room for maneuver in educating the poor. One would be to provide tuition grants to children who opted out of the public-controlled schools, equal to what would be spent on them if they stayed in. These tuition grants could be used to pay the bills in private schools. There are not, of course, enough private schools today to handle all the potential applicants from the slums, but more would spring up if money were available. But even without tuition grants it should be possible to create much more diversity and decentralization in the schools. School boards could, for example, contract with various groups to manage particular schools in their own system.

A university might be given contract to run a model school system in the slums, as suggested by the Panel on Educational Research and Development of the President's Science Advisory Committee. This is apparently to be tried in New York.

A local business group might also take over the management of a school. (If Litton Industries can run a Job Corps camp, it can surely run a school.)

A group of teachers might incorporate itself to manage a school contract from the citywide board. This could be done at no expense within the present system, using present personnel and facilities, and it might have appreciable advantages. Suppose, for example, that the New York City Board of Education were to rent its facilities to their present staffs and provide them with a management contract subject to annual review. Ultimate control over the school could be vested in the teachers, who would hire administrators. Hiring and firing teachers, budget-making, programming and so forth would all be decided on the spot. If the school did a poor job—which some surely would—the contract could be terminated. A group of parents, working through an elected board, might also take over a school. This alternative, which should be especially appealing to the New Left and to the prophets of "community action," is perhaps better described as a new kind of public control than as private control. In effect, it would mean replacing responsibility to the taxpayer-stockholder with responsibility to the consumer—a kind of educational cooperative.

All these alternatives aim at a radical decentralization of both power and responsibility. All would liberate the schools from the dead hand of central adminstration, from minute accountability to the public for every penny, every minute, and every word. They all recognize that so far as the slum child is concerned, the present system of "socialized education" has failed, and that some kind of new departure, either "capitalist" or "syndicalist," is needed.

Either tuition grants or management contracts to private organizations would, of course, "destroy the public school system as we know it." When one thinks of the remarkable past achievements of public education in America, this may seem a foolish step. But we must not allow the memory of past achievements to blind us to present failures. Nor should we allow the rhetoric of public school men to obscure the issue. It is natural for public servants to complain about private competition, just as private business complains about public competition. But if the terms of the competition are reasonable, there is every reason to suppose that it is healthy. Without it, both public and private enterprises have a way of ossifying. And if, as some fear, the public schools could not survive in open competition with private ones, then perhaps they *should* not survive.

A NON-GRADED SCHOOL: THE UNIVERSITY ELEMENTARY SCHOOL OF U. C. L. A. (1965)

From John I. Goodlad, "Meeting Children Where They Are," *Saturday Review,* vol. XLVII pp. 57–59, 72–74.

The University Elementary School of the University of California, Los Angeles, is a nongraded school. Children normally enter before the age of four and move upward through their twelfth year without encountering the grade levels so characteristic of our educational system. They are not promoted from grade to grade; nor do they repeat grades. There are no grades.

This school stands with a small but growing company of schools now abandoning the grade labels—grades one, four, seven, or eleven—in favor of what educators call a continuous progress plan. These nongraded schools are not alike, any more than graded schools are alike. The educators responsible for them are not agreed on what nongrading is or could be. But they all have one feature in common: the grade labels have been removed from a substantial portion of the school. University Elementary School at UCLA is a completely gradeless school.

There is no magic in the removal of grade labels. If this is all that takes place, we have the same old school under a new name and a fraud has been perpetrated. There are fads in education as in everything else. Not to be caught up nowadays in nongrading, team teaching, programed instruction, or educational television is to be regarded in some educational circles as to be woefully out of touch. Consequently, there are those administrators who have merely removed the labels and then declared a nongraded school to be in existence. Others have replaced three or four grade levels with twelve or more rigidly arbitrary achievement levels. Fortunately, some schools are being redesigned in a much more fundamental way.

Until recently, nongrading was thought of as an organizational device for permitting youngsters to move through a common body of material at somewhat differing rates of speed, according to their individual readiness to proceed. Most thinking and most nongraded schools are geared to this conception. But differentiated progress through what are still essentially graded assignments represents, at best, only significant tampering with a concept of education that has been seriously questioned by educational reformers from Rousseau to Bruno Bettelheim and A. S. Neill.

Nongrading, as used and defined in the balance of this paper, is both a concept and a plan within a larger view of education embracing a few simple but nonetheless compelling principles of child development, learning, school function, and pedagogical practice.

First, children are different, much more different than we have up to now recognized. We have been shamefully remiss in taking these differences into account in or planning and teaching.

Second, in seeking to provide intelligently for these differences, educational diagnosis of and prescription for the individual is essential. Mass techniques and common expectations for all are inimical to these highly sensitive human processes.

Third, there must be alternatives from which to fill the prescriptions. A monolithic school structure providing only pass or fail as the alternatives in regulating pupil progress simply does not square with the range of alternatives necessary to coping imaginatively with human variability.

Fourth, the proper question to ask in starting a child off on his school career is not, "Is this child ready for school?" but, "What is this child ready for?" This is the most pregnant idea, and is, indeed, at the heart of nongrading.

Fifth, criterion standards replace normative standards as the measure of pupil progress. Normative standards are sloppy standards based on group performance. They tend to result in unjustified rewards for high but inadequate performance on the part of the able and relentless, punishing failure for the slow and deprived. It has been estimated that 25 per cent of children in school receive 75 per cent of the failing grades based on normative standards. These children ultimately come to regard themselves as failures—not just in school but in life itself. Most of this loss to mankind could have been prevented by asking and carefully answering the qustion. "What is this child ready for?"

Criterion standards arrange a sequence of difficulty or a meaningful progression in work assignments. Instead of pronouncing the child to be at the fourth-grade level, which tells us very little and most of that misleading, these standards seek to provide a profile of where the child is now functioning with respect to the skills and concepts comprising the sequence of learning. These are really tougher standards, each child pitting himself against the rigor of the material rather than the uncertainties of group competence and variability. Unfortunately, we are still at a relatively primitive stage in the development of these criterion measures but rapid progress is being made in projects designed to change the curricula of America's schools.

Sixth, sound learning is cumulative. That is, the child's progression should not suffer from what psychologists call retroactive and proactive interference. A percentage problem for the child who has no conception of parts and wholes, let alone the number base on which per cent depends, contaminates his present mathematical knowledge and interferes with what follows. Such is the unhappy, cumulative product of several "bare passes" in a graded system.

The graded school was brought into being at a time when we knew little about individual differences in learning. The assumption then, in the middle of the nineteenth century, was that the content of instruction could be divided into roughly equal packages and mastered, a year at a time, by children of the same age. Soon, there came to be graded content, graded textbooks, graded children, graded teachers, and graded expectations for schooling. Graded tests and graded norms came later. The entire graded machinery was efficient in classifying the hordes of children pouring into our schools in increasing numbers throughout the balance of the nineteenth century and into the twentieth.

But the children didn't fit. Some simply could not master the work of a grade in a year; others romped through it. Good teaching raised the level throughout; poor teaching lowered it. A formidable gap between the swift and the slow remained.

Nonpromotion (grade failure) and double promotion (grade skipping) were used—and still are used—to narrow the gap within any one grade. Neither has proved effective. The nonpromoted child, repeating the grade, rarely is stimulated anew. Studies reveal that nonpromoted children generally do worse than children of like ability and past performance who are promoted to the next grade. In fact, some nonpromoted children fail to equal their own performance of the previous year on the second time around.

The answer, however, is not simply to promote the slow-learning child. Inadequate or faulty comprehension, if not checked, leads to an accumulation and compounding of inadequacy. Promotion and nonpromotion are the ineffective adjustment mechanisms of the graded system. The answer appears to be to transform or replace the system.

The nongraded school is one replacment for the graded system. It is not simply a corrective mechanism. The component parts of grading and nongrading are not interchangeable. The two systems are built on differing assumptions, arouse differing expectations, and demanded differing teacher behavior. They require differing language for their description and interpretation but, unfortunately, a language of nongrading has not yet developed. We are forced to think and talk about nongrading using the terms characteristic of grading and, as a consequence, we never quite escape gradedness.

Let us not abandon the graded school out of hand. Let us, instead, create alternatives. There can be no meaningful comparisons of what we now have without alternatives. Let us not create alternatives capriciously, however. Let us instead build alternatives which can be argued vigorously from supporting data.

The facts of individual differences among learners support the nongraded alternative. The usual fourth grade class contains children achieving at second, third, fourth, fifth, and sixth grades in some aspects of their school work—and even occasionally above and below these levels. The average spread in achievement is four years. In a fifth grade class it is five; in a sixth, six years in tested achievement, and so on. These are not fourth or fifth or sixth grades except in name. They are composites of many grades, each graded class overlapping graded classes above and below. In a field such as reading, the picture is even more startling. Children in a fifth grade class commonly range in reading from the second or third to the ninth or tenth.

The commonsense protest here is that, given ideal school conditions, these slow pupils could be pulled up substantially. True, but given equally ideal conditions for the able, they too would move up beyond these performances.

A commonsense solution to managing this vast range of attainments, frequently posed by lay critics of the schools, is to group those of like achievement in a single class. (The term used often but incorrectly for this achievement grouping is ability grouping.) But some additional evidence gives us pause. The variability in attainments with one child sometimes parallels the variability in an entire class. A child, like a class, is not a second, fourth, or sixth grader. Johnny can be in the fifth grade for arithmetic computation, the sixth for arithmetic reasoning, the seventh for spelling, the eighth for word meaning, the ninth for paragraph meaning, and the tenth for language—and yet be officially registered in the sixth grade. In the same class is Jean, whose scores range from low third to high seventh; Bill, from high second to high fifth; and Pat, from fourth to tenth. (These figures, incidentally, are taken from actual class roles.) Children are downright ornery. They refuse to grow up all of a piece.

Under a plan of grouping for likeness in achievement, Johnny, Jean, Bill, and Pat would join a new group for each subject and rarely would be together in the same groups. Their class groups, to be closely homogeneous (that is, comparable in attainment), would be composed of children from throughout the building, brought together because of their assumed readiness for identical learnings. A monstrous scheduling problem is involved. This can readily be managed through modern computer techniques.

The main problem is not logistics. Three other matters come in for attention: the composition of the class groups brought together in this fashion, the degree of homogeneity actually produced, and the accomplishments of students in such groups.

Strange partners often come together. Is a class made up of pupils ranging from seven to twelve years of age but alike in reading attainment a teachable reading group? Are the same materials for all likely to be appropriate? The answer to both questions, of course, is no. A new and at least equally perplexing problem of dealing with individual differences has been created. This is a caricature, admittedly, but it serves to sharpen the fact that grouping children for likeness in one trait creates groups of vast differences in most other traits.

Still another problem arises from the fact that students grouped for likeness on a trait are not alike on sub-elements of that trait. When two things look alike, this usually means that the viewer is not looking deeply or carefully enough. Children grouped for likeness in reading achievement, for example, usually have comparable test scores representing a combination of paragraph meaning and word recognition. But when one examines these children for six or eight separate factors involved in reading, he discovers that these "homogeneously" grouped youngsters are really very different on each of them. The grouping pattern performs a disservice because it lulls the teachers into proceeding as though the group were once when in reality it is marked diverse in the components which must be provided for in the productive teaching of reading. Patterns of school organization should reveal, not hide, human variability.

Presumably, students of like ability are brought together to enhance their learning. The evidence is not convincing. Studies in England, Sweden, and the United States show no significant advantages in achievement for homogeneous groups over mixed or heterogeneous groups. The findings in any given study are either inconclusive or, if statistically significant, are offset by another study concluding the exact opposite. Grouping of any kind is productive only when designed to serve a specific purpose and when accompanied by special provisions of an intimate and highly individualized sort.

The potentiality of complex grouping patterns fades and the crucial significance of individualizing instruction looms large. Needed is a system of such flexibility and responsiveness that it is scarcely a system at all. Such a system must reveal individuality, not disguise or obscure it. Once revealed, human variability most assuredly will demand alternatives. The nongraded school is but a part, albeit a significant one, of the total educational system need for the identification and proper nurturing of precious, individual, human talent.

It will be more helpful now to talk specifically about one nongraded school than to talk in general about the alternatives in content, grouping, pedagogy, and expectations for children available through nongrading. In 1960, UCLA's University Elementary School consisted of seventeen graded rooms: three nursery school, two kindergarten, and two each subsequent grade through the sixth. Each was largely self-contained; that is, teachers worked alone in providing the daily diet of reading, arithmetic, language arts, social studies, and science but called upon help as desired for art, music, health, and physical education.

Today, five years later, University Elementary School consists of nine nongraded clusters of children and teachers, each cluster ranging in size from as few as twenty-five to as many as seventy-five children. Each child is assigned to one of these clusters and, subsequently, to sub-clusters within these larger ones, on the basis of diagnosis and prescription. Instead of the alternatives being pass or fail, the alternatives are several in number, no one of which is grade repetition or skipping. The clusters were different in number and organization last year; they will be different again next year. The school evolves as the staff clarifies beliefs and subjects them to test.

Most clusters are staffed by teams of full-time and part-time teachers. This team teaching has facilitated the inclusion of part-time personnel, some of them students in the university, in a way that was not possible five years ago. Although the budget is only slightly larger, because of normal salary increases, 50 per cent more people are on the payroll. Not all teachers are in teams. Some maintain about the same pattern of self-sufficiency that existed throughout the school five years ago. Teachers, too, are individuals and deserve alternatives.

Team teaching is not essential to nongrading. There are nongraded schools with self-contained classrooms and team-taught schools with grade levels. But team teaching as a way of clustering children and teachers fits nicely with nongrading as a way of guiding students upward through the school. They are compatible, flexible patterns of school and classroom organization which provide a useful array of alternatives for dealing with pupil variability. Since University Elementary School developed both at about the same time, the two are almost indistinguishably interwoven in practice and, consequently, in this description.

Let no one think that change comes naturally to a laboratory school, especially if its primary function has been demonstration. Such a school is in the public eye. To change what has long been demonstrated and from what have come success and recognition is to suggest that the practices being replaced were never good when, in reality, they may have been first-rate for their time. Further, time for planning change is hard to come by. In a laboratory school, the work load of teaching children, advising future teachers, assisting many university faculty members in the conduct of their research, demonstrating various procedures, and interpreting programs to endless streams of visitors is almost unbelievably demanding. To effect basic changes while keeping the ship afloat is an unsettling experience.

The route from yesterday to today was often a tortuous one. It included changing the function of this laboratory school from demonstration to inquiry, innovation, experimentation, and research in schooling. It began with two aspects of teacher dissatisfaction which were traced to a common source. First, class membership remained rather constant from year to year, as is typical in a graded school. Consequently, children were always the oldest or youngest and rather consistently followers or leaders. They had little opportunity to shift roles and explore new relationships. Second, certain learning ills persisted for some children into the upper elementary years. The problem was less pronounced than in most schools but it was particularly frustrating for these teachers because the school was highly regarded for its instruction, and rightfully so. Teachers did everything possible within the graded organization characteristic of schools generally but often were unable to overcome what appeared to be unfortunate but irrevocable pupil placement. The placement adjustment for inadequate learning appeared to be retention and grade repetition, a solution which these teachers regarded as disagreeable and noncorrective.

They were boxed in by the graded system, a system that they had often stretched to the near-breaking point but had always retained. It is unwise to break away from long-established practice when no reasonably clear alternative is in sight. The search for an acceptable alternative led to better understanding of what was hidden by the graded structure, the fact that the seventeen classrooms were graded in name but not in the attainment of pupils. The graded structure now looked less sacred and inviolable than it had before. Some teachers who had read or otherwise learned about nongrading wanted to abolish the graded system then and there. This decision was not to come for another year.

By collapsing the next three years, we come to the present. The school is now viewed as having three broad levels of function and expectations, each successive level overlapping the previous one both in function and expectations and in the age of children assigned to it.

The early childhood level enrolls children from under four to over six. The primary function is to develop a sturdy, wholesome self-concept. Children are expected to interact productively and satisfyingly with the children, adults, and things of their daily environment. Teachers are there to assist them in working at these relationships. Concern for this wholesome self-concept carries over into the lower elementary level where diagnosis and prescription for needs in this area continue. But now the central function becomes progressive development in the fundamental skills of self-directed learning, especially reading. The age spread is now from about six to eight or nine, but age is not a primary factor in placement. The upper elementary level of function normally embraces children from eight or nine to eleven or twelve years of age. Again, attention to wholesome self-development continues, particularly as it relates to inadequate learning skills demanding special attention. The central goal now, however, is to develop the ability to understand and use man's approaches to studying social and natural phenomena. Hopefully, children will leave the school with a desire to continue learning as well as considerable self-directing proficiency in the process.

These three levels of function are not organizational units of the school, although at one point in the school's recent evolution they were. The nine broad clusters of children are not evenly distributed among them. One cluster, for example, enrolling sixty-five children from age seven to age eleven, obviously cuts across both lower and upper elementary levels, reaching toward the bottom of the former, and well up in the latter. The three-levels concept of function underlying University Elementary School simply emphasizes that the function of elementary education is not unitary throughout but, rather, shifts in emphasis from the early childhood to the early adolescent years.

Each cluster of children, whether large or small, whether team-taught or self-contained, has a wide spread in age. For example, a cluster entirely within the lower elementary level might contain children of age six, seven, and eight. Another conceived to be entirely within this same lower elementary level of function might contain children from seven to nine. One cutting across lower and upper elementary conceptions of function might spread from age seven to twelve.

This system of school organization virtually forces teachers to recognize and provide for individual differences. Several ages together serve as a blinking light reminding teachers that the students are not all alike. A single age group could lull them into forgetting the wide range of differences actually residing in it. With a little care, a mixed age group can be put together so that the overall individual differences are little or no greater than in a single age group. But experience suggests that the revelation of one kind of difference—namely, in age—creates pressure to deal with differences generally.

The learning environment in a cluster of children provides a wide range of activities appropriated to the functions involved. A cluster of forty children from age four through six, for example, shares two rooms that formerly were separate classrooms but that have now been merged by knocking out part of an intervening wall. It is not unusual for them to share other indoor spaces with neighboring clusters and the simultaneous sharing of outdoor spaces is standard practice. The skilled observer would see a certain rhythm to the daily activities. At a given moment, a sub-group is talking about a walk from which the children have just returned; another is busily engaged in a variety of jumping and balancing activities; another is sitting at a table with reading materials; and little clusters of two and three are deeply involved in still other tasks. What one child is doing now, another will be doing an hour from now. The range and variety are in part possible because, in expanding total cluster size, additional personnel also are added.

Each of the tasks mentioned above is believed to be prelude to or part of reading. Each child is working at a point thought to be appropriate for him and, most of the time, selected by him. Progression through such tasks is far from ordered, partly because some of them are parallel rather than sequential and partly because research has not yet defined the most productive sequences. Further, a productive sequence for one child usually only partly overlaps a productive sequence for another. Individual diagnosis and prescription are essential. The child is not incapable of self-diagnosis and prescription, especially if the range of alternatives is broad, visible, and attractive and he is helped to see what these alternatives are designed to accomplish.

Progress through any sequence is only very loosely related to age. The number of years a human being has lived is a poor yardstick for determining what he is ready to learn. Each of the sub-groups above contained fours, fives, and sixes, for whom the task at hand was appropriate. The sub-groups assembled for the next tasks of the day also would contain this age distribution but the children comprising the group would not be entirely the same. Here we see sharply revealed a key difference between grading and nongrading. The graded school is geared rather closely to age and to arbitrary provision of what children of that age (and grade) are to learn. The nongraded school is geared to readiness to learn, which, in turn, is determined from continuing diagnosis.

Another key difference is flexibility in expectations for children. The graded school presents a series of graded expectations. Contrary to much popular opinion, these are not rigorous expectations for all. But they are unfair. As pointed out earlier, they punish the weak and fail to challenge the strong.

University Elementary School provides a broad range of expectations—broad enough to reach from the floor to the ceiling of individual attainment—within each level of function. A child is not expected to reach a set level of reading by the age of six. Nor is he retained in an early childhood cluster of children until he does. But he will have engaged in activities considered basic to reading (many of which, unfortunately, are not seen as such by the layman) as well as in many other kinds of learnings. On moving to join older clusters of children, where these children will now be the youngest rather than the oldest, some will be among the most proficient readers in the new environment, some among the slowest. New groupings for reading will occur to take these individual differences into account. Staff and resources are now geared to make special provision for reading, with a range of expectations far in excess of those normally assumed under the label, "grade."

A child in University Elementary School seldom remains less than a year or more than three years with a cluster of children and teachers, depending on the size of that cluster, the age spread in it, and the diagnosis of that child. In principle, a child is moved whenever placement in another cluster appears to be desirable. In practice, however, every effort is made to keep a child in a cluster of children for at least a year, on the assumption that this continuity contributes to his sense of identity in a world of increasing anonymity. A child in a cluster for three years will have seen children come and go each year, will have had a long-term continuing relationship with some of these children and with several teachers, and will have enjoyed the experience of being at first one of the youngest and then one of the oldest members of the group.

Placement for each subsequent year grows out of a series of meetings taking place in the spring of each year. There are total faculty meetings in which general policies are reiterated and refined. There are single cluster meetings in which teachers who have been closely associated with these children, sometimes for as long as three years, pool data and observations concerning each child. There are cross-cluster conferences in which children likely to be assigned to one of several possible alternative clusters are discussed in relation to the teachers and to the expectations of each cluster. The data come from many sources but particularly from children's present teachers, parents, the school principal, and the children themselves.

At no time is there a squaring of each child's performance with a predetermined set of common expectancies for all four-year-olds or all nine-year-olds. Criteria are derived from the functions of the level of schooling; adequacy from a study of the child's performance over a long period of time. These are decisions for teachers to make, teachers who are close to the data. The principal participates as a member of the team, not as a final arbiter "passing on" each decision.

When the decision is to move a child from his present placement to a new one, the question is, "Which alternative?" In a carefully organized nongraded school, there should be a minimum of three alternatives from which to choose. Each of these alternatives will differ in several strategic ways, the most significant of which are the differences among the teachers. It is the responsibility of the total staff, with the principal's guidance, to determine just how these alternatives will differ: in anticipated learning activities, in the teachers to be in charge, in group size, and in actual group membership. All of these can be and should be manipulated in seeking to set up productive clusters of teachers and children for each subsequent year. Consequently, at University Elementary School, final placements of children are held up until the composition of each tentative cluster has been carefully examined. Frequently, on the basis of this examination, clusters initially proposed are modified through reassigning children.

Teachers find this process to be excruciatingly difficult at first. They must consider much more than the relatively simple alternatives: to promote or not to promote. They need to know a great deal about the children with whom they have been working—parental expectations and their effects, peer group associations, feelings in success and failure, ability to tolerate restrictions or permissiveness, and so on—and about their colleagues. They are uncertain about the criteria to use, largely because, as a total staff or as sub-groups of that staff, they have not previously discussed the matter. And, to their surprise and frustration, they usually discover that they possess far too little useful information about the children with whom they have been working. In brief, they are confronted with a new and highly challenging professional task and, understandably, can be somewhat unnerved by it.

Supported and encouraged, however, most teachers learn the behavior required and practice it with growing satisfaction. At University Elementary School, the second round of spring meetings was a marked improvement over the first. Teachers came armed with data and hammered out the criteria in the process of making pupil placement. The third round was strikingly professional. But now a new kind of frustration emerged. The teachers wanted data going beyond their own observations, sensitive test data in all areas of child development—data derived from criterion measures, not normative data derived from graded standards. Such data are conspicuously absent in education. To create a demand for them is to speed their coming. Nongraded schools, of the type conceived here, create this demand.

Needed in a nongraded school is a person knowledgeable in both education and the informative sciences. He might well be the guidance counselor. His job is to set up a system for the collection, organization, storage, and retrieval of data designed to assist teachers in their vital decisions of diagnosis and prescription. He must join the teachers in these processes, learning more about them, bringing data to bear, and refining the information processing system as needed. The necessity for collecting masses of data, for maintaining them over long periods of time, for assembling them in many different ways, and for quick retrieval suggests the potentiality of a computer serving several schools or school systems simultaneously. Computers are now being used experimentally for similar purposes in research projects scattered across the country.

Complex? Yes, at first, simply because these are not familiar modes of thought to most people. It is not easy to escape more than a century of gradedness. The early phases of comprehending non-gradedness are something like a first experience with English money. One is forever trying to translate pence, shillings, and pounds into cents, quarters, and dollars (and those half-crowns are maddening!). Or, perhaps better, it is comparable to the way most of us struggle initially and awkwardly with a foreign language. We seek to translate French literally into English rather than to think and to communicate in French. What a revelation it is when the intervening translation disappears and we find ourselves thinking, reading, and speaking French!

Similarly, before the potentialities of this redefined and redesigned school open up we must come to think in non-graded terms. To translate nongrading into graded nomenclature is to stay within the limited possibilities of yesterday's schools. Until fully functioning nongraded models have been carefully developed, meaningful discourse about and comparisons of nongrading and grading will be impossible. But even with models of both standing side by side, experimental comparison will be difficult and, for persons holding differing conceptions of education, probably impossible. For grading and nongrading are fundamentally differing expressions of schooling, based on fundamentally differing conceptions of what schools are for and of how learners should progress in them. Ask not if this child is ready for school but what this child is ready for.

University Elementary School is still becoming. The promise of the future far outstrips the accomplishments of the past. Three years have elapsed since the faculty committed itself to nongrading and jokingly promised to fine its members for each use of the word, "graded." The school is not yet fully nongraded; it never will be. For, as quickly as one goal is attained, others come into view. As former Chancellor Lawrence Kimpton once said about the University of Chicago over which he presided, "This probably isn't a very good place for the pursuit of happiness, but it's a wonderful place to find happiness in pursuit."

THE NEW TEACHER: THE TEACHER-EMPIRICIST (1965) From W. James Popham, *The Teacher Empiricist* (Woodland Hills, Calif., 1965), pp. 7–10.

There are a number of ways of viewing the instructional act. Teaching can be thought of primarily as an artistic endeavor in which the instructor, much as a virtuoso, performs for his class. With this conception of the teacher-artist it is difficult, if not impossible, to subject the instructional efforts of the teacher to much systematic improvement. Since, by definition, the nature of an artist's endeavors defy precise objective evaluation.

It is also possible to approach the instructional act as one totally amenable to rigorous empirical improvement. This view of instruction as a technology suggests the behavior of the teacher can be systematically improved in time so that he is increasingly more effective. According to this idea of teaching, the activities of the instructor can be analyzed and subsequently improved by gathering evidence regarding variations in instructor behavior resulting in the most improvement in student learning.

Total commitment to either view is probably extreme for there are elements of truth in both. There are many things a teacher does bordering on virtuosity and which would be almost impossible to analyze or modify. On the other hand, much teacher behavior can be treated in a highly technical fashion. Teacher education programs should focus on these technical aspects in their efforts to increase the competence of the would-be teacher. It should be recognized there are a number of ingredients in "effective teaching" over which the teacher educator has no control. For example, a certain degree of native intellectual ability is necessary in order for one to function effectively in the classroom. Yet, once the teaching candidate has met admissions criteria there is little the teacher education program can do to make him more intelligent. Similarly, certain personality patterns have been ingrained in the behavior of the teaching candidate by the time he enters his pre-service course work and it would be foolhardy to think any collection of courses and/or student teaching experiences would invariably effect such profound personality structures.

Common Non-Empirical Approaches

Just how does an individual begin to teach when faced with his first class? In what manner does the beginning student teacher decide how he will behave in front of his students? Or when faced with his first full day of teaching, how does the beginning instructor plan what he will do in five different classes? A common answer to these questions is that the teacher engages in activities which seem "teacher-like" in nature. He will often recall the way he was taught over the years and may attempt to emulate an admired teacher. He may decide to rely heavily upon lectures, or class discussions, or individual reports, etc. His decisions, however, will often be based upon a rather simple motive—to fill the class hours with activities which appear to be instructional. It is not that the beginning teacher is attempting to deceive his students, but he often has the idea activites which appear to be instructional in nature will somehow yield desirable results. He falls into a pattern of "teaching" a particular way and, after a year or two of use, the behavior pattern takes on some kind of intrinsic merit. It is "good" because it has been done before. Often the teacher fails to realize the reason it may have been done in the first place was just to fill up time.

An Instructional Paradigm

Rather than approaching instruction as so many beginning teachers do, it is recommended a more rational scheme be employed. In the following paragraphs an instructional paradigm (model) is described designed to assist the beginning teacher in selecting learning activities and in subsequently improving them.

The instructional paradigm advocated here emphasizes the intellectual decision-making the teacher engages prior to and after instruction. It is more of a planning and assessment model than an actual "teaching procedures" scheme. It seems reasonable the teacher educator can have more influence over the rational instructional decisions the prospective teacher makes rather than over some of the idiosyncratic ways in which he behaves once he is in the classroom. In subsequent paragraphs the major elements of the paradigm will be briefly described. The approach embodied in this model is deceptively simple. It consists of four major components. First, the objectives of instruction are specified. Second, the student is preassessed in order to determine his current status with respect to the instructional objectives. Third, activities for the students and the teacher are selected in order to best promote the pupils' achievement of the objectives. Fourth, the student's attainment of the objectives is evaluated. . . .

There are obviously things which educators know about instruction other than the relatively modest collection of principles in this model. But in his study of teaching methods the neophyte instructor runs a great risk of superficially "covering the waterfront". In general, the begining teacher benefits far more by mastering a few principles than by gathering fragmentary instructional knowledge from all that is known regarding how students learn.

*　　*　　*

SPECIFYING INSTRUCTIONAL OBJECTIVES[1]

Most educators admit educational objectives are important. They will readily agree the teacher does not really know what to do without instructional goals. That is, he does not really know what to plan for in his classes. Unfortunately, however, most instructional objectives are stated in a fashion so vague and ambiguous as to reduce their utility. When objectives are phrased in very broad terms, there are many possible interpretations which could be made regarding what the objective means. It is almost impossible to identify what the instructor really has in mind. For example, when a teacher says he wants students to "become familiar" with a certain concept, we do not know how the pupil will manifest this familiarity unless the instructor goes on to state just what the student should do or be able to do in order to evidence the desired familiarity.

Behavioral Statements

Meaningful instructional objectives, therefore, must be stated in terms of student behavior, they must specify the type of behavior a student will engage (or be able to engage) when he has satisfactorily achieved the objective. For instance, the teacher might assert first, in a rather general way, that the student will "understand" a particular principle and then clarify this goal by giving a more specific objective. This objective should indicate that understanding will be manifested when the student will be able to describe in writing the five major elements of the principle and give one original example of each.

In other words, the more explicit the instructor can be regarding the statement of instructional objectives, the better. The only kind of specificity which really helps

EDUCATION
IN THE
UNITED STATES

3292

[1] An excellent treatment of how to state instructional objectives is provided by Mager, Robert, *Preparing Objectives for Programmed Instruction*, Fearon Press, San Francisco, 1962.

with respect to empirically improving teacher behavior is to specify goals in terms of student behavior changes. "Behavior" in this sense is defined rather broadly. It does not need to be behavior only on a test but perhaps behavior in an informal situation (e.g., observed politeness) or even behavior in a situation specifically contrived by the instructor to reflect a more basic kind of commitment. For instance, the literature instructor is often concerned with the degree his students are really interested in the literature he has been treating. He may set up situations in which students are free to volitionally choose reading material and then note the degree the choices coincide with preferences advocated in his class. The most common behavior used with behaviorally stated objectives is test behavior, although there are numerous other ways to assess both the objectives in the intellectual as well as attitudinal realms. These latter approaches take considerable ingenuity on the part of the teacher.

Minimal Standards

It is also extremely important to specify minimally acceptable standards for the performance of the student. These standards should be described in advance of the instruction. With clear criterion levels the teacher can attempt to gear his instruction so the students are able to behave as well as initially specified prior to instruction. In other words, he should certify in advance how well the student must do on the behavior measures in order for his instruction to be considered satisfactory. It is extremely difficult to establish precisely how well a student should do on examinations or other behavioral measures, particularly for the beginning teacher. However, in time, it is usually possible to reach a more or less defensible decision regarding the minimum proficiency students should display on assessment devices. The teacher can then pit his instructional effectiveness against these standards.

In some cases the minimum standards are rather well established by the fact the student goes on to an advanced class which requires certain prerequisite knowledge and skills. In other professional-type courses the necessary proficiency of the student can be validated against the actual performance requirements of the job. For example, the medical school has an enormously important criterion with respect to their program when they consider the life or death of their doctor's patients. Therefore, in certain surgery courses it is necessary to establish 100 per cent accuracy on particular kinds of skill tests, whereas in other fields less than perfect accuracy may be required. At first, however, the student teacher need not be too concerned if the minimum proficiency levels for his objectives are somewhat elusive.

Important Conditions

A third characteristic of a well stated objective is that it specifies any important conditions under which the terminal behavior will be manifested. In otherwords, any "givens" or restrictions that will actually make a difference in expected student performance after instruction should be identified. To illustrate—if the student is to take an open book test, this should be so described. If, in a mathematics class the student is required to use certain mathematical formulae rather than others, this should also be so described. Although somewhat less important than behavioral statements and minimum proficiency levels, the description of conditions can be quite significant in some cases.

*   *   *

TEACHING DISADVANTAGED CHILDREN IN THE PRE-SCHOOL

(1967)   From Carl Bereiter, "Instructional Planning in Early Compensatory Education," *Phi Delta Kappan* (March, 1967), pp. 355-56, 358-59.

$\mathbf{T}$he history of teaching shows cycles of vigorous times followed by periods of stultification and rigidity. During the vigorous times people are concerned with what children are learning. During the dull times people are concerned with putting children through the motions that, previously, had been more finely tuned to the production of learning. In our present haste to provide preschool programs for disadvantaged children, we are in danger of leaping directly to a blind concentration upon what children should do without going through the productive phase of considering what children should learn and devising methods that will bring this learning about. This is occurring, ironically, at a time when in other areas of education we are in a stage of vigorous growth, in which the question of what children should learn is being reexamined more deeply and in more detail than ever before and in which new methods are being developed with a clearer view to the attainment of learning objectives and less reliance upon pedagogical ritual.

But wait. Is there not a great deal of research going on to determine the needs of disadvantaged children and to test ways of meeting these needs? To be sure. But this is not the same thing as instructional planning. It leaves out the essential step of converting "deficits," "needs," and "conditions" into specific learning objectives and then developing instructional methods to achieve these learning objectives, rather than trying to treat the deficits, needs, and conditions directly, which is something that education cannot hope to do except by a remarkable stroke of luck.

This kind of instructional planning is what Siegfried Engelmann and I have been trying to do in an experimental program at the University of Illinois. We have, for instance, tried to convert the general goal of improving language abilities into a series of specific concepts and language operations to be taught. These were arrived at in the same way that curriculum planners go about determining the content of science and mathematics courses—not by empirical means but by a consideration of what concepts and skills were necessary or most powerful in relation to future tasks. We have done the same kind of thing with reading and arithmetic. Although tbse latter subjects had already been worked over by curriculum planners, the analysis of tasks into their component concepts and skills has not been carried down to a low enough level to permit a clear specification of the first steps in learning for naive four-year-olds. Thus it was necessary to design "sub-zero" curricula, as it were, in reading and arithmetic; but we have tried to do this in as direct and specific a fashion as is done for higher-level mathematics instruction, rather than contenting ourselves with more indefinite kinds of "readiness" training.

Curriculum planning for young disadvantaged children—that is, the specification of what should be taught and in what order—has been discouraged by a kind of medical orientation to disadvantaged children on the one hand and by strong anti-instructional biases on the other. The medical orientation has led to regarding cultural deprivation as an ailment or complex of ailments that need to be diagnosed and cured. For people who hold to this orientation, the important question to ask of any proposed curriculum is whether it will get to the heart of the ailments and cure them—and the answer has to be negative, because no curriculum ever cured anything. More generally, the medical orientation leads to a fruitless concern over whether a given curriculum is the "right one" for disadvantaged children. How do we know, for instance, that the particular language concepts and operations that we have elected to teach are the ones that disadvantaged children really need to learn? This unanswerable question does not seem to come up when one is planning curricula for ordinary children. The planner of a junior high school biology course knows that there are many alternative choices of content and that there is plenty of room for argument against any particular selection, but he is under no illusion that there exists, somewhere in the unprobed psyches of his students, a key that would tell him which is the "right one." He simply tries to do the best he can with the knowledge and imagination at his disposal. If curriculum planners had to worry about finding a key to the "right one," curriculum innovation would remain at a standstill.

The anti-instructional bias is tied to a number of widely held convictions about not "forcing" young children, about the importance of play and free exploration, the primacy of social or nonverbal learning, and so on. There is no logical reason why these convictions should militate against the defining of instructional objectives, however, since specifying *what* children should learn does not in itself rule out or entail any particular ways of treating children. On the other hand, it can bring about a showdown, in which the advocates of a certain method must either demonstrate how their method can produce the designated learnings or else come up with some alternate set of learnings which their method can accomplish and which can be defended in open competition. This kind of showdown is badly needed, but it is not likely to occur so long as achievement objectives of any kind are met with hostility.

The second part of instructional planning is finding a practical way of getting all children to learn the specified content. It is on this point that our experimental program has aroused the most controversy. In fact, *all* of the controversy seems to have centered on this point, which is unfortunate. It is unfortunate because constructive debate on educational methods cannot really be carried on without a consideration of what one is trying to teach. Opponents should either claim that they can teach the same things in better ways or that other things should be taught. Simply arguing about teaching methods without reference to what the children are to learn is rather like arguing the merits of different means of transportation without reference to where one is going.

We have chosen to teach in the most direct manner possible, striving in each lesson to make it clear to the children what they are supposed to be learning, what the criteria of learning are, how what they are learning now relates to what they have learned previously, and what good it does them to learn it—that is, what they can do with what they have learned. With disadvantaged four-year-olds, very little of this can be communicated to them through explanation. They have to be shown through example, through the structure of the tasks themselves, and through careful control of the teacher's responses. The methods we have developed are appropriate for a live teacher working with small and relatively homogeneous groups. Other methods of teaching the same content could be used. Individual tutorial methods, for example, would call for somewhat different procedures. With more heterogeneous groups one might make more use of modeling behavior and of children's helping one another. Some of the teaching could be automated, although this is difficult for teaching verbal responses. The use of television or other unresponsive media would create new problems but also new possibilities. A more potent system of contingent rewards might lessen the need for dramatizing the intrinsic value of what is being learned. It might also be possible, though it appears to us much more difficult and time-consuming, to make greater use of discovery methods. Given the same content to be learned, however, these alternate methods would have to be judged on economy and effectiveness.

Debate over the "right" method of teaching is likely to be as unproductive as debate over the "right" content. The best method of teaching a given body of content is likely to be the one that is the most thoroughly developed at the time, although for the long haul one should probably put his money on the method that has the greatest potentiality for development. I would venture the guess, for instance, that in the first trials of our program we would have gotten better results with the same basic program by incorporating into it a "token reward economy" of the kind favored by behavioristic psychologists. Had we maintained a more consistently high level of motivation through inadequately designed parts of the program, children would have been more likely to learn in spite of defective methods of presentation and gaps in the sequence of learning steps. But to the extent that this occurred, we should have been unable to discern what the gaps and defects were. As it was, lagging motivation and halts in learning provided sensitive indicators of trouble spots in the curriculum, and as these weaknesses were remedied, the need for an ancillary reward system with its added burden and possible troublesome side effects has all but vanished. We could be wrong, however. There is room for the development of a variety of methods of teaching young disadvantaged children, and there is a good chance that any serious and extended effort at the development of such methods will yield results that are of benefit to the others.

The key word in the preceding sentence is "development." By circumventing the problem of defining explicit curriculum content and explicit methods for teaching it, early childhood educators cut themselves off from possibilities for program development. They may create a program that is pretty good, as judged by terminal or long-range measures, but they have no systematic way of making it better or even telling whether it can be made better. That is why the evaluations of Project Head Start are so difficult to get excited about. We are naturally curious to know what the Head Start programs have accomplished; but, on the premise that they must do some good while falling short of perfection, we cannot expect the results to tell us anything that would lead to substantive program changes. At best they may encourage people to keep up the good work or try harder.

A preschool program that is capable of true development rather than haphazard change must have instructional objectives and methods that are sufficiently well defined and closely wedded that it is at least possible to judge the effectiveness of individual activities and units. The smaller the units that can be evaluated, the greater the possibilities for development. Ideally, one should be able to evaluate single sentences and questions spoken by the teacher, particular examples and demonstrations, and the sequencing of items within small units. Data for such evaluations are not likely to be of very high quality, but for developmental purposes it seems preferable to have low quality data, even merely impressionistic data, on a minute-to-minute basis than to have very high quality psychometric data that can be obtained only after the program has run to completion.

It is worth noting, in the regard, that for the evaluation of preschool programs high quality data are not presently available at all. A few mental ability tests of high reliability, such as the Stanford-Binet Intelligence Test, are available, but is not known whether changes on these measures have any validity. Their use as evaluative criteria is therefore questionable. There are no achievement tests on the market which are appropriate for preschool use. The Preschool Achievement Test, as well as the standard readiness tests, appear to be nothing more than general scholastic aptitude tests, and so their use as evaluative criteria is subject to the same reservations as the use of other aptitude tests. In our work we have made use of the Wide Range Achievement Test, which has norms extending down through the kindergarten level for reading, arithmetic, and spelling; but this test does not provide very precise measurement and covers only a very narrow range of content. The reason that there are no preschool achievement tests is that there have been no achievement objectives. It is getting the cart ahead of the horse to produce achievement tests before curricula with achievement objectives are in wide use, but in the present case it would not be a bad idea. My colleague, Siegfried Engelmann, has developed one such test, the Concept Inventory, which assesses the kinds of language concepts and skills that we have built our language curriculum around. As far as I know, it is the only language test for young children that can properly be called an achievement rather than an aptitude test—a test, in other words, which could be used to assess how successfully a program had taught language operations rather than merely showing how capable the children are with verbal tasks.

In so far as we can judge from the crude achievement measures available, our program has been quite successful in fostering academic achievement in young disadvantaged children. Our first experimental class, which was composed of typically deprived urban Negro children, obtained mean grade level scores on the Wide-Range Achievement Test of 1.6 in reading, 2.6 in arithmetic, and 1.7 in spelling at the end of the kindergarten year, having completed two years of preschool training. By present indications the second group, which is now in the middle of its kindergarten year, should do considerably better than this in reading; and the third group, which is now in its first year of work, is progressing faster than earlier groups in all areas.

The long-range effects of preschool training are, of course, a matter of great social concern. For the planner of preschool programs, however, the matter is not a simple one of waiting for the pudding that brings the proof. On the one hand, the preschool educator cannot be responsible for the failures of the elementary schools to follow through on achievements made during the preschool period. He must be sure, however, that the achievements are genuine and not illusory. A preschool program might produce gains in I.Q. or other psychological indices, but if these gains disappear in later years and have no apparent effect on school performance, this is not necessarily the fault of the elementary schools. It may simply indicate that the gains did not reflect any significant learning or improvement in educability. Only when there is evidence of genuine learning can it be claimed that something has been accomplished which the schools should take account of.

On the other hand, the preschool educator has not only the responsibility of teaching disadvantaged children material relevant to the content of later instruction but also the responsibility of teaching the children skills and habits that will enable them to make use of this material under the conditions of elementary school life, which usually include large classes, a considerable amount of independent seatwork, and frequently teaching of a not very skillful kind. As the children in our original experimental class now make their way through the first grade in. a variety of different classroom situations, we are beginning to recognize some of the things that should have been included in our curriculum but weren't or were not emphasized enough. For instance, one of the requirements of many first-grade classes, for which our children (and, it would appear, children in most other heavily staffed preschool classes) were not adequately trained, is that of carrying out extended seatwork assignments with minimal supervision and help. Middle-class children may well learn the necessary habits and skills for this kind of activity through solitary play extended over a number of years. They gradually work their way up from activities that are immediately and continually rewarding to ones that yield dividends only after a considerable period of effort. A preschool program, however, lacks both the time and the appropriate conditions for establishing these habits through undirected play—and in any event it is questionable whether the result is worth the time it would take to achieve it through this means. But the necessary learnings can be formulated as instructional objectives and once this is done it should be possible to find more efficient means of teaching them. For instance, a schedule of increasingly spaced token rewards for solitary effort would seem to be an appropriate training procedure. The advantage of a well-defined instructional program for picking up loose ends such as these is that, when you know what children have learned, it is much easier to detect what they have not learned.

I have said practically nothing in this discussion about problems or methods unique to disadvantaged children. This is not to imply that preschool programs for disadvantaged children need be no different from those for more privileged children. What is implied, however, when one approaches preschool education as an instructional problem, is that the same achievements are expected of all children, these achievements having been dictated not by empirical norms or the needs of individual children but by the requirements of future learning tasks. If disadvantaged children need special programs, it is because they are unable to meet some of the achievement criteria under the same conditions as other children. If, for instance, there are certain criteria of language mastery that middle-class children appear to meet through nothing more than informal language activities, but disadvantaged children do not, then there is an evident need for building into the educational program of disadvantaged children some special kinds of teaching to bring these achievements about. It may be presumed, however, that other kinds of children may also need the same special teaching. Why children might happen to be in a condition to need it is not a very relevant issue. It is unnecessary to treat the disadvantaged child as a stereotype possessed of certain characteristics by virtue of his social status. It is enough to know what reequired learnings a child lacks and to have available the means of producing them. A great deal of the agony over "defining the disadvantaged" and "meeting their needs" seems to be unnecessary and leads only to further agonizing over the issue of cultural differences versus cultural handicaps, and similar false dilemmas.

At the present time preschool education is largely restricted to children who either hardly need it at all or else need it so badly that practically anything that is done for them is of some help. This is not a very favorable condition for progress in instructional methodology. We would do better to look ahead to the time when preschool education will be available to all children. If at that time we have no clearer conception of achievement goals for early education and no more effective ways for reaching them than we have today, we will have a pretty poor bill of goods to offer the public. If, on the other hand, we are able to define a reasonable set of concepts, skills, and habits that can serve as a foundation upon which to build later school curricula, and if we have developed reliable and efficient means of teaching these things to children who lack them, then we shall be in a position to offer a variety of preschool programs to which children may be assigned on the basis of what they need to learn rather than on the basis of their skin color, aptitude test scores, or the incomes of their parents. The sooner we are in a position to do this, the sooner we shall be able to stop floundering and start moving toward the development of more effective programs for today's needy children.

JOSEPH FEATHERSTONE DESCRIBES INNOVATIONS IN BRITISH INFANT SCHOOLS (1967) From Joseph Featherstone "Schools For Children," *New Republic* (August 19, 1967), pp. 17–21.

My wife and I have just spent a month in England visiting classes in primary schools, talking to children and teachers. Friends told us about good things happening in British classrooms, but we were scarcely prepared for what we found; in recent decades there has been a profound and sweeping revolution in English primary education, involving new ways of thinking about how young children learn, classroom organization, the curriculum and the role of the teacher. We saw schools in some good local educational authorities: Bristol, Nottingham, Leicestershire, Oxfordshire and a few serving immigrant areas in cities like London.

In the first part of what follows, I'm going to be as specific as I can about how classes work in a good English school, how the room is laid out, what sort of things are in it, how the teacher and the children spend the day and, in some detail, how a child learns to read, as an example of the kind of learning that goes on. I know that teachers in this country, particularly good ones, are rightly suspicious of most talk on education, because so little of what they hear ever relates to actual classroom practice. I hope I can be specific enough. The relevance of these classrooms to us is another, more difficult question which I'll leave for later. I don't have any easy answers.

Primary schools divide into "infant" and "junior" schools. Much of this report will focus on the infant schools, which take children from the age of five to seven, and in some authorities eight. (As in Israel, children begin compulsory schooling at the early age of five in England.) It is in the infant schools that people learn to read and write and to work with numbers. Junior schools take children from seven or eight to 11, when they go on to secondary school. Infant and junior schools sometimes occupy the same building, and some authorities—Oxfordshire, for example—have a policy of putting them together in one unit, like an American elementary school.

It is important to understand that what goes on in the good infant schools is much the same. The approach is similar, though the quality of teaching and children's work varies greatly.

Westfield Infant School is a one-story structure, like any of a thousand American buildings, on a working-class housing estate in Leicestershire. If you arrive early, you find a number of children already inside, reading, writing, painting, playing music, tending to pets. Teachers sift in slowly, and begin working with students. Apart from a religious assembly (required by English law) it's hard to say just when school actually begins, because there is very little organized activity for a whole class to do together. The puzzled visitor sees some small group work in mathematics ("maths") or reading, but mostly children are on their own, moving about and talking quite freely. The teacher sometimes sits at her desk, and the children flock to her for consultations, but more often she moves about the room, advising on projects, listening to children read, asking questions, giving words, talking, sometimes prodding.

The hallways, which are about the size of those in our schools, are filled with busy children, displays of paintings and graphs, a play grocery store where children use play money and learn to count, easels, tables for collections of shells and plants, workbenches on which to pound and hammer nails and boards, big wooden boxes full of building blocks.

Classrooms open out onto the playground, which is also much in use. A contingent of children is kneeling on the grass, clocking the speed of a tortoise, which they want to graph against the speeds of other pets and people. Nearby are five-year-olds, finishing an intricate, tall tower of blocks, triumphantly counting as they add the last one, "23, 24." A solitary boy is mixing powders for paint; on a large piece of paper attached to an easel, with very big strokes, he makes an ominous, stylized buiding that seems largely to consist of black shutters framing deep red windows. "It's the hospital where my brother is," he explains, and pulls the visitor over to the class-library corner, where a picture book discusses hospitals. He can't read it yet (he's five), but says he is trying. And he is; he can make out a number of words, some pretty hard, on different pages, and it is clear that he has been studying the book, because he wants badly to know about hospitals. At another end of the hall there is a quieter library nook for the whole school. Here two small boys are reading aloud; the better reader is, with indifferent grace, correcting the grateful slower boy as he stumbles over words.

The rooms are fairly noisy—more noisy than many American teachers or principals would allow—because children can talk freely. Sometimes the teacher has to ask for quiet. With as many as 40 in some classes, rooms are crowded and accidents happen. Paint spills, a tub overflows, there are recriminations. Usually the children mop up and work resumes.

The visitor is dazed by the amount and variety and fluency of the free writing produced: stories, free-verse poems, with intricate images, precise accounts of experiments in "maths" and, finally, looking over a tiny little girl's shoulder, he finds: "Today we had visitors from America. . . ."

After a time, you overcome your confusion at the sheer variety of it all, and you begin making more definite observations. The physical layout of the classrooms is markedly different from ours. American teachers are coming to appreciate the importance of a flexible room, but even in good elementary schools this usually means having movable, rather than fixed, desks. In these classes there are no individual desks, and no assigned places. Around the room (which is about the size of one of ours) there are different tables for different kinds of activities: art, water and sand play, number work. (The number tables have all kinds of number lines— strips of paper with numbers marked on them in sequence on which children learn to count and reason mathematically—beads, buttons and odd things to count; weights and balances; dry and liquid measures; and a rich variety of apparatus for learning basic mathematical concepts, some of it homemade, some ready-made. The best of the commercial materials were familiar: Cuisenaire rods, the Dienes multibase material, Stern rods and attribute or logical blocks. This sort of thing is stressed much more than formal arithmetic.)

Wendy and Puppets

Every class has a library alcove, which is separated off by a room divider that also serves as a display shelf for books. Some library corners have a patch of carpet and an old easy chair. Every room has a "Wendy House," a play corner with dolls and furniture for playing house. Often there is a dress-up corner, too, with different kinds of cast-off adult clothes. The small children love the Wendy houses and dress-up corners, but you see older ones using them as well. Some classes have puppet theatres for putting on improvised plays with homemade puppets—although many make do with the legs of one table turned upside down on top of another for a makeshift stage. Often, small children perform dance dramas involving a lot of motion and a minimum of words.

Gradually it becomes clear how the day proceeds in one of these rooms. In many infant and some junior schools the choice of the day's routine is left completely up to the teacher, and the teacher, in turn, leaves options open to the children. Classes for young children, the visitor learns, are reaching a point in many schools where there is no real difference between one subject in the curriculum and another, or even between work and play. A school day run on these lines is called, variously, the "free day," the "integrated curriculum," or the "integrated day." The term scarcely matters.

In a school that operates with a free day, the teacher usually starts in the morning by listing the different activities available. A lot of rich material is needed, according to the teachers, but the best stuff is often homemade; and, in any case, it isn't necessary to have 30 or 40 sets of everything, because most activities are for a limited number of people. "Six children can play in the Wendy House," says a sign in one classroom. The ground rules are that they must clean up when they finish, and they mustn't bother others.

A child might spend the day on his first choice, or he might not. Many teachers confess they get nervous if everybody doesn't do some reading and writing every day; others are committed in principle to letting children choose freely. In practice, a lot of teachers give work when they think it's needed. In this, as in any other way of doing things, teachers tailor their styles to their own temperament and the kind of children they have. But the extent to which children really have a choice and really work purposefully is astonishing.

How they learn reading offers a clear example of the kind of individual learning and teaching going on in these classrooms, even in quite large ones. (The mathematics work shows this even better, but I'll talk of math in another context.) Reading is not particularly emphasized, and my purpose is singling it out is purely illustrative, though the contrast between English classes and most American ones, where reading is a formidable matter, is vivid and depressing.

At first it is hard to say just how they do learn reading, since there are no separate subjects. A part of the answer slowly becomes clear, and it surprises American visitors used to thinking of the teacher as the generating force of education: children learn from each other. They hang around the library corners long before they can read, handling the books, looking at pictures, trying to find words they do know, listening and watching as the teacher hears other children's reading. It is common to see nonreaders studying people as they read, and then imitating them, monkey doing what monkey sees. Nobody makes fun of their grave parodies, and for good reasons.

A very small number of school in two or three authorities have adopted what they call "family," or "vertical," grouping, which further promotes the idea of children teaching children. In these schools, each class is a cross-section of the whole school's population, all ages mixed together. This seems particularly successful in the early school years, when newcomers are easily absorbed, and older children help teach the young ones to clean up and take first steps in reading. Family grouping needs smaller classes, teachers say, because it requires close supervision to make sure small children don't get overshadowed and big ones are still challenged. Teachers using it swear by the flexibility it provides.

Teachers use a range of reading schemes, sight reading, phonics, and so forth, whatever seems to work with a child. (Only about five percent of English schools use the Initial Teaching Alphabet, an improved alphabet, not a method of reading, that has proved successful with poor readers and adults both in England and in this country; heads of good schools we visited thought that ITA was unnecessary with a truly flexible reading program, but that in a rigid scheme, it gave the slow reader another chance, and thus a break.)

Books in Profusion

Increasingly in the good infant schools, there are no textbooks and no class readers. There are just books, in profusion. Instead of spending their scanty book money on 40 sets of everything, wise schools have purchased different sets of reading series, as well as a great many single books, at all levels of difficulty. Teachers arrange their classroom libraries so they can direct students of different abilities to appropriate books, but in most classes a child can tackle anything he wants. As a check, cautious teachers ask them to go on their own through a graded reading series—which one doesn't matter.

However a child picks up reading, it will involve learning to write at the same time, and some write before they can read; there is an attempt to break down the mental barrier between the spoken, the written and the printed word. When a child starts school, he gets a large, unlined notebook; this is his book for free writing, and he can put what he wants in it. On his own, he may draw a picture in it with crayon or pencil, discuss the picture with the teacher, and dictate a caption to her, which she then writes down for him: "This is my Dad." He copies the caption, writing just underneath. In this way he learns to memorize the look and sound of his dictated words and phrases, until he reaches a point where, with help, he can write sentences. Often his notebook serves as his own first reading book.

He also gets a smaller notebook, his private dictionary, in which he enters words as he learns them. "I got a new word," a five-year-old brags to the visitor. Children are always running to the teacher for words, as they find they have more and more to write. Good teachers don't give in without a struggle; the children have to guess the first letter and sound the word out before they get it. Thus they pick up phonetic skills informally, although some teachers do use sight cards at the outset with their children. Gradually as a child amasses a reading and writing vocabulary, he reaches a fluent stage and you see six-year-olds writing stories, free-verse poems, accounts of things done in class, for an audience that includes other children as well as the teacher.

As a rule, teachers don't pay much attention to accuracy or neatness until a child is well on in his writing. They introduce grammar and spelling after a time, but not as separate subjects or ends in themselves: they are simply ways to say what you want better and more efficiently. Under these methods, where the children choose the content to their writing, there seems in fact to be more attention paid to content than externals, such as punctuation, spelling and grammar. In the good schools, these are presented as what they are, living ways to get a meaning across, to be understood. Even some unimaginative teachers, who quibble with children about other work, can respect the content of the free writing books and take it seriously. This emphasis on self-chosen content has produced a flowering of young children's literature in schools working with many kinds of teachers and children. There is growing recognition that different people flourish on different kinds of writing; storytellers and poets are not necessarily the same as those who can do elegant and graceful writing about mathematics. Impressive examples of free writing and poetry similar to what we saw are contained in the West Riding Education Committee's anthology, *The Excitement of Writing.* Samples of "maths" writing are included in the Schools Council's *Mathematics in the Primary Schools*, a wonderfully instructive book on many accounts. Books made and illustrated by the children are coming to be a regular part of the curriculum in some schools.

I've focused on reading, although of course children spend their time doing other things, and the teachers in the schools we saw would be annoyed at the manner in which I've singled out one academic subject. The very best often argued that art was the key. Miss Nash, the head of Sea Mills School in Bristol said firmly that if the art is good, all else follows. All else does follow, richly, at Sea Mills, when the infants sat us down and performed a concert of skillful poetry and songs they made up on musical instruments.

But my purpose was to show not reading, but the changed role of the classroom teacher. Formal classroom teaching—the instructor standing up front, talking to the group, or even the first-grade room divided up into reading groups which the teacher listens to separately as she tries desperately to keep order has disappeared from many infant and a number of junior schools. It has disappeared because it is inflexible, because it imposes a single pattern of learning on a whole group of children—thus forcing the schools to "track," or to group classes by ability—because it ignores the extent to which children teach each other, and because in many workaday schools other methods are working better. Ordinary teachers, trained formally, take to the new role when they can see with their own eyes that the result is not chaos.

Informality Is Hard Work

These methods mean more work for the teacher, not less. In informal conditions, it is essential for the teacher to keep detailed and accurate accounts of what a child is learning, even though at any given moment she might not know what he's up to. Children help by keeping their own records: in some schools, they have private shelves where they store writing books, accounts of experiments and work in "maths," lists of the books they've read, and dates when they checked in with the teacher to read aloud. If American parents could ever see some of the detailed histories kept of each child's separate path, including his art work, they would feel, quite rightly, that a report card is a swindle.

When the class seldom meets as a unit, when children work independently, discipline is less of a problem. It does not disappear as a problem, but it becomes less paramount. The purposeful self-discipline of these children is, we were told, just as surprising to middle-aged Englishmen as it is to Americans. It is a recent development, and by no means the product of luck: much hard work and thought go into the arrangement of these classrooms and their rich materials. When they work at it, teachers find they can make time during the day for children who need it. "I can give all my attention to a child for five minutes, and that's worth more to him than being part of a sea of faces all day," said a teacher in an East London school overlooking the docks. Other teachers say they can watch children as they work and ask them questions; there is a better chance of finding out what children really understand.

What we saw is no statistical sample. The practices of the good schools we visited in different kinds of communities are not universal; but there are reasons for thinking that they are no longer strikingly exceptional. The schools we saw are, for the most part, staffed by ordinary teachers; they are not isolated experiments, run by cranks and geniuses. A government advisory body—the Plowden Committee—published a massive, and to American eyes, a radical report early this year, in which it indicated that about a third of England's 23,000 primary schools have been deeply influenced by the new ideas and methods, that another third are stirring under their impact, and that the remaining third are still teaching along the formal lines of British schools in the thirties, and of American schools now.

The change is most widespread and impressive in the infant schools, and becomes more scattered on the junior level. Junior schools in some authorities are playing stunning variations on the free themes developed by the infant schools; but, in general, change in the junior schools is slower, more diffident and faces more problems.

Many formal schools—English and American—are probably doing a more effective job, in conventional terms, than many of these schools. It doesn't do to dogmatize. For example, by and large, in terms of measurable achievement on conventional tests, children in traditional, formal classes in England do slightly better than children from the freer classes. (The survey is submitted by the Plowden Report.) The difference is greatest in mechanical arithmetic, and least in reading. These are facts, but there are reasons for discounting them, apart from evidence that the differences disappear in later school years. Formal schools teach children to take conventional tests; that is their function, and it would be surprising if all their efforts didn't produce some results. In view of the lack of test training in the freer schools, the students' results seem to me surprisingly high. It is perfectly clear that the mathematics taught in the informal schools—mathematical relationships in which process of thought counts for more than arithmetical skill—and the English—free writing, rather than grammar and so on—put their students at a disadvantage on achievement tests, whose authors would probably be the first to admit this. England and America badly need new kinds of tests. My own very strong impression is that in areas easy to define and probably not hard to test—ability to write, for example, or understanding of the math they were doing—the children in the good schools I saw, including slum schools, were far ahead of students in good schools in this country.

The external motions teachers go through in the schools matter less than what the teachers are and what they think. An organizational change—the free day, for example, or simply rearranging classroom space—is unlikely to make much difference unless teachers really believe that in a rich environment young children can learn a great deal by themselves and that most often their own choices reflect their needs. But when you see schools where teachers do believe in them, it is easy to share the Plowden Report's enthusiasm for informal, individual learning in the early years of school. (The Plowden Committee is in a sense the official voice of the primary school revolution.) The infant schools are a historical accident—nobody years ago gave much thought to why children should begin school at five—but British teachers are now realizing their advantages. With kindergarten and the first few years fused together, children have an extended time in which to learn to read and write and work with numbers. This is especially effective if the pattern of learning is largely individual; if the teacher is important, but she doesn't stand in the way or try to take over the whole job. Many of the difficulties that plague formal first-grade classes disappear; children aren't kept back from learning, nor are they branded as problems if they take their time.

A few American kindergartens and Head Start classes have tried to alter the rigid rules of the game, but they are just voices in the wilderness. And the cry doesn't carry very far. An Englishman told me of a good Head Start class run on individual lines; when he peeked into the next room it was the first-grade class and there were the children, sitting in rows, all copying the letter 'E.'

ON TEACHER EXPECTATIONS AND CLASSROOM LEARNING (1968)
From Robert Rosenthal and Lenore Jacobson, *Pygmalion in the Classroom* (New York, 1968), pp. vii–viii, 180–82.

People, more often than not, do what is expected of them. Much of our behavior is governed by widely shared norms or expectations that make it possible to prophesy how a person will behave in a given situation, even if we have never met that person and know little of how he differs from others. At the same time, however, there is considerable variability of behavior so that often we can more accurately prophesy the behavior of a person we know well than we can prophesy the behavior of a stranger. To a great extent, our expectations for another person's behavior are accurate because we know his past behavior. But there is now good reason to believe that another factor increases our accuracy of interpersonal predictions or prophecies. Our prediction or prophecy may in itself be a factor in determining the behavior of other people. When we are led to expect that we are about to meet a pleasant person, our treatment of him at first meeting may, in fact, make him a more pleasant person. If we are led to expect that we shall encounter an unpleasant person, we may approach him so defensively that we make him into an unpleasant person. That, in general, is the concern of this book. It is about interpersonal self-fulfilling prophecies: *how one person's expectation for another person's behavior can quite unwittingly become a more accurate prediction simply for its having been made.*

The existing evidence for the effects of these interpersonal self-fulfilling prophecies will be summarized and, in greater detail, new evidence will be presented. This new evidence is from an educational context, and it is addressed to the question of whether a teacher's expectation for her pupils' intellectual competence can come to serve as an educational self-fulfilling prophecy.

To anticipate briefly the nature of this new evidence it is enough to say that 20 percent of the children in a certain elementary school were reported to their teachers as showing unusual potential for intellectual growth. The names of these 20 percent of the children were drawn by means of a table of random numbers, which is to say that the names were drawn out of a hat. Eight months later these unusual or "magic" children showed significantly greater gains in IQ than did the remaining children who had not been singled out for the teachers' attention. The change in the teachers' expectations regarding the intellectual performance of these allegedly "special" children had led to an actual change in the intellectual performance of these randomly selected children.

There are many determinants of a teacher's expectation of her pupils' intellectual ability. Even before a teacher has seen a pupil deal with academic tasks she is likely to have some expectation for his behavior. If she is to teach a "slow group," or children of darker skin color, or children whose mothers are "on welfare," she will have different expectations for her pupils' performance than if she is to teach a "fast group," or children of an upper-middle-class community. Before she has seen a child perform, she may have seen his score on an achievement or ability test or his last year's grades, or she may have access to the less formal information that constitutes the child's reputation. There have been theoretical formulations, and there has been some evidence, most of it anecdotal, that the teacher's expectation, however derived, can come to serve as an educational self-fulfilling prophecy. After a consideration of the new experimental evidence bearing on these formulations, the implications for educational research and practice will be considered.

＊　　＊　　＊

On the basis of other experiments on interpersonal self-fulfilling prophecies, we can only speculate as to how teachers brought about intellectual competence simply by expecting it. Teachers may have treated their children in a more pleasant, friendly, and encouraging fashion when they expected greater intellectual gains of them. Such behavior has been shown to improve intellectual performance, probably by its favorable effect on pupil motivation.

Teachers probably watched their special children more closely, and this greater attentiveness may have led to more rapid reinforcement of correct responses with a consequent increase in pupils' learning. Teachers may also have become more reflective in their evaluation of the special children's intellectual performance. Such an increase in teachers' reflectiveness may have led to an increase in their special pupils' reflectiveness, and such a change in cognitive style would be helpful to the performance of the nonverbal skills required by the IQ test employed.

To summarize our speculations, we may say that by what she said, by how and when she said it, by her facial expressions, postures, and perhaps by her touch, the teacher may have communicated to the children of the experimental group that she expected improved intellectual performance. Such communications together with possible changes in teaching techniques may have helped the child learn by changing his self-concept, his expectations of his own behavior, and his motivation, as well as his cognitive style and skills.

It is self-evident that further research is needed to narrow down the range of possible mechanisms whereby a teacher's expectations become translated into a pupil's intellectual growth. It would be valuable, for example, to have sound films of teachers interacting with their pupils. We might then look for differences in the way teachers interact with those children from whom they expect intellectual growth compared to those from whom they expect less. On the basis of films of psychological experimenters interacting with subjects from whom different responses are expected, we know that even in such highly standardized situations, unintentional communications can be incredibly subtle and complex (Rosenthal, 1966). Much more subtle and much more complex may be the communications between children and their teachers, teachers not constrained by the demands of the experimental laboratory to treat everyone equally to the extent that it is possible to do so.

The implications of the research described herein are of several kinds. There are methodological implications for the conduct of educational research, and these were discussed in the last chapter. There are implications for the further investigation of unintentional influence processes especially when these processes result in inter-personally self-fulfilling prophecies, and some of these have been discussed. Finally, there are some possible implications for the educational enterprise, and some of these will be suggested briefly.

Over time, our educational policy question has changed from "who ought to be educated?" to "who is capable of being educated?" The ethical question has been traded in for the scientific question. For those children whose educability is in doubt there is a label. They are the educationally, or culturally, or socioeconomically, deprived children and, as things stand now, they appear not to be able to learn as do those who are more advantaged. The advantaged and the disadvantaged differ in parental income, in parental values, in scores on various tests of achievement and ability, and often in skin color and other phenotypic expressions of genetic heritage. Quite inseparable from these differences between the advantages and the disadvantaged are the differences in their teachers' expectations for what they can achieve in school. There are no experiments to show that a change in pupils' skin color will lead to improved intellectual performance. There is, however, the experiment described in this book to show that change in teacher expectation can lead to improved intellectual performance.

Nothing was done directly for the disadvantaged child at Oak School. There was no crash program to improve his reading ability, no special lesson plan, no extra time for tutoring, no trips to museums or art galleries. There was only the belief that the children bore watching, that they had intellectual competencies that would in due course be revealed. What was done in our program of educational change was done directly for the teacher, only indirectly for her pupils. Perhaps, then, it is the teacher to whom we should direct more of our research attention. If we could learn how she is able to effect dramatic improvement in her pupils' competence without formal changes in her teaching methods, then we could teach other teachers to do the same. If further research shows that it is possible to select teachers whose untrained interactional style does for most of her pupils what our teachers did for the special children, it may be possible to combine sophisticated teacher selection and placement with teacher training to optimize the learning of all pupils.

As teacher-training institutions begin to teach the possibility that teachers' expectations of their pupils' performance may serve as self-fulfilling prophecies, there may be a new expectancy created. The new expectancy may be that children can learn more than had been believed possible, an expectation held by many educational theorists, though for quite different reasons (for example, Bruner, 1960). The new expectancy, at the very least, will make it more difficult when they encounter the educationally disadvantaged for teachers to think, "Well, after all, what can you expect?" The man on the street may be permitted his opinions and prophecies of the unkempt children loitering in a dreary schoolyard. The teacher in the schoolroom may need to learn that those same prophecies within her may be fulfilled; she is no casual passer-by. Perhaps Pygmalion in the classroom is more her role.

THE "TALKING TYPEWRITER" (1968)   From Omar Khayyam Moore and Alan Ross Anderson, "The Responsible Environments Project," in Robert D. Hess and Roberta M. Bear, eds., *Early Education: Current Theory, Research, And Action* (Chicago, 1968), pp. 171, 177–79.

Our purpose is to describe the Responsive Environments Project: to provide an analysis of its structure, to state its goals, and to give an informal progress report on some of its aspects.

The long-range objective of the Project, which is part of the Learning Research and Development Center at the University of Pittsburgh, is the creation of an experimentally grounded theory of human problem-solving and social interaction. The present proximate goals are: (a) To construct new formal systems which, hopefully, will be of use in formulating such a theory; (b) to design equipment in accordance with the principles of the theory, both to facilitate testing the theory and for educational applications; (c) to formulate heuristic principles which may prove helpful in guiding empirical investigations; and, finally, (d) to test parts of the theory as they are formulated. Our discussion is organized in terms of these four objectives.

*   *   *

One of the aims of the Project has been to provide specifications for particular responsive environments with responsive devices, with a view toward accelerating learning. We have chosen what we take to be the most fundamental aspect of the socialization process as material for the initial experimental study of the general notion, namely, the acquisition of a natural language, in both spoken and written form. In the remainder of this section we will describe one example from the potentially very large family of responsive devices currently under investigation: the "talking typewriter."

This device, co-invented by Moore and Kobler (1963; Kobler and Moore, 1966), is in current production under the name of the *Edison Responsive Environment*. One of the things for which it was designed was to enable a person with no knowledge of a particular natural language to learn both the spoken and written forms of that language. It can be used equally well to teach very young children how to cope with the written form of the language they speak (and most of our experience has been with children learning to read and write English), and also to enable adults to learn languages with which they are unfamiliar. If the reader himself wishes to learn Russian, the steps would be roughly as follows (of course, the machine would have to be equipped with the Cyrillic alphabet):

Step 1. The machine is set so that the user may strike any key, after which the keyboard locks until the voice-box gives the user the name and/or the phonetic value of the character. Repeated explorations of the keyboard lead to both visual and auditory command of the alphabet.

Step 2. The machine is reset so that the voice-box names a letter, and the user is to find the corresponding character and strike the appropriate key. Arrangements can be made such that if the machine names a letter—or gives its phonetic value, or both—only the appropriate key can be activated, the rest of the keyboard being locked.

Step 3. The machine is reset so as to display some word, perhaps with an appropriate picture on a screen to the right of the keyboard. A typical sequence of events at this stage might run as follows:

(a) The projection screen displays a picture of a table and directly above the paper carriage there is displayed the Russian word for "table."

(b) The keyboard is locked so that only the keys for the letters of a word in order can be depressed, so that the user may strike the operable keys, and the voice-box will give the phonetic value of each in turn.

(c) The voice-box then repeats the spelling, pronounces the word, and allows the user time to repeat and record the word.

(d) The voice-box may make additional remarks about some words, calling attention to irregularities, etc.

Steps 1-3 simply constitute an example; the talking typewriter can be treated in a variety of subtly different ways, for an indefinitely large number of words. Sentences may be treated relatively to words, in the same way that words are treated relatively to letters; the situation is the same for paragraphs, considered as clusters of sentences.

At each stage, flexibility is maintained. The machine can give or take dictation, with or without the projection screen; the keyboard can be locked or not as the programmer—or the user—wishes, and so on.

To prepare a program the programmer need only do three things, since the keyboard and the recording device are themselves usable as encoding devices. The programmer simply (a) types in the desired material, (b) speaks as desired into the recording system, (c) manipulates a small number of buttons which coordinate the results of (a) and (b), together with any material to be used on the projection screen or exhibitor. The flexibility and simplicity of the encoding procedures make additions or deletions in the program possible with very little time and effort. It is in fact possible to make daily changes with a view to following the interests and progress of the user. The program is not a monolithic affair which begins at the beginning and grinds its way relentlessly to the end. Parts may be skipped or abridged, depending on the user's prior knowledge. And if a user already has some familiarity with the spoken form of the language (as is the case in the uses far most extensively investigated—allowing pre-school children to learn to read and write), a large part of what can be learned with the help of the machine is already known, so that the amount to be done by both programmer and user is reduced substantially.

We turn finally to the relationship between the talking typewriter and the notion of a responsive environment. There can be no doubt that the instrument is a "responsive device" in the sense considered under the classification of machines above. Experimental evidence to be discussed below makes it abundantly clear that the machine is "efficacious" in changing the cognitive status of its users.

It should be equally clear that a booth containing such a responsive device, if surrounded by the appropriate autotelic conventions, is a responsive environment in the sense described at the outset of this section. It allows the user a number of actions which may be explored or used systematically; the environment responds promptly and systematically; the pace is determined by the user; the situation permits discoveries by the user; and what is learned is generalizable to other situations in which communication skills are required.

3) *Projections.* Ten years ago there were no automated responsive environments in existence; there were no responsive devices designed specifically for the purpose of facilitating learning, though the concept was available. We envisage, if cooperation between behavioral scientists, formal scientists, and engineers continues, a shelf full of responsive devices from which we may choose those instruments best suited for particular purposes—much as we now have a shelf full of logical systems adaptable to various analytic purposes.

COMPUTER-ASSISTED INSTRUCTION (1968) From Patrick Suppes. "Computer Technology and the Future of Education," *Phi Delta Kappan* (April 1968), pp. 420–23.

Current applications of computers and related information-processing techniques run the gamut in our society from the automatic control of factories to the scrutiny of tax returns. I have not seen any recent data, but we are certainly reaching the point at which a high percentage of regular employees in this country are paid by computerized payroll systems. As another example, every kind of complex experiment is beginning to be subject to computer assistance either in terms of the actual experimentation or in terms of extensive computations integral to the analysis of the experiment. These applications range from bubble-chamber data on elementary particles to the crystallography of protein molecules.

As yet, the use of computer technology in administration and management on the one hand, and scientific and engineering applications on the other, far exceed direct applications in education. However, if potentials are properly realized, the character and nature of education during the course of our lifetimes will be radically changed. Perhaps the most important aspect of computerized instructional devices is that the kind of individualized instruction once possible only for a few members of the aristocracy can be made available to all students at all levels of abilities.

Because some may not be familiar with how computers can be used to provide individualized instruction, let me briefly review the mode of operation. In the first place, because of its great speed of operation, a computer can handle simultaneously a large number of students—for instance, 200 or more, and each of the 200 can be at a different point in the curriculum. In the simplest mode of operation, the terminal device at which the student sits is something like an electric typewriter. Messages can be typed out by the computer and the student in turn can enter his responses on the keyboard. The first and most important feature to add is the delivery of audio messages under computer control to the student. Not only children, but students of all ages learn by ear as much as by eye, and for tutorial ventures in individualized instruction it is essential that the computer system be able to talk to the student.

A simple example may make this idea more concrete. Practically no one learns mathematics simply by reading a book, except at a relatively advanced level. Hearing lectures and listening to someone else's talk seem to be almost psychologically essential to learning complex subjects, at least as far as ordinary learners are concerned. In addition to the typewriter and the earphones for audio messages, the next desirable feature is that graphical and pictorial displays be available under computer control. Such displays can be provided in a variety of formats. The simplest mode is to have color slides that may be selected by computer control. More flexible, and therefore more desirable, devices are cathode-ray tubes that look very much like television sets. The beauty of cathode-ray tubes is that a graphical display may be shown to the student and then his own response, entered on a keyboard, can be made an integral part of the display itself.

This is not the place to review these matters in detail; but I mean to convey a visual image of a student sitting at a variety of terminal gear—as it is called in the computer world. These terminals are used to provide the student with individualized instruction. He receives information from audio messages, from typewritten messages, and also from visual displays ranging from graphics to complex photographs. In turn, he may respond to the system and give his own answers by using the keyboard on the typewriter. Other devices for student response are also available, but I shall not go into them now.

So, with such devices available, individualized instruction in a wide variety of subject matters may be offered students of all ages. The technology is already available, although it will continue to be improved. There are two main factors standing in our way. One is that currently it is expensive to prepare an individualized curriculum. The second factor, and even more important, is that as yet we have little operational experience in precisely how this should best be done. For some time to come, individualized instruction will have to depend on a basis of practical judgment and pedagogical intuition of the sort now used in constructing textbook materials for ordinary courses. One of the exciting potentialities of computer-assisted instruction is that for the first time we shall be able to get hard data to use as a basis for a more serious scientific investigation and evaluation of any given instructional program.

To give a more concrete sense of the possibilities of individualized instruction, I would like to describe briefly three possible levels of interaction between the student and computer program. Following a current usage, I shall refer to each of the instructional programs as a particular system of instruction. At the simplest level there are *individualized drill-and-practice systems*, which are meant to supplement the regular curriculum taught by the teacher. The introduction of concepts and new ideas is handled in conventional fashion by the teacher. The role of the computer is to provide regular review and practice on basic concepts and skills. In the case of elementary mathematics, for example, each student would receive daily a certain number of exercises, which would be automatically presented, evaluated, and scored by the computer program without any effort by the classroom teacher. Moreover, these exercises can be presented on an individualized basis, with the brighter students receiving exercises that are harder than the average, and the slower students receiving easier problems.

One important aspect of this kind of individualization should be emphasized. In using a computer in this fashion, it is not necessary to decide at the beginning of the school year in which track a student should be placed; for example, a student need not be classified as a slow student for the entire year. Individualized drill-and-practice work is suitable to all the elementary subjects which occupy a good part of the curriculum. Elementary mathematics, elementary science, and the beginning work in foreign language are typical parts of the curriculum which benefit from standardized and regularly presented drill-and-practice exercises. A large computer with 200 terminals can handle as many as 6,000 students on a daily basis in this instructional mode. In all likelihood, it will soon be feasible to increase these numbers to a thousand terminals and 30,000 students. Operational details of our 1965–66 drill-and-practice program at Stanford are to be found in the forthcoming book by Suppes, Jerman, and Brian.[1]

At the second and deeper level of interaction between student and computer program there are *tutorial systems*, which take over the main responsibility both for presenting a concept and for developing skill in its use. The intention is to approximate the interaction a patient tutor would have with an individual student. An important aspect of the tutorial programs in reading and elementary mathematics with which we have been concerned at Stanford in the past three years is that every effort is made to avoid an initial experience of failure on the part of the slower children. On the other hand, the program has enough flexibility to avoid boring the brighter children with endlessly repetitive exercises. As soon as the student manifests a clear understanding of a concept on the basis of his handling of a number of exercises, he is moved on to a new concept and new exercises. (A detailed evaluation of the Stanford reading program, which is under the direction of Professor Richard C. Atkinson, may be found in the report by Wilson and Atkinson.[2] A report on the tutorial mathematics program will soon be available. The data show that the computer-based curriculum was particularly beneficial for the slower students.)

At the third and deepest level of interaction there are dialogue systems aimed at permitting the student to conduct a genuine dialogue with the computer. The dialogue systems at the present time exist primarily at the conceptual rather than the operational level, and I do want to emphasize that in the case of dialogue systems a number of difficult technical problems must first be solved. One problem is that of recognizing spoken speech. Especially in the case of young children, we would like the child to be able simply to ask the computer program a question. To permit this interaction, we must be able to recognize the spoken speech of the child and also to recognize the meaning of the question he is asking. The problem of recognizing meaning is at least as difficult as that of recognizing the spoken speech. It will be some time before we will be able to do either one of these things with any efficiency and economy.

I would predict that within the next decade many children will use individualized drill-and-practice systems in elementary school; and by the time they reach high school, tutorial systems will be available on a broad basis. Their children may use dialogue systems throughout their school experience.

If these predictions are even approximately correct, they have far-reaching implications for education and society. As has been pointed out repeatedly by many people in many different ways, the role of education in our society is not simply the transmission of knowledge but also the transmission of culture, including the entire

[1] P. Suppes, M. Jerman, and D. Brian, *Computer-assisted Instruction at Stanford: The 1965–66 Arithmetic Drill-and-Practice Program.* New York: Academic Press, 1968.

[2] H. A. Wilson and R. C. Atkinson, *Computer-based Instruction in Initial Reading: A Progress Report on the Stanford Project.* Technical Report No. 119, August 25, 1967, Institute for Mathematical Studies in the Social Sciences, Stanford University.

range of individual, political, and social values. Some recent studies—for example, the Coleman report—have attempted to show that the schools are not as effective in transmitting this culture as we might hope; but still there is little doubt that the schools play a major role, and the directions they take have serious implications for the character of our society in the future. Now I hope it is evident from the very brief descriptions I have given that the widespread use of computer technology in education has an enormous potential for improving the quality of education, because the possibility of individualizing instruction at ever deeper levels of interaction can be realized in an economically feasible fashion. I take it that this potentiality is evident enough, and I would like to examine some of the problems it raises, problems now beginning to be widely discussed.

Three rather closely related issues are particularly prominent in this discussion. The first centers around the claim that the deep use of technology, especially computer technology, will impose a rigid regime of impersonalized teaching. In considering such a claim, it is important to say at once that indeed this is a possibility. Computer technology could be used this way, and in some instances it probably will. This is no different from saying that there are many kinds of teaching, some good and some bad. The important point to insist upon, however, is that it is certainly not a *necessary* aspect of the use of the technology. In fact, contrary to the expectations sometimes expressed in the popular press, I would claim that one of the computer's most important potentials is in making learning and teaching more personalized, rather than less so. Students will be subject to less regimentation and lockstepping, because computer systems will be able to offer highly individualized instruction. The routine that occupies a good part of the teacher's day can be taken over by the computer.

It is worth noting in this connection that the amount of paper work required of teachers is very much on the increase. The computer seems to offer the only possibility of decreasing the time spent in administrative routine by ordinary teachers. Let us examine briefly one or two aspects of instruction ranging from the elementary school to the college. At the elementary level, no one anticipates that students will spend most of their time at computer consoles. Only 20 to 30 percent of the student's time would be spent in this fashion. Teachers would be able to work with classes reduced in size. Also, they could work more intensely with individual students, because some of the students will be at the console and, more importantly, because routine aspects of teaching will be handled by the computer system.

At the college level, the situation is somewhat different. At most colleges and universities, students do not now receive a great deal of individual attention from instructors. I think we can all recognize that the degree of personal attention is certainly not less in a computer program designed to accommodate itself to the individual student's progress than in the lecture course that has more than 200 students in daily attendance. (In our tutorial Russian program at Stanford, under the direction of Joseph Van Campen, all regular classroom instruction has been eliminated. Students receive 50 minutes daily of individualized instruction at a computer terminal consisting of a teletype with Cyrillic keyboard and earphones; the audio tapes are controlled by the computer.)

A second common claim is that the widespread use of computer technology will lead to excessive standardization of education. Again, it is important to admit at once that this is indeed a possibility. The sterility of standardization and what it implies for teaching used to be illustrated by a story about the French educational system. It was claimed that the French minister of education could look at his watch at any time of the school day and say at once what subject was being taught at each grade level throughout the country. The claim was not true, but such a situation could be brought about in the organization of computer-based instruction. It would technically be possible for a state department of education, for example, to require every fifth-grader at 11:03 in the morning to be subtracting one-fifth from three-tenths, or for every senior in high school to be reciting the virtues of a democratic society. The danger of the technology is that edicts can be enforced as well as issued, and many persons are rightly concerned at the spectre of the rigid standardization that could be imposed.

On the other hand, there is another meaning of standardization that holds great potential. This is the imposition of educational standards on schools and colleges throughout the land. Let me give one example of what I mean. A couple of years ago I consulted with one of the large city school systems in this country in connection with its mathematics program. The curriculum outline of the mathematics program running from kindergarten to high school was excellent. The curriculum as specified in the outline was about as good as any in the country. The real source of difficulty was the magnitude of the discrepancy between the actual performance of the students and the specified curriculum. At almost every grade level, students were performing far below the standard set in the curriculum guide. I do not mean to suggest that computer technology will, in one fell stroke, provide a solution to the difficult and complicated problems of raising the educational standards that now obtain among the poor and culturally deprived. I do say that the technology will provide us with unparalleled insight into the actual performance of students.

Yet I do not mean to suggest that this problem of standardization is not serious. It is, and it will take much wisdom to avoid its grosser aspects. But the point I would like to emphasize is that the wide use of computers permits the introduction of an almost unlimited diversity of curriculum and teaching. The very opposite of standardization can be achieved. I think we would all agree that the ever-increasing use of books from the sixteenth century to the present has deepened the varieties of educational and intellectual experience generally available. There is every reason to believe that the appropriate development of instructional programs for computer systems will increase rather than decrease this variety of intellectual experience. The potential is there.

The real problem is that as yet we do not understand very well how to take advantage of this potential. If we examine the teaching of any subject in the curriculum, ranging from elementary mathematics to ancient history, what is striking is the great similarity between teachers and between textbooks dealing with the same subject, not the vast differences between them. It can even be argued that it is a subtle philosophical question of social policy to determine the extent to which we want to emphasize diversity in our teaching of standard subjects. Do we want a "cool" presentation of American history for some students and a fervent one for others? Do we want to emphasize geometric and perceptual aspects of mathematic more for some students, and symbolic and algebraic aspects more for others? Do we want to make the learning of language more oriented toward the ear for some students and more toward the eye for those who have a poor sense of auditory discrimination? These are issues that have as yet scarcely been explored in educational philosophy or in discussions of educational policy. With the advent of the new technology they will become practical questions of considerable moment.

The third and final issue I wish to discuss is the place of individuality and human freedom in the modern technology. The crudest form of opposition to widespread use of technology in education and in other parts of our society is to claim that we face the real danger of men becoming slaves of machines. I feel strongly that the threat to human individuality and freedom in our society does not come from technology at all, but from another source that was well described by John Stuart Mill more than a hundred years ago. In discussing precisely this matter in his famous essay *On Liberty*, he said,

> the greatest difficulty to be encountered does not lie in the appreciation of means towards an acknowledged end, but in the indifference of persons in general to the end itself. If it were felt that the free development of individuality is one of the leading essentials of well-being; that it is not only a co-ordinate element with all that is designated by the terms civilization, instruction, education, culture, but is itself a necessary part and condition of all those things; there would be no danger that liberty should be undervalued, and the adjustment of the boundaries between it and social control would present no extraordinary difficulty.

Just as books freed serious students from the tyranny of overly simple methods of oral recitation, so computers can free students from the drudgery of doing exactly similar tasks unadjusted and untailored to their individual needs. As in the case of other parts of our society, our new and wondrous technology is there for beneficial use. It is our problem to learn how to use it well. When a child of six begins to learn in school under the direction of a teacher, he hardly has a concept of a free intelligence able to reach objective knowledge of the world. He depends heavily upon every word and gesture of the teacher to guide his own reactions and responses. This intellectual weaning of children is a complicated process that we do not yet manage or understand very well. There are too many adults among us who are not able to express their own feelings or to reach their own judgments. I would claim that the wise use of technology and science, particularly in education, presents a major opportunity and challenge. I do not want to claim that we know very much yet about how to realize the full potential of human beings; but I do not doubt that we can use our modern instruments to reduce the personal tyranny of the individual over another, wherever that tyranny depends upon ignorance.

KENNETH CLARK ON ALTERNATIVE PUBLIC SCHOOL SYSTEMS

(**1968**)   From Kenneth B. Clark, "Alternative Public School Systems," *Harvard Educational Review*, vol. XXXVIII, pp. 100, 111–13.

It is now clear that American public education is organized and functions along social and economic class lines. A bi-racial public school system wherein approximately 90 per cent of American children are required to attend segregated schools is one of the clearest manifestations of this basic fact. The difficulties encountered in attempting to desegregate public schools in the South as well as in the North point to the tenacity of the forces seeking to prevent any basic change in the system.

The class and social organization of American public schools is consistently associated with a lower level of educational efficiency in the less privileged schools. . . .

*   *   *

Problems of Educational Monopoly

It is possible that all attempts to improve the quality of education in our present racially segregated public schools and all attempts to desegregate these schools will have minimal positive results. The rigidity of present patterns of public school organization and the concomitant stagnation in quality of education and academic performance of children may not be amenable to any attempts at change working through and within the present system.

*   *   *

The above measures, however, will not suffice. The following are suggested as possible, realistic, and practical competitors to the present form of urban public school systems:

Regional State Schools. These schools would be financed by the states and would cut across present urban-suburban boundaries.

Federal Regional Schools. These schools would be financed by the Federal Government out of present state aid funds or with additional federal funds. These schools would be able to cut through state boundaries and could make provisions for residential students.

College- and University-Related Open Schools. These schools would be financed by colleges and universities as part of their laboratories in education. They would be open to the public and not restricted to children of faculty and students. Obviously, students would be selected in terms of constitutional criteria and their percentage determined by realistic considerations.

Industrial Demonstration Schools. These schools would be financed by industrial, business, and commercial firms for their employees and selected members of the public. These would not be vocational schools—but elementary and comprehensive high schools of quality. They would be sponsored by combinations of business and industrial firms in much the same way as churches and denominations sponsor and support parochial or sectarian schools.

Labor Union Sponsored Schools. These schools would be financed and sponsored by labor unions largely, but not exclusively, for the children of their members.

Army Schools. The Defense Department has been quietly effective in educating some of the casualties of our present public schools. It is hereby suggested that they now go into the business of repairing hundreds of thousands of these human casualties with affirmation rather than apology. Schools for adolescent drop-outs or educational rejects could be set up by the Defense Department adjacent to camps— but not necessarily as an integral part of the military. If this is necessary, it should not block the attainment of the goal of rescuing as many of these young people as possible. They are not expendable on the altar of anti-militarism rhetoric.

With strong, efficient, and demonstrably excellent parallel systems of public schools, organized and operated on a quasi-private level, and with quality control and professional accountability maintained and determined by Federal and State educational standards and supervision, it would be possible to bring back into public education a vitality and dynamism which are now clearly missing. Even the public discussion of these possibilities might clear away some of the dank stagnation which seems to be suffocating urban education today. American industrial and material wealth was made possible through industrial competition. American educational health may be made possible through educational competition.

If we succeed, we will have returned to the dynamic, affirmative goal of education; namely, to free man of irrational fears, superstitions, and hatreds. Specifically, in America the goal of democratic education must be to free Americans of the blinding and atrophying shackles of racism. A fearful, passive, apologetic, and inefficient educational system cannot help in the attainment of these goals.

If we succeed in finding and developing these and better alternatives to the present educational inefficiency, we will not only save countless Negro children from lives of despair and hopelessness; and thousands and thousands of white children from cynicism, moral emptiness, and social ineptness—but we will also demonstrate the validity of our democratic promises. We also will have saved our civilization through saving our cities.

THE OPEN CLASSROOM (1969)   From Herbert R. Kohl, *The Open Classroom* (New York, 1969), pp. 20–22, 28–33.

A teacher in an open classroom needs to cultivate a state of *suspended expectations*. It is not easy. It is easy to believe that a dull class is dull, or a bright class is bright. The words "emotionally disturbed" conjure up frightening images. And it is sometimes a relief to discover that there are good pupils in the class that is waiting for you. Not reading the record cards or ignoring the standing of the class is an act of self-denial; it involves casting aside a crutch when one still believes one can't walk without it. Yet if one wants to develop an open classroom within the context of a school which is essentially totalitarian, such acts of will are necessary.

What does it mean to suspend expectations when one is told that the class one will be teaching is slow, or bright, or ordinary? At the least it means not preparing to teach in any special way or deciding beforehand on the complexity of the materials to be used during a school year. It means that planning does not consist of finding the class's achievement level according to the record cards and tailoring the material to those levels, but rather preparing diverse materials and subjects and discovering from the students as the year unfolds what is relevant to them and what isn't.

Particularly it means not reading I.Q. scores or achievement scores, not discovering who may be a source of trouble and who a solace or even a joy. It means giving your pupils a fresh chance to develop in new ways in your classroom, freed from the roles they may have adopted during their previous school careers. It

RE-APPRAISAL
1951–1973

3317

means allowing children to become who they care to become, and freeing the teacher from the standards by which new pupils had been measured in the past.

There are no simple ways to give up deeply rooted expectations. There are some suggestions, however:

—talk to students outside class
—watch them play and watch them live with other young people.
—play with them—joking games and serious games
—talk to them about yourself, what you care about
—listen

In these situations the kids may surprise you and reveal rather than conceal, as is usual in the classroom, their feelings, playfulness, and intelligence.

✻   ✻   ✻

Rules and Routines

It is difficult for beginning teachers to establish control because they have not yet sensed that control comes as much through imposing rules and routines as it does from the personal authority of the teacher. Not having had a class of their own yet, they can't imagine the degree to which routine (and not curriculum, not learning, not teaching) can be used to control and contain the behavior of students. When my wife first taught, she was overwhelmed by the number of things she had to do that seemed to have nothing to do with teaching. She had to call the roll; line up her pupils; organiz fire drills; pass out and collect papers, books, and pencils; lead the pledge to the flag; collect milk and lunch money, and so on. Failing to perceive how these extraneous activities contributed to maintaining control in the classroom, she was exasperated. A second-year teacher, sensing her frustration, reassured her that after the first year it wasn't so bad. "In fact, " she said, "after the first year teaching is just like being a secretary." Once you get your routines straight you can control space and time in your environment. The content or quality of what you are doing is irrelevant.

It is not only routines and rules that shore up the authoritarian classroom. Textbooks and workbooks have the same function. The first year it may be difficult to get the knack of using them, but after that one can do the same thing year after year—read the same stories, ask the same questions, get the same answers. It may get boring but is also gets easier. Chance occurrences are minimized.

In an open classroom it is different. Each school year is unique for both the students and the teacher. The first day is not filled with the mastery of routines and the pronouncement of rules. It is not possible to anticipate which rules or routines will emerge as convenient or necessary for a particular class. Nor is it desirable to announce rigid rules and routines when they may prove irrelevant or cumbersome later in the year, and one may want to abandon them. Just as one has to suspend expectations with respect to individual students, so with respect to rules and routines one must suspend one's fear of chaos.

One must face one's fear that young people will run wild if they are not held down or controlled. The spectre of chaos haunts many teachers, probably because they don't believe in their own strength or ability to handle the power they assume. Yet there is no need to impose rules or pull rank. It is possible to assume that rules and routines are necessary only as they emerge as indispensable for the group's functioning. If students find ways to line up and sit down, hang up their coats, choose and change their seats with a minimum of problems, why bother to restrict them by rigid routines? If discussion can develop without the students raising their hands, why bother with the procedure? As teachers are more willing to take chances with new ways of acting they may find it increasingly possible to be themselves and relax with young people.

However, hanging up coats in the morning, for example, may become a real problem if students fight over hooks or take things from each other's pockets or throw coats on the floor. In these circumstances something must be done—the problem can't be ignored without destroying respect for the teacher as an honest and strong person. But that does not mean that the teacher should legislate the problem of coats out of existence. The people in the class must deal with it as their problem and come to some resolution.

The students involved can, for example, settle the matter in private with the teacher adjudicating. The problem can also be settled by the class in a general discussion or a mock trial. There are theatrical and playful ways to deal with the problem of coathooks too. The teacher can suggest that the whole class try to hang their coats on one hook, or do without hooks for a day, or find other places in the classroom to store their coats. Then the question of storing coats can be discussed in a general way or in relationship to the coat games. The initial incident can be forgotten or made to seem insignificant.

All this may take time—time that will be taken away from reading and science and social studies and other supposedly basic work. One must learn to respond to what happens spontaneously in the classroom and to put aside one's other plans. This is as true with matters of curriculum as with "discipline" problems. For example, a short story may refer to an earthquake in passing and the class may be more interested in discussing earthquakes than in finishing the story. Or in studying motion in physics some students may want to look into motion in dance or track. A math lesson on probability theory can lead to a crap game and even to a historical study of the origins of dice. A discussion of the French Revolution can lead by association to a study of instruments of execution, of penal institutions, and finally the role of law in an unjust society. A teacher has to learn to go with the class, to respond to their desire to learn about things and not cut off their enthusiasm in the service of getting through the curriculum. It is necessary to take time to solve problems communally. The democratic development of routines and rules and restrictions is as crucial to the development of freedom in an open classroom as the arbitrary imposition of them is central to control in an authoritarian class.

The concept of order in an open classroom is not the same as that current in the schools where rules and routines are developed to avoid disagreements. In most classrooms there is no place for argument or conflict, nor is there time for teachers and pupils to learn how to live with and listen to each other. There is no give-and-take. The students direct their talk to the teacher, and obey the teacher's rules. Conflict, defiance, or disagreement are disciplinary problems and offenders must by punished. In an open classroom there is considerable give-and-take, argument, disagreement, even conflict. These are organic elements in the life of the group, to be dealt with and resolved by the group and arbitrated by the teacher. The teacher is a mediator and not a judge or executioner.

Students may have disputes about where they want to sit, or how to line up. It may take a while for them to learn to talk or listen to each other or to the teacher. But in the classroom—as in life—it is more dangerous to legislate disagreement out of existence than to accept and integrate it into the whole.

The first day of school does not have to consist of proclaiming rules and practicing routines. There are other things a teacher can do on the first day. It depends upon his style and personality, the subject he is teaching, the age of the students—any number of things. The important point, however, is that in an open classroom the teacher is no more required to behave like a "teacher" than the students are required to be submissive children. The teacher needn't always be at the front of the room and lead, nor does he have to speak "proper" English, nor defend a rigid system of "right" and "wrong." He can be in the classroom the same complex person he is in life and relieve himself of the strain of assuming what he thinks to be the appropriate persona. He needn't be afraid of the students learning his first name, nor of talking with the class about his "private" life and experiences, his confusions, defeats, and triumphs. He can use his own experiences to help his students deal with theirs.

Often on the first day students are asked to write an essay on themselves, or a theme on "what I did last summer." Such assignments may be well intentioned, but they miss something crucial. The students are asked to write about themselves and their experiences. What about the teacher? Shouldn't the students have as much opportunity to assess the teacher's words as he theirs? One way of beginning a school year is by telling the pupils about yourself—where you came from where you are, and where you think you are going. Then it may make more sense to the students to talk of themselves in reasonably open and honest ways.

Another thing that can be done the first day is to introduce the students to the room you will share with them for the year. Show them the furniture and books in the room and tell them of other resources available. Show them the supplies and equipment in the room, open the doors to them. Ask students what they would like to do with what is available. Suggest that they add to the richness of the environment by bringing in things they care about. Talk about what you are interested in doing yourself. There is no need to preach a non-authoritarian sermon and many reasons for not doing it. Students generally distrust all sermons, regardless of their message. An open classroom develops through the actions of the teacher and not because of his words.

ACCOUNT OF OPEN ADMISSIONS EXPERIMENT AT THE CITY UNIVERSITY OF NEW YORK (1970)   From Rebecca Strauss, "Open Admissions 1970: The Audacious Experiment," *Teachers College Record*, vol. LXXII, pp. 513–18.

My grandmother, that rigorous combination of Victorian rectitude and Dresden efficiency, regarded her grandchildren's generation with dismay. We lacked, in her eyes, the essential ingredient for success—what she called, in her version of American slang, "the have to." We had it too easy, the pressure to achieve was too inconsistent, we had no wall at our backs to make us struggle with the determination born of no alternative. This lack of brutal necessity, in her view, could only produce a state of vitiated accomplishment, a diffusion of purpose, a lack of commitment.

While her perspective has more in common with a Hobbes-like view of mankind than seems palatable to many of us, the "have to" has served as a mighty spur for many an individual effort and many a group response. In this category I think it safe to include the extraordinary educational revolution known as the Open Admissions Program (OAP) of the City University of New York.

The situation in New York since the spring of 1969 bears recalling. Everywhere young people were protesting the world in which they found themselves. The ills of society, so frustratingly complex and intangible, had become crystallized for the college population in the malfunction of their immediate environment—the college campus. No metropolitan institution of higher learning entirely escaped the turmoil, and no system was harder hit than CUNY. CUNY, with its far-flung alliance of community colleges, senior colleges, and a graduate center, reflects within its own walls, and in the geographic location of its many campuses, all the irritations and tensions of the current scene.

While the very size of CUNY made it an obvious target for dissidence and dissatisfaction, the role of CUNY as the only metropolitan institution of public higher education gave it a public responsibility unfelt by the private sector. CUNY, in short, was faced by the need for a fundamental revision of its educational design or the prospect of continued agitation and possible destruction. Whatever moral, legal, or intellectual rationale exists for Open Admissions—and there is much—the "have to" was certainly the catalyst.

Accelerating the Goals

The Board of Higher Education, which serves as the board of trustees to the entire university (nineteen colleges—two to open in September, a graduate center, a medical school, 170,000 students) responded to the unrest with a historic educational mandate. In July, 1969, the Board announced its intention to accelerate the educational goals it has posited in the Master Plan for 1975: to initiate Open Admissions five years earlier, thus promising to every June, 1970, high school graduate admission to CUNY in September, 1970. The Board declared its decision to be a matter of "educational desirability, social equity and economic necessity."

With less than a year lead-off time, the gigantic bureaucratic conglomerate known as CUNY creaked and groaned and whirled itself into the fulfillment of the dream. The doors opened in September, 1970, to 35,000 freshmen, approximately a quarter of whom would not have been there but for the change in admissions policy, to a greatly enlarged faculty operating in new and expanded facilities—and with collective fingers crossed.

Historical Notes

Because historic memory is short, it is helpful to recall that in a curious way 1970 became the logical fulfillment of the 1847 conviction of Townsend Harris, president of the New York City Board of Education, "to open the doors to all—let the children of the rich and poor take their seats together and know of no distinction save that of industry, good conduct and intellect." His plan to create a free academy of higher education was realized in May, 1847. In a citywide referendum the voters—19,305 for and 3,409 against, with a clear majority in every ward—adopted a law "creating an institution of higher education open to all without regard to race, creed or financial ability."

Thus began City College of New York in 1849 with 143 students. Dr. Horace Webster, its first president, addressed the student body, defining the task as follows:

"The experiment is to be tried whether the highest education can be given to the masses; whether the children of the whole people can be educated; and whether an institution of learning, of the highest grade, can be successfully controlled by the popular will; not by the privileged few, but by the privileged many."

The year 1849 speaks to 1970 in the most uncompromising terms; the mandate is the same: to educate all the young people who seek higher education—in nineteenth century parlance—"the privileged many." That the opportunity so created was indeed seized by the young people of the City is borne out by the history of CUNY which spans 121 years and reflects in microcosm the very growth of the City itself. For each new wave of immigrants, free public higher education was the high road up and out; up from the impoverished class, out from the ghetto, into the mainstream of American life.

The admissions policy of the colleges which finally came to comprise the City University often reflected economic conditions rather than educational convictions. Cutoff points (grades below which high school graduates could not be admitted) fluctuated due to size and cost limitations from the era of 1900–1920, when all high school graduates were automatically admitted, to 1960 when an 87 percent high school average was used in the four senior colleges. In all the commotion about Open Admissions, it is interesting that a little over a hundred years ago the following prerequisites were set for college admission:

> No student can be admitted to the college unless he resides in the City, be fourteen years of age, have attended the Common Schools in the City twelve months and pass a good examination in: spelling, reading, writing, English grammar, arithmetic, algebra, geography, history of the United States, elementary bookkeeping.

The 1970 plan for Open Admissions contains new elements unprecedented in CUNY's own history or the history of the state universities where the idea of admitting all high school graduates to higher education has been part of the American educational scene for a long time. Of new critical significance are a policy undergirded by free tuition; a change in grading and course work that enables a student to succeed at a slower pace with remedial and compensatory services to help him achieve; a commitment that the "revolving door" technique of "take them in and fail them out" will not be used either overtly or covertly; an extended system of counseling designed to anticipate and help solve personal and academic difficulties for a very new kind of college population; and finally, a firm determination that there shall be no dilution of the educational experience—that the diploma must have integrity and that the University must also continue to attract and educate the well-prepared and proven able.

Recruitment

Curiously enough, the first major hurdle in the Open Admissions Program was the recruitment of students. It is perhaps the most savage comment on the City high schools that the majority of students—and these were, after all, those who had shown enough fortitude to complete high school—had no hope of higher education; the whole idea of college rarely entered their thinking or the thinking of their teachers or advisors. And so, despite the enormous financial and educational opportunity offered by CUNY, it was necessary to go to the students, their parents, the schools, social agencies and organizations to spread the word. Over and over the admissions office had to state that CUNY *meant* open admissions, believed in it, and would support it. A distrustful, angry generation had to be persuaded that there was an alternative to violence and hopelessness.

While recruitment was certainly not totally effective and while the old spectre of high school counselor ineptitude, indifference, or downright discrimination continued to haunt too many places, and while student ignorance about this new opportunity remained in some areas, it is nevertheless a real measure of success that 55,000 applications were completed and places offered.

Of the 35,000 students who accepted and actually registered, 80 percent received their first choice of college and/or program of study—a tremendous tribute to the skill of the admissions staff backed by the sophisticated computer operation of the University. To show in some detail how the high school record and rank were used, the following is excerpted from the admissions application form for 1970:

CHOOSING A COLLEGE IN CUNY

The final step in completing your application is to select the six colleges or programs for which you wish to apply.

Under the new admissions policy of the University, applicants will be considered for their choices on the basis of either their high school academic average, or their rank in their high school class. Using these two factors, ten admissions groups have been established as shown in the chart below:

Group	Students With Academic* Averages Between	Students Whose Rank In Their High School Is In or
1	90-100	or 90-99 percentile (top tenth)
2	87.5-89.9	or 80-89 percentile (second tenth)
3	85-87.4	or 70-79 percentile (third tenth)
4	82.5-84.9	or 60-69 percentile (fourth tenth)
5	80-82.4	or 50-59 percentile (fifth tenth)
6	77.5-79.9	or 40-49 percentile (sixth tenth)
7	75-77.4	or 30-39 percentile (seventh tenth)
8	72.5-74.9	or 20-29 percentile (eighth tenth)
9	70-72.4	or 10-19 percentile (ninth tenth)
10	69.9 or under	or 0-9 percentile (last tenth)

* Also called College Admissions Average

All applicants will be placed in the highest group for which they are eligible. For example, if your high school rank places you in Group 4 (fourth tenth of your class) but your high school academic average is in Group 2 (88 percent average) you will be placed in Group 2 for admissions purposes.

All applicants meeting the admissions criteria of high school diploma, residence, and health will be offered admission to the University. Students in the higher admissions groups will be more likely to be admitted to their first-choice senior or community colleges and programs than students in the remaining admissions groups. Applicants in Groups 1, 2, and 3 are most likely to be admitted to their first-choice college and program. Applicants in Groups 4 and 5 are most likely to be admitted to a senior college program, if they wish, although not necessarily the college of their first choice. Applicants in Groups 6, 7, 8, 9, and 10 may be admitted to senior college programs if space is available, but are more likely to be admitted to a community college transfer or career program. Because many students in Group 6 through 10 may not be admitted to senior colleges, students in these groups are advised to include community college programs among their six choices of college and program.

The University will offer their first choice of college to as many students as possible. Additional students will be placed in the program of their choice, even if their college choice cannot be honored.

While admissions financing and space location are administered centrally by CUNY, educational decisions are primarily made by each faculty for its own campus. There is certainly much exchange of views and considerable central office guidance, but the colleges maintain decided educational autonomy. Each of the colleges involved in Open Admissions devised its own plan for handling both the new style of student and the vast increase in the actual numbers of the entering class.

These plans varied considerably as to sophistication, experience, and even determination to succeed. The central office served as a task force to counsel, encourage, and demand an Open Admissions blueprint, but the implementation of its style was a reflection of the thinking and commitment (or lack) of the faculty and administration of each college. Most of the colleges have had the advantage of pilot programs to educate high risk students and have acquired much critical experience. In the senior colleges, the SEEK (Search for Education Elevation and Knowledge) program and in the community college, the College Discovery programs, have been in existence long enough to play a significant role in the design and operation of Open Admissions. The colleges where these programs have been most successful appear, at least initially, to have accepted and planned for Open Admissions most skillfully. Only time will tell if good implementation is also an outcome of the influence of these pilot programs.

Underway, from the very start of the programs last fall, has been an independent, privately funded, massive evaluation study. There is a clear and sensitive understanding on the part of the University that the findings, good or bad, are critical not only to the University itself but to higher education across the nation. No measurements are yet available, but constant self-examination proceeds at each campus with continuous exchange with the central staff over potential or actual problems. Difficulties would have arisen even if the lead-off time for planning had been long, the money abundant, the space needs met generously and the faculty unanimous in good will and skill. Clearly none of the foregoing conditions existed.

What is clear already, however, is that a major university has had the audacity to try to interrupt the cycle of failure, hopelessness, and poverty among the young people of our City by providing a real chance to "go up and out." Laid to rest is the question of *should* University admission be opened to all high school graduates. What the University faces is *how* to make the opportunity work well for all who enter its doors.

The task that the University has set for itself is the task of society, for as the Vice Chancellor for Academic Affairs, Timothy Healy, wrote so eloquently in the *Saturday Review* a year ago: "In no sense can the University do the whole job, nor should it try. But what it can do is potent indeed. It can short-circuit the terrible rhythm of disappointment and rage that locks our inner-city youths out of productive careers, that robs them of a stake in their city, and that can create a new race of barbarians more terrible in their visitations than the Goths and Vandals because not only do they not care, but the whole sophisticated apparatus has taught

EDUCATION
IN THE
UNITED STATES

3324

them not to care."[1]

Few involved in the Open Admissions enterprise have illusions of total success. Educated guesses on probable attrition range widely because no one knows all the factors, personal, educational, or societal, that might contribute to failure or to success. By September, 1971, we will be in a better position to begin to assess what has happened and to make recommendations and changes. Today there is little talk of what is meant by "open" on the campuses or in the City. What started as a revolution has in a short time become, if not exactly commonplace, at least accepted.

Nationwide comparatively little time is being devoted to anguishing over the philosophy of open admissions; attention, instead, is focused on its implementation and viability. Colleges and universities across the nation are sending investigators to see what is going on at CUNY. New York City may have more young people involved and the size of its educational arena may be larger, but no major city in the nation can remain untouched by either the issues or the proposed solutions which are lumped under the rubric of Open Admissions. In the Victor Hugo sense, it is truly an "idea whose time has come."

STEPHEN WRIGHT ON BLACK STUDIES (1970) From Stephen J. Wright, "Black Studies and Sound Scholarship," *Phi Delta Kappan*, vol. LI, pp. 365–67.

Very few, if any, developments in all of education are as freighted with confusion, controversy, emotion, and pressure for haste as black studies. Yet institutions of higher learning are being called upon to make long-term commitments to faculty recruited for the emerging programs of black studies, to make heavy investments in the books and periodicals needed to support them, and to institute radical new policies incident to their administration and operation, some of which would not be considered seriously for any other department or division—the demand for departmental "autonomy" being an example. The consequences of this situation could, during the coming decade, be an educational disaster. It is imperative, therefore, that the situation be critically, dispassionately, and reflectively examined.

Issues and Problems

The really fundamental issues—as distinguished from the problems of implementation such as recruiting staff, developing the specific types of courses, procuring the necessary library holdings, etc.—are those of definition, objectives, rationale, and the general nature and character of the program. The central question is whether the program as a whole (or its component parts), is to be treated as a discipline or as a constellation of disciplines.

The purpose of this article is to examine these issues and a few of the important problems and to suggest some approaches that may, hopefully, contribute to a more

[1]Timothy Healy, "The Challenge of Open Admission: Will Every Man Destroy the University?" *Saturday Review*, December 20, 1969, pg. 54.

orderly and a more viable development of this very significant and urgently needed field. This examination is based on the following fundamental assumptions:

1. That the basic subjects that constitute the program of black studies are disciplines, or parts of disciplines in the usual academic meaning of the term; that they involve no mystique and can, therefore, be taught and "learned" by those academically competent to do so. (This assumption in no sense excludes appropriate and relevant field experiences.)

2. That competence to teach and learn in the area of black studies is not a function of race, creed, or color.

3. That there are sufficient materials and problems to justify minors, majors, and graduate study, but that they need to be arranged in a scholarly manner and taught in an effective way.

4. That programs of black studies can be organized and developed in both predominantly black and predominantly white institutions of higher learning.

5. That black studies should not be substituted, in any total sense, for the education necessary to understand and function effectively in the larger American society.

6. That individuals pursuing, or individuals who have pursued, a sound program of black studies are capable of making their own judgments and applications with respect to the knowledge and appreciations they gain.

7. That the black people of the nation will not become a "fifty-first state," living separately as a "nation" within a nation, but that they will, increasingly, become involved in all aspects of the economic, political, educational, and cultural life of the nation, while maintaining their cultural identity as do several other minorities— Jews, for example.

Such a set of assumptions will doubtless offend those black Americans who desire a more doctrinaire or propagandistic approach. Those espousing such an approach are deeply concerned, of course, with the commitment of black students to the problems of the masses of black people. While I am equally concerned with the commitment of black students to the problems of the masses of black people, it is my position that there can be no program of substance or of lasting value that is not built firmly on the tenets of sound scholarship. If a black studies program built on sound scholarship is taught by those who bring dedication, competence, and enthusiasm to it, then those who experience it as students are very likely to be infected by that enthusiasm and will, on their own, develop the commitment to apply appropriate aspects of their knowledge and appreciation both to themselves and to the masses of the black people. But of equal importance is the fact that such students will be able to think for themselves and continue their own education in the field without the inhibiting influence of any imposed position.

*   *   *

Rationale

While a number of programs of black studies have been established solely as a response to insistent student demands, there is a sound rationale for their establishment:

1. The black experience, in any fair and substantial sense, has simply been omitted from the curriculum of higher education in America and, without it,

neither black students nor white students are educated for the hard realities of their times. In fact, the same rationale used to introduce non-Western studies into the curriculum is applicable to black studies:

Until quite lately higher education in the United States of America has been almost completely under the sway of an illusion shared by nearly everybody of European descent since the Middle Ages—the illusion that the history of the world is the history of Europe and its cultural offshoots; that Western experience is the sum total of human experience; that Western interpretations of that experience are sufficient, if not exhaustive; and that the resulting value systems embrace everything that matters.

. . . This illusion has been shattered by confrontation with a world of new and renascent nations striving to satisfy the submerged needs of their awakening peoples and to secure a place of dignity and respect in the international community. The need to do what we can, if only for the sake of self-preservation, to steer this restless world into paths of peaceful and orderly development, has forced the American people to look outward. And, looking outward, we have begun to see ourselves more clearly and to recognize our illusion as the product of ignorance, which breeds racial snobbery and intellectual parochialism.

2. The black student has a very special need for a sound program of black studies, for it serves at least two essential purposes: a) It helps him, perhaps more than anything else, to answer his persistent questions concerning his identity. "A man must come to see himself in relation to his total environment in space and time, and so to locate himself on the map of human experience." b)It provides him with the information and the appreciation he needs, almost desperately, to perform his leadership responsibilities. For any effective leadership, especially of a minority people, must be based upon a knowledge of their past and a comprehensive knowledge of their present condition, out of which a sense of their aspirations and destiny grows.

3. The white student also has an urgent need for systematic exposure to at least the fundamental aspects of a black studies program. At the present time, every ninth person in the United States is black, and the burden of the information and experience of the typical white student lead him, fallaciously, to the position of being either anti-black, indifferent, or patronizing. The position results inevitably from biased or inadequate information. Such positions, during the decades immediately ahead, can lead only to disaster.

The report of the Harvard University faculty committee on African and Afro-American studies summarizes the rationale aptly when it states:

Quite a number of courses recognize the existence of black men in the development of America; quite a bit of expertise is already available. However, merely recognizing black men as integral segments of certain overall social processes is not good enough. We are dealing with 25 million of our own people with a special history, culture, and range of problems. It can hardly be doubted that the study of black men in America is a legitimate and urgent academic endeavor. If this be so and if we are determined to launch this field of study successfully, far-sighted goals and programs are required. These goals and programs should maintain and even raise academic standards; should avoid experience isolation; and finally, should have meaning for all serious students—black and white.

Stated another way, whatever deeply concerns man and promises significantly to benefit man is an appropriate matter for systematic study. Moreover, if this criterion were rigidly applied to many of the courses now included in the curriculum of higher education in America, those that would be eliminated would leave more than enough room for black studies.

Objectives

The basic objectives of programs of black studies are inherent in the rationale for their establishment. These objectives should, nevertheless, be clearly stated, for they serve as guides for the selection of courses, experiences, and materials. In addition, they provide the basis for evaluating the programs.

The specific objectives for programs of black studies should include:

1. Acquainting the students with the history, literature, art, and music of black men—African and American.

2. Providing young black Americans with valid and reliable information concerning the social, economic, educational, and political problems confronting black people in the United States as a basis for their leadership responsibilities in and for the black community.

3. Providing young white Americans with essentially the same type of information indicated in No. 2 above as a de-mythologizing experience and as a basis for the understandings they will need to live responsibly in a multi-racial society.

4. Examining the extent, causes, nature of, and possible remedies for racism in America.

5. Developing teachers and scholars in the field of black studies.

6. Stimulating research in the field of black studies.

Problems

The establishment of programs of black studies on what has amounted to a crash basis has generated, understandably, a plethora of problems—not the least of which is the presence of too many nonexperts in the development process. Undoubtedly, the most critical and urgent problem is the paucity of qualified teachers. And the only way to relieve this situation is to train teachers on a crash basis. The National Endowment for the Humanities has helped significantly with its institutes, but such institutes need to be conducted for longer periods and a significant number of adequately financed fellowships need to be established. A related and essential need is for the development of a few centers with the resources to train the teachers. Obviously, the quickest way to get highly qualified teachers is to limit the fellowships initially to post-doctoral study. Atlanta University has already announced what appears to be a promising program at the master's level, with a doctoral program offered in cooperation with Emory University.

The problem of providing the necessary library materials will offer some difficulty for a few years. Fortunately, however, several companies have begun to reprint a number of the out-of-print volumes. The Kraus Reprint Company has undertaken a major program in this area. The Arno Press has also begun a promising program. Also, films of the Schomburg Collection in New York are available.

ON EDUCATION VOUCHERS (1971)   From Judith Areen and Christopher Jencks,
"Education Vouchers: A Proposal for Diversity and Choice," *Teachers College Record*, vol.
LXXII, pp. 327–35.

E̲ver since Adam Smith first proposed that the government finance
education by giving parents money to hire teachers, the idea has enjoyed recurrent
popularity. Smith's ideal of consumer sovereignty is built into a number of
government programs for financing higher education, notably the G.I. Bill and the
various state scholarship programs. Similarly a number of foreign countries have
recognized the principle that parents who are dissatisfied with their local public
school should be given money to establish alternatives.[1] In America, however,
public financing for elementary and secondary education has been largely confined
to publicly managed schools. Parents who preferred a private alternative have had
to pay the full cost out of their own pockets. As a result, we have almost no
evidence on which to judge the merit of Smith's basic principle, namely, that if all
parents are given the chance, they will look after their children's interest more
effectively than will the state.

During the late 1960's, a series of developments in both public and nonpublic
education led to a revival of interest in this approach to financing education. In
December, 1969, the United States Office of Economic Opportunity made a grant to
the Center for the Study of Public Policy to support a detailed study of "education
vouchers." This article will summarize the major findings of that report and outline
briefly the voucher plan proposed by the Center.[2]

The Case of Choice

Conservatives, liberals, and radicals all have complained at one time or another that
the political mechanisms which supposedly make public schools accountable to
their clients work clumsily and ineffectively.[3] Parents who think their children are
getting inferior schooling, can, it is true, take their grievances to the local school
board or state legislature. If legislators and school boards are unresponsive to the
complaints of enough citizens, they may eventually be unseated. But mounting an
effective campaign to change local public schools takes an enormous investment of

---

[1] Estelle Fuchs, "The Free Schools of Denmark," *Saturday Review*, August 16, 1969.

[2] For a complete description of the Center proposal *see Education Vouchers: A Report on
Financing Education by Payments to Parents*. Prepared by the Center for the Study of Public
Policy, Cambridge, Massachusetts, December, 1970.

[3] For other discussions of the need to encourage alternatives to the present public schools,
see Kenneth Clark, "Alternative Public School Systems," *Equal Educational Opportunity*.
Cambridge: Harvard University Press, 1969; James S. Coleman, "Toward Open Schools," *The
Public Interest*, Fall, 1967; Anthony Downs, "Competition and Community Schools," written
for a Brookings Institution Conference on the Community School held in Washington, D.C.,
December 12–13, 1968, Chicago, Illinois, revised version, January, 1969; Milton Friedman,
"The Role of Government in Education," *Capitalism and Freedom*. Chicago: University of
Chicago Press, 1962; Christopher Jencks, "Is the Public School Obsolete?" *The Public
Interest*, Winter, 1966; Robert Krughoff, "Private Schools for the Public," *Education and
Urban Society*, Vol. II, November, 1969; Henry M. Levin, "The Failure of the Public Schools
and the Free Market," *The Urban Review*, June 6, 1968; Theodore Sizer and Phillip Whitten,
"A Proposal for a Poor Children's Bill of Rights," *Psychology Today*, August, 1968; E. G.
West, *Education and the State*. London: Institute of Economic Affairs, 1965.

time, energy, and money. Dissatisfied though they may be, few parents have the political skill or commitment to solve their problems this way. As a result, effective control over the character of the public schools is largely vested in legislators, school boards, and educators—not parents.[4]

If parents are to take genuine responsibility for their children's education, they cannot rely exclusively on political processes. They must also be able to take individual action on behalf of their own children. At present, only relatively affluent parents retain any effective control over the education of their children. Only they are free to move to areas with "good" public schools, where housing is usually expensive (and often unavailable to black families at any price). Only they can afford nonsectarian, private schooling. The average parent has no alternative to his local public school unless he happens to belong to one of the few denominations that maintain low-tuition schools.

Not only does today's public school have a captive clientele, but it in turn has become the captive of a political process designed to protect the interests of its clientele. Because attendance at a local public school is nearly compulsory, its activities have been subjected to extremely close political control. The state, the local board, and the school administration have established regulations to ensure that no school will do anything to offend anyone of political consequence. Virtually everything of consequence is either forbidden or compulsory. By trying to please everyone, however, the schools have often ended up pleasing no one.

A voucher system seeks to free schools from the restrictions which inevitably accompany their present monopolistic privileges. The idea of the system is relatively simple. A publicly accountable agency would issue a voucher to parents. The parents could take this voucher to any school which agreed to abide by the rules of the voucher system. Each school would turn its vouchers in for cash. Thus parents would no longer be forced to send their children to the school around the corner simply because it was around the corner.

Even if no new schools were established under a voucher system, the responsiveness of existing public schools would probably increase. We believe that one of the most important advantages of a voucher system is that it would encourage diversity and choice *within the public system*. Indeed, if the public system were to begin matching students and schools on the basis of interest, rather than residence, one of the major objectives of a voucher system would be met without even involving the private sector. Popular public schools would get more applicants, and they would also have incentives to accommodate them, since extra students would bring extra funds. Unpopular schools would have few students, and would either have to change their ways or close up and reopen under new management.

As this last possibility suggests, however, there are great advantages to involving the private sector in a voucher system if it is properly regulated. Only in this way is the overall system likely to make room for fundamentally new initiatives that come from the bottom instead of the top. And only if private initiative is possible will the

---

[4]School management has been increasingly concentrated in the hands of fewer educators and school boards. The number of school districts, for example, declined from 127,531 in 1930, to less than 20,440 in 1968. The number of public elementary schools dropped from 238,000 to less than 73,000 in the same period. The concentration is particularly striking in urban areas. The New York City School Board alone is responsible for the education of more students than are found in the majority of individual states. Los Angeles has as many students as the state of South Carolina; Chicago as many as Kansas; Detroit as many as Maine. Nearly half of all the students in public schools are under the control of less than 4 percent of the school boards. *See* U.S. Department of Health, Education, and Welfare, Digest of Educational Statistics (1969).

public sector feel real pressure to make room for kinds of education that are politically awkward but have a substantial constituency. If the private sector is involved, for example, parents can get together to create schools reflecting their special perspectives or their children's special needs. This should mean that the public schools will be more willing to do the same thing—though they will never be willing or able to accommodate all parental preferences. Similarly if the private sector is involved, educators with new ideas—or old ideas that are now out of fashion in the public schools—would also be able to set up their own schools. Entrepreneurs who thought they could teach children better and more inexpensively than the public schools would have an opportunity to do so. None of this ensures that every child would get the education he needs, but it would make such a result somewhat more likely than at present.

Beyond this, however, differences of opinion begin. Who would be eligible for vouchers? How would their value be determined? Would parents be allowed to supplement the vouchers from their own funds? What requirements would schools have to meet before cashing vouchers? What arrangements would be made for the children whom no school wanted to educate? Would church schools be eligible? Would schools promoting unorthodox political views be eligible? Once the advocates of vouchers begin to answer such questions, it becomes clear that the catch phrase around which they have united stands not for a single panacea, but for a multitude of controversial programs, many of which have little in common.

Revised Vocabulary

To understand the voucher plan recommended by the Center, it is useful to begin by reconsidering traditional notions about "public" and "private" education. Since the nineteenth century, we have classified schools as "public" if they were owned and operated by a governmental body. We go right on calling colleges "public," even when they charge tuition that many people cannot afford. We also call academically exclusive high schools "public," even they have admissions requirements that only a handful of students can meet. We call neighborhood schools "public" despite the fact that nobody outside the neighborhood can attend them, and nobody can move into the neighborhood unless he has white skin and a down payment on a $30,000 home. And we call whole school systems "public," even though they refuse to give anyone information about what they are doing, how well they are doing it, and whether children are getting what their parents want. Conversely, we have always called schools "private" if they were owned and operated by private organizations. We have gone on calling these schools "private," even when, as sometimes happens, they are open to every applicant on a nondiscriminatory basis, charge no tuition, and make whatever information they have about themselves available to anyone who asks.

Definitions of this kind conceal as much as they reveal, for they classify schools entirely in terms of who runs them, not how they are run. If we want to describe what is really going on in education, there is much to be said for reversing this emphasis. We would then call a school "public" if it were open to everyone on a nondiscriminatory basis, if it charged no tuition, and if it provided full information about itself to anyone interested. Conversely, we would call any school "private" if it excluded applicants in a discriminatory way, charged tuition, or withheld information about itself. Admittedly, the question of who governs a school cannot be ignored entirely when categorizing the school, but it seems considerably less important than the question of how the school is governed.

Adopting this revised vocabulary, we propose a regulatory system with two underlying principles:

—No public money should be used to support "private" schools.

—Any group that operates a "public" school should be eligible for public subsidies.

The Proposal

Specifically, the Center has proposed an education voucher system (for *elementary* education) which would work in the following manner:

1. An Educational Voucher Agency (EVA) would be established to administer the vouchers. Its governing board might be elected or appointed, but in either case it should be structured so as to represent minority as well as majority interests. The EVA might be an existing local board of education, or it might be an agency with a larger or smaller geographic jurisdiction. The EVA would receive all federal, state, and local education funds for which children in its areas were eligible. It would pay this money to schools only in return for vouchers. (In addition, it would pay parents for children's transportation costs to the school of their choice.)

2. The EVA would issue a voucher to every family in its district with children of elementary school age. The value of the basic voucher would initially equal the per pupil expenditure of the public schools in the area. Schools which took children from families with below-average incomes would receive additional incentive payments. These "compensatory payments" might, for example, make the maximum payment for the poorest child worth double the basic voucher.

3. To become an "approved voucher school," eligible to cash vouchers, a school would have to:
   a. Accept each voucher as full payment for a child's education, charging no additional tuition.
   b. Accept any applicant so long as it had vacant places.
   c. If it had more applicants than places, fill at least half these places by picking applicants randomly and fill the other half in such a way as not to discriminate against ethnic minorities.
   d. Accept uniform standards established by the EVA regarding suspension and expulsion of students.
   e. Agree to make a wide variety of information about its facilities, teachers, program, and students available to the EVA and to the public.
   f. Maintain accounts of money received and disbursed in a form that would allow both parents and the EVA to determine where the money was going. Thus a school operated by the local board of education (a "public" school) would have to show how much of the money to which it was entitled on the basis of its vouchers was actually spent in that school. A school operated by a profit-making corporation would have to show how much of its income was going to the stockholders.
   g. Meet existing state requirements for private schools regarding curriculum staffing, and the like.

Control over policy in an approved voucher school might be vested in an existing local school board, a PTA, or any private group. Hopefully, no government restrictions would be placed on curriculum, staffing and the like, except those already established for all private schools in a state.

4. Just as at present, the local board of education (which might or might not be the EVA) would be responsible for ensuring that there were enough places in publicly managed schools to accommodate every elementary school age child who did not want to attend a privately managed school. If a shortage of places developed for some reason, the board of education would have to open new schools or create more places in existing schools. (Alternatively, it might find ways to encourage privately managed schools to expand, presumably by getting the EVA to raise the value of the voucher.)

5. Every spring each family would submit to the EVA the name of the school to which it wanted to send each of its elementary school age children next fall. Any children already enrolled in a voucher school would be guaranteed a place, as would any sibling of a child enrolled in a voucher school. So long as it had room, a voucher school would be required to admit all students who listed it as a first choice. If it did not have room for all applicants, a school could fill half its places in whatever way it wanted, choosing among those who listed it as a first choice. It could not, however, select these applicants in such a way as to discriminate against racial minorities. It would then have to fill its remaining places by a lottery among the remaining applicants. All schools with unfilled places would report these to the EVA. All families whose children had not been admitted to their first-choice school would then choose an alternative school which still had vacancies. Vacancies would then be filled in the same manner as in the first round. This procedure would continue until every child had been admitted to a school.

6. Having enrolled their children in a school, parents would give their vouchers to the school. The school would send the vouchers to the EVA and would receive a check in return.

Some Caveats

The voucher system outlined above is quite different from other systems now being advocated; it contains far more safeguards for the interests of disadvantaged children. A voucher system which does not include these or equally effective safeguards would be worse than no voucher system at all. Indeed, an unregulated voucher system could be the most serious setback for the education of disadvantaged children in the history of the United States. A properly regulated system, on the other hand, may have the potential to inaugurate a new era of innovation and reform in American schools.

One common objection to a voucher system of this kind is that many parents are too ignorant to make intelligent choices among schools. Giving parents a choice will, according to this argument, simply set in motion an educational equivalent of Gresham's Law, in which hucksterism and mediocre schooling drive out high quality institutions. This argument seems especially plausible to those who envisage the entry of large numbers of profit-oriented firms into the educational marketplace. The argument is not, however, supported by much evidence. Existing private schools are sometimes mere diploma mills, but on the average their claims about themselves seem no more misleading, and the quality of the services they offer no

RE-APPRAISAL
1951–1973

lower, than in the public schools. And while some private schools are run by hucksters interested only in profit this is the exception rather than the rule. There is no obvious reason to suppose that vouchers would change all this.

A second common objection to vouchers is that they would "destroy the public schools." Again, this seems far-fetched. If you look at the educational choices made by wealthy parents who can already afford whatever schooling they want for their children, you find that most still prefer their local public schools if these are at all adequate. Furthermore, most of those who now leave the public system do so in order to attend high-cost, exclusive private schools. While some wealthy parents would doubtless continue to patronize such schools, they would receive no subsidy under the proposed system.

Nonetheless, if you are willing to call every school "public" that is ultimately responsible to a public board of education, then there is little doubt that a voucher system would result in some shrinkage of the public sector and some growth of the "private" sector. If, on the other hand, you confine the label "public" to schools which are equally open to everyone within commuting distance, you discover that the so-called public sector includes relatively few public schools. Instead, racially exclusive suburbs and economically exclusive neighborhoods serve to ration access to good "public" schools in precisely the same way that admissions committees and tuition charges ration access to good "private" schools. If you begin to look at the distinction between public and private schooling in these terms, emphasizing accessibility rather than control, you are likely to conclude that a voucher system, far from destroying the public sector, would greatly expand it, since it would force large numbers of schools, public and private, to open their doors to outsiders.

A third objection to vouchers is that they would be available to children attending Catholic schools. This is not, of course, a necessary feature of a voucher system. The courts, a state legislature, or a local EVA could easily restrict participation to nonsectarian schools. Indeed, some state constitutions clearly require that this be done. The federal Constitution may also require such a restriction, but neither the language of the First Amendment nor the legal precedent is clear on this issue. The First Amendment's prohibition against an "establishment of religion" can be construed as barring payments to church schools, but the "free exercise of religion" clause can also be construed as requiring the state to treat church schools in precisely the same way as other private schools. The Supreme Court has never ruled on a case of this type (e.g., G.I. Bill payments to Catholic colleges or Medicare payments to Catholic hospitals). Until it does, the issue ought to be resolved on policy grounds. And since the available evidence indicates that Catholic schools have served their children no worse than public schools,[5] and perhaps slightly better, there seems no compelling reason to deny them the same financial support given other schools.

The most worrisome objection to a voucher system is that its success would depend on the EVA's willingness to regulate the marketplace vigorously. If vouchers were used on a large scale, state and local regulatory efforts might be uneven or even nonexistent. The regulations designed to prevent racial and economic discrimination seem especially likely to get watered down at the state and local level, or else to remain unenforced. This argument applies, however, to any educational reform, and it also applies to the existing system. If you assume any

[5]Andrew Greeley and Peter Rossi. *The Education of Catholic Americans.* Chicago: Aldine, 1966.

given EVA will be controlled by overt or covert segregationists, you must also assume that this will be true of the local board of education. A board of education that wants to keep racist parents happy hardly needs vouchers to do so. It only needs to maintain the neighborhood school system. White parents who want their children to attend white schools will then find it quite simple to move to a white neighborhood where their children will be suitably segregated. Except perhaps in the South, neither the federal government, the state government, nor the judiciary is likely to prevent this traditional practice.

If, on the other hand, you assume a board which is anxious to eliminate segregation, either for legal, financial, or political reasons, you must also assume that the EVA would be subject to the same pressures. And if an EVA is anxious to eliminate segregation, it will have no difficulty devising regulations to achieve this end. Furthermore, the legal precedents to date suggest that the federal courts will be more stringent in applying the Fourteenth Amendment to voucher systems than to neighborhood school systems. The courts have repeatedly thrown out voucher systems designed to maintain segregation, whereas they have shown no such general willingness to ban the neighborhood school. Outside the South, then, those who believe in integration may actually have an easier time achieving this goal with voucher systems than they will with the existing public school system. Certainly, the average black parent's access to integrated schools would be increased under a voucher system of the kind proposed by the Center. Black parents could apply to any school in the system, and the proportion of blacks admitted would have to be at least equal to the proportion who applied. This gives the average black parents a far better chance of having their children attend an integrated school than at present. There is, of course, no way to compel black parents to take advantage of this opportunity by actually applying to schools that enroll whites. But the opportunity would be there for all.

The Proposed Demonstration

The voucher plan described above could in theory be adopted by any local or state jurisdiction interested in increasing diversity in schools and parental choice in selection of schools. In the long run it is not much more expensive than the present system. But the Center has recommended to OEO that a demonstration project be financed first, carefully regulated to ensure that the proposed rules are followed, and carefully monitored to test the effects of dispensing public education funds in the form of vouchers. The Center has recommended that at least 10,000 elementary school students be included in the demonstration site, and that the demonstration city (or part of a city) should contain a population which is racially and economically heterogeneous. Ideally some alternative schools should already exist in the selected area, and the prospects for beginning other new schools should be reasonable.

In March, 1970, staff and consultants of the Center embarked on an extensive investigation of the feasibility of conducting a demonstration project. Superintendents of schools in all cities with a population in excess of 150,000 in the 1960 census, which were not under court or administrative order to desegregate their school systems, were contacted by mail. Expressions of interest were followed up. Meetings were held in interested cities around the country. Local and state school administrators were contacted, as were interested school officials, teachers' groups, parents' organizations, and nonpublic schools.

As of November 1, 1970, five communities had decided to apply for preliminary planning funds. If one or more of these cities decides to conduct a demonstration of the voucher program, we may have a chance at last to test what contributions a voucher program could make to improving the quality of education available to children in this country. If, on the other hand, the National Education Association and the American Federation of Teachers have their way, we shall have no test at all.

ACCOUNT OF A PRIVATE CORPORATION OPERATING A PUBLIC ELEMENTARY SCHOOL IN GARY, INDIANA (1971) From *Wall Street Journal*, June 2, 1971.

GARY, IND.—Banneker School is one of 36 elementary schools in this grimy industrial city, but it differs from the others. If its 840 pupils don't master reading and math as well as others their age across the country, the school system gets its money back.

That's because Banneker is run by a private company, Behavioral Research Laboratories Inc. (BRL) of Palo Alto, Calif., under contract to the Gary board of education. The school district pays the company about $670,000 a year, or $800 for each student, the district's cost of educating each pupil last year. Out of that the company pays for teachers' salaries, for educational materials and even for rent of the school building. It must refund the full $800 for every child who doesn't perform up to national standards in reading and math at the end of the three-year agreement. Anything left over is BRL's profit.

Gary is the only U.S. city that has turned over an entire school to a company to run on a money-back guarantee basis, but many others are trying the concept on a more limited scale. More than 40 school districts, including those in New York, Philadelphia, Dallas and Seattle, have entered into so-called performance contracts covering some 40,000 students this year, and the U.S. Office of Education estimates that an additional 150 systems are studying the concept. A year ago only one such contract existed, covering 350 students in Texarkana, Ark.

The practice is controversial. The 228,000-member American Federation of Teachers views it as a threat to job security. Some educators object because they believe the practice will focus teaching efforts on reading and math, where performance is easily measured, and that music, art, social studies and other important areas will be neglected. Others fear that companies will turn schools into something akin to factories.

"Education isn't a profit-and-loss sheet or a mass-production measurement," says one California school board member. "These are human minds we're dealing with, not machines that can be revved up or slowed down to meet someone's idea of 'performance.'"

But many educators argue that performance contracting deserves a chance. School spending has risen sharply in recent years, they say, but they contend the present system hasn't worked. This was the case in Gary, they argue. "Three of every four sixth-graders couldn't read (at acceptable levels), and in view of that we didn't feel we could continue to ask the public for more money," says Dr. Alfonso D. Holliday II, school board president. "We were at rock bottom and had to try new approaches to educate our children."

Growing teacher-union militancy also is prompting interest in performance contracting. Many school board members believe teachers today are more interested in pay than in education. "In the face of that, board members contend that teachers have an inescapable performance obligation that must be translated into measurable performance levels that are written clearly into contracts," says Harold Webb, head of the National School Boards Association.

Performance contractors aren't using any teaching techniques that are revolutionary or that schools themselves haven't tried. They rely heavily on individualized instruction with each child proceeding at his own pace, not that of a class. They group children by ability, not age. Teachers work in teams, and parents are hired to help in the classrooms.

But the companies contend that whenever a school tried such an approach before it was on a piecemeal basis that reduced effectiveness. The companies think they can succeed by discarding the old system entirely.

"We're an outside group with no tradition to weigh us down, so we can take completely fresh approaches," says George Stern, BRL president. "Also we have an economic incentive that the teachers don't have. We think we can make a profit and perform a service at the same time."

Most of the 15 or so companies engaged in performance contracting are relatively new to the education field—only three of them existed in 1965. Some were started to run industry training programs. A few, like Thiokol Chemical Corp., entered the field to use know-how gained from running federal Job Corps training centers. Some make teaching machines, and still others, like BRL, publish textbooks and other educational materials.

BRL, formed in 1961 by Allen Calvin, a former psychology professor who now is chairman of the company, took on the Gary project both to make money and to try out its educational materials and concepts in a school that it controlled. "You can put all the materials in the world into a classroom, but unless they're used correctly they might as well not be there," says Mr. Stern. "Banneker offered us the chance to implement and supervise the entire system."

BRL hopes to run other public schools. "We think it would be good for education, for the children and for BRL," Mr. Stern says. The company contracted this year to teach reading to 15,000 Philadelphia pupils and to 200 children in Monroe, Mich., but it doesn't run a school in either city.

Banneker is not run like an ordinary school. For one thing, it uses fewer teachers—24 compared with 34 last year. For another, they aren't known as teachers, but as "curriculum managers," and they are aided in class by "learning supervisors." BRL hired 28 supervisors from the community and pays them $4,000 a year, considerably less than the $10,000 that the average Banneker teacher earns. The supervisors aren't trained as teachers; many are parents chosen because of their interest in education.

Instead of a principal, Banneker has a "school manager." "We created this position because we wanted someone directly involved with the education of the children," Mr. Stern explains. "Normally, a principal isn't directly involved. He shuffles papers, acts as a public relations representative, greets parents, handles discipline and supervises the staff." At Banneker, all of this is done by a "learning director," Clarence L. Benford, a former Banneker principal. (The "curriculum managers" also are all former Banneker teachers.)

The school manager's job is to plan and organize the educational program, keep performance records to see how the pupils are doing, and, in short, to see that the system works. For this, BRL brought in a former systems analyst for space projects at Lockheed Corp., Donald G. Kendrick, because it wanted someone with industry experience in setting goals, devising systems to reach them and meeting deadlines.

"This project is like building a missile," he says. "Every child is a component; you have to keep an eye on each one to see how he's functioning. We start with the basic assumption that any child can learn and that if he doesn't something must be wrong with the system. If he fails, we must take a look at the system to see what went wrong, reevaluate it and adapt it to the students' needs. Under the old method nobody did that—nobody went back to see why a student failed. If we don't, we lose $800.

The heart of the system is three programs developed by BRL and based on texts compiled by M. W. Sullivan, a linguist. They are Project Read, a 21-book series; Project Math, a 37-book series, and Project Learn, a combination of the two along with other materials. A science program published by Xerox Corp. also is used.

The prime task of curriculum managers—and thus the title—isn't to lecture but rather is to organize these workbooks, supplemented by tapes and film strips, into short lessons through which a student works his way pretty much on his own.

The school gets along with fewer teachers because most learning takes place from the materials. To learn vocabulary words a child writes answers in a workbook. The correct answers are given on the same page, and he checks his work immediately. He works on his own this way for 24 pages. Then the curriculum manager or learning supervisor gives him a short quiz. Other workbooks teach other skills. Depending on his speed, a child may work through from two to 10 such programed texts in each subject in a year.

"We're trying to motivate students to succeed, not fail," says Mr. Stern. "Under this system a pupil can go slowly without being made to feel as if he's a failure. We instruct teachers not to reprimand a child for going slowly. We want to give him the idea that he is a very worthwhile person."

Motivating the teachers also is important to BRL. The company offers them overtime if they stay after class hours to work on ways to help slow learners. A teacher can earn as much as $3,000 a year extra, boosting earnings to around $13,000.

BRL expects eventually to make a profit at Banneker. It has budgeted $400,000 a year for salaries and fringe benefits, $55,000 for rent of the building and miscellaneous items and $50,000 for programed teaching materials. In addition, it will pay $40,000 to an independent research organization for administering the year-end math and reading tests to determine each child's progress. That leaves approximately $125,000 as profit, or about $150 for each pupil—assuming no refunds.

But BRL officials concede they have made mistakes in setting up the program, and expenses have run higher than anticipated. "As a result, we'll probably only break even at Banneker this year," says Mr. Stern.

The program seems successful educationally, though results of the final reading and math tests won't be known until next month. Preliminary tests were given to a sample of students last January; on the average they had advanced about four months in reading proficiency and five months in math after only three months of instruction. "We think a school is doing well when students gain three months' proficiency after three months instruction," says Gordon L. McAndrew, Gary school superintendent. "Few Gary schools do that well."

Parents and teachers seem satisfied, too. "The youngsters are doing beautifully," says Annabelle T. Kilgore, who has taught at Banneker for 11 years. "They can go at their own rate, and this keeps them interested,"

Mrs. Cleo Franklin says her 11-year-old twin daughters have greater initiative to study and succeed than last year. "And they have confidence that was lacking before."

Some school systems have encountered difficulties with performance contracting, however. A project to teach reading to 600 students in two New York City schools probably won't produce a profit partly because the company involved, Learning Foundations Inc. of Athens, Ga., isn't using any teachers, only parents. "We will never attempt another project like this without teachers," says Joel Kaye, who is in charge of the company's performance contracting. "You must have them because there are curriculum decisions that have to be made and classroom management problems that go beyond the scope of a parent, no matter how well trained." The absence of teachers has led to some students being kept in learning groups unsuited for their abilities.

Last year in Texarkana, Ark., the company that was hired to teach reading and math to 350 students was accused of rigging the results of its work. The school district says the company, Dorsett Educational Systems of Norman, Okla., a maker of teaching machines, taught the test to the students, thereby ensuring that they would do well on the final exam and that the company would receive the maximum payment.

Lloyd Dorsett, company president, admits some test teaching did occur, though he disputes how much. He contends that his company wasn't given guidelines on what would or wouldn't be permitted in this respect until after the final test last June. The contract wasn't renewed for a second year, and Dorsett was paid $105,000 out of a maximum $135,000. Texarkana is continuing the contract this year with another company.

RE-APPRAISAL
1951-1973

The Federal Government and Education

PRESIDENT DWIGHT EISENHOWER ON THE CREATION OF THE DEPARTMENT OF HEALTH, EDUCATION, AND WELFARE (1953) From House Document No. 102, 83d Cong., 1st Sess. (1953), pp. 1–2.

To the Congress of the United States:

I transmit herewith Reorganization Plan No. 1 of 1953, prepared in accordance with the provisions of the Reorganization Act of 1949, as amended.

In my message of February 2, 1953, I stated that I would send to the Congress a reorganization plan defining a new administrative status for Federal activities in health, education, and social security. This plan carries out that intention by creating a Department of Health, Education, and Welfare as one of the executive departments of the Government and by transferring to it the various units of the Federal Security Agency. The Department will be headed by a Secretary of Health, Education, and Welfare, who will be assisted by an Under Secretary and two Assistant Secretaries.

The purpose of this plan is to improve the administration of the vital health, education, and social-security functions now being carried on in the Federal Security Agency by giving them departmental rank. Such action is demanded by the importance and magnitude of these functions, which affect the well-being of millions of our citizens. The programs carried on by the Public Health Service include, for example, the conduct and promotion of research into the prevention and cure of such dangerous ailments as cancer and heart disease. The Public Health Service also administers payments to the States for the support of their health services and for urgently needed hospital construction. The Office of Education collects, analyzes, and distributes to school administrators throughout the country information relating to the organization and management of educational systems. Among its other functions is the provision of financial help to school districts burdened by activities of the United States Government. State assistance to the aged, the blind, the totally disabled, and dependent children is heavily supported by grants-in-aid administered through the Social Security Administration. The old-age and survivors insurance system and child development and welfare programs are additional responsibilities of that Administration. Other offices of the Federal Security Agency are responsible for the conduct of Federal vocational rehabilitation programs and for the enforcement of food and drug laws.

There should be an unremitting effort to improve those health, education, and

RE-APPRAISAL
1951–1973

3341

social-security programs which have proved their value. I have already recommended the expansion of the social-security system to cover persons not now protected, the continuation of assistance to school districts whose population has been greatly increased by the expansion of defense activities, and the strengthening of our food and drug laws.

But good intent and high purpose are not enough; all such programs depend for their success upon efficient, responsible administration. I have recently taken action to assure that the Federal Security Administrator's views are given proper consideration in executive councils by inviting her to attend meetings of the Cabinet. Now the establishment of the new Department provided for in Reorganization Plan No. 1 of 1953 will give the needed additional assurance that these matters will receive the full consideration they deserve in the whole operation of the Government.

*   *   *

DWIGHT D. EISENHOWER.

THE WHITE HOUSE, *March 12, 1953*

THE WHITE HOUSE CONFERENCE ON EDUCATION (1956)   From *A Report to the President; the Committee for the White House Conference on Education, Full Report, April 1956* (Washington D.C., 1956), pp. 4–5, 8–13.

From the work of the Committee for the White House Conference on Education, one fundamental fact emerges: schools now affect the welfare of the United States more than ever before in history, and this new importance of education has been dangerously underestimated for a long time.

Some of the reasons for the rapidly increasing importance of the schools have been often noted. Ignorance is a far greater handicap to an individual than it was generation ago, and an uneducated populace is a greater handicap to a nation. This trend is obviously going to continue and quicken.

An equally important and less frequently mentioned reason for the growing importance of education is the plain fact that the schools have become the chief instrument for keeping this Nation the fabled land of opportunity it started out to be. In other decades, the opportunities of America lay primarily in escape from the rigid class barriers of Europe, the availability of free land at the frontier, and the excitement of a violently growing nation, where farms often became villages and villages became cities within the span of one human life. When the frontier was closed, it would have been easy for opportunities to dry up in this Nation, and for rigid class barriers to develop. It has been primarily the schools which have prevented this from happening. As long as good schools are available, a man is not frozen at any level of our economy, nor is his son. Schools free men to rise to the level of their natural abilities. Hope for personal advancement and the advancement of one's children is, of course, one of the great wellsprings of human energy. The schools, more than any other agency, supply this hope in America today. By providing a channel for ambition, they have taken the place of the frontier, and in a highly technical era, have preserved the independent spirit of a pioneer nation. The schools stand as the chief expression of the American tradition of fair play for everyone, and a fresh start for each generation.

It is this fundamental conception of schools designed to give a fresh start to each generation that has broadened the ideals of education in America so much in the past 25 years. It is no longer thought proper to restrict educational programs to the skills of the mind, even though those skills remain of fundamental importance. Schools also attempt to improve children's health, to provide vocational training, and to do anything else which will help bring a child up to the starting line of adult life as even with his contemporaries as native differences in ability permit.

The most practical aspect of this new concept of education is that it calls for the most careful mining and refining of all human talents in the land—it is in itself a kind of law against waste. This new educational ideal represents the fullest flowering of the long western tradition of emphasizing the dignity of the individual. Many difficulties, of course, attend its development, but the members of this Committee believe that in essence it is noble and right, and that in the long run it will prove to be one of the great strengths of America.

It is, of course, obvious that much progress has been made toward realizing this new educational ideal in the United States during the recent past. It is the belief of this Committee, however, that improvement has been nowhere near fast enough. The onrush of science has outstripped the schools. What is even more important, ideals of human conduct have in some areas advanced as rapidly as technology. Many a school which seemed good enough a generation ago now seems a disgrace to the community where it stands.

The schools have fallen far behind both the aspirations of the American people and their capabilities. In the opinion of this Committee, there is growing resolve throughout the Nation to close the gap between educational ideals and educational realities. . . .

What Should Our Schools Accomplish?

What should our schools accomplish? No attempt has been made to answer from the point of view of ultimate philosophical objectives which could be read into the question. The Committee has deliberately limited its considerations to the responsibilities of elementary and secondary schools in the contemporary American scene. As a lay group, the Committee has felt it inappropriate to undertake a discussion of curriculum content in specific detail. It has sought instead to reaffirm those current objectives of our schools that it believes to be desirable and to suggest those new emphases which will enable our schools to adjust to the changing needs of our society.

It is relatively easy to observe what the schools *try* to accomplish. The list is startling to anyone who remembers schools a generation back, even more startling to historians who recall the original task assigned to schools: the teaching of reading and ciphering. What schools try to do varies widely. People in suburbs demand different services from those expected by residents in rural areas. In spite of this, it is not difficult to draw up a list of purposes shared by most schools, however widely the technique for fulfilling them may vary. For good or ill, most modern school systems are normally asked to provide something like the following:

1. A general education as good as or better than that offered in the past with increased emphasis on the physical and social sciences.
2. Programs designed to develop patriotism and good citizenship.
3. Programs designed to foster moral, ethical, and spiritual values.
4. Vocational education tailored to the abilities of each pupil and to the needs of community and Nation.
5. Courses designed to teach domestic skills.
6. Training in leisure-time activities such as music, dancing, avocational reading, and hobbies.
7. A variety of health services for all children, including both physical and dental inspections, and instruction aimed at bettering health knowledge and habits.
8. Special treatment for children with speech or reading difficulties and other handicaps.
9. Physical education, ranging from systematic exercises, physical therapy, and intramural sports, to interscholastic athletic completion.
10. Instruction to meet the needs of the abler students.
11. Programs designed to acqaint students with countries other than their own in an effort to help them understand the problems America faces in international relations.
12. Programs designed to foster mental health.
13. Programs designed to foster wholesome family life.
14. Organized recreational and social activities.
15. Courses designed to promote safety. These include instruction in driving automobiles, swimming, civil defense, etc.

The Growth Of School Goals

During the past two generations, this list of school goals has grown with increased speed. This is a phenomenon which has excited both admiration and dismay. After several decades of experimentation, should this broadening of the goals be recognized as legitimate?

This Committee answers *Yes*. Nothing was more evident at the White House Conference on Education than the fact that these goals, representing as they do an enormously wide range of purposes, are the answer to a genuine public demand. These goals have, after all, been hammered out at countless school board meetings during the past quarter-century throughout the land. The basic responsibility of the schools is the development of the skills of the mind, but the overall mission has been enlarged. Schools are now asked to help children to acquire any skill or characteristic which a majority of the community deems worthwhile. The order given by the American people to the schools is grand in its simplicity: in addition to intellectual achievement, foster morality, happiness, and any useful ability. The talent of each child is to be sought out and developed to the fullest. Each weakness is to be studied and, so far as possible, corrected. This is truly a majestic ideal, and an astonishingly new one. Schools of that kind have never been provided for more than a small fraction of mankind.

Although it is new, this ideal of schools which do everything possible for all children is a natural development in the United States. The moving spirit of this Nation has been from the beginning a sense of fairness. Nowadays equality of opportunity for adults means little without equality of educational opportunity for children. Ignorance is a greater obstacle than ever to success of most kinds. The schools have become a major tool for creating a Nation without rigid class barriers. *It is primarily the schools which allow no man's failure to prevent the success of his son.*

In still another way, this new ideal for the schools is a natural development of this country: it recognizes the paramount importance of the individual in a free society. Our schools are asked to teach skills currently needed by the Nation, but never at the expense of the individual. This policy of encouraging each child to develop his individual talents will be of the greatest use to the Nation, for in the long run, if no talent is wasted in our land, no skill will be lacking. . . .

Recommendations

1. As the duties of the schools expand, the establishment of priorities in education should be studied by every board of education. This Committee believes that the development of the intellectual powers of young people, each to the limit of his capacity, is the first responsibility of schools. Beyond this basic task, all kinds of instruction are not equally important for all children, and their importance varies from community to community. This Committee also recognizes the need to invoke priorities in extracurricular activities. Athletics must be controlled, for instance, so that they serve young people rather than use them to enhance the competitive standing of a school or community. A primary responsibility of any local school authority is to establish priorities of significance among basic general education, specialized education of all kinds, and extracurricular activities.

In this era of international stress, the United States has unusual demands for good scientists and engineers, in addition to other specialists. There is a necessity for broad understanding of the meaning of citizenship in the United States. America must have citizens who know something of other nations and are equipped to understand their own Nation's role in international affairs. These special needs can be assigned a high priority by schools which are pursuing the broad list of objectives currently demanded by the people. In adding new, worthwhile activities to the curriculum, nothing of value has to be subtracted if a proper sense of proportion is maintained and enough resources are provided.

2. Overspecialization of vocational education should be avoided. There are almost 50,000 trades in this country, and specialized instruction for all of them cannot be provided. Broadly conceived programs of vocational education must be maintained which are not likely to be outmoded rapidly by technological change and which offer basic instruction that can be useful in many jobs.

3. Just as good schools permit flexibility in this whole Nation by allowing individuals to achieve the level of accomplishment their abilities deserve, the school system must be flexible within itself. Pupils should be able to shift from one program to another as they grow and change in interests and abilities. This Committee thinks that for every child to have, throughout his school career, the chance to change to the kind of education found best for him is more important than the time saved by choosing a few pupils early in their lives for accelerated, specialized programs, as is often done in Europe. The American people have time as well as the physical resources to allow this kind of flexibility.

4. Educational programs which fully exercise and develop the abilities of especially brilliant students must be maintained. A system which wastes the talents of those who have the most to offer has no part in the new American ideal for the schools. Social equality can be maintained by the schools without hampering the intellectual progress of the unusually able. Increased stress must be placed on meeting the challenge of those students who have the capacity for the greatest intellectual growth. Improved provision for these talented young people should be the next great advance in our public school system. This Committee believes it possible to achieve this goal and still handle the tidal wave of new students which is expected. The real and fundamental manpower scarcity at the present time is a scarcity of quality and not of numbers. Consequently, the identification and careful handling of talented youth are urgent and commanding requirements.

5. School leaders should *help* foster all desirable characteristics in children, but they should not be tempted to consider themselves the only agency in the field. The major influence upon children is their home and the whole community in which they are raised. It is right for people to expect the schools to help forward all worthy causes, but entirely wrong to abnegate responsibility in hope that the schools will take up the slack. Schools can never take the place of a warm family life, a vigorous church, and a wholesome community, although they must be strong allies. Where other good influences are lacking, schools should and do try to repair the damage, but they cannot do the job alone.

In conclusion, this Committee believes that the new goals for the schools demanded by the American people reflect a determination to leave nothing that can be done for each generation of children undone. Far from seeking the abandonment of the ideals of the past, the people have called for a quickened pursuit of those ideals. At the same time, they have decided to use the schools in a variety of new ways, sometimes as an ally of other agencies, sometimes as a replacement for other agencies which have failed. Controversy has often surrounded questions of procedure and relative importance, but the nobility of intent implicit in this new concept is beyond doubt. There is far more to be proud of in today's schools than there is to criticize. Their weaknesses usually stem from a lack of means, rather than any defect in their goal. Efforts to work out ways in which school, family, church, and many other agencies can best work together for the fullest development of every child must be a continuous process in every community. To avoid a general dilution of education, the multiplication of school duties must be accompanied by a proportionate increase of school resources. We must never lose sight of the insistent need to increase the excellence of our schools while increasing their scope; the two goals are not incompatible except under conditions of bad management or inadequate resources. The problems of the schools are great, but they never should be allowed to obscure the worthiness of their goals. In the judgment of this Committee, the people will probably continue to insist that all needs of all children be met, one way or another. The attempt to provide schools capable of playing their full part in making that ideal a reality may well prove to be one of the wisest decisions ever made by the American people.

EXECUTIVE ORDER ESTABLISHING THE PEACE CORPS SIGNED BY PRESIDENT JOHN F. KENNEDY (1961) From "Statement by the President upon Signing Order Establishing the Peace Corps, March 1, 1961," *Public Papers of the Presidents* (Washington, D.C., 1961), pp. 134–35.

I have today signed an Executive Order[1] providing for the establishment of a Peace Corps on a temporary pilot basis. I am also sending to Congress a message proposing authorization of a permanent Peace Corps. This Corps will be a pool of trained American men and women sent overseas by the U.S. Government or through private institutions and organizations to help foreign countries meet their urgent needs for skilled manpower.

It is our hope to have 500 or more people in the field by the end of the year.

The initial reactions to the Peace Corps proposal are convincing proof that we have, in this country, an immense reservoir of such men and women—anxious to sacrifice their energies and time and toil to the cause of world peace and human progress.

In establishing our Peace Corps we intend to make full use of the resources and talents of private institutions and groups. Universities, voluntary agencies, labor unions and industry will be asked to share in this effort—contributing diverse sources of energy and imagination—making it clear that the responsibility for peace is the responsibility of our entire society.

We will only send abroad Americans who are wanted by the host country—who have a real job to do—and who are qualified to do that job. Programs will be developed with care, and after full negotiation, in order to make sure that the Peace Corps is wanted and will contribute to the welfare of other people. Our Peace Corps is not designed as an instrument of diplomacy or propaganda or ideological conflict. It is designed to permit our people to exercise more fully their responsibilities in the great common cause of world development.

Life in the Peace Corps will not be easy. There will be no salary and allowances will be at a level sufficient only to maintain health and meet basic needs. Men and women will be expected to work and live alongside the nationals of the country in which they are stationed—doing the same work, eating the same food, talking the same language.

But if the life will not be easy, it will be rich and satisfying. For every young American who participates in the Peace Corps—who works in a foreign land—will know that he or she is sharing in the great common task of bringing to man that decent way of life which is the foundation of freedom and a condition of peace.

[1]Executive Order 10924, 26 F. R. 1789.

PRESIDENT KENNEDY'S SPECIAL MESSAGE TO THE CONGRESS ON EDUCATION (1961)

From "Special Message to the Congress on Education, February 20, 1961, "*Public Papers of the Presidents: John F. Kennedy, 1961; No. 46* (Washington D.C., 1961), pp. 107–10.

To the Congress of the United States:

Our progress as a nation can be no swifter than our progress in education. Our requirements for world leadership, our hopes for economic growth, and the demands of citizenship itself in an era such as this all require the maximum development of every young American's capacity.

The human mind is our fundamental resource. A balanced Federal program must go well beyond incentives for investment in plant and equipment. It must include equally determined measures to invest in human beings—both in their basic education and training and in their more advanced preparation for professional work. Without such measures, the Federal Government will not be carrying out its responsibilities for expanding the base of our economic and military strength.

Our progress in education over the last generation has been substantial. We are educating a greater proportion of our youth to a higher degree of competency than any other country on earth. One-fourth of our total population is enrolled in our schools and colleges. This year 26 billion dollars will be spent on education alone.

But the needs of the next generation—the needs of the next decade and the next school year—will not be met at this level of effort. More effort will be required—on the part of students, teachers, schools, colleges and all 50 states—and on the part of the Federal Government.

Education must remain a matter of state and local control, and higher education a matter of individual choice. But education is increasingly expensive. Too many state and local governments lack the resources to assure an adequate education for every child. Too many classrooms are overcrowded. Too many teachers are underpaid. Too many talented individuals cannot afford the benefits of higher education. Too many academic institutions cannot afford the cost of, or find room for, the growing numbers of students seeking admission in the 60's.

Our twin goals must be: a new standard of excellence in education—and the availability of such excellence to all who are willing and able to pursue it.

I. Assistance To Public Elementary And Secondary Schools

A secondary educational system requires the proper balance, in terms of both quality and quantity, of three elements: students, teachers and facilities. The quality of the students depends in large measure on both the quality and the relative quantity of teachers and facilities.

Throughout the 1960's there will be no lack in the quantity of students. An average net gain of nearly one million pupils a other areas of responsibility—will encourage all states to expand their facilities to meet the increasing demand and enrich the quality of education offered, and gradually assist our relatively low-income states in the elevation of their educational standards to a national level.

The bill which will follow this message has been carefully drawn to eliminate disproportionately large or small inequities, and to make the maximum use of a limited number of dollars. In accordance with the clear prohibition of the

Constitution, no elementary or secondary school funds are allocated for constructing church schools or paying church school teachers' salaries; and thus non-public school children are rightfully not counted in determining the funds each state will receive for its public schools. Each state will be expected to maintain its own effort or contribution; and every state whose effort is below the national average will be expected to increase that proportion of its income which is devoted to public elementary and secondary education.

This investment will pay rich dividends in the years ahead—in increased economic growth, in enlightened citizens, in national excellence. For some 40 years, the Congress has wrestled with this problem and searched for a workable solution. I believe that we now have such a solution; and that this Congress in this year will make a land-mark contribution to American education.

II. Construction Of College And University Facilities

Our colleges and universities represent our ultimate educational resource. In these institutions are produced the leaders and other trained persons whom we need to carry forward our highly developed civilization. If the colleges and universities fail to do their job, there is no substitute to fulfill their responsibility. The threat of opposing military and ideological forces in the world lends urgency to their task. But that task would exist in any case.

The burden of increased enrollments—imposed upon our elementary and secondary schools already in the fifties—will fall heavily upon our colleges and universities during the sixties. By the autumn of 1966, an estimated one million more students will be in attendance at institutions of higher learning than enrolled last fall—for a total more than twice as high as the total college enrollment of 1950. Our colleges, already hard-pressed to meet rising enrollments since 1950 during a period of rising costs, will be in critical straits merely to provide the necessary facilities, much less the cost of quality education.

The country as a whole is already spending nearly $1 billion a year on academic and residential facilities for higher education—some 20 percent of the total spent for higher education. Even with increased contributions from state, local and private sources, a gap of $2.9 billion between aggregate needs and expenditures is anticipated by 1965, and a gap of $5.2 billion by 1970.

The national interest requires an educational system on the college level sufficiently financed and equipped to provide every student with adequate physical facilities to meet his instructional, research, and residential needs.

I therefore recommend legislation which will:

(1) Extend the current College Housing Loan Program with a five year $250 million a year program designed to meet the Federal Government's appropriate share of residential housing for students and faculty. As a start, additional lending authority is necessary to speed action during fiscal 1961 on approvable loan applications already at hand.

(2) Establish a new, though similar, long-term, low-interest rate loan program for academic facilities, authorizing $300 million in loans each year for five years to assist in the construction of classrooms, laboratories, libraries, and related structures—sufficient to enable public and private higher institutions to accommodate the expanding enrollments they anticipate over the next five years; and also to assist in the renovation, rehabilitation, and modernization of such facilities.

III. Assistance to College and University Students

This nation a century or so ago established as a basic objective the provision of a good elementary and secondary school education to every child, regardless of means. In 1961, patterns of occupation, citizenship and world affairs have so changed that we must set a higher goal. We must assure ourselves that every talented young person who has the ability to pursue a program of higher education will be able to do so if he chooses, regardless of his financial means.

Today private and public scholarship and loan programs established by numerous states, private sources, and the Student Loan Program under the National Defense Education Act are making substantial contributions to the financial needs of many who attend our colleges. But they still fall short of doing the job that must be done. An estimated one-third of our brightest high school graduates are unable to go on to college principally for financial reasons.

While I shall subsequently ask the Congress to amend and expand the Student Loan and other provisions of the National Defense Education Act, it is clear that even with this program many talented but needy students are unable to assume further indebtedness in order to continue their education.

I therefore recommend the establishment of a five-year program with an initial authorization of $26,250,000 of state-administered scholarships for talented and needy young people which will supplement but not supplant those programs of financial assistance to students which are now in operation.

Funds would be allocated to the states during the first year for a total of twenty-five thousand scholarships averaging $700 each, 37,500 scholarships the second year, and 50,000 for each succeeding year thereafter. These scholarships, which would range according to need up to a maximum stipend of $1000, would be open to all young persons, without regard to sex, race, creed, or color, solely on the basis of their ability—as determined on a competitive basis—and their financial need. They would be permitted to attend the college of their choice, and free to select their own program of study. Inasmuch as tuition and fees do not normally cover the institution's actual expenses in educating the student, additional allowances to the college or university attended should accompany each scholarship to enable these institutions to accept the additional students without charging an undue increase in fees or suffering an undue financial loss.

*　　*　　*

PRESIDENT JOHN KENNEDY'S CALL FOR A NATIONAL EDUCATION IMPROVEMENT ACT (1963) From "Special Message to the Congress on Education, January 29, 1963," *Public Papers of the Presidents: John F. Kennedy, 1963* (Washington, D.C., 1963), pp. 105–8, 112–16.

Education is the keystone in the arch of freedom and progress. Nothing has contributed more to the enlargement of this Nation's strength and opportunities than our traditional system of free, universal elementary and secondary education, coupled with widespread availability of college education.

For the individual, the doors to the schoolhouse, to the library and to the college lead to the richest treasures of our open society: to the power of knowledge—to the training and skills necessary for productive employment—to the wisdom, the ideals, and the culture which enrich life—and to the creative, self-disciplined understanding of society needed for good citizenship in today's changing and challenging world.

For the Nation, increasing the quality and availability of education is vital to both our national security and our domestic well-being. A free nation can rise no higher than the standard of excellence set in its schools and colleges. Ignorance and illiteracy, unskilled workers and school dropouts—these and other failures of our educational system breed failures in our social and economic system: delinquency, unemployment, chronic dependence, a waste of human resources, a loss of productive power and purchasing power and an increase in tax-supported benefits. The loss of only 1 year's income due to unemployment is more than the total cost of 12 years of education through high school. Failure to improve educational performance is thus not only poor social policy, it is poor economics.

At the turn of the century, only 10 per cent of our adults had a high school or college education. Today such an education has become a requirement for an increasing number of jobs. Yet nearly 40 per cent of our youths are dropping out before graduating from high school; only 43 per cent of our adults have completed high school; only 8 per cent of our adults have completed college; and only 16 per cent of our young people are presently completing college. As my Science Advisory Committee has reported, one of our most serious manpower shortages is the lack of Ph. D.'s in engineering, science, and mathematics; only about one-half of 1 per cent of our school-age generation is achieving Ph. D. degrees in all fields.

This Nation is committed to greater investment in economic growth; and recent research has shown that one of the most beneficial of all such investments is education, accounting for some 40 per cent of the Nation's growth and productivity in recent years. It is an investment which yields a substantial return in the higher wages and purchasing power of trained workers, in the new products and techniques which come from skilled minds and in the constant expansion of this Nation's storehouse of useful knowledge.

In the new age of science and space, improved education is essential to give new meaning to our national purpose and power. In the last 20 years, mankind has acquired more scientific information than in all of previous history. Ninety per cent of all the scientists that ever lived are alive and working today. Vast stretches of the unknown are being explored every day for military, medical, commercial and other reasons. And finally, the twisting course of the cold war requires a citizenry that understands our principles and problems. It requires skilled manpower and brainpower to match the power of totalitarian discipline. It requires a scientific effort which demonstrates the superiority of freedom. And it requires an electorate in every State with sufficiently broad horizons and sufficient maturity of judgment to guide this Nation safely through whatever lies ahead.

In short, from every point of view, education is of paramount concern to the national interest as well as to each individual. Today we need a new standard of excellence in education, matched by the fullest possible access to educational opportunities, enabling each citizen to develop his talents to the maximum possible extent.

Our concern as a Nation for the future of our children—and the growing demands of modern education which Federal financing is better able to assist—make it necessary to expand Federal aid to education beyond the existing limited number of special programs. We can no longer afford the luxury of endless debate over all the complicated and sensitive questions raised by each new proposal on Federal participation in education. To be sure, these are all hard problems—but this Nation has not come to its present position of leadership by avoiding hard problems. We are at a point in history when we must face and resolve these problems.

*   *   *

But all this has not been enough. And the Federal Government—despite increasing recognition of education as a nationwide challenge, and despite the increased financial difficulties encountered by States, communities, and private institutions in carrying this burden—has clearly not met its responsibilities in education. It has not offered sufficient help to our present educational system to meet its inadequacies and overcome its obstacles.

I do not say that the Federal Government should take over responsibility for education. That is neither desirable nor feasible. Instead its participation should be selective, stimulative and, where possible, transitional.

A century of experience with land-grant colleges has demonstrated that Federal financial participation can assist educational progress and growth without Federal control. In the last decade, experience with the National Science Foundation, with the National Defense Education Act, and with programs for assisting federally affected school districts has demonstrated that Federal support can benefit education without leading to Federal control. The proper Federal role is to identify national education goals and help local, State, and private authorities build the necessary roads to reach those goals. Federal aid will enable our schools, colleges and universities to be more stable financially and therefore more independent.

These goals include the following:

First, we must improve the *quality* of instruction provided in all of our schools and colleges. We must stimulate interest in learning in order to reduce the alarming number of students who now drop out of school or who do not continue into higher levels of education. This requires more and better teachers—teachers who can be attracted to and retained in schools and colleges only if pay levels reflect more adequately the value of the services they render. It also requires that our teachers and instructors be equipped with the best possible teaching materials and curriculums. They must have at their command methods of instruction proven by thorough scientific research into the learning process and by careful experimentation.

Second, our educational system faces a major problem of *quantity*—of coping with the needs of our expanding population and of the rising educational expectations for our children which all of us share as parents. Nearly 50 million people were enrolled in our schools and colleges in 1962—an increase of more than 50 per cent since 1950. By 1970, college enrollment will nearly double, and secondary schools will increase enrollment by 50 per cent—categories in which the cost of education, including facilities, is several times higher than in elementary schools.

Third, we must give special attention to increasing the *opportunities* and *incentives* for all Americans to develop their talents to the utmost—to complete their education and to continue their self-development throughout life. This means preventing school dropouts, improving and expanding special educational services, and providing better education in slum, distressed and rural areas where the educational attainment of students is far below par. It means increased opportunities for those students both willing and intellectually able to advance their education at the college and graduate levels. It means increased attention to vocational and technical education, which have long been underdeveloped in both effectiveness and scope, to the detriment of our workers and our technological progress.

In support of these three basic goals, I am proposing today a comprehensive, balanced program to enlarge the Federal Government's investment in the education of its citizens—a program aimed at increasing the educational opportunities of potentially every American citizen, regardless of age, race, religion, income, and educational achievement.

This program has been shaped to meet our goals on the basis of three fundamental guidelines:

(a) An appraisal of the entire range of educational problems, viewing educational opportunity as a continuous lifelong process, starting with preschool training and extending through elementary and secondary schools, college, graduate education, vocational education, job training and retraining adult education, and such general community educational resources as the public library;

(b) A selective application of Federal aid—aimed at strengthening, not weakening, the independence of existing school systems and aimed at meeting our most urgent education problems and objectives, including quality improvement; teacher training; special problems of slum, depressed, and rural areas; needy students; manpower shortage areas such as science and engineering; and shortages of educational facilities; and

(c) More effective implementation of existing [education] laws. . . .

To enable the full range of educational needs to be considered as a whole, I am transmitting to the Congress with this message a single, comprehensive education bill—the National Education Improvement Act of 1963. For education cannot easily or wisely be divided into separate parts. Each part is linked to the other. The colleges depend on the work of the schools; the schools depend on the colleges for teachers; vocational and technical education is not separate from general education. This bill recalls the posture of Jefferson: "Nobody can doubt my zeal for the general instruction of the people. I never have proposed a sacrifice of the primary to the ultimate grade of instruction. Let us keep our eye steadily on the whole system."

In order that its full relation to economic growth, to the new age of science, to the national security, and to human and institutional freedom may be analyzed in proper perspective, this bill should be considered as a whole, as a combination of elements designed to solve problems that have no single solution.

This is not a partisan measure—and it neither includes nor rejects all of the features which have long been sought by the various educational groups and organizations. It is instead an attempt to launch a prudent and balanced program drawing upon the efforts of many past Congresses and the proposals [of] many Members of both Houses and both political parties. It is solely an educational program, without trying to solve all other difficult domestic problems. It is clearly realistic in terms of its cost—and it is clearly essential to the growth and security of this country.

*   *   *

The welfare and security of the Nation require that we increase our investment in financial assistance for college students both at undergraduate and graduate levels. In keeping with present needs and our traditions of maximum self-help, *I recommend that the Congress enact legislation to—*

(1) *Extend the National Defense Education Act student loan program, liberalize the repayment forgiveness for teachers, raise the ceiling on total appropriations and eliminate the limitation on amounts available to individual institutions.*

(2) *Authorize a supplementary new program of Federal insurance for commercial loans made by banks and other institutions to college students for educational purposes.*

(3) *Establish a new work-study program for needy college students unable to carry too heavy a loan burden, providing up to half the pay for students employed by the colleges in work of an educational character—as, for example, laboratory, library, or research assistants.*

(4) *Increase the number of National Defense Education Act fellowships to be awarded by the Office of Education from 1,500 to 12,000, including summer session awards.*

(5) *Authorize a thorough survey and evaluation of the need for scholarships or additional financial assistance to undergraduate students so that any further action needed in this area can be considered by the next Congress.*

(6) In addition, as part of this program to increase financial assistance to students . . . expand the number of [National Science Foundation] fellowships and new teaching grants for graduate study from 2,800 in 1963 to 8,700 in fiscal 1964.

* * *

The teacher training support programs of the National Science Foundation and the Office of Education have demonstrated their value.

I recommend, therefore—

That the National Science Foundation program for training institutes for teachers in the natural sciences, mathematics, engineering, and social sciences be expanded to provide for upgrading the knowledge and skills of 46,000 teachers. . . .

That new legislation be enacted to (a) broaden authority for teacher institutes financed by the Office of Education, now restricted to school guidance counselors and language teachers, to other academic fields; (b) authorize a program of project grants to help colleges and universities improve their teacher preparation programs by upgrading academic courses and staff, by encouraging the selection and retention of their most talented prospective teachers, and by attracting and training teachers from new sources such as retired military personnel or women whose family responsibilities permit them to teach; and (c) authorize training grants through colleges and universities for teachers and other educational personnel requiring specialized training, with particular emphasis on the training of teachers of the mentally retarded and other handicapped children, teachers of gifted or culturally deprived children, teachers of adult literacy, librarians, and educational researchers.

IV. Strengthening Public Elementary
and Secondary Education

Improved research and teacher training are not enough, if good teachers do not choose to teach. Yet present salary schedules in some cases are too low at the start to compete against other positions available to college graduates. In almost all cases, they are too low at the top to retain our ablest young teachers. Without sufficient incentive to make teaching a lifetime career, teachers with valuable training and experience but heavy family responsibilities too often become frustrated and drop out of the profession. Their children may never try to enter. Although teachers' salaries have generally improved in the Nation in recent years, there are still districts which have starting salaries below $3,000.

Good teachers, moreover, need good schools. Last year, over 1,500,000 children were in overcrowded classrooms and an estimated 2 million others were studying amid grossly substandard health and safety conditions. In many areas school dropouts, or the education of the economically disadvantaged, the culturally deprived, the physically or mentally handicapped, and the gifted require specially designed programs which simply are not available.

I am not the first, but I hope to be the last, President to be compelled to call these needless shortcomings to the Nation's attention. These are national problems crossing State boundaries, and deserving of national attention. In our mobile population—where every year one out of five families moves, sometimes across the street, but often across State lines—every family has reason to make teaching in every State a more rewarding and productive profession, and to help every State strengthen its public elementary and secondary education, particularly in those school districts that are financially unable to keep up.

Yet let us face the fact that the Federal Government cannot provide all the financial assistance needed to solve all of the problems mentioned. Instead of a general aid approach that could at best create a small wave in a huge ocean, our efforts should be selective and stimulative, encouraging the States to redouble their efforts under a plan that would phase out Federal aid over a 4-year period.

I recommend, therefore, a 4-year program to provide 1.5 billion dollars to assist States in undertaking under their own State plans selective and urgent improvements in public elementary and secondary education including: (1) increasing starting and maximum teacher salaries, and increasing average teacher salaries in economically disadvantaged areas; (2) constructing classrooms in areas of critical and dangerous shortage; and (3) initiating pilot, experimental, or demonstration projects to meet special educational problems, particularly in slums and depressed rural and urban areas.

I also recommend extension of the National Defense Education Act programs which contribute to improving the quality of elementary and secondary education. Grants for testing, guidance, and counseling programs should be expanded and continued beyond the 1964 expiration date. This program has great relevance for the detection of incipient problems which inhibit learning and for development of the talents of our youth. National Defense Education Act assistance for science, mathematics, and foreign language laboratory equipment—which is essentially for adequate educational programs using newly developed teaching methods—should also be continued beyond 1964.

Finally, in regard to elementary and secondary schools, *I recommend a 4-year continuation of those portions of the federally affected area laws which expire June 30, 1963.* These statutes now assist some 4,000 school districts located in every

State, which together enroll one-third of all public elementary and secondary school pupils in the Nation. Almost 60,000 critically needed classrooms have been constructed at a cost of $1.15 billion to house more than 1,700,000 pupils; and school operating budgets have been supplemented by more than $1.7 billion. For fiscal 1964 the present provisions would be extended. Limited modifications of the existing provisions, which would take effect beginning in 1965, would overcome certain inequities demonstrated by past experience. Also, the District of Columbia should be added to the jurisdictions eligible to participate.

V. Vocational and Special Education

Since the wartime administration of President Woodrow Wilson, Congress has recognized the national necessity of widespread vocational education. Although revised and extended frequently since 1917, the national vocational education acts are no longer adequate. Many once-familiar occupations have declined or disappeared and wholly new industries and jobs have emerged from economic growth and change. The complexities of modern science and technology require training at a higher level than ever before.

For this reason, 2 years ago I requested the Secretary of Health, Education, and Welfare to convene an expert and representative committee to review and evaluate the present vocational education laws and to make recommendations for their modernization. The report of that committee shows the need for providing new training opportunities—in occupations which have relevance to contemporary America—to 21 million youth now in grade school who will enter the labor market without a college degree during the 1960's. These youth—representing more than 80 per cent of the population between the ages of 16 and 21—will be entering the labor market at a time when the need for unskilled labor is sharply diminishing. It is equally necessary to provide training or retraining for the millions of workers who need to learn new skills or whose skills and technical knowledge must be updated.

Both budgetary action and enactment of new legislation is called for. In my 1964 budget *I have recommended funds which would permit doubling the number of workers to be trained by the Manpower Development and Training Act programs.* These programs have, in their brief existence, already enrolled more than 18,000 men, women, and out-of-school youths who are being trained in occupations where jobs are available.

In addition, I recommend legislation to—

(a) *Expand the scope and level of vocational education programs supported through the Office of Education by replacing the Vocational Education Act of 1946 with new grant-in-aid legislation aimed at meeting the needs of individuals in all age groups for vocational training in occupations where they can find employment in today's diverse labor markets, and*

(b) *Provide employment and training opportunities for unemployed youth in conservation and local public service projects.* . . .

VI. Continuing Education

Education need not and should not end upon graduation at any level. An increasing number of Americans recognize the need and the value of continuing education. The accountant, the salesman, the merchant, the skilled and semiskilled worker, all interested in self-improvement, should all be afforded the apportunity of securing up-to-date knowledge and skills. Only one American in eight has even taken as much as one college course. Yet the State universities and land-grant colleges which offer the majority of extension or part-time courses enroll less than a half million people. Due to inadequate finances and facilities, these colleges can offer only a very limited adult education program.

I recommend legislation authorizing Federal grants to States for expanding university extension courses in land-grant colleges and State universities. Despite our high level of education opportunity and attainment, nearly 23 million adult Americans lack an eighth-grade education. They represent a staggering economic and cultural loss to their families and the Nation. *I recommend again, as part of this comprehensive bill, a program to assist all States in offering literacy and basic education courses to adults.*

The public library is also an important resource for continuing education. But 18 million people in this Nation still have no access to any local public library service and over 110 million more have only inadequate service.

Advanced age, lack of space, and lack of modern equipment characterize American public library buildings in 1963. Their rate of replacement is barely noticeable: 2 per cent in a decade. There are now no Carnegie funds available for libraries, nor have there been for 40 years.

The public library building is usually one of the oldest governmental structures in use in any community. In one prosperous midwestern State, for example, 30 per cent of all public library buildings were built before the year 1910, and 85 per cent were erected before 1920. Many other States are in a similar situation.

I recommend enactment of legislation to amend the Library Services Act by authorizing a 3-year program of grants for urban as well as rural libraries and for construction as well as operation.

VII. Conclusion

In all the years of our national life, the American people, in partnership with their governments, have continued to insist that "the means of education shall forever be encouraged," as the Continental Congress affirmed in the Northwest Ordinance. Fundamentally, education is and must always be a local responsibility, for it thrives best when nurtured at the grassroots of our democracy. But in our present era of economic expansion, population growth, and technological advance, State, local, and private efforts are insufficient. These efforts must be reinforced by national support if American education is to yield a maximum of individual development and national well-being.

The necessity of this program does not rest on the course of the cold war. Improvement in education is essential to our Nation's development without respect to what others are doing. Nevertheless, it is worthwhile noting that the Soviet Union recognizes that educational effort in the 1960's will have a major effect on a nation's power, progress, and status in the 1970's and 1980's. According to a recent report prepared for the National Science Foundation, Soviet institutions of higher education are graduating three times as many engineers and four times as many physicians as the United States. While trailing behind this country in aggregate annual numbers of higher education graduates, the Soviets are maintaining an annual flow of scientific and technical professional manpower more than twice as large as our own. At the same time, they have virtually eliminated illiteracy, with a 23-fold increase since the turn of the century in the proportion of persons with an education beyond the seventh grade. This Nation's devotion to education is surely sufficient to excel the achievements of any other nation or system.

The program here proposed is reasonable and yet far reaching. It offers Federal assistance without Federal control. It provides for economic growth, manpower development, and progress toward our educational and humanitarian objectives. It encourages the increase of the knowledge, skills, attitudes, and critical intelligence necessary for the preservation of our society. It will help keep America strong and safe and free. I strongly recommend it to the Congress for high priority action.

THE HIGHER EDUCATION FACILITIES ACT (1963)   From *Public Law 88-204*, 88th Congress, December 16, 1963.

An act to authorize assistance to public and other nonprofit institutions of higher education in financing the construction, rehabilitation, or improvement of needed academic and related facilities in undergraduate and graduate institutions.

Be it enacted by the Senate and House of Representatives of the United States of America in Congress assembled, That this Act may be cited as the "Higher Education Facilities Act of 1963,"

FINDINGS AND DECLARATION OF POLICY

SEC. 2. The Congress hereby finds that the security and welfare of the United States require that this and future generations of American youth be assured ample opportunity for the fullest development of their intellectual capacities, and that this opportunity will be jeopardized unless the Nation's colleges and universities are encouraged and assisted in their efforts to accommodate rapidly growing numbers of youth who aspire to a higher education. The Congress further finds and declares that these needs are so great and these steps so urgent that it is incumbent upon the Nation to take positive and immediate action to meet these needs through assistance to institutions of higher education, including graduate and undergraduate institutions, junior and community colleges, and technical institutes, in providing certain academic facilities.

Title I—Grants for Construction of Under-Graduate Academic Facilities

APPROPRIATIONS AUTHORIZED

SEC. 101. (a) The Commissioner of Education (hereinafter in this Act referred to as the "Commissioner") shall carry out during the fiscal year ending June 30, 1964, and each of the four succeeding fiscal years, a program of grants to institutions of higher education for the construction of academic facilities in accordance with this title.

(b) For the purpose of making grants under this title, there is hereby authorized to be appropriated the sum of $230,000,000 for the fiscal year ending June 30, 1964, and each of the two succeeding fiscal years; but for the fiscal year ending June 30, 1967, and the succeeding fiscal year, only such sums may be appropriated as the Congress may hereafter authorize by law. In addition to the sums authorized to be appropriated under the preceding sentence, there is hereby authorized to be appropriated for the fiscal year ending June 30, 1965, and the succeeding fiscal year, for making such grants the difference (if any) between the sums authorized to be appropriated under the preceding sentence for preceding fiscal years and the aggregate of the sums which were appropriated for such preceding years under such sentence.

(c) Sums appropriated pursuant to subsection (b) of this section shall remain available for reservation as provided in section 109 until the close of the fiscal year next succeeding the fiscal year for which they were appropriated.

ALLOTMENTS

SEC. 102. Of the funds appropriated pursuant to section 101 for any fiscal year, 22 per centum shall be allotted among the States in the manner prescribed by section 103 for use in providing academic facilities for public community colleges and public technical institutes. The remainder of the funds so appropriated shall be allotted among the States in the manner as prescribed in section 104 for use in providing academic facilities for institutions of higher education other than public community colleges and public technical institutes.

ALLOTMENTS TO STATES FOR PUBLIC COMMUNITY COLLEGES AND PUBLIC TECHNICAL INSTITUTES

SEC. 103. (a) The funds to be allotted for any fiscal year for use in providing academic facilities for public community colleges and public technical institutes shall be allotted among the States on the basis of the income per person and the number of high school graduates of the respective States. Such allotments shall be made as follows: The Commissioner shall allot to each State for each fiscal year an amount which bears the same ratio to the funds being allotted as the product of—
   (1) the number of high school graduates of the State, and
   (2) the State's allotment ratio (as determined under subsection (d))
bears to the sum of the corresponding products for all the States.

(b) The amount of each allotment to a State under this section shall be available, in accordance with the provisions of this title, for payment of the Federal share (as determined under sections 108(b)(3) and 401(d)) of the development cost of approved projects for the construction of academic facilities within such State for public community colleges and public technical institutes. Sums allotted to a State for the fiscal year ending June 30, 1964, shall remain available for reservation as provided in section 109 until the close of the next fiscal year, in addition to the sums allotted to such State for such next fiscal year.

(c) All amounts allotted under this section for the fiscal year ending June 30, 1965, and the succeeding fiscal year, which are not reserved as provided in section 109 by the close of the fiscal year for which they are allotted, shall be reallotted by

RE-APPRAISAL
1951–1973

3359

the Commissioner, on the basis of such factors as he determines to be equitable and reasonable, among the States which, as determined by the Commissioner, are able to use without delay any amounts so reallotted for providing academic facilities for public community collegs or public technical institutes. Amounts reallotted under this subsection shall be available for reservation until the close of the fiscal year nêxt succeeding the fiscal year for which they were orginally allotted.

(d) For purposes of this section—

(1) The "allotment ratio" for any States shall be 1.00 less the product of (A) .50 and (B) the quotient obtained by dividing the income per person for the States by the income per person for all the States (not including Puerto Rico, the Virgin Islands, American Samoa, and Guam), except that (i) the allotment ratio shall in no case be less than .33 1/3 or more than .66 2/3, (ii) the allotment ratio for Puerto Rico, the Virgin Islands, American Samoa, and Guam shall be .66 2/3, and (iii) the allotment ratio of any State shall be .50 for any fiscal year if the Commissioner finds that the cost of school construction in such State exceeds twice the median of such costs in all the States as determined by him on the basis of an index of the average per pupil cost of constructing minimum school facilities in the States as determined for such fiscal year under section 15(6) of the Act of September 23, 1950, as amended (20 U.S.C. 645), or, in the Commissioner's discretion, on the basis of such index and such other statistics and data as the Commissioner shall deem adequate and appropriate; and

(2) The allotment ratios shall be promulgated by the Commissioner as soon as possible after enactment of this Act, and annually thereafter, on the basis of the average of the incomes per person of the States and of all the States for the three most recent consecutive calendar years for which satisfactory data are available from the Department of Commerce.

(3) The term "high school graduate" means a person who has received formal recognition (by diploma, certificate, or similar means) from an approved school for successful completion of four years of education beyond the first eight years of schoolwork, or for demonstration of equivalent achievement. For the purposes of this section the number of high school graduates shall be limited to the number who graduated in the most recent school year for which satisfactory data are available from the Department of Health, Education, and Welfare. The interpretation of the definition of "high school graduate" shall fall within the authority of the Commissioner.

ALLOTMENTS TO STATES FOR INSTITUTIONS OF HIGHER EDUCATION OTHER THAN PUBLIC COMMUNITY
COLLEGES AND PUBLIC TECHNICAL INSTITUTES

SEC. 104. (a) Of the funds to be allotted for any fiscal year for use in providing academic facilities for institutions of higher education other than public community colleges and public technical institutes (1) one-half shall be allotted by the Commissioner among the States so that the allotment to each State under this clause will be an amount which bears the same ratio to such one-half as the number of students enrolled in the institutions of higher education in such State bears to the total number of students enrolled in such institutions in all the States; and (2) the remaining one-half shall be allotted by him among the States so that the allotment to each State under this clause will be an amount which bears the same ratio to such remainder as the number of students enrolled in grades nine to twelve (both inclusive) of schools in such States bears to the total number of students in such grades in schools in all the States. For the purposes of this subsection, (A) the number of students enrolled in institutions of higher education shall be deemed to be equal to the sum of (i) the number of full-time students and (ii) the full-time equivalent of the number of part-time students as determined by the Commissioner in accordance with regulations; and (B) determinations as to enrollment under either clause (1) or clause (2) of this subsection shall be made by the Commissioner on the basis of data for the most recent year for which satisfactory data with respect to such enrollment are available to him.

(b) The amount of each allotment to a State under this section shall be available, in accordance with the provisions of this title, for payment of the Federal share (as determined under sections 108 (b)(3) and 401 (d)) of the development cost of approved projects for the construction of academic facilities within such State for institutions of higher education other than public community colleges and public technical institutes. Sums allotted to a State for the fiscal year ending June 30, 1964, shall remain available for reservation as provided in section 109 until the close of the next fiscal year, in addition to the sums allotted to such State for such next fiscal year.

(c) All amounts allotted under this section for the fiscal year ending June 30, 1965, and the succeeding fiscal year, which are not reserved as provided in section 109 by the close of the fiscal year for which they are allotted, shall be reallotted by the Commissioner, on the basis of such factors as he determines to be equitable and reasonable, among the States which, as determined by the Commissioner, are able to use without delay any amounts so reallotted for providing academic facilities for institutions of higher education other than public community colleges and public technical institutes. Amounts reallotted under this subsection shall be available for reservation until the close of the fiscal year next succeeding the fiscal year for which they were originally allotted.

PRESIDENT JOHN KENNEDY'S MESSAGE TO CONGRESS ON CIVIL RIGHTS (1963) From "Civil Rights—Message from the President of the United States," *Congressional Record—House* (Washington, D.C., 1963), pp. 3245-47.

To the Congress of the United States:

"Our Constitution is colorblind," wrote Mr. Justice Harlan before the turn of the century, "and neither knows nor tolerates classes among citizens." But the practices of the country do not always conform to the principles of the Constitution. And this message is intended to examine how far we have come in achieving first-class citizenship for all citizens regardless of color, how far we have yet to go, and what further tasks remain to be carried out—by the executive and legislative branches of the Federal Government, as well as by State and local governments and private citizens and organizations.

One hundred years ago the Emancipation Proclamation was signed by a President who believed in the equal worth and opportunity of every human being. That proclamation was only a first step—a step which its author unhappily did not live to follow up, a step which some of its critics dismissed as an action which "frees the slave but ignores the Negro." Through these long 100 years, while slavery has vanished, progress for the Negro has been too often blocked and delayed. Equality before the law has not always meant equal treatment and opportunity. And the harmful, wasteful and wrongful results of racial discrimination and segregation still appear in virtually every aspect of national life, in virtually every part of the Nation.

The Negro baby born in America today, regardless of the section or State in which he is born, has about one-half as much chance of completing high school as a white baby born in the same place on the same day; one-third as much chance of completing college; one-third as much chance of becoming a professional man; twice as much chance of becoming unemployed; about one-seventh as much chance of earning $10,000 per year; a life expectancy which is 7 years less; and the prospects of earning only half as much.

No American who believes in the basic truth that "all men are created equal, that they are endowed by their Creator with certain unalienable rights," can fully excuse, explain, or defend the picture these statistics portray. Race discrimination hampers our economic growth by preventing the maximum development and utilization of our manpower. It hampers our world leadership by contradicting at home the message we preach abroad. It mars the atmosphere of a united and classless society in which this Nation rose to greatness. It increases the costs of public welfare, crime, delinquency, and disorder. Above all, it is wrong.

Therefore, let it be clear, in our own hearts and minds, that it is not merely because of the cold war, and not merely because of the economic waste of discrimination, that we are committed to achieving true equality of opportunity. The basic reason is because it is right.

The cruel disease of discrimination knows no sectional or State boundaries. The continuing attack on this problem must be equally broad. It must be both private and public—it must be conducted at National, State, and local levels—and it must include both legislative and executive action.

In the last 2 years, more progress has been made in securing the civil rights of all Americans than in any comparable period in our history. Progress has been made—through executive action, litigation, persuasion, and private initiative—in achieving and protecting equality of opportunity in education, voting, transportation, employment, housing, government, and the enjoyment of public accommodations.

But pride in our progress must not give way to relaxation of our effort. Nor does progress in the executive branch enable the legislative branch to escape its own obligations. On the contrary, it is in the light of this nationwide progress, and in the belief that Congress will wish once again to meet its responsibilities in this matter, that I stress in the following agenda of existing and prospective action important legislative as well as administrative measures.

*　　*　　*

II. EDUCATION

Nearly 9 years have elapsed since the Supreme Court ruled that State laws requiring or permitting segregated schools violate the Constitution. That decision represented both good law and good judgment—it was both legally and morally right. Since that time it has become increasingly clear that neither violence nor legalistic evasions will be tolerated as a means of thwarting court-ordered desegregation, that closed schools are not an answer, and that responsible communities are able to handle the desegregation process in a calm and sensible manner. This is as it should be, for, as I stated to the Nation at the time of the Mississippi violence last September:

"Our Nation is founded on the principle that observance of the law is the eternal safeguard of liberty, and defiance of the law is the surest road to tyranny. The law which we obey includes the final rulings of the courts, as well as the enactments of our legislative bodies. Even among law-abiding men, few laws are universally loved—but they are uniformly respected and not resisted.

"Americans are free to disagree with the law but not to disobey it. For in a government of laws and not of men, no man, however prominent or powerful, and no mob, however unruly or boisterous, is entitled to defy a court of law. If this country should ever reach the point where any man or group of men, by force or threat of force, could long defy the commands of our courts and our Constitution, then no law would stand free from doubt, no judge would be sure of his writ, and no citizen would be safe from his neighbors."

The shameful violence which accompanied but did not prevent the end of segregation at the University of Mississippi was an exception. State-supported universities in Georgia and South Carolina met this test in recent years with calm and maturity, as did the State-supported universities of Virginia, North Carolina, Florida, Texas, Louisiana, Tennessee, Arkansas, and Kentucky in earlier years. In addition, progress toward the desegregation of education at all levels has made other notable and peaceful strides, including the following forward moves in the last 2 years alone:

Desegregation plans have been put into effect peacefully in the public schools of Atlanta, Dallas, New Orleans, Memphis, and elsewhere, with over 60 school districts desegregated last year—frequently with the help of Federal persuasion and consultation, and in every case without incident or disorder.

Teacher training institutes financed under the National Defense Education Act are no longer held in colleges which refuse to accept students without regard to race, and this has resulted in a number of institutions opening their doors to Negro applicants voluntarily.

The same is now true of Institutes conducted by the National Science Foundation.

Beginning in September of this year, under the aid to impacted area school program, the Department of Health, Education, and Welfare will initiate a program of providing onbase facilities so that children living on military installations will no longer be required to attend segregated schools at Federal expense. These children should not be victimized by segregation merely because their fathers chose to serve in the Armed Forces and were assigned to an area where schools are operated on a segregated basis.

In addition, the Department of Justice and the Department of Health, Education, and Welfare have succeeded in obtaining voluntary desegregation in many other districts receiving impacted area school assistance; and, representing the Federal interest, have filed lawsuits to end segregation in a number of other districts.

The Department of Justice has also intervened to seek the opening of public schools in the case of Prince Edward County, Va., the only county in the Nation where there are no public schools, and where a bitter effort to thwart court decrees requiring desegregation has caused nearly 1,500 out of 1,800 school-age Negro children to go without any education for more than 3 years.

In these and other areas within its jurisdiction, the executive branch will continue its efforts to fulfill the constitutional objective of an equal, nonsegregated, educational opportunity for all children.

Despite these efforts, however, progress toward primary and secondary school desegregation has still been too slow, often painfully so. Those children who are being denied their constitutional rights are suffering a loss which can never be regained, and which will leave scars which can never be fully healed. I have in the past expressed my belief that the full authority of the Federal Government should be placed behind the achievement of school desegregation, in accordance with the command of the Constitution. One obvious area of Federal action is to help facilitate the transition to desegregation in those areas which are conforming or wish to conform their practices to the law.

Many of these communities lack the resources necessary to eliminate segregation in their public schools while at the same time assuring that educational standards will be maintained and improved. The problem has been compounded by the fact that the climate of mistrust in many communities has left many school officials with no qualified source to turn to for information and advice.

There is a need for technical assistance by the Office of Education to assist local communities in preparing and carrying out desegregation plans, including the supplying of information on means which have been employed to desegregate other schools successfully. There is also need for financial assistance to enable those communities which desire and need such assistance to employ specialized personnel to cope with problems occasioned by desegregation and to train school personnel to facilitate the transition to desegregation. While some facilities for providing this kind of assistance are presently available in the Office of Education, they are not adequate to the task.

I recommend, therefore, a program of Federal, technical and financial assistance to aid school districts in the process of desegregation in compliance with the Constitution.

Finally, it is obvious that the unconstitutional and outmoded concept of "separate but equal" does not belong in the Federal statute books. This is particularly true with respect to higher education, where peaceful desegregation has been underway in practically every State for some time. I repeat, therefore, this administration's recommendation of last year that this phrase be eliminated from the Morrill Land Grant College Act.

* * *

CONCLUSION

The various steps which have been undertaken or which are proposed in this message do not constitute a final answer to the problems of race discrimination in this country. They do constitute a list of priorities—steps which can be taken by the executive branch and measures which can be enacted by the 88th Congress. Other measures directed toward these same goals will be favorably commented on and supported, as they have in the past—and they will be signed, if enacted into law.

In addition, it is my hope that this message will lend encouragement to those State and local governments—and to private organizations, corporations, and individuals—who share my concern over the gap between our precepts and our practices. This is an effort in which every individual who asks what he can do for his country should be able and willing to take part. It is important, for example, for private citizens and local governments to support the State Department's effort to end the discriminatory treatment suffered by too many foreign diplomats, students, and visitors to this country. But it is not enough to treat those from other lands with equality and dignity—the same treatment must be afforded to every American citizen.

The program outlined in this message should not provide the occasion for sectional bitterness. No State or section of this Nation can pretend a self-righteous role, for every area has its own civil rights problems.

Nor should the basic elements of this program be imperiled by partisanship. The proposals put forth are consistent with the platforms of both parties and with the positions of their leaders. Inevitably there will be disagreement about means and strategy. But I would hope that on issues of constitutional rights and freedom, as in matters affecting our national security, there is a fundamental unity among us that will survive partisan debate over particular issues.

The centennial of the issuance of the Emancipation Proclamation is an occasion for celebration, for a sober assessment of our failures, and for rededication to the goals of freedom. Surely there could be no more meaningful observance of the centennial than the enactment of effective civil rights legislation and the continuation of effective executive action.

JOHN F. KENNEDY.

THE WHITE HOUSE, *February 28, 1963.*

REPORT OF THE PANEL OF CONSULTANTS ON VOCATIONAL EDUCATION (1963) From U.S. Department of Health, Education, and Welfare, Office of Education, *Education For A Changing World of Work,* Report of the Panel of Consultants on Vocational Education (Washington D.C., 1963), pp. xv–xx.

By 1970, the American labor force—those working or seeking work at any time during the year—will total 100 million people. There will be 87 million Americans working full time, the year round. Of these, 58 million are working now, 26 million will be young workers entering the labor force during the 1960–70 decade, and 3 million will be women entering or reentering the labor force.

The Panel of Consultants on Vocational Education has considered the educational needs of all nonprofessional workers. Many now at work will need training during this decade to keep pace with new methods, new materials, new opportunities. Many others will require retraining as their jobs disappear due to automation or economic change. The local-State-Federal vocational and technical education program, which is the subject of this report, can provide appropriate training and retraining for them.

It is especially important that the 26 million young workers who will start work in this decade adapt to the needs of a changing economy. The 8 out of 10 students now in elementary schools who will not complete 4 years of college may gain occupational competence in many ways: through on-the-job training organized by employers; through apprenticeship and journeymen training, or other trade union programs; in public and private technical institutes or in vocational and general high schools; from the armed services; by individual study and work; and especially through the public program of vocational and technical education.

The 3 million wives, mothers, and widows who will shift from fulltime housework to jobs during the decade ending in 1970 will also need marketable skills. Public vocational and technical education programs can help these women improve old skills and gain the new ones needed in a changing world of work.

The local-State-Federal public program of vocational and technical education was inaugurated in 1917 with enactment of the Smith-Hughes Act. Subsequent legislation expanded and extended the original program. Today it benefits about 4 million students (half of whom are adults), and involves more than $250 million in local, State, and Federal funds expended in an estimated two-thirds of the high schools and many colleges and universities.

Every State and territory now offers federally aided vocational education programs. Each State has a vocational education board to set policy. Federal funds can be used for program operation but not for the construction of buildings; nearly all the Federal funds are used by the States as partial reimbursement for teachers' salaries. In all but the most recent programs—those under the Area Redevelopment Act and the Manpower Development and Training Act—States must match Federal funds dollar for dollar. In general, State and local expenditures far exceed the matching requirements. The types of reimbursable vocational instruction are specified in several Federal statutes, as well as the age and job status of the students.

Federal law limits funds for vocational instruction of both young people and adults to the following broad categories, among which current enrollment is distributed as follows:

Vocational category	Enrollment (1960-61)
Agriculture	805,322
Distributive occupations	306,083
Homemaking	1,610,334
Trades and industry	963,609
Practical nursing	47,264
Technician training	122,952

A major concern of the Panel had been to study the strengths and limitations of these local-State-Federal programs, including the implications of automation, technological advance, population mobility, discrimination, urbanization, and the administration of the programs.

The Panel is convinced that vocational and technical education are sound investments in people. Data indicate that graduates of high school vocational education programs are less likely to be unemployed than other high school graduates, that vocational education graduates do in fact work in the occupations for which they prepare, and that vocational education increases their subsequent earnings. The Panel is satisfied that the local-State-Federal partnership in vocational and technical education is capable of imparting virtually any specific production service or technical skill that may be required by national or international crises or emergencies. The evidence includes the program's record of training production workers during World War II, the rising number of technicians being trained under the National Defense Education Act, and the increasing number of practical nurses and other health workers graduating annually from vocational education courses.

However, the Panel found that vocational education is not available in enough high schools. In a special study made by the Panel of 3,733 public high schools in 6 representative States, only 5 percent offered distributive education courses, only 9 percent offered trade and industrial courses, and less than half offered courses in homemaking or vocational agriculture. Even in the largest cities, less than one-fifth of the high school students are enrolled in vocational education programs, although two-thirds of those completing the high school curriculum will not complete 4 years of college education.

The Panel also found that vocational education programs are not preparing people for enough kinds of jobs. One study which compared vocational education enrollments with subsequent occupational employment found that only 10 boys studied vocational agriculture for every 100 males employed in that field. The ratios were even less satisfactory in wholesale and retail trade (1:200) and manufacturing and construction (2:444). In only nine States can one learn to be an office machine repairman through the federally reimbursed vocational education program. Similarly, only 11 States offer federally reimbursed courses in electric appliance repair, only 6 teach heating and ventilating mechanics through this program, and only 11 prepare people for work as drycleaners, spotters, or pressers.

Post-high-sehool technical training is an especially critical need, the Panel found. Estimates of the number of new technicians needed in every year of the present decade range from 67,800 to 200,000. Technician training is presently offered under a variety of auspices, public and private, with the federally reimbursed programs authorized for title VIII of the National Defense Education Act producing a major share of the graduates.

The Panel's general recommendations are that, in a changing world of work, vocational education must—

- Offer training opportunities to the 21 million noncollege graduates who will enter the labor market in the 1960's.
- Provide training or retraining for the millions of workers whose skills and technical knowledge must be updated, as well as those whose jobs will disappear due to increasing efficiency, automation, or economic change.
- Meet the critical need for highly skilled craftsmen and technicians through education during and after the high school years.
- Expand vocational and technical training programs consistent with employment possibilities and national economic needs.
- Make educational opportunities equally available to all, regardless of race, sex, scholastic aptitude, or place of residence.

The Panel believes that the Federal Government must continue to work with States and local communities to develop and improve the skills of its citizens. In place of the occupational categories specified in the present statutes, the Panel recommends that the local-State-Federal partnership increase support of vocational and technical education for—

I. High school students preparing to enter the labor market or become homemakers.

II. Youth with special needs who have academic, socioeconomic, or other handicaps that prevent them from succeeding in the usual high school vocational education program.

IV. Youth and adults unemployed or at work who need training or retraining to achieve employment stability.

V. Adequate services and facilities to assure quality in all vocational and technical education programs.

The Panel urges that occupational preparation be available to all American youth. The world of work requires many more young people well trained to enter employment in agriculture, the skilled trades, business, industry, merchandising, service occupations, and technical and health fields, as well as homemaking. Since the American population is highly mobile, responsibility for occupational preparation must be considered by every high school, but the need for vocational and technical education is especially evident in urban centers, which offer the greatest number of employment opportunities.

For young people in high school who are preparing to enter the labor market or to become homemakers, the Panel recommends that present vocational education programs be expanded. Training for office occupations should be included among the federally reimbursed vocational education programs. Preemployment training for the distributive occupations should be eligible for Federal support in addition to the present cooperative (work-school) programs. The vocational agriculture program, under Federal reimbursement, should permit instruction for occupations related to agriculture as well as for actual farming.

For high school age youth with academic, socioeconomic, or other handicaps that prevent them from suceeeding in the usual high school vocational education program, the Panel recommends that instruction be highly individualized. Specially qualified and highly motivated teachers with occupational competence, who understand the needs of disadvantaged youth, should be employed for this purpose. Occupational information of practical significance and expert vocational counseling must be made available to their students. Diversity and flexibility must characterize these programs; experimental or pilot projects to develop more effective instruction should be fully supported by Federal funds.

For youth and adults who are full-time students preparing to enter the labor market, having completed or left high school, the Panel recommends that the Federal Government increase its support of full-time, post-high-school vocational and technical training. An advancing technology constantly demands more skilled craftsmen and highly skilled technicians in occupations requiring scientific knowledge. Vocational and technical education must prepare many more technicians and skilled craftsmen for employment in industry, business, agriculture, and the health fields.

Both the area vocational schools and the specialized vocational schools in large urban centers provide a diversity of occupational training programs to large numbers without the usual restrictive residence requirements. Many more of these schools are needed, especially for training highly skilled craftsmen and technicians. Technician training is also available in community or junior colleges, agricultural and technical institutes, and vocational-technical schools. Expanding their output is also a national need of urgent importance.

For youth and adults unemployed or at work who need training or retraining to achieve employment stability, the Panel recommends that part-time, short-term training courses be expanded. Millions of workers also require updating and upgrading—lifelong learning—in an era of changing materials, processes, tools, and techniques. Courses in many more fields, including the office and service occupations, should be made available to both groups. More equipment and facilities must be provided to extend educational opportunities to many more workers, especially those living in communities where training is a critical need. Apprentice and journeymen training opportunities should be expanded by mutual action of employers and unions.

For services required to assure quality in all vocational and technical education programs, the Panel recommends that—

- Teacher and leadership training programs be improved and enlarged. Institutions of higher education, especially land-grant colleges and State universities, should provide for the professional growth of vocational and technical teachers.
- Basic education material oriented to specific occupations be available for all programs. For this purpose, instructional materials laboratories should be established in appropriate institutions and financed and coordinated through the Division of Vocational and Technical Education, U.S. Office of Education.
- Occupational information and guidance services be available for all students. State and national leadership for these programs should be supported and coordinated by the Division of Vocational and Technical Education, U.S. Office of Education.
- Research and development in vocational and technical education be encouraged, supported and coordinated at the national level. The results of this research and development should be made available on a nationwide basis.

To finance expanding programs of vocational and technical education, support from all sources must expand as enrollments expand, as dropouts diminish, and as adult training and retraining become more urgent. Local and State governments should increase the $500 million they now provide annually for operation, administration, and construction costs. The Federal Government should provide at least $400 million as its investment in the 6 million young people and adults who currently benefit from vocational and technical education. This should include for the 1963–64 school year:

	Million
I. For youth in high school who are preparing to enter the labor market or to become homemakers	$200
II. For high school youth with academic, socioeconomic, or other handicaps that prevent them from succeeding in the usual high school vocational education program	10
III. For youth and adults who have completed or left high school and are full-time students preparing to enter the labor market	50
IV. For youth and adults unemployed or at work who need training or retraining to achieve employment stability	100
V. For services required to assure quality in all vocational and technical education programs	40

RE-APPRAISAL
1951–1973

3369

THE CIVIL RIGHTS ACT OF 1964   From U.S. Commission on Civil Rights, Civil Rights Digest, *Special Bulletin* (August, 1964), Appendix.

Title IV—Public Education

Under this title the U.S. Office of Education is authorized to:

a. conduct a national survey to determine the availability of equal educational opportunity;

b. provide technical assistance, upon request, to help States, political subdivisions or school districts carry out school desegregation plans;

c. arrange training institutes to prepare teachers and other school personnel to deal with desegregation problems;

d. make grants enabling school boards to employ specialists for in-service training programs.

In addition, the Attorney General is authorized to file civil suits seeking to compel desegregation of public schools, including public colleges.

Before filing such a suit the Attorney General must have received a signed complaint from a pupil or parent and must have determined that the complainant, according to standards set forth in the Act, is unable to bring the action. The Attorney General is also required to notify the school board and give it a reasonable period of time to correct the alleged condition before filing suit.

*   *   *

Title VI—Federally Assisted Programs

Under this title every Federal agency which provides financial assistance through grants, loans or contracts is required to eliminate discrimination on the grounds of race, color or national origin in these programs.

For example, this title would require the following:

a. hospitals constructed with Federal funds would have to serve all patients without regard to race, color or national origin;

b. elementary and secondary schools constructed, maintained and operated with Federal funds would have to admit children without regard to race, color or national origin;

c. State employment services financed by Federal funds would have to refer qualified job applicants for employment without discrimination;

d. schools for the deaf and the blind operated with Federal funds would have to serve the deaf and blind of any color;

e. colleges and universities receiving funds for their general operation or for the construction of special facilities, such as research centers, would have to admit students without discrimination;

f. construction contractors receiving funds under Federal public work programs would have to hire employees without discrimination.

Action by a Federal agency to carry out the requirements of this title may include the terminating of programs where discrimination is taking place or refusal to grant assistance to such a program.

Each agency is required to publish rules or regulations to carry out the purposes of the title. These rules and regulations are subject to the approval of the President.

Compliance actions are subject to the following conditions:

a. notice must be given of alleged failure to comply and an opportunity for a hearing must be provided;

b. in the event assistance is to be cut off, a written report must be submitted to Congress 30 days before the cut-off date;

c. compliance action may be appealed to the courts.

Social security and veteran's benefits, and other Federal benefits distributed directly to individuals are not affected by this law.

Federal assistance in the form of insurance or guaranty—for example, FHA insured loans—are not covered by this title (however, the President's Executive Order prohibiting discrimination in Federally aided housing remains in effect).

PRESIDENT LYNDON JOHNSON'S CALL UPON CONGRESS TO PASS ELEMENTARY AND SECONDARY EDUCATION ACT (1965) From House Document No. 45, 89th Cong., 1st Sess. (1965), pp. 1–3.

To the Congress of the United States:

In 1787, the Continental Congress declared in the Northwest Ordinance:

"Schools and the means of education shall forever be encouraged."

America is strong and prosperous and free because for 178 years we have honored that commitment.

In the United States today—

One-quarter of all Americans are in the Nation's classrooms.

High school attendance has grown eighteenfold since the turn of the century—six times as fast as the population.

College enrollment has advanced eightyfold. Americans today support a fourth of the world's institutions of higher learning and a third of its professors and college students.

In the life of the individual, education is always an unfinished task.

And in the life of this Nation, the advancement of education is a continuing challenge.

There is a darker side to education in America:

One student out of every three now in the fifth grade will drop out before finishing high school—if the present rate continues.

Almost a million young people will continue to quit school each year—if our schools fail to stimulate their desire to learn.

Over 100,000 of our brightest high school graduates each year will not go to college—and many others will leave college—if the opportunity for higher education is not expanded.

RE-APPRAISAL
1951–1973

The cost of this neglect runs high—both for the youth and the Nation:

3371

Unemployment of young people with an eighth grade education or less is four times the national average.

Jobs filled by high school graduates rose by 40 percent in the last 10 years. Jobs for those with less schooling decreased by nearly 10 percent.

We can measure the cost in even starker terms. We now spend about $450 a year per child in our public schools. But we spend $1,800 a year to keep a delinquent youth in a detention home, $2,500 a year for a family on relief, $3,500 a year for a criminal in State prison.

The growing numbers of young people reaching school age demand that we move swiftly even to stand still.

Attendance in elementary and secondary schools will increase by 4 million in the next 5 years; 400,000 new classrooms will be needed to meet this growth. But almost one-half million of the Nation's existing classrooms are already more than 30 years old.

The post-World War II boom in babies has now reached college age. And by 1970, our colleges must be prepared to add 50 percent more enrollment to their presently overcrowded facilities.

In the past, Congress has supported an increasing commitment to education in America. Last year, I signed historic measures passed by the 88th Congress to provide—

Facilities badly needed by universities, colleges, and community colleges;
Major new resources for vocational training;
More loans and fellowships for students enrolled in higher education; and
Enlarged and improved training for physicians, dentists, and nurses.

I propose that the 89th Congress join me in extending the commitment still further. I propose that we declare a national goal of

Full Educational Opportunity

Every child must be encouraged to get as much education as he has the ability to take.

We want this not only for his sake—but for the Nation's sake.

Nothing matters more to the future of the country: not our military preparedness, for armed might is worthless if we lack the brainpower to build a world of peace; not our productive economy, for we cannot sustain growth without trained manpower, not our democratic system of government, for freedom is fragile if citizens are ignorant.

We must demand that our schools increase not only the quantity but the quality of America's education. For we recognize that nuclear age problems cannot be solved with horse-and-buggy learning. The three R's of our school system must be supported by the three T's—teachers who are superior, techniques of instruction that are modern, and thinking about education which places it first in all our plans and hopes.

Specifically, four major tasks confront us—

to bring better education to millions of disadvantaged youth who need it most;

to put the best educational equipment and ideas and innovations within reach of all students;

to advance the technology of teaching and the training of teachers; and

to provide incentives for those who wish to learn at every stage along the road to learning.

Our program must match the magnitude of these tasks. The budget on education which I request for fiscal year 1966 will contain a total of $4.1 billion. This includes $1.1 billion to finance programs established by the 88th Congress. I will submit a request for $1.5 billion in new obligational authority to finance the programs described in this message. This expenditure is a small price to pay for developing our Nation's most priceless resource.

In all that we do, we mean to strengthen our State and community education systems. Federal assistance does not mean Federal control—as past programs have proven. The late Senator Robert Taft declared:

> Education is primarily a State function—but in the field of education, as in the fields of health, relief, and medical care, the Federal Government has a secondary obligation to see that there is a basic floor under those essential services for all adults and children in the United States.

In this spirit, I urge that we now push ahead with the No. 1 business of the American people—the education of our youth in preschools, elementary and secondary schools, and in the colleges and universities.

ON THE TEACHER CORPS (1968)   From *About the Teacher Corps,* pamphlet (Washington, D.C., 1968).

For most of America's children, the schoolroom is a clean, well-lighted place peopled with friends who share the excitement of learning and the stimulation of a well-trained, professional teacher. For most children. But not all. More than one-fifth of America's children go to schools that—because of isolation and inaccessibility, or because of ghetto-bred violence and despair—cannot attract, cannot hold, well-trained teachers. Children at these schools arrive in hand-me-down clothes—undernourished, underprepared, apathetic, often hostile.

Educators know it takes more than professional skill to reach this kind of youngster, more than dedication to tackle these tough teaching assignments. That these children can be reached, can be taught, has been proved time and again by cadres of dedicated, determined professionals. But there aren't enough of them. Far too often the schools these youngsters attend are the last resort for the job-hunting teacher—trained or untrained—who has been turned down elsewhere.

What's a principal to do? He can't get anyone else. Often he can't even get these poorly qualified people. A new Federal program—the Teacher Corps—is trying to find an answer.

With the cooperation of 54 universities and 124 school systems in 28 States, this work-study teacher-training program aims at finding college graduates dedicated to the principle of service, "force-feeding" them special professional skills in an intensive summer program, and speeding them into internship in the schools that need them most.

The Teacher Corps has had 2,000 teacher-interns in the field since June 1966. Across the country they work in teams of five to eight under the supervision of an experienced teacher who is their team leader. As interns they are exposed to every kind of teaching situation—from one-to-one tutorial work with 13-year-olds who are total nonreaders to full responsibility for an advanced placement class; from playground supervision to regular work in classes for the mentally retarded.

While they intern, Corpsmen take courses in ghetto sociology, Appalachian subculture, or Sioux history—depending on where they teach. Evenings and weekends they visit students at home, work in neighborhood Teen Posts, start Blue Bird groups; they go into the community to more fully comprehend their difficult young students.

Every Teacher Corps program is different. Where teams go, what they do, and how they do it is up to the schools that employ them.

Although the Federal Government pays 90 percent of the intern salaries, teacher Corpsmen are employees of the school systems in which they work—they are hired, fired, assigned, or reassigned by the local administrators.

About the Teacher Corps . . .

MEMBERSHIP:

Teacher Corps membership is open to graduates of accredited colleges and Universities as well as specially qualified third- and fourth-year under-graduates. Preference is generally given to applicants without prior teacher training or experience.

Experienced teachers who serve as team leaders to groups of interns should have a master's degree (or its equivalent) plus 5 years' general teaching experience or 3 years' experience teaching disadvantaged youngsters.

SALARY:

Corps interns receive a $75 weekly living allowance plus $15 for each dependent. Full tuition and fees leading to a degree are paid by the Teacher Corps.

Experienced team leaders are paid according to the local salary scale for persons of equivalent education, experience, and responsibility. The Teacher Corps pays up to 90 percent of salary costs.

APPLICATION:

To apply for Teacher Corps service, contact any of the participating colleges, universities, or local school systems; your chief state education officer; see your college placement officer; or write TEACHER CORPS, Washington, D.C. 20202.

Prospective Corps members should list geographic preferences in their applications, and the Teacher Corps will try to honor such requests. Applications sent to Teacher Corps Washington are placed in a national pool from which local project directors select suitable candidates. Final selection and assignment remain with the local school system and the university project director who select or reject Corpsmen for their programs. Applicants may reject any assignment offered them. This does not disqualify them from selection for other programs.

TRAINING:

Training is conducted at colleges and universities across the country. During the 1967—68 academic year 54 colleges and universities served as Teacher Corps training sites. In most cases training centers are located close to a poverty area. Most training programs are administered by the school of education at the participating college or university.

Teacher Corps training is a two-stage process including 8—13 weeks of preservice, or orientation, training at the university followed by 21 months of inservice training in the public schools, poverty community, and at the university.

DEGREES OFFERED:

Most Teacher Corps interns participate in a 2-year graduate program leading to a master's degree, usually in education. A small percentage of training institutions offer other degrees in areas directly related to education—such as educational psychology, urban education, or counseling and guidance—or subject fields such as English, history, or social studies. The majority of schools grant a master's in elementary or secondary education or a master of arts in teaching (M.A.T.).

LENGTH OF SERVICE:

Teacher Corps interns serve for 2 years. An intern cannot extend his service beyond 2 years; however, it is hoped that after Teacher Corps service interns will accept regular teaching assignments in needy schools, and frequently in the very schools in which they have served.

TRANSPORTATION TRAVEL ALLOWANCE:

Corpsmen are responsible for making their own travel arrangements. Provisional Corpsmen receive a flat travel allowance to their preservice training site. They are not authorized to move household goods and dependents at Federal expense at this time. Once a provisional member gains permanent standing, heads of household may move their families, and they will be reimbursed for transportation of household goods and dependents. Anyone deselected at the close of preservice or terminated during inservice will receive a travel allowance. A person who resigns during inservice is not automatically entitled to travel or moving expenses. Corps members receive an appropriate travel allowance at the completion of their 2 years of Teacher Corps service.

Each Corps member is responsible for locating and financing his own housing. Residence in or near the poverty area is preferred.

TRANSFER, RESIGNATION, EARLY TERMINATION:

A Teacher Corpsman can be terminated at any time during his 2 years of service either by local school officials or his training university. All early terminations are subject to review by Teacher Corps Washington. An intern may also resign at any time; however, the Teacher Corps expects Corps members to enter with an honest intention to complete the full 2 years of service. Transfers from one program to another are discouraged except in special cases involving health or hardship. Generally, universities will not accept more than 6 hours of graduate credit earned at some other institution.

MARRIAGE AND PREGNANCY:

Married couples are encouraged to file joint applications for Teacher Corps service though only one person need apply. Applications should be submitted at the same time in a single envelope. If both husband and wife are selected for service, they will be assigned to the same program. Each local school system has its own policy regarding pregnancy and the intern must adhere to the policy of the system in which she is serving.

THE DRAFT:

A Corps member's draft status is, of course, determined by his local draft board. Most Corps members now have 2A occupational deferments as teachers, rather than the 2S deferments abolished in February for new graduate students. However, it must be emphasized that the granting of a 2A deferment for teaching, or any other profession, is a decision made by each local draft board on the basis of "essential community need" and can in no way be guaranteed by the Teacher Corps.

STUDENT LOANS:

The law prohibits Teacher Corps interns from participating in any Federal student loan programs while they are enrolled in the Teacher Corps. Teacher Corps service does not count as teaching-time applied against NDEA loans.

INSURANCE, HEALTH BENEFITS, SOCIAL SECURITY:

Teacher Corpsmen are protected by the Federal Employees Compensation Act, which provides limited compensation for disability and death, medical care, and rehabilitation services for injuries suffered on the job. Most school districts have medical insurance plans in which Corpsmen may participate.

The intern's salary is subject to social security and the local school system's pension plan deductions. Some deductions may be returnable upon leaving the school system.

Projects with special programs serving Spanish-speaking youngsters give preference to applicants who are proficient in Spanish or to applicants willing to undertake intensive language training at Teacher Corps expense.

Programs serving Indian populations would be inclined to select applicants with an interest in the culture and language of the American Indian.

AFTER THE TEACHER CORPS:

The Teacher Corps has a career information service for Corps members who cannot be employed by the school systems in which they have served. This service provides terminating Corps members with information about job opportunities in poverty-area schools around the country.

U.S. COMMISSIONER OF EDUCATION JAMES E. ALLEN NAMES TARGET FOR THE 70's: THE RIGHT TO READ (1969)

From Report of a Hearing Before the General Subcommittee on Education of the U.S. House of Representatives Committee on Education and Labor, *American Education* (December 1969), pp. 2–7.

Chairman Pucinski: Commissioner Allen, we are very pleased to have you here this morning. As you know, our subcommittee has started a series of hearings on the educational needs of elementary and secondary schools for the 70's. . . . We are hopeful that from these hearings can come information and opinions that will give all of us the chance to look down-range the next 10 years to anticipate the problems and the needs of our schools and to do something meaningful about them. It seems to me one of the great problems we have had in education is that we are always chasing the problem instead of anticipating it.

Dr. Allen: Thank you very much, Mr. Chairman and members of the committee. I am delighted for this opportunity to appear before you to discuss matters of very deep concern to our Nation and to all of us in the field of education. . . . We in the Office of Education, Department of Health, Education, and Welfare, are presently working on a statement of goals for the 70's. We would welcome the opportunity to discuss the statement with you when we have completed it.

This morning I would like to bring to your attention one of these problems, so grave in its import for our Nation that it must, in my judgment, receive immediate attention. I refer to our failure in the teaching of reading, a failure that can no longer be tolerated.

In an address two weeks ago before the annual meeting of the National Associaton of State Boards of Education, I called upon the educational and lay leaders of America to join me in a nationwide effort to see to it that by the end of the 1970's no boy or girl shall be leaving our schools without the skill and the desire to read to the full limits of his capability.

Imagine, if you can, what life would be like if you could not read, or if your reading skills were so meager as to limit you to the simplest of writings, and if for

RE-APPRAISAL
1951–1973

3377

you the door to the whole world of knowledge and the inspiration available through the printed word had never opened.

For more than a quarter of our population this is true. For them education, in a very important way, has been a failure, and they stand as a reproach to all of us who hold in our hands the shaping of the opportunity for education. These individuals have been denied a right—a right as fundamental as the right to life, liberty, and the pursuit of happiness—to right to read.

Education has come to mean many things and to encompass a wide range of information and experience, but certainly it must still include, as it did in the beginning, the ability to read. Those who do not gain this ability in the course of their early education lack a skill necessary to all other areas of learning and are being denied a fundamental educational right.

From a variety of statistical information accumulated by the Office of Education regarding reading deficiencies throughout the country, these shocking facts stand out:

1. One out of every four students nationwide has significant reading deficiencies.

2. In large city school systems up to half of the students read below expectation. For example, toward the end of the period during which I was Commissioner of Education in New York, we measured reading in the State and found that 46 percent of the sixth-graders in the City of New York were reading well below minimum State competency level.

3. There are more than 3 million illiterates in our adult population.

4. About half of the unemployed youth, ages 16-21, are functionally illiterate.

5. Three-quarters of the juvenile offenders in New York City are two or more years retarded in reading. I am sure similar statistics would apply to other cities.

6. In a recent U.S. Armed Forces program called Project 100,000, 68.2 percent of the young men fell below grade seven in reading and academic ability.

The tragedy of these statistics is that they represent a barrier to success that for many young adults produces the misery of a life marked by poverty, unemployment, alienation, and, in many cases, crime.

It must be recognized also, however, that for the majority who do not acquire the basic reading skills, there can be another barrier which limits the fulfillment of their right to read. This barrier exists when the skill of reading is not accompanied by the desire to read. We fail, therefore, just as much in assuring the right to read when a student's desire is absent as when his skills are missing.

It is inexcusable that in this day when man has achieved such giant steps in the development of his potential, when many of his accomplishments approach the miraculous, there still should be those who cannot read.

It is my view, therefore, that there is no higher nationwide priority in the field of education than the provision of the right to read for all, and that the Office of Education and the Department of Health, Education, and Welfare can do no greater service for the cause of education than to spearhead a nationwide attack to eliminate this failure of our education effort. It is my belief that *we should immediately set for ourselves the goal of assuring that by the end of the 1970's the right to read shall be a reality for all—that no one shall be leaving our schools without the skill and the desire necessary to read to the full limits of his capability.*

This is education's "moon"—the target for the decade ahead. With the same zeal, dedication, perseverance, concentration, and resources that made possible man's giant step of last July 20, this moon too can be reached.

I chose to set forth this target at the meeting of the National Association of

State Boards of Education because State boards bear the responsibility for shaping basic educational policies for the primary and secondary schools of our Nation. The responsibility for the provision of educational opportunity, traditionally and legally, rests with the States.

The public education system of our Nation has developed on the premise that education belongs to the people and its control shall be in the hands of lay boards. It is State boards, therefore, and State education agencies that have the original responsibility and authority, within the framework established by their respective legislatures, for the setting and enforcement of standards, and for the evaluation of performance. It is they also who must be accountable for educational stewardship within their respective States. They are at the center of any effort to raise the level of achievement of our educational system.

In asking State boards of education to accept the obligation of ensuring that every child in our Nation will learn to read, I have requested that each State begin immediately to consider how this goal can be achieved, to assemble resources, to plan, and to report to me what actions have been taken under State leadership so that the school year 1969–70 can be recorded as the year when we set in motion the nationwide effort that will erase this intolerable deficit in American education.

State boards are, of course, not alone in this responsibility, for it falls also upon all those who participate in the administration and operation of the educational enterprise. Therefore, in presenting the challenge of this target to State school boards I am also presenting it to groups such as the Education Commission of the States, the Council of Chief State School Officers, State education departments, local school boards and their staffs, the American Association of School Administrators, the National Education Association and the American Federation of Teachers and their State and local affiliates, the National Congress of Parents and Teachers, students and their organizations—indeed, to all individuals and organizations comprising the total educational endeavor of our Nation.

Essential also, of course, will be the intensive participation of the colleges and universities and their schools of teacher education.

But to hit the target by the end of the 70's, to achieve a goal of such enormous dimensions, involvement will have to reach far beyond the forces of education. Necessary will be the committed participation and support of the Congress; State and local political leaders and legislative bodies; business, industry, and labor; civic and community groups; publishers; advertising organizations (if advertising agencies can sell soap, they can sell reading); television, radio, and the press; research and scientific organizations; foundations; the entertainment industry; the sports world; and, perhaps most essential of all, the understanding and support of an enlightened and enthusiastic public.

In other words, *I am calling for a total national commitment to and involvement in the achievement of the "right to read" goal.*

While the main task of carrying out the activities necessary to achieve the goal of the right to read for all by the end of the 70's will fall upon the States and localities, the Federal Government has a vital supportive role to play. It is not the role of the Federal Government to make specific plans or to prescribe the programs and methods to be used. The diverse needs and conditions of the various States and their communities require the flexibility of approach that our decentralized system makes possible.

The main contribution *that can be made at the Federal level* will be the coordination of the effort, the marshalling of forces and resources on a nationwide basis, and the provision of the technical, administrative, and financial assistance required, all done in a spirit of total and fervent commitment.

Some significant steps already have been taken by the Office of Education that will have impact on our national "right to read" goal. We are focusing a significant portion of our research and development resources on the reading problem. These efforts can be divided into five major sets of activities.

One emerging long-range effort for which we have high hopes is the application of planning procedures developed in the National Cancer Institute, the purpose of which is to concentrate an attack on a specific problem. This convergence technique is now being used to develop a clear map of what is known about the process of reading. This map will provide us with a guide for targeting research dollars toward a greater understanding of the reading process.

A second research project will focus in fiscal year 1970 on the development of operational models for bilingual learning with particular emphasis on Mexican-American and inner-city children.

A third approach to reading is found in the Children's Television Workshop supported by the Office of Education in cooperation with private foundations and other Federal agencies. This project is aimed at developing cognitive skills in preschool children with the emphasis on language development and prereading skills.

The fourth and fifth major program efforts in reading and language development are to be found in the regional educational laboratories, the National Laboratory on Early Childhood Education, and the Office of Education-supported research and development centers. More than 40 percent of the activities of these institutions is devoted to research and development on language learning and other basic skills areas. The laboratories are currently working on 11 different kinds of instructional systems designed to aid all elementary school students, but particularly disadvantaged young people in the mastery of basic reading, writing, listening, quantitative and problem-solving skills.

The total Office of Education investment in fiscal year 1970 for all of these programs is over $16 million.

The decade of the 70's will see the 200th anniversary of our Nation. A most appropriate celebration, a celebration that would honor the spirit of the democratic concept and recognize the fundamental importance described to education from the beginning our our Nation would be to secure for all of our citizens that right to read which so long ago made possible the feasibility of a democratic society and continues to undergird its strength.

The importance which is attached to this goal by the Administration is highlighted by the announcement that Mrs. Richard M. Nixon, our Nation's First Lady, would serve as Honorary Chairman of a Nationwide Citizens' Committee on the Right to Read, which will lead this effort. I am most grateful that Mrs. Nixon, a devoted mother and former teacher, has accepted leadership for which I consider to be one of the most significant efforts in the improvement of our country's schools.

Continuing toleration of the failure to give everyone the ability to read breaks faith with the commitment to equality of opportunity which is the foundation of our public education system. Having arrived at a time that holds forth the possibility of eliminating this failure, we must, in all justice, seize the opportunity with the utmost vigor and determination.

Remarkable success has been achieved by our educational system, but so long as there is one boy or girl who leaves school unable to read to the full extent of his capability, we cannot escape the charge of failure in carrying out the responsibility entrusted to us.

We are currently planning how to mount this effort on a nationwide basis. There will be some little time before this program is completed, but I hope before long to be able to announce other steps that are being undertaken or being planned at the national level to assist the States and localities in helping to overcome this deficiency.

The Honorable Augustus F. Hawkins: Just who is involved in this commitment? . . . are you speaking for the Administration in making this national commitment?

Dr. Allen: I am speaking for the Administration. We hope, of course, we are going to be able to solicit the support of all segments of our society in this effort. I don't look upon this by any means solely as a Federal project. . . .

Mr. Hawkins: In the fiscal 1970 recommendations for the Office of Education the Administration reduced the Department's operating level budget by approximately $374,517,000. Do you agree with that reduction in the operational level? In what way does this square with the national commitment to help people read?

Dr. Allen: If we cannot cut back inflationary trends then the kinds of monies that ought to be put into education will not bring the kinds of results that we should expect. . . . I think for the time being we are under some constraints. The budget has been developed with emphasis on the disadvantaged, insofar as can be provided within these constraints. It is my hope that we can use the funds available to us at the Federal and State levels to reorder the priorities wherever possible to concentrate on this very basic area, on this number one priority, as I look upon it, of an educational system.

Mr. Hawkins: In what specific way is the commitment to be implemented?

Dr. Allen: We are going to implement it by asking the States and localities to give special attention to the field of reading, by asking labor, industry, business, and other parts of society to help support this effort . . . we are taking a look at the various Federal funds—and they are very considerable at the present time—that can be used to help reading and the teaching of reading, to see ways in which we can point these even more toward this effort, within the purpose for which these funds have been allocated or appropriated. . . .

Indeed, I am not saying at the moment there will be need for more Federal funds to do this job. We are spending $45 to $50 billion in Federal, State, and local funds in American education right now for the elementary and secondary schools. I want to make certain that these funds are going to reach this basic problem of reading, to eliminate this weakness in our educational system. I think that one of the things we can do is point up the importance of this and encourage school boards and others to give special attention to it.

Chairman Pucinski: If I understand your statement correctly, Mr. Commissioner, you hope to place a greater emphasis in title I on the verbal skills. . . . Is that correct? Is that an example of how you intend to redirect present Federal programs in order to achieve this reading goal?

Dr. Allen: That is right.

The Honorable William D. Hathaway: . . . We should have some uniform professional opinion on reading through research before we go out and start getting the school to go ahead with it. The present state of research just last year was that there was still a tossup whether the sight reading or phonic reading method was better.

Dr. Allen: There is a controversy over the subject of teaching reading. I don't want to get involved in that because I think the teacher in the local community must decide what system works best for the children in his care.

. . . Let me add one other point here concerning why I have felt it is important to urge the Nation to get behind this goal. There is a lack of confidence on the part of a great many people in this country in the ability of the public schools to do the job that needs to be done. . . . We in education talk in terms of compensatory education; we talk in terms of a lot of language which we understand and which may mean something to us but doesn't mean very much to the people on the street. I have a hope that the subject of reading is such that we can get support and enthusiasm for it. It is something we can measure. Each year we can show a parent whether or not his child is learning to read better.

I think we can help to restore confidence in the ability of the public school system to teach, particularly to teach the disadvantaged. I hope we can gain support to the extent that the current trend toward voting down of bond issues, voting down of budgets, and slowness of voting educational support at all levels will be changed, and there will be a feeling of confidence on the part of the public that we can do the job that we are saying we are prepared to do.

PRESIDENT RICHARD NIXON'S PROPOSAL FOR A HIGHER EDUCATION OPPORTUNITY ACT (1970) From *Chronicle of Higher Education,* vol. IV, pp. 1–4.

No qualified student who wants to go to college should be barred by lack of money. That has long been a great American goal; I propose that we achieve it now.

Something is basically unequal about opportunity for higher education when a young person whose family earns more than $15,000 a year is nine times more likely to attend college than a young person whose family earns less than $3,000.

Something is basically wrong with federal policy toward higher education when it has failed to correct this inequity, and when government programs spending $5.3-billion yearly have largely been disjointed, ill-directed, and without a coherent long-range plan.

Something is wrong with our higher education policy when—on the threshold of a decade in which enrollments will increase almost 50 per cent—not nearly enough attention is focused on the two-year community colleges so important to the careers of so many young people.

Something is wrong with higher education itself when curricula are often irrelevant, structure is often outmoded, when there is an imbalance between teaching and research and too often an indifference to innovation.

To help right these wrongs, and to spur reform and innovation throughout higher education in America today, I am sending to the Congress my proposed Higher Education Opportunity Act of 1970.

In this legislation, I propose that we expand and revamp student aid so that it places more emphasis on helping low-income students than it does today.

I propose to create the National Student Loan Association to enable all students to obtain government-guaranteed loans, increasing the pool of resources available for this purpose by over one billion dollars in its first year of operation, with increasing aid in future years.

I propose to create a career education program funded at $100-million in fiscal

1972 to assist states and institutions in meeting the additional costs of starting new programs to teach critically-needed skills in community colleges and technical institutes.

I propose to establish a National Foundation for Higher Education to make grants to support excellence, innovation, and reform in private and public institutions. In its first year, this would be funded at $200-million.

There is much to be proud of in our system of higher education. Twenty-five years ago, two Americans in ten of college age went to college; today, nearly five out of ten go on to college; by 1976, we expect seven out of ten to further their education beyond secondary school.

This system teaching 7-million students now employs more than half a million instructors and professors and spends approximately $23-billion a year. In its most visible form, the end result of this system contributes strongly to the highest standard of living on earth, indeed the highest in history.

One of the discoveries of economists in recent years is the extraordinary, in truth the dominant, role which investment in human beings plays in economic growth. But the more profound influence of education has been in the shaping of the American democracy and the quality of life of the American people.

The impressive record compiled by a dedicated educational community stands in contrast to some grave shortcomings in our post-secondary educational system in general and to the federal share of it in particular.

• Federal student loan programs have helped millions to finance higher education; yet the available resources have never been focused on the neediest students.

• The rapidly rising cost of higher education has created serious financial problems for colleges, and especially threatens the stability of private institutions.

• Too many people have fallen prey to the myth that a four-year, liberal-arts diploma is essential to a full and rewarding life, whereas in fact other forms of post-secondary education—such as a two-year community college or technical training course—are far better suited to the interests of many young people.

• The turmoil on the nation's campuses is a symbol of the urgent need for reform in curriculum, teaching, student participation, discipline, and governance in our post-secondary institutions.

• The workings of the credit markets, particularly in periods of tight money, have hampered the ability of students to borrow for their education, even when those loans are guaranteed by the federal government.

• The federal involvement in higher education has grown in a random and haphazard manner, failing to produce an agency that can support innovation and reform.

We are entering an era when concern for the quality of American life requires that we organize our programs and our policies in ways that enhance that quality and open opportunities for all.

No element of our national life is more worthy of our attention, our support, and our concern than higher education. For no element has greater impact on the careers, the personal growth, and the happiness of so many of our citizens. And no element is of greater importance in providing the knowledge and leadership on which the vitality of our democracy and the strength of our economy depends.

This Administration's program for higher education springs from several deep convictions:

• Equal educational opportunity, which has long been a goal, must now become a reality for every young person in the United States, whatever his economic circumstances.

• Institutional autonomy and academic freedom should be strengthened by federal support, never threatened with federal domination.

• Individual student aid should be given in ways that fulfill each person's capacity to choose the kind of quality education most suited to him, thereby making institutions more responsive to student needs.

• Support should complement rather than supplant additional and continuing help from all other sources.

• Diversity must be encouraged, both between institutions and within each institution.

• Basic reforms in institutional organization, business management, governance, instruction, and academic programs are long overdue.

Aside from veterans' programs and social security benefits, the federal government provides aid to students through four large programs: the educational opportunity grants, college work-study grants, National Defense student loans, and guaranteed student loans.

In fiscal 1970 these programs provided an estimated $577-million in federal funds to a total of 1.6-million individual students. For fiscal 1971, I have recommended a 10 per cent increase in these programs, to $633-million, for today's students must not be penalized while the process of reform goes on. But reform is needed.

Although designed to equalize educational opportunity, the programs of the past fail to aid large numbers of low-income students.

With the passage of this legislation, every low-income student entering an accredited college would be eligible for a combination of federal grants and subsidized loans sufficient to give him the same ability to pay as a student from a family earning $10,000.

With the passage of this legislation, every qualified student would be able to augment his own resources with federally-guaranteed loans, but federal subsidies would be directed to students who need them most.

Under this plan, every student from a family below the $10,000 income level—nearly 40 per cent of all students presently enrolled—would be eligible for federal aid. When augmented by earnings, help from parents, market-rate loans, or other public or private scholarship aid, this aid would be enough to assure him the education that he seeks.

The Secretary of Health, Education, and Welfare would annually determine the formula that would most fairly allocate available federal resources to qualified low-income students. Because subsidized loans multiply the available resources, and because the lowest-income students would receive more than those from families with incomes near $10,000, the effect would be a near-doubling of actual assistance available to most students with family incomes below $7,500.

If all eligible students from families with an annual income of $4,500 had received grants and subsidized loans under the existing student aid programs, they would have received an average of $215 each. Under our proposal, all eligible students from families of $4,500 annual income would be guaranteed a total of $1,300 each in grants and subsidized loans. This would constitute the financing floor; it will be supplemented by earnings, other scholarships, and access to unsubsidized loans.

The Higher Education Opportunity Act of 1970 would strongly improve the ability of both educational and financial institutions to make student loans. Although most students today are eligible for guaranteed student loans, many cannot obtain them. Because virtually all guaranteed loans are made by banks, a student is forced to assemble his financial aid package at two or more institutions—his bank and his college—and colleges are denied the ability to oversee the entire financial aid arrangements of their own students.

In order to provide the necessary liquidity in the student loan credit market, I am asking the Congress to charter a National Student Loan Association. This institution would play substantially the same role in student loans that the Federal National Mortgage Association plays in home loans.

The corporation would raise its initial capital through the sale of stock to foundations, colleges, and financial institutions. It would issue its own securities—education bonds—which would be backed by a federal guarantee. These securities would attract additional funds from sources that are not now participating in the student loan program.

The corporation would be able to buy and sell student loans made by qualified lenders—including colleges as well as financial institutions. This would serve to make more money available for the student loan program, and it would do so at no additional cost to the government.

The Secretary of Health, Education, and Welfare, in consultation with the Secretary of the Treasury, would set an annual ceiling on these transactions. In fiscal 1972, I estimate that the NSLA would buy up to $2-billion in student loan paper.

Expanding credit in this manner would make it possible to terminate the payments now made to banks to induce them to make student loans in this tight money market. We would let the interest rates on these loans go to a market rate but the presence of the federal guarantee would assure that this rate would result in one- to two-per cent interest reduction for each student.

By removing the minimum repayment period we would not only enable students to pay back loans as quickly as they wish but we would make it possible for students to refinance their loans as soon as interest rates are lower.

We would continue to relieve all students of interest payments while they are in college but would defer rather than totally forgive those payments. This would be more than compensated for by extending the maximum repayment period from 10 to 20 years, easing the burden of repaying a student loan until the borrower is well out of school and earning a good income.

The added funds made available from these changes, which should exceed one-half billion dollars by 1975, would be redirected to aid for lower-income students.

By increasing the maximum annual individual loans from $1,500 to $2,500, we would enhance the student's ability to avail himself of an education at any institution that will admit him.

Thus, the ability of all students to obtain loans would be increased, and the ability to borrow would be strongly increased for students from low-income families. The financial base of post-secondary education would be correspondingly strengthened. It is significant that this would be done at no cost to the federal taxpayer.

A traditional four-year college program is not suited to everyone. We should come to realize that a traditional diploma is not the exclusive symbol of an educated human being, and that "education" can be defined only in terms of the fulfillment, the enrichment, and the wisdom that it brings to an individual. Our young people are not sheep to be regimented by the need for a certain type of status-bearing sheepskin.

Throughout this message, I use the term "college" to define all post-secondary education—including vocational schools, four-year colleges, junior and community colleges, universities, and graduate schools.

Any serious commitment to equal educational opportunity means a commitment to providing the right kind of education for an individual.

● A young person graduating from high school in one of the states that lacks an extensive public junior college system—more commonly and appropriately known as community colleges—today has little opportunity to avail himself of this immensely valuable but economical type of post-secondary education.

● A youth completing 12th grade in a city without an accessible technical institute is now deprived of a chance for many important kinds of training.

● A 40-year-old woman with grown children who wants to return to school on a part-time basis, possibly to prepare for a new and rewarding career of her own, today may find no institution that meets her needs or may lack the means to pay for it.

We must act now to deal with these kinds of needs. Two-year community colleges and technical institutes hold great promise for giving the kind of education which leads to good jobs and also for filling national shortages in critical-skill occupations.

Costs for these schools are relatively low, especially since there are few residential construction needs. A dollar spent on community colleges is probably spent as effectively as anywhere in the educational world.

These colleges, moreover, have helped many communities forge a new identity. They serve as a meeting ground for young and old, black and white, rich and poor, farmer and technician. They avoid the isolation, alienation, and lack of reality that many young people find in multiversities or campuses far away from their own community.

At the same time, critical manpower shortages exist in the United States in many skilled occupational fields such as police and fire science, environmental technology, and medical para-professionals. Community colleges and similar institutions have the potential to provide programs to train persons in these manpower-deficient fields. Special training like this typically costs more than general education and requires outside support.

Accordingly, I have proposed that Congress establish a career education program, to be funded at $100-million in fiscal 1972.

The purpose of this program is to assist states and colleges in meeting the additional costs of starting career education programs in critical skill areas in community and junior colleges and technical institutes. The Department of Health, Education, and Welfare would provide formula grants to the states, to help them meet a large part of the costs of equipping and running such programs, in critical-skill areas as defined by the Secretary of Labor.

One of the unique achievements of American higher education in the past century has been the standard of excellence that its leading institutions have set. The most serious threat posed by the present fiscal plight of higher education is the

possible loss of that excellence.

But the crisis in higher education at this time is more than simply one of finances. It has to do with the uses to which the resources of higher education are put, as well as to the amount of those resources, and it is past time the federal

government acknowledged its own responsibility for bringing about, through the forms of support it has given and the conditions of that support, a serious distortion of the activities of our centers of academic excellence.

For three decades now the federal government has been hiring universities to do work it wanted done. In far the greatest measure, this work has been in the national interest, and the nation is in the debt of those universities that have so brilliantly performed it. But the time has come for the federal government to help academic communities to pursue excellence and reform in fields of their own choosing as well, and by means of their own choice.

Educational excellence includes the state college experimenting with dramatically different courses of study, the community college mounting an outstanding program of technical education, the predominantly black college educating future leaders, the university turning toward new programs in ecology or oceanography, education, or public administration.

Educational excellence is intimately bound up with innovation and reform. It is a difficult concept, for two institutions with similar ideas may mysteriously result in one superb educational program and one educational dead end. It is an especially difficult concept for a federal agency, which is expected to be even-handed in the distribution of its resources to all comers.

And yet, over the past two decades, the National Science Foundation has promoted excellence in American science, and the National Institutes of Health has promoted excellence in American medical research.

Outside of science, however, there is no substantial federal source for assistance for an institution wishing to experiment or reform. There is a heightened need in American higher education for some source for such support.

To meet this need, I have proposed the creation by Congress of a National Foundation for Higher Education. It would have three principal purposes:

• To provide a source of funds for the support of excellence, new ideas, and reform in higher education, which could be given out on the basis of the quality of the institutions and programs concerned.

• To strengthen colleges and universities or courses of instruction that play a uniquely valuable role in American higher education or that are faced with special difficulties.

• To provide an organization concerned, on the highest level, with the development of national policy in higher education.

There is a need to stimulate more efficient and less expensive administration, by better management of financial resources that can reduce capital investment needs, and the use of school facilities year-round. There is also need for better, more useful curricula, while developing a new dimension of adult education.

There is a need to give students far greater opportunities to explore career direction through linking education with the world of work.

There is a need to develop avenues for genuine and responsible student participation in the university. Colleges of today and tomorrow must increase communications and participation between the administration and students, between faculty and students, where they are presently faulty, weak, or non-existent.

The National Foundation for Higher Education would be organized with a semi-autonomous board and director appointed by the President. It would make grants to individual institutions, to states and communities, and to public and private agencies. Its grants would emphasize innovative programs and would be limited to five years each.

A number of small, categorical programs presently located in the Department of Health, Education, and Welfare would be transferred to the foundation. In addition to the more than $50-million now being spent in those programs, $150-million would be requested for the foundation in fiscal 1972. Beginning with this $200-million budget, this foundation would have the capacity to make a major impact on American higher education.

From the earliest times higher education has been a special concern of the national government.

A year ago I asserted two principles which would guide the relations of the federal government to the students and faculties and institutions of higher education in the nation:

"First, the universities and colleges are places of excellence in which men are judged by achievement and merit in defined areas. . . . Second, . . . that violence or the threat of violence may never be permitted to influence the actions or judgments of the university community."

I stated then, and I repeat now, that while outside influences, such as the federal government, can act in such a way as to threaten those principles, there is relatively little they can do to guarantee them.

This is a matter not always understood. No one can be forced to be free. If a university community acts in such a way as to intimidate the free expression of opinion on the part of its own members, or free access to university functions, or free movement within the community, no outside force can do much about this. For to intervene to impose freedom, is by definition to suppress it.

For that reason I have repeatedly resisted efforts to attach detailed requirements on such matters as student discipline to programs of higher education. In the first place they won't work, and if they did work they would in that very process destroy what they nominally seek to preserve.

As we enter a new decade, we have a rare opportunity to review and reform the federal role in post-secondary education. Most of the basic legislation that now defines the federal role will expire in the next 15 months. The easy approach would be simply to ask the Congress to extend these old programs. But the need for reform in higher education is so urgent that I am asking the Congress for a thoroughgoing overhaul of federal programs in higher education.

The Higher Education Opportunity Act of 1970 would accomplish this purpose. In addition, it would consolidate and modernize a number of other federal programs that affect higher education. Through it, I propose to systematize and rationalize the federal government's role in higher education for the first time.

In setting such an ambitious goal, we must also arouse the nation to a new awareness of its cost, and make clear that it must be borne by state, local, and private sources as well as by federal funds. In fiscal year 1972, I anticipate that the new programs authorized by the Higher Education Opportunity Act alone will cost $400-million more than the federal government is presently spending for post-secondary education. If our goal is to be attained, there must be comparable growth in the investment of other public and private agencies.

The time has come for a renewed national commitment to post-secondary education and especially to its reform and revitalization. We must join with our creative and demanding young people to build a system of higher education worthy of the ideals of the people in it.

RICHARD NIXON

3388   THE WHITE HOUSE, March 19, 1970

THE NATIONAL INSTITUTE OF EDUCATION (1971) From Sidney P. Marland, "A New Order of Educational Research And Development," *Phi Delta Kappan* (June, 1971), pp. 576–79.

A recent witness at a House subcommittee hearing on the National Institute of Education expressed his conviction that federally sponsored educational research and development would be far more productive if it were removed from Office of Education jurisdiction and placed in the NIE. In a federal agency such as the USOE, he reasoned, interests change from commissioner to commissioner; and experimental failure, the quintessence of the research route to invention, tends to become unacceptable in the vagaries of bureaucratic life.

I am not persuaded that the Office of Education sheds more darkness than light in the land, and yet I agree with his point. If educational research and development is going to be the success it really must be in this country, then it cannot exist in the compromised anonymity of the conventional federal bureaucracy. The time has clearly come, as President Nixon proposes, to establish a focus for educational research and experimentation in the United States. To achieve a genuine impact on education's problems, we must create the setting and the atmosphere in which the crucial and delicate work of research and development can thrive, funded generously, isolated from political and administrative whim, and dedicated to one purpose alone—the discovery and application of new alternatives in education.

First, the National Institute of Education will be a separate agency within HEW, detached from the office of Education. It will report through the Commissioner of Education to the Secretary of HEW. The NIE will be responsible for the planning and direction of research and development at all levels of schooling, while the USOE will administer operational programs, as it does now. The USOE will, furthermore, be strongly linked with the NIE for the necessary input of ideas and needs, and for the follow-up dissemination of NIE products.

The director of the institute will be a presidential appointee, according the position the status to recruit a national figure, commanding the respect to attract the very best scientists, educational practitioners, public administrators, and others essential to the high importance of the NIE. Above all, the NIE's director must be capable of developing solutions to pressing educational problems. He need not be overly concerned with administration and congressional relations because these are areas in which the Secretary of HEW and the Commissioner of Education can play a strong supportive role for the NIE without cluttering its affairs with unnecessary governmental restraints.

The director will be assisted by a National Advisory Council on Research and Development. The council will be involved in setting general policy for the NIE and in coordinating its efforts with outside agencies such as the National Science Foundation, the Office of Economic Opportunity, the National Institute of Mental Health, the Office of Child Development, and so on. Some personnel would rotate from the NIE to the Office of Education and back again to maintain close cooperation between the two sister agencies, bringing real-world experience to NIE planning and a high level of knowledge and motivation to the operations of the USOE.

At least two kinds of functioning groups will exist within the institute—task forces addressing major problems, and study groups seeking to understand the nature of the processes of education at a deeper level. Both will consist of permanent NIE staff people, plus outside consultants and short-term fellows of the institute.

Two parallel efforts will supplement the task forces and study groups—an intramural program of research and development, and a researcher-training program operating through institutes, fellowships, and training contracts.

However the staff is organized, certain personnel patterns characteristic of learning research and development agencies will emerge. These distinctive patterns will be made possible in large part by the NIE's authority to hire and compensate technical and professional staff exempt from civil service classification and compensation regulations. This authority, I should stress, will only apply when there is a specific reason to use it; hence very likely many of the staff members will be hired under the civil service system. The special authority is not likely to be used for those engaged in support functions for the agency, such as budget, personnel, and contracts.

The concept of civil service exemption authority builds upon the experience of other successful research and development institutions, such as the National Science Foundation and the National Institutes of Health. As these agencies have found, drawing the highest quality staff for research and development requires staffing patterns and compensation levels specially adapted to the career patterns and professional traditions of the scholarly community. Exemption permits, for example, a system of short-term, noncareer appointments. Distinguished academicians and educators whose permanent career commitment is to a university, school system, or industry could join the NIE staff for even shorter periods to work on a single project. In addition, the authority would permit streamlined hiring procedures particularly suited for short-term, high-level personnel.

With flexibility in recruiting and the ability to pay salaries commensurate with the type of talent that is sought, we hope to attract to the NIE the most significant names in education. But beyond our distinguished colleagues in education, we would also expect to attract their counterparts from many other disciplines such as sociology, biochemistry, psychiatry, medicine, anthropology, and so on.

What will these scholars and academicians do at the NIE? This question is presently absorbing the attention of a good many thinkers and planners, and we feel a broad pattern of priorities is emerging from these deliberations, the principal areas to which the fully functioning NIE will address its organized talents.

Let me stress that such speculation in no way implies limiting the scope of the organization. In truth, as we envision the NIE, the entire universe of educational concerns will be its concern. The NIE will have the range of capabilities required to match the wonderfully varied, endlessly changing, hundred-sided activities of education. It will deal with concrete problems such as education of the disadvantaged, career education, and higher education. But the men and women of the NIE will not be harnessed to immediacy; their purpose will be as broad as the very nature of learning itself. They will look deeply into the learning process in all its physical, biological, and psychological aspects, to explore in an unfettered atmosphere of pure investigation the far reaches of man's capacity to create knowledge and transmit it. The knowledge base upon which education now rests, our ablest scholars agree, is still in its infancy. We propose to increase it systematically.

More concretely, I would like to sketch for you briefly some of the objectives and plans we have in mind in establishing the institute.

First, it will seek new knowledge and new insights into educational experience. It will do basic research into the learning process in all its sociological and physiological variables. We will want to undertake studies that may not lead to immediate changes in practice, such as the examination of the effects of chemical stimulation upon learning, as well as studies that are likely immediately to influence present policy and practice. The institute will certainly be concerned with increasing the productivity of teachers; it will look for ways to utilize technology to enhance the teacher's life; it will look for ways to make education available and deliverable to all who want it, whatever their circumstances.

Second, the NIE will seek useful alternatives in educational practice in order to offer the people of this country a far wider range of new procedures, new operations, and new products than they presently enjoy. One choice in anything is simply not enough. An elementary school curriculum that works perfectly well in Boston, for example, could be wholly incorrect, ineffective, and perhaps even damaging in San Antonio, Texas. And we must recognize in our schools, at every level, that there is no single ladder for individual fulfillment and success. If boys who love to fix cars are becoming unhappy office managers, somebody is wasting money, talent, and happiness—precious commodities that we waste at our individual and collective peril. We have much to learn about human needs and the capacity of our institutions of learning to help their individuals meet those needs.

Administrative and management issues and problems will be apt topics for the NIE's investigation as we try to establish closer ties between the costs of education and its beneficiaries. For example, we could conceivably develop and extend to the entire nation a plan such as the one Ohio State University will soon begin operating in which students will be allowed to pay for college out of the future earnings of all students. Or perhaps business and industry could assume a specific new tax for higher education, a talent tax that corresponds to the number of college graduates annually engaged.

Third, we see the institute strengthening the nation's research and development capability through the stimulation and training of new scholars. The new respectability of educational research will, I believe, greatly increase the number of competent professional persons engaged in the field. Even in the unlikely event of Congress's appropriating a billion dollars this year for educational research and development, expenditure of such a huge sum, while compatible with other fields of research, might actually cause more harm than good because there are not enough competent people to do the work at this level of investment. And even if we were able to collect together all the talented people in this country who would like nothing better than to work for the improvement of education, we have neither the organization nor the network of communications to absorb their efforts fruitfully.

The NIE will take the responsibility for coordinating educational research and development efforts throughout the entire federal government, as well as for providing general leadership and support to training now taking place within universities and laboratories. The institute will also administer grants, institutes, and fellowships as methods of supporting and encouraging the growth of competence in people committed to educational research and development.

Fourth, the institute will undertake the invention and perfection of ways to deliver educational innovations we know are successful. Whatever sort of breakthrough we achieve in teaching and learning, it will be useless unless it is linked with a system for delivery that works. That is why I maintain that the NIE holds the genius of that central system, flowing collegially, constructively, and systematically through the education network into the classrooms of America. Systematizing the art and science of teaching is one of the principal reasons for the NIE. The art and science of teaching are very human things, changing with the people affected and with the time and place. The NIE must be, more than ordinarily, a humane institution.

We know there are many sound innovations in education, methods that have proved their effectiveness over and over again. I refer to such techniques as peer tutoring, individual progress programs, and the use of paraprofessionals in the classroom. But we also know that too many school systems are skilled at protecting themselves from the invasion of good ideas and as a consequence, good techniques such as those I just alluded to—and many more—are serving only a fraction of the school children of this nation, illuminating only a fraction of the darkness.

The NIE's dissemination efforts will build upon and utilize the facilities and experience of the National Center for Educational Communication, the Office of Education's dissemination arm, and other delivery systems. Parallel with the growth of the NIE, I see a reshaping of the total commitment of the Office of Education to accelerating nationwide use of tested educational improvements resulting from NIE and other efforts. We can no longer accept a situation in which we can deliver a new mouthwash to 200 million Americans in a matter of weeks while a new system of education to freshen the quality of our minds moves with glacial inperceptibility. The dissemination of the NIE's products and processes is one of the principal reasons for the close articulation with the USOE and its vast human network of states, local systems, and classrooms.

To summarize our thinking about the role of the NIE, we believe that the lion's share of the agency's budget would be devoted to mobilizing the ablest scholars and directing their talents to comprehensive research and development programs seeking solutions to education's most serious problems. Some of these solutions will build on the best current techniques—and many will probe radically new approaches to learning. All will lean heavily on development and on the invention of effective means of translating ideas into readily deliverable materials and practices which are workable—and working—in the field. The institute's independent, creative atmosphere and flexible organization will enable its staff to take a hard look at the common assumptions and hallowed traditions of the profession and expose us to ourselves where we are found wanting, suggesting solutions.

Teams of people with different expertise—research and development personnel, educators, teachers, public officials, engineers, economists, statisticians, artists—will be organized around basic problems. They will plan research and development programs designed to yield new knowledge, materials, and methods and coordinated to provide powerful leverage on each problem. For example, finding successful approaches to educating the disadvantaged might mean supporting a range of projects from basic language studies to designing alternatives to formal schooling for alienated ghetto teen-agers.

As many of you know, when I became commissioner in December several new staff members joined me in the Office of Education. Among them is Harry Silberman, director of the National Center for Educational Research and Development, the Office of Education's present research operation. A principal concern of his has been to reorganize the NCERD in preparation for transfer of most of its functions to the institute while continuing to operate the USOE research and development effort until the NIE becomes a reality. Silberman is already assembling able and lively people to reinforce the NCERD-NIE component during this period of development.

The NIE must be responsive to the Office of Education's role in serving American education broadly. The Office of Education, for its part, must be in a position to help formulate the questions the NIE would address. Further, the USOE must strengthen and expand the delivery system for promoting implementation of the practical results of educational research and development in the field. There is a large new role for the USOE in this context which I call leadership and some call technical assistance. Stated simply, it is that a new idea will be delivered and sustained not only by memoranda and journal articles but by people on call.

To summarize, the NIE would assume most activities now conducted by the National Center for Educational Research and Development. The NIE would become responsible for programs in basic research, ongoing development activities, the research and development centers and regional education laboratories, research training, and construction of research and development facilities.

The Office of Education would retain its responsibility for evaluation and policy-oriented research relating to USOE programs and the gathering and dissemination of statistics. While the NIE would be charged with designing new delivery systems for research products, the USOE would oversee demonstration and dissemination activities and support and deploy whatever new system the NIE might develop.

We look to the NIE to bridge the education and related research and development activities of all federal agencies, activities largely unconnected at the moment. The NIE would act as a clearinghouse for information on relevant programs and provide an intellectual meeting ground where personnel of various government agencies can reason together about educational problems, supporting each other, avoiding duplication and cross-purposes. For example, extraordinary institutional materials have been developed by the Department of Defense. No systematic arrangement exists for their adaptation and articulation in the school systems of the country.

Before closing, I would like to touch briefly on the projected relationship between the institute and another Administration initiative, the National Foundation for Higher Education. These instruments, while very different, have been confused in the minds of some, perhaps because they are both being advanced in legislation at the same time.

In the broadest sense, the foundation will be a new federal vehicle to help higher education reform itself and renew itself and to help it cope with the realities of increasing enrollment, new social expectation, and accelerating technological change. It will be a device to help colleges and universities decide rationally what they want to become and, when they have organized their plans, to provide seed money to help get them under way.

The need for institutional change is forcefully argued in the recently released Newman Report on Higher Education. It states, "The system [of higher education], with its massive inertia, resists fundamental changes, rarely eliminates outmoded programs, ignores the differing needs of students, seldom questions its educational goals, and almost never creates new and different types of institutions." While I do not go along with all of these generalizations as applying to all higher education, the issue is drawn for everyone to consider.

The foundation, we believe, will help turn that situation around by providing aid to develop new kinds of institutions as well as to strengthen those we already have, and by working toward development of a national policy for higher education. While the NIE devises and tests new educational methods at all levels of instruction as a research body, the foundation will encourage the demonstration and adoption of promising practices in higher education that we already know about but haven't fully applied. It will indeed be a foundation, not a research activity. The NIE will deal with broadly based problems and practices, at all levels of education, while the foundation will target on the needs and issues of higher education alone.

The same coordination mechanisms linking the NIE to the Office of Education—boards of directors, staff exchanges, and reporting through the commission—would join the NIE to the foundation.

The great problems of education have a peculiar endurance. Ignorance lives on today, as it has throughout recorded history, in companionship with learning. The nonreader on the lower East Side of New York City is but the newest recruit to that tragic fraternity, and the child who rejects our educational offerings and consequently cannot benefit from them is very nearly as commonplace as the child who flowers and flourishes to the fullest under education's benefits. And to these antique conundrums of society must be added year after year the pressures and problems unique to our time and place in history and to society's ever-rising expectations. One thinks of drugs, environment, and changing career demands, to name a few.

And yet, I think there is a difference today from, say, 25 years ago or perhaps even 10 years. There is a far wider perception and a deeper understanding of our problems as being detrimental not simply to an individual boy or girl who cannot read, but to an entire nation whose nonreaders and other deprived members constitute a menacing subculture undermining and mocking the security and progress of the rest, and challenging most profoundly our ideals of justice and opportunity for all. This condition gnaws at the conscience of the "successful" more than ever before.

For many reasons, then, practical as well as idealistic, we have begun to attack our educational problems and to probe our educational potential. Our approach is impassioned, as the search for truth and justice must always be. But it is now intended to be systematic and, with the coming reality of the National Institute of Education, intelligent, humane, and productive as well.

The National Institute of Education is an embodiment of very large national aspirations and, with enough money, talent, and fortitude in the face of inevitable periodic disappointment, I believe the institute will bring those aspirations to fulfillment.

In a nation that has attached scientific inquiry with great profit to nearly all of its major interests—medicine, industry, commerce, communications—it is time that education, perhaps the overriding concern of Americans as we rank our values, should come to adulthood.

For permission to reprint copyrighted material, the author wishes to thank the following:

ALDINE PUBLISHING CO. and ROBERT D. HESS and ROBERTA MEYER BEAR for an excerpt from Robert D. Hess and Roberta Meyer Bear, eds., *Early Education* (1968):

AMERICAN ASSOCIATION OF COMMUNITY AND JUNIOR COLLEGES for an excerpt from R. Richardson, Jr. and P. Elsner, "A New Role for the Junior College," *Junior College Journal* (1965):

AMERICAN ASSOCIATION FOR JEWISH EDUCATION for an excerpt from A. M. Dushkin and U. F. Engelman, *Jewish Education in the United States* (1959):

AMERICAN ASSOCIATION OF UNIVERSITY PROFESSORS for an excerpt from Ann Sutherland Harris, "The Second Sex in Academe," *Bulletin* (vol LVI):

THE AMERICAN FOUNDATION, INC. and MRS. CURTIS BOK for an excerpt from Edward Bok, *The Americanization of Edward Bok* (1920):

APPLETON-CENTURY-CROFTS for excerpts from Samuel Everett, ed., *A Challenge to Secondary Education* (1935); William Kilpatrick, ed., *The Educational Frontier* (1933):

THE ATLANTIC MONTHLY COMPANY, Boston, Mass., for an excerpt from Albert Lynd, "Quakery in the Public Schools," *The Atlantic Monthly* (1950):

BASIC BOOKS, INC. for an excerpt from Theodore Caplow and Reece J. McGee, *The Academic Marketplace* (1958):

ARTHUR BESTOR for an excerpt from Arthur Bestor, *Educational Wastelands* (1953):

KARL BIGELOW for an excerpt from Karl Bigelow, "The Passing of the Teachers College," *Teachers College Record* (1957):

LURTON BLASSINGAME for an excerpt from Leonard Covello, *The Heart Is a Teacher* (1958):

BOARD OF JEWISH EDUCATION for an excerpt from Mordecai Kaplan and Bernard Cronson, "Report of Committee on Jewish Education of the Kehilla . . . New York, 1910," *Jewish Education*, XX (1949):

MABEL D. BOBBITT for an excerpt from J. Franklin Bobbitt, *How to Make a Curriculum* (1924):

CAMBRIDGE UNIVERSITY PRESS for excerpts from C. P. Snow, *The Two Cultures and the Scientific Revolution* (1959); Sir Thomas More, *Utopia*, J. Rawson Lumby, ed. (1940):

CARNEGIE FOUNDATION FOR THE ADVANCEMENT OF TEACHING for an excerpt from Abraham Flexner, *Medical Education in the United States and Canada* (1910):

THE CLARENDON PRESS for an excerpt from Lance G. E. Jones, *Negro Schools in the Southern States* (1928):

COLUMBIA UNIVERSITY PRESS for an excerpt from Erasmus, *The Education of a Christian Prince*, Lester K. Born, trans. (1936):

THE COUNCIL FOR EXCEPTIONAL CHILDREN for an excerpt from Frank Hewett, "A Hierarchy of Education Tasks for Children with Learning Disorders," *Exceptional Children* (1964):

CURTIS BROWN, LTD. for an excerpt from Betty and Ernest Lindley, *A New Deal for Youth* (1938):

THE CURTIS PUBLISHING CO. for an excerpt from James Meredith, "I'll Know Victory or Defeat," *The Saturday Evening Post* (November 10, 1962):

DODD, MEAD AND COMPANY, INC. for an excerpt from Wilfrid Lay, *Man's Unconscious Conflict* (1917, 1948):

E. P. DUTTON AND CO., INC. for excerpts from John and Evelyn Dewey, *Schools of Tomorrow* (1915, 1962); Hyman Rickover, *Education and Freedom* (1959):

MARIE C. EICHELSER for an excerpt from Abraham Flexner, *Universities: American, English, German* (1930):

SOPHIE ELAM for an excerpt from Sophie Elam, "Acculturation and Learning Problems of Puerto Rican Children," *Teachers College Record* (1960):

FARRAR, STRAUS AND GIROUX, INC. for an excerpt from Abraham Heschel, *The Insecurity of Freedom* (1966):

ANNA FREUD for an excerpt from Anna Freud, "Psychoanalysis and the Training of the Young Child," *Psychoanalytic Quarterly* (1935):

HARCOURT BRACE JOVANOVICH, INC. for excerpts from T. S. Eliot, *Notes Toward a Definition of Culture* (1949); Robert S. and Helen M. Lynd, *Middletown* (1929, 1957); Robert S. and Helen M. Lynd, *Middletown in Transition* (1937, 1965); George S. Counts *School and Society in Chicago* (1928, 1956):

HARPER AND ROW, PUBLISHERS, INC. for excerpts from Jacques Barzun, *The House of Intellect* (1959); "Introduction" by John Dewey in Elsie Ripley Clapp, *The Uses of Resources in Education* (1952); Rudolf Flesch, *Why Johnny Can't Read–And What You Can Do About It* (1955); Aldous Huxley, *Brave New World* (1932); Gunnar Myrdal, *An American Dilemma* (1944); Frank Thompson, *The Schooling of the Immigrants* (1920):

HARRISON–BLAINE OF NEW JERSEY, INC. for an excerpt from Alexander Bickel, "Desegregation: Where Do We Go From Here?," *New Republic* (February 7, 1970):

HART PUBLISHING CO., NEW YORK for an excerpt from A. S. Neill, *Summerhill: A Radical Approach to Child Rearing* (1960):

HARVARD EDUCATIONAL REVIEW for excerpts from Arthur Jensen, "How Much Can We Boost I.Q. and Scholastic Achievement?," *Harvard Educational Review* (1969); William Brazziel, "A Letter from the South," *Harvard Educational Review* (1969); Kenneth Clark, "Alternative Public School Systems," *Harvard Educational Review* (1968); B. F. Skinner, "The Science of Learning and the Art of Teaching," *Harvard Educational Review* (1954):

HARVARD UNIVERSITY PRESS for an excerpt from George Ives, trans., *The Essays of Montaigne* (1925):

JOHN S. HOLLISTER, Project Administrator of the CONANT STUDIES OF AMERICAN EDUCATION, for an excerpt from James Conant, *The Education of American Teachers* (1963):

HOLT, RINEHART AND WINSTON, INC. for excerpts from Benjamin S. Bloom, et. al., Compensatory Education for Cultural Deprivation (1965); R. Rosenthal and L. Jacobson, *Pygmalion in the Classroom* (1968); Lillian Wald, *The House on Henry Street* (1915):

HORIZON PRESS for an excerpt from Paul Goodman, *Compulsory Mis–Education* (1964):

HOUGHTON MIFFLIN CO. for excerpts from Mary Antin, *The Promised Land* (1912); William Kilpatrick, *The Montessori System Examined* (1914): James Koerner, *The Miseducation of American Teachers* (1963):

HUMANITIES PRESS, INC. for excerpts from Susan Isaacs, *Social Development in Young Children* (1933); Wolfgang Kohler, *The Mentality of Apes* (1925); Jean Piaget, *The Child's Conception of Physical Causality* (1930); Alfred Adler, *The Practice and Theory of Individual Psychology* (1929); Karl Mannheim, *Diagnosis of Our Time* (1943):

INSTITUTE FOR INSTRUCTIONAL IMPROVEMENT, INC. for an excerpt from Harold Clark and Harold Sloan, *Classrooms in the Military* (1964):

INTELLECT for excerpts from Gilbert Love, "College Students Are Beating the Depression," *School and Society* (1933); W. Henry Cooke, "The Segregation of Mexican–American School Children in Southern California," *School and Society* (1948); Frank Lenz, "Education of the Immigrant," *Educational Review* (1916):

INTERNATIONAL PUBLISHERS for excerpt from Ivan Pavlov, *Lectures on Conditioned Reflexes*, W. H. Gantt, translator (1928):

CARL T. IRWIN for an excerpt from Elizabeth Irwin and Louis Marks, *Fitting the School to the Child* (1924):

JOURNAL OF THE AMERICAN ACADEMY OF ARTS AND SCIENCE for an excerpt from Edward Shils, "Mass Society and Its Culture," *Daedalus* (LXXXIX):

KAPPA DELTA PI, AN HONOR SOCIETY IN EDUCATION, for an excerpt from Isaac Kendel, "Can the School Build a New Social Order?," *Kadelpian Review* (1933):

LIVERIGHT PUBLISHING CO. for excerpts from Joseph Featherstone, *Schools Where Children Learn* (1917); William Kilpatrick, *Education and the Social Crisis* (1932, 1960):

MACMILLAN PUBLISHING CO., INC. for excerpts from Jane Addams, *Twenty Years at Hull House* (1910, 1938); John Dewey, *Democracy and Education* (1916, 1944); Walter Lippmann, *American Inquisitors* (1928, 1956); Alfred North Whitehead, *The Aims of Education and Other Essays* (1929, 1957):

MCGRAW–HILL BOOK COMPANY for an excerpt from F. De la Fontainerie, trans., *French Liberalism and Education in the 18th Century* (1932); Kurt Lewin, *A Dynamic Theory of Personality: Selected Papers* (1935):

THE MERRILL–PALMER INSTITUTE for an excerpt from J. McVicker Hunt, "The Psychological Basis for Using Pre-School Enrichment as an Antidote for Cultural Deprivation," *Merrill–Palmer Quarterly* (1962):

MICHIGAN STATE UNIVERSITY PRESS for an excerpt from John Wales, *Schools of Democracy* (1962):

HELEN T. MOSHER for an excerpt from Lewis Terman, *The Measurement of Intelligence* (1916):

THE VIKING PRESS for excerpts from Thorstein Veblen, *The Higher Education in America* (1918, 1946); August Aichhorn, *Wayward Youth* (1935, 1963):

WARWICK AND YORK, INC. for an excerpt from William Bagley, "An Essentialist's Platform for the Advancement of American Education," *Educational Administration and Supervision* (1938):

JAMES A. WECHSLER for an excerpt from *Revolt on the Campus* (1935):

THE WESTMINSTER PRESS and the SCM PRESS, LTD. for an excerpt from John Calvin, *Theological Treatises*, volume XXII, The Library of Christian Classics; translated with introductions and notes by The Rev. J. K. S. Reid (1954):

JOHN WILEY AND SONS, INC. for excerpts from Willard Waller, *The Sociology of Teaching* (1932); Benjamin Bloom, *Stability and Change in Human Characteristics* (1964); August Hollingshead, *Elmtown's Youth* (1949):

THE H. H. WILSON COMPANY for an excerpt from Y. R. Macias, "The Chicano Movement," *Wilson Library Bulletin* (1969):

YALE UNIVERSITY PRESS for excerpts from Robert Hutchins, *The Higher Learning in America* (1936); David Riesman, et.al., *The Lonely Crowd* (1950); Leo Simmons, ed., *Sun Chief: The Autobiography of a Hopi Indian* (1942)

INDEX

Particular Parts of Learning
(Petty), 246-249
"Advice to a Young Tradesman,
Written by an Old One,"
491-492
Aegidius, 194
Aeneid (Virgil), 415, 696
Aertsen, Rynier, 546
Aeschylus, 1221
Aesop, 164, 461, 511
Aesop's Fables, 46-47, 164, 168,
170, 285, 406, 417, 461, 511
in Greek, 160-161
Aesop's Fables (Jones), 298-299
Affaragoa, 625-626
Affection
as teacher qualification, 1358
between children and teacher,
833
and discipline, 1368
and infant education, 1205-
1206
Africa, study of, 2498
*After the War: A Southern Tour,
May 1, 1865, to May 1,
1866* (Reid), 1636
Agamemnon, 1877
Agassiz, Alexander, 1461, 1718
Agassiz, Louis, 1402, 1457-1458,
1458, 1459, 1459-1460, 1462,
1545, 1596
Age
and admission to Massachusetts
State Normal Schools, 1336
of applicants to New York
State Normal School, 1344
of child labor, 2193-2194
of children in Pennsylvania
coal mines, 2144-2145
in child's perception of reality,
2027
classes organized by, 1319-1320
classification by, 960
of college admission, 675
and curriculum, 2266
and elective system, 1555,
1556-1557
at entrance to school, 1588,
2054, 2199
and individual differences, 2242
and intelligence tests, 251-2252,
2254, 2256
and learning, 628
of learning to read, 2436, 2497
ratio between mental age and,
2257
and teacher's status, 2004,
2006-2007
"Age of Great Cities, The," 1083
Agesilaus, 603
Agrarianism, 1015, 1058
and ignorance, 1104
Agricola, 162, 259
Agricultural Adjustment Act,
2599
Agricultural community, schools
in. See Rural Schools
Agricultural courses, 185, 775
in college curriculum, 803,
1507
and college reform, 1514
at Hampton Institute, 1656

at Hofwyl, Switzerland, 853-
856
at Indian mission school, 1723
teaching of, 112
Agricultural and Mechanical
College, Alabama, 1649
Aguilar, Grace, 1198
Ahabash Achim congregation,
1202
Aholiab, 123
Aichhorn, August, 2002-2003
Aiken, Wilford M., 2613-2617
Aiken, William, 1676
*Aims of Education and Other
Essays, The* (Whitehead),
2070-2075
Ainsworth, 512
Air Corps, education in, 2840-
2843
Aitken, George A., 314-317
Alabama
agricultural colony in, 2163
during Depression, 2528
law prohibiting teaching of
slaves in, 1623
Negro education in, 1664-1665,
1666
treatment of Northern teachers
in, 1664
Alain, 2121
Albany, New York
Normal Schools at, 1344-1348
teaching licenses in, 353
Albany Female Academy,
description of, 1591-1594
Alcestis, 186
Alcott, Bronson, 1204-1208, 1208-
1210
Boston school of, 1210-1212
on infant education, 1204-1208
on Massachusetts North
primary school, 1210-1213
on teachers, 1208-1210
Alder v. Board of Education,
2734, 2736
Aldus, 151
Alexander, Fred M., 2602-2603
Alexander, Hugh Q., 3006-3009
Alexander, M. W., 2267
Alexander the Great, 43, 161,
163, 179, 211, 414, 1222
Algebra, 83, 439, 441, 443, 510
beginning, 3238
Committee of Fifteen on,
1968-1969
in grammar school curriculum,
948, 1927, 1928, 1929
in Prussian schools, 1089
in secondary school curriculum,
1936, 1939
in teacher seminaries in
Prussia, 933
Alger, Horatio, 1392-1397
Algorism, in new math, 3238
"All-America Schools," 3140
Allan, Robert, 513
Allen, Dr. Nathan, 1183, 1591
Allen, Ira W., 1497
Allen, James E., 3377-3382
Allen, John, 726
Allen, W. O., 325
Allen, William, 637-638, 903
Allen v. Louisiana, 3092

Allgeyer v. Louisiana, 3091
Alliteration, 1807
Almquist, Alan F., 1732-1734
Alphabet, 46, 262, 288-289, 560,
561-562, 3302
ITA
learning of, 294-297, 835-836,
1291
Montessori, 2314-2315
in Prussian schools, 1086-1087
teaching of, 880
Alphonso, King, 220, 230
Alsea sub-agency, 1737
"Alternative Public School
Systems" (Clark), 3315-3317,
3329n
Alvarado, Ernestine, 2929-2930
Alvarez, 290
Amasiah, 122
Ambrose, Saint, 155
America. See United States
American Annals of Education,
978, 979, 1306-1307, 1310-
1311, 1324-1325
American Association for the
Advancement of Science,
1457, 2390
American Association of Colleges
for Teacher Education, 2676-
2678
American Association of School
Administrators, Educational
Policies Commission, 2623n
American Association of Teachers
Colleges, 2676-2677
American Association of
University Professors
Bulletin, 2724, 2883-2889,
3220-3222
General Declaration of
Principles, 2876-2881
"Joint Statement on Rights and
Freedoms of Students," 2883-
2889
opposition to loyalty oaths for
teachers, 2724
organization of, 2875-2876
*Report of the Committee on
Academic Freedom and
Tenure*, 2876-2881
American Association of
University Women, 3222
American Bar Association,
Committee on the Bill of
Rights of the, 3054
American character
and American education, 2110-
2115, 2118
and child-rearing methods,
2115-2119
and development of United
States, 1904-1905
and idealism, 2159
and immigrants, 995
and Puritanism, 2103
American Character, The
(Brogan), 2110-2115
American cities
Jewish education in, 1200-1202
poor and rich areas, 2124
See also Cities
American City, 2275-2278
American City Bureau, 2390

American Civil Liberties Union, 2795, 3054
American College Personnel Association, 2541
American colleges
competition from state universities, 1527
and English model, 1512
See also Colleges
American Colleges and the American Public, The (Porter), 1471-1477
American colonies
education in, 3070, 3076
Indian-White relations in, 602
American Council on Education, 2542-2547
on teacher training, 2703-2705
American Council of Learned Societies. *See* ACLS
American Creed, and Negro education, 3003, 3005
American culture
disaffection from, 3188-3192
and ethnic groups, 2378-2381
femininity in, 2116-2117
and individualism, 2461-2462
masculinity in, 2116-2117
and motion pictures, 2388-2391
sex roles in, 2116-2117
siblings in, 2116-2117
See also Culture
American Dilemma, An (Myrdal), 3000-3006, 3106n
American education, 2965-2969, 3377-3382
and American character, 2110-2115
compared with English education, 2104-2108
compared with French education, 2119-2122
compared with German education, 941-945
European views of, 2101-2129
and first Montessori school in America, 2310-2316
and immigrants, 2111
and infant schools, 978
Maurois on, 2119-2122
Mead on, 2123
Mosely Commission on, 2104-2108
reform movement in, 2101-2104
Sadler on, 2101-2104
social and political role of, 2110-2111
Soviet view of, 2124-2129
See also entries under Education
American Education Fellowship, new policy proposal for, 3169-3172
American family, ideal, 2116
American Federation of Labor, and industrial education, 2268-2269
American Federation of Teachers, 2938
and private corporations running public schools, 3336
and voucher plan, 3336

American Federationist, 1870-1871
American flag
in American schools, 2112-2113
in classrooms, 2126
at Indian Schools, 1757-1758
See also Flag salute
American High School To-Day, The (Conant), 3160-3161
American high schools
critique of, 2520-2523
psychological selection of pupils by, 2509
selective character of, 2505-2510
typical day in, 2108-2110
See also High schools
American Historical Association, 1946
Report of the Commission on the Social Studies, 2590-2594, 2674-2676
American Inquisitors: A Commentary on Dayton and Chicago (Lippmann), 2719-2722
American Instructor: or, Young Man's Best Companion, The (Slack), 540
American Jewish Historical Society, 353-354, 450-451
American Journal of Education, 59-60, 399-400, 402, 1068-1069, 1325-1326, 1399, 1605-1606, 1781-1786
American Journal of Nursing, 2305-2306
American Journal of Psychiatry, 2465-2466, 2783-2786
American Journal of Science and Arts, 1441-1451
American language, necessity for, 766-769
American Legion, 2731
American Library Association, 2492n
American Life and the School Curriculum: Next Steps Toward Schools of Living, 2574-2576
American Lyceum, proposed constitution for, 1605-1606
American Medical Association, 2771n
American Medical Directory, 2769
American Missionary Association, 1741-1742
American People, The (Gorer), 2115-2119
American Revolution, and students at Harvard, 718
"American Scholar, The," 1225-1229
American schools
buildings and furniture, 961
discipline in, 965
drawing in, 962-963
educational reform of, 966-972
elocution in, 963
instructional methods in, 965-966
manual instruction in, 962-963

organization of, 960-961
patriotism in, 964-965, 2107
religion in, 2111-2112
teachers' salaries in, 2111
See also entries under Education
American Selection. . . (Webster), 1571-1572
American Spelling book, The (Webster), 769-773, 1377-1381
American Sunday School Union, 979
American Teacher, The (Elsbree), 557
American women
compared with English women, 947
Lieber on, 941
See also Education of women
American Youth Commission, 2626-2632, 2627n
Americanization, 2162
of adult immigrants, 2173-2174
attitudes toward, 2371-2373
of Bok, 2156-2160
consequences of, 2175-2178
criticism of, 2225
and education, 955, 2111-2113, 2114-2115, 2190
and evening school for adult immigrants, 2180-2182
and Japanese language schools, 2974
and melting pot concept, 2178-2179
of Mexican-American children, 2930-2934
Stowe on, 993-994
in West, 991-992
See also Assimilation
Americanization of Edward Bok: The Autobiography of a Dutch Boy Fifty Years After, The, 2156-2160
Americans, Crevecoeur on, 812-817
"American's Creed," 2111-2112
Americans in Their Moral, Social, and Political Relations, The (Grund), 941-945
Amerikanischer Zeitung, 999-1000
Amerman, Abraham A., 1339
Amherst College, 1151
founding of, 1467-1468
Amnesty, to student strikers, 2940
Amsterdam, petitions by Jews in, 353-355
Anastasi, A., 3179n
Anatomy, 185, 247
in secondary school curriculum, 1936, 1939
at University of Virginia, 1488, 1490
See also Phrenology
Ancient languages
and child study method, 1849
in college curriculum, 1502
at Harvard College, 1462
Jefferson on, 1484-1485
retention in college curriculum, 1471-1472

at University of Virginia, 1488, 1489
  See also Greek; Latin; etc.
Anderson, Alan Ross, 3308-3310
Anderson, John, 2091
Anderson, Lewis Flint, 827-831
Anderson, Meta L., 2405
Anderson, Robert, 3140
Andrews, George W., 3006-3009
Angell, James B., 600, 1414, 1930-1946
Anger
  study of, 1840
  of teacher, 76
Anglo-German relations, in Pennsylvania, 630-631
Anglo-Latinus (Herme), 290
Anglo-Saxon Superiority (Demolins), 1950
Animal behavior
  general laws of, 2235-2236
  and law of effect, 2246-2247
Animal intelligence, 2011-2016
  association psychologists on, 2011-2012
  and insight, 2015-2016
  Thorndike on, 2233-2236
Animal Intelligence (Thorndike), 2233-2236
Animal psychology, and human psychology, 1428
Animals
  and city children, 2502-2503
  classification of, 1334
  in classroom, 248-249
  object teaching lessons on, 1783-1784
  and superego, 2001
  See also Animal behavior; Animal intelligence
Animism, in mental development of child, 2026
Annals of the American Academy of Political and Social Science, 2192-2195
Annals of the Boston Primary School Committee, 976-977
Annals of Congress, 15th Cong., 2d Sess., 1723-1724
Annals of Public Education in the State of New York from 1626 to 1746 (Pratt), 353, 545-546
Anne (Queen of England), 651
Anniversary Discourse (Peixotto), 1184-1185
Announcements
  of opening of female academy in Warrenton, North Carolina, 1572
  of opening of Negro School in Raleigh, N. C., 1620
  of school for Negro girls in Baltimore, 1622
Annual Circular of the Executive Committee, 1850, 1344-1348
Annual reports
  of Board of Commissioners of Common Schools in Connecticut, 1291-1292
  of Board of Education of Massachusetts, 1326-1327
  of the Board of Education, for

the Year Ending March 31, 1861, 1780-1781
  of Board of Regents of University of Michigan, 1516-1517
  of Carlisle Indian School, 1745-1748
  of Commissioner of Education, 999-1000, 1032, 1195-1199, 1200-1203, 1404-1405, 1407-1409
  of Commissioner of Indian Affairs, 1754-1756, 1756-1760
  of Connecticut Board of Commissioners, 1317-1318
  of the Controllers of the Public Schools of the First District of the State of Pennsylvania, 1826, 982-983
  of educational officers, 959
  of Massachusetts Board of Education, 932-934, 1076-1080
  of New Britain, Connecticut Normal School, 1340-1344
  of North Carolina superintendent of Common Schools, 1012-1014
  of Secretary of Board of Education of Connecticut, 1323-1324
  of Secretary of Board of Education of Massachusetts, 990, 1083-1094, 1311-1315, 1315-1317, 1335-1337, 1337-1339
  of Superintendent of Common Schools, New York State, 1027-1029, 1294-1296
  of the Superintendent of Instruction of the State of Michigan for 1855, 1516-1517
Annuities, for relocated Indians, 1730-1731
"Answer By Charles V. Hamilton, An," 3227-3228
Answer to the "Rejoinder" of Twenty-nine Boston Schoolmasters (Mann), 1094-1095
"Answer to Some Cases of Conscience Respecting the Country," (Stoddard), 618
Antagonism, between teacher and pupil, 2395-2396
Anthony, Richard, 1051-1052
Anti-Catholicism, in Massachusetts Bay, 367-368
Antichrist, 126
Antient and Roman Histories (Rollins), 502
Antin, Mary, 2167-2170, 2178
Antioch College, 2422
  catalogue for 1854, 1497-1502
  curriculum at, 1498-1499
  Mann's baccalaureate address at, 1112-1115
Antipater, 758
Antiquity (Potter), 351
Anti-Semitism, 354-355
  in Rome, 1198-1199

Anti-social conduct, and social work in public schools, 2400
Antoninus, 179
Anxieties
  and play, 2080
  signal of, 2001
Apaches, 1737, 1738
Aphorisms, of Francis Bacon, 213-216
Apophthegms, 170
Apostles, 54, 124, 126, 131, 135
  and New Testament, 41
Apostles' Creed, 53
Apostolic Letters, 65
  "Communes Litteras," 2043n
Apparatus
  and Montessori method, 3263
  at New York State Normal School, 1346
  at State Normal School at New Britain, Connecticut, 1342
  for state university, 1523
  for teaching geography, 1928
  See also Equipment
Apperception
  and concentration, 1880
  in Herbartian pedagogy, 1872-1876
  and phases of correlation, 1888
  and recitation, 1920
Appleton, 1746
Applewhait, Henry, 344
Application
  in Herbartian method, 1878
  in Teacher Corps, 3374
Applied geography, in secondary school curriculum, 1936, 1939
Appointment of professors, criteria for, 1458-1459
"Apprentices to the School" (Bourne), 2329-2331
Apprenticeship
  in America, 935
  in Boston, 389
  at Carlisle Indian School, 1746-1747, 1750-1751
  in Connecticut, 392, 402
  in Maine, 390
  in Massachusetts, 391-392
  in New England, 390-391
  in New Jersey, 358-359
  to school teachers, 555-556, 2666
  in 17th century Virginia, 343-344
  See also Apprenticeship contracts; Apprenticeship law; Indenture
Apprenticeship and Apprenticeship Education in Colonial New England and New York (Seybolt), 389, 403, 404
Apprenticeship contracts, 449-450
Apprenticeship law
  in Virginia, 342
  of 1563, 318-321
Appropriations. *See* Federal aid to education
Apthonius, 286
Aptness in teaching

272, 306, 513, 777, 1067, 1350, 1483-1484, 1497
in French secondary school curriculum, 1924
Cicill, Sir William, 176
Cincinnati, Ohio
conflict over religious education in public schools in, 952
German immigrants in, 992
Jewish education in, 1202
Negro enrollment in, 3044
school buildings, 3046
Circuit Court of Champaign County, Illinois, 3067-3068
Circuit Court of Mississippi, 3093-3097
Circular and Catalogue of the Albany Female Academy, 1836, 1591-1594
Circulars of Information, 954-959
Cities
crime in, 986
description of, 2316-2317
Citizens, education of, 1486
Citizens' Compensatory Education Advisory Committee, 2938
Citizen's Manual for Public Schools, A (Smith), 3146-3149
Citizenship
and Americanization, 1768, 2381-2382
as teaching requirement, 797
and children of immigrants, 1126-1127
and curriculum, 2432-2434
and education, 1025, 1104-1107, 2224, 2281
and educational goals, 2281
in high school, 2516
and school segregation, 1643
and secondary school training, 1923
and self-governing assemblies, 2493
City College of New York, 3178n
establishment of, 3321-3322
City and Country School, New York City, 2316-2318, 2499, 2500
City life, and learning, 1839-1840
City school systems
centralization of, 1983-1989
compared with rural schools, 1921-1922
City University of New York, open admissions at, 3320-3325
Civics, in high school curriculum, 2520
Civil engineering, in college curriculum, 1513
Civil government, in secondary school curriculum, 1936, 1939
Civil history, in Prussian schools, 1089
Civil rights
Jefferson on, 784
Kennedy's message to Congress on, 3361-3365

Civil Rights Act of 1964, 3223
title IV, 3370
title VI of, 3049, 3370-3371
title VII of, 3220
Civil Rights Commission, 3041, 3046, 3047
Report of the California State Advisory Committee to the U.S. Commission on Civil Rights,
"Civil Rights—Message from the President of the United States," 3361-3365
Civil Service, 2978
and Feinberg Law, 2734
and teachers in Japanese internment camps, 2978
Civilian Conservation Corps, 2556
educational program of, 2558-2567
evaluation of, 2562-2567
Civilization of Indians
and "Benevolent Associations," 1724
and House of Representatives policy, 1725-1727
and "Indian Civilization Fund," 1723-1724
role of public schools in, 1100
Civilization's Inferno, Or Studies in the Cellar (Flower), 2136-2138
Clap, Thomas, 673, 687-691
Clapp, Elsie Ripley, 3127-3131
Clark, Donald, 2909
Clark, Edward, 446
Clark, Harold F., 2841-2843
Clark, Justice, 2735-2736, 2741, 2882-2883, 3080-3081, 3108-3113
Clark, Kenneth B., 3043, 3106n, 3315-3317, 3329n
Clark, Matthew St. Clair, 979
Clark, Thomas, 387, 1456
Clark, Walter, 346, 514-516
Clark University, child study at, 1840-1841
Clarke, Edward H., on education of women, 1596-1598
Clarke, Jonas, 408
Class Day, at Harvard College, 1466
Class distinctions, 1217, 1220
attitudes toward college preparatory students vs. vocational students, 2634-2635
and college education. *See* Industrial universities
and curriculum, 2055-2056
and education, 1025, 1057-1058, 1103-1104, 2082-2085, 2229-2231, 2230-2231
in England and U.S. compared, 2106
and public schools, 1001-1002
and social problems, 2085-2088
and University Extension, 1616
Class size, 1322
in British infant school, 3300
in disadvantaged areas, 3025-3026

and recitation, 1920-1921
Classes
homogeneous, 879-880, 1493-1494
of Hull House, 2292-2293
in Lancasterian system, 987
organization of, 879-880
in progressive and traditional schools, 2457
separation into, 46
Classics, 473
at Phillips Exeter Academy, 1237, 1238
translations of, 1221-1223
Yale resolution on retention of, 1441-1451
See also Ancient languages
Classification of pupils
and democratic society, 1952-1953
by grade, 1319-1323
and intelligence tests, 2254-2255, 2427-2428
in Negro schools in South, 1639-1640
Classified Digest of the Records for the Society for Propagation of the Gospel in Foreign Parts, 1701-1900 (Pascoe), 326
Classis, Rev., 586
Classroom atmosphere
in Indianapolis progressive public school, 1894-1896
in progressive vs. mechanical schools, 1897-1898
in St. Louis public schools, 1894
Classrooms
in Alcott's school, 1210-1211
in American elementary schools, 2125
animals in, 248-249
in California school rules, 1043
at Carlisle Indian School, 1750
in Civilian Conservation Corps Camps, 2558-2559
at elementary school of School of Education at University of Missouri, 2478
of Hebrew Sunday school, 1191-1192
in Massachusetts schoolhouses, 1081-1082
at New York City Ethical Culture Society Workingman's School, 1791-1792
overcrowded, 3355
at Owen's New Lanark school, 902
in progressive schools, 3144
and seats "Reserved For Colored," 3098-3099
in U.S. schools, 961
See also Classroom atmosphere; Schoolrooms
Classrooms in the Military (Clark and Sloan), 2841-2843
Class-spirit, and correspondence teaching, 1609-1610
Clavis, 291
Claxton, P. P., 2992-2993

"Day of Doom, The"
(Wigglesworth), 371-376
de Amicitia (Cicero), 165
de Carlo, Charles, 3221
de Crevecoeur, Michel-Guillaume
Jean, 812-817
De facto segregation
McCone report on, 3023-3036
in North, 3020-3023
De Fellenberg, Emmanuel, 853-
856
De Foe, 477
De Garmo, Charles, 1872-1876,
1877-1878, 1884-1888
de Guimps, Roger, 832-837
de La Fontainerie, F., 106-108,
110-115
De La Howe, John, 773-776
De Lima, Agnes, 2479-2481
de Madariaga, 2522
de natura Deorum (Tullie), 285
de Officiis (Cicero), 163, 165
De Oratore (Cicero), 270
de Saint-Esteve, Constant, 837n
de Villevielle, Count Louis, 854
Deaf and dumb children, 471
Deafness, and child labor, 2140
Dean of Christ Church, Oxford,
165
Dean of Westminster, 165
Dearden, John Cardinal, 2908
Death, Horace Mann on, 1114-
1115
Death sentence, for incorrigible
children, 370-371
Debates, of Phi Beta Kappa
Society, 724
Debating skills, 479-480
Debating societies, in American
schools in 1874, 1906
Debt, Benjamin Franklin on, 494
Debtors prison, 1059
Decapolis, 144
Decentralization
and tuition grants for private
schools, 3281
in urban schools, 3262
of U.S. schools, 951, 958-960
Decius, 180
Declamation, 1236
"Declaration on Christian
Education," 2044-2053
Declaration of Independence,
754, 964, 2176
Declaration, by New York State
Normal School pupils, 1345,
2046n, 2050n, 2050n
Declaration of the Rights of Man,
112
Decorations, in progressive
schools, 3144
Decree on the Apostolate of the
Laity, 2049n
Decree on the Bishops' Pastoral
Office in the Church," 2048n
Decree on the Instruments of
Social Communication,
2048n
Decroly, 2255
Decurions, 72
Dedham, Massachusetts, free
school in, 396
Dedham Town Records, 396

Dedication, of the state normal
school at Bridgewater, Mass.,
1335
Defense Department, 3316
Deficient children
and didactic material, 1996-
1997
and Montessori method, 1996-
1997
"Definition of the Activity
Movement To-Day"
(Kilpatrick), 2573-2574
"Deflating The Schools"
(Carlson), 2534-2538
Defoe, Daniel, 314-317
DeForest, Robert W., 2141-2143
Degand, 2255
Dejordy, Alma, 200-208
Delacroix, M. H., 2024
Delaware
and *Brown* v. *Board of
Education*, 3102-3108
during Depression, 2536
Delaware Court of Chancery,
3102n-3103
Delaweare, Mrs., 446
"Deliberate speed" formula, 3223
Delineator, 2355-2357
Delinquent parents, 2408-2409
Dell, Floyd, 2413-2414
Delsarteans, 1604
deLucena, Abraham, 354
"Demands of Sociology upon
Pedagogy" (Small), 2185-
2188
Demas, 122
Demetrius, 122
Democracy
and American Creed, 3004
and classification of pupils,
1952-1953
and communism, 2584-2585
de Tocqueville on, 935-939
and education, 953, 2102-2103,
2229-2231, 2450, 2584-2587,
2803-2806, 3173-3174
education in, 2122
and educational growth of
adolescents, 2611-2613
and essentialist platform, 2650-
2655
and free education, 1062-1063
and Gary system, 2341
goal of education in, 2280-2281
and high schools, 2521-2522
and higher education, 1508-
1509
and homogeneous classes, 1929-
1930
and indoctrination of beliefs,
2644-2645
and life adjustment education,
2627
and majority rule, 2719-2722
and masses and select
minorities, 2032-2033
and melting pot concept, 1275-
2178
misinterpreted in American
schools, 2640-2643
and progressive education,
2647
and Project method, 2274

in school, 1828-1829
and school as a social center,
2229
and social control, 2081-2082
and social education, 2188-
2192
and treatment of Mexican
immigrants, 2930
at University of Michigan,
1516-1517
and vocational education, 2360
Webster on, 769-770
Democracy in America
(Tocqueville), 935-939
Democracy and Education
(Dewey), 2232-2233, 2467
Democracy and Social Ethics
(Addams), 2188-2192
"Democracy versus The Melting
Pot" (Kallen), 2175-2178
Demolins, 1950
Demonstration in Navajo
Education, Inc., 2967
Demoralization, in children,
2007-2010
"Demoralized Children" (Adler),
2007-2010
Demosthenes, 168, 186, 267, 306,
1067, 2273, 2766
Denison College, religious revival
at, 1451
*Denison: The Story of an Ohio
College* (Chessman), 1451
Dennett, John, 343
Dennett, Margaret, 343
Dennett, Sarah, 343
Dennett, Thomas, 343
Dennison, 1738
Denominational colleges, 2760-
2763
Density, child's conceptions
about, 2028-2029
Denver High School, 1930
Department of Agriculture, 3192
and Civilian Conservation
Corps, 2558
Department of Education
*Report of the Commissioner of
Education for the Year
1892-1893*, 1930-1944
Department of Health,
Education, and Welfare,
3194, 3378
and desegregation, 3363-3364
Eisenhower on the creation of,
3341-3342
and National Foundation for
Higher Education, 3387
Office of Education, 3027-3033,
3365-3369
Department of Housing and
Urban Development, 3040
Department of the Interior, and
Office of Education, 1407
See also U.S. Bureau of
Education
Department of Justice, and
desegregation, 3363-3364
Department of Labor, Children's
Bureau, 2357-2358
Department of Mexican
Education, 2933-2934

and TEPS conferences, 2707-2711
and voucher plan
See also Experimental schools
Educational research, and International Bureau of Education, 2001
Educational Review, 1885, 1951-1959, 2101-2104, 2180-2182, 2748-2752, 2752-2757
Educational theory. *See* Educational philosophy
Educational Voucher Agency (EVA), 3332-3333, 3334-3335
Educational Wastelands: The Retreat from Learning. . . (Bestor), 3131-3135
Educational Writings of John Locke, The (Adamson), 233-238, 238-240
"Educators Should Be Warned by the Pasadena Revolt" (Chodorov), 3126-3127
Edwards, Charles, 344
Edwards, Jonathan, 421-430, 680-681
Edwards, Richard, 1349-1353
Edwards, Tyron, 422-424
Edy, John, 391
Effect of Prejudice and Discrimination on Personality Development (Clark), 3106n
"Effective Child Labor Law, An" (Kelley), 2192-2195
Efficiency
of school management, 2257-2260
and use of time in education, 2264
Effingham, Lord, 650
Egg, development of, 865
Eggleston, Edward, 1299-1300
Ego, function of, 2000-2002
Egocentrism
in mental development of child, 2026-2027
and play, 2081
Ego-love, and object-love, 2002
Egypt, study of, 2485
Eighteenth Amendment, 2383
Eighth Annual Report of the Secretary of the Board of Education, 1315-1317
Eighth Biennial Report of the Superintendent of Public Instruction of the State of Illinois, 1713-1716
"Eight-Year Study," of early admittance to colleges, 2613-2617
Einheitsschule, curriculum in, 1924
Einhorn, 1198
Eisenhower, Dwight
on the creation of Department of Health, Education, and Welfare, 3341-3342, 3011-3013, 3015, 3011-3013
sends federal troops to Little Rock, 3110
Eisenstein, Judy, 2865
Elam, Sophie L., 3177-3180

Elan, C. T., 437
Elderly, and Hull House, 2293
Eleazer Wheelock's Indian School, 619-624
Elections
at Harvard, 1465-1466
and parochial school issue, 1140-1141
Elective programs, 1493
and college reform, 1506
criticism of, 1558-1563
in elementary and secondary school, 2745-2748
at Harvard, 2745-2748, 1554-1557
in high schools, 960-961
and individual differences, 1549-1550
and individuality, 2103
in Los Angeles high schools, 2939
at Manual Training School of Washington University, 1860
at Oberlin College, 1498-1499
at Princeton, 1561-1563
in secondary schools, 2285-2286
"Elective System at Harvard, The" (Moore), 2745-2748
Electoral candidates, positions on education of, 1052
Electric typewriter, reading learning with, 3247
Elegy (Gray), 1964
An Elegy on Ezekiel Cheever (Mather), 548-553
Elementa Rhetorices (Dugard), 290
"Elementary Education" (Harris), 1919-1922
Elementary English Review, 2492n
Elementary Instruction (Sheldon), 1786-1787
Elementary School Journal, 2490n, 2492n, 2569-2572, 3136
"Elementary School Teacher, The," 2269-2271
Elementary schools
Catholic, 2899-2900
economy of time in, 2261-2266
emphasis on reading skills in, 2217-2219
federal aid to, 3348-3349
in Great Britain. *See* Infant schools; Junior schools
and Herbartian curriculum, 1884-1888
homogeneous grouping in, 2572-2573
and initiation of reading instruction, 2569-2572
and junior high schools, 2326
Kennedy's recommendations on, 3355-3356
Latin in, 967-968
in Prussia, 929-931, 1510, 1511
P.S. 188 on New York City's East Side, 2302-2304
of the school of education at University of Missouri, 2477-2479

Soviet educator on, 2124-2129
teacher-training for, 1971-1980
of University of Chicago, 2295-2302
See also Grammar school
Elementary and Secondary Education Act of 1965, 3035, 3048, 3371-3373
Elements (Euclid), 446
Elements of Moral Science, The, 1477-1480
Elements of Phrenology (Combe), 884-886
Elements of Social Science (Fairchild), 2382n
Elijah, 430
Eliot, Andrew, 718
Eliot, Charles William, 1718, 1923, 1930-1946, 2745, 2765
in defense of Committee of Ten Report on secondary education, 1951-1959
on education of women, 1595
on elective system at Harvard University, 1554-1557
on grammar school curriculum, 1926-1930
inaugural address as president of Harvard, 1546-1554
and Progressive Education Association, 2422
Eliot, George, 2165, 2291
Eliot, Jared, 673
Eliot, John, 612-615, 615-616, 655
Eliot, T. S., 2082-2085, 2088
Eliot, Dr. Thomas, 2400
Eliphalet Pearson to the Trustees, 517
Elites
as leaders of masses, 2085-2088
education of, 2958-2059
in U.S., 3181-3182
Elizabeth (Queen of England), 128, 165, 266-268
Bacon on, 209
epistle from Marian exiles to, 122-125
Ellender, Allen J., 3006-3009
Ellicott, George, 600
Elliott, Carl, 3006-3009
Elliott, Edward C., 1567-1568
Ellis, C. C., 981
Ellis, Frederick E., 1166-1171
Ellis, John, 384-385
Ellis, John Tracy, 1160-1161, 1163-1165
Elmtown's Youth (Hollingshead), 2633-2637
Elocution
in American schools, 963
in elementary school curriculum, 1969
in Prussian elementary schools, 931
See also Speech; Speech lessons
Eloquence, 456
Elsbree, Willard, 557
Elsner, Paul, 2849-2851
Ely, John, 981
Ely, Richard T., 2138
Elyot, Thomas, 156-163

for women, 445
Everett, Edward, 1062-1063, 1070-1071, 1076-1080
Everett, Samuel, 2595-2598, 2599, 2602-2603
Evers, Medgar, 3017
Everson v. Board of Education, 3063-3067, 3069-3071, 3080, 3082
Evils Suffered By American Women and American Children: The Causes And The Remedy, The (Beecher), 1318-1319
Evolution
  Darwin's theories of, 915-920
  and meaning of education, 1925-1926
Ewart, Joseph A., 2324
Ewing Street (Chicago), 2138
Examinations, 191
  for admission to Massachusetts State Normal Schools, 1336
  for admission to Normal School, 1328, 1330
  at Albany Female Academy, 1594
  at Boston High School for Girls, 1251
  boycott of, 2059, 2060
  in college, 1506-1507
  in correspondence system, 1609
  critique of, 1818
  Dewey on, 2214
  at elementary school of School of Education of University of Missouri, 2479
  for entrance to teacher seminaries in Prussia, 932-933
  at female seminary, 1578-1579
  of first-grade children, 1833-1840
  in French high schools, 2120
  for grammar schools, 1253-1258
  Hall on, 1949
  in Herbartian system, 1875
  in Michigan high schools, 2122-2123
  at Notre Dame University, 1161
  at Philadelphia Hebrew Sunday school, 1192
  psychological effects of, 1430
  and Quincy system, 1814-1815
  at Sabbath school, 1203
  at State Normal School at New Britain, Connecticut, 1342
  study methods for, 1603-1604
  and superficiality, 1813
  and supervision of the schools, 1900
  for teacher certification, 1323-1324
  in teacher training school, 1979-1980
  for teachers, 1814
  for teachers, and classroom performance, 1312
  at University of California, 1535

Exceptional students, 3254-3260
  and cultural deprivation, 3275
  development of abilities of, 3345-3346
Excitement of Writing, The, 3303
Excursions. *See* Field trips
Exercise. *See* Physical training
Exercitatio Linguae Latinae (Vives), 164
Exercitationes (Gassendi), 671
Exeter Academy, 2510
Exhortation to the Diligent Study of Scripture, An (Erasmus), 49
Exile's Return (Cowley), 2415-2416
Existence, struggle for, 917
Exodus, 140-142
Expectations
  of college attendance by Negroes, 2509
  and interest, 860
  and social class, 2506-2507
Expenditures
  of Bureau of Refugees, Freedmen, and Abandoned Lands, 1411
  at Hampton Institute, 1656
Expenditures on education
  in California, 1048
  in inner-city schools, 3046-3048
  and Negro schools, 2998-2999
  in New York City, 2303
  of poor, 3276-3277
  in suburbs and inner cities, 3187
  in U.S. and England compared, 2105
  See also Cost accounting
Experience
  and art, 2487
  and education, 108, 2435-2436
  learning by, 99
  and progressive education, 2451, 2456
  and subject matter, 2442-2444
Experience And Education (Dewey), 2648-2650
Experiential story writing, 3258
Experimental philosophy, 473
Experimental psychology, and Montessori method, 1996-1999
Experimental schools
  City and Country School of New York City, 2316-2318
  first Montessori school in America, 2310-2316
  in Gary, Indiana, 2324-2331
  in Indianapolis, 2326-2329
  in Menomonie, Wisconsin, 2344-2345
  at New York State Normal School, 1347
  role of, 1351-1352
  Rough Rock Demonstration School, 2965-2969
  See also Progressive education; Progressive schools
Exploratory task level, 3257-3258
Expulsion
  in American high schools, 2110
  from "Children's House," 2000

at Columbia University, 698
in Massachusetts school, 1338
from Phi Beta Kappa Society, 721
at South Carolina College, 1435
from United Nations, 2043
at Yale College, 677, 678
External events, and ego, 2000
Extracurricular activities, 3345
  Harvard Committee on Secondary Education on, 2620
  in Jewish schools, 2927
  and progressive education, 2455
Eyes, of newborn infants, 867-868
Eyre, Lyttleton, 723
Ezekiel Cheever, Schoolmaster (Boston, 1904) (Gould), 548-553
Ezra, 122
Fables (Croxall), 500
"Factories' Bill," 1083, 1084
Factory children, *See* Child labor
Factory, compared with school, 2515
Factory law of 1893, 2139-2140
Faculty
  of Antioch College, 1497
  of Brown University, 706
  and curricula changes, 1450
  and Free Speech Movement, 2860
  in multiversity, 2825-2826
  of Notre Dame University, 1160
  of university, 2073-2075
  at University of California, 1535
  at University of Michigan, 1518
Failure
  in Essentialist platform, 2653
  and lockstep system, 2275
  and visual problems, 2402-2403
  in Winnetka, Illinois schools, 2491
"Failure of the Public Schools and the Free Market, The" (Levin), 3329*n*
"Fair Harvard," 1721
Fairchild, Henry Pratt, 2381-2386
"Faithful Narrative of the Surprising Work of God in the Conversion of Many Hundred Souls in Northampton, A. . .," 425-427
Familiar Sketches of the Phillips Exeter Academy (Cunningham), 517-518, 518-522
Families (Family), 2001
  allocution to fathers of, 2043*n*
  in America, 936-937
  and attendance at high school, 2507-2508
  impact on high school achievement, 2635-2637
  incomes, National Youth Administration and, 2557-2558

wandering, during depression, 2530
See also Family life; Parents
Family consultation centers, 2551
Family education, role of, 1915
Family Expositor (Doddridge), 517
Family grouping, 3302
Family life
  and Americanization of Chinese immigrants, 1767
  in Children's Charter, 2551-2552
  among East Side Jews, 2913-2914
  education for, 2549-2551
  and Jewish immigrants, 2151-2152
  and mental illness, 2396-2398
  and school rules, 3057
  and social relationships, 2609
Family size
  and high school attendance, 2507-2508
  and intelligence quotients, 2509
Family spirit, in educational establishment, 835
Fantasy
  and activity, 3266-3267
  and play, 2034, 2080, 2081
Faraday, 2758
Farber, Jerry, 2864-2867
Farish, Hunter D., 457-467, 719
Farity, Charles, 1626
Farm
  at Indian School, 1759-1760
  as school, 1759-1760
Farm children. *See* Rural schools
Farming, and rural education, 2352
Farnaby, 290
Farnifold, John, 643, 645
Farquharson, Francis, 468
Farrington, Frederick, 73-74
Farrington v. *Tokushige*, 2976
Fascism
  and Civilian Conservation Corps, 2566
  and unemployed intellectuals, 2817
Fashion, in education of girls, 245
Father Henson's Story of His Own Life (Fisher), 1619
Father-image, of school, 2394-2395
Father(s)
  occupation, in IEA study of mathematics achievement, 2054
  and parents associations, 2307
  relations with sons, 845-846, 2913-2914
Fauquier, Governor, 453
Fears
  and child training, 2005-2006
  and demoralization, 2007-2008
  and discipline, 89
  in education, 826
  instincts of, 2244
  of lightning, 2396
  study of, 1840
  and teaching, 268

and upbringing, 94-95
Featherstone, Joseph, 3299-3305
Federal aid to education, 1006-1009, 2807
  and Blair Bill, 1692-1695
  call for, 1691-1692
  and Civil Rights Act of 1964, 3370-3371
  and Civilian Conservation Corps, 2558-2567
  and Commission on National Aid to Vocational Education, 2360-2363
  during depression, 2535
  and Elementary and Secondary Education Act, 3372-3373
  and Higher Education Facilities Act, 3358-3361
  and Higher Education Opportunity Act, 3382-3388
  Kennedy on, 3348-3358
  and National Youth Administration, 2555-2558
  and reading deficiencies, 3377-3382
  and Smith-Hughes Act, 2364-2368
  and Smith-Lever Act, 2363-2364
  and vocational education, 3369
  Walker on, 1686-1690
  See also Federal government
Federal Board for Vocational Education, 2364
Federal Bureau of Education, 2420
"Federal Catechism" (Webster), 769-770
Federal Communications Commission, and educational radio programs, 2841
"Federal Corporation in Unemployment Relief, Hearing Before a Subcommittee of the Committee on Manufacturers," 2531-2534
Federal Employees Compensation Act, 3376
Federal Gazette, 597-599
Federal government
  and creation of Department of Health, Education and Welfare, 3341-3342
  and education, 1408, 1410-1414, 2355-2368, 2549-2567, 3341-3393
  and establishment of Peace Corps, 3347
  housing policy, 3034
  and implementation of Supreme Court desegregation decision, 3038-3040
  and Indian education, 1740-1745, 1754-1760
  and proposal for National Institute of Education, 3389-3393
  and schools, 957-958
  and Teacher Corps, 3373-3377
  and vocational education, 3365-3369

See also White House Conference on Education
Federal regional schools, 3316
Federal Security Administrator, and creation of Department of Health, Education and Welfare, 3342
Federal Security Agency, 2623n
Federal and State Constitutions, Colonial Charters, and Other Organic Laws of the United States, The (Moore), 793-794, 797, 809, 1021, 1650-1651
Federal and State Constitutions. . ., The (Thorpe), 1647, 1647-1648, 1651, 1652
Federal troops
  in Little Rock, Arkansas, 3013-3016, 3110
  at University of Mississippi, 3018-3019
Federal university. *See* National University
Federalist, The, 2799
Federated Institutes Dependent on Ecclesiastical Authority, 2043n, 2050n
Federation of Catholic Universities, 2052n
Federation of Women's Clubs, 3058
Feeble-minded children
  and intelligence tests, 2250, 2257
  and public schools, 2403-2406
  See also Retarded children
Fees, for lectures by professors, 1457
Feinberg Law, 2724-2727, 2734-2736
Felkin, Emmie, 857-861
Felkin, Herman M., 857-861
Fellner, E., 999
Fellows
  of Brown University, 705
  of Harvard College, 660
  of Yale College, 673-674, 679
Fellowships, 248
Felsenthal, Rabbi Bernard, 1194-1195, 1201
Felton (president of Harvard), 1464
Female equality, in Greenwich Village philosophy, 2415, 2416
Female Guardian Society of America, 2154
Female seminaries
  benefits of, 1579-1580
  description of, 1575-1579
  proposed in New England, 1583
  purpose of, 1584-1585
Female teachers, 1093, 1580-1581, 3221
  advantages of, 1317-1318
  in England and U.S. compared, 2106
  and female seminary training, 1579-1580
  increase in number of in Massachusetts, 1315-1316

Folk dancing, and organic education, 2496
Folk singing, and organic education, 2496
Folks, Homer, 2355-2356
Following the Color Line (Baker), 2992-2993
Fonesca, 195
Fontaine, Rev. Peter, 574-575
Fontenelle, 1484
Food
    at "Soup School" for Italian immigrants, 2153-2155
    in Soviet Union, 3154
Food fadism, and weaning experiences in infancy, 2412
Foote, 1772
Forbes, Abner, 1703
Force
    child's conceptions about, 2028
    in mental development of child, 2026
Ford, Lieutenant E., 1738
Ford, Paul Leicester, 530-533, 596-597, 739-744, 783-785 1483-1485
Ford, Washington, 408-410
Ford Foundation, 3277
    grant to higher education, 2818-2820
Foreign Associates, of National Academy of Education, 2680
"Foreign colonies," 2382
Foreign languages. *See* Language learning; Languages; and under individual names of Foreign studies. *See* European education for Americans
Foreign trade, in manufactured articles, 2362-2363
Forensicks, 1236
Forerunners of the International Bureau of Education (Ressello), 2011
Forest Grove Indian School, 1752
Forest Park Community College, St. Louis, 2850
Forestry and Soil Erosion Service, 2558
"Foreword," *The Graduate Study of Education* (Sizer), 2686-2687
Forfeits, at Boston High School for Girls, 1250
Forgery, in South Carolina College rules, 1433
Form system, 2108
Formal lessons, 89-80
Formal thinking operations, and cognitive development, 3249-3250
Forms, and education, 830-831
Fornication, in South Carolina College rules, 1433
Forrester, E. L., 3006-3009
Forster School, Somerville, Mass., 2324
Forsyth, Alex, 407
Fort Berthold, 1739
Fort Worth, Texas, Association of Junior Colleges Convention at, 2845
Fortas, Justice, 2739-2742

Forte-Piana, 458
Fortesque, Charles, 440
Fortification, 185, 244, 442, 443
Forum, The, 1842-1844, 2217-2219
Fossils, and child study, 1841
Foster, John, 343, 914
Foster, Joseph, 903
Foster, Mrs., 1034
Foster, Nathan, 1051-1052
Fouace, Stephen, 643, 645
"Fougueux," 1115
Fould, 1198
Foundations, Bacon, on, 210-211
Foundations of Method (Kilpatrick), 2442-2444
Founding Fathers, and church-state controversy, 3077-3078
"Founding of the Hampton Institute, The," 1653-1654
Founding of Harvard College, The (Morison), 657-660
Fountain, L. H., 3006-3009
Fouquet, 839n, 840n
Fourteenth Amendment, 2729, 2739, 3077, 3099
    effect on public education, 3104
    Equal Protection Clause of, 3102
    and segregation, 3087-3090
    See also Church-state controversy
Fourteenth Yearbook: Part I, Minimum Essentials In Elementary School Subjects, 2261-2266
Fourth Annual Report of the Secretary of the Board of Education, 1311-1315
Fourth Report of the Boston Record Commissioners, 397-399
Fox, Justus, 524
Foxcroft dining club, 1720
Foxley, Barbara, 90-106
Frame gilding, and child labor, 2140
France
    education in, 106-108, 110-115
    Jews in, 1198-1199
    moral codes in, 2385
    Second Empire, 1463
    secondary schools in, 1924
    vocational education, 2363
France, University of, 2119
France-Soir, 2061
Frankfurter, Justice, 2732, 2883, 3054-3058, 3069-3071, 3074, 3078, 3108-3113
    on Feinberg Law, 2726
Franklin, Benjamin, 434-435, 510, 1746, 1964, 2758
    on achievement of wealth, 492-495
    business advice of, 491-492
    on college education, 482-484
    on curriculum of academy, 495-500
    on education of German immigrants, 637-638
    on education of Indian children, 626-627

    education of, 476-480
    on education in Philadelphia, 504-509
    on German immigrants, 630-631
    on morality, 487-490
    plan for academy by, 495-500
    on religion, 484-487
    on slave trade, 597-599
    on virtues, 488-490
    See also Philadelphia Academy
Franklin, Cleo, 3339
Franklin, James, 477
Franklin, Matthew, 985-986
Franklin, Thomas, 985-986
Franklin County, Virginia, 1658-1659
Fraser, Bishop, 960
Fraternities. *See* Phi Beta Kappa Society
Frazier, James B., Jr., 3006-3009
Frederick the Great, 928, 1388-1390
Free association, 1602
Free day, in British infant schools, 3301
Free enterprise, and education, 1904
Free Exercise Clause, 3077, 3080-3081
Free Inquirer, The, 1215-1219
Free lunches, during Depression, 2527
Free Negroes, Mississippi law forbidding education of, 1621
    See also Education of Negroes; Manumission of slaves; Negroes
Free play
    importance of, 1806
    and organic education, 2497
Free press, Jefferson on, 751-752
Free School System of the United States, The (Adams), 950-954
Free schools
    in Brookline, Massachusetts, 403
    in Connecticut, 403
    fines used in support of, 404
    in Hampton, New Hampshire, 401
    Jefferson on, 741
    in Massachusetts, 396-397
    for Negro children in New York, 589
    and nonresidents, 404-405
    petition from North Boston for, 405
    in Philadelphia, 761-762
    proposals for, 757
    Virginia petition for, 642
"Free Schools of Denmark, The" (Fuchs), 3329n
Free Schools: A Documentary History of the Free School Movement in New York State (Finegan), 352, 544-545
"Free Seminaries of Brooklyn" (Whitman), 1296-1297
"Free Sons of Israel," 1200
Free Speech Movement, at University of California, Berkeley, 2859-2863

Free University of California,
  proposals for, 2863
Freedman's organizations, 1411
Freedmen's Bureau
  act establishing, 1635
  description of schools under
    supervision of, 1641-1642
Freedmen's school, 1635-1636
Freedom
  of American children, 946
  and art teaching, 2489
  and computers, 3314-3315
  and Dalton Plan, 2466-2467
  and education, 756, 1015,
    1068-1069, 3156-3160
  and elective system, 1554,
    1558-1559
  and Essentialist platform, 2651-
    2652
  from guilt feelings, 3265
  in high school, 3216
  in open classroom, 3319
  and progressive education,
    2449, 2456, 2458-2459, 2579-
    2580, 2645-2646, 2648-2649
  and pupil initiative, 2450
  in school, 2230
  and student self-government,
    2473-2477
  at Summerhill, 3270
Freedom of association
  for students, 2885-2886
  for teachers, 2724-2736
"Freedom of Choice" Plan, 3117-
  3120
Freedom of speech
  Jefferson on, 752
  for teachers, 2736-2738
Freehand drawing, by American
  teachers, 962
Freeman, Douglas S., 2814n
Free-trade philosophy, and
  neglect of education, 1002
Frelich, Jacob, 524
Frelinghuysen, 979
French Constitution, 112
French education
  compared with American
    education, 1924-1925, 2119-
    2122
  and March 22nd Movement,
    2059-2061
  and standardization, 3313-3314
French high schools
  examinations in, 2120
  General Competition in, 2119
French language, 173, 452, 510,
  523
  in college curriculum, 1505
  in Dalton Plan, 2469
  at Manual Training School of
    Washington University, 1860
  in secondary school curriculum,
    1936, 1939
  teachers of, 2706
  in university curriculum, 804
French lessons, in New York, 443
*French Liberalism and Education
  in the Eighteenth Century*
  (de la Fontainerie), 106-108,
  110-115
French Revolution, 2119
  discussion of, 3319

and education, 2121
French Secondary Schools
  (Farrington), 73-74
"Frenchman Appraises United
  States Schools, A" (Maurois),
  2119-2122
Fresno Buddhist School, 2976n
Freud, Anna, on psychoanalysis
  and education, 2004-2007
Freud, Sigmund, 3253, 3270
  on psychical apparatus, 2000-
    2002
  on psychoanalysis and child
    training, 2002-2003
Frick, 969, 970, 971, 1886
Friedlander, 1198
Friedman, Milton, 3277, 3329n
Friends. *See* Quakers
Frietchie, Barbara, 2112-2113
Froebel, Friedrich, 842-846, 846-
  848, 848-849, 850, 1856,
  1858, 2230, 2437
  and child study, 1846
  compared with Herbart, 1891
  education philosophy of, 851-
    853
  on free play, 1805-1808
  kindergarten gifts of, 1802-
    1805, 1807
  and Montessori method, 2322
  on play with children, 851-852
  and teacher's role, 1997
  See also Froebel's method
Froebel School, Gary, Indiana,
  2340
Froebel Union, 1797
Froebel's gifts, 1908
Froebel's method, 1908
  Peabody on, 1792-1798
  and teacher requirements,
    1798-1799
  and teacher training, 1788-1789
Froelicher, Francis M., 2422
Frontier days, rural school in,
  2599
Frost, Amarieas, 716
Frost, Robert, 3148
Frothingham, O.B., 1213-1215
Froude, 1545
Frugality, Webster on, 773
Fry, John, 524
Fry, Joshua, 452
Fuchs, Estelle, 3329n
Fulbright, J. W., 3006-3009
"Function of the Mental Hygiene
  Clinic in the Schools and
  Colleges, The" (Blanton),
  2481-2482
"Function of the University In
  the Training of Teachers,
  The" (Russell), 2662-2665
Functional Method (Leslie), 3137
*Functions of Secondary
  Education*, 2627n
Fund raising
  for education in Virginia, 1001
  for Hebrew College, 1186
  for Indian education, 1741-
    1742
  for Jewish education, 1182
  for Jewish schools, 1184-1185
  and lotteries, 1060

by Montessori Educational
  Association, 2321
by New York Free-School
  Society, 1122
and philanthropists, 1326
for Progressive Education
  Association, 2418-2419
for rural schools, 2349
for school in North Carolina,
  980
for Silver Street Kindergarten,
  1802
by Society for Establishing a
  Free School in the City of
  New York, 984-986
for South Carolina Normal
  School, 1349
for Summerhill, 2068-2069
for Teachers College,
  Columbia University, 1421
See also Financing; Funds
"Fundamental Assumptions in the
  Report of the Committee of
  Ten, The" (Eliot), 1951-1959
Funds
  Catholic petitions for, 1155-
    1157
  for civilization of Indians, 1728
  for education, 1413
  for female seminary for
    teachers, 1583
  for Industrial Education
    Association, 1422-1423
  for public schools in
    California, 1048
  for State Normal School for
    New Britain, Connecticut,
    1340
  See also Fund raising
Funerals, as teacher's duty, 546
Furniture. *See* School furniture
Furnivall, F. J., 171-175, 299-304
"Future for the Tests, A"
  (Lippmann), 2425-2428
Gaba, 163
Gabain, Marjorie, 2023-2029
Gage, Thomas, 593
Gaging, 446
Galbraith, J. K., 3191
Galbraith, John A., 2909
Galbraith, Major, 1739
Galbreath, L. H., 1851
Galen, 163
Galenes, 151
Galilee, 144, 149
Galileo, 1231
  on Copernican theory, 80-81
Gall, Dr., 884-885
Gallaudet, T. H., 1306-1307
Galleries, in classroom, 249
Gallup polls, 2856
Gambling, in Yale College laws,
  677
Games
  in American high schools, 2110
  and child study method, 1847
  at Indian Schools, 1758-1759
  symbolism of, 1805-1808
  See also under individual
    names of
Gammel, H. P. N., 1016-1019
Gansyoort Farmers Market, 2502
Garden of Eden, 138-140

teacher training programs, 3164
in American schools, 2118
and Batavia Plan, 2270-2271
and child study, 1843
Dewey on, 2214
at elementary school of School of Education at University of Missouri, 2478
at Ethical Culture School, 2480
at Harvard College, 1462
impact on high school achievement, 2635-2637
at Indian Schools, 1757
in Park Forest schools, 3141
and progressive schools, 2449
in progressive and traditional schools, 2457
Soviet education on, 2126-2127
in suburban high schools, 3218
Gradgrind, Thomas, 908-911
Graduate school, women at, 3221-3222
Graduate students, at Teachers College, Columbia University, 2659-2660
Graduates, of experimental college plan, 2616-2617
from Columbia University, 696
from grammar school, 960
from normal school
See also Bachelor of Arts; Master of Arts
Graduation certificates, from Phillips Exeter Academy, 522-523
Graecae linguae (Clavis), 291
Graeme, 347
Grafton, Mary, 544
Grafton, Richard, 544
Graham, William A., 1676
Grainger, Samuel, 439
Grammar, 46, 47, 48, 55, 150, 160, 172, 180, 184, 185, 188, 264, 270-271, 278, 285, 361, 446, 456, 458, 497, 500, 501-502, 522
before age seven, 159
in British infant schools, 3303
and child study method, 1848
in college curriculum, 66, 2797-2798
in elementary school curriculum, 1964-1965, 1969
examination in, 1256-1257
of Indian languages, 607-608
and Latin, 967-968
and Latin studies, 1927
at Manual Training School of Washington University, 1860
at Notre Dame University, 1160
at Phillips Exeter Academy, 1236-1237
and play of combinations, 860
in Prussian elementary schools, 931
psychological basis of, 1917
rules for teachers of, 71-72
in Society of Jesus universities, 67
textbooks, 539

in university curriculum, 195, 906
at University of Virginia, 1488, 1489
Grammar (Lilie), 290
Grammar books, 208
Grammar schools
curriculum for, 500-504, 1926-1930
curriculum and teaching methods in, 289-298
in Dorchester, Massachusetts, 397-399
English teaching in, 287-289
entrance requirements, 297
examinations for, 1253-1258
in post-revolutionary U.S., 739-744
purpose of, 284-286
rules for professor of, 71-72
of William and Mary College, 653
See also Elementary schools and under individual names of
Grand jury men, 402-403
"Grand Man," 1915
Grand River agency, 1739
Grande (chimpanzee), 2012
Grant, George M., 3006-3009
Grant, Ulysses S., 1676
on public funds for religious schools, 1165-1166
Grant, W. Horsley, 2017-2020
Grappin, Dean, 2060, 2061
Gratian, 134
Gratification, and learning problems, 3254-3260
Gratz, Rebecca, 222, 222; 223-229, 1191-1192, 1200
Gray, Samuel, 645
Gray, W. A., 1772
Gray, William S., 2492n
Gray Standardized Oral Reading Check Test, 2571
Graydon, Alexander, 510-513
Great Awakening: Documents Illustrating the Crisis. . .,
The (Miller and Heimert), 682-685
Great Barrington high school, 1720
Great Britain
apprenticeship law in, 318-321
charity school in
child study societies in, 1841
education in, compared with American education, 2104-2108
education in, Plowden Report on, 2092-2095
and education of German immigrants in American colonies, 634-635
education of poor of, 987
elites in, 3182n
infant schools in, 3299-3305
Jews in, 1198-1199
Pestalozzianism in, 1780
primary schools in, 2095-2097
and Rhodes scholarships, 2063-2065
Great Didactic of John Amos

Comenius, The (Keatinge), 258-265
Grecian antiquities, at Princeton University, 709
Grecians, 125
Greek education, 508-509, 1054, 1067, 1868
compared with United States, 937
and physical training, 42-43
Greek grammar, 165, 291, 458, 517
in college curriculum, 2797-2798
recited, 72
Greek language, 40, 55, 67, 172, 183-184, 191, 262, 267, 347, 348, 350, 351, 403, 406, 413, 441, 456, 461, 499, 510, 517, 523, 554, 653, 657, 658
at Albany Female Academy, 1594
for Bibles, 63, 132, 134-135
and child study method, 1848-1849
in college curriculum, 1505, 1507, 1547-1548
and elective system, 2747
in Jesuit curriculum, 73-74
learning of, 150
Locke on, 236-237
Marian exiles on, 126-127
at Princeton University, 709
in secondary school curriculum, 1940
Thoreau on, 1221-1222
in university curriculum, 56
in Virginia schools, 749-750
See also Ancient languages; Greek grammar; Greek literature
Greek literature, 40, 150-151, 154-155, 185
censorship of, 68
Greek Test (Hesiod), 351
Greek Testament, 193, 285, 291, 348, 675
Greeke Commentaries (Budaeus), 272
Greeley, Andrew, 3279
Green, Bishop Joseph, 2909
Green, Edwin L., 1433-1434
Green, Enoch, 457
Green, Jacob, 686
Green, Robert, 344
Green v. School Board of New Kent County, 3117-3120
Greene, George W., 1545
Greenwich Village idea, 2415-2416
Greenwich Village Voice, 3270
Greenwood, 479
Greenwood, I. M., 1835
Gregg system, 3137
Gregory, 290
Griffin, John, 1482-1483
Griffin v. County School Board of Prince Edward, 3113-3116
Grimkes, 2986
"Grimm's Fairy Tales," 1876
Grimshaw, Aaron, 473
Grinnell, Peter, 1051-1052
Griscom, John, 853-856

Griswold, Mississippi, 1830
Griswood, Grace, 344
Gross National Product (GNP), in IEA study of mathematics achievement, 2055
Group activities. See Activity movement
Group consciousness, 2461-2462
Group demoralization, 2009
Group hostility, and play, 2081
Group life, and Dalton Plan, 2467
Group play, at Little Red School House, 2502-2503
Group projects, and Project method, 2273
Grouping
   and comprehensive education, 2056-2057
   "family" or "vertical," 3302
Grout, Paul, 1140
Growing Up Absurd (Goodman), 3188-3192
Growth
   in early childhood, 3252
   and education, 2232-2233, 2282
Grube's method, 1746
Grund, Francis J., 941-945
Grundy, Felix, 979
Guainacapa, 604
Guardian, 503
Guidance programs, 2605
   in Middletown high schools, 2606
   in secondary schools, 2284
Guide to the Kindergarten. . . (Peabody), 1794-1798
Guild, Reuben A., 704-706
Guilday, Peter, 1158-1159, 1162-1163, 2893-2897
Guilt feelings
   freedom from, 3265
   and motherhood, 2115
Guiraud, 837n
Gulliver's Travels, 1969
Gun powder, in South Carolina College rules, 1433
Gunnery, 442, 443
Gurdjieff, George Ivanovich, 2415n
Guyot, 1402
Gwyn, Hugh, 343
Gymnasium
   curriculum in, 1924
   in Gary, Indiana schools, 2333
   in Prussia, 1512, 1513
Gymnastics
   in Prussian teachers seminaries, 1511
   at University of Virginia, 1491
   See also Physical training
Habersham, Joseph, 789
"Habit Clinics for Children of the Pre-School Age" (Thom), 2465-2466
Habit formation, 2407
   and "conduct curriculum," 2474-2477
   and "habit clinics" for preschool children, 2465-2466
   and infant care, 2358
   laws of, 2246-2247

"Habit Inventory," in Teachers College kindergarten, 2474-2477
Habits, 94
   and Americanization of Chinese immigrants, 1767
   and educational change, 508-509
   and moral obligation, 1478
   See also Habit formation
Hackett, Mr., 543
Hadarim, 2924
Haddad, William, 2909
Haddon, William, 266, 267, 269, 513
Hagar, D. B., 1399
Hagiographa, 2919
Haigue, William, 359
Hailmann, W. N., 842-846
Hakluyt, Richard, 331-334
Hale, Dr. Benjamin, 1455
Hale, Samuel, 716
Hale, William T., 3236
Haley, James A., 3006-3009
Halezy, 1198
Halifax Medical College, 2774n
Hall, Clifton C., 1070-1071
Hall, Clifton L., 513, 1252
Hall, Clifton S., 1779
Hall, Francis, 714, 722, 723
Hall, Frederick, 1020-1021
Hall, G. Stanley, 2205-2206
   criticism of Committee of Ten report on secondary education, 1946-1951
   Eliot responds to, 1951-1959
   on ideal school based on child study, 1845-1851
   on knowledge of children entering primary schools, 1833-1840
   See also Child study
Hall, Richard, 543
Hall, Samuel R.
   on teaching, 1357-1359
Hall, Sidney B., 2602-2603
Hall, Thomas, 448, 726
Hall passes, 3202
Hall v. St. Helena Parish School Board, 3115
Halley, Dr., 418
Ham, Charles H., 1857-1859
Hamilton, Alexander, 808
Hamilton, Archibald, 446
Hamilton, Gail, 1597
Hamilton, James, 637-638
Hamilton, John, 685
Hamilton v. Regents, 3055
Hamlet, 2462-2463
Hampton, Bernard, 266
Hampton Court Conference, 133-134
Hampton Institute, 1660, 2988
   Booker T. Washington at, 1661-1664
   and Carlisle Indian School, 1745
   catalogue of, 1655-1657
   curriculum at, 1655-1656
   description of, 1654
   discipline at, 1657
   founding of, 1653-1654

and Indian education, 1740-1745, 1749, 1752
   industrial training in, 3004
Hampton and Its Students (Armstrong and Ludlow), 1654, 1655-1657
Hampton Normal School. See Hampton Institute
Hancock, General, 1744, 1745
Hancock, Mary, 346
Hancock, Thomas, 346
Handbook of University Extension (James), 1613-1616
Handicrafts, 262
Handwriting, 497
   in Prussian schools, 1090
Haney, George E., 3192-3197
Haney, James P., 2266, 2267
Hannan, Philip M., 2907
Hansen, Allen O., 991-992
Hanus, Paul, 2257-2260
Hapgood, Hutchins, 2914-2915
Happiness
   and education, 2084
   in school, 2437-2438
Hard Times (Dickens), 907-911
Hardey, Charles, 708
Harding, President, 2383
Hardy, Georgiana, 2937
Hardy, John, 391, 392
Hardy, Porter, Jr., 3006-3009
Hardy, Samuel, 722, 723, 726
Hardy, W. J., 363
Haring, 3256
Harlan, Justice, 2735-2736, 3089-3090, 3093, 3108-3113, 3361
Harlem, 3218, 3219-3220, 3277, 3279
Harmony, in teacher seminaries in Prussia, 933
Harper, William Rainey, 2262n, 2873-2875
   on correspondence teaching, 1608-1613
Harper's Magazine, 1791
Harper's Weekly, 1414-1415, 1644-1645
Harpsicord, 458
Harquebus, 172
Harrington, Johns, 2936-2942
Harris, Ann Sutherland, 3220-3222
Harris, Dr., 969, 970, 971-972
Harris, James, 1700
Harris, Oren, 2006-3009
Harris, Owen, 438
Harris, Reed, 2791-2795
Harris, Rhoda, 2503
Harris, Roger, 344
Harris, Seymour E., 2814-2818
Harris, Townsend, 3321
Harris, William Torrey, 1613, 1930-1946
   on moral education, 1909-1914
   on psychology and education, 1917-1919
   on recitation methods, 1919-1922
   on social purposes of education, 1914-1917
   on value of kindergarten, 1907-1908
Harrison, Benjamin, 643, 645

Harrison, Burr P., 3006-3009
Harrison, Frederic, 924
Harrison, Harvey, 349
Harrison, Major, 349
Harrison, Mrs., 249
Harrols, Susan P., 1655
Harrower, John, 468-473
Harrower, Mrs. John, 471-472
Hart, Albert Bushnell, 1718, 1719
Hart, Hastings H., 2355-2356
Hartford Connecticut Female
    Seminary
    catalogues of, 1582-1583
    Catherine Beecher on purpose
        of, 1580-1582
    curriculum at
Hartford, Connecticut, free
    schools in, 403
Hartley, Stephen, 447
Hartley House, 2317
Hartlib, Samuel, 186, 243-244,
    248
*Hartlib, Dury and Comenius:
    Gleanings from Hartlib's
    Papers* (Turnbull), 243-244
Hartman, Gertrude, 2421, 2438-
    2441, 2444-2446, 2483-2486,
    2486-2489
Hartsook, Ralph, 1299, 1300
Hartwell, Henry, 643, 645
Harvard College, 484, 691-692,
    2119
    Adams on, 1460-1467
    advice to students at, 663-671
    charter of, 660-661
    class of 1858, 1461
    criticism of elective system at,
        1558-1563
    curriculum at, 662, 663-666,
        1462, 1561
    discipline at, 965
    elections at
    and Eliot, 655
    Eliot's inaugural address as
        president of, 1546-1554
    fines at, 716-717
    first rules of, 657
    founding of, 656, 1467, 2845
    Lawrence Scientific School of,
        1514
    Master of Art theses at, 715-
        716
    opposition to proposed college
        in West Massachusetts, 700-
        704
    Phi Beta Kappa Society at,
        725-726
    Presidential address at, 671
    and Protestant sects, 1468
    religious education at, 681-685
    sex discrimination at, 3221
    statutes of, 658-660
    student politics at, 718
    Whitefield on, 681-685
    See also Harvard University
*Harvard College in the
    Seventeenth Century*
    (Morison), 662-666, 671
Harvard Committee on the
    Graduate Study of
    Education, 2686-2687
Harvard Committee on Secondary

Education, 2618-2622, 2802-
    2806
Harvard Educational Review,
    3202-3209, 3210-3214, 3229-
    3235, 3315-3317
Harvard Graduate Magazine,
    2745-2748
Harvard Graduate School, 2752
Harvard Graduate School of
    Education, 3140, 3211
    staff of, 2702
Harvard Psychological
    Laboratories, 3230
Harvard University
    Booker T. Washington's address
        at, 1675-1676
    elective system at, 1554-1557
    faculty committee on African
        and Afro-American studies,
        3327
    Jewish students at, 1183
    reform plan for, 1492-1494
    in 1888, 1718
    See also Harvard College
Harvard University Archives, 718
Harvey, Sarah, 346
Harvey, Thomas, 346
Haskell, 1330
Haslet, James, 524
Hastings, Hugh, 352, 356
Hasty Pudding Club, 1466, 1718-
    1719
Hathaway, William D., 3381
Havighurst, 3253
Havilah, 139
Hawaii, missionary plan in, 1653
Hawkes, Dean Herbert E., 2793,
    2794, 2795
Hawkins, Augustus F., 3381
Hawkins, Hugh, 1568
Hawkins, Miss, 1330
Hawthorne, 1964, 2291
Hay, John, 1464
Hayes, Carlton, 2111
Haygood, Atticus G., 1680
Hayne, 290, 979, 1772-1775
Hays, Brooks, 2006-3009
Hays, Isaac, 449-450
Hays, Will H., 2388-2391
Hayt, Ezra A., 1742, 1743
Hazard, Samuel, 686
*Hazard's Register of
    Pennsylvania*, 1064, 1064-
    1067
Hazlewood, 584
Head, configurations of. *See*
    Phrenology
Head Master, 165, 169
Head monitor, at Boston High
    School for Girls, 1250
Head Start. *See* Project Head
    Start
Head teacher, in new British
    primary schools, 2096
Health, 244, 249, 251-252
    of American women, 1598
    and Batavia Plan, 2270
    at Boston High School for
        Girls, 1249
    in California, 1530-1531
    and educational goals, 2281
    of homeless children, 2530
    in Indian schools, 2958

and mental development, 233-
    234
    at Mount Holyoke Seminary,
        1590-1591
    and New York tenements, 2143
    in North Boston slums, 2137-
        2138
    and physical education courses,
        1101-1102
    and progressive education,
        2447
    and school nurse, 2305-2306
    and schoolhouses, 1082
    of working children in
        Chicago, 2140-2141
Health benefits
    and Teacher Corps, 3376
"Health Briefs," 2528
Health care, in Children's
    Charter, 2553
Health education
    in comprehensive high school,
        2287, 2288
    Harvard Committee on
        Secondary Education on,
        2621
Health program, White House
    Conference Committee
    Report on, 2554
Health record, 2360
Health Service, in universities,
    2785
Healy, Dr., 2481
Healy, Timothy, 3324, 3325n
Hearing, of wild boy, 839
Heart is the Teacher, The
    (Covello), 2153-2155
Heath, John, 719, 720, 722
Heathohn J., 723
Heating, of public school in
    Pennsylvania, 1297
Hebb, 3253
Hebert, F. Edward, 3006-3009
Hebrew Bible, 1191
Hebrew College
    proposal for, 1185-1188
    sites for, 1186-1187
Hebrew Congregation in
    Newport, Rhode Island, 811-
    812
Hebrew education, Annual
    Report of Commissioner of
    Education on, 1195-1199
"Hebrew Education" (Noah),
    1195-1199
Hebrew grammar, 169
    textbooks, 538
Hebrew hymns, 1192
Hebrew language, 67, 172, 186,
    262, 285, 347, 348, 350, 418,
    460, 654, 658
    for Bible, 63, 132, 134-135
    in college curriculum, 1505
    and Jewish American children,
        2914
    in Jewish schools, 1184, 1195,
        1196-1197, 2926-2927, 2928
    Marian exiles on, 126-127
    in university curriculum, 56, 57
    See also Ancient languages
Hebrew literature, 40
Hebrew Orphan Asylum,
    Cleveland, 1201

Higher Education Opportunity Act (1970), 3382-3388

Higher Learning in America, The (Hutchins), 2796-2799

Higher Learning in America, The (Veblen), 2778-2780

Highet, Gilbert, 2705-2707

"High-School Costs" (Bobbitt), 2260-2261

Hilgard, Ernest, 1800, 1802, 3164

Hill, Colonel, 349

Hill, Frank Ernest, 2558-2562

Hill, Henry, 524

Hill, Lister, 3006-3009

Hill, Merton E., 2930-2934

Hill, Patty, 2317, 2473-2477

Hillard, George S., 1703

Hillsdale College, 2763

Hinckley, Francis E., 1567

Hindustan, intermarriage in, 1752

Hine, Lewis W., 2147-2150

Hinsdale, B. A., 1414, 1415-1418

Hippocrates, 151, 1490

Hiram, 123

Hirschfelder, Dr. J., 1800, 1802

"Hist. Nat. des Animaux sans Vertebres" (Lamarck), 915

Historians, Greek, 151

Historical Account of the Incorporated Society for the Propagation of the Gospel in Foreign Parts, An (Humphreys), 577-580, 580-584

Historical Collection of Essex Institute, 391-392

Historical Collections (Burton), 477

Historical sciences, professorship of, 1482

"Historical Sketch of Teachers College From its Foundation to 1897" (Harvey), 1420-1425

History of education courses in, 1419
in teacher training courses, 1973, 1975-1976, 1982

History of Education in New Jersey (Murray), 1339

History of Education in Pennsylvania (Wickersham), 359, 558-559

History of Eton College, A, (Maxwell-Ltle), 164-165

History examinations, 1253-1254

History of the Grammar School in Roxburie, A (Dillaway), 397

History of Harvard University, A (Pierce), 715-716

History of Harvard University, The (Quincy), 700-704, 716-717

History of New England from 1630-1649, The (Winthrop), 383

History of Oberlin College, A (Fletcher), 1495-1497, 1496-1497

History of the Parish of Trinity Church in the City of New York, A (Dix), 589

"History of Pedagogy" (Compayre), 1419

History and Present State of Virginia, The (Wright), 605-606

History of the Public School Society of the City of New York (Bourne), 983-986, 986-988, 1119-1122, 1122, 1123-1125, 1126-1127, 1133-1136, 1136-1139, 1143-1146

History of the Public School System of California (Swett), 1032-1033, 1033, 1046-1050

History of the Reformation of Religion in Scotland, The (Knox), 54-57

History of the Royal Society of London for the Improving of Natural Knowledge, The (Sprat), 216-220

History of San Jose, The (Hall), 1020-1021

History teaching, 42, 162, 191, 351, 388, 455, 456, 498, 499, 502, 503, 510, 523, 1236
in American schools, 968-969
in American schools in 1874, 1906
at Beaver Country Day School, 2498-2499
books for, 203-204, 1876
in college curriculum, 1505, 1507, 1548
at Cook County Normal School, 1830
in Dalton Plan, 2469
Dewey on, 2214-2215
and dramatization, 2483-2484
in elementary school curriculum, 1966, 1969
in French secondary school curriculum, 1925
in German and American schools, 943
at Hampton Institute, 1655
in Herbartian system, 1877-1878, 1883, 1890
in high school curriculum, 2520
and life activities, 922-923
at Manual Training School of Washington University, 1860
and moral education, 1886
in normal schools, 1334
at Notre Dame University, 1160
professorship of, 1482
in Prussian teachers seminaries, 1511
psychological basis of, 1917
reforms in, 969-970
in secondary school curriculum, 1936, 1939
in Society of Jesus universities, 67
textbook for, 1372-1373
in university curriculum, 803, 906
at University of Virginia, 1488
in Virginia schools, 749-750
History textbooks, of nineteenth century, 1391-1392

History of the United States (Hale), 1139

History of the University of Michigan (Hinsdale), 1414

History of the University of South Carolina, A (Green), 1433-1434

Hitchcock, Edward, 1583-1585, 1585-1589

Hitchcock, Roswell D., 1654

Hite, Isaac, 722

Hitler, 2566

Hoadley, Charles J., 672-674

Hoar, Hon. G. F., 1412

Hoar, Jonathan, 716

Hoar, Leonard, 663-666

Hoar Bill (1870), 1683-1686

Hobart College, education at, 1454-1457

Hobbes, 242

Hobby, Charles, 439

Hoboes, compared with homeless children, 2529

Hodgson, Shadworth, 2208

"Hodson's Life," 1234

Hoffman, John, 559-560

Hoffman, Virginia, 2967

Hofstadter, Richard, 2867

Hofwyl, Switzerland, agricultural school at, 853-856

Hogg, W. Q., 2831n

Hohenlinden (Campbell), 1964

Holbrook, Josiah, proposal for constitution for American Lyceum, 1605-1606

Holbrook's apparatus, 1311

Holdsworth, Richard, 187

Holidays, 465-466
in American schools, 964
at Indian schools, 1759
in Jewish schools, 2920, 2928
of Providence public schools, 1285
in rural schools, 2349

Holladay, Antho., 344

Holland, Spessard L., 3006-3009

Holliday, Dr. Alfonso D. II, 3337

Hollingshead, August B., 2633-2637

Hollis, Thomas, 718

Hollis Papers, 718

Hollywood, and slang, 2114

Holmes, Dr. Bayard, 2141

Holmes, Oliver Wendell, 1461, 1718, 2112, 2717-2718, 3055

Holmes, Pauline, 732-738

Holmes, Rev. Thomas, 1497

Holmes, Theodore, 359

Holy Bible, The, 128-129, 137
See also Bible

Holy Congregation for the Propagation of the Faith, 1171

Holy Cross, priests of, 1160

Holy Day of Obligation, 3072

Holy Ghost, 53, 123

Holy Name Society, 2905

Holy Scriptures, 545

Holy See, 904

Holy spirit, 58, 131

Holyoke, Edward, 715

Home economics

in comprehensive high school, 2288

in heterogenous high school classes, 2624

Home education, 836

advice to mothers on, 3150-3153

of infants, 1354-1356

in Switzerland, 821-826

in tenement homes, 2204

vs. school education, 1368-1370

Home Ins. Co. v. *New York*, 3091

Home life

and Catholic schools, 2895-2896

correlation of the school with, 1879-1880

and emphasis on school life, 2520, 2521*n*

and habit clinics, 2465

influence of kindergartens on, 2161

of Negro and white students, 3029

of poor children, 2201-2202

of tenement children, 2134

See also Environment

Home Missionary operations in Illinois, 1468

Home-and-school-visitor, 2204

Home visitation, and kindergartens, 2160

Homeless children, during Depression, 2529-2531

"Homeless Wanderers Create a New Problem for America" (Baker), 2529-2531

Homer, 150, 161, 163, 168, 186, 285, 347, 351, 406, 413, 414, 461, 503, 1067, 1221, 1233, 1238, 2121

Homework, 2440

and Cook County "arithmetic creed," 1831

Homogeneous classes, 513, 2057

in American education, 2120

critique of, 2572-2573

and democratic theory, 1929-1930

"Honest Abe," 1638

Honorarium, for lectures at universities, 1483

Hooker, Mathew, 396

Hoole, Charles, 289-298, 309-311

Hooper, William, 407

Hoosier Schoolmaster, The (Eggleston), 1299-1300, 2697

Hoover, President

educational policies of, 2604

and White House Conference on Child Health and Protection, 2551-2553

Hopi children, education of, 2949-2955

Hopkins (governor of Hartford, Connecticut), 383

Hopkins, Mark, 2988

Hopkins Grammar School, New Haven, 2108

rules of, 399-400

Hopscotch, at Indian schools, 1758-1759

Horace, 164, 170, 285, 349, 351, 406, 414, 463, 503, 512, 513, 522, 1067, 1233

in French secondary school curriculum, 1925

Horace Mann: Educational Statesman (Williams), 1110-1111

Horace Mann in Ohio (Hubbell), 1497-1502

Horace Mann School, 2474

Horman, 270

Horn Silver Mining Co. v. *New York*, 3091

Horney, 3253

Horological school course, 1948

Horsemanship, 172, 243

Horticulture, in Prussian teachers seminaries, 1511

Hosmer, Miss, 1212

Hospitals

Jewish, 1201

and wandering children, 2530

Hostility, of pupils, 834, 2705

"Hot line," 3199

"Hot Sulphur Springs," 1040

House of Burgesses, 547

House Document no. 1004, 2360-2363

House on Henry Street, The (Wald), 2203-2205

House of Intellect, The (Barzun), 3150-3153

House of Representatives

Act establishing United States Bureau of Education, 1406-1407

Buchanan's veto message on Morrill Bill to, 1526-1527

Committee on Education of, 1338

Committee on Indian Affairs of, 1725-1727

Indian Committee of, 1743

Memorial of the National Association of State and City School Superintendents to, 1404-1405

prayer, 3079

signers of Southern Manifesto, 3008-3009

Household arts, Dewey on, 2221-2222

Housekeeping

at Indian School, 1759-1760

at Mount Holyoke Female Seminary, 1590-1591

in Reconstruction South, 1632

Housekeeping Center, of Henry Street Settlement, 2203-2204

Housing

in Chicago slums, 2135-2136

in New York City slums, 2141-2143

in North Boston slums, 2136-2138

in Soviet Union, 3154

and Teacher Corps, 3376

Housing discrimination, and school segregation, 3034, 3035, 3040

Housing integration, and Americanization of Chinese immigrants, 1767

Housing problems, in high school curriculum, 2624

Hovey, James, 716

How, Chew. *See Gong Lum* v. *Rice*

How, Robert, 446-447

How, Samuel B., 1183

"How Gertrude Teaches Her Children," (Pestalozzi), 827

"How Much Can We Boost I.Q. and Scholastic Achievement?" (Jensen), 3202-3209

"How Not to Teach Teachers" (Koerner), 3162-3168

How the Other Half Lives (Riis), 2133-2135

How Prohibition Works (Crowell), 2384*n*

How Sleep the Brave (Collins), 1964

How to Make a Curriculum (Bobbitt), 2428-2435

"How to Make Our Ideas Clear" (Peirce), 2208

"How Youth Differ," 2623*n*

Howard of Effingham, 644

Howard, General O. O., 1411, 1641-1642

Howard, M. William, 180

Howard, Robert, 1629

Howe, Albert, 1655

Howe, Dr., 1331

Howe, Harold, 3042

Howell, "Bill," 1456

Howes, Miss, 2266

Howison, 2208

Howland, John, 1051-1052

Hoyle, Thomas, 606

Hoyt, Dr., 1412

Hoyt, Miss, 1034

Hubbard, Elbert, 2419

Hubbell, George Allen, 1497-1502

Huber, Wm. D., 2267

Huddleston, Geroge, Jr., 3006-3009

Hude, James, 686

Hudson County Water Co. v. *McCarter*, 3055

Hughes, Bishop John, 1127, 1140-1141

Hughes, Chief Justice, 3083, 3097-3098, 3102, 3113

Hugo, Victor, 3325

Hull, George, 1076-1080

Hull House, 2141, 2225, 2228-2229

adult education at, 2832-2835

early days at, 2291-2293

immigrants at, 2163-2167

Hull House Labor Museum, 2164, 2166, 2225

Hull-House Maps and Papers (Ely), 2138-2141

Hullfish, Dr. H. Gordon, 3176

Human development, 115-116

continuity of, 843-844

laws of, 828-829

and play, 845

Human Development Corporation, 2850

Human Intellect, The, 1477

Scientific Management—
Underlying Principles"
(Hanus), 2257-2260
Improvisation, in progressive
schools, 2650
"In The Schools of America:
Notes of a Soviet Educator"
(Malkova), 2124-2129
Inaugural Address of President
Charles W. Eliot, October
19, 1869, 1595
"Inaugural Address," (Van Hise),
2757-2760
Inbecility, and memory ability,
1995
Incapables, 1953-1954
Incentives, 262
improvement of, 3352-3353
Income, average per capita, 2808
Income distribution, in American
cities, 2124
Incompetents, and teacher
certification, 1324
Incorrigibles, 76, 370
school for, 560
Indenture, of teacher, 555-556
Indenture contract, 328
Independence, and play, 2081
Independent Gazetteer, The, 761
Independent and Weekly Review,
2384n
India Teas, Harvard students
protest against, 718
Indian agencies, schools of, 1746
Indian agents, on education, 1738
Indian boarding schools, critique
of, 2955-2956, 2958-2959
"Indian Civilization Fund,"
act establishing, 1723-1724
Indian Coil method, 2445
Indian education
Arthur on, 1753-1754
at boarding schools in Oregon,
1734-1735
at Choctaw Academy, 1728-
1729
critique of, 2955-2956
and founding of Carlisle Indian
School, 1740-1745
and government schools, 1754-
1756
and "Indian Civilization Fund,"
1723-1724
and mission schools, 1723
need for reform of, 2957-2960
in New Hampshire, 709
and Plains Indians, 1731-1732
report of Commissioner of
Education on, 1735-1740
at Rough Rock Demonstration
School, 2965-2969
and rules for Indian schools,
1756-1760
and school segregation in
California, 2978-2979
and segregation, 2964
survey of, 2960-2969
and vocational training, 1729
and William and Mary College,
652, 746
See also Equal educational
opportunity; Indian schools

"Indian Education in the United
States" (Beatty), 2960-2964
Indian and His Problem, The
(Leupp), 2955-2956
Indian land, purchase of, 618,
607
Indian languages, 616-617, 607
banning of, 1757-1758
description of, 607-608
Indian Massacres, 338
Indian missionaries, 621-622
Indian Peace Commission, 1737,
1740
Indian prisoners, 1742
and Carlisle Indian School,
1745-1746, 1752-1754
Indian reservations
conditions on, 1736-1737
establishment of, 1730-1731,
1732-1734
forced removal to, 1752-1754
Indian School at Carlisle
Barracks, 1748-1752
Indian schools
at Keams Canyon, 2949-2955
in Lebanon, Connecticut, 619-
624
location of, 629
number of, 1754-1755
on Pacific Coast, 1736-1737
report on, 1728
of William and Mary College,
654
Indian Service, 2958
day schools, 2959
and Indian Education, 2962-
2963
Indian Territory, 1745, 1752-1754
Indian treaties
in California, 1732-1734
educational provisions in, 1734-
1735
problems caused by, 1752-1754
in Virginia, 625-626
Indian Treaties Printed By
Benjamin Franklin, 1736-
1762 (Van Doren), 625-626
Indian women, education of, 620-
621, 622
Indiana
educational provision in
constitution of, 1021
statutes authorizing racially
separate public schools, 3035
Indianapolis, Indiana, public
schools in, 1894-1896, 2106,
2326-2329
Indians
conversion of, 612-615
customs of, 609
education of, 360, 575-576
Jackson's plan for removal of,
1730-1731
laws for conversion of, 618-619
Massachusetts court order for
conversion of, 611
of mountain territories, 1739
of the Pacific Coast, 1736-1737
Penn on, 607-611
physical description of, 607
and religious education, 335-
338
In South Carolina, 572-574

See also Education of Indians
Indian-white relations
Eliot on, 612-615
and intermarriage, 605-606
and land purchases, 618
in Massachusetts, 616-617
and massacre of 1622 in
Virginia, 603-605
Penn on, 608, 609
Wahunsonacock on, 602
Individual ability
and homogeneous classes, 1929-
1930
and teaching methods, 260
Individual culture,
and college studies, 1474-1475
Individual differences, 563
of character, 1357-1358
critique of, 3147-3148
and curriculum, 66
and education, 2587
and elective courses, 1549-1550
and graded classes, 1320
and homogeneous grouping,
2572
and instructional methods, 1313
in mental development, 864
and moral training, 100-101
and role of tutor, 159
studies of, 2242-2243
and talent, 107
See also Pestalozzianism
Individual instruction, 2490
and Batavia Plan, 2269-2271
and computers, 3310-3315
cost of, 2278
and discipline, 2277
and Montessori method, 2320-
2321
and performance contractors,
3337
in rural schools, 2277
vs. lockstep method, 2275-2277
See also Quincy method
Individual needs, in high school
of future, 2596-2597
"Individual system as developed
in the San Francisco State
Teachers College" (Ward),
2490n
Individual tastes, and college
studies, 1474-1475
Individualism, 2855
and activity movement, 2644
end of age of, 2591
of Europe, 2461-2462
in Port Huron Statement, 2855
in progressive schools, 2645-
2646
and rise of masses, 2032-2033
See also Individuality
Individuality
in American education, 2103
and capitalism, 2612-2613
and child study, 1841
and "elective studies," 2103
in Herbartian system, 1875
and nongrading, 3282-3290
and physiological method of
education, 861-862
and play, 2080-2081
and progressive education,
2454-2455, 2456

Achievement in Mathematics (Husen), 2053-2059
International Thomistic Congress, sixth, 2052n
Internationalism, and Royal Society, 218-219
Internment camps, for Japanese, 2977-2978
Interpersonal relations
between literary and scientific intellectuals, 2089-2092
of demoralized child, 2009-2010
"Intimations of Immortality of Childhood" (Wordsworth), 1795
Intraindividual differences, and grouping, 2057
"Introduction" (Wilson), 2261-2266
Introductorium (Shirley), 291-192
Intuition, nature of, 3242-3243
Iosiah, 123
Iowa
during Depression, 2535
physicians in, 2773n
Iowa Indians, 1745
Iowa, State University of
and adult education, 2840
during Depression, 2557
IQ. *See* Intelligence quotients
Ireland, Archbishop John, on public schools, 1176-1181
Irish
attitudes at Harvard toward, 1720
and Scotch, 2384
Irish hierarchy, and Catholic schools, 1163
Irish immigrants, 995-997, 2162
Iron Curtain countries, 2095
Iroquois, 627, 629
Irresponsibility, and deprived children, 2095
Irving, Washington, 1964
Irwin, Elizabeth A., 2435-2438, 2499, 2500, 2501, 2503
"Is The Public School Obsolete?" (Jencks), 3329n, 3329n
Isaac, 618
Isaacs, 1198, 3255
Isaacs, Susan, 2079-2081
Isaiah, 48
Ishmael, Rabbi, 2922
Ishmaelites, 1737
Isocrates, 168, 285, 351, 406
Israel, Fred L., 1730-1731
Israel, study of, in Jewish schools, 2927
Israelites, 126
and slavery, 591
Issues of Secondary Education, 2627n
Italian Association of Catholic Teachers, 2046n, 2047n
Italian immigrants
in Chicago, 2138-2139, 2163, 2189-2190
and prohibition, 2383-2384
and public schools, 2196
"soup school" for, 2153-2155
Italian language, 173, 184, 446

Italian Social Week, 2047n, 2049n
Italicus, Silius, 170
Itard, Jean-Marc-Gaspard, 837-842
Ittner, Anthony, 2267
Ivers, James, 438
Jackman, 1890
Jackson, 3011
Jackson, Andrew, 2588
plan for removal of Indians, 1730-1731
Jackson, Justice, 3058-3064, 3069-3071, 3074-3075, 3081
Jackson, Stonewall, 2112-2113
Jackson State College, 3017
Jacob, 131, 132, 590, 618, 754
Jacobinism, 924
Jacobs, Rev. George, 1200
Jacobs, Julius, 1800
Jacobson, Lenore, 3305-3308
Jacotot, 1875
Jamal, N. K., 3218-3220
James, Edmund J., 1525-1526
James, Edmund S., 1613-1616
James, George F., 1613-1616
James, William, 1718, 1719, 2207-2211, 2796
on child study, 1852-1855
on mental health of female students, 1602-1604
on psychology, 1426-1430
James I (king of England), 335
See also King James Bible
James River Company, 806-807
Jameson, J. Franklin, 586
James-Town, 605
Janin, Jules, 1198
Japan
attitudes toward black Americans in, 3017
in IEA study of mathematics achievement, 2054, 2055
moral codes in, 2385
vocational education in, 2363
Japanese Educational Association of America, 2977
Japanese immigrants, in San Francisco, 2973-2974
Japanese Immigration Hearings, 2974n, 2975n, 2976n, 2977n
"Japanese Language Associations," 2977
Japanese language schools
in California, 2974-2977
prohibited in internment camps, 2971
Japanese-American Yearbook, 2976n
Jaques, Samuel, 556
Jarvis, Josephine, 846-848, 848-849
Jaycox, Emma, 2490n
Jefferson, Thomas, 452-453, 596-597, 1471, 1483-1485, 1687, 2112
"Bill for Establishing Religious Freedom," 783-785
criticism of schools by, 1483-1485
educational plan for Virginia, 748-750
on a free press, 751-752

on ignorance, 750-751
on the natural aristocracy among men, 752-756
on reforms for William and Mary College, 745-747
on religion, 781-783
on studying abroad, 798-799
Jefferson Market, 2501
Jefferson School, Gary, Indiana, 2330
Jeffries, David, 554
Jeffries, John, 407
Jehovah's Witnesses, 2112
and flag salute cases, 3054-3064
Jehuda Hallevi, 1198
Jencks, Christopher, 3276-3281, 3329-3336, 3329n
Jenk, H. F., 548
Jenkins, William, 976
Jenner, 1297
Jennings, W. Pat, 3006-3009
Jensen, Arthur R., answer to, 3210-3214
Jeoffries, Jeffrie, 644
Jerman, M., 3312n
Jernegan, Marcus W., 390-391, 394-395
Jerome, Saint, 41, 62, 132, 134, 135, 155
Jerusalem, 144
Jervis, 1114
Jesse, Richard H., 1930-1946
Jesuits. *See* Society of Jesus
Jesus Christ, 49-50, 55, 124, 125, 126, 129, 143-149, 149, 489, 566, 782-783, 1231
and catechism for children, 51-54
and children, 255
doctrines of, 1484
and teaching Catholic youth, 1166
Jewelry, and progressive education curriculum, 2448
Jewish education, 2915-2918
aims of, 2919-2921
in American cities, 1200-1202
in Boston, Massachusetts, 1200
in Chicago, Illinois, 1201
in Cincinnati, 1202
meaning of, 2921-2923
in New York City, 2915-2918
in Philadelphia, 1200
Shearith Isreal congregation on, 1182
in St. Louis, Missouri, 1201, 1202-1203
in United States, 2923-2928
Jewish Education in a Pluralist Society: Samson Benderly and Jewish Education in the United States, 2919-2921
Jewish Education in the United States (Dushkin and Engelman), 2923-2928
Jewish Education in the United States (Gartner), 1194-1195
Jewish Experience in America, The (Karp), 538
Jewish Foster Home, 1200
Jewish girls, education of, 1193-1194

Keatinge, M. W., 258-265, 263-265
Keelor, Miss, 2440, 2441
Keen, Robert, 708
Keep, 1745, 1746
Kehew, Mary Morton, 2267
Kehoe, L., 1128-1132
Kekerman, 190
Keliher, Alice V., 2572-2573
Keller, Helen, 1995
Kelley, Florence, 2138-2141
  on child labor laws, 2192-2195
Kellogg, Sheldon G., 1771
Kelly, J., 1128-1132
Kemp, William, 627-629
Kendrick, Donald G., 3338
Kennedy, David, 441
Kennedy, John F., 3079, 3207
  call for National Education
    Improvement Act
  executive order establishing
    Peace Corps, 3347
  message to Congress on civil
    rights, 3361-3365
  on school segregation, 3363
  "Special Message to Congress
    on Education," 3348-3358
Kennedy, Robert, 441
Kennet, 351
Kent (Chancellor), 1594
Kentucky
  Pestalozzianism in school in,
    1779
  physicians in, 2772n
  satire on college for women in,
    1573
  school segregation in, 3091-3093
  women teachers in, 1318
Kenwick, Bishop Francis Patrick,
    1146-1147
Kenworthy, Marion E., 2409-2412
Kephart, 3258
Kepler's law, 2210
Keppel, 1114
Kern, 970
Kerr, Clark, 2823
Kerr, John, 1451
Kessen, William, 3248-3250
Key, Francis Scott, 979, 2112
Keyes, 1212, 2266
Keyishan v. Board of Regents of
  the University of the State
  of New York 2733-2735
Kick Wheel, 2445
"Kid brother," 2117
"Kid on the Housetop, The"
  (Aesop), 299
Kiersted, Mary Smith Cornelius,
    555
Kilgore, Annabelle T., 3339
Kilpatrick, William Heard, 2272-2274, 2322-2324, 2442-2444,
    2573-2574, 2582-2583, 2584-2587, 2587, 2588, 2600,
    3151n
Kimber, M. C., 1655
Kimberly, Dennis, 1701-1702
Kimpton, Lawrence, 3290
Kindergarten teachers
  requirements of, 1792-1794,
    1798-1799

at Silver Street Kindergarten,
    1799, 1800-1801
  training of, 1788-1789
"Kindergarten: An Uplifting
  Social Influence in the Home
  and the District, The"
  (Gilder), 2160-2161
"Kindergarten Work in
  California," 1798-1799
Kindergartens
  activities in, 1794-1798
  behavior clinics in, 2482
  child study method and, 1848
  in Children's Charter, 2552
  and compensatory education,
    3275-3276
  equipment and activities in,
    1802-1805
  and Froebel, 853
  Froebel's plan for, 846-848
  at Hull House, 2292, 2293
  and immigrant children, 2160-2161
  Kindergarten and
    Workingman's School of the
    New York City Society for
    Ethical Culture, 1789-1792
  at Little Red 'School House,
    2500, 2501-2503
  and misuse of Froebel's
    principles, 1808
  and moral training, 1856
  program for teachers of, 2714
  role of, 1907-1908
  Silver Street Kindergarten,
    1799-1802
  and symbolic meaning of play,
    1805-1808
  teacher training for, 1788-1789
  at Teachers College, Columbia
    University, 2317, 2473-2477
  in U.S., 959
  in U.S. and Soviet Union, 2125
Kindness, and young children,
    1355
Kinesthetic word tracing, 3258
King, Benjamin S., 1620
King, Clarence, 1464
King, Henry C., 1930-1946
King James Bible
  dedication to, 128-129
  Exodus, 140-142
  Genesis, 137-140
  Gospel According to St. John,
    148-149
  Gospel According to St.
    Matthew, 143-147
  preface to, 130-136
  Psalm twenty-four, 143
  Psalm twenty-three, 142-143
Kings College. See Columbia
  University
Kingsbury, Susan M., 335-338,
    603-605
Kinnersley, Mr., 510, 511
Kinsey, John, 686
Kiowa agency, 1745
Kiowa Indians, 1745
Kite, Elizabeth S., 1993-1995
Klemm, L., 999
Knight, Edgar W., 339-341, 446-449, 474-475, 513, 575-576,
    576, 584-586, 606, 643-647,

650, 724, 853-856, 927-928,
    1012-1014, 1070-1071, 1252,
    1779
Knight, Edmund Andros, 548
Knight, Samuel, 151-155
Knight, Sarah Kemble, 385-386
Knight, William, 2827-2831
Knowing faculties, cultivation of,
    891
Knowledge
  as teacher qualification, 1359
  assimilation of. See
    Apperception of knowledge
  canalization of, 1947
  of child entering school, 1833-1840, 1892
  of common school studies by
    teachers, 1311
  distribution of, 1567
  enjoyment of, 42
  and generalizations, 863
  German concept of, 1537
  and human power, 213
  humanization of, 925
  importance of applying, 2280
  and life activity, 923-924
  necessary and useful, 108
  and sense training, 862-863
  structure of, 3240-3245
  and universities, 1566
Knox, John, 54-57, 57-58
Knox, Samuel, 776-780
Kobler, 3308
Koch, 2758
Koerner, James D., 3162-3168
Kohl, Herbert R., 3317-3320
Kohler, Wolfgang, 2011-2016
Kolben, 630
Konsul (chimpanzee), 2012
Kosciusko, 3017, 3020
Kossuth, 1114
Kotschnig, 2817
Kraus, 1789
Kraus, Mrs., 1789
Kraus-Boelte School, New York
  City, 1788-1789
Kraus Reprint Company, 3328
Krughoff, Robert, 3329n
Kuhlman, Clementine, 3248-3250
Kursheedt, I. B., 1182
Kussmaul, 868
"L' Osservatore Romano," 2047n,
    2049n, 2052n
La Chalotais, Louis-Rene de
  Caradeuc, 106-108
La Fontaine, 107, 1484
La Raza Studies, 2947
La Soupa Scuola. See "Soup
  School"
Laban, 754
Labaree, Benjamin, 995
Labaree, Leonard W., 434-435,
    480-481, 482-484, 491-492,
    492-495, 626-627, 630-634,
    637-638
Labode, 1738
Labor problems, and manual
  training, 1865, 1869
Labor supply, and industrial
  education, 2269
Labor unions
  opposition to manual training,
    1870-1871

attitudes toward, 1856-1857
benefits of, 1860-1867, 1866
Butler on, 1867-1869
and child study method, 1847
at Cook County Normal
    School, 1830
Dewey on, 2219-2223
in elementary school
    curriculum, 1967, 1969
of feebleminded, 2405
in ideal school, 1857-1859
in Indianapolis public school,
    2327, 2328
in junior high school, 2324
in Menomonie, Wisconsin
    Schools, 2344-2345
as mental training, 1867-1869
and Negroes, 2509
opposition of organized labor
    to, 1870-1871
for Southern Negroes, 1682
at Summerhill, 2067
and technical training, 2828n
and University of Chicago
    Elementary School, 2296
in U.S. and England compared,
    2105-2106
See also Industrial training
Manual Training in Education
    (Woodward), 1866
Manual Training School, The
    (Woodward), 1859-1860,
    1860-1865
Manual training schools, 1430
of Washington University, St.
    Louis, 1859-1860
"Manual vs. Technical Training"
    (O'Donoghue), 1870-1871
Manufactures, in university
    curriculum, 803
Manufacturing centers,
    development of, 1904
Maps, 185, 193, 503
and child study method, 1849
in classroom, 249
at Concord, Mass. school, 1213
at Indian Schools, 1759
in infant school, 902
at Prairie View, Kansas
    schoolhouse, 1302
Maquire, Matthew, 445
Marbles, at Indian schools, 1758-
    1759
Marburg, University of, 1539
Marbury v. *Madison*, 3112
Marcus, Jacob R., 706-707
Mardirosian, Rev. Vahac, 2942
Margaret, 825, 826
Margate Intermediate School,
    Palo Verdes, Calif., 3199-
    3201
"Marginal object," 1427
"Maria Montessori and A. S.
    Neill: A Redbook Dialogue,"
    3262-3270
Marian exiles, 125-128
epistle to Queen Elizabeth
    from, 122-125
Maricopas, 1737
Marine Corps, military schools,
    2841-2843
Marketing, in rural high schools,
    2601

Marks. *See* Grading
Marks, Louis, 2435-2438, 2500
Marland, Sidney P., 3389-3393
Marmion (Scott), 1964
Marqusee, Michael, 3216-3218
Marriage
in America, 936-937
among Indians, 608, 609
as reason for leaving school,
    2545-2546
as themes of traditional
    children's games, 1805
and co-education, 876
preparation for, 2549-2551
reasons for, 1318
and Teacher Corps, 3376
Mars, 79
Marsh, Dean, 2563
Marsh, Jonathan, 673
Marshall, Chief Justice, 2736-
    2738, 3112
Marshall, J. F. B., 1655
Marshall, James, 556
Marshall, John, 1437-1441
Martin, Nicholas, 343
Martineau, Harriet, 945-946
Marwedel, Emma, 1798-1799,
    1800
Marx, Karl, 1462, 1719, 3155
Mary (queen of England), 642,
    643, 651
Maryland
average income per person in,
    3028
and *Brown* v. *Board of
    Education*, 3106-3108
Catholic education in, 357-358
physicians per person in, 2771
religious toleration in, 356-357
See also Georgetown University
Masculinity, in American culture,
    2116-2117
Masefield, John, 2483-2484
Mashburn, 606
Mason, Sir J., 266, 267
Mason, Sue, 2482
Mass education, and uniformity,
    946-947
Mass media, impact on children,
    3183-3186
Mass psychoses, 2082
Mass society
culture in, 3180-3182
disorganizing effects of, 2082
"Mass Society And Its Culture"
    (Shils), 3180-3182
Massachusetts
academies in, 1239-1241
academy movement in, 516-517
apprenticeship in, 391-392
Catholic school enrollment in,
    2907
compulsory school law of
    1852, 1115-1116
court order for conversion of
    Indians in, 611
creation of state board of
    education in, 1070-1072
education laws in, 393-396,
    397-399
free schools in, 396-397
government in, 754

Indian-White relations in, 616-
    617
Mann on public schools in,
    1095-1099
petition for freedom by
    Negroes in, 592-593
population density in, 1103
public schools in, 1083-1094,
    1100-1110
punishment in, 376-377
punishment of incorrigible
    children in, 370-371
school committees in, 1076-
    1077
school laws in, 794-797, 1148,
    1252-1253
school libraries in, 1078
slavery in, 589-591
teacher education in, 1077-
    1078
women teachers in, 1318
Massachusetts Acts and Resolves,
    1711
Massachusetts Bay
anti-Catholic law of, 367-268
request for college for, 655
See also Harvard College
Massachusetts Board of
    Education, 1083-1094, 1095-
    1099, 1100-1110
first annual report of the, 1076-
    1080
Mann leaves, 1110-1112
recommendation of
    establishment of normal
    schools by, 1326-1327, 1073-
    1075, 1073-1075, 1077, 1079,
    1081-1082
*Seventh Annual Report of . . .
    The Secretary of the Board*,
    932-934
*Tenth Annual Report . . . of
    the Secretary of the Board*,
    1337-1339
Massachusetts Historical Society,
    718
Collections, 416-418, 592-593
Massachusetts public schools
authority of teacher in, 1337-
    1339
criticism of, 1153-1155, 1286-
    1289
employment of female teachers
    in, 1315-1317
establishment of, 1333
government control of, 1304-
    1305
Mann's contribution to, 1111-
    1112
philanthropic donations for,
    1326
textbooks in, 1079
Massachusetts State Legislature
and academies, 1239
law ending school segregation,
    1711
Massachusetts State Normal
    School, regulations of, 1335-
    1337
Massachusetts Supreme Court,
    decision on constitutionality
    of school segregation, 1708-
    1711

Massachusetts Teacher, The, 995-997
Massachusetts Teachers' Association, 1399
Masses
  and culture, 924-925
  and Populist movement in England, 2085-2088
  reaction to class distinctions, 2087-2088
  rise of, in Europe, 2030-2033
Mast, Mir Camar Uddin, 1221
Master of Arts degree
  at Columbia University, 696
  requirements for, 1505
  of William and Mary College, 654
Master of Arts theses, at Harvard College, 715-716
Master of Trinity College, Cambridge, 165
Masters, Nathall, 390
Masters
  absences of, 171
  of University of Oxford, 176, 177
  in Westminster School, 165-166
  of William and Mary College, 646
Master's degree, in education, 2716
Mastery task level, 3259
Masturbation, 3265-3266
Masurek, 2164
"Mater et Magistra," 2045n, 2046m
Material success, and manual training, 1864
Materialism, American, 2107
Materials
  for art, 2488
  for art teaching, 2414
  for black studies programs, 3328
  in British infant schools, 3300-3301
  at City and Country School, New York City, 2317
  handling of, 254-255
  in Los Angeles high schools, 2941
  and Montessori method, 2313
  See also Equipment
Mathematical instruments, 438
Mathematical Principles of Natural Philosophy, The (Motte), 221-222, 222-230
Mathematics, 42, 83, 243, 446, 456, 473, 513, 522, 654, 710, 1548
  application to life, 931
  and *A B C of Anschauung,* 860
  at Beaver Country Day School, 2499
  books on, 202-203
  in British infant schools, 3301
  in college curriculum, 1502, 1505, 1507, 1513
  in core-curriculum plan, 2603
  in Dalton Plan, 2469
  early introduction of, 3149n
  and elective system, 2747

  in German and American schools, 943
  at Hampton Institute, 1655
  in high school curriculum, 2518, 3161
  international study of achievement in, 2053-2059
  at Manual Training School of Washington University, 1859
  and mental improvement, 240
  in Middletown high schools, 2606
  in new British primary schools, 2096
  at Notre Dame University, 1161
  and Pestalozzianism, 1779
  at Princeton University, 709
  professorship of, 1482
  in Prussian teachers seminaries, 1511
  in secondary school curriculum, 1940
  in Society of Jesus universities, 67
  teaching of, 464-465
  in university curriculum, 56, 57, 803, 906
  at University of Virginia, 1488
  See also New math
Mathematics in the Primary Schools, 3303
Mather, Cotton, 408-415, 414-415, 418, 548-553
Mather, Increase, 377-379, 417, 418, 477, 671
Mather, Miss S. A., 1745
Mather, Samuel, 407, 660
Mathews, Thomas, 357
Mathewson, F. E., 2267
Matisse, 2413
Matrimonial engagements, and coeducation, 1496
Matthew, Saint, 48, 143-147, 1166-1167
Matthews, D. R., 3006-3009
Matthews, May, 2317
Matthews, William, 714
Maturity, and education, 2232-2233
Maurois, Andre, on American education, 2119-2122
Maury, Ann, 574-575
Maury, Rev. James, 452, 453-457
Maxfield, John, 441
Maximus, Valerius, 164, 169
Maxwell, Dr., 2204
Maxwell-Ltle, Sir Henry Churchill, 164-165
May, Samuel Joseph, 1542
May Affair, in England (1958), 2085-2088
Mayer, 600
Mead, George, 714
Mead, Margaret, 2115, 2116-2117, 3177n
  Cultural Patterns and Technological Change 3177n
Meaning of Education and other Essays and Addresses, The (Butler), 1922-1926
Means, Jack, 1299-1300
Mearns, Hughes, 2438-2441

"Measurable differences in books suitable for different grades," (Washburne), 2492n
Measurement, of educational products, 2247-2249
Measurement of Intelligence, The (Terman), 2249-2257
Mechanical education, 264
  in college curriculum, 1505, 1507
  and grading of classes, 1921, 1922
  at Hampton Institute, 1656
  at Manual Training School of Washington University, 1860
  and moral training, 1910, 1911-1912
  Rice's critiques of, 1892-1901
  See also Manual training
Mechlin, Samuel, 524
Medals
  for excellence in studies, 882
  at state university, 1524
Medical care, 3273
  and medical education, 2768
Medical examinations. *See* Physical examinations
Medical Inspector, and school nurse, 2305
Medical Journal, 2305
Medical method, of intelligence measurement, 1993
Medical Register (Polk), 2769n
"Medical School Inspection," 2305
Medical schools
  and behavior problems, 2401
  in New York, 1458
  reform of, 2768-2777
  See also Medicine
Medical sciences, professorship of, 1482
Medicine
  in college curriculum, 1505
  in Society of Jesus universities, 67
  in university curriculum, 56, 57
  at University of Virginia, 1488, 1490
Medulla, Dr. Ames, 664
Medulla oblongata, 886
"Meeting Children Where They Are" (Goodlad), 3282-3290
Meiklejohn, Alexander, 2766-2768
Meister, Wilhelm, 2187
Mela, 185
Melamdim, 2924
Melancholia, 1602-1603
Melancthon, 45, 290
Melby, Ernest O., 3173-3176
Melting pot concept, 2175-2178
  criticism of, 2175-2179, 2381-2386
Melting-Pot Mistake, The (Fairchild), 2381-2386
"Memoir of Rebecca Gratz and the Hebrew Sunday School of Philadelphia," 1191-1192
Memoir of Samuel Slater (White), 976
Memoirs of a Huguenot Family (Maury), 574-575
Memoirs of a Life Chiefly Passed

in Pennsylvania. . .
(Graydon), 510-513
*Memoirs of the Life and Death
of the Pious and Ingenious
Mrs. Jane Turell* (Turell),
387-389
Memorable Things of Socrates
(Xenophon), 479
*Memorial of the First Centenary
of Georgetown College, D.C.,
Comprising a History of
Georgetown University*
(Shea), 713-714
*Memorials of Thomas Davidson,
the Wandering Scholar*
(Knight), 2827-2831
Memorization, 47, 170, 197
in American schools, 963-964
of psalms, 48
of psalms and hymns, 264
special training in, 2238-2239
See also Memory
Memory, 246, 247, 260, 361
Bacon on, 212
and doctrine of concentration,
1880-1881
in infant development, 869-871
and intelligence, 1995
and intelligence tests, 1994
and isolation, 838
and languages, 749
and manual training, 1862
and powers of invention, 1443
and science learning, 254
See also Recitations
Mencken, 2113
Mendelssohn, Moses, 1198
*Mendez v. Westminster School
District*, 2810n
Menelaus, 1877
Menomonees, 1745
Menomonie, Wisconsin schools,
2344-2345
Mensuration, 439, 440, 441, 446,
1236
at Manual Training School of
Washington University, 1860
at Notre Dame University,
1161
of superficies, 443
Mental age
of Americans, 2427
and intelligence tests, 2253
and reading evaluation, 2570
and reading instruction, 2570-
2572
and retardation, 2257
and social class, 2255-2256
Mental constitution, inheritance
of, 2406-2407
Mental development
Combe on, 887-893
and conception of physical
causality, 2023-2029
and curriculum, 1472
and education, 2232-2233
and freedom, 2449
and health, 233-234
in Herbartian theory, 1881-
1883
and infant teaching, 1368-1369
influences on, 1226

and instructional methods, 827-
828, 1818-1820
and intelligence tests, 2249-
2250
Locke on, 230-232
and object teaching, 1782
and phrenology, 884-893
and play equipment, 1802-1805
Preyer on, 863-871
and transfer of training, 2236-
2240
Wundt on, 871-875
See also Psychology
Mental health, 2396-2400, 2409
in childhood, 2396-2400
of college students, 2784-2786
and education, 2435-2438
of girl students, 1602-1604
and habit clinics, 2465-2466
Harvard Committee on
Secondary Education on,
2618-2620
in infancy, 2409-2412
and instincts, 2005-2006
and progressive education,
2454-2455
in universities, 2783-2786
Mental hygiene. *See* Mental
health
Mental Hygiene of Childhood
(White), 2397
Mental hygiene clinics, in
Minneapolis public schools,
2481-2482
"Mental Hygiene In A University"
(Thompson), 2783-2786
Mental illness
and family life, 2396-2398
and personality make-up, 2398
Mental life, and psychical
apparatus, 2000
Mentality of Apes, The (Kohler),
2011-2016
Mentally defective children. *See*
Feebleminded; Retardation
Mercer, Charles F., 1001-1002
Merchant Taylor's School
(London), 707
Merchants accounts, 440, 441,
444, 447, 473, 510
Merck and Company, 3189
Mercury, 79
Mercy, Webster on, 771
Meredith, James, 3017-3020
Meredith, Mrs. James, 3020
Meredith, John Howard, 3020
Meredith, William, 1183
Meriam, Junius L., 2477-2479
Meriam, Lewis, 2957-2960
Merit, order of, 882
Meritocracy, rise of, 2085-2088
Merits, at Boston High School for
Girls, 1250
Merrill, 3252
Merrill-Palmer Quarterly, 3245-
3247
"Message to the New York State
Legislature, 1842," 1141-
1143
Messages from the Governors
(Lincoln), 1141-1143
Messages and Papers of the

Presidents (Richardson),
1752-1754
Messengers, at Boston High
School for Girls, 1251
Metal-stamping works, and child
labor, 2140
Metamorphosis (Ovid), 48, 164,
168, 193, 351, 406, 543, 550
Metaphysics, 68, 184, 194-195,
654, 658
books on, 202
and pragmatic method, 2207
science and, 2209
in Society of Jesus universities,
67
Metcalf, Joel, 1051-1052
Metcalf, Thomas, 1886
Meteorology, in secondary school
curriculum, 1936, 1939, 1940
*Method, Meditations, and
Selections from the
Principles of Descartes, The*
(Descartes), 81-86
*Method of Teaching and
Studying the Belles Lettres,
The* (Rollin), 496
Methodist Episcopal Church, on
public funding of parochial
schools, 1133-1136
Methodology. *See* Instructional
methods
Metrica. *See* Prosody
Metrical composition, in
university curriculum, 907
Meumann, 2255
Mexican-Americans
Americanization of, 2930-2934
experiences in United States,
2929-2930
and Los Angeles high school
strike, 2937-2942
and Los Angeles public
schools, 2942-2944
and segregation, 2810n
and segregation in California,
2934-2936
"Mexican Immigration To The
United States" (Alvarado),
2929-2930
Mexico, conquest of, 604
Meyer, Cotton, 821-822
Meyer, Maria, 821-822
Meyer v. State of Nebraska,
2717-2718, 2741, 3052
Meyerbeer, 1198
Micah, 366
Michigan
Catholic school enrollment in,
2908
educational reform proposal
for, 1510-1515
high schools, 2122-2123
proposal for mission school for
Indian children in, 1723
public schools in, 1024-1026,
1511-1512
rate bill and warrant for
collection in, 1030
taxation during Depression in,
2536
See also Detroit, Michigan
Michigan Board of Public
Instruction, 1155-1157

Michigan Children's Aid Society, 2963
Michigan Educational Association, 2122, 2909
Michigan, University of, 2295
democracy at, 1516-1517
influence on Cornell University, 1542
teacher education at, 1414-1418
White on, 1517-1519
Mickstur, Isaak, 391
Microtechne, 151
Middle Ages, attitudes toward education during, 1845-1846
Middle Atlantic States Philosophy of Education Association, 3151
Middle class
advantages of, 3274-3275
attacks on, 1462-1463
and family education, 2204
and progressive education, 2578-2579
Middle-class aspirations, of Negroes, 3219-3220
"Middle language," 3243
Middletown (Lynd and Lynd), 2515-2520, 2689-2692
Middletown, Connecticut, 435-436, 2604-2606
Middletown in Transition (Lynd and Lynd), 2604-2606
Midrashim, 2919
Midwest
school segregation in, 3027
schools in, 1299-1302, 2106
Mifflin, Benjamin, 1052
Mifflinburg Academy, 1298
Migrant education, problems of, 3192-3197
Migration, of Southern Negroes, 2994-2995
Mildmaye, Sir Walter, 266, 267
Milhaud, 2210
Military careers, glorification of, 1318-1319
Military conscription
in Prussia, 928
teachers' exemption from, 926
Military discipline, Quaker attitude toward, 903-904
Military forces
and Civilian Conservation Corps, 2565-2566
and national government, 1410
Military schools, 2840, 2841-2843
West Point, 1481
Military sciences, professorship of, 1482
Military training, 172-173, 174, 243
and apprenticeship, 358-359
at Carlisle Indian School, 1748
Mill, John Stuart, 911-913, 1599, 3315
Millard, Joseph, 714
Miller, Clyde R., 2541-2542
Miller, Francis, 3009
Miller, Fred J., 2267
Miller, Herbert Adolphus, 2182-2184
Miller, Joaquin, 1600

Miller, John, 380
Miller, Kelly, 2986
Miller, Leslie W., 2267
Miller, Perry, 379, 380-381, 381-383, 385-386, 414-415, 618, 656-657, 682-685
Miller, Persis K., 2420
Miller, Phyllemon, 344
Miller, Samuel, 985-986
Milligan, Dr. Josephine, 2141
"Millions of B.A.'s But No Jobs," 2814-2818
Mills, Wilbur D., 3006-3009
Milne, A. A., 2483
Milner, Thomas, 643, 645
Milton, John, 182-187, 486, 496, 503, 1546, 1613, 1964
Milton's Tractate on Education (Browning), 182-187
Mind of the Child, The (Preyer), 863-871
Mind and Hand: Manual Training the Chief Factor in Education (Ham), 1857-1859
Mine inspectors, and child labor, 2144-2145
Mineralogy
in Prussian schools
at University of Virginia
at Universtiy of Virginia, 1488
Minersville, Pennsylvania. See Minersville School District v. Gobitis
Minersville School District v. Gobitis, 3054-3058, 3058, 3060-3064
Minimal standards, 3293
Minister for National Education (France), 2119
Minister of Public Instruction (Prussia), 1090
Ministers, and religious instruction, 60
Ministry, education for, 1467-1471
Ministry of Public Instruction, of Ecclesiastical and Medical Affairs, 927
Minneapolis public schools, mental hygiene clinics in, 2481-2482
Minnesota
child study questionnaire used in, 1851-1852
free food plan in, 2146-2147
physicians in, 2773n
"Minnesota Child-Study Association" (Galbreath), 1851-1852
Minority, formation of, 2031
Minority rights, and Catholic schools, 1179-1180
Minors
in Dalton Plan, 2469
in teachers colleges, 2705
Minton, Justice, 2724-2726
Minturn, Benjamin G., 985-986
"Minutes of the Pennsylvania Colonial Council," 359
Miscegenation
and Chinese migration, 1766
and integrated schools, 1769
See also Intermarriage

Misconduct, 2401
"Miseducation of the Negro, The" (Woodson), 2999-3000
Mishnah, 2919
Mission Church, of Santa Barbara, 1037-1038
Mission Indians, 1754
Mission of San Buenaventura, 1037
Mission of San Miguel, California, 1040
Mission of Santa Margarita, California, 1040
Missionaries
attitudes toward education of Negroes, 575-576
and conversion of slaves, 580-584
and education of Negro children, 584-585
to Indians, 627-629
Mississippi
law forbidding education of Negroes in, 1621
and Peabody Fund, 1677-1678
school desegregation in, 3224
Sunday schools in, 979
Mississippi, University of, desegregation of, 3363
Meredith at, 3017-3020
Missouri, Catholic school enrollment in, 2907
Missouri Ex Rel. Gaines v. Canada, 3097-3098, 3102, 3104
Missouri, Kansas & Texas Railway v. McCann, 3092
Missouri River party, 1740
Missouri Teachers' Association, 1399
Missouri, University of, elementary school of School of Education at, 2477-2479
Mitchel, 2339
Mitchell, Clara, 2295
Mitchell, James T., 729
Mitchell, John, 2267
Mitchell, Jonathen, 660, 664
Mitchell, Lucy Sprague, 2499-2503
Mitchell, Samuel, 468
Mittleberger, Gottlieb, 437
Mobile, Alabama, meeting of Department of Superintendence in, 2262, 2263
Mobility, in Los Angeles ghettos, 3024-3025
Model First Reader (Webb), 1746
Model school
at Massachusetts State Normal School, 1337
and normal school, 1331
at State Normal School of New Britain, Connecticut, 1342
See also Lancastrian system
"Modell of Christian Charity, A", 365-367
"Modern Slaves: The Student as Nigger" (Farber), 2864-2867
Mohawks, 623
Mohr, Louise, 2490n

Moliere, 2121, 2706
Molineus, 190
Mollineaux, Lady, 473
Moloch, 255
Molyneux, Robert, 714
Monarchy
  of American colleges, 1555-1556
  school governed as, 1363
Money making, proverbs on, 914-915
Money rewards, and reading learning
Monis, Judah, 538
Monitor-general, 879
Monitorial system, Lancaster's, 878-884
  See also Lancasterian System
Monitors, 165-170
  of absentees, 879
  of attendance, 1250
  of dictation at Boston High School for Girls, 1250
  in Lancastrian System, 981, 982, 988-989
  responsibilities of, 883-884, 400
  of ruling, 878
  of sections at Boston High School for Girls, 1250
  of slates, 879
"Monkey" laws, 2740, 2742
Monographs of the Society for Research in Child Development, 3248-3250
Monro, 885
Monroe, Will S., 255-257
Monroe doctrine, 2102
Montana, Indians in, 1739
Monte District, California, public schools in, 1035
Montecito District, California, public schools of, 1038
Montefiore, 1198
Montesquieu, 839n, 840n, 954
Montessori Bulletin, 2320
Montessori Educational Association
  organization of, 2318-2321
  purpose, 2319, 3255-3256
Montessori, Maria, 1996-2000, 2080, 2311, 2316, 2319
Montessori, Mario, dialogue with A. S. Neill, 3262-3270
Montessori method, 1996-1999
  criticism of, 2322-2324
  and intelligence tests, 2250
  See also "Children's Houses"
Montessori Method, The (Montessori), 1996-2000
Montessori schools
  first in America, 2310-2316, 2319
  Neill on, 3262-3270
  in U.S. and Italy compared, 604
Montessori System Examined, The (Kilpatrick), 2315
Montezuma, 2322-2324
Montgomery, Luanne, 3014
Montgomery, Alabama, Negro physician in, 1665
Monthly Labor Review, 3192

Moody, Eleazer, 536-537
Moody, Matthew, 448
Moon, and gravity, 222, 226
Moor, Omar Khayyam, 3308-3310
Moore, Benjamin P., 793-794, 797
Moore, Charles A., 2267
Moore, Charles S., 2745-2748
Moore, George, 589-591
Moore, O. K., 3247
Moor's Indian-Charity School, 619-623
Moquis, 1737
Morache, Estter, 449
Morache, Salomon, 449-450
Moraine Park School, 2420, 2422
"Moral Catechism" of Webster, Noah, 771-773
Moral character
  as teacher qualification, 1315
  and teacher certification, 1324
Moral code, and nationality, 2385-2386
Moral culture, 1210-1212
Moral discernment, as teacher qualification, 1358-1359
Moral education, 408-409, 411, 502
  at Choctaw Academy, 1728
  and discipline, 859
  and domestic economy lesson, 1377-1378
  Emerson on, 1232
  and family ties in U.S., 957
  at female seminary, 1575
  Harris on, 1909-1914
  at Harvard College, 657, 659
  Herbartian position on
  in Jewish schools, 1885-1887
  and lack of family nurture, 1905
  and literature, 415
  and manual training, 1857, 1862-1863, 2920-2921
  New York Free-School Society on, 1866
  and phrenology, 890-891
  of poor children, 1119
  in Prussian elementary schools, 894-897
  role of Church in, 2049
  Rousseau on, 98-101
  in spelling book, 1379-1381
  Vatican II on, 2045
"Moral Education in the Common Schools" (Harris), 931
Moral philosophy, 68, 162, 172, 503, 523
  in college curriculum, 1505
  at Princeton University, 709
  in university curriculum, 56, 57
Moral Philosophy (Wayland), 1333
Moral qualities, and Darwin's theories, 918-919
Moral rules, at Columbia University, 697-698
Moral science
  Porter on, 1477-1480
  and preparation for professional and public life, 1479

in Society of Jesus universities, 67
Moral and Spiritual Values in the Public Schools, 2623n
Moral training
  in children's charter, 2551-2552
  and co-education, 877
  in college, 1475
  Committee of Fifteen on, 1967
  and discipline, 1916-1917
  in home and school, 2213-2214
  in kindergarten, 1856, 1907
  Parker on, 1825-1826
  and physiological education, 863
  in schools of Public School Society of New York, 1125-1126
Morality, 257, 264, 498, 628, 653
  in charity school, 324-325
  in country schools, 776
  and education of girls, 87-88
  and European education, 799
  Franklin on, 487-490
  in indenture contract, 328
  as science, 109
  teaching of, 66
  and university students, 197-199
  Webster on, 771-773
Moravian Brethren, 607
Moray, Sir Robert, 217
Mordecai, Jacob, 1572
Mordecai, Rosa, 1191-1192
More, Sir Thomas, 150-151, 164
Morell, 948
Moreno, Edward, 2941
Morgan, Arthur E., 2422
Morgan, Francis, 343
Morgan, Lloyd, 1427
Morisanus, 194
Morison, John, 722, 723, 726
Morison, Samuel Eliot, 657-660, 662-666, 671
Mormons, 1036
Morning ablution, of teacher, 1361
Morphett, Mabel, 1526-1527
Morrill Act, text of, 3364
Morris, Richard B., 390
Morrison, Francis, 641
Morrison, James H., 3006-3009
Morrison, Samuel Eliot, 1595
Morse, Miss Lucia, 2421
Mortality, and wandering children, 2530
Mosellanus, 47
Mosely, Alfred, 2104-2108
Mosely Commission, on American education, 2104-2108
Moses, 124, 140-141, 142, 186, 562
Mosley, Joseph, 714
Mosley v. Mattingly, 1772
"Most Pressing Problems Concerning the Elementary Course of Study" (de Garmo), 1884-1888
Most Reverend Francis Patrick Kenrick, Third Bishop of Philadelphia, 1830-1851, The (Nolan), 1146-1147

NEA: The First Hundred Years
(Wesley), 1398
Neal, Dr. John P., 2791
Neale, Leonard, 714
Neatness, as teacher qualification, 1360-1361
Neau, Elias, 581-582
Nebraska
immigrants in, 2382
public schools, 2717-2718
Nebraska State Legislature, banning of foreign languages in schools by, 2717-2718
Necho, King of Egypt, 124
Needle-work, 438, 439
at female seminary, 1577-1578
at Indian Schools, 1759
Negro in Chicago: A Study of Race Relations and a Race Riot, The, 2993-2996
Negro children, of French parentage, 1638
See also Education of Negroes; Negroes
Negro colleges, opposition to, 1701-1702
Negro education. *See* Education of Negroes
Negro intelligence, Jensen on, 3206-3207
Negro physician, in Montgomery, Alabama, 1665
Negro population, expansion of, 3043-3046
Negro problem, and education, 1681
See also Education of Negroes
Negro protest, in South, 3002
Negro Schools in the Southern States (Jones), 2997-2999
Negro students
dropouts during Depression, 2543
at Harvard, 1718-1722
at West Point, 1716-1718
Negro teachers
in Chicago, 2996
in the deep South, 1628-1631
in South, 3001-3002
Negro in the United States, The (Frazier), 3106n
Negroes
barriers to higher education of, 2809-2811
conversion to Christianity, 577-580, 586
duties of, 2991
education of. *See* Education of Negroes
and education of Southern whites, 1003-1004
and high school enrollment, 2508-2509
in IGC classes, 2128
and object-naming tests, 1835-1838
in oyster and shrimp canneries, 2150
passing as white, 1721
religious instruction for, 592
South Carolina laws on, 572-574
taxes paid by, 1691

in wars against Indians, 2949
See also Slaves
Neigebauer, 928
Neighborhood schools, 2117
elimination of, 3280
and P.A.T., 3020-3023
and private schools, 3280
and voucher plan, 3330-3336
Neill, Edward, 335
Neill, A. S., 2066-2070, 3261
dialogue with Montessori, 3262-3270
Nelson, Lord, 1114-1115
Nephthalim, 144
Nepos, 1238
"Neptune," 1115
Nervous system
and conditioned reflexes, 2017-2020
excitement of, 866
and infant development, 869-870
See also Mental development; Sense development
Nervousness
and Batavia Plan, 2270
of infants, 2359
Ness, Lieut. William, 3014
Neuropsychiatric Institute School (NPI) at the University of California, Los Angeles, 3254-3260
Neurotic child, and habit clinics, 2465-2466
New Amsterdam, teachers in, 544-545
New Britain, Connecticut, State Normal School of, 1340-1344
New Deal for Youth: The Story of the National Youth Administration, A (Lindley and Lindley), 2555-2558
New Departure in College Education, Being a Reply to President Eliot's Defense of it in New York, The (McCosh), 1558-1563
New Departure in the Common Schools of Quincy, The (Adams), 1809-1812
New Digest of the Statute Laws of Louisiana, A, 1621
New Discovery of the Old Art of Teaching Schoole, in Four Small Treatises, A (Campagnac), 289-298
New education. *See* Progressive education
New Education Fellowship, statement of principles of, 2065-2066
New England
apprenticeship in, 390-391
attitude toward education in, 954-955
child labor in, 1060-1061
education in, 543-544, 1460
public schools in, 1062-1063
teachers in Reconstruction South from, 1632-1634
New England Association of Colleges and Preparatory

Schools, *Addresses and Proceedings*, 1418-1420
New England District School, 1283-1285
"New England Female Seminary for Teachers," 1583-1585
New England Freedmen's Aid Society, 1635-1636
New England Primer. . ., The (Ford), 530-533
New England Weekly Journal, 591-592
"New England's First Fruits," 656-657
New English Weekly, 2415n
New Era, The, 2065-2066
New Guide to the English Tongue (Dilworth), 539
New Hampshire
academy movement in, 517-523
and Dartmouth College case, 1435-1441
establishment of free school in, 401
Indian education in, 709
Phillips Exeter Academy at, 1236-1241
See also Dartmouth College
New Haven, Connecticut, 1457
free schools in, 403
opposition to a proposed Negro college in, 1701-1702
See also Yale College
New Horizons Report, 2710
New Jersey
apprenticeship in, 358-359
Catholic school enrollment in, 2907
education in, 513
public schools in, 1068-1069
teacher qualifications in, 557
teachers' contracts in, 1339
See also Princeton University
New Jersey Historical Society, 358-359
New Jersey legislature, and busing to religious schools, 3065
New Kent School, New Kent County, Va., 3117-3120
New Lanark, Owen's school at, 893-897, 900-904
New left, Port Huron Statement on, 2858
New math, 3235-3239
New Mexico
statutes authorizing racially separate schools in, 3035
support for public education in, 1022-1024
New Mexico Indians, 1737-1738
New Netherlands
education in, 352-353
hiring of teacher in, 352
petition for school in, 353
New Oraibi, 2949
"New Order of Educational Research And Development, A," 3389-3393
New Orleans, Louisiana
description of mixed schools in, 1644-1646
Negro schools in, 1636-1641

See also School rules
Pendleton, Charles, 2490n
Pendleton, Edmund, 1687
Pendleton, Senator, 1743
Peninsula Council for Youth, 3199
Penmanship, 473
  at Manual Training School of Washington University, 1860
  in Prussian teachers seminaries, 1511
  See also Writing
Penn, Thomas, 632-633
Penn, William, 359, 361-362, 607-611
Pennell, C. S., 1497
Pennell, Miss R. M., 1497
Pennsylvania
  Catholic school enrollment in, 2907-2908
  constitutional provision for schools in, 797
  description of district in Union County, 1297-1299
  education of German immigrants in, 633, 634-637
  education in, 560-565, 758-760
  education laws in, 359
  German immigration to, 630-631
  Indian education in, 1754
  loyalty oaths for teachers in, 729-731
  movement for public schools in, 1064-1067
  physicians per person in, 2771
  plan for public schools in, 360-361
  religion in, 437
  slavery in, 587-588
  teaching methods in, 558-559
Pennsylvania constitution, on free schools for poor, 975
Pennsylvania Gazette, 556-557, 558
Pennsylvania Legislature, on public schools, 1064
Pennsylvania Magazine of History and Biography, 587-588
Pennsylvania Packet, The, 452
Pennsylvania School Journal, 1297-1299, 1298
Pennsylvania State College, and adult education, 2840
Pennsylvania Statutes at Large from 1802-1805, 975
Pennsylvania Supreme Court, on teacher fitness, 2728-2730
"Pennsylvania Trustees of the German Society to the Society," 637-638
Pennsylvania, University of, during Depression, 2540
Pennsylvanian, 1148
"Penny Lunches," 2204
Pensions, for teachers, 926
Pentateuch, 2919
Pentz, Daniel C., 1140
Perception
  development of, 866
  and intelligence, 1994-1995
  and play materials, 1803

training of infants in, 1369-1371
Pereira, Benjamin, 450-451
Pererius, 194
Perez, Albino, 1022-1024
Performance, specification of minimally acceptable standards for, 3293
Performance contracting, 3336-3339
Periegetis (Dionysious), 351
Perine v. Chesapeake & Delaware Canal Co., 3091
Periodicals
  established, 1333
  for teachers, 926
  See also Journals
Peripatetics, 223
Perkins, B. D., 985-986
Pernambuco, 354
Perry, Bliss, 1229-1231
Perry, Micajah, 644
Persian language, 150
Persians, 125
Persistence, and creative work, 2440
Persius, 285
Personal adjustment, Harvard Committee on Secondary Education on, 2618-2620
Personal appearance
  in Bonnal school, 825
  at Carlisle Indian School, 1749, 1751
  at de Fellenberg's agricultural school, 855
  of ideal women, 1571
  in textbooks for immigrants, 2174
  See also Cleanliness
Personal habits, education in, 1101-1102
Personal unity, and concentration and reflection, 860
Personality, alteration of, 234
Personality development
  education as, 2602
  and fantasy, 3267
  and Montessori schools, 3264
  and progressive education, 2454-2455
Personality in the Making (Witmer and Kotinsky), 3106n
Personality problems, of college students, 2784-2786
Perspective, 497, 510
Perspective drawing, in elementary school, 949
Peru, conquest of Indians of, 604
Pessimism and fear, 2007-2008
Pestalozzi (Anderson), 827-831
Pestalozzi, Johann Heinrich, 821-826, 827-831, 832-837, 968, 1184, 1228, 1350, 1818, 1858, 1889, 2437
  and education at Stanz, 832-837
  influence of, 855
  See also Pestalozzianism
Pestalozzi: His Life and Work (de Guimps), 832-837
Pestalozzianism

in Kentucky school, 1779
  and "Object teaching," 1781-1787
  in Oswego, New York public schools, 1780-1781
Peter, Sir William, 266, 267
Peters, Richard, 637-638
Petitions
  against school segregation in Boston, 809-810
  for college in Massachusetts Bay, 558
  of Detroit Catholics for school funds, 1702-1703
  to establish college in Virginia, 641-645, 1155-1157
  for free schools in Rhode Island, 1051-1052
  for an Indian school, 1744
  of Jews in Rome, 651
  for mandamus, 1199
  of New York Catholics, 3093-3097
  by New York Free-School Society, 1122, 1128-1139
  for use of Catholic Bible in public schools, 1123
Petosa, Felicia, 3023
Petosa, John, 3023
Pets, 1806-1807
Petty, William, 246-249
Pfahler, W. F., 2267
Pfister, Oscar, 2393-2394
Phalareus, Demetrius, 162, 186
Phalerii, 290
Phantasy. See Fantasy
Ph.D.'s
  critiques of, 2752-2757
  theses written for, 2702
  for women, 3221-3222
Phi Beta Kappa Society, 1718
  beginnings at William and Mary College, 719-723
  Harvard chapter of, 725-726
  subjects debated in, 724
Phi Delta Kappan, 2867-2871, 2936-2942, 3294-3299, 3310-3315, 3325-3328, 3389-3393
Philadelphia, Pennsylvania
  academy movement in, 523-526
  business schools in, 444
  call for free education in, 1054-1056
  during Depression, 2541
  education in, 504-509
  first school in, 359
  free schools in, 761-762
  Hebrew Sunday-school in, 1190, 1191-1192
  Jewish education in, 1200
  Lancastrian school in, 981-983
  meeting of Department of Superintendence in, 2262
  meeting to organize National Teachers' Association in, 1398-1403
  petition for use of Catholic Bible in public schools of, 1146-1147
  public schools of, 1148
  questions on education to candidate from, 1052
  Whitefield visits, 434-435

Philadelphia Academy, 510-513
advertisement for, 510
Philadelphia High School, 2108
Philadelphia National Gazette,
on public schools, 1057-1058
Philadelphia Society for the
Establishment and Support
of Charity Schools, 980-981
Philanthropic school societies, in
England and U.S. compared,
2110
Philanthropy
and denominational colleges,
2760-2763
and Ford Foundation's grant to
higher education, 2818-2820
and Negro education in South,
3001, 3006
and Silver Street Kindergarten,
1799-1802
and state universities, 1531-
1532
and Summerhill, 2068-2069
Philbrick, 1632
Philbrick's tablets, 1213
Philip of Macedonie, King, 149,
161, 267, 2273
Philippines, 2104
Philipps, Caleb, 439
Philistines, 136
Phillips, Elizabeth, 522
Phillips, Hen, 396
Phillips, J. H., 2992-2993
Phillips, John, 516, 517, 522
Phillips, Jonas, 809-810
Phillips, Naphtali, 1182
Phillips, Samuel, 516
Phillips, William, 516
Phillips Andover Academy
charter of, 516
schedule at, 517
teacher training at, 1324-1326
Phillips Exeter Academy
charter of, 517-518
college preparatory course,
1237-1238
constitution of, 518-522
English course at, 1236-1237
graduation certificates from,
522-523
influence on public schools,
1239-1241
*Phillips Exeter Academy: A
History, The* (Crosbie), 522-
523, 1236-1238
Philological Association, 1946
Philology, in university
curriculum, 803
Philosopher's stone, 131
Philosophical Union, University
of California, 2208
"Philosophie Zoologique"
(Lamarck), 915
Philosophy, 55, 510
in college curriculum, 1507,
1548
and elective system, 2747
and founding of Royal Society
of London, 217
and idols and false notions,
215-216
method of teaching, 1548
in normal schools, 1334

at Princeton University, 709
in university curriculum, 56
See also Natural philosophy
"Philosophy of Catholic
Education, The"
(McGucken), 2897-2901
Philosophy (Newton), 222
Philosophy school, of William
and Mary College, 654
"Philosophy of the Winnetka
Curriculum, The"
(Washburne), 2489
Phonetics
neglect of, 3136-3138
and sandpaper letters, 2314
Phrenology
Combe on, 884-893
and education, 889-893
Physical activity, 98
Physical causality, child's
conception of, 2023-2029
Physical confinement, in New
York City public schools,
1893
Physical defects, and retarded
children, 2199-2200
Physical Degeneracy (Allen),
1591
Physical development
during adolescence, 2205-2206
in childhood, 103-104
and progressive education,
2424
of wild boy, 838
Physical education teachers,
diplomas for, 2715
Physical efficiency, and
curriculum, 2431-2432
Physical examinations, 2360
of child labororers, 2141
Physical fitness, 182
Physical geography, in secondary
school curriculum, 1940
Physical growth, in Gary, Indiana
schools, 2333-2334
Physical health, and learning,
102-104
*Physical and Metaphysical Works
of Lord Bacon, The* (Devey),
209-213, 213-216
Physical nearness, and
impressions of objects, 829
Physical punishment, 883
See also Corporal punishment
Physical science, in college
curriculum, 1505
Physical training, 42-43, 247, 252,
273-275, 497, 2359
in California school rules, 1043
at Carlisle Indian School, 1751
and child study method, 1849-
1850
in curriculum for feebleminded
children, 2405
in elementary school
curriculum, 1967, 1969
Emerson on, 1235
in high school, 2516
in Massachusetts public
schools, 1101-1103
at Mount Holyoke Female
Seminary, 1588-1589

at University Elementary
School, 2300
Physically handicapped, in
Children's Charter, 2552
Physicians
per person, 2768-2769
shortages of, 2768-2772
Physico-mathematics, at
University of Virginia, 1488
Physics, 55, 173, 185, 244, 388,
654
in American schools, 969
books on, 202
and elective system, 2747
in Gary, Indiana Schools, 2331
in grammar school curriculum,
1927, 1928, 1929
and preternatural causes, 228
in Prussian teachers seminaries,
1511
in secondary school curriculum,
1936, 1939
in Society of Jesus universities,
67
status of, 213
in university curriculum, 56, 57
at University of Virginia, 1488
Physics (Aristotle), 2797
Physiological method of
education, of Seguin, 861-
863
Physiological psychology,
Wundt's principles of, 871-
875
See also Phrenology
Physiology
in college curriculum, 1507
in elementary school in Salem,
Massachusetts, 948-949
and infant education, 1204-
1205
in normal schools, 1334
in public schools, 1102-1103
research on, 2017-2020
in secondary school curriculum,
1936, 1939
"Physiology of the Embryo,"
(Preyer), 864
Piaget, Jean, 3246-3247, 3253
on child's conception of
physical causality, 2023
on cognitive development,
3248-3250
Pickering, Marvin L., 2736-2738
*Pickering v. Board of Education
of Township High School*,
2736-2738
Picolomeneus, 194
Picture-books, role of, 827
Pierce, Benjamin, 715-716
Pierce, Cyrus, 1328-1331
Pierce, John, 1024-1026
*Pierce v. Society of the Sisters of
the Holy Names of Jesus
and Mary*, 3051-3052, 3057,
3083
Pierpont, John, 1247
Pierson, John, 686
Piety, as teacher qualification,
1358-1359
Pigeon behavior studies, 3230
Pigeon-English, 1766
Pigott, Nath, 591-592

Pilcher, John L., 3006-3009
Pilgrim Fathers, 1095-1096
Pilgrim's Progress, The (Bunyan), 312-313, 477
Pillory, 883
Pimos Indians, 1737
Pine Bluff, Arkansas, 1675
Pine Grove, 1632-1634
Pine Ridge, 1754
Pine Ridge Agency, 1745
Pinel, 838
Pingree, Miss L. B., 1833
Pintner-Cunningham Primary Mental Test, 2571
Pioneer Day, 2349
Pioneer: A History of the Johns Hopkins University (Hawkins), 1568
Pioneers of Women's Education in the United States (Goodsell), 1580-1582
"Pirates" Own Book, The," 1455
Pison, 139
Pitt, 1504
Pittsburgh, University of
during Depression, 2541
Learning Research and Development Center at, 3308-3310
Pius IV, Pope, 133
Pius XI, Pope, 2048, 2050n, 2050n
encyclical letter on Christian education, 2020-2023
Pius XII, Pope, 2045n, 2047n, 2051n n
allocution to the Association of Catholic Teachers of Bavaria, 2048n
Pizzarro, Francis, 604
Placement, in nongraded school, 3288-3289
Plagius, 483
Plains Indians, education of children by, 1731-1732
"Plan of February 1818," 976-977
"Plan for an Industrial University, for the State of Illinois" (Turner), 1520-1525
Plane trigonometry, 1236
Planetary theory. *See* Astronomy
Planets, and gravity, 224
Planning for American Youth, 2627n
Plantagenets, 2089
Planters' Bank, 1677-1678
Planters' Bank bonds, 1677
Plants, object teaching lessons on, 1783-1784
Plasteline, 2445
Plastic art, in education, 2444-2446
"Plastic Art" (Levin), 2444-2446
Plato, 150, 158, 163, 186, 242, 267, 269, 414, 415, 671, 1223, 1350, 1463, 1483-1484, 1858, 2121, 2797, 2798n, 3157
attitude toward education, 1925
and Christian thought, 2897
in French secondary school curriculum, 1925

ideal of the cultured man, 1360
ideal ruler, 2765
Plato club, at Hull House, 2833
Platonic Christianity, 1484
Platonic republicanism, 1484
Platt, H. G., 1771
Plautus, 47
Play, 262-263
and art, 2486-2489
and balls, 848-849
between adults and children, 851-852
in British infant schools, 3301
and child study method, 1847
developmental role of, 845
and education of Indian children, 2955
Emerson on, 1233
and infant education, 1204-1205
with infants, 2359
in kindergartens, 1794-1798
and personality development, 2079-2081
role of, 846-848
symbolic meaning of, 1805-1808
at Westminster School, 170
Play corner, in British infant schools, 3301
Play equipment, and mental development, 1802-1805, 1759
Playfair, 1629
Playground movement, 2492
Playgrounds, 2359
in American schools, 961
at Indian Schools, 2333
"Play-level" of curriculum, 2492
Playmates, selection of, 157
Plays, at Westminster School, 171
"Plea for Western Colleges" (Post), 1451-1454
Pleasure
and education, 89
and ego, 2001
and learning, 1213, 1312
Pledge of allegiance, 2112n, 3079
See also Flag salute
Plessy v. *Ferguson,* 3007, 3087-3090, 3096, 3102, 3103, 3104, 3105
Plimpton Collection, 529
Plinius Secundus, 181
Pliny, 106, 185, 1966, 2112
Plowden, Edmond, 714
Plowden Report, 2092-2095, 3304, 3305
Plutarch, 150, 168, 185, 256-257, 477
Plymouth colony, school law of 1677 of, 401
Plymouth Colony Records, 401
Pocahontas, 605
"Pocho," 2944
Poems on Various Subjects, Religious and Moral (Wheatley), 594
Poetry, 186, 191, 388
in British infant schools, 3303
and dramatization, 2483-2484
Mather on, 414-415

and progressive education curriculum, 2448
in Society of Jesus universities, 67
in university curriculum, 907
Poetry writing, 48, 415, 2445-2446
in Latin, 406, 407
Poets, 285
books of, 205-206
Jewish, 1198
Poff, Richard H., 3006-3009
Poincare, 2210
"Point-scale method," 2254
Poland, forced nationalization in, 2373
Police
at Central High School, Little Rock, 3009-3011
and drug problem in Palos Verdes, 3201
at Nanterre, 2059, 2060
and school safety, 3202
Political action, and education, 1015-1016
Political beliefs, of teachers. *See* Academic freedom
Political consciousness, and Nanterre movement, 2060
Political economy
in American schools, 968-969
in college curriculum, 1507
at Harvard College, 1462
at Manual Training School of Washington University, 1860
at University of Virginia, 1488
Political education
in public schools, 1104-1107
in Soviet schools, 3155
See also Political economy
Political function, of American schools, 2111
Political life, role of intellectuals in, 3180-3182
Political opinions, of applicants to New York State Normal School, 1344
Political philosophy, 1236
Political proselytism, in schools, 1105-1106
Political relations, activities relating to, 921
Political rights, of Chinese immigrants, 1768
Political Science. *See* Political economy
Politics, 186, 264
and economics, 2608-2609
and education, 2104
and immigrant population, 2175
in public schools, 2672-2674
and riots against Gary schools, 2338-2340
and school system, 1900
and student life at Harvard, 718
study of, 498
in university curriculum, 56, 57
Polk, 2769n
Polk Street, Chicago, 2164
Polk Street Night-School, (Chicago), 2138-2139

Poll tax
for Alabama public schools, 1648
in Louisiana, 1652
Pollock, 1745
Polytechnic School of Munich, 1416
Ponca Indians, 1740, 1745
Ponca school, 1739
Pontius Pilate, 53
Poole, Captain, 1739
Poor children
Brookline's free school for, 403
and call for White House Conference on Children, 2355-2357
of East Side, New York tenements, 2133-2135
education of, 544
and hunger, 2145-2147
in North Boston slums, 2137
problems of, 2201-2203
in Quaker schools, 568
See also Child labor; Education of poor
Poor laws, for Virginia children, 342-343
Poor Richard, 493-495
Poor Richard Improved, 492-495
Poore, Benjamin P., 809, 1021, 1650-1651
Poor-relief law (1601), 321-323
Popes, 458, 497, 503, 1596
and Catholic schools, 1163
See also under individual names of
Popham, W. James, 3290-3294
Popular Science Monthly, 2208, 2776n
Population
high-school, 2510-2512
in Massachusetts, 1103, 1316
Mexican American, in California, 2943
in poor neighborhoods, 2094
of secondary-schools, 2279-2280
of sweaters' district of New York City, 2152
See also Population growth
Population Act (England), 897
Population growth
and American democracy, 3157-3158
and higher education, 1508
and immigration to West, 991
and Jews, 1185-1186
in New York City, 1122
and public schools, 1332-1333
and rise of masses, 2030-2031
in U.S., 955
Populists, in England, 2085-2088
Port Huron Statement, 2853-2859
Port Royal, during Reconstruction, 1632-1634
Port Royalists on Education, The (Barnard), 75-77
Portage, Ohio, School Examiners for County of, 1310
Porter, Noah, 1471-1477, 1477-1480, 1569
Portland, Oregon public schools, 3152

Portuguese, in North Boston slums, 2137
Positions Concerning the Training Up of Children (Mulcaster), 272-279
Posselius, 413
Possewine, 665
Post, Truman M., 1451-1454
Postal Guide, physicians in, 2773n
Postgraduate studies
in education, 2686-2687
purpose of, 1918
Posture, 825
for art work, 2488
Potential
and phrenology, 887-893
realization of, 843
Pott, Schueneman, 1800
Potter, William A., 1422
Pound, Thad C., 1743
Poverty
and children, 2145-2147, 2201-2203
and compensatory education, 3270-3276
and demoralization of children, 2007-2008
and education, 45, 1103-1104
and intelligence, 2250
intergenerational, 2510
and Negro education, 2984
and retardation, 3246
Poverty (Hunter), 2201-2203
Power, Rev. John, 1137-1139
Power, 442
craving for, 2008, 2009-2010
in public schools, 2672-2674
of teachers, 2580-2582
Power of Christian Benevolence Illustrated in the Life and Labors of Mary Lyon, The (Hitchcock), 1583-1585, 1585-1589
Powhatan. See Wahunsonacock
Practical and Theoretical Problems in Instinct and Habits (Watson), 2396n
Practice
in Herbartian method, 1878
and theory, 1447
Practice teaching
in teacher training courses, 1973-1974
tests of success, 1979-1980
See also Student Teaching
Practice and Theory of Individual Psychology, The, 2007-2010
Practice-school, Committee of Fifteen on, 1977-1978
Pragmatism, meaning of, 2207-2211
Pragmatism: A New Name for Some Old Ways of Thinking (James), 2207-2211
Prairie View, Kansas, schoolhouse at, 1301-1302
Praise, of art work, 2441
Pratt, Anna B., 2400-2403
Pratt, Caroline, 2316-2318
Pratt, Daniel, 353, 545-546
Pratt, John, 447

Pratt, Lieutenant, 1749, 1751
Pratt, Mrs., 1752
Pratt, Richard Henry, 1740-1745
and Carlisle Indian school, 1740-1748
Prayer for Colleges, A Premium Essay, Written For "The Society for the Promotion of Collegiate and Theological Education at the West" (Tyler), 1467-1471
Prayers, 250, 400, 408, 544, 545
for child, 57-58
in class, 69
at college commencement exercises, 699
of Franklin, 486-487
in Jewish schools, 2927
in public schools, 3075-3079
and punishment, 75
in school, 47, 154, 324, 560-561
at University of Michigan, 1518
at Westminster School, 166, 167, 169
Preachers
in Pennsylvania, 437
Whitefield, 681-685
See also Sermons
Prebendaries, 165, 171
Preceptors, 72
of Providence public schools, 1286
Predelinquent children, 2400
Prediction, of behavior, 2235
Predispositions, and education, 2244-2246
Prefects, 167
Pregnancy
and Indian women, 609
and Teacher Corps, 3376
Prejudice
against immigrants, 2379
in Chicago public schools, 2995
and Indian education, 1741
and school integration, 1715-1716
at West Point, 1716-1718
Premiums, at Albany Female Academy, 1594
"Preparation for the Study of Medicine, The" (Lewis), 2776n
Preparatory schools, 1489, 1493
for Antioch College, 1497
in Prussia, 1512
Preparing Objectives for Programmed Instruction (Mager), 3292n
Preschools, 3245-3247
compensatory education in, 3294-3299
evaluation of programs for, 3296-3298
"habit clinics" for, 2465-2466
Present State of Virginia, The (Jones), 648-649
Preservation of the species, instinct of, 2002
President Arthur's First Annual Message, December 6, 1881, 1752-1754

and United States Bureau of
Education, 1404-1414
See also Teacher education
Professionals
oversupply of, 2817-2818
unemployed during Depression,
2542
women as, 3222
See also Professions
Professions
Jews in, 1198-1199
of women, 1580-1581
Professors
and American Association of
University Professors, 2875-
2881
choice of, for Cornell
University, 1545
at German universities, 1538-
1539, 1540, 1541-1542
at Hebrew College, 1187
at multiuniversity, 2825-2826
and Nanterre movement, 2060
relations with students, 2864-
2867
selection of, 2783
at state university, 1524
and teacher-training seminaries,
1305
at Universities of State of New
York, 793
at University of Georgia, 789
at University of Virginia, 1490-
1491
in U.S., 1457-1459
of William and Mary College,
646
See also Professors' salaries;
Professorships
Professors salaries, 2782
at Cornell University, 1545
Professorships
at Catholepistemiad, 1482
resident, 1545
Profit, in public schools run by
private corporations, 3338
"Program for American Youth,
A" (Watson), 2595-2598
"Program of individualization, A"
(Washburne), 2490n
"Program for the Prevention of
Delinquency,"
Commonwealth Fund of
New York, 2400
Programmed instruction, in
public schools run by private
corporations, 3338
Progressive Education, 2455-2460,
3176
Progressive education, 2416-2423,
2423-2424, 3169-3172
adoption of doctrines of, 3176
Ascham on, 266-272
and common man, 2646-2647
and Council for Basic
Education, 3146-3149
Counts on, 2578-2582
critiques of, 3123-3127, 3150-
3153
and Dalton Laboratory Plan,
2466-2473
defense of, 3169-3172, 3173-
3176

description of, 2417, 2446-2449
Dewey on, 2219-2223, 2455-
2460, 2648-2650, 3127-3131
evaluations of, 2460-2463,
2645-2647
and habit clinics, 2465-2466
"New articles of faith" of,
2449-2455
as organic education, 2496-
2497
organized attacks on, 3128
and reinforcement techniques,
3231
and social reconstruction, 2577-
2582
and Three Rs, 3174
as tool of socialism, 3127
See also Progressive schools
Progressive Education
Association, 2446-2449
founding of, 2416-2423
statement of principles of,
2423-2424
See also American Education
Fellowship
Progressive Education at the
Crossroads (Bode), 2645-2647
"Progressive Education And The
Science of Education"
(Dewey), 2455-2460
Progressive schools, 2448
as leader in educational
movements, 2425
Beaver Country Day School,
Brookline, Mass., 2498-2499
caricature of, 3138-3139
child-interest based curriculum
in, 2452-2453
compared with mechanical
schools, 1896-1899
creative self-expression in, 2453
elementary school of School of
Education at University of
Missouri, 2477-2479
Ethical Culture School, 2479-
2481
freedom of activity in, 2451
freedom in, 2449, 2458-2459
in Indianapolis, 1894-1896
kindergarten at Teachers
College, Columbia
University, 2473-2477
Little Red School House, New
York City, 2499-2503
of Park Forest, 3139-3143
personality and social
adjustment in, 2454-2455
self-government in, 2450
Shady Hill School, Cambridge,
Mass., 2483-2486
teacher-pupil relationships in,
2450
teacher's role in, 3143-3146
Walden School, New York
City, 2486-2489
of Winnetka, Illinois, 2489-
2496
Prohibitions, for young children,
1355
Project Head Start, 3296, 3305
Research and Evaluation
Branch of, 3212

"Project Method, The"
(Kilpatrick), 2272-2274
Proletariat, children of, 2007
Prologue (Chaucer), 2518
Promise of American Politics, The
(Smith), 2612n
Promised Land, The (Antin),
2167-2170
Promotions, in progressive and
traditional schools, 2457
Pronunciation, 497
at Carlisle Indian School, 1746
lessons in, 1379-1381, 1382-
1383
in readers, 1388-1390
and spelling, 764
Property, destruction of, 1104
See also School property
Property taxes
in Georgia, 1691
for public boarding schools,
1218-1219
Prophets, 135, 562, 2919
"Proposal for a Poor Children's
Bill of Rights, A" (Sizer and
Whitten), 3329n
Proposals relating to the
Education of Youth in
Pennsylvania (Franklin), 504
Prosody, 47, 48
Prospectus of the Ref. Mr. Peer's
School, 1779
Prosser, Dr. Charles A., 2629,
2631, 2632
Prosser Resolution, 2629n
Prostitution, and school
integration, 1769-1770
Protein malnutrition, and
intelligence, 3211
Protestant colleges, need for,
1452-1454
Protestant Episcopal Church,
1740
opposition to Catholic petition
for school funds, 1156-1157
Protestantism
and colleges, 1467-1471
and education, 954-955
and education of German
immigrants, 634-637
and higher education, 904-905
and need for colleges in West,
1452-1454
and public funding of Catholic
schools, 1133-1136
and state schools, 1177-1178
Proust, 2706
Proverbs (Sirach), 562
Proverbs, on money making, 914-
915
Proverbs of Solomon, 48
Providence Association of
Mechanics and
Manufacturers, petition for
free schools in Rhode Island,
1051-1052
Providence, Rhode Island
letter from Roger Williams to,
368-370
school regulations of, 1285-
1286
Sunday school for child
laborers in, 976

Provincialism, 1224
Prudentius, 154
Prussian Academy of Science, 2012
Prussian education, 927-928, 1065, 1083-1094
  and American college reform movement, 1510-1515, 1519
  compulsory, 1002
  elementary, 929-931
  as model for American reform, 1515-1516
  of teachers, 932-934, 1510-1511
  See also Prussian schools
Prussian schools
  drawing in, 1089
  Mann on, 1094-1095
  reading in, 1087-1088
  teachers in, 1089-1094
  writing in, 1086-1087, 1088-1089
Psalm of Life (Longfellow), 1964
Psalms, 48, 169, 545, 559
  twenty-fifth, 58
  twenty-fourth, 143
  twenty-third, 142-143
Psalters Spelling Books, 585
Pseudolus (Plautus), 47
Psychiatrist, in university, 2784
Psychic development of child, lack of knowledge in schools of, 2009
Psychical apparatus, Freud on, 2000-2002
"Psychoanalysis and the Training of the Young Child" (Freud, Anna), 2004-2007
Psychoanalytic Quarterly, 2004-2007
Psychoanalytic theory
  and developmental stages, 3253
  and education, 2002-2007, 2393-2396
  and play activities, 2080
Psychobiological environment, and psychological environment, 2035-2036
"Psychogenesis," (Preyer), 864
Psychologic Foundations of Education (Harris), 1917-1919
Psychological adjustment, in Greenwich Village philosophy, 2415, 2416
"Psychological Basis for Using Pre-School Enrichment As An Antidote For Cultural Deprivation The" (Hunt), 3245-3247
Psychological Effects of Enforced Segregation: A Survey of Social Science Opinion, The (Deutscher and Chein), 3106n
Psychological field forces, 2036-2037
Psychological influence, of environment, 2033-2037
Psychological method of measuring intelligence, 1993-1995
Psychological Review, 2236
Psychological testing, 3043

Psychological training, 830
  and education, 834-835
  and education of poor, 855-856
  in gaining sense impressions, 827-828
Psychologist, in kindergarten, 2474
Psychology
  application to curriculum, 1917-1919
  and approach to adult education, 2378
  and child as behaving oganism, 1428-1429
  compared with physiological psychology, 871, 872
  and correlation of studies, 1960-1961
  and education, 1852-1855, 2240-2243
  for high school teachers, 1981-1982
  of identification with masses or minority, 2031-2032
  and mental health of girl students, 1602-1604
  and progressive education, 1897
  and stream of consciousness, 1426-1427
  in teacher training courses, 1973, 1974
  See also Child study
Psychology of adolescence (Hall), 1951
"Psychology of the Elementary Curriculum, The" (Dewey), 2265n
Psychology Today, 3329n
Psychometry, and pedagogy, 1996
Psycho-sensory exercises, 1996-1997
Ptholomee, King of Egypt, 78, 132, 162, 220
Puberty, 103
Public accomodations discrimination, and Plessy v. Ferguson, 3087-3090
Public boarding schools, need for, 1215-1220
Public control, and slum schools, 3277
Public Education Association of New York City, 2309-2310, 2500
Public Education and Religious Liberty. See PEARL
Public Education in Rhode Island (Carroll), 1051-1052
Public health, in Gary, Indiana, schools, 2335-2336
Public Health Service, Surgeon General of, 2528
Public Interest, The, 3276-3281, 3329n
Public Kindergarten Society of San Francisco, 1800, 1801-1802
Public Laws of the State of Rhode Island, 786-787
Public library, 504
  of Boston, Mass., 2102
  Kennedy on, 3357

Public opinion
  and admission of women to colleges, 1519
  against public schools, 1004-1005
  on college curriculum, 1487
  on cost of college education, 1503-1504
  and education, 2102
  on education of women, 1595
  on employment of female teachers, 1316, 1317
  on establishment of public schools, 1005-1006
  and public schools in South Carolina, 1014-1016
  of schools in California, 1048-1049
  and vocational education, 2361
Public Papers of the Presidents, 3347, 3348-3358
Public Records of the Colony of Connecticut, The (Hoadley), 370, 402-403, 672-674
Public ridicule, as punishment, 883-884
"Public School Education of Second Generation Japanese in California" (Bell), 2974-2977
"Public School and the Immigrant Child, The" (Addams), 2195-2198
Public School Society of New York
  act incorporating, 1124-1125
  and Catholics, 1129-1139
  establishment of, 1123-1125
  moral and religious exercises in schools of, 1125-1126
  opposition to petition by New York City Catholics, 1132-1133
  Power on, 1137-1139
Public School System of the United States, The (Rice), 1829-1831
Public Schools, 38-39, 1188-1191, 1894
  alternatives to, 3315-3317
  of America and Europe compared, 1418
  Archbishop Ireland on, 1176-1181
  in Baltimore, 2420
  ban on teaching of Darwinism in, 2718-2719
  Bible reading in, 3080-3081
  in California, 1033, 1042-1045
  Catholic children in, 1163-1165
  and class distinctions, 1001-1002
  compared with normal schools, 1349-1353
  compared with private schools, 776-778
  compared with public boarding schools, 1217-1218, 1219-1220
  in Connecticut, 1069-1070
  Constitutional amendment on, 1166

3480

Organization of Public Instruction" (Condorcet), 110-115
Report of a Hearing Before the General Subcommittee on Education of the U.S. House of Representatives Committee on Education and Labor, 3377-3382
"Report of the Investigating Committee," 1569-1570
"Report of the Joint Committee of the Two Houses of the Pennsylvania Legislature on the Subject of a System of General Education," 1064
Report of the Panel of Consultants on Vocational Education, 3365-3369
Report to the President; the Committee for the White House Conference on Education, Full Report, April 1956, A, 3342-3346
"Report of the Special Committee of the Board of Supervisors of San Francisco," 1769-1770
Report on the State of Public Education in Prussia (Cousin), 927-928
"Report of the Sub-Committee On Grammar Schools of the School Committee of the City of Boston," 1253-1258
Report of a Sub-Committee of the School Committee Recommending Various Improvements In The System of Instruction in . . . this City, 989-990
"Report of the Superintendent of Public Instruction of the State of Michigan," 1024-1026
Reporters, at Little Rock, Arkansas, 3014-3015
Reports of Cases Argued and Decided in the Supreme Court of the United States, 1435-1437
Reports on European Education (Knight), 853-856, 927-928
Reports of the General Agent of the Peabody educational Fund, 1678-1680
Reports of the Selectmen and Other Officers of The Town of Concord From March 7, 1859, to March, 5, 1860, . . ., 1210-1213
Repository, for state university, 1523
Reproval, by parents, 88-89
Republic (Plato), 1483-1484, 2797
Republic and the Person, The (Chalmers), 2123
Republican government
  and American language, 763-766
  and education, 758-760, 954
  and general intelligence, 1104-1107

and necessity for American language, 766-769
school as, 1363-1365
and teacher training, 1304
Republican party, Negro support of, 1665-1666
Repulsion, and attraction, 2002
Rereading, 192
Research
  on family life, 2550-2551
  and universities, 2073-2074
Resenkranz, 1415
Residential segregation. *See* Housing discrimination
Residential zoning, 3224
Resignation, from Teacher Corps, 3376
"Resolute Beneficial Society," and school for Negro children in Washington, D.C., 1700-1701
Resolves of the General Court of Massachusetts (1837), 1070-1071
Respect
  for child, 2468
  for law in moral training, 1913-1914
Responsibility, and mental health, 1604
"Responsible Environments Project, The" (Moore and Anderson), 3308-3310
Responsive Environments Project, 3308-3310
Ressello, Pedro, 2011
Rest periods, 2359
Retarded children
  and Batavia Plan, 2270
  and behavior, 2401
  causes of, 2199-2200
  education of, 2198-2201
  examination by psychiatrist of, 2360
  and IQ, 2253-2254
  and late entrance, 2199
  and mental age, 2257
  and poverty, 3246
  remedies for, 2200-2201
  and sex differences, 2200
"Retentivity," in IEA study of mathematics achievement, 2054, 2058, 2059
Retirement, of school staff, 2259
Rev. B. Booth's Academy, 473
Review, at home, 70
Revised School Law, of California, 1042-1050
Revivalism, at Denison College, 1451
Revolt on Campus (Wechsler), 2791-2795
Revolt of the Masses, The (Ortega y Gasset), 2030-2033
Rewards, 414
  and adult education, 3269
  at Boston High School for Girls, 1249
  for first-graders, 560
  at Indian mission school, 1723
  Lancaster on, 882
  in Lancasterian system, 988
  Parker on, 1826
Reyerse, Adriaen, 546

Reynolds, Dr., 413, 1212
Reynolds, Grindall, 1051-1052
Reynolds, June, 3021, 3022
Reynolds v. United States, 3055
Rhemes and Doway (Cotton), 61-64
Rhemus, 290
Rhetoric, 48, 55, 162, 172, 186, 270, 290-291, 361, 406, 452, 456, 501-502, 503, 510, 523, 654, 1236
  in college curriculum, 66, 1505, 1507, 2798
  at Notre Dame University, 1161
  at Princeton University, 709
  in secondary school curriculum, 1936, 1939
  in Society of Jesus universities, 67
  at University of Virginia, 1489
Rhoad, William, 1732-1734
Rhoads, Bobby, 3016
Rhode, Hugh, 303-304
Rhode Island
  abolition of slavery in, 786-787
  Catholic school enrollment in, 2908
  compulsory school attendance in, 952
  illiteracy in, 1060
  public schools, 1319-1323
Rhode Island College. *See* Brown University
Rhodes scholars, 2110
Rhodes scholarships, establishment of, 2063-2065
Ricardo school, 1719
Rice, Dr. Arthur, 2909
Rice, Joseph Mayer, 1829-1831
  on Indianapolis public schools, 1894-1896
  on New York City and St. Louis public schools, 1892-1894
  on progressive *vs.* old education, 1896-1899
  on school supervision, 1899-1901
Rich, Josiah, 1136-1137
Richard, Father Gabriel, 1723
Richard of the Lion heart, 1067
Richards, B. W., 983
Richards, C. R., 2267
Richards, James P., 3006-3009
Richardson, Alexander, 664
Richardson, Alfred T., 1731-1732
Richardson, H. H., 1461, 1464
Richardson, James D., 1526-1527, 1752-1754
Richardson, Richard C., Jr., 2849-2851
Richmond Hill, Queens, 3023
Richmond, Virginia, meeting of Department of Superintendence in, 2262
Richmond, William, 1051-1052
Rickert, Edith, 299-304
Rickets, during Depression, 2528
Rickover, Hyman G., 3156-3160
Ridgeley, 460
Riesman, David, 3143-3146
Riggs, George W., 1676

Schneider v. *State of New Jersey,* 3056
Scholars
  contributions of, 2758-2759
  duties of, 1227-1228
  Emerson on, 1225-1229
  pedantry in, 219
  solitary state of, 1228-1229
  twofold election of, 166
  of University of Oxford, 176, 177
Scholarship
  and high school reforms, 2122-2123
  and teaching, 1360
Scholarship of Teachers in Secondary Schools, The (Fitzpatrick and Hutson), 2787*n*
Scholarships, 45
  for high school, 2595
  Rhodes, 2063-2065
  for training of social workers, 2400
  at University of California, 1536
Scholastic achievement
  American and European standards of, 2118-2119
  of Negroes and whites compared, 3206-3207
  and Rhodes scholarships, 2064
  See also Academic achievement
Scholastics, of Society of Jesus, 65-67
"Scholemaster, The" (Ascham), 266-272
Schomburg Collection, 3328
School administration. *See* Administration
"School as a Social Center, The" (Dewey), 2224-2229
School attendance. *See* Attendance
School bells, at University of Michigan, 1518-1519
School for the Blind, Moscow, 3155
School boards
  and city school system, 1985-1986
  in Prussia, 927-928
  representation on, 2673-2674
  at St. Louis Sabbath school, 1202-1203
  in U.S., 958-959, 960
  See also Board of Education
School buildings
  at Antioch College, 1500
  at Carlisle Indian School, 1749
  in Cincinnati, 3046
  and Dalton Plan, 2471
  in Detroit, 3046
  at elementary school of School of Education at University of Missouri, 2478
  in England and U.S. compared, 2107
  at Ethical Culture School, 2480
  for female seminary, 1575
  in Gary, Indiana, 2333
  at Hampton Institute, 1654

of ideal school, 1857
at Indian Schools, 1757-1758, 2963
at Little Red School House, 2500
of Machzikay Talmud Torah School, 2911
at Phillips Andover Academy, 1324-1325
in poor neighborhoods, 2093-2094
of progressive schools, 2449
small units used as, 3262
for State Normal School of New Britain, Connecticut, 1340
for state university, 1523
at University of Michigan, 1518
for University of Virginia, 1485-1486
in U.S., 961-962
wasted use of, 2332-2333
White House Conference Committee Report on, 2554
See also Schoolhouse(s)
School In The Camps: The Educational Program of the Civilian Conservation Corps, The (Hill), 2558-2562
School census, in Los Angeles County, 1036
School and the Child, The (Dewey), 2265*n*
School clinics, 2360
School Committee of Boston, petition to, 1702-1703
School committees, in Massachusetts, 1076-1077
"School Council," 1986
School Days in the Fifties (Giffin), 1820, 1831-1832
School desegregation
  at Central High School Little Rock, Arkansas, 3009-3016
  failure of, 3223-3227
  in Illinois, 1713-1716
  implementation of, 3106-3113
  and Jensen's theories, 3210-3214
  in Louisiana, 1644-1646
  Meredith on, 3017-3020
  in North, 3020-3023, 3315
  and private schools, 3113-3116
  at state universities, 3363
  in South, 3315
  and Southern Manifesto, 3006-3009
School director, Committee of Fifteen on role of, 1986-1987
School economy, in teacher training courses, 1973, 1975, 1982
School enrollment
  in Boston in 1738, 407
  in California, 1033
  in Hebrew school, 2911-2912
  of Indian children, 2961
  in inner-city, 3043-3046
  in Jewish schools, 2923-2925
  in Los Angeles County, 1036
  in Los Angeles ghettos, 3024-3025
  in Santa Barbara County, 1039

in Santa Clara County, 1041
School Examiners for the County of Portage, Ohio, 1310
School furniture
  in American schools, 961-962, 2125
  at elementary school of School of Education at University of Missouri, 2478
  impact of, 1961-1962
School of Good Manners, Composed for the Help of Parents in Teaching their Children How to Carry It in Their Places During Minority, The (Moody), 531-537
"School for Hebrew, A," 2911-2912
School and the Immigrant, The (Miller), 2182-2184
School Improvement League, 2349-2350
School inspection, by Boston school board, 407-408
School Journal, 2211-2217
School Law of California; Rules and Regulations of the State Board of Education, . . ., 1763, 2974*n*
School laws. *See* Education laws
School libraries, 113
  exclusion of religious books from, 1153-1154
  Jewish, 2927
  in Massachusetts, 1078
  selection of books for, 1153
  See also Libraries
School Life, 3192-3197
School management
  concentrated, 3330*n*
  and cost-accounting, 2260-2261
  efficiency of, 2257-2260
  by private corporation, 3336-3339
"School manager," 3337-3338
School museum, 113
"School News, The," 1747
School newspapers, 2493, 2559
School nurse, 2359
  in New York City, 2305-2306
  selection of, 157, 159
School organization. *See* Organization
School physicians, 2359
School property
  in California school rules, 1043
  destruction of, 1651
  in Los Angeles County, 1036
  religious instruction on, 3067-3075
  in San Jose, California, 1041
  in San Luis Obispo, 1040
  in Santa Clara County, 1041
  valuation of, in San Bernardino, California, 1037
School psychiatrist, 2360
School reform. *See* Educational reforms
School regulations
  in Dorchester, Massachusetts, 397-399

of Hopkins grammar school, 399-400
See also School rules
School Review, 2260-2261, 2262n
"School Riots And the Gary System" (Bonner), 2337-2340
School rules
of American Lyceum, 1606
and authority of teachers, 1337-1339
in British infant schools, 3301
in California public schools, 1042-1045
of the "Children's Houses," 1999-2000
and coeducation, 1496
of Columbia University, 696-699
for country schools, 774
on dress. *See* Dress rules
at Harvard College, 657
of high school for girls in Boston, 1247-1252
for Indian schools, 1756-1760
and Jewish students, 1183
of Massachusetts State Normal School, 1335-1337
in New Amsterdam, 544-545
in open classroom, 3318-3320
of Providence, Rhode Island schools, 1285-1286
of Regents of University of State of New York, 790-793
at South Carolina College, 1433-1444
for St. Louis Sabbath school, 1202-1203
of Teacher Corps, 3375-3377
of Yale College, 675-679
for young children, 1355
School schedule
in American elementary schools, 2126
in American high schools, 2108-2110
in British infant schools, 3301
in California, 1048
in California public schools, 1042, 1047
in Dalton Plan, 2466
of first school in San Francisco, 1033
flexible, 2096-2097
in Gary, Indiana schools, 2333-2334
at Hampton Institute, 1657
for infant, 2358
at Mount Holyoke Female Seminary, 1590
in new British primary schools, 2096
New York Free School Society on, 1121
in Oswego, New York public schools, 1780
in progressive schools, 2449
of Providence public schools, 1285
at Summerhill, 2066-2070
for teacher training, 1978-1979
and teacher's organizational ability, 1314

and time alloted per subject, 1969-1971
at Tuskegee Institute, 1670
at University Elementary School, 2299-2302
School and Schoolmaster, The, 1298
School segregation
and academic achievement, 3029-3033
in Alabama Constitution, 1648
attitudes of Southern whites and Negroes toward, 1697-1699
Bateman on, 1713-1716
and *Brown v. Board of Education of Topeka*, 3102-3108
in California, 1761, 1772-1775, 2934-2936, 2978-2979
California Supreme Court decision on, 1763-1765
and Chinese children, 1769-1772
Coleman Report on, 3027-3033
Constitutional provision against in Louisiana, 1644
and housing discrimination, 3034, 3035, 3040
and Indians, 2964
for Indians and Negroes, 1741
Kennedy on, 3363
in Louisiana Constitution, 1652
Massachusetts law abolishing, 1711
Massachusetts Supreme Court decision on, 1708-1711
Negro petition against, 1702-1703
in New York State, 1712-1713
New York State law repealing, 1713
in North Carolina Constitution, 1647
and Oriental children in San Francisco, 2971, 2972-2973
Report of National Advisory Commission on Civil Disorder on, 3041-3050
results of, 3036-3037
in South, 3001-3005
in South Carolina Constitution, 1651
Sumner on, 1642-1644, 1703-1707
Supreme Court decisions on, 3091-3120
in Tennessee Constitution, 1648
U.S. Commission on Civil Rights on, 3033-3040
School social workers, need for, 2400-2403
See also Social workers
School and Society (Dewey), 2541-2542, 2103-2104, 2219-2223, 2299, 2539-2541, 2934-2936
School and Society in Chicago (Counts), 2672-2674
School superintendent
of Alleghany County, New York, 1294-1296

choice of textbooks by, 965
at Concord, Mass., 1210-1212
of Michigan, 1024-1026
of Ohio, 1027-1029
School supervision
elementary school of School of Education at University of Missouri, 2477-2479
and Gary system, 2342
Rice on, 1899-1901
in St. Louis public schools, 1894
School systems
during Depression, 2531-2538, 2542-2547
IEA study of achievement in mathematics, 2053-2059
national vs. local, 950-951
use of educational films by, 2390
School taxes, 474, 757-758, 761-762
in Boston, 1699, 404
in California, 1046
and Catholic schools, 1127-1133
in Massachusetts, 1070
in New York City, 1144-1145
in New York State, 1141
opposition to, 1058
and parochial schools, 1155-1157
in San Bernardino, California, 1036-1037
in San Luis Obispo, 1040
in Santa Barbara County, 1039
School terms
at Albany Female Academy, 1594
in college, 1506-1508
Committee of Fifteen on, 1967-1968
length of, 952
shortening of, 1926-1927
School uniforms, 325
Schoolhouse at Prairie View, The (Barber), 1301-1302
Schoolhouse(s)
at Concord, Mass., 1213
Mann on, 1081-1082
in Massachusetts, 1076
at Prairie View, Kansas, 1301-1302
of public school in Pennsylvania, 1297
Schooling of the Immigrants, The (Thompson), 2371-2373
Schoolmaster, 172
Schoolmaster of a Great City, A (Patri), 2170-2173
Schoolrooms
of first American Montessori school, 2312
in Prussian schools, 1086
silence in, 1911-1912
See also Classrooms
Schools
advertisements by, 446-449
alternative to public schools, 3315-3317
attitude toward, 1461-1462
based on child study, 1845-1851

3489

in Bonnal, Switzerland, 824-826
changing goals of, 3344-3345
Children's Bureau on, 2359-2360
constitutional provision for, 793-797
and construction of new social order, 2639-2640
correlation of home life with, 1879-1880
critique of existence of, 3150-3153
and curative pedagogy, 2010
deterioration of, 38
and family education, 1915
father-image of, 2394-2395
first in Philadelphia, 359
form of government for, 1363-1366
goals of, 3343-3344
and hungry children, 2145-2147
ideal. See Ideal schools
for Indians, 606-607
Knox on necessity of, 54-57
and mental hygiene training, 2398-2400
at New Lanark, 893-897
non-graded, 3282-3290
opposition to, 44-45
in poor neighborhoods, 2093-2095
at Port Royal, 1633-1634
and psychological needs of pupils, 2399-2400
purpose of, 1825
relation of achievement to characteristics of, 3031-3033
as republican governments, 1363-1365
request for in New Netherlands, 353
in Salem, Massachusetts, 947-950
self-government in, 1365-1366
setting for, 360
site for, 184, 243, 497
social atmosphere in, 1828-1829
as social centers, 2224-2229
as social institutions, 2213-2214, 2296-2297
as social settlements, 2326-2329
of Society for Promoting Christian Knowledge, 325
of Society for the Propagation of the Gospel in Foreign Parts, 474-475
urban and rural compared, 1905
Vatican II on role of, 2048
in Virginia colony, 345
See also Academies; Country schools; Free schools; Rural schools
"Schools For Children" (Featherstone), 3299-3305
Schools Council, 3303
Schools of Democracy (Wales), 2122-2123
Schools for the poor. See Education of poor
Schools of practice
at State Normal School of

New Britain, Connecticut, 1342
and State Normal Schools, 1340
television viewing by children in, 3184
Schools of To-Morrow (Dewey and Dewey), 2229-2231, 2326-2329
Schramm, Wilbur, 3183-3186
Schrieke, 3006
Schulordnung, The, 560-565
Schulrath, 927, 928
Schulzwang, 1537
Schurz (Secretary of the Interior), 1750, 1751
and Indian education, 1742, 1743
Schutter, Charles H., 3149
Science of education
compared with other sciences, 1351
and universities, 1415-1418
Science of Education, The (Herbart), 857-861
Science and Human Behavior (Skinner), 3231n
"Science of Learning and the Art of Teaching, The" (Skinner), 3229-3235
Science of mind. See Psychology
Science of teaching, 1973
in college curriculum, 1507
for high school teachers, 1981-1982
See also Teacher education
Science(s), 259, 360, 2215, 2757-2760
and activity, 1478
advancement of, 212
and bureaucracy, 3189
at Chautauqua, 1607
and child study method, 1849
in college curriculum, 66, 1547-1548
contributions of, 2758
at Cook County Normal School, 1830-1831
in core-curriculum plan, 2603
in Dalton Plan, 2469
definition of, 109
and elective system, 2747
and foreign universities, 801
at Gymnasium, 1513-1514
in high schools, 3161
in Indianapolis progressive public school, 1895
indifference toward, 1614
and life activities, 922-924, 2298
at Manual Training School of Washington University, 1859-1860
means of learning, 254-255
and metaphysics, 2209
in mid-nineteenth century, 1457-1460
in new British primary schools, 2096
patronage for, 210-211
in progressive and traditional schools, 2457
reforms in, 969-970

and religion, 1564
rules of teaching, 253
in Society of Jesus universities, 67
at teacher-training seminaries, 1303, 1310
in University of Chicago Elementary School, 2298
Scientific intellectuals, vs. literary intellectuals, 2088-2092
Scientific laws, and pragmatism, 2210
Scientific method
Descartes on, 81-86
and education, 2804
Scientific publications, European, 1460
Scientists, status of, 1457-1460
Scipio, 163
Scoggens, 281
Scopes case, 2739
Scotch, and Irish, 2384
Scotland, corporal punishment in, 1312-1313
Scott, Emmett J., 1671-1672, 1672-1675
Scott, John, 556
Scott, W. Kerr, 3006-3009
Scott, Walter, 1233, 1964
Scotus, 241-242
Scripps interests, 2390
Scriptures, 44, 186, 410-411, 562, 659
on children, 256
for common people, 119-121
in normal schools, 1334
at Philadelphia Hebrew Sunday school, 1192
reading of, 250
rules for professor of, 71
translation into vernacular, 61-64
See also Religious education
Sculpting. See Plastic arts
Sea Mills School, Bristol, 3303
Sears, Barnas, 1678-1680
Sears, Dr., 1413
Searson, John, 441
Seating arrangements, 400
in Bonnal school, 825
at Boston High School for Girls, 1249
in progressive schools, 3143-3144
by size, 1301
Seats, in progressive schools, 2449
Seaver, 1861
Second Annual Report of the Secretary of the Board of Education, 1081-1082
Second Biennial Report of the Superintendent of Schools, 1046-1050
Second Reader (Appleton), 1746
"Second Report" (Sears), 1678-1680
"Second Sex in Academe, The" (Harris), 3220-3222
Second Vatican Council. See Vatican II
Secondary education

comprehensive high school as standard for, 2286-2289
criticism of Committee of Ten report on, 1946-1951
division into junior and senior periods, 2282-2283
and elementary education, 2283
Harvard Committee on, 2618-2622
and higher education, 2283
Kennedy's recommendations on, 3355-3356
need for reorganization of, 2279-2280
Report of Commission on Reorganization of, 2278-2290
specializing and unifying functions of, 2284-2286
time allotted to, 2262
See also High schools; Junior high schools; Secondary schools
Secondary Education For Industrialism (Counts), 2510-2514
Secondary Education for Youth in Modern America (Douglas), 2627n
Secondary school teachers, teaching certificate for, 2715
Secondary schools
Catholic, 2900-2901
Committee of Ten report on, 1951-1959
curriculum of, 113
federal aid to, 3348-3349
function of, 1922-1925
goals of, 2280-2282
Negro students, 3028-3029
report of Committee of Ten on, 1930-1944
teacher training for, 1980-1982
See also High schools; Junior high schools; Secondary education
"Secret Diary of William Byrd of Westover, The," 347-350
Secretary, 286
at American Lyceum, 1605
of Board of Education of Connecticut, 1323-1324
of Board of Education of Massachusetts, 1326, 1333-1339
duties of, 1071-1075, 1100-1110
Secretary of Health, Education, and Welfare, 3341, 3356, 3384
Secretary of the Interior, 1526
and federal aid to education, 1686, 1695
Secretary of Labor, 2357
Secretary of the Treasury, and federal aid to education, 1686
Secretary of War
and establishment of military academy at West Point, 1481
and Freedman's Bureau, 1635
Sectarian colleges
defense of, 687-691

and Massachusetts school law of 1827, 1148
opposition to, 691-694
See also Parochial schools
Secular schools, 952-953
Sedentary habits, and mental development, 890
Sedgwick (Miss), 946
Sedulius, 154
"Seeming," distinguished from "being," 2025
Segredo, Giovanni Francesco, 81
Segregation
in colleges, 2809-2811
of German emigrants, 940
and law schools, 3100-3102
of social classes, 853-854, 856
in state universities, 3097-3099, 3098-3099
Supreme Court decisions on, 3087-3120
"Segregation of Loyal and Disloyal Japanese," 2977-2978
"Segregation of Mexican-American School Children in Southern California, The" (Cooke), 2934-2936
Seguin, Edward, 861-863
Selden, Armistead I., Jr., 2006-3009
Select Epistles of Cicero (Sturmius), 168
Select Orations (Tully), 696
Selected Chapters from the Autobiography of Andrew D. White, 1454-1457, 1542-1545
"Selected List of Books on American Ethnic Groups for Secondary School Libraries, A," 2941
Selected Sermons of Jonathan Edwards (Gardiner), 428-430
Selections from the Prose Works of Ralph Waldo Emerson (Perry), 1229
Selective Character of American Secondary Education, The (Counts), 2505-2510
Self-activity, excessive, 1907
Self-confidence
and fear, 2007-2008
and poverty, 2007-2008
Self-control
and Montessori philosophy, 2312
training in, 1967
Self-correction, and use of didactic materials, 1997
Self-criticism
and "acting out," 2484
and Gary system, 2343
Self-culture
in moral training, 1912
and University Extension, 1614
Self-defense, 173
Self-determination, and education, 842
Self-education, 477-480
of Banneker, 599-601
in college, 1474
of Douglass, 1624-1627
of Negro teacher, 1628, 1629

Self-examination, and efficient school management, 2258, 2259
Self-expression
cultivation of, 2103
in Greenwich Village philosophy, 2415, 2416
Self-fulfilling prophecies, and teacher expectations, 3305-3308
Self-government
in college, 1562
in kindergarten, 2473-2477
in progressive schools, 2450
in schools, 1365-1366
Self-help, 913-915
Self-Help (Smiles), 913-915
Self-improvement
and college students, 1474-1475
of teachers, 1309-1310, 2706
Self-preservation
activities relating to, 921
instinct of, 2002
Self-reliance
Emerson on, 1229-1231
and individual instruction, 2276
Self-trust, and consistency, 1231
Seligman, Joseph, 1791
Seligson, Tom, 3216-3220
Seller, 479
Selman, Richard, 328
Selman, William, 328
Selyns, Rev. Henricus, 586
Seminary
for Indians, 629
for Lancastrian teachers, 982-983
Semiprofessional training, at junior colleges, 2847-2848
Senate Journal, 1024-1026
Senate of Rome, 131
Senate Subcommittee on Migratory Labor, 3192
Senate, U.S.
Act establishing United States Bureau of Education, 1406-1407
hearing on payless paydays for teachers in Chicago, 2531-2534
Memorial of the National Association of State and City School Superintendents to, 1404-1405
Miscellaneous Documents, 2977-2978
Senators, signers of Southern Manifesto, 3008
Senatus Academicus, of University of Georgia, 789
Seneca, 185, 262
Senekas, 628
Senensis, Sextus, 665
Sensation
and fields of consciousness, 1427
and ideas, 231
and intelligence, 1994-1995
Sense development
and concept formation, 869-871
and diet, 889

and mental development, 872-874

Sense experiences, 95-96

Sense ideas, doctrine of, 874-875

Sense perceptions, of wild boy, 839-842

Sense of touch, and sandpaper letters, 2314

Sense training, 862-863, 2221, 2239
  and Montessori method, 2323-2324

Sense-impressions
  as foundation of knowledge, 831
  training in, 827, 829-831

Senses
  development of, 866-869
  and education, 1085-1086
  inward, 311
  and Montessori method, 2321
  and science learning, 254

Sensory motor operations, in cognitive development, 3248

Sensory perception, and ego, 2000

Sentenia, 351

Sentiments, cultivation of, 890-891

"Separate but equal" doctrine, 2997-2999, 3103, 3106
  Kennedy on, 3364

Separation of church and state
  and moral training in public schools, 1909-1910
  in North Carolina, 781

Septuagint, 135

Sequel to the So Called Correspondence Between the Rev. M. H. Smith and Horace Mann, 1154-1155

Sergeant, 622

Serial maze, 3229

"Sermon on the Duty Sending Children to School"(Luther), 43-45

Sermon on the Mount, 1826

Sermons
  on conversion of the Negroes, 586
  by Edwards, 428-430
  by Tennent, 430-434
  by Whitefield, 434-435

Sermons on Sacramental Occasions by Divers Ministers, 431-434

Servant schoolmasters, advertisements for, 558

Servants, education of, 402-403

Servius, 415

Session Laws of Tennessee, 2718-2719

"Setting," 2057

Settlement houses
  Henry Street Settlement, 2203-2205
  Hull House, 2163-2167, 2291-2293

Seventh Annual Report of the Board of Regents of the University of Michigan, 1516-1517

Seventh Annual Report of the

Secretary of the Board, 1083-1094

Seventh Annual Report of the Superintendent of Schools, 1033

"Several Sources of the Odium and Discouragement Which the College of William and Mary in Virginia Lies Under, The," 647

Sewall, Margaret, Jr., 392

Sewall, Samuel, 589-591

Sewall, Stephen, 392

Sewall, Susannah, 392

Seward, William H., 1126-1127

Sewing, 2215
  in elementary school curriculum, 1969

Sex differences, 87-88
  and dropouts during Depression, 2543
  and education of women, 1596-1598
  and higher education, 2748-2752
  and individual differences, 2242
  and need for Jewish education, 2924
  and retardation, 2200
  and right to education, 2045
  at Summerhill, 2067-2068

Sex education, of American girls, 1599-1602

Sex in Education; or, a Fair Chance for Girls (Clarke), 1596-1598

Sex problems, of college students, 2784-2786

Sex roles
  in American culture, 2116-2117
  and employment of women, 3222
  and Puerto Rican children, 3178-3179

Sexias, Moses, 811

Sexual activity
  and basic instincts, 2002
  and Indian school, 2952-2953

Sexuality
  and procreation, 752-753
  of wild boy, 840

Seybolt, Robert F., 389, 403, 404-408, 438-440, 440-443, 443, 444, 445, 510, 553-554, 555, 558

Shackle, 883

Shadows, child's conceptions about, 2028-2029

Shady Hill School, Cambridge, Mass., dramatics at, 2483-2486

Shaftesbury, 479

Shakespeare, 1463, 1600, 1613, 1614, 1964, 2090, 2121
  in French secondary school curriculum, 1925

Shakespeare club, at Hull House, 2833

Shaler, Nathaniel, 1718

"Shared time" policy, 2909

Sharpstein, 1771

Shaw, Adele Marie, 2344-2345

Shaw, C. J. See Sarah C. Roberts v. The City of Boston

Shaw, Chief Justice, 3092, 3096-3097

Shaw, Mrs. Quincy, 1833

Shay's Rebellion, 751-752

Shea, John Gilmary, 713-714

Shearith Israel Congregation, on Jewish education, 1182

Sheldon, Edward, 1780, 1781-1787

Shelley v. Kraemer, 3101

Shelton v. Tucker, 2730-2732

Shepard, Frederick J., 360-361

Shephard, Reverend Thomas, 667-671

Sherman, General, 1233, 1744

Shermy, 479

Shils, Edward, 3180-3182

Shippen, Edward, 686

Shirley, 290, 291-292

Shoemaking, at Carlisle Indian School, 1750-1751

Shops, at Indian schools, 1750-1751, 1759-1760

Short, William, 722, 723, 726

Short Introduction of Grammar, A (Lily), 305-308

"Shortening and Enriching the Grammar School Course" (Eliot), 1926-1930

"Shortening the Years of Elementary Schooling" (Dewey), 2262n

Shorthand, 439

Shoshones, 1730

"Should the Higher Education of Women Differ from That of Men?" (Thomas), 2748-2752

"Should the Visiting Teacher be a New Official?" (Pratt), 2400-2403

Shuey, Audrey, 3207, 3210

Shuford, George A., 3006-3009

Shumaker, Ann, 2438-2441, 2444-2446, 2449, 2483-2486, 2486-2489

Shurtleff, Nathaniel B., 367-368, 370-371, 376-377, 393-394, 611

Shutte, John, 353

Siblings, in American culture, 2116-2117

Sick pay, for teachers, 926

Sick-leave rate, for women, 3222

Sidis boys, 2250

Sidney, Algernon, 497

Sight, development of, 867-868

Sigismund, King of the Romanes, 180

Sigma Phi, 1456

Sigwart, 2210

Sikes, Robert L. F., 3006-3009

Silberman, Harry, 3392

Silence
  and moral training, 1911-1912, 1916-1917
  and progressive education, 2455
  in progressive schools, 2449
  at school for Italian immigrants, 2155

"Silence Dogood, No. 4," 482-484

Specializing functions, of secondary education, 2284-2286

Spectacle de la Nature, 502

Spectator, The, 478, 501, 503, 2791, 2792, 2793, 2793-2794

Speech, 273, 285, 300, 301, 304, 501, 501-502, 510-511, 518, 1638
 and autistic children, 3256
 in curriculum for feebleminded children, 2405
 in Germany and U.S. compared, 941-942
 instruction in, 184-185
 lessons in readers, 1382-1383, 1386-1387
 of Negro children, 1388-1390, 1390-1391

Speed, Adolphus, 243-244

Speer, 1739

Spelling, 288-289, 561, 881-882
 and alphabet learning, 835-836
 in British infant schools, 3303
 at Carlisle Indian School, 1746
 and child study method, 1848
 early teaching of, 2297
 in elementary school curriculum, 1969, 1971
 in Lancastrian school, 981
 at Manual Training School of Washington University, 1860
 in New England District School, 1283-1284
 preparation for, 827
 reform of, 763-766
 as training in mental analysis, 1962

Spelling books, nineteenth century, 1377-1379

"Spelling curriculum based on research, A" (Washburne), 2490n, 2492n

Spencer, Herbert, 920-924, 1302, 1427

Spencer, Philip, 1454-1455

Speyer School, 2473

Spherical geometry, 444

Spillane, Mickey, 3148

Spinal curvature, and child labor, 2140

Spinning, 835

Spinoza, 1198

"Spiral curriculum," 3242, 3243-3245

Spirit of the Ghetto, The (Hapgood), 2914-2915

Spiritual Milk for Boston Babes in either England Drawn out of the Breasts of both Testaments for their Souls Nourishment (Cotton), 529

Split personality, and individual instruction, 2495

Sports
 and Americanization of immigrants, 2114-2115
 at Indian Schools, 1758-1759
 and Rhodes scholarships, 2064

Spotted Tail, 1746

Sprat, Thomas, 216-220

Spreckelmeyer, Richard L., 3149

Springfield Republican and Journal, 1573

Spurzheim, Dr. J. G., 885

Sputnik, 2090-2091, 3149

Spy system, in college, 1562

St. Gaudens, Augustus, 1464

St. George's Episcopal Church (N.Y.C.), 2293-2295

St. Ignatius and the Ratio Studiorum (Fitzpatrick), 64-68, 69-72

St. James' Church, 1132

St. Jameses Park, 220

St. John's College, Cambridge, guidance for students at, 187-199

St. John's Gospel, 696

St. Louis, Missouri
 Jewish education in, 1201
 meeting of Department of Superintendence in, 2262
 Negro high school students in, 2509
 Sabbath school in, 1202-1203

St. Paul, Minnesota, 1173

St. Paul's School, 151-155
 admission requirements, 155-156

St. Peter's Basilica, 2905

St. Sernin, Canton of, 837

St. Vincent de Paul Society of the United States, 2355

Stability and Change in Human Characteristics (Bloom), 3250-3254

Staff
 of Children's Bureau, 2357-2358
 at Civilian Conservation Corps Camps, 2564
 and efficient school management, 2258, 2259-2260
 of Harvard Graduate School of Education, 2702
 in slum schools, 2093-2094
 at Summerhill, 207
 of Teachers College, Columbia University, 2700

Stalin, 3155

Stalinism, and Students for a Democratic Society, 2854

Stammering, and weaning experiences in infancy, 2412

Standard deviation, of Negroes IQ tests, 3206-3207

Standard of living
 of professors, 1459
 in Soviet Union, 3154

Standardization
 and computer technology, 3313-3314
 and French education, 3313-3314

Standing Commission on the National Intelligence, 2086

Stanford Revision and Extension of the Binet-Simon Measuring Scale of Intelligence, The, 2256n

Stanford University, 3164
 computer-assisted instruction at, 3310-3315

graduates of junior colleges at, 2845-2846, 2974-2977

Stanford-Binet tests, 3206
 and reading evaluation, 2570

Stanz, Switzerland, education of poor at, 832-837

Stapfer, 832

Staples Experimental English class, 3216

Starbuck, Miss, 1329

Starkey, 357

Starr, Comfort, 660

Starr, Harris E., 1569

Starr, Miss, 2291

"Star-Spangled Banner, The," 2112, 3079

State
 and church, 1171-1173
 and education, 1057-1058
 educational duties of, 2048-2049
 separation of Church and, 2896-2897

State Board of Education, 2712
 of California, 1042-1045
 creation in Massachusetts of, 1070-1072

State bonds, 1459

State Branch Normal College, Pine Bluff, Arkansas, 1675

State of California, Governors Commission On the Los Angeles Riots, 3023-3026

State of California Laws, 2722-2723

State certification requirements, 3165

State Departments of Education, and initiation of state information service, 2712

"State and Education, The," 1068-1069

State Fund, in California, 1046

State Legislatures
 California, 1761-1762
 and public boarding schools, 1218
 and reforms of teachers education, 2712-2713
 and teacher-training seminaries, 1303-1304

State of New York, University of the
 regents of, 790-793

State Normal School, San Francisco, California, 2276

State qualifications
 legality of, 2728-2730
 and membership in "subversive" organizations, 2724-2727

State Records of North Carolina, The (Clark), 346, 514-516

State School Fund, in Los Angeles County, 1036

"State Schools and Parish Schools—Is Union Between Them Impossible?" (Ireland), 1176-1181

State superintendents of schools
 duties of, 1684-1685
 first annual report in North Carolina, 1012-1014

North Carolina law providing
for, 1009-1012
of Santa Barbara schools, 1038
State Teachers' Associations, call
for organization of National
Teachers' Association by,
1398, 1399
State teachers colleges, decline in
number of, 2676-2679
*State of the Union Messages of
the Presidents, 1790-1966,
The* (Israel), 1730-1731
State universities
call for in California, 1531-
1532
desegregation at, 3363
establishment in New York,
790-793
first, 787-789
Illinois State legislature
resolution on, 1525-1526
and Morrill Act, 1526-1530,
1528-1530
and National youth
Administration, 2555-2558
and Organic Act creating
University of California,
1533-1536
plan for, 1522-1525
public financing of, 1004-1005
segregation in, 3097-3099
University of Wisconsin, 2757-
2760
See also Industrial universities
and under individual names
of
State-church controversy
and Bible reading in public
schools, 3080-3081
and flag salute cases, 3054-
3064
and prayers in public schools,
3075-3079
and right to operate religious
school, 3051-3052
and textbooks for parochial
schools, 3052-3053, 3082-
3085
"Statement by the President upon
Signing Order Establishing
the Peace Corps, March 1,
1961," 3347
*Statement of the Theory of
Education in the United
States of America as
Approved by Many Leading
Educators, A*, 1904-1906
States
and equal opportunity for legal
education, 3097-3098
and implementation of
Supreme Court desegregation
decision, 3038-3040
and organization of schools,
959-960
standards of teacher education,
2693
and vocational education, 2361-
2362
See also States rights and under
individual states
States rights

and school desegregation, 3108-
3113
and Southern Manifesto, 3006-
3009
Statistical tables, 943
Statistics, in Gary, Indiana,
schools, 2335
Stature, and heredity and
environment, 2092
Status quo, and changes, 2428
Status of teachers, 2695-2698,
3002
Statutes, of College of William
and Mary, 650-654
*Statutes at Large of
Pennsylvania, 1682-1801,
The* (Mitchell and Flanders),
729
*Statutes At Large of
Pennsylvania, 1782*, 523-526
*Statutes at Large of South
Carolina, The* (Cooper and
McCord), 572-574, 1349,
1624
*Statutes at Large of the State of
New York*, 1712-1713
*Statutes at Large, Treaties, and
Proclamations, of the United
States of America, The*
(Sanger), 1528-1530, 1635
*Statutes at Large of Virginia,
1619-1782* (Hening), 339,
342-343, 345, 571, 641-642,
785-786
"Statutes and Laws of the
University in Cambridge,
Massachusetts," 1492
Stead, W. T., 2063-2065
Stealing, 324-325
and demoralization, 2009
in Yale College laws, 677
Stebbins, Rev. Horatio, 1800,
1802
Steffen, William, 999-1000
Stengel, Stuart, 2929
Stennis, John, 3006-3009
Stereometry, 441
Stereotype, of teacher, 2695-2698
Sterling v. *Constantin*, 3113
Stern, George, 3337
Stern rods, 3301
Steuart, Alexander, 468
Stevens, Alzina P., 2138-2141
Stevens, Benjamin, 715
Stevens, Thaddeus, on public
schools, 1064-1067
Steward, Eliz., 346
Stewardson, Thomas, 981
Stewart, Justice, 2730-2732, 2735-
2736, 3078-3079
Stickney (Board of Indian
Commissions), 1749
Stierius Golius, 190
Stiles, Ezra, 592
Stimulus, and mental
development, 865
Stith, William, 348, 726
Stock, at Indian School, 1759-
1760
Stockwood, 290
Stoddard, Anthony, 407, 673, 681
Stoddard, Lothrop, 2427
Stoddard, Solomon, 618

Stodder, 1328, 1330
Stoics, 671
Stokes, Thomas, 328
Stone, Chief Justice, 2112
Stone, Rev. T. D. P., 1340
Stone, Samuel, 380
Stoner girl, 2250
Storer, Dr. H., 1702
Stories (Keep), 1746
Stork, John, 720
Story, Justice, 1492
Story hour, 1879
*Story of John Adams, a New
England Schoolmaster, The*
(Brown and Brown)
*Story of My Life and Work: An
Autobiography, The*
(Washington), 1668-1670,
1675-1676
Story telling, 262, 408, 501
biblical, 410
and organic education, 2496-
2497
Story of a Varied Life, The
(Rainsford), 2293-2295
*Story of the White House
Conferences on Children and
Youth, The*, 2551-2553
Stoughton, Jonathan, 392
Stoughton, Thomas, 392
Stout, 2266, 2344
Stowe, Calvin, 929-931, 993-994
Stowe, Professor, 1085
Stoy, 970, 1884
Strachey, James, 2000-2002
Stranger in America, The
(Lieber), 939-940, 941
Strauss, Rebecca, 3320-3325
Strayer, Dr. George D., 2531-
2532
Stream of consciousness, 1426-
1427
"Streaming," 2057
Street beggars, 997
"Street urchins," 2039
Streit, Peggy, 3020-3023
Strikes
in London, 2085-2088
at Nanterre University, 2059-
2061
Strong, E. K., Jr., 2975*n*
Strutt, 976
Stuart, Archibald, 726
Stuart, John, 720, 722, 723
Stuart, William, 726
Studebaker, John W., 2600
Student activism, and Columbia
University strike of 1932,
2791-2795
Student affairs, improper
disclosure of, 2885
Student apathy, 2857
Student government
and activity movement, 2575
Harvard Committee on
Secondary Education on,
2620
in New York City public
school, 2302
Student life
in American colleges, 1473-
1476
at Harvard College, 657

and *Adler* v. *Board of Education,* 2724-2727
and aid to parochial schools, 2906, 2908-2909
and *Beilan* v. *Board of Education of Philadelphia,* 2728-2730
and *Berea College* v. *Commonwealth of Kentucky,* 3091-3093
and *Board of Education of Central School District* v. *Allen,* 3082-3085
and *Brown et al.* v. *Board of Education of Topeka et al.,* 3102-3108
and *Cochran* v. *Louisiana State Board of Education,* 3052-3053
and *Cooper* v. *Aaron,* 3108-3113
and Dartmouth College case, 1435-1441
desegregation decision, 3006-3009, 3102-3108
and *Engel* v. *Vitale,* 3075-3079
and *Everson* v. *Board of Education,* 3063-3067
in *Flag Salute* cases, 3054-3064
on flag worship, 2112
and *Garner* v. *Los Angeles Board,* 2724-2725
and *Gong Lum* v. *Rice,* 3093-3097
and *Griffin* v. *County School Board of Prince Edward,* 3113-3116
and *Illinois ex rel. McCollum* v. *Board of Education,* 3067-3071
on Japanese language schools, 2976
and *Keyishan* v. *Board of Regents of the University of the State of New York,* 2733-2735
and *McLaurin* v. *Oklahoma State Regents,* 3098-3099
on *Meyer* v. *State of Nebraska,* 2717-2718
and *Minersville School District* v. *Gobitis,* 3054-3058
and *Missouri Ex Rel. Gaines* v. *Canada,* 3097-3098
and Oklahoma loyalty oaths, 2882-2883
and *Pickering* v. *Board of Education of Township High School,* 2736-2738
and *Pierce et al.* v. *Society of Sisters,* 3051-3052
and *Plessy* v. *Ferguson,* 3087-3090
on racial issue, 3087-3120
on released time for religious instruction, 3067-3075
and religion in public schools, 1149-1150
on religious issue in schools, 3051-3085
and school integration, 3012-3013
on school prayers, 3075-3079

and *Shelton* v. *Tucker,* 2730-2732
and *Sweatt* v. *Painter,* 3100-3102
and *West Virginia State Board of Education* v. *Barnette,* 3058-3064
and *Zorach* v. *Clauson,* 3071-3075
Supreme Judicial Court of Massachusetts, 3096-3097
Surgeon General, of Public Health Service, 2528
Surgical pedagogy, 1884
Surmaster, role of, 152-153
Survey, 2147-2150
"Survey by the National Association of Visiting Teachers and Home and School Visitors, A," 2400
Surveying, 438, 440, 441, 443, 444, 446, 510, 1236
at Notre Dame University, 1161
in Prussian schools, 1089
Susenbrotus, 164, 169
Suspension
at Sabbath school, 1203
at South Carolina College, 1435
Sutherland, Jacob, 1594
Sutherland, Justice, 2717-2718
Swackhamer, Conrad, 1140
Swaddling, 93-94
Swain, Elizabeth, 346
Swain, John, 346
Swearing, 324-235, 563-564, 1364
in Montessori schools, 3269
in Yale College laws, 677
Sweaters' district, 2151, 2152
Sweatshops, and child labor, 2140
Sweatt v. *Painter,* 3099, 3100-3102, 3104, 3105
Sweden
in IEA study of mathematics achievement, 2054, 2055
schools in, 1418
Swedenborgians, 1915
Swedish Sloyd system, 1430
Sweezy v. *New Hampshire,* 2734
Swett, John, 1032-1033, 1033, 1046-1050, 1800, 1802
Swift, Jonathan, 240-243, 458, 503, 1964
Swift, Mary, 1328
Swift (Miss), 1329
Swimming pools, in Gary, Indiana schools, 2333
Swinburne, 1600
Swindlers, and emigrants, 939
Switzerland, education reform in, 832-837
Syllabi, for child study work, 1840
Syllables
learning of, 288-289, 836
recognition of, 2490
Syluius, Aeneas, 365
Symbolic culture, 1908
Symbolic Education (Blow), 1805-1808
Symbolism
in block play, 1795-1796

and concepts, 2501-2502
and flag salute, 3059-3060
and play, 1805-1808
Sympathy, cultivation of, 861
Syms, Benjamin, will of, 339-341
Synagogues, in Philadelphia, 1200
See also Hebrew schools
Synod of Dort, 59-60
Syntax, 47, 48
and child study method, 1848
Synthetical judgment, 1875
Syria, 144
Syrian dialect, 186
Table manners. *See* Manners
Tacitus, 351, 604
Taft, Chief Justice, 3093-3097
Tailoring department, at Carlisle Indian School, 1747
Taine, 1427
Talaeus, 290
Talbot, Sir Gilbert, 217
Talent, 107
and education, 107, 109
inheritance of, 2406-2407
and poverty, 111
"Talented Tenth, The" (Du Bois), 2987-2990
Taliaferro, 751
Talking
in British infant school, 3300
in class, 564-565
in school, 882-883
"Talking typewriter," 3308-3310
Talks on Pedagogics: An outline of the Theory of Concentration (Parker), 1820-1824, 1825-1829
Talks to Teachers on Psychology: And to Students on Some of Life's Ideals (James), 1426-1430, 1602-1604, 1852-1855
Talmud, 2919, 2920
in Jewish schools, 1197
Talmud Torah school, 2916
Tammany Hall, 2339-2340
Taney, Chief Justice, 3112
Tannersville, New York, 2559
Tape v. *Hurley,* 1771-1772
Tappan, Henry P.
attack on college reform proposal of, 1515-1516
on democratic character of University of Michigan, 1516-1517
role at University of Michigan, 1517-1519
on university reform, 1510-1515
Tarbell, H. S., 1971-1980, 1980-1982
Tarborough (N.C.) Free Press, 1622
Tarquine, King, 158
Tarrytown, New York, first Montessori school in, 2310-2316, 2319
Tartars, 44
Tascala, 604
Taste, sense of, of wild boy, 841
Taussig, Frank, 1718, 1719
Taxes
and busing of children to religious schools, 3063-3067

collection of, 1104-1105
during Depression, 2535-2536
and education, 1904
for education in Texas, 1016-1019
Franklin on, 493
for free schools in Pennsylvania, 975
and North Carolina school system, 1647
on parents, 1218
for parochial school aid, 2906
for public boarding schools, 1218-1219
for public schools, 1004-1005, 1015
and school expenditures in slums and suburbs, 3276-3277
for support of racially segregated private schools, 3113-3116
and textbooks for parochial schools, 3052-3053, 3082-3085
and Virginia public schools, 1650-1651
See also School taxes
Taylor, Abraham, 444
Taylor, Eva G. R., 331-334
Taylor, James, 1930-1946, 2941
Taylor, Thomas, 1052
Taylor, William M., 1654
Teacher (Abbott), 1334
Teacher certification, 2710
annullment of, 1324
and authority, 1337-1338
in Connecticut, 1323-1324
proposal for, 1307
for secondary school teachers, 2715
Teacher education. See Teacher training
Teacher Empiricist, The (Popham), 3290-3294
Teacher expectations
and learning, 3305-3308
in open classroom, 3317-3320
Teacher initiative, vs. child initiative, 2450
Teacher: Moral Influences Employed in the Instruction and Government of the Young, The (Abbott), 1362-1366
Teacher qualifications
character traits as, 1357-1359
for female teachers, 1316-1317
Mann on, 1311-1315
Parker on, 1825-1826
and personal habits, 1360-1362
and Ph. Ds, 2752-2757
and psychological knowledge, 1852-1855
in schools for German immigrants, 636
See also State qualifications
Teacher seminaries, in Prussia, 932-934
Teacher supervision, 71
Teacher training, 45-46, 106
and academies, 1240
all-university approach to, 2714

American Council on Education on, 2703-2705
American Historical Association on, 2674-2676
in Catholic colleges, 2052-2053
for Catholic school teachers, 2050-2051
Committee of Ten on, 1943-1944, 1945
Conant on, 2711-2716
critique of, 3131-3135, 3162-3168
and decline of teachers colleges, 2676-2679
and desegregation, 3363
Dewey on, 2665-2670, 3130
for elementary school, 1971-1980
and federal support programs, 3354
at female seminaries, 1583-1585
Flexner report on, 2699-2702
and founding of Teachers College, Columbia University, 1420-1425
and freehand drawing, 962
graduate studies, 2686-2687
in Herbartian pedagogy, 1873-1875
of high school teachers, 1980-1982
and individual instruction, 2276
and institutional rivalries, 2670-2672
for kindergarten, 1788-1789
and length of training-school course, 1978-1979
in Massachusetts, 1077-1078
Massachusetts Board of Education proposal for, 1326-1327
of Middletown teachers, 2689-2690
in Montessori method, 1998, 2311
at Mount Holyoke Female Seminary, 1585-1589
and Negro education, 2988-2989
at Phillips Andover Academy, 1324-1326
proposals for, 1303-1310
in Prussia, 1510-1511
and psychoanalysis, 2003
role of Normal Schools in, 1349-1353
at school for teachers in Ohio, 1310-1311
and Smith-Hughes Act, 2368
from social point of view, 2588
and social work, 2403
status of, 2692-2695
and subject-matter preparation, 2704-2705
and teacher corps, 3373-3377
and teacher expectations, 3307-3308
at Teachers College, Columbia University, 2654-2665
at Teachers College kindergarten, 2473-2477

theory and practice in, 2665-2670
at University of Michigan, 1414-1418
in U.S., 953, 959
White House Conference Committee Report on, 2554
for women, 1317-1318, 1319
See also Normal schools
Teachers
as absolute monarch, 1363
academic freedom for, 1569-1570
advertisements by, 446-449, 452
advertisements for, 447-448, 449
in Alabama, 1664
Alcott on, 1208-1210
of Alleghany County, New York, 1294-1296
in American high schools, 2110
appointments of, 960
for art, 2487-2488
assignment of, 2712
attitudes toward college preparatory students vs. vocational students, 2634-2635
attitudes toward intelligence quotient, 2127-2128
attitudes toward students, 3042-3043
attitudes toward teaching, 2338
authority of, 292-293
authority of, in Massachusetts, 1337-1339
and Batavia Plan, 2270
and behavior problems, 2401
best, 1565
in Bonnal school, 824-826
at Boston High School for Girls, 1248, 1251
of Boston, quarrel with Mann, 1094-1095
in Brooklyn, New York, 1292-1294
in California public schools, 1047
in California school rules, 1042-1043
of Catholic children in public schools, 1163-1164, 1171
in Catholic schools, 2051
for charity school, 324
at Chautauqua, 1607
in Chicago, 2993-2994
and child study method, 1850
and child study movement, 1842-1844
child study questionnaire for, 1851-1852
in city school system, 1987-1988
at Civilian Conservation Corps Camps, 2559
and class size, 1322
in Cleveland evening school for immigrants, 2183-2184
at Concord, Mass. primary school, 1212
at Congregational school, 2917

in Connecticut, 1069-1070, 1291-1292
control by, 3254-3260
at Cook County Normal School, 1830
in correspondence system, 1609-1610, 1612
for country schools, 774
demand for, 1308
in deprived areas, 2094-2095
Dicken's portrayal of, 907-911
duties of, 412-413
at elementary school of School of Education at University of Missouri, 2477
in evening schools for adult foreigners, 2180-2181
and feeding of hungry pupils, 2527
female. See Female teachers
firing of, 548
at first Negro school in Virginia, 1659-1660
for freed slaves, 1635-1636
in Gary, Indiana schools, 2333-2334, 2338
German school laws on, 926
German-American, 999-1000
in Germany and U.S. compared, 943
as guide, 2473-2477
at Hampton Institute, 1654, 1655, 1663
at Harvard University in 1888, 1718
for Hebrew school, 450-451
hiring in New Netherlands, 352
Hoosier schoolmaster, 1299-1300
incompetent, 926
at Indian schools, 622, 2968-2969
in infant schools, 902, 1206-1208
initial probationary period of employment, 2713
in inner-city schools, 3042-3043
installation of, in Bonnal, 824-825
instructions for, 327-328
in Japanese internment camps, 2978
in Japanese language schools in California, 2976-2977
Jewish, 2921
in Jewish schools of the United States, 2925-2926
at Jewish Sunday schools, 2917-2918
Lancastrian, 982-983
lay adults as, 3261
loyalty oaths for, 2722-2744
Loyola's rules for, 69-72
and majority opinion, 2719-2722
in Massachusetts public schools, 1287-1288, 1289
membership in "subversive" organizations, 2724-2727
mental hygiene courses for, 2482
in Middletown, 2689-2692
for migrant children, 3194-3195

in Monte District, California, 1035
in Montecito District school, 1038
in Negro schools in South, 1636-1637
in New Amsterdam, 544-545
of New Education Fellowship, 2065-2066
for New Lanark school, 902
in nongraded schools, 3285-3286
number of, in California, 1033
obedience to superiors, 69
and "object" lesson on numbers, 1786-1787
overdominating, 857
paper work required of, 3313
and parents. See Parent-teacher associations
in Park Forest schools, 3140
personal cleanliness of, 1360-1361
personal conduct of, 466-467
personal habits of, 1360-1362
and Pestalozzianism, 1781
at Philadelphia Academy, 511-512
as philosopher, 2187
and political partisanship, 1105-1106
probation for, 933
professionalization of. See Professionalization of teachers
in Prussian schools, 1087-1088, 1089-1094
in public high schools in Massachusetts, 1253
in public school in Pennsylvania, 1298-1299
in public schools run by private corporations, 3338
and punishment, 75-77
and Quincy method, 1812
and Quincy number lesson, 1815, 1816-1817
and reactions of students, 1429-1430
and recitation, 1920-1921
in Reconstruction South, 1632-1634
referrals to social worker, 2402
relations between academicians and, 2707-2711
relationship with students, 833-835
religious requirements for, 554-555
requirements for, 276, 557, 3167-3168
responsibilities of, 857-861
role of. See Teacher's role
at Rough Rock Demonstration School, 2965-2970
runaway, 556-557
in rural high schools, 2601
of rural school, 2351
in Salem, Massachusetts, 947-948
in San Jose, California, 1041
in Santa Clara County, 1041
as scholar, 1360

and school grading, 1319-1323
of Scottish or Scotch-Irish ancestry, 2101
selection of, for Indians, 628
selection of, in Massachusetts, 797
selection of, at Phillips Exeter Academy, 519-520
in self-governed school, 1365-1366
servant schoolmasters, 558
sex of, 1850
for slaves, 581-582
of "Soup School" for Italian immigrants, 2153-2155
at St. Louis Sabbath school, 1202-1203
at St. Paul's School, 152
status of, 2004, 2006-2007
status in community, 2695-2698
strikes by, 3197-3198
strikes, in fall of 1968, 3226
strikes, in Salt Lake City, 3197-3198
at Summerhill, 2069-2070
and superego, 2001
at Talmud Torah school, 2916
technical skills of, 1819-1820
tone of, 823
and understanding of stream of consciousness, 1426-1427
unemployed during Depression, 2542
unfit, 828
at University of Chicago Elementary School, 2295, 2296
at University Extension, 1615
in U.S., 958-959
use of blackboards by, 961-962
use of psychoanalysis by, 2003
in Virginia colony, 457-467
in Winnetka, 2569-2570
Teachers aide, in Bonnal school, 825
Teachers' associations. See National Teachers' Association; State Teachers associations
Teachers College, Columbia University, 2237, 2317, 3164, 3212
course of study at, 2659-2665
Flexner on, 2699, 2700-2701
founding of, 1420-1425
kindergarten at, 2473-2477
staff of, 2700
Teachers College Record, 1420-1425, 2272-2274, 2654-2662, 2676-2679, 3320-3325, 3329-3336
Teachers Colleges
decline in number of, 2676-2679
Flexner report on, 2699-2702
Mosely Commission on, 2106
Teachers conferences, 926
Teachers congresses, in Scotland, 2101-2104
Teachers' contracts
in Lancaster, Pennsylvania, 559-560

at Hampton Institute, 1656-1657
in Japanese language schools in California, 2976
at Lancaster's school for poor children, 878
in Massachusetts Normal Schools, 1335-1336
at Negro school, 1620
in New Amsterdam, 544-545
at New Lanark school, 900
in New York Public Schools, 1124
at Notre Dame University, 1161
at Oberlin College, 1495
in Pennsylvania schools for the poor, 975
at Philadelphia Academy, 510
in post-revolutionary grammar schools, 744
in private high schools, 2510
in racially segregated private schools, 3114-3115
at school for Negro girls in Baltimore, 1622
at St. Paul's School, 153
at state university, 1524
for students at New York State Normal School, 1345
at Yale College, 675
Tuitte, John, 714
Tullis v. *Lake Erie & Western Railroad*, 3092
Tully, 155, 192, 284, 285, 406, 657, 675, 696
Turell, Ebenezer, 387-389
Turell, Jane, 387-389
Turfey, Mary, 438
Turkey, moral codes in, 2385
Turks, 44, 67
Turnbull, George H., 243-244, 244-245, 496
Turner, Jonathan B., on industrial universities, 1520-1525
Turn-over rates, for women, 3222
Turpin, Tom, 348-349
Tuskegee Idea, 1671-1672
Tuskegee Institute, 1660, 1667, 2988
daily program at, 1670
Fisher on, 1673-1675
industrial training in, 3004
Tuskegee and its People (Scott), 1671-1672, 1672-1675
Tutorial systems, computer, 3312
Tutor(s)
advice to, 462-467
diary of, 468-473
education of, 460-461
older children as, 2337
role of, 159-160
of University of Georgia, 789
Twelfth Annual Report of . . . the Secretary of the Board, 1100-1110
Twenty Years at Hull House (Addams), 2135-2136, 2163-2167, 2291-2293, 2832-2835
Twitchell, Ralph Emerson, 1022-1024
Two Cultures and the Scientific

Revolution, The (Snow), 2088-2092
Two Hundred Years: The History of the Society for Promoting Christian Knowledge, 1698-1898 (Allen and McClure), 325
Two Lives: The Story of Wesley Clair Mitchell and Myself (Mitchell), 2499-2503
Tyler, Amelia, 1655
Tyler, W. S., 1467-1471
Typewriting, in junior high school, 2324
"Typhoid Mary," 2825
UICSM program, 3238
Ulysses, 161, 186
Umatilla agency, 1737
Uncleanliness, punishment for, 883-884
Unconditioned reflex, 2019
Unconscious of the child, and school, 2394-2396
Undergraduates, course of instruction for, 1445-1446
Undernourishment, effects of, 2528-2529
See also Hunger
Understanding, 108-109
Unemployment, among college graduates, 2541-2542, 2538-2539, 2817
"Unemployment in the Learned Professions" (Kotschnig), 2817
Ungnadius, Lord, 133
Ungraded classes, vs. graded classes, 1921
Unification, in comprehensive high school, 2284-2287
Unit guides, in high school of future, 2598
Unitarianism, and Harvard College, 1460, 1471
United Hebrew Charities, 1200
United Nations, 3172
Charter of, 3013
Declaration of Rights of Men, 2045n
Educational, Scientific, and Cultural Organization, 2041-2044
General Assembly, Pope Paul VI's allocution to, 2047n
United States
assimilation of immigrants in, 939-940
and education, 1412-1413
in IEA study of mathematics achievement, 2054, 2055
as land of opportunity, 3342-3343
national education system in, 776-780
and Rhodes scholarships, 2064
school organization in, 2056
stages in development of, 1904-1905
uniformity in, 946-947
United States bonds, 1459
United States Bureau of Education, 957
act establishing, 1406-1407

call for establishment of, 1404-1405
United States Court of Appeals for the Eighth Circuit, 3108-3113
United States Court of Appeals for the Fourth Circuit, 3113-3116
United States *Gazette*, 1058
United States Immigration Commission Reports, 2974n
United States Office of Economic Opportunity, 3329
United States v. *Peters*, 3112
Universal education
establishment of, 1884
in South, 1002-1004
Universal suffrage. *See* Suffrage
Universities
as corporations, 1550-1552, 2778-2780
business principles used in, 2778-2780
curriculum of, 56-57
departments of education, 3131-3135
education as course of study at, 1414-1425
and elective system, 2745-2748
French and American compared, 2120-2121
Flexner report on, 2787-2791
in Germany and America compared, 1537-1542
governing boards of, 2780-2783
Jewish students at, 1198-1199
and junior high school movement, 2325
Knox on, 55-57
and medical education, 2768-2777
mental hygiene in, 2783-2786
and model schools in slums, 3281
Newman on, 904-907
Notre Dame, 1160-1161
origin of, 2072
and Ph.Ds, 2752-2757
in Prussia, 927
radicalism at. *See* Radicalized University; Student activism
relationships between, 212
schools of education in, 2699-2702
selection of faculty for, 2073-2075
and Society of Jesus, 65-67
summer schools of, 1943, 1945
time allotted to, 2262n, 2263
Whitehead on function of, 2070-2075
women in, 2748-2752
See also Catholic universities; Colleges; State universities
Universities: American, English, German (Flexner), 2699-2702, 2787-2791
University of Chicago Decennial Publications, 2873-2875
"University Education" (Spalding), 1173-1176
University extension, 2828
critique of, 2838-2841

functions of, 1613-1616
Kennedy on, 3357
University High School, 3236
University of the Pacific, 1041
University Problems, 1564-1565
University Record, 2295-2298
Universities, reform of, and new left, 2859
Universities at, research, 2820-2823
"University School, The" (Dewey), 2295-2298
University towns, 1457
Unpleasure and ego, 2001
"Unsearchable Riches of Christ Considered in Two Sermons . . ." (Tennent), 431-434
Unwanted child, 2397-2398
Up from Slavery (Washington), 1658-1664
UPI survey of Catholic education, 2906-2908
Urban Review, The, 3329n
Urban schools
disparity between suburban schools and, 3034-3035
in Great Britain, 3299-3305
See also Inner-city schools
U.S. Army
education in, 2841-2843
in Little Rock, Arkansas, 3013-3016
U.S. Bureau of the Census
on schooling, 2807
U.S. Bureau of Education, 954-959, 966-972, 999-1000, 1032, 1195-1199, 1200-1203, 2278-2290, 2626-2632
Annual Report of the Commissioner of Education, 1407-1409, 1641-1642, 1735-1740
Bulletin No. 4, 1920, 2373-2378
Circular of Information, 1909-1914
The Indian School at Carlisle Barracks, 1748-1752
Report of the Commissioner of Education for the Year 1870, 1765-1769
Report of the Commissioner of Education, 1892-1893, 1648-1649
U.S. Bureau of Indian Affairs, 2966, 2967, 2969
Annual Report of the Commissioner of Indian Affairs, 1880, 1745-1748
Annual Report of the Commissioner of Indian Affairs, 1881, 1754-1756
Annual Report of the Commissioner of Indian Affairs, 1890, 1756-1760
U.S. Census Bureau, 2769n
U.S. Commission on Civil Rights, 3370-3371
U.S. District Court for the Eastern District of Pennsylvania, 3080-3081
U.S. News & World Report, 3011-3013, 3013-3016

U.S. Supreme Court
and aid to parochial schools, 2906, 2908-2909
Use of Resources in Education, The (Clapp), 3127-3131
Uses of the University, The (Kerr), 2823-2826
Ushers, 168, 169, 653
elimination of, 877
Utah Education Association's House of Delegates, 3197-3198
Utah Indians, 1739
Utes, 1737-1739
Utley, Robert M., 1740-1745
Utopia (More), 150-151
Utopians, 151
Uzbek Republic, education in, 3155
Uzgiris, Dr. Ina, 3246
Vacations, 70
at Albany Female Academy, 1594
at Carlisle Indian School, 1747-1748
at Columbia University, 698-699
at Hebrew College, 1187
length of, 1923
at New York State Normal School, 1346
of State Normal School of New Britain, Connecticut, 1341
and violation of child labor laws, 2195
Valences, of the environment, 2035-2037
Valente, William, 2907-2908
Valentin, Gabriel Gistav, 1457-1460
Valentine, T. W., 1399
Valerius Maximus, 290, 351
Valla, 195
Van Amburgh, 1300
Van De Riet, 3207
Van Doren, Carl, 625-626
van Eckkelen, Johannes, 546
Van Hise, Charles R., 2757-2760
Van Liew, C. C., 1881-1882
Van Sickle, J. H., 2992-2993
Van Waters, Miriam, 2408-2409
Van Zuren, Casparus, 546
Vanderbilt University, during Depression, 2557
Vanderen, John, 524
Vanderlip, Frank A., 2267, 2311, 2319
Vanderlip, Mrs. Frank A., 2319
Vandwyck, Cornelius Barent, 546
Vardaman (senator), 3002
Varro, 185
Vassar College, 1721
and adult education, 2840
Vatican II
and Catholic education, 2902-2906
on Christian education, 2044-2053
on higher education, 2052-2053
Vaughan, Herbert E., 3236
Veblen, Thorstein, 2778-2780
Vegetarianism, 479

Vehrly, 854-856
Veiller, Laurence, 2141-2143
Veitch, John, 81-86
Ventilation, 1297
in England and U.S. compared, 2107
at Lexington, Mass. Normal School, 1330
in New York tenements, 2142
in schoolhouses, 1081-1082
Venus, 79
Verdi, 2275
Ver Planck, 699
Vermont, constitutional provision for schools in, 794
Vernacular School, Comenius on, 263-265
Verulam, Lord, 246
Vesalius, 3189
Vespers. *See* Prayers
Veterans, and "G.I. Bill of Rights," 2799-2802
Veterans' Administration, and Civilian Conservation Corps, 2558
Viart, Lydia, 446
Vickary, Miss, 2310
Vida, 415
Villages, education in, 112, 113
Villavicencio, Rafael, 1020-1021
Villette, Gray, 3009
Vincennes, Bishop of, 1160
Vincent, John H., 1608
Vindication of the Rights of Woman, A (Wollstonecraft), 876-878
Vineyards of California, 1034, 1035
Vinson, Chief Justice, 3006-3009, 3098-3099
Violence
in Little Rock, Arkansas, 3009-3016
in schools, 3201-3202
Violence In The City—An End or A Beginning?, 3023-3026
Violin lessons, 448
in teacher seminaries in Prussia, 933
Virgil, 44, 155, 161, 165, 168, 210, 213, 242, 285, 351, 406, 414, 415, 503, 512, 513, 550, 669, 675, 696, 1067, 1233, 1238, 1597
in French secondary school curriculum, 1924
"Virgil Club," 2518
Virgile, 158
Virgin Mary, 53
Virginia
advantages of college in, 648-649
apprenticeship in, 342-344
and *Brown* v. *Board of Education,* 3102-3108
charter of, 334
education in, 453-473, 750-751
education of Indians in, 606, 1741-1742
education of Negroes in, 585-586
first Negro school in, 1659-1660

"freedom of choice" plan in, 3117-3120
Indian massacre of 1622 in, 603-605
Indian treaties in, 625-626
Jefferson's educational plan for, 747-750
law prohibiting teaching of slaves in, 1623
Literary Fund for education in, 1001
petition to establish college in, 641-642
propagation of gospel among heathens in, 335-338
proposal for college in, 335-338
reasons for colonizing, 331-334
religious instruction in, 339
report on schools in, 345
resistance to school desegregation in, 3113-3120
slavery in, 574-575
statute on baptism of slaves in, 571
statute for religious freedom in, 785-786
workhouse law for poor children in, 342-343
workhouse laws in, 345
Virginia Assembly
  incorporation of Hampton Institute by, 1653
  and teachers' licenses, 547
Virginia Company of London, 603-605, 334
Virginia Constitution, educational provisions in, 1650-1651
Virginia Gazette, The, 447-449
Virginia high schools, core-curriculum plan in, 2602-2603
Virginia House of Delegates, resolution on national university by, 806
Virginia Legislature
  and public schools, 1687
  and University of Virginia, 1491
Virginia Magazine of History and Biography, The, 647
Virginia, University of, 1519
  curriculum at, 1486-1491
  elective studies at, 1493
  and Protestant sects, 1468
  Rockfish Gap Report on, 1485-1491
Virginia Vetusta During the Reign of James the First (Neill), 335
Virtues, 257, 263
  education in, 235-236
  Franklin on, 488-490
  of ideal women, 1571
Vision, development of, and color discrimination, 868-869
Visit to Some American Schools and Colleges, A (Jex-Blake), 947-950
Visiters. See Board of Visiters
Visiting teacher, 2309-2310
  See also School social worker

"Visiting Teacher, The," 2309-2310
Visiting Teachers' Survey in 1921, 2401-2402
Visitors
  and admission to State Normal Schools, 1341
  at Albany Female Academy, 1593
  at Notre Dame University, 1161
VISTA, 2967
Visual Instruction Association of America, 2390
Visual problems
  and failure, 2402-2403
Vitruvius, 185
Vives, John Lewis, 164
Vives, Ludovico, 168
Vocabulary, 500
  limitation of, 96
  and reading, 2490
Vocabulary of the Massachusetts (or Natick) Indian Language (Cotton), 616-617
Vocal music
  in American schools in 1874, 1906
  in elementary school curriculum, 1969
  at Notre Dame University, 1161
  See also Singing
Vocational Aptitudes of Second-Generation Japanese in the United States (Strong), 2975n
Vocational choice, 2281
  in elementary school, 2302-2303
Vocational curricula
  in American schools, 2118-2119
  and behavior problems, 2401
  at Choctaw Academy, 1729
  and Civilian Conservation Corps, 2560-2561
  and college curriculum, 2784
  in comprehensive high school, 2287
  federal aid to, 2360
  and federal government, 3365-3369
  in Gary, Indiana schools, 2329-2331, 2339
  and high school curriculum, 2518-2520
  and intelligence, 2509
  for Indian children, 2962-2964
  Kennedy on, 3356
  on Los Angeles high schools, 2939
  Nixon on, 3386
  for out-of-school youth, 2546-2547
  overspecialization of, 3345
  and Smith-Hughes Act, 2364-2368
  See also Industrial education
Vogel, Dr., 1093-1094
Vogel, Mabel, 2490n, 2492n
Vogt, C., 1457
Voice training, for teachers, 1819
Volney, 1151
Volstead Act, 2383

Voltaire, 2121
Volunteers
  in compensatory pre-school programs, 3276
  at Hull House, 2291
von Altenstein, Baron, 927
von Hapsburg, Rudolph, 1876
Von Marenholz-Bulow, Baroness Bertha, 851-853
von Uexkull, 2035
Vossius, 290
Voucher system, 2909
Vrim, 124
Vulcan, 211
Waaubon, 612, 613
Wabash College, founding of, 1468
Wadleigh High School, New York, 2108
Wadsworth, Daniel, 673
Wadsworth, Gen., 1331
Wage slavery and individuality, 2612-2613
"Wage-Earning Children" (Kelley and Stevens), 2138-2141
Wages
  of children, 2140
  of employees of U.S. Bureau of Education, 1407
  and excess of college graduates, 2817
  and manual training, 1871
Wagon-making, at Carlisle Indian School, 1747, 1750-1751
Wahunsonacock, 602, 605
Wake, Dr., 651
Wald, Lillian D., 2203-2205
Walden, or Life in the Woods (Thoreau), 1220-1224
Walden School, New York City, 2486-2489
Waldenses, 365
Wales, John N., 2122-2123
Walker, 406-407, 1465
Walker, General Francis A., 1422
Walker, George Leon, 435-436
Walker, Gilbert, on federal aid to education, 1686-1690
Walker, John, 448, 903
Walker, Mrs. John, 448
Walker, Obadiah, 496
Walking, learning of, 1821
Wall Street Journal, 3336-3339
Wallace, George, 3226
  at University of Mississippi, 3018
Wallace, W. B., 1772
Waller, Willard, 2695-2698
"Walnut Tree, The" (Aesop), 298
Walsh, Michael, 1140
Wampooas, 615
Wampum, 610, 625-626
War Department, 1742
  and Freedmen's Bureau, 1635
War Relocation Authority, and Japanese interment camps, 2977
Ward, Mary, A., 2490n
Ward, Samuel, 706
Ward v. Flood, 1763-1765, 1772
Wardman Park Hotel, Washington, D.C., 2628
Ware, Jr., 1329

Waring, Marsham, 714
Warm Spring agency, 1737
Warner, Benjamin, 980
Warner, Charles F., 2267
Warren, John, 358
Warren, Justice, 1748-1752, 2729, 3102-3108
Warren G. Harding High School, 2111
Warren v. Mayor of Charlestown, 3092
Warrenton, North Carolina, female academy at, 1572
Washburne, Carleton, 2490n, 2489-2496, 2569-2572
Washington, Booker T., 1664-1667
Address at Harvard University, 1675-1676
Atlanta Exposition Address of, 1668-1670
DuBois on, 2984-2987
education of, 1658-1664, 2989
family of, 1658-1659
at Hampton Institute, 1661-1664
on Negro education in South, 1664-1667
on Tuskegee idea, 1671-1672
Washington, George, 3079
on education, 1408
Farewell Address of, 964, 2102
on national university, 806-808
on religious freedom, 811-812
Washington, John H., 1673
Washington, D.C., 2722, 3218
Montessori school in, 2319-2320
Negro school enrollment in, 3046
Negro schools in, 1700-1701, 2997-2998
physicians in, 2769n
school safety in, 3201-3202
school segregation in, 1642-1643
Washington Monthly, The, 3201-3202
Washington Post, 3211-3212
Washington Public Library, 2418
Washington University, St. Louis, 2540
manual training school of, 1859-1860
Washington's birthday, 964, 2349
"Washington's Farewell Address to the People of the United States," 964, 2102
Water colors, for art, 2488
Waterhouse, Dr. Benjamin, 782-783
Waterhouse, Edward, 603-605
Waterloo (Byron), 1964
Watkin, E. I., 2900n
Watson, Foster, 156-163
Watson, Goodwin, 2545-2598
Watson, John B., 2396, 2406-2408
Watt's Hymns, 1191
Watts riots, and McCone Report, 3023-3026
Waverley Institution, 2405
Wayland, Francis

on higher education and democracy, 1508-1509
on normal schools, 1333
proposal for reform of Brown University, 1506-1508
on reform of American colleges, 1502-1505
Wayward Youth (Aichhorn), 2002-2003
Wealth, achievement of, 492-495
Wealthy classes
and public schools in Ohio, 1027, 1028
withdrawal of children from public schools by, 1241
Weaning, 2411-2412
Weare, W., 518
Weather, and absences, 1329
Webb, Alexander S., 1422
Webb, Dr., 1331
Webb, Harold, 3337
Webster, Daniel
and Dartmouth College case, 1435-1437
on public schools, 1062-1063
Webster, Dr. Horace, 3321
Webster, Noah, 1149, 1150, 1377-1381, 1571
on European education for Americans, 800-803
on morality, 771-773
on necessity for an American language, 766-769
on spelling reforms, 763-766
Webster's spelling book, 1626, 1659-1660
Wechsler, James, 2791-2795
Wechsler scales, 3206
Weekly Essays on Sundry Subjects, More Particularly Adapted to the Province of New York . . ., 691-694
Weekly Post-Boy. See New York Gazette
Weekly Reader, The, 3144
Weight, child's conceptions about, 2028-2029
Weiland, 3255
Weiman v. Updegraff, 2882-2883
Weir, George, 1140
Weiser, Conrad, 625, 637-638
Welch, Dr. William H., 2528-2529
Welch, Paul, 3009-3011
Wellesley, 2748
Wells, S. A., 1242-1244
Welsh, William, 1740
Wendell, Barrett, 1718
Wendell, Jacob, 407
Wendlin, 194
"Wendy House" in British infant schools, 3301
Were You Ever a Child? (Dell), 2413-2414
Werowocomoco, Virginia, 602
Wertenbaker, Thomas Jefferson, 685-687
Wertheimer, M., 2016
Werther, 2833
Wesley, Edgar B., 1398
Wesleyan University, charter, 2763
Wessely, 1198

West, Daniel, 708
West, E. G., 3329n
West, James E., 2355-2357
West, Mrs. Max, 2358-2359
West
Americanization of immigrants in, 991-992
school segregation in, 3027
West India Company, Jews petition to, 354-355
West Point Academy
act establishing a military academy at, 1481
curriculum at, 1504
Negro cadet at, 1716-1718
West Riding Education Committee, 3303
West Virginia legislature, flag salute laws, 3058-3064
West Virginia State Board of Education v. Barnette, 3058-3064, 3081
Western Reserve University, Cleveland
during Depression, 2539-2540
founding of, 1468
Westfield Infant School, Leicestershire, 3299-3301
Westfield Normal School, Leicestershire, 948
Westminster Hall, 269
Westminster School, statutes of, 165-171
Wetmore, 699
Wetmore, Samuel, 1676
W.H. Jones & Brother, 1672-1673
Whaley, Mrs., 449
What the High Schools Ought to Teach, 2627n
"What Is Progressive Education?" (Snyder), 2446-2449
"What Kind of School Is a CCC Camp?" (Coe), 2562-2567
"What the Liberal College Is" (Meiklejohn), 2766-2768
"What Youth Have in Common," 2623n
Wheeler, Ignatius, 714
Wheeler, (senator), 2531-2534
Wheelock, Eleazer, 619-624, 707-709, 1636
"When Should Children Begin to Read" (Morphett and Washburne), 2569-2572
Whetstone agency, 1739
Whipple, Bishop, 1740
Whistler, 2114
Whitaker, Rev. Nathanial, 707-708
White, Andrew D., 1454-1457, 1517-1519, 1454-1457
on Cornell, 1542-1545
on University of Michigan, 1517-1519
White, E. E., 1404-1406
White, George Savage, 976
White, Goodrich C., 3082-3084
White, Justice, 2735-2736, 3082-3084
White, Phillips, 522
White, Samuel, 715
White, William A., 2396-2400
White House Conference on

Child Health and Protection, 2549-2555
White House Conference on Children and Youth, 3192
  call for the first, 2355-2357
White House Conference on Education (1956), 3342
White League in Louisiana, 1645-1646
Whitefield, George, 434-436, 681-685
Whitehead, Alfred North, 2121
  on function of universities, 2070-2075
Whitely, Jacob, 472
Whites
  attitude of Hopi Indians toward, 2949
  attitudes toward Negro education, 3003-3005
  and black studies, 3328
  and integration of Northern schools, 3020-3023
  and Negro education, 1680-1681, 3000-3001
  reaction to school desegregation, 3224-3225
  and school segregation, 1643
  and segregation, 2810
White-Williams Foundation of Philadelphia, 2400
Whitman, Samuel, 673
Whitman, Walt
  on corporal punishment, 1292-1294
  on public schools, 1296-1297
Whitney, John, 391
Whittaker, Justice, 3108-3113
Whittelsey, Samuel, 673
Whitten, Jamie L., 3006-3009
Whitten, Phillip, 3329n
Whittier, 1964, 2112-2113
Whittington, 270
Whittlesey, 979
Whittling, 2414
Why Johnny Can't Read—and What You Can Do About It (Flesch), 3136-3138
"Why They Fight for P.A.T." (Streit), 3020-3023
Whyte, William H, 3139-3143
Wichita, Kansas, 1745
Wickedness, punishment for, 826
Wickersham, J. P., 359, 558-559
Wickliffe, 979
Wide-Awake Gift: A Know-Nothing Token for 1855, The, 997-999
Wide-Range Achievement Test, 3297
Wiener boys, 2250
Wieting, C. Maurice, 2599-2562
Wigglesworth, Michael, 371-376
Wightman, Joseph M., 977
Wilberforce College, 1673
Wilcox, Mark, 714
Wild boy of Aveyron, education of, 837-842
Wild Boy of Aveyron, The (Itard), 837-842
"Wild children of Russia," 2529, 2530
Wilde, Oscar, 2114

Wiley, Calvin H., 1012-1014
Will County, Illinois, 2736-2738
Willard, Emma, on education of women, 1573-1580
Willard, Samuel, 377
Willenshandlungen, 874-875
Willey, Senator, 1413
William, Earl of Dartmouth, 594
William Graham Sumner (Starr), 1569
William, King, 326, 642, 643, 651
William and Mary College, 452-453, 725, 741, 744, 798
  after American Revolution, 748
  beginnings of the Phi Beta Kappa Society at, 719-723
  charter of, 645-647
  curriculum of, 747
  debates of Phi Beta Kappa Society at, 724
  Jefferson's plan for reforming, 745-747
  petition for establishment of, 642, 643-645
  problems of, 647
William and Mary College Quarterly Historical Magazine, 342-344, 719-726
Williams, E. I. F., 1110-1111
Williams, Ebenezer, 673
Williams, John Bell, 3006-3009
Williams, Laura C., 2417, 2418
Williams, R. S., 1038
Williams, Roger, 368-370
Williamson, David, 557
Willis, Edwin E., 3006-3009
Willis, Francis, 343
Willis, Samuel, 557
Willoughby, Harold R., 119-121
Willpower, training of, 1916-1917
Wills, 339-341, 357-358
Wilmington, California, 1034
  public schools in, 1035
Wilson, H. B., 2261-2266
Wilson, Irvin A., 2531-2534
Wilson, J. D., 924-925
Wilson, John, 442
Wilson, Logan, 2820
Wilson, Woodrow, 3356
Wilson Library Bulletin, 2944-2948
Winchell, Walter, 3148
Winnesa Chippewas, 1740
Winnetka Graded Book List (Washburne and Vogel), 2492n
Winnetka, Illinois
  curriculum in public schools of, 2489-2496
  reading teaching in, 2569-2572
"Winnetka social science investigation, The" (Mohr), 2490n
Winsor, Justin, 1718
Winstead, Arthur, 3006-3009
Winston, 2266
Winter, Ella, 2011-2016
Winter, Nathan H., 2919-2921
"Winter Free School," 1287
Winter term, at New York State Normal School, 1346

Winthrop, Adam, 407
Winthrop, John, 365-367, 381-383
Winthrop, Margaret, 381-383
Winthrop, Robert C., 1676, 1678
Winthrop Papers, The, 365-367
Wirkwelt, 2035
Wirt, 979, 2332-2333, 2337
Wirtemberg, common schools of, 930-931
Wisconsin
  Catholic school enrollment in, 2908
  physicians in, 2773n
Wisconsin legislature, on normal schools, 2671
Wisconsin, University of, 2757-2760
  and academic freedom, 1569-1570
  during Depression, 2541
Wisdom, 236, 309
Wise, Isaac M., 1202
Wissenschaft, 1537
Wissler, Clark, 2237
Withers, 242
Witherspoon, John, 709-713
Wolfe, 1964
Wolin, Sheldon S., 2859-2863
Wollstonecraft, Mary, on co-education, 876-878
Woman and the Higher Education (Brackett), 1573-1580
Women
  admission to University of Michigan, 1519
  and Civilian Conservation Corps, 2566
  degradation of, 1316
  problems of, 1318-1319
  role among Indians, 608
  in Soviet Union, 3154
  as teachers, 953
  Webster's ideal, 1571-1572
  See also Education of women; Female teachers, 3221
Women workers, 3222
  as teachers, 1318
Women's Bureau of the Department of Labor, 3222
Women's circles (England), 2086
Women's clubs
  and parents associations, 2307
  representation on school boards, 2674
Women's Party, 2420
"Wonder children," 2250
Wood, 1334, 1329
Wood, Walter M., 2267
Woodbridge, William, 1482-1483
Woodbury, 1328
Woods, Robert A., 2267
Woods Hole, 3243
Woodson, Carter G., 2999-3000
Woodstock, 2440
Woodward, A. B., 1482-1483
Woodward, Calvin M., 1859-1867
Woodward, William H., 1437
Woodwork, and progressive education curriculum, 2448
Woodworth, Robert S., 2236-2240

Zeno, 671
Zerubbabel, 122
Ziller, 970-971, 1876
Zoilus, 414

Zoning ordinances, racial, 3034
Zook, Commissioner, 2563
Zoology
    out-of-door instruction in, 1941

in Prussian schools, 1089
in secondary school curriculum,
    1936, 1939
at University of Virginia, 1488
Zorach v. *Clauson*, 3071-3075ZZZ